PROBLEM SOLVER® in

REGISTERED TRADEMARK

STRENGTH OF MATERIALS and MECHANICS OF SOLIDS

Staff of Research and Education Association,

Dr. M. Fogiel, Director

REA

Research and Education Association
505 Eighth Avenue
New York, N. Y. 10018

PROBLEM SOLVER® IN
STRENGTH OF MATERIALS
AND MECHANICS OF SOLIDS

Printed in the United States of America

Library of Congress Catalog Card Number 85-60134

International Standard Book Number 0-87891-522-2

Revised Printing, 1985

WHAT THIS BOOK IS FOR

Students have generally found "strength of materials" and "solid mechanics" a difficult subject to understand and learn. Despite the publication of hundreds of textbooks in this field, each one intended to provide an improvement over previous textbooks, students continue to remain perplexed as a result of the numerous conditions that must often be remembered and correlated in solving a problem. Various possible interpretations of terms used in "strength of materials" and "solid mechanics" have also contributed to many of the difficulties experienced by students.

In a study of the problem, REA found the following basic reasons underlying students' difficulties with "strength of materials" and "solid mechanics" taught in schools:

(a) No systematic rules of analysis have been developed which students may follow in a step-by-step manner to solve the usual problems encountered. This results from the fact that the numerous different conditions and principles which may be involved in a problem, lead to many possible different methods of solution. To prescribe a set of rules to be followed for each of the possible variations, would involve an enormous number of rules and steps to be searched through by students, and this task would perhaps be more burdensome than solving the problem directly with some accompanying trial and error to find the correct solution route.

(b) Textbooks currently available will usually explain a given principle in a few pages written by a professional who has an insight in the subject matter that is not shared by students. The explanations are often written in an abstract manner which leaves the students confused as to the application of the principle. The explanations given are not sufficiently detailed and extensive to make the student aware of the wide range of applications and different aspects of the principle being studied. The numerous possible variations of principles and their applications are usually not discussed, and it is left for the students to discover these for themselves while doing the exercises. Accordingly, the average student is expected to rediscover that which has been long known and practiced, but not published or explained extensively.

(c) The examples usually following the explanation of a topic are too few in number and too simple to enable the student to obtain a thorough grasp of the principles involved. The explanations do not provide sufficient basis to enable a student to solve problems that may be subsequently assigned for homework or given on examinations.

The examples are presented in abbreviated form which leaves out much material between steps, and requires that students derive the omitted material themselves. As a result, students find the examples difficult to understand--contrary to the purpose of the examples.

Examples are, furthermore, often worded in a confusing manner. They do not state the problem and then present the solution. Instead, they pass through a general discussion, never revealing what is to be solved for.

Examples, also, do not always include diagrams/graphs, wherever appropriate, and students do not obtain the training to draw diagrams or graphs to simplify and organize their thinking.

(d) Students can learn the subject only by doing the exercises themselves and reviewing them in class, to obtain experience in applying the principles with their different ramifications.

In doing the exercises by themselves, students find that they are required to devote considerably more time to "strength of materials" and "solid mechanics" than to other subjects of comparable credits, because they are uncertain with regard to the selection and application of the theorems and principles involved. It is also often necessary for students to discover those "tricks" not revealed in their texts (or review books), that make it possible to solve problems easily. Students must usually resort to methods of trial-and-error to discover these "tricks", and as a result they find that they may sometim spend several hours in solving a single problem.

(e) When reviewing the exercises in classrooms, instructors usually request students to take turns writing solutions on the board and explaining them to the class. Students often find it difficult to explain the solutions in a manner that holds the interest of the class, and enables the remaining students to follow the material written on the board. The remaining students seated in the class are, furthermore, too occupied with copying the material from the board, to listen to the oral explanations and concentrate on the methods of solution.

This book is intended to aid students in "strength of materials" and "solid mechanics" in overcoming the difficulties described, by supplying detailed illustrations of the solution methods which are usually not apparent to students. The solution methods are illustrated by problems selected from those that are most often assigned for class work and given on examinations. The problems are arranged in order of complexity to enable students to learn and understand a particular topic by reviewing the problems in sequence. The problems are illustrated with detailed step-by-step explanations, to save students the large amount of time that is often needed to fill in the gaps that are usually found between steps of illustrations in textbooks or review/outline books.

The staff of REA considers "strength of materials" and "solid mechanics" a subject that is best learned by allowing students to view the methods of analysis and solution techniques themselves. This approach to learning the subject matter is similar to that practiced in various scientific laboratories, particularly in the medical fields.

In using this book, students may review and study the illustrated problems at their own pace; they are not limited to the time allowed for explaining problems on the board in class.

When students want to look up a particular type of problem and solution, they can readily locate it in the book by referring to the index which has been extensively prepared. It is also possible to locate a particular type of problem by glancing at the material within the boxed portions. To facilitate rapid scanning of the problems, each problem has a heavy border around it. Furthermore, each problem is identified with a number immediately above the problem at the right-hand margin.

To obtain maximum benefit from the book, students should familiarize themselves with the section, "How To Use This Book," located in the front pages.

To meet the objectives of this book, staff members of REA have selected problems usually encountered in assignments and examinations, and have solved each problem meticulously to illustrate the steps which are difficult for students to comprehend. Special gratitude is expressed to them for their efforts in this area, as well as to the numerous contributors who devoted brief periods of time to this work.

Gratitude is also expressed to the many persons involved in the difficult task of typing the manuscript with its endless changes, and to the REA art staff who prepared the numerous detailed illustrations together with the layout and physical features of the book.

The diffucult task of coordinating the efforts of all persons was carried out by Carl Fuchs. His conscientious work deserves much appreciation. He also trained and supervised art and production personnel in the preparation of the book for printing.

Finally, special thanks are due to Helen Kaufmann for her unique talents in rendering those difficult border-line decisions and in making constructive suggestions related to the design and organization of the book.

Max Fogiel, Ph.D.
Program Director

HOW TO USE THIS BOOK

This book can be an invaluable aid to students in "strength of materials" and "solid mechanics" as a supplement to their textbooks. The book is subdivided into 18 chapters, each dealing with a separate topic. The subject matter is developed beginning with deformation of bodies, and extending through bending moments, shear, stress & strain relations, beam deflections, torsion, and columns. Included are also sections on statically indeterminate members, dynamic loading, structural analysis, failure criteria, timber design, and design of reinforced concrete structures. An extensive number of applications have been included, since these appear to be most troublesome to students.

TO LEARN AND UNDERSTAND A TOPIC THOROUGHLY

1. Refer to your class text and read the section pertaining to the topic. You should become acquainted with the principles discussed there. These principles, however, may not be clear to you at that time.

2. Then locate the topic you are looking for by referring to the "Table of Contents" in front of this book, "The Strength of Materials and Mechanics of Solids Problem Solver."

3. Turn to the page where the topic begins and review the problems under each topic, in the order given. For each topic, the problems are arranged in order of complexity, from the simplest to the more difficult. Some problems may appear similar to others, but each problem has been selected to illustrate a different point or solution method.

To learn and understand a topic thoroughly and retain its content, it will generally be necessary for students to review the problems several times. Repeated review is essential in order to gain experience in recognizing the principles that should be applied, and in selecting the best solution technique.

TO FIND A PARTICULAR PROBLEM

To locate one or more problems related to a particular subject matter, refer to the index. In using the index, be certain to note that the numbers given there refer to problem numbers, not page numbers. This arrangement of the index is intended to facilitate finding a problem more rapidly, since two or more problems may appear on a page.

If a particular type of problem cannot be found readily, it is recommended that the student refer to the "Table of Contents" in the front pages, and then turn to the chapter which is applicable to the problem being sought. By scanning or glancing at the material that is boxed, it will generally be possible to find problems related to the one being sought, without consuming considerable time. After the problems have been located, the solutions can be reviewed and studied in detail. For this purpose of locating problems rapidly, students should acquaint themselves with the organization of the book as found in the "Table of Contents".

In preparing for an exam, locate the topics to be covered on the exam in the "Table of Contents," and then review the problems under those topics several times. This should equip the student with what might be needed for the exam.

CONTENTS

CHAPTER 1

INTRODUCTION TO MECHANICS OF DEFORMABLE BODIES

DEFORMABLE BODIES

• PROBLEM 1-1

A 90-ft. flagpole is made of 6 in. diameter steel pipe. It is attached to its foundation by a ball-and-socket joint and is supported in the upright position by four 1/4 in. diameter high-strength steel wires, as shown in Fig. 1. When there is no wind, the tension in the wires is negligible. In a hurricane the wind blows hard from the south, and its effects can be represented by a horizontal force of 900 lb. at the mid-height of the pole.

Estimate how far the top of the pole moves from its original position, which is perpendicular to the base.

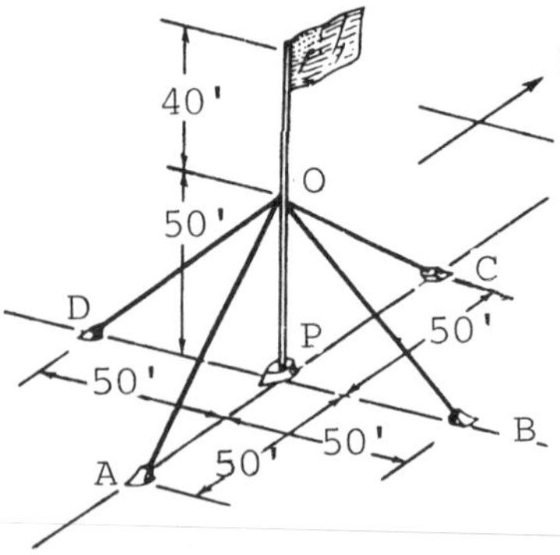

Fig. 1.

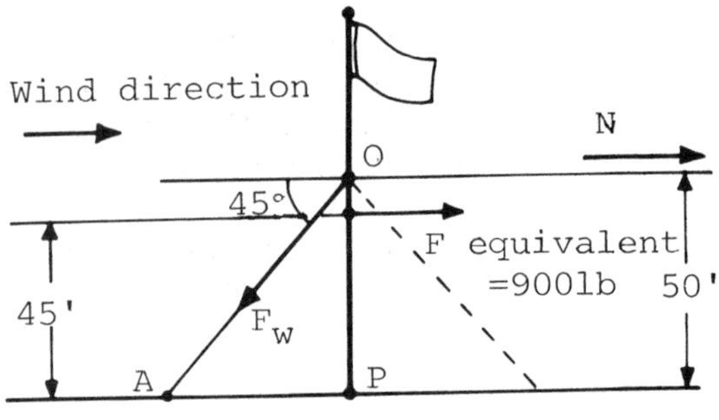

Fig. 2.

Solution: We are given an equivalent loading for the wind of 900 lb. from the south, acting at the midpoint of the pole. Since the force is from the south, the wires running east and west from the flagpole will exert a negligibly small force on the flagpole, since they will not be stressed appreciably. We can, therefore, ignore the effects of the wires $\overline{OB}$ and $\overline{OD}$ in Figure 1. The wire $\overline{OC}$ in Figure 1 can apply no force at O, since it is initially unstressed (i.e., when no wind is present) and any force applied against a southern wind by $\overline{OC}$ would have to be compressive. (Wires are one-way rigidity devices and cannot sustain compression.) Thus, the only wire supplying a force at point O is $\overline{OA}$. The force supplied by the wire must be directed along the line $\overline{OA}$. Wires can exert forces only through simple tension, as opposed to beams, which can also supply forces due to flexure.

Setting the sum of moments about point P in Fig. 2 equal to zero, we have:

$$\Sigma M \overset{+}{\circlearrowright} = 0 = (F_w \cos 45°)(50') - (F_{equiv.})(45')$$

$$0 = 35.355F_w - 45(900 lb.)$$

$$F_w = 1145.5 \text{ lb.}$$

Note that length of OA is

$$L = \sqrt{(50')^2 + (50')^2} = 70.71' = 848.52".$$

We can now calculate the extension of the wire. By definition:

$$\sigma = \frac{F}{A} \qquad \varepsilon = \frac{\delta}{L} \qquad E = \frac{\sigma}{\varepsilon}$$

$$\therefore E = \frac{\frac{F}{A}}{\frac{\delta}{L}} = \frac{FL}{A\delta}.$$

Divide both sides by E and multiply both sides by δ:

$$\delta = \frac{FL}{AE}$$

$$\delta_w = \frac{F_w L}{AE} = \frac{(1145.5 \text{ lb.})(848.52")}{\pi \frac{\left(\frac{1}{4}"\right)^2}{4}(30 \times 10^6 \text{ psi})}$$

$$\delta_w = 0.660".$$

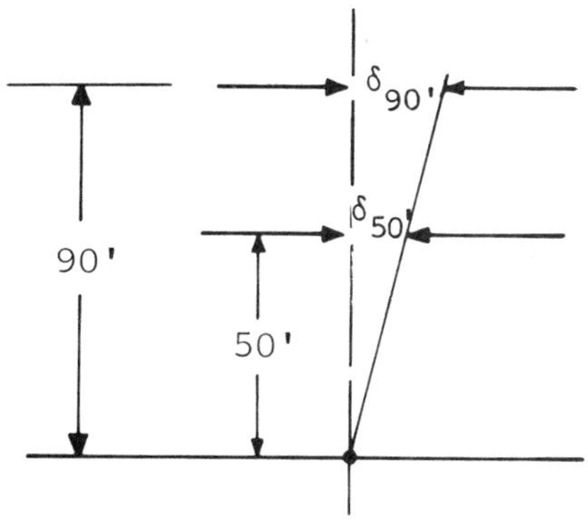

Fig. 3.

This is the extension along the wire. Looking at Fig. 2, we see that the lateral movement of the flagpole at 50' will be

$$\delta_{50'} = \delta_w \cos 45° = (.660")(.7071) = .4667".$$

We want to know how far the top of the flagpole moves. From Fig. 3 we note from similar triangles that

$$\delta_{90'} = \frac{90}{50}\,\delta_{50'} = \frac{9}{5}(.4667").$$

Therefore, the movement of the top of the pole is

$$\delta_{90'} = 0.840".$$

• PROBLEM 1-2

A bolt is threaded through a tubular sleeve, and the nut is turned up just tight by hand as shown in Fig. 1. Using wrenches, the nut is then turned further, the bolt being put in the tension and the sleeve in compression. If the bolt has 16 threads per inch, and the nut is given an extra quarter turn (90°) by the wrenches, estimate the tensile force in the bolt if both the bolt and sleeve are of steel and the cross-sectional areas are:

Bolt area = 1.00 in.^{2};
Sleeve area = 0.60 in.^{2}.

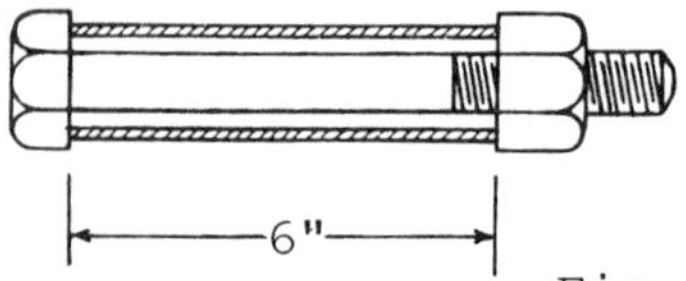

Fig. 1.

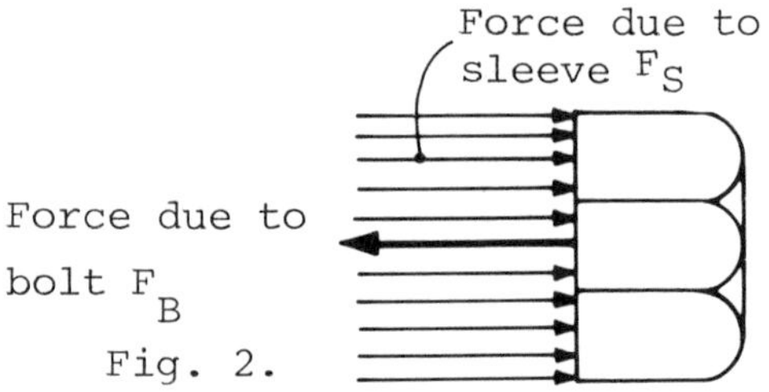

Fig. 2.

Solution: We will first apply equilibrium conditions to the nut. Figure 2 shows a free-body diagram.

From $\Sigma F = 0$, we have

$$F_S = F_B \,. \tag{1}$$

Since there are 16 threads to the inch, one full turn produces a movement 1/16" to the left. The quarter turn applied moves the nut 1/4(1/16)" = 1/64 in. This is the total deflection and must equal the deflection of the bolt plus the deflection of the sleeve. This is expressed mathematically as

$$\delta_T = \delta_{\text{sleeve, comp.}} + \delta_{\text{bolt, tension}} = \frac{1}{64}\text{ in.} \tag{2}$$

For simple extension or compression in one dimension, we have

$$\delta = \frac{FL}{AE} \qquad \text{or} \qquad F = \frac{AE\delta}{L} . \tag{3}$$

From (3) and (1), we have

$$F_B = \frac{A_B E_B \delta_B}{L_B} = \frac{A_s E_s \delta_s}{L_s} = F_s \tag{4}$$

where B subscripts refer to the bolt, and s subscripts refer to the sleeve. Substituting values into (4), we obtain

$$\frac{(1 \text{ in.}^2)(E_B)(\delta_B)}{6''} = \frac{(.6 \text{ in.}^2)(E_s)(\delta_s)}{6''} .$$

Since bolt and sleeve are both steel, $E_B = E_s$ and cancel out. Therefore

$$\delta_B = .6\delta_s \tag{5}$$

From (2),

$$\delta_s + .6\delta_s = \frac{1}{64} \text{ in.} = 1.6\delta_s$$

$$\delta_s = .0097656 \text{ in.}$$

From (5), $\delta_B = .00586$ in.

We can now use (3) to solve for F:

$$F = F_B = \frac{(1 \text{ in.}^2)(30 \times 10^6 \text{ psi})(.00586 \text{ in.})}{6''}$$

$$F_B = 29{,}300 \text{ lb.}$$

• PROBLEM 1-3

Figure 1 shows a truss with the loads given. The truss material is aluminum, which has a Young's modulus of 10×10^6 psi. All the outer members of the truss have a cross-sectional area of 4 in.^{2}, and each of the three inner members has an area of 2 in.^{2}. Determine how much the length of each member changes due to the loads shown in Fig. 1.

Solution: This is a truss problem. It is desired to find the change in length of each member of the truss, due to the external and internal forces which act on this structure. It is helpful to draw the force equilibrium

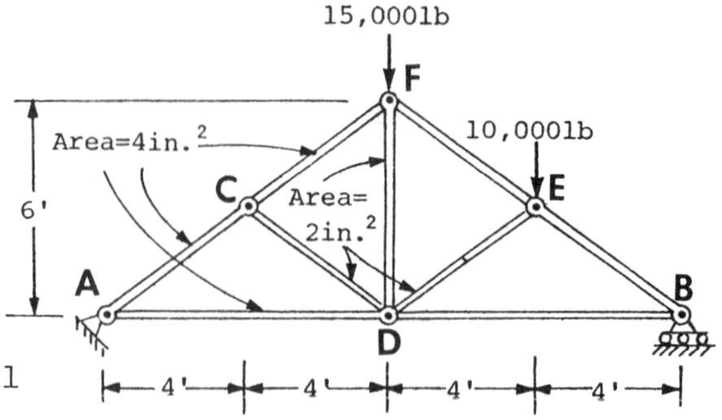

Fig. 1

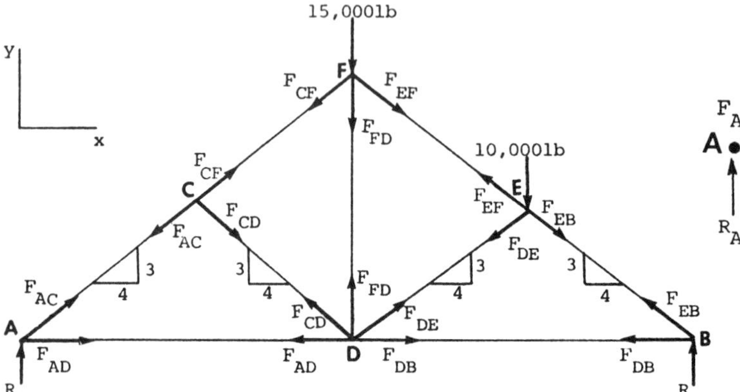

Fig. 2

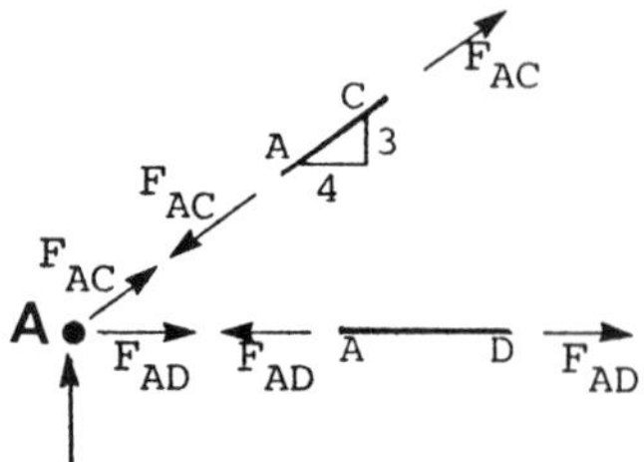

Fig. 2a

diagram shown in Fig. 2. All of the applied, reaction, and internal forces acting on the pins are indicated. The applied and reaction forces are shown acting in their true directions, while the internal forces are assumed to be directed away from the pins on which they act (see Fig. 2). This corresponds to tensile forces acting on each of the members of the truss. The true directions of the internal forces will be determined.

To begin, the procedure for finding the deformations is to determine: (1) the unknown external reactions (using the conditions for static equilibrium), (2) the internal forces for each member, and (3) the change in length of each member (using Hooke's Law). Then by considering the geometric compatibility of the truss, the deformed shape of the whole truss is found.

(1) Use the conditions for static equilibrium to find the reaction forces on the truss. The conditions for static equilibrium for a body require the sum of the external forces acting on the body to be equal to zero. Also, the moment about any point in the body must be zero. Using this information, the reaction forces R_A and R_B can be found (see Fig. 2).

Look at the reaction due to the support at A. The reaction has two components: horizontal and vertical. Since there are no forces acting on the truss in the horizontal direction, the horizontal component of the reaction at A is zero, leaving only the vertical component as the reaction, R_A.

The reactions are evaluated using the equations of static equilibrium as follows:

$$\Sigma F_y = 0 \quad \uparrow +$$

$$R_A + R_B - 15{,}000 - 10{,}000 = 0$$

$$R_A + R_B = 25{,}000 \qquad (1)$$

$$\Sigma M_A = 0 \quad +\circlearrowleft$$

$$R_B(16) - 10{,}000(12) - 15{,}000(8) = 0$$

$$R_B = \frac{120{,}000 + 120{,}000}{16}$$

$$R_B = 15{,}000 \text{ lb.}$$

Substitute this value into (1):

$$R_A + 15{,}000 = 25{,}000$$

$$R_A = 10{,}000 \text{ lb.}$$

(2) The internal forces for each member are now found. Look at Fig. 2. The force in each member is found using $\Sigma F_x = 0$ and $\Sigma F_y = 0$. Take each pin and add the forces acting on it in the vertical and horizontal directions. By setting the sums of the forces equal to zero, equations are developed that can be solved to get the magnitudes of the forces. If a force is found to be negative, it acts in the direction opposite to that assumed in Fig. 2.

An expanded picture of the forces acting on pin A is shown in Fig. 2A.

$$\Sigma F_y = 0 \quad \uparrow +$$

$$F_{AC} \sin(\tan^{-1} \tfrac{3}{4}) + R_A = 0$$

$$F_{AC}(\tfrac{3}{5}) + 10{,}000 = 0$$

$$F_{AC} = -16{,}670 \text{ lb.}$$

Hence, F_{AC} acts in the direction opposite to that assumed in Fig. 2. Therefore member AC is under compression.

$$\Sigma F_x = 0 \quad \rightarrow +$$

$$F_{AC}\cos(\tan^{-1} \tfrac{3}{4}) + F_{AD} = 0$$

$$-16{,}670(\tfrac{4}{5}) + F_{AD} = 0$$

$$F_{AD} = 13{,}330 \text{ lb.}$$

Look at pin C (see Fig. 2).

$$\Sigma F_x = 0 \rightarrow +$$

$$-F_{AC}\cos(\tan^{-1} \tfrac{3}{4}) + F_{CF}\cos(\tan^{-1} \tfrac{3}{4}) + F_{CD}\cos(\tan^{-1} \tfrac{3}{4}) = 0$$

$$-(-16,670)(\tfrac{4}{5}) + F_{CF}(\tfrac{4}{5}) + F_{CD}(\tfrac{4}{5}) = 0$$

$$F_{CF} + F_{CD} = -16,670 \qquad (2)$$

$$\Sigma F_y = 0 \uparrow +$$

$$F_{CF}\sin(\tan^{-1} \tfrac{3}{4}) - F_{AC}\sin(\tan^{-1} \tfrac{3}{4}) - F_{CD}\sin(\tan^{-1} \tfrac{3}{4}) = 0$$

$$F_{CF}(\tfrac{3}{5}) - F_{AC}(\tfrac{3}{5}) - F_{CD}(\tfrac{3}{5}) = 0$$

$$F_{CF} + 16,670 - F_{CD} = 0$$

$$F_{CF} - F_{CD} = -16,670. \qquad (3)$$

Solve (2) and (3) by adding the equations together:

$$2F_{CF} + 0 = 2(-16,670)$$

$$F_{CF} = -16,670 \text{ lb.}$$

$$F_{CD} = 0 \text{ lb.}$$

Notice that F_{CF} and F_{AC} are equal in magnitude and opposite in direction, because $F_{CD} = 0$.

Now look at support B (see Fig. 2).

$$\Sigma F_y = 0 \uparrow +$$

$$F_{EB}\sin(\tan^{-1} \tfrac{3}{4}) + R_B = 0$$

$$F_{EB}(\tfrac{3}{5}) + 15,000 = 0$$

$$F_{EB} = -25,000 \text{ lb.}$$

$$\Sigma F_x = 0 \rightarrow +$$

$$-F_{EB}\cos(\tan^{-1} \tfrac{3}{4}) - F_{DB} = 0$$

$$25,000(\tfrac{4}{5}) - F_{DB} = 0$$

$$F_{DB} = 20,000 \text{ lb.}$$

Look at pin E.

$$\Sigma F_x = 0 \leftarrow +$$

$$-F_{EB}\cos(\tan^{-1}\tfrac{3}{4}) + F_{EF}\cos(\tan^{-1}\tfrac{3}{4}) + F_{DE}\cos(\tan^{-1}\tfrac{3}{4}) = 0$$

$$25,000(\tfrac{4}{5}) + F_{EF}(\tfrac{4}{5}) + F_{DE}(\tfrac{4}{5}) = 0$$

$$F_{EF} + F_{DE} = -25,000 \text{ lb.} \qquad (4)$$

$$\Sigma F_y = 0 \uparrow +$$

$$F_{EF}\sin(\tan^{-1}\tfrac{3}{4}) - F_{EB}\sin(\tan^{-1}\tfrac{3}{4}) - F_{DE}\sin(\tan^{-1}\tfrac{3}{4}) - 1000 = 0$$

$$F_{EF}(\tfrac{3}{5}) - F_{EB}(\tfrac{3}{5}) - F_{DE}(\tfrac{3}{5}) = 10,000$$

$$F_{EF} + 25,000 - F_{DE} = 10,000(\tfrac{5}{3})$$

$$F_{EF} - F_{DE} = -8,330 \text{ lb.} \qquad (5)$$

Solve (4) and (5) by adding the two equations together:

$$2F_{EF} + 0 = -8,330 - 25,000$$

$$F_{EF} = -16,670 \text{ lb.}$$

Substituting the value of F_{EF} into (4) and solving for F_{ED} results in:

$$F_{ED} = -8330 \text{ lb.}$$

Now look at pin F.

$$\Sigma F_y = 0 \downarrow +$$

$$15,000 + F_{FD} + F_{CF}\sin(\tan^{-1}\tfrac{3}{4}) + F_{EF}\sin(\tan^{-1}\tfrac{3}{4}) = 0$$

$$15,000 + F_{FD} - 16,670(\tfrac{3}{5}) - 16,670(\tfrac{3}{5}) = 0$$

$F_{FD} = 5,000$ lb.

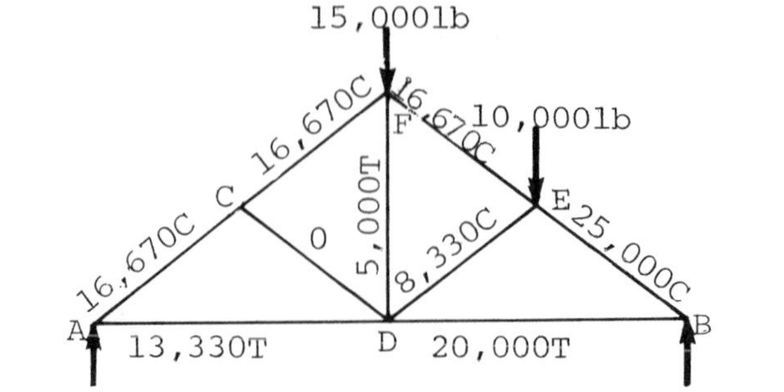

Fig. 3.

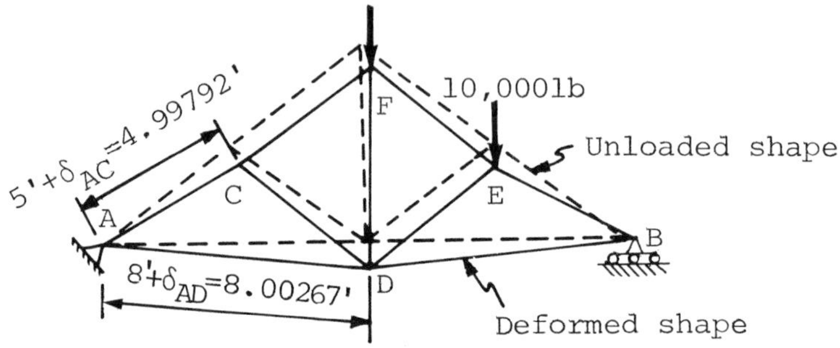

Fig. 4.

All the bar forces have now been calculated. They are shown on Fig. 3, where the symbols "T" and "C" are used to indicate whether the force is tensile (+) or compressive (-).

The deformations due to the forces just calculated have to be geometrically compatible. The members of the truss make up a series of triangles and the truss is the sum of these triangles. If the pins are frictionless and allow free rotation, then the three members which form any one triangle also will form a triangle if the three members change their lengths. Furthermore, adjacent triangles can distort independently of each other in this problem, since the roller support at B is free to move horizontally to accommodate the distortion of the triangles which make up the truss. From this we conclude that each member of the truss is free to lengthen or shorten without any restraint being imposed by the other members of the truss. The overall behavior of the truss is indicated in Fig. 4, where the deflections have been greatly exaggerated for purposes of illustration.

With most engineering materials, the relationship between force and deformation for small deformations is linear. This is known as Hooke's Law. This linear relationship follows immediately from the basic definitions of stress and strain:

$$\sigma = \frac{F}{A}, \qquad \varepsilon = \frac{\delta}{L}, \qquad E = \frac{\sigma}{\varepsilon}$$

Substituting for σ and ε results in:

$$E = \frac{FL}{A\delta}$$

The deformation is therefore:

$$\delta = \frac{FL}{AE} \tag{6}$$

Everything on the right hand side of Eq.(6) is known. The forces have been calculated, Young's modulus, E, the member lengths, L, and areas, A, are all given. These values are substituted into Eq.(6) to find the deformation in each member as follows:

$$\delta_{AC} = \left(\frac{FL}{AE}\right)_{AC} = \frac{-16{,}670\text{lb.}(5\text{ft.})}{4\text{in.}^2(10\text{x}10^6\text{lb./in.}^2)}$$
$$= -0.00208 \text{ ft. (compression)}$$

$$\delta_{AD} = \left(\frac{FL}{AE}\right)_{AD} = \frac{13{,}330(8)}{4(10\text{x}10^6)} = 0.00267 \text{ ft. (extension)}$$

$$\delta_{CD} = \left(\frac{FL}{AE}\right)_{CD} = 0 \text{ (no deformation)}$$

$$\delta_{CF} = \left(\frac{FL}{AE}\right)_{CF} = \frac{-16{,}670(5)}{4(10\text{x}10^6)} = -0.00208 \text{ ft. (compression)}$$

$$\delta_{FD} = \left(\frac{FL}{AE}\right)_{FD} = \frac{5000(6)}{2(10\text{x}10^6)} = 0.00150 \text{ ft. (extension)}$$

$$\delta_{EF} = \left(\frac{FL}{AE}\right)_{EF} = \frac{-16{,}670(5)}{4(10\text{x}10^6)} = -0.00208 \text{ ft. (compression)}$$

$$\delta_{DE} = \left(\frac{FL}{AE}\right)_{DE} = \frac{-8{,}330(5)}{2(10\text{x}10^6)} = -0.00208 \text{ ft. (compression)}$$

$$\delta_{EB} = \left(\frac{FL}{AE}\right)_{EB} = \frac{-25{,}000(5)}{4(10\text{x}10^6)} = -0.00313 \text{ ft. (compression)}$$

$$\delta_{DB} = \left(\frac{FL}{AE}\right)_{DB} = \frac{20{,}000(8)}{4(10\text{x}10^6)} = 0.00400 \text{ ft. (extension)}$$

The change in length of each member has now been determined. Thus it is seen that this relatively complex problem can be solved by repeated application of basic principles.

• PROBLEM 1-4

Determine the relative displacement of points A and D of the steel rod of variable cross-sectional area shown in Fig. 1 when it is subjected to the four concentrated forces P_1, P_2, P_3, and P_4 equal to 40, 100, 80, 20 kips respectively. Let Modulus of Elasticity, E = 30×10^6 psi.

Solution: For such a problem, a check must first be made

FIG. 1

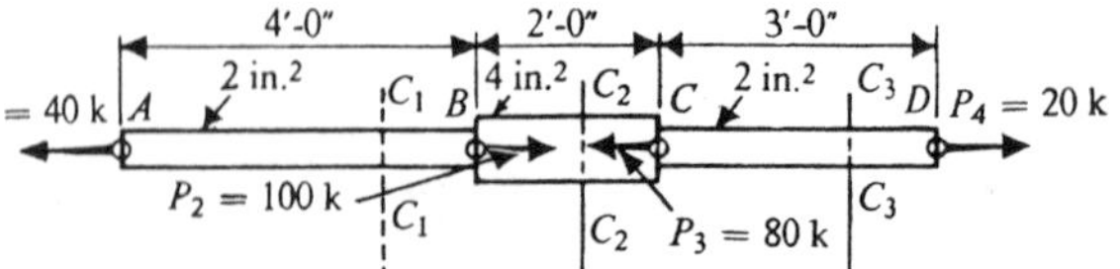

FIG. 2

FIG. 3

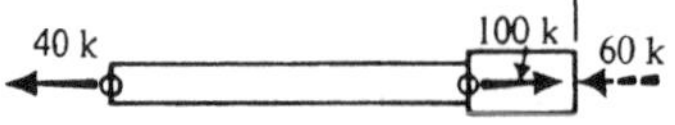

FIG. 4

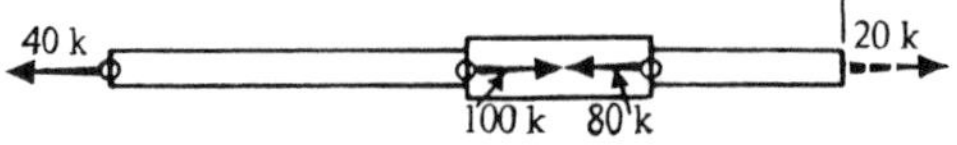

FIG. 5

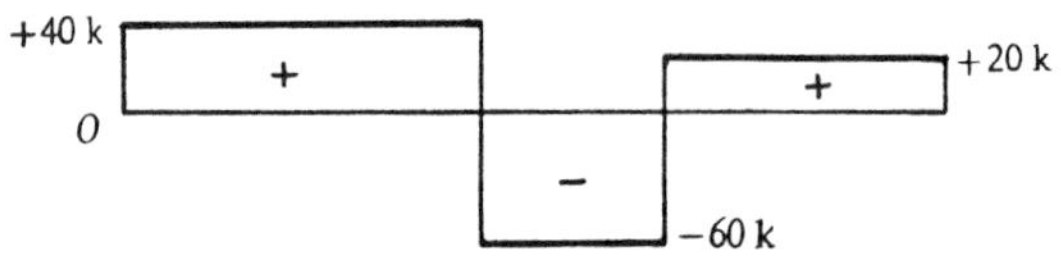

to ascertain that the body as a whole is in equilibrium, i.e.

$$\Sigma F_x = 0 \overset{+}{\rightarrow}$$

$$-P_1 + P_2 - P_3 + P_4 = -40 + 100 - 80 + 20 = 0$$

and $\quad \Sigma F_y = 0 \overset{+}{\uparrow} \qquad 0 = 0$

so the rod as a whole is in equilibrium. Next, the variation of P along the length of the bar must be studied. This may be done conveniently with the aid of sketches as shown in Figs. 2, 3, and 4, which show that no matter where a section C_1-C_1 is taken between points A and B, the force in the rod is P = +40 kips. Similarly, between B and C, P = -60 kips, and between C and D, P = +20 kips. An axial-force diagram for these quantities is in Fig. 5. The variation of A is in Fig. 1. Neither P nor A is a continuous function along the rod since both have jumps or sudden changes in their values. Hence, in integrating, unless singularity functions are used, the limits of integration must be "broken." Thus applying the equation of deflection and noting that for the origin at A the constant $C_1 = 0$, one has

$$u = \int_0^L \frac{P(x)\,dx}{A(x)E} = \int_A^B \frac{P_{AB}dx}{A_{AB}E} + \int_B^C \frac{P_{BC}dx}{A_{BC}E} + \int_C^D \frac{P_{CD}dx}{A_{CD}E}$$

So the total relative displacement of points A and D is the sum of relative displacement of points (A,B), (B,C), and (C,D). In the last three integrals the respective P and A are constants between the limits shown. The subscripts of P and A denote the range of applicability of the function; thus P_{AB} applies in the interval AB, etc.

$$u = \sum \frac{PL}{AE}$$

$$u = \frac{(40\text{kips})(1000\frac{\text{pounds}}{\text{kips}})(4\text{-ft.})(12\frac{\text{in.}}{\text{ft.}})}{(2\text{-in.}^2)(30 \times 10^6 \text{ psi})}$$

$$+ \frac{(40\text{-}100\text{kips})(1000\frac{\text{lbs.}}{\text{kips}})(2\text{-ft})(12\frac{\text{in.}}{\text{ft.}})}{(4\text{-in.}^2)(30 \times 10^6 \text{ psi})}$$

$$+ \frac{(-60+80\text{kips})(1000\frac{\text{lbs.}}{\text{kips}})(3\text{-ft})(12\frac{\text{in}}{\text{ft}})}{(2\text{-in.}^2)(30 \times 10^6 \text{ psi})}$$

$$u = 0.032 - 0.012 + 0.012 = 0.032 \text{ in.}$$

This operation adds, or superposes, the individual deformations of the three "separate" rods. Each of these rods is subjected to a constant force. The positive sign of the answer indicates that the rod elongates as a positive sign is associated with tensile forces. The equality of the absolute values of the deformations in lengths BC and CD is purely accidental. Note that in spite of the relatively large stresses present in the rod, the value of u is small. Finally, do not fail to observe that units of all quantities have been changed to be consistent. Forces originally given in kips have been changed into pounds, lengths into inches.

• PROBLEM 1-5

Figure 1 shows the pendulum of a clock which has a 3-lb. weight suspended by three rods of 30-in. length. Two of the rods are made of brass and the third of steel. How much of the 3-lb. suspended weight is carried by each rod?

Solution: Our model of the system is shown in Fig. 2. We assume that the support at the top and the weight at the bottom are stiff and act as rigid members. Because of the symmetry of the rod arrangement and the loading, each brass rod will carry the same load and all three rods will elongate the same amount. There are four unknowns, two forces and two deflections. With one force relation, one geometrical condition and two relations between forces and deformations, we can solve for the four unknowns.

We first find the force equilibrium. $\Sigma M = 0$ is satisfied because of the symmetry of the force system. $\Sigma F = 0$ is satisfied by

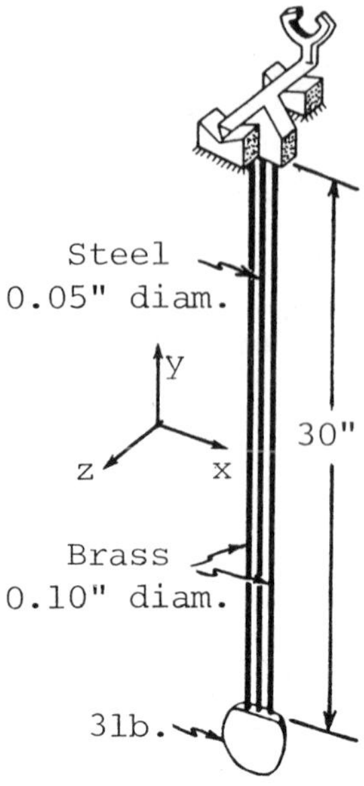

Fig. 1.

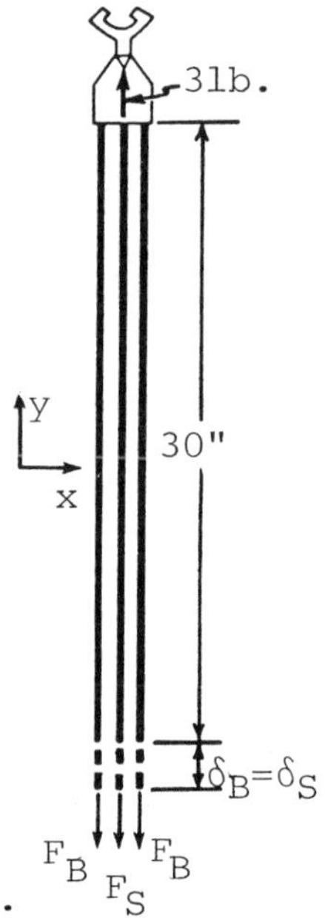

Fig. 2.

$$\Sigma F_y = 3 - F_s - 2F_B = 0. \qquad \text{(a)}$$

Now find the geometric compatibility. The rods extend equal amounts, and so

$$\delta_s = \delta_B. \qquad \text{(b)}$$

To find the relation between forces and deformations, use Hooke's Law to obtain

$$\delta_s = \frac{F_s L_s}{A_s E_s} \qquad \delta_B = \frac{F_B L_B}{A_B E_B} . \qquad \text{(c)}$$

Combining (b) and (c) yields

$$F_s = \frac{A_s}{A_B} \frac{E_s}{E_B} \frac{L_B}{L_s} F_B$$

$$= \frac{(0.05)^2}{(0.10)^2} \frac{(30\text{x}10^6)}{(15\text{x}10^6)} \frac{30}{30} F_B = 0.50F_B. \qquad \text{(d)}$$

Combining (a) and (d) yields

$$3 - 0.5F_B - 2F_B = 0$$

$$2.5F_B = 3$$

$$F_B = 1.20 \text{ lb.}$$

$$F_S = 0.50\ F_B$$

$$F_S = 0.50(1.20)\ \text{lb.}$$

$$F_S = 0.60\ \text{lb.}$$

From (a):

$$F_B = 1.20\ \text{lb.}$$

• PROBLEM 1-6

A triangular frame supporting a load of 5,000 lbs. is shown in Figure 1. The size of members and the type of connections are specified. Find the displacement at the point D due to the 5,000-lb. load carried by the chain hoist.

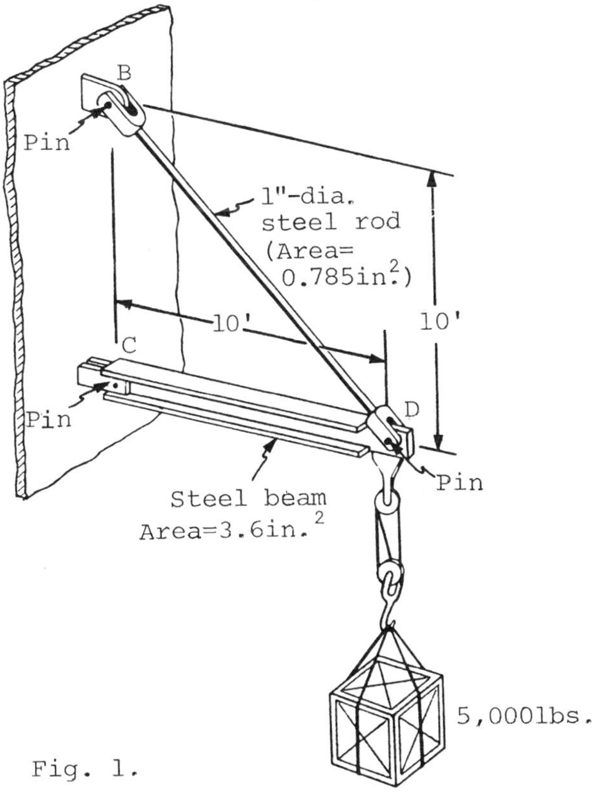

Fig. 1.

Solution: In this problem, the members of the frame are subjected to forces and deformation will occur as a result of these internal forces. The deformations of these members will be restricted by geometrical compatibility. Several assumptions must be made in solving this problem. First, assume that the weight of the frame and the hoist are negligible. Next, assume that the pinned joints are frictionless.

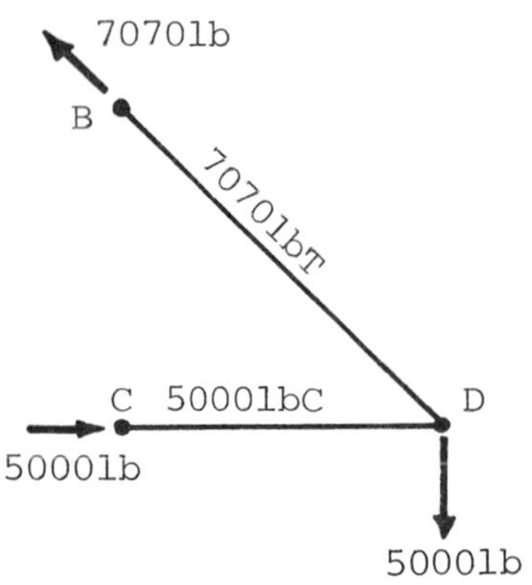

Fig. 2.

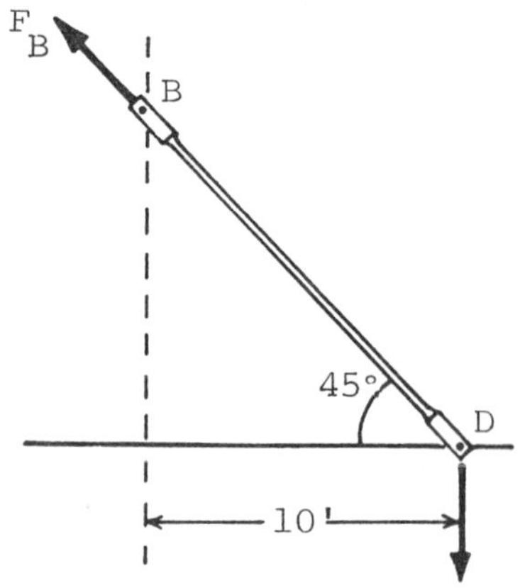

Fig. 3.

In the free-body diagram of Fig. 2 there will be forces F_B and F_C at the wall-support points, but no moments (because of the assumption that the pinned joints are frictionless). The directions of F_B and F_C are known here since all members of the truss are two-force members. The line of action of the forces is in the direction of the member. Any other configuration of force lines would imply that bending moments existed in the beams. In the free-body diagram of bar BD in Fig. 3, there are only two forces acting on the member; therefore F_B must be along the line BD in order to achieve equilibrium. Returning to the entire frame in Fig. 2, it can be concluded that since the three forces acting on the frame have to intersect at a point, F_C must also be collinear with CD as shown. Taking the entire frame as a free-body diagram, the force equilibrium is

$$\Sigma F_y \uparrow + = 0, \quad F_B \sin 45° - 5{,}000 \text{ lb.} = 0$$

$$F_B = \frac{5{,}000}{\sin 45°}$$

$$F_B = 7.070 \text{ lb. (tension)}$$

$$\Sigma F_x \rightarrow + = 0, \quad F_C - F_B \cos 45° = 0$$

$$F_C = F_B \cos 45° = 7.070 \cos 45°$$

$$= 5{,}000 \text{ lb. (compressive).}$$

Notice that the force F_B acts away from the pin at D, so it is tensile, and the force F_C acts toward the pin at D, making it compressive.

By Hooke's Law, the deformations of the members BD and CD due to the forces acting on the ends of the members are obtained. These deformations are:

$$\delta_{BD} = \left(\frac{FL}{AE}\right)_{BD} = \frac{7.070(14.14)(12)}{0.785(30\text{x}10^6)} = 0.0510 \text{ in.}$$

$$\delta_{CD} = \left(\frac{FL}{AE}\right)_{CD} = \frac{-5,000(10)(12)}{3.6(30\text{x}10^6)} = -0.0056 \text{ in.}$$

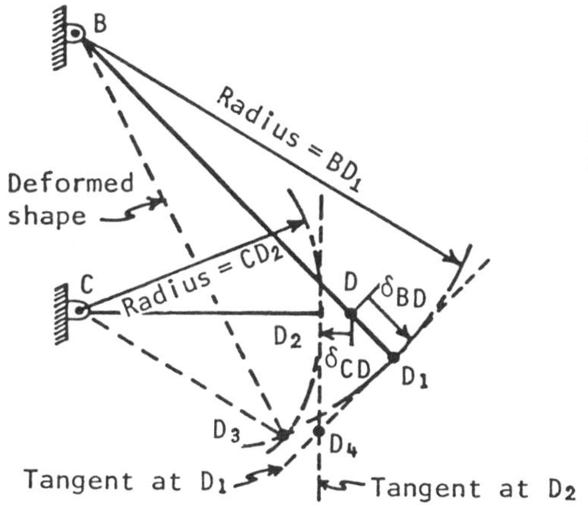

Fig. 4

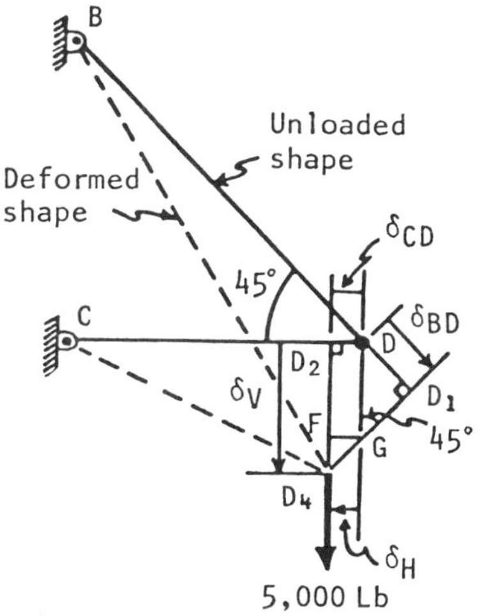

Fig. 5

Geometric compatibility of the deformations requires that the bars BD and CD move in such a way that, while the bars change lengths by the amounts calculated above they remain straight and also remain fastened together at D. The mechanism by which this can be accomplished is illustrated in Fig. 4. Assume, for the moment, that the bars are uncoupled at D and allowed to change lengths by δ_{BD} and δ_{CD} so that the bars now are of lengths BD_1 and CD_2 , respectively. We see from the sketch that we can bring the ends D_1 and D_2 into coincidence without further change in the lengths of the bars by rotating the bars BD_1 and CD_2 about B and C as centers. Thus, due to the action of the 5,000-lb. load, the point D moves to D_3 , and the deformed shape of the structure is as shown in the dotted position in Fig. 4.

Locating the point D_3 at the intersection of the two arcs in Fig. 4 is a rather lengthy calculation. Fortunately, since the deformations of the bars are only very small fractions of the lengths (these deformations are exaggerated greatly in Fig. 4), we can, with great accuracy, replace the arcs by the tangents to the arcs at D_1 and D_2 and obtain the intersection D_4 as an approximation to the location of D_3.

Employing this approximation of replacing the arcs with tangents, we illustrate in Fig. 5 the calculation of the horizontal and vertical displacements by which the point D moves to D_4. We begin by laying off δ_{BD} and δ_{CD} to locate the points D_1 and D_2. At D_1 and D_2 we erect the perpendiculars (tangents) D_1G and D_2F; these perpendiculars intersect in the desired point D_4. From the geometry of Fig. 5 we then can write

$$\delta_H = \delta_{CD} = 0.0056 \text{ in.}$$

$$\delta_V = D_2F + FD_4 = DG + FG$$

$$= \sqrt{2}\,\delta_{BD} + \delta_{CD} = 0.0778 \text{ in.}$$

• PROBLEM 1-7

The stiff horizontal beam AB in Fig. 1 is supported by two soft copper rods AC and BD of the same cross-sectional area but of different lengths. The load-deformation diagram for the copper is shown in Fig. 2. A vertical load of 34,000 lb is to be suspended from a roller which rides on the horizontal beam. Where can the roller be located so that the beam AB will still be horizontal in the deflected position? If the load is increased from 34,000 lb. to 68,000 lb., would the location still be the same?

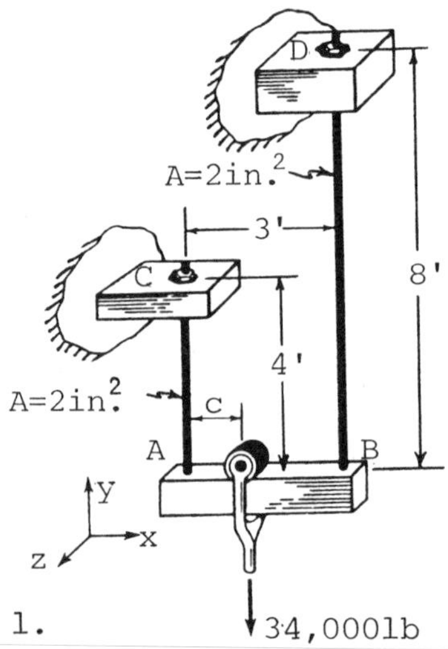

Fig. 1.

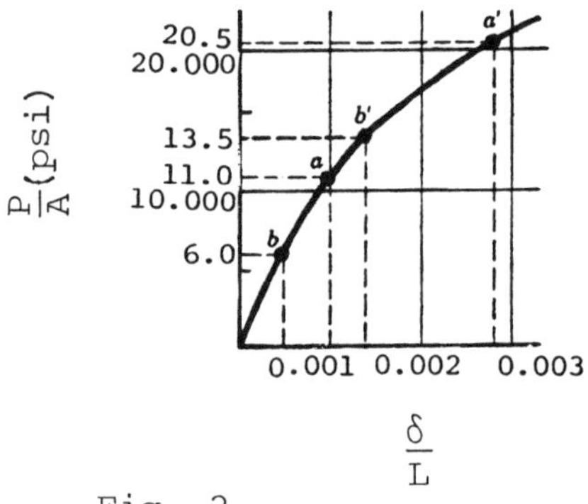

Fig. 2.

Solution: Assume that the points A and B deflect vertically to A' and B', as shown in Fig. 3. The beam is considered to be rigid. Also assume that there are no horizontal forces or couples acting between the beam and the bars. Now find the force equilibrium. The sum of forces and moments are zeros for the free body of the beam in Fig. 3.

$$\Sigma F_Y = F_A + F_B - 34,000 = 0 \qquad \text{(a)}$$

$$\Sigma M_{A'} = 3F_B - c(34,000) = 0.$$

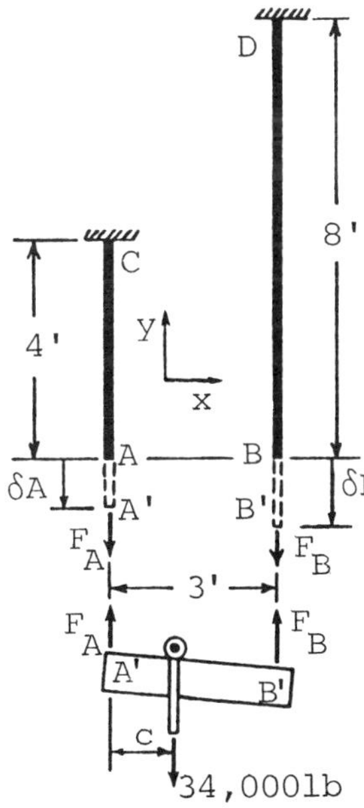

Fig. 3

Now find the geometric compatibility. Since the beam moves down without rotating,

$$\delta_A = \delta_B \qquad \text{(b)}$$

Using this equality, from the lengths of the bars in Fig. 1 it is seen that

$$\frac{\delta_A}{L_A} = \frac{\delta_B}{L_A} = \frac{\delta_B}{48} = 2\frac{\delta_B}{96} = 2\frac{\delta_B}{L_B} \; . \qquad \text{(c)}$$

Next, find the relation between force and deformation. The diagram in Fig. 2 gives the relation between force and elongation. For example, if we enter the diagram with F_B/A_B = 10,000 psi, we find δ_B/L_B = 0.0009. (d)

The relations (a), (c), and (d) represent the analysis of the physics of the problem. Now combine (a), (c), and (d) mathematically to find the correct location of the roller. Dividing the first of Eqs.(a) by A_A yields

$$\frac{F_A}{A_A} + \frac{F_B}{A_A} = \frac{34{,}000}{A_A} \; .$$

Substituting $A_A = A_B = 2$ in.^{2}, the following relation is obtained:

$$\frac{F_A}{A_A} + \frac{F_B}{A_B} = 17{,}000 \text{ psi.} \qquad \text{(e)}$$

Now select an arbitrary value of δ_B/L_B. Then, using (c) to obtain δ_A/L_A , enter the diagram in Fig. 2 and obtain F_B/A_B and F_A/A_A. Then check to see if these values satisfy (e). If (e) is not satisfied, make a new guess for δ_B/L_B and obtain new values for F_A/A_A and F_B/A_B. Proceeding in this way, we find the points a and b in Fig. 2. From these points,

$$\frac{F_A}{A_A} = 11{,}000 \text{ psi} \qquad F_A = 22{,}000 \text{ lb.}$$

$$\frac{F_B}{A_B} = 6{,}000 \text{ psi} \qquad F_B = 12{,}000 \text{ lb.} \qquad \text{(f)}$$

$$\frac{\delta_A}{L_A} = 0.001 \text{ in./in.} \qquad \delta_A = \delta_B = 0.048 \text{ in.}$$

Substituting this value for F_B in the second of Eqs.(a), the required location of the roller is obtained:

$$c = 1.06 \text{ ft.} \qquad \text{(g)}$$

If the analysis is repeated for a load of 68,000 lb., the solution would be represented by the points a' and b' in Fig. 2, with the results

$$F_A = 41{,}000 \text{ lb.}$$

$$F_B = 27{,}000 \text{ lb.} \qquad \text{(h)}$$

$$\delta_A = \delta_B = 0.13 \text{ in.}$$

$$c = 1.19 \text{ ft.}$$

It is not surprising that this value of c differs from the previous result, since a nonlinear material does not produce equal increments of elongation for equal increments of load. For example, in Fig. 2 a value of P/A of 10,000 psi produces a δ/L of 0.0009, whereas the next increment of 10,000 psi produces an increment in δ/L of 0.0017.

• PROBLEM 1-8

In a test on an engine, a braking force is supplied through a lever arm EF to a steel brake band CBAD which is in contact with half the circumference of a 24-in.-diameter flywheel. The brake band is 1/16 in. thick and 2 in. wide and is lined with a relatively soft material which has a kinetic coefficient of friction of f = 0.4 with respect to the rotating flywheel. How much elongation will there be in section AB of the brake band when the braking force is such that there is a tension of 9,000 lb. in the section BC of the band?

Solution: A free-body sketch of section AB of the brake band is shown in Fig. 3. There will be forces acting at all points of contact between the band and the drum. These forces are shown as components normal and tangential to

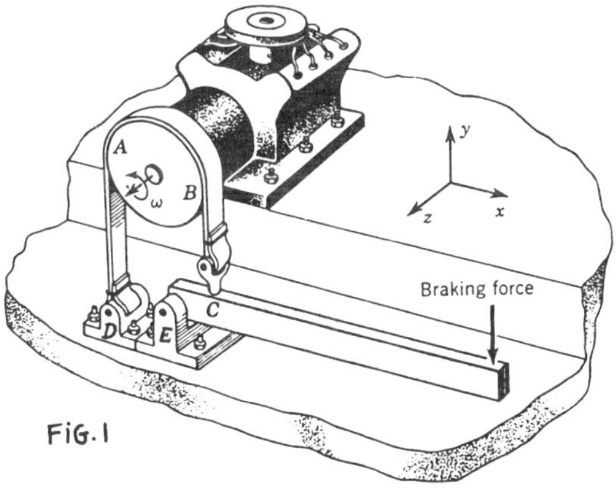

FiG.1

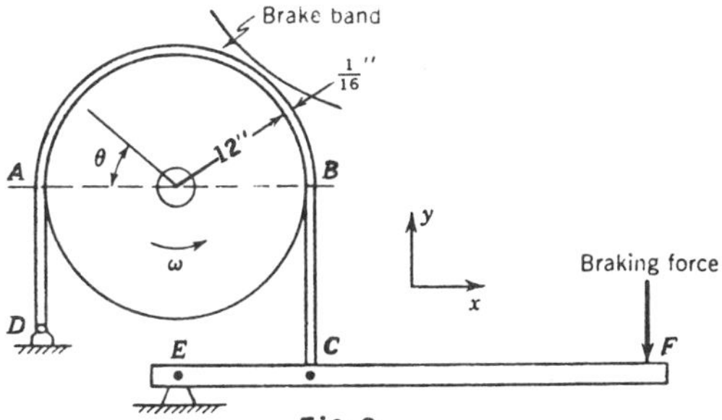

FiG.2

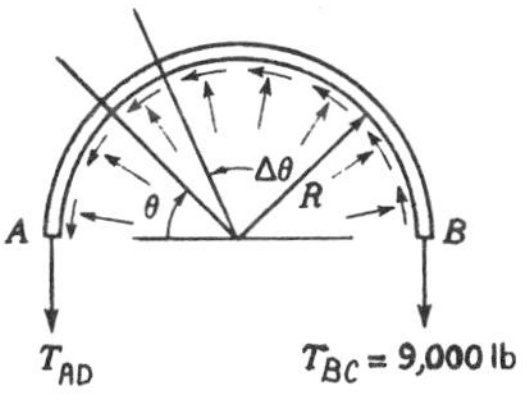

FiG.3

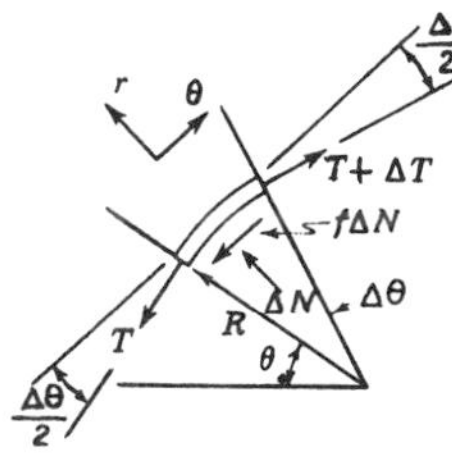

FiG.4

the surface of contact, where we assume the tangential component is caused by friction between the flywheel and the lining and thus is shown acting in the same direction as the motion of the flywheel past the band. Figure 4 shows a free-body sketch of an element of the band. It is assumed that the force in the band is a tangential force T which varies along the circumference, changing by an amount ΔT over the length $R\Delta\theta$. The total radial component of force on the element is given the symbol ΔN, and the tangential component caused by the friction then is $f\Delta N$. We shall assume that the force T is carried entirely by the steel band and not at all by the lining, which was described as being relatively soft.

It is important to emphasize that because the tension varies along the brake band we will derive a differential equation for its variation along the band. We do this by considering the differential element shown in Fig. 4 and letting the size of the element shrink to zero. By letting the element size become small to the point of vanishing, we find the conditions which must be satisfied at a point on the band.

First find the force equilibrium. All the forces on the small element in Fig. 4 may be considered concurrent, and thus equilibrium is satisfied when $\Sigma F = 0$. All forces are parallel to the $r\theta$ plane, and $\Sigma F = 0$ can be satisfied conveniently by requiring that the sum of the force components in the r and θ directions be zero.

$$\Sigma F_r = \Delta N - T \sin \frac{\Delta\theta}{2} - (T + \Delta T) \sin \frac{\Delta\theta}{2} = 0 \qquad \text{(a)}$$

$$\Sigma F_\theta = (T + \Delta T) \cos \frac{\Delta\theta}{2} - T \cos \frac{\Delta\theta}{2} - f\Delta N = 0 \qquad \text{(b)}$$

Considering the free body in Fig. 4, we note that the angle $\Delta\theta$ is small (in the limit, zero). For small angles it is frequently convenient to make the following approximations:

$$\sin \theta \approx \theta$$

$$\tan \theta \approx \theta$$

$$\cos \theta \approx 1$$

Using these approximations, Eq. (a) becomes

$$\Delta N - T \frac{\Delta\theta}{2} - (T + \Delta T) \frac{\Delta\theta}{2} = 0$$

$$\Delta N - T \frac{\Delta\theta}{2} - T \frac{\Delta\theta}{2} + \frac{\Delta T \cdot \Delta\theta}{2} = 0.$$

We ignore $\frac{\Delta T \cdot \Delta\theta}{2}$ because it has an additional differential element, and obtain

$$\Delta N = T\Delta\theta. \qquad \text{(c)}$$

Eq. (b) becomes

$$(T + \Delta T) - T - f\Delta N = 0$$

$$\Delta T = f \cdot \Delta N$$

$$\Delta T = f \cdot T \cdot \Delta\theta$$

$$\frac{\Delta T}{\Delta\theta} = fT. \qquad \text{(d)}$$

In the limit as $\Delta\theta \to 0$ this becomes the derivative

$$\frac{dT}{d\theta} = fT. \qquad \text{(d')}$$

Integrating (d) and satisfying the boundary condition that $T = T_{AD}$ at $\theta = 0$, we obtain

$$\frac{dT}{d\theta} = fT$$

$$\int_{T_{AD}}^{T} \frac{1}{T}\, dT = \int_{0}^{\theta} f\, d\theta$$

$$\ln T \Big|_{T_{AD}}^{T} = f\theta$$

$$\ln T - \ln T_{AD} = f\theta$$

$$\ln \frac{T}{T_{AD}} = f\theta$$

$$\frac{T}{T_{AD}} = e^{f\theta}$$

$$T = T_{AD} e^{f\theta} \qquad \text{(e)}$$

where e is the base of natural logarithms. We now can calculate T_{AD} from the condition that $T = T_{BC} = 9{,}000$ lb. at $\theta = \pi$, and $f = 0.4$. Then,

$$9{,}000 \text{ lb.} = T_{AD} e^{0.4\pi}$$

$$T_{AD} = \frac{9{,}000}{e^{0.4\pi}}$$

$$T_{AD} = 2560$$

$$T = 2560 e^{0.4\theta} \text{ lb.} \qquad \text{(f)}$$

Now determine the relation between force and deformation by applying Hooke's Law to obtain:

$$\Delta\delta = \frac{FL}{AE}$$

$$\Delta\delta = \frac{TR\Delta\theta}{AE} \,. \qquad \text{(g)}$$

We see that the elongation varies with position along the band. To calculate total deflection, we need to consider the integral of the incremental variations along the band. Now consider the geometric compatibility. The total elongation of the brake band from A to B, δ_{AB}, is the sum of the tangential elongations $\Delta\delta$ of the small elements of length $R\Delta\theta$ shown in Fig. 4. In the limit as $\Delta\theta \to 0$ this sum becomes the following integral:

$$\delta_{AB} = \int_{\theta=0}^{\theta=\pi} d\delta = \int_{\theta=0}^{\theta=\pi} \frac{TRd\theta}{AE} . \qquad \text{(h)}$$

Substituting (e) and integrating, we obtain an estimate of the elongation of the section AB:

$$\delta_{AB} = \frac{T_{AD}R}{AE} \int_0^{\pi} e^{f\theta}\, d\theta = \frac{T_{AD}R}{AEf} (e^{f\pi} - 1)$$
$$= \frac{2560(12)(e^{0.4\pi}-1)}{0.125(30x10^6)(0.4)} = 0.051 \text{ in.} \qquad \text{(i)}$$

• PROBLEM 1-9

The rod AB of constant cross-sectional area A and length L is fixed at one end. Force P is applied at the free end of the bar (Fig. 1). Determine the displacement of point A relative to point B, due to P. The elastic modulus of the material is E.

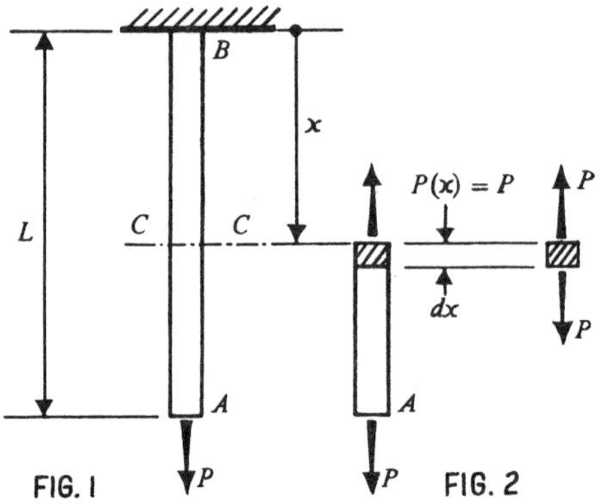

FIG. 1 FIG. 2 FIG. 3

Solution: Neglecting the weight of the beam, the deflection is due only to force P. Drawing the free body diagram (Fig. 2) of an arbitrary section C-C, at any infinitesimal element in the bar the force is P and cross section is A (Fig. 3).

Using the strain-displacement relationship,

$$\varepsilon = \frac{du}{dx}$$

and Hooke's Law, $\varepsilon = \frac{F}{AE}$, one finds

$$\frac{du}{dx} = \frac{F}{AE} \qquad \text{or} \qquad du = \frac{F}{AE}\, dx.$$

By integrating, with F = P, the applied force,

$$u = \int_0^x \frac{P}{AE}\, dx$$

$\frac{P}{AE}$ is constant, so the displacement is

$$u = \frac{P}{AE} x + C_1.$$

Using boundary conditions,

$$\text{at } x = 0,\ u(0) = 0 \Rightarrow C_1 = 0,$$

and the equation of displacement becomes

$$u = \frac{PL}{AE} \quad \text{at } x = L \text{ (at free end)}.$$

The above relation indicates that the deflection of the rod AB is directly proportional to force P and length, and is inversely proportional to area A and modulus of elasticity E.
Another method of solution is to first determine the strain from the stress-strain relationship.

Recall that $\sigma = E\varepsilon$ (a)

where $\sigma \equiv$ axial stress and $\varepsilon \equiv$ axial strain. In this case

$$\sigma = \frac{P}{A}$$

where $A \equiv$ cross-sectional area

$$\varepsilon = \frac{P}{AE}$$

and $\varepsilon = \frac{\Delta}{L}$ where $\Delta \equiv$ displacement.

Therefore $\frac{\Delta}{L} = \frac{P}{AE}$

$$\Delta = \frac{PL}{AE}$$

• PROBLEM 1-10

Find the deflection of point A of the rod AB (Fig. 1), due to its own weight. Assume that the rod AB weighs p_o lb. per inch, and has a constant cross-sectional area, A.

Solution: In this case P(x) (weight of the rod at any distance x from point A) is variable. It is conveniently expressed as $p_o x$ if the origin is taken at A. Applying

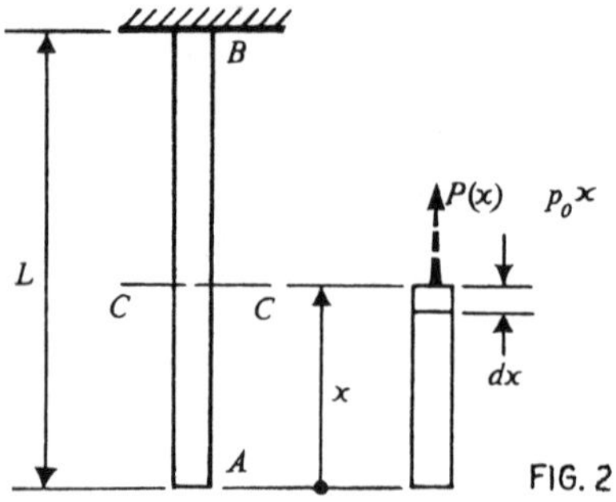

FIG. 1 FIG. 2

the equation for deflection,

$$u = \int_0^x \frac{P(x)dx}{A(x)E}$$

where $A(x) \equiv$ cross-sectional area
$E \equiv$ modulus of elasticity,
and both are constant.

$$\therefore \quad u = \frac{1}{AE}\int_0^x P_o x dx$$

$$u = \frac{P_o x^2}{2AE} + C_1$$

At the boundary B, where x = L, the displacement is zero, i.e., u(L) = 0. This condition must be used to evaluate the constant of integration:

$$u(L) = 0 = \frac{P_o L^2}{2AE} + C_1$$

$$\therefore \quad C_1 = -\frac{P_o L^2}{2AE}$$

So

$$u = \frac{P_o x^2}{2AE} - \frac{P_o L^2}{2AE}$$

$$u = -\frac{P_o}{2AE}(L^2 - x^2)$$

at point A where x = 0 the deflection u is

$$u = -\frac{P_o L^2}{2AE}$$

The negative sign indicates that the displacement u is in the opposite direction to that of positive x. If W designates the total weight of the rod, the absolute maximum deflection is WL/2AE.

A thin ring of internal radius r, thickness t, and width b is subjected to a uniform pressure p (psi) over the entire internal surface, as shown in Fig. 1. A view looking down the axis of the ring is sketched in Fig. 2. Determine the forces in the ring and the deformation of the ring due to the internal pressure.

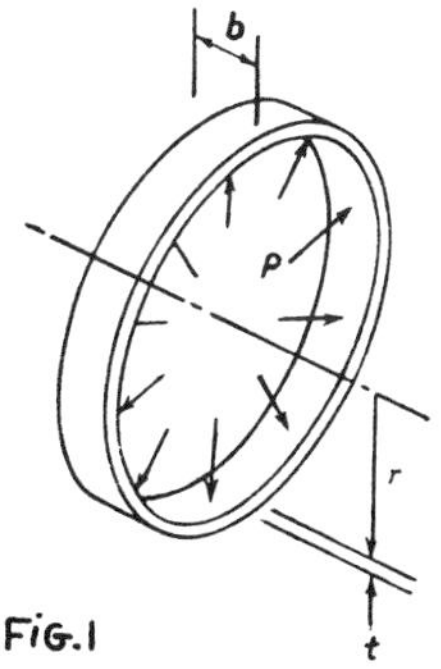

FIG.1

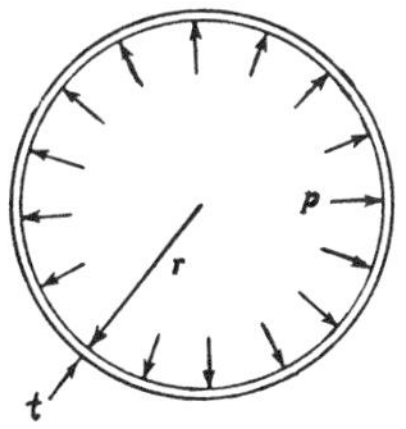

FIG.2

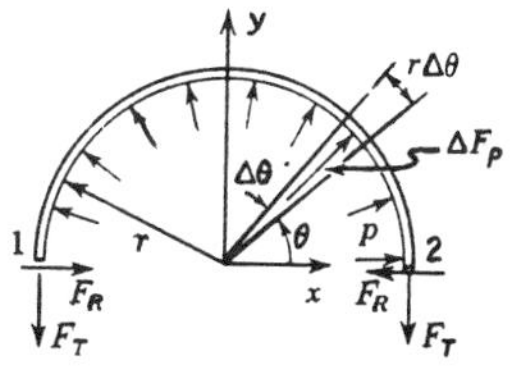

FIG.3

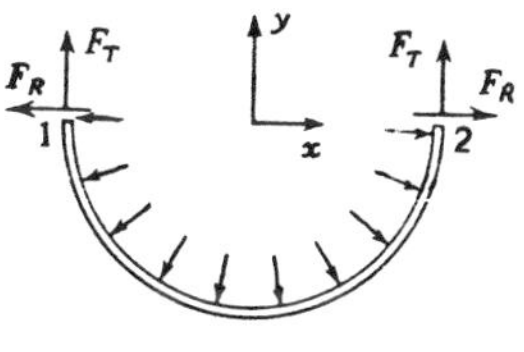

FIG.4

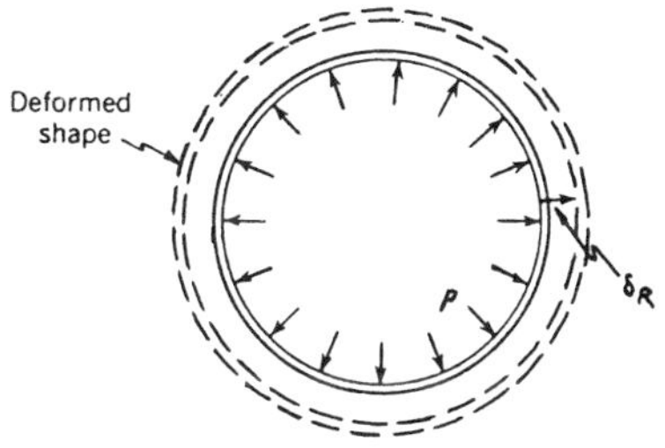

FIG.5

Solution: The model which we assume to represent the behavior of the hoop is shown in Fig. 3, which is a free body obtained by cutting the hoop on a diameter. By symmetry, we assume that the section forces at every point on the ring are the same, and that at the cut sections 1 and 2 there are acting tangential and radial forces F_T and F_R which resist the internal pressure. Note that if, at the section 1, we arbitrarily assign to F_T and F_R the directions shown in Fig. 3, then the directions shown at section 2 in the same sketch follow automatically from the symmetry of the hoop and its loading.

The directions of the forces F_T and F_R in Fig. 4 follow directly from those in Fig. 3 according to Newton's third law, which states that action and reaction forces are equal in magnitude and opposite in direction. We observe that the forces F_T act in similar manner on the two halves of the hoop, but the forces F_R act inward on the upper half and outward on the lower half. This action of the forces F_R violates the symmetry which we expect to find in the two halves of the hoop. We can resolve this paradox in only one way; we must conclude that the radial forces F_R are zero, and that on any radial cut made across the hoop there is acting only a tangential force F_T.

Returning now to the free body of Fig. 3, we see that moment equilibrium is satisfied about the hoop center. Also, force equilibrium in the x direction is satisfied as a result of the symmetry, and thus to ensure equilibrium we need only require force balance in the y direction. Considering an arc length $r\Delta\theta$ on the inner surface of the ring, there will be acting on this arc a radial force

$$\Delta F_p = p[b(r\Delta\theta)]. \tag{a}$$

The component in the y direction of this radial force is

$$\Delta F_y = \Delta F_p \sin\theta = p[b(r\Delta\theta)]\sin\theta. \tag{b}$$

In the limit as $\Delta\theta \to 0$ the sum of the forces ΔF_y acting on the free body of Fig. 3 becomes the integral in the following force-balance equation

$$\Sigma F_y = \int_{\theta=0}^{\theta=\pi} pbr \sin\theta \, d\theta - 2F_T = 0. \tag{c}$$

$$2F_T = pbr \int_{\theta=0}^{\theta=\pi} \sin\theta \, d\theta$$

$$= -pbr \cos\theta \Big|_{\theta=0}^{\theta=\pi}$$

$$= -pbr[\cos\pi - \cos\theta]$$

$$= 2pbr$$

$$F_T = prb \tag{d}$$

It is interesting to note that the quantity $[(r\Delta\theta)\sin\theta]$ in (b) is the projection on the x axis of the arc length $r\Delta\theta$. Thus the force ΔF_y can be seen to be numerically equal to the pressure p acting over the projected area which is seen when we look in the y direction. Since this is true for each element of arc length, it must also be true for the entire half hoop for which the projected area is 2rb, and our equilibrium equation for the half hoop can be written directly as

$$\Sigma F_y = p(2rb) - 2F_T = 0 \tag{e}$$

$$F_T = prb.$$

The hoop may be thought of as a flat plate of thickness t, width b, and length $2\pi(r + t/2)$, where $(r + t/2)$ is the mean radius, and $2\pi(r + t/2)$ is the circumferencial length of the hoop. This plate is subjected to a tensile force F_T given by (d). Using this model, we can calculate the increase in the circumference of the hoop, δ_T, where $\delta_T = \frac{FL}{AE}$, by Hooke's Law.

$$\delta_T = \frac{F_T[2\pi(r + t/2)]}{(bt)E} = \frac{2\pi pr^2}{tE}\left(1 + \frac{t}{2r}\right). \qquad \text{(f)}$$

Since the circumference of a circle of radius r is equal to $2\pi r$, an increase in circumference of δ_T must be accompanied by a radial expansion δ_R, as shown in Fig. 5, where

$$2\pi R = L_T$$

$$2\pi\delta_R = \delta_T$$

$$\delta_R = \frac{\delta_T}{2\pi}. \qquad \text{(g)}$$

Substituting (f), we find

$$\delta_R = \frac{pr^2}{tE}\left(1 + \frac{t}{2r}\right). \qquad \text{(h)}$$

If we have a thin hoop we can neglect t/2r compared to unity, and thus arrive at the following result which is used in engineering calculations involving thin hoops.

$$\delta_R = \frac{pr^2}{tE} \qquad \text{(i)}$$

• PROBLEM 1-12

A very light and stiff wood plank of length 2L is attached to two similar springs of spring constant k, as shown in Fig. 1. The springs are of length h when the plank is resting on them. Suppose that a man steps up on the middle of the plank and begins to walk slowly toward one end. How far can he walk before one end of the plank touches the ground? That is, we want to know the distance b in Fig. 2, when the right end E of the plank is just in contact with the ground. Note that the springs can exert tension as well as compression.

Solution: Fig. 3 shows the free-body diagram of the plank. We show no force at the right end E because we are interested in the limiting case where the plank just comes in contact with the ground. We represent the man by his weight W located at the distance b from the center. Because the plank is described as being light, we neglect its weight; it follows as a consequence of this assump-

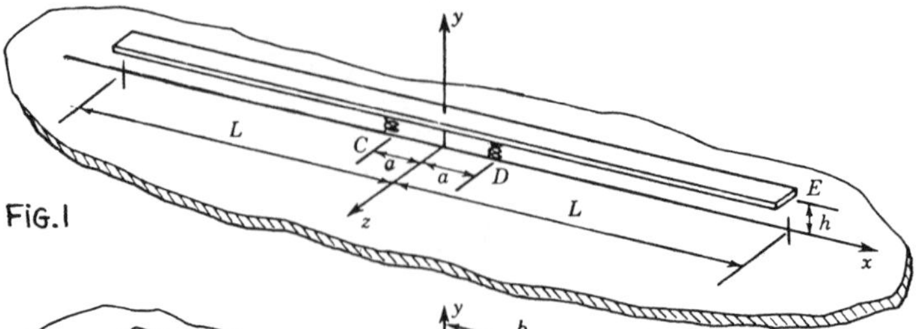

FIG. 1

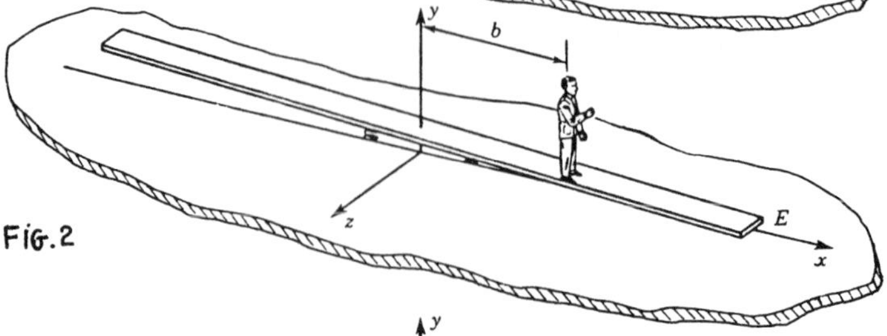

FIG. 2

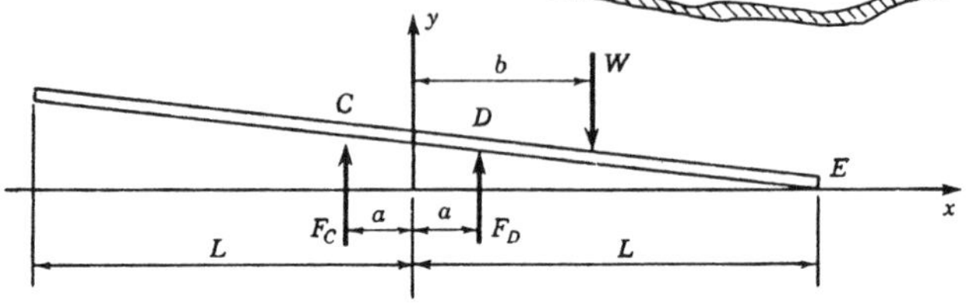

FIG. 3

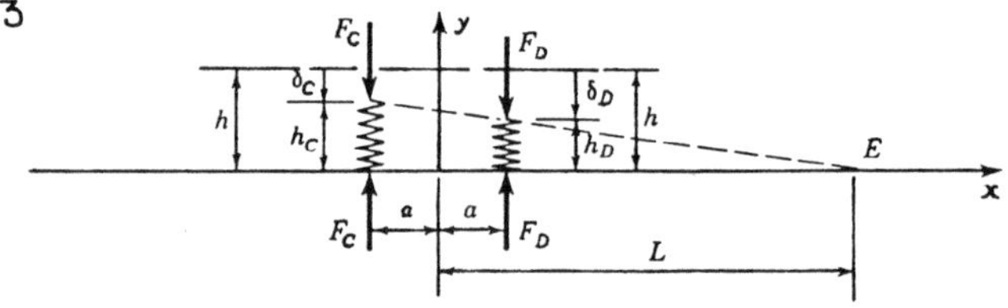

FIG. 4

tion that the springs in Fig. 1 are exerting no force on the plank, and thus h is the free length of each spring. Finally, we have assumed that the stiffness of the plank is such that we can consider it to remain absolutely straight so the deflections of the springs are as illustrated in Fig. 4.

There are seven unknowns. By using two equilibrium conditions, three of geometric compatibility, and two relations between forces and deflections, we can solve for all seven unknowns.

To find the force equilibrium, apply the conditions

$$\Sigma F = 0$$

$$\Sigma M = 0$$

to the free body of the plank in Fig. 3. We find that the first of these is satisfied when

$$\Sigma F_y = F_C + F_D - W = 0 \qquad \text{(a)}$$

and the second is satisfied when

$$\Sigma M_C = 2aF_D - (a+b)W = 0. \qquad \text{(b)}$$

The springs in Fig. 4 satisfy the equilibrium requirements of two-force members.

We now study the geometry of deformation and determine the requirements of geometric compatibility. When the plank remains straight, we see from the similar triangles in Fig. 4 that the lengths of the springs have the following ratio:

$$\frac{h_C}{h_D} = \frac{L + a}{L - a}. \tag{c}$$

Also, the deflections of the springs are

$$\begin{aligned} \delta_C &= h - h_C \\ \delta_D &= h - h_D. \end{aligned} \tag{d}$$

Find the relations between forces and deflections. Since both springs have the same spring constant, the force deflection relations are

$$\begin{aligned} F_C &= k\delta_C \\ F_D &= k\delta_D. \end{aligned} \tag{e}$$

Substitute (d) into (e):

$$F_C = k(h - h_C) \tag{f}$$

$$F_D = k(h - h_D). \tag{g}$$

Substitute (b) into (g):

$$F_D = \frac{(a+b)W}{2a} = k(h - h_D)$$

$$h_D = h - \left(\frac{a+b}{2ak}\right)W = \left(\frac{2akh - a - b}{2ak}\right)W$$

Substitute the above into (c):

$$h_C = \left(\frac{L+a}{L-a}\right) \cdot \left(\frac{2akh-a-b}{2ak}\right)W.$$

Substitute this into (f):

$$F_C = k\left[h - \left(\frac{L+a}{L-a}\right) \cdot \left(\frac{2akh-a-b}{2ak}\right)W\right]$$

$$F_D = k\left[h - \left(\frac{2akh-a-b}{2ak}\right)W\right].$$

Substitute F_C and F_D into (a) to obtain

$$k\left[h - \left(\frac{L+a}{L-a}\right) \cdot \left(\frac{2akh-a-b}{2ak}\right)W\right] + k\left[h - \frac{2akh-a-b}{2ak}\,W\right] = W.$$

Simplifying this, we obtain

$$b = \frac{a^2}{L}\left(\frac{2kh}{W} - 1\right). \tag{h}$$

It is also of interest to calculate the spring deflections in terms of the value of b determined by Eq. (h). These become

$$\begin{aligned} \delta_C &= \frac{W}{2k}\left(1 - \frac{b}{a}\right) \\ \delta_D &= \frac{W}{2k}\left(1 + \frac{b}{a}\right). \end{aligned} \tag{i}$$

We see that δ_D is always positive in the sense defined in Fig. 4. δ_C is positive so long as $b < a$. When $b = a$, the man is directly over the spring D, and, as would be expected, all the load is taken by the spring D, and the deflection and force in the spring C are zero. When $b > a$, then δ_C is negative (i.e., the spring extends). In Fig. 3 we assumed that $b > a$ and that the spring C is compressed. If after making these assumptions in a particular case the result from (h) was that $b > a$, then we would find from our algebra that both δ_C and F_C were negative; we would interpret these negative results to mean that the actual δ_C and F_C were in directions opposite to those defined as positive in Fig. 4.

• PROBLEM 1-13

A light rigid bar ABC is supported by three springs, as shown in Fig. 1. Before the load P is applied, the bar is horizontal. The distance from the center spring to the point of application of P is λa, where λ is a dimensionless parameter which can vary between $\lambda = -1$ and $\lambda = 1$. Determine the deflections in the three springs as functions of the load position parameter λ. Obtain a general solution for arbitrary values of the spring constants and display the results for the particular set $k_A = 1/2k$, $k_B = k$, and $k_C = 3/2k$.

Solution: The system is modeled by a rigid weightless bar and three linear-elastic springs. We now determine the equilibrium requirements.

Free-body diagrams for the springs and for the bar are

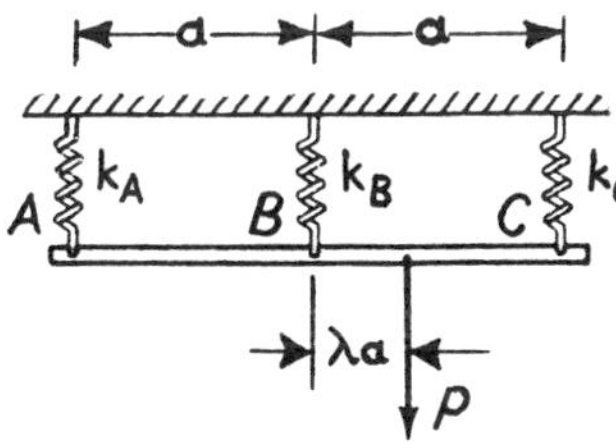

Fig. 1

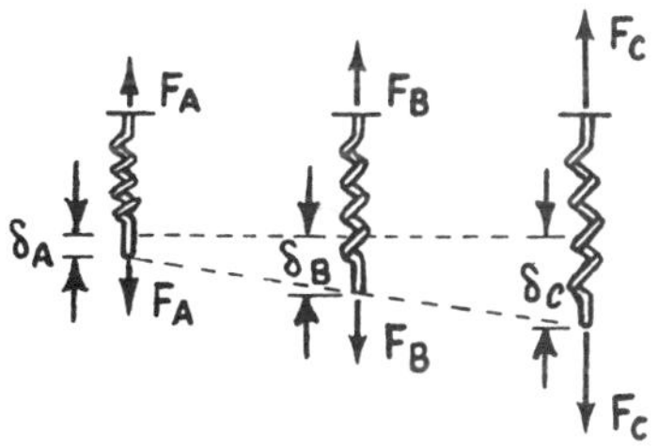

Fig. 2

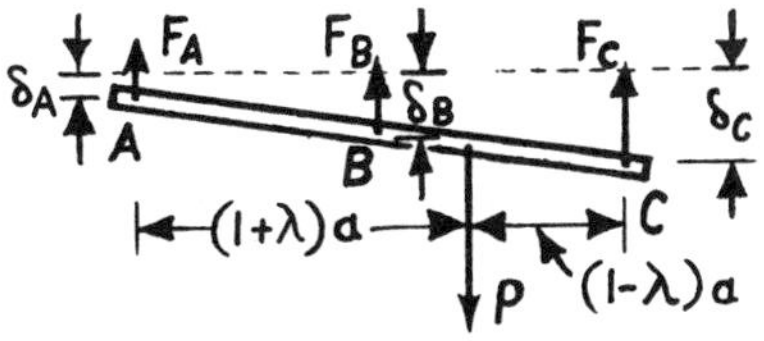

Fig. 3

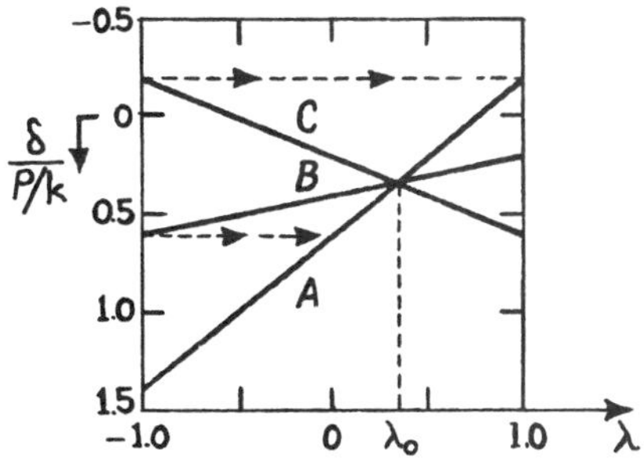

Fig. 4

shown in Fig. 2 and Fig. 3. We note that there are three unknown parallel forces acting on the bar in Fig. 3 and only two independent equilibrium requirements; i.e., the problem is statically indeterminate. The best we can do is to use the equilibrium conditions to express two of the forces in terms of the third. If we take the middle force F_B as our primary unknown, we can conveniently obtain F_A and F_C in terms of F_B by requiring balance of moments about C and A, respectively.

$$\Sigma M_C = 0 \qquad 2aF_A = (1 - \lambda)aP - aF_B \tag{a}$$

$$\Sigma M_A = 0 \qquad 2aF_C = (1 + \lambda)aP - aF_B.$$

In order for the springs to remain connected to the bar, it is necessary for the spring deflections in Fig. 2 to be the same as the corresponding bar deflections in Fig. 3. Since the bar ABC is rigid, it is necessary that the points A, B, and C in Fig. 3 remain collinear. Because two points determine a straight line, one of the three deflections can be expressed in terms of the other two. Thus, if the end deflections δ_A and δ_C are given, the midpoint deflection must be

$$\delta_B = 1/2(\delta_A + \delta_C). \tag{b}$$

We now ascertain the relations between the forces and deformations. For the linear springs in Fig. 2, we have

$$\delta_A = \frac{F_A}{k_A} \qquad \delta_B = \frac{F_B}{k_B} \qquad \delta_C = \frac{F_C}{k_C}. \tag{c}$$

From (a) we have:

$$F_A = \left(\frac{1 - \lambda}{2}\right)P - \frac{1}{2}F_B$$

$$F_C = \left(\frac{1 + \lambda}{2}\right)P - \frac{1}{2}F_B.$$

Substitute these two equations into (c) as follows:

$$\delta_A = \left[\left(\frac{1 - \lambda}{2}\right)P - \frac{1}{2}F_B\right]\frac{1}{k_A}, \qquad \delta_B = \frac{F_B}{k_B}$$

$$\delta_C = \left[\left(\frac{1 + \lambda}{2}\right)P - \frac{1}{2}F_B\right]\frac{1}{k_C}. \qquad \text{(d)}$$

Substitute these three deflections into (b).

$$\delta_B = \frac{F_B}{k_B} = \frac{1}{2}\left\{\frac{1}{2k_A}\left[(1-\lambda)P - F_B\right] + \frac{1}{2k_C}\left[(1+\lambda)P - F_B\right]\right\}$$

$$\frac{1}{k_B}F_B = \frac{1}{4k_A}(1-\lambda)P - \frac{1}{4k_A}F_B + \frac{1}{4k_C}(1+\lambda)P - \frac{1}{4k_C}F_B$$

$$F_B\left(\frac{1}{k_B} + \frac{1}{4k_A} + \frac{1}{4k_C}\right) = P\left[\frac{1}{4k_A}(1-\lambda) + \frac{1}{4k_C}(1+\lambda)\right]$$

$$F_B = \frac{\frac{1}{4k_A}(1-\lambda) + \frac{1}{4k_C}(1+\lambda)}{\left(\frac{1}{k_B} + \frac{1}{4k_A} + \frac{1}{4k_C}\right)}P.$$

Multiply the numerator and denominator by $4k_A \cdot k_B \cdot k_C$ to obtain

$$F_B = \frac{k_Bk_C(1-\lambda) + k_Ak_B(1+\lambda)}{(4k_Ak_C + k_Bk_C + k_Ak_B)}P.$$

Substitute F_B into (d) and simplify:

$$\delta_A = P\frac{2k_C - \lambda(k_B + 2k_C)}{k_Ak_B + 4k_Ak_C + k_Bk_C}$$

$$\delta_B = P\frac{k_A + k_C + \lambda(k_A - k_C)}{k_Ak_B + 4k_Ak_C + k_Bk_C}$$

$$\delta_C = P\frac{2k_A + \lambda(k_B + 2k_A)}{k_Ak_B + 4k_Ak_C + k_Bk_C}$$

For the particular case $k_A = \frac{1}{2}k$, $k_B = k$ and $k_C = \frac{3}{2}k$. We obtain:

$$\delta_A = P \cdot \frac{3k - \lambda(k + 3k)}{\frac{1}{2}k \cdot k + 4 \cdot \frac{1}{2}k \cdot \frac{3}{2}k + k \cdot \frac{3}{2}k}$$

$$= P \cdot \frac{(3 - 4\lambda)}{\left(\frac{1}{2} + 3 + \frac{3}{2}\right)k}$$

$$= P \cdot \frac{(3 - 4\lambda)}{(5k)}$$

$$\therefore \qquad \frac{\delta_A}{P/k} = \left(\frac{3 - 4\lambda}{5}\right).$$

Similarly,

$$\delta_B = P \cdot \frac{\frac{1}{2}k + \frac{3}{2}k + \lambda\left(\frac{1}{2}k - \frac{3}{2}k\right)}{\frac{1}{2}k \cdot k + 4 \cdot \frac{1}{2}k \cdot \frac{3}{2}k + k \cdot \frac{3}{2}k}$$

$$= P \cdot \frac{(2 - \lambda)}{\left(\frac{1}{2} + 3 + \frac{3}{2}\right)k} = P\,\frac{(2 - \lambda)}{5k}$$

$$\frac{\delta_B}{P/k} = \left(\frac{2 - \lambda}{5}\right)$$

and

$$\delta_C = P\,\frac{2\left(\frac{1}{2}k\right) + \lambda\left(k + 2 \cdot \frac{1}{2}k\right)}{\left(\frac{1}{2}k\right) \cdot (k) + 4\left(\frac{1}{2}k\right)\left(\frac{3}{2}k\right) + (k)\left(\frac{3}{2}k\right)}$$

$$= P \cdot \frac{k + \lambda(2k)}{\left(\frac{1}{2} + 3 + \frac{3}{2}\right)k^2} = P\,\frac{(1 + 2\lambda)}{5k}$$

$$\left(\frac{\delta_C}{P/k}\right) = \left(\frac{1 + 2\lambda}{5}\right).$$

Figure 4 shows how these deflections vary with the load position parameter λ for the particular case $k_A = \frac{1}{2}k$, $k_B = k$, and $k_C = \frac{3}{2}k$. Note that when the load is at the position indicated by λ_o in Fig. 4, all three spring deflections are equal. This means that the bar deflects without tipping when the load is applied at this position.

A machine part carrying a load F terminates in a piston which fits into a cavity, as shown in Fig. 1. Within the cavity are two springs arranged coaxial with each other. Each spring has the characteristic that the force required to deflect it is proportional to the amount of deflection. The spring constants of the two springs in the cavity are k_A and k_B. When the springs are unloaded, each has the same length L. How much of the load F is carried by the spring with constant k_A?

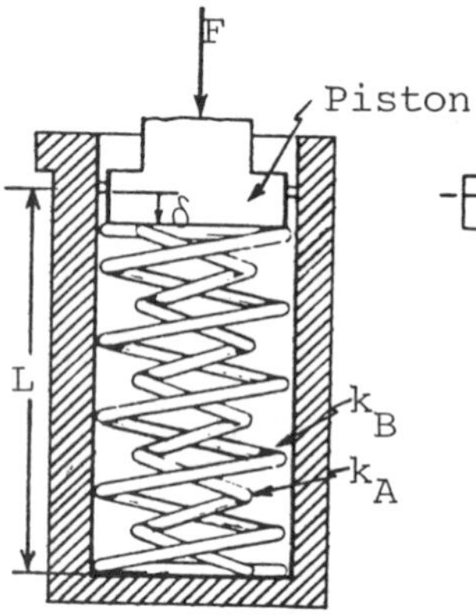

Fig. 1.

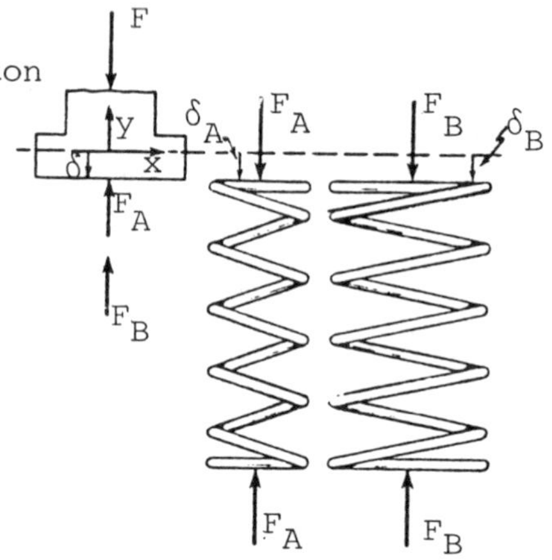

Fig. 2.

Solution: The first step in the analysis is to select our model. This is a relatively simple step in this situation; the model consists simply of the piston and the two springs, as shown in the sketches in Fig. 2. We have assumed that the springs have been made with flat ends such that the compressing force, which is distributed around the periphery of the spring, can be considered to act along the spring axis. We have also assumed that gravity effects can be ignored without substantially changing the problem.

To ensure that a body is in equilibrium we isolate that body from its surrounding environment and replace the environment with the forces which are the sole effect of the environment on the body. Fig. 2 shows free-body sketches of the piston and of the two springs. Equilibrium of a given free body requires that the vector sum of the forces and moments on the free body is equal to zero. Thus, for each of the three free bodies in Fig. 2, we must have

$$\Sigma F = 0$$

$$\Sigma M = 0.$$

Considering first the piston, we see that the forces acting on it all have the same line of action and thus $\Sigma M=0$. Since we have only forces in the y direction, the equation $\Sigma F = 0$ is satisfied when

$$\Sigma F_y = F_A + F_B - F = 0. \qquad \text{(a)}$$

By taking equal and opposite forces at the ends of each spring in Fig. 2, we have satisfied the conditions $\Sigma M = 0$ and $\Sigma F = 0$ for the springs.

We want to find the requirements for geometric compatibility with the restraints. It will be necessary to express these requirements in a quantitative or analytical manner. In the problem at hand the action of the piston is to cause both springs to move the same amount as the piston, and thus the requirement for geometric compatibility is simply

$$\delta_A = \delta_B = \delta. \qquad \text{(b)}$$

In order to deal precisely with the manner in which the deformation of a physical body is related to the forces acting on it, we must express this relation quantitatively, either by equations or by graphs. For this problem the force-deflection relation is a simple one. The force in each spring is linearly proportional to the deflection of the spring, and the constant of proportionality is the spring constant. Thus,

$$\begin{aligned} F_A &= k_A \delta_A \\ F_B &= k_B \delta_B. \end{aligned} \qquad \text{(c)}$$

We note that the spring constant has the units of force per unit length, e.g., lb/in., or newton/m. With Eqs.(a), (b), and (c) we have in quantitative form all the information we can write down about the force balance, the geometric fit, and the force-deflection characteristics of the system shown in Fig. 1. We have at this stage completed the physical part of the analysis. We now manipulate these equations mathematically, eliminating the deflections, to obtain the desired result.

From (a) we have $F = F_A + F_B.$

Substitute (c) into (a) to obtain $F = k_A\delta_A + k_B\delta_B.$

Substitute (b) into the above:

$$F = (k_A + k_B)\delta. \qquad \text{(d)}$$

Dividing (c) by (d) yields

$$\frac{F_A}{F} + \frac{k_A}{k_A + k_B}.$$

The total deflection of the piston is therefore

$$\delta = \frac{F_A}{k_A} = \frac{F}{k_A + k_B}.$$

A group of students, 22 in all, have a tug of war using a manila rope of 1/2-in. diameter. They start with a rope initially 50 ft. long and dispose themselves as shown in Fig. 1. A team wins when it pulls its end of the rope over the edge of the field. When the rope is stretched, there must be a clearance of 4 ft. at each end between the end of the rope and the edge of the field. The teams estimate that each man can pull with a force of 100 lb. A 1-ft. length of rope has a spring constant of 29,400 lb/in., including the effect of the untwisting of the rope. How long should they make the field?

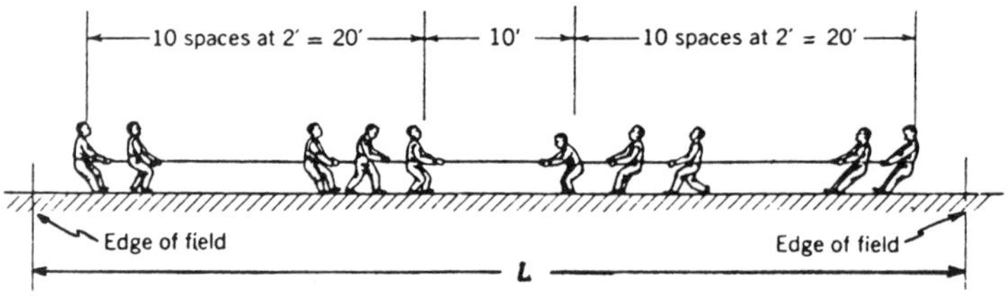

Fig. 1.

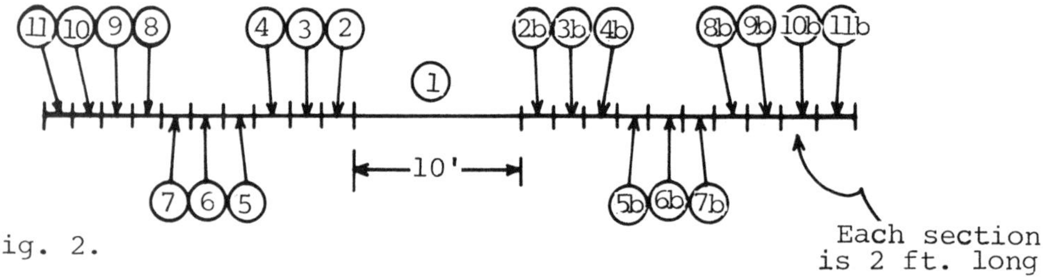

Fig. 2.

Solution: We must first find the tensile force in each of the 21 sections of the rope. A free-body diagram of section (1) is as shown:

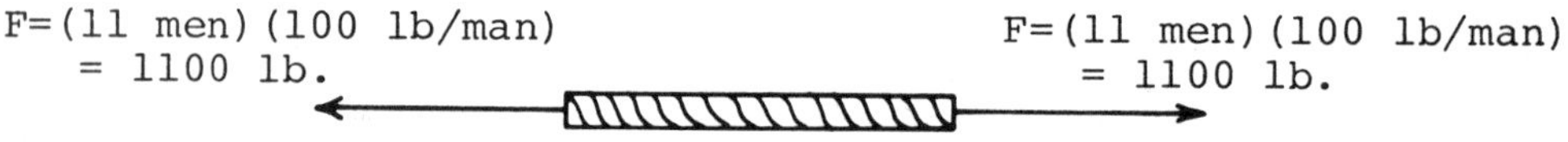

The load on this section is 1100 lb.

Now, analyze sections (2) and (2b). A free-body diagram of (2b) is as follows:

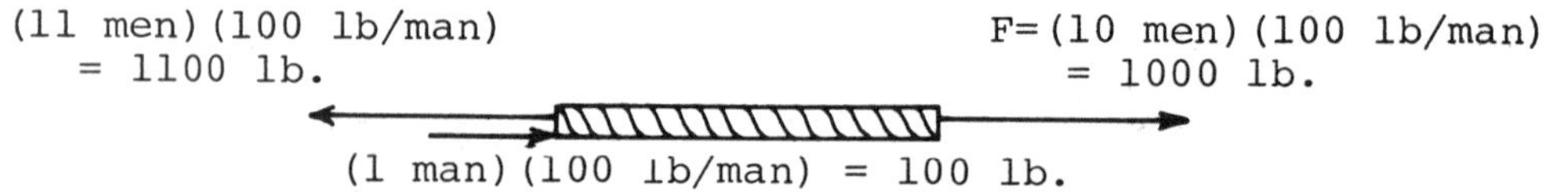

For section (2) we have

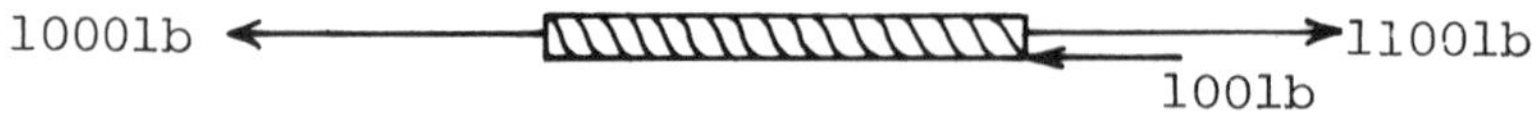

Thus, both sections (2) and (2b) reduce to

Likewise, sections (3) and (3b) reduce to:

that is, a net loading of 900 lb.

This can easily be continued to the ends of the rope. The next step in the solution is to find the extension in each section of the rope.

The extension of a 1-ft. length of rope is

$$\delta_{1'} = \frac{F}{k} = \frac{F}{29{,}400 \text{ lb.}} \text{ (in.)}.$$

The spring constant k is defined as

$$k \equiv \frac{AE}{L};$$

therefore, doubling the length of the rope section would halve the spring constant. Thus, for all the 2-foot sections of rope,

$$\delta_{2'} = \frac{F}{k/2} = \frac{F}{14{,}700 \text{ lb.}} \text{ (in.)}.$$

Likewise, the extension for the 10-foot section can be shown to be

$$\delta = \frac{F}{k/10} = \frac{F}{2940 \text{ lb.}} \text{ (in.)}.$$

The total extension of the fifty foot rope is the extension in the center 10' length, $\delta_{(1)}$, plus the extensions in all the 2' lengths as follows:

$$\delta_T = \delta_1 + \delta_2 + \delta_3 \; . \; . \; . \; . \; . \; . + \delta_{2b} + \delta_{3b} \; . \; . \; . \; . \; .$$

Noting that $\delta_2 = \delta_{2b}$; $\delta_3 = \delta_{3b}$; etc., we find

$$\delta_T = \frac{1100 \text{ lb}}{2940 \text{ lb}}\text{(in.)} + \left[\frac{2(1000)+2(900)+2(800)+2(700)+2(600)+2(500)+2(400)+2(300)+2(200)+2(100)}{14{,}700 \text{ lb.}}\right]\text{in.}$$

$$\delta_T = .3741'' + .7483'' = 1.122'' = .0935 \text{ ft.}$$

The length of the field is

$$L_f = 50' + 4' + 4' + \delta_T = 58' + .0935 \text{ ft.}$$

$$L_f = 58.0935 \text{ ft.}$$

(The extension is small compared to the total field length.)

CHAPTER 2

AXIAL FORCE, SHEAR AND BENDING MOMENT

SHEAR AND BENDING MOMENT DIAGRAMS

• PROBLEM 2-1

Plot a shear force and bending moment diagram for a simply supported beam with a uniformly distributed load, Fig. 1.

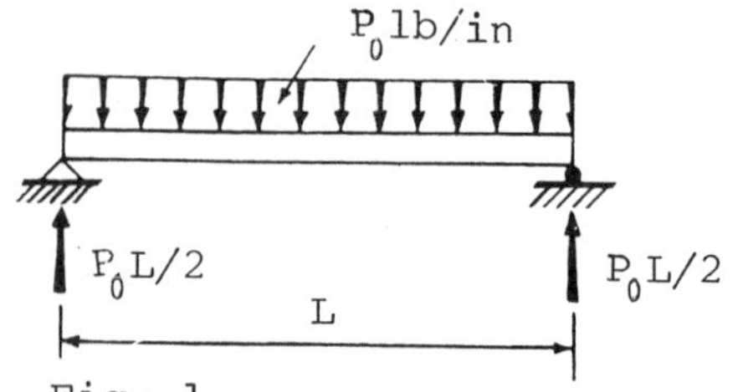

Fig. 1.

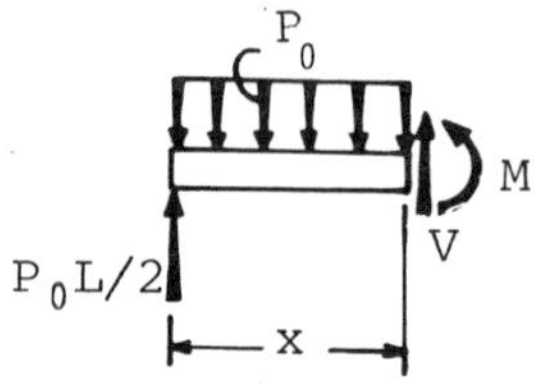

Fig. 2.

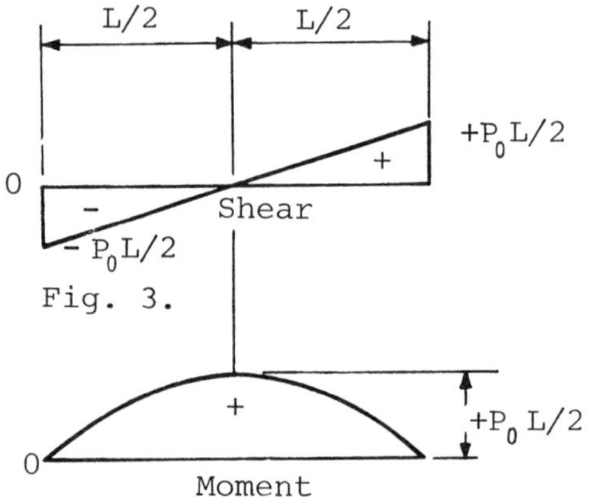

Fig. 3.

Fig. 4.

Solution: First determine the reactions at the support, i.e. $\sum M = 0$ about any support.

$$= P_0 \times \ell \times \frac{L}{2} - R\ell$$

$$\therefore R = \frac{P_0 L}{2}$$

Since the beam is loaded uniformly throughout the length, we need only consider an arbitrary section taken at a distance x from the left support.

Assume a shear force V and a bending moment M acting at the section in positive direction. The free body in Fig. 2 should be in equilibrium

$$\sum F_y = 0 \quad +\uparrow, \quad V + \frac{P_0 L}{2} - P_0 \cdot x = 0$$

$$V = -\frac{P_0 L}{2} + P_0 \cdot x$$

$$\sum M = 0 \quad \circlearrowleft +, \quad M + P_0 x\left(\frac{x}{2}\right) - \frac{P_0 L}{2}(x) = 0$$

$$M = \frac{P_0 Lx}{2} - \frac{P_0 x^2}{2}$$

Note that, on taking moment, the uniform force P_0 in Fig. 2 is equivalent to a single force $P_0 \cdot x$ acting at a point distant $\frac{x}{2}$ from the left support.

The plots of the V and the M functions are shown in Fig. 3 and Fig. 4.

• PROBLEM 2-2

Sketch shear force and bending moment diagrams. Indicate sign convention employed and label important values.

Solution: To sketch the shear force and bending moment diagrams, first establish the shear force and bending moment expressions. In order to do this, the reaction force and bending moment at the wall need to be determined. The sign convention used in this problem will be forces in the positive y direction will be positive and bending moments in the clockwise direction will be positive.

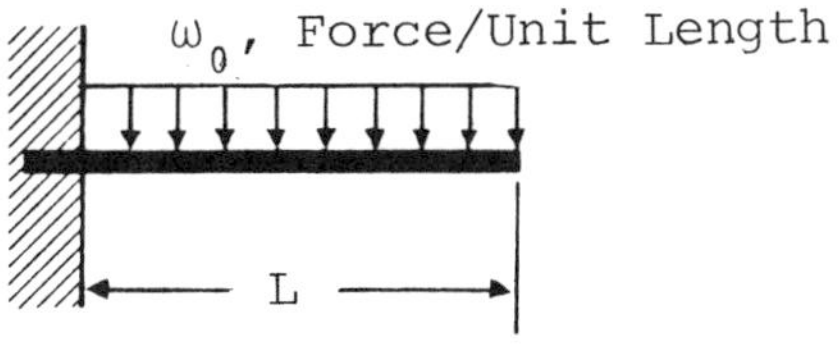

Fig. 1.

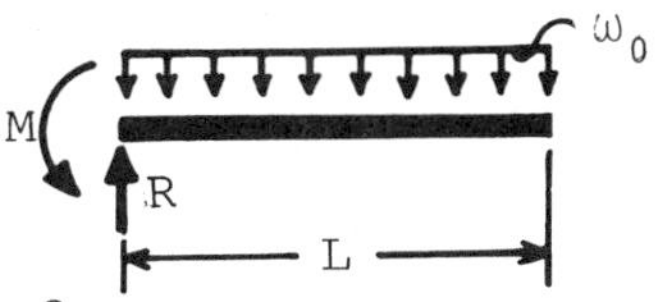

Fig. 2.

Let R ≡ Reaction at the support
M ≡ Moment at the support.

For equilibrium,

$$\sum F = 0$$

$$+\uparrow \qquad \therefore R - \omega_0 L = 0$$

$$\therefore R = \omega_0 L$$

$$\sum M = 0$$

$$\circlearrowright + \qquad \therefore M - \omega_0 L \cdot \frac{L}{2} = 0$$

$$\therefore M = \frac{\omega_0 L^2}{2}$$

Now consider a free body diagram:

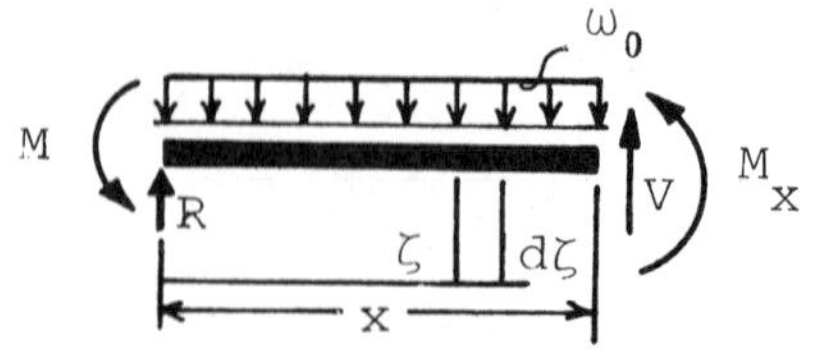

Fig. 3.

$\sum F = 0 \quad +\uparrow \quad \therefore R + V - \omega_0 x = 0$

$$\therefore V = -\omega_0 L + \omega_0 x$$

$$V = \omega_0 x - \omega_0 L.$$

This is the expression for shear force. But the expression relating shear force and bending moment, in keeping with the sign convention used in this problem, is

$$M = -\int vdx$$

In order to find the general equation for the moment at any given value of x, x is treated as a constant in the upper limit of integration and a dummy variable is used in its place as the variable of integration.

$$M_x = -\int_0^x \omega_0 (y - L)dy$$

$$= -\omega_0\left(\frac{x^2}{2} - Lx\right) + C.$$

When $\quad x = 0 \; ; \quad M_x = -M$

This can be seen by analyzing the free body diagram for the point x = 0:

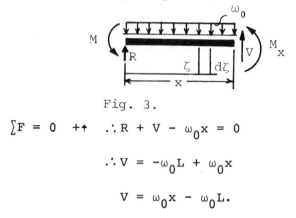

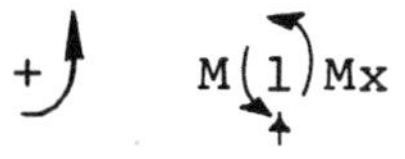

$\sum M$ about x = 0 is zero

$$M_x + M = 0$$

$$M_x = -M = -\frac{\omega_0 L^2}{2}$$

$$x = 0 \quad M_x = -\omega_0\left(\frac{(0)^2}{2} - L(0)\right) + C$$

$$M_x = C.$$

But

$$M_x = -\frac{\omega_0 L^2}{2}$$

$$\therefore C = -\frac{\omega_0 L^2}{2}$$

$$\therefore M_x = -\omega_0\left(\frac{x^2}{2} - Lx\right) - \frac{\omega_0 L^2}{2}$$

$$M_x = -\frac{\omega_0}{2}(x - L)^2.$$

This same answer can be obtained by analyzing the free body diagram, shown in Fig. 3.

$$\sum M \text{ about } x \text{ is zero}$$

$$\circlearrowleft + \qquad M_x + \omega_0 x^2/2 - R + M = 0.$$

Substituting for R and M and solving for M_x yields:

$$M_x = -\omega_0 x^2/2 + \omega_0 x - \omega_0 L^2/2.$$

Dividing through by $-\omega_0/2$ and rewriting the squared terms:

$$M_x = -\omega_0/2(x - L)^2.$$

The equation for the shear is then:

$$V = \omega_0 x - \omega_0 L,$$

and for the bending moment:

$$M_x = -\frac{\omega_0}{2}(x - L)^2.$$

To graph the shear, notice that its equation is the equation of a straight line with a slope of ω_0 and a y-intercept of $-\omega_0 L$. When x is equal to L, V is zero.

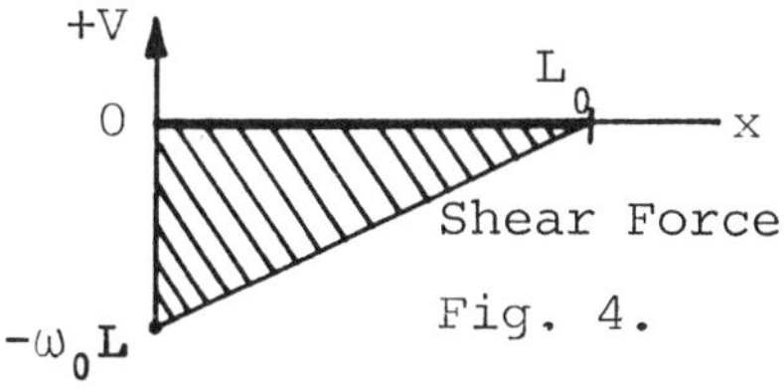

Shear Force diagram

Fig. 4.

The equation for the bending moment is that of a parabola opening downward with its apex on the x axis at x = L. The y intercept is found by setting x = 0:

$$x = 0 \quad M_x = -\frac{\omega_0}{2}(0 - L)^2 = -\frac{\omega_0 L^2}{2}$$

It is now known that the parabola crosses the y axis at $-\omega_0 L^2/2$ and touches the x axis at x = L. Substitute various values of x into the bending moment equation to find several points in between in order to be able to sketch the curve:

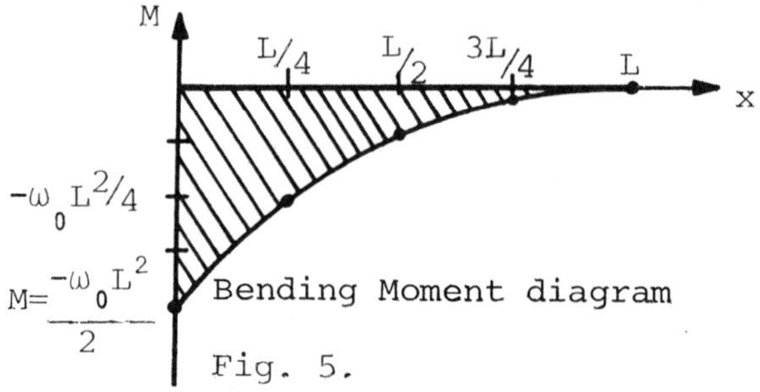

Bending Moment diagram

Fig. 5.

x	M_x
0	$-\omega_0 L^2/2$
L/4	$-\omega_0 L^2/4 - \omega_0 L^2/32$
L/2	$-\omega_0 L^2/8$
3L/4	$-\omega_0 L^2/32$

• PROBLEM 2-3

Construct the shear force and bending moment diagrams for the cantilever beam shown in Fig. 1.

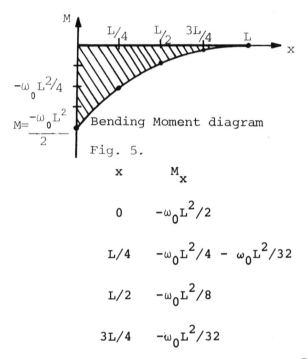

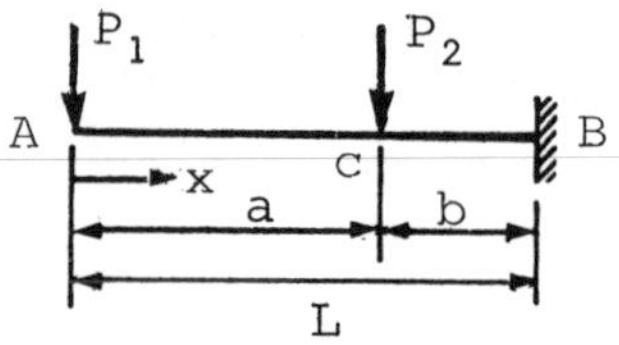

Fig. 1.

<u>Solution</u>: The beam AB is divided into two parts, AC and CB, by the forces P_1 and P_2. We must consider the two regions separately in order to examine the internal forces. If the structure is not broken into cross-sections, the determination of the internal forces is impossible. If we choose x measured from A, the regions we consider will be $0 < x < a$ and $a < x < L$.

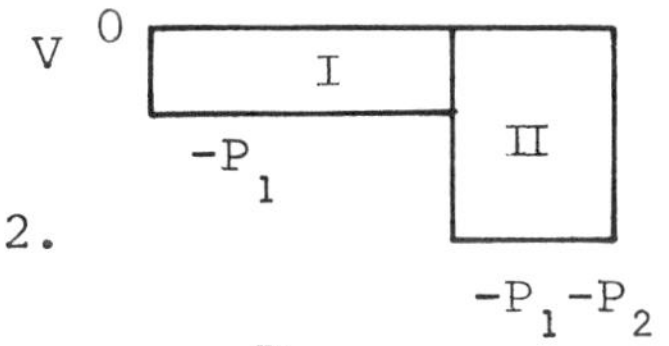

Fig. 2.

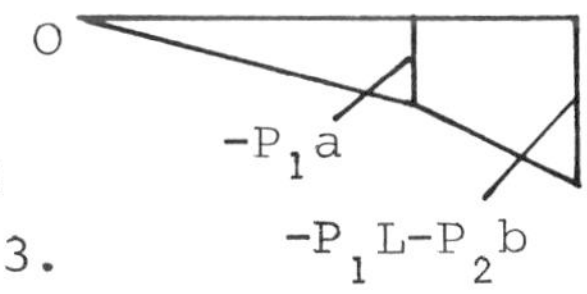

Fig. 3.

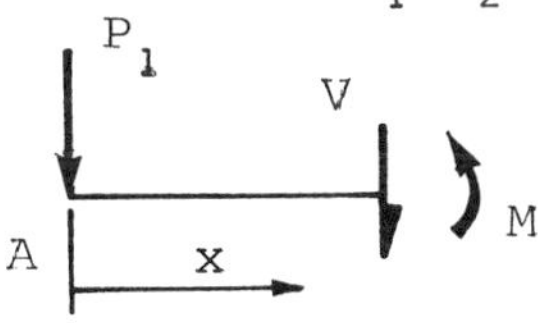

Fig. 4. Fig. 4.

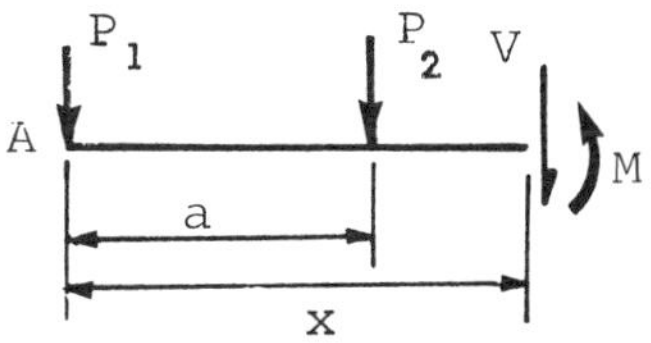

Fig. 5.

Consider the region $0 < x < a$ (see Fig. 4). By applying the equilibrium equation in the vertical direction, we obtain

$$\Sigma F_y = 0 \quad +\downarrow \qquad V + P_1 = 0$$

$$V = -P_1$$

By taking moment about the cut section, we obtain

$$\Sigma M_x \; +\circlearrowleft = 0$$

$$M + P_1 \cdot x = 0$$

$$M = -P_1 \cdot x$$

Consider the region $a < x < L$ (see Fig. 5). By force equilibrium equation in vertical direction, we obtain

$$V + P_1 + P_2 = 0$$

$$V = -P_1 - P_2.$$

By taking moment about the cut section, we obtain

$$\Sigma M = 0$$

$$M + P_2 \cdot (x - a) + P_1 \cdot x = 0$$

$$M = -P_1 x - P_2 (x - a).$$

The corresponding shear force and bending moment diagrams (Fig. 2 and 3) can be drawn by combining the shear and bending moment in the two regions. The bending moment values at $x = a$ and $x = L$ can be determined in two ways. The obvious way is to plug values for a and L into the BM equation. The second method is called the summation procedure. By using the relation $M = \int V dx$, we can find the moment at any point by finding the area below the shear force diagram.

Ex. To find moment at C: (see Fig. 2)

Moment at C = Area I = length × width

$$= a(-P_i)$$

Moment at B = Area I + II = $-P_1a$ + (length × width)

$$= -P_1a + (b \cdot (-P_1 - P_2))$$

$$= -P_1a + (-P_1b) - P_2b$$

$$= -P_1(a + b) - P_2b$$

$$= -P_1L - P_2b.$$

• PROBLEM 2-4

A cantilever beam which is free at end A and fixed at end B is subjected to a distributed load of linearly varying intensity q (see Fig. 1). Find the shear force V and bending moment M at a distance x from the free end.

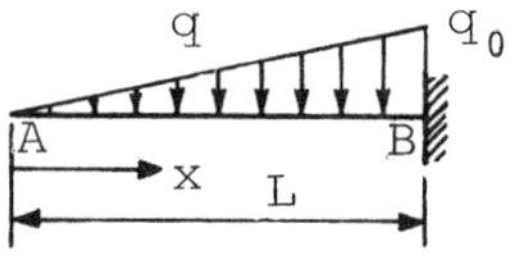

Fig. 1.

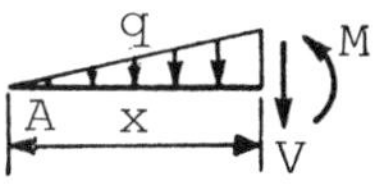

Fig. 2.

Solution: We begin by cutting through the beam at a distance x from the left-hand end and isolating part of the beam as a free body (Fig. 2). The shear force V and bending moment M are assumed to be positive. The intensity of the distributed load at that point is seen to be $q = q_0x/L$, and therefore the total downward load on the free body of Fig. 2 is equal to $\frac{1}{2}(x)(q_0 \frac{x}{L})$. Hence, we find from equilibrium in the vertical direciton that

$$V = -\frac{q_0x^2}{2L}. \qquad (a)$$

We see from this equation that at the free end A (x = 0) the shear force is V = 0, and at the fixed end B (x = L) the shear force is $V = -q_0L/2$.

To find the bending moment in the beam, we write an equation of moment equilibrium about an axis through the cut section. Note that the resultant force acts through the centroid of the triangle, which is (1/3) x away from the cut section.

$$\frac{q_0x^2}{2L} \cdot \frac{1}{3} \cdot x + M = 0 \qquad M = -\frac{q_0x^3}{6L} \qquad (b)$$

Again considering the two ends of the beam, we see that the bending moment is zero when $x = 0$ and equal to $-q_0L^2/6$ when $x = L$.

• PROBLEM 2-5

a) Determine the shear-force and bending-moment equations for Fig. 1, and b) draw the shear and bending moment diagram for part a.

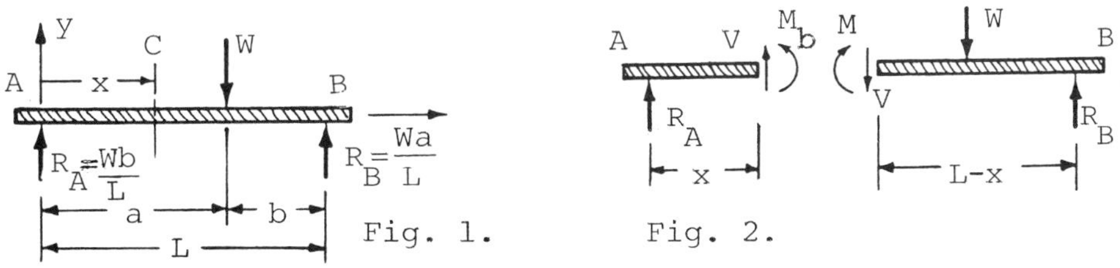

Fig. 1. Fig. 2.

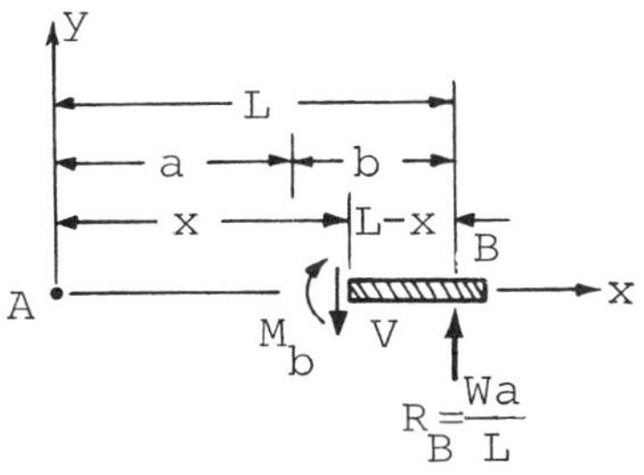

Fig. 3.

Solution: a) Cut a section through the beam distance x away from point A, establish a coordinate axis for the beam as shown in Fig. 1, and then consider the parts $0 < x < a$ and $a < x < (a + b)$ separately. To find the reaction forces at the supports A and B:

$$\sum M_A = 0 \curvearrowleft + , \quad R_B \cdot L - W \cdot a = 0$$

$$R_B = \frac{Wa}{L}$$

$$\sum M_B = 0 \curvearrowright +, \quad R_A \cdot L - W \cdot b = 0$$

$$R_A = \frac{Wb}{L}$$

Check $\sum F_y = 0$

$$R_A + R_B - W = 0$$

$$\frac{Wa}{L} + \frac{Wb}{L} = W$$

$$\frac{W}{L}(a + b) = W$$

$$W = W.$$

In Fig. 2, the shear force V and bending moment M_b are assumed in positive direction as shown. Apply equilibrium to the left portion of the beam:

$$\sum F_y = 0 \quad \uparrow + \qquad R_A + V = 0$$

but

$$V = -\frac{Wb}{L}$$

$$\therefore \; R_A = \frac{Wb}{L}$$

$$\sum M = 0 \quad \curvearrowleft + , \qquad M_b - R_A \cdot x = 0$$

$$M_b = R_A \cdot x = \frac{Wbx}{L}$$

For a < x < L, make a cut as shown in Fig. 3. The shear and moment would have a direction as shown in Fig. 3.

$$\sum F_y = 0 \quad \uparrow + , \qquad R_B - V = 0$$

$$\therefore \quad V = R_B = \frac{Wa}{L}$$

$$\sum M = 0 \quad \curvearrowright + , \qquad -M_b + R_B \cdot (L - x) = 0$$

$$M_b = \frac{Wa}{L}(L - x).$$

Fig. 4

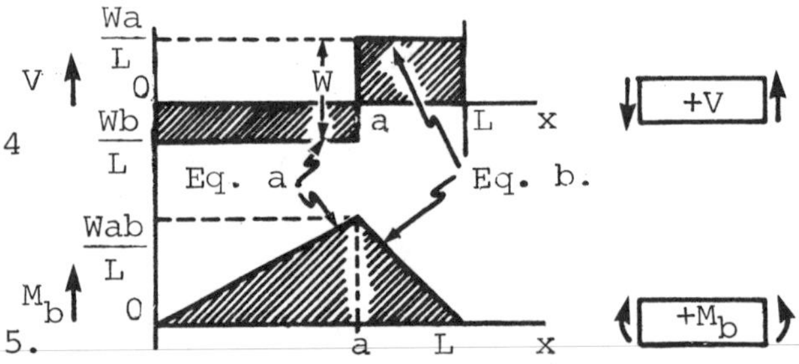

Fig. 5.

SHEAR-FORCE AND BENDING-MOMENT DIAGRAMS FOR BEAM

b) The plotted values of V vs. x and M vs. x, which are the shear force and bending moment diagrams, are shown in Fig. 4 and Fig. 5 with the sign conventions on their right hand sides.

Construct shear and bending-moment diagrams for the beam loaded with the forces shown in Fig. 1.

Fig. 1

Fig. 2

Fig. 3

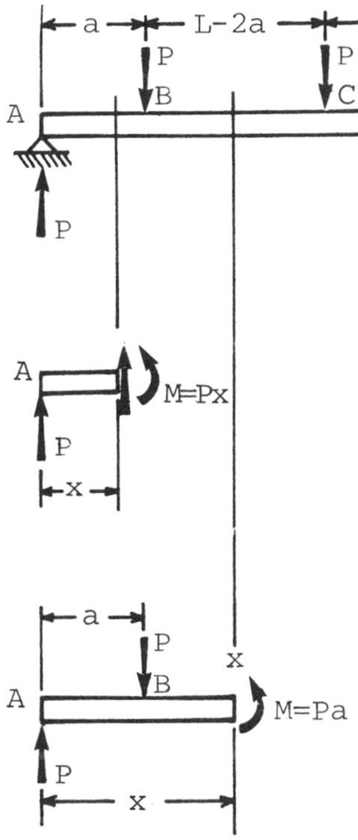

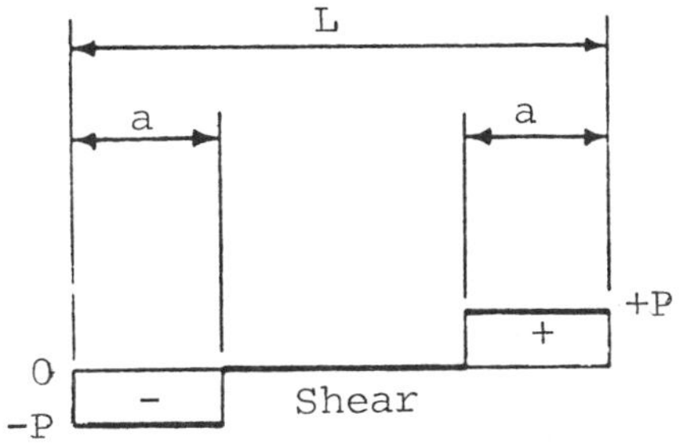

Fig. 4.

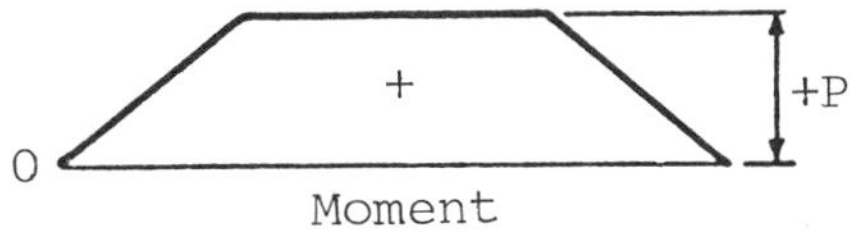

Fig. 5.

Solution: The entire beam is divided into three sections, AB, BC and CD. By making cuts on the sections between AB, BC and CD and considering the free body diagrams, we can solve for the forces and moments on each section.

By symmetry, the reactions at A and at D are both equal to P. Considering the free-body diagram in Fig. 2, let axial force, the shear, and the bending moment be F, V and M respectively. $0 < x < a$ By applying equilibrium to the free-body diagram in Fig. 2, we obtain, for $0 < x < a$,

$$\sum F_y = 0 \quad \uparrow + , \qquad P + V = 0$$

$$V = -P$$

$$\sum F_x = 0 \rightarrow + \qquad F = 0$$

At point x $\sum M = 0$ ↻+ , $M - P \cdot x = 0$

$$M = P \cdot x$$

The shear, regardless of the distance from the support, remains constant and is $-P$. The bending moment varies linearly from the support, reaching a maximum of $+P \cdot a$. $a < x \leq L - 2a$.

An arbitrary section at a distance x between the two applied forces is shown in Fig. 3. Force equilibrium:

$\sum F_y = 0$ ↻+ , $P - P + V = 0$

$$V = 0$$

No shearing force is necessary to maintain equilibrium.

At point x: $\sum M = 0$ + , $M_x - P \cdot x + P \cdot (x-a) = 0$

$$M_x = Px - Px + P \cdot a$$

$$M_x = P \cdot a$$

The bending moment is independent of x. It remains a constant throughout this zone BC.

$L - a < x \leq L;$

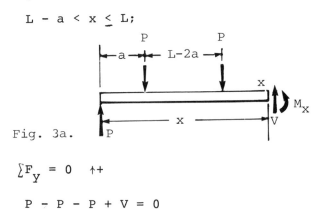

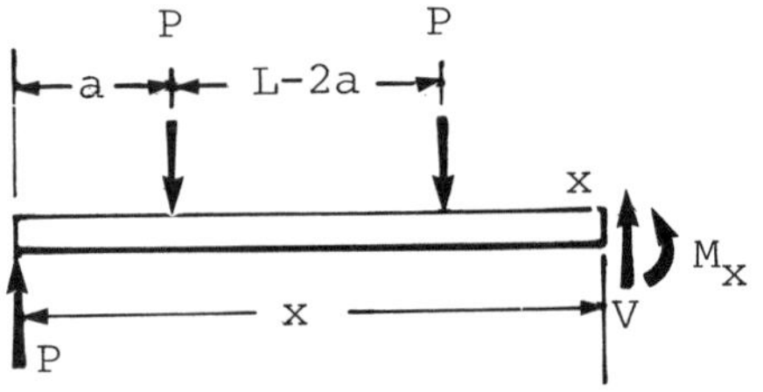

Fig. 3a.

$\sum F_y = 0$ ↑+

$$P - P - P + V = 0$$

$P = V$ ∴ The shear force is now positive due to the load present at C, and remains constant.

$\sum M_x = 0$ +↺

$$P(x - (L-2a+a)) + P(x-a) - P(x) + M_x = 0$$

$$M_x = -Px + PL - Pa - Px + Pa + Px$$

$M_x = P(L - x)$ ∴ The bending moment for this section shows a negative slope which brings the net moment to zero as seen in Fig. 3. This shows that the boundary conditions are satisfied; $m(0) = 0$; $M(L) = 0$.

Finally, the shear and moment diagrams are shown in Fig. 4 and Fig. 5.

Construct the shear force and bending moment diagrams for the beam shown in the figure.

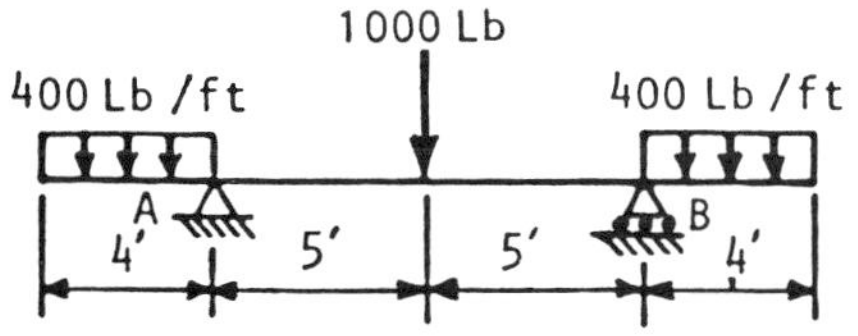

Fig. 1.

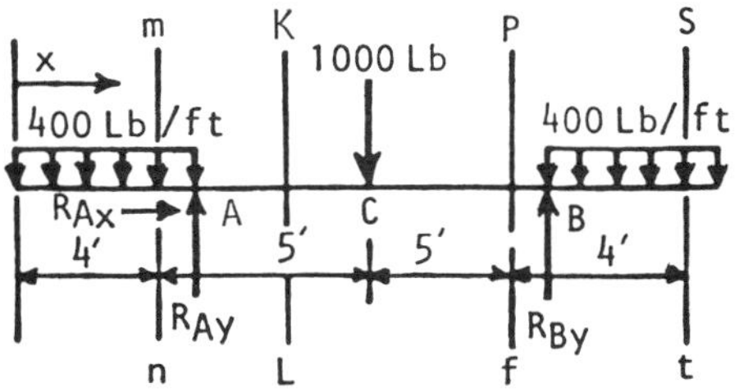

Fig. 2.

Solution: The loading diagram is shown in Figure 2. Reactions at the supports are calculated to be:

$$\sum F_x = 0 \qquad R_{Ax} = 0$$

$$\sum M_A = 0 \quad +\curvearrowright$$

$$400(4)(10 + 2) - R_{By}(10) + 1000(5) - 400(4)(2) = 0$$

$$R_{By} = \frac{19,200 + 5000 - 3200}{10} = 2100 \text{ lbs}$$

Because the loading is symmetric $R_{Ay} = R_{By} = 2100$ lbs.

Check for whether the beam is in equilibrium

$$\sum F_y = 0$$

$$R_{Ay} + R_{By} - (400)(4) - (400)(4) - 1000 = 0$$

$$2100 + 2100 - 1600 - 1600 - 1000 = 0$$

Beam is in vertical equilibrium and calculated values of R_{Ay} and R_{By} are correct.

The free-body diagram for a portion of the beam to the left of section mn is shown in Fig. 3.

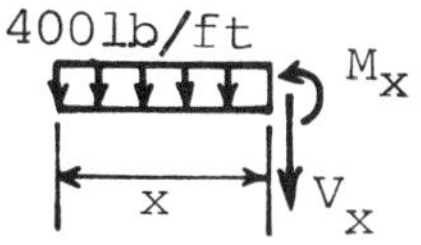

Fig. 3.

$0 < x \leq 4$

$$V_x + 400x = 0 \Rightarrow V_x = -400x$$

$$M_x + 400(x)\left(\frac{x}{2}\right) = 0 \Rightarrow M_x = -400\,\frac{x^2}{2} = -200x^2$$

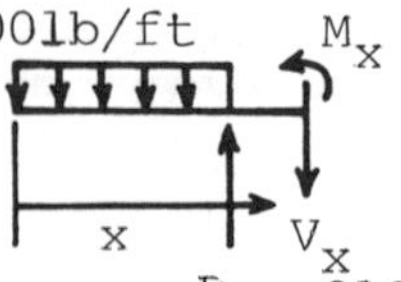

Fig. 4.

$4 < x \leq 9$

$V_x - 2100 + 400(4) = 0$

$V_x = 500$ lbs.

$M_x + 400(4)(x - 4 + 2) - 2100(x - 4) = 0$

$M_x = 2100x - 8400 - 1600x + 3200$

$M_x = 500x - 5200.$

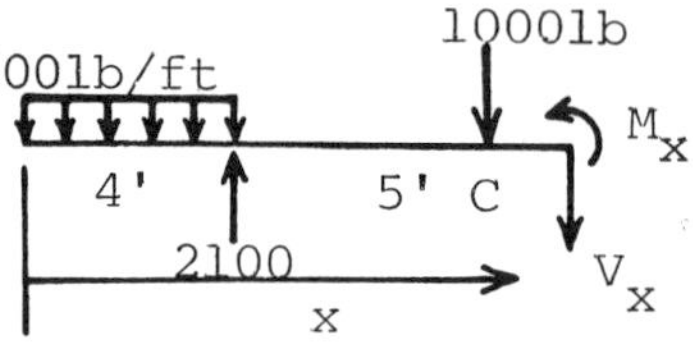

Fig. 5.

$9 < x \leq 14$

$V_x + 1000 - 2100 + 400(4) = 0$

$V_x = 2100 - 1000 - 1600 = -500$ lbs

$M_x + 1000(x-9) - 2100(x-4) + 400(4)(x-4+2) = 0$

$M_x = -1000x + 9000 + 2100x - 8400 - 1600x + 3200$

$M_x = -500x + 3800$

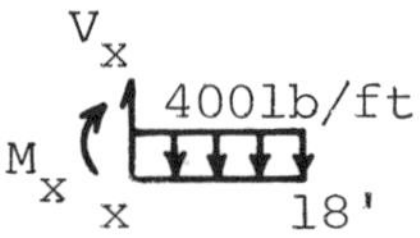

Fig. 6.

For this section of the beam it is simpler to look at the free body diagram of the portion to the right of the cut rather than on the left-hand side, as was done for the previous sections.

$V_x - 400(18 - x) = 0 \qquad V_x = -400x + 7200$

$M_x + 400(18 - x)(18 - x)/2 = 0 \quad M_x = -200(18 - x)^2$

Multiplied out:

$M_x = -200x^2 + 7200x - 64,800$

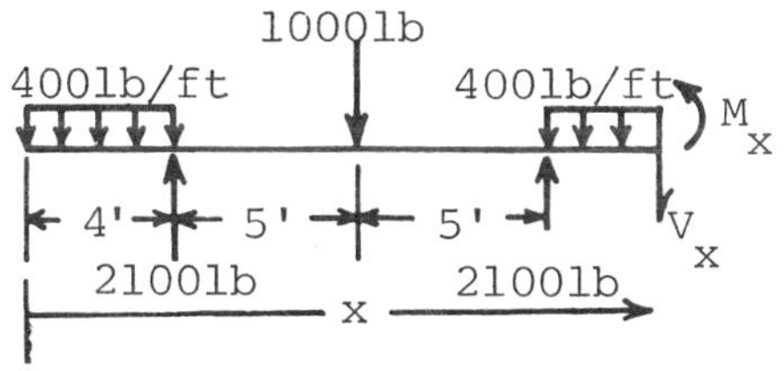

Fig. 7

This section of the beam, $14 < x \leq 18$, can also be analyzed by looking at the loads to the left of the cut. Summing the forces from right to left:

$$V_x + 400(x - 14) - 2100 + 1000 - 2100 + 400(4) = 0$$

$$V_x = -400x + 7200$$

Summing the moments:

$$M_x + 400(x - 14)(x - 14)/2 - 2100(x - 14) + 1000(x - 9)$$
$$- 2100(x - 4) + 400(4)(x - 4/2) = 0$$

$$M_x = -200x^2 + 7200x - 64800$$

The shear force and bending moment diagrams are then plotted by substituting for x in the various expressions for V_x and M_x (Figs. 8 and 9).

Fig. 8 SHEAR FORCE DIAGRAM

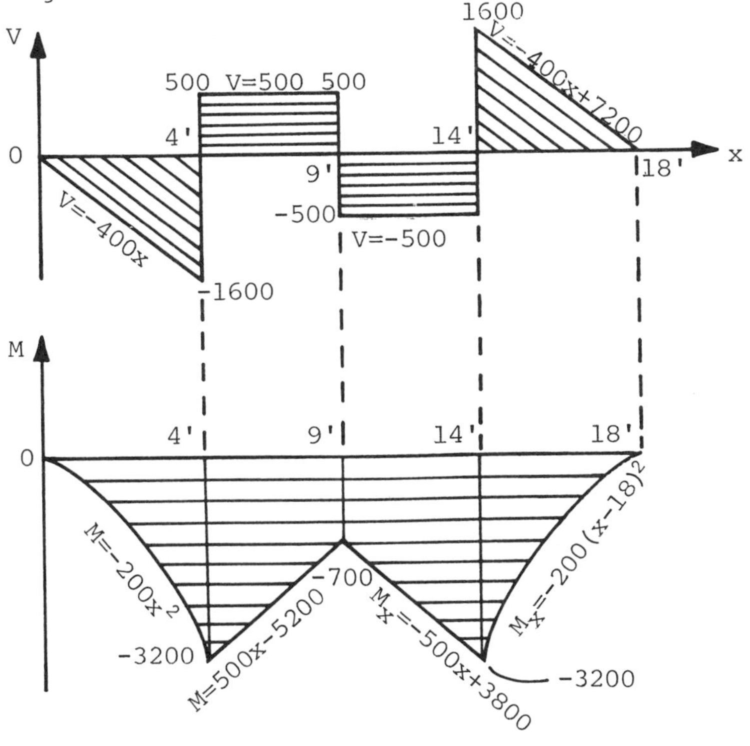

Fig. 9 BENDING MOMENT DIAGRAM

• PROBLEM 2-8

Determine the shear force and bending moment diagrams for a simple beam with a uniform load of intensity q acting over a part of the span (Fig. 1).

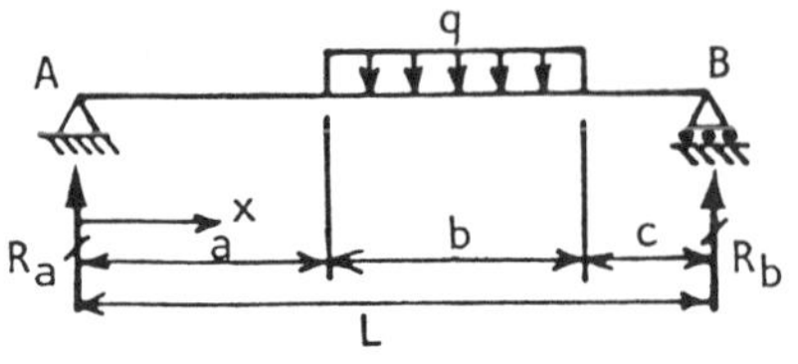

Fig. 1

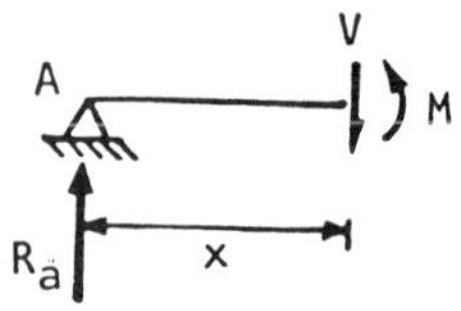

Fig. 2

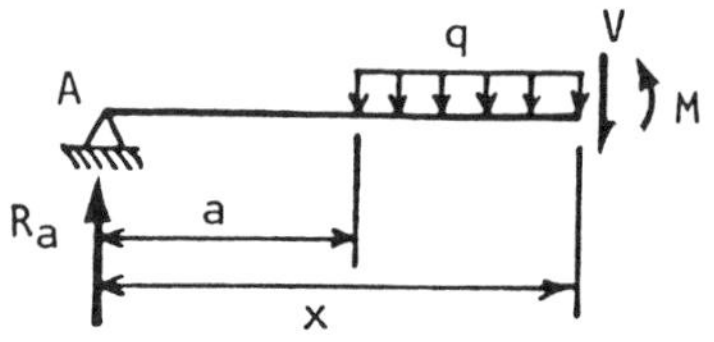

Fig. 3

Solution: We begin by finding the reactions for the entire beam

$$\sum F_y = 0 \quad +\uparrow, \qquad R_a + R_b = q \cdot b \qquad \text{(h)}$$

$$M_B = 0 \curvearrowright + , \qquad \therefore \; R_a \; L - (q \cdot b)(\frac{b}{2} + c) = 0$$

$$R_a = \frac{q \cdot b}{L}(c + \frac{b}{2}) \qquad \text{(i)}$$

Substituting (i) into (h), we obtain

$$R_b = \frac{q \cdot b}{L}(a + \frac{b}{2}) \qquad \text{(j)}$$

To find the shear forces and bending moments we must consider separately the three regions of the beam. For the unloaded portion at the left end of the beam ($0 < x < a$) as shown in Figure 2, we find from static equilibrium

$$\sum F_y = 0 \quad +\uparrow \qquad \sum M = 0 \curvearrowright +$$

$$V = R_a \qquad M = R_a x \qquad \text{(l)}$$

For a cross section within the loaded portion of the beam (Fig. 3) the shear force is obtained by subtracting from the reaction R_a the load $q(x - a)$ acting on the beam to the left of the cross section. The bending moment in the same region is obtained by subtracting the moment of the load to the left of the cross section from the moment of the reaction R_a (see Fig. 3). In this manner we find

$$V = R_a - q(x - a) \qquad \text{(m)}$$

$$M = R_a x - q(x - a)(x - a)/2 \qquad \text{(n)}$$

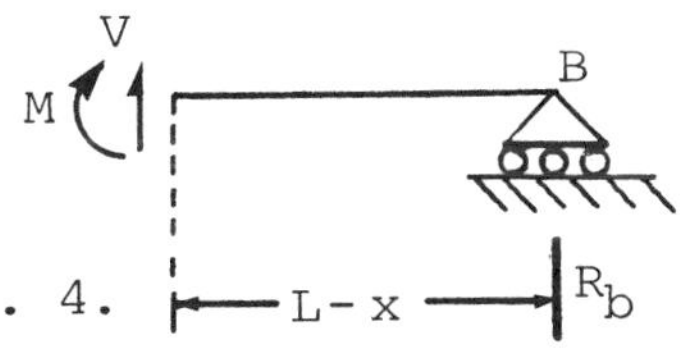

Fig. 4.

For the unloaded portion of the beam at the right end we find from Fig. 4 that

$$V = -R_b \qquad M = R_b(L - x). \tag{o}$$

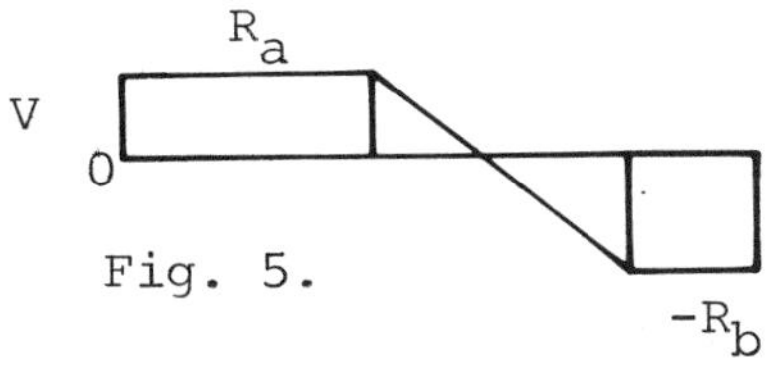

Fig. 5.

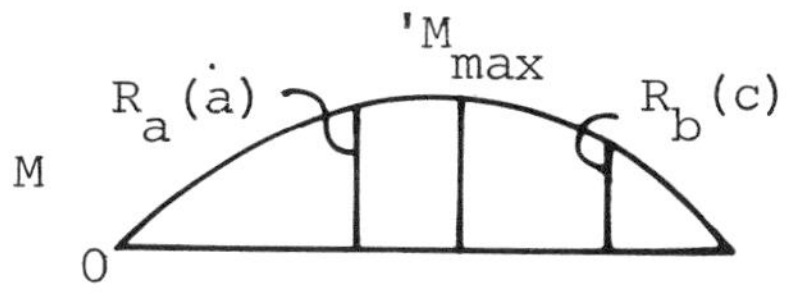

Fig. 6.

By using expressions (l) to (o), we can readily construct the shear force and bending moment diagrams. The former diagram (see Fig. 5) consists of two horizontal lines corresponding to the unloaded portions of the beam and an inclined line corresponding to the uniformly loaded region. The bending moment diagram (Fig. 6) consists of the two inclined straight lines corresponding to the unloaded portions of the beam and a parabolic curve corresponding to the loaded portion. The inclined lines are tangent to the parabolic curve at the points where they meet. This conclusion follows from the fact that there are no abrupt changes in the magnitude of the shear force at these points.

• PROBLEM 2-9

A simply supported beam is subjected to various loadings. Derive the shear force and bending moment equations.

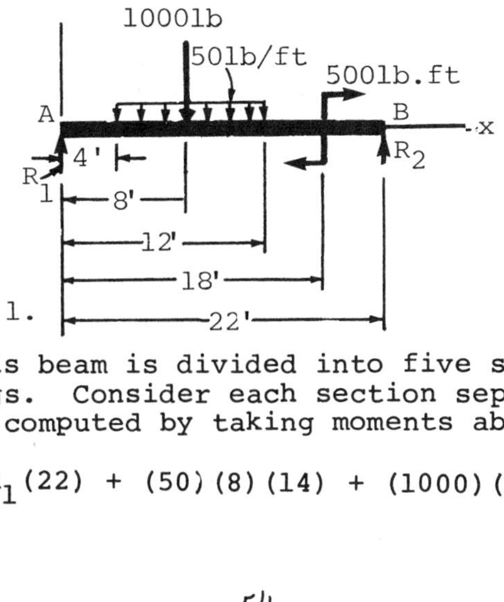

Fig. 1.

Solution: This beam is divided into five sections by different loadings. Consider each section separately. The reactions are computed by taking moments about point B.

$\underline{\Sigma M_B = 0:}$ $\quad -R_1(22) + (50)(8)(14) + (1000)(14) - 500 = 0$

$$\therefore R_1 = 868 \text{ lb}$$

$\sum M_A = 0$:

$$R_2(22) - 500 - (50)(8)(8) - (1000)(8) = 0$$

$$\therefore R_2 = 532 \text{ lb}$$

check: $\sum F_y = 0$.

Then $R_1 - 1000 - 50(8) + R_2 = 0$

$$868 - 1000 - 400 + 532 = 0$$

$$0 = 0$$

In Fig. 2(a) we have shown a free-body diagram exposing sections between the left support and the uniform load. Summing forces and taking moments about a point in the section, where we have drawn V and M as positive according to our convention, we get:

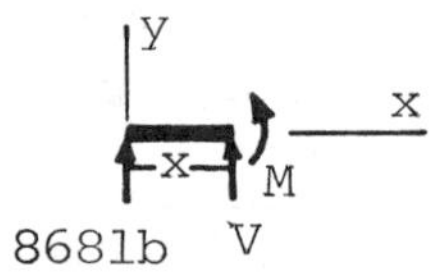

2(a)

$0 < x < 4$:

$$\sum F_y = 0 \qquad 868 + V = 0$$

$$\therefore V = -868 \text{ lb}$$

$$\sum M = 0 \qquad -868x + M = 0$$

$$\therefore M = 868x \text{ ft-lb.}$$

The next interval is between the beginning of the uniform load and the point force. Thus, observing Fig. 2(b), we get:

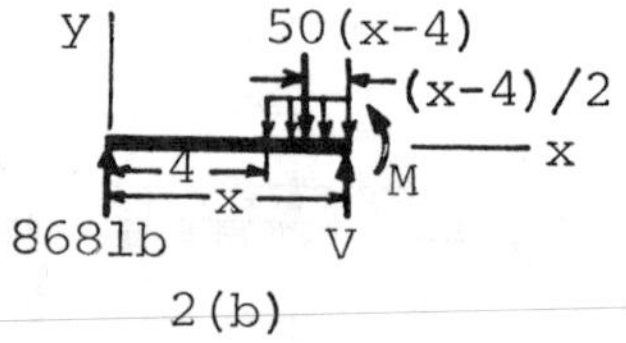

2(b)

$4 < x < 8$:

$$\sum F_y = 0 \qquad 868 - 50(x - 4) + V = 0$$

$$\therefore V = 50x - 1068 \text{ lb}$$

$$\sum M = 0 \qquad -868x + \frac{50(x - 4)^2}{2} + M = 0$$

$$\therefore M = -25x^2 + 1068x - 400 \text{ ft-lb}$$

We now consider the interval between the point force and the end of the uniform load. Thus, observing Fig. 2(c) we get:

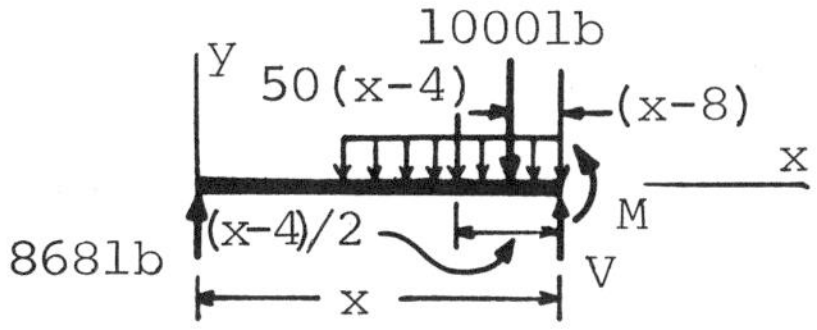

2(c)

8 < x < 12:

$\sum F_y = 0 \quad 868 - 50(x - 4) - 1000 + V = 0$

$\therefore V = 50x - 68$ lb

$\sum M = 0 \quad -868x + \frac{50(x - 4)^2}{2} + 1000(x - 8) + M = 0$

$\therefore M = -25x^2 + 68x + 7600$ ft-lb.

The next interval is between the end of uniform loading and the point couple. We can now replace the uniform loading by its resultant of 400 lb. as shown in Fig. 2(d). Thus,

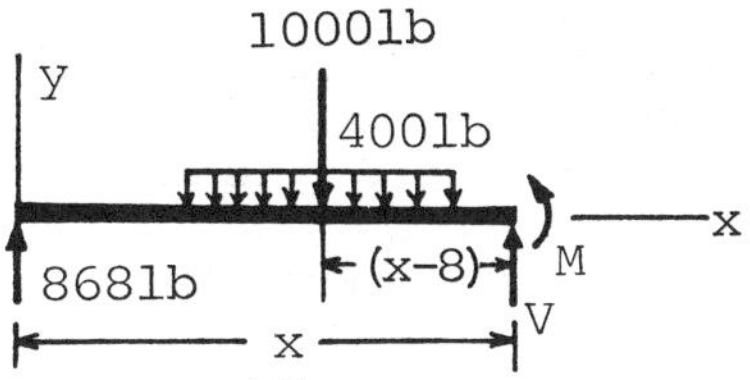

2(d)

12 < x < 18:

$\sum F_y = 0 \quad 868 - 400 - 1000 + V = 0$

$\therefore V = 532$ lb

$\sum M = 0 \quad -868x + 1400(x - 8) + M = 0$

$\therefore M = -532x + 11,200$ ft-lb.

The last interval goes from the point couple to the right support. It is to be pointed out that the point couple does not contribute directly to the shear force and so we could have used the above formulation for V for the interval 18 < x < 22. However, the couple does contribute directly to the bending moment and thus the additional interval is required. Accordingly, using Fig. 2(e), we get

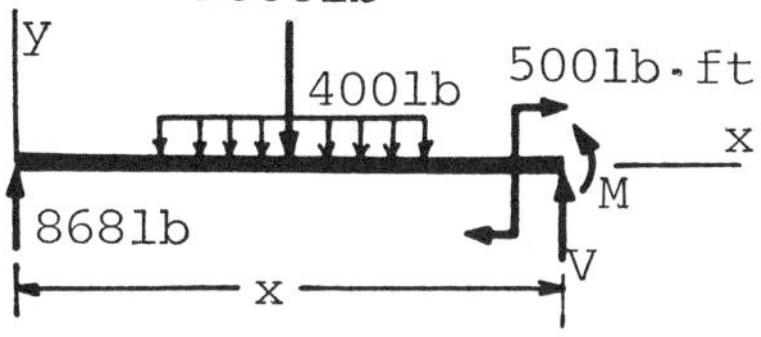

2(e)

$\underline{18 < x < 22}$:

$$V = 532 \text{ lb} \quad \text{(as in previous interval)}$$

$$\sum M = 0, \quad -868x + 1400(x - 8) - 500 + M = 0$$

$$M = -532x + 11{,}700 \text{ ft-lb}$$

• PROBLEM 2-10

Determine the numerically maximum bending moment in the beam ABC loaded as shown in the figure.

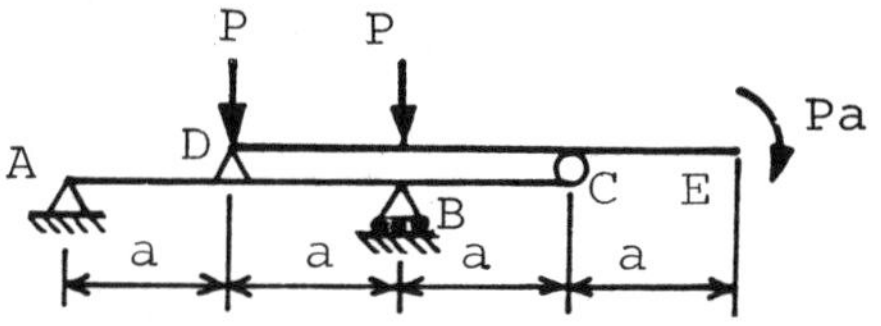

Fig. 1.

Solution: In this problem, the forces and bending moment are applied to one beam, DE, and transferred to a second beam, ABC. It is desired to find the bending moment of greatest magnitude in the second beam, ABC. The convention used in this problem for external applied moments is: counter clockwise moments are considered positive, and clockwise moments are considered negative.

A symmetrical beam will be bent just as much by a moment in one direction as by a moment in the other direction. When the problem asks for "numerically maximum bending moment", the largest moment, regardless of sign, is desired. In order to find this, the first beam must be analyzed to find the forces it exerts on the second beam at the points of contact, D and C.

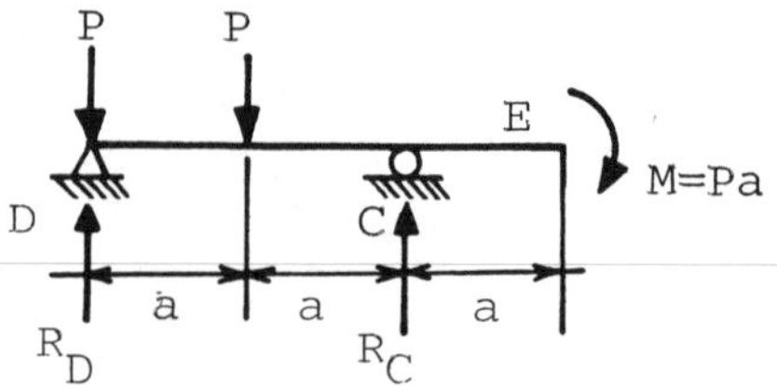

Fig. 2.

Consider the free body diagram of the first beam, DE. In reaction to the applied loads and moment, forces are exerted on the beam at the supports D and C. Moment equilibrium is used to find these reaction forces.

$$\sum M \text{ about } D = 0$$

$$(+\circlearrowleft) \quad P(0) - P(a) + R_C(2a) - Pa = 0$$

The load, P, and reaction force, R_D, acting on point D have no moment arm with respect to D and thus contribute zero moment about point D. R_C is the only unknown that remains. Combining the Pa terms and dividing both sides by 2a:

$$R_C = \frac{2Pa}{2a} = P$$

$$\sum M \text{ about } C = 0$$

$$\overset{\curvearrowleft}{+} \quad P(2a) - R_D(2a) + P(a) + R_C(0) - Pa = 0$$

As before, since R_C has a moment arm of zero length with respect to point C, it contributes no moment about C. Again as before, solving for the reaction that remains:

$$R_D = \frac{2aP}{2a} = P$$

If the reaction forces found are correct, they should just counteract the applied loads.

Check for equilibrium of beam DE,

$$\text{i.e. } \sum F_y = 0$$

$$P + P = R_C + R_D$$

Substituting in for R_C and R_D:

$$P + P = P + P.$$

The beam is in equilibrium and the calculated values of R_D and R_C are correct.

The forces at the points of contact, C and D, between the two beams have been found. Now the second beam, ABC, can be analyzed.

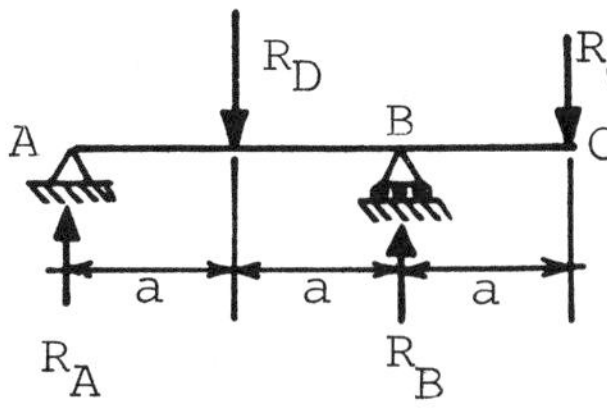

Fig. 3.

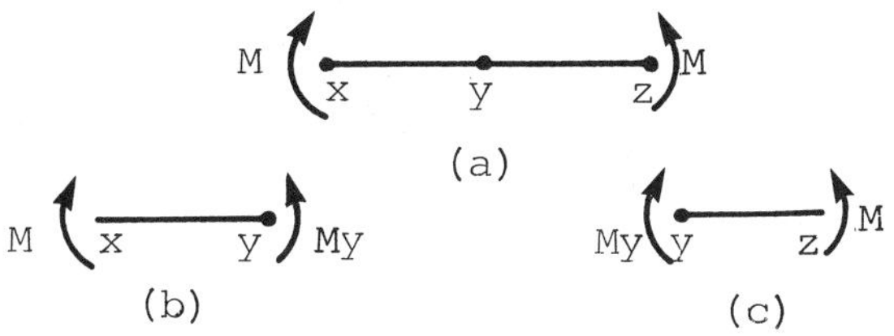

Fig. 4.

Consider the free body diagram for beam ABC (Fig. 3).

Notice that the reactions of beam DCE now act as the applied forces on beam ABC at the points of contact of the two beams. In reaction to the applied forces, forces are exerted on the beam ABC at the supports A and B. These reaction forces are found by moment equilibrium.

$\sum M$ about A = 0   See Fig. 3.

$$\overset{+}{\circlearrowleft} \quad \therefore -aR_D - 3aR_C + 2aR_B = 0$$

Since R_A has zero moment arm with respect to point A, it contributes no moment about A. Dividing both sides by 2a:

$$R_B = \frac{1}{2}R_D + \frac{3}{2}R_C$$

Substituting for R_D and R_C gives

$$R_B = \frac{1}{2}P + \frac{3}{2}P$$

$$R_B = 2P.$$

$\sum M$ about B = 0

$$\overset{+}{\circlearrowleft} \quad \therefore -2aR_A - aR_C + aR_D = 0$$

$$\therefore R_A = \frac{R_D}{2} - \frac{R_C}{2}$$

Substituting for R_D and R_C gives:

$$R_A = \frac{P}{2} - \frac{P}{2} = 0$$

Looking at Figure 3, it can be understood why R_A is zero. R_D and R_C are equal forces at equal distance from the support B, so they balance each other.

As an additional check, force equilibrium in the vertical direction can be verified:

$$\sum F_y = 0$$

$$R_D + R_C = R_B + R_A$$

Substituting in the values

$$P + P = 2P + 0.$$

Now that all the forces on the second beam ABC are known, the internal bending moment at every point along the beam can be found. This is done by cutting the beam into sections and analyzing the free body diagram for each section.

If the same convention used above for complete beams was used for beams cut into sections, the same point in a beam could have both a positive and a negative moment depending on whether the section to the right or to the left of the cut was analyzed.

Consider the beam XYZ in Fig. 4a. For purposes of analysis the beam is cut at point Y and the internal reaction moment at Y is found. Using the convention for external applied moments, Fig. 4b is analyzed:

+ $\sum M = 0$ Sum of the moments about Y is zero.

$$-M + M_Y = 0$$

$$M_Y = +M.$$

Fig. 4c is analyzed:

+ $\sum M = 0$ Sum of the moments about Y is zero.

$$M_Y + +M = 0$$

$$M_Y = -M$$

So at the point Y, the internal moment is both positive and negative M. To resolve this difficulty, a new sign convention is needed. When analyzing bending moments about the left-hand end of a section, all bending moments, applied external and internal reacting, are positive clockwise and negative counterclockwise. When analyzing moments about right hand ends of beam sections the convention is: counterclockwise moments are considered positive, and clockwise moments are considered negative.

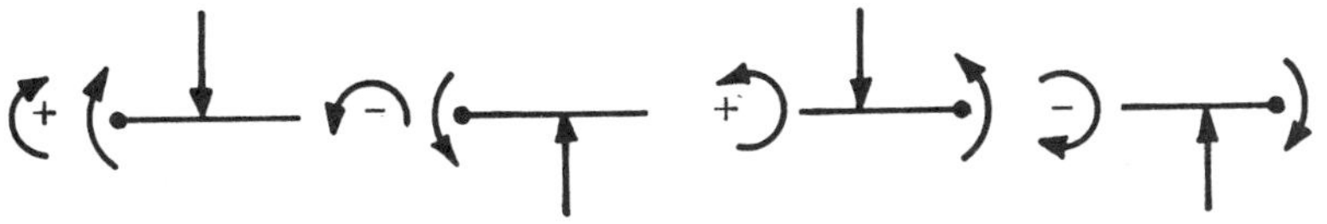

Left hand end of section   Right hand end of section

Fig. 5.

Analyzing the free body diagram in Fig. 4b using the above sign convention for moment about right-hand end of section:

$\sum M = 0$ Sum of the moments about Y is zero.

+ $M_Y - M = 0$

$$M_Y = M$$

Analyzing Fig. 4c using convention for moment about left-hand end:

$\sum M = 0$ Sum of the moments about Y is zero.

+ $M_Y - M = 0$

$$M_Y = M$$

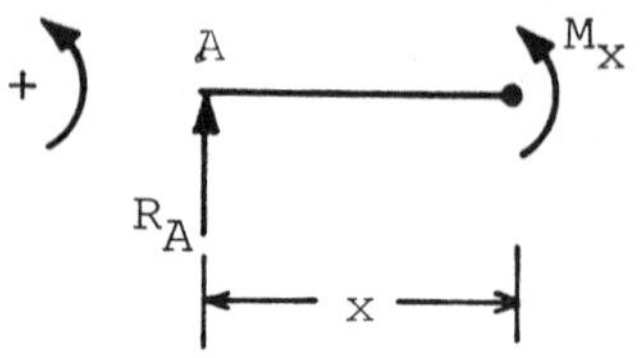

Fig. 6.

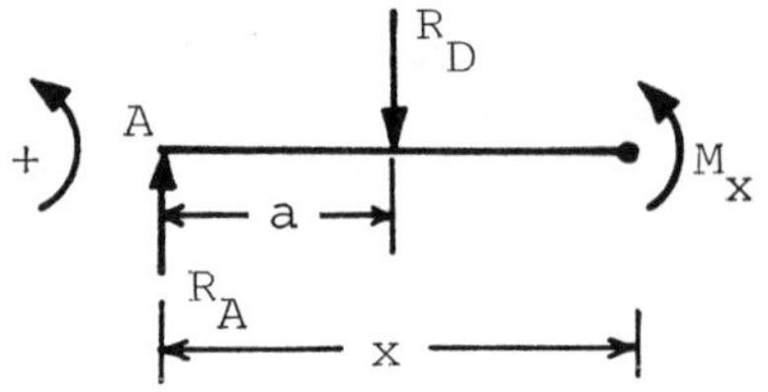

Fig. 7.

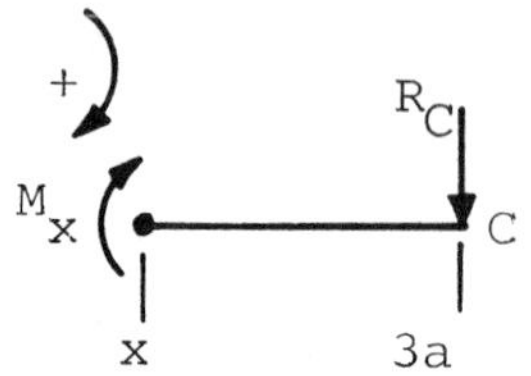

Fig. 8.

It is seen that this convention gives consistent results.

Moment equations for beam ABC:

$0 < x \le a$

$\sum M = 0$ about point x.

$$M_x - xR_A = 0$$

Substituting for R_A gives

$$M_x = 0$$

$a < x \le 2a$

$\sum M = 0$ about point x.

$$M_x - R_A x + R_D(x - a) = 0$$

Substituting for R_A and R_D gives

$$M_x = 0 - P(x - a).$$

For the last part of the beam, the section to the right of the cut is analyzed.

$2a < x \le 3a.$

$\sum M = 0$ about point x.

$$M_x + R_C(3a - x) = 0$$

Substituting for R_C gives

$$M_x = -P(3a - x)$$

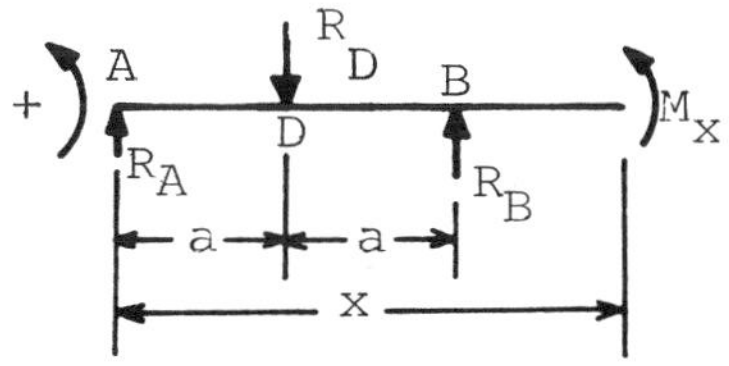

Fig. 9.

Check by analyzing the section to the left of the cut.

$\Sigma M = 0$ about point x.

$$M_x - R_B(x - 2a) + R_D(x - a) - R_A(x)$$

Substituting in:

$$M_x = 2P(x - 2a) - P(x - a) + 0(x)$$

$$M_x = Px - 3Pa$$

Compare this to the answer above

$$Px - 3Pa = -P(3a - x)$$

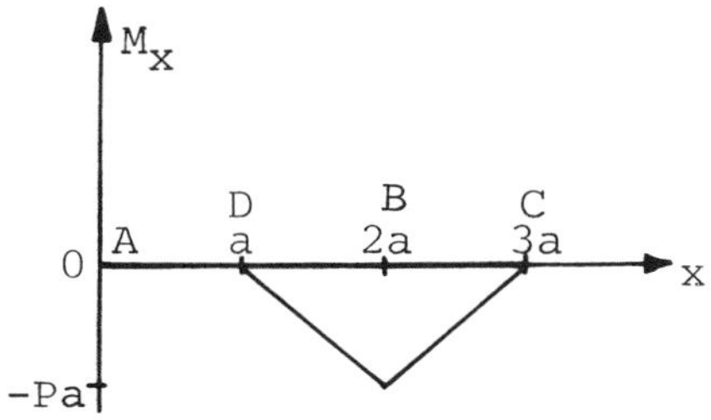

Fig. 10.

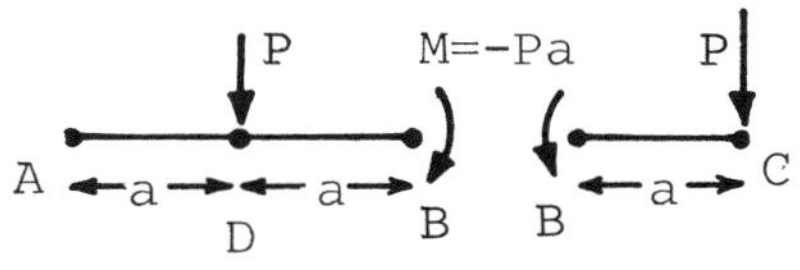

Fig. 11.

To find the maximum moment, draw a moment diagram.

$0 < x \leq a$	$a < x \leq 2a$	$2a < x \leq 3a$
$M_x = 0$	$M_x = -P(x - a)$	$M_x = -P(3a - x)$
	$M_{max} = -P(2a - a)$	$M_{max} = -P(3a - 2a)$
	$M_{max} = -Pa$	$M_{max} = -Pa$

The bending moment varies between zero and -Pa.

$$|M_{max}| = Pa \text{ at point B.}$$

This means that if beam ABC were cut at point B the resulting moment would be as in Fig. 11.

Evaluate the shear and bending-moment equations for the beam shown in Fig. 1.

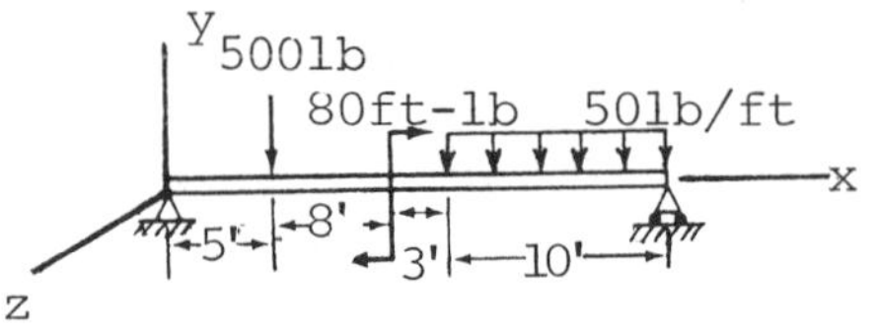

Fig. 1.

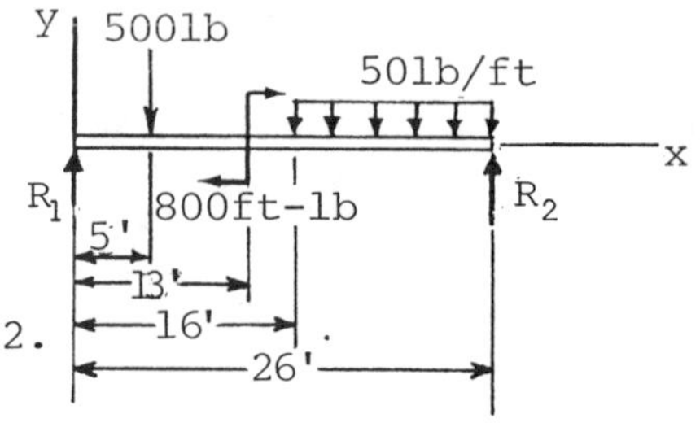

Fig. 2.

Solution: We need to find the reaction forces at the two supports and evaluate the shear and bending moment from the free body diagram of each section. Each segment is examined separately.

A free-body diagram of the beam is shown in Fig. 2. We can immediately compute the supporting forces as follows:

$\sum M_2 = 0$:

$$-R_1(26) + (500)(21) - 800 + (500)(5) = 0$$

$$\therefore R_1 = 469.2 \text{ lb}$$

$\sum M_1 = 0$:

$$R_2(26) - (500)(21) - 800 - (500)(5) = 0$$

$$\therefore R_2 = 530.8 \text{ lb}$$

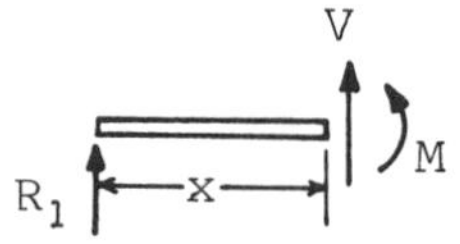

Fig. 3.

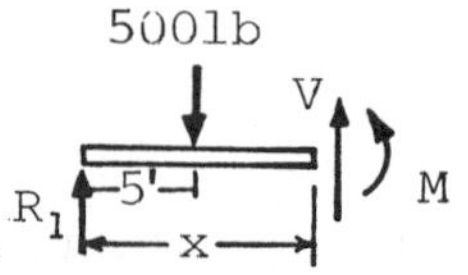

Fig. 4.

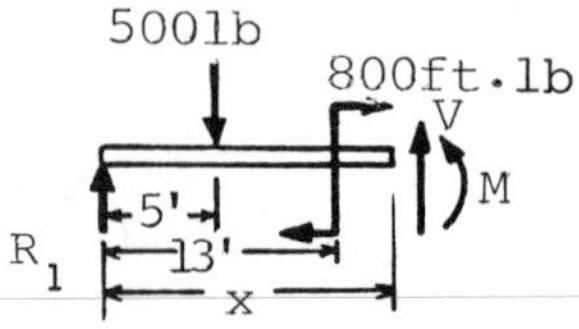

Fig. 5.

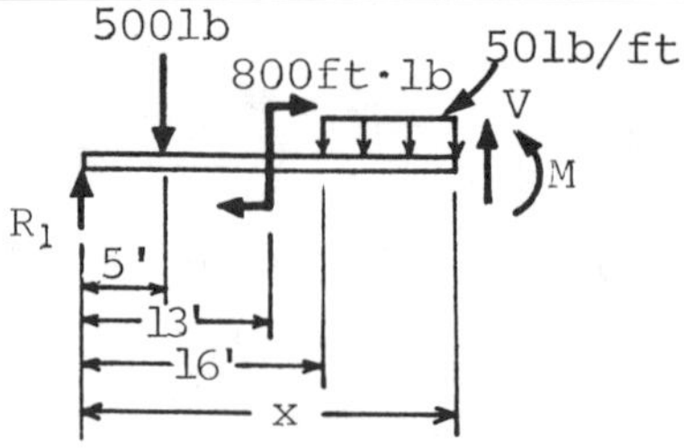

Fig. 6.

We may now directly give the shear force V and bending moment M while viewing Fig. 2. Thus: (see Fig. 3)

$0 < x < 5$:

$$V = -R_1 = -469.2 \text{ lb}$$

$$M = 469.2x \text{ ft-lb.}$$

$\underline{0 < x < 13}$: (see Fig. 4)

$$V = -469.2 + 500 = 30.8 \text{ lb}$$

$$M = 469.2x - 500(x - 5) = -30.8x + 2500 \text{ ft-lb.}$$

$\underline{0 < x < 16}$: (see Fig. 5)

$$V = 30.8 \quad \text{(same as previous interval)}$$

$$M = 469.2x - 500(x - 5) + 800 = - 30.8x + 3300 \text{ ft-lb}$$

$\underline{0 < x < 26}$: (see Fig. 6)

$$V = -469.2 + 500 + 50(x - 16) = -769.2 + 50x \text{ lb}$$

$$M = 469.2x - 500(x - 5) + 800 - \frac{50(x - 16)^2}{2}$$

$$= -25x^2 + 769.2x - 3100$$

• PROBLEM 2-12

Determine shear, axial-force, and bending-moment diagrams for the cantilever loaded with an inclined force at the end, Fig. 1.

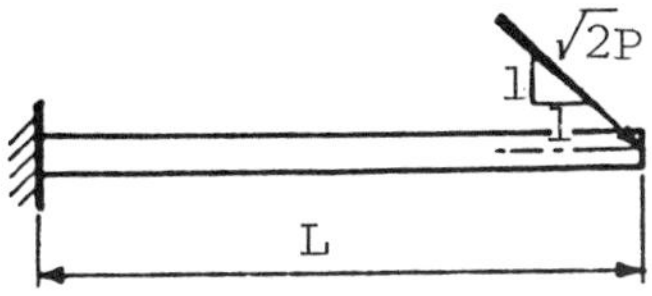

Fig. 1.

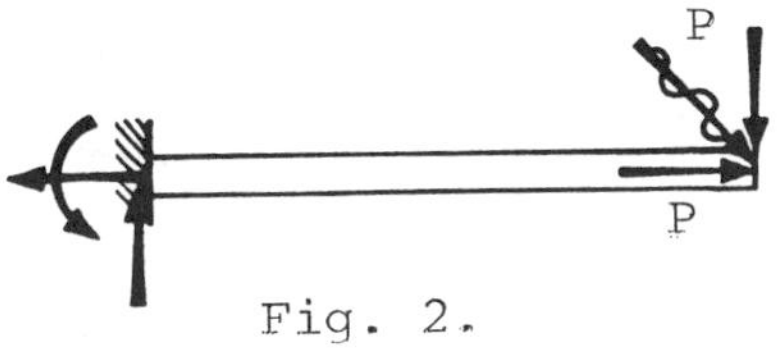

Fig. 2.

Solution: We can solve this problem by considering the right section or the left section of the beam after cut at an arbitrary section. Since the right section is free-ended and the applied force is known, it is easier to consider the right section. In this case, we do not have to find the reactions at the wall. The inclined force is replaced by its vertical and horizontal components shown in Fig. 2.

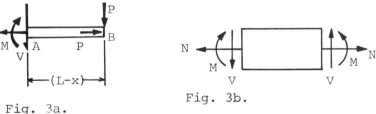

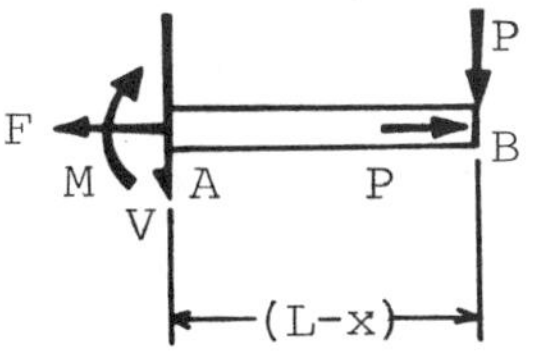

Fig. 3a.

Fig. 3b.

For a section at a distance x from the left support, the right section is shown in Fig. 3a. The axial force (F), shear (V) and bending moment (M) are drawn in the diagram in a positive sense according to the convention shown in Fig. 3b.

Force equilibrium:

$\sum F_x = 0 \ \rightarrow +$, $\quad P - F = 0$

$F = P$

$\sum F_y = 0 \ \uparrow +$, $\quad -P - V = 0$

$V = -P$

$\sum M_A = 0 \ \circlearrowleft +$, $\quad -P(L - x) - M = 0$

$M = -P(L - x)$

FIG. 4

FIG. 5

FIG. 6

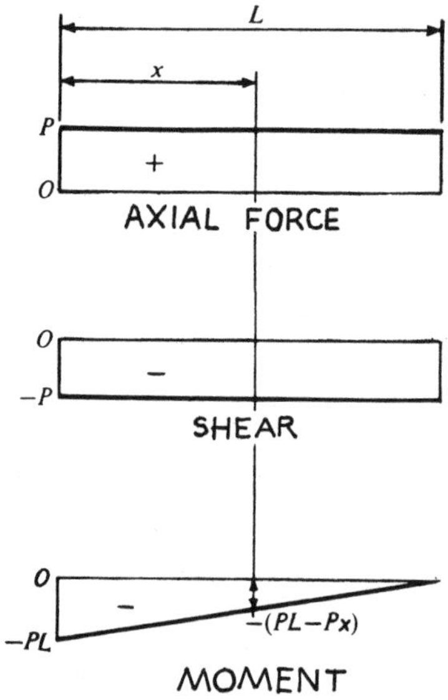

The three diagrams are plotted in Fig. 4, Fig. 5 and Fig. 6.
Notice, the shear force diagram is a negative constant, so from the relation $-V = \frac{dM}{dx}$, the slope of the moment diagram is positive.

• **PROBLEM 2-13**

Construct shear, axial-force, and bending-moment diagrams for the weightless beam shown in Fig. 1 subjected to the inclined force P = 5 kips.

FIG. 1

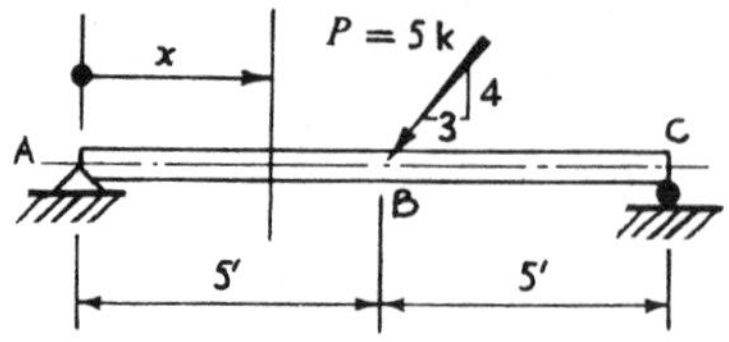

Solution: The beam is divided into two parts by the 5k force. Consider the two portions separately. By making sections between AB and BC, and considering the free body to the left or the right of the sections, we shall be able to solve for the forces and moments on each section. Resolve the 5k load into its horizontal and vertical components.

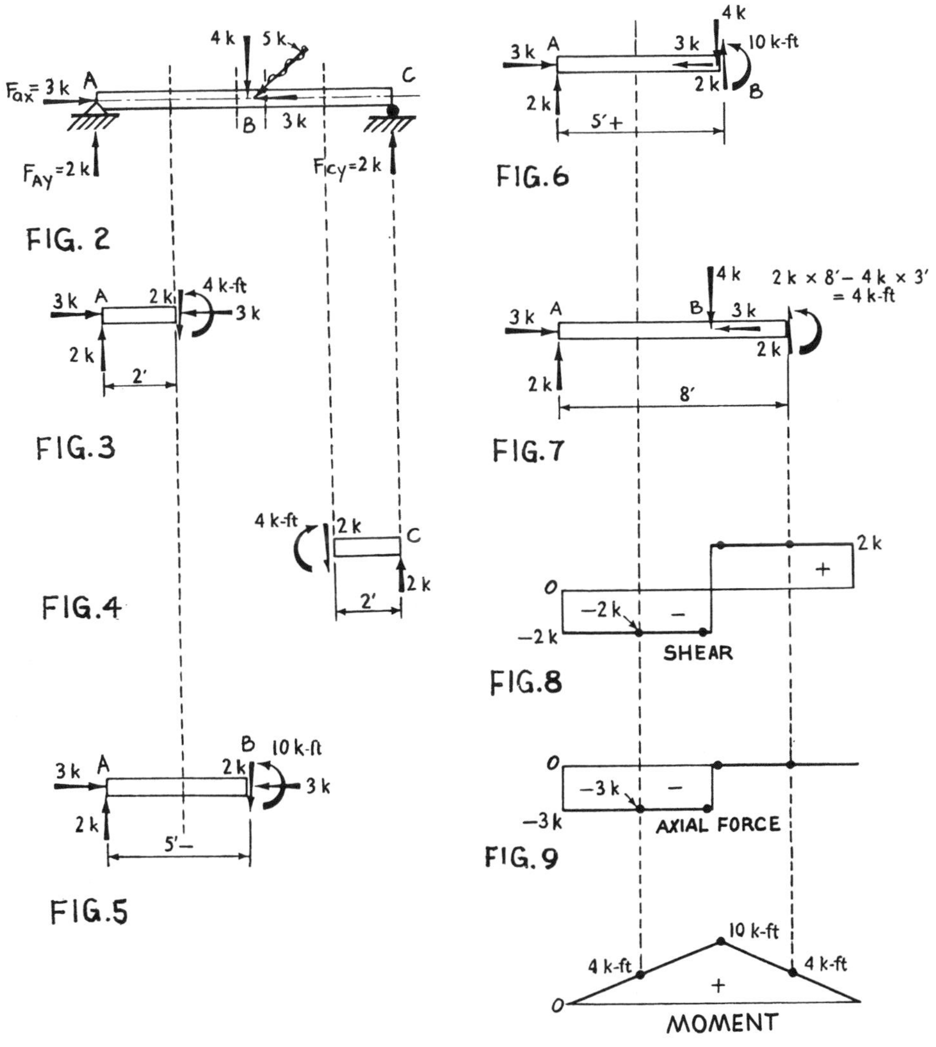

FIG. 10

A free-body diagram of the beam is shown in Fig. 2. Solving for reactions at supports:

By equilibrium,

$$\sum F_x = 0 \quad \rightarrow + \qquad F_{Ax} - 3k = 0$$

$$F_{Ax} = 3k$$

$$\sum F_y = 0 \quad \uparrow + \qquad F_{Ay} + F_{Cy} = 4k$$

By symmetry. $F_{Ay} = F_{Cy}$.

Therefore, $F_{Ay} = F_{Cy} = 2k$.

Solve for shear V, axial force F and bending moment M at section 2 feet from A (see Fig. 3).

By equilibrium consideration,

$$\sum F_y = 0 \quad \uparrow + , \qquad -V + 2k = 0$$

$$V = 2k.$$

$$\sum F_x = 0 \quad \rightarrow + , \qquad F + 3k = 0$$

$$F = -3k$$

$$\sum M = 0 \circlearrowright + , \qquad M - (2k \times 2 \text{ ft.}) = 0$$

$$M = 4 \text{ k-ft}.$$

The result is shown in Fig. 3.

Similarly, by making a cut at a section 2 feet away from point C (see Fig. 4), we can find the shear, axial force and bending moment by applying equilibrium to the free body diagram. The result is shown in Fig. 4.

For the cut section at point B, we have to consider the points just to the right of B and just to the left of B, as shown in Fig. 5 and Fig. 6. By applying equilibrium to the free body diagram as before, we can find the shear, axial force and bending moment.

Fig. 8, Fig. 9 and Fig. 10 are the plots of shear, axial force and bending moment of the beam, using the results obtained previously. Note that the shear force and axial force from A to B, and from B to C do not vary. The shear changes sign at point B, as does the axial force, which drops to zero at point B. This is because no other forces are applied between AB,and BC and the bending moment has to vary linearly between AB and BC because $V = -\frac{dM}{dx}$. When V is constant, the slope of M is also constant, as shown in Fig. 10.

• PROBLEM 2-14

Construct shear and bending-moment diagrams for the beam loaded as shown in Fig. 1 using the summation procedure. Find the location of the inflection points for the beam.

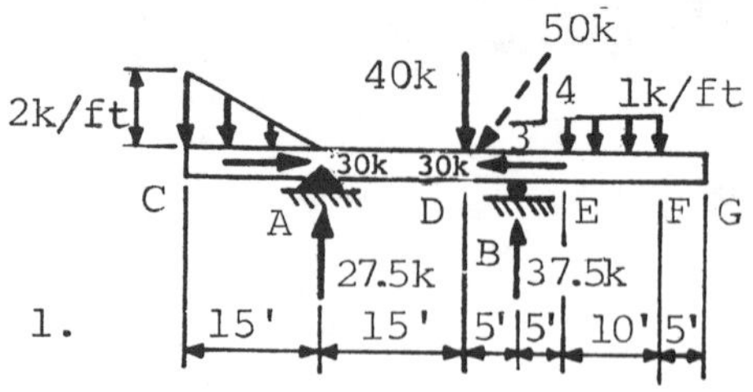

Fig. 1.

Solution: In order to use summation procedure, find all the forces applied to this beam, including the reactions at the supports. Resolve the inclined force into its horizontal and vertical components. To find reaction forces at supports, apply equilibrium:

$$\sum F_x = 0 \quad \overset{\rightarrow}{+}\,, \qquad R_{Ax} - 30 = 0$$

$$R_{Ax} = 30k$$

At point A,

$$\sum M_A = 0 \quad \circlearrowleft + \,,$$

$$-(1\text{ k/ft.} \cdot 10\text{ ft})(5' + 5' + 5' + 15')$$

$$-\ (40k)(15') + R_{By}(15' + 5')$$

$$+\ (\tfrac{1}{2} \times 2\text{ k/ft} \times 15\text{ ft})(\tfrac{2}{3} \times 15') = 0$$

$$-\ 300\text{ k-ft} - 600\text{ k-ft} + 20'\ R_{By} + 150\text{ k-ft} = 0$$

$$20'\ R_{By} = 750\text{ k-ft}$$

$$R_{By} = \frac{750}{20}\text{ k}$$

$$R_{By} = 37.5\text{ k (acting upwards)}$$

At point B, $\sum M_B = 0$

$$(40k) \times (5') + (15k)(5' + 15' + 10') - R_{Ay}(15' + 5')$$

$$-\ (114\text{ ft})(10')(5' + 5') = 0$$

$$200 + 450 - 20\ R_{Ay} - 100 = 0$$

$$R_{Ay} = 27.5\text{ k}$$

Check:

$$\sum F_y = 0$$

$$R_{Ay} + R_{By} - 40 - 10 - 15 = 0$$

$$27 \cdot 5 + 37 \cdot 5 - 65 = 0.$$

$$0 = 0.$$

With reactions known, the summation of forces is begun from the left end of the beam to obtain the shear diagram, Fig. 2. By the formulas $\frac{dV}{dx} = -w$ and $\frac{dM}{dx} = -V$, the shear force can be obtained by observing the change of applied load along the beam and the moment diagram from the shear force diagram. At first, the downward distributed load is large, then it decreases. Hence, the shear diagram in the zone CA at first has

2

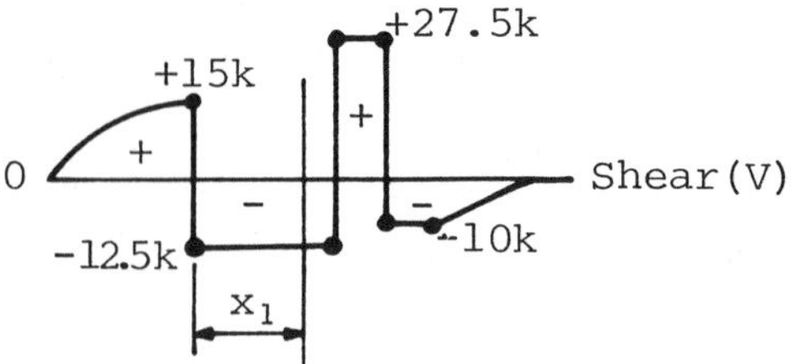

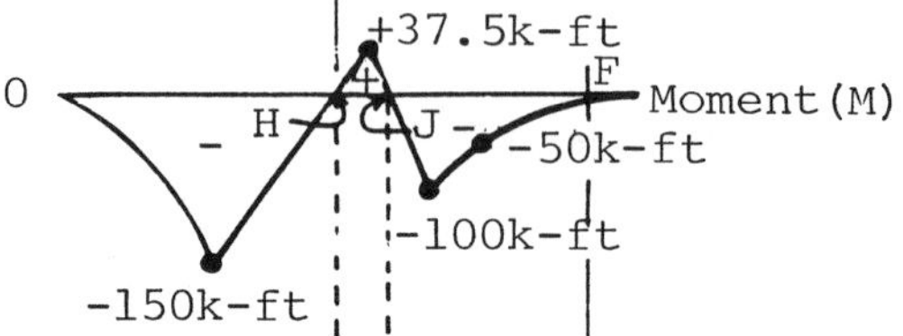

Fig. 3

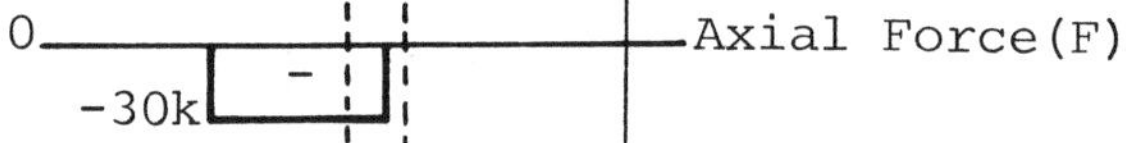

Fig. 4

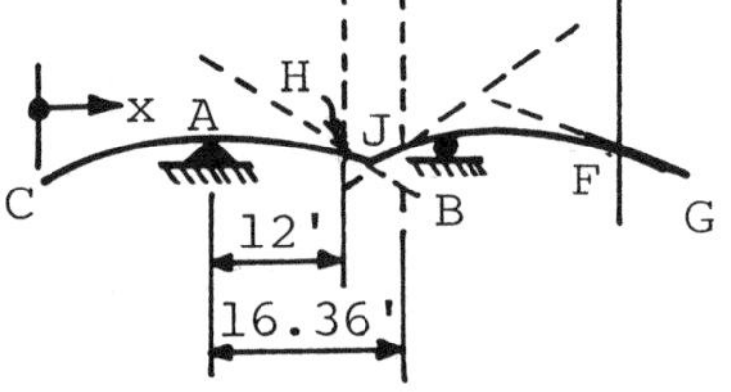

Fig. 5

a large, positive slope, which gradually decreases resulting in a curved line, which is concave downward. In this case, a downward load is positive. The total downward force from C to A is 15 kips (total load = area $\Delta = 1/2 \times 2$ k/ft $\times$ 15 ft = 15 kips), which is the positive ordinate of the shear diagram, just to the left of the support A. At A, upward reaction of 27.5 kips moves the ordinate of the shear diagram downward to -12.5 kips. This value of the shear applies to a section through the beam just to the right of the support A. The total change in the shear at A is equal to the reaction.

No forces are applied to the beam between A and D, hence there is no change in the value of the shear. At D, the 40 kip downward component of the concentrated force raises the value of the shear to +27.5 kips. Similarly, the value of the shear is lowered to -10 kips at B by the presence of reaction 37.5 k acting upward. Since between E and F the uniformly distributed load acts downward, an increase in shear takes place at a constant rate of 1 kip per foot. Thus at F the shear becomes zero, which serves as the final check.

To construct the moment diagram shown in Fig. 3 by the summation method, areas of the shear diagram in Fig. 2 must be continuously summed from the left end and taken with the opposite signs to yield the moment. For the segment CA the shear gradually increases to the right; therefore in the moment diagram a curve concave downward results. The slope of the curve gradually increases in negative sense. The moment at A is equal to the area of the shear diagram for the segment CA with reversed sign. This area is enclosed by a curved line, and it may be determined by integration. This procedure often is tedious, and, instead of using it, the bending moment at A may be obtained from the fundamental definition of a moment at a section.

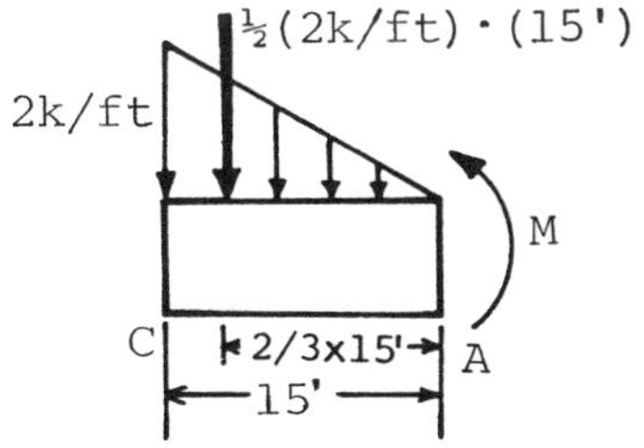

$$\sum M_A = 0 \curvearrowleft + ,$$

$$M + \frac{1}{2}(2)(15) \times (\frac{2}{3} \times 15) = 0$$

$$M = -150 \text{ k-ft}$$

Hence we obtain moment at point A. The remaining areas of the shear diagram in this example are easily determined. Due attention must be paid to the signs of these areas. It is convenient to arrange the work in tabular form. At the right end of the beam, the customary check is obtained.

M_A .....-1/2(15)2(10) =	-150.0 kip-ft	(moment around A)
+ 12.5(15) =	+187.5	(-1) × (shear area A to D)
M_D..................	+ 37.5 kip-ft	
- 27.5(5) =	-137.5	(-1) × (shear area D to B)
M_B..................	-100.0 kip-ft	
+ 10(5) =	+ 50.0	(-1) × (shear area B to E)
M_E..................	- 50.0 kip-ft	
+ 1/2(10)10 =	+ 50.0	(-1) × (shear area E to F)
Check: ....M_F =	0.0 kip-ft	

The diagram for the axial force is in Fig. 4. The compressive force acts only in the segment AD of the beam.

By definition, an inflection point corresponds to a point on a beam where the bending moment is zero. Since $M = -\int V(x)dx$, we only have to find the point where total area in V(x) diagram becomes zero. Thus, since the moment at A is -150 kip-ft, the point of zero moment occurs when the shear-diagram area with the reversed sign from A to H equals this moment, i.e., $-150 + (-1)(-12.5x_1) = 0$

Hence the distance AH = 150/12.5 = 12 ft, or x = 27 ft.

Similarly, beginning with a known positive moment of +37.5 kip-ft at D, the second inflection point is known to occur when a portion of the shear-diagram area with the reversed sign between D and J reduces this value to zero. Again, writing an expression to find where the moment reduces to zero:

$$+37.5 \text{ k-ft} + (-1)(27.5 \text{ k})(x_2) = 0$$

$$x_2 = \frac{37.5}{27.5} = 1.36' = DJ$$

Hence, the distance DJ = 37.5/27.5 = 1.36 ft, or the distance AJ = 15 + 1.36 = 16.36 ft.

• PROBLEM 2-15

Construct shear and moment diagrams for the member shown in Fig. 1. Neglect the weight of the beam.

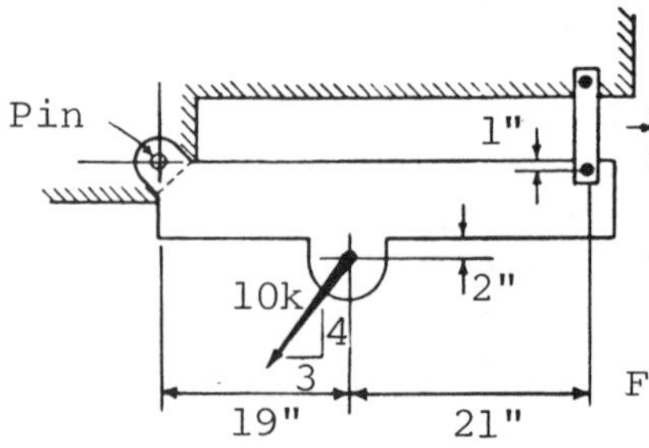

Fig. 1.

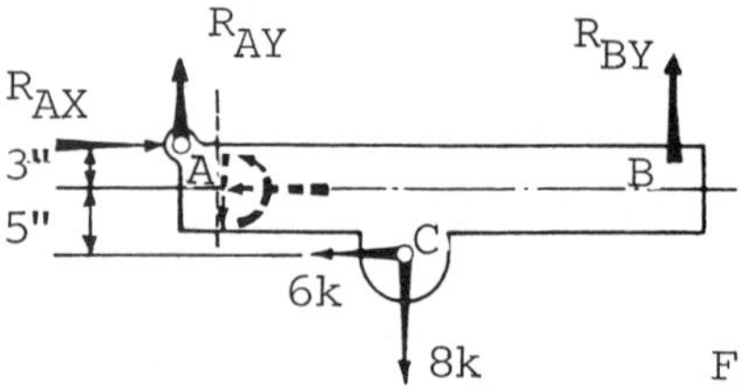

Fig. 2.

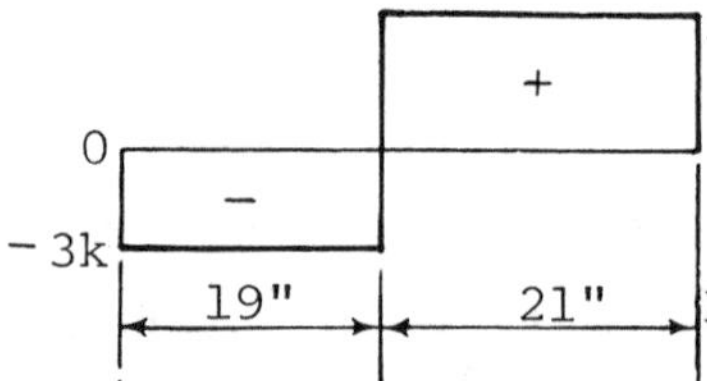

Fig. 3.

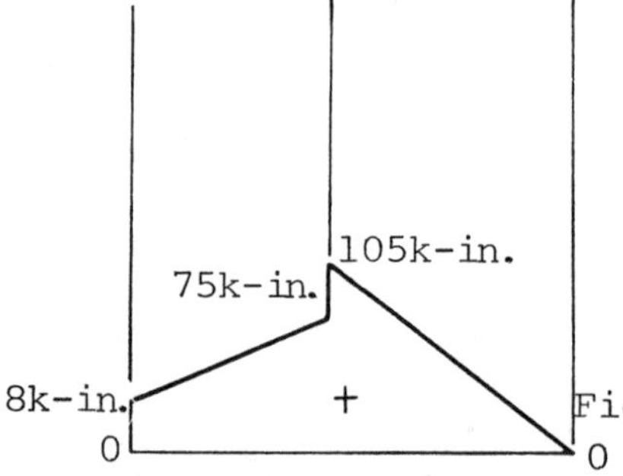

Fig. 4.

Solution: In this case, definite dimensions are assigned for the depth of the beam. The beam, for simplicity, is assumed to be rectangular in its cross-sectional area, consequently its longitudinal axis lies 3 in. below the top of the beam. Note carefully that this beam is not supported on its axis.

Find the reaction forces at the supports and then consider the section forces and moments by free body diagram.

A free-body diagram of the beam with the applied force at C resolved into components is shown in Fig. 2. Taking moment about the pin:

$$\Sigma M_A = 0 \circlearrowleft + , \qquad R_{By} \cdot (40) - 8 \cdot (19) - 6 \cdot (8) = 0$$

$$R_{By} \cdot (40) = 200$$

$$R_{By} = 5k$$

$\sum F_y = 0 \quad \uparrow + , \qquad R_{By} + R_{Ay} = 8$

$$5 + R_{Ay} = 8$$

$$R_{Ay} = 3k.$$

$\sum F_x = 0 \quad \rightarrow + , \qquad R_{Ax} - 6 = 0$

$$R_{Ax} = 6k$$

In constructing the shear diagram, we notice that at A, there is a vertical reaction of 3 lbs upwards, therefore, the shear is -3k at A. It remains constant between A and C since no external force acts on the beam. At point C, there is an external force of 8k acting downwards. This induces an increase in the shear force by 8k to the right of point C. The final value +5k will remain constant between C and B. This value will be cancelled out by the 5k reaction upwards at point B.

In constructing the moment diagram in Fig. 4, particular care must be exercised. As was emphasized earlier, the bending moments may always be determined by considering a segment of a beam, and they are most conveniently computed by taking moments of external forces around a point on the centroidal axis of the beam. Thus, by passing a section just to the right of A and considering the left segment, it may be seen that a positive moment equal to 6k · 3", or 18 k-in, is resisted by the beam at this end. Hence the plot of the moment diagram must start with an ordinate of +18 kip-in. The other point of the beam where a concentrated moment occurs is C. Here the horizontal component of the applied force induces a clockwise moment of 6(5) = 30 kip-in. around the neutral axis. Just to the right of C this moment must be resisted by an additional positive moment. This causes a discontinuity in the moment diagram. The summation process of the shear-diagram areas applies for the segments of the beam where no external moments are applied. The necessary calculations are carried out below in tabular form.

M_A........+6(3) = + 18 kip-in.

+3(19) = $\underline{+\ 57}$ (-1) × (shear area A to C)

Moment just to left of C = + 75 kip-in.

+6(5) = $\underline{+\ 30}$ (external moment at C)

Moment just to right of C = + 105 kip-in.

-5(21) = $\underline{-\ 105}$ (-1) × (shear area C to B)

Check: $M_B = 0$

(a) For the structure shown in the diagram, find the forces in members JR, AD, CD, and DE.
(b) Find the bending moment, the axial force, and the shear force at the center of beam EJ. Neglect deformation considerations of the beam in computing the bending moment.

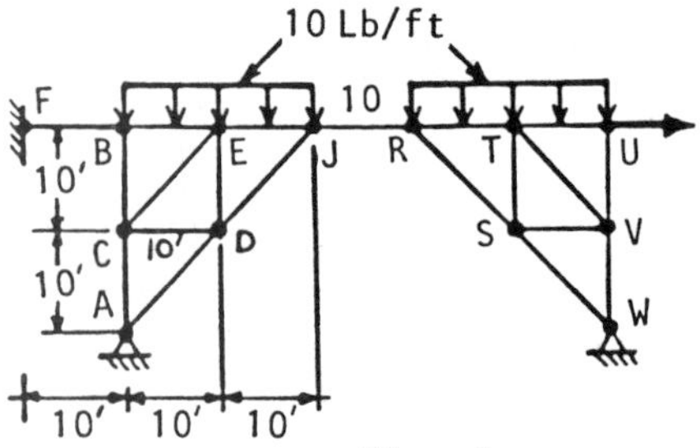

Fig. 1

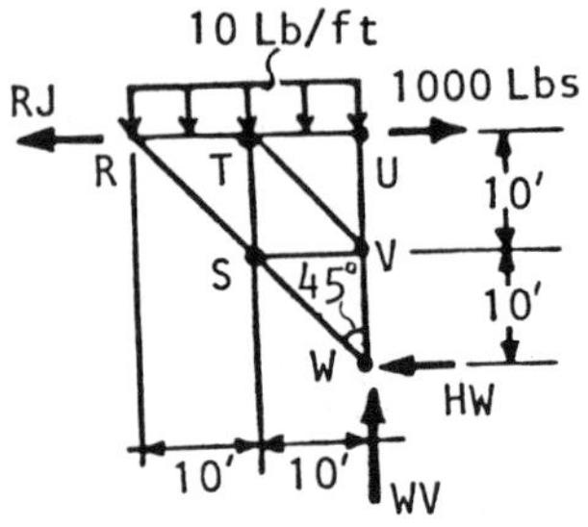

Fig. 2

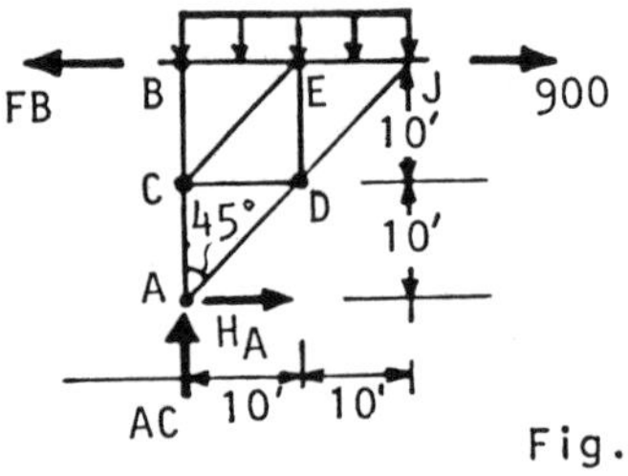

Fig. 3

Solution: To determine the forces in the members, break up the structure at convenient locations. Fig. 2 shows all the forces acting on a section of the structure to the right of a cut in member JR. For this structure to be in equilibrium, a force equivalent to the force in member JR has to be applied at the cut.

Since joint W is a hinge (all the joints in the structure are considered as hinges because the structure is a truss), then $\sum M = 0$ at joint W for all the externally applied forces.

Therefore, $20JR + 20 \times 10 \times \frac{20}{2} - 1000 \times 20 = 0$

$$\therefore JR = 900$$

Fig. 3 shows all the forces acting on a section of the structure cut between JR and AB. Using the same reasoning as before: $\sum M = 0$ at joint A for all the externally applied forces, therefore

$$20FB - 20 \times 10 \times \frac{20}{2} - 900 \times 20 = 0$$

$$\therefore FB = 1000 \text{ lbs.}$$

$\sum F_V = 0$ for all externally applied forces on the structure, therefore, $AC - (20 \times 10) = 0$

$$AC = 200 \text{ lbs.}$$

$\sum F_H = 0$ for all externally applied forces on the structure, therefore $900 + H_A - FB = 0$.

Substituting for FB and solving, we have $H_A = 100$ lbs.

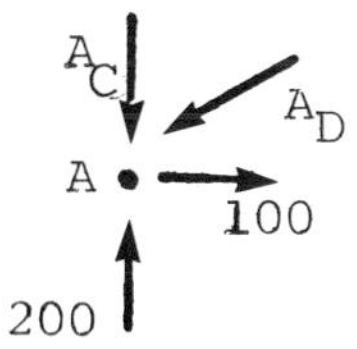

Fig. 4.

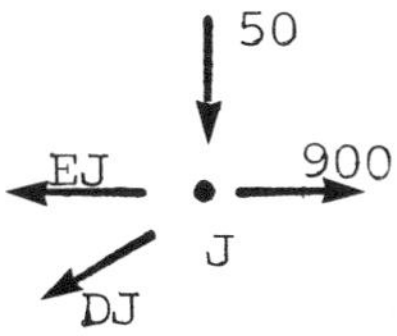

Fig. 5.

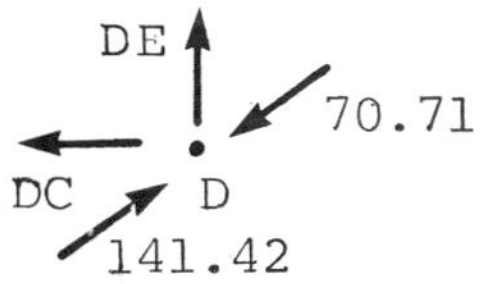

Fig. 6.

Now to solve for the forces in the members within the structure, consider joint equilibrium, i.e., at each joint $\sum F_H = 0$ and $\sum F_V = 0$.

Joint A: $\sum F_H = 0$

$$\therefore \quad 100 - AD \cos 45 = 0$$

$$\therefore \quad AD = 141.42 \text{ lbs compressive}$$

Joint J:

When considering equilibrium of the joints, the uniformly distributed load is considered as point loads acting at the joints.

$$\sum F_V = 0$$

$$\therefore \quad -50 - DJ \cos 45 = 0$$

$$\therefore \quad DJ = -70{\cdot}71 \text{ lbs.}$$

The negative sign means the force is acting in the opposite direction to the chosen direction, and is compressive.

$$\sum F_H = 0$$

$$\therefore \quad 900 - EJ - DJ \cos 45 = 0$$

Substituting for DJ and solving we have

$$EJ = 950 \text{ lbs tensile}$$

Joint D:

Substituting for R_j in the equation for the moment we have

$$M = (5 \times 50) - (10 \times 5 \times \tfrac{5}{2})$$

$$= 125 \text{ ft-lbs.}$$

Consider a free body diagram at the middle of the beam (Fig. 6a).

$$\sum F_V = 0$$

$$R_j - \left(10 \times 5\right) - V = 0$$

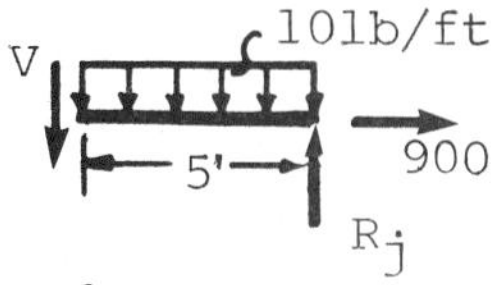

Fig. 6a.

Substituting for R_j and solving, we have

$$V = 0.$$

$\sum F_V = 0$

$$\therefore \quad DE + 141.42 \cos 45 - 70 \cdot 71 \cos 45 = 0$$

$$\therefore \quad DE = -50 \text{ lbs compressive}$$

b) Now consider beam EJ (Fig. 7).

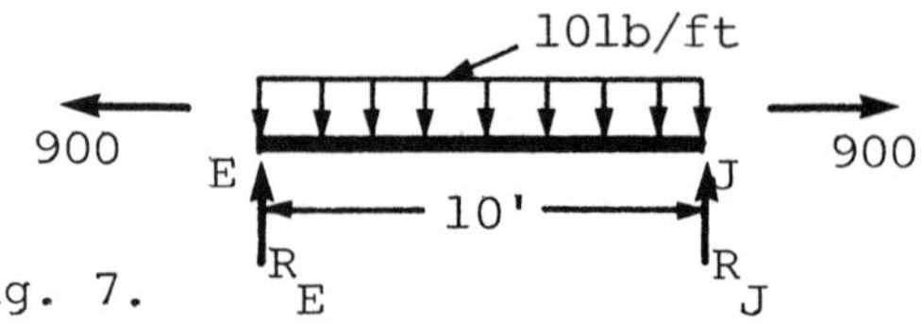

Fig. 7.

The bending in the middle of the beam is

$$5 \times R_j - (10 \times 5 \times \frac{5}{2})$$

R_j can be computed from equilibrium conditions of member EJ or by resolving the force in member JD in the vertical direction.

$$R_j = \frac{10 \times 10}{2} = 70 \cdot 71 \cos 45$$

$$= 50 \text{ lbs.}$$

• PROBLEM 2-17

A cantilever beam is subjected to uniform torque loading for one part of the beam, and axial loading having the distribution shown, for another part of the beam. Find the moments and forces in the beam.

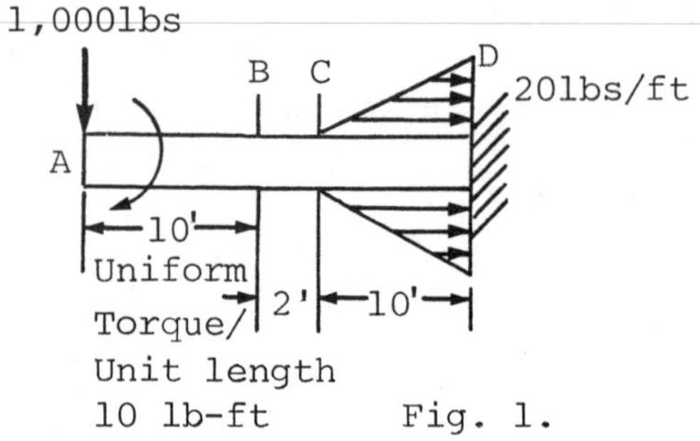

Fig. 1.

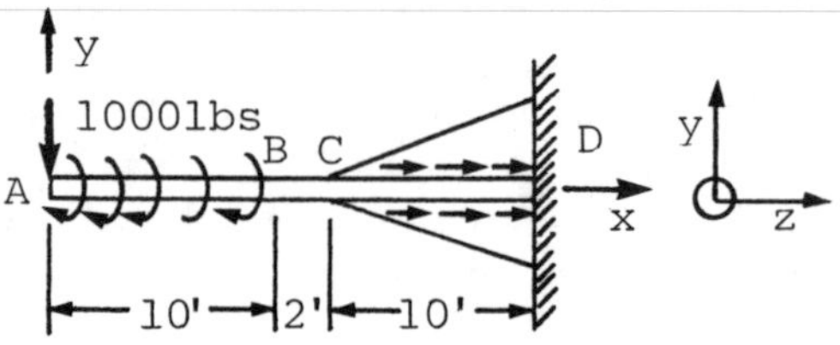

Fig. 2.

Solution: It is helpful to divide the beam into parts, and then to find the various forces and moments by analyzing the free body diagram of each part. First, establish a coordinate system as shown in Fig. 2. Then consider the beam in sections.

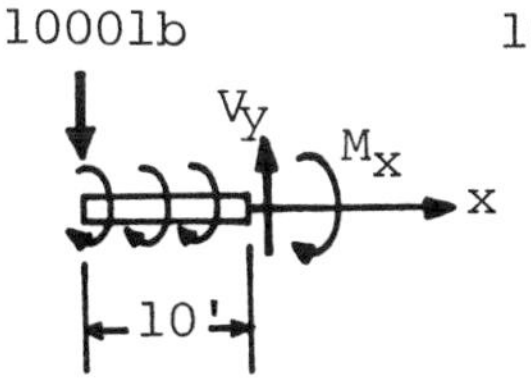

Fig. 3

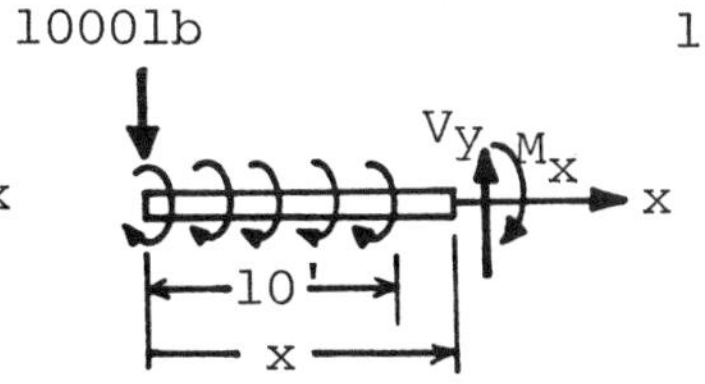

Fig. 4

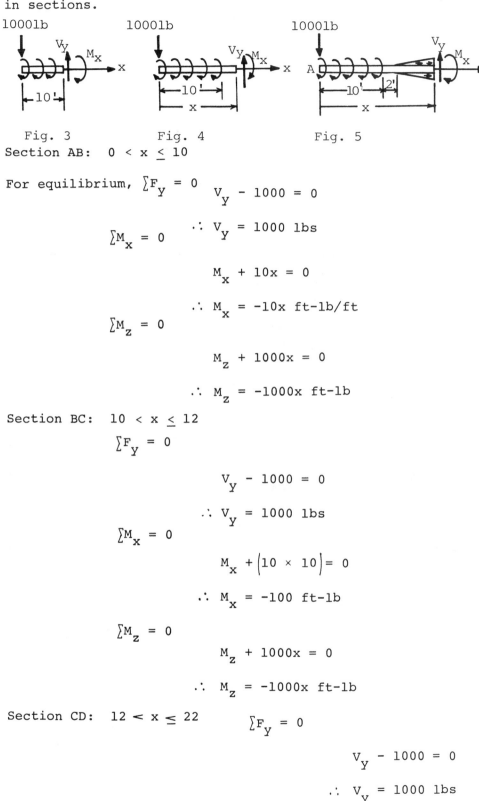

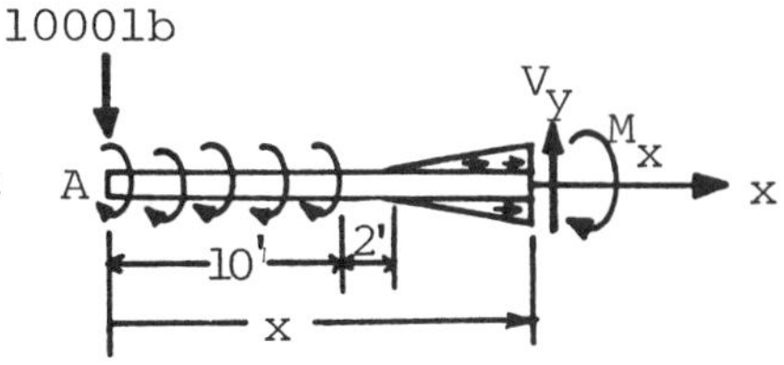

Fig. 5

Section AB: $0 < x \leq 10$

For equilibrium, $\sum F_y = 0$

$$V_y - 1000 = 0$$

$$\therefore V_y = 1000 \text{ lbs}$$

$\sum M_x = 0$

$$M_x + 10x = 0$$

$$\therefore M_x = -10x \text{ ft-lb/ft}$$

$\sum M_z = 0$

$$M_z + 1000x = 0$$

$$\therefore M_z = -1000x \text{ ft-lb}$$

Section BC: $10 < x \leq 12$

$\sum F_y = 0$

$$V_y - 1000 = 0$$

$$\therefore V_y = 1000 \text{ lbs}$$

$\sum M_x = 0$

$$M_x + (10 \times 10) = 0$$

$$\therefore M_x = -100 \text{ ft-lb}$$

$\sum M_z = 0$

$$M_z + 1000x = 0$$

$$\therefore M_z = -1000x \text{ ft-lb}$$

Section CD: $12 < x \leq 22$ $\sum F_y = 0$

$$V_y - 1000 = 0$$

$$\therefore V_y = 1000 \text{ lbs}$$

$$\sum M_x = 0$$

$$M_x + \left|10 \times 10\right| = 0$$

$$\therefore M_x = -100 \text{ ft-lb}$$

$$\sum M_z = 0$$

$$M_z + 1000x = 0$$

$$\therefore M_z = -1000x \text{ ft-lb}$$

$$\sum F_x = 0$$

The load causing the horizontal force in this section is the frictional force, f.

First, write an expression for the loading intensity, f.

$$f = \frac{20(x - 12)}{10} = 2(x - 12)\text{lb/ft}$$

$$H + 2(x - 12)\frac{(x - 12)}{2} = 0$$

$$\therefore H = -(x - 12)^2$$

$$= (-x^2 + 24x - 144)\text{lbs.}$$

• PROBLEM 2-18

A bent rod is subjected to the loads shown. Find the shear force, bending moment, and axial force for the three sections of the rod.

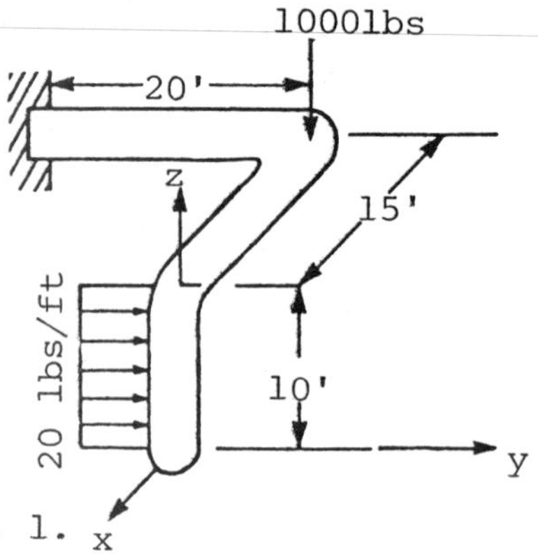

Fig. 1.

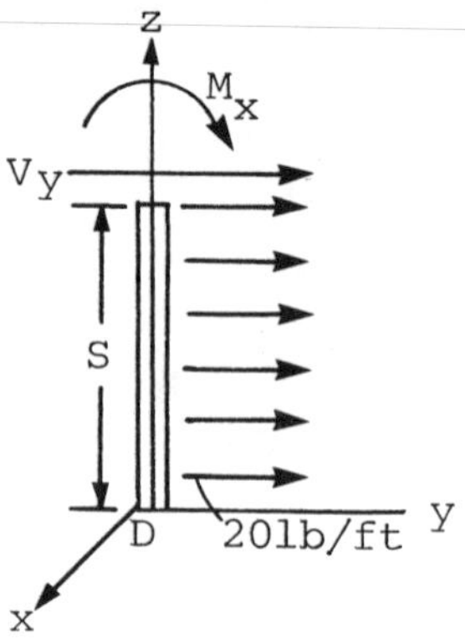

Fig. 2.

Solution: This is a three-dimensional problem and can be solved using either vector notation or several coordinate systems, one for each section AB, BC, and CD of the beam. All three have the same orientation, but the origins are different. Here the solution will be presented using several co-ordinate systems. The origin of the first coordinate system will be at D with the orientation shown. The second will be at C and the third at B.

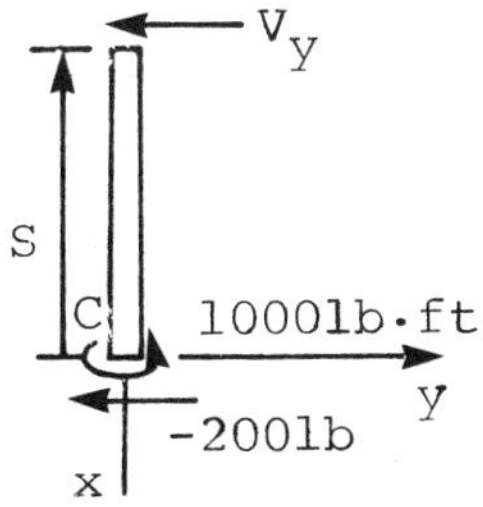

Fig. 3.

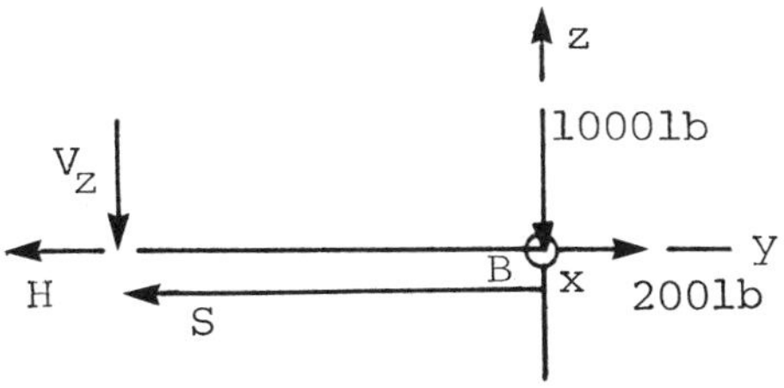

Fig. 4.

Draw a free body diagram for each section as shown in Figs. 2, 3 and 4, showing the forces and moment acting at a cut along that section.

CD: $0 < s \leq 10$, (Fig. 2)

For equilibrium: $\sum F = 0$

$$\therefore V_y + 20s = 0$$

$$\therefore V_y = -20s$$

$$M_x = \int V_y ds$$

$$= \int -20s\, ds + C$$

$$= -10s^2 + C$$

At $s = 0$, $M = 0$ $\therefore C = 0$

$$M_x = -10s^2$$

Note that M_x is moment about the x-axis. Moment about the y-axis M_y and moment about the z-axis M_z do not exist.

To determine which moment exists, use the rule of thumb; i.e., if the four fingers of the right hand are wrapped around the point at which moment is considered in such a way as to produce an imaginary bend similar to the one produced by the moment acting on the beam, then the moment acts about the axis in the direction of the thumb.

BC: $10 < s \leq 25$, (Fig. 3)

$$\sum F_y = 0$$

$$\therefore V_y - 200 \text{ lbs} = 0 \qquad V_y = 200 \text{ lbs}$$

Moment in the x-direction:

$$\sum M_x = 0$$

$$\therefore M_x - 1000 \text{ lb-ft} = 0$$

$$\therefore M_x = 1000 \text{ lb-ft}$$

Using the rule of thumb as explained above, the only other moment that exists is about the z-axis and this is due to the 200 lbs force acting in the y-direction.

$$\therefore M_z = \int V_y \, ds \qquad = \int 200 \, ds = 200s + C$$

At $s = 10$, $M_z = 0$

$$\therefore 0 = 2000 + C \Rightarrow C = -2000$$

$$\therefore M_z = (200s - 2000) \text{lb-ft.}$$

BA: $25 < s \leq 45$, (Fig. 4)

Notice that here, we have a 200 lb force acting in the y-direction which corresponds to an axial force on this member and will be designated as H.

$$\sum F_y = 0$$

$$\therefore 200 - H = 0$$

$$H = 200 \text{ lbs}$$

$$\sum F_z = 0$$

$$\therefore V_z + 1000 = 0$$

$$V_z = -1000 \text{ lbs}$$

A moment M_z is transferred from section CB and its value is constant throughout the length of AB:

$$M_z = (200 \times 25 - 2000) \text{lb-ft}$$

$$= 3000 \text{ lb-ft.}$$

The only other moment that exists is about the x-axis.

$$M_x = \int V_z \, ds$$

$$= -\int 1000 \, ds + C$$

$$= -1000s + C.$$

When s = 25, M_x = 1000

$$\therefore 1000 = -1000 \times 25 + C$$

$$C = 26{,}000 \text{ and}$$

$$M_x = (-1000s + 26{,}000)\text{lb-ft.}$$

• PROBLEM 2-19

In the circular beam shown, the shear force, bending moment, and axial force vary as a function of θ. Calculate their relationships.

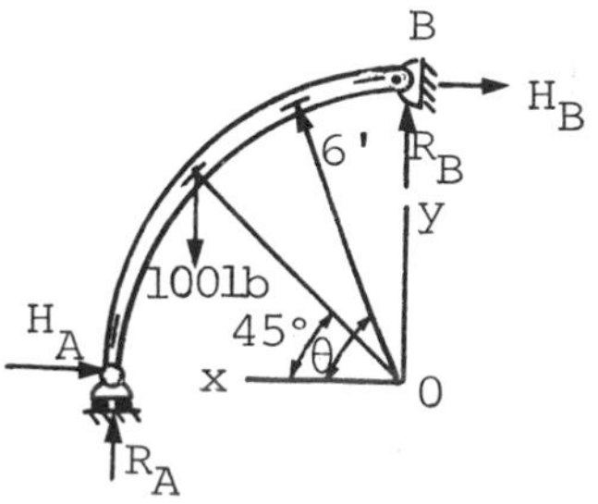

Fig. 1.

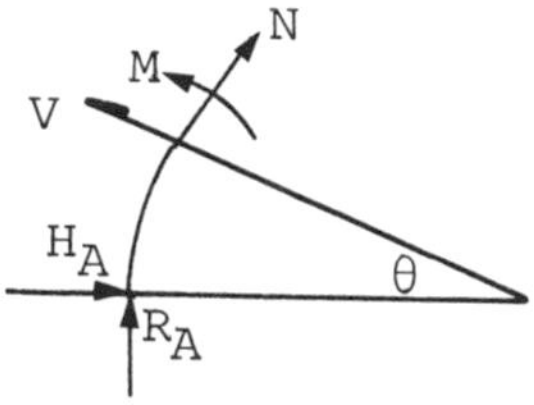

Fig. 2.

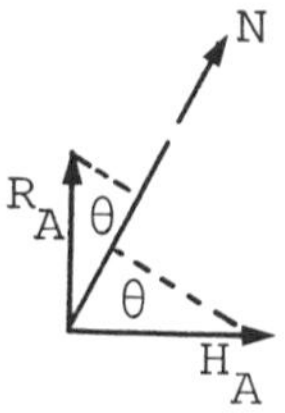

Fig. 2a.

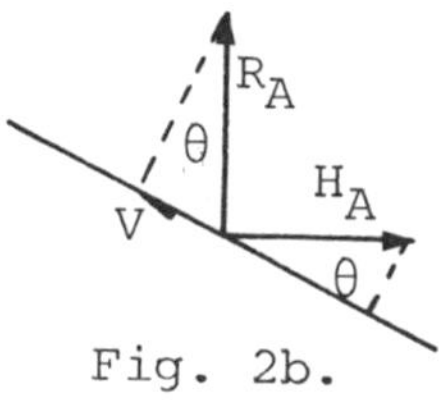

Fig. 2b.

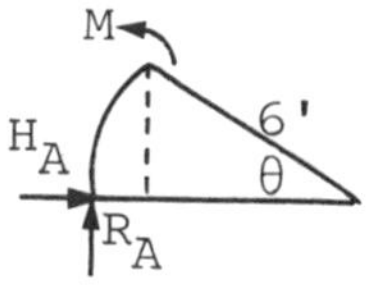

Fig. 2c.

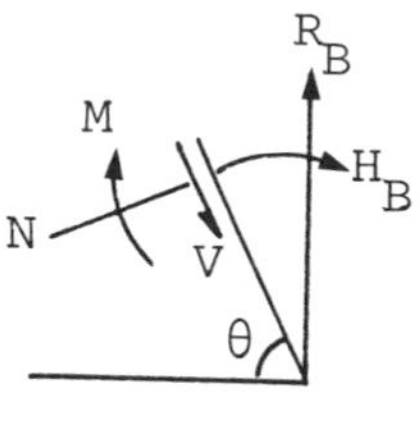

Fig. 3.

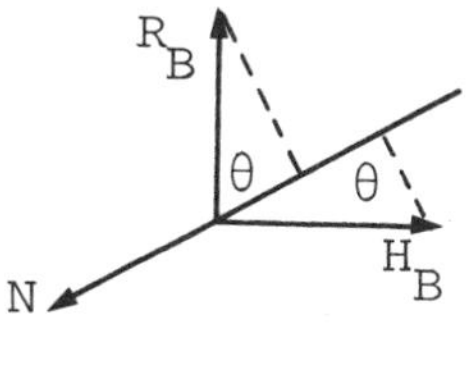

Fig. 3a.

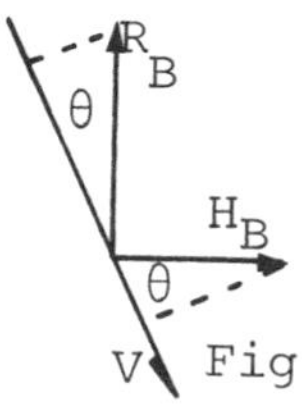

Fig. 3b.

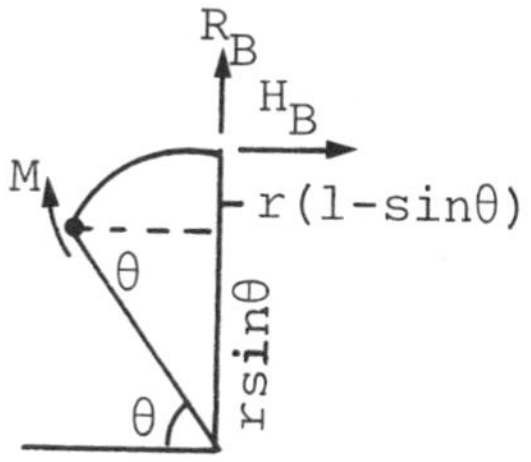

Fig. 3c.

Solution: The principle of equilibrium applied to a straight beam can also be applied to a curved beam.

The force system acting on the curved beam is as shown in Fig. 1, while Figures 2 and 3 show forces acting within the member.
First determine the reactions at A and B.

For equilibrium:

$\sum F = 0$ in the horizontal direction,

$\therefore H_A + H_B = 0.$ (1)

$\sum F = 0$ in the vertical direction,

$\therefore R_A + R_B - 100 = 0.$ (2)

$\sum M = 0$ at hinge A (see Fig. 4).

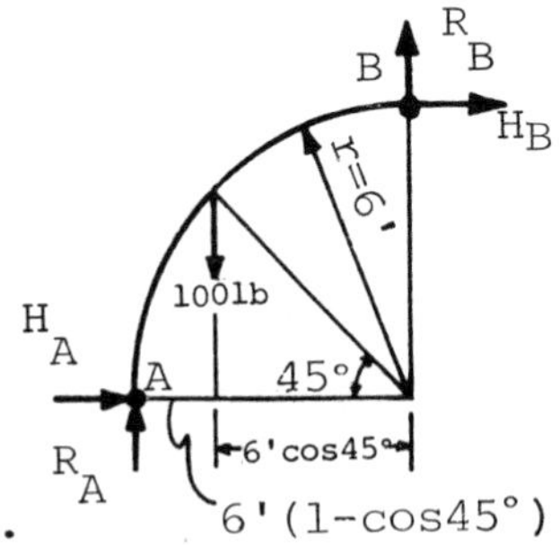

Fig. 4.

$+\circlearrowright \quad 100 \times 6(1 - \cos 45) - 6R_B - 6H_B = 0$

Dividing through by 6:

$100(1 - \cos 45) - R_B - H_B = 0$ (3)

$\sum M = 0$ at hinge B.

$+\circlearrowright \quad 6R_A - 100 \times 6 \cos 45 - 6H_A = 0$

$R_A - 100 \cos 45 - H_A = 0$ (4)

Solving these 4 equations with 4 unknowns gives:

From (1): $H_A = -H_B$

From (2): $R_A = 100 - R_B$

Solving for R_A and H_A in (4) gives

$$(100 - R_B) - 100 \cos 45 + H_B = 0$$

Subtractin H_B from both sides:

$$-H_B = (100 - R_B) - 100 \cos 45 \quad (5)$$

Substituting right side of (5) into (3) for $-H_B$ gives:

$$100(1 - \cos 45) - R_B + (100 - R_B - 100 \cos 45) = 0$$

$$2R_B = 100 - 100 \cos 45 + 100 - 100 \cos 45$$

$$R_B = 100 - 100 \cos 45$$

$$R_B = 29.3$$

Solving for R_A:

$$R_A = 100 - R_B = 100 - 29.3 = 70.7$$

Solving for H_B:

$$-H_B = (100 - R_B) - 100 \cos 45$$

$$H_B = -100 + R_B + 100 \cos 45$$

$$H_B = -100 + 29.3 + 100 \cos 45$$

$$H_B = -100 + 29.3 + 70.7$$

$$H_B = 0$$

$$H_A = H_B = 0$$

Now introduce an x-y coordinate system at the cut and resolve the forces to determine the values of N, V and M. The sign convention used in this problem is as shown in Figure 5.

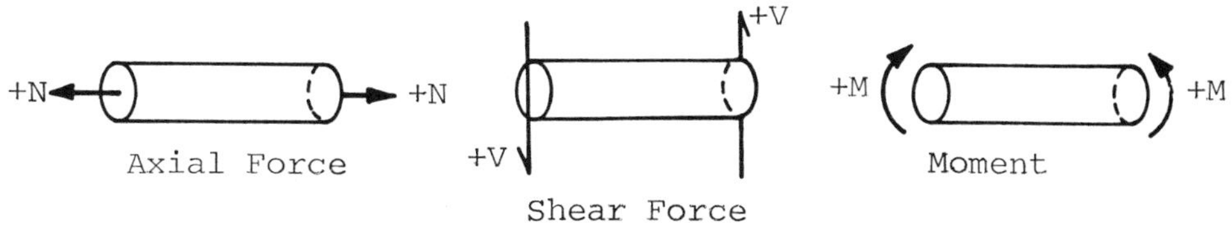

Fig. 5.

$0 < \theta < 45°$ (see Figs. 2 and 2a - 2c)

$$N = -R_A \cos \theta - H_A \sin \theta$$

$$N = -70.7 \cos \theta$$

$$V = -R_A \sin \theta + H_A \cos \theta$$

$$V = -70.7 \sin \theta$$

$$M = R_A r(1 - \cos \theta) - H_A r \sin \theta$$

$$M = (70.7)6(1 - \cos \theta) = 424(1 - \cos \theta)$$

$45 < \theta < 90$ (see Figs. 3, 3a-3c)

$$N = R_B \cos\theta + H_B \sin\theta$$

$$N = 29.3 \cos\theta$$

$$V = +R_B \sin\theta - H_B \cos\theta$$

$$V = +29.3 \sin\theta$$

$$M = R_B\, r \cos\theta - H_B\, r(1 - \sin\theta)$$

$$M = (29.3)(6)\cos\theta = 176 \cos\theta.$$

• PROBLEM 2-20

Consider a curved beam whose centroidal axis is bent into a semicircle of radius r = 10" as shown in Fig. 1. If this member is being pulled by a force P shown, find the axial force, the shear, and the bending moment at a section A-A which makes angle $\alpha = 45°$ with the line of the force P. The centroidal axis and the applied forces all lie in the same plane.

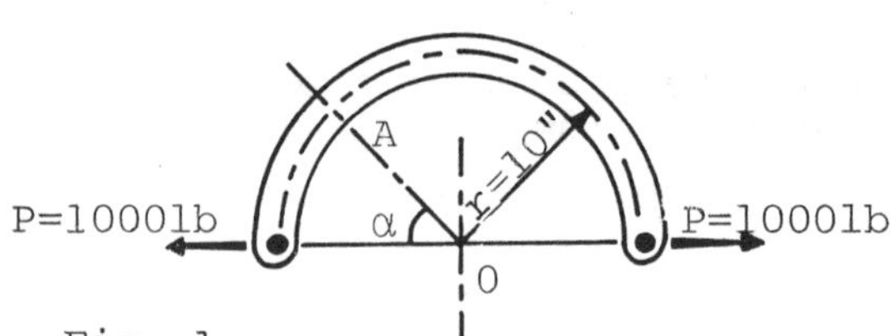

Fig. 1.

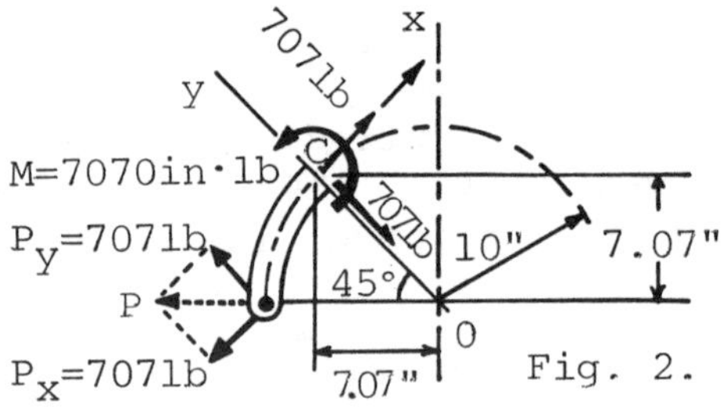

Fig. 2.

Solution: This problem can be solved using a similar method as that used for straight beams. Applying conditions of equilibrium to the free body, a segment of the beam is isolated as shown in Fig. 2. The applied force P is resolved into components parallel and perpendicular to the cut. These directions are taken respectively as the y and x axes. The x and y components of P are:

$$P_x = -P \sin\alpha$$

$$P_y = P \cos\alpha$$

From $\sum F_x = 0$, the axial force at the cut is $P \sin\alpha$. From $\sum F_y = 0$, the shear is $-P\cos\alpha$. The bending moment M at section A-A is obtained by taking the moment about point C.

$$\sum M_C = 0 \;\curvearrowleft +, \qquad M - P\,r \sin\alpha = 0$$

$$M = P\,r \sin\alpha$$

$\therefore$ M = 1000 lb (7.07 in.) = 7070 in-lbs

Note that the moments at the ends will vanish for $\alpha = 0°$ and $\alpha = 180°$. For $\alpha = 90°$, the shear vanishes and the axial force becomes equal to the applied force P. Likewise the maximum bending moment is associated with $\alpha = 90°$.

DIFFERENTIAL EQUILIBRIUM RELATIONSHIP

• PROBLEM 2-21

Give the shear force and the bending moment equations for the beam shown in the diagram and sketch shear force and bending moment diagrams.

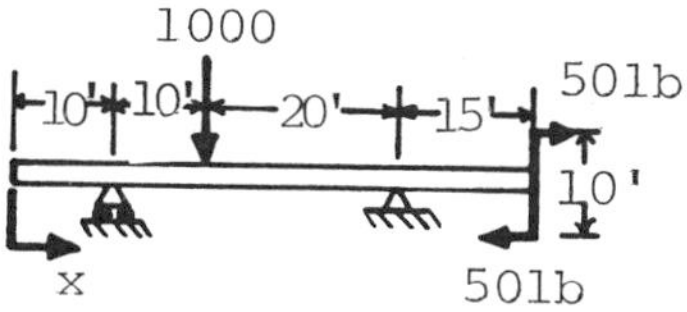

Fig. 1.

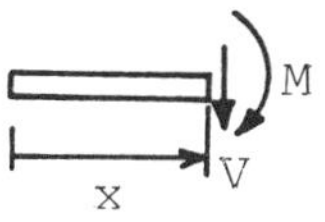

Fig. 2.

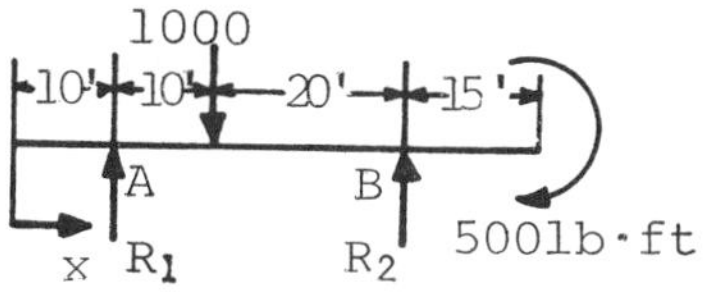

Fig. 3.

Solution: Since the beam is subject to several different forces and bending moments, it is helpful to divide the beam into several pieces and analyze each separately. Consider the beam in four sections, $0 < x \le 10$, $10 < x \le 20$, $20 < x \le 40$, and $40 < x \le 55$.

(a) $0 < x \le 10$ (Fig. 2)

No load is acting on this section of the beam, therefore,

$$V = 0 \quad \text{and} \quad M = -\int V\,dx + C$$

$$= 0$$

(b) $10 < x \le 20$ (Fig. 3)

First determine the reaction at the supports. This is done using moment equilibrium.

$\sum M = 0$ about point A (+ clockwise)

$$1000 \times 10 - 30R_2 + 500 = 0$$

$$\therefore R_2 = 350 \text{ lbs}$$

$\sum M = 0$ about point B (+ clockwise)

$$-1000 \times 20 + 30R_1 + 500 = 0$$

$$\therefore R_1 = 650 \text{ lbs}$$

These values can be checked by verifying vertical equilibrium.

$\sum F_y = 0 \qquad R_1 + R_2 - 1000 = 0$

$$350 + 650 - 1000 = 0.$$

$$1000 - 1000 = 0.$$

$$0 = 0.$$

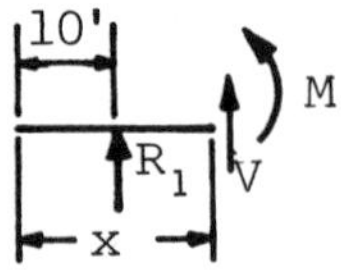

Fig. 4

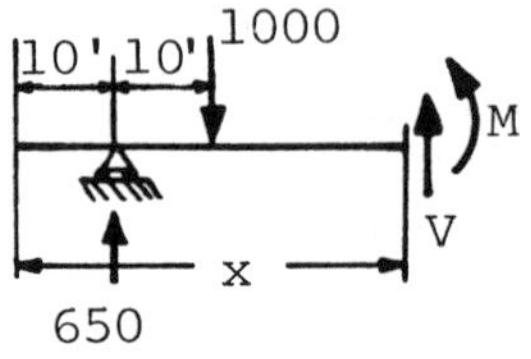

Fig. 5

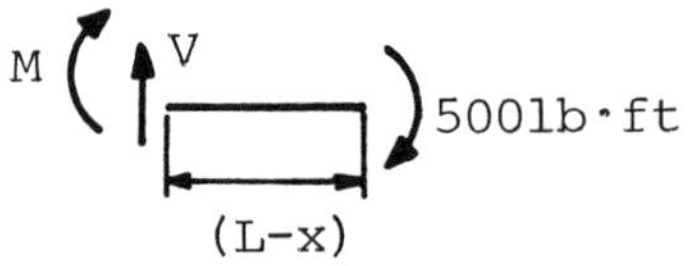

Fig. 6

Now consider a free body diagram (Fig. 4).

For equilibrium:

$\sum F = 0 \; ; \qquad R_1 + V = 0$

$$\therefore \; V = -650 \text{ lbs}$$

But $\qquad M = -\int V\,dx$

$$= -\int -650\,dx = 650x + C.$$

To determine C, consider the boundary conditions. At $x = 10$, $M = 0$

$$0 = 6500 + C$$

$$\therefore \; C = -6500 \text{ lb-ft}$$

$$\therefore \; M = (650x - 6500)\text{lb-ft counter clockwise}$$

(c) $20 < x \leq 40$ (Fig. 5)

$\sum F = 0 \; ;$

$$V + 650 - 1000 = 0$$

$$\therefore \; V = 350 \text{ lbs}$$

$$M = -\int V\,dx = -\int 350\,dx = -350x + c$$

At $x = 40$, $M = 0$

$$\therefore \; 0 = -350 \times 40 + C - 500$$

$$C = 13{,}500$$

$$M = (-350x + 13{,}500)\text{lb-ft}$$

(d) $40 < x \leq 55$

For simplicity, consider a section to the right of B (Fig. 6).

$\sum F = 0$

$$\therefore V = 0$$

$\sum M = 0$

$$\therefore M = 500 \text{ lb-ft}$$

The shear force and bending moment diagrams are shown in Figs. 7 and 8 respectively.

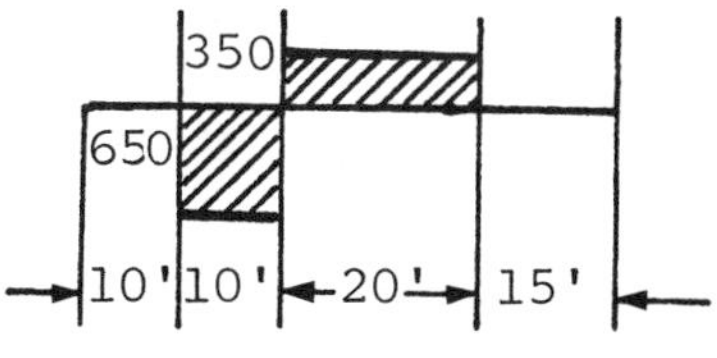

Fig. 7. Shear force diagram

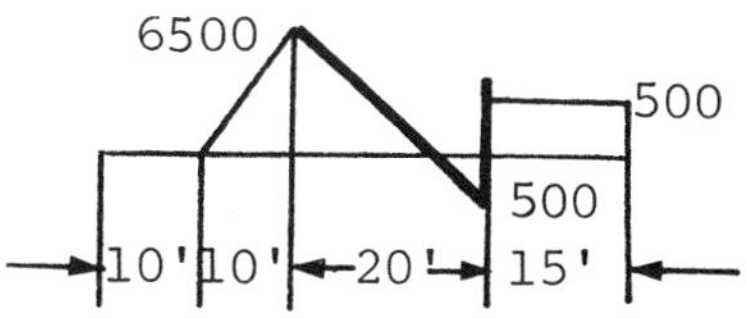

Fig. 8. Bending moment diagram

• PROBLEM 2-22

A pole held in the ground is subjected to the wind load shown. Find the shear force and bending moment equations and sketch the corresponding diagrams.

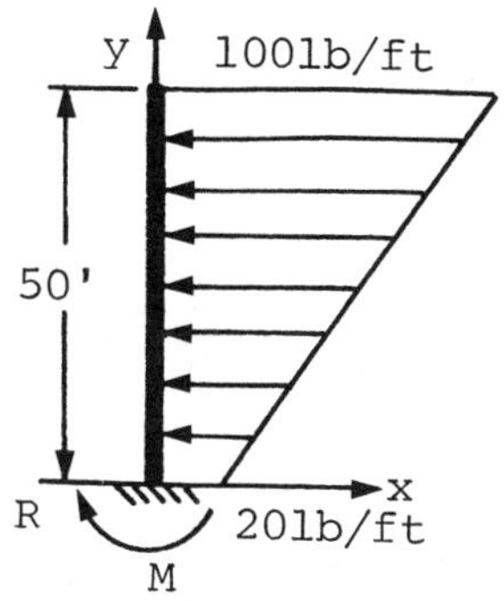

Fig. 1.

Solution: Express p(y), the experession for the load, as a function of y.

Since the loading varies linearly, the expression should be a straight line passing through the points (20,0) and (100,50). Since it is desired to integrate along the y axis, the equation of the line will be found in terms of y.

The two point equation of a line for x in terms of y is:

$$x - x_1 = \left(\frac{x_2 - x_1}{y_2 - y_1}\right)(y - y_1)$$

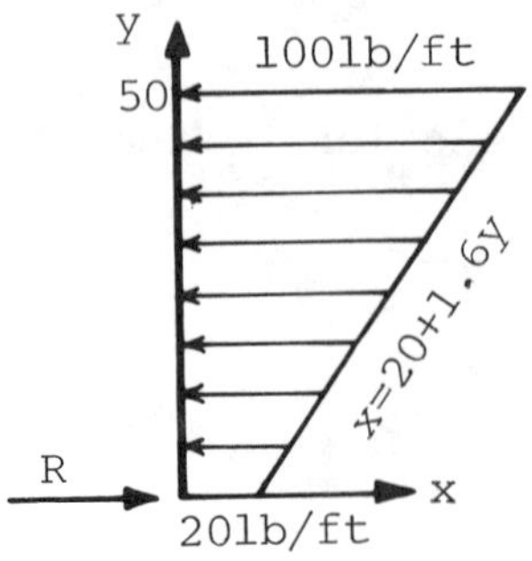

Fig. 2.

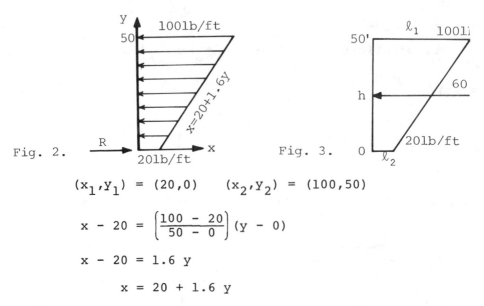

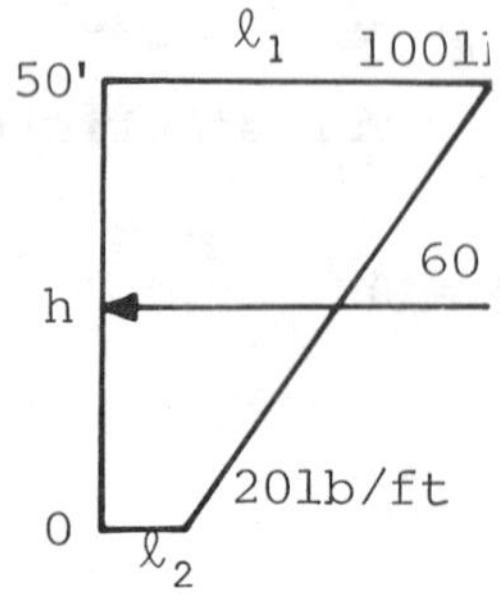

Fig. 3.

$$(x_1,y_1) = (20,0) \qquad (x_2,y_2) = (100,50)$$

$$x - 20 = \left(\frac{100 - 20}{50 - 0}\right)(y - 0)$$

$$x - 20 = 1.6\ y$$

$$x = 20 + 1.6\ y$$

Then determine the reaction at the support. From equilibrium:

$\sum F = 0$

The reaction force at the base is equal and opposite to the distributed load. The distributed load can be divided up into an infinite number of concentrated loads, each acting on a signle point. In calculus, these are called differential forces. For example, the load acting on the point $y = 25$ is equal to $20 + 1.6(25) = 60$ lb. These concentrated loads can be added together to find the resultant force, (see Fig. 2). This can be done by integrating as follows:

$$R - \int_0^{50} (20 + 1.6y)dy = 0$$

$$R = 20y + 0.8y^2 \Big|_0^{50}$$

$$= 3000 \text{ lb}$$

This is the same as finding the area. The area can also be found using the formula for a trapezoid from geometry (see Fig. 3):

$$A = \frac{1}{2}(\ell_1 + \ell_2)h$$

Notice this is the same as multiplying the average load by the height,

$$A = \frac{1}{2}(100 + 20)50$$

$$A = 3000$$

Determine the moment at the built-in end. Each of the infinite number of concentrated loads has a moment arm. For example, the force acting at the point y = 25 has a moment arm of 25'. The magnitude of the force is 20 + 1.6(25) = 60 lb. The moment about the base due to this force is (20 + 1.6y)y = (20 + 1.6(25))25 = (60)25 = 1500 ft-lb.

All of the moments can be added up using calculus as follows:

$\sum M = 0 \quad +\circlearrowleft$

$$M - \int_0^{50} (20 + 1.6y)y\, dy = 0$$

$$M = \int (20y + 1.6y^2)\, dy$$

$$= \left[10y^2 + \frac{16}{3}y^3\right]\Bigg|_0^{50}$$

$$= 91{,}666\cdot67 \text{ ft-lb}$$

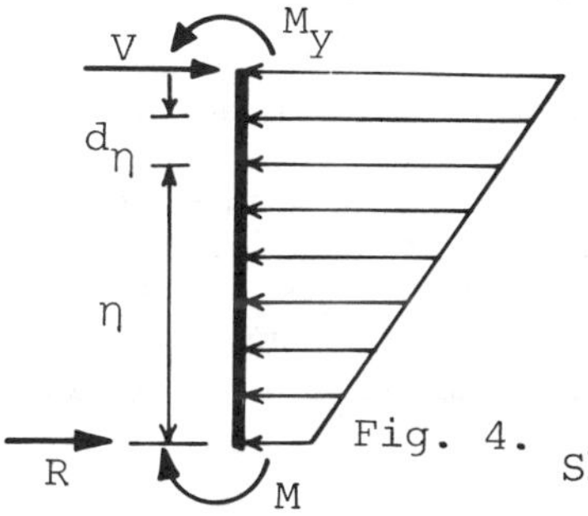

Fig. 4.

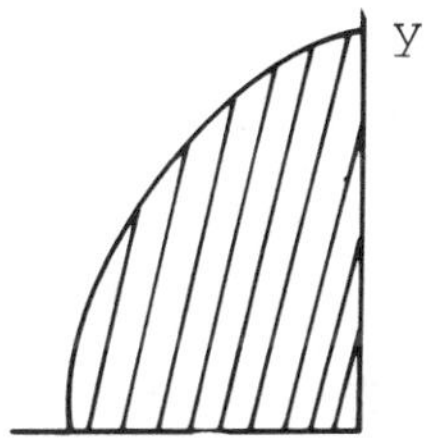

Fig. 5.
Shear Force Diagram

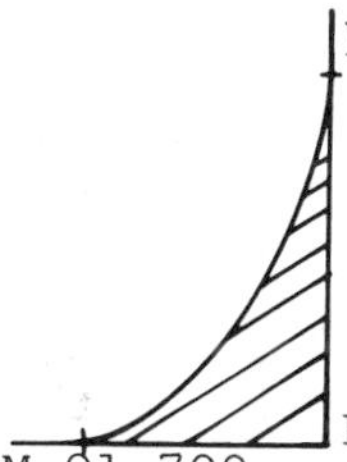

Fig. 6.
Bending Moment Diagram

Now consider a free body diagram (Fig. 4). The shear force V is going to vary as a function of y. In order to get a general expression for the sum of the distributed load at any point, y, temporarily call the y axis the η axis in order to evaluate the integral.

To determine V:

$\sum F = 0$

$$V + R - \int_0^{y} (20 + 1.6\eta)d\eta = 0,$$

where η is a dummy variable.

Integrating and substituting for R gives

$$V = -3000 + (20y + 0.8y^2).$$

From the expression relating moment and shear force,

i.e. $\quad M = -\int V\, dy,$

we have

$$M_y = -\int(-3000 + 20y + 0.8y^2)dy$$

$$= 3000y - 10y^2 - 0.267y^3 + C$$

To determine C, consider the boundary conditions.

At $y = 0$, $M_y = -M$

$$\therefore -91,666\cdot67 = c$$

$$\therefore M_y = 3000y - 10y^2 - 0.267y^3 - 91,666\cdot67$$

Various values of y are substituted into the shear force and bending moment expressions to obtain the shear force and bending moment diagrams as shown in Figs. 5 and 6, respectively. Notice that the slope of the moment diagram is equal to the shear because the derivative of the moment is the shear.

• PROBLEM 2-23

A simply supported I beam is shown in the diagram. A hole must be cut through the web to allow passage of a pipe which runs horizontally at right angles to the beam.
(a) Where, within the marked 24-ft section, would the hole least affect the moment-carrying capacity of the beam?
(b) In the same section, where should the hole go to least affect the shear-carrying capacity of the beam?

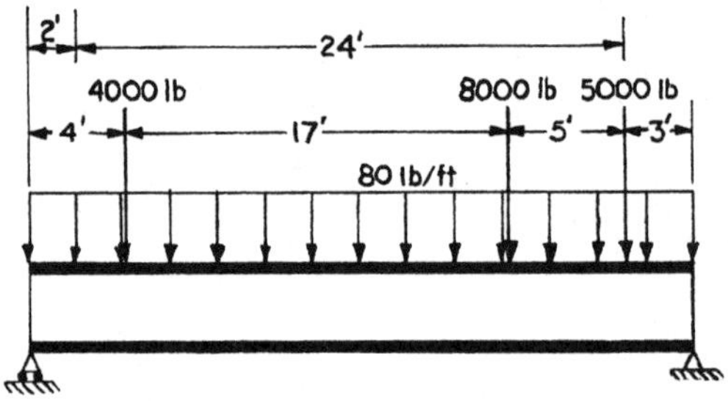

FIG. 1

Solution: The hole will least affect the moment-carrying capacity of the beam at a point where the moment in the beam is minimum.

To determine where the moment is minimum, first determine the reactions at the supports. (see Fig. 2)
Because the supports are pinned,

$\sum M = 0$ at A (+ clockwise)

$$\therefore 0 = 80 \times 29 \times \frac{29}{2} + 4000 \times 4 + 8000 \times 21 + 5000 \times 26 - 29R_B$$

$$R_B = 11,987.6$$

$\sum M = 0$ at B (+ clockwise)

$$0 = 29R_A - 80 \times 29 \times \frac{29}{2} - 4000 \times 25 - 8000 \times 8 -$$

$$- 5000 \times 3$$

$$R_A = 7332.4$$

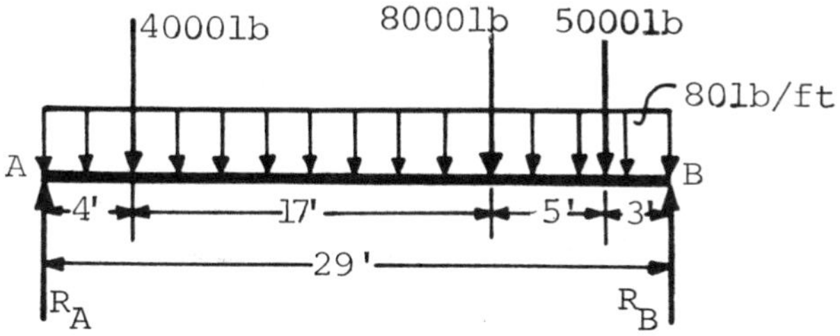

Fig. 2.

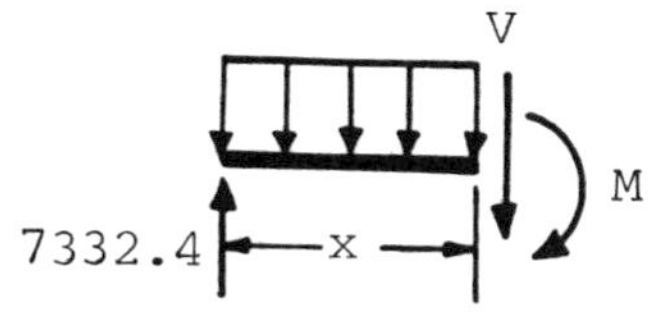

Fig. 3.

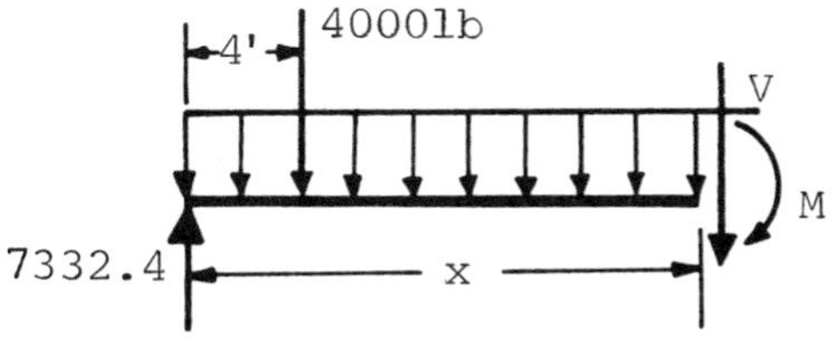

Fig. 4.

Now formulate the moment equation for each section of the beam. (A point where there is a change of loading or geometry is considered the end or the beginning of a section.)

$0 < x \leq 4$, (see Fig. 3)

$\sum F = 0$

$$\therefore 7332.4 - 80x - V = 0$$

Shear force at the cut, $V = 7332.4 - 80x$. But

$$M = -\int V\,dx$$

$$= -\int 7332.4 - 80x = 40x^2 - 7332.4x + C$$

At $x = 0$, $M = 0$ $\therefore C = 0$

$$M = 40x^2 - 7332.4x$$

$4 < x \leq 21$, (see Fig. 4)

$\sum F = 0$

$$\therefore 7332.4 - 4000 - 80x - V = 0$$

$$V = -80x + 3332.4$$

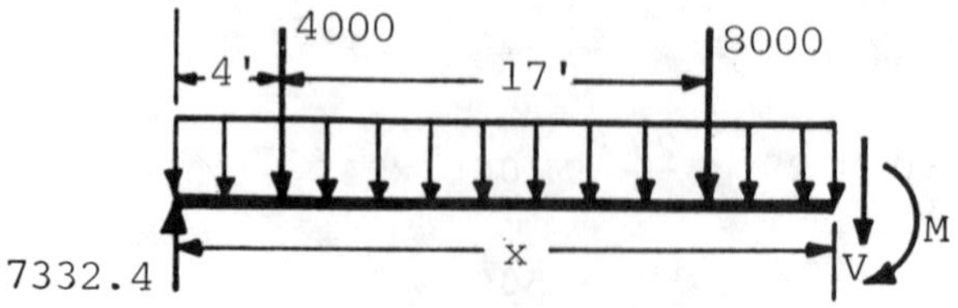

Fig. 5.

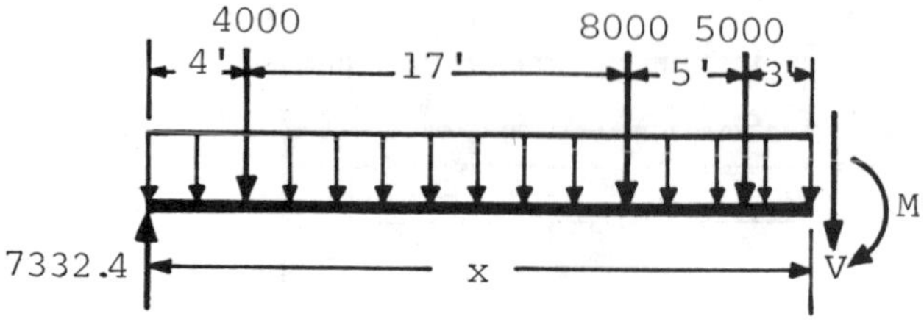

Fig. 6.

$$M = -\int V\,dx$$

$$= \int 80x + 4000 - 7332.4$$

$$= 40x^2 + 4000(x - 4) - 7332.4x$$

$21 < x \leq 26$, (see Fig. 5)

$\sum F = 0$

$$7332.4 - 4000 - 8000 - 80x - V = 0$$

$$V = -(4667.6 + 80x)$$

$$M = \int 80x + 8000 + 4000 - 7332.4$$

$$= 40x^2 + 8000(x - 21) + 4000(x - 4) - 7332.4x$$

$26 < x \leq 29$, (see Fig. 6)

$\sum F = 0$

$$7332.4 - 4000 - 8000 - 5000 - 80x - V = 0$$

$$V = -(9667.4 + 80x)$$

$$M = \int 80x + 5000 + 8000 + 4000 - 7332.4$$

$$= 40x^2 + 5000(x - 26) + 8000(x - 21)$$

$$+ 4000(x - 4) - 7332.4x$$

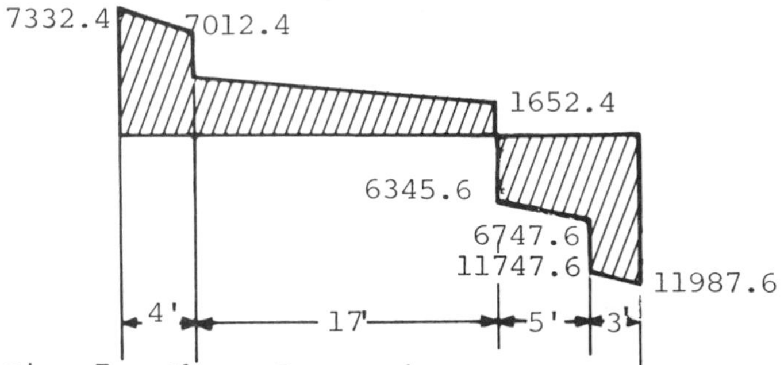

Fig. 7. Shear Force Diagram

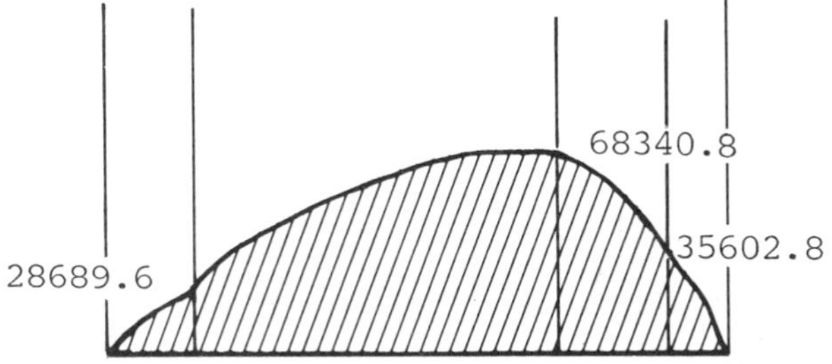

Fig. 8. Bending Moment Diagram

We have now formulated the shear force and bending moment equations. To be able to visualize this problem better, plot the shear force and bending moment diagrams (Figs. 7 and 8).

From the shear force diagram, it will be noticed that the point where the absolute value of the shear is minimum is 8' from the right support.

Therefore, the hole will have the least effect on the shear-carrying capacity of the beam if placed slightly to the left of this point. This is because at a point 8' from the right support the absolute value of the shear changes from 1652.4 to 6345.6, while at a point just to the left of this, the shear takes on a value slightly above 1652.4 lbs.

From the bending moment diagram, we can see that the moment is everywhere increasing as the distance from the supports increases. Since the minimum value within the marked range is at a point 2' from the left support, this consequently is where the hole will least affect the moment-carrying capacity of the beam.

• PROBLEM 2-24

By using differential relations of shear and moments subject to the prescribed boundary conditions, determine the functions for shear and moment for a simply supported beam loaded as in Fig. 1. Show the results in shear and moment diagrams. Find the largest moment in this beam. The total applied upward load is W lb.

Solution: First we must find an expression to represent the loading. Since the load varies uniformly, let the load intensity p at x be kx lb per inch. The load intensity at

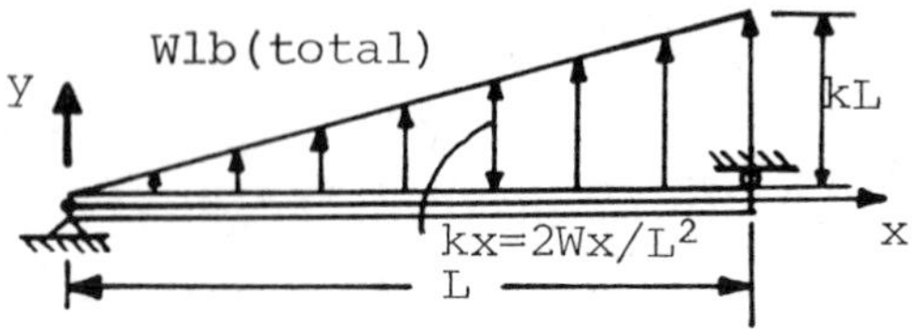

Fig. 1.

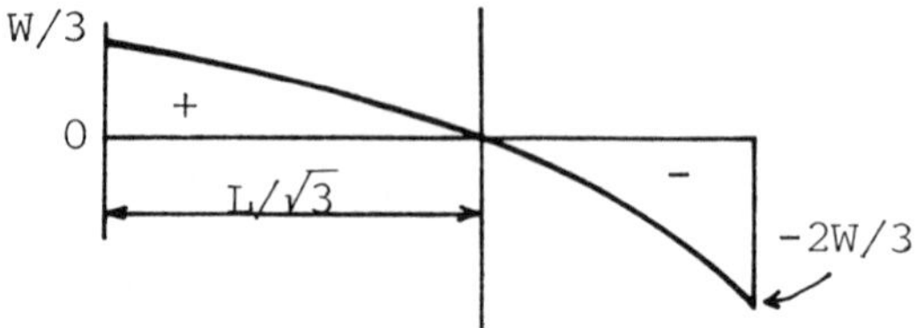

Fig. 2.

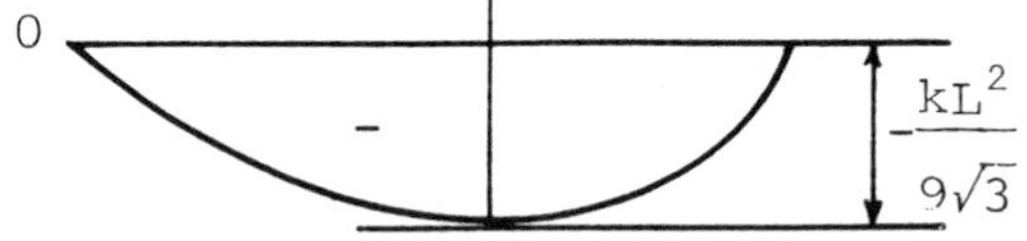

Fig. 3.

the right end becomes kL lb/inch. The total load $W = kL^2/2$ (where L is the length of the beam). Therefore, $k = 2W/L^2$. Using the constant k just found, one can express the loading function p in terms of the applied load W. On this basis,

$$\frac{d^2M}{dx^2} = p = +kx = +\frac{2W}{L^2}x$$

where the constant k is positive since the applied load acts in an upward direction. Integrating this differential equation twice, one obtains

$$\frac{dM}{dx} = +\frac{kx^2}{2} + C_1 \quad \text{and} \quad M = +\frac{kx^3}{6} + C_1x + C_2$$

Since $dM/dx = -V$, if the reaction on the left were known, the constant C_1 could be evaluated from the first of the above equations. However, it can be noted directly from the boundary conditions that since there is no moment restraint at x = 0 & x = L, M = 0 at x = 0 and at x = L, i.e., M(0) = 0 and M(L) = 0. Therefore since

$$M(0) = 0, \quad C_2 = 0$$

and, similarly, since M(L) = 0,

$$kL^3/6 + C_1L = 0 \quad \text{or} \quad C_1 = -kL^2/6$$

Notice, since $V = -\frac{dM}{dx} = -\frac{kx^2}{2} - C_1$, and where x = 0, the shearing force V or the reaction at the left side, is C_1, pointing downwards. Here it was found by solving a boundary-value problem without the use of the conventional procedure used in statics.

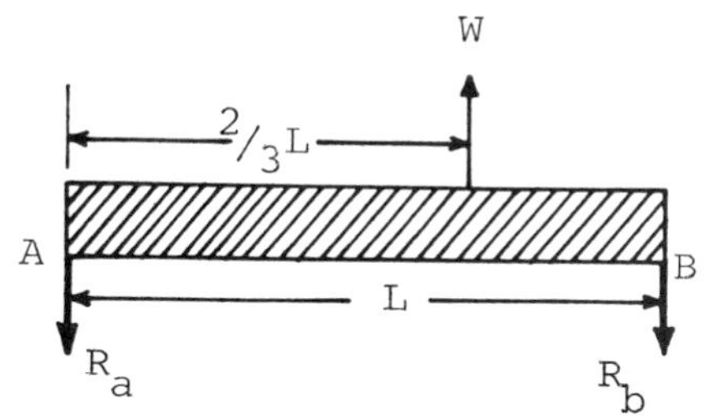

Fig. 4.

Checking our reaction forces using statics, shows the convenience of using the single shear force equation. By reducing the distributed load to a concentrated load, acting through the centroid of the triangular load distribution, a free body diagram of the beam is possible. Using laws of statics, the reactions at A and B are found

$$\sum F_y = 0 \qquad W - R_a - R_B = 0 \tag{1}$$

$$\sum M_A = 0 \quad +\!\circlearrowright \quad (\tfrac{2}{3}L)W - (L)R_B = 0$$

$$R_B = \tfrac{2}{3}W \tag{2}$$

Using (1) in (2):

$$W - R_a - \tfrac{2}{3}W = 0$$

$$R_a = \tfrac{1}{3}W$$

These reactions agree with the ones obtained from the shear equation. The statics' procedure involves two equations, two unknowns, substitutions, etc. for a solution. The shear force equation is a very useful tool.

After C_1 and C_2 are determined, the expressions for the shear and moment are known:

$$V = -dM/dx = -(kx^2/2) + (kL^2/6)$$

and $$M = +(kx^3/6) - (kL^2x/6)$$

In Fig. 2 and Fig. 3, the shear and moment diagrams are shown. The shear force relation is quadratic, giving a starting point for the diagram. Knowing certain points (boundary conditions and intercepts) a good approximation of the graph is possible without a point for point plot. The bending moment diagram can be obtained from taking boundary points and an intermediate maxima-minima.

Using maxima-minima from the calculus, the largest moment occurs at $dM/dx = -V = -kx^2/2 + kL^2/6 = 0$; i.e., at $x_1 = L/\sqrt{3}$. By substituting this value of x_1 into the expression for moment, one finds that the largest moment $M = -kL^3/(9\sqrt{3})$.

A simply supported beam has various loadings applied to it. Find and sketch the shear force and bending moment diagrams.

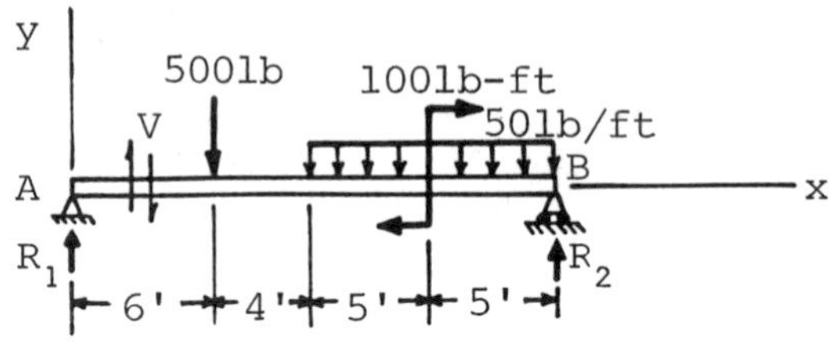

Fig. 1

Solution: Let vertical reactions at A and B be R_1 and R_2. There is no horizontal reaction at B because of the movable support. By applying equilibrium horizontally, we can see that there is no horizontal reaction at A either. The supporting forces R_1 and R_2 are found by rules of statics. Thus,

$\underline{\sum M_B = 0:}$ +

$$-R_1(20) + (500)(14) + (50)(10)(10/2) - 100 = 0$$

$$\therefore R_1 = 470 \text{ lb}$$

$\underline{\sum M_A = 0:}$

$$R_2(20) - (500)(6) - (50)(10)(15) - 100 = 0$$

$$\therefore R_2 = 530 \text{ lb}$$

Check: $\sum F_y = 0$

$$R_1 - 500 - 50(10) + R_2 = 0$$

$$470 - 500 - 500 + 530 = 0$$

$$0 = 0.$$

We can directly state the shear and bending-moment equations on observing Fig. 2 and substituting the value of R_1 obtained from above. Note sign convention (Fig. 4).

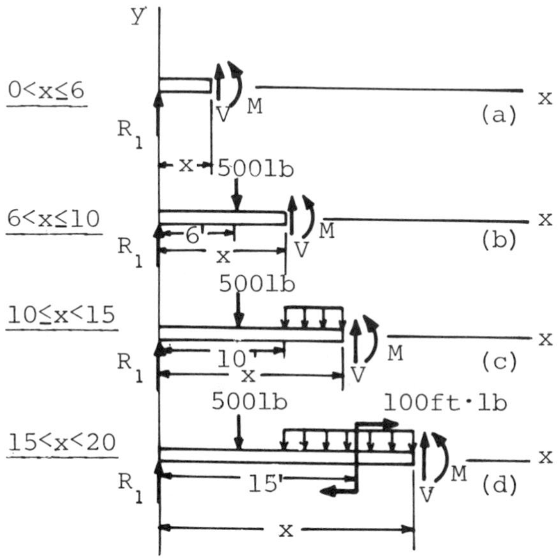

Fig. 2.

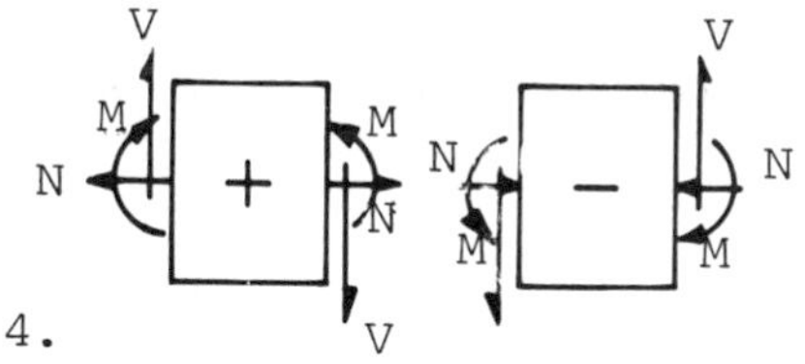

Fig. 4.

<u>$0 < x < 6$</u>:

$$\sum F_y = 0 \quad +\uparrow \quad V = -R_1 = -470 \text{ lb}$$

$$\sum M = 0 \quad \circlearrowleft + \quad M = R_1 x = 470x \text{ ft lb}$$

<u>$6 < x \leq 10$</u>

$$\sum F_y = 0 \quad +\uparrow \quad V = -R_1 + 500 = 30 \text{ lb}$$

$$\sum M = 0 \quad \circlearrowleft + \quad M = R_1 x - 500(x - 6) = -30x + 3000 \text{ ft lb}$$

<u>$10 \leq x \leq 15$</u>:

$$\sum F_y = 0 \quad +\uparrow \quad V = -R_1 + 500 + 50(x - 10) = 50x - 470 \text{ lb}$$

$$\sum M = 0 \quad \circlearrowleft + \quad M = R_1 x - 500(x - 6) - 50(x - 10)\frac{(x - 10)}{2}$$

$$= -25x^2 + 470x + 500 \text{ ft lb}$$

$\underline{15 \leq x \leq 20:}$

$$\sum F_y = 0 \quad \uparrow + \quad V = -R_1 + 500 + 50(x - 10) = 50x - 470 \text{ lb}$$

$$\sum M = 0 \quad \circlearrowleft + \quad M = R_1 x - 500(x - 6) - \frac{50(x - 10)^2}{2} + 100$$

$$= -25x^2 + 470x + 600 \text{ ft lb}$$

In sketching the diagrams we shall employ the differential equations of equilibrium and their integrals i.e.,

$$\frac{dV_y}{dx} = -W(x) \quad , \quad V_y = -\int w(x)dx$$

and

$$\frac{dM_z}{dx} = -V_y \quad , \quad M_z = -\int M_z \, dx$$

We accordingly first draw the loading diagram in Fig. 3(a), ane we shall then sketch the shear-force and bending-moment diagrams without the aid of the above equations, evaluating key points as we go.

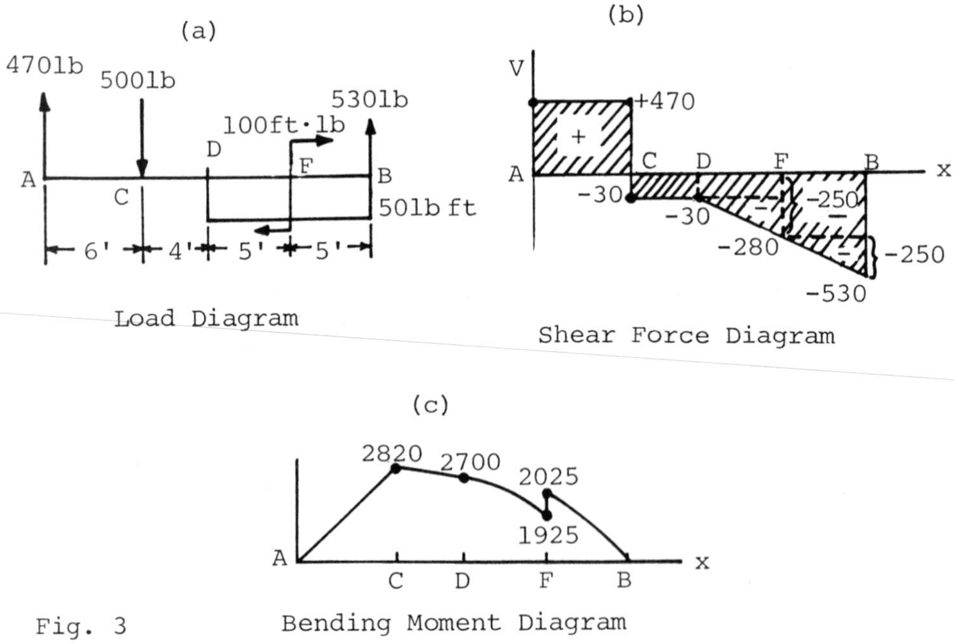

Fig. 3

Note that as we start on the shear diagram that the 470-lb supporting force induces a negative shear of -470 lb just to the right of the support. Now from A to C the area of loading is zero and so there is no change in the value of shear between A and C. Hence, V = -470 lb just before C, as shown in Fig. 3(b). Also, since w = 0 between A and

C, the slope of the shear curve should be zero in accordance with

$$\frac{dV_y}{dx} = \omega = 0$$

And so we have a horizontal line for V between A and C. Now as we cross C the 500-lb downward force will induce a positive increment of shear of value 500 on sections to the right of it. Accordingly, V jumps from -470 to +30 lb as we cross C. Between C and D there is no loading so that $V_D = V_C$ and we have a 30-lb shear force at point D. Again, since w = 0 in this interval, the slope of the shear curve is zero and we have a horizontal line for the shear curve between C and D. Since there is no concentrated load at D, there is no sudden change in shear as we cross this point. Next the change in shear between D and B is minus the area of the loading curve in this interval in accordance with $V_y = -\int w\,dx$. But this area is (-50)(10) = -500. Hence, from

$$V_{y_2} = V_{y_1} - \int_1^2 w\,dx$$

The value of V_B (just to the left of the support) is V_D -(-500) = 530 lb. Also, since w is negative and constant between D and B, the slope of the shear curve should be positive and constant in accordance with

$$\frac{dV_y}{dx} = -w_y$$

Hence, we can draw a straight line between V_D = 30 lb and V_B = 530 lb. As we now cross the right support force we see that it induces a negative shear of 530 lb on sections to the right of the support and so at B the shear curve comes back to zero.

We can proceed with the bending-moment curve. With no point couple present at A, the value of M_A must be zero.

The change in moment between A and C is then minus the area underneath the shear curve in this interval. We can then say from

$$M_2 = M_1 - \int_1^2 V_y\,dx$$

that $M_C = M_A$ - (-470)(6) = 0 + 2820 = 2820 ft-lb, and we denote this in the moment diagram. Furthermore the value of V is a negative constant is the interval, and accordingly

$\frac{dM_z}{dx} = -V_y$ the slope of the moment curve is positive and constant.

The positive slope can also be seen from the moment equation $(0 < x < 6)$ which is a positive linear function: $M = R_1x = 470x$. We can then draw a straight line between M_A and M_C. Between C and D the area for the shear diagram is 120 ft-lb and so we can say that $M_D = M_C - (120) = 2820 - 120 = 2700$ ft-lb. Again with V constant and positive in the interval the slope of the moment curve must be negative and constant in the interval and has been so drawn. Also, looking at the respective moment equations, $M = -30x + 3000$, indicates a negative slope. Between D and F the area under the shear curve is readily seen to be $(30)(5) + 1/2(5)(250) = 775$ ft-lb. Hence, the bending moment goes from 2700 ft-lb at D to 1925 ft-lb at F. Now the shear curve is positive and increasing in value as we go from D to F. This means that the slope of the bending-moment curve is negative and becoming steeper negatively as we go from D to F and has been so drawn in the diagram. As we go by F we encounter the 100-ft-lb point couple and we can say that this point couple induces a positive 100-ft-lb moment on sections to the right of point F. Accordingly, there is a sudden increase in bending moment of 100 ft-lb at F, as has been shown in the diagram. The area of the shear diagram between F and B is readily seen from Fig. 3(b) to be $(280)(5) + 1/2(5)(250) = 2025$ ft-lb. We see then that the bending moment goes to zero at B. Since the shear is positive and increasing between F and B, then we conclude that the slope of the bending moment curve is negative and becoming more steep negatively as we approach B. We have thus drawn the shear and bending-moment diagram and have labeled all key points.

• PROBLEM 2-26

Parabolic loading is applied to a cantilever beam, in addition to the other loads shown. Find the shear force and bending moment equations, and sketch the corresponding diagrams.

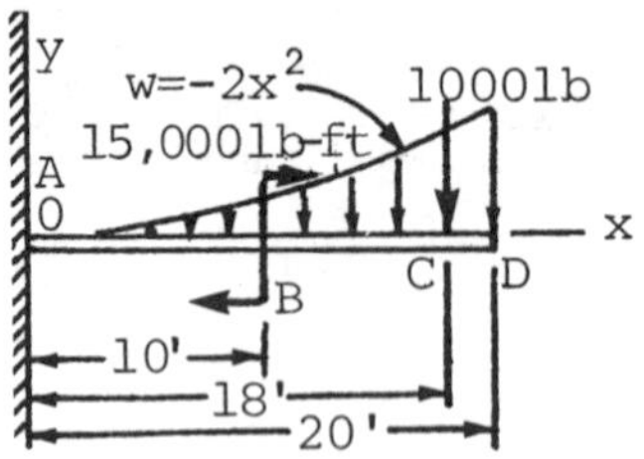

Fig. 1.

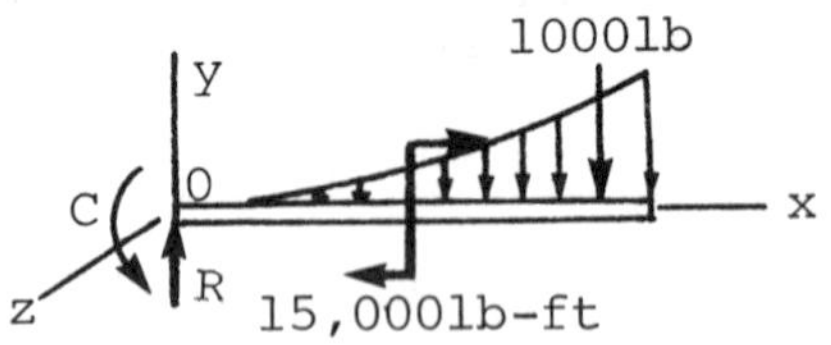

Fig. 2.

Solution: First find the reaction force of the wall on the beam and moment on the section of the beam adjacent to the wall. We shall consider these as external supports for the beam (see Fig. 2). Because these quantities are to be handled as external loads, we do not apply the sign convention of shear and bending moments to them.

Before applying equilibrium conditions, the distributed load must be converted to a concentrated force acting through the centroid of the parabola. The magnitude of the total load is found by taking the area under the loading function using integration. That is, taking an elemental width dx and the height of the function w(x), at a distance x from 0, as $w(x) = -2x^2$, the total load w is $\int_0^{20} -2x^2 dx$. The moment due to this, resultant about point 0, can be found two ways. The definition applied for a distributed loading problem is $M_0 = \int w(x)\, x dx$. This method is practical for this problem because of the varying loads and moments applied also to the beam. In the alternate method, the distributed load acts as a concentrated load at the centroid of the parabola. This will be used as a check.

From equilibrium conditions, the reactions are found:

$\underline{\sum F_y = 0:}$

$$R - 1000 - \int_0^{20} 2x^2 dx = 0$$

$$R - 1000 - 2\left(\frac{x^3}{3}\right)\Bigg|_0^{20} = 0$$

$$\therefore R = 6333.3 \text{ lbs}$$

$\underline{\sum M_0 = 0:}$ $+\circlearrowright$

$$-C + 15{,}000 + (1000)(18) + \int_0^{20} 2x^3 dx = 0$$

$$\therefore C = 113{,}000 \text{ ft-lb}$$

The concentrated resultant force w was found from $\int_0^{20} -2x^2 dx = -6333.6$. This acts $\bar{x}$ distance from 0 where $\bar{x}$ is $\frac{3}{4}(20)$ ft. or 15 ft. Write $\sum M_0 = 0$ $+\circlearrowleft$

$$C - 15{,}000 \text{ lb-ft} - 1000 \text{ lb}(18 \text{ ft}) - 5333.3(15) = 0$$

$$C = 113{,}000 \text{ lb-ft.}$$

We may next give the shear and bending-moment equations:

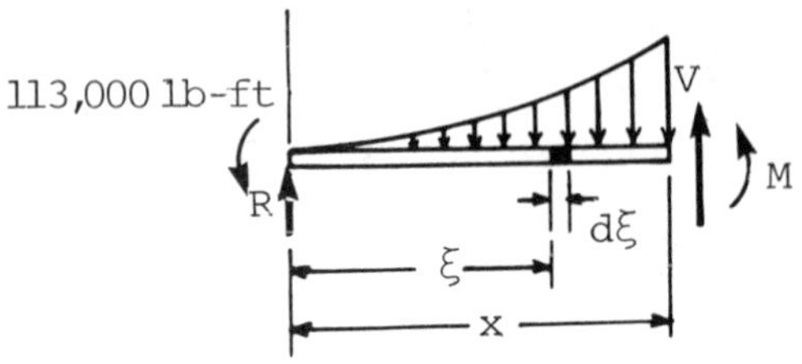

Fig. 3.

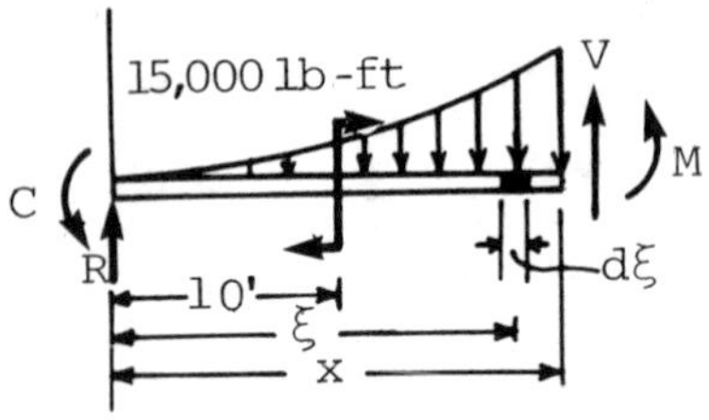

Fig. 4.

<u>$0 < x < 10$</u>: (see Fig. 3)

$$\sum F_y = 0 , \quad V = 6333.3 + \int_0^x 2\xi^2 d\xi$$

$$= \frac{2x^3}{3} - 6333.3 \qquad \text{(a)}$$

assuming that the resultant of the parabolic loading is at a point, ξ away from left reaction.

$$\sum M = 0 , \quad M = -113{,}000 + 6333.3\,x - \int_0^x 2\xi^2 (x - \xi) d\xi$$

$$= \frac{x^4}{6} + 6333.3x - 113{,}000 \qquad \text{(b)}$$

<u>$10 < x < 18$</u>: (see Fig. 4)

$$\sum F_y = 0 , \quad V = -6333.3 + \int_0^x 2\xi^2 d\xi$$

$$= \frac{2x^3}{3} - 6333.3 \qquad \text{(c)}$$

$$\sum M = 0 , \quad M = -113{,}000 + 6333.3x - \int_0^x 2\xi^2 (x - \xi) d\xi + 15{,}000$$

$$= -\frac{x^4}{6} + 5333.3x - 80{,}000 \qquad \text{(d)}$$

<u>$18 < x \le 20$</u>: (see Fig. 5)

$$\sum F_y = 0 , \quad V = -6333.3 + \int_0^x 2\xi^2 d\xi + 1000$$

$$= \frac{2x^3}{3} - 5333.3 \qquad \text{(e)}$$

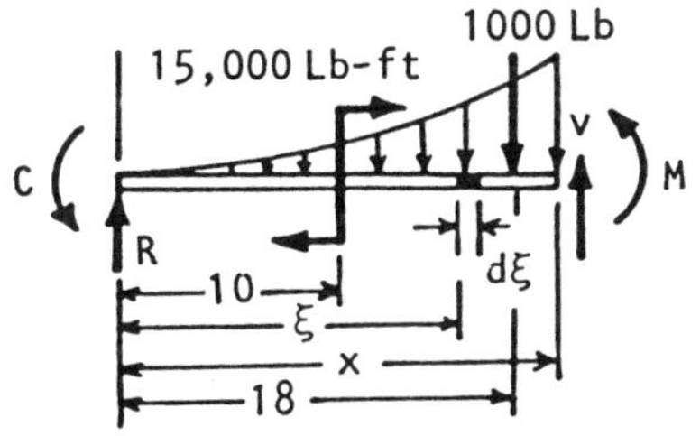

Fig. 5

$$\sum M = 0 , \quad M = -113,000 + 6333.3x - \int_0^x 2\xi^2(x - \xi)d\xi + 15,000$$

$$- 1000(x - 18)$$

$$= -\frac{x^4}{6} + 6333.3x - 98,000 \qquad \text{(f)}$$

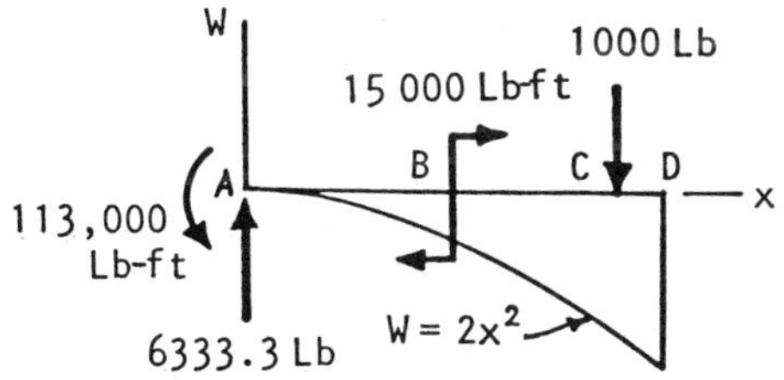

Loading Diagram. Fig. 6

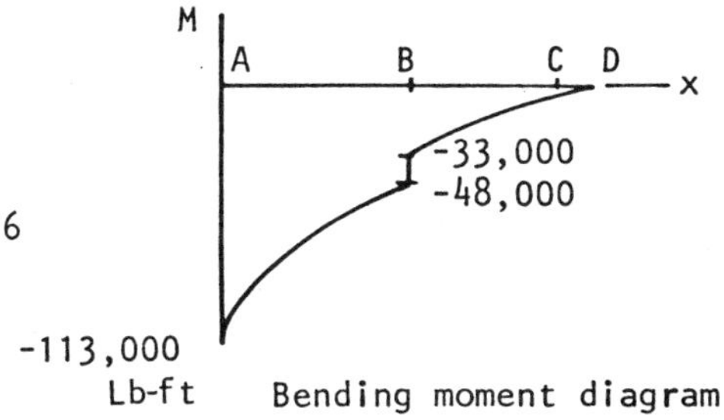

Bending moment diagram.

Fig. 8

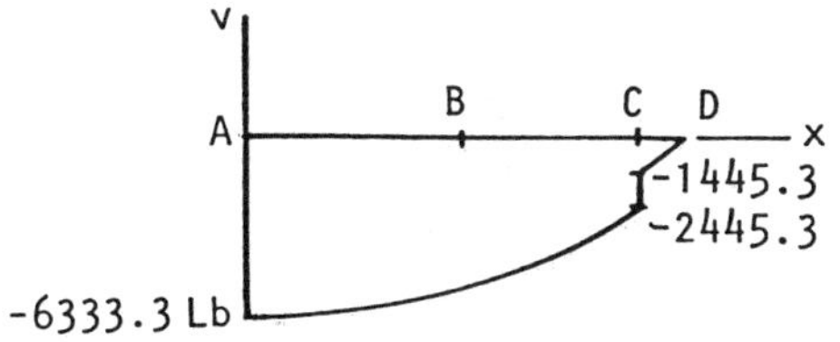

Shear force diagram. Fig. 7

To sketch the diagrams and thus ascertain the positions of the key points, we use the above equations and the slope relations. The loading diagram has been redrawn (Fig. 6). The shear force is -6333.3 lbs to the right of the support at A and from Eq. (c) we see that, just to the left of where the 1000-lb load is applied at C (i.e., at x = 18), the shear force is -2445.3 (see Fig. 7). Between A and C the loading w is negative and increasing negatively. Hence, by the differential relations $\frac{dV}{dx} = -P$, the shear curve has a positive slope which is becoming steeper. At C the 1000-lb load contributes a sudden +1000 shear-force increment. According to Eq. (e), at D (i.e., at x = 20), the shear force must be zero. Between C and D the loading is negative and increasing negatively. The slope of the shear diagram then is positive and becoming steeper. Clearly, the greatest shear force is -6330 lb at the base.

As for the bending-moment diagram we have at A the instantaneous contribution of -113,000 ft-lb from the couple at the support. At B to the left of the point couple (at x = 10) we have from Eq. (b) the value of -48,000 ft-lb (see Fig. 8). Between A and B the shear force is negative and getting smaller negatively. Hence, by the differential relations, $\frac{dM}{dx} = -V$. Accordingly, the slope of the bending moment is positive and flattening. As we cross B there is a sudden +15,000-ft-lb. increment of bending moment resulting from the applied point couple. At D (i.e., at x = 20) the bending moment is clearly zero. Between B and D the shear force is negative and decreasing negatively with a discontinuous jump at C. Accordingly, between B and D the slope of the moment diagram is positive and flattening with a discontinutiy in slope (a cusp) at C. The greatest bending moment, like the shear, is at the base.

• PROBLEM 2-27

For the crank and piston arrangement shown, plot the components V_y, V_z, M_y, M_z for shaft portion A-B.

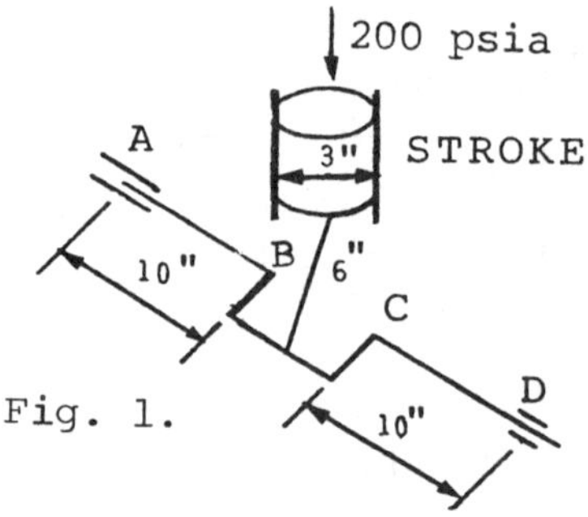

Fig. 1.

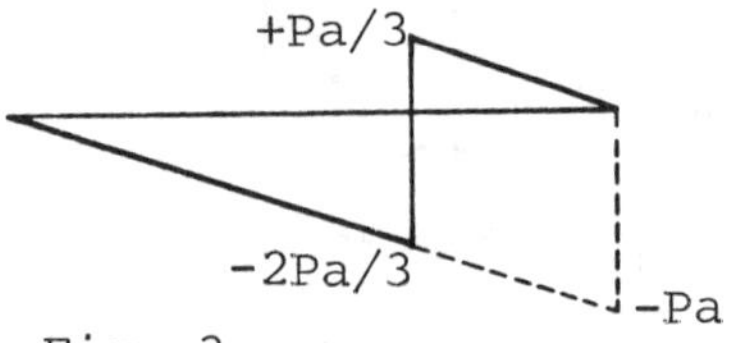

Fig. 3.

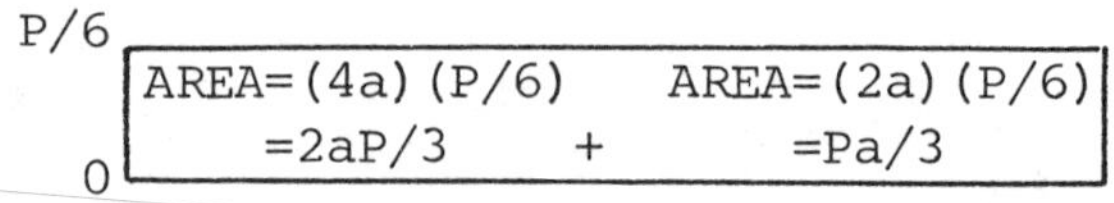

Fig. 2.

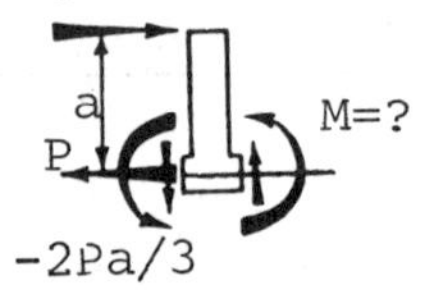

Fig. 4.

Solution: First find the reaction forces at the supports, and then consider the free body of left half of a cut section of the beam to get bending-moment.

Taking moments about point A,

$$\sum M = 0 \quad \curvearrowleft + , \quad R_{Cy} \cdot 6a - P \cdot a = 0$$

$$R_{Cy} = \frac{P}{6}.$$

Taking moments about point C,

$$\sum M = 0 \quad \curvearrowleft + , \quad -R_{Ay} \cdot 6a - P \cdot a = 0$$

$$R_{Ay} = -\frac{P}{6}$$

Checking the forces in the vertical direction:

$$F_y = 0$$

$$\frac{P}{6} - \frac{P}{6} = 0.$$

At A the reaction acts down, at C it acts up. From $F_x = 0$ it is known that at A a horizontal reaction equal to P acts to the left. The shear diagram is drawn next, Fig. 2. It has a constant, positive ordinate for the whole length of the beam because there is no vertical force acting in between A and C. After this, by using the summation process i.e., $M = -\int V\,dx$ which is derived from $V = -\frac{dM}{dx}$, the moment diagram shown in Fig. 3 is constructed. The moment at the left end of the beam is zero since the support is pinned. The total change in moment from A to B is given by the area of the shear diagram between these sections taken with the reversed sign; it equals -2Pa/3. Because $V = -\frac{dM}{dx}$, the moment diagram in the zone AB has a constant, negative slope. For further analysis, an element is isolated from the beam as shown in Fig. 4. The moment on the left side of this element is known to be -2Pa/3, and the concentrated moment caused by the applied force P about the beam's centroidal axis is Pa. Hence, for equilibrium,

$\sum M = 0$, $$M + \frac{2P\ a}{3} - P \cdot a = 0$$

$$M = \frac{1}{3}P \cdot a.$$

At B an upward jump of +Pa is made in the moment diagram, and so just to the right of B the ordinate is +Pa/3. Beyond B, the summation of the shear diagram area is continued. The area between B and C taken with the reversed sign is equal to -Pa/3. This value closes the moment diagram at the right end of the beam, and thus the boundary conditions are satisfied. Note that the inclined lines in the moment diagram are parallel because $\frac{dM}{dx} = -V$ where V is contant throughout the whole beam, giving a constant slope $\frac{-dM}{dx}$.

• PROBLEM 2-28

Consider a one-cylinder compressor as shown in the diagram. The pressure of the piston face is 200 psia. The bore is 3 in. and the stoke is 4 in., while the length of the connecting rod is 6 in. For the position shown, plot V_y and V_z for member AB. Also plot M_y and M_z for member AB.

Solution: For the position shown, first compute the force acting, P, and the angle through which it acts θ from the data given (see Fig. 2).

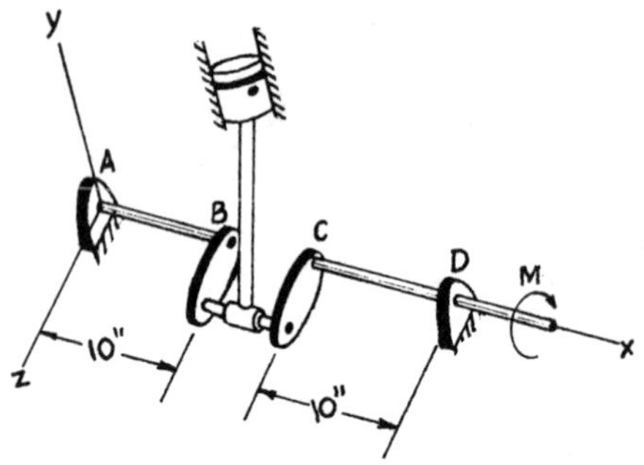

FIG.1

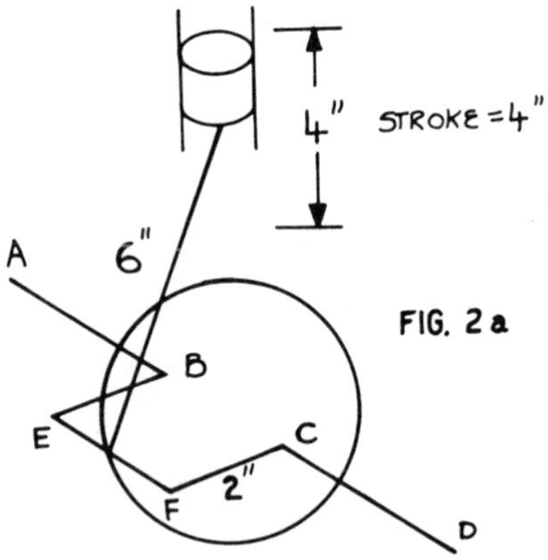

FIG. 2a

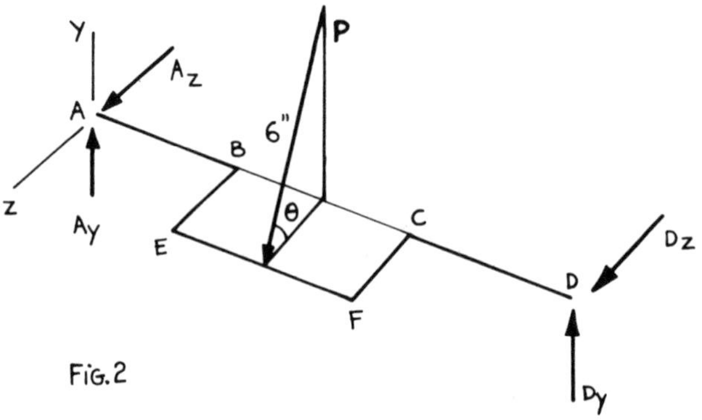

FiG.2

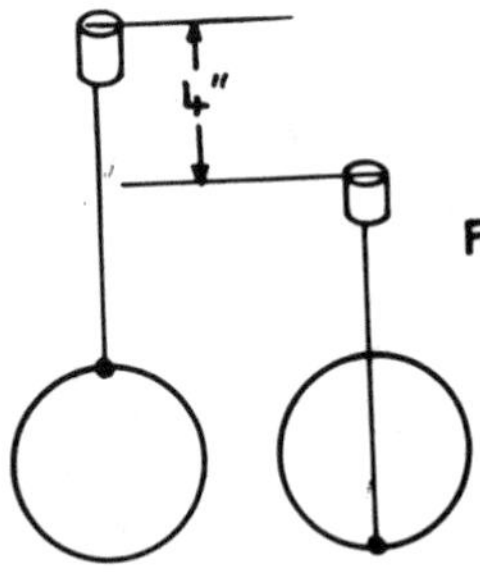

FIG. 2b

The stroke is 4 in. (See figures 2a and 2b.) This means that the diameter of the circle through which the end of the arm of the crank shaft moves is 4 in. The length of the arm is then the radius of the circle, 2 in. The angle is then the arc cos (2/6). Evaluated, $\theta = 70.53^0$. Part of the data given is the pressure of the piston face = 200 psia and the bore = 3 in.

$$\text{But} \quad \text{Pressure (stress)} = \frac{\text{Force}}{\text{Area}}$$

$$\therefore \quad \text{Force } P = 200 \times \frac{\pi \times 3^2}{4}$$

$$P = 1413.72 \ \text{lbs.}$$

To determine the support reactions A_y, A_z, D_y, and D_z, consider equilibrium of the structure in the y and z directions.

$\sum F_y = 0$,

$$A_y + D_y = P \sin\theta.$$

From symmetry, $A_y = D_y$

$$\therefore \quad 2A_y = P \sin\theta.$$

Substituting for P and θ,

$$A_y = D_y = \frac{1413.72 \times .943}{2}$$

$$= 666.6 \text{ lbs.}$$

$\sum F_z = 0$:

$$A_z + D_z = -P \cos \theta.$$

Substituting for P and θ,

$$D_z = A_z = \frac{-1413.72 \times .33}{2}$$

$$= -233.26.$$

Now consider section AB $0 < x \leq 10$ (Fig. 3).

$\sum F_y = 0$:

$$\therefore A_y + V_y = 0$$

$$V_y = -666.6 \text{ lbs}$$

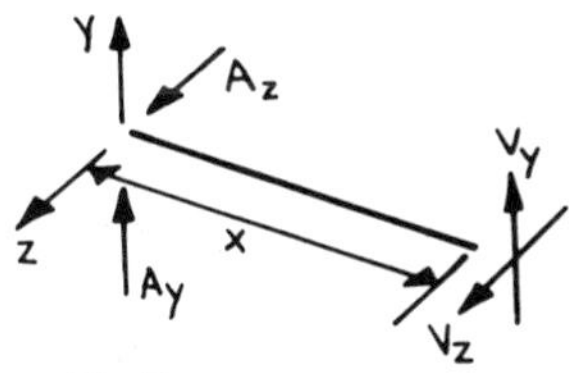

FiG.3

$\sum F_z = 0$:

$$A_z + V_z = 0$$

$$V_z = 233.3 \text{ lbs}$$

But $$M = -\int V\,dx$$

$$\therefore M_y = \int 666.6\,dx$$

$$= 666.6x + C.$$

At $x = 0$, $M_y = 0$ $\therefore C = 0$

and $$M_y = 666.6x.$$

Similarly, $$M_z = -\int 233.3dx$$

$$= -233.3x + D.$$

At $x = 0$, $M_z = 0$ $\therefore D = 0$

and $$M_z = -233.3x.$$

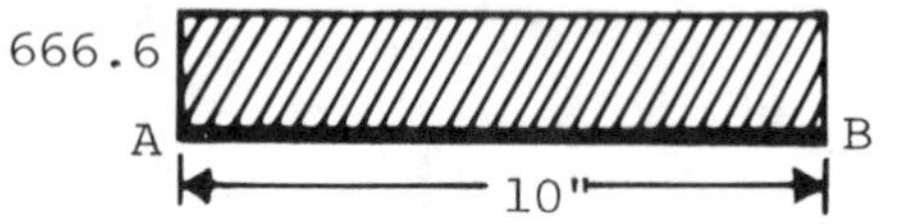

Plot of V_y vs x for member AB

Fig. 4.

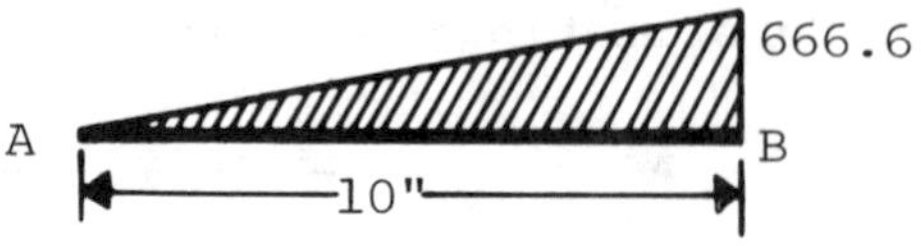

Plot of M_y vs x

Fig. 6.

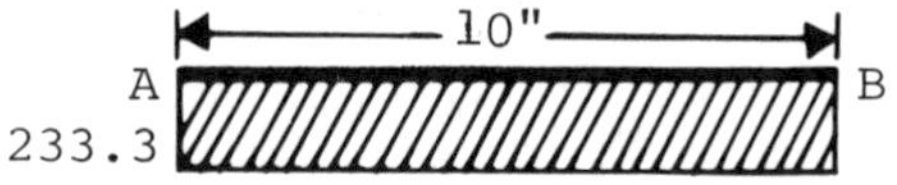

Plot of V_z vs x for AB

Fig. 5.

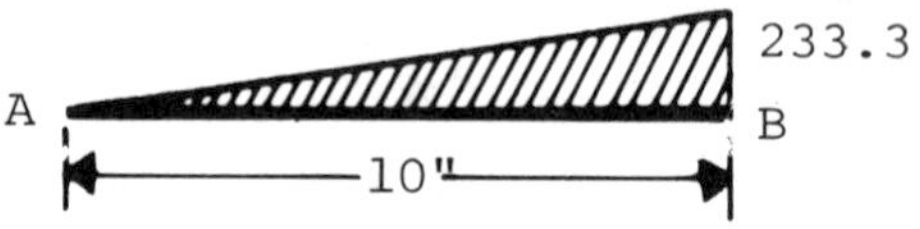

Plot of M_z vs x

Fig. 7.

The shear force and bending moment diagrams for member AB are shown in Figs. 4 through 7 respectively.

• PROBLEM 2-29

Fig. 1 shows a 5-ft-square gate which is retaining the water at half the length of the gate as shown. If it is assumed that the total pressure load on the gate is transmitted to the supports at A, B, D, and E by means of symmetrically located simply supported beams AB and DE, find the maximum bending moment in the beams. The bottom edge DA of the gate is 2 ft below the water line, and $\gamma = 62.4$ lb/ft^3.

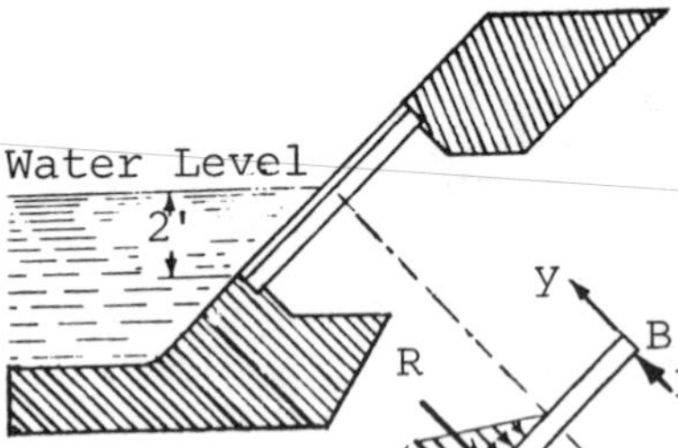

Fig. 1.

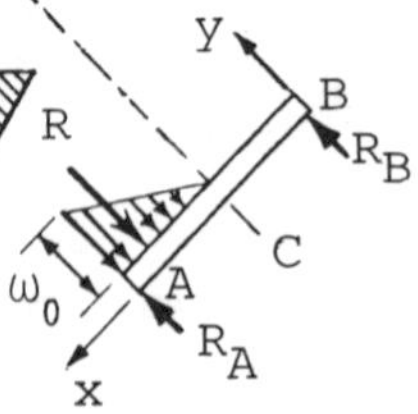

Fig. 2.

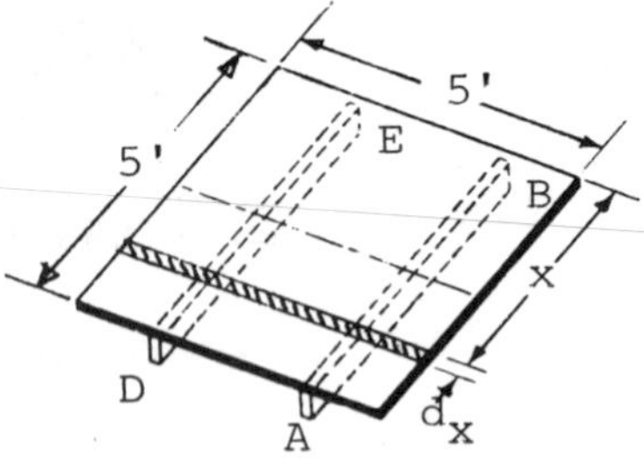

Fig. 3.

Solution: The fluid pressure acts normal to the gate, is uniform on lines parallel to DA, and varies linearly from zero pressure (above atmospheric) at the middle of the gate to a maximum pressure p_A along the bottom edge where

$$p_A = \gamma z_A = (62.4)(2) = 124.8 \text{ lb/ft}^2 \qquad \text{(a)}$$

To obtain the loading on the beams we assume that the pressure loading on the shaded strip in Fig. 2 is carried equally by the two beams. If the pressure at this location is p(x), the total load on this strip would be = $(5 \cdot dx)p(x)$. The load on one beam = $\frac{1}{2} \cdot 5 \cdot p(x) \cdot dx$. The load per unit lenght $\omega(x)$ carried by one of the beams is

$$\omega(x) = \frac{\frac{5}{2}p(x)dx}{dx}$$

$$= \frac{5}{2}p(x). \qquad \text{(b)}$$

This implies that $\omega(x)$ varies along the length of a beam in the same fashion as p(x), as indicated in Fig. 3 for the beam AB. If we establish an x-y coordinate system on the beam AB as shown in Fig. 3, the loading can then be represented by the expression

$$q(x) = \frac{-\omega_0}{\left(\frac{5}{2}\right)}\left(x - \frac{5}{2}\right)\left[u\left(x - \frac{5}{2}\right)\right]$$

$$= -\frac{2}{5}\omega_0\left[x - \frac{5}{2}\right]u\left(x - \frac{5}{2}\right) \qquad \text{(c)}$$

where $u\left(x - \frac{5}{2}\right)$ is a unit step function starting at $x = \frac{5}{2}$.

Note that: $$u\left[x - \frac{5}{2}\right] = \begin{cases} 0 & \text{for } -\infty < x < \frac{5}{2} \\ 1 & \text{for } \frac{5}{2} < x < +\infty. \end{cases}$$

ω_0 is obtained by evaluating (b) at the bottom of the gate

$$\omega_0 = \frac{5}{2}p_A = 312 \text{ lb/ft} \qquad \text{(d)}$$

The resultant R of this loading is $\left(\frac{1}{2}\omega_0\right)\frac{5}{2} = \frac{5}{4}\omega_0$, and its line of action passes through the centroid of the loading diagram which is $\frac{1}{3}\left(\frac{5}{2}\right) = \frac{5}{6}$ ft from A.

Integrating (c) using $V(x) = -\int q(x)dx$ gives

$$-V_{(x)} = -\frac{2\omega_0}{5}\int\left(x - \frac{5}{2}\right)\left[u\left(x - \frac{5}{2}\right)\right]dx + C_1$$

$$= -\frac{2\omega_0}{5}\int_{-\infty}^{x}\left(\xi - \frac{5}{2}\right)\left[u\left(\xi - \frac{5}{2}\right)\right]d\xi + C_1$$

$$= -\frac{2\omega_0}{5}\left\{\int_{-\infty}^{\frac{5}{2}}\left(\xi - \frac{5}{2}\right)\left[u\left(\xi - \frac{5}{2}\right)\right]d\xi + \int_{\frac{5}{2}}^{x}\left(\xi - \frac{5}{2}\right)\left[u\left(\xi - \frac{5}{2}\right)\right]d\xi\right\}$$

$$+ C_1$$

$$= -\frac{2\omega_0}{5}\left\{0 + u\left(x - \frac{5}{2}\right)\int_{\frac{5}{2}}^{x}\left(\xi - \frac{5}{2}\right)d\xi\right\} + C_1$$

$$= -\frac{2}{5}\omega_0\left[u\left(x - \frac{5}{2}\right)\right]\frac{\left(x - \frac{5}{2}\right)^2}{2} + C_1$$

$$= -\frac{1}{5}\omega_0\left(x - \frac{5}{2}\right)^2 u\left(x - \frac{5}{2}\right) + C_1 \qquad \text{(e)}$$

Now

$$V(0) = -R_B = -C_1 \qquad \text{(f)}$$

and R_B is computed by taking moments about A and using the resultant, R, to get

$$5R_B = R\left(\frac{5}{6}\right)$$

$$R_B = \frac{5}{24}\omega_0 \qquad \text{(g)}$$

Integrating (e) using $M_b(x) = -\int V(x)dx$, we get

$$M_b(x) = -\frac{1}{5}\omega_0\int\left(x - \frac{5}{2}\right)^2 u\left(x - \frac{5}{2}\right)dx + C_1x + C_2.$$

By similar method as above, the first integral can be evaluated

$$M_b(x) = -\frac{\omega_0}{15}\left(x - \frac{5}{2}\right)^3 u\left(x - \frac{5}{2}\right) + \frac{5}{24}\omega_0 x + C_2 \qquad \text{(h)}$$

and $C_2 = 0$ in order that the moment vanish at $x = 0$. Now the maximum bending moment is located in this case between A and C at the point where $V = 0$, because $V = -\frac{dM}{dx}$, and M is maximum when $\frac{dM}{dx}$ is equal to zero. Solving (e) for x_0 such that $V(x_0) = 0$ gives

$$-\frac{1}{5}\omega_0\left(x_0 - \frac{5}{2}\right)^2 u\left(x_0 - \frac{5}{2}\right) + \frac{5}{24}\omega_0 = 0.$$

For a solution of x_0, the first term cannot be equal to zero. Therefore, $u\left(x_0 - \frac{5}{2}\right) = 1$, and

$$-\frac{1}{5}\omega_0\left(x_0 - \frac{5}{2}\right)^2 = -\frac{5}{24}\omega_0$$

$$\left(x_0 - \frac{5}{2}\right)^2 = \frac{25}{24}$$

$$x_0 - \frac{5}{2} = \frac{5}{2\sqrt{6}}$$

$$x_0 = \frac{5}{2} + \frac{5}{2\sqrt{6}}$$

$$x_0 = \frac{5}{2}\left(1 + \frac{1}{\sqrt{6}}\right)$$

$$= 3.52 \text{ ft.}$$

Substitution into (h) gives for the maximum bending moment

$$M_b(x_0) = 207 \text{ ft-lb.} \qquad \text{(i)}$$

APPLICATION OF SINGULARITY FUNCTIONS

• PROBLEM 2-30

Find V(x) and M(x) for a beam loaded as in Fig. 1. Use singularity functions and treat it as a boundary-value problem.

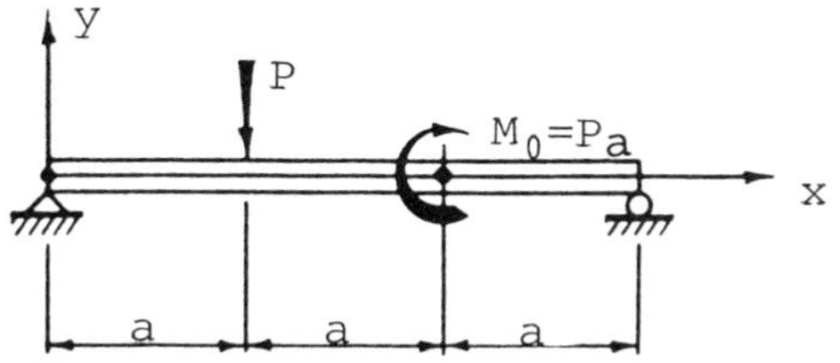

Fig. 1.

Solution: The types of loading in this system consist of a point load P and a couple of moment M_0 = Pa. We need singularity functions to represent this loading system. The point load can be written as Direc-delta function $-P[\delta(x - a)]$ where $\delta(x - a)$ is a unit Direc-delta function, the integral of which represnets a unit function $u(x - a)$. Similarly, the couple can be written as a doublet function

$Pa \cdot \eta(x - 2a)$ where $\eta(x - 2a)$ is a unit doublet function, the integral of which represents a unit Direc-delta function $\delta(x - 2a)$. The loading function $p(x)$ can be written in symbolic form. From the conditions $M(0) = 0$ and $M(L) = 0$, with $L = 3a$, the constants of integration can be found:

$$d^2M/dx^2 = p = -P[\delta(x - a)] + Pa[\eta(x - 2a)]$$

$$dM/dx = -V = \int -P[\delta(x - a)]dx + \int Pa[\eta(x - 2a)]dx$$

$$= -P[u(x - a)] + Pa\,[\delta(x - 2a)] + C_1$$

$$M = \int -P[u(x - a)]dx + \int Pa[\delta(x - 2a)]dx + \int C_1 dx + C_2$$

$$= \int_{-\infty}^{x} -P[u(\zeta - a)]d\zeta + Pa\,u(x - 2a) + C_1 x + C_2$$

where ζ is an integration variable. First term,

$$\int_{-\infty}^{x} -P[u(\zeta - a)]d\zeta = \int_{-\infty}^{a} -P[u(\zeta - a)]d\zeta$$

$$+ \int_{a}^{x} -P[u(\zeta - a)]d\zeta$$

$$= 0 + -P[u(x - a)] \int_{a}^{x} d\zeta$$

The first integral is zero because of the nature of unit function. In the second integral, the unit function can be extracted out from the integral.

Now we have

$$M = -P[u(x - a)] \int_{a}^{x} d\zeta + Pa\,u(x - 2a) + C_1 x + C_2$$

$$= -P[u(x - a)](x - a) + Pa[u(x - 2a)] + C_1 x + C_2$$

The boundary conditions $M(0) = 0$ and $M(3a) = 0$ lead to

$$-P[u(x - a)]\Big|_{x=0}(0 - a) + Pa[u(x - 2a)]\Big|_{x=0} + C_1(0) + C_2 = 0$$

$$0 \quad + \quad 0 \quad + 0 \quad + C_2 = 0 \qquad C_2 = 0$$

(Remember $u(x-a) = \begin{cases} 0 & \text{for } x < a \\ 1 & \text{for } x \geq a \end{cases}$, therefore the first and second terms become zero.)

$$M(3a) = 0$$

$$-P[u(x-a)]\Big|_{x=3a}(3a-a) + Pa[u(x-2a)]\Big|_{x=3a} + C_1(3a) + C_2 = 0$$

$$-P(1)(2a) + Pa(1) + C_1(3a) = 0$$

$$-P(2a) + Pa + C_1(3a) = 0$$

$$C_1 = \frac{Pa}{3a} = \frac{P}{3}.$$

$$M = -P[u(x-a)](x-a) + Pa[u(x-2a)] + \frac{P}{3}x$$

$$V = P[u(x-a)] - Pa[\delta(x-2a)] - \frac{P}{3}$$

Since M and V are also zeros when $x < 0$, we can modify the last terms of M and V as

$$M = -P[u(x-a)](x-a) + Pa[u(x-2a)] + \frac{P}{3}[u(x-0)](x-0)$$

$$V = +P[u(x-a)] - Pa[\delta(x-2a)] - \frac{P}{3}[u(x-0)$$

• PROBLEM 2-31

Using singularity function, determine V(x) and M(x) caused by the loading in Fig. 1.

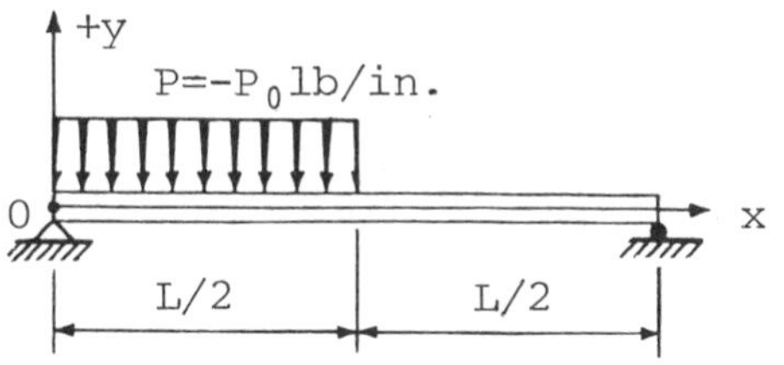

Fig. 1.

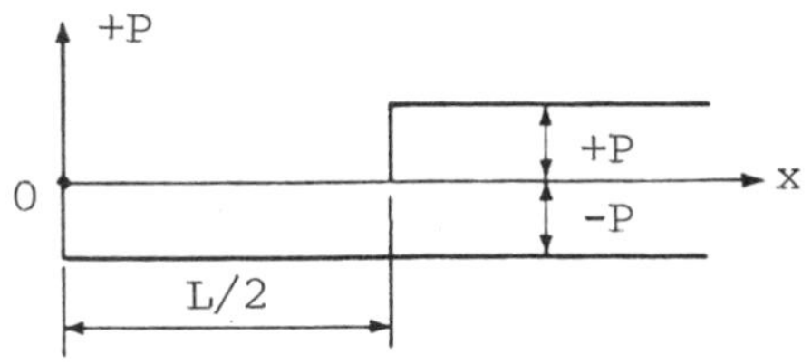

Fig. 2. Load Diagram

Solution: In order to represent the type of loading in this system, we need singularity function, which consists of unit step function and Direc-delta function. The unit step function $u(x-\xi)$ means that, when the number x is less than ξ, the function is zero and when x is greater than ξ, it is equal to one. The applied load p(x) acts downward and begins at x = 0. Therefore, a term $p = -p_0$, or $-p_0[u(x - 0)]$ must exist, where u(x - 0) is a unit step function starting from x = 0 to +∞. This function, however, propagates across the whole span, see Fig. 2. To terminate the distributed load at x = L/2 as required in this problem, another func-function $+p_0[u(x - L/2)]$ must be added. The two expressions together represent correctly the applied load.

For this simply supported beam the known boudnary conditions are M(0) = 0 and M(L) = 0. These are used to determine the reactions:

$$\frac{d^2M}{dx^2} = +p = -p_0[u(x - 0)] + p_0[u(x - L/2)]$$

$$\frac{dM}{dx} = -V = -p_0 \int_{-\infty}^{x} u(x - 0)dx + p_0 \int_{-\infty}^{x} u(x - L/2)dx + C_1$$

$$= -p_0\left[\int_{-\infty}^{0} u(x - 0)dx + \int_{0}^{x} u(\zeta - 0)d\zeta\right]$$

$$+ p_0\left[\int_{-\infty}^{\frac{L}{2}} u\left(x - \frac{L}{2}\right)dx + \int_{\frac{L}{2}}^{x} u\left(\zeta - \frac{L}{2}\right)d\zeta\right] + C_1$$

$$= -p_0\left[0 + \{u(x - 0)\}\int_{0}^{x} d\zeta\right] + p_0\left[0 + \left\{u\left(x - \frac{L}{2}\right)\right\}\int_{\frac{L}{2}}^{x} d\zeta\right] + C_1$$

$$= -p_0(x)[u(x - 0)] + p_0\left(x - \frac{L}{2}\right)\left[u\left(x - \frac{L}{2}\right)\right] + C_1.$$

In this step, we have used ζ as the integration variable and the boudnary of integration form -∞ to x.

$$M(x) = \frac{dM}{dx}(x) = -p_0(x)[u(x - 0)] + p_0\left(x - \frac{L}{2}\right)\left[u\left(x - \frac{L}{2}\right)\right] + C_1$$

$$M(x) = -p_0\int x[u(x - 0)]dx + p_0\int\left(x - \frac{L}{2}\right)\left[u\left(x - \frac{L}{2}\right)\right]dx + C_1x + C_2$$

$$= -p_0 \int_{-\infty}^{x} \zeta[u(\zeta - 0)]d\zeta + p_0 \int_{-\infty}^{x} \left(\zeta - \frac{L}{2}\right)\left[u\left(\zeta - \frac{L}{2}\right)\right]d\zeta + C_1x + C_2$$

$$= -p_0\left\{\int_{-\infty}^{0} \zeta[u(\zeta - 0)]d\zeta + \int_{0}^{x}\zeta[u(\zeta - 0)]d\zeta\right\}$$

$$+ p_0\left\{\int_{-\infty}^{\frac{L}{2}} \left(\zeta - \frac{L}{2}\right)\left[u\left(\zeta - \frac{L}{2}\right)\right]d\zeta\right.$$

$$\left. + \int_{\frac{L}{2}}^{x}\left(\zeta - \frac{L}{2}\right)\left[u\left(\zeta - \frac{L}{2}\right)\right]d\zeta\right\} + C_1x + C_2$$

$$= -p_0\left\{0 + u(x - 0)\int_0^x \zeta d\zeta\right\} + p_0\left\{0 + u\left(x - \frac{L}{2}\right)\int_{\frac{L}{2}}^{x}\left(\zeta - \frac{L}{2}\right)d\zeta\right\}$$

$$+ C_1x + C_2$$

$$= -p_0\ u(x - 0)\left[\frac{\zeta^2}{2}\right]_0^x + p_0\ u\left(x - \frac{L}{2}\right)\left[\frac{\left(\zeta - \frac{L}{2}\right)^2}{2}\right]_{\frac{L}{2}}^{x} + C_1x + C_2$$

$$= -p_0\ u(x - 0)\ \frac{x^2}{2} + p_0\ u\left(x - \frac{L}{2}\right)\left[\frac{\left(x - \frac{L}{2}\right)^2}{2}\right] + C_1x + C_2$$

Boundary condition: $M(0) = 0$

$$C_2 = 0$$

$$M(L) = 0$$

$$-p_0\ \frac{L^2}{2} + p_0\ \frac{L}{8} + C_1L = 0.$$

Hence, $C_1 = +\frac{3}{8}\ p_0L$

and $V(x) = p_0(x)[u(x - 0)] - p_0\left(x - \frac{L}{2}\right)\left[u\left(x - \frac{L}{2}\right)\right] - \frac{3}{8}p_0L$

$$M(x) = -p_0[u(x - 0)]\frac{x^2}{2} + \frac{p_0}{2}\left(x - \frac{L}{2}\right)^2\left[u\left(x - \frac{L}{2}\right)\right] + \frac{3}{8}p_0Lx.$$

After the solution is obtained, these relations are more easily read by rewriting them in conventional form:

$$\left.\begin{aligned} V &= -\frac{3}{8}p_0L + p_0x \\ M &= +\frac{3}{8}p_0Lx - \frac{1}{2}p_0x^2 \end{aligned}\right\} \quad \text{when} \quad 0 < x \le (L/2)$$

$$\left.\begin{aligned} V &= -\frac{3}{8}p_0L + \frac{1}{2}p_0L = +\frac{1}{8}p_0L \\ M &= \frac{1}{8}p_0L^2 - \frac{1}{8}p_0Lx \end{aligned}\right\} \quad \text{when} \quad (L/2) \le x < L$$

• PROBLEM 2-32

Consider the beam shown in Fig. 1 with simple transverse supports at A and B and loaded with a uniformly distributed load $q = -\omega_0$ over a portion of the length. Find the shear-force and bending-moment diagrams by (a) differential relationships; (b) singularity functions.

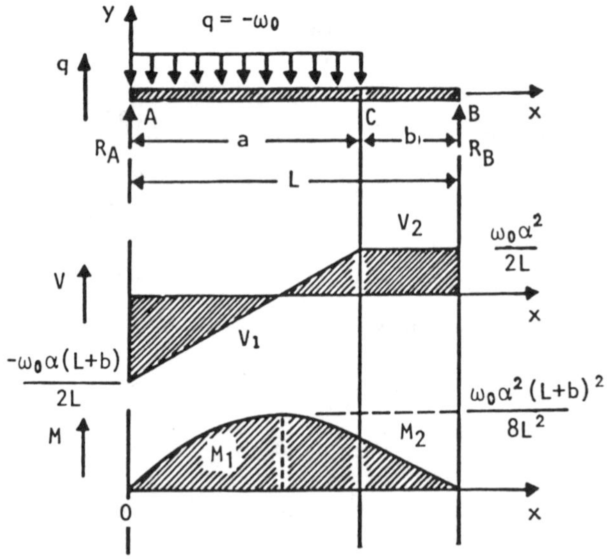

Fig. 1

Fig. 2

Fig. 3

Solution: (a) Differential relationships:

Since the loading q is not for the whole beam, the beam is divided into two parts AC and CB. We have to consider these two parts separately. Let subscripts 1 and 2 indicate values of variables in the loaded and unloaded segments of the beam.

Using $\frac{dV}{dx} = -q$ in each segment and integrating gives

$$\frac{dV_1}{dx} - \omega_0 = 0 \qquad \frac{dV_2}{dx} = 0 \tag{a}$$

$$V_1 - \omega_0 x = C_1 \qquad V_2 = C_2$$

Next we write $\frac{dM}{dx} = -V$ in each segment, using the V's from (a)

$$\frac{dM_{b1}}{dx} + \omega_0 x + C_1 = 0 \quad \frac{dM_{b2}}{dx} + C_2 = 0 \tag{b}$$

and integrating again gives

$$M_{b1} + \frac{1}{2}\omega_0 x^2 + C_1 x = C_3 \qquad M_{b2} + C_2 x = C_4 \tag{c}$$

We have two boundary conditions available for the moments. There is no moment restraint at each end of the beam, hence

$$M_{b1} = 0 \text{ at } x = 0 \qquad M_{b2} = 0 \text{ at } x = L \tag{d}$$

However, we need two additional conditions in order to determine the remaining two arbitrary constants. These follow from equilibrium requirements at the junction of the two segments

$$\begin{aligned} V_1 &= V_2 \quad \text{at } x = a \\ M_{b1} &= M_b 2 \quad \text{at } x = a \end{aligned} \tag{e}$$

Inserting these boundary conditions into (a) and (c) leads to

$$M_{b1}(x = 0) = 0, \qquad \therefore C_3 = 0 \tag{f}$$

$$M_{b2}(x = L) = 0, \qquad \therefore 0 + C_2(L) = C_4 \tag{g}$$

$V_1 = V_2$ at $x = a$,

$$\omega_0(a) + C_1 = C_2$$

$$C_1 = C_2 - \omega_0 \cdot a \tag{h}$$

$M_{b1} = M_{b2}$ at $x = a$,

$$C_3 - \frac{1}{2}\omega_0 x^2 - C_1 x = C_4 - C_2 x \quad \text{at} \quad x = a$$

$$0 - \frac{1}{2}\omega_0 (a)^2 - C_1(a) = C_4 - C_2(a)$$

Substitute (h) into the above equation

$$-\frac{1}{2}\omega_0 a^2 - (C_2 - \omega_0 a)a = C_4 - C_2 a$$

$$-\frac{1}{2}\omega_0 a^2 - C_2 a + \omega_0 a^2 = C_4 - C_2 a$$

$$C_4 = \frac{1}{2}\omega_0 a^2$$

From (g), $$LC_2 = \frac{1}{2}\omega_0 a^2$$

$$\therefore C_2 = \frac{1}{2}\frac{\omega_0 a^2}{L}$$

from (f),

$$C_1 = \frac{1}{2}\frac{\omega_0 a^2}{L} - \omega_0 a$$

$$= \frac{1}{2}\omega_0 a\left(\frac{a}{L} - 2\right)$$

$$= \frac{1}{2}\omega_0 a\left(\frac{L - b}{L} - 2\right)$$

$$= -\frac{1}{2}\omega_0 a\,\frac{(L + b)}{L}$$

The shear-force and bending-moment diagrams can be constructed from

$$V_1 = \omega_0 x - \frac{\omega_0 a}{2L}(L + b) \qquad 0 \leq x \leq a$$

$$V_2 = \frac{1}{2}\frac{\omega_0 a^2}{L} \qquad a \leq x \leq L \tag{i}$$

and

$$M_{b1} = +\frac{\omega_0 a}{2L}(L + b)x - \frac{1}{2}\omega_0 x^2 \qquad 0 \leq x \leq a$$

$$M_{b2} = \frac{1}{2}\omega_0 a^2 - \frac{1}{2}\frac{\omega_0 a^2 x}{L} \qquad a \leq x \leq L \tag{j}$$

as shown in Figs. 2 and 3.

(b) Singularity functions method:

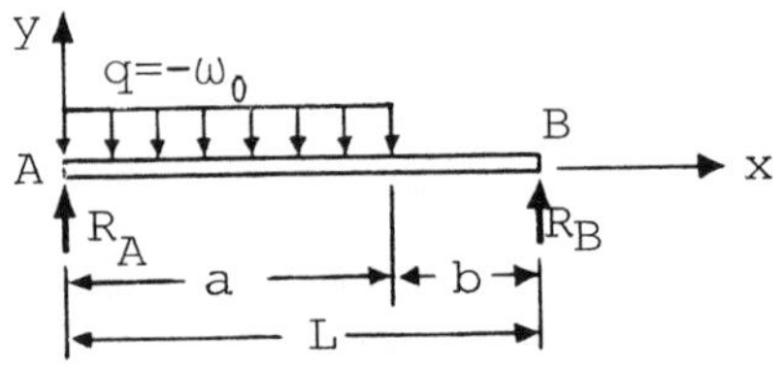

Fig. 4.

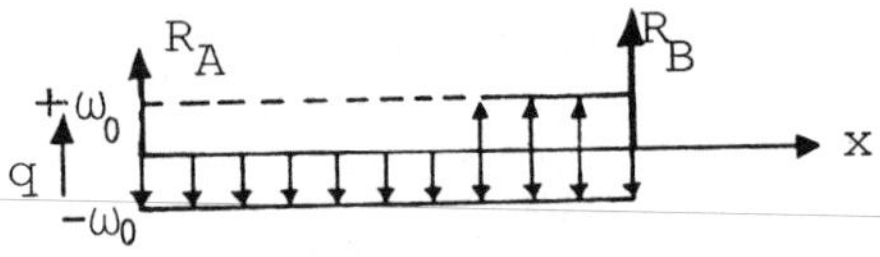

Fig. 5.

By using singularity function, we could represent the loading of the system by a single equation. The two functions used in this problem are Direc-delta function and unit step function. The Direc-delta function $\delta(x - a)$ is used to represent unit load at $x = a$. The unit step function $u(x - a)$ is used to represent a unit uniform load from $x = a$ to ∞.

In Fig. 2, the load intensity q is given in a form which permits easy translation into the singularity functions. The load $q = -\omega_0$ which stops at $x = a$ in Fig. 4 is shown continuing on to B, but at $x = a$ the supplementary load $q = \omega_0$ is started. This cancels the other load, leaving no net distributed load after $x = a$. Now, we write the load-intensity function

$$q(x) = -\omega_0[u(x - 0)] + \omega_0[u(x - a)] \qquad \text{(k)}$$

which is valid for $0 < x < L$. Substituting (a) into $\frac{dV}{dx} = -q$ and integrating we find

$$\frac{dV}{dx} = \omega_0[u(x - 0)] - \omega_0[u(x - a)]$$

$$V = \omega_0 \int u(x)dx - \omega_0 \int u(x - a)dx + C_1$$

The integral $\int [u(x - a)]dx = \int_{-\infty}^{x} u(\zeta - a)d$ (where ζ is an integration variable)

$$= \int_{-\infty}^{a} [u(\zeta - a)]d\zeta + \int_{a}^{x} [u(\zeta - a)]d\zeta$$

$$= 0 + u(x - a) \int_{a}^{x} d\zeta$$

Apply the fact that

$$u(x - a) = \begin{cases} 0 & \text{for} \quad -\infty < x < a \\ 1 & \text{for} \quad a < x < \infty \end{cases}$$

Therefore

$$V(x) = \omega_0[u(x)] \int_{0}^{x} d\zeta - \omega_0[u(x - a)] \int_{a}^{x} d\zeta + C_1$$

$$= \omega_0 x u(x) - \omega_0(x - a)[u(x - a)] + C_1 \qquad \text{(l)}$$

In particular, $V(0) = C_1$, but this is just $-R_A$, which is easily found from a moment-balance equation about point B as follows:

$\sum M_B = 0$ (+ ↺),

$$R_A \cdot L - \omega_0 \cdot a\left(\frac{a}{2} + b\right) = 0$$

$$R_A = \frac{\omega_0 a}{2} \frac{(a + 2b)}{L}$$

$$-R_A = -\frac{\omega_0 a}{L}\left(b + \frac{a}{2}\right) \quad \text{(m)}$$

Integrating (1) with C_1 known gives:

$$\frac{dM}{dx} = -V(x)$$

$$M = -\int V(x)dx + C_2$$

$$= -\omega_0 \int xu(x)dx + \omega_0 \int (x - a)[u(x - a)]dx - C_1x + C_2$$

by similar way,

$$= -\omega_0\ u(x) \int_0^x \zeta\ d\zeta + \omega_0\ u(x - a) \int_a^x (\zeta - a)d\zeta - C_1x + C_2$$

$$= -\omega_0\ u(x)\frac{x^2}{2} + \omega_0[u(x - a)]\left[\frac{(\zeta - a)^2}{2}\right]_a^x - C_1x + C_2$$

$$= -\omega_0 \frac{x^2}{2} u(x) + \omega_0\frac{(x - a)^2}{2}[u(x - a)] - C_1x + C_2$$

$$= -\omega_0 \frac{x^2}{2} u(x) + \frac{\omega_0}{2}(x - a)^2[u(x - 0)] - \frac{\omega_0 a}{2} \frac{(a + 2b)}{L}x + C_2 \quad \text{(n)}$$

where $C_2 = 0$ since $M_b(0) = 0$.

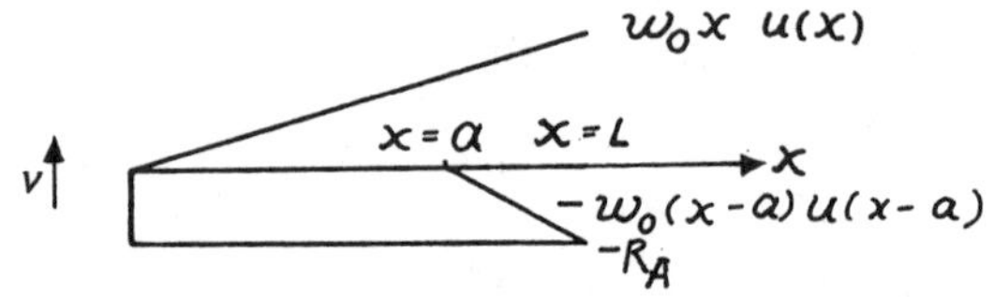

FIG. 6

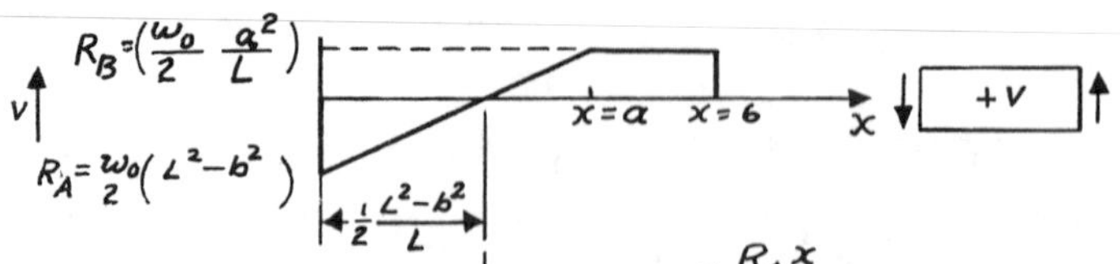

FIG 7

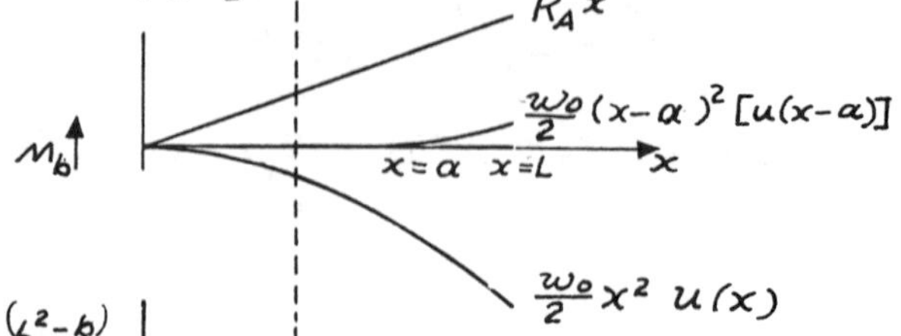

FIG. 8

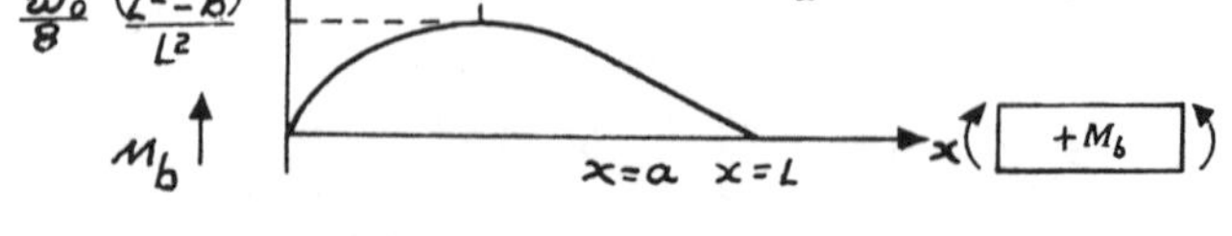

FIG. 9

The shear-force and bending-moment diagrams are easily constructed using (l) and (n) with C_1 and C_2 known. To help the reader interpret (b), each term has been sketched separately in Fig. 6 before showing the resultant shear-force diagram in Fig. 7. In similar fashion each term of (n) has been sketched separately in Fig. 8 before showing the resultant bending-moment diagram in Fig. 9.

There are many alternative techniques for solving problems like this one. The method we have shown involved the separate evaluation of a support reaction which was used in evaluating an arbitrary constant of integration. An alternate procedure involves the introduction of the support reactions into the loading term as unknowns and their determination from the two boundary conditions on the moments at the ends of the beam.

Let us work through this example again, this time including the reactive forces in the loading term q(x). We write the load-intensity function

$$q(x) = R_A\delta(x) - \omega_0[u(x - 0)] + \omega_0[u(x - a)] + R_B\delta(x - L) \quad \text{(o)}$$

This representation is valid for all x, since it gives $q = 0$ when x is outside of the segment between A and B. Since $V = 0$ at $x = -\infty$,

$$\frac{dV(x)}{dx} = -q$$

$$-V(x) = \int_{-\infty}^{x} q\, dx = R_A\, u(x) - \omega_0\, u(x)(x - 0)$$

$$+ \omega_0[u(x - a)](x - a) + R_B[u(x - L)] \quad \text{(p)}$$

A second integration using $\frac{dM(x)}{dx} = -V$ and the fact that $M_b = 0$ at $x = -\infty$, yields

$$M_b(x) = -\int_{-\infty}^{x} V\, dx = R_A x\, u(x) - \omega_0\, u(x)\int_0^x \zeta\, d\zeta$$

$$+ \omega_0[u(x - a)]\int_a^x (x - a)dx$$

$$+ R_B[u(x - L)](x - L)$$

$$= R_A x\, u(x) - \omega_0 x\, u(x) + \omega_0\frac{(x - a)^2}{2}[u(x - 0)]$$

$$+ R_B(x - L)[u(x - L)]. \quad \text{(q)}$$

If R_A and R_B were known, (p) and (q) would furnish the complete solution for the shear force and bending moment. It is not difficult to obtain the reactions from a separate calculation, and in some cases this may prove to be the simplest procedure. We can, however, use our results to determine the reactions by making use of our observation that there should be no internal forces and moments outside of the segment AB. If we take x just slightly larger than x = L, the shear force (p) should vanish, that is,

$$R_A - \omega_0 L + \omega_0(L - a) + R_B = 0 \qquad (r)$$

$$R_A + R_B = \omega_0 a$$

and the bending moment (q) should also vanish, that is,

$$R_A L - \frac{\omega_0}{2}L^2 + \frac{\omega_0}{2}(L - a)^2 = 0$$

$$(s)$$

$$R_A = \frac{\omega_0}{2}\,\frac{L^2 - b^2}{L}$$

Equations (r) and (s) furnish two relations for determining the two reactions R_A and R_B. Note that these relations are, in fact, the conditions for equilibrium of the entire beam. Vertical-force balance is indicated by (r), and balance of moments about point B is indicated by (s). What this means is simply that the satisfaction of the equilibrium requireemnts for every differential element of the beam implies satisfaction of the equilibrium requirements of the entire beam.

• PROBLEM 2-33

For the simply supported beam shown, find the shear-force and bending moment equations. Figure 2 shows the hypothetical infinite beam.

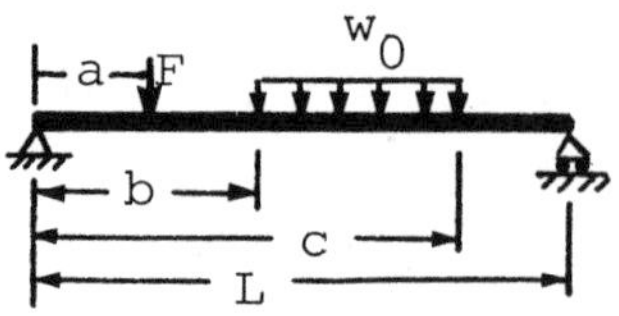

Fig. 1.

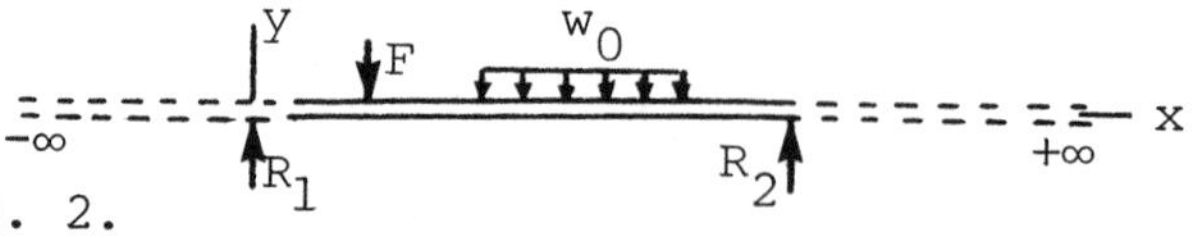

Fig. 2.

Solution: We begin by determining the intensity of loading for the entire beam. For simplicity, we shall consider the contribution of each force separately.

There are three kinds of singularity functions: Direc-delta function $\delta(x - \xi)$ which represents a single unit load at $x = \xi$, unit step function $u(x - \xi)$ which represents a uniform unit load distribution for $-\infty < x < \xi$, and doublet function which is not used here. We thus have

For Force R_1: $$\omega_1(x) = R_1\left[\delta(x - 0)\right] \tag{a}$$

For Force F: $$\omega_2(x) = -F\left[\delta(x - a)\right] \tag{b}$$

For uniform loading:
$$\omega_3(x) = -\omega_0\left[u(x - b)\right] + \omega_0\left[u(x - c)\right] \tag{c}$$

For Force R_2: $$\omega_4(x) = R_2\left[\delta(x - L)\right] \tag{d}$$

Then the total intensity of loading $\omega(x)$ is
$$\begin{aligned}\omega(x) &= R_1\left[\delta(x - 0)\right] - F\left[\delta(x - a)\right] - \omega_0\left[u(x - b)\right] \\ &\quad + \omega_0\left[u(x - c)\right] + R_2\left[\delta(x - L)\right]\end{aligned} \tag{e}$$

For shear:
$$\begin{aligned}\frac{dV_y}{dx} = -\omega(x) &= -R_1\left[\delta(x - 0)\right] + F\left[\delta(x - a)\right] \\ &\quad +\omega_0\left[u(x - b)\right] - \omega_0\left[u(x - c)\right] - R_2\left[\delta(x - L)\right]\end{aligned} \tag{f}$$

Integrate the differential equation by bringing dx to the right-hand side of the equation, and, using ζ as the integration variable.

$$\begin{aligned}V_y(x) - V_y(-\infty) &= -R_1\int_{-\infty}^{x}[\delta(\zeta - 0)]d\zeta + F\int_{-\infty}^{x}[\delta(\zeta - a)]d\zeta \\ &\quad + \int_{-\infty}^{x}\omega_0[u(\zeta - b)]d\zeta - \int_{-\infty}^{x}\omega_0[u(\zeta - c)]d\zeta \\ &\quad - \int_{-\infty}^{x}R_2[\delta(\zeta - L)]d\zeta \\ &= -R_1[u(x - 0)] + F[u(x - a)]\end{aligned}$$

$$+ \int_{-\infty}^{b} \omega_0[u(\zeta - b)]d\zeta + \int_{b}^{x} \omega_0[u(\zeta - b)]d\zeta$$

$$- \int_{-\infty}^{c} \omega_0[u(\zeta - c)]d\zeta - \int_{c}^{x} \omega_0[u(\zeta - c)]d\zeta - R_2\, u(x - L)$$

$$= -R_1[u(x)] + F[u(x - a)]$$

$$+ 0 + \omega_0[u(x - b)] \int_{b}^{x} d\zeta - 0 - \omega_0[u(x - c)] \int_{c}^{x} d\zeta$$

$$- R_2[u(x - L)]$$

$$= -R_1[u(x)] + F[u(x - a)] + \omega_0(x - b)[u(x - b)]$$

$$- \omega_0(x - c)[u(x - c)] - R_2[u(x - L)] \qquad (g)$$

But from our boundary conditions given by (g) we must conclude that $V_y(-\infty) = 0$.

$$V_y = -R_1[u(x)] + F[u(x - a)] + \omega_0[u(x - b)](x - b)$$
$$- \omega_0[u(x - c)](x - c) - R_2[u(x - L)] \qquad (h)$$

We may now evaluate the bending moment by employing the second of our basic differential equations. Thus,

$$\frac{dM_z}{dx} = -V_y = R_1[u(x)] - F[u(x - a)] - \omega_0[u(x - b)](x - b)$$
$$+ \omega_0[u(x - c)](x - c) + R_2[u(x - L)] \qquad (i)$$

Transferring dx to the right-hand side of the equation and changing to integration variable ζ we again integrate from $-\infty$ to x. Thus,

$$M_z(x) - M_z(-\infty) = \int_{-\infty}^{x} R_1[u(\zeta - 0)]d\zeta - \int_{-\infty}^{x} F[u(\zeta - a)]d$$

$$- \omega_0 \int_{-\infty}^{x} [u(\zeta - b)](\zeta - b)d\zeta \quad - \omega_0 \int_{-\infty}^{x} [u(\zeta - c)](\zeta - c)d\zeta$$

$$+ R_2 \int_{-\infty}^{x} [u(\zeta - L)]d\zeta$$

But $u(x - \xi) = 0$ for $x < \xi$ therefore $\int_{-\infty}^{\xi} u(x - \xi)dx = 0$

The above expression becomes,

$$= \int_0^x R_1[u(\zeta - 0)]d\zeta - \int_a^x F[u(\zeta - a)]d\zeta$$

$$- \omega_0 \int_b^x [u(\zeta - b)](\zeta - b)d\zeta$$

$$+ \omega_0 \int_c^x [u(\zeta - c)](\zeta - c)d\zeta$$

$$+ R_2 \int_L^x [u(\zeta - L)]d\zeta$$

$$= R_1\left(\mu(x)\right)\int d\zeta - F\left(u(x - a)\right)\int_a^x d\zeta$$

$$- \omega_0[u(x - b)] \int_b^x (\zeta - b)d\zeta$$

$$+ \omega_0[u(x - c)] \int_c^x (\zeta - c)d\zeta$$

$$+ R_2[u(x - L)] \int_L^x d\zeta \qquad \text{(j)}$$

Since the boundary conditinons are $+\infty$ and $-\infty$ with moments and shear forces equal to zero, then the constants of integration are zero. Let us now consider the third and fourth integrals. When the integrand is of the form $\zeta - b$ and the lower limit has the value b we can integrate in the following simple way:

$$\int_b^x (\zeta - b)d\zeta = \left.\frac{(\zeta - b)^2}{2}\right|_b^x = \frac{(x - b)^2}{2} \qquad \text{(k)}$$

You may readily show that this shortcut is correct by carrying out the integration on the left-hand side in the usual way. We may then generalize the procedure as follows:

$$\int_b^x (\zeta - b)^n d\zeta = \frac{(x - b)^{n+1}}{n + 1} \tag{l}$$

This procedure will be of great help when we extend the methods herein presented for use in the solution of the deflection of beams. Thus, carrying out the integrations of Eq. (j), we get

$$\begin{aligned} M_z = \; & R_1[u(x)]x - F[u(x - a)](x - 0) \\ & - \omega_0[u(x - b)]\frac{(x - b)^2}{2} \\ & + \omega_0[u(x - c)]\frac{(x - c)^2}{2} \\ & + R_2[u(x - L)](x - L) \end{aligned} \tag{m}$$

The shear equation [Eq. (h)] and the bending-moment equation [Eq. (m)] have a total of two unknown quantities: They are the supporting forces R_1 and R_2. These unknowns can be computed from the boundary conditions. Thus, to the right of the beam, M_z and V_y are again zero. For $x = L^+$ we see that we are to the right of all the step functions in Eq. (h), including the one at $x = L$. Putting in the value of unity for the step functions, we then get

$$V_y = 0 = -R_1 + F + \omega_0(L - b) - \omega_0(L - c) - R_2 \tag{n}$$

And for the bending-moment equation, we get

$$M_z = 0 = R_1 L - F(L - a) - \omega_0\frac{(L - b)^2}{2} + \omega_0\frac{(L - c)^2}{2} \tag{o}$$

We now have two simultaneous equations: (n) and (o) from which we may solve for the two unknowns R_1 and R_2. We shall not proceed further with the computations but shall merely state the shear-force and bending-moment equations in terms of R_1 and R_2. Thus,

$$\begin{aligned} V_y = \; & -R_1[u(x)] + F[u(x - a)] + \omega_0[u(x - b)](x - b) \\ & - \omega_0[u(x - c)](x - c) - R_2[u(x - L)] \end{aligned} \tag{p}$$

$$\begin{aligned} M_z = \; & R_1[u(x)]x - F[u(x - a)](x - a) - \omega_0[u(x - b)]\frac{(x - b)^2}{2} \\ & + \omega_0[u(x - c)]\frac{(x - c)^2}{2} + R_2[u(x - L)](x - L) \end{aligned} \tag{q}$$

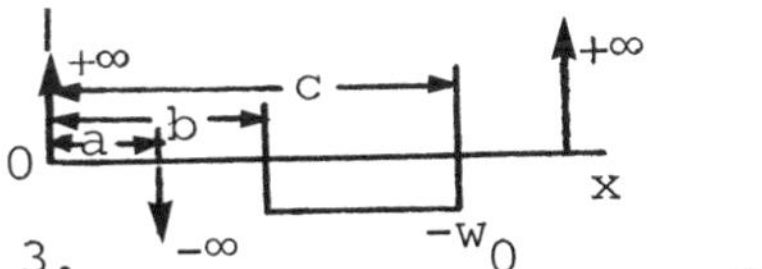

Fig. 3.

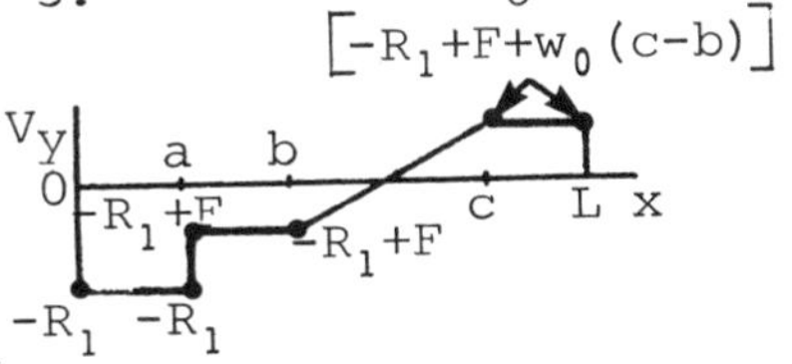

Fig. 4.

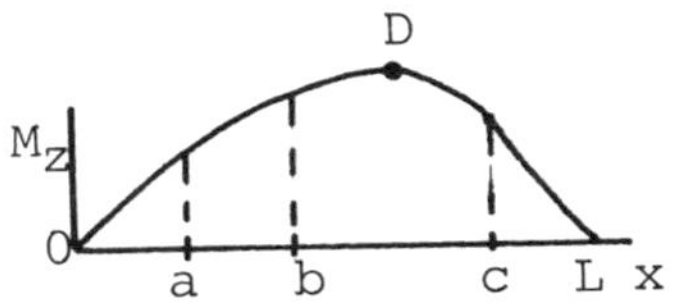

Fig. 5.

A sketch of the loading, shear, and bending moment diagrams are supplied for better understanding. Notice in the loading of forces R_1, R_2, and F, the magnitudes are infinite. This comes from the delta function concept. Also take note of the interval b - c in the shear diagram. The slope is constant because of the relation $\frac{dV}{dx} = -\omega$, where ω is a constant distributed load. The moment diagram is simply the slope of the shear diagram from the relation $\frac{dM}{dx} = -V$. The place where the shear force diagram crosses the x-axis from +ve to -ve or from -ve to +ve (V = 0) indicates the location of maximum moment. Understanding the diagrams helps in understanding the equations.

• PROBLEM 2-34

A cantilever beam has a partial uniform load and a horizontal force F as shown in Fig. 1. Determine the axial and shear forces along the beam as well as the bending moment along the beam by using singularity functions.

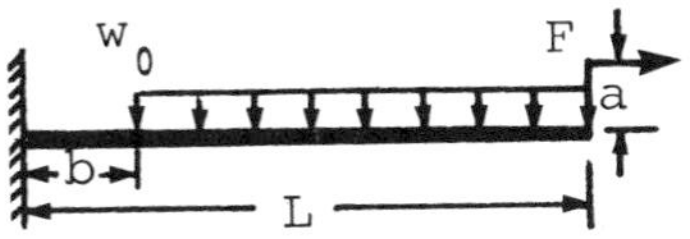

Fig. 1.

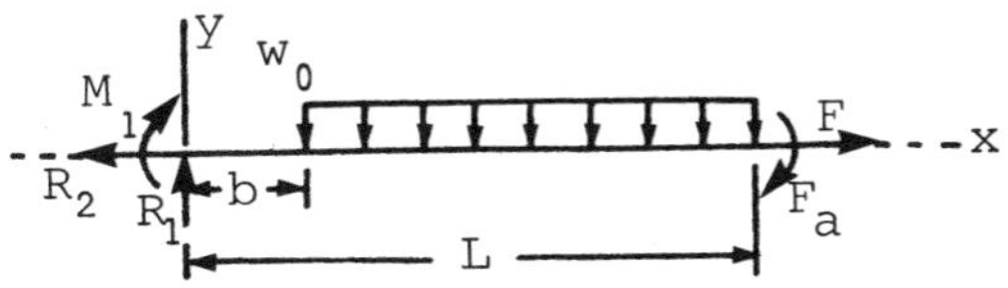

Fig. 2.

Solution: Singularity functions are used to represent the type of loading in this system. There are three kinds of singularity functions: Direc-delta function $\delta(x - c)$ which represents a unit load at x = c, unit step function u(x - c) which represents a unit uniform load between x = c to ∞, and Doublet function $\eta(x - c)$ which represents a unit couple at point x = c.

The force F may be replaced by a force along the centerline of the beam and a moment (couple) Fa. The hypothetical infinite beam is shown in Fig. 2 with the equivalent force, and the point forces R_1, R_2 and couple M_1 which replace the supporting force system.

Fig. 3.

The axial force F applies constant tension throughout the length of the beam. To find the shear force and bending moment equations,

$$w(x) = R_1[\delta(x)] + M_1[\eta(x)] - w_0[u(x - b)] \qquad \text{(a)}$$

$$+ w_0[u(x - L)] + Fa\,[\eta(x - L)]$$

Using the differential equation for shear

$$\frac{dV_y}{dx} = -w(x)$$

$$\frac{dV_y}{dx} = -R_1[\delta(x)] - M_1[\eta(x)] + w_0[u(x - b)] \qquad \text{(b)}$$

$$- w_0[u(x - L)] - Fa[\eta(x - L)]$$

Integrating term by term, we get for example,

$$\int \delta(x)dx = u(x),$$

because the area under a Direc-delta function is unity by definition. And

$$\int u(x - b)dx = \int_{-\infty}^{x} u(\zeta - b)d\zeta \quad \text{where } \zeta \text{ is an integration variable}$$

$$= \int_{-\infty}^{b} [u(\zeta - b)]d\zeta + \int_{b}^{x} [u(\zeta - b)]d\zeta$$

$$= 0 + u(x - b) \int_{b}^{x} d\zeta$$

because $u(\zeta - a) = \begin{cases} 0 & \text{for} \quad -\infty < \zeta < z \\ 1 & \text{for} \quad a < \zeta < \infty \end{cases}$

The first term is then equal to zero and the second term contains a constant which can be drawn out of the integral sign as shown above.

$$V_y = -R_1[u(x)] - M_1[\delta(x)] + w_0[u(x - b)] \int_0^x d\zeta \qquad \text{(c)}$$

$$- w_0[u(x - L)] \int_L^x d\zeta - Fa[\delta(x - L)]$$

Carrying out the quadratures, we get

$$V_y = -R_1[u(x)] - M_1[\delta(x)] + w_0[u(x - b)](x - b) \qquad \text{(d)}$$

$$- w_0[u(x - L)](x - L) - Fa[\delta(x - L)]$$

The differential equation for the bending moment now becomes

$$\frac{dM_z}{dx} = -V_y$$

$$\frac{dM_z}{dx} = R_1[u(x)] + M_1[\delta(x)] - w_0[u(x - b)](x - b) \qquad \text{(e)}$$

$$+ w_0[u(x - L)](x - L) + Fa[\delta(x - L)]$$

Integrating, we get

$$M_z = R_1 \int u(x)dx + M_1 \int [\delta(x)]dx - w_0 \int [u(x - b)](x - b)dx$$

$$+ w_0 \int [u(x - b)](x - L)dx + Fa \int [\delta(x - L)]dx$$

$$= R_1 u(x) \int_0^x dx + M_1[u(x)] - w_0 u(x - b) \int_b^x (x - b)dx$$

$$+ w_0 u(x - L) \int_L^x (x - L)dx + Fa[u(x - L)]$$

$$M_z = R_1[u(x)]x + M_1[u(x)] - w_0[u(x - b)]\frac{(x - b)^2}{2} \qquad \text{(f)}$$

$$+ w_0[u(x - L)]\frac{(x - L)^2}{2} + Fa[u(x - L)]$$

The boundary condition at $x = L^+$ gives us

$$V_y(x = L) = 0 \quad \text{and} \quad M_z(x = L) = Fa.$$

By simplifying the equations, we get

$$=-R_1 + w_0(L - b) = 0 \tag{g}$$

$$R_1L + M_1 - w_0\frac{(L - b)^2}{2} + Fa = 0 \tag{h}$$

We may readily solve for R_1 and M_1 from the foregoing equations. Inserting these values into Eqs. (d) and (f) then gives us the desired shearforce and bending-moment equations.

The shear-force and bending-moment curves are shown in figure 3.

• PROBLEM 2-35

For the beam shown, derive V, M, and their corresponding diagrams.

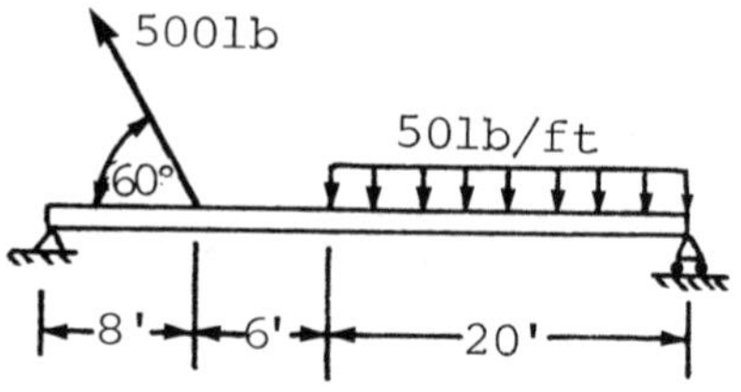

Fig. 1.

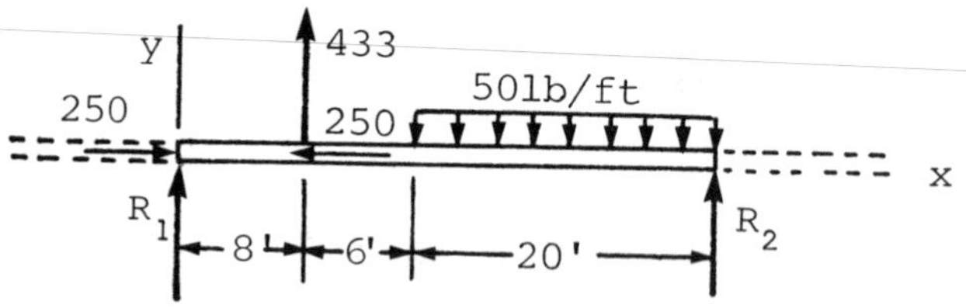

Fig. 2.

Solution: This problem will be solved using singularity functions. The notation, "b[u(x - a)]", means from $-\infty$ to a the function is zero, at a, the function jumps to a value of b, and from a to $+\infty$ the value of the function is b. The notation, "b [δ(x - a)] ", means the function has the value of b at the point x = a and is zero everywhere else.

Resolve the force applied at 60° into its components in the x and y directions in order that the other forces and moments may be conveniently calculated. The component

in the x direction is -500 lb·cos 60°, or -250 lb, and in the y direction, 500 lb·sin 60°, or 433 lb. The beam with all the forces acting in the horizontal and vertical directions is shown in Fig. 2.
For simplicity, consider the contribution of each force separately

$$w_1(x) = R_1[\delta(x - 0)]$$

$$w_2(x) = 433[\delta(x - 8)]$$

$$w_3(x) = -50[u(x - 14)] + 50[u(x - 34)]$$

$$w_4(x) = R_2[\delta(x - 34)]$$

The intensity of loading $w(x) = w_1(x) + w_2(x) + w_3(x) + w_4(x)$.

$$w(x) = R_1[\delta(x - 0)] + 433[\delta(x - 8)] - 50[u(x - 14)] + 50[u(x - 34)] + R_2[\delta(x - 34)]$$

But shear force $V = -\int w(x)dx$

Let ζ be a dummy variable

$$V = -\int_{-\infty}^{x} R_1[\delta(\zeta - 0)]d\zeta - \int_{-\infty}^{x} 433[\delta(\zeta - 8)]d\zeta + \int_{-\infty}^{x} 50[u(\zeta - 14)]d\zeta - \int_{-\infty}^{x} 50[u(\zeta - 34)]d\zeta - \int_{-\infty}^{x} R_2[\delta(\zeta - 34)]d\zeta$$

$$= -\int_{0}^{x} R_1[\delta(\zeta - 0)]d\zeta - \int_{8}^{x} 433[\delta(\zeta - 8)]d\zeta + \int_{14}^{x} 50[u(\zeta - 14)]d\zeta - \int_{34}^{x} 50[u(\zeta - 34)]d\zeta - \int_{34}^{x} R_2[\delta(\zeta - 34)]d\zeta$$

$$\therefore V = -R_1[u(x - 0)] - 433[u(x - 8)] + 50[u(x - 14)](x - 14)$$

$$- 50[u(x - 34)](x - 34) - R_2[u(x - 34)].$$

Also, moment $M = -\int Vdx$

$$\therefore M = \int_0^x R_1[u(\zeta - 0)]d\zeta + \int_8^x 433[u(\zeta - 8)]d\zeta$$

$$- \int_{14}^x 50[u(\zeta - 14)](\zeta - 14)d\zeta$$

$$+ \int_{34}^x 50[u(\zeta - 34)](\zeta - 34)d\zeta \quad + \int_{34}^x R_2[u(\zeta - 34)]d\zeta$$

$$\therefore M = R_1x[u(x - 0)] + 433[u(x - 8)](x - 8)$$

$$- 50[u(x - 14)]\frac{(x - 14)^2}{2} + 50[u(x - 34)]\frac{(x - 34)^2}{2}$$

$$+ R_2[u(x - 34)](x - 34).$$

The equation for shear and moment have two unknowns R_1 and R_2 which can be solved for from the boundary conditions.

For $x = 34$

$$V = 0 = -R_1 - 433 + 50(34 - 14) - 50(34 - 34) - R_2$$

$$= -R_1 + 567 - R_2$$

$$R_2 = -R_1 + 567$$

$$M = 0 = 34R_1 + 433(34 - 8) - 50\frac{(34 - 14)^2}{2}$$

$$+ 50\frac{(34 - 34)^2}{2} + R_2[34 - 34)$$

$$\therefore 0 = 34R_1 + 11258 - 10000$$

$$R_1 = -37 \text{ lbs}$$

$$\therefore R_2 = -R_1 + 567 = 604 \text{ lbs}$$

Now construct the shear force and bending moment diagrams Figs. 3 and 4.

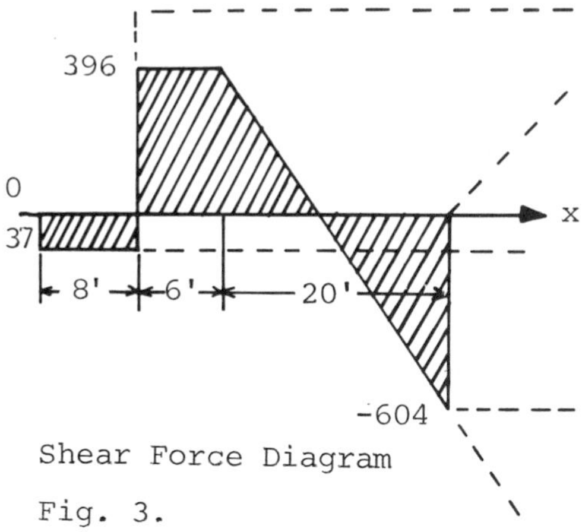

Shear Force Diagram

Fig. 3.

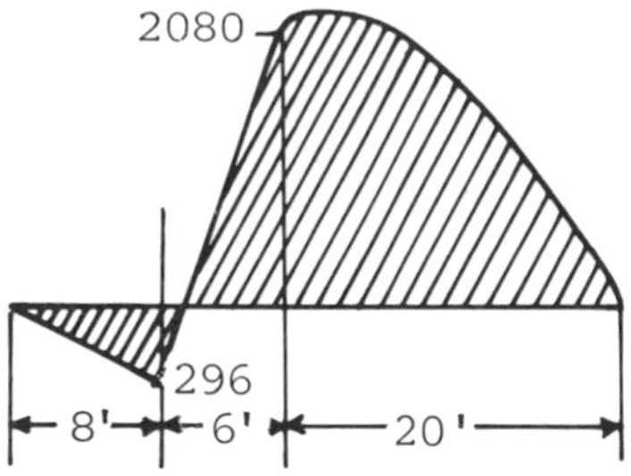

Bending Moment Diagram

Fig. 4.

• PROBLEM 2-36

Express the loads shown in the diagram as w(x) with the aid of singularity functions.

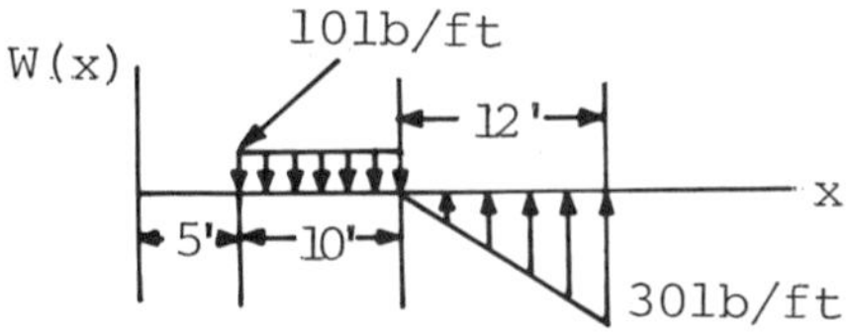

Fig. 1.

<u>Solution</u>: There are 3 types of singularity functions (1) Dirac-delta function, $\delta(x - c)$ which represents a unit load at $x = c$, (2) Unit step function $u(x - c)$ which represents a unit uniform load between $x = c$ to ∞ and (3) Dublet function $\eta(x - c)$ which represents a unit couple at point $x = c$.

First consider the uniformly distributed load. The type of singularity function suitable for this is the unit step function

$$\therefore w(x) = -10[u(x - 5)$$

This represents a uniformly distributed load from x = 5 ft to ∞.

So we have to cancel the loading from x = 15 ft to infinity by adding another function but with negative sign from x = 15' to ∞.

$\therefore$ We have

$$\omega_1(x) = -10[u(x - 5)] + 10[u(x - 15)]$$

Then consider the triangular loading which goes from 0 at x = 15 to 30 at x = 27.

So we have

$$\omega(x) = + \frac{(x - 15)}{12} \cdot 30[u(x - 15)]$$

by similar reasoning to above, add another function which goes from x = 27 to ∞ as shown in Fig. 2.

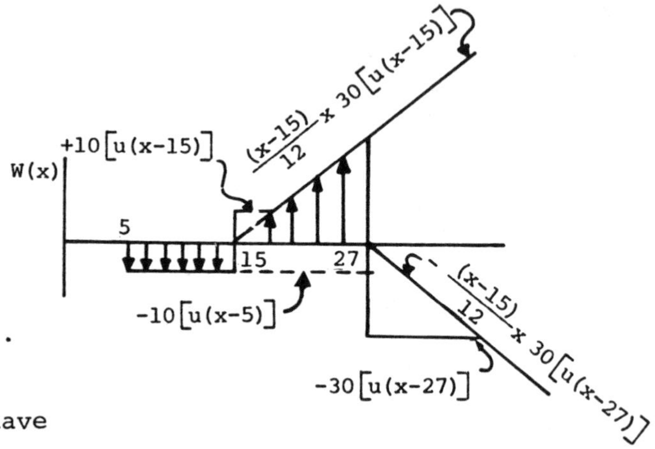

Fig. 2.

Now we have

$$\omega_2(x) = \frac{(x - 15)}{12} \times 30[u(x - 15)] - \frac{(x - 15)}{12} \times 30[u(x - 27)] - 30[u(x - 27)]$$

So total loading expression is given by the addition of $\omega_1(x)$ and $\omega_2(x)$

$$\therefore w(x) = -10[u(x - 5)] + 10[u(x - 15)] + \frac{(x - 15)}{12} \times 30[u(x - 15)] - \frac{(x - 15)}{12} \times 30[u(x - 27)] - 30[u(x - 27)]$$

• PROBLEM 2-37

A beam, shown in Fig. 1, is loaded with a triangular loading distribution, the total weight of which is 500 lbs. Compute the shear-force and bending-moment equations. Determine the supporting forces from your equations.

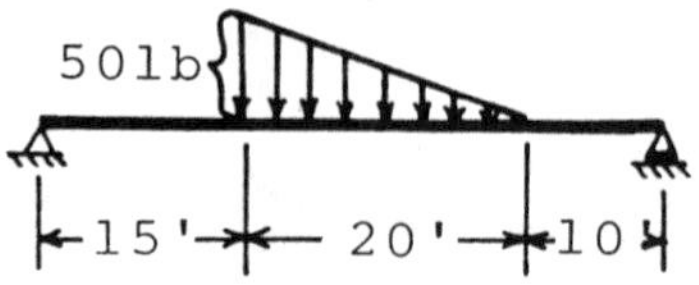

Fig. 1.

Solution: This problem is solved using singularity functions. The notation, "b[u(x - a)]", means that the function is zero from $-\infty$ to a, and has the value b, from a to $+\infty$. This is called the unit step function. The integral of the step function is b[u(x - a)](x - a). The derivative of the unit step function is b[δ(x - a)]. This is called the delta function. It is used in equations of loading intensity that will be integrated to find the shear. The relation between shear and loading intensity for the sign convention used in this problem, is

$$\frac{dV}{dx} = w$$

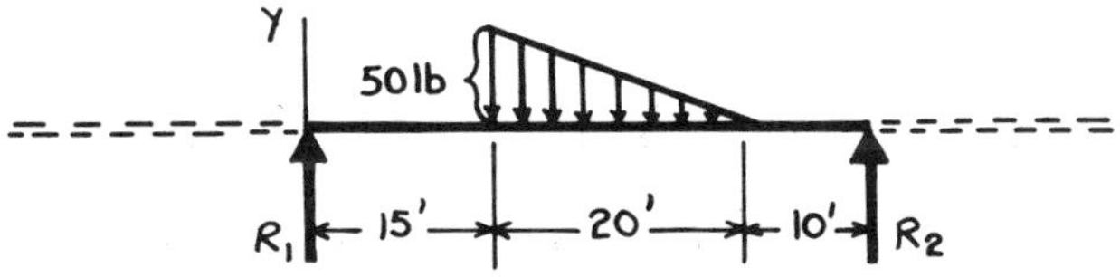

FIG. 2

First draw the beam with all the forces acting as shown in Fig. 2.

For simplicity, consider the contribution of each force separately.

Force R_1

$$w_1(x) = R_1\left[\delta(x - 0)\right]$$

Triangular loading

$$w_2(x) = + \frac{(x - 15)}{20} \times 50[u(x - 15)]$$

$$- \frac{(x - 35)}{20} \times 50[u(x - 35)] - 50[u(x - 15)]$$

Force R_2

$$w_3(x) = R_2[\delta(x - 45)]$$

The total intensity of loading w(x) then becomes

$$w(x) = R_1[\delta(x - 0)] + \frac{5}{2}(x - 15)[u(x - 15)]$$

$$- \frac{5}{2}(x - 35)[u(x - 35)] - 50[u(x - 15)]$$

$$+ R_2[\delta(x - 45)]$$

but differential equation for shear is $\frac{dV}{dx} = -\omega(x)$

$$\frac{dV}{dx} = -R_1[\delta(x - 0)] - \frac{5}{2}(x - 15)[u(x - 15)]$$

$$+ \frac{5}{2}(x - 35)[u(x - 35)] + 50[u(x - 15)]$$

$$- R_2[\delta(x - 45)]$$

Using dummy variable ζ, integrate the above expression

$$V = \int_{-\infty}^{x} -R_1[\delta(\zeta - 0)] - \int_{-\infty}^{x} \frac{5}{2}(\zeta - 15)[u(\zeta - 15)]$$

$$+ \int_{-\infty}^{x} \frac{5}{2}(\zeta - 35)[u(\zeta - 35)] + \int_{-\infty}^{x} 50[u(\zeta - 15)]$$

$$- \int_{-\infty}^{x} R_2[\delta(\zeta - 45)]d\zeta$$

but $u(x - \zeta) = 0$ for $x < \zeta$

therefore $\int_{-\infty}^{\zeta} u(x - \zeta)d\zeta = 0$

∴ We have

$$V = \int_{0}^{x} -R_1[\delta(\zeta - 0)]d\zeta - \int_{15}^{x} \frac{5}{2}(\zeta - 15)[u(\zeta - 15)]d\zeta$$

$$+ \int_{35}^{x} \frac{5}{2}(\zeta - 35)[u(\zeta - 35)]d\zeta + \int_{15}^{x} 50[u(\zeta - 15)]d\zeta$$

$$- \int_{45}^{x} R_2[\delta(\zeta - 45)]d\zeta$$

$$= -R_1[u(x - 0)] - \frac{5}{4}(x - 15)^2[u(x - 15)]$$

$$+ \frac{5}{4}(x - 35)^2[u(x - 35)]$$

$$+ 50(x - 15)[u(x - 15)] - R_2[u(x - 45)]$$

Eq. (1)

But relationship between M and V is

$$M = -\int Vdx$$

$$M = \int_0^x R_1[u(\zeta - 0)]d\zeta + \int_{15}^x \frac{5}{4}(\zeta - 15)^2[u(\zeta - 15)]d\zeta$$

$$- \int_{35}^x \frac{5}{4}(\zeta - 35)^2[u(\zeta - 35)]d\zeta - \int_{15}^x 50(\zeta - 15)[u(\zeta - 15)]d\zeta$$

$$+ \int_{45}^x R_2[u(\zeta - 45)]d\zeta$$

$$= R_1x[u(x - 0)] + \frac{5}{12}(x - 15)^3[u(x - 15)]$$

$$- \frac{5}{12}(x - 35)^3[u(x - 35)]$$

$$- 25(x - 15)^2[u(x - 15)]$$

$$+ R_2(x - 45)[u(x - 45)] \qquad \text{Eq. (2)}$$

Now we have equations for V and M with two unknowns R_1 and R_2. But at $x = 45$, $V = 0$ $M = 0$

Substituting into equations (1) and (2) we have

$$0 = -R_1 - \frac{5}{4} \cdot 30^2 + \frac{5}{4} \cdot 10^2 + 50 \cdot 30 - R_2$$

$$\therefore \qquad R_2 = 500 - R_1$$

$$0 = 45R_1 + \frac{5}{12} \cdot 30^2 - \frac{5}{12} \cdot 10^3 - 25 \cdot 30^2 + 0R_2$$

$$\therefore \qquad R_1 = 259.26 \text{ lbs}$$

$$R_2 = 500 - 259.26$$

$$= 240.74$$

Determine the shear force and bending-moment equations for the simply supported beam shown in Fig. 1 using singularity functions. Acting on the beam is a triangular intensity of loading with a maximum value of w_0, as well as a point force F.

In Fig. 2 we have shown the hypothetical infinite beam that we shall work with, where the supporting forces R_1 and R_2 will be considered as unknown point forces.

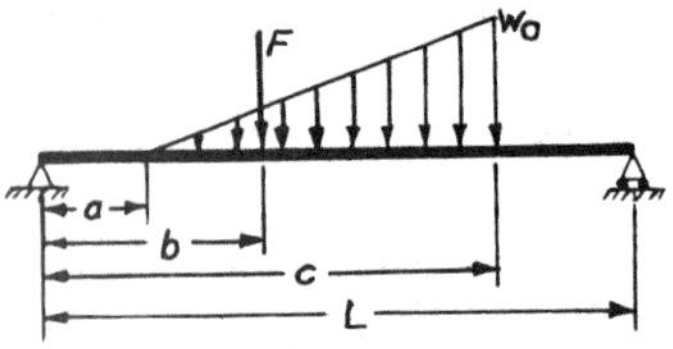

FIG.1

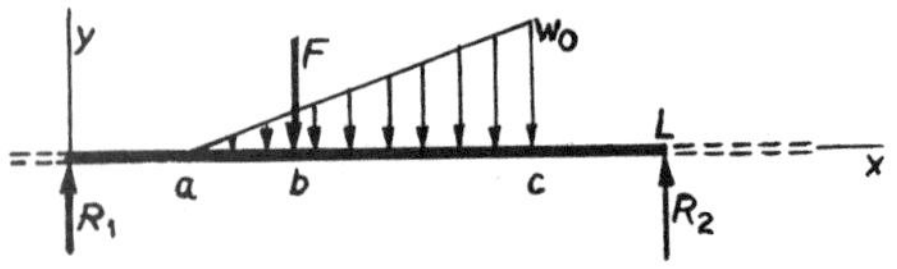

FIG. 2

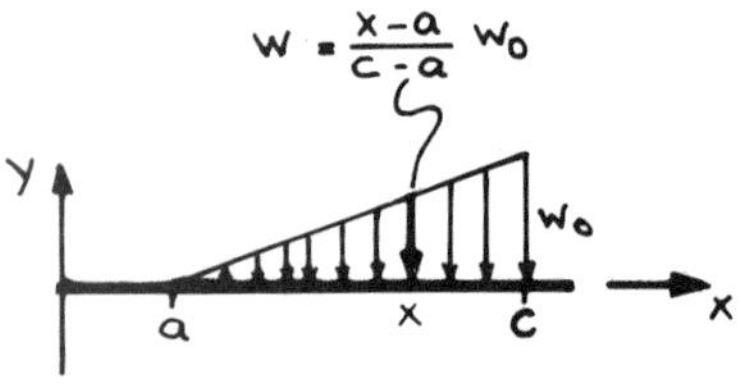

FIG.3

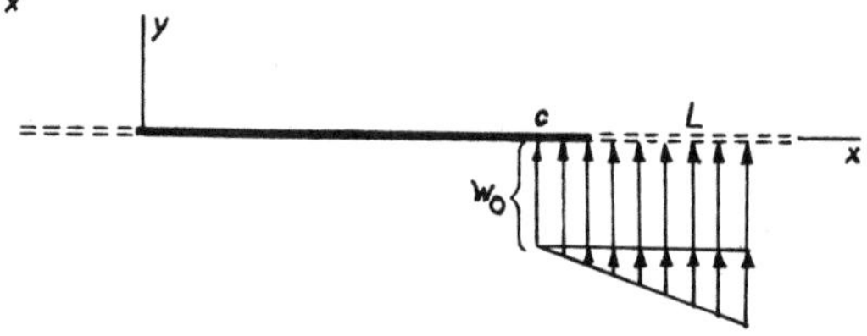

FIG.4

Solution: First of all, we have to find singularity functions to represent the type of loading in this system. Unit step function u(x - a) is used to represent uniform unit loading from x = a to infinity. Another type of singular functions called Direc-delta function $\delta(x - b)$ is used to represent a single unit load at x = b.

Let us first consider the triangular loading. We may use the concept of similar triangles to give w for this loading as:

$$w = -\frac{x - a}{c - a}w_0[u(x - a)] \qquad (a)$$

where the negative sign means the load is pointing downwards and $\frac{x - a}{c - a}w_0$ is obtained from similar triangles shown in Fig. 3. The loading starts at a and continues to $+\infty$, increasing linearly as it goes. To obtain the type of triangular loading given in the problem, we have to eliminate the loading from x = 0 to infinity. We shall apply a set of positive loading distributions starting at x = c and continuing to $+\infty$. The required distributions are shown in Fig. 4. They consist of a uniform distribution having an intensity w_0

and a triangular loading distribution which is identical except for sign and position to the original one. To express w for the new triangular loading, we can return to Eq. (a) and make two changes. First we use a plus sign instead of a negative sign, and, second, we employ x - c instead of x - a. For the two new loadings starting at x = c we have, accordingly:

$$w = + \frac{x - c}{c - a} w_0 [u(x - c)] + w_0 [u(x - c)]$$

We can now give the loading function w for the whole beam as follows:

$$w = R_1 [\delta(x)] - F[\delta(x - b)] - \frac{w_0}{c - a}[u(x - a)](x - a)$$

$$+ \frac{w_0}{c - a}[u(x - c)](x - c) + w_0 [u(x - c)] + R_2 [\delta(x - L)] \tag{b}$$

Employing the first of the differential equations of equilibrium, i.e.,

$$\frac{dV_y}{dx} = -w, \text{ we get}$$

$$\frac{dV_y}{dx} = -R_1 [\delta(x)] + F[\delta(x - b)] + \frac{w_0}{c - a}[u(x - a)](x - a)$$

$$- \frac{w_0}{c - a}[u(x - c)](x - c) - w_0 [u(x - c)]$$

$$- R_2 [\delta(x - L)] \tag{c}$$

Integrating, we have for example:

$$\int \delta(x - a)dx = u(x - a)$$

and $\int [u(x - a)](x - a)dx$

$$= \int_{-\infty}^{x} [u(\zeta - a)](\zeta - a)d\zeta \quad \text{where } \zeta \text{ is a dummy variable,}$$

$$= \int_{-\infty}^{a} [u(\zeta - a)](\zeta - a)d\zeta + \int_{a}^{x} [u(\zeta - a)](\zeta - a)d\zeta$$

$$= 0 + u(x - a) \int_{a}^{x} (\zeta - a)d\zeta$$

$$\text{because } u(\zeta - a)\begin{cases} = 0 & \text{at} \quad -\infty < \zeta < a \\ = 1 & \text{at} \quad a < \zeta < \infty \end{cases}$$

Since $u(\zeta - a) = 1$ is a constant at $a < \zeta < \infty$ it could be taken out of the integration and the dummy variable switched to variable x again.

Therefore, integrating the equation (c), we get

$$V_y = -R_1[u(x)] + F[u(x - b)] + \frac{w_0}{c - a}[u(x - a)] \int_a^x (\zeta - a)d\zeta$$

$$- \frac{w_0}{c - a}[u(x - c)] \int_c^x (\zeta - c)d\zeta - w_0[u(x - c)] \tag{d}$$

$$\times \int_c^x d\zeta - R_2[u(x - L)]$$

All quadratures can be handled by the simple procedure presented earlier. We then get

$$V_y = -R_1[u(x)] + F[u(x - b)] + \frac{w_0}{c - a}[u(x - a)]\frac{(x - a)^2}{2}$$

$$- \frac{w_0}{c - a}[u(x - c)]\frac{(x - c)^2}{2} - w_0[u(x - c)](x - c)$$

$$- R_2[u(x - L)] \tag{e}$$

The differential equation for M_z then becomes

$$\frac{dM_z}{dx} = -V_y$$

$$\frac{dM_z}{dx} = R_1[u(x)] - F[u(x - b)] - \frac{w_0}{c - a}[u(x - a)]\frac{(x - a)^2}{2}$$

$$+ \frac{w_0}{c - a}[u(x - c)]\frac{(x - c)^2}{2} + w_0[u(x - c)](x - c) \tag{f}$$

$$+ R_2[u(x - L)]$$

Integrating, we get

$$M_z = R_1[u(x)] \int_0^x d\zeta - F[u(x - b)] \int_b^x d\zeta - \frac{w_0}{c - a}[u(x - a)]$$

$$\times \int_a^x \frac{(\zeta - a)^2}{2} d\zeta + \frac{w_0}{c - a}[u(x - c)] \int_c^x \frac{(\zeta - c)^2}{2} d\zeta \qquad (g)$$

$$+ w_0[u(x - c)] \int_c^x (\zeta - c) d\zeta + R_2[u(x - L)] \int_L^x d\zeta$$

Carrying out the quadratures, we get

$$M_z = R_1[u(x)]x - F[u(x - b)](x - b)$$

$$- \frac{w_0}{c - a}[u(x - a)]\frac{(x - a)^3}{6} + \frac{w_0}{c - a}[u(x - c)]\frac{(x - c)^3}{6} \qquad (h)$$

$$+ w_0[u(x - c)]\frac{(x - c)^2}{2} + R_2[u(x - L)](x - L)$$

We may now apply the boundary conditions to determine the two unknowns of the problem, namely R_1 and R_2. The boundary conditions just to the right of the right support require that $V_y = 0$ and $M_z = 0$ at $x = L$. We get

$$\text{from (e)}, \ -R_1 + F + \frac{w_0}{c - a}\frac{(L - a)^2}{2} - \frac{w_0}{c - a}\frac{(L - c)^2}{2}$$

$$- w_0(L - c) - R_2 = 0 \qquad (i)$$

$$\text{from (h)}, \ R_1L - F(L - b) - \frac{w_0}{c - a}\frac{(L - a)^3}{6} + \frac{w_0}{c - a}\frac{(L - c)^3}{6}$$

$$+ w_0\frac{(L - c)^2}{2} = 0 \qquad (j)$$

We can solve for R_1 from Eq. (j) and returning to Eq. (i) we can then get R_2 easily. Assuming that R_1 and R_2 are now known, we can express the shear-force and bending-moment equations in the following way

$$V_y = -R_1[u(x)] + F[u(x - b)] + \frac{w_0}{c - a}[u(x - a)]\frac{(x - a)^2}{2}$$

$$- \frac{w_0}{c - a}[u(x - c)]\frac{(x - c)^2}{2} \qquad (k)$$

$$- w_0[u(x - c)](x - c) - R_2[u(x - L)]$$

$$M_z = R_1[u(x)]x - F[u(x-b)](x-b) - \frac{w_0}{c-a}[u(x-a)]\frac{(x-a)^3}{6}$$

$$+ \frac{w_0}{c-a}[u(x-c)]\frac{(x-c)^3}{6} + w_0[u(x-c)]\frac{(x-c)^2}{2} \qquad (1)$$

$$+ R_2[u(x-L)](x-L).$$

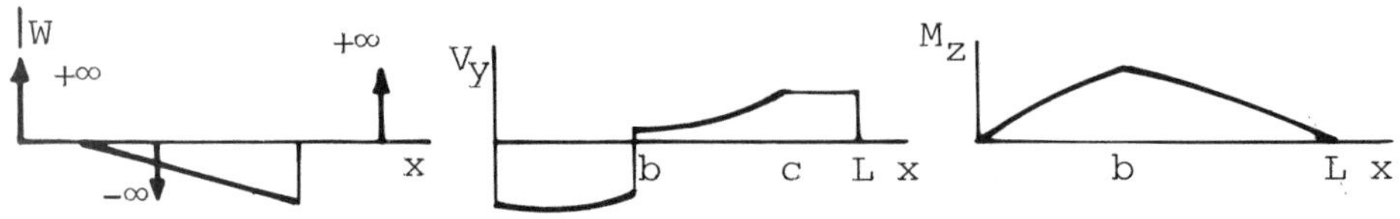

Fig. 5.

The load intensity, shear-force, and bending-moment diagrams for this problem are shown in Fig. 5.

• PROBLEM 2-39

> The loading on a beam is assumed to have the shape shown in Fig. 1. Find the location of the supports A and B such that the bending moment at the midpoint is zero.

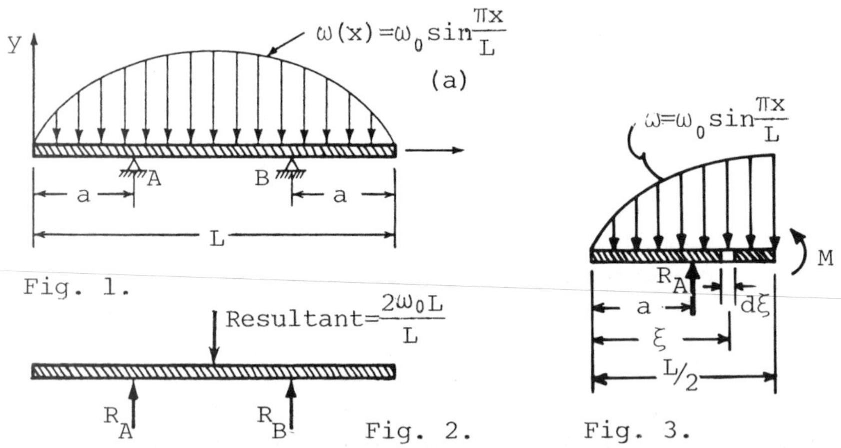

Fig. 1. Fig. 2. Fig. 3.

Solution: This problem can be done in two ways; the first method is by free-body equilibrium and the second by singularity functions.

In the first method, we find the bending moment at the mid-point by free-body equilibrium, and equate that moment to zero.

As our first step, the reactive forces at A and B will be found. From symmetry, $R_A = R_B = (1/2)R$ where R is the resultant of the load-distribution curve

$$R = \int_0^L \omega(x)\,dx$$

$$= \omega_0 \int_0^L \sin \frac{\pi x}{L} dx$$

$$= \frac{2\omega_0 L}{\pi}$$

Now, we look at the free body diagram. (Fig. 3)
Taking moment about the mid-point, we have

$$M = 0 \curvearrowleft + \ , \ M - R_A(\frac{L}{2} - a) + \int_0^{\frac{L}{2}} w_0 \sin \frac{\pi\xi}{L}(\frac{L}{2} - \xi)d\xi = 0$$

$$M = \frac{w_0 L}{\pi}(\frac{L}{2} - a) - \int_0^{\frac{L}{2}} w_0 \sin \frac{\pi\xi}{L}(\frac{L}{2} - \xi)d\xi = 0$$

$$\frac{w_0 L}{\pi}(\frac{L}{2} - a) - w_0 \int_0^{\frac{L}{2}} \frac{L}{2} \sin \frac{\pi\xi}{L} d\xi + w_0 \int_0^{\frac{L}{2}} \xi \sin \frac{\pi\xi}{L} d\xi = 0$$

using the method of integration by parts where

$$\int udV = uV - \int Vdu$$

is this case $\xi = u \Rightarrow d\xi = du$ and $\sin \frac{\pi\xi}{L} d\xi = dV$

$$\int_0^{\frac{1}{2}} dV \cdot u = u \cdot V \Big|_0^{\frac{1}{2}} - \int_0^{\frac{1}{2}} du \cdot V$$

$$\frac{w_0 L^2}{2\pi} - \frac{w_0 La}{\pi} + w_0 \frac{L}{2}\frac{L}{\pi} \cos \frac{\pi\xi}{L}\Big]_0^{\frac{1}{2}} + w_0 \int_0^{\frac{1}{2}} \xi \cdot \frac{L}{\pi} d\left(-\cos \frac{\pi\xi}{L}\right) = 0$$

$$\frac{w_0 L^2}{2\pi} - \frac{w_0 La}{\pi} + \frac{w_0 L^2}{2\pi}(-1) - \frac{w_0 L}{\pi}\left[\xi \cdot \cos \frac{\pi\xi}{L}\Big|_0^{\frac{1}{2}} - \int_0^{\frac{1}{2}} \cos \frac{\pi\xi}{L} d\xi\right] = 0$$

$$- \frac{w_0 La}{\pi} - \frac{w_0 L}{\pi}\left[0 - \frac{L}{\pi} \sin \frac{\pi\xi}{L}\Big|_0^{\frac{L}{2}}\right] = 0$$

$$- \frac{w_0 La}{\pi} - \frac{w_0 L}{\pi}\left(- \frac{L}{\pi}\right) = 0$$

$$a = \frac{L}{\pi}$$

In the second method, we use singularity function to represent the load intensity distribution, and integrate it twice to get the general moment equation.

The load intensity function can be written in the form,

$$q(x) = -w_0 \sin \frac{\pi x}{L}[u(x)] + \frac{w_0 L}{\pi}\delta(x - a) + \frac{w_0 L}{\pi}\delta[x - (L - a)] \qquad \text{(c)}$$

where u(x) is unit step function starting from x = 0, and $\delta(x - a)$ is Direc-delta function which represent a single force at x = a. Now,

$$\frac{dV}{dx} = -q(x)$$

therefore, $$V = -\int q(x)dx.$$

$$= + w_0 u(x) \int_0^x \sin \frac{\pi \xi}{L} d\xi - \frac{w_0 L}{\pi} \int \delta(x - a)dx - \frac{w_0 L}{\pi} \int \delta[x - (L - a)]dx + C_1$$

$$= -w_0 u(x)\frac{L}{\pi} \cos \frac{\pi \xi}{L}\Big|_0^x - \frac{w_0 L}{\pi}u(x - a) - \frac{w_0 L}{\pi}u[x - (L - a)] + C_1$$

$$= - \frac{w_0 L}{\pi} \cos \frac{\pi x}{L}u(x) + w_0 u(x)\frac{L}{\pi} - \frac{w_0 L}{\pi}u(x - a) - \frac{w_0 L}{\pi}u[x - (L - a)] + C_1$$

But V = 0 at x = 0 , therefore, by substituting x = 0 ,

$$- \frac{w_0 L}{\pi} \cos(0)\ u(0) + w_0 u(0)\ \frac{L}{\pi} - 0 - 0 + C_1 = 0$$

But u(0) = 1 by definition of unit step function

$$- \frac{w_0 L}{\pi}(1) + \frac{w_0 L}{\pi} + C_1 = 0$$

$$C_1 = 0$$

$$V = -\frac{w_0L}{\pi}\cos\frac{\pi x}{L}u(x) + \frac{w_0L}{\pi}u(x) - \frac{w_0L}{\pi}u(x-a)$$

$$-\frac{w_0L}{\pi}u[x-(L-a)]$$

Integrating V again, we get, by $M = -\int V(x)dx$

$$M = +\frac{w_0L}{\pi}\int \cos\frac{\pi x}{L}u(x)dx - \frac{w_0L}{\pi}\int u(x)dx$$

$$+\frac{w_0L}{\pi}\int u(x-a)dx + \frac{w_0L}{\pi}\int u[x-(L-a)]dx$$

$$= +\frac{w_0L}{\pi}u(x)\frac{L}{\pi}\sin\frac{\pi x}{L}\Big|_0^x - \frac{w_0L}{\pi}\cdot u(x) + \frac{w_0L}{\pi}[u(x-a)](x-a)$$

$$+\frac{w_0L}{\pi}[x-(L-a)]u[x-(L-a)]$$

when $x = \frac{L}{2}$ (note that $\frac{L}{2} > a$ and $\frac{L}{2} < (L-a)$)

$$M = +\frac{w_0L}{\pi}(1)\frac{L}{\pi}\sin\frac{\pi}{2} - \frac{w_0L}{\pi}\frac{1}{2}(1) + \frac{w_0L}{\pi}[1]\left(\frac{L}{2}-a\right)$$

$$+\frac{w_0L}{\pi}\left[\frac{L}{2}-(L-a)\right](0)$$

$$= +\frac{w_0L^2}{\pi^2} - \frac{w_0L^2}{2\pi} + \frac{w_0L^2}{2\pi} - \frac{w_0La}{\pi} \qquad = \frac{w_0L^2}{\pi^2} - \frac{w_0La}{\pi}$$

For $M = 0$ then ,

$$\frac{w_0L^2}{\pi^2} = \frac{w_0La}{\pi} \qquad a = \frac{L}{\pi}$$

• PROBLEM 2-40

In the loaded cantilever beam shown, a force is applied to it through a triangular plate welded at a point on the beam. Find the shear force and bending moment equations and sketch their corresponding diagrams.

Solution: This problem is solved using singularity functions. The notation, "b[u(x - a)]", means that the function is zero from $-\infty$ to a, and has the value b from a to $+\infty$. This is called the unit step function. The integral of the step function is b[u(x - a)](x - a). The derivative

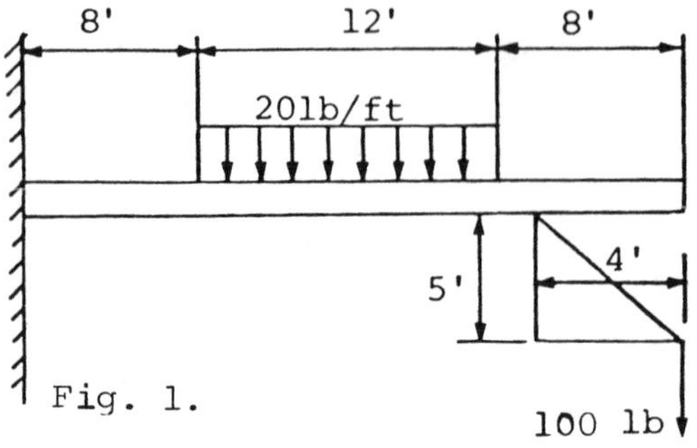

Fig. 1.

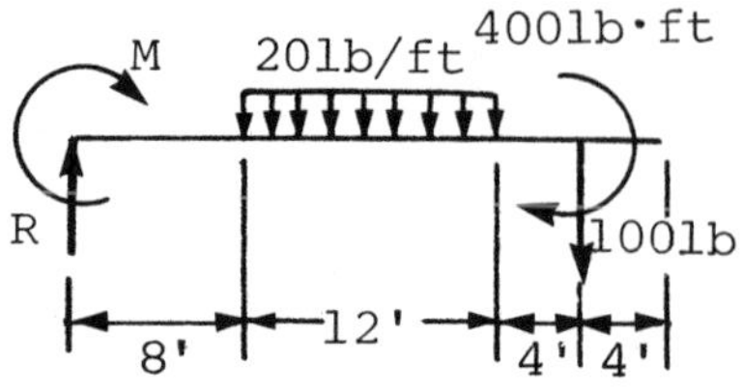

Fig. 2.

of the unit step function is $b[\delta(x - a)]$, the delta function, and the second derivative of the unit step is $b[\eta(x - a)]$, the doublet function.

They are used in equations of loading intensity that will be integrated to find the shear and integrated again to find the moment.

The relationships between the loading intensity and the shear, and the loading intensity and the moment, for the sign convention used in this problem is:

$$w = \frac{dV}{dx}$$

$$w = \frac{d^2M}{dx^2}$$

Figure 2 shows the cantilever beam with all the forces acting. Note that the 100 lbs force on the attachment has been reduced to a 100 lbs force and 400 lbs moment acting at the point of connection between the attachment and the beam.

To get the shear force and bending moment equations, first express the intensity of loading as follows·

$$w(x) = R[\delta(x - 0)] + M[\eta(x - 0)] - 20[u(x - 8)] + 20[u(x - 20)] - 100[\delta(x - 24)] + 400[\eta(x - 24)]$$

But $V = -\int w(x)\,dx$

$$\therefore V = \int_0^x -R[\delta(\zeta - 0)]d\zeta - \int_0^x M[\eta(\zeta - 0)]d\zeta + \int_8^x 20[u(\zeta - 8)]d\zeta - \int_{20}^x 20[u(\zeta - 20)]d\zeta + \int_{24}^x 100[\delta(\zeta - 24)]d\zeta - \int_{24}^x 400[\eta(\zeta - 24)]d\zeta$$

$$V = -R[u(x - 0)] - M[\delta(x - 0)] + 20(x - 8)[u(x - 8)]$$
$$- 20(x - 20)[u(x - 20)] + 100[u(x - 20)]$$
$$- 400[\delta(x - 24)]$$

$$M = -\int V dx \qquad \therefore M_x = \int_0^x R[u(\zeta - 0)]d\zeta + \int_0^x M[\delta(\zeta - 0)]d\zeta$$
$$- \int_0^x 20(\zeta - 8)[u(\zeta - 8)]d\zeta + \int_{20}^x 20(\zeta - 20)[u(\zeta - 20)]d\zeta$$
$$- \int_{24}^x 100[u(\zeta - 24)]d\zeta + \int_{24}^x 400[\delta(\zeta - 24)]d\zeta$$

$$M_x = xR[u(x - 0)] + M[u(x - 0)] - 10(x - 8)^2[u(x - 8)]$$
$$+ 10(x - 20)^2[u(x - 20)] - 100(x - 24)[u(x - 24)]$$
$$+ 400[u(x - 24)].$$

Now determine M and R from the boundary conditions, i.e., at $x = 28$; $V = 0$; $M = 0$

$$\therefore 0 = -R + 20 \times 20 - 20 \times 8 + 100$$
$$R = 340 \text{ lbs}$$
$$0 = 28 \times 340 + M - 10 \times 20^2 + 10 \times 8^2 - 100 \times 4 + 400$$
$$\therefore M = -6160 \text{ lb-ft}$$

Therefore the shear force and bending moment equations are

$$V = -340[u(x - 0)] + 6160[\delta(x - 0)] + 20(x - 8)[u(x - 8)]$$
$$- 20(x - 20)[u(x - 20)] + 100[u(x - 24)] - 400[\delta(x - 24)]$$
$$M_x = 340x[u(x - 0)] - 6160[u(x - 0)] - 10(x - 8)^2[u(x - 8)]$$
$$+ 10(x - 20)^2[u(x - 20)] - 100(x - 24)[u(x - 24)]$$
$$+ 400[u(x - 24)]$$

The shear force and bending moment diagrams are shown in Figs. 3 and 4 respectively.

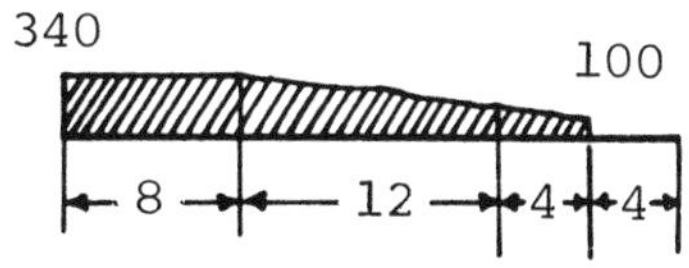

Shear Force Diagram

Fig. 3.

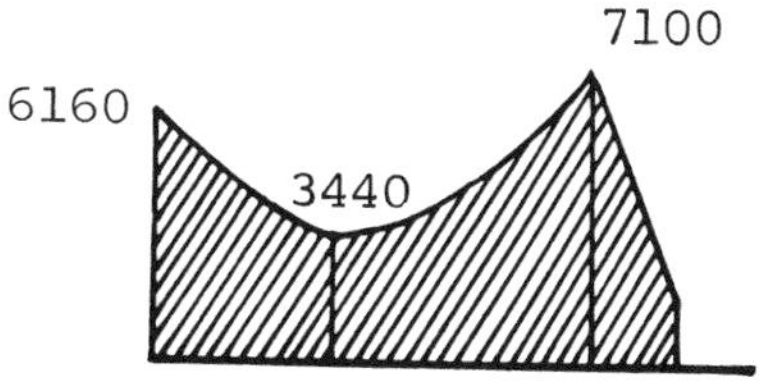

Bending Moment Diagram

Fig. 4.

• PROBLEM 2-41

A beam has two cantilever sections extending from a fixed support. Find the shear force and bending moment equations for the sections.

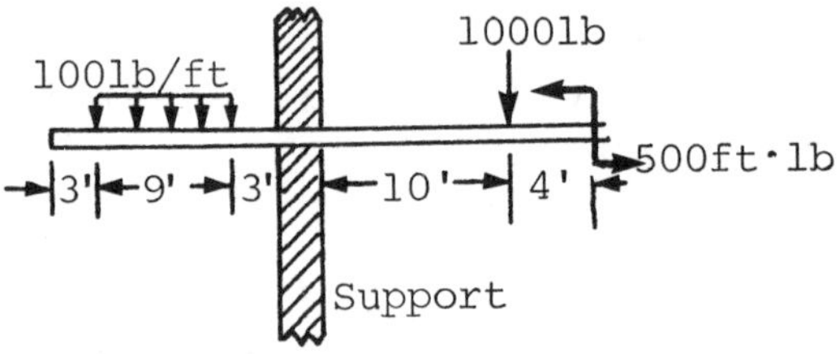

Fig. 1.

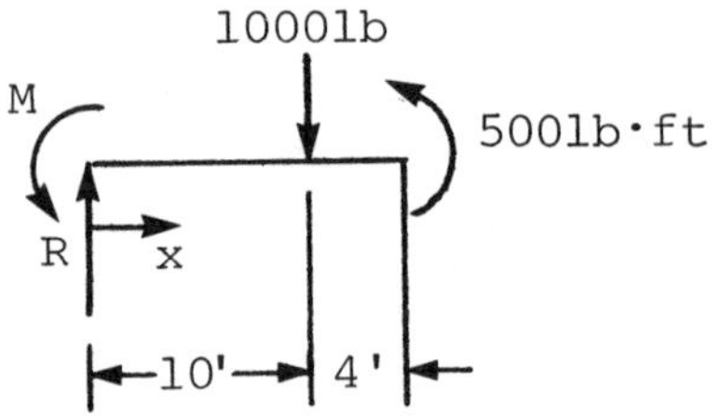

Fig. 2.

Solution: Because of the thickness of the support, this beam can be considered as two separate cantilevers.

Consider the cantilever on the right side. This is shown in Fig. 2 with all the forces acting.

The intensity of loading is

$$\omega(x) = R[\delta(x - 0)] + M[\eta(x - 0)] - 1000[\delta(x - 10)] + 500[\eta(x - 14)]$$

But $V = -\int \omega(x)dx$

$$V = \int_0^x -R[\delta(\zeta - 0)]d\zeta - \int_0^x M[\eta(\zeta - 0)]d\zeta + 1000\int_0^x [\delta(\zeta - 10)]d\zeta - 500\int_{14}^x [\eta(\zeta - 14)]d\zeta$$

$$\therefore V = -R[u(x - 0)] - M[\delta(x - 0)] + 1000[u(x - 10)] - 500[\delta(x - 14)]$$

$$M_x = -\int V\,dx$$

$$M_x = \int_0^x R[u(\zeta - 0)]d\zeta + \int_0^x M[\delta(\zeta - 0)]d\zeta - 1000\int_{10}^x [u(\zeta - 10)]d\zeta + \int_{14}^x 500[\delta(x - 14)]d\zeta$$

$$= xR[u(x - 0)] + M[u(x - 0)] - 1000(x - 10)[u(x - 10)] + 500[u(x - 14)]$$

The unknowns R and M are determined from the known boundary conditions, i.e.,

$$\text{at} \quad x = 14 \; ; \quad V = 0 \; , \quad M_x = 500$$

Substituting these into the expressions for V and M_x we have

$$0 = -R + 1000$$

$$\therefore R = 1000 \text{ lbs}$$

$$500 = 14 \times 1000 + M - 1000 \times 4$$

$$\therefore M = -9500 \text{ ft-lb}$$

Therefore the shear force and bending moment expressions are

$$V = -1000[u(x - 0)] + 9500[\delta(x - 0)] + 1000[u(x - 10)] - 500[\delta(x - 14)]$$

$$M_x = x1000[u(x - 0)] - 9500[u(x - 0)] - 1000(x - 10)[u(x - 10)] + 500[u(x - 14)]$$

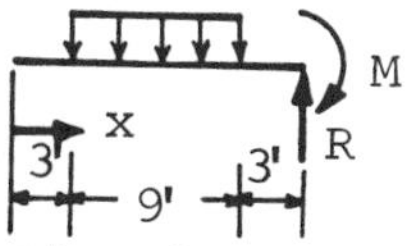

Fig. 3.

Now consider the cantilever on the left side. This is shown in Fig. 3 with all the forces acting
The intensity of loading is

$$\omega(x) = -100[u(x - 3)] + 100[u(x - 12)] + R[\delta(x - 15)] + M[\eta(x - 15)]$$

$$\text{But} \quad V = -\int \omega(x)dx$$

$$V = 100 \int_3^x [u(\zeta - 3)]d\zeta - 100 \int_{12}^x [u(\zeta - 12)]d\zeta - \int_{15}^x R[\delta(\zeta - 15)]d\zeta - \int_{15}^x M[\eta(\zeta - 15)]d\zeta$$

$$V = 100(x - 3)[u(x - 3)] - 100(x - 12)[u(x - 12)]$$
$$- R[u(x - 15)] - M[\delta(x - 15)]$$

$$M_x = -\int V\,dx$$

$$M_x = -\int_3^x 100(\zeta - 3)[u(\zeta - 3)]d\zeta + \int_{12}^x 100(\zeta - 12)[u(\zeta - 12)]d\zeta$$
$$+ \int_{15}^x R[u(\zeta - 15)]d\zeta$$
$$= \int_{15}^x M[\delta(\zeta - 15)]d\zeta$$

$$M_x = -50(x - 3)^2[u(x - 3)] + 50(x - 12)^2[u(x - 12)]$$
$$+ R(x - 15)[u(x - 15)]$$
$$+ M[u(x - 15)]$$

As in the previous case, the unknowns R and M are determined from the known boundary conditions, i.e.,

at $x = 15$; $V = R$; $M_x = -M$

Substituting these into the expression for V and M_x we have

$$R = 100(15 - 3) - 100(15 - 12)$$
$$= 900 \text{ lbs}$$

$$M = -(-50(15 - 3)^2 + 50(15 - 12)^2)$$
$$= +6750 \text{ ft-lb}$$

Therefore the shear and bending moment expressions are

$$V = 100(x - 3)[u(x - 3)] - 100(x - 12)[u(x - 12)]$$
$$- 900[u(x - 15)] - 6750[\delta(x - 15)]$$

$$M_x = -50(x - 3)^2[u(x - 3)] + 50(x - 12)^2[u(x - 12)]$$
$$+ 900(x - 15)[u(x - 15)]$$
$$+ 6750[u(x - 15)]$$

FORCES AND MOMENTS IN SLENDER MEMBERS

• PROBLEM 2-42

Calculate the internal forces and moments acting at sections 1 and 2 in the structure shown.

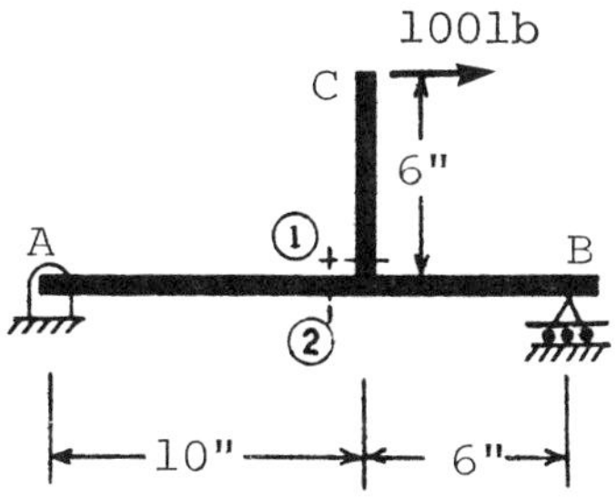

Fig. 1.

Fig. 2.

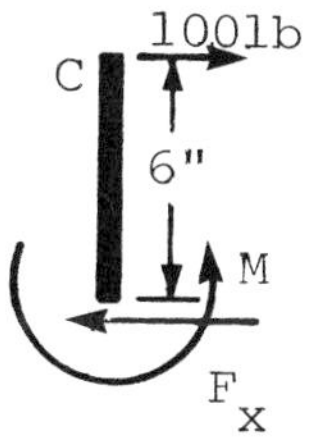

Solution: Consider a cut at section 1 and draw a free body diagram indicating the internal forces and moments as shown in Fig. 2.

For equilibrium

$$\sum F = 0$$

$$\therefore \; F_x - 100 = 0$$

$$\therefore \; F_x = 100 \text{ lb}$$

$\sum M = 0$ about the cut

$$\therefore \; M = 6 \times 100 = 0$$

$$\therefore \; M = 600 \text{ lb-in}$$

To get the internal forces and moment at section 2, first determine the reactions at the supports. See Fig. 3

F = 0 (horizontal forces)

$$\therefore \; -H_A + 100 = 0$$

$$\therefore \; H_A = 100 \text{ lbs}$$

$\sum M = 0$ at support A +↻

$$\therefore \; 100 \times 6 - 16R_B = 0$$

$$\therefore \; R_B = 37.5 \text{ lbs}$$

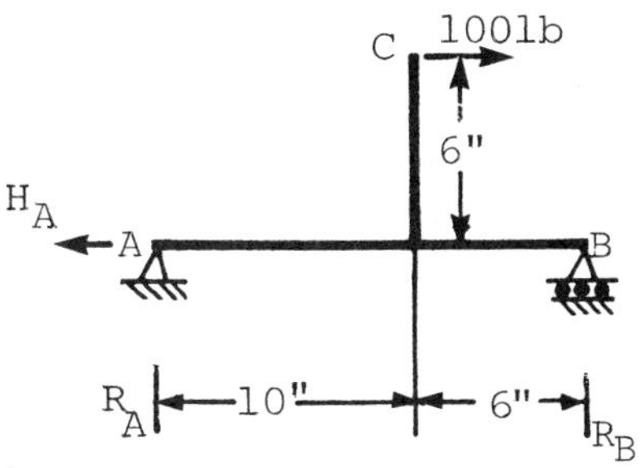

Fig. 3.

$\sum M = 0$ at support B +↻

$$100 \times 6 + 16R_A = 0$$

$$\therefore R_A = -37.5 \text{ lbs}$$

Now consider a cut through section 2 and draw a free body diagram as shown in Fig. 4.

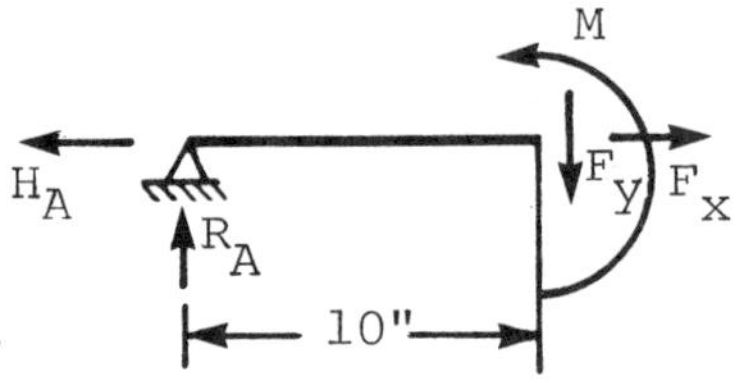

Fig. 4.

$\sum F_y = 0$

$$\therefore R_A - F_y = 0$$

$$\therefore F_y = R_A = -37.5 \text{ lbs}$$

$\sum F_x = 0$

$$\therefore F_x - H_A = 0$$

$$\therefore F_x = H_A = 100 \text{ lbs}$$

$\sum M = 0$ about the cut +↻

$$-M + 10R_A = 0$$

$$\therefore M = -10 \times 37.5$$

$$= 375 \text{ lb-in clockwise}$$

• PROBLEM 2-43

A curved bar ABC is subjected to loads in the form of two equal and opposite forces P, as shown in the figure. The axis of the bar forms a semicircle of radius r. Determine the axial force N, shear force V, and the bending moment M at a cross section defined by the angle θ (see figure).

Solution: The principles of equilibrium applied to a straight beam can also be applied to a curved beam to resolve the forces acting on it.

The force system acting on the semicircular beam is as shown in Fig. 1 and a free body diagram at a section of the beam is shown in Fig. 2.

This free body diagram illustrates the forces acting at any section within the member. These are the shear

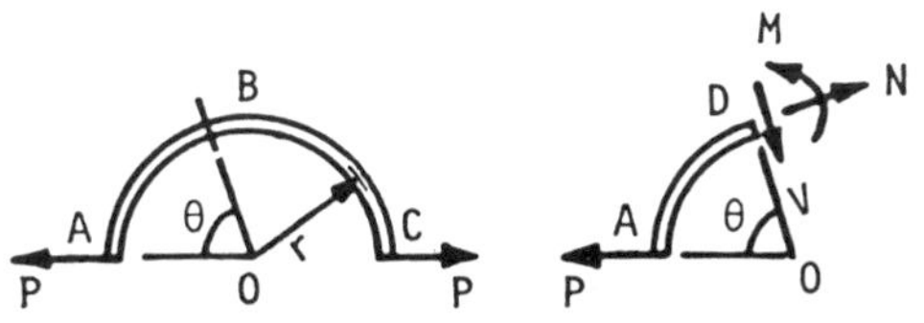

Fig. 1 Fig. 2

force, V, axial force, N, and bending moment M.

First establish an x - y co-ordinate system at the cut (Fig. 3)

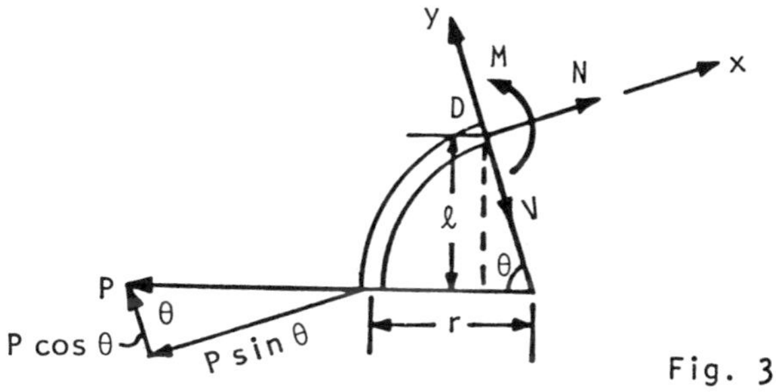

Fig. 3

For equilibrium

$\sum F = 0$ in the x direction

$$\therefore \; N - P\sin\theta = 0$$

$$N = P\sin\theta$$

$\sum F = 0$ in the y direction

The convention is that V is positive in the downward, negative y direction.

$$\therefore \; -V + P\cos\theta = 0$$

$$V = P\cos\theta$$

$\sum M = 0$ about point D

$$M = P \times \ell \quad \text{(where } \ell \text{ is the moment arm)}$$

$$\ell = r\sin\theta$$

$$M = Pr\sin\theta$$

• PROBLEM 2-44

Determine the axial force, the shear force, and the bending moment acting at any section θ in the circular arc AB.

<u>Solution:</u> The system of forces acting on the circular arc is as shown in Fig. 2.

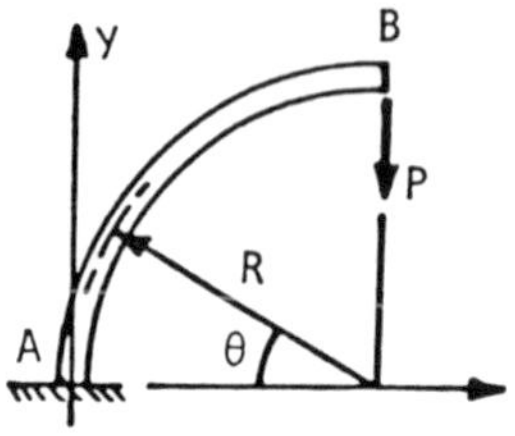

Fig. 1

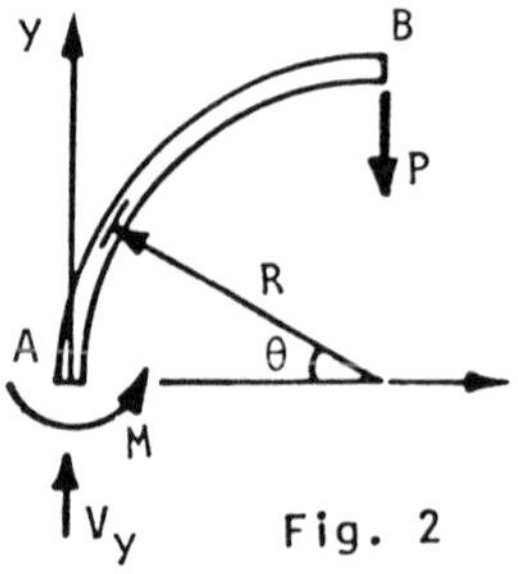

Fig. 2

First determine the moment and raction at the support.

$\sum F = 0$

$$\therefore V_y - P = 0$$

$$V_y = P$$

$\sum M = 0$ at A

$$M - PR = 0$$

$$\therefore M = PR$$

Now consider a cut at any point on the circular arc which sustains an angle θ with the center.

Establish an r - a co-ordinate system at the cut as shown in Fig. 3.

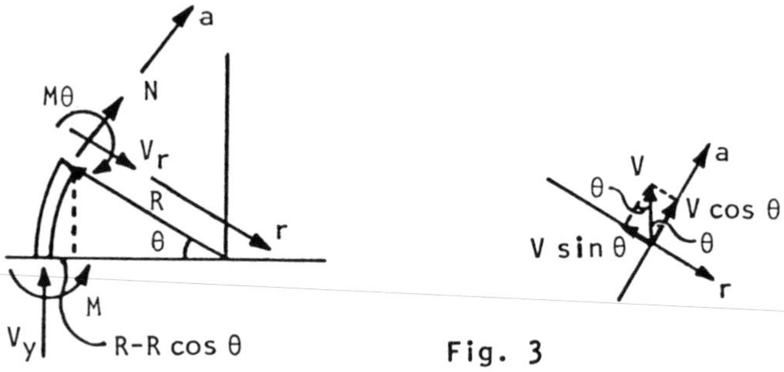

Fig. 3

For equilibrium

$\sum F_a =$ $\quad \therefore N + V_y \cos\theta = 0$

$$\therefore N = -P\cos\theta$$

The axial force is -P cos θ, the minus sign indicates compression.

$\sum F_r = 0$

$$V_r - V_y \sin\theta = 0$$

$$V_r = P \sin \theta$$

The shear force is P sin θ towards the center of the arc.

$\sum M = 0$ at cut +)

$$M_\theta - M + V_y(R - R \cos \theta) = 0$$

$$M_\theta = M - V_y R(1 - \cos \theta)$$

Substituting for M and V_y

$$\therefore M = PR - PR(1 - \cos \theta)$$

$$= PR \cos \theta$$

The bending moment is PR cos θ, clockwise.

• PROBLEM 2-45

Shown in Fig. 1 is a piece of refinery piping AB anchored at B and bent into a quadrant of a circle of center O and radius a. Find the force and moment diagrams for this segment of pipe when a transverse load P is acting as shown.

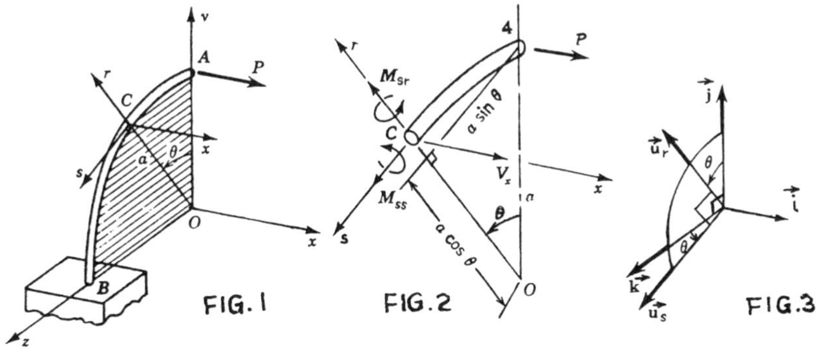

FIG. 1 FIG. 2 FIG. 3

Solution: This is a three-dimensional problem. Therefore, we have to consider equilibrium in all three directions. For convenience we can use vector notation to solve 3 dimensional problem. The same basic procedure is used as before. A cut is made at C, and the segment AC is isolated as a free body in Fig. 2. To help describe the forces and moments, we have introduced the rectangular coordinate system (x,r,s) at the face of the cut. Here s = aθ is arc length along the pipe, and r is radial distance from 0. (M_{xy} is a moment acting on the surface with the normal in x direction and the direction of the moment by "Right hand rule" pointed to y.) The force P at the free end A can be held in equilibrium by the force V_x and the torques M_{ss} and M_{sr} acting on the section C, providing

$$\sum F = P\vec{i} + V_x\vec{i} = 0 \qquad (a)$$

$$\sum M_C = M_{ss}\vec{u}_s + M_{sr}\vec{u}_r + \vec{r}_{CA} \times (P\vec{i}) = 0 \qquad (b)$$

The last term of (b) is the cross multiply of vector distance to vector force which forms a vector moment by definition of moment. $\vec{i}$, $\vec{u}_r$, and $\vec{u}_s$ are unit vectors in the x, r, and s directions and $\vec{r}_{CA}$ is the vector distance from C to A. In order to express $\vec{r}_{CA}$ in terms of the unit vectors, we may note from Fig. 1 and rules on addition of vectors that

$$\vec{r}_{CA} = \vec{r}_{OA} - \vec{r}_{OC} = a\vec{j} - a\vec{u}_r \qquad (c)$$

where $\vec{j}$ is the unit vector in the y direction, and that, from Fig. 3, and transformation of vectors.

$$\vec{j} = \vec{u}_r \cos\theta - \vec{u}_s \sin\theta \qquad (d)$$

Therefore from (c)

$$\begin{aligned}\vec{r}_{CA} &= a(\vec{u}_r \cos\theta - \vec{u}_s \sin\theta) - a\,\vec{u}_r \\ &= a(1 - \cos\theta)\vec{u}_r - a \sin\theta\, \vec{u}_s \qquad (e)\end{aligned}$$

Equation (e) may also be obtained directly from Fig. 2. Upon substitution of (e) into (b), we find

$$\begin{aligned}\sum M_C &= M_{ss}\vec{u}_s + M_{sr}\vec{u}_r + [-a(1 - \cos\theta)\vec{u}_r - a \sin\theta\, \vec{u}_s] \times (P\vec{i}) \\ &= M_{ss}\vec{u}_s + M_{sr}\vec{u}_r - Pa(1-\cos\theta)(\vec{u}_r \times \vec{i}) - Pa \sin\theta(\vec{u}_s \times \vec{i}) \\ &= M_{ss}\vec{u}_s + M_{sr}\vec{u}_r - Pa(1 - \cos\theta)(-\vec{u}_s) - Pa \sin\theta(\vec{u}_r) \\ &= M_{ss}u_s + M_{sr}u_r + P[a(1 - \cos\theta)u_s - a \sin\theta\ u_r] = 0 \quad (f)\end{aligned}$$

Setting the coefficient of each unit vector separately equal to zero in (a) and (f) yields

$$V_x = -P$$

$$M_{sr} - Pa \sin\theta = 0$$

therefore $M_{sr} = Pa \sin\theta$

$$M_{ss} + Pa(1 - \cos\theta) = 0$$

therefore $M_{ss} = -Pa(1 - \cos\theta)$ (g)

These are the shear force, bending moment, and twisting moment acting at the general angle θ. Figure 4 shows their variation with arc length $s = a\theta$ along with sketches of the sign conventions employed.

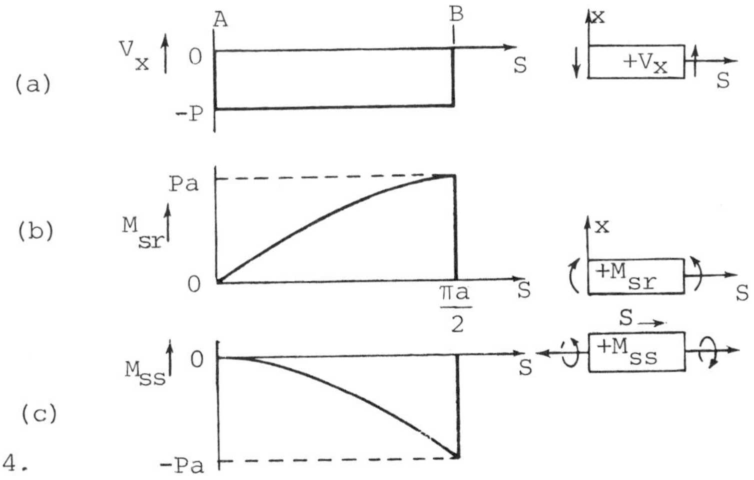

Fig. 4.

To clarify the directions and positive or negative values used in the diagrams, this sign convention might be useful

<u>Shear Force</u>

Convention

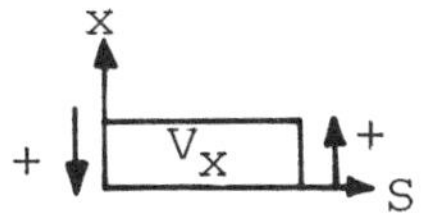

Free body:

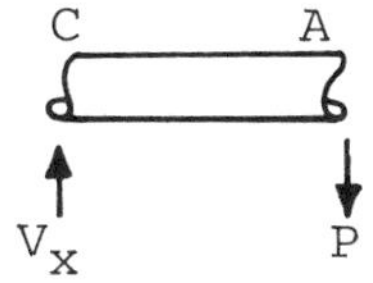

Negative values for V_x and P are seen also in the S.F. Diag.

<u>Bending Moment-M_{sr}</u>

Convention:

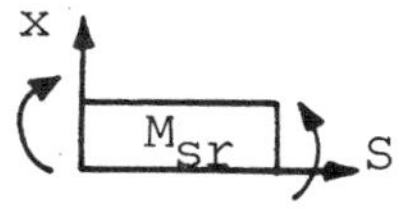

Free body:

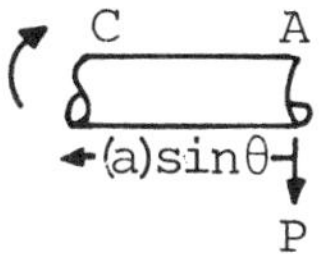

If the piping rotated about C, then the rotation would be positive

<u>Twisting Moment-M_{ss}</u>

Convention:

Looking into the convention at the (+) end gives positive as CCW. The twist in the pipe looking at the (+) end gives a CW twist which is negative

Free body

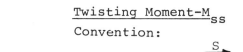

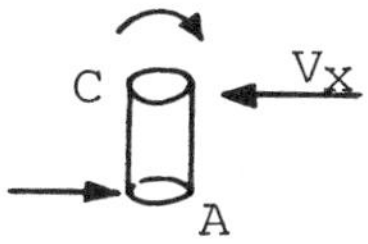

A 5-in diameter 20° spur gear is attached to the end of a 5-in long cantilevered shaft. A smaller gear (ratio 3:1) transmits a 100 ft-lb torque. Sketch the shear-force, bending-moment, and twisting-moment diagrams for the cantilevered shaft, labeling important values.

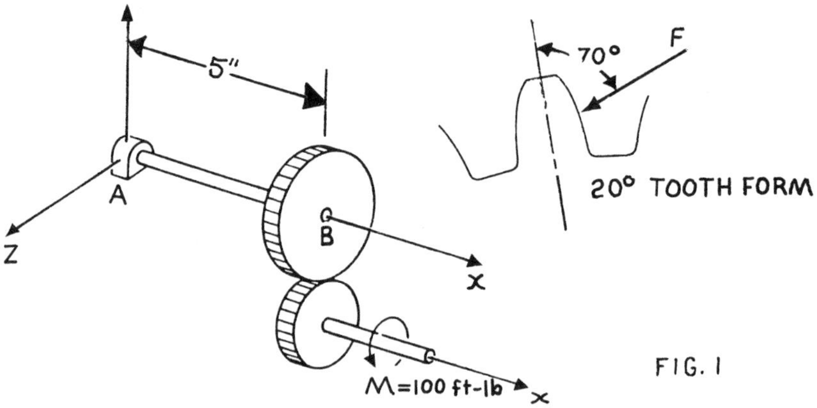

FIG. 1

Solution: To solve the problem, first the torque and the force on the large gear due to the small gear must be found.
Torque transmitted by the smaller gear = 100 ft-lb

= 1200 in-lb.

This torque is the twisting moment, M_t.

Since gear ratio is 3:1

∴ Twisting moment in the cantilever shaft is

$$M_t = 3 \times 1200$$

$$= 3600 \text{ lb-in}$$

This is constant throughout the length of the shaft. Recall that the gear ratio is 3:1

∴ Diameter of smaller gear $= \frac{5}{3}$"

Now consider Fig. 2 which shows the smaller gear with all the forces acting.
For equilibrium, $\sum M = 0$ about 0

$$\therefore 0 = RF \sin 70 - 1200$$

$$\therefore F = \frac{1200}{R \sin 70}$$

where R is the radius of the smaller gear $= \frac{5}{6}$"

$$\therefore F = 1532.41$$

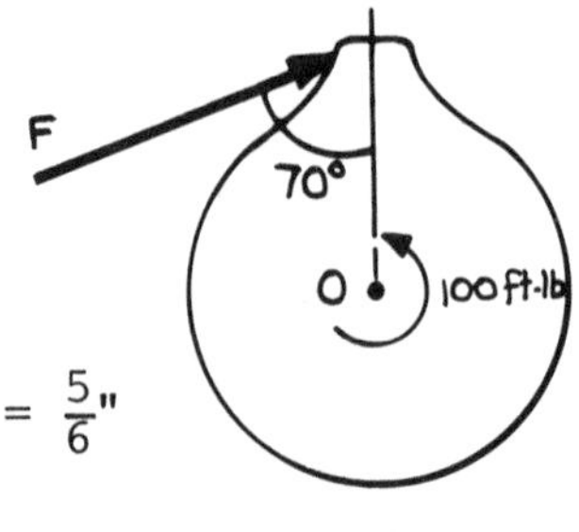

FIG. 2

Bending moment in the cantilever shaft, M_b:

$$M_b = F(5 - x)$$

$$= 1532.41(5 - x)$$

Maximum bending moment occurs when $x = 0$

$$\therefore (M_b)_{max} = 7662 \text{ in-lb}$$

The shear force, bending moment and twisting moment diagrams are shown in Fig. 3, 4 and 5 respectively.

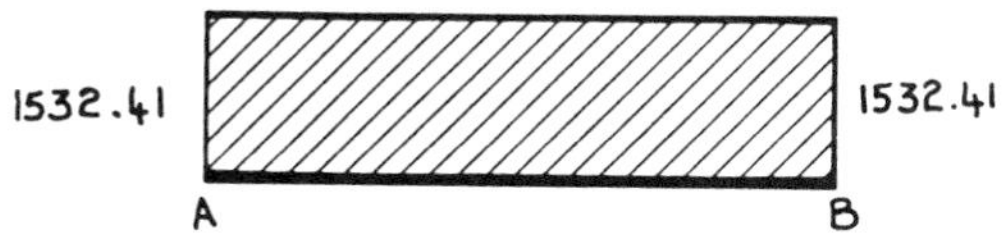

FIG.3 SHEAR FORCE DIAGRAM

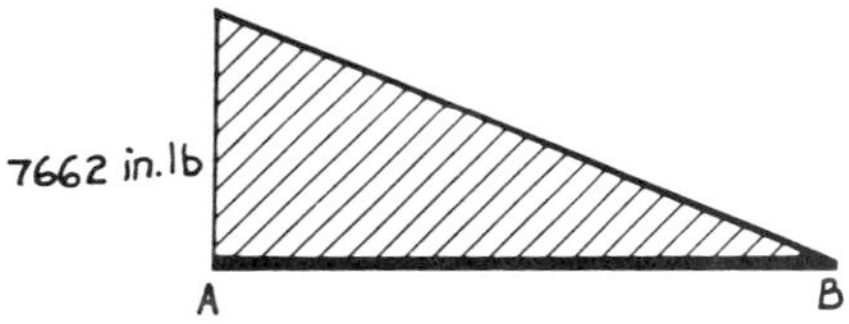

FIG.4 BENDING MOMENT DIAGRAM

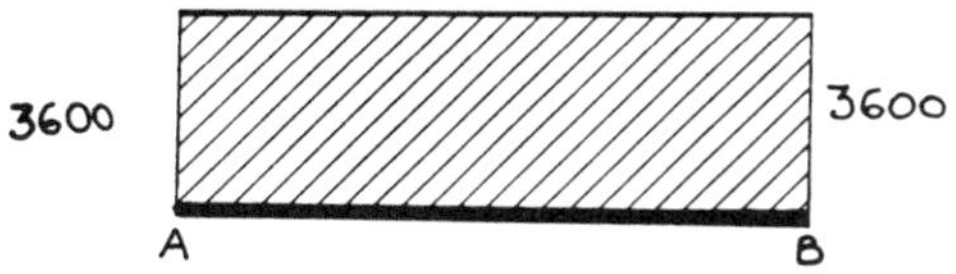

FIG.5 TWISTING MOMENT DIAGRAM

• PROBLEM 2-47

A number of small, two-wheeled boat trailers have a suspension system similar to that shown. Estimate the maximum twisting and bending moments in the 18 in bar and the 24 in bar when the wheels are carrying loads of 500 lb each. A wheel with a 5.00-8 tire has an outside diameter of 5 in + 8 in + 5 in = 18 in.

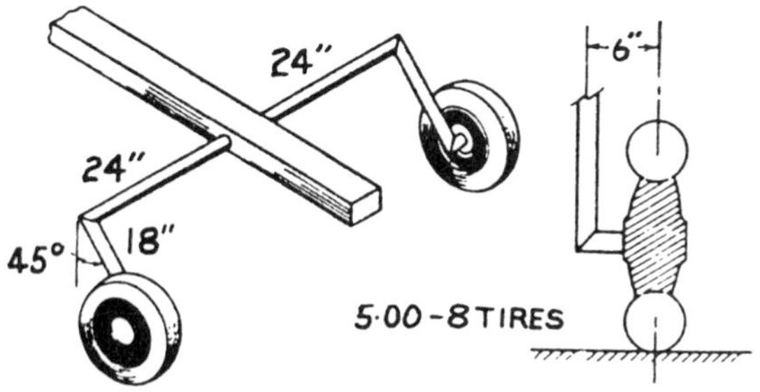

FIG. 1

Solution: Structure is symmetrical both in geometry and in loading so consider only the section either to the right or the left of the middle piece.

Figure two shows members to the right of the middle piece with the 500 lb force acting.

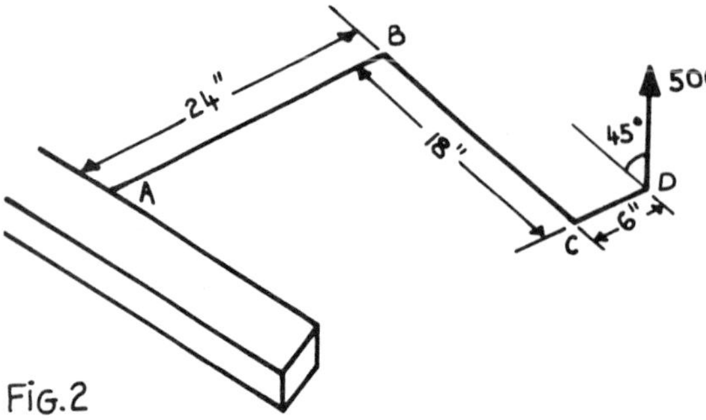

FiG.2

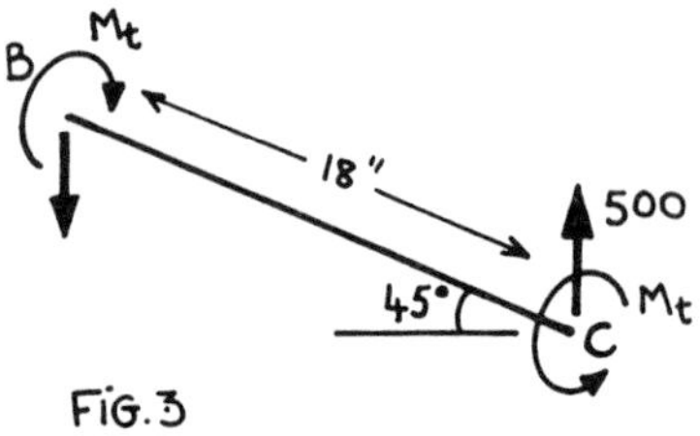

FiG.3

Now consider the 18" member, Fig. 3.
The maximum bending moment occurs at B. Taking moment about B we have

$$(M_b)_{max} = 500 \times 18 \cos 45°$$

$$= 6363.93 \text{ in-lb.}$$

The twisting moment is constant throughout the length of the member. Its value can be calculated by considering point C: Fig. 4.
At Joint C; $\sum M = 0$ (equilibrium of joints)

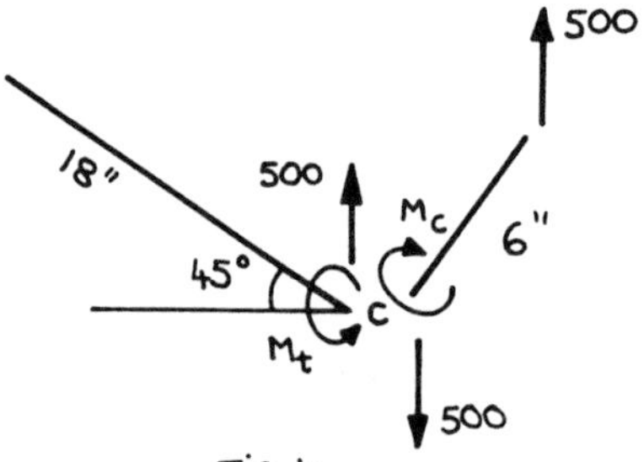

FiG.4

$$\therefore M_C - M_T = 0$$

$$\therefore M_T = M_C$$

but $M_C = 500 \times 6 \cos 45$

$$\therefore M_t = 2121.32 \text{ in-lbs}$$

Using the same argument for the 24" member, the maximum bending moment occurs at point A. Taking moment about A, we have

$$(M_b)_{max} = 500(24 + 6)$$

$$= 15000 \text{ in-lb}$$

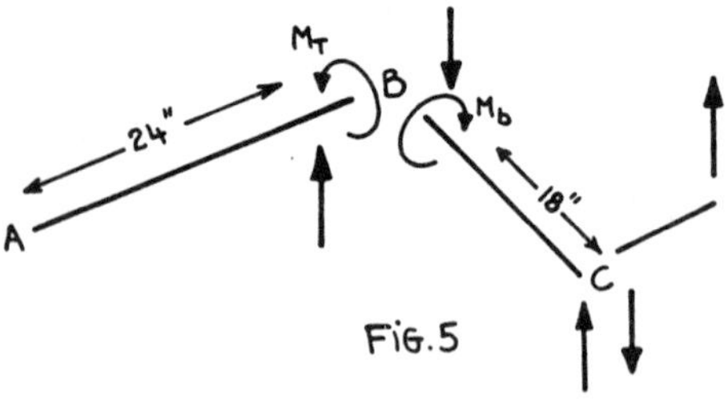

FiG.5

The twisting moment is also constant throughout the length of this member.
Consider joint B

$\sum M = 0$ at B $\quad \therefore M_T = M_B \quad = 6363.76$ in. lb.

A crankshaft for a single-cylinder engine is shown in bearings at each end. It is in equilibrium under the action of the connecting-rod force and the shaft torque M_0. The engine has:

$$\text{Bore} = 2\frac{1}{2} \text{ in}$$

$$\text{Stroke} = 3 \text{ in}$$

Connecting rod length=5 in.

Show diagrams for shear, bending moment and twisting moment for the two end sections of the crankshaft.

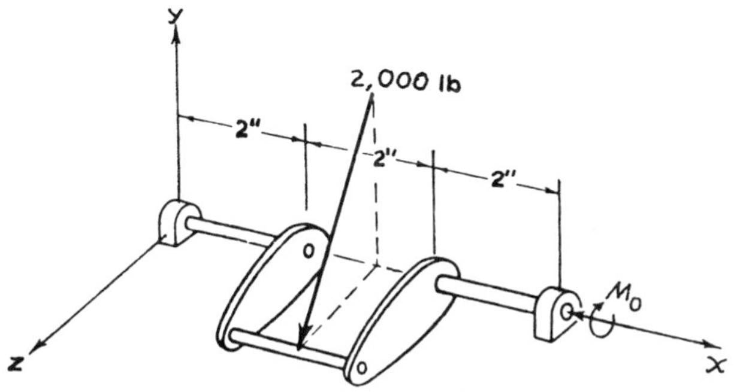

FIG.1.

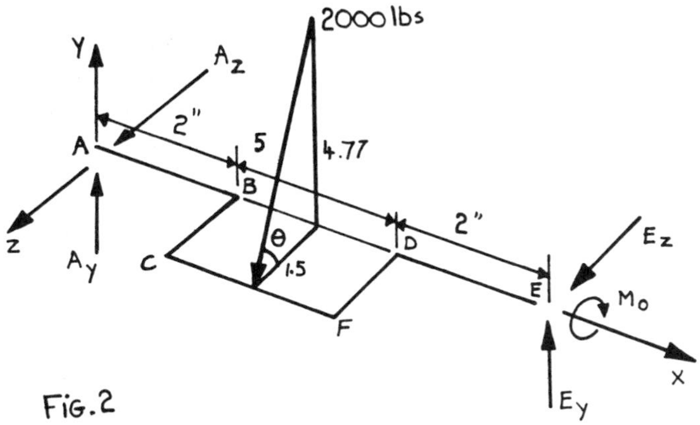

FiG.2

Solution: The force diagram is shown in Fig. 2. The stroke length is given as 3 in. Therefore the length of the crankshaft arm is 1.5 in. The angle θ is then arc cos(1.5/5) = 72.54°. By the Pythagorean Theorem, the vertical height is:

$$\ell = \sqrt{(5)^2 - (1.5)^2} = 4.77$$

Consider equilibrium in the y and z directions

$\sum F_y = 0$

$$A_y + E_y = (2.000)\left(\frac{4.77}{5}\right)$$

from symmetry, $A_y = E_y$

$$\therefore 2A_y = (2,000)\left(\frac{4.77}{5}\right)$$

$$E_y = A_y = 954 \text{ lbs}$$

$\sum F_z = 0$

$$A_z + E_z = (-2,000)\left(\frac{1.5}{5}\right)$$

Also from symmetry,

$$A_z = E_z$$

$$\therefore 2E_z = (2000)\left(\frac{1.5}{5}\right)$$

$$A_z = E_z = -300 \text{ lbs}$$

Consider section AB $0 < x \leq 2$

$\sum F_y = 0$

$$\therefore A_y + V_y = 0$$

$$\therefore V_y = -954 \text{ lbs}$$

$\sum F_z = 0$

$$\therefore A_z + V_z = 0$$

$$\therefore V_z = 300 \text{ lbs}$$

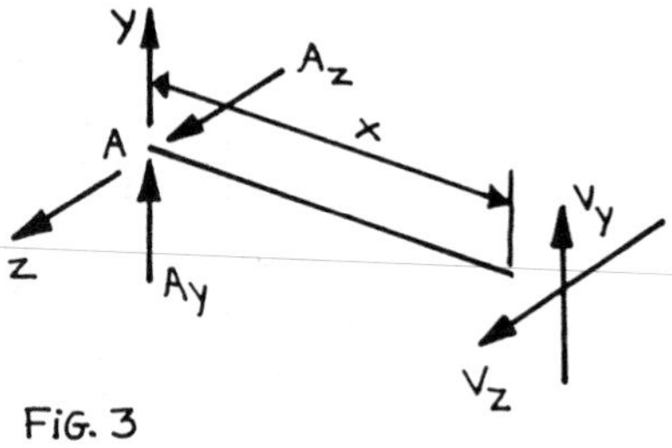

FIG. 3

The shear at any point in the section is the resultant of these two

$$\therefore V = \sqrt{(954)^2 + (300)^2}$$

$$= 1000 \text{ lbs}$$

On this section, the forces that cause bending are those in the y and z directions

But $\qquad M = -\int V dx$

$$\therefore \qquad M_{by} = \int 954dx$$

$$= 954x + C$$

at $\quad x = 0, \; M_{by} = 0 \qquad C = 0$

$$M_{by} = 954x$$

$$M_{bx} = -\int 300dx$$

$$= -300x + D$$

at $\quad x = 0, \; M_{bx} = 0 \qquad D = 0$

$$M_{bx} = -300x$$

These moments are maximum at point B

i.e. when $\quad x = 2''$

$\therefore \quad$ At point B ;

$$M_{bx} = -600 \quad ; \quad M_{by} = 1908$$

The net bending moment is the resultant of these two

$$\therefore \quad M_b = \sqrt{(1908)^2 + (600)^2}$$

$$= 2000 \text{ in lb}$$

The calculated values of M_b and V also hold true for section DE because of symmetry.

The twisting moment acts only on DE because of the applied moment M_0 at point E which keeps it in equilibrium

Now consider section DE. See fig. 4.

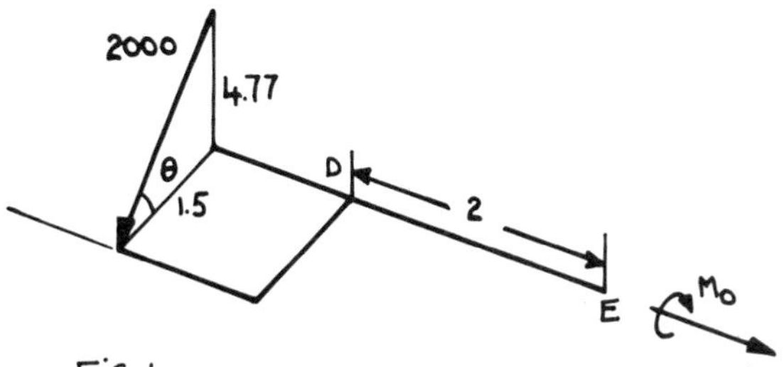

FIG. 4

The twisting moment on DE is a moment about the x-axis and is equivalent to M_x.

Taking moment at any section on DE for the forces to

the left of DE:

$$M_t = M_x = (2000)\left(\frac{4.77}{5}\right)(1.5)$$

$$= 2862 \text{ in lb}$$

Note: A structure is said to be symmetrical in a particular plane only if the geometry and loading are symmetrical.

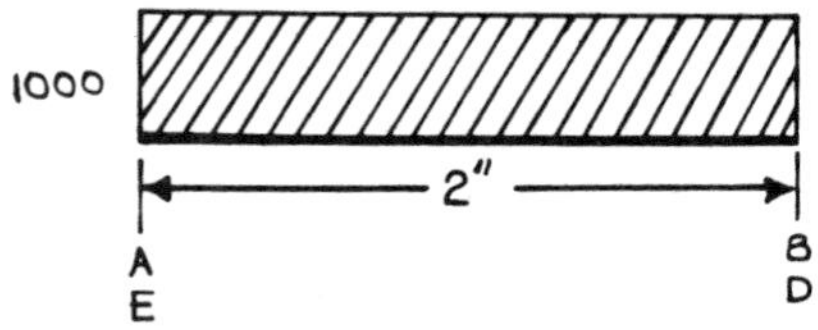

FIG. 5

SHEAR FORCE DIAGRAM FOR MEMBERS AB AND DE

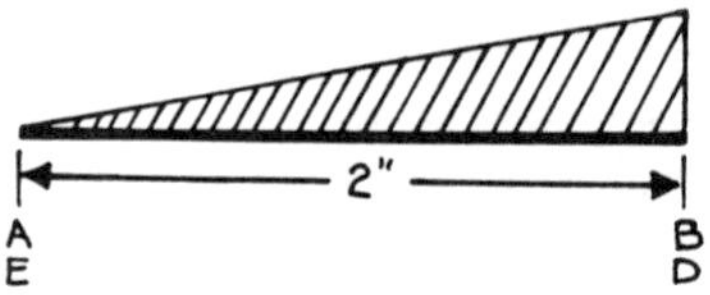

FIG. 6

BENDING MOMENT DIAGRAM FOR MEMBERS AB AND DE

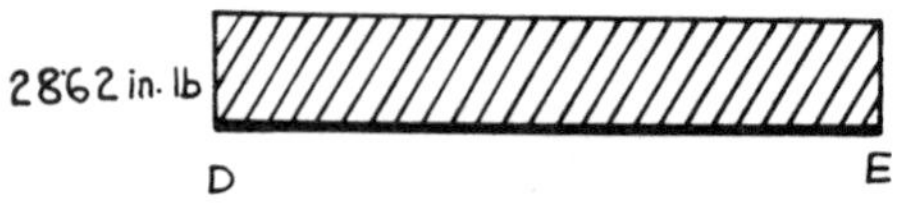

FIG. 7

TWISTING MOMENT DIAGRAM FOR MEMBER DE

In this case, the structure is symmetrical in the y and z planes but is not symmetrical in the x plane.

The shear and bending moment diagrams for members AB and DE are identical and are shown in Figs. 5 and 6 respectively.

The twisting moment diagram for member DE is shown in Fig. 7.

CHAPTER 3

STRESS

STRESS DUE TO AXIAL FORCE

• PROBLEM 3-1

Consider the loads of Fig. 1 to be axially applied at sections B, C, and D to the concrete structure supported at A. The cross-sectional areas are: For CD, 12 sq in., for BC, 3.6 sq in., and for AB, 16 sq in. Determine the axial stress in the concrete:

(a) On a section in the CD interval.
(b) On a section in the BC interval.
(c) On a section in the AB interval.

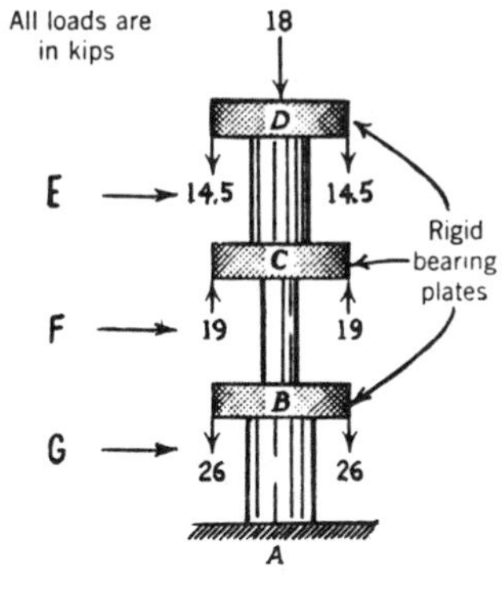

FIG. 1

Solution: Forces in the members can be found from equilibrium. Since there are no geometrical constraints $\sigma_{member} = F/A$.

First, sketching free-body diagrams of the concrete members E, F and G:

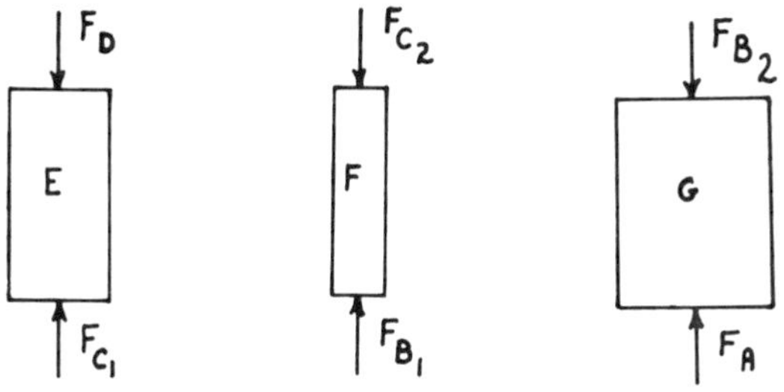

FIG. 2

From figures 1 and 2 all the forces acting on the members are:

$$F_D = F_{C_1} = 18 + 2 \times 14.5 = 47 \text{ kips C.}$$

$$F_{C_2} = F_{B_1} = 47 - 2 \times 19 = 9 \text{ kips C.}$$

$$F_{B_2} = F_A = 9 + 2 \times 26 = 61 \text{ kips C.}$$

To find axial stresses

$$\sigma_{DC} = \frac{F_D}{A_{CD}} = \frac{47}{12} = 3.92 \text{ ksi C.}$$

$$\sigma_{CB} = \frac{F_{C_2}}{A_{DC}} = \frac{9}{3.6} = 2.5 \text{ ksi C.}$$

$$\sigma_{BA} = \frac{F_{B_2}}{A_{BA}} = \frac{61}{16} = 3.81 \text{ kips C.}$$

• PROBLEM 3-2

In Fig. 1, the axial stresses are 1150 psi C in the wood post B, and 19,000 psi T in the steel bar A. Determine the load P.

C = Compression
T = Tension

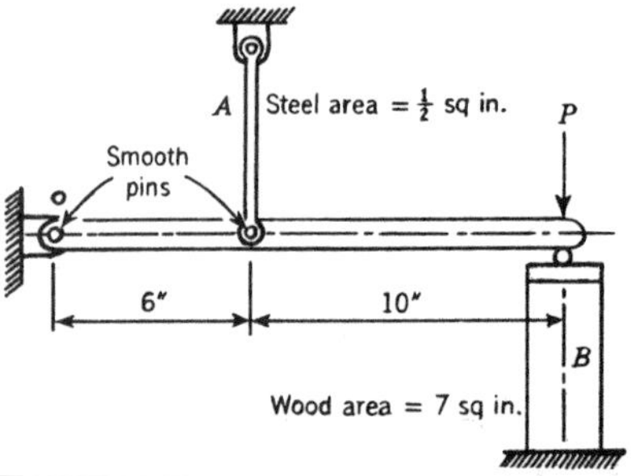

FIG. 1

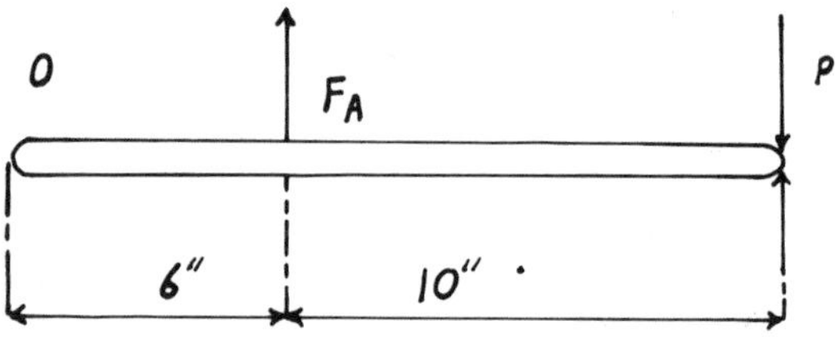

FIG. 2

F_B

Solution: First find the forces acting on the members A and B where the force equals the area of the member times the given stresses:

$$F_A = A_A \sigma_A = 0.5 \times 1900 = 9500 \text{ lb T.}$$

$$F_B = A_B \sigma_B = 7 \times 11500 = 8050 \text{ lb C.}$$

A sketch of the free-body diagram of the main member appears in Fig. 2. Using the equilibrium condition equation, from Fig. 2:

$$\Sigma M_0 = 0 + \curvearrowright$$

$$P \times 16 - F_A \times 6 - F_B \times 16 = 0$$

$$P \times 16 - 9500 \times 6 - 8050 \times 16 = 0$$

$$P = \frac{185800}{16} = 11612.5 \text{ lb}\downarrow$$

or

$$P = 11.61 \text{ kips}\downarrow$$

The beam BE in Fig. 1 is used for hoisting machinery. It is anchored by two bolts at B, and at C it rests on a parapet wall. The essential details are given in the figure. Note that the bolts are threaded as shown in Fig. 4 with d = 0.620 in. at the root of the threads. If this arrangement is used to lift equipment of 1 ton (2,000 lb), determine the stress in the bolts BD and the bearing stress at C. Assume that the weight of the beam is negligible in comparison with the loads handled.

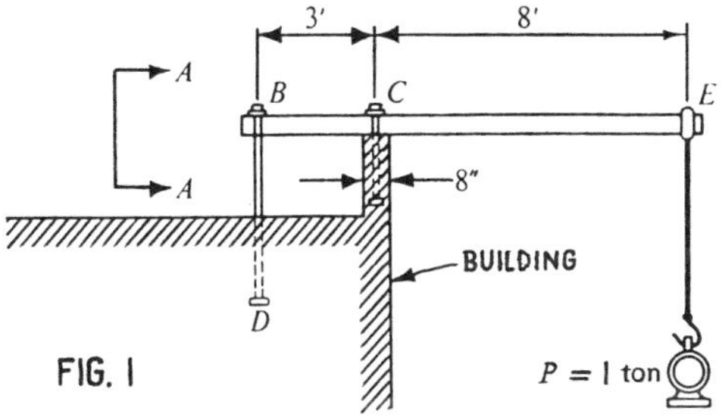

FIG. 1

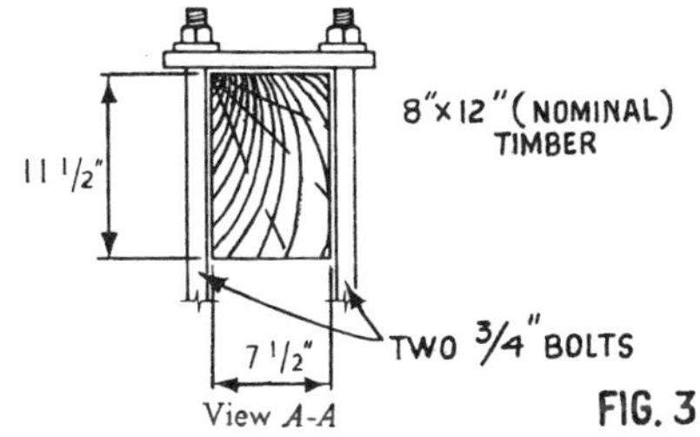

FIG. 3

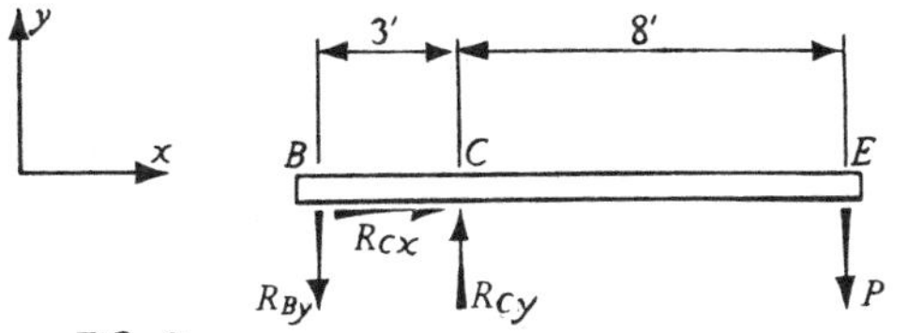

FIG. 2

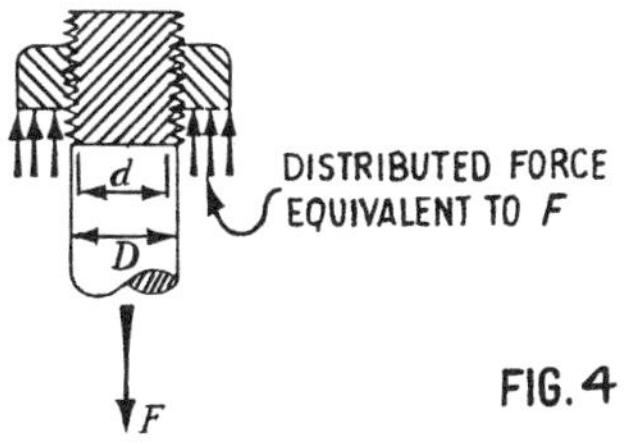

FIG. 4

Solution: To solve this problem, the actual situation is idealized, and a free-body diagram is made on which all known and unknown forces are indicated. This is shown in Fig. 2. The vertical reactions at B and C are unknown. They are indicated respectively as R_{B_y} and R_{C_y}, where the first subscript identifies the location and the second the line of action of the unknown force. As the long bolts BD are not effective in resisting the horizontal force, only an unknown horizontal reaction at C is assumed and marked as R_{Cx}. The applied known force P is shown in its proper location. After a free-body diagram is prepared, the equations of statics are applied and solved for the unknown forces.

$$\Sigma M_B = 0. \; +\curvearrowright \qquad 2000(8 + 3) - R_{C_y}(3) = 0 .$$

$$R_{C_y} = \frac{22,000}{3} = 7333.33 \text{ lbs}\uparrow$$

$$\Sigma M_C = 0. \; +\curvearrowright \qquad 2000(8) - R_{B_y}(3) = 0.$$

$$R_{B_y} = \frac{16,000}{3} = 5333.33 \text{ lbs}\downarrow$$

Check: $\Sigma F_y = 0. \; +\uparrow$

$$7333.33 - 5333.33 - 2000 = 0$$

$$\Sigma F_x = 0 . \quad R_{C_x} = 0 .$$

These steps complete and check the work of determining the forces. The various areas of the material that resist these forces are determined next.

Cross-sectional area of one 3/4 in. bolt: $A = \pi(0.75/2)^2 = 0.442 \text{ in.}^2$. This is not the minimum area of a bolt; threads reduce it. (Fig. 4).

The cross-sectional area of one 3/4 in. bolt at the root of the threads is

$$A_{net} = \pi(0.620/2)^2 = 0.302 \text{ in.}^2$$

Force on each bolt (two bolts at point B) is:

$$P = \frac{R_{By}}{2} = 2666.66 \text{ lbs.}$$

Maximum normal tensile stress in each bolt is:

$$\sigma_{max} = \frac{P}{A_{net}}$$

$$\sigma_{max} = \frac{2666.66 \text{ lbs}}{0.302 \text{ in.}^2} = 8830 \text{ psi} .$$

Tensile stress at the shank of each bolt is:

$$\sigma = \frac{2666.66 \text{ lbs}}{0.442 \text{ in.}^2} = 6033.2 \text{ psi} .$$

To determine the bearing stress at point C the contact area should be calculated.

A(Area at contact) = $7.5(8.0) = 60 \text{ in.}^2$ (from the dimensions given in Fig. 3)

$$\sigma_{bearing} = \frac{R_{Cy}}{A_C} = \frac{7,333.33}{60} = 122.22 \text{ psi} .$$

• PROBLEM 3-4

The dynamic system shown in Fig. (1) has a rotating shaft (AB) with a constant angular velocity of 600 rpm. A rod of negligible weight (CD in the Fig.) is attached to shaft AB and at point D, a 10-lb. weight is fastened. Select the size of the rod CD so that the stress in it will not exceed 10,000 psi. (neglect the friction due to spin of weight at D on the plane, and the weight of the rod AB).

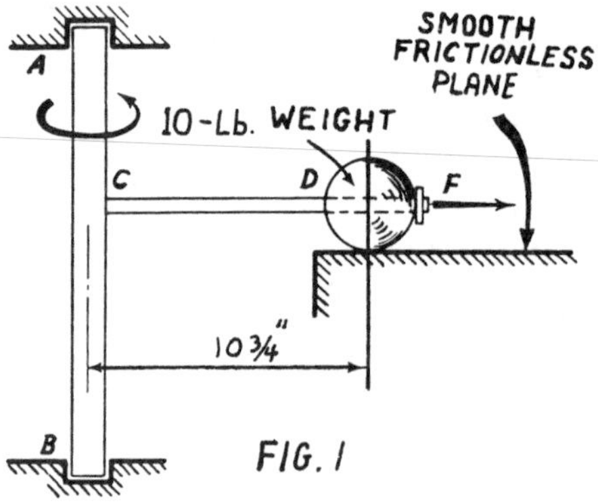

FIG. 1

Solution: For the given motion the body W = 10 lb. is accelerated toward the center of rotation with an acceleration of $\omega^2 R$, where R is the distance CD.

angular velocity ω = (600 rpm)(2π)/60 sec. = 20π radian/sec.

The force F is obtained by the relation:

$$F = ma = \frac{W}{g}\omega^2 R$$

where $m = \frac{w}{g} = \frac{10 \text{ lbs}}{32.2(12'')} = 0.025 \text{ lbs/in/sec}^2$

$$F = 0.025 \text{ lbs/in/sec}^2 (20\pi)^2 (10.75 \text{ in.}) = 1{,}098.32 \text{ lbs.}$$

Force F is acting on rod CD at the cross-sectional area:

$$F = \sigma_{allow.} A_{net} \Rightarrow A_{net} = \frac{F}{\sigma_{allow.}} = \frac{1{,}098.32 \text{ lbs}}{10{,}000 \text{ psi}}$$

$$= 0.1090\square''$$

A 3/8" in. round bar which has a cross-sectional area of

$$\tfrac{1}{4}(3/8)^2(\pi) = 0.110\ \square'' > 0.109\ \square''$$

will provide the required cross-sectional area for the stress to remain less than 10,000 psi.

$$\sigma_{actual} = \frac{1{,}098.32 \text{ lbs}}{A(\text{area of } 3/8''\text{bar})} = 9950 \text{ psi.}$$

• PROBLEM 3-5

Select members FC and CB in the truss of Fig. 1 to carry an inclined force P of 150 kips applied at joint G, with an allowable tensile stress of 20 kpsi.

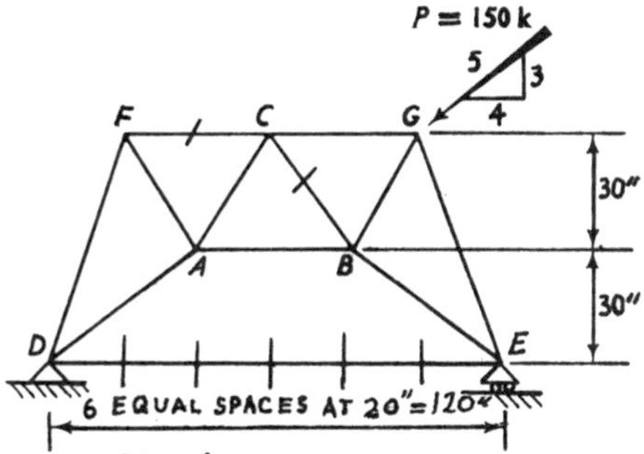

FIG. 1

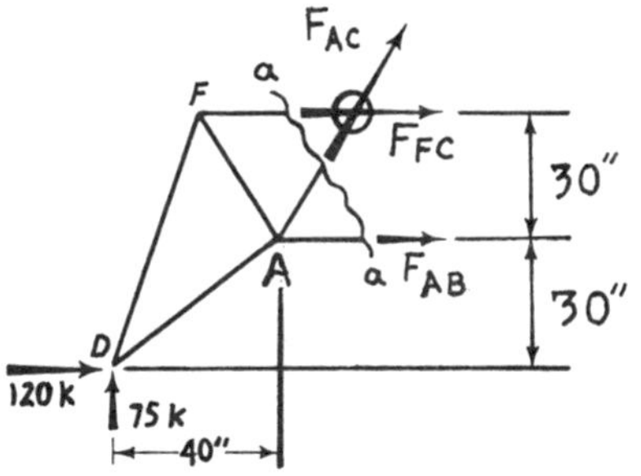

FIG. 3

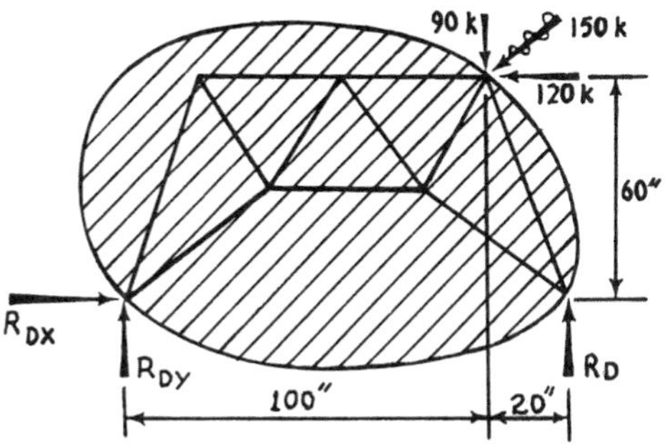

FIG. 2

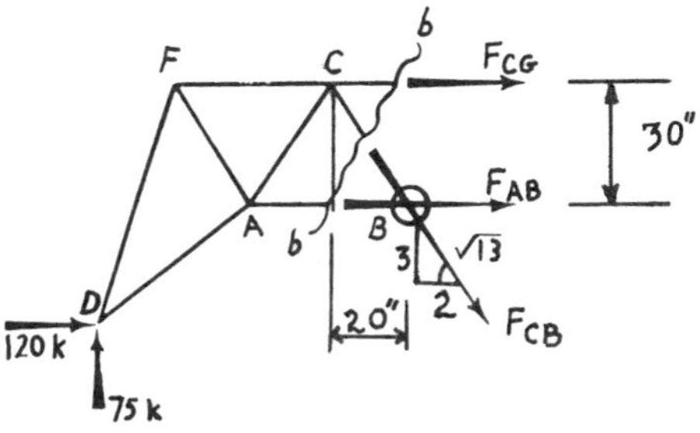

FIG. 4

Solution: If all members of the truss were to be designed, forces in all members would have to be found. In practice this is often done by constructing a Maxwell-Cremona diagram or analyzing the truss by the method of joints. However, if only a few members are to be designed or checked, the method of sections is quicker.

It is generally understood that a planar truss such as shown in the figure is stable in the direction perpendicular to the plane of the paper. Practically this is accomplished by introducing braces at right angles to the plane of the truss. In this example the design of compression members is avoided as this will be treated in the chapter on columns.

To determine the forces in the members to be designed, the reactions for the whole structure are computed first. This is done by completely disregarding the interior framing. Only reaction and force components definitely located at their points of application are indicated on a free-body diagram of the whole structure, Fig. 2. After the reactions are determined, free-body diagrams of a part of the structure are used to determine the forces in the members considered, Figs. 3 and 4.

Using free-body in Fig. 2:

$$\Sigma F_x = 0 \qquad R_{Dx} - 120 = 0 \qquad R_{Dx} = 120 \text{ kips}$$

$$\Sigma M_E = 0. \; +\circlearrowright \quad R_{Dy}(120) - 150(3/5)(20) - 150(4/5)(60) = 0$$

$$R_{Dy} = 75 \text{ kips}$$

$$\Sigma M_D = 0. \; +\circlearrowright - R_{Ey}(120) + 150(3/5)(100) - 150(4/5)(60) = 0$$

$$R_{Ey} = 15 \text{ kips}$$

Check: $\Sigma F_y = 0 , \quad + 75 - 90 + 15 = 0$

Section a-a is drawn to find the magnitude F_{FC}. Using free-body in Fig. (3) taking the moment about point A eliminates the two other unknown forces F_{AC}, F_{AB} which both pass through point A, and the only unknown force is F_{FC}.

$$\Sigma M_A = 0 \quad \circlearrowright + , \qquad +F_{FC}(30) + 75(40) - 120(30) = 0 ,$$

$$F_{FC} = + 20 \text{ kips}$$

$$A_{FC} = F_{FC}/\sigma_{allow} = 1 \text{ in.}^2 \qquad \text{(use } \tfrac{1}{2}\text{-in.-by-2-in.bar)}$$

where $\sigma_{allowable} = 20{,}000$ psi $= 20$ ksi . Using free-body in Fig. 4 section b-b is drawn to determine the magnitude of F_{CB}; it is apparent from the figure that F_{CG} and F_{AB} are both in the x direction and by use of the static equilibrium equation in the y direction, the only unknown is F_{CB_y}

$$\Sigma F_y = 0 , \qquad -(F_{CB})_y + 75 = 0 , \qquad (F_{CB})_y = +75 \text{ kips}$$

The relative lengths of the projection of CB in the x and y directions are respectively, 2 and 3. Using Pythagoras' theorem, the relative length of CB is

$$\sqrt{3^2 + 2^2} = \sqrt{13}$$

$$F_{CBy} = F_{CB} \frac{3}{\sqrt{13}}$$

or

$$F_{CB} = \frac{\sqrt{13}}{3} F_{CBy} = \frac{\sqrt{13}}{3}(75) = 90.2 \text{ kips}$$

$$A_{CB} = F_{CB}/\sigma_{allow.} = 90.2/20 = 4.51 \text{ in}^2$$

(use two bars $1\frac{1}{8}$ in. by 2 in.)

Member GF of the pin-connected truss in Fig. 1 has a cross-sectional area of 2.4 sq in. (a) Determine the axial stress in GF. The lengths shown are center to center of pins. (b) If member CF of the pin-connected truss is a 7/8-in. diameter rod, determine the axial stress in CF. The lengths shown are center to center of pins.

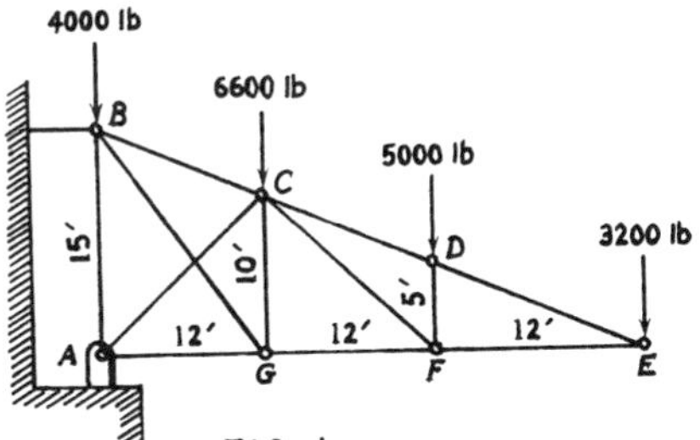

FIG. 1

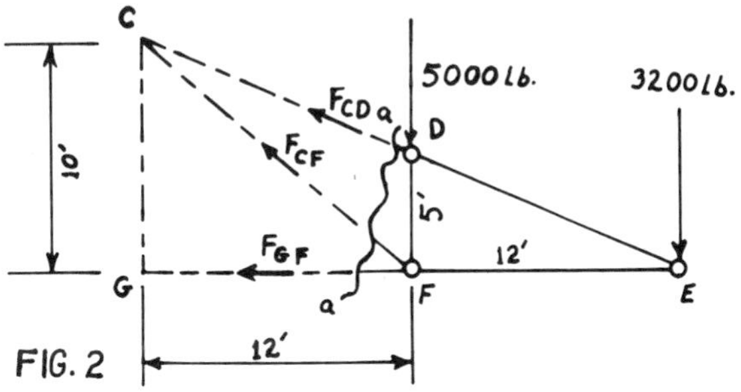

FIG. 2

Solution: In general, to determine the forces in the truss members, the reactions for the whole structure should be calculated. Since the truss in this problem is a cantilever truss the member forces can be found without finding the reaction.

(a) to find the axial force in GF, make a section cut a-a as shown in Fig. 2, and apply the equilibrium equation:

$$\Sigma M_C = 0 \quad +\circlearrowright$$

By taking the moment about point C, F_{CD} and F_{CF} will not contribute since their lines of action go through C. Therefore the only unknown is F_{GF}.

$$F_{GF} \times 10 + 5000 \times 12 + 3200 \times 24 = 0$$

$$F_{GF} = -13680 = 13680 \text{ lb, compression}$$

and axial stress in GF.

$$\sigma_{GF} = \frac{F_{GF}}{A_{GF}} = \frac{13680}{2.4} = 5700 \text{ psi C.}$$

(b) to find the axial force in CF, again from Fig. 2,

$$\Sigma M_D = 0 \quad +\circlearrowright$$

the vertical component of F_{CF} passes through the point D and contributes no moment. The horizontal component of F_{CF} is $F_{CF} \times 12/15.62$ therefore:

$$\left(F_{CF} \times \frac{12}{15.62}\right) \times 5 - 13680 \times 5 + 3200 \times 12 = 0$$

$$F_{CF} = 7810 \text{ lb. Tension .}$$

Axial stress in CF: $$\sigma_{CF} = \frac{F_{CF}}{A_{CF}}$$

where $$A_{CF} = \frac{\pi d^2}{4} = \frac{\pi(7/8)^2}{4} = .601 \text{ in.}$$

$$\sigma_{CF} = \frac{7810}{.6} = 12{,}990 \text{ psi T.}$$

In Figure 1, a 10' high, thin-walled cone is supporting a load of 100 lb. It is desired to analyze the normal stress in the cone wall half way down from the top. At this half way point, find the normal stress, n_1, pointing towards the apex of the cone, and the normal stress in the vertical direction, n_2.

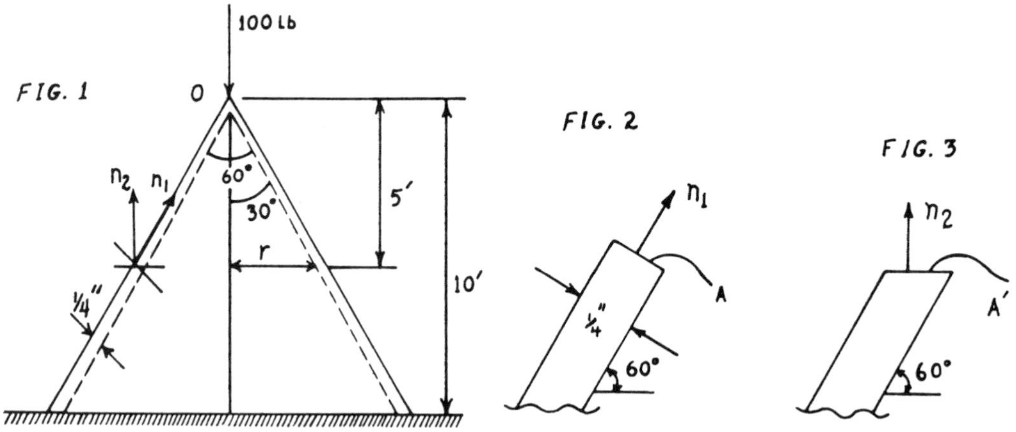

Solution: The first step is to draw a diagram of the interface in each case. This is done in Figs. 2 and 3.

If the cone is cut 5 ft' (vertically) from 0 (see Fig. 1), in the manner shown in Fig. 2, the area A around the cut will be

$$A = 2\pi rt ,$$

where t is the thickness, .25". From Fig. 1 it can be seen that

$$r = 5' \tan 30° .$$

The area is then

$$A = 2\pi(5 \text{ ft} \times 12 \text{ in/ft})\tan 30°(.25 \text{ in.}) .$$

$$A = 54.4 \text{ in}^2 .$$

We are now ready to set up a force balance. From Fig. 4,

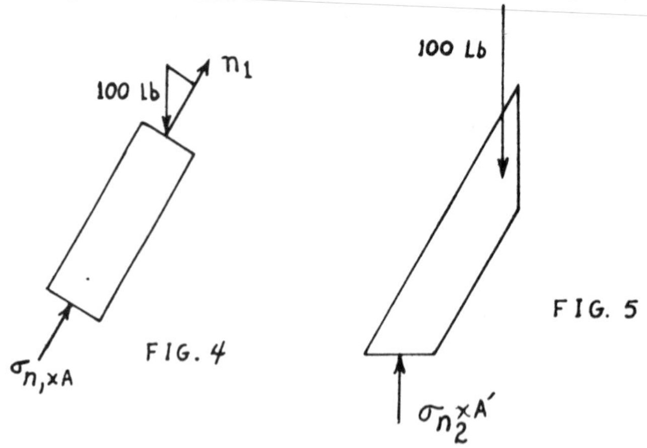

$$\Sigma F_{n_1} = (\sigma_{n_1} \times A) - 100 \sin 60° = 0$$

$$\sigma_{n_1} \times A = 100 \sin 60^\circ$$

$$\sigma_{n_1} = \frac{100 \sin 60^\circ}{A} = \frac{(100)(.866)}{54.4} = 1.59 \text{ psi}$$

If the cone is cut as in Figure 3, the total area of the cut will be

$$A' = 2\pi(r)\left[(\tfrac{1}{4}")\left(\frac{1}{\cos 60^\circ}\right)\right] .$$

since the radius is the same as in the previous case,

$$A' = 2\pi(34.64")\left[\frac{1}{(4)(.866)}"\right] = 62.83 \text{ in.}^2$$

From Fig. 5, we write

$$\Sigma F = 0 = \sigma_{n_2} A' - 100 \text{ lb}$$

$$\frac{100 \text{ lb.}}{A'} = \sigma_{n_2}$$

$$\sigma_{n_2} = \frac{100 \text{ lb}}{62.83 \text{ in.}^2} = 1.59 \text{ psi} .$$

• PROBLEM 3-8

The concrete pier shown in Fig. 1 is loaded at the top with a uniformly distributed load of 600 lb per square foot. Investigate the state of stress at a level of 4 ft. above the base. Concrete weighs approximately 150 lb per cubic foot.

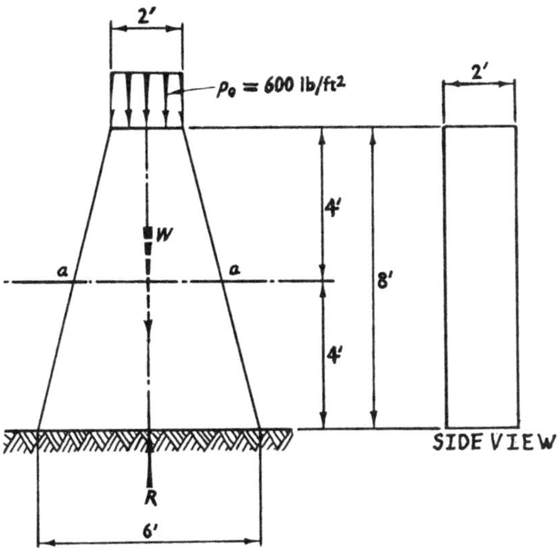

FIG.1

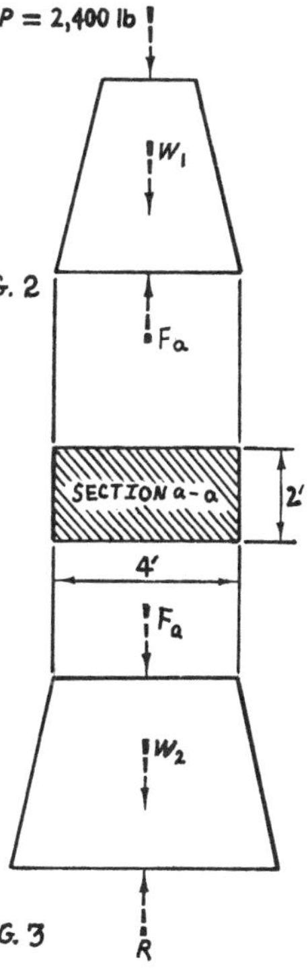

FIG. 2

FIG. 3

Solution: In this problem the weight of the structure itself is appreciable and must be included in the calculations.

Weight of the whole pier:

$$W = (\text{vol. of concrete pier})(\text{number of lbs/cu.ft of concrete})$$

$$= (\text{height X width}_y \text{ X average width}_x)\ (\text{lb/cu ft of concrete})$$

$$W = (2 + 6)2(8)150/2 = 9{,}600 \text{ lb.}$$

Total applied force:

$P = 600(2)2 = 2{,}400$ lb (converting uniform load to concentrated load).

From $\Sigma F_y = 0$, reaction at base:

$$R = W + P = 12{,}000 \text{ lb.}$$

These forces are shown in the diagrams schematically as concentrated forces acting through their respective centroids. Then, to determine the stress at the desired level, the body is cut into two separate parts. A free-body diagram for either part is sufficient to solve the problem. For comparison the problem is solved both ways.

Using the upper part of the pier as a free-body, Fig. 2, the weight of the pier above the cut is:

$$W_1 = (2 + 4)2(4)150/2 = 3{,}600 \text{ lb.}$$

From $\Sigma F_y = 0$, the force at the cut is: $F_a = P + W_1 = 6{,}000$ lb. The normal stress at the level a-a is

$$\sigma_a = \frac{F_a}{A} = \frac{6{,}000}{2(4)} = 750 \text{ lb per square foot or } \frac{750}{144} = 5.2 \text{ psi.}$$

This stress is compressive as F_a acts on the cut.

Using the lower part of the pier as a free body, Fig. 3, the weight of the pier below the cut is:

$$W_2 = (4 + 6)2(4)150/2 = 6{,}000 \text{ lb.}$$

From $\Sigma F_y = 0$, the force at the cut is:

$$F_a = R - W_2 = 6{,}000 \text{ lb.}$$

$$\sigma_{a-a} = \frac{F_a}{\text{Area}} = \frac{6{,}000 \text{ lbs}}{(2')(4')} = 750 \text{ PSF}$$

or

$$\frac{750}{144} = 5.2 \text{ psi.}$$

NORMAL STRESS

• PROBLEM 3-9

Given the loaded bar shown in Figs. (a) and (b), determine the normal and shear stress components for the orientation of area in each case.

Solution: Shown in Fig. (a) is a uniform bar subjected to a tensile force P whose line of action coincides with the centerline of the bar. A cross section A is shown away from the applied loads. The force intensity transmitted through this section is uniform over the section. With section A normal to P, there will be only a normal stress present on A. Neglecting the force of gravity, this stress, τ_n, is given every-

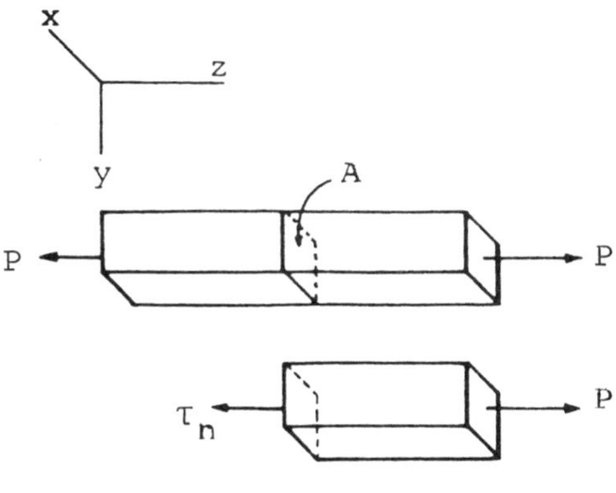

Fig. A.

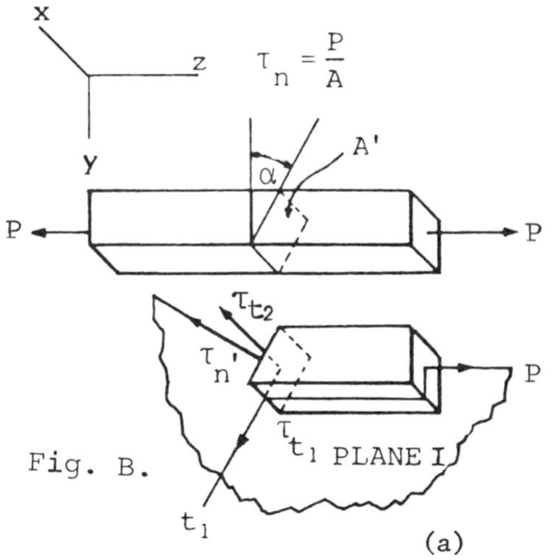

Fig. B.

where on the section as

$$\tau_n = \frac{P}{A} \qquad \text{(a)}$$

Now consider another section of area A' such as is shown in Fig. (b). Here again the force intensity over the section is uniform. There is, however, a new normal stress $\tau_{n'}$, and, for directions parallel to the edges of the section, shear stresses τ_{t_1} and τ_{t_2} . Note that the force P and the stresses $\tau_{n'}$ and τ_{t_1} are coplanar (plane I); it is then apparent that τ_{t_2} lying normal to plane I must be zero from considerations of equilibrium in that direction. Then,

$$\Sigma F_x = 0 \qquad P - \tau_{n'}A' \cos\alpha - \tau_{t_1}A'\sin\alpha = 0 \qquad \text{(b)}$$

$$\Sigma F_y = 0 \qquad -\tau_{n'}A' \sin\alpha + \tau_{t_1}A' \cos\alpha = 0 \qquad \text{(c)}$$

From (c), we have

$$\tau_{n'} \sin\alpha = \tau_{t_1} \cos\alpha$$

$$\tau_{t_1} = \frac{\sin\alpha}{\cos\alpha}\,\tau_{n'} \;.$$

Substituting into (b), we find:

$$P = \tau_{n'}A' \cos\alpha + \frac{\sin^2\alpha}{\cos\alpha}A'\,\tau_{n'}$$

but $A' \cos\alpha = A$, so that

$$\frac{P}{A} = \tau_{n'} + \tan^2\alpha\,\tau_{n'} = (1 + \tan^2\alpha)\tau_{n'}$$

$$\tau_{n'} = \frac{P}{A}\left(\frac{1}{\sec^2\alpha}\right) = \frac{P}{A}\cos^2\alpha \qquad \text{(d)}$$

$$\tau_{t_1} = \frac{\sin\alpha}{\cos\alpha}\,\tau_{n'} = \frac{P}{A}\sin\alpha\cos\alpha = \frac{1}{2}\frac{P}{A}\sin 2\alpha \qquad \text{(e)}$$

Notice that the normal and shear stresses vary with the orientation α of the section.

• PROBLEM 3-10

A bracket of negligible weight shown in Fig. 1 is loaded with a force P of 3 kips. For interconnection purposes the bar ends are clevised (forked). Pertinent dimensions are shown in the figure. Find the normal stresses in the members AB and BC and the bearing and shearing stresses for the pin C. All pins are 0.375 in. in diameter.

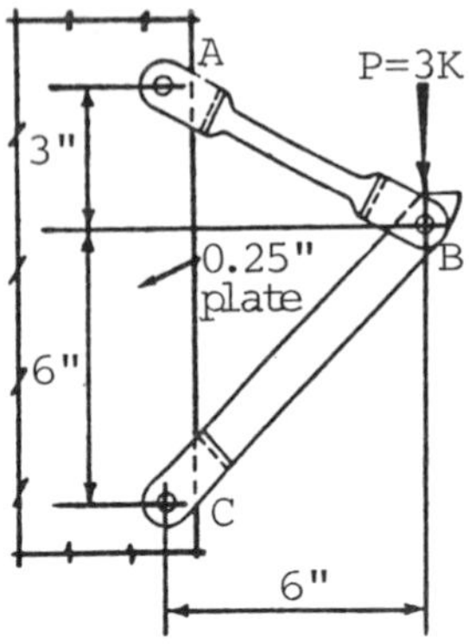

Fig. 1

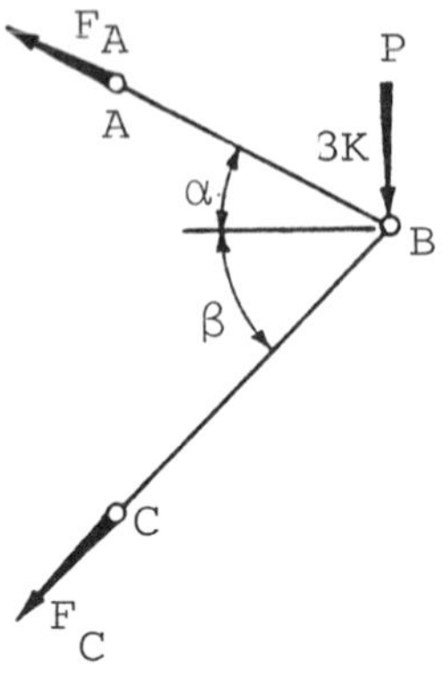

Fig. 2

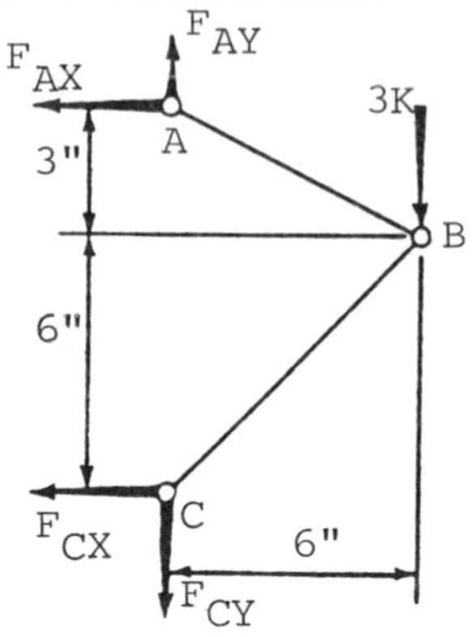

Fig. 3

Solution: The first step is to draw a free-body diagram of the bracket (Fig. 2). Except for the load $P = 3$ kips at point B there are no intermediate forces acting on the bars. The magnitude of the forces are unknown and are labeled F_A and F_C in Fig. 2. In order to determine F_A, F_C, the angles α, β (from Fig. 2) are calculated.

$$\tan\beta = \frac{6''}{6''} = 1.0 \rightarrow \beta = 45^\circ$$

$$\tan\alpha = \frac{3}{6''} = 0.5 \rightarrow \alpha = 26.5^\circ$$

Using the static equilibrium equations:

$\Sigma F_y = 0$. (From Fig. 3)

$$F_A \sin\alpha - F_C \sin\beta = 3 \tag{1}$$

$\Sigma F_x = 0$.

$$-F_C \cos\beta - F_A \cos\alpha = 0 . \tag{2}$$

Two simultaneous equations, solving for F_A, F_C

$$F_C = -F_A \frac{\cos\alpha}{\cos\beta}$$

Substituting back into equation (1)

$$F_A \sin\alpha + F_A \frac{\cos\alpha}{\cos\beta} \sin\beta = 3$$

$$F_A(\sin\alpha\cos\beta + \cos\alpha\sin\beta) = 3\cos\beta$$

$$F_A = \frac{3\cos\beta}{\sin(\alpha+\beta)} = 2.23 \text{ k}$$

$$F_C = -2.23 \frac{\cos 26.5^\circ}{\cos 45} = 2.83 \text{ k} .$$

Note that $\sin(A \pm B) = \sin A \cos B \pm \cos A \sin B$. Stress in main bar AB:

$$\sigma_{AB} = \frac{F_A}{A}$$

$$A = (0.50)(0.25) = 0.125 \text{ in}^2$$

(dimensions from Figures 4 and 5)

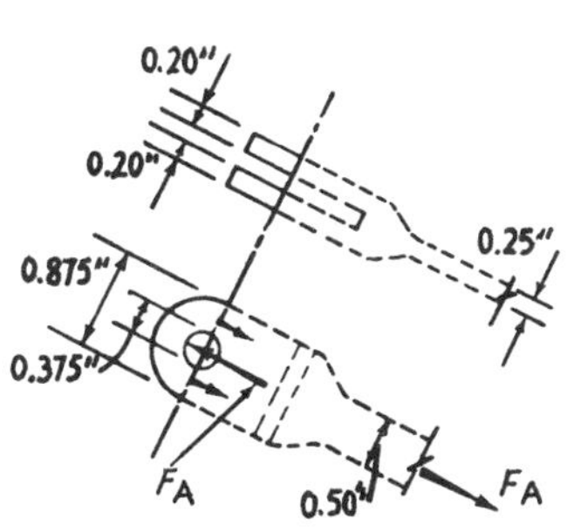

FIG. 4

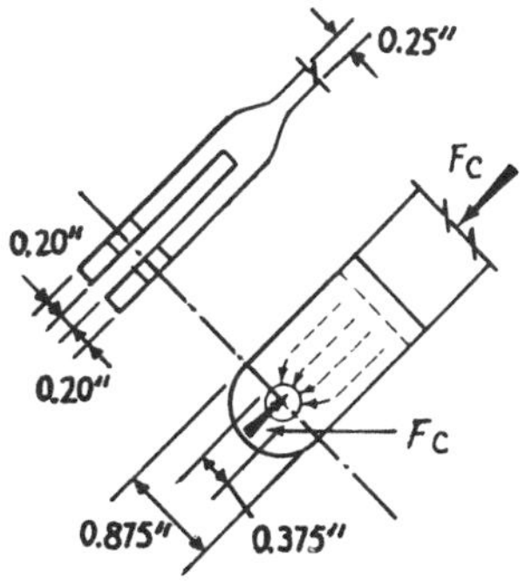

FIG. 5

$$\sigma_{AB} = \frac{2.23k}{0.125\ \square''} = 17.84 \text{ ksi tension.}$$

Stress in main bar BC:

$$\sigma_{BC} = \frac{F_C}{A}$$

$$A = (0.876'')(0.25'') = 0.219 \text{ in}^2$$

$$\sigma_{BC} = \frac{2.83}{0.219} = 12.92 \text{ ksi}$$

Stress in clevis part of bar AB:

$$\sigma_{AB}(\text{clevis}) = \frac{F_A}{A_{net}}$$

The net area of the clevis end of the bar is found from Figs. 4 and 5. The thickness in one direction is shown as 0.2" for two forks. In the other direction, by cutting through the pin, normal to the bar the dimension is 0.875" minus the width of the pin hole, 0.375"

$$A_{net} = 2(0.20'')(0.875 - 0.375) = 0.2$$

$$\sigma_{AB} = \frac{2.23}{0.2} = 11.15 \text{ ksi}$$

To find bearing stress between pin C and clevis:

$$\sigma_b = \frac{F_C}{A(\text{in contact})} = \frac{2.83 \text{ kips}}{(0.375)(0.20)(2)} = 18.86 \text{ ksi}$$

The area in contact is found by taking the width, 0.2", multiplied by the projection of the pin surface normal to the bar, 0.375". Pin C is also in bearing with the main plate, so the bearing stress is:

$$\sigma_b = \frac{F_C}{A} = \frac{2.83}{0.375)(0.25'')} = 30.18 \text{ ksi}$$

The shear stress of the pin at point C is double shear, then

$$\tau = \frac{F_C}{A} = \frac{2.83}{2\pi(.375/2)^2} = 12.81 \text{ ksi} .$$

• PROBLEM 3-11

A 1-in^2. rod L in. long is supended vertically as shown in Fig. 1. The weight per unit volume of the material is γ . Determine the normal stress in this rod using differential equations of equilibrium.

Solution: Since the only force applied is in the axial direction, $F_y = 0$. The shear stress, $\tau_{xy} = F_y/A$, is therefore zero. If $T_{xy} = 0$, then

$\partial T_{xy}/\partial y$ will also be zero.

$$\frac{\partial\sigma_x}{\partial x} + \frac{\partial T_{xy}}{\partial y} + x = 0 .$$

$$\frac{\partial\sigma_x}{\partial x} + X = 0$$

where X is the body force of the material $= \gamma$

$$\partial\sigma_x = -\gamma\partial x .$$

Integrating both sides of the equation yields

$$\sigma_x = -\gamma x + C_1$$

due to the boundary condition at $x = L$, $\sigma_x = 0$

$$\sigma_x(L) = -\gamma(L) + C_1 = 0 .$$

$$C_1 = \gamma L$$

$$\sigma_x = -\gamma x + \gamma L \Rightarrow \sigma_x = \gamma(L - x) .$$

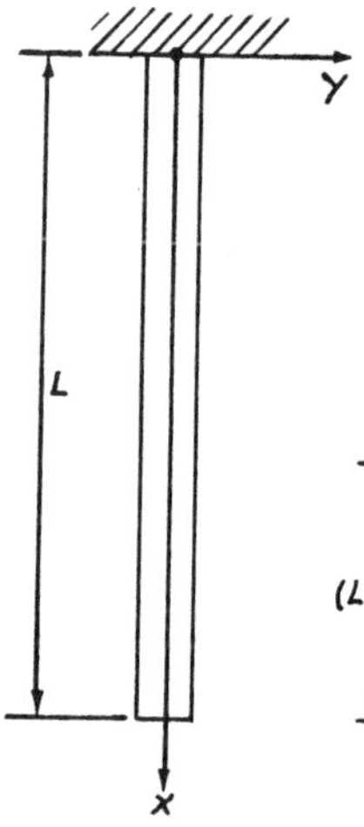

FIG. 1

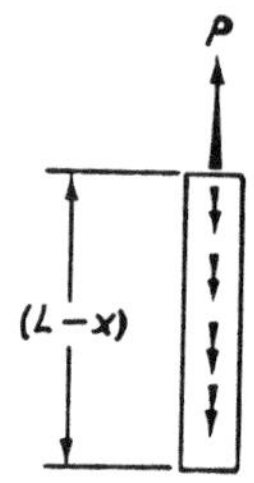

FIG. 2

The result obtained can be easily checked by cutting the rod (L - x) inches above the free end, Fig. (2)

$$\sigma_{(L-x)} = \frac{P}{A} \Rightarrow \sigma_{(L-x)} = \frac{(L-x)(\text{Area})\gamma}{\text{Area}} = \gamma(L - x)$$

Note that in more general problems deformations must be considered simultaneously in the analysis.

• PROBLEM 3-12

A 4 by 4-in. wood-post BC is connected to a 1-in. diameter steel eye-bar AB to form a hoist. A load of w = 7000 lbs is applied at point B on the hoist.

a) Determine the axial stresses in members AB and BC.

b) Determine the cross shearing stress in the 1-in. diameter bolt at point A.

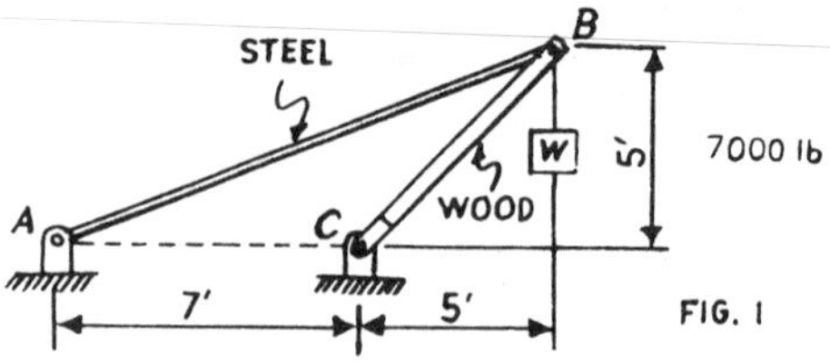

FIG. 1

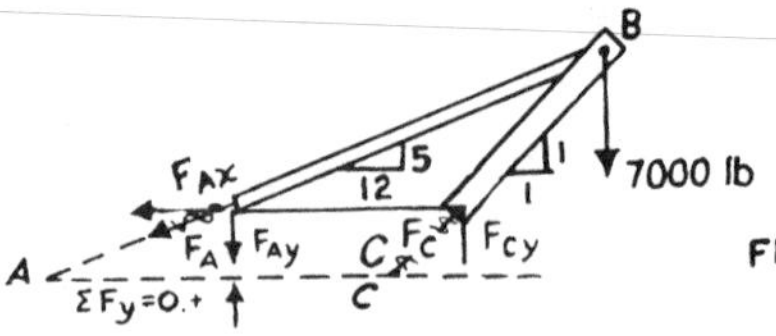

FIG. 2

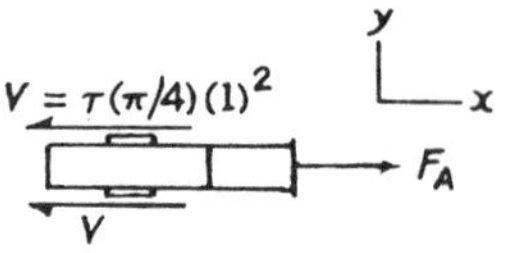

FIG. 3

Solution: a) Members AB, BC are subjected to axial loading using the equilibrium condition equations from Fig. 2. The vertical component of F_A is found by trigonometry to be $(5/13)F_A$. The horizontal component acts through the point C so it does not cause any moment.

$$\Sigma M_C = 0. \quad +\circlearrowright$$

$$(7000 \text{ lbs})(5\text{-ft}) - F_A(5/13)(7\text{-ft}) = 0 .$$

$$F_A = 13{,}000 \text{ lbs in tension}$$

$$\sigma_{AB} = \frac{F_A}{A} = \frac{13{,}000 \text{ lbs}}{(1)^2 \pi/4} = 16{,}552.1 \text{ psi}$$

$$\Sigma F_y = 0. \quad + \uparrow$$

$$-13{,}000(5/13) - 7000 + F_C(\sqrt{2}/2) = 0 .$$

$$F_C = \frac{2(5{,}000 + 7000)}{\sqrt{2}} = 16970.56 \text{ lbs}$$

$$\sigma_{BC} = \frac{16970.56}{4 \times 4} = 1060.66 \text{ psi} .$$

Check:

$$\Sigma M_A = 0. \quad + \circlearrowright$$

$$7000(12\text{-ft}) - F_C(\sqrt{2}/2)(7\text{-ft}) = 0 .$$

$$F_C = \frac{7000(12)2}{7\sqrt{2}} = 16970.56 \text{ lbs.}$$

b) From Fig. 3 it is apparent that the bolt at A is in double shear, so the shearing force $V = F_{AB}/2$ and the shearing stress is $\tau = V/A$.

$A = (1\text{-in})^2 \ \pi/4$ = x-sectional area of the bolt

$$\tau = \frac{13{,}000}{2(1)^2 \pi/4} = 8276 \text{ psi.}$$

• PROBLEM 3-13

The coupling of Fig. 1 is connected by two ½-in. diameter flange bolts (one on each side). Specifications for the bolts require that the axial tensile stress not exceed 12.0 ksi and the cross shearing stress not exceed 8.0 ksi. Determine the maximum value of the coupling load P that can be applied without exceeding either of the given requirements. Note: The cross-sectional area of the bolts at the root of the threads is 0.126 sq. in.

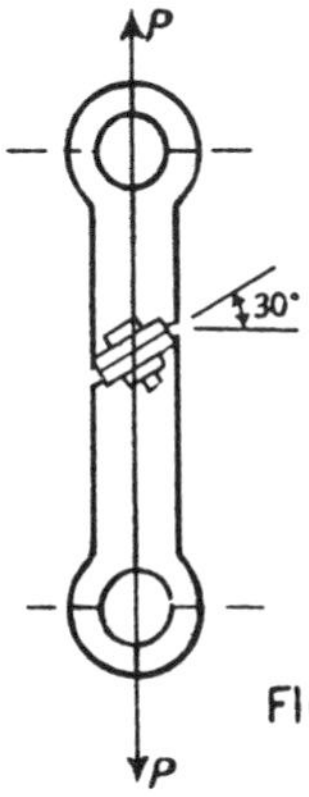

FIG. 1

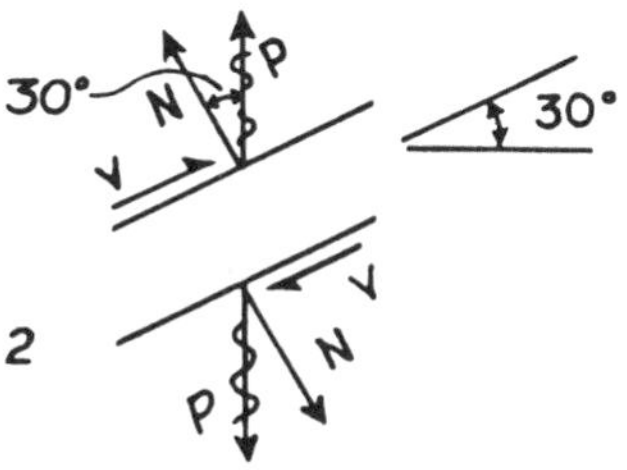

FIG. 2

Solution: To find the maximum value of the coupling load P, first sketching the free-body diagram of coupling at the connected section, Fig. (2), and resolve the load P into components normal and tangent to the connected plane:

$$N = P \cos 30°$$

$$V = P \sin 30°$$

Since N should not exceed the allowable axial tensile force, and V should not exceed the allowable shearing force,

$$P \cos 30° = N \le (12 \times 0.126) \times 2$$

$$P \sin 30° = V \le (8 \times 0.126) \times 2$$

or

$$P \le \frac{12 \times 0.126 \times 2}{\cos 30°} = 3.49 \text{ ksi} \qquad (1)$$

$$P \le \frac{8 \times 0.126 \times 2}{\sin 30°} = 4.032 \text{ ksi} \qquad (2)$$

The smaller value will control , so

$$P_{allowable} = 3.49 \text{ ksi} .$$

• PROBLEM 3-14

An axial force is applied to a shaft which rotates against a thrust bearing surface, shown in Fig. 1. Assume that the force intensity is distributed uniformly over the bearing surface, and that the coefficient of friction is 0.3. Calculate the stresses on the end of the shaft at point A.

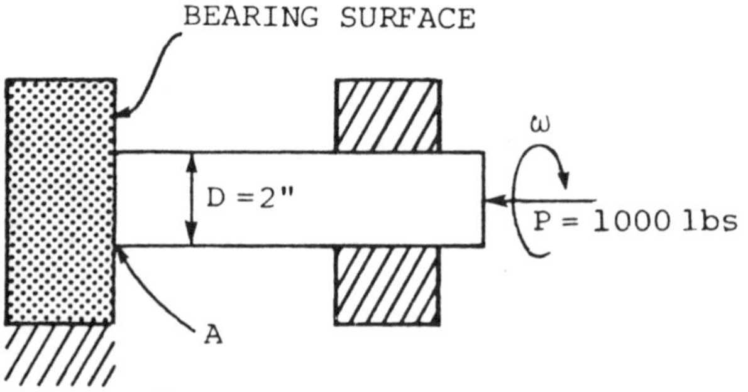

Fig. 1.

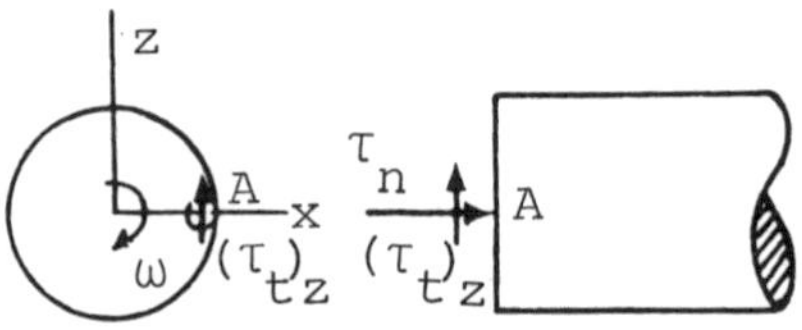

Fig. 2.

Solution: Fig. 2 shows a view of the end surface of the rod as seen from below and an interface at point A. To find the normal stress, note that the pressure p over the entire contact surface is uniform and must equal

$$p = \frac{\text{Force}}{\text{Area}} = \frac{P}{\pi D^2/4} = \frac{1000}{\pi 2^2/4} = 318 \text{ psi}$$

The normal stress τ_n at all interfaces over the contact surface is then 318 psi.

The shear stress is found as follows: In Figure 2, point A is moving straight down in the negative z direction. That means the frictional force, f, of the surface against the rod at point A is in the positive Z direction. At point A there is no component of the frictional force in the x direction. Therefore, the shear stress in the x direction, τ_{t_x} , is zero.

The coefficient of friction is defined as the ratio of the frictional force to the normal force.

$$\mu = \frac{f}{N} .$$

The frictional force, f, is then:

$$f = \mu N .$$

By differentiating both sides the force on a point is found,

$$df = \mu dN .$$

At A, df points in the z direction. The shear stress at point A is therefore in the z direction, τ_{t_z}. The stress at a point is:

$$\tau = \frac{dF}{dA} .$$

At point A:

$$\tau_{t_z} = \frac{df}{dA} .$$

Above, df was found to be μdN.

$$\tau_{t_z} = \mu \frac{dN}{dA} .$$

But the normal stress at point A is equal to dN/dA. This was calculated to be 318 psi.

Substituting in:

$$\tau_{t_z} = \mu \frac{dN}{dA} = .3 \times 318 = 95.4 \text{ psi} .$$

The stresses computed for the element are shown in Fig. 2.

• PROBLEM 3-15

A small diameter shaft is centered inside a larger diameter tube with a piece of rubber between the two and fastened to their surfaces. (a) Calculate the shear stress in the rubber as a function of radius. Compute the normal stress on cross-sectional planes of the tube below the connecting rubber.

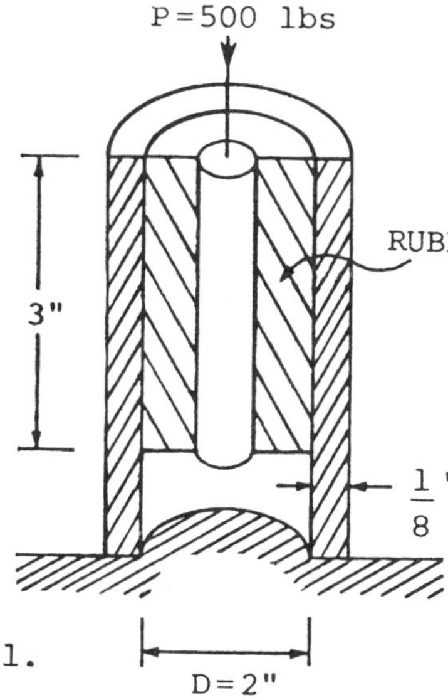

Fig. 1.

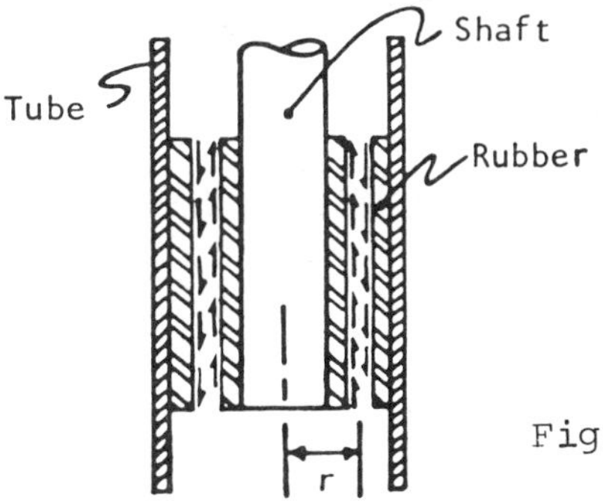

Fig. 2.

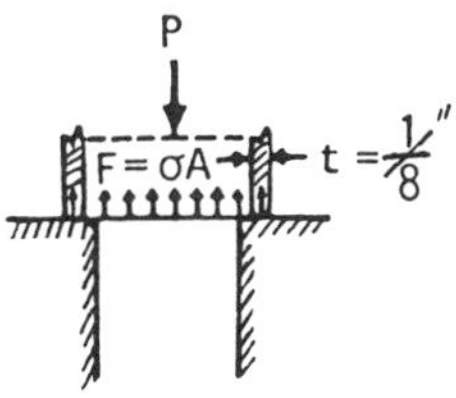

Fig. 3.

Solution: The load P acting downward on the shaft will be balanced by an equivalent force acting upward, which will have to be transmitted from the ground, through the tube and through the rubber. Fig. 2 shows the shear forces acting on a cylindrical cross-section of the rubber.

$$\Sigma F_{vertical} = 0$$

$$\tau \times A - P = 0 . \qquad (a)$$

The area at this cylindrical cross-section is

$$A = 2\pi r \times 3 = 6\pi r .$$

So, from (a):

$$\tau = \frac{P}{A} = \frac{500 \text{ lb}}{6\pi r} = \frac{26.5}{r} \text{ psi} .$$

The same load P must also be supported by the tube. A normal stress in the tube, acting over the tube's cross-sectional area, will supply the necessary reactive force. Figure 3 shows the normal forces acting on the tube.

From equilibrium, $P = \sigma A$

$$\sigma = \frac{P}{A}, \text{ where } A = 2\pi(R_{avg.})t$$

$$R_{avg.} = R_i + t/2$$

So,

$$\sigma = \frac{500 \text{ lb}}{2\pi(1'' + 1/16'')1/8''} = 599 \text{ psi} .$$

• PROBLEM 3-16

A rubber sleeve is attached by its internal surface to a steel shaft. The sleeve outer surface is attached to the interior of a tube (Fig. 1), to produce a flexible coupling for transmitting a torque from shaft to tube through the rubber. Compute the shear stress on a cylindrical surface in the rubber as a function of the cylinder radius.

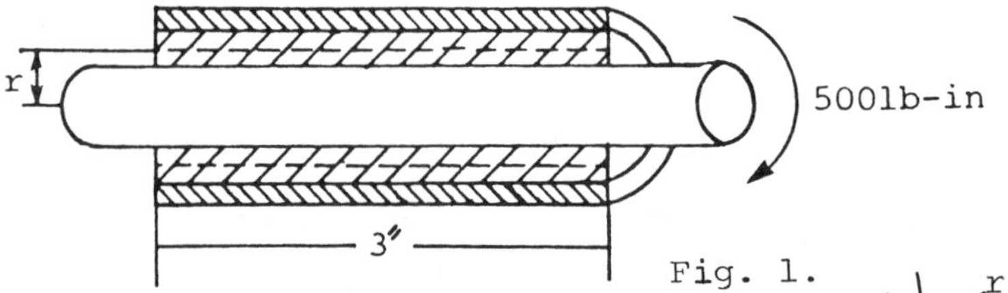

Fig. 1.

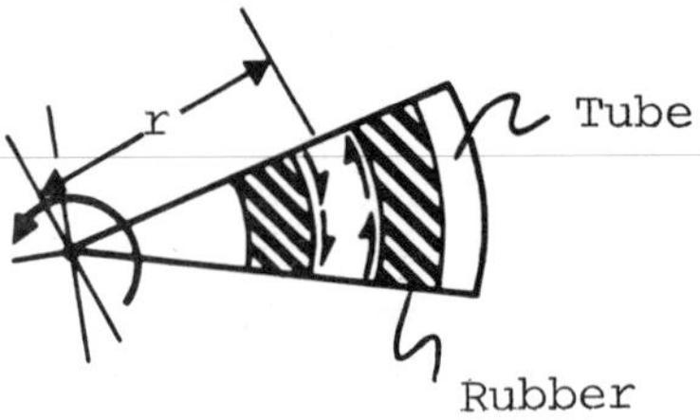

Fig. 2.

Solution: The shear stresses for a small arc of the rubber is shown in Figure 2. Shear Force, $F_s = \tau A = \tau(2\pi r)L$.

The torque is the force times the radius at which it is applied. The torque applied by the shaft to the rubber is reacted to by the rubber with equal torque.

Reactive torque in rubber

$$T_r = (F_s)r = \tau(2\pi r^2)L . \qquad (a)$$

Since the torque will be transmitted through the rubber to the tube,

$$T_r = T = 500 \text{ in.-lb} \qquad \text{(b)}$$

Substituting (a) into (b),

$$\tau(2\pi r^2)(3'') = 500 \text{ in.-lb}$$

$$\tau = \frac{26.5}{r^2} \text{ psi .}$$

• PROBLEM 3-17

At a given point in a machine element, the following stresses were evaluated: 8000 psi T and zero shear on a horizontal plane and 4000 psi C on a vertical plane. Determine the stresses at this point on a plane having a slope of 3 vertical to 4 horizontal.

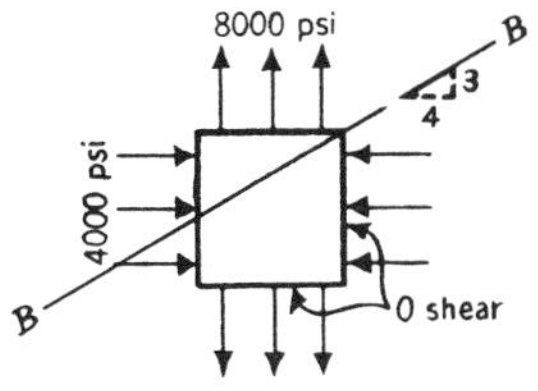

FIG. (a)

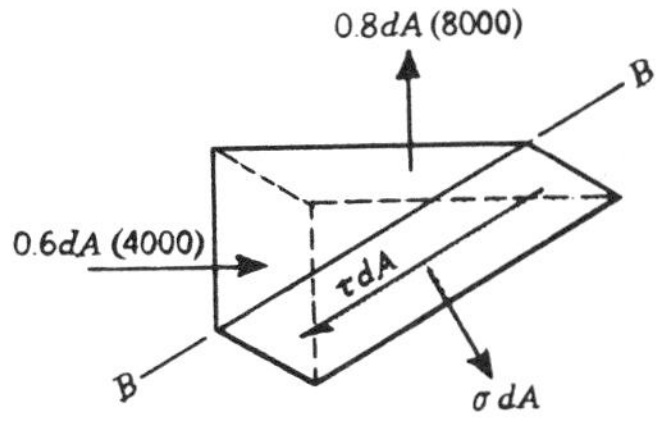

FIG. (b)

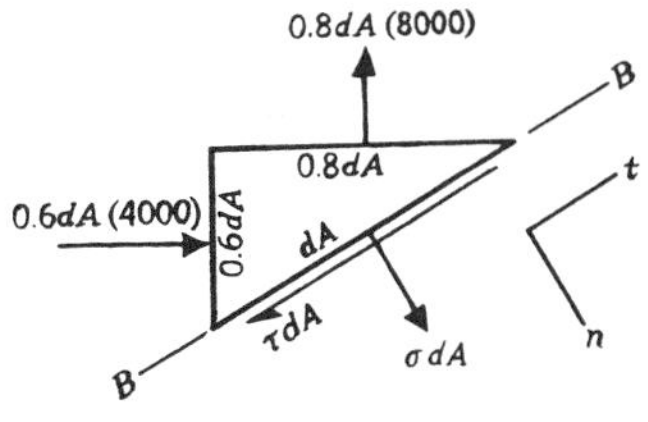

FIG. (c)

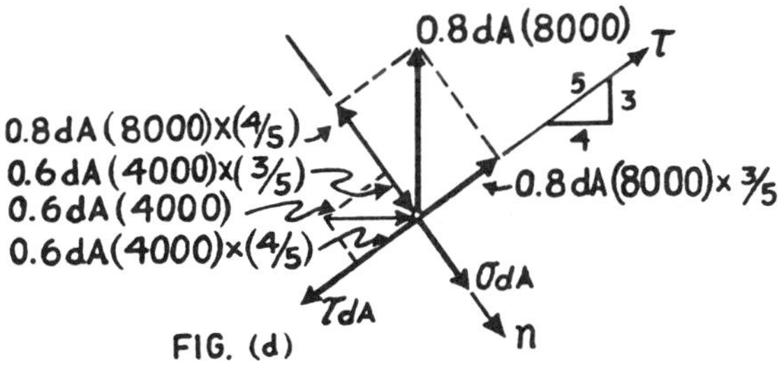

FIG. (d)

Solution: As an aid to visualization of the data, it is suggested that the differential block of Fig. a be drawn (a stress picture, not a free-body diagram). The next step is to draw a free-body diagram subjected to ordinary force vectors. Various satisfactory free-body diagrams can be used such as the wedge-shaped element defined by the three given planes in Fig. b, in which the shaded area indicates the plane on which the stresses to be evaluated are acting. To this area is assigned arbitrarily the magnitude dA, and the corresponding areas of the horizontal and vertical faces of the element are 0.8 dA and 0.6 dA, respectively. The forces acting on these areas will be as indicated in the diagram. It must be emphasized that force vectors act on these areas. For practical purposes, the two-dimensional free-body diagram of Fig. c will be adequate. Summing forces in the n direction yields the following:

$$\Sigma F_n = 0, \quad \sigma\, dA + 0.6\, dA\,(4000)(0.6) - 0.8\, dA(8000)(0.8) = 0,$$

from which

$$\sigma = 3680 \text{ psi T.}$$

When forces are summed in the t direction, the shearing stress is found to be

$$-\tau\, dA + 0.6\, dA(4000)(0.8) + 0.8\, dA(8000)(0.6) = 0$$

$$\tau = 5760 \text{ psi .}$$

Note that the normal stress should be designated as tension or compression. The presence of shearing stresses on the horizontal and vertical planes, had there been any, would merely have required two more forces on the free-body diagram; one parallel to the vertical face and one parallel to the horizontal face.

• PROBLEM 3-18

At a point in a structural member subjected to plane stress there are stresses on horizontal and vertical planes through the point as shown in Fig. a.

(a) Determine the principal stresses and the maximum shearing stress at the point.

(b) Locate the planes on which these stresses act and show the stresses on a complete sketch.

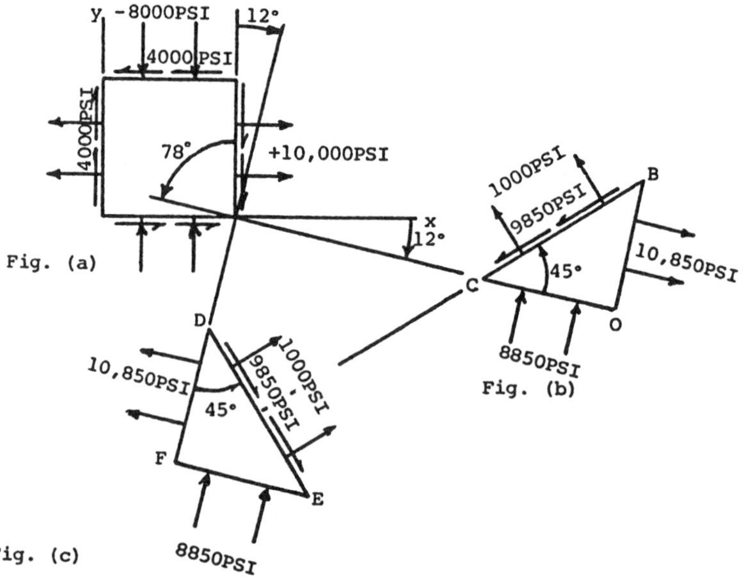

Solution: (a) On the basis of the established sign convention, σ_x is positive, whereas σ_y and τ_{xy} are negative.

$$\sigma_x = +10{,}000 \text{ psi}, \quad \sigma_y = -8000 \text{ psi}, \quad \text{and} \quad \tau_{xy} = -4000 \text{ psi}.$$

The principal stresses may be calculated from

$$\sigma_p = \frac{\sigma_x + \sigma_y}{2} \pm \sqrt{\left(\frac{\sigma_x - \sigma_y}{2}\right)^2 + (\tau_{xy})^2} \qquad \text{(I)}$$

Substituting values into (I) yields

$$\sigma_p = \frac{10{,}000 - 8000}{2} \pm \sqrt{\left(\frac{10{,}000 + 8000}{2}\right)^2 + (-4000)^2}$$

$$= 1000 \pm 9850$$

$$= 10{,}850 \text{ psi T} \quad \text{and} \quad 8850 \text{ psi C}$$

$$\sigma_z = 0 .$$

Since σ_{p_1} and σ_{p_2} are of opposite sign, the maximum shearing stress is

$$\tau_{max} = \frac{\sigma_1 - \sigma_2}{2} = \frac{10,850 - (-8850)}{2} = 9850 \text{ psi.}$$

(b) $$\tan 2\theta_p = \frac{\tau_{xy}}{\left(\frac{\sigma_x - \sigma_y}{2}\right)}$$

The convention for using this equation is that positive θ signifies a counterclockwise rotation from the x and y planes to the principal stress planes, and negative θ a clockwise rotation.

$$\tan 2\theta_p = -4000/9000 = -0.4444,$$

from which $$2\theta_p = -23.96^\circ$$

and $$\theta_p = -11.98^\circ \text{ or } 12^\circ \curvearrowright .$$

The required sketch is shown in Fig. b or c. Note that the planes of maximum shear, CB and DE, are perpendicular to each other, and at 45° angles to the no-shear (principal) planes.

The sum of the normal stresses on any two orthogonal planes is a constant for plane stress. Planes CB and DE are orthogonal and the normal stresses on them are obviously equal. Therefore,

$$2\sigma_n = \sigma_x + \sigma_y = 10,000 - 8000 = 2000$$

and $$\sigma_n = 1000 \text{ psi on the planes of maximum shear.}$$

• PROBLEM 3-19

A 5-ft structural steel bar ½ by 4 in. in cross section is to support an axial tensile load with allowable normal and shearing stresses of 18,000 psi and 8000 psi respectively and with an allowable elongation of 0.035 in. Determine the maximum permissible load.

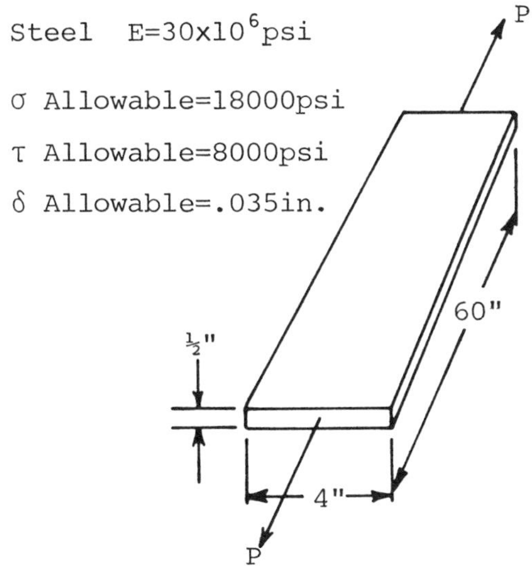

Fig. 1.

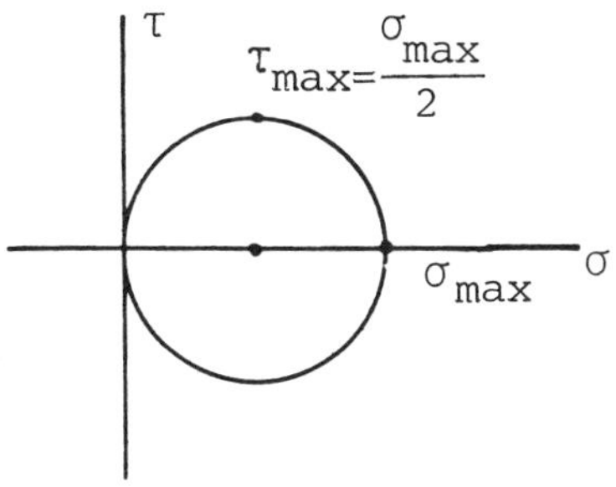

Fig. 2.

Solution: There are three factors here, maximum allowable normal stress, maximum allowable shear stress, and maximum allowable elongation. For each of the three factors, there is a corresponding load which will cause that particular maximum to be reached in the steel bar. The smallest of these three loads is P, the value of the steel bar's maximum allowable load. As soon as P is exceeded, the beam fails.

First, find the relationship between σ_{max} and τ_{max} from a Mohr's circle diagram. The Mohr's circle for the case of a bar undergoing tension is shown in Figure 2.

The maximum shear stress is half of the maximum normal stress. Thus, if $\sigma = 18{,}000$ psi,

$$\tau = \frac{18{,}000}{2} = 9000 \text{ psi}$$

and $\tau_{allow.}$ has been exceeded.

So, the maximum allowable shear stress will be exceeded before the maximum allowable normal stress.

The normal stress that corresponds to the maximum allowable shear stress is:

$$\sigma = 2(8000 \text{ psi}) = 16{,}000 \text{ psi.}$$

From the definition of normal stress:

$$\sigma = \frac{P}{A}$$

$$P = (16{,}000 \frac{\text{lb}}{\text{in}^2})(4'')(\tfrac{1}{2}'') = 32{,}000 \text{ lb.}$$

This force can also be calculated using shear stress alone. The maximum shear stress occurs on the plane with an orientation of 45°

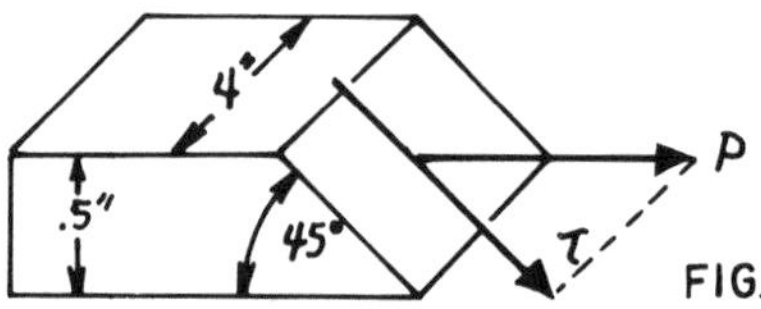

FIG. 3

$$\tau = \frac{F}{A} = \frac{P \sin 45^\circ}{(.5''/\sin 45^\circ)4''} = \frac{.707\,P}{(.707)4''}$$

$$\tau = \frac{P}{4}$$

$$P = 4\tau = 4(8000)$$

$$P = 32{,}000 \text{ lb.}$$

It still remains for us to determine whether the extension for this load exceeds the allowable elongation.

$$\delta = \frac{PL}{AE} = \frac{(32{,}000 \text{ lb})(60'')}{(2 \text{ in.}^2)(30 \times 10^6 \text{ in/in}^2)} = .032 \text{ in.}$$

This is within the allowable range of elongation, therefore,

$$P_{max} = 32{,}000 \text{ lb.} = 32.0 \text{ kips}$$

MOHR'S CIRCLE FOR STRESS

• PROBLEM 3-20

Find the principal stress and the orientation of the principal axes of stress for the following cases of plane stress.

(a) $\sigma_x = 4{,}000$ psi

$\sigma_y = 0$

$\tau_{xy} = 8{,}000$ psi

(b) $\sigma_x = -12{,}000$ psi

$\sigma_y = 5{,}000$ psi

$\tau_{xy} = -10{,}000$ psi

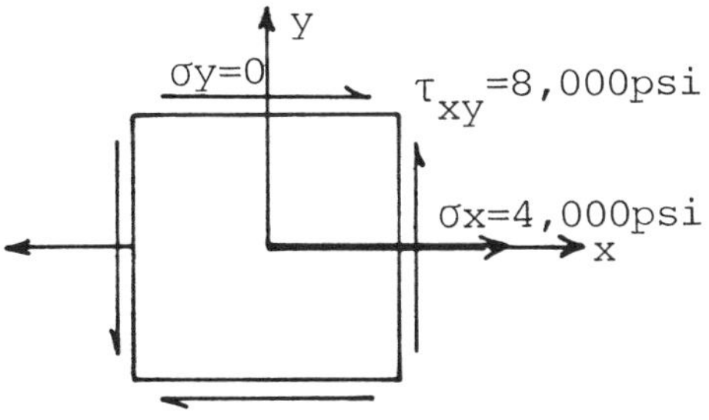

Fig. 1a.

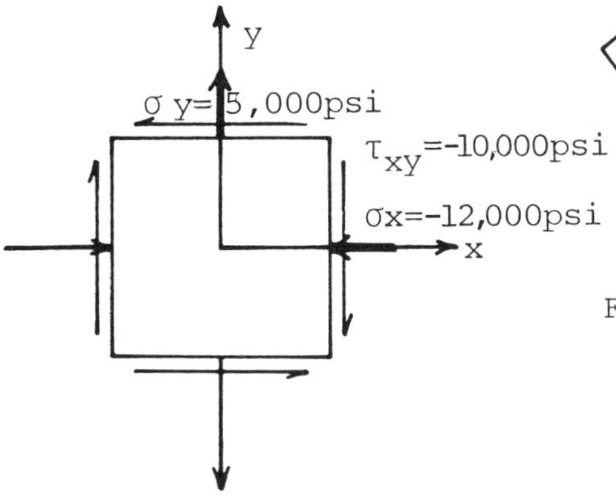

Fig. 1b.

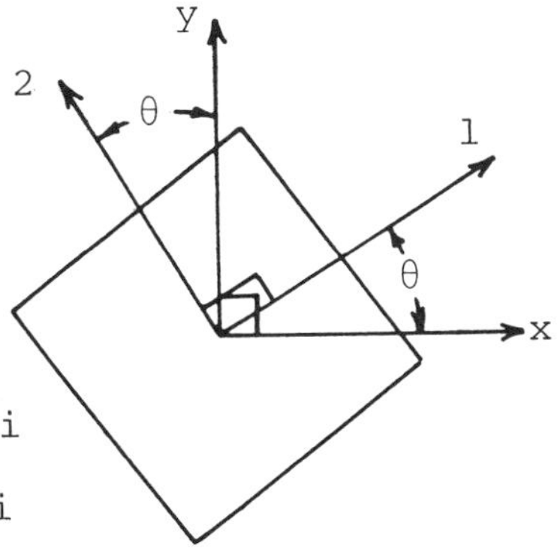

Fig. 1c.

Solution: We have a stress field given for plane stress as shown in Figure 1c .

We are given the normal and shear stresses with respect to the x-y coordinate axes. We want to determine the principal strains σ_1 and σ_2 and the angle θ through which the x-y axes must rotate so that they coincide with the 1-2 axes. We will make use of Mohr's circle analysis.

(a)

$$\sigma_x = 4{,}000 \text{ psi}$$

$$\sigma_y = 0$$

$$\tau_{xy} = 8{,}000 \text{ psi}$$

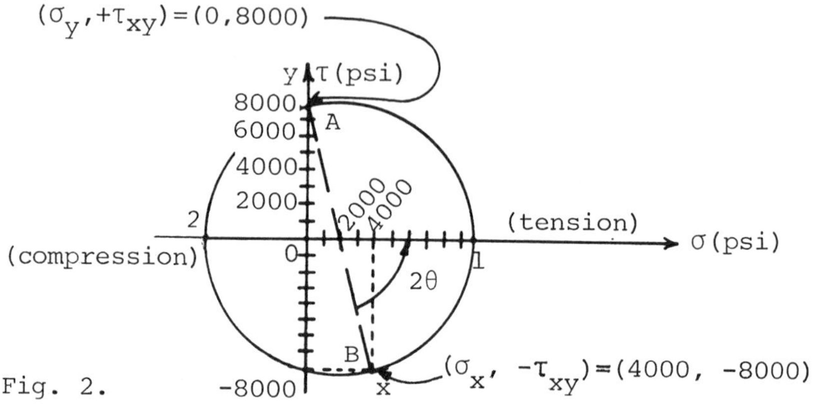

Fig. 2.

The Mohr's circle is laid out as shown in Figure 2.

First, point A is plotted at $\sigma = \sigma_y$, $\tau = \tau_{xy}$. Point B is plotted at $\sigma = \sigma_x$, $\tau = -\tau_{xy}$. This is the standard convention for construction of the Mohr's circle.

The center of the circle, C, is the point on the σ axis half way between σ_y and σ_x, as can be seen from Figure 2. Saying the same thing in symbols, the value of C can be obtained by the following equation:

$$\frac{\sigma_y + \sigma_x}{2} = C .$$

Substituting in the values given at the beginning of the problem:

$$\frac{0 + 4000}{2} = C = 2000$$

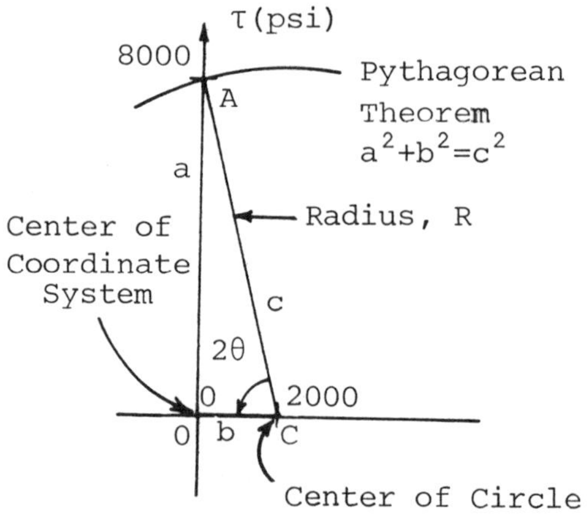

Fig. 3.

The radius is found by the Pythagorean theorem: (See Figure 3) The length of the vertical side of the triangle is the value of τ_{xy}, 8000. The length of the horizontal side can be expresses as

$$\frac{\sigma_x - \sigma_y}{2} = \frac{4000 - 0}{2} = 2000 .$$

$$R = \sqrt{(8000)^2 + (2000)^2} = 8250 \text{ psi} .$$

The principal stresses are those normal stresses for which there are no corresponding shear stresses. Thus from Figure 2,

$$\sigma_1 = 2000 + R$$

$$\sigma_1 = 10{,}250 \text{ psi}$$

$$\sigma_2 = 2000 - R = -6250 \text{ psi}$$

The angle that the x-y coordinate system has to rotate to coincide with the principal stress coordinate system is called θ. Positive θ means a counter-clockwise rotation of the x-y coordinate system into the principal stress coordinate system. Negative values of θ indicate clockwise rotation.

2θ is the angle between two axes on the Mohr's circle whose physical angle is θ. (Note that because this is true, the x and y axes are 180° apart on the Mohr circle as opposed to 90° in the physical situation.)

Therefore,

$$2\theta = \arctan\left(\frac{8000}{2000}\right) = 76^\circ$$

$$\theta = 38^\circ$$

This means that if the x-y coordinate axes were rotated 38° clockwise, and everything else was kept stationary, the stress in the x direction would change from 4,000 psi to 10,250 psi, the stress in the y direction would change from 0 to -6,250 psi, and the shear, τ_{xy} would go from 8,000 psi to zero.

(b) As in (a), we first construct the Mohr's circle:

As mentioned in part (a), σ_x is plotted with $-\tau_{xy}$. In this case $\tau_{xy} = -10{,}000$, so $-\tau_{xy} = +10{,}000$. The center of the circle is found as before:

$$C = \frac{\sigma_y + \sigma_x}{2} = \frac{5000 + -12000}{2} = -3500.$$

The Pythagorean theorem is again used to find the radius. The length of the vertical side of the triangle is $\tau_{xy} = -10{,}000$ or 10,000 since we are just interested in magnitude. The length of the horizontal side is:

$$\frac{\sigma_x - \sigma_y}{2} = \frac{-5000 - 12000}{2} = -8500,$$

and the magnitude is 8,500. The radius is:

$$R = \sqrt{(10{,}000)^2 + (8{,}500)^2} = 13{,}100$$

Therefore,

$$\sigma_1 = -3500 + 13{,}100 = 9600 \text{ psi}$$

$$\sigma_2 = -3500 - 13{,}100 = -16{,}600 \text{ psi}$$

Finding θ is slightly more involved than in the last case. As can be

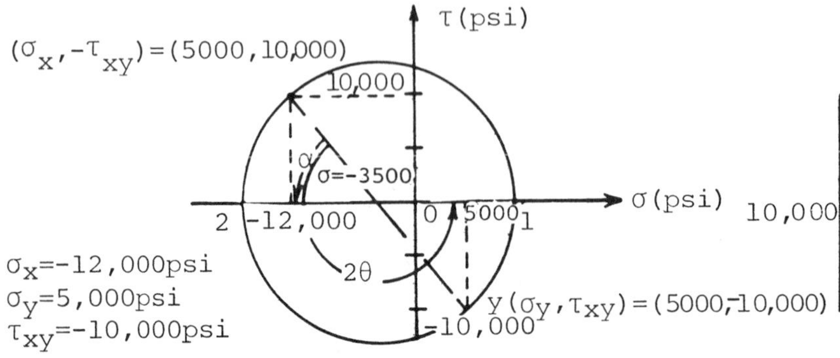

Fig. 4.

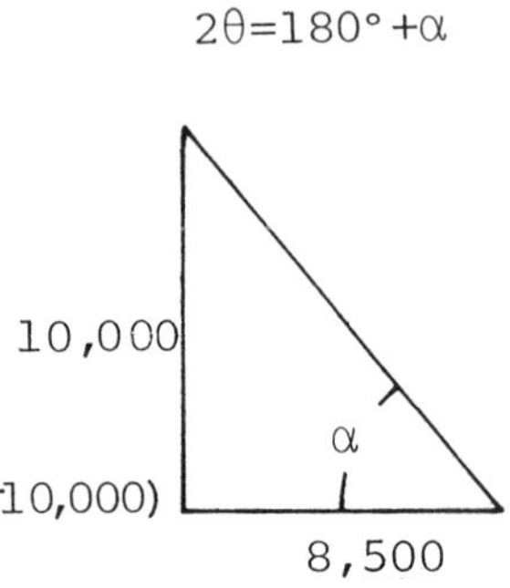

Fig. 5.

seen from Figure 4, 2θ is equal to 180° plus the angle α.

$$2\theta = 180^\circ + \alpha$$

The lengths of the sides of the triangle have already been found.

$$\alpha = \text{arc tan}\,\frac{10000}{8000} = 49.6^\circ .$$

Substituting the value of α into the equation:

$$2\theta = 180^\circ + 49.6^\circ = 229.6^\circ$$

$$\theta = 114.8^\circ .$$

This means that if the x-y coordinate axes were rotated 114.8° counterclockwise, and everything else was kept stationary, σ_x would go from -12,000 psi to 9,600 psi, σ_y would go from 5,000 psi to -16,600 psi, and τ_{xy} would go from -10,000 psi to zero.

Check: Since the sum of the normal stresses is always constant:

$$\sigma_x + \sigma_y = \sigma_1 + \sigma_2$$

From part (a):

$$\sigma_x = 4{,}000 \text{ psi} \qquad \sigma_1 = 10{,}250$$

$$\sigma_y = 0 \qquad \sigma_2 = -6250$$

$$\sigma_x + \sigma_y = 4000 + 0 \qquad \sigma_1 + \sigma_2 = 10{,}250 - 6250$$

$$4000 = 4000 .$$

From part (b):

$$\sigma_x + \sigma_y = \sigma_1 + \sigma_2$$

$$-12{,}000 + 5{,}000 = 9{,}600 - 16{,}600$$

$$7000 = 7000 .$$

A more involved check involves going back to the equations the Mohr circle is based on.

$$\sigma_{p_1,p_2} = \frac{\sigma_x + \sigma_y}{2} \pm \sqrt{\left(\frac{\sigma_x - \sigma_y}{2}\right)^2 + \tau_{xy}^2} .$$

For part (a):

$$\sigma_x = 4000 \quad \sigma_y = 0 \quad \tau_{xy} = 8000 \quad \sigma_1 = 10250 \quad \sigma_2 = -6250$$

$$\sigma_{1,2} = \frac{4000}{2} \pm \sqrt{\left(\frac{4000}{2}\right)^2 + (8000)^2}$$

$$= 2000 \pm 8250$$

$$\sigma_1 = 10250 \qquad \sigma_2 = -6250 .$$

For part (b):

$$\sigma_x = -12000, \quad \sigma_y = 5000, \quad \tau_{xy} = -10,000, \quad \sigma_1 = 9600, \quad \sigma_2 = -16,600$$

$$\sigma_{1,2} = \frac{-12000 + 5000}{2} \pm \sqrt{\left(\frac{-12000 - 5000}{2}\right)^2 + (-10,000)^2}$$

$$\sigma_{1,2} = -3500 \pm 13,100$$

$$\sigma_1 = 9600 \qquad \sigma_2 = -16,600$$

The angle θ can be verified using the following equation:

$$\tan 2\theta = \frac{\tau_{xy}}{(\sigma_x - \sigma_y)/2} .$$

For part (a):

$$\tan 2\theta = \frac{8000}{(4000)/2} = 4$$

$$2\theta = \text{arc} \tan 4 = 76^\circ$$

$$\theta = 38^\circ$$

For part (b):

$$\tan 2\theta = \frac{-10,000}{(-12,000 - 5,000)/2} = \frac{-10,000}{-8500}$$

minus over minus. Remember to add 180° .

$$2\theta = \text{arc} \tan \frac{-10,000}{-8500} = 49.6^\circ + 180^\circ = 229.6^\circ$$

$$\theta = 114.8^\circ .$$

THIN-WALLED CYLINDERS AND SPHERES

• PROBLEM 3-21

> Equal and opposite torques are applied to the ends of a tube which may be considered thin-walled. Calculate the stresses in the wall on a cross-sectional plane between the ends.

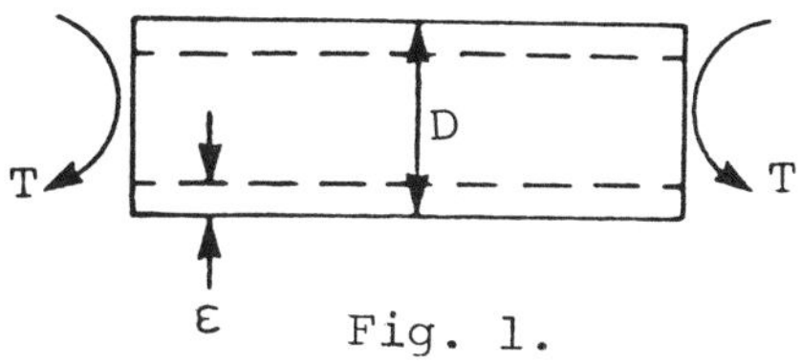

Fig. 1.

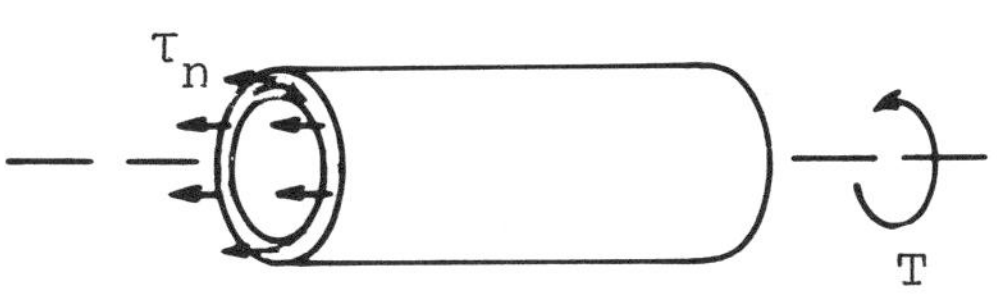

Fig. 2.

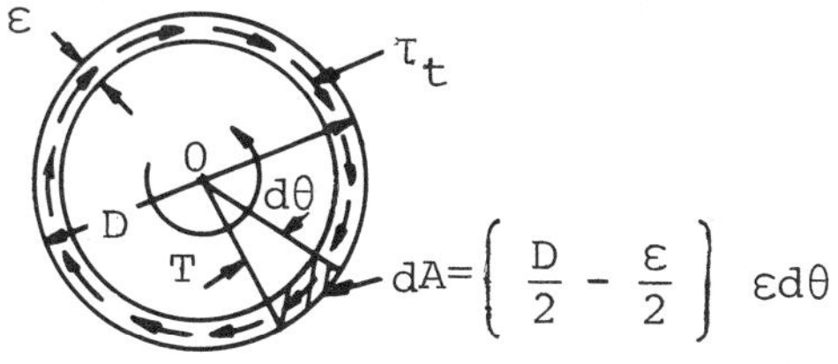

Fig. 3.

Solution: Imagine "cutting" the cylinder over a cross section and forming a free body of the portion on one side of the cut (see Fig. 2.) Assume for a moment that a normal stress τ_n exists for the section. Because the cylinder wall is very thin, τ_n may be considered constant in value across the thickness of the wall, and additionally, because of axial symmetry, τ_n does not vary along the circumference. Accordingly τ_n is then constant over the entire section. Using the static equilibrium equation, from Figure 2:

$$\Sigma F_{axil} = 0 \quad + \leftarrow$$

$$\tau_n \pi(D - \epsilon)\epsilon = 0 \qquad \text{since} \quad \pi(D - \epsilon)\epsilon \neq 0$$

therefore

$$\tau_n = 0 .$$

Furthermore, by choosing directions that are radial and transverse to the section (i.e., out from the center 0 in Fig. 3 or tangent to the midcircle, respectively) we may assume that the shear stress in the radial direction is zero since the radial stress cancels through symmetry, and that only the transverse shear stress τ_t is nonzero. Finally, because the cylinder is thin, τ_t is taken as uniform over the thickness of the cylinder, and, because of the axial symmetry, τ_t is also uniform in the transverse direction of the section. Thus, τ_t is constant for the entire cross section. Summing the moments about the axis of the cylinder by using the static equilibrium equation, from Figure 3:

$$\Sigma M_{0(axil)} = 0 \quad + \circlearrowright$$

dA is found by using arclength x thickness. The mean radius is D/2 - ϵ/2, the subtended angle is $d\theta$, and the thickness is ϵ.

$$\iint_A \left(\frac{D}{2} - \frac{\epsilon}{2}\right)\tau_t \, dA - T = 0$$

$$T = \iint_A \left(\frac{D}{2} - \frac{\epsilon}{2}\right)\tau_t \, dA = \int_0^{2\pi} \tau_t\left[\left(\frac{D}{2} - \frac{\epsilon}{2}\right)\right]^2 \epsilon d\theta = 2\pi\tau_t\left(\frac{D}{2} - \frac{\epsilon}{2}\right)^2 \epsilon$$

therefore

$$\tau_t = \frac{2T}{\pi(D - \epsilon)^2 \epsilon} .$$

• PROBLEM 3-22

A compressed air tank that may be considered thin-walled is subjected to an internal pressure. Use an infinitesimal element ABCD as a free body from the tank wall, and calculate the stresses on the surfaces of the element.

Solution: Examine face BC by considering a free body of part of the tank, as shown in Fig. (b). Because there is only a net force from the pressure in the axial direction of the cylinder, there is only normal

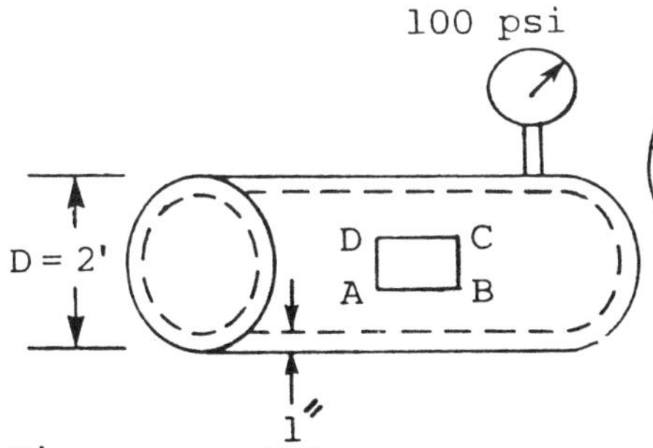

Fig. a.

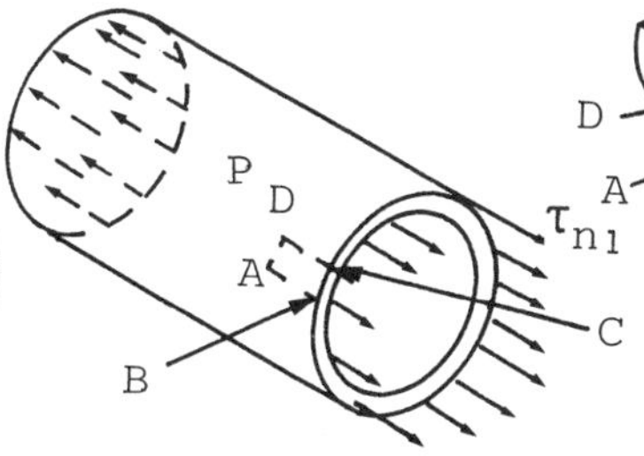

Fig. b.

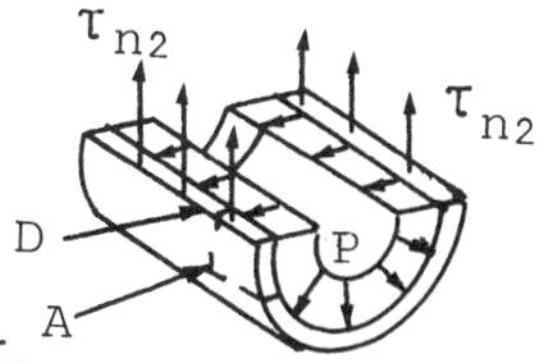

Fig. c.

stress over the cut section of the cylinder, as has been indicated in the diagram. Furthermore, because the wall of the tank is thin compared to the diameter, assume that the stress τ_{n_1} is uniform across the thickness. Finally for reasons of axial symmetry of geometry and loading, this stress is uniform around the cross section. Now from considerations of equilibrium in the axial direction (Force pulling on cylindrical cross-section) = (force due to pressure on cylinder ends), that is

$$(\tau_{n_1})(2\pi R)(t) = p(\pi r_i^2) .$$

Using mean radius,

$$R = \frac{D - t}{2} , \quad \text{and} \quad r_i = \frac{D}{2} - t ,$$

substituting in:

$$\tau_{n_1} \pi(D - t)t = p\pi\left(\frac{D}{2} - t\right)^2$$

therefore

$$\tau_{n_1} = \frac{p\left(\frac{D}{2} - t\right)^2}{(D - t)t} = \frac{(100)(12 - \frac{1}{4})^2}{(23.75)(\frac{1}{4})} = 2325 \text{ psi} \qquad \text{(a)}$$

Hence, on face BC there is a uniform stress of 2325 psi. This must also be true for face AD.

To expose face DC next, consider a half-cylinder of unit length such as is shown in Fig. (c). Because it is far from the ends and because the wall is thin, assume that the stress τ_{n_1} shown is uniform over the cut section. Assume that the area considered is far from the ends so that end disturbances (due to non-symmetry, for example) are not present. Also, if a very thin wall is assumed, there will be no distribution of forces over the area, but rather a single value. A pressure p is shown acting normal to the inside wall surface. (The stress τ_{n_1} computed above is not shown to avoid cluttering the diagram.) Now consider Figure (d) for equilibrium in the vertical direction.

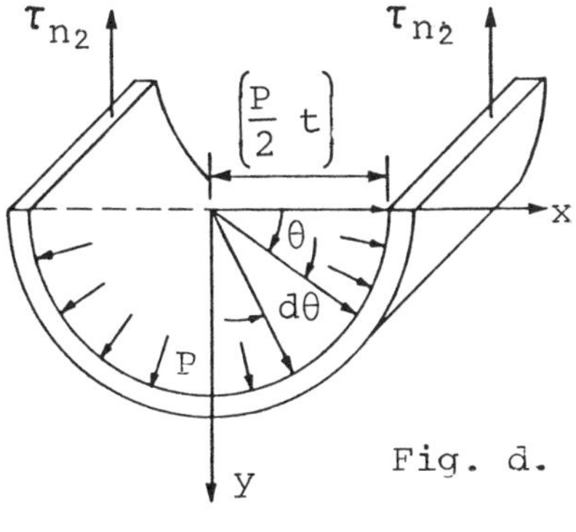

Fig. d.

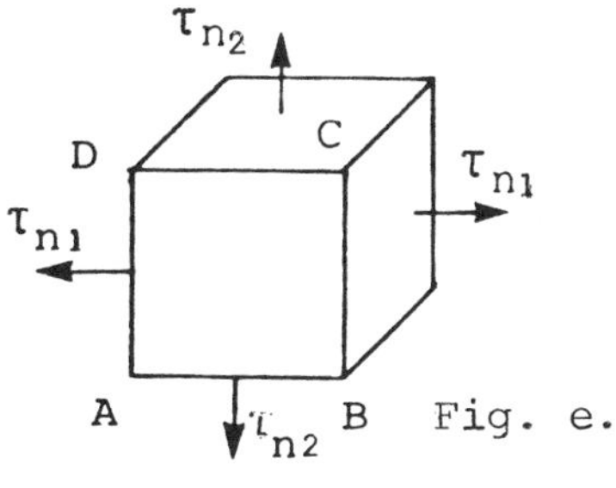

Fig. e.

$$2F_{n_2} = \int_A p\, dA \sin\theta$$

$$2[(\tau_{n_2})(t)(\text{length})] = (\text{length})\int_0^{\pi} pr_i\, d\theta \sin\theta$$

For a unit length, this becomes:

$$2[(\tau_{n_2})(t)(1)] = \int_0^{\pi} p\left(\frac{D}{2} - t\right) d\theta\,(1)\sin\theta$$

therefore

$$\tau_{n_2} = \frac{1}{2t}\left[p\left(\frac{D}{2} - t\right)\right](-\cos\theta)\Big|_0^{\pi}$$

$$= \frac{p\left(\frac{D}{2} - t\right)}{t} = 4700 \text{ psi} \qquad \text{(b)}$$

Also, from studies of hydrostatics, the force in a particular direction from a uniform pressure on a curved surface equals the pressure times the projected area of this surface in the direction of the desired force. Thus, for the case at hand the projected area is that of a rectangle $1 \times (D - 2t)$ so that the

$$\text{Force} = p \times (\text{Area})_{\text{projected}} = p[1 \times (D - 2t)] = p(D - 2t)$$

and

$$\tau_{n_2} = \frac{\text{Force}}{\text{cross-sectional area}} = \frac{p(D - 2t)}{(2)(1)(t)} = \frac{p(D/2 - t)}{t}$$

which is the same as (b).

The stress τ_{n_2} is called the hoop stress. It is about twice the axial stress τ_{n_1}. Element ABCD with the stresses present is shown in Figure (e).

• PROBLEM 3-23

A thin-walled pressure vessel is subjected to an internal gauge pressure. Determine the normal stresses on an infinitesimal element.

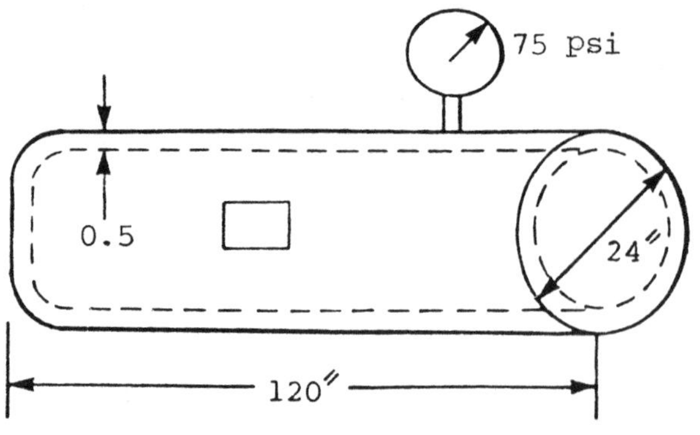

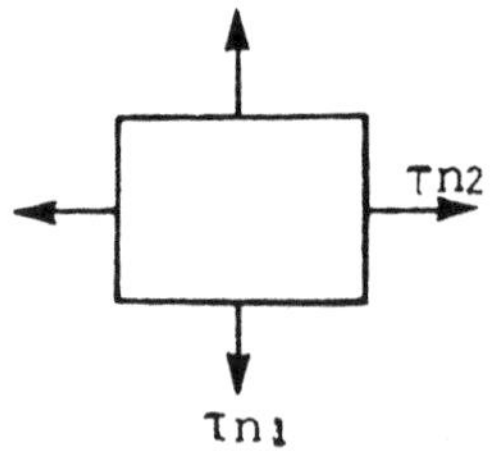

Solution: The equations for the normal stresses $(\tau_n)_1$ and $(\tau_n)_2$ for a thin cylinder acted on by internal pressure p, at a point far from the ends of the cylinder are

$$\tau_{\theta\theta} = (\tau_n)_2 = \frac{pr}{t} \tag{1}$$

and

$$\tau_{zz} = (\tau_n)_1 = \frac{pr}{2t} . \tag{2}$$

The internal pressure is 75 psi above atmospheric pressure. This is the same as the net internal pressure, or the equivalent internal pressure if the external pressure were zero. Since this is the pressure used to derive (1) and (2), we can use it without modification for this problem.

From (1),

$$(\tau_n)_2 = \frac{(75 \text{ psi})(12'')}{(\frac{1}{2}'')} = 1800 \text{ psi} . \tag{3}$$

From (2),

$$(\tau_n)_1 = \frac{(75 \text{ psi})(12'')}{2(\frac{1}{2}'')} = 900 \text{ psi} . \tag{4}$$

It is seen from (3) and (4) that both components of normal stress are much larger in value than the pressure that caused them. This can be accounted for by the fact that the internal pressure acts over a large area to create certain forces that must be balanced by forces in the cylinder acting over small areas. This produces rather large stresses in the cylinder.

Also note that the axial stress $(\tau_n)_1$ is half as large as the tangential stress $(\tau_n)_2$.

Equations (1) and (2) should be used only where $t \ll r$ and away from the ends of the cylinder.

• PROBLEM 3-24

Calculate the membrane stresses σ_φ , σ_θ for a cylindrical tank of radius r and wall thickness h if it carries a uniform internal pressure p.

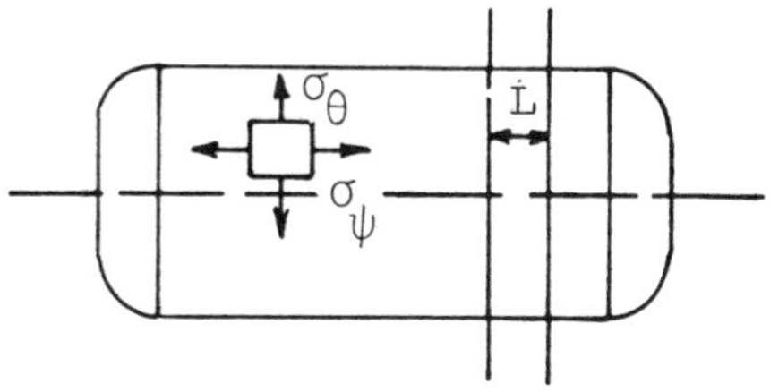

Fig. 1.

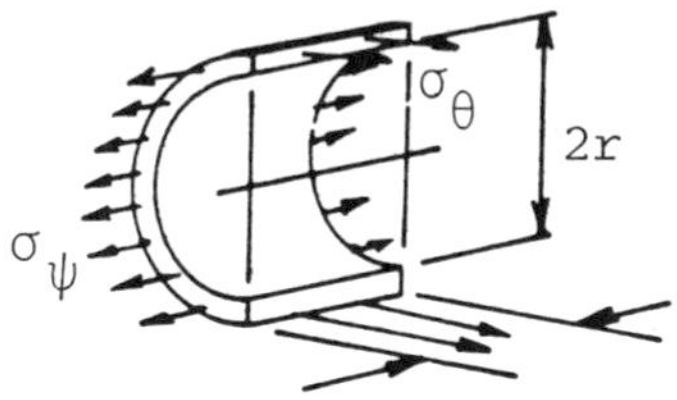

Fig. 2.

Fig. 3.

Solution: In this case, cylindrical vessel has $r_1 = \infty$ and $r_2 = r$

$$\frac{\sigma_\varphi}{\infty} + \frac{\sigma_\theta}{r_2} = \frac{p}{h}$$

$$\sigma_\theta = \frac{pr_2}{h} = \frac{pr}{h} .$$

To find the other principal stress σ_φ in the longitudinal direction, cut the cylinder in two by a section normal to its axis of revolution and consider the equilibrium of that portion to one side of the section (shown in Fig. 4).

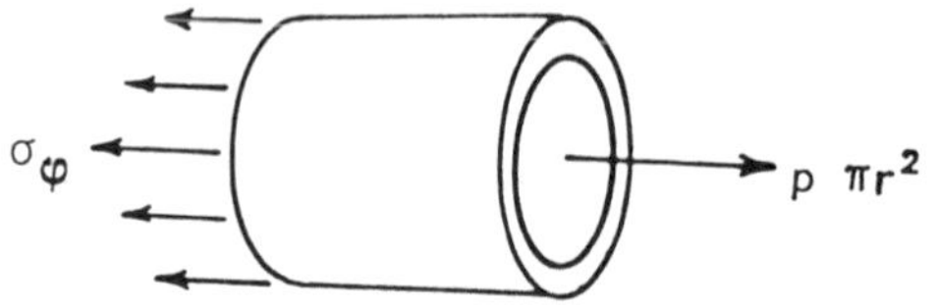

Fig. 4

The resultant thrust on the end of the tank is $p\pi r^2$ and it must be balanced by a uniform longitudinal stress σ_φ around the circumference of the cylinder. Thus,

$$\sigma_\varphi(2\pi rh) = \pi r^2 p$$

$$\sigma_\varphi = \frac{\pi r^2 p}{2\pi rh} = \frac{pr}{2h}$$

Comparing σ_θ, and σ_φ, it is found that for a circular cylindrical tank subjected to uniform internal pressure, the longitudinal stress σ_φ is half as large as the hoop stress σ_θ.

• PROBLEM 3-25

A cylindrical thin-walled pressure vessel 25 in. in diameter has a welded spiral seam as indicated in Figure 1. If the vessel is subjected to an internal pressure of 200 psi, determine the normal and shearing forces which must be carried per linear inch of the weld.

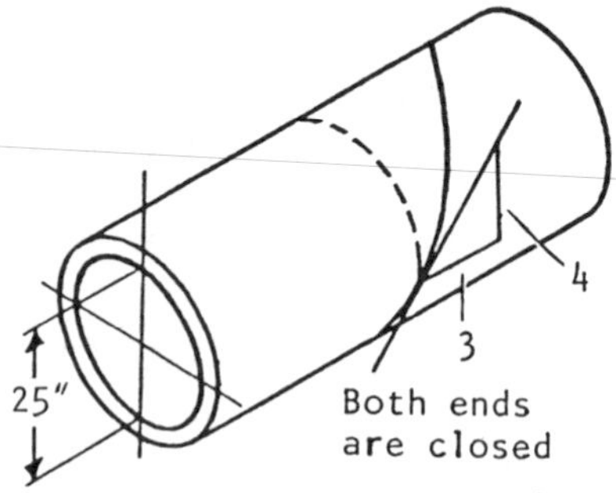

Fig. 1

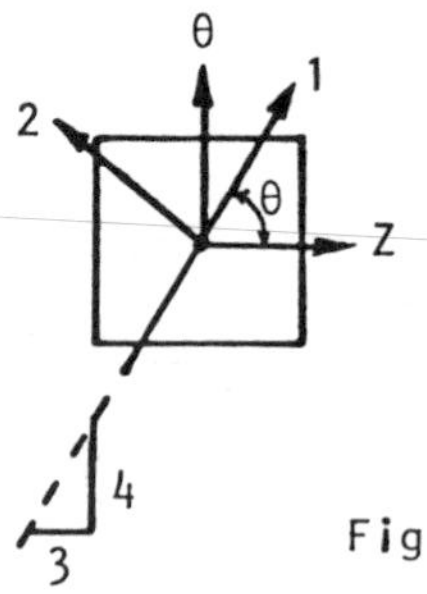

Fig. 2a

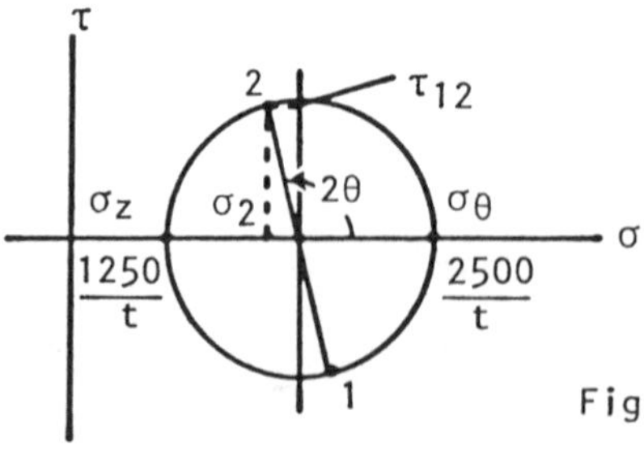

Fig. 2a

Solution: For a thin-walled cylinder with closed ends under the influence of an internal pressure p:

$$\text{axial normal stress, } \sigma_Z = \frac{pr}{2t} \qquad (1)$$

and

$$\text{tangential normal stress, } \sigma_\theta = \frac{pr}{t} . \qquad (2)$$

These equations have been derived for internal pressures given in terms of gauge pressures (absolute pressure minus atmospheric pressure). Since the question does not state whether the 200 psi is gauge or absolute, we will assume 200 psig, that is, gauge pressure. Then, from (1)

$$\sigma_Z = \frac{(200\text{ psi})(12.5'')}{2t} = \frac{1250}{t}\text{ psi}$$

$$\sigma_\theta = \frac{(200\text{ psi})(12.5'')}{t} = \frac{2500}{t}\text{ psi} .$$

This state of stress is shown in Figure 2b.

From Figure 2a, note that the necessary change in orientation to get from θ - Z coordinates to 1 - 2 coordinates is

$$\theta = \text{arc tan } 4/3 = 53.1^\circ .$$

Now rotate $2\theta = 106.2^\circ$ counterclockwise around the Mohr's circle of Figure 2b. From Fig. 2a, note that σ_2 is the normal stress that tends to separate the seam. From Fig. 2b one can find that the distance from zero to the center of the circle is the average of the farthest and nearest points on the perimeter:

$$\frac{\sigma_\theta + \sigma_Z}{2} .$$

The distance from the center of the circle to σ_2 is the length of the radius times $\cos(2\theta)$. The length of the radius is half the distance between two points on the perimeter at opposite ends of a diameter:

$$R = \frac{\sigma_\theta - \sigma_Z}{2} .$$

Putting it all together results in:

$$\sigma_2 = \frac{\sigma_\theta + \sigma_Z}{2} + R\cos(2\theta)$$

$$= \frac{\sigma_\theta + \sigma_Z}{2} + \frac{\sigma_\theta - \sigma_Z}{2}\cos(2\theta) .$$

This is the same as the basic equation for normal stress on a plane at an angle θ to the x-y plane:

$$\sigma = \frac{\sigma_x + \sigma_y}{2} + \frac{\sigma_x - \sigma_y}{2}\cos 2\theta + \tau_{xy}\sin 2\theta .$$

In the equation for σ_2 above, τ is zero.

$$\sigma_2 = \frac{\frac{2500}{t} + \frac{1250}{t}}{2} + \frac{\frac{2500}{t} - \frac{1250}{t}}{2}(\cos 106.2^\circ)$$

$$\sigma_2 = \frac{1700}{t}\text{ psi} .$$

The normal force tending to tear the seam is

$$F_n = (\sigma_2)(\text{Area}_{\text{seam}}) = \left(\frac{1700}{t}\right)(Lt) = 1700\text{ L} .$$

Thus, the normal force per linear inch of the seam which must be carried by the weld is

$$f_n = 1700 \text{ lb/in} \quad \text{(tension)}$$

From Fig. 2b, the shear stress tending to tear the seam is determined. The magnitude of τ_{12} is the radius times $\cos 2\theta$.

The radius was found above to be:

$$R = \frac{\sigma_\theta - \sigma_Z}{2}$$

Putting it together:

$$\tau_{12} = \frac{\sigma_\theta - \sigma_Z}{2} (\sin 2\theta) \quad .$$

This is the same as the basic equation for shear stress on a plane at an angle θ to the x-y plane:

$$\tau = \frac{\sigma_y - \sigma_x}{2} \sin 2\theta + \tau_{xy} \cos 2\theta \ .$$

In the equation for τ_{12} above, the shear term is zero.

$$\tau_{12} = \frac{\frac{2500}{t} - \frac{1250}{t}}{2} (\sin 106.2) = \frac{600}{t} \text{ psi}$$

The shearing force that must be carried by the seam is:

$$F_s = (\tau_{12})(\text{Area}_{\text{seam}}) = \left(\frac{600}{t}\right)(Lt) = 600 \text{ L} \ .$$

Therefore, the shear force per linear inch of the seam which must be carried by the weld is:

$$f_s = 600 \text{ lb/in.}$$

• PROBLEM 3-26

Calculate the membrane stress σ_φ, σ_θ for a thin-walled spherical shell of radius r and wall thickness of h which is subjected to a uniform internal pressure of intensity p.

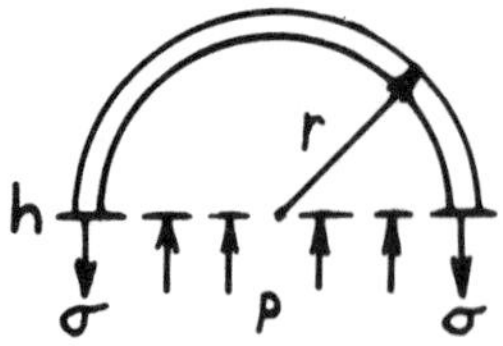

FIG. 1

Solution: Since the shell is spherical, a section taken through the center in any direction will be the same by symmetry. Therefore, $\sigma_\theta = \sigma_\varphi = \sigma$. Likewise, the radius is equal in all directions. From Figure 1, the force exerted by the pressure p is equal to p multiplied by the projected area of the spherical surface (which is a circle of radius r) $= p \times \pi r^2$. The projected area times the pressure normal to that surface can be used, since on the spherical surface the tangential components cancel out. This force must be equilibrated by the force caused by the stress in the shell, $\sigma \times$ circumferential length $\times$ shell thickness.

$$\pi r^2 p = \sigma \pi r h$$

or

$$\sigma = \frac{pr}{2h}$$

$$\sigma_\varphi / r_1 + \sigma_\theta / r_2 = p/h \ .$$

• PROBLEM 3-27

From Fig. 1, calculate, a) the maximum normal stress in the Horton sphere of diameter 60-ft. and wall thickness of 1.13 in. with welded joints by a gas at a pressure of 75 psi, b) the force transmitted by the internal pressure to a 10-in. length of the vertical meridian joint of the shell.

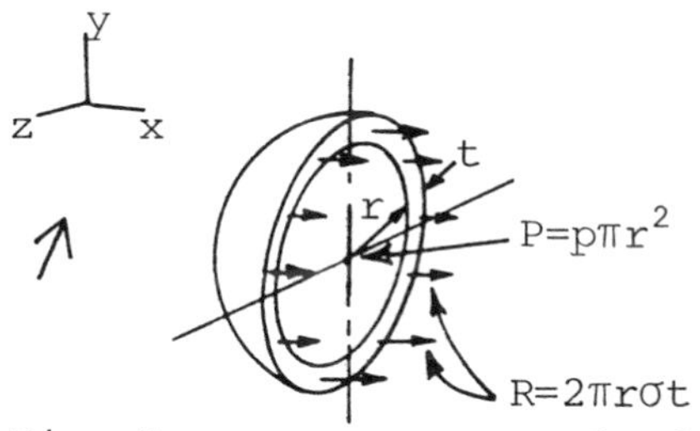

Fig. 1.

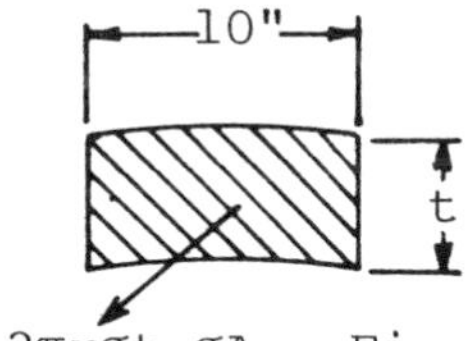

Fig. 2.

Solution: a) Applying the formula for a pressure vessel:

$$\frac{\sigma_\varphi}{r_1} + \frac{\sigma_\theta}{r_2} = \frac{p}{t} \ .$$

For a sphere $\sigma_\varphi = \sigma_\theta = \sigma$, $r_1 = r_2 = r$ by symmetry. So,

$$\frac{2\sigma}{r} = \frac{p}{t} \Rightarrow \sigma_{max} = \frac{pr}{2t}$$

$$\sigma_{max} = \frac{75(30)(12)}{2(1.13)} = 11{,}946.9 \text{ psi} \ .$$

b) Force resisted by the joints from internal pressure

$$F = \sigma A \qquad A = (t)(10)$$

$$F = \sigma(t)(10)$$

$$F = 11{,}946.9(1.13)(10) = 135{,}000 \text{ lbs.}$$

• PROBLEM 3-28

Determine the membrane stresses in a spherical dome of radius a caused by its own weight of q lb. per square inch, Fig. 1.

Solution: The surface area of the dome above an arbitrary angle φ is found first. Multiplying this area by q yields the resultant R which acts downward, i.e., R must be taken as negative. This force is equal to the vertical component of σ_φ, times the cross-sectional area at the arbitrarily cut section. The cross-sectional area of the shell is

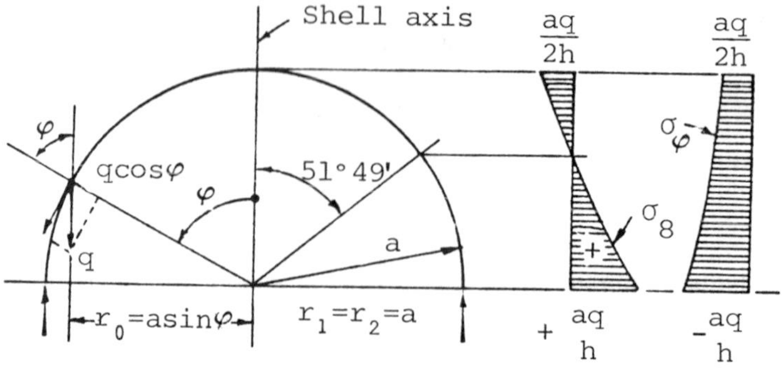

Fig. 1.

$2\pi r_0 h$. Since the vertical component of σ_φ is $\sigma_\varphi \sin \varphi$, then:

$$\sigma_\varphi (2\pi r_0 h \sin \varphi) = R \quad \text{for equilibrium}$$

$$\sigma_\varphi = \frac{R}{2\pi r_0 h \sin^2 \varphi} = \frac{R}{2\pi a h \sin^2 \varphi}$$

since $r_0 = r_2 \sin \varphi = a \sin \varphi$. The surface area of the dome is $\int_0^\varphi 2\pi r_0 \cdot a d\varphi$. Performing the integration yields

$$S = -2\pi a^2 \int_0^\varphi \sin \varphi \, d\varphi$$

$$= -2\pi a^2 (1 - \cos \varphi) .$$

The vertical force resultant due to the weight of the dome is gS down ward.

$$R = -g \cdot 2\pi a^2 (1 - \cos \varphi) .$$

Therefore,

$$\sigma_\varphi = \frac{-2\pi a^2 q(1 - \cos \varphi)}{2\pi a h \sin^2 \varphi}$$

or

$$\sigma_\varphi = - \frac{aq}{h(1 + \cos \varphi)} .$$

To determine the hoop stress σ_θ , use the equation:

$$\frac{\sigma_\varphi}{r_1} + \frac{\sigma_\theta}{r_2} = \frac{p_z a}{h}$$

since $r_1 = r_2 = a$, $p_z = -q \cos \varphi$,

$$\sigma_\theta = \frac{p_z a}{h} - \sigma_\varphi = - \frac{q \cos \varphi \, a}{h} + \frac{aq}{h(1 + \cos \varphi)}$$

$$\sigma_\theta = \frac{aq}{h} \left(\frac{1}{1+\cos \varphi} - \cos \varphi \right)$$

These results are plotted in Fig. 1. It is interesting to note the change in sign of σ_φ which means that up to $\varphi = 51°49'$ no hoop tension develops in the dome. This is an important fact for materials weak in tension and accounts for the successful use of domes in roof construction during the medieval era.

A transmission pipe line for oil has two pressure gauges spaced apart by the given distance shown in Fig. 1. The readings of the gauges register a pressure drop which is assumed to be uniform along the pipe line. Calculate the stresses on the inside wall of the pipe at a cross-section that is equidistant from the two gauges.

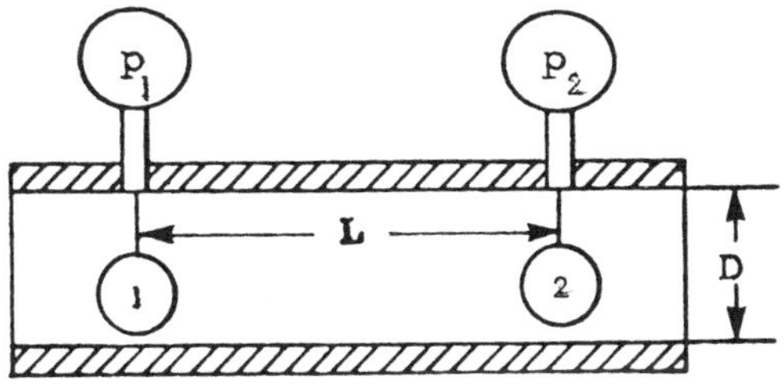

Fig. 1.

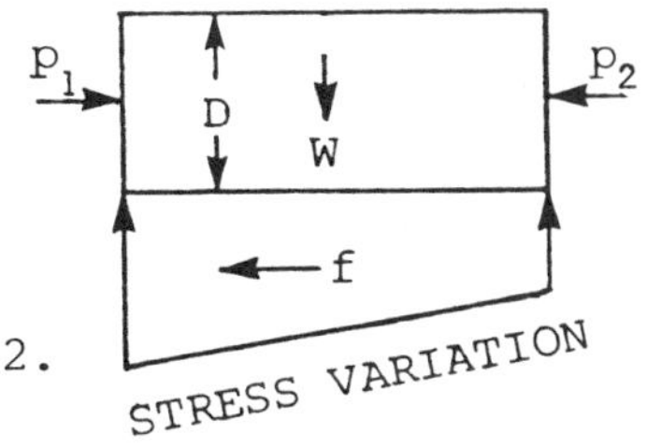

Fig. 2.

Solution: Since it is equal to the pressure, the normal stress on the pipe surface halfway between sections 1 and 2 is $\frac{1}{2}(p_1 + p_2)$. That is,

$$\tau_n = \tfrac{1}{2}(p_1 + p_2)\text{psf}\ .$$

To get the shear stress, consider as a free body the chunk of oil in the pipe at some time t between sections 1 and 2, as shown in Fig. 2. The pressures p_1 and p_2 act uniformly over the end sections, as has been shown. Pressure variation due to gravity can be neglected. Also, p varies linearly with x along the periphery of the body. The total friction force f on the periphery opposes the motion of the chunk of fluid. The end forces are equal to the cross-sectional area times the respective pressures. Since the chunk of fluid is not accelerating, set the forces in the x direction equal to zero as follows:

$$p_1 \frac{\pi D^2}{4} - f - p_2 \frac{\pi D^2}{4} = 0$$

$$(p_1 - p_2)\frac{\pi D^2}{4} - f = 0$$

therefore

$$f = (p_1 - p_2)\frac{\pi D^2}{4}$$

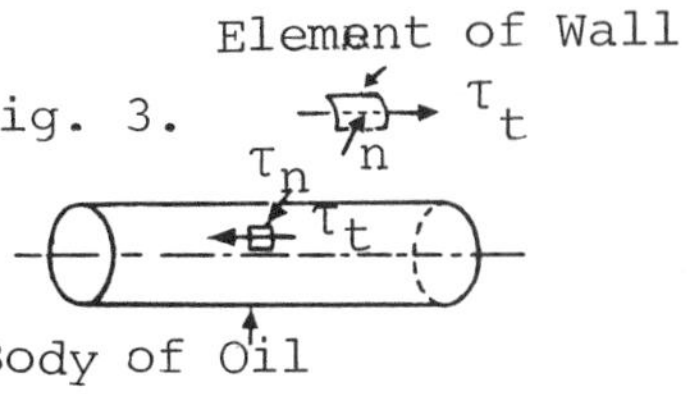

Fig. 3.

The force f is uniformly distributed over the peripheral surface of the fluid and, hence, there is a uniform shear stress τ_{t_x} over the surface given as

$$\tau_{t_x} = \frac{f}{\pi DL} = (p_1 - p_2)\frac{\pi D^2/4}{\pi DL}$$

$$= \frac{(p_1 - p_2)D}{4L}$$

Thus, for surface elements on the periphery of the oil there is a uniform shear stress in the axial direction - i.e., along the direction of the axis of the pipe, but clearly there is zero shear stress transverse to this direction. This is shown for a typical area element in Figure 3. Note that these stresses act on the oil at the wall of the pipe. The corresponding stresses on the pipe are oppositely directed in accordance with Newton's third law. This is also shown in Figure 3.

CHAPTER 4

STRAIN

NORMAL STRAIN

• PROBLEM 4-1

Axial tensile forces are applied to a bar with uniform cross-section of a square. Assuming that the volume remains constant for the elongation shown, determine the normal strains.

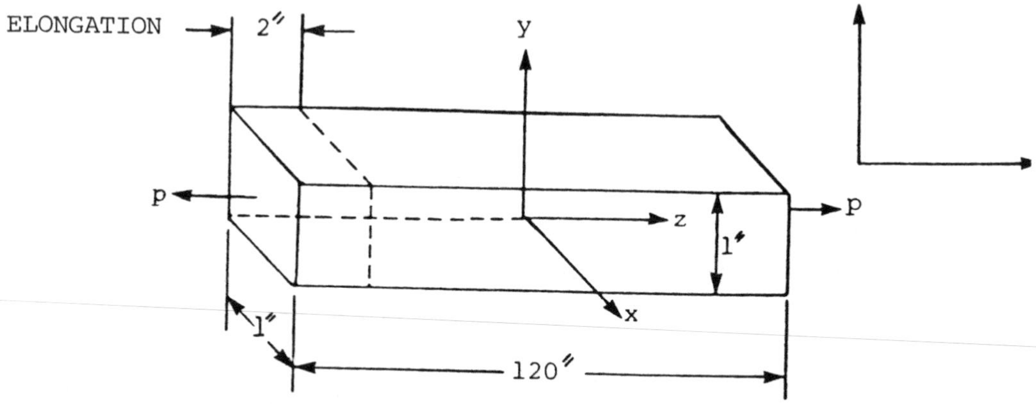

Solution: In this problem, the deformation is uniform and it is called uniform strain. The ratio of the elongation to original length, (ϵ), is the same for corresponding sides of all elements in the bar having edges parallel to the xyz axes regardless of the size of the element.

$$\epsilon_{zz} = \frac{\Delta L}{L} = \frac{2\text{-in.}}{10'(12)} = 0.1667 \text{ in./in.}$$

Since the total volume of the bar stays constant, then, unit volume before and after deformation is

$$v(\text{before}) = (10\text{-ft})(12\text{-in./ft})(1\text{-in})^2$$

$$v(\text{after}) = (120\text{-in.} + 2\text{-in.})(1 + \delta)^2$$

where δ is the change in length of the sides of the cross-section (see Fig. 2). The value for δ is the same for the height and width since $\delta_x = \epsilon x$, $\delta y = \epsilon y$ and dimensions $x = y$ for the square cross-section.

$$(120)(1)^2 = (122)(1 + \delta)^2$$

$$(1 + \delta)^2 = \frac{120}{122}$$

$$\delta = \sqrt{\frac{120}{122}} - 1$$

$$\delta = -0.00823 \text{ in.}$$

$$\epsilon_{xx} = \epsilon_{yy} = \frac{\Delta L}{L} = \frac{-0.00823 \text{ in.}}{1 \text{ in.}} = -0.00823 \text{ in./in.}$$

• PROBLEM 4-2

A rigid (does not bend) 14,300-lb plate is supported as shown in Fig. 1. Posts B and D are hard rubber 4 by 5 by 8 in. Post C is a 2 by 2 by 7.84-in. timber. Given that all three posts are compressed when the load (plate) is applied, determine the relation between the axial strains in the two materials.

FIG. 1

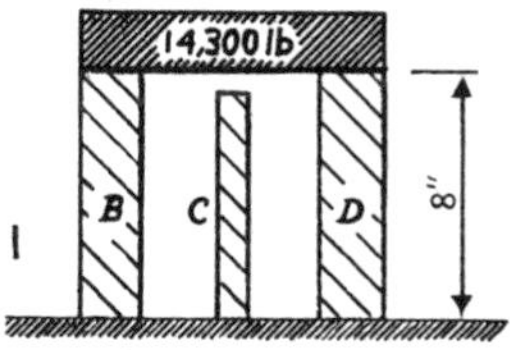

Solution: To find the relationship between ϵ_B, ϵ_D, and ϵ_C, there are two strains we must consider. The first occurs while the plate is supported only by posts B and D. The second occurs when all three posts support the plate. The strain developed in posts B and D for the first case is simply $\Delta L/L$, where ΔL is the distance to the top of post C.

$$\epsilon_i = \frac{.16''}{8''} = .02$$

Post C develops no strain in this case.

In the second case, since the plate does not bend, the posts must all shorten by the same amount, ΔL_2. So

$$\epsilon_B = \frac{\Delta L_2}{L_B} = \epsilon_D \quad \text{and} \quad \epsilon_C = \frac{\Delta L_2}{L_C} .$$

To find ϵ_B in terms of ϵ_C we note

$$\Delta L_2 = \epsilon_C L_C .$$

So

$$\epsilon_B = \frac{\epsilon_C L_C}{L_B} .$$

Substituting values for L_C and L_B

$$\epsilon_B = \epsilon_C \frac{7.84}{8} = .979\epsilon_C .$$

To this we must add the value of ϵ_B from case 1, so

$$\epsilon_B = \epsilon_D = .979\epsilon_C + .02$$

SHEAR STRAIN

• PROBLEM 4-3

A cube-shaped member of flexible rubber has adhesive opposite surfaces attached to two surfaces A-B and C-D and hinged members E-F and G-H. A-B and C-D are movable relative to one another from position in Fig. 1 to position in Fig. 2. Compute the shear angle and corresponding shear strains at any point in the rubber.

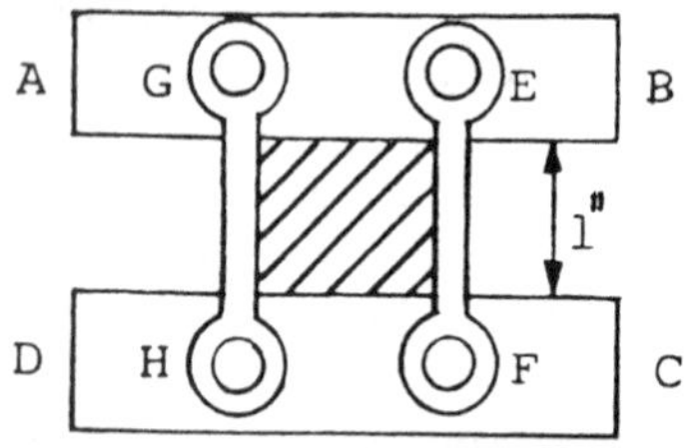

Fig. 1.

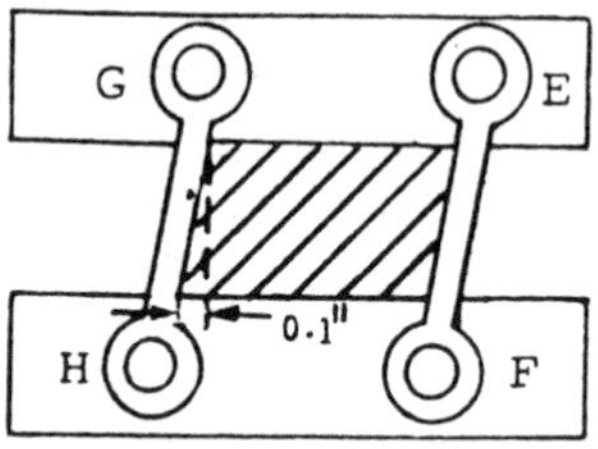

Fig. 2.

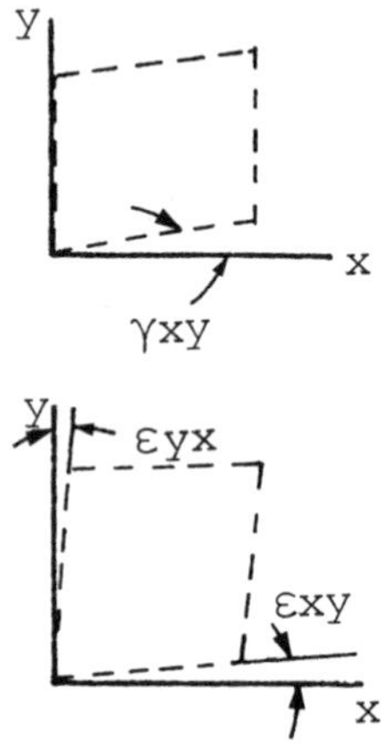

Fig. 3.

Solution: We have shown the rubber block in its deformed geometry in Fig. 2. We have here again a case of uniform strain since all pairs of vanishingly small line segments parallel to the x and y axes undergo the same loss of perpendicularity as a result of the deformation and thus develop the same shear angle γ_{xy}. Indeed, we may consider finite edges ad and ab (Fig. 1) during deformation since they remain straight, undergoing the same change in right angles as any pair of line segments dx and dy. Accordingly, noting that we have positive shear strain, we conclude that

$$\gamma_{xy} = \tan^{-1}\left(\frac{.1}{1}\right)$$

Since for small angles the tangent may be taken equal to the angle itself in radians, we have

$$\gamma_{xy} = .1$$

Consequently, we may say for the shear strains that

$$\epsilon_{xy} = .05; \ \epsilon_{yx} = .05$$

since

$$2\epsilon_{ij} = \gamma_{ij}$$

and

$$\epsilon_{ij} = \epsilon_{ji}$$

These results are shown in Fig. 3.

• PROBLEM 4-4

A thin-walled tube is subjected to equal and opposite torques at its ends which rotate relative to each other due to the torques. Compute the shear strain at a point on the tube surface.

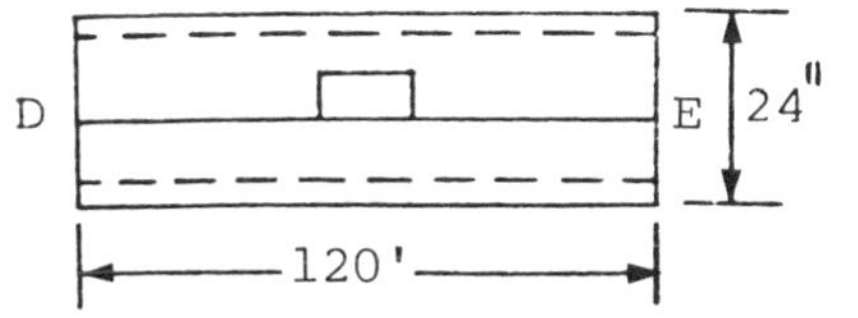

Fig. 1.

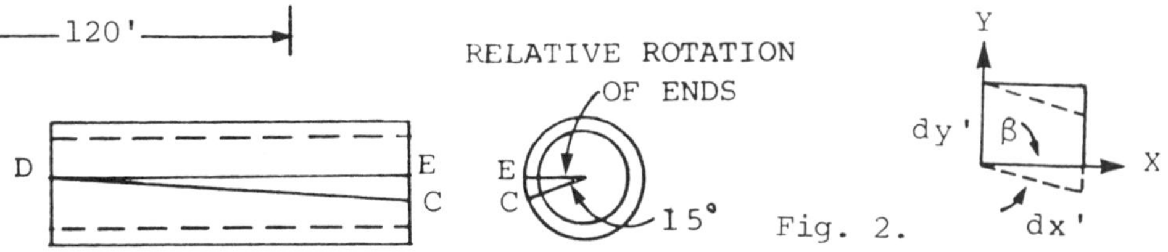

Fig. 2.

Solution: Referring to Fig. 1, an element line DE moves to position DC in Fig. 2 due to the torques. Assuming DC as a straight line, then line element dx in the deformed state when projected back to the xy plane has rotated an angle β, given as

$$-\beta = \tan^{-1}\frac{\delta}{L} = \tan^{-1}\left(\frac{r\Delta\varphi}{L}\right) = \tan^{-1}\left[\frac{(1)[(15/360 \times 2\pi)]}{10}\right] = .0262$$

δ in the cross-section is the arc subtended by $\Delta\varphi = r\Delta\varphi$ where r = radius and $\Delta\varphi$ is change in the angle in radians. On the other hand, we can expect that line element dy' in the deformed state when projected back to the xy plane has undergone no rotation. Consequently, for the segment dx and dy chosen we have negative shear strain, given as

$$\gamma_{xy} = -.0262$$

$$\epsilon_{xy} = -.01310$$

$$\epsilon_{yx} = -.01310$$

Since $2\epsilon_{ij} = \gamma_{ij}$ and $\epsilon_{ij} = \epsilon_{ji}$.

• PROBLEM 4-5

A motor metal shaft is held within a metal tube by a rubber sleeve firmly attached along the surface of the shaft and inner surface of the tube. If the shaft is rotated about its axis 6° relative to the sleeve as shown in plane section Fig. 2, what is the shear strain in the rubber?

Solution: Since the shear strain is defined as one-half the change in angle in the plane considered, we must locate the plane which is undergoing shear. The shaft is rotating and there is no movement in the z-direction so shear occurs in the x-y plane. Since $\tan\gamma_{xy} = r\theta/L$ in this case, from Figure 2 we see that

$$\tan\gamma_{xy} = -\frac{(\frac{1}{2})6^\circ}{\frac{1}{4}} = -\frac{\frac{1}{2}(6)(2\pi)}{(\frac{1}{4})(360)} \text{ (radians)}$$

$$\tan\gamma_{xy} \cong \gamma_{xy}$$

since the angles involved are small, and

$$\gamma_{xy} = -\frac{\pi}{15} = -0.2094 .$$

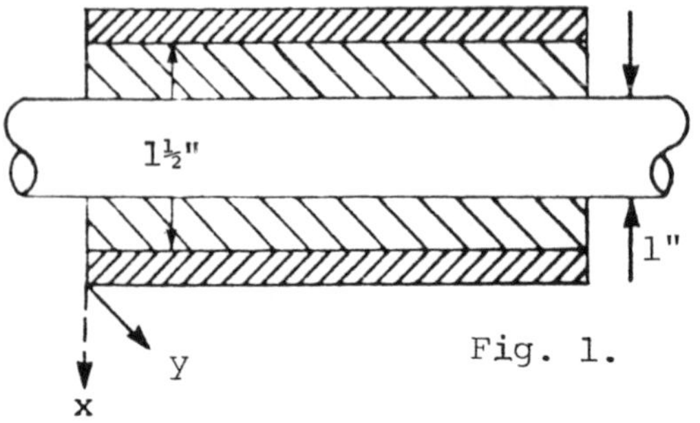

Fig. 1.

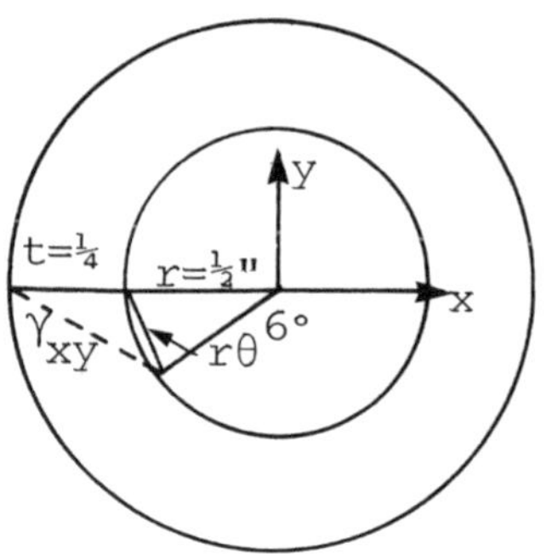

Fig. 2.

• PROBLEM 4-6

Sealed ends of two thin-walled tubes of different diameter are connected together at a plane which is rotated, while the other ends of the tubes are held fixed. Compute the shear strains in the tubes.

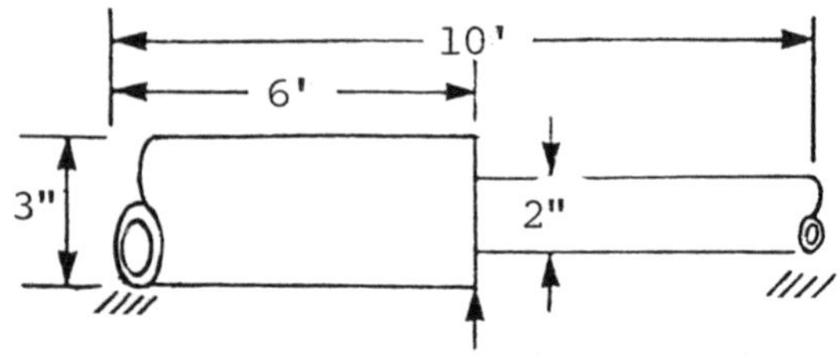

JOINT IS ROTATED 8°

Fig. 1.

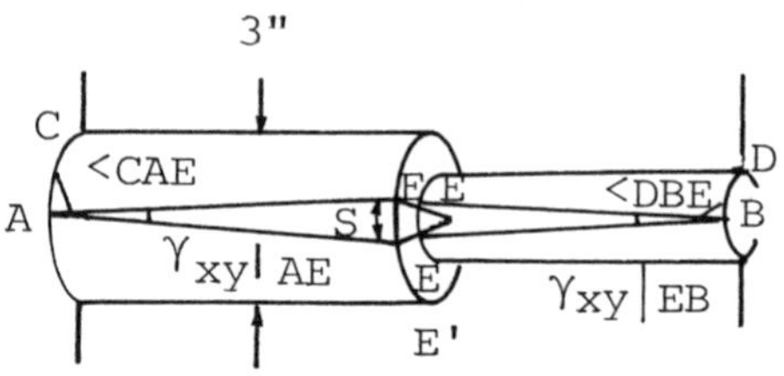

Fig. 2.

Solution: The rigid connecting plate assures that all the rotation is taken in the cylinders, while the immovable walls constrain the rotation at the walls to be zero. Line AE of the 3" diameter cylinder has rotated 8° as shown in Figure 2, so that the arclength, s, of this rotation is

$$s = \frac{D\theta^{\circ}}{2} = \frac{D\theta}{2}\left(\frac{2\pi}{360}\right) = \frac{D\theta\pi}{360}$$

where D is the cylinder diameter and equals 3"

$$= \frac{(3'')(8)\pi}{360} = \frac{\pi''}{15}$$

Positive shear strain γ_{xy} is taken as a decrease in angle <CAE . In this case <CAE has increased so that

$$\tan(\gamma_{xy}) = -\ s/L$$

since γ_{xy} is small, we can make the approximation $\tan(\gamma_{xy}) \cong \gamma_{xy}$

so

$$\gamma_{xy} = - s/L$$

We know that $\gamma_{xy} = 2\epsilon_{xy} = 2\epsilon_{yx}$ so

$$\epsilon_{xy} = \gamma_{xy}/2 = - s/2L$$

Inserting values for arclength s and length L for the 3" diameter cylinder we have

$$\epsilon_{xy}\Big|_{AE} = - \frac{(\pi/15)\text{ in.}}{2 \times 6 \text{ ft} \times 12 \text{ in/ft}}$$

$$= -.001454 \quad .$$

The shear strain in cylinder EB is found in a similar fashion. The arclength

$$s = \frac{D\theta^\circ}{2} = \frac{D\pi\theta}{360} = (2)(8)\left(\frac{\pi}{360}\right) = \frac{2\pi}{45}$$

$\gamma_{xy}\big|_{EB}$ is, by convention, positive for a decrease in angle $<DBE$. But $<DBE$ has increased so, again γ_{xy} is negative

$$\gamma_{xy} = - \frac{s}{L}$$

$$\epsilon_{xy} = - \frac{s}{2L}$$

$$= - \frac{2\pi/45}{2 \times 4 \times 12}$$

$$= - .001454 \ .$$

• PROBLEM 4-7

A closed large diameter, thin wall, metal tube is subjected to torques at its ends which cause the ends to rotate relative to each other by θ. Pressure within the tube, at the same time, forces the tube to elongate by L_1 and the diameter to expand by δ. Compute the strains at a point on the tube wall.

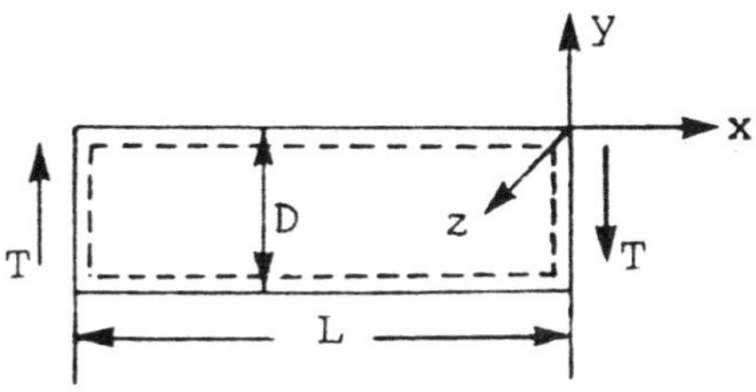

Fig. 1.

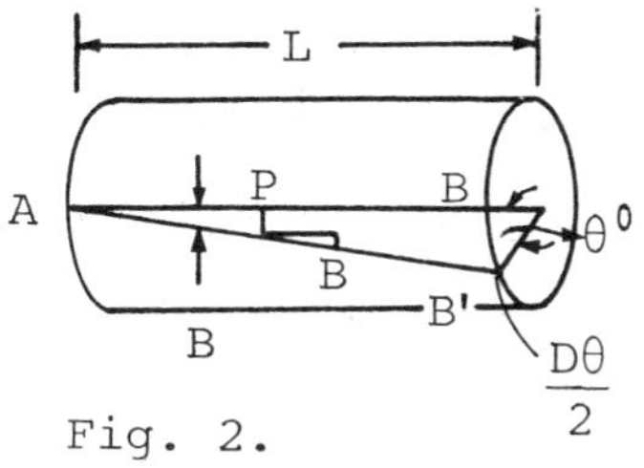

Fig. 2.

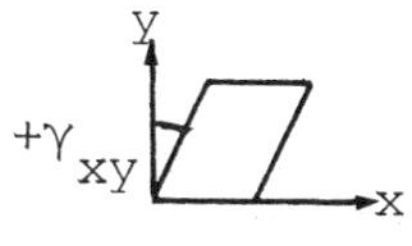

Fig. 3.

Solution: By definition, ϵ_{xx} is the change in length (Δx) over the original length in the x-direction (Lx),

$$\epsilon_{xx} = \frac{\Delta x}{Lx}$$

Since the ends have separated an amount L_1,

$$\Delta x = L_1 \quad \text{and} \quad Lx = L$$

so $\epsilon_{xx} = \frac{L_1}{L}$. Similarly, ϵ_{yy} is the change in length over the original length in the y-direction.

$$\epsilon_{yy} = \frac{\Delta y}{Ly}$$

The original dimension in the y-direction is simply the diameter D and the change in the y-direction is given as the change in the diameter, δ . So $\epsilon_{yy} = \delta/D$. It is interesting to note that, since the diameter is independent of direction, as is the change δ, the strain in the y-z plane is also independent of direction and is equal to δ/D . The engineering shear strain, γ_{xy}, is defined as the change in angle in the x-y plane, positive as shown in Figure 3. When defining the strain field ϵ_{ij}, γ_{xy} is considered to contribute equally to ϵ_{xy} and ϵ_{yx} , so

$$\epsilon_{xy} = \epsilon_{yx} = \tfrac{1}{2}\gamma_{xy} .$$

To find ϵ_{xy}, we must consider the effects of the torques T on the cylinder. It is helpful to consider one end, A, as fixed, while the other rotates the prescribed amount θ° as in Figure 2. Here, we assume that θ is small, so that we may assume θ to be equal to its sine and tangent. When end B is rotated, the line AB becomes line AB', and for small deformation may be considered a straight line. Line AB' has rotated by an angle β, clockwise, which can be found by geometry:

$$\tan\beta = \frac{D\theta}{2L}$$

where $D\theta/2$ is the arclength subtended by the rotation, θ. For small β, $\tan\beta \cong \beta$ so $\beta = D\theta/2L$. Positive shear strain is shown in Figure 3. By this sign convention $\beta = -\gamma_{xy}$ so $\gamma_{xy} = -D\theta/2L$ therefore $\epsilon_{xy} = -D\theta/4L$. Since $\theta^{\circ} = \theta(2\pi/360)$ radians

$$\epsilon_{xy} = -\frac{D(2\pi\theta)}{4L(360)}$$

$$= -\frac{D\pi\theta}{720L} .$$

STRAIN COMPONENTS

• PROBLEM 4-8

Given the displacement field

$$\vec{u} = (x^2\vec{i} + 3y\vec{j} + 10\vec{k}) \times 10^{-2} \text{ ft.}$$

What are the strain components at position (1,2,0)?

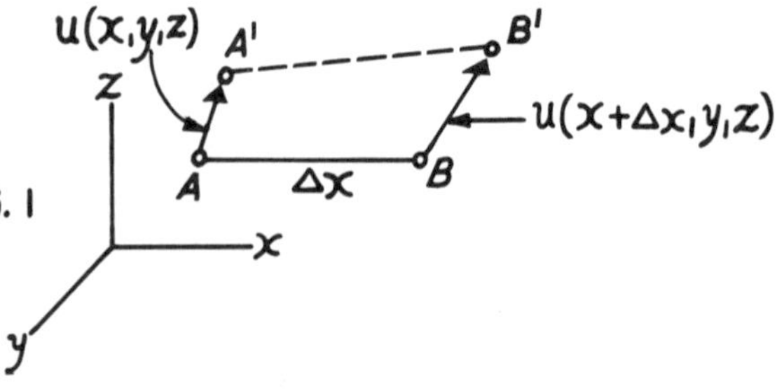

FIG. 1

Solution: By using the strain displacement relationship

$$\epsilon_{ij} = \tfrac{1}{2}\left(\frac{\partial u_i}{\partial j} + \frac{\partial u_j}{\partial i}\right)$$

we can express the strain components as functions

$$\epsilon_{xx} = \tfrac{1}{2}\left(\frac{\partial u_x}{\partial x} + \frac{\partial u_x}{\partial x}\right) = \tfrac{1}{2}\left(2\,\frac{\partial u_x}{\partial x}\right)$$

of position:

$$\epsilon_{xx} = \frac{\partial u_x}{\partial x} = \frac{\partial}{\partial x}(x^2) = 2x$$

$$\epsilon_{yy} = \frac{\partial u_y}{\partial y} = \frac{\partial}{\partial y}(3y) = 3$$

$$\epsilon_{zz} = \frac{\partial u_z}{\partial z} = \frac{\partial}{\partial z}(10) = 0$$

$$\epsilon_{xy} = \epsilon_{yx} = \tfrac{1}{2}\left(\frac{\partial u_x}{\partial y} + \frac{\partial u_y}{\partial x}\right) = \tfrac{1}{2}\left(\frac{\partial}{\partial y}(x^2) + \frac{\partial}{\partial x}(3y)\right) = 0$$

$$\epsilon_{xz} = \epsilon_{zx} = \tfrac{1}{2}\left(\frac{\partial u_x}{\partial z} + \frac{\partial u_z}{\partial x}\right) = \tfrac{1}{2}\left(\frac{\partial}{\partial z}(x^2) + \frac{\partial}{\partial x}(10)\right) = 0$$

$$\epsilon_{yz} = \epsilon_{zy} = \tfrac{1}{2}\left(\frac{\partial u_y}{\partial z} + \frac{\partial u_z}{\partial y}\right) = \tfrac{1}{2}\left(\frac{\partial}{\partial z}(3y) + \frac{\partial}{\partial y}(10)\right) = 0$$

The only non-zero strains are ϵ_{xx} and ϵ_{yy}. By substituting the values of the position of the point into the strain expressions, we get:

$$\epsilon_{xx} = 2x = 2 \times (1) \times 10^{-2} = .002$$

$$\epsilon_{yy} = 3 \times 10^{-2} = .003\ .$$

To understand how the strain-displacement equation is obtained, consider the element Δx in Figure 1. The displacement vectors are shown for ends A and B of the element and transform Δx to the deformed geometry A'B'. Since $\epsilon_{xx} = \Delta L/L$, for this point A

$$\epsilon_{xx} = \lim_{\Delta x \to 0}\left[\frac{A'B' - \Delta x}{\Delta x}\right]$$

because A'B' - Δx is the change in length. If the angle between A'B' and AB are small, we can use the projection of A'B' in the x-direction instead of A'B'.

$$\epsilon_{xx} = \lim_{\Delta x \to 0}\left[\frac{(A'B')_x - \Delta x}{\Delta x}\right]$$

Notice that $(A'B')_x$ is equal to Δx plus the net movement in the x-direction of the end points of the segment Δx as a result of deformation.

$$(A'B')_x = \Delta x + [u_x(x+\Delta x,y,z) - u_x(x,y,z)]$$

and

$$\epsilon_{xx} = \lim_{\Delta x \to 0}\left[\frac{u_x(x+\Delta x,y,z) - u_x(x,y,z)}{\Delta x}\right]$$

Now, the right-hand side is the definition of the partial derivative with respect to x so

$$\epsilon_{xx} = \frac{\partial u_x}{\partial x} .$$

The other strain components can be found in a similar manner.

• PROBLEM 4-9

Given the following displacement field,

$$u = [(x^2 + 3)i + (3y^2 z)j + (x + 3z)k] \times 10^{-2}$$

what are the strain components at point A (0,2,3)?

Solution: Note that the displacement field is given in vector notation with i corresponding to the x direction, j corresponding to the y direction and k corresponding to the z direction. First we determine the strain components as functions of position (i.e., the strain field). From the strain-displacement relationship

$$\epsilon_{ij} = \tfrac{1}{2}\left(\frac{\partial u_i}{\partial j} + \frac{\partial u_j}{\partial i}\right)$$

(for small strain only).

$$\therefore \epsilon_{xx} = \frac{\partial u_x}{\partial x} = \frac{\partial}{\partial x}[(x^2 + 3) \times 10^{-2}] = 2x \times 10^{-2}$$

$$\epsilon_{yy} = \frac{\partial u_y}{\partial y} = \frac{\partial}{\partial y}[(3y^2 z) \times 10^{-2}] = 6yz \times 10^{-2}$$

$$\epsilon_{zz} = \frac{\partial u_z}{\partial z} = \frac{\partial}{\partial z}[(x + 3z) \times 10^{-2}] = 3 \times 10^{-2}$$

$$\epsilon_{xy} = \epsilon_{yx} = \tfrac{1}{2}\left(\frac{\partial u_x}{\partial y} + \frac{\partial u_y}{\partial x}\right) = \tfrac{1}{2}(0 + 0) \times 10^{-2} = 0$$

$$\epsilon_{xz} = \epsilon_{zx} = \tfrac{1}{2}\left(\frac{\partial u_x}{\partial z} + \frac{\partial u_z}{\partial x}\right) = \tfrac{1}{2}(0 + 1) \times 10^{-2} = \tfrac{1}{2} \times 10^{-2}$$

$$\epsilon_{yz} = \epsilon_{zy} = \tfrac{1}{2}\left(\frac{\partial u_y}{\partial z} + \frac{\partial u_z}{\partial y}\right) = \frac{1}{2}(3y^2 + 0) \times 10^{-2}$$

To find the magnitude of strain at point A, values of x,y,z for this point are substituted into the strain equations

$$\epsilon_{xx} = 0 \qquad \epsilon_{xy} = \epsilon_{yx} = 0$$

$$\epsilon_{yy} = .36 \qquad \epsilon_{xz} = \epsilon_{zx} = .005$$

$$\epsilon_{zz} = .03 \qquad \epsilon_{yz} = \epsilon_{zy} = .06$$

• PROBLEM 4-10

The relationship given below prevails in a structural member. Calculate the length of the line A-B after deformation.

$$\epsilon_{ij} = \begin{pmatrix} x^2 + 2yx & 3 + 10zx & z^3 + 10xy \\ 3 + 10zx & 5y + z^2 x & x^2 + 2yz^2 \\ z^3 + 10xy & x^2 + 2yz^2 & x^2 + y^2 \end{pmatrix} \times 10^{-2}$$

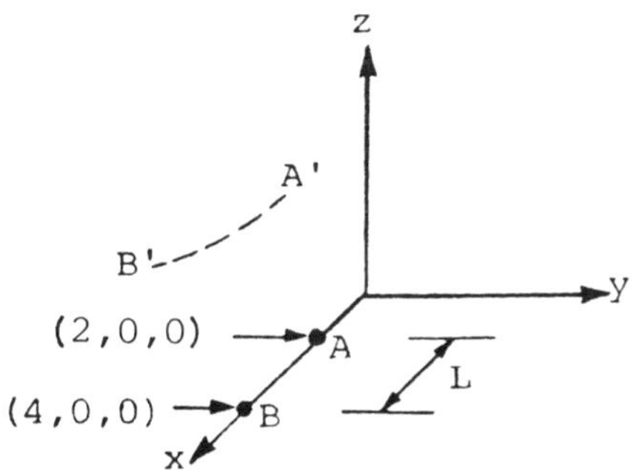

Solution: From our physical interpretation of normal strain the change in length of a line element dx in the original geometry is $\epsilon_{xx}\,dx$. The change in length ΔL of the line AB can then be given as follows:

$$\epsilon_{xx} = \frac{\Delta L}{L}$$

so, for a line element $dx = dL$ in x direction

$$\Delta L = \int_{x=2}^{x=4} \epsilon_{xx}\,dx$$

ϵ_{ij} is written in terms of its components

$$\epsilon_{ij} = \begin{pmatrix} \epsilon_{xx} & \epsilon_{xy} & \epsilon_{xz} \\ \epsilon_{yx} & \epsilon_{yy} & \epsilon_{yz} \\ \epsilon_{zx} & \epsilon_{zy} & \epsilon_{zz} \end{pmatrix}$$

From the given matrix distribution

$$\epsilon_{xx} = (x^2 + 2yx) \times 10^{-2}$$

Along the x axis we take $y = 0$ and substituting this into the expression for ϵ_{xx} we have

$$[\epsilon_{xx}]_{x\ axis} = (x^2) \times 10^{-2}$$

Thus,

$$\Delta L = \left[\int_2^4 (x^2)dx\right] \times 10^{-2} = \frac{x^3}{3}\Big|_2^4 \times 10^{-2} = .187 \text{ ft.}$$

The new length L' of AB will now be

$$L' = L + \Delta L = 2.187 \text{ ft.}$$

Note that AB in the deformed geometry is no longer a straight line.

• PROBLEM 4-11

> A cylindrical column has a specific gravity γ that varies along its length, and is suspended from a ceiling. If the material behaves linearly, i.e.the normal stress σ,equals E x the normal strain ε, a) What is the total deflection of the end A of the member as a result of the weight? b) Find the deflection using a displacement field approach.

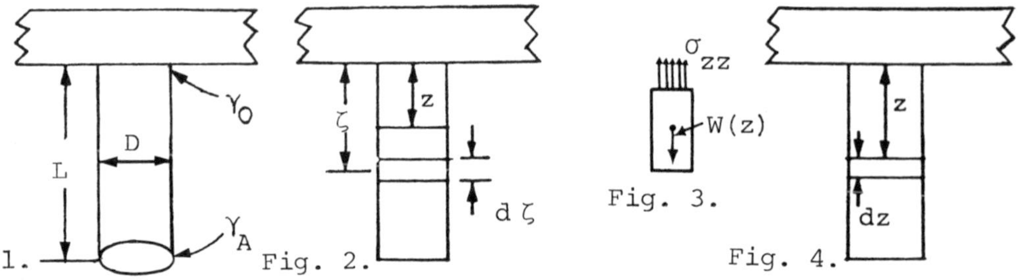

Fig. 1. Fig. 2. Fig. 3. Fig. 4.

<u>Solution</u>: Our method of approach will be to find the strain ϵ_{zz} at any position z. Then we can ascertain the elongation of the entire rod by an integration procedure. As a first step, we determine γ as a function of position z as follows; since γ varies linearly with z, the mathematical expression is $\gamma = c_1 z + c_2$ using the boundary conditions $\gamma(0) = \gamma_0$, $\gamma(L) = \gamma_A$

$$\gamma_0 = c_1 \cdot 0 + c_2 \qquad \gamma_A = c_1 \cdot L + c_2$$

$$c_2 = \gamma_0 \qquad \gamma_A = c_1 \cdot L + \gamma_0$$

$$c_1 = \frac{\gamma_A - \gamma_0}{L}$$

so,

$$\gamma = \gamma_0 + \frac{z}{L}(\gamma_A - \gamma_0) \tag{a}$$

We shall need the stress σ_{zz} at any section z (see Fig. 2). The stress at z, considering the material below (shown crosshatched) as a free body (Fig. 3), supports the weight of this material and may be considered uniform over the section. Accordingly, we shall need the weight of that part of the cylinder below position z; we shall then consider z in the next few steps as a fixed parameter. We have shown a slice of material in the cylinder below section z and have used the "dummy" variable ζ (zeta) to locate this element (see Fib. 2) and $d\zeta$ to give its thickness. In summing the weights of these slices, the dummy variable ζ runs from z (the top of the crosshatched region) to L. Accordingly, for the weight, which we shall denote as $W(z)$, we have

$$W(z) = \int_z^L \gamma \frac{\pi D^2}{4} d\zeta \tag{b}$$

Now γ at any position ζ below the top can be given from Eq. (a) with z replaced by ζ. Accordingly, we have

$$W(z) = \int_z^L \left[\gamma_0 + \frac{\zeta}{L}(\gamma_A - \gamma_0)\right] \frac{\pi D^2}{4} d\zeta$$

$$= \frac{\pi D^2}{4}\left[\gamma_0(L - z) + \frac{\gamma_A - \gamma_0}{2L}(L^2 - z^2)\right] \tag{c}$$

Notice that the dummy variable ζ "integrates out" and disappears, leaving the right-hand side as a function of the parameter z. To get the stress we employ the free body shown in Fig. 3. and the fact that

$$\sigma_{zz} = \frac{F}{A}$$

where F ≡ Force which in this case = W

A ≡ cross-sectional area.

Then from equilibrium we have

$$\sigma_{zz} = \frac{1}{\frac{\pi D^2}{4}} W(z) = \gamma_0(L - z) + \frac{\gamma_A - \gamma_0}{2L}(L^2 - z^2) . \qquad (d)$$

Also, for ϵ_{zz} we have from Hooke's Law (i.e., stress-strain relationship)

$$\sigma_{zz} = E\,\epsilon_{zz}$$

where E ≡ Young's Modulus

$$\epsilon_{zz} = \frac{1}{E}\sigma_{zz} = \frac{1}{E}\left[\gamma_0(L - z) + \frac{\gamma_A - \gamma_0}{2L}(L^2 - z^2)\right] \qquad (e)$$

Now we have ϵ_{zz} at any position z, and we can consider z to be a variable rather than a parameter in the remainder of the discussion.

In Fig. 4 we have shown a slice dz of the cylinder. The increase in length in the z direction of this slice, $\Delta(dz)$

$$\Delta dz = \epsilon_{zz} dz = \frac{1}{E}\left[\gamma_0(L - z) + \frac{\gamma_A - \gamma_0}{2L}(L^2 - z^2)\right]dz$$

To get the elongation of the entire rod we sum the elongations of all the elements in the rod - i.e., we integrate from z = 0 to z = L. Thus,

$$\Delta_A = \frac{1}{E}\int_0^L \left[\gamma_0(L - z) + \frac{\gamma_A - \gamma_0}{2L}(L^2 - z^2)\right] dz$$

$$\frac{L^2}{E}\left[\frac{1}{3}\gamma_A + \frac{1}{6}\gamma_0\right]$$

For the displacement field approach, we use the differential strain-displacement equation in the z direction:

$$\frac{\partial u_z}{\partial z} = \epsilon_{zz} .$$

Since u_z does not depend on x and y, since the forces in the x and y directions are zero, we can use an ordinary derivative:

$$\frac{\partial u_z}{\partial z} = \epsilon_{zz}$$

Now, by using equation (e) we have,

$$\frac{\partial u_z}{\partial z} = \frac{1}{E}\left[\gamma_0(L - z) + \frac{\gamma_A - \gamma_0}{2L}(L^2 - z^2)\right]$$

Separate the variables by multiplying by dz and integrate both sides of the equation

$$u_z = \int_0^z \frac{1}{E}\left[\gamma_0(L - z) + \frac{\gamma_A - \gamma_0}{2L}(L^2 - z^2)\right] dz$$

$$= \frac{1}{E}\left[\gamma_0(Lz - \frac{z^2}{2}) + \frac{\gamma_A - \gamma_0}{2L}(L^2 z - \frac{z^3}{3})\right] + c$$

where c is a constant of integration. Since the displacement at the support is zero, $u(0) = 0 = c$.

To find the displacement at A we must find $u(L) = \Delta_A$

$$= \frac{1}{E}\left[\gamma_0(L^2 - \frac{L^2}{2}) + \frac{\gamma_A - \gamma_0}{2L}(L^3 - \frac{L^3}{3})\right]$$

$$= \frac{L^2}{E}\left[\frac{\gamma_A}{3} + \frac{\gamma_0}{6}\right]$$

which is the same result as before.

• PROBLEM 4-12

A circular rod hangs by its own weight as shown in Figure 1. The material behaves linear-elastically, with modulus of elasticity, E, and has a specific weight, γ, which is constant throughout the rod. Using a displacement field approach, find the deflection at any section z. What is the total deflection of the end A of the member as a result of its weight?

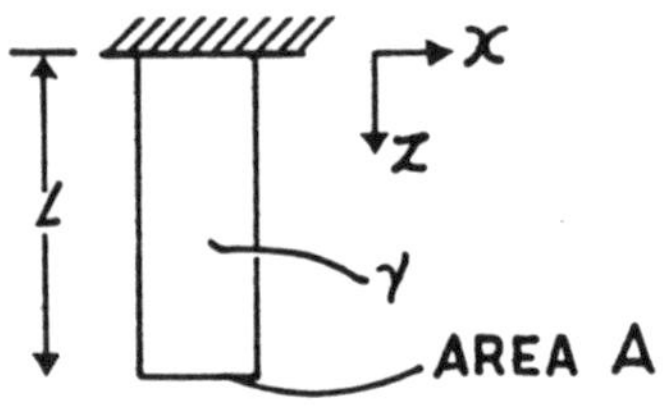

FIG. 1

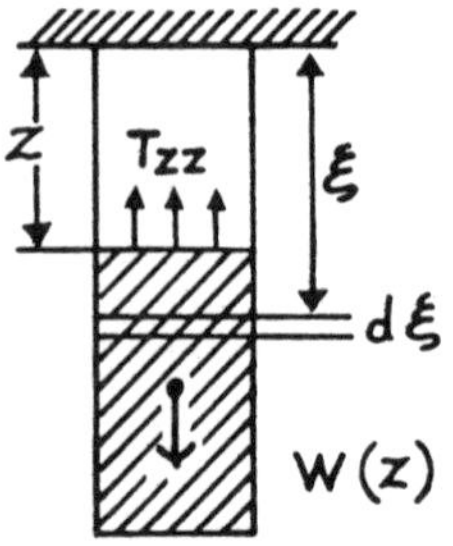

FIG. 2

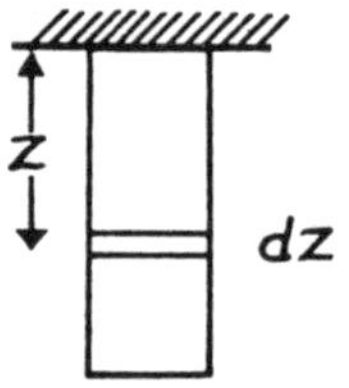

FIG. 3

Solution: The strain field ϵ_{ij} can be expressed in terms of the displacement field, u :

$$\epsilon_{ij} = \frac{1}{2}\left(\frac{\partial u_i}{\partial j} + \frac{\partial u_j}{\partial i}\right) \quad (1)$$

The deflection due to the weight of the rod is in the z-direction so we want to find u_z . By using (1) we get

$$\epsilon_{zz} = \frac{\partial u_z}{\partial z}$$

or using the integral form:

$$u_{z_0} = \int_0^{z_0} \epsilon_{zz}\, dz$$

Once we find the expression for the strain, we obtain the deflection by performing the integration. We will need the stress τ_{zz} at any section z (see Figure 2). The stress at z by equilibrium must support the weight of the material below the section. So we must find the weight of the cylinder below section z. Consider z for the moment as a fixed parameter. We now locate an element in the section under consideration with the dummy variable ζ and the thickness of the element by $d\zeta$. The integration over this section runs from z (at the top of the section) to L. Therefore, the weight

$$W(z) = \int_z^L \gamma \frac{\pi D^2}{4} d\zeta$$

since $W = \gamma \cdot$ volume $= \gamma \cdot$Area $\times$ height

$$W(z) = \gamma \frac{\pi D^2}{4} \zeta \Big|_z^L$$

$$= \gamma \frac{\pi D^2}{4}(L - z)$$

The dummy variable at this point integrates out, giving the weight as a true function of z. The stress by equilibrium

$$\tau_{zz} = \frac{W(z)}{A} \qquad A = \text{Area}$$

$$= \gamma \frac{\frac{\pi D^2}{4}(L - z)}{\frac{\pi D^2}{4}}$$

$$= \gamma(L - z)$$

Since the material is linear-elastic

$$\epsilon_{zz} = \frac{\tau_{zz}}{E} = \frac{\gamma}{E}(L - z)$$

Now, the increase in length of a slice dz, shown in Figure 3 is

$$\Delta dz = \epsilon_{zz} dz = \frac{\gamma}{E}(L - z)dz$$

To get the deflection of the point z_0 we sum the elongations of all the elements up to z_0 - i.e., we integrate from $z = 0$ to z_0. Thus,

$$\Delta_{z_0} = \frac{1}{E}\int_0^{z_0} \gamma(L - z)dz$$

$$= \frac{\gamma}{E}(Lz - \frac{z^2}{2}) \Big|_0^{z_0}$$

$$= \frac{\gamma}{E}(Lz_0 - \frac{z_0^2}{2})$$

The deflection at Δ can be found by setting $z_0 = L$, so

$$\Delta_{total} = \frac{\gamma}{E}(L^2 - \frac{L^2}{2})$$

$$= \frac{\gamma L^2}{2E}$$

• PROBLEM 4-13

A conical structure hangs down from a ceiling to which its base is attached. If E for the material is 10^7psi, and the density (specific weight) is 200 lbs/ft^3, compute the extension of the cone tip due to its own weight.

Solution: To find the total deflection of the end A, we find the expression for strain for any section z of the cone, and then integr-

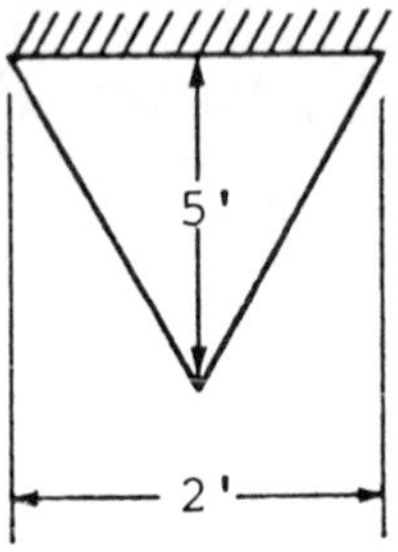

Fig. 1.

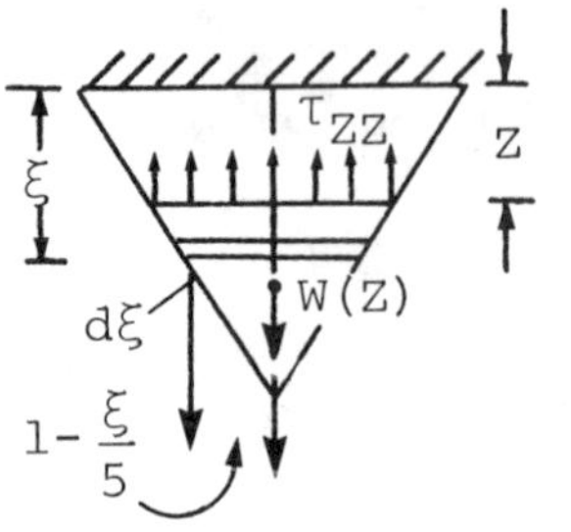

Fig. 2.

ate over the total length of the cone.

For a section as shown in Fig. 2 the product of the stress and cross-sectional area at z must equal the weight of the material below z. We next determine this weight by temporarily considering z as a fixed parameter. We now locate an element in the section below z with a dummy variable, ζ; denote the thickness of the element by $d\zeta$, and the radius of the element by $(1 - \zeta/s)$. The weight of the element is equal to its volume times the specific weight γ. The volume of the disc-shaped element is equal to $\pi r^2 t$ where r is its radius and t its thickness. In this case the element's radius = $(1 - \zeta/5)$ and its thickness is $d\zeta$. Its volume is therefore $\pi(1 - \zeta/5)^2 d\zeta$ and its weight is therefore $\gamma\pi(1 - \zeta/5)^2 d\zeta$. To find the weight of material below z we must integrate this expression from z, the top of the section, to 5', the end of the cone.

$$w(z) = \int_z^{5'} \gamma\pi(1 - \zeta/5)^2 \, d\zeta$$

$$w(z) = \frac{-5\gamma\pi}{3}(1 - \zeta/5)^3 \Big|_z^5$$

$$w(z) = \frac{-5\gamma\pi}{3}\left[(1 - 5/5)^3 - (1 - z/5)^3\right]$$

$$= \frac{-5\gamma\pi}{3}\left[0 - (1 - z/5)^3\right]$$

$$w(z) = \frac{5\gamma\pi}{3}(1 - z/5)^3$$

So, the dummy variable disappears and the weight is a function of z. The stress $\tau_{zz}(z)$ is the weight below z (w(z)) divided by the cross-sectional area at z(A(z)), where both w and A vary with z.

$$\tau_{zz}(z) = \frac{w(z)}{A(z)} = \frac{\frac{5\pi\gamma}{3}(1 - z/5)^3}{\pi(1 - z/5)^2}$$

$$= (5\gamma/3)(1 - z/5)$$

Since the material is linear-elastic

$$\epsilon_{zz} = \frac{5\gamma}{3E}(1 - 2/5) .$$

The deflection of a segment dz is given by definition as $\Delta dz = \epsilon_{zz}(z)dz$. To get the total deflection we sum up the elongations for all segments dz - i.e., we integrate over the entire length.

$$\Delta_{total} = \frac{5\gamma}{3E}\int_0^5 (1 - z/5)dz$$

$$= \frac{25\gamma}{6E}(1 - z/5)^2 \Big|_0^5$$

$$= - \frac{25\gamma}{6E}(0 - 1)$$

$$= \frac{25\gamma}{6E}$$

By substituting the values for γ and E we get

$$\Delta_{total} = \frac{25 \times (200\ lb/ft^3)(1\ ft^2)}{(6 \times 10 \times 10^6 lb/sq.in) \times (144\ sq.in/ft^2)}$$

$$= .579 \times 10^{-7}\ ft.$$

MOHR'S CIRCLE FOR STRAIN

• PROBLEM 4-14

Linear strains ϵ_a, ϵ_b, ϵ_c are measured by the strain gages in a 45° rosette, as shown in Figure 1. Assuming $\epsilon_a < \epsilon_b < \epsilon_c$, construct Mohr's circle.

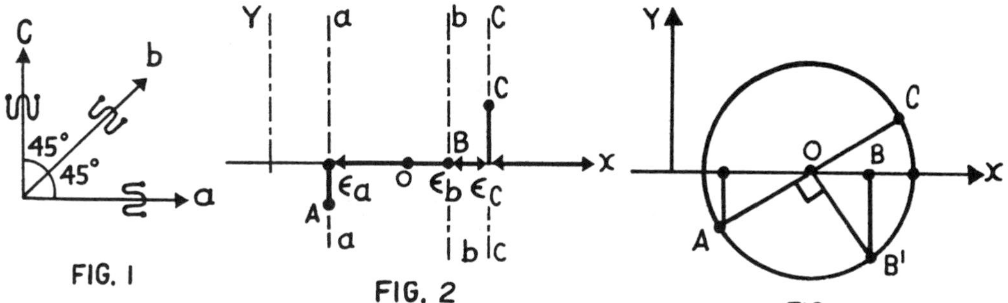

FIG. 1 FIG. 2 FIG. 3

Solution: In drawing any Mohr's circle, the abscissa, or x-axis, is the normal strain, while the ordinate, y-axis, is the shear strain. Therefore, mark the values ϵ_a, ϵ_b, ϵ_c on the x-axis. Draw three vertical lines aa, bb, cc through the values ϵ_a, ϵ_b, ϵ_c. If any of the measured strains are negative, the corresponding vertical lines will lie to the left of the origin.

To locate the center of the circle, find the average value of the perpendicular normal strains ϵ_a and ϵ_c, labeled pt 0 in Figure 2.

To construct the circle, we must find the diameter of the circle. The normal strain at 45° is

$$\epsilon_{45°} = \frac{\epsilon_a + \epsilon_c}{2} + \frac{\epsilon_a - \epsilon_c}{2}\cos(2 \times 45°)$$

$$+ \epsilon_{ac}\sin(2 \times 45°)$$

$$= \frac{\epsilon_a + \epsilon_c}{2} + \epsilon_{ac}$$

This shows that ϵ_b which is equal to $\epsilon_{45°}$ has a value equal to the value at the center of the circle plus the shear strain for the perpendicular axes a and c. Therefore, the distance from 0 to pt. B is equal to the vertical distance from the x-axis at c to a pt. on the circle above the x-axis and is equal to the vertical distance from the x-axis at a to a pt. on the circle below the x-axis, as in Figure 2.

The shear strain at a is negative because of the sign convention, counterclockwise rotation or increase in angle is negative. Since the a and c axes are 90° apart, the angle between them in Mohr's circle is 180°. Therefore, the line connecting them goes through the center of the circle and line AC is a diameter of Mohr's circle. This circle will cut the intermediate vertical bb at a point B' such that OB is perpendicular to line AC, corresponding to a 45° angle in the rosette. (See Figure 3).

• PROBLEM 4-15

Following results were received from a strain rosette composed of three wire resistance gages making angles of 0°, 60°, and 120° with the x axis.

$$\epsilon_0 = +100(10^{-5}),\quad \epsilon_{60} = -65(10^{-5}),\quad \epsilon_{120} = +75(10^{-5}).$$

Compute the principal strains and the maximum shearing strain.

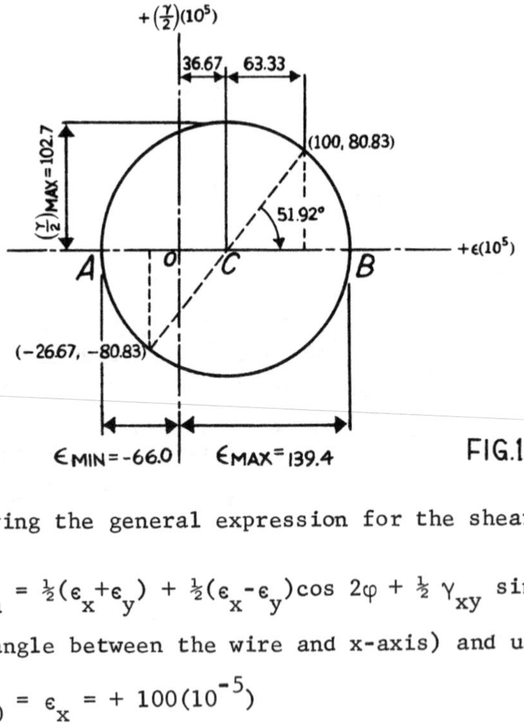

FIG.1.

Solution: By applying the general expression for the shearing and principal strains.

$$\epsilon_a = \tfrac{1}{2}(\epsilon_x+\epsilon_y) + \tfrac{1}{2}(\epsilon_x-\epsilon_y)\cos 2\varphi + \tfrac{1}{2}\gamma_{xy}\sin 2\varphi$$

(where φ is the angle between the wire and x-axis) and using the data,

$$\epsilon_0 = \epsilon_x = +100(10^{-5})$$

Substituting into the expression for ϵ_a (in units of 10^{-5} in per in) we have at 60° angle

$$-65 = \frac{100+\epsilon_y}{2} + \frac{100-\epsilon_y}{2}(\cos 120°) + \frac{\gamma_{xy}}{2}(\sin 120°)$$

$$= \frac{100+\epsilon_y}{2} + \frac{100-\epsilon_y}{2}\left(-\tfrac{1}{2}\right) + \frac{\gamma_{xy}}{2}(\sqrt{3}/2) \qquad (1)$$

at 120° angle

$$75 = \frac{100 + \epsilon_y}{2} + \frac{100 - \epsilon_y}{2} \cos 240^\circ + \frac{\gamma_{xy}}{2} \sin 240^\circ$$

$$75 = \frac{100 + \epsilon_y}{2} + \frac{100 - \epsilon_y}{2}(-\tfrac{1}{2}) + \frac{\gamma_{xy}}{2}(-\sqrt{3/2}) \qquad (2)$$

(units in 10^{-5})

There are 2 equations and 2 unknowns. The above equations are solved simultaneously, and

$$\epsilon_y = -26.67 \times 10^{-5}, \quad \gamma_{xy} = -161.66 \times 10^{-5}$$

To find the principal strains and maximum shearing strain, the Mohr's circle is constructed for the above strain plane with coordinates ϵ_x, $\gamma_{xy}/2$, and ϵ_y, $\gamma_{xy}/2$ (as shown in Fig. 1). The line connecting the two points intersects the x-axis at point C (0,36.67) which then is the center of the Mohr's circle. Using the values of strain given at 60° and 120°, the radius can be found.

$$\epsilon_{max} = OB = 139.4\ (10^{-5})$$

$$\epsilon_{min} = OA = -66.0\ (10^{-5})$$

$$\gamma_{max} = 2(\text{radius}) = \pm\ 205.4\ (10^{-5})\ .$$

CHAPTER 5

STRESS AND STRAIN RELATIONS

DISPLACEMENT DUE TO AXIAL LOADING

• **PROBLEM** 5-1

Consider a carefully conducted experiment in which an aluminum bar of 2 1/4 in. diameter is stressed in a testing machine as in the Fig. At a certain instant the applied force P is 32 kips while the measured elongation of the rod is 0.00938 in. in a 12-in. gage length and the dimension of the diameter is decreased by 0.000585 in. Calculate the two physical constants ν (Poisson's ratio) and E (modulus of elasticity) of the material.

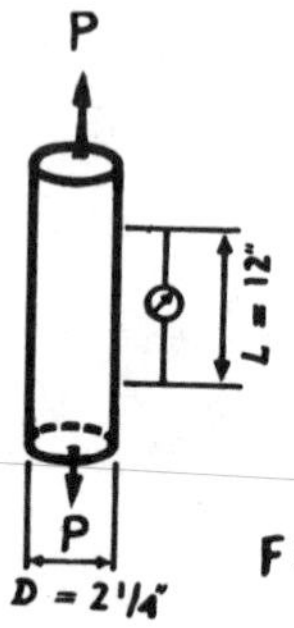

FIG.

Solution: Transverse strain:

$$\varepsilon_t = \frac{\Delta_t}{D} = \frac{-0.000585}{(2.25)} = -0.000260 \text{ in. per in.}$$

where Δ_t is tht total change in dimension of the diameter of the rod and the negation sign indicates the reduction in diameter of the bar (contraction).

Axial strain:

$$\varepsilon_a = \frac{\Delta}{L} = \frac{0.00938}{12} = 0.000782 \text{ in. per in.}$$

Poisson's ratio:

$$\nu = \frac{\varepsilon_t}{\varepsilon_a} = \frac{0.000260}{0.000782} = 0.333.$$

As the area of the rod $A = \pi(2.25/2)^2 = 3.976 \text{ in.}^2$ and σ is the stress due to the load P over the area of the bar, then

$$\sigma = \frac{P}{A} = \frac{32 \text{ kips}}{3.976 \text{ in.}^2} = 8.0483 \text{ ksi} = 8048.3 \text{ psi}$$

$$E = \frac{\sigma}{\varepsilon_a} = \frac{8048.3 \text{ psi}}{.00078 \text{ in./in.}} = 10.29 \times 10^6 \text{ psi.}$$

• PROBLEM 5-2

A 2-in. cube of steel is subjected to a uniform pressure of 30,000 psi acting on all faces. Determine the change in dimension between two parallel faces of the cube. Let $E = 30 \times 10^6$ psi and $\nu = 1/4$.

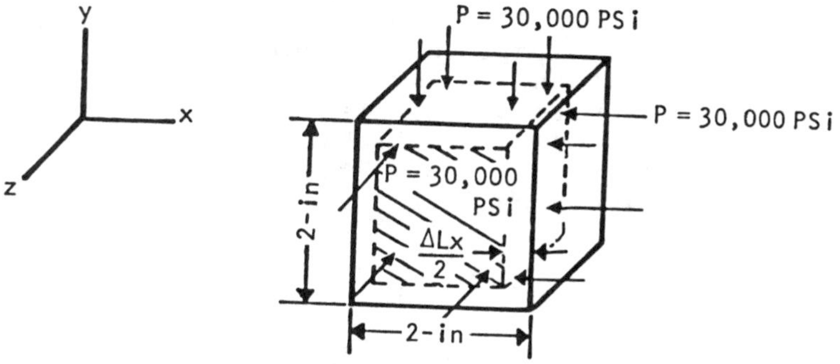

Solution: To determine strain, note that pressure is a compressive stress, and recognizing that the strains remain constant within the interval considered,

$$\varepsilon_x = \frac{1}{E}(\sigma_x - \nu\sigma_y - \nu\sigma_z) \text{ or}$$

$$\varepsilon_x = \frac{1}{E}\sigma_x - \frac{\nu}{E}\sigma_y - \frac{\nu}{E}\sigma_z$$

$$\varepsilon_x = \frac{(-30,000)}{(30)10^6} - \frac{(-30,000)}{4(30)10^6} - \frac{(-30,000)}{4(30)10^6}$$

$$= -(5)10^{-4} \text{ in. per in.}$$

The change in dimension between two parallel faces in a cube is the same for any two parallel faces around it.

$$\varepsilon_x = \frac{\Delta L_x}{L_x}$$

$$\Delta L_x = \varepsilon_x L_x = -(5)10^{-4} \times (2\text{-in.}) = -10^{-3} \text{ in.}$$

ΔL_x is negative because it is a compressive pressure and signifies a contraction.

• PROBLEM 5-3

A rubber cylinder A of diameter d is compressed in a steel cylinder B by a force P (see figure). Determine the pressure p between the rubber and the steel if P = 1000 lb, d = 2 in., and Poisson's ratio for rubber is 0.45.

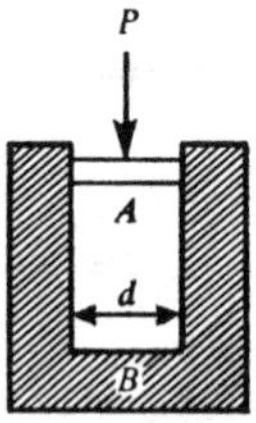

Solution: When the force P is applied to the rubber cylinder, it will compress. If the cylinder were unrestrained, it would react to the longitudinal shortening by expanding in the lateral direction. However, since it is restrained, it will exert a pressure on the steel cylinder equal to the stress in the rubber cylinder which would cause the unrestrained expansion.

Use the two dimensional stress-strain relation:

$$\varepsilon_{yy} = \frac{1}{E}(\tau_{yy} - \nu\tau_{xx}).$$

By equilibrium, $\tau_{yy} = 0$ because there is no applied force in the lateral direction

$$\tau_{xx} = -\frac{P}{A} \quad \text{(compression)}$$

$$= -\frac{1000}{\pi(1)^2}$$

$$= -\frac{1000}{\pi}.$$

Therefore, $$\varepsilon_{yy} = \frac{1}{E}\left(-.45\left(-\frac{1000}{\pi}\right)\right)$$

$$= \frac{450}{\pi E}.$$

The stress which causes this strain is just

$$\tau = \varepsilon \times E = P$$

$$P = \frac{450}{\pi} = 143.2 \text{ psi.}$$

A long, thin plate of width b, thickness t, and length L is placed between two rigid walls a distance b apart and is acted on by an axial force P, as shown in Figure 1. We wish to find the deflection of the plate parallel to the force P. We also wish to find the component of normal strain in the thin direction.

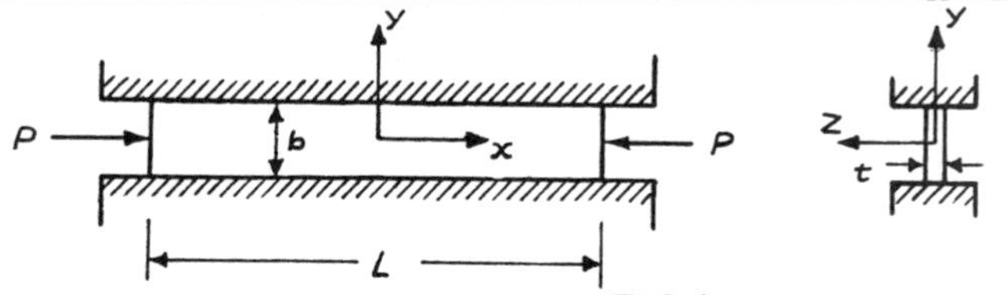

FIG. 1

(1) ACTUAL PROBLEM (2) IDEALIZED MODEL

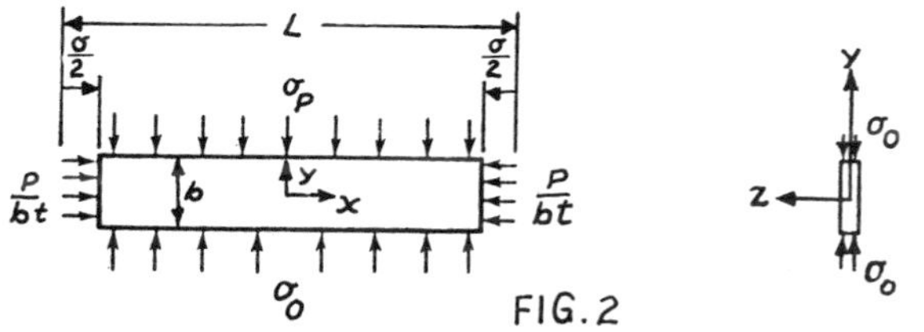

FIG. 2

Solution: The following assumptions are made to solve the problem, using the idealized model in Figure (2):

1. The axial force P results in an axial normal stress uniformly distributed over the plate area, including the end areas.
2. There is no normal stress in the thin direction. (Note that this implies a case of plane stress in the xy plane.)
3. There is no deformation in the y direction, that is, $\varepsilon_y = 0$. (Note that this implies a case of plane strain in the xz plane.)
4. There is no friction force at the walls (or, alternatively, it is small enough to be negligible).
5. The normal stress of contact between the plate and wall is uniform over the length and width of the plate.

Equilibrium with the external loads is satisfied when the stresses existing in the plate are

$$\sigma_x = -\frac{P}{bt} \qquad \sigma_y = -\sigma_0 \qquad \sigma_z = 0$$
$$\tau_{xy} = \tau_{yz} = \tau_{zx} = 0. \tag{a}$$

These stresses also satisfy the equilibrium equations, and therefore we assume them to be the stresses acting throughout the plate.

Since the walls are rigid, the plate cannot expand in the y direction, and therefore

$$\varepsilon_y = 0. \tag{b}$$

Also, in terms of the deflection parallel to the force P, δ, taken as a positive quantity, we can write

$$\varepsilon_x = -\frac{\delta}{L}. \tag{c}$$

In view of (a) and because the temperature is constant, Hook's law, which states that each component of stress is proportional to each component of strain, is applicable.

$$\varepsilon_x = \frac{1}{E}(\sigma_x - \nu(\sigma_y + \sigma_z))$$

$$\varepsilon_y = \frac{1}{E}(\sigma_y - \nu(\sigma_x + \sigma_z))$$

$$\varepsilon_z = \frac{1}{E}(\sigma_z - \nu(\sigma_x + \sigma_y))$$

but, since $\sigma_z = 0$

$$\varepsilon_x = \frac{1}{E}(\sigma_x - \nu\sigma_y) \quad \varepsilon_y = \frac{1}{E}(\sigma_y - \nu\sigma_x) \quad \varepsilon_z = -\frac{\nu}{E}(\sigma_x + \sigma_y) \tag{d}$$

$$\gamma_{xy} = \gamma_{yz} = \gamma_{zx} = 0$$

where ν is Poisson's ratio and E is Young's modulus.

Solving equation (d) for $\varepsilon_y = \frac{1}{E}(\sigma_y - \nu\sigma_x) = 0.$

$$\therefore \quad \sigma_y = \nu\sigma_x$$

but $\sigma_x = -\frac{P}{bt}$ (from eq. (a))

$$\therefore \quad \sigma_y = \nu\sigma_x = -\nu\frac{P}{bt}. \tag{e}$$

From eq. (c), $\varepsilon_x = -\frac{\delta}{L} = \quad = -\varepsilon_x L$

but $\qquad \varepsilon_x = \frac{1}{E}(\sigma_x - \nu\sigma_y)$

$$\therefore \quad \delta = -\frac{L}{E}(\sigma_x - \nu\sigma_y)$$

and $\sigma_y = \nu\sigma_x$.

Therefore, $\qquad \delta = -\frac{L}{E}(\sigma_x - \nu^2\sigma_x)$

$$\delta = -\frac{L}{E}(\sigma_x)(1 - \nu^2).$$

Knowing that $\sigma_x = -\frac{P}{bt} = \frac{\sigma_y}{\nu}$ then,

$$\delta = -\frac{L}{E}(-\frac{P}{bt})(1 - \nu^2) = +\frac{PL}{Ebt}(1 - \nu^2) \qquad \text{(f)}$$

We note that the presence of the rigid walls reduces the axial deflection of the plate by the factor $(1 - \nu^2)$.
To get ε_z:

$$\varepsilon_z = -\frac{\nu}{E}(\sigma_x + \sigma_y) \qquad \text{(from eq. (d))}.$$

$$\varepsilon_z = -\frac{\nu}{E}(-\frac{P}{bt} - \nu\frac{P}{bt}) \quad \text{from eqs. (a) and (e)}$$

$$\varepsilon_z = -\frac{\nu}{E}(-\frac{P}{bt})(1 + \nu)$$

$$\varepsilon_z = +\nu(1 + \nu)\frac{P}{Ebt}\,. \qquad \text{(g)}$$

The equation (f) can be written as

$$\delta = (1 + \nu)(1 - \nu)\frac{PL}{Ebt}$$

from which

$$(1 + \delta) = \frac{\delta}{L}\frac{Ebt}{P}(\frac{1}{1-\delta})$$

Substitute the value of $(1+\delta)$ into equation (g) to obtain

$$\varepsilon_z = \nu(\frac{\delta}{L})(\frac{Ebt}{P})(\frac{1}{1-\delta})\frac{P}{Ebt}$$

or,

$$\varepsilon_z = \frac{\nu}{1-\nu}\frac{\delta}{L}\,.$$

(Note that no load is applied in the z direction. The z-component of normal strain, ε_z, is due to the Poisson effect.)

• PROBLEM 5-5

A rod-shaped member has two separate loads applied along its length. The member is suspended at an end from a ceiling. Compute the displacement of the free (bottom) end.

<u>Solution</u>: Neglecting the weight of the member, we have 2 separate loads, each of which acts upon given segments of the rod. It will be convenient to analyze the bar in three separate sections: Starting at the top of the bar, draw a

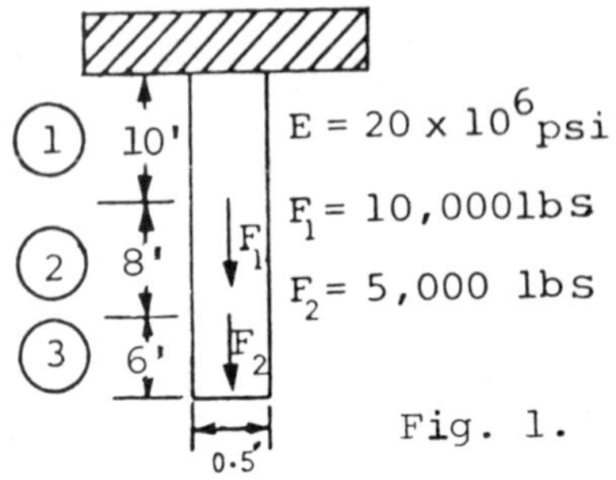

Fig. 1.

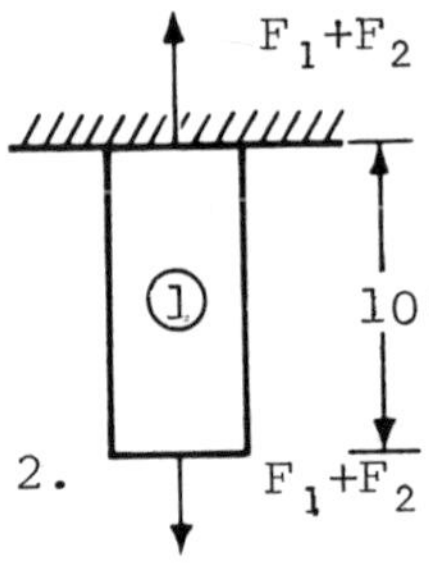

Fig. 2.

Fig. 3.

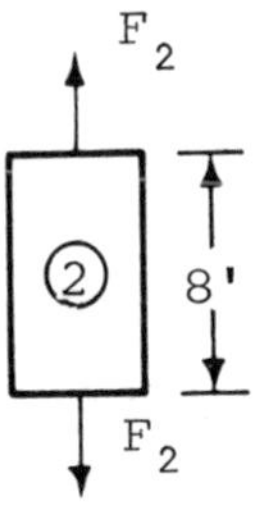

free-body diagram of the 10-foot section. For this purely extensional problem, the total extension of the section is given by

$$\delta_1 = \frac{FL}{AE} = \frac{(15{,}000 \text{ lb})(10 \text{ ft})}{\left(\pi\frac{(6")^2}{4}\right)(20 \times 10^6 \text{ psi})}$$

$$\delta_1 = 2.6526 \times 10^{-4} \text{ ft.}$$

For section 2, we have:

$$\delta_2 = \frac{(5000 \text{ lb})(8 \text{ ft})}{\left(\pi\frac{(6")^2}{4}\right)(20 \times 10^6 \text{ psi})}$$

$$\delta_2 = 7.0736 \times 10^{-5} \text{ ft.}$$

Neglecting the weight of the rod, section 3, the 6-foot section, is completely unloaded and will contribute nothing to the overall extension of the rod. Thus, the displacement at the end of the rod is

$$\delta_{TOT} = \delta_1 + \delta_2$$

$$= 2.6526 \times 10^{-4} + 7.0736 \times 10^{-5}$$

$$= 3.36 \times 10^{-4} \text{ ft.}$$

• PROBLEM 5-6

Consider a nylon cord with a diameter of $\frac{1}{4}$ in. and a length of 5 ft. If this material has a modulus of elasticity of 3×10^4 psi and a Poisson ratio of 0.4, what is the stress and the diameter when pulled by a force of 500 lb? Compute the spring constant for the load of 500 lb.

Solution: The basic measurement in stress-strain relations, a one-dimensional tensile test, yields two sets of information. The actual stress, $\tau_{xx\ actual}$, is computed using the actual cross-sectional area of the specimen, which decreases as the load increases. The engineering stress, $\tau_{xx\ eng}$, is calculated using the initial area of the specimen.

For small loads the cross-sectional area decreases very little, and the engineering stress remains quite close to the actual stress. However, if loads become high, the area will decrease appreciably, causing the engineering stress to diverge noticably from the actual stress. Due to the difficulty in measuring the change in area, and the simplicity of calculating τ_{eng}, this stress is the more common.

In this example, the Poisson ratio is 0.4, meaning that the diameter of the cord will decrease rather quickly with increasing load $\left(\varepsilon_{yy} = -\nu\left(\frac{F}{EA_0}\right)\right)$. Also, the load applied is quite high for a cord of the given diameter and Young's modulus, so we will consider the actual stress.

To find the actual stress, we must first find the actual area of the cord. In other words, we must take into account the decrease in diameter due to the Poisson effect.

We begin with the two-dimensional stress-strain relation

$$\varepsilon_{yy} = \frac{1}{E}(\tau_{yy} - \nu\tau_{xx})$$

$\tau_{yy} = 0$ so

$$\varepsilon_{yy} = -\frac{\nu\tau_{xx}}{E}$$

$$\varepsilon_{xx} = \frac{\tau_{xx}}{E}.$$

The change in diameter, Δd, which is in the y-direction in this case is given by

$$\Delta d = d \cdot \varepsilon_{yy}.$$

The new diameter, $d + \Delta d$, then is

$$d + \Delta d = d + d \cdot \varepsilon_{yy}$$

giving the actual area

$$A = \frac{\pi d^2}{4} = \frac{\pi(d + d\varepsilon_{yy})^2}{4}.$$

Therefore, the acutal stress is

$$\tau_{xx} = \frac{F}{A} = \frac{F}{\frac{\pi(d+d\varepsilon_{yy})^2}{4}}.$$

Substituting for ε_{yy}:

$$= \frac{4F}{\pi\left(d - \frac{\nu\tau_{xx}d}{E}\right)^2}.$$

Inserting all known values, we have

$$\tau_{xx} = \frac{4(500)}{\pi\left(\frac{1}{4} - \frac{.4\tau_{xx} \cdot \frac{1}{4}}{3 \cdot 10^4}\right)^2}$$

$$= \frac{2000}{\pi\left(\frac{1}{4} - \frac{\tau_{xx}}{3 \cdot 10^5}\right)^2}.$$

With this expression for stress, we must use an iterative approach. We begin by calculating the engineering stress

$$\tau_{xx} = \frac{500}{\pi(.25)^2}$$

$$= 2546.48 \text{ psi.}$$

We substitute this value for τ_{xx} in the right-hand side of the equation and get a new value for τ_{xx}

$$\tau_{xx} = 10{,}914 \text{ psi.}$$

Now, substitute this value in the right-hand expression and continue in this manner until the value begins to approach a limit. For example, the 2nd and 3rd values are 10,914 and 13,950 respectively, an increase of 27.8%. The sixteenth and seventeenth values are 17,075 and 17,076, an increase of .005%. So, τ_{xx} = 17,076 psi. Note the large discrepancy between engineering stress and actual stress in this case. The diameter is found using the expression

$$d + \Delta d = d - \frac{d\nu\tau_{xx}}{E}$$

$$= .25 - \frac{.25(.4)(17{,}076)}{3 \cdot 10^4}$$

$$= .193 \text{ in.}$$

The spring constant, K, is a constant of proportionality relating the applied load to elongation.

$$F = k\Delta\ell.$$

Now, $\Delta\ell = t_{xx} \cdot \ell$

and $t_{xx} = \frac{\tau_{xx}}{E}$.

But $\tau_{xx} = \dfrac{4F}{\pi\left(d - \dfrac{\nu\tau_{xx}d}{E}\right)^2}$

so, by making these substitutions,

$$F = \frac{K\ell}{E}\left[\frac{4F}{\pi\left(d - \dfrac{\nu\tau_{xx}d}{E}\right)^2}\right]$$

or
$$K = \frac{E\pi\left(d - \dfrac{\nu\tau_{xx}d}{E}\right)^2}{4\ell}$$

$$= \frac{(3 \cdot 10^4)\pi\left(.25 - \dfrac{.4(17{,}076)(.25)}{3 \cdot 10^4}\right)^2}{4 \cdot 5 \cdot 12}$$

$$= 14.64 \text{ lb/in.}$$

• PROBLEM 5-7

An element in a state of biaxial stress is subjected to stresses $\sigma_{xx} = -\sigma_{yy} = 10{,}000$ psi. (See. Fig. 1.) What are the principal normal strains ε_a, ε_b, and the maximum shear strain γ, if the modulus of elasticity $E = 10 \times 10^6$ psi and Poisson's ratio $\nu = 0.25$?

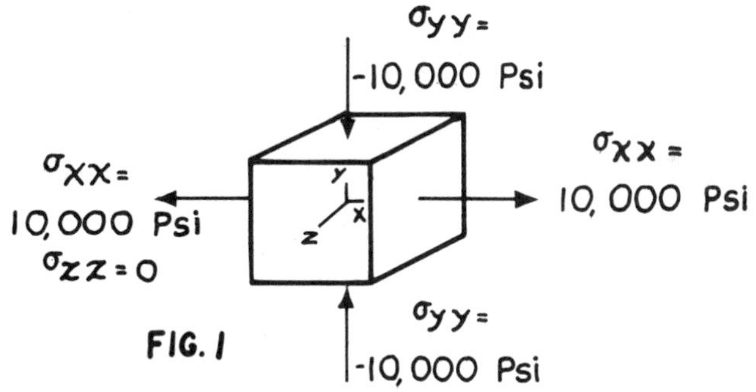

FIG. 1

Solution: To find the principal strains, we first must find the strains in the x and y direction due to the applied stresses. Using the three-dimensional Hooke's Law, and noting that σ_{zz} is equal to zero, we have

$$\varepsilon_{xx} = \frac{1}{E}(\sigma_{xx} - \nu\sigma_{yy})$$

$$\varepsilon_{yy} = \frac{1}{E}(\sigma_{yy} - \nu\sigma_{xx})$$

$$\varepsilon_{xx} = \frac{1}{10 \cdot 10^6}(10,000 - .25(-10,000))$$

$$= .00125$$

$$\varepsilon_{yy} = \frac{1}{10 \cdot 10^6}(-10,000 - .25(10,000))$$

$$= -.00125.$$

We proceed to find the principal strains by using the formula

$$\varepsilon_{a,b} = \frac{\varepsilon_{xx} - \varepsilon_{yy}}{2} \pm \sqrt{\left(\frac{\varepsilon_{xx} - \varepsilon_{yy}}{2}\right)^2 + \varepsilon_{xy}^2}$$

with the values $\varepsilon_{xx} = -\varepsilon_{yy} = .00125$; $\varepsilon_{xy} = 0$:

$$\varepsilon_a = \frac{.00125 - .00125}{2} + \sqrt{\left(\frac{.00125 - (-.00125)}{2}\right)^2 + 0^2}$$

$$= .00125$$

$$\varepsilon_b = \frac{.00125 - .00125}{2} - \sqrt{\left(\frac{.00125 - (-.00125)}{2}\right)^2 + 0^2}$$

$$= -.00125.$$

The formula for shear strain in rotated coordinates is

$$\varepsilon_{x'y'} = \frac{\varepsilon_{yy} - \varepsilon_{xx}}{2} \sin 2\theta + \varepsilon_{xy} \cos 2\theta .$$

To find the maximum shear strain we let

$$\frac{d\varepsilon_{x'y'}}{d\theta} = 0 = \left(\frac{\varepsilon_{yy} - \varepsilon_{xx}}{2}\right) 2 \cos 2\theta - 2\varepsilon_{xy} \sin 2\theta$$

Since $\varepsilon_{xy} = 0$

$$0 = \left(\frac{\varepsilon_{yy} - \varepsilon_{xx}}{2}\right) 2 \cos 2\theta .$$

$\frac{\varepsilon_{yy} - \varepsilon_{xx}}{2}$ is a given value so $\cos 2\theta$ must equal zero. This occurs at 45° and 135°.

$$\varepsilon_{x'y'} \text{ at } 45° = \left(\frac{-.00125 - .00125}{2}\right) \sin(2 \times 45°)$$

$$= -.00125$$

$$\varepsilon_{x'y'} \text{ at } 135° = \left(\frac{-.00125 - .00125}{2}\right)\sin(2 \times 135°)$$

$$= .00125.$$

Therefore, the maximum shear strain $\gamma = 2t_{x'y'} = .0025.$

• PROBLEM 5-8

> The shank of a bolt is subjected to an axial force F. A sleeve is located between the bolt head and a fixed ceiling. Calculate the displacements of D and C.

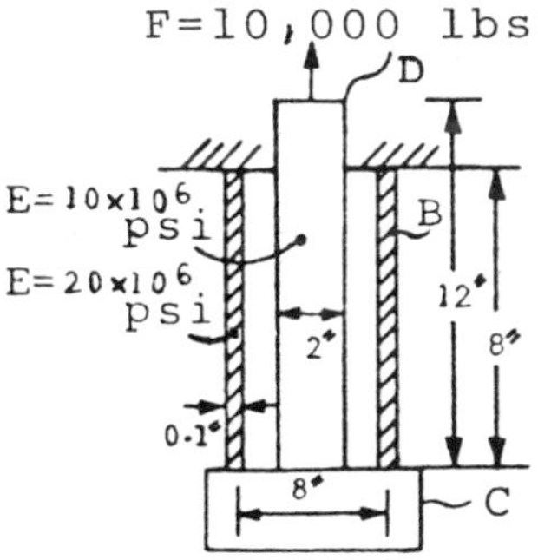

Fig. 1.

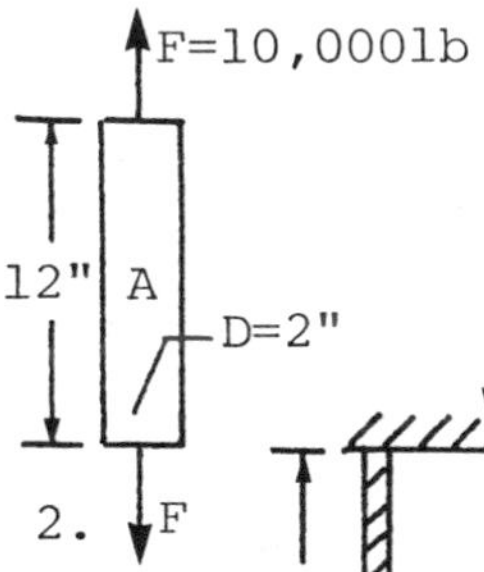

Fig. 2.

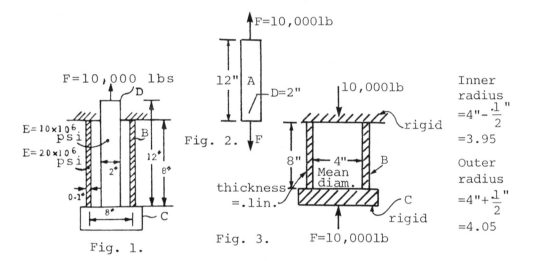

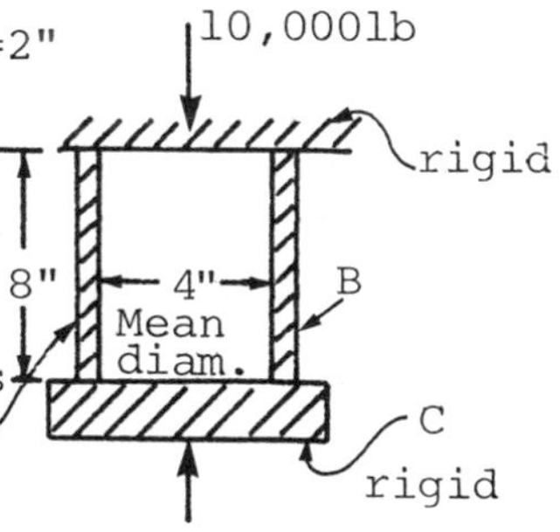

Fig. 3.

Inner radius $= 4" - \frac{.1}{2}" = 3.95$

Outer radius $= 4" + \frac{.1}{2}" = 4.05$

Solution: First, draw a free-body diagram of rod A: For this one-dimensional simple extension problem, the total elongation, δ_A, is given by:

$$\delta_A = \frac{FL_A}{A_A E_A},$$

where A_A = area of rod A; E_A = modulus of elasticity of rod A, and L_A = length of rod A. Therefore,

$$\delta_A = \frac{(10{,}000 \text{ lb})(12")}{\pi\left(\frac{2^2}{4}\right)\left[10 \times 10^6 \text{ psi}\right]} = 3.8197 \times 10^{-3} \text{ in.}$$

This is the extension of rod A. We now want to find how far sleeve B will compress under the applied load. Draw a free-body diagram of sleeve B:

The length change, δ_B, is calculated the same way as δ_A, except that the member is now in compression, so that it will be shortened by an amount δ_B.

$$\delta_B = \frac{FL_B}{A_B E_B} = \frac{(10,000\ \text{lb})(8")}{\left[\pi\left(\frac{4.05^2 - 3.95^2}{4}\right)\text{in}^2\right](20 \times 10^6\ \text{psi})}$$

$$\delta_B = 6.3662 \times 10^{-3}\ \text{in.}$$

Thus, it is apparent from Fig. 1 that plate C will rise by .0063662".

From compatability considerations: Upward movement of end D, Δ, is given by $\Delta = \delta_A + \delta_B$ = .0038197" + .0063662". Thus, end D moves upward by an amount Δ = .0101859 in.

• PROBLEM 5-9

A structure for suspending a load F is composed of two rods of different materials connected together. a) Calculate the deflection at the end of the structure due to the load. b) Assuming the indicated yield points, find the load for which yielding will occur. c) Determine the permanent deformation of the end if the load is removed after the end was first deformed by .05 ft due to the load.

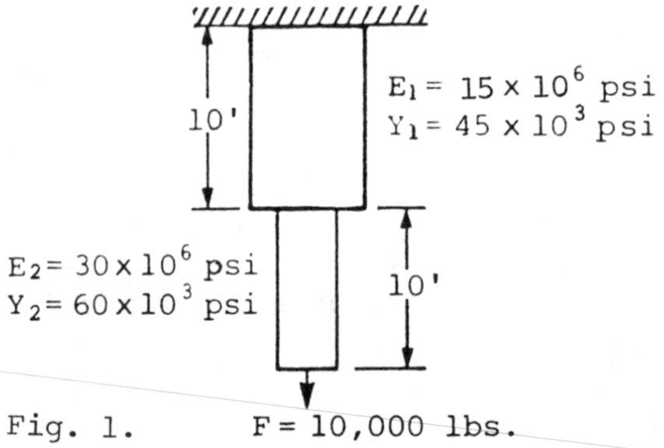

Fig. 1.

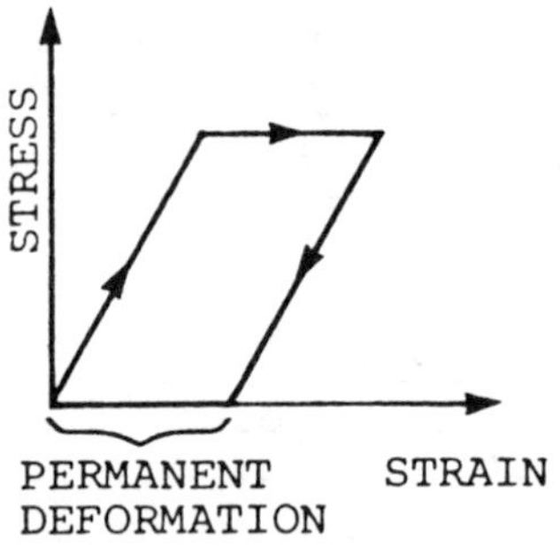

Fig. 2.

Solution: From equilibrium considerations at sections away from C, B, and A where there are stress concentrations, we may say for the stress τ_{zz} if we neglect the weight of the members:

$$(\tau_{zz})_1 = \frac{F}{A_1} = \frac{10,000}{\pi\frac{2^2}{4}} = 3183\ \text{psi}$$

$$(\tau_{zz})_2 = \frac{F}{A_2} = \frac{10,000}{\pi\frac{1^2}{4}} = 12,730\ \text{psi.}$$

To get the total deflection we now compute the strain ε_{zz} assuming that it is uniform throughout each rod. We now use the constitutive law (Hooke's law) for elastic materials as follows:

$$(\varepsilon_{zz})_1 = \frac{(\tau_{zz})_1}{E_1} = \frac{3183}{15 \times 10^6} = .212 \times 10^{-3}$$

$$(\varepsilon_{zz})_2 = \frac{(\tau_{zz})_2}{E_2} = \frac{12,730}{30 \times 10^6} = .424 \times 10^{-3}$$

Knowing the strain ε_{zz} of each material, the elongation of each cylinder due to the 10,000 lb load can be determined.

$$\delta_1 = \int_0^{10} (\varepsilon_{zz})_1 \, dz = (\varepsilon_{zz})_1 L_1$$

$$= (.212 \times 10^{-3})(10) = .212 \times 10^{-2} \text{ ft}$$

$$\delta_2 = \int_{10}^{20} (\varepsilon_{zz})_2 \, dz = (\varepsilon_{zz})_2 L_2$$

$$= (.424 \times 10^{-3})(10) = .424 \times 10^{-2} \text{ft.}$$

The deflection δ_1 and δ_2 are completely compatible with each other for all values of δ_1 and δ_2. The entire deflection δ_T of point A as the result of the force F is then

$$\delta_T = \delta_1 + \delta_2 = .636 \times 10^{-2} \text{ ft.}$$

b) Considering the materials separately we have

$$Y_1 = 45,000 = \frac{F_1}{\frac{\pi(2)^2}{4}}$$

$$\therefore F_1 = 141,400 \text{ lb}$$

$$Y_2 = 60,000 = \frac{F_2}{\frac{\pi(1)^2}{4}}$$

$$\therefore F_2 = 47,100 \text{ lb}$$

Clearly, the maximum load permitted for no yielding would be just smaller than 47,100 lb.

c) The maximum possible deflection of end A with elastic action everywhere occurs when F is just under 47,1000 lb, as computed above. We can thus say that

$$(\delta_{max})_{El} = \left[\frac{(\tau_{zz})_1}{E_1}\right](L_1) + \left[\frac{(\tau_{zz})_2}{E_2}\right](L_2)$$

$$= \left[\frac{\frac{47{,}100}{\frac{\pi(2)^2}{4}}}{15\times10^6}\right](10) + \left[\frac{\frac{47{,}100}{\frac{\pi(1)^2}{4}}}{30\times10^6}\right](10)$$

$$= 1.000 \times 10^{-2} + 2.00 \times 10^{-2}$$

$$= 3.00 \times 10^{-2} \text{ ft.}$$

It is clear that for a deflection of 5.00×10^{-2} ft there must be yielding for the system. The lower member reaches the yield conditions first when the deflection is 3×10^{-2} ft and then with constant stress "flows" to generate the additional deflection of 2×10^{-2} ft, while the upper member undergoes no further change whatever from the elastic extension of 1.000×10^{-2} ft. This may seem strange, but you must realize that it is a consequence of the "perfectly plastic" idealization we have made. Thus, the force needed is just over 47,100 lb causing an elastic elongation in member 1 of 1.000×10^{-2} ft and an elastic elongation in member 2 of 2.00×10^{-2} ft plus a plastic elongation in member 2 of 2.00×10^{-2} ft. When the load is released, member 1 will recover elastically completely, but member 2 will retain a permanent elongation of 2.00×10^{-2} ft. The stress-strain curve for member 2 is shown in Fig. (2) for this action.

• PROBLEM 5-10

A reinforcing hoop is placed on a barrel having a smooth cylindrical surface at that location. The hoop is a composite of a steel outer part and aluminum inner part. The hoop is tightened by closing the gap between its ends by turning the bolt in the nut. Compute the stresses in the inner and outer parts.

Solution: We will assume that the hoop pieces are thin enough that the stress will be the same throughout the thickness of each material. We will then use the average radius of each part of the hoop to calculate its length.

$$L_{STEEL} = 2\pi(8.20") = 0.3" = 51.2"$$

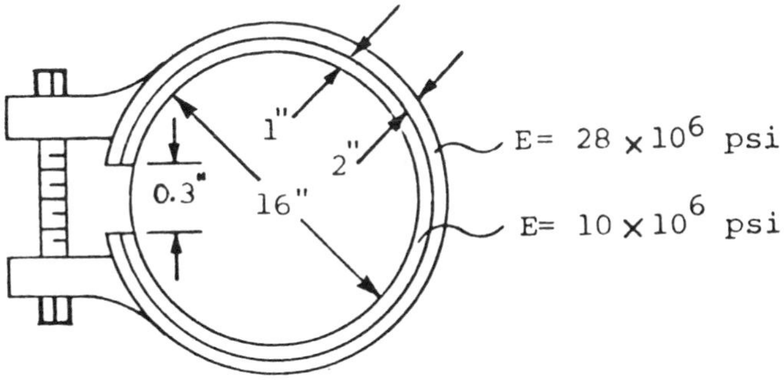

$$\varepsilon_{STEEL} = \frac{\delta_{STEEL}}{L_{STEEL}}.$$

The band will be stretched by 0.3 inches, so

$$\varepsilon_{STEEL} = \frac{0.3"}{51.2"} = .00586$$

$$\sigma_{STEEL} = (E_{STEEL})(\varepsilon_{STEEL}) = (28 \times 10^6)(.00586)$$

$$\sigma_{STEEL} = 164,000 \text{ psi}$$

Likewise, for the aluminum part:

$$L_{A\ell} = 2\pi(8.05") - 0.3" = 50.28"$$

$$\varepsilon_{A\ell} = \frac{0.3"}{50.28"} = .00597$$

$$\sigma_{A\ell} = (E_{A\ell})(\varepsilon_{A\ell}) = (10 \times 10^6)(.00597).$$

$$\sigma_{A\ell} = 59,700 \text{ psi}.$$

• PROBLEM 5-11

A substantially horizontal member BOC is held in position by two links that are pivoted at their ends and have the same diameters and materials. The angular rotation of the member is not to exceed a predetermined amount. Calculate the least diameter of the links for the indicated yield stress and safety factor.

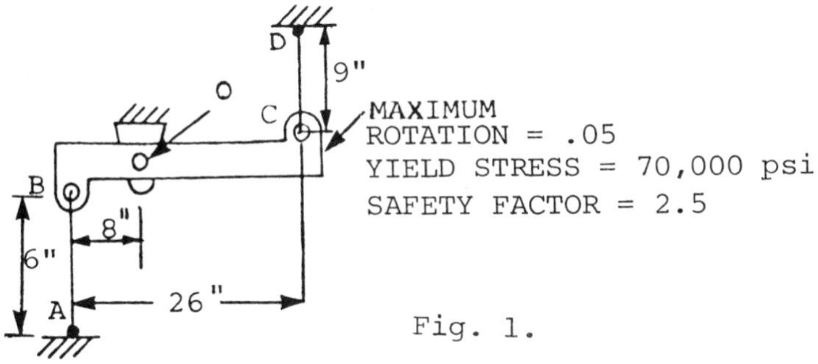

Fig. 1.

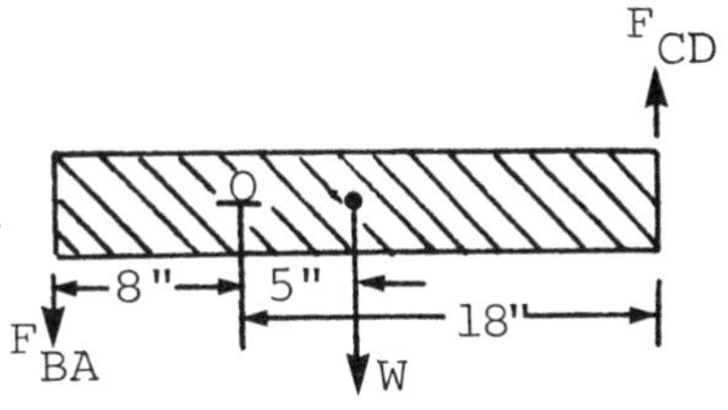

Fig. 2.

Solution: By permitting the block to rotate the full amount of .05° we shall be ensuring a minimum diameter of the rods. However, in such a procedure we must check to see if the stresses in the rods exceed the allowable stress for the design. We shall proceed in the aforestated manner.

From equilibrium, in setting moments about point 0 equal to zero, knowing that the weight of the block (100,000 lbs) acts at the centroid of the block which is $\frac{18+8}{2} - 8" = 5$ in. away from point 0 (Fig. 2).

$\Sigma M_0 = 0$ +↻

$$-F_{BA}(8 \text{ in}) - F_{CD}(18 \text{ in}) + 100{,}000(5 \text{ in}) = 0 \qquad \text{(a)}$$

Using the constitutive law for elastic behavior we have

$$\delta_{BA} = \frac{F_{BA}}{AE}(L_{BA}) = \frac{F_{BA}(\text{lb})}{A(\text{in.}^2)}\left(\frac{6"}{18 \times 10^6 \frac{\text{lb}}{\text{in.}^2}}\right) = \frac{F_{BA}}{A}\left(\frac{1}{3} \times 10^{-6}\right) \text{in.} \qquad \text{(b)}$$

$$\delta_{CD} = \frac{F_{CD}}{AE}(L_{CD}) = \frac{F_{CD}(\text{lb})}{A(\text{in.}^2)}\left(\frac{9"}{18 \times 10^6 \frac{\text{lb}}{\text{in.}^2}}\right) = \frac{F_{CD}}{A}\left(\frac{1}{2} \times 10^{-6}\right) \text{in.} \qquad \text{(c)}$$

For maximum allowable rotation of the block the change in length of AB will equal 8 in × sin(.05°), or in radians, $8 \times \sin\frac{(.05)2\pi}{360}$. The change in length of CD will be $18 \sin\frac{(.05)2\pi}{360}$. For small angles, $\sin\theta \cong \theta$ so for compatibility,

$$\delta_{BA} = (8)\frac{.05}{360}(2\pi) = .00698 \text{ in.} \qquad \text{(d)}$$

$$\delta_{CD} = (18)\frac{.05}{360}(2\pi) = .01570 \text{ in.} \qquad \text{(e)}$$

Substituting for δ_{BA}, δ_{CD} in equations (b), (c), we get

$$\frac{F_{BA}}{A} = .02094 \times 10^6 \text{ psi} \qquad \text{(f)}$$

$$\frac{F_{CD}}{A} = .03140 \times 10^6 \text{ psi.} \qquad \text{(g)}$$

Equations (a), (f), and (g) comprise three equations for the three unknowns F_{BA}, F_{CD}, and A. Solving for F_{BA} and F_{CD} in terms of A in Eqs. (f) and (g) and substituting these results into Eq. (a) we get

$$8[(.02094) \times 10^6 A] + 18[(.0314) \times 10^6 A] = 500{,}000$$

$$\therefore A = .682 \text{ in.}^2$$

The corresponding diameter is then

$$D = .932 \text{ in.}$$

Now compute the forces F_{BA} and F_{CD}. From Eqs. (f) and (g) we get

$$F_{BA} = (.02094)(10^6)(.682) = 14{,}280 \text{ lb}$$

$$F_{CD} = (.03140)(10^6)(.682) = 21{,}400 \text{ lb}$$

becuase the force in CD is greater than BA, while both have the same diameter, the maximum stress occurs in rod CD and is

$$\sigma_{max} = \frac{21{,}400}{.682} = 31{,}400 \text{ psi.}$$

This is greater than the allowable stress of

$$\frac{70{,}000}{2.5} = 28{,}000 \text{ psi}$$

where 2.5 is the factor of safety, and so we conclude that we cannot permit the deflection of .05°. The stress level rather than the deflection becomes the controlling factor. We then assign the stress in rod CD to be 28,000 psi. Note that by assigning the maximum permissible stress to rod CD, we shall be minimizing the diameter of the rods under the constraint that the allowable stress not be exceeded. Equations (a), (b), and (c) with $F_{CD}/A = 28{,}000$ still apply, but in Eqs. (d) and (e) we must replace the angle .05° by an unknown quantity β. These equations are now restated as follows:

$$8F_{BA} + 18F_{CD} = 500{,}000 \tag{h}$$

$$\delta_{BA} = \left(\frac{F_{BA}}{AE}\right)L_{BA} = \frac{F_{BA}}{A}\left(\frac{1}{3} \times 10^{-6}\right) \text{in.} \tag{i}$$

$$\delta_{CD} = \left(\frac{F_{CD}}{AE}\right)L_{CD} = (28{,}000)\left(\frac{1}{2} \times 10^{-6}\right) = .014 \text{ in} \tag{j}$$

$$\delta_{BA} = 8\left(\frac{\beta}{360}\right)(2\pi) = .1396\beta \tag{k}$$

$$\delta_{CD} = 18\left(\frac{\beta}{360}\right)(2\pi) = .314\beta. \tag{l}$$

We have here as unknowns F_{BA}, F_{CD}, δ_{BA}, δ_{CD}, and β -- five unknowns for which we have five equations. From Eqs. (k) and (l) we see that

$$\delta_{CD} = \frac{.314}{.1395}\delta_{BA} = 2.25\delta_{BA}.$$

Using the result of Eq. (j) for δ_{CD} , we get for δ_{BA} from above

$$.014 = 2.25\delta_{BA}$$

$$\therefore \delta_{BA} = .00622 \text{ in.}$$

From Eq. (i) we get

$$.00622 = \frac{F_{BA}}{A}\left(\frac{1}{3} \times 10^{-6}\right)$$

$$\therefore \frac{F_{BA}}{A} = 18{,}660 \text{ psi.} \qquad \text{(m)}$$

In Eq. (h) we now divide through by A. We thus have

$$8\left(\frac{F_{BA}}{A}\right) + 18\left(\frac{F_{CD}}{A}\right) = \frac{500{,}000}{A}.$$

Replacing F_{BA}/A by 18,660 as per Eq. (m) and F_{CD}/A by 28,000, for the above equation we get

$$(8)(18{,}660) + (18)(28{,}000) = \frac{500{,}000}{A}$$

$$\therefore A = .765 \text{ in.}^2.$$

Hence, the minimum diameter is

$$D_{min} = .987 \text{ in.}$$

In practice we use the closest stock diameter larger than the above diameter.

• PROBLEM 5-12

A 30-in.-long aluminum rod is enclosed within a steel-alloy tube,(Figs. 1,2). The two materials are bonded together. If the stress-strain diagrams for the two materials can be idealized as shown, respectively, in Figure 4, what end deflection will occur for P_1 = 80 kips and for P_2 = 125 kips? The cross-sectional areas of steel A_s and of aluminum A_a are the same and equal to 0.5 in.^{2}.

Solution: Drawing the free body diagram of the bar for an arbitrary section, (Fig. 3), the distribution of the load P on the cross-section of the bar is not known for two different materials, so the problem is internally statically indeterminate. The requirements of equilibrium (statics) remain valid, but additional conditions are necessary to solve the problem. One of the auxiliary conditions comes from the requirements of the compatibility of deformations. However, since the requirements of statics involve forces and deforma-

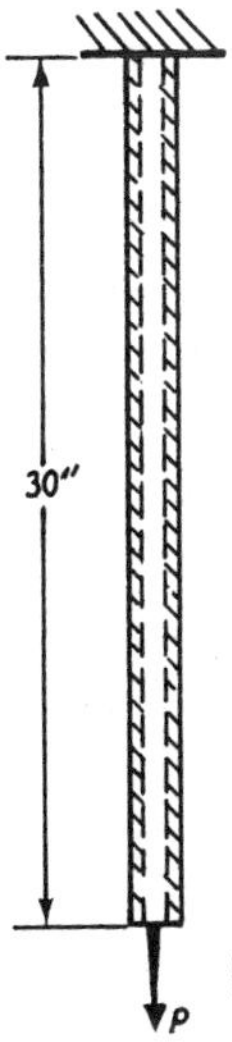

FIG. 1

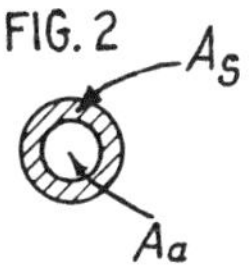

FIG. 2

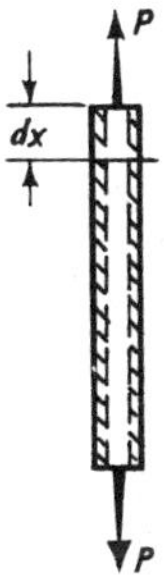

FIG. 3

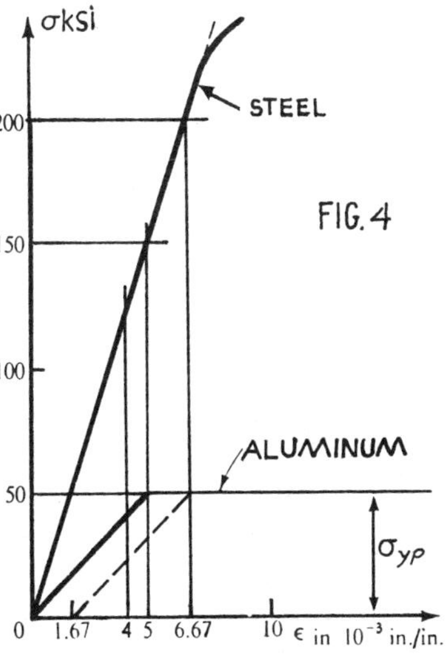

FIG. 4

tions involve displacements, a connecting condition based on the property of materials must be added.

Let subscripts a and s on P, ε, and σ identify these quantities as being for aluminum and steel, respectively. Then, noting that the applied force is supported by a force developed in steel and aluminum and because the two materials are bounded together, at every section the displacement or the strain of the two materials is the same, and tentatively assuming elastic response of both materials, one has

Equilibrium: $P_a + P_s = P_1$ or P_2

Deformation: $u_a = u_s$ or $\varepsilon_a = \varepsilon_s$

Material properties: $\varepsilon_a = \sigma_a/E_a$ and $\varepsilon_s = \sigma_s/E_s$

From Fig. 4 the slope of each curve is $\frac{\sigma}{\varepsilon}$ which is the elastic modulus of material, $E_s = 30 \times 10^6$ psi, $E_a = 10 \times 10^6$ psi. Thus

$$\varepsilon_a = \varepsilon_s = \frac{\sigma_a}{E_a} = \frac{\sigma_s}{E_s} = \frac{P_a}{A_a E_a} = \frac{P_s}{A_s E_s}$$

$$\frac{P_a}{A_a E_a} = \frac{P_s}{A_s E_s} \quad \text{solving for } P_s$$

$$P_s = P_a \left(\frac{A_s E_s}{A_a E_a} \right)$$

Since $A_s = A_a$

$$P_s = P_a \frac{E_s}{E_a} \quad \text{or} \quad P_s = P_a \left(\frac{30 \times 10^6}{10 \times 10^6} \right)$$

$$P_s = 3P_a.$$

Substituting back in the qquation $P_a + P_s = 80^k$

$$P_a + 3P_a = 80 \Rightarrow P_a = 20^k$$

$$P_s = 60^k.$$

Deflection of the bar is

$$u = \frac{PL}{AE} \quad \text{or} \quad \frac{P_s L}{A_s E_s} = \frac{P_a L}{A_a E_a} = \frac{20(10^3)30}{0.5(10)(10^6)} = 0.12 \text{ in.}$$

This corresponds to a strain of $0.120/30 = 4 \times 10^{-3}$ in. per inch. In this range both materials respond elastically, which satisfies the material-property assumption made at the beginning of this solution. In fact, as may be seen from Fig. 4, since for the linearly elastic response the strain can reach 5×10^{-3} in. per inch for both materials, by direct proportion the applied force P can be as large as 100 kips.

At P = 100 kips the stress in aluminum reaches 50 ksi. According to the idealized stress-strain diagram no higher stress can be resisted by this material, although the strains may continue to increase. Therefore, beyond P = 100 kips, the aluminum rod can be counted upon to resist only $P_a = A_a \sigma_{yp} = 0.5 \times 50 = 25$ kips. The remainder of the applied load must be carried by the steel tube. For $P_2 = 125$ kips, 100 kips must be carried by the steel tube. Hence $\sigma_s = 100/0.5 = 200$ ksi. At this stress level $\varepsilon_s = 200(30 \times 10^3) = 6.67 \times 10^{-3}$ in. per inch. Therefore, the tip deflection

$$u = \varepsilon_s L = 6.67 \times 10^{-3} \times 30 = 0.200 \text{ in.}$$

Note that it is not possible to determine u from the strain in aluminum since no unique strain corresponds to the stress of 50 ksi, which is all that the aluminum rod can carry. However, in this case the elastic steel tube contains the plastic flow. Thus, the strains in both materials are the same, i.e., $\varepsilon_s = \varepsilon_a = 6.67 \times 10^{-3}$ in. per inch, see Fig. 4.

If the applied load $P_2 = 125$ kips were removed, both materials in the rod would rebound elastically. Thus if one imagines the bond between the two materials broken, the steel tube would return to its initial shape. But a permanent set (stretch) of $(6.67 - 5) \times 10^{-3} = 1.67 \times 10^{-3}$ in. per inch would occur in the aluminum rod. This incompatibility of strain cannot develop if the two materials are bonded together. Instead, residual stresses develop, which maintain the same axial deformations in both materials. In this case, the aluminum rod remains slightly compressed, and the steel tube is slightly stretched.

To determine the stress concentration factor k in a plate with an elliptical opening therethrough is subjected to photoelastic measurement to find the stress at the indicated point on the ellipse. Compute the strain tensor at this point.

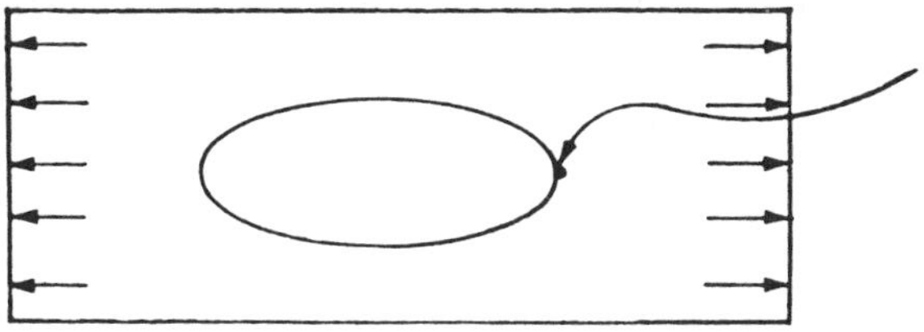

Solution: Since the material is linear-elastic with modulus of elasticity, E, from Hooke's law we know that the stress is proportional to the strain:

$$\tau_{ii} = E\varepsilon_{ii}$$

and

$$\tau_{ij} = 2G\varepsilon_{ij} \qquad i \neq j$$

$$G = \frac{E}{1 + 2\nu}.$$

Because the plate is in a state of plane stress, we must use the two-dimensional form of Hooke's law for the normal strains:

$$\varepsilon_{xx} = \frac{1}{E}[\tau_{xx} - \nu\tau_{yy}]$$

$$\varepsilon_{yy} = \frac{1}{E}[\tau_{yy} - \nu\tau_{xx}]$$

The shear stresses act independently of each other, so they are unaffected.

Substituting $\tau_{xx} = 2000$ psi and all other stresses equal to zero, we get:

$$\varepsilon_{xx} = \frac{1}{50 \cdot 10^6}[2000],$$

$$= 40 \times 10^{-5}$$

$$\varepsilon_{yy} = \frac{1}{50 \cdot 10^6}[-(.2)(2000)]$$

$$= -8 \times 10^{-5}.$$

The shear stresses are all zero, so $\frac{\tau_{ij}}{G}$ will be zero.

Therefore, the strain tensor is

$$\varepsilon_{ij} = \begin{bmatrix} 40 & 0 & 0 \\ 0 & -8 & 0 \\ 0 & 0 & -8 \end{bmatrix} \times 10^{-5}$$

• PROBLEM 5-14

The principal strains in the plane of a flat aluminum plate which is loaded in its plane are

$$\varepsilon_1 = 3.2 \times 10^{-4}$$

$$\varepsilon_2 = -5.4 \times 10^{-4}.$$

Find the stresses σ_x, σ_y, σ_z and τ_{xy}, where the x, y axes are located as shown in the sketch.

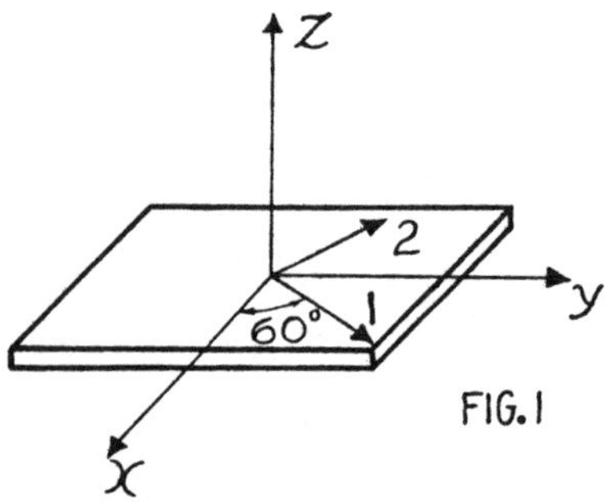

FIG. 1

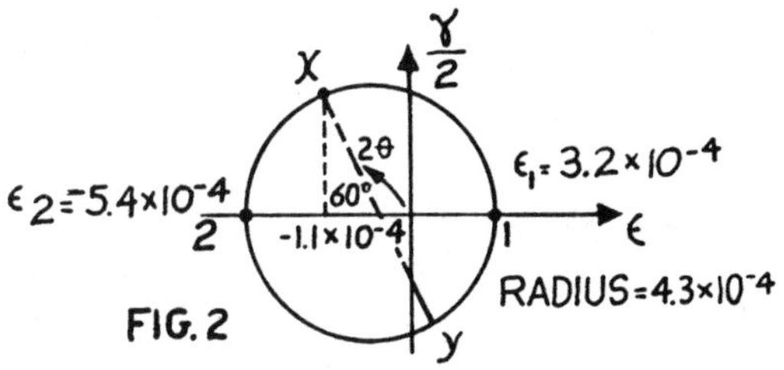

FIG. 2

Solution: The principal strains are those for which the shear strains are zero. Since there are only 2 non-zero components of strain, we have the case of plane strain. We will take $E = 11 \times 10^6$ psi and $\nu = \frac{1}{3}$ for aluminum.

The first step in the solution is to construct a Mohr's circle for strain. We are given principal strains, which are plotted on the ε axis in Fig. 2. The center of the circle is halfway between points 1 and 2. From Fig. 1, we see that axis 1 must be rotated 60° clockwise to get to axis x, and 2 must be rotated 60° clockwise to get to axis y. By the Mohr's circle convention, we always rotate 2θ in the reverse direction from the physical situation. In this case we rotate 120° counter-clockwise. After rotation, we find

$$\varepsilon_x = (4.3 \cos 120° - 1.1) \times 10^{-4} = -3.25 \times 10^{-4}$$

$$\varepsilon_y = (4.3 \cos (-60°) - 1.1) \times 10^{-4} = +1.05 \times 10^{-4}$$

and $\dfrac{\gamma_{xy}}{2} = (4.3 \times 10^{-4}) \sin 60° = 3.724 \times 10^{-4}$

or $\gamma_{xy} = 7.448 \times 10^{-4}.$

Now, we can use stress-strain relationships for plane strain to obtain the desired stresses:

$$\sigma_x = \frac{E}{(1 + \nu)(1 - 2\nu)}[(1 - \nu)\varepsilon_x + \nu\varepsilon_y]$$

$$\sigma_x = \frac{11 \times 10^6}{(\frac{4}{3})(\frac{1}{3})}\left[\frac{2}{3}(-3.25 \times 10^{-4}) + \frac{1}{3}(1.05 \times 10^{-4})\right]$$

$$\sigma_x = -4495 \text{ psi}$$

$$\sigma_y = \frac{E}{(1 + \nu)(1 - 2\nu)}[\nu\varepsilon_x + (1 - \nu)\varepsilon_y]$$

$$\sigma_y = \frac{11 \times 10^6}{(\frac{4}{3})(\frac{1}{3})}\left[\frac{1}{3}(-3.25 \times 10^{-4}) + \frac{2}{3}(1.05 \times 10^{-4})\right]$$

$$\sigma_y = -947.9 \text{ psi.}$$

$$\tau_{xy} = \gamma G,$$

where $$G = \frac{E}{2(1 + \nu)}$$

$$G_{A\ell} = \frac{11 \times 10^6 \text{ psi}}{2(1 + \frac{1}{3})} = 4.125 \times 10^6 \text{ psi}$$

$$\tau_{xy} = (4.125 \times 10^6)(7.448 \times 10^{-4})$$

$$\tau_{xy} = 3072 \text{ psi.}$$

$$\sigma_z = \frac{\nu E}{(1 + \nu)(1 - 2\nu)}(\varepsilon_x + \varepsilon_y)$$

$$\sigma_z = \frac{(\frac{1}{3})(11 \times 10^6)}{(\frac{4}{3})(\frac{1}{3})}(-3.25 \times 10^{-4} + 1.05 \times 10^{-4})$$

$$\sigma_z = -1813.9.$$

The necessary components of stress have been found. We can check these values by checking the value of the first stress invariant for x-y coordinates against the value of the invariant for 1-2 coordinates. The first stress invariant is given by

$$I_1 = \sigma_1 + \sigma_2 + \sigma_3.$$

First, we will find these stresses for the 1-2 directions.

$$\sigma_1 = \frac{E}{(1+\nu)(1-2\nu)}[(1-\nu)\varepsilon_1 + \nu\varepsilon_2]$$

$$\sigma_1 = \frac{11 \times 10^6}{(\frac{4}{9})}\left[\frac{2}{3}(3.2 \times 10^{-4}) + \frac{1}{3}(-5.4 \times 10^{-4})\right]$$

$$\sigma_1 = +825 \text{ psi.}$$

$$\sigma_2 = \frac{E}{(1+\nu)(1-2\nu)}\left[(\nu\varepsilon_1 + (1-\nu)\varepsilon_2\right]$$

$$\sigma_2 = \frac{11 \times 10^6}{\frac{4}{9}}\left[\frac{1}{3}(3.2 \times 10^{-4}) + \frac{2}{3}(-5.4 \times 10^{-4})\right]$$

$$\sigma_2 = -6270 \text{ psi.}$$

$$\sigma_3 = \frac{\nu E}{(1+\nu)(1-2\nu)}(\varepsilon_1 + \varepsilon_2)$$

$$\sigma_3 = \frac{(\frac{1}{3})(11 \times 10^6)}{(\frac{4}{9})}\left(3.2 \times 10^{-4} + (-5.4 \times 10^{-4})\right)$$

$$\sigma_3 = -1814 \text{ psi.}$$

Thus, $I_1 = \sigma_1 + \sigma_2 + \sigma_3 = +825 - 6270 - 1814.$

$$I_1 = -7259 \text{ psi.}$$

Check:

I_1 should also equal $\sigma_x + \sigma_y + \sigma_z$:

$$I_1 = -4495 - 948 - 1814 = -7257.$$

Thus, the two invariant values are the same to 3 digits.

• PROBLEM 5-15

A suspended tapered member has applied to it a load F. Compute the deflection at the bottom end due to its own weight and the load.

Solution: We shall assume here that the only nonzero stress on any section away from the ends is a uniform stress τ_{zz} with all other stresses equal to zero. That is, we assume a one-dimensional stress distribution with the stress a function of the coordinate z only. Such an assumption is useful

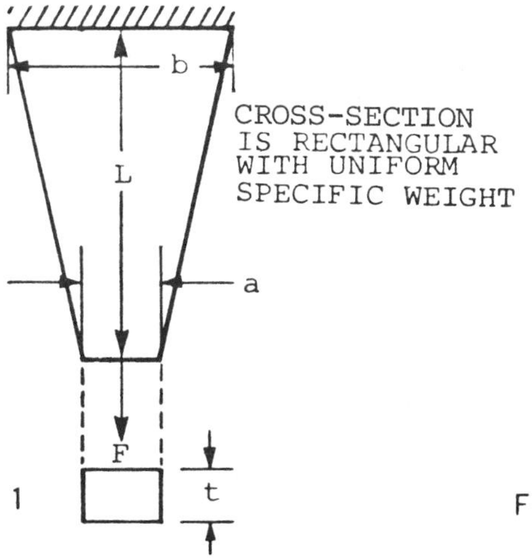

Fig. 1

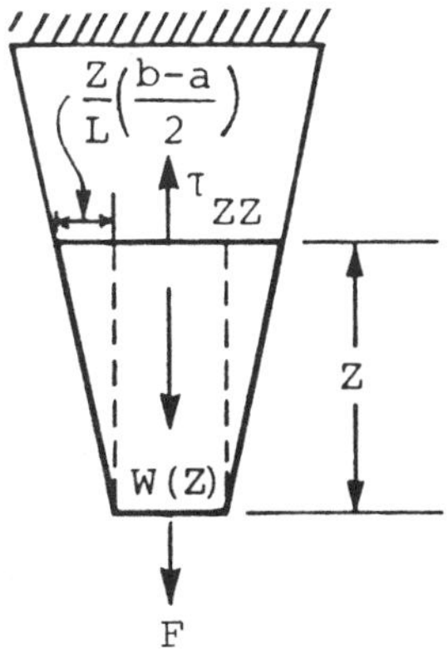

Fig. 2

only if the taper of the member in the direction of loading is not large. We take the material to be homogeneous with a constant modulus of elasticity E.

The equations of equilibrium are first satisfied by computing τ_{zz} at any section as follows (see Figure 2 for the free-body diagram):

$$(\tau_{zz})(A) = F + W(z)$$

$$(\tau_{zz})(t)\left[a + \frac{z}{L}(b - a)\right] = F + \gamma\left\{atz + 2\left[\frac{1}{2}\left(\frac{z}{L}\,\frac{b-a}{2}\right)zt\right]\right\}.$$

Hence, for τ_{zz} we have

$$\tau_{zz} = \frac{F + \gamma zt\left[a + \frac{b-a}{2}\,\frac{z}{L}\right]}{t\left[a + \frac{z}{L}(b - a)\right]} \qquad \text{(a)}$$

Now use the constitutive law for elastic materials to determine the strain. That is, $\varepsilon_{zz} = \frac{\tau_{zz}}{E}$. Thus,

$$\varepsilon_{zz} = \frac{F + \gamma zt\left[a + \frac{b-a}{2}\,\frac{z}{L}\right]}{Et\left[a + \frac{z}{L}(b - a)\right]}$$

Using the definition of strain we can get the elongation δ as follows considering incremental elements dz. Thus,

$$\delta = \int_0^L \varepsilon_{zz}dz = \int_0^L \frac{F + \gamma zt\left[a + \frac{b-a}{2}\,\frac{z}{L}\right]}{Et\left[a + \frac{z}{L}(b - a)\right]}\,dz$$

We may best carry out the quadrature as follows:

$$\delta = \int_0^L \frac{F}{A + Bz}dz + \int_0^L \frac{Cz}{A + Bz}dz + \int_0^L \frac{Gz^2}{A + Bz}dz$$

where

$$A = Eat \qquad C = \gamma ta$$

$$B = \frac{Et(b - a)}{L} \qquad G = \gamma t\frac{b - a}{2L}$$

Using standard integration forms, on inserting limits we get

$$\begin{aligned}\delta &= F\left\{\frac{1}{B}\ln(A + BL) - \frac{1}{B}\ln A\right\} \\ &+ C\left\{\frac{1}{B^2}[A + BL - A\ln(A + BL)] - \frac{A}{B^2}(1 - \ln A)\right\} \\ &+ G\left\{\frac{1}{B^3}\left[\frac{1}{2}(A + BL)^2 - 2A(A + BL) + A^2\ln(A + BL)\right]\right. \\ &\left.- \frac{A^2}{B^3}\left[-\frac{3}{2} + \ln A\right]\right\}.\end{aligned} \tag{b}$$

The position for maximum stress (outside the stress concentrations at the loading point and the support) will next be investigated. Note that for increasing z the load over the section increases because of the gravitational effect, but the area over which this load acts increases. There are then two opposing effects here determining the stress level. To compute $(\tau_{zz})_{max}$ we first take the partial derivative with respect to z in Eq. (a) and set it equal to zero to establish the value of z for $(\tau_{zz})_{max}$. Thus, using Eq. (a) we have

$$\begin{aligned}\frac{\partial\tau_{zz}}{\partial z} = 0 &= -\left\{F + \gamma zt\left[a + \frac{b - a}{2}\frac{z}{L}\right]\right\}\frac{\frac{t}{L}(b - a)}{t\left[a + \frac{z}{L}(b - a)\right]^2} \\ &+ \frac{\gamma at + \frac{\gamma t}{L}(b - a)z}{t\left[a + \frac{z}{L}(b - a)\right]}\end{aligned} \tag{c}$$

This becomes a quartic algebraic equation in z which for given data may be solved by approximate methods or by trial and error for the desired root. We may then readily establish $(\tau_{zz})_{max}$ by using Eq. (a).

THIN-WALLED PRESSURE VESSELS

• PROBLEM 5-16

> Calculate the axial and transverse normal strains on the outside surface of the compressed air tank, at a distance from the ends. Also, compute the diameter change at that location.

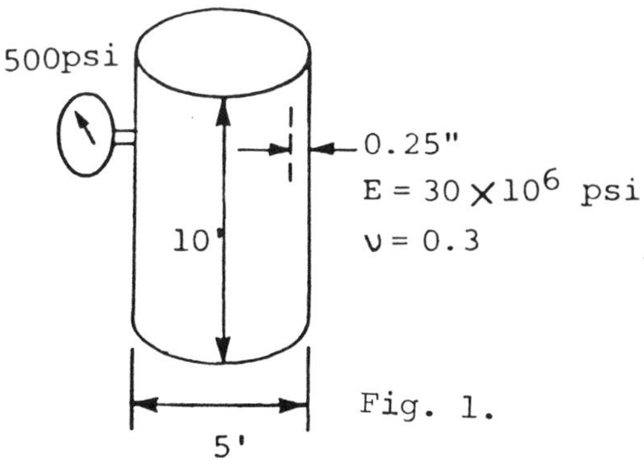

Fig. 1.

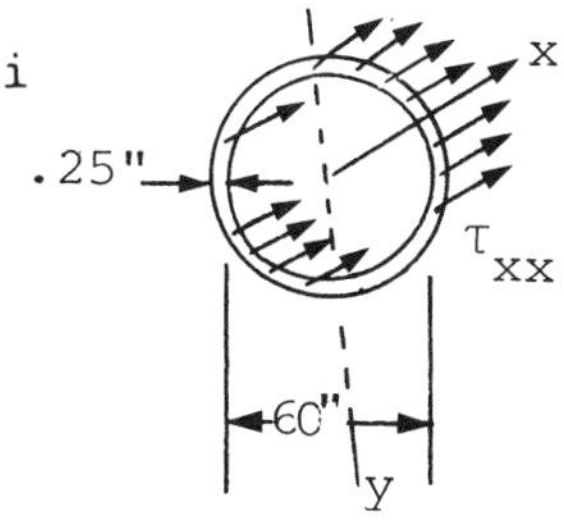

Fig. 2.

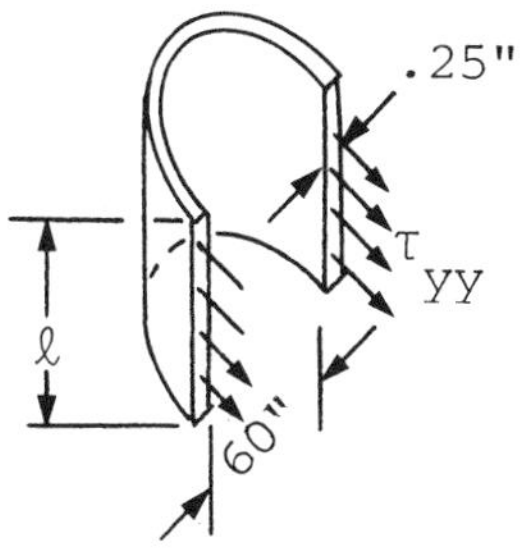

Fig. 3.

Solution: Because of the internal pressure acting in all directions, we must use the two-dimensional stress-strain relation

$$\varepsilon_{ii} = \frac{1}{E}(\tau_{ii} - \nu\tau_{jj}).$$

To find τ_{xx}, the axial stress in the wall of the tank, we apply the equation of equilibrium to the section shown in Figure 2

$$p \times \text{Area} = \tau \times A_{wall}$$

$$A_{wall} = \frac{\pi(60.5)^2}{4} - \frac{\pi(60)^2}{4}$$

$$= 47.32 \text{ in.}^2$$

$$\text{Area} = \frac{\pi 60^2}{4} = 2827.4 \text{ in.}^2$$

$$\tau_{xx} = \frac{(500)(2827.4)}{47.32} \text{ psi}$$

$$= 29{,}875 \text{ psi.}$$

The transverse stress is calculated by applying equilibrium to the section shown in Figure 3.

$$p \times \ell \times d = 2\tau\ell \times t$$

$$\tau_{yy} = \frac{pd}{2t}$$

$$= \frac{500(60)}{2(.25)}$$

$$= 60{,}000 \text{ psi.}$$

Now, we can find the strains by substituting the values of τ_{xx} and τ_{yy} in the stress-strain relation.

$$\varepsilon_{xx} = \frac{1}{E}(29875 - .3(60000))$$

$$= .000395$$

$$\varepsilon_{yy} = \frac{1}{E}(60000 - .3(29875))$$

$$= .0017.$$

The change in diameter is a change in the transverse direction so

$$\Delta d = \varepsilon_{yy} \cdot d$$

$$= .0017 \times 60''$$

$$= .102''$$

$$= .0085 \text{ ft.}$$

• PROBLEM 5-17

A long, thin-walled cylindrical tank of length L just fits between two rigid end walls when there is no pressure in the tank. Estimate the force exerted on the rigid walls by the tank when the pressure in the tank is p and the material of which the tank is made obeys Hooke's Law.

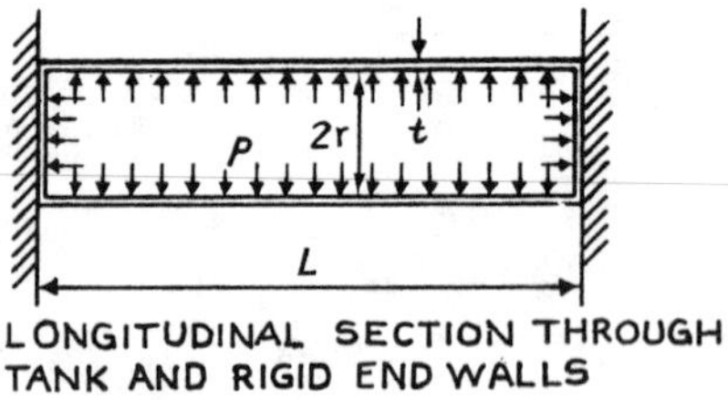

FIG. 1

Solution: When the pressure in the tank is zero, there is no stress or strain in the system. However, when the internal pressure p is present, the tank will try to expand, i.e., it will want to increase its dimensions and will have a strain E. But, the walls do not allow this. The strain must remain zero. To satisfy compatibility, a force is exerted on the ends of the tank causing a shortening which will exactly balance the lengthening due to the internal pressure

$$\Delta \ell_p = \Delta \ell_F$$

$$\Delta \ell_p = \varepsilon_p \times L = \frac{L}{E}(\tau_{xx} - \nu\tau_{yy})$$

$$\Delta \ell_F = \varepsilon_F \cdot L = \frac{FL}{AE}$$

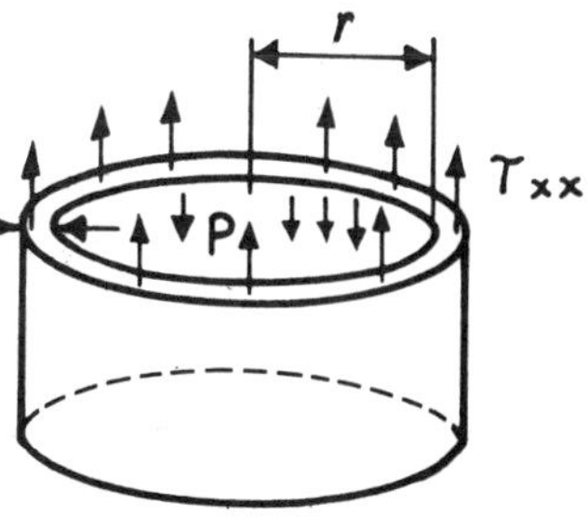

FIG. 2

so $$\frac{FL}{AE} = \frac{L}{E}(\tau_{xx} - \nu\tau_{yy})$$

$\therefore$ $$F = A(\tau_{xx} - \nu\tau_{yy}).$$

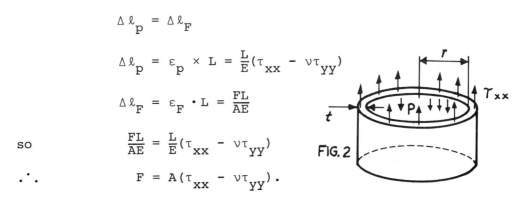

To find τ_{xx}, we consider a transverse cross-section as in Figure 2. By equilibrium,

$$p \times A = \tau_{xx} \times 2\pi r \times t$$

where $A = \pi r^2$

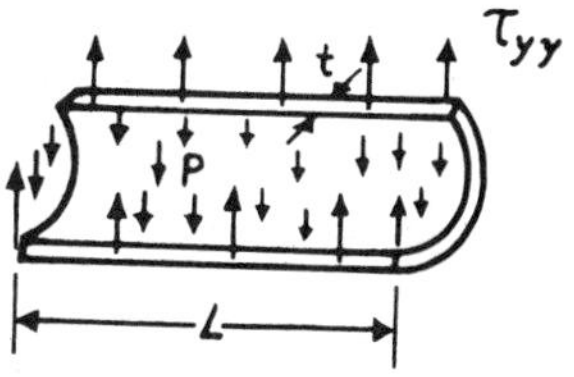

FIG. 3

$$\tau_{xx} = \frac{pr}{2t}.$$

τ_{yy} is determined by applying equilibrium to a longitudinal cross-section as in Figure 3:

$$p \times 2r \times L = 2 \times \tau_{yy} \times t \times L$$

$$\tau_{yy} = \frac{pr}{t} = 2\tau_{xx}.$$

By substituting into the expression for force, we get

$$F = \pi r^2(\tau_{xx} - \nu \times 2\tau_{xx})$$

$$F = \pi r^2(1 - 2\nu)\frac{pr}{2t}.$$

• PROBLEM 5-18

A long, thin-walled cylindrical tank has a radius r and a wall thickness t. Its ends are closed, and when a pressure p is put in the tank, a strain gage mounted on the outside surface in a direction parallel to the axis of the tank measures a strain of ε_0. What is the pressure in the tank?

FIG. 1

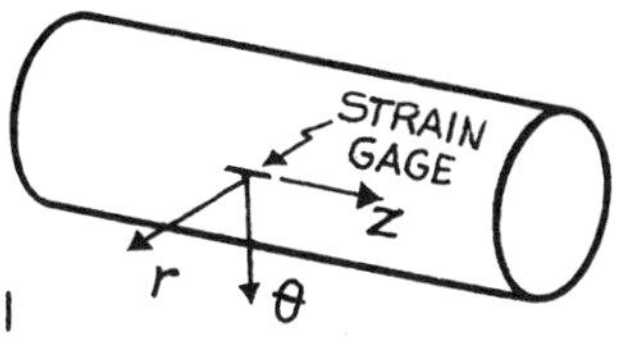

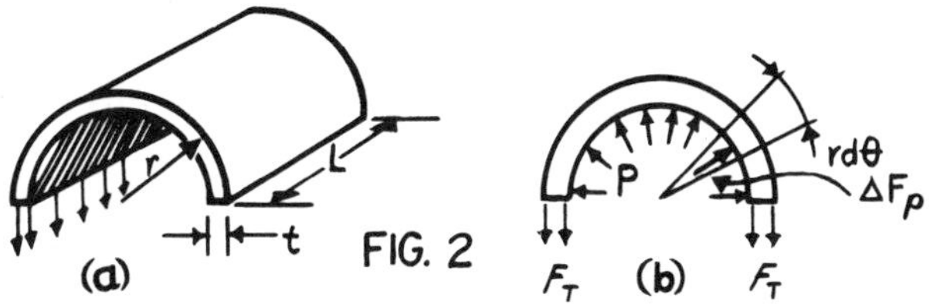

FIG. 2

Solution: First formulate a stress field for the pressurized cylinder of Figure 1. There will be a component of normal stress in the z-direction, due to the pressure acting on the ends of the cylinder. The force acting on the end is (pressure × area) or

$$(P)(\pi r^2) = F.$$

The stress produced by this force will be given by

$$\sigma_z = \frac{F}{(\text{Area})_{\text{walls}}} = \frac{\pi r^2 P}{2\pi r t} = \frac{Pr}{2t}. \qquad \text{(a)}$$

There will also be a component of normal stress in the transverse, or θ-direction

To find the value of σ_θ, let us draw a free-body diagram of the cylinder.

From Fig. 2(b), we see that the value of an incremental pressure force, ΔF_P, will be given by

$$\Delta F_P = P[(L)(rd\theta)].$$

The vertical component of this force is

$$\Delta F_{P_{\text{vert.}}} = PLr \sin\theta \, d\theta.$$

From $\sum \vec{F} = 0$, we have

$$\int_{\theta=0}^{\theta=2\pi} LPr \sin\theta \, d\theta - 2F_T = 0$$

$$2F_T = 2LPr \; ; \quad F_T = LPr.$$

The transverse stress is given by

$$\sigma_\theta = \frac{F_T}{\text{Area}} = \frac{LPr}{Lt} = \frac{Pr}{t}. \qquad \text{(b)}$$

There will also be a small normal stress in the radial direction, but for a long, very thin cylinder, the area acted upon in this direction is comparatively large.

Thus, $\sigma_r \cong 0.$

Given this stress field in three dimensions, and the value of ε_{zz}, we will now proceed to solve for P.

$\varepsilon_z = \varepsilon_0$, as measured by a strain gage. Thus,

$$\varepsilon_z = \frac{1}{E}(\sigma_z - \nu\sigma_\theta) = \varepsilon_0.$$

From (a) and (b);

$$E\varepsilon_0 = \left[\frac{Pr}{2t} - \nu\left(\frac{Pr}{t}\right)\right]$$

$$tE\varepsilon_0 = P\left[\frac{r}{2} - \nu r\right]$$

$$P = \frac{2tE\varepsilon_0}{r - 2\nu r}$$

$$\therefore \quad P = \frac{2tE\varepsilon_0}{(1 - 2\nu)r}.$$

• PROBLEM 5-19

A thin-walled cylinder with closed ends and a thin-walled sphere of the same diameter and wall thickness are put under the same internal pressure. Find the ratio of the change in diameter of the cylinder to the change in diameter of the sphere.

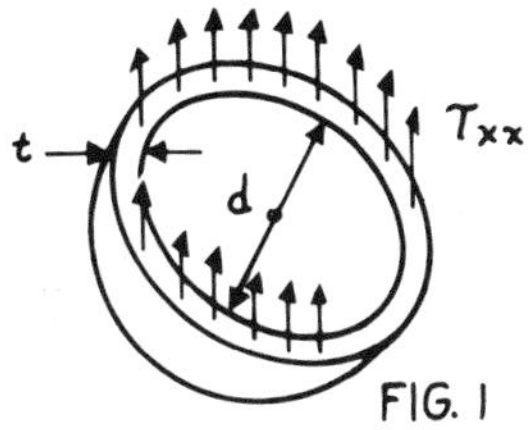

FIG. 1

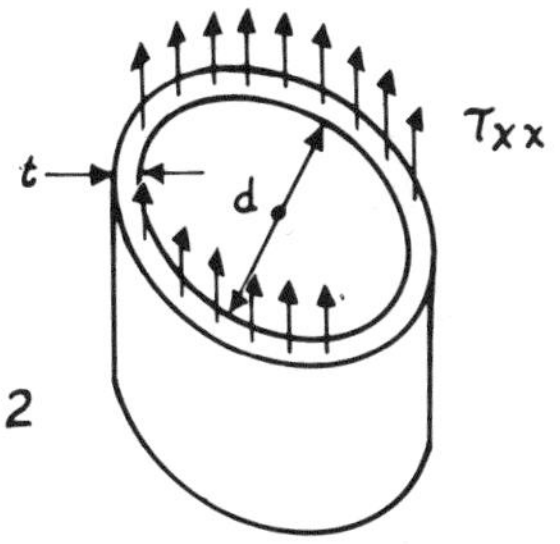

FIG. 2

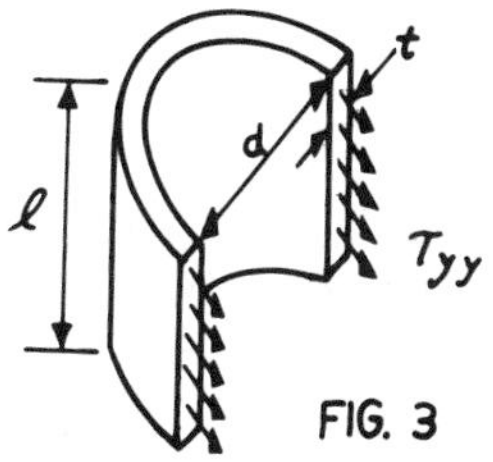

FIG. 3

Solution: To simplify this problem, we first consider the fact that the diameters are the same for the cylinder and the sphere. We want to find

$$\frac{\Delta d_{cylinder}}{\Delta d_{sphere}}.$$

But since $d_{cyl.} = d_{sphere}$ we can divide both numerator and denominator by d:

$$\frac{\frac{\Delta d_{cyl.}}{d}}{\frac{\Delta d_{sphere}}{d}}.$$

We notice that $\frac{\Delta d}{d}$ is simply the definition of strain so we can find the ratio of the change in diameters by finding the ratio of the strains.

Using the two-dimensional stress-strain relation

$$\varepsilon_{xx} = \frac{1}{E}(\tau_{xx} - \nu\tau_{yy})$$

we must find the stresses in the x and y directions for both the cylinder and the sphere.

We can again reduce the amount of work by making use of symmetry in the sphere. Any cross-section taken through the center will be the same (see Figure 1) so $\tau_{xx} = \tau_{yy}$ for a constant internal pressure p. We find τ_{xx} by using the definition of stress, $\tau = \frac{F}{A}$ and equilibrium: the force due to pressure must be equilibrated by force due to internal stress.

$$\text{Area(pressure)} = \frac{\pi d^2}{4}$$

$$\text{Area(stress)} = 2\pi\left(\frac{d}{2}\right) \times t = \pi dt$$

$$p\frac{\pi d^2}{4} = \tau(\pi dt)$$

so,

$$\tau_{xx} = \frac{p\pi d^2}{4\pi\, dt}$$

$$= \frac{pd}{4t} = \tau_{yy}.$$

For the cylinder, we must consider each direction separately. If the y-axis is taken as the longitudinal axis of the cylinder, τ_{yy} is found by considering Figure 2, and equilibrium:

$$p\frac{\pi d^2}{4} = \tau(\pi dt)$$

$$\tau_{yy} = \frac{pd}{4t}.$$

Using Figure 3,

$$\text{Area(pressure)} = \ell d$$

$$\text{Area(stress)} = 2\ell t$$

$$p\ell d = 2\tau\ell t \qquad \text{by equilibrium}$$

$$\tau_{xx} = \frac{pd}{2t} = 2\tau_{yy}$$

so

$$\varepsilon_{cylinder} = \frac{1}{E}\left(2\cdot\frac{pd}{4t} - \nu\frac{pd}{4t}\right)$$

$$\varepsilon_{sphere} = \frac{1}{E}\left(\frac{pd}{4t} - \nu\frac{pd}{4t}\right)$$

$$\frac{\varepsilon_{cylinder}}{\varepsilon_{sphere}} = \frac{\frac{1}{E}\left(\frac{pd}{4t}\right)(2 - \nu)}{\frac{1}{E}\left(\frac{pd}{4t}\right)(1 - \nu)} = \frac{2 - \nu}{1 - \nu}$$

A load F is applied to the free end of a tube with thin walls bent at right angle. At the indicated location on the tube, strain gauges provide values for ε_{xx} and ε_{zz}. Compute the stress tensor components τ_{ij} and ε_{yy} at that location.

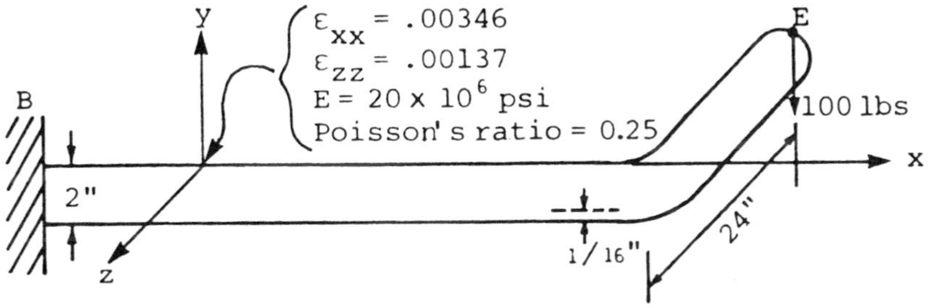

Solution: To determine the stress tensor at point A, we must first determine what effect the 100 lb load at point E has on the pipe length BC. If we examine the pipe at point C we see that the load creates a moment of 2400 in-lb which will cause a shear stress in the x-z plane. At C there is no vertical force applied so that τ_{yy} must equal zero by equilibrium. Since the moment is in the xz plane, the shear stresses in the y direction will also be zero.

Therefore, we know the stress tensor will be

$$[\tau_{ij}]_{\text{pt A}} = \begin{bmatrix} \tau_{xx} & 0 & \tau_{xz} \\ 0 & 0 & 0 \\ \tau_{zx} & 0 & \tau_{zz} \end{bmatrix}.$$

To find the normal stresses we use the multi-dimensional stress-strain relation:

$$\varepsilon_{ii} = \frac{1}{E}(\tau_{ii} - \nu(\tau_{jj} + \tau_{kk}))$$

along with the readings for ε_{xx} and ε_{zz} from the strain gauges.

$$\varepsilon_{xx} = .00346 = \frac{1}{20 \times 10^6}(\tau_{xx} - .25(0 + \tau_{zz}))$$

$$\varepsilon_{zz} = .00137 = \frac{1}{20 \times 10^6}(\tau_{zz} - .25(0 + \tau_{xx}))$$

$$6.92 \times 10^4 = \tau_{xx} - .25\tau_{zz} \quad (1)$$

$$2.74 \times 10^4 = \tau_{zz} - .25\tau_{xx}. \quad (2)$$

By multiplying equation (2) by 4 and adding to (1) we can find τ_{zz}.

$$6.92 \times 10^4 = \tau_{xx} - .25\tau_{zz}$$

$$10.96 \times 10^4 = -\tau_{xx} + 4\tau_{zz}$$

$$17.88 \times 10^4 = 3.75\tau_{zz}$$

$$\tau_{zz} = 47680 \text{ psi.}$$

Substituting this value of τ_{zz} into (1)

$$6.92 \times 10^4 = \tau_{xx} - .25(47680)$$

$$\tau_{xx} = 81120 \text{ psi.}$$

To find τ_{xz} and τ_{zx} we must consider the torsion of a thin-walled tube.

We have an expression for shear stress

$$\tau_{xz} = \frac{M_x r}{J}$$

where M_x is the moment about the x-axis
r is the radius of the tube
J is the polar moment of inertia.

The variation of shear stress through the thickness of the tube is found by varying r from r_{inner} to r_{outer}. We will consider an average value, the shear stress in the mid-plane of the tube with $r = r_{inner} + \frac{t}{2} = (1 - \frac{1}{16}) + (\frac{1}{16})\frac{1}{2}$

$$r = \frac{15}{16} + \frac{1}{32}$$

$$= \frac{31''}{32}.$$

M_x is found by noting that the 100 lb load is applied at 24" from the elbow, so

$$M_x = F \cdot d = 100 \text{ lb} \times 24''$$

$$= 2400 \text{ in-lb.}$$

The polar moment of inertia for a tube is simply the J for the outer diameter solid shaft minus J for the inner diameter solid shaft. $J = \frac{\pi r_0^4}{2}$ for a solid shaft.

$$J = \frac{\pi(1)^4}{2} \quad \frac{\pi\left(\frac{15}{16}\right)^4}{2}$$

$$= .357 \text{ in}^4.$$

So $$\tau_{xz} = \frac{(2400 \text{ in-lb})\left(\frac{31}{32}\right)\text{in}}{.357 \text{ in.}^4}$$

$$= 6512 \text{ psi} = \tau_{zx}.$$

Therefore, the stress tensor is

$$\tau_{ij} = \begin{bmatrix} 81,120 & 0 & 6512 \\ 0 & 0 & 0 \\ 6512 & 0 & 47,680 \end{bmatrix} \text{psi.}$$

To find ε_{yy} we merely substitute our τ_{xx} and τ_{zz} into the stress-strain relation

$$\varepsilon_{yy} = \frac{1}{E}(0 - .25(81,120 + 47,680)$$

$$= -\frac{.25}{20 \times 10^6}(128800) = -.00161.$$

• PROBLEM 5-21

In a thick-walled cylinder under internal pressure, the radial and transverse stresses are given as

$$\tau_{rr} = \frac{a^2 P_i}{b^2 - a^2}\left(1 - \frac{b^2}{r^2}\right) \quad \text{(a)}$$

$$\tau_{\theta\theta} = \frac{a^2 P_i}{b^2 - a^2}\left(1 + \frac{b^2}{r^2}\right) \quad \text{(b)}$$

Compute the strains ε_{rr}, $\varepsilon_{\theta\theta}$, $\varepsilon_{r\theta}$ at the indicated position within the wall of the cylinder.

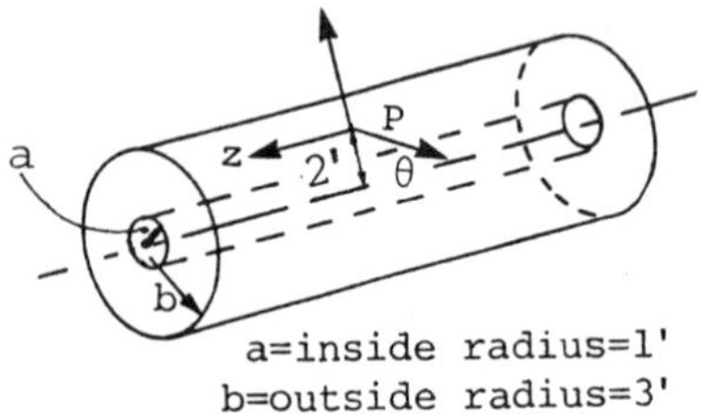

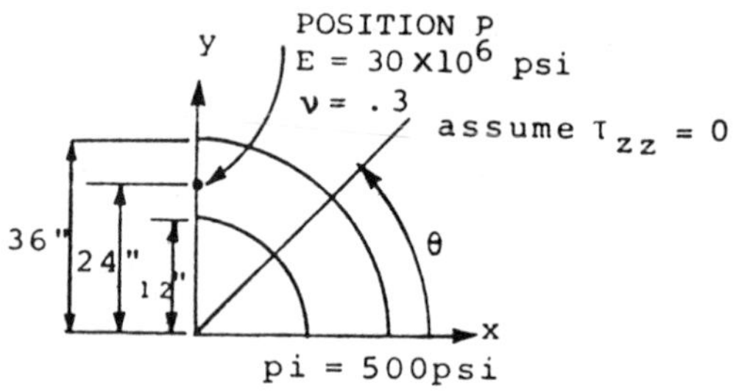

Solution: By using the expressions for τ_{rr}, $\tau_{\theta\theta}$, and the data given, the three components of normal stress can be obtained. These can be used, along with stress-strain relations in three dimensions, to obtain the desired strains.

First, calculate the normal stresses: from (a) at the point P

$$\tau_{rr} = \frac{(1\ \text{ft})^2(500\ \text{psi})}{(3\ \text{ft})^2 - (1\ \text{ft})^2}\left(1 - \frac{3^2}{2^2}\right)$$

$$\tau_{rr} = -78.125\ \text{psi.}$$

The negative value of τ_{rr} indicates the expected compression of the cylinder in the r-direction by the internal pressure.

From (b),

$$\tau_{\theta\theta} = \frac{(1)^2(500)}{3^2 - 1^2}\left(1 + \frac{3^2}{2^2}\right)$$

$$\tau_{\theta\theta} = 203.125\ \text{psi.}$$

The positive value of $\tau_{\theta\theta}$ indicates the expected tension in the transverse direction as the cylinder is forced to expand.

Because we are assuming the ends to be free, $\tau_{zz} = 0$.

We now have the three values of normal stress, and we can now proceed to determine the strains. The shear stresses, $\tau_{r\theta}$, $\tau_{\theta z}$, and τ_{rz} are all zero because we are considering only hydrostatic pressure (no viscous shear forces are present).

$$\tau_{rz} = \tau_{\theta z} = \tau_{r\theta} = 0 \tag{c}$$

The necessary three-dimensional stress-strain relations for cylindrical coordinates are as follows:

$$\varepsilon_{rr} = \frac{1}{E}(\tau_{rr} - \nu\tau_{\theta\theta} - \nu\tau_{zz}) \tag{d}$$

$$\varepsilon_{\theta\theta} = \frac{1}{E}(\tau_{\theta\theta} - \nu\tau_{rr} - \nu\tau_{zz}) \tag{e}$$

$$\varepsilon_{zz} = \frac{1}{E}(\tau_{zz} - \nu\tau_{\theta\theta} - \nu\tau_{zz}) \tag{f}$$

where ν = Poisson's ratio, given as .3 and E = Young's modulus, given as 30×10^6 psi.

Substituting these values and the normal-stress values previously obtained, we get from (d):

$$\varepsilon_{rr} = \frac{1}{30 \times 10^6 \text{ psi}}(-78.125 \text{ psi} - (.3)(203.125 \text{ psi}) - (.3)(0))$$

$$\varepsilon_{rr} = -4.6 \times 10^{-6}$$

from (e): $$\varepsilon_{\theta\theta} = \frac{1}{30 \times 10^6}[(203.125) - (.3)(-78.125) - 0]$$

$$= 14.58 \times 10^{-6}$$

from (f) $$\varepsilon_{zz} = \frac{1}{30 \times 10^6}[0 - (.3)(203.125) - (.3)(-78.125)]$$

$$\varepsilon_{zz} = -1.25 \times 10^{-6}.$$

To find $\varepsilon_{r\theta}$, recall that

$\varepsilon_{r\theta} = \frac{\tau_{r\theta}}{G}$, where G is the shear modulus.

But, from (c), $\tau_{r\theta} = 0$.

$\therefore \quad \varepsilon_{r\theta} = 0.$

Looking at our results, we find that there are three non-zero components of strain, but only 2 non-zero stress components. This corresponds to the definition of plane stress. The problem could have identically been solved using the plane stress relations:

$$\varepsilon_{rr} = \frac{1}{E}(\tau_{rr} - \nu\tau_{\theta\theta})$$

$$\varepsilon_{\theta\theta} = \frac{1}{E}(\tau_{\theta\theta} - \nu\tau_{rr})$$

$$\varepsilon_{zz} = \frac{-\nu}{E}(\tau_{\theta\theta} + \tau_{rr})$$

• PROBLEM 5-22

In pre-stressed concrete, reinforcing bars have applied to them compressive stresses to counteract tensile loads which the concrete cannot sustain well. Reinforcing hoops of circular cross-section are to be applied to a concrete tank to pre-stress the concrete into compression. Compute the spacing between hoops if tension in the concrete is to be prevented.

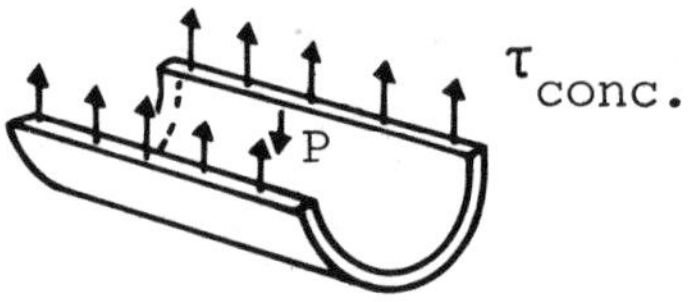

Fig. 2.

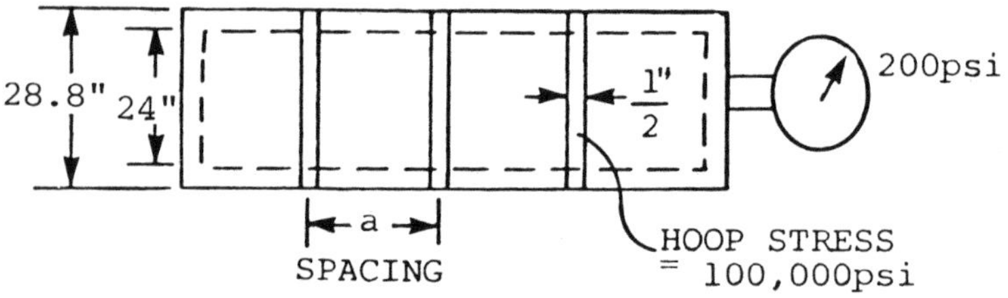

Fig. 1.

Solution: The hoop spacing, a, must be such that the stress in the hoop exactly equilibrates the stress developed in the length of the concrete tank due to the internal pressure.

To find the stress in the concrete, we consider the section shown in Figure 2. By equilibrium we know that the resultant force due to the internal pressure must equal the resultant force due to the stress in the concrete.

$$p \cdot \text{diameter} \times \text{length} = 2 \times \tau_{conc.} \times \text{thickness} \times \text{length}$$

$$(200 \text{ psi})(12 \text{ in}) = 2(2.4 \text{ in})\tau_{conc.}$$

$$\tau_{conc.} = 500 \text{ psi.}$$

Therefore, the resultant force due to the concrete stress over a length, a, is

$$F_L = 2\tau_{conc.} \times 2.4 \times a$$

$$= 2400 \text{ a lb.}$$

Fig. 3.

The force supplied by one hoop must equal 2400 a lb in order for the concrete to be free of stress. By considering the section of Figure 3 we can determine the hoop force.

$$F_h = (100{,}000 \text{ psi})\pi\left(\frac{1}{4}\right)^2 \qquad r_h = \frac{1}{4} \text{ in.}$$

Therefore,

$$2400 \text{ a lb-in} = \frac{100{,}000\pi \text{ psi}}{8 \text{ in}^2}$$

$$a = 8.18 \text{ in.}$$

THERMAL DEFORMATION

• **PROBLEM** 5-23

In the member shown in Figure 1, the temperature variation as a function of z is given as $T(z) = 60 + .2z^2$ after being initially at 50° uniformly throughout the member. What is the thermal strain at z = 3 ft. and what is the change in length of the whole system? Take $\alpha = 8 \times 10^{-6}/°F$.

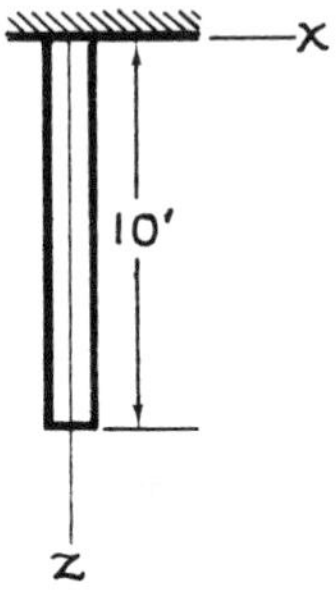

FIG. 1

Solution: Since the bar is hanging freely, i.e., there are no restraints which will cause stress in the bar, we know that

$$\varepsilon = \alpha \Delta T.$$

ΔT can be found as a function of z, as follows.

$$T_i(z) = 50° \qquad \text{initial distribution}$$

$$T_f(z) = 60° + .2z^2 \qquad \text{final distribution}$$

so
$$\Delta T(z) = T_f(z) - T_i(z)$$

$$= 60 + .2z^2 - 50$$

$$= 10 + .2z^2.$$

Therefore, $\varepsilon(z) = (8 \cdot 10^{-6})(10 + .2z^2)$

the thermal strain at z = 3 ft is found by substituting z = 3 into $\varepsilon(z)$

$$\varepsilon(3) = (8 \cdot 10^{-6})(10 + .2(3)^2)$$

$$= 9.44 \cdot 10^{-5}.$$

To find the change in length of the bar, we consider a segment of the bar, dz. The elongation of this segment, $\Delta_{dz} = \varepsilon_{zz} \cdot dz$. To obtain the elongation of the entire bar we sum the elongations of all the segments in the bar; in other words, integrate from z = 0 to 10 ft.

$$\Delta L = \int_0^{10} 8 \cdot 10^{-6}(10 + .2z^2)dz$$

$$= 8 \cdot 10^{-6}(10z + \frac{.2}{3}z^3)\Big|_0^{10}$$

$$= 8 \cdot 10^{-6}(100 + \frac{.2}{3} \cdot 1000 - 0)$$

• PROBLEM 5-24

A rod held between two walls is heated from 30° to 200°F. What is the stress in the rod if $\alpha = 10 \times 10^{-6}/°F$ and the walls move apart a distance of .001 ft? Take $E = 20 \times 10^6$ psi.

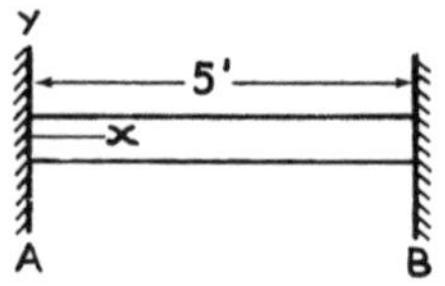

FIG.1

Solution: Neglecting the weight of the member, we have a one-dimensional problem. Using the one-dimensional, temperature-dependent Hooke's law:

$$\varepsilon_{xx} = \frac{1}{E}(\tau_{xx}) + \alpha\Delta T \qquad (a)$$

$$\varepsilon_{xx} = \frac{\Delta L}{L} = \frac{.001 \text{ ft.}}{5 \text{ ft.}}$$

$$\Delta T = 200°F - 30°F = 170°F$$

$$\therefore \quad \frac{.001}{5} = \frac{1}{20 \times 10^6 \text{ psi}}(\tau_{xx}) + \frac{10 \times 10^{-6}}{°F}(+170°F).$$

Computing, we obtain

$$\tau_{xx} = -30,000 \text{ psi.}$$

Notice that large compressive stresses can be created by a temperature increase.

Fig. 1 shows a bar AB 120 in. long. The cross-section is $\frac{1}{2}$ in. square at A and $1\frac{1}{2}$ in. square at B, and the bar is uniformly tapered. Find the extension of the bar due to tensile end forces of 2000 lb. Also find the flexibility and stiffness coefficients for this bar. The material is homogeneous and for the stresses of this problem it obeys Hooke's Law with $E = 20 \times 10^6$ psi.

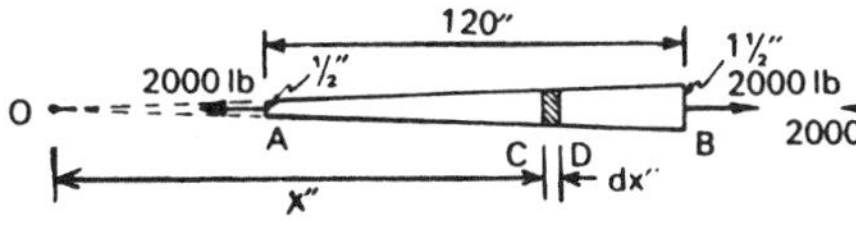

FiG.1

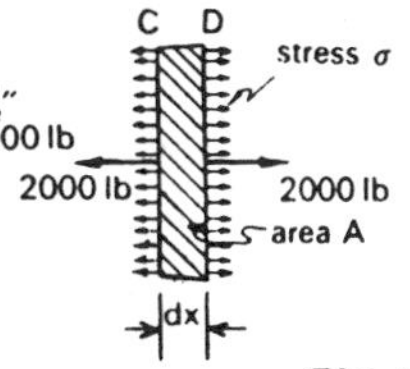

FiG.2

Solution: Consider first the extension of a typical element (Fig. 2). In the case of tapered bars it greatly simplifies the algebra if the distance x is measured form the origin of taper (0 in Fig. 1). Let point 0 be at x_0 away from A. By similar triangles,

$$\frac{x_0}{\frac{1}{2}''} = \frac{x_0 + 120}{1\frac{1}{2}''}$$

$$\frac{3}{2}x_0 = \frac{1}{2}x_0 + 60$$

$$\left(\frac{3}{2} - \frac{1}{2}\right)x_0 = 60$$

$$x_0 = 60.$$

0 is found to be 60 in beyond A.

Then at C, x inches from 0, the width of the bar is $\frac{x}{\frac{60}{\frac{1}{2}}} = \frac{x}{120}$ in and the area of cross-section is

$$A = \left(\frac{x}{120}\text{ in.}\right)\left(\frac{x}{120}\text{ in.}\right) = \frac{x^2}{14,400}\text{ in.}^2.$$

The elemental extension is then, by using Hooke's law

$$de = \frac{F/dx}{EA} = \frac{2000\ dx}{20 \times 10^6}\ \frac{14,000}{x^2}$$

$$= \frac{1.44\ dx}{x^2}\text{ in.}$$

The total extension is

$$e = \int_A^B \frac{1.44\ dx}{x^2} = \int_{60}^{180} \frac{1.44\ dx}{x^2} = 1.44\left(-\frac{1}{x}\right)\Bigg|_{60}^{180}$$

Stiffness coefficient is just another name for the Hooke's law spring constant

$$k = \left(\frac{P}{\delta}\right) \text{(lb./in.)}$$

The flexibility coefficient is the reciprocal of the stiffness coefficient

$$f = \frac{1}{k} = \left(\frac{\delta}{p}\right) \text{(in./lb.)}$$

To find the flexibility coefficient of this bar directly we could carry out the above with end forces of 1 lb. This would give

$$f = \frac{0.016}{2000} = 8 \times 10^{-6} \text{ in/lb.}$$

The stiffness coefficient of the bar is

$$k = \frac{1}{f} = 0.125 \times 10^{6} \text{ lb/in.}$$

Thus, the force required to extend the bar 1 in. is 0.125×10^6 lb. (provided the material still obeys Hooke's Law.)

• PROBLEM 5-26

A bar of length 120 in. is prevented from expansion or contraction by rigid end restraints. Find the stress induced by a temperature rise of 60°F. $\alpha = 8 \times 10^{-6}$ per °F and $E = 20 \times 10^6$ psi.

Solution: The total extension of the bar, if it was not restrained would be calculated using this equation:

$$e = \frac{fL}{AE} + \alpha L \Delta t \tag{1}$$

where;
- e = elongation of the bar
- f = force
- L = length of the bar
- A = cross-sectional area of the bar
- Δt = change in temperature
- α = coefficient of expansion
- E = Modulus of elasticity

Rewriting Eq. (1) knowing that $\frac{f}{A} = \sigma$ and expansion is zero due to the end restraints yields

$$0. = \frac{\sigma L}{E} + \alpha L \Delta t$$

$$0. = \frac{\sigma L}{20 \times 10^6} + 8 \times 10^{-6} \times 60L.$$

Solving for σ, $\rightarrow \sigma L = -(8 \times 10^{-6} \times 60L)(20 \times 10^6)$

$$\sigma = -9600 \text{ psi}.$$

The negative sign indicates compressive stress.

• PROBLEM 5-27

A 2-in. diameter 20-ft long duralumin rod is secured at the ends to supports that permit a change in length of the bar of 0.06 in. The following properties apply: modulus of elasticity $10(10^6)$ psi, coefficient of thermal expansion $13(10^{-6})$ per degree F, and Poisson's ratio 0.333. When the temperature is 80 F, there is no stress in the rod. For a temperature of -20 F, determine:

(a) The maximum normal stress in the rod.
(b) The maximum shearing stress in the rod.
(c) The change in diameter of the rod.

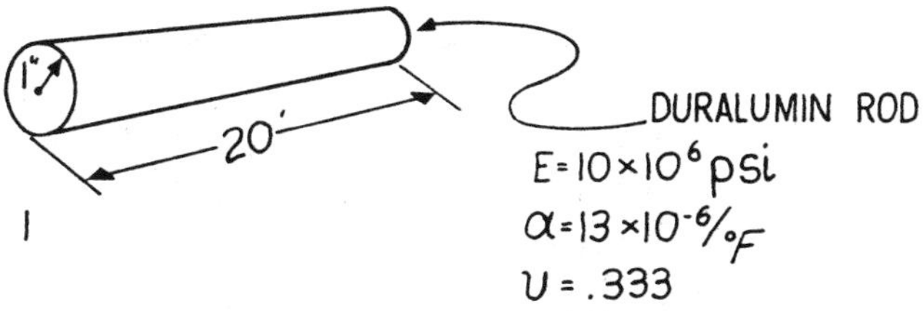

FIG. 1

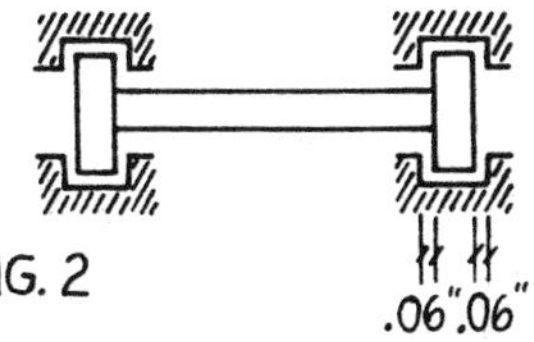

FIG. 2

MAX. DEFLECTION IS ±.06"

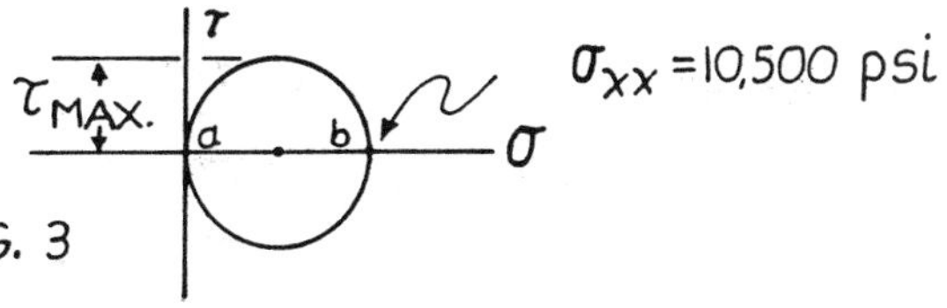

FIG. 3

Solution: (a) It is given that $\delta_{max} = \pm .06"$. Since there is no stress in the rod at 80°F, measure ΔT from this temperature. Using the temperature-dependent, one dimensional form of Hooke's Law:

$$\varepsilon_{xx} = \frac{1}{E}(\tau_{xx}) + \alpha \Delta T.$$

We first determine whether the bar's extension will exceed .06" if not restricted.

$$\varepsilon_{xx}(\text{hypothetical}) = \alpha\Delta T = \left(13 \times \frac{10^{-6}}{°F}\right)(-100°F)$$

$$\varepsilon_{xx}(\text{hypothetical}) = -.0013$$

$$\delta_{(\text{hypothetical})} = (L)(\varepsilon_{xx_h}) = (240")(-.0013) = -0.312".$$

Since this is larger than the allowable extension, there will be a limiting force imposed. Thus, using $\varepsilon = \frac{\tau}{E}$ since the temperature effects have been considered:

$$-\left(\frac{.06"}{240"}\right) = \frac{1}{E}(\tau_{xx}) - \frac{.312"}{240"}$$

$$\tau_{xx} = E(.00105) = 10,500 \text{ psi.}$$

(b) To find the maximum shearing stress, we will use a Mohr's circle analysis. This is the case of simple tension: $\tau_{xx} = 10,500$ psi. Since there is no force or restraint in the y-direction, $\tau_{yy} = 0$.

From Figure 3 the maximum shearing stress is given by the maximum ordinate, which will be the value of the radius of Mohr's circle. The radius of the circle is $\frac{\tau_{xx} - \tau_{yy}}{2}$

$$\tau_{max} = \frac{\sigma_{max}}{2} = \frac{10,500}{2} = 5250 \text{ psi.}$$

(c) To find the change in diameter, first calculate the strain in this direction, i.e., along the y-axis. There are two contributions to this strain, that due to the temperature effect and that due to Poisson's ratio.

The strain due to temperature is the same as that in the x-direction: $\varepsilon_{yy} = -.0013$ since the material is assumed to be homogeneous. Using $\varepsilon_{yy} = -\nu\varepsilon_{xx}$, the second component is

$$\varepsilon_{yy} = -.333 \times .00105$$

$$= -.000349.$$

Adding these components yields

$$\varepsilon_{yytotal} = -.00165.$$

Therefore, the change in diameter is

$$\Delta D = \varepsilon_{yy} \times D$$

$$= -.00165 \times 2"$$

$$= -3.3 \times 10^{-3} \text{ in.,}$$

where the negative sign implies a decrease.

In the diagram are shown a steel rod and an aluminum sleeve held between two immovable supports A and B. If the temperature is raised from 60° to 100°F, what is the thermal stress in the materials and what is the force developed on the supports? Take α to be 6.5×10^{-6}/°F for the steel rod and 12×10^{-6}/°F for the aluminum sleeve. E for the rod is 30×10^6 and for the sleeve is 10×10^6 psi.

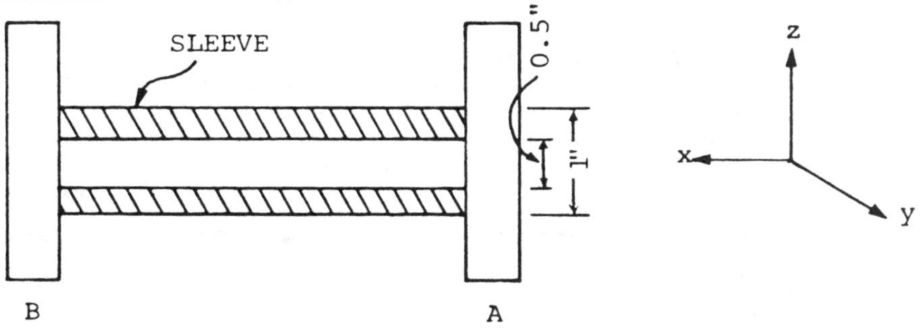

Solution: Since the supports are immovable, there can be no strain in the x-direction. Thus,

$$\varepsilon_{xx} = 0.$$

Using the one-dimensional, temperature-dependent Hooke's law:

$$\varepsilon_{xx} = \frac{1}{E}(\tau_{xx}) + \alpha\Delta T = 0,$$

where α is the coefficient of linear expansion,

$$-\frac{1}{E}(\tau_{xx}) = \alpha\Delta T$$

or $$\tau_{xx} = -E\alpha\Delta T.$$

But, $$\tau_{xx} = F_x/A.$$

So $$F_x = -AE\alpha T. \qquad (1)$$

Substituting in (1) for each material: For the steel rod,

$$F_{x_{ROD}} = -\left[\frac{\pi\left(\frac{1}{2}"\right)^4}{4}(30 \times 10^6 \text{ psi})\left(6.5 \times \frac{10^{-6}}{°F}\right)(+40°F)\right]$$

$$F_{x_{ROD}} = -1531.5 \text{ lb.}$$

For the aluminum sleeve,

$$F_{x_{SLEEVE}} = -\left[\frac{\pi\left(1''^2 - \frac{1}{2}''^2\right)}{4}(10 \times 10^6 \text{ psi})\left(12 \times \frac{10^{-6}}{°F}\right)(+40°F)\right]$$

$$F_{x_{SLEEVE}} = -2827.4 \text{ lb.}$$

$$F_{x_{TOTAL}} = F_{x_{SLEEVE}} + F_{x_{ROD}} = (-2827.4) + (-1531.5)$$

$$= -4359 \text{ lb.}$$

The negative sign indicates compression of the members, so the force developed on the supports acts upward on the top support and downward on the lower support. The force in each case is 4359 lb.

• PROBLEM 5-29

Cooling fluid circulates through a pipe braced between two walls, and cools the pipe from 60°F to 0°F. Calculate the forces on the walls due to change in pipe length.

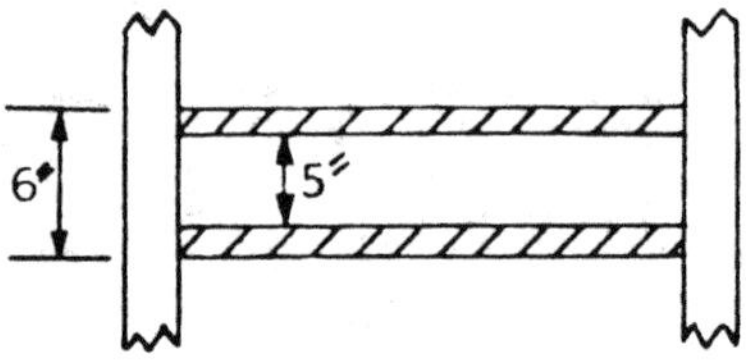

coefficient of linear expansion $= 6.5 \times 10^{-6}/°F$

Fig. 1.

Solution: Away from the end supports, we can assume for the stress resulting from temperature change a one-dimensional stress distribution in the z direction. Because of the constraint in the z direction imposed by the walls and because of the uniformity of temperature and geometry in the z direction, compatibility requires that $\varepsilon_{zz} = 0$.

Hence, using the one-dimensional temperature-dependent Hooke's law as the constitutive law (for a solid with linear stress-dependence on temperature) for ε_{zz} we get

$$\tau_{zz} = -E\alpha\Delta T$$

where τ_{zz} is stress due to change in temperature
E = modulus of elasticity
α = coeff.of expansion
Δt = change in temperature.

The tensile force P on the supports is now available from

equilibrium considerations. Thus,

$$P = \tau_{zz}A = -E\alpha\Delta TA.$$

We may evaluate τ_{zz} and P numerically. Taking $E = 30\times10^6$ psi for steel, we have

$$\tau_{zz} = -(30 \times 10^6)(6.5 \times 10^{-6})(-60) = 11{,}700 \text{ psi}$$

$$\therefore P = 11{,}700\frac{\pi(6^2 - 5^2)}{4} = 101{,}100 \text{ lb.}$$

We see that considerable forces can be developed by thermal effects.

• PROBLEM 5-30

An aluminum sleeve is held between the head and the nut of a steel bolt. The temperature is raised 40°F from 60°F after the nut is turned 45° against the sleeve from loose contact therewith. Calculate the stresses in the sleeve and the bolt.

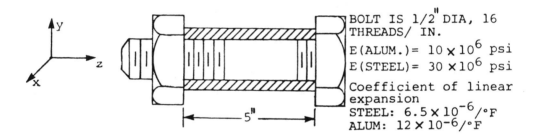

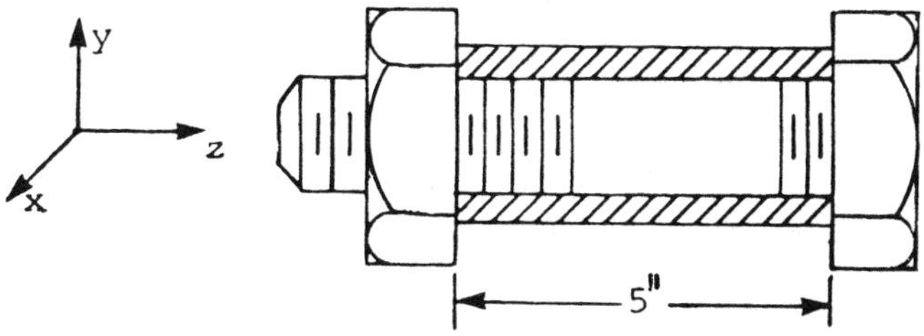

BOLT IS 1/2" DIA, 16 THREADS/ IN.
E(ALUM.) = 10×10^6 psi
E(STEEL) = 30×10^6 psi
Coefficient of linear expansion
STEEL: 6.5×10^{-6}/°F
ALUM: 12×10^{-6}/°F

Solution: We shall first compute stresses caused by turning the nut alone. Such stresses will be denoted by subscript 1. Then we shall compute the stresses caused by thermal action only. We shall denote the thermal stresses with subscript 2.

Accordingly, we note that turning the nut results in a tensile stress $[(\tau_{xx})_1]_B$ in the bolt. Using Hooke's law as the constitutive law, the strain in the bolt is then

$$[(\varepsilon_{zz})_1]_B = \frac{[(\tau_{zz})_1]_B}{E_B} \quad \text{(a)}$$

As for the sleeve, let us employ compatibility considerations at this time. The change in length of the sleeve must equal the distance moved by the nut. Were there no strain in the steel bolt then the nut would move a distance equal to the number of turns of the nut times the advance of the nut per turn (i.e., the so-called lead). However, the bolt will extend and decrease the movement of the nut by the amount $[(\tau_{zz})_1]L_B/E_B$. Thus, the net movement of the nut upward is $\{(\text{Turns})/(\text{Lead}) - [(\tau_{zz})_1]_B L/E_B\}$. The net change in length of the sleeve must accordingly be

$$\Delta L = -(\text{Turns})(\text{Lead}) + \frac{[(\tau_{zz})_1]_B}{E_B} L$$

$$= -(\tfrac{1}{8})(\tfrac{1}{16}) + \frac{[(\tau_{zz})_1]_B}{30 \times 10^6} L \qquad \text{(b)}$$

The strain in the sleeve is then found by dividing Eq. (b) by L. Thus

$$[(\varepsilon_{zz})_1]_S = \frac{\Delta L}{L} = \frac{(\frac{1}{8})(\frac{1}{16}")}{5"} + \frac{[(\tau_{zz})_1]_B}{E_B L}L = -.001563$$

$$+ \frac{[(\tau_{zz})_1]_B}{30 \times 10^6} \qquad \text{(c)}$$

The stress in the sleeve is now easily expressed as

$$[(\tau_{zz})_1]_S = \left\{-001563 + \frac{[(\tau_{zz})_1]_B}{30 \times 10^6}\right\} 10 \times 10^6$$

$$= -15{,}630 + \tfrac{1}{3}[(\tau_{zz})_1]_B \qquad \text{(d)}$$

Equilibrium now demands that the force of the bolt be balanced by the force in the sleeve.

$$[(\tau_{zz})_1]_S \frac{\pi}{4}\left[1^2 - (\tfrac{1}{2})^2\right] + [(\tau_{zz})_1]_B \frac{\pi}{4}\left(\frac{1}{2}\right)^2 = 0 \qquad \text{(e)}$$

Substituting from Eq. (d) for $[(\tau_{zz})_1]_S$, on canceling terms we get

$$3\{-15{,}630 + \tfrac{1}{3}[(\tau_{zz})_1]_B\} + [(\tau_{zz})_1]_B = 0$$

Solving for $[(\tau_{zz})_1]_B$ we get

$$[(\tau_{zz})_1]_B = 23{,}400 \text{ psi} \qquad \text{(f)}$$

$[(\tau_{zz})_1]_B$ is positive, indicating the expected tension of the bolt.

From Eq. (d) we get

$$[(\tau_{zz})_1]_S = -15,630 + 7815 = -7815 \text{ psi}$$

$[(\tau_{zz})_1]_S$ is negative, indicating the expected compression of the aluminum sleeve.

Next, consider the stress owing to temperature change. We have the following equations using the constitutive law with $(\tau_{zz})_2$ representing here only the thermally induced stress:

<u>For bolt</u>:

$$[(\varepsilon_{zz})_2]_B = \frac{1}{E_B}[(\tau_{zz})_2]_B + \alpha_B \Delta T$$

$$= \frac{[(\tau_{zz})_2]_B}{30 \times 10^6} + 2.60 \times 10^{-4} \qquad \text{(g)}$$

<u>For sleeve</u>:

$$[(\varepsilon_{zz})_2]_S = \frac{[(\tau_{zz})_2]_S}{10 \times 10^6} + 4.80 \times 10^{-4} \qquad \text{(h)}$$

Compatibility requires that

$$[(\varepsilon_{zz})_2]_B = [(\varepsilon_{zz})_2]_S \qquad \text{(i)}$$

Hence, from Eqs. (g) and (h), we can say that

$$\frac{[(\tau_{zz})_2]_B}{30 \times 10^6} + 2.60 \times 10^{-4} = \frac{[(\tau_{zz})_2]_S}{10 \times 10^6} + 4.80 \times 10^{-4}$$

This leads to the following equation:

$$[(\tau_{zz})_2]_B = 3[(\tau_{zz})_2]_S + 6600 \qquad \text{(j)}$$

Furthermore, equilibrium requires that

$$[(\tau_{zz})_2]_S \frac{\pi}{4}\left[1^2 - \left(\frac{1}{2}\right)^2\right] + [(\tau_{zz})_2]_B \frac{\pi}{4}\left(\frac{1}{2}\right)^2 = 0$$

Hence,

$$3[(\tau_{zz})_2]_S = -[(\tau_{zz})_2]_B \qquad \text{(k)}$$

Now, substituting from Eq. (k) into Eq. (j), we have

$$[(\tau_{zz})_2]_B = -[(\tau_{zz})_2]_B + 6600$$

Hence,

$$[(\tau_{zz})_2]_B = 3300 \text{ psi} \qquad \text{(l)}$$

Also from Eq. (k), we have

$$[(\tau_{zz})_2]_S = -1100 \text{ psi} \qquad \text{(m)}$$

The total stress for the bolt and sleeve can now be given. We get

$$[(\tau_{zz})_B]_{total} = 23{,}400 + 3300 = 26{,}700 \text{ psi}$$

$$[(\tau_{zz})_S]_{total} = -7815 - 1100 = -8915 \text{ psi}$$

• PROBLEM 5-31

An outer aluminum ring slides freely over an inner steel ring at an initial temperature T_0. After reducing the temperature to $(T_0 - 80)$°F, calculate the stresses in the rings.

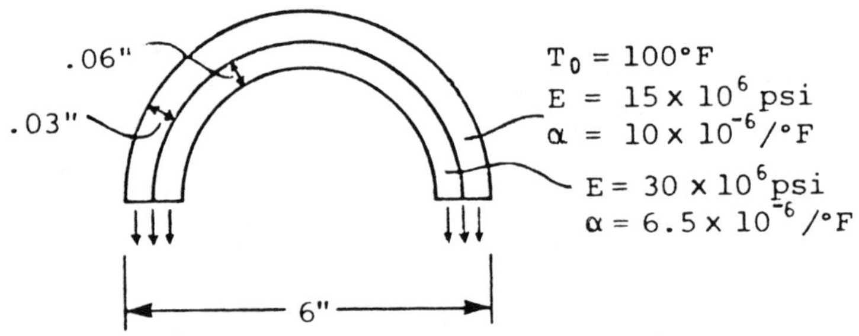

Solution: In this example there are no applied forces. The stresses in the materials arise solely because of the temperature effects. A change in temperature causes a change in length (diameter in this case) equal to $\alpha \Delta T L$, where α is the coefficient of expansion, ΔT is the change in temperature, and L is the original length.

When the temperature drops the steel ring is going to shrink at the interface by $\alpha_{st} \Delta T L_I$. The aluminum is also going to shrink. If the aluminum were unrestrained it would change an amount $\alpha_A \Delta T L_I$, which is greater than $\alpha_{st} \Delta T L_I$, because $\alpha_A > \alpha_{st}$. So the steel will prohibit the aluminum ring's full shrinkage. This will cause stresses in both materials; the aluminum ring is pushing in on the steel, causing compression, and this pushing causes tension in the aluminum.

We can express the change in diameter by

$$\Delta L_{st} = \alpha_{st} \Delta T L_I + \frac{\tau_{st}}{E_{st}} L_I$$

$$\Delta L_A = \alpha_A \Delta T L_I + \frac{\tau_A}{E_A} L_I .$$

But from compatibility, the change in length must be equal for both materials.

$$\alpha_{st} \Delta T L_I + \frac{\tau_{st}}{E_{st}} L_I = \alpha_A \Delta T L_I + \frac{\tau_A}{E_A} L_I$$

$$\tau_{st} = \left[(\alpha_A - \alpha_{st}) \Delta T + \frac{\tau_A}{E_A} \right] E_{st}$$

Substituting the given values

$$\tau_{st} = \left[(10 - 6.5) \cdot 10^{-6} \times (-80) + \frac{\tau_A}{15 \cdot 10^6} \right] 30 \cdot 10^6$$

$$\tau_{st} = -8400 + 2\tau_A .$$

We obtain our second equation from equilibrium since the external applied force is zero, we know that

$$\tau_{st} \times A_{st} + \tau_{al} \times A_{al} = 0$$

$$A_{st} = \pi (r^2_{outer} - r^2_{inner})$$

$$= \pi [(3 - .03)^2 - (3 - .03 - .06)^2]$$

$$= \pi [2.97^2 - 2.91^2]$$

$$= (.3528)$$

$$A_{al} = \pi [3^2 - (3 - .03)^2]$$

$$= \pi (.1791) .$$

$$\tau_{st} \times \pi \times .3528 = \tau_{al} \times \pi \times .1791$$

$$\tau_{st} = - \frac{.1791}{.3528} \tau_{al}$$

$$= -.5\tau_{al} .$$

Substituting for τ_{st} in our compatibility equation, we solve for τ_{al}.

$$- \frac{1}{2} \tau_{al} = 2\tau_{al} - 8400$$

$$\frac{5}{2} \tau_{al} = 8400$$

$$\tau_{al} = 3360 \text{ psi}$$

$$\tau_{st} = -.5\tau_{al} = -1680 \text{ psi}$$

$$\tau_{al} = 3360 \text{ psi.}$$

Note that the stress in the steel ring has a negative sign and that the stress in the aluminum ring has a positive sign. This is consistent with an earlier note that the aluminum ring would be in tension (positive stress) and that the steel ring would be in compression (negative stress).

• PROBLEM 5-32

A steel tire is to be heated and placed on a 72.00-in. diameter locomotive drive wheel. At 80 F the tire has an inside diameter of 71.94 in. The coefficient of thermal expansion for the steel is $6.5(10^{-6})$ per degree F, and its yield strength for 0.2 per cent offset is 60 ksi. Determine:

(a) The temperature increase required for the inside diameter of the tire to be 72.04 in. to facilitate placing it on the wheel.

(b) The maximum tensile stress in the tire when it has cooled to -20 F, assuming that the diameter of the wheel does not change.

(c) The factor of safety with respect to failure by slip for the stress obtained in part (b).

Solution: a) We use the stress-strain relation including thermal effects for this problem.

$$\varepsilon = \frac{1}{E}\tau + \alpha\Delta T.$$

We know that strain, by def., is change in length over original length.

$$\varepsilon = \frac{\Delta d}{d}$$

and since there is no restraint on the tire during heating, the stress will be zero. Therefore,

$$\frac{\Delta d}{d} = \alpha\Delta T$$

or

$$\Delta T = \frac{\Delta d}{\alpha d}$$

The change in diameter $\Delta d = 72.04 - 71.94 = .1$ in.

$$\alpha = 6.5 \times 10^{-6}/°F$$

$$d = 71.94 \text{ in}$$

So $\Delta T = \dfrac{.1 \text{ in}}{(6.5 \times 10^{-6})/°F \times 71.94 \text{ in}}$

$= 213.9°F.$

b) To solve part b, we now consider the diameter of the wheel to remain constant. Since $\Delta d = 0$, the strain will be zero, and stress will develop in the tire due to the restraint.

$$0 = \frac{\tau}{E} + \alpha\Delta T$$

$$\Delta T = -20 - 213.8°F$$

so

$$\tau = -\alpha E \Delta T$$

$$= -(6.5 \times 10^{-6})(30 \cdot 10^{6})(-233.8)$$

$$\tau = 45.6 \text{ ksi} \quad \text{(tension)}$$

c) Failure by slip will occur when the stress in the tire reaches the yield stress, because at yield stress, the material will begin to deform with no further stress. The yield stress is 60 ksi, so the factor of safety with respect to failure is the ratio of yield stress to actual stress.

$$\text{Factor of safety} = \frac{60k}{45.6k} = 1.315.$$

VISCOELASTIC BEHAVIOR

• PROBLEM 5-33

A uniform viscoelastic bar AB having a cross-sectional area of 1 in.^{2} and length 12 in. is suspended from one end A. If $E = 10 \times 10^6$ psi, $\eta = 100 \times 10^8$ psi-sec and γ is 400 lb/ft.^{3}. What is the movement of end B after 1000 sec as a result of the weight and viscoelastic action? What is the rate of movement of end B?

Solution: Using the Maxwell model for a viscoelastic material the expression for strain rate is:

$$\dot{\varepsilon} = \frac{\dot{\tau}}{E} + \frac{\tau}{\eta}$$

where $\dot{f} = \dfrac{df}{dt}$.

Since we are finding the deflection due to the weight, which is constant, $\dot{\tau} = 0$ and therefore $\dot{\varepsilon} = 0 + \frac{\tau}{\eta}$. The stress distribution due to the weight can be found by using a dummy variable which runs from the top of a given cross-section to the bottom of the bar.

The weight W(z) is found to be

$$W(z) = \frac{\gamma_0 (L - z)}{A}$$

where γ_0 is the density
A is the area
L is the length

$$\tau(z) = \frac{W(z)}{A} = \gamma_0 (L - z).$$

Substituting the given values

$$\tau(z) = 400(\text{lb/ft}^3) \times (\text{ft}^3/12^3\text{in}^3)(L - z)$$

$$= \frac{400}{12^3}(L - z)\,\text{lb/in}^3$$

Therefore

$$\dot{\varepsilon} = \frac{400(L - z)\ \text{lb/in}^3}{12^3 \cdot 100 \cdot 10^8\ \text{psi-sec}}$$

$$= \frac{400}{12^3}\ 10^{-10}(L - z).$$

The total strain, ε, is equal to the elastic strain plus the viscoelastic strain, which is the strain rate $\times$ time.

$$\varepsilon(z) = \frac{\tau(z)}{E} + \dot{\varepsilon}t$$

$$= \frac{400}{12^3} \cdot 10^{-7}(L - z) + \frac{400}{12^3} \cdot 10^{-10}(L - z)t.$$

To find the deflection at B after 1000 sec. we must integrate the strain over the entire length

$$\Delta_B = \int_0^L \varepsilon(x)dz = \int_0^{12} \frac{400}{12^3} \cdot 10^{-7}(12 - z)dz$$

$$+ \int_0^{12} \frac{400}{12^3} \cdot 10^{-10}(12 - z) \cdot 10^3 dz$$

$$= 2\int_0^{12} \frac{400}{12^3} \cdot 10^{-7}(12 - z)dz.$$

After integrating:

$$= \frac{800}{12^3} \cdot 10^{-7} \left(12z - \frac{z^2}{2} \right) \Bigg|_0^{12}$$

$$= \frac{800}{12^3} \cdot 10^{-7} \left(\frac{12^2}{2} \right)$$

$$= 3.35 \times 10^{-4} \text{ in.}$$

The rate of movement of B is the change in position of pt. B with time.

$$\Delta_B = \int_0^{12} \left(\frac{\tau}{E} + \dot{\varepsilon} t \right) dz.$$

Therefore, differentiating with respect to time,

$$\dot{\Delta}_B = \int_0^{12} 0 + \dot{\varepsilon} dz$$

$$= \int_0^{12} \dot{\varepsilon} dz$$

$$= \int_0^{12} \frac{400}{12^3} \cdot 10^{-10} (12 - z) dz$$

$$= \frac{400}{12^3} \cdot 10^{-10} \left(12z - \frac{z^2}{2} \right) \Bigg|_0^{12}$$

$$= \frac{400}{12^3} \cdot 10^{-10} \left(\frac{12^2}{2} \right)$$

$$\dot{\Delta}_B = 1.66 \times 10^{-9} \text{ in/sec.}$$

• PROBLEM 5-34

If a Maxwell solid is initially strained an amount ε_0 causing an initial stress of σ_0 , and the strain ε_0 is maintained, how does the stress vary with time?

FIG. 1

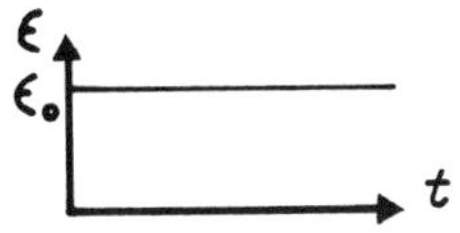

FIG. 2

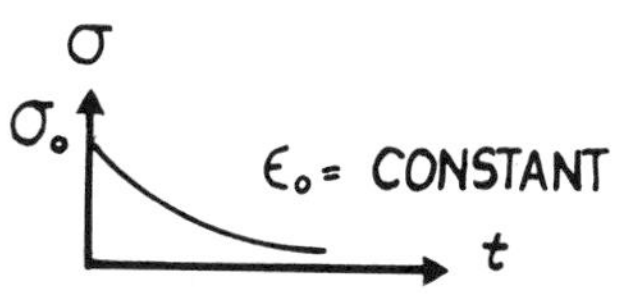

Solution: Here the strain rate $\dot{\varepsilon} = 0$ or $\frac{d\varepsilon}{dt} = 0$ (see Fig. 1) since no change in strain is permitted. So, in order to determine the variation of stress with time, the differential form of stress-strain relationship should be used. Note that the initial stress condition at t = 0 is σ_0.

$$\frac{d\sigma}{dt} + \frac{E}{\eta}\sigma = 0$$

Solving this equation with a constant of integration A,

$$\sigma = Ae^{-(E/\eta)t} \text{ , and, since } \sigma(0) = \sigma_0 \text{ ,}$$

$$\sigma = \sigma_0 e^{-(E/\eta)t}$$

If the result is plotted for various values of stress and time, the plot would show how the stress gradually decreases with time and tends toward zero asymptotically. (Fig. 2).

• PROBLEM 5-35

An overhead oil storage drum is suspended at three points ABC. Assume a Maxwell model for the rods where they behave viscoelastically. Calculate the rate of drum rotation.

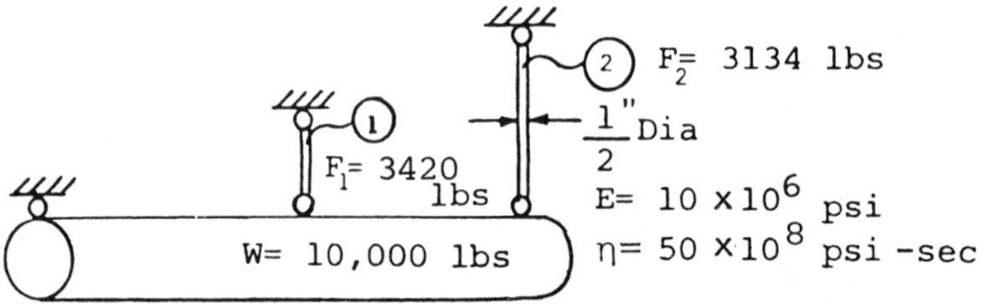

Solution: The rotation of the drum, ϕ, can be found by trigonometry.

$$\tan\phi = \frac{\Delta L_{1A}}{L_{1A}}$$

where L_{1A} = distance from A to bar 1.

By similar triangles, and to satisfy compatibility,

$$\tan\phi = \frac{\Delta L_{2A}}{\Delta L_{2A}}$$

where L_{2A} = distance from A to bar 2.

If we assume ϕ to be small we can use the approximation

$$\tan \phi \cong \phi$$

or $$\phi = \frac{\Delta L_{1A}}{L_{1A}} = \frac{\Delta L_{2A}}{L_{2A}}$$

The rate of rotation is the time derivative of the rotation

$$\dot{\phi} = \frac{\Delta\dot{L}_1}{L_{1A}} = \frac{\Delta\dot{L}_2}{L_{2A}}$$

Therefore, we must find the rate of elongation in the bars. We know, by definition, that

$$\Delta L = \varepsilon L,$$

so taking the time derivative

$$\Delta\dot{L} = \dot{\varepsilon} L.$$

In a Maxwell-model, the strain rate is given by

$$\dot{\varepsilon} = \frac{\dot{\tau}}{E} + \frac{\tau}{\eta}$$

but since the force applied is the weight of the drum, which is constant, $\dot{\tau}$ must equal zero.

$$\therefore \qquad \dot{\varepsilon} = \frac{\tau}{\eta} \text{ or } \frac{F}{A\eta}$$

Therefore $$\Delta\dot{L}_1 = \frac{F_1 L_1}{A\eta}$$

$$\Delta\dot{L}_2 = \frac{F_2 L_2}{A\eta}$$

where F_1 and F_2 are forces due to elastic action only.

$$\dot{\phi} = \frac{F_1 L_1}{A\eta L_{1A}}$$

$$= \frac{F_2 L_2}{A\eta L_{2A}}$$

We will consider first bar 1.

$$F_1 = 3420 \text{ lb}$$

$$L_1 = 60 \text{ in}$$

$$A = \pi\left(\frac{1}{4}\right)^2$$

$$\eta = 50 \times 10^8$$

$$L_{1A} = 72 \text{ in}$$

$$\dot{\phi} = \frac{(3420)(60)}{\pi\left(\frac{1}{4}\right)^2 (50 \times 10^8)(72)}$$

$$= 2.903 \times 10^{-6} \text{ rad/sec.}$$

Considering bar 2, we should get the same rate of rotation, because the drum is rigid and the angle will be the same for both bars.

$$\dot{\phi} = \frac{(3134)(120)}{\pi\left(\frac{1}{4}\right)^2 (50 \times 10^8)(132)}$$

$$= 2.903 \times 10^{-6} \text{ rad/sec.}$$

• PROBLEM 5-36

A viscoelastic shaft corresponding to Maxwell model is suspended from a ceiling and surrounded by an elastic sleeve. A metal disk is connected to both members at their free ends. If a force is applied to the disc at t = 0, calculate the stresses in the shaft. and sleeve as a function of time.

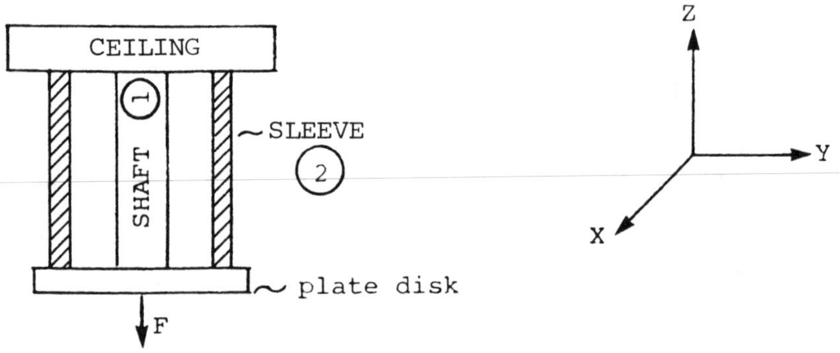

Solution: Equilibrium requires that

$$F_1 + F_2 = F_{Total}$$

where F_1, F_2 are the forces in the shaft and sleeve, respectively. Using the equation $F = \tau_{zz}A$ the above relation is rewritten in the form:

$$(\tau_{zz})_1 A_1 + (\tau_{zz})_2 A_2 = F \qquad \text{(a)}$$

Considering the areas as essentially constant for the loads involved, we can say after t = 0 on differentiating the terms in the above equation with respect to time that

$$\frac{d(\tau_{zz})_1}{dt} A_1 + \frac{d(\tau_{zz})_2}{dt} A_2 = 0 \qquad \text{(b)}$$

The requirement of compatibility indicates that the strain ε_{zz} in each member must be equal to each other at all times, due to the fact that the shaft and sleeve are connected to a rigid wall on one side and a rigid plate on the other side. The original lengths are equal and the rigid end constraints require $\Delta L_1 = \Delta L_2$ so

$$\frac{\Delta L_1}{L_1} = \frac{\Delta L_2}{L_2}$$

or

$$(\varepsilon_{zz})_1 = (\varepsilon_{zz})_2$$

and accordingly we can say that

$$\frac{d(\varepsilon_{zz})_1}{dt} = \frac{d(\varepsilon_{zz})_2}{dt} \qquad \text{(c)}$$

We next consider the material behavior of the members -- that is, the constitutive laws. For the viscoelastic material, we can deduce with the aid of the spring-dashpot model that when the load is suddenly developed the dashpot has no time to respond and acts initially as a rigid connector. Accordingly, the force P_1 in the viscoelastic shaft initially causes entirely elastic action in the shaft. Thus, upon initial application of the load the forces P_1 and P_2 in the members are those for elastic bodies with elastic moduli E_1 and E_2, respectively. As time progresses from t = 0, the dashpot extends and the force carried by the shaft decreases with the result that the elastic sleeve supports increasingly more of the total force F. For the subsequent strain rate of each member using the appropriate constitutive law, we then have

$$(\varepsilon_{zz})_2 = \frac{(\tau_{zz})_2}{E_2}, \quad \text{then}$$

$$\frac{d(\varepsilon_{zz})_2}{dt} = \frac{d(\tau_{zz})_2}{E_2 dt} \qquad \text{(d)}$$

$$\frac{d(\varepsilon_{zz})_1}{dt} = \frac{d(\tau_{zz})_1}{E_1 dt} + \frac{(\tau_{zz})_1}{\eta_1} \qquad \text{(e)}$$

Substituting the above results into Eq. (c) we get

$$\frac{d(\tau_{zz})_2}{E_2 dt} = \frac{d(\tau_{zz})_1}{E_1 dt} + \frac{(\tau_{zz})_1}{\eta_1} \qquad (f)$$

Now eliminate $d(\tau_{zz})_2/dt$ in Eq. (f) using Eq. (b).

$$\frac{d(\tau_{zz})_1}{dt}A_1 + \frac{d(\tau_{zz})_2}{dt}A_2 = 0$$

$$\frac{d(\tau_{zz})_2}{dt} = -\frac{d(\tau_{zz})_1}{dt}\left(\frac{A_1}{A_2}\right)$$

$$-\frac{d(\tau_{zz})_1}{E_2 dt}\left(\frac{A_1}{A_2}\right) = \frac{d(\tau_{zz})_1}{E_1 dt} + \frac{(\tau_{zz})_1}{\eta_1}$$

or,

$$\frac{d(\tau_{zz})_1}{E_2 dt}\left(\frac{A_1}{A_2}\right) + \frac{d(\tau_{zz})_1}{E_1 dt} + \frac{(\tau_{zz})_1}{\eta_1} = 0$$

$$\therefore \quad \left[\frac{A_1}{E_2 A_2} + \frac{1}{E_1}\right]\frac{d(\tau_{zz})_1}{dt} + \frac{(\tau_{zz})_1}{\eta_1} = 0.$$

Separating the variables (multiplying by $dt/(\tau_{zz})_1$) we get,

$$\left[\frac{A_1}{E_2 A_2} + \frac{1}{E_1}\right]\frac{d(\tau_{zz})_1}{(\tau_{zz})_1} + \frac{dt}{\eta_1} = 0$$

Integrating,

$$\left[\frac{A_1}{E_2 A_2} + \frac{1}{E_1}\right] \ln(\tau_{zz})_1 + \frac{t}{\eta_1} = C$$

$$\ln(\tau_{zz})_1 = \left(C - \frac{t}{\eta_1}\right)\left[\frac{1}{\frac{A_1}{E_2 A_2} + \frac{1}{E_1}}\right] = \left(C - \frac{t}{\eta_1}\right)\left[\frac{1}{\frac{E_1 A_1 + E_2 A_2}{E_1 E_2 A_2}}\right]$$

$$\ln(\tau_{zz})_1 = \left(C - \frac{t}{\eta_1}\right)\left[\frac{E_1 E_2 A_2}{E_1 A_1 + E_2 A_2}\right]$$

Applying the exponential function to both sides, we get

$$(\tau_{zz})_1 = C' e^{\{[-E_1 E_2 A_2/\eta_1 (E_1 A_1 + E_2 A_2)]t\}} \qquad (g)$$

Just after the application of the load (we denote the time then as $t = 0+$) the stresses in both the viscoelastic shaft and the sleeve result from elastic action only, as pointed out earlier. We can solve for such instantaneous stresses by methods illustrated earlier. We shall denote the instantaneous stress at t = 0+ in the viscoelastic shaft as $[(\tau_{zz})_1]_{E1}$. Subjecting Eq. (g) to this initial condition, we see on inspection that the integration constant is simply $[(\tau_{zz})_1]_{E1}$ and so we have

$$(\tau_{zz})_1 = [(\tau_{zz})_1]_{E1} e^{\{[-E_1E_2A_2/\eta_1(E_1A_1+E_2A_2)]t\}} \qquad \text{(h)}$$

We see here that the stress in the shaft relaxes exponentially from the initial maximum value computed for complete elastic action. The stress in the sleeve then builds up in accordance with the following equation, developed using Eqs. (h) and (a):

$$(\tau_{zz})_2 = \frac{F}{A_2} - \frac{A_1}{A_2}[(\tau_{zz})_1]_{E1}\, e^{\{[-E_1E_2A_2/\eta_1(E_1A_1+E_2A_2)]t\}} \qquad \text{(i)}$$

It is seen that if F/A_2 exceeds Y_2 the sleeve will in due time approach its yield stress.

• PROBLEM 5-37

Two coaxial tubes, the inner one of 1020 CR steel and cross-sectional area A_s and the outer one of 2024-T4 aluminum alloy and of area A_a, are compressed between heavy, flat end plates, as shown. Determine the load-deflection curve of the assembly as it is compressed into the plastic region by an axial force P.

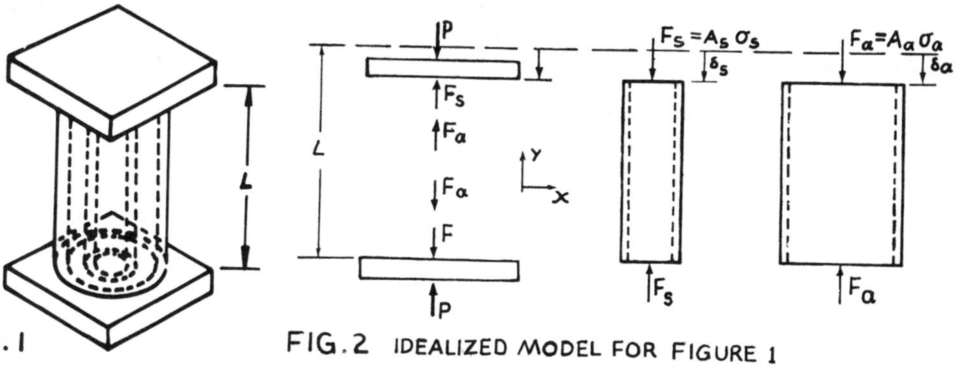

FIG. 1 FIG. 2 IDEALIZED MODEL FOR FIGURE 1

Solution: First construct an idealized model of the situation, as shown in Figure 2. We assume in Fig. (2), that the end plates are so stiff that both tubes are shortened exactly the same amount.

From Fig. (2) we see that, because of geometric compatibility, we must have the following relation betweeen the strains:

$$\varepsilon_s = \varepsilon_a = \varepsilon = \frac{\delta}{L} \qquad \text{(a)}$$

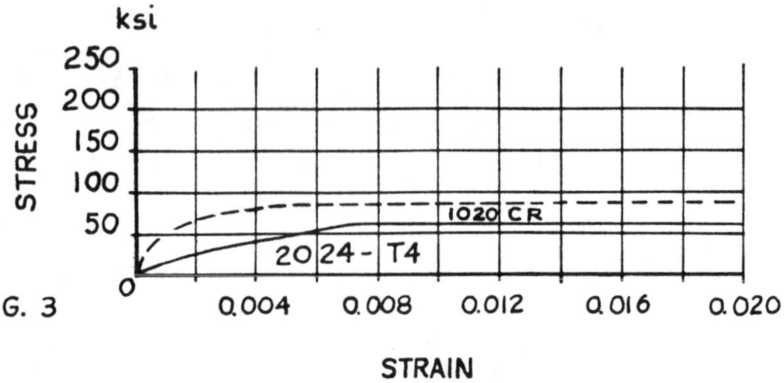

FIG. 3

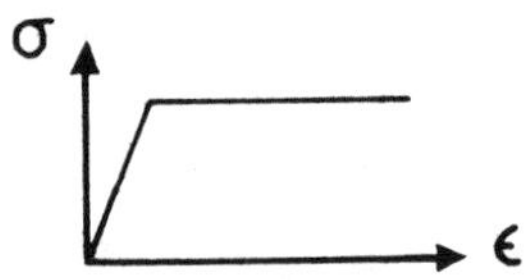

ELASTIC, PERFECTLY PLASTIC-MATERIAL (IDEALIZED MODEL)

FIG. 4

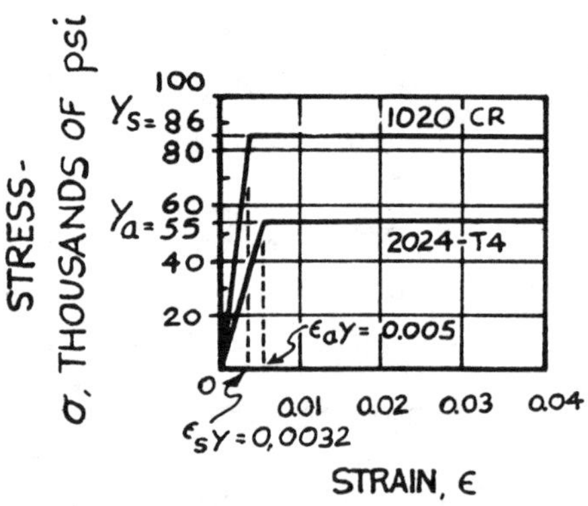

FIG. 5
IDEALIZED STRESS-STRAIN CURVES

We wish to carry the test through the elastic region to the point where both materials are in the plastic region. Looking at the curves for 1020 CR steel and 2024 T4 aluminum alloy in Figure 3, we conclude that we can, with reasonable accuracy, idealize both these curves as being of the elastic-perfectly plastic type of Figure 4, although the 1020 CR steel is described by this model somewhat better than the 2024-T4 aluminum alloy. These idealized stress-strain curves are shown in Fig. 5. From Fig. 5, we see that there are three regions of strain which are of interest as we compress the assembly.

In the range $0 \leq \varepsilon \leq 0.0032$,

$$\sigma_s = E_s \varepsilon_s = E_s \varepsilon$$

$$\sigma_a = E_a \varepsilon_a = E_a \varepsilon \tag{b}$$

where

$$E_s = \frac{86{,}000}{0.0032} = 27 \times 10^6 \text{ psi}$$

$$E_a = \frac{55{,}000}{0.005} = 11 \times 10^6 \text{ psi.}$$

In the range $0.0032 \leq \varepsilon \leq 0.005$,

$$\sigma_s = Y_s = 86{,}000 \text{ psi} \tag{c}$$

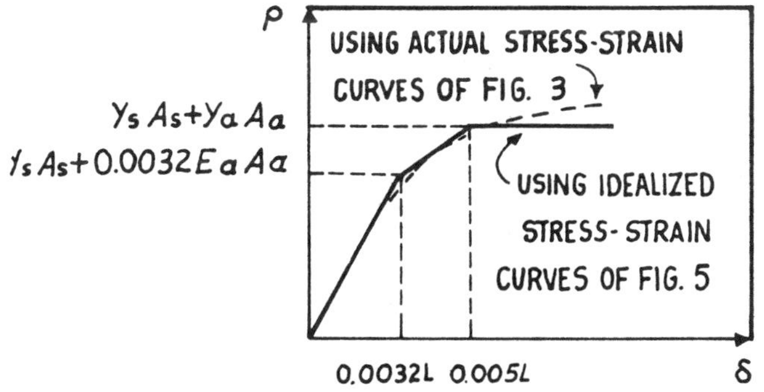

FIG. 6 LOAD-DEFORMATION CURVES

$$\sigma_a = E_a \varepsilon_a = E_a \varepsilon \qquad (c)$$

In the range $0.005 \leq \varepsilon$,

$$\sigma_s = Y_s = 86{,}000 \text{ psi}$$
$$\sigma_a = Y_a = 55{,}000 \text{ psi} \qquad (d)$$

EQUILIBRIUM

In Figure 2 the top plate is in equilibrium when

$$\sum F_y = \sigma_s A_s + \sigma_a A_a - P = 0 \qquad (e)$$

where A_s and A_a are the cross-sectional areas of the metal in the steel and aluminum tubes.

Combining (e) with (b), (c), and (d) in succession, we obtain the load-deformation curve of Fig. (6). It should be borne in mind that this is the load-deformation curve for the idealized materials of Fig. 5. If we repeat the analysis replacing (b), (c), and (d) by the actual stress-strain curves of the materials from Figure 3 we will obtain the dotted curve shown in Fig. (6), which is only slightly different from the result using the idealized curves.

PLASTIC DEFORMATION

• PROBLEM 5-38

Cylinder B, and cylinder A, to which B is welded, are considered elastic $E = 20 \times 10^6$ psi, perfectly plastic with a yield stress of 100,000 psi. (a) What is the maximum force that can be imposed without causing permanent set? (b) What is the maximum movement of end D without permanent set? (c) What force is needed to double this deflection? Neglect the weight of the members.

Solution: (a) The maximum possible force that can be imposed without causing permanent set (plastic deformation)

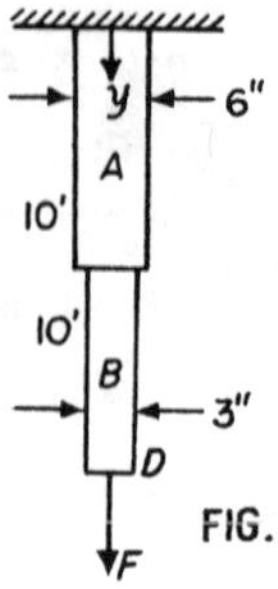

FIG.

is the product of the yield stress and the cross-sectional area of the member.

$$\text{That is,}\quad \frac{F_{max.}}{A} = (\tau_{yy})_{max}$$

$$\text{or}\quad F_{max.} = A(\tau_{yy})_{max} \tag{1}$$

For cylinder A,

$$F_{max.} = \left(\pi\frac{(6")^2}{4}\right)[100{,}000 \text{ psi}] = 2.827 \times 10^6 \text{ lb}$$

For cylinder B,

$$F_{max.} = \left(\pi\frac{(3")^2}{4}\right)[100{,}000 \text{ psi}] = 7.07 \times 10^5 \text{ lb}$$

Thus, cylinder B will begin plastic deformation at 7.07×10^5 lb, and the maximum allowable force (for totally elastic deformation) is

$$F_{allow.} = 7.07 \times 10^5 \text{ lb.}$$

(b) The maximum movement of end D will occur at $F = 7.07 \times 10^5$ lb. The extension for this simple, one-dimensional case is

$$\delta = \frac{FL}{AE} \tag{2}$$

for each member, where L is the length of the member, and A is its cross-sectional area.

Thus, for cylinder A, the maximum extension is

$$\delta_A = \frac{(7.07 \times 10^5 \text{ lb})(120")}{\left(\pi\frac{(6")^2}{4}\right)(20 \times 10^6 \text{ psi})} = 0.150"$$

Likewise, the maximum extension of cylinder B

$$\delta_B = \frac{(7.07 \times 10^5)(120)}{\left[\pi\frac{(3)^2}{4}\right](30 \times 10^6 \text{ psi})} = 0.400".$$

The movement at end D is merely the sum of these two extensions. That is,

$$\delta_{TOT} = \delta_A + \delta_B = 0.550".$$

(c) Just after F_{max} is exceeded, plastic deformation will begin. For a perfectly plastic material, no additional tensile force will be required. The material of cylinder B will "flow" continuously until the deflection is doubled. (This could theoretically continue until the cylinder is infinite in length.)

Thus, no additional force is necessary to double the extension of the system.

$$F_{necessary} = 7.07 \times 10^5 \text{ lb.}$$

Note also that cylinder A undergoes no further extension after plastic deformation starts in B, because no additional stress is introduced after this point.

• PROBLEM 5-39

A chain hoist is attached to the ceiling through two tie rods at an angle θ to the vertical, as shown in the figure. The tie rods are made of cold-rolled steel with yield strength Y, and each has an area A.

(a) What is the load at which both rods become plastic, so that large-seale plastic deformation begins?

(b) By how much would this load be increased if a third rod of area A were added, as shown by the dotted line?

(c) What is the load-deflection relation when the deflections are elastic in all three rods?

(d) If the three-member frame is loaded until all three rods become fully plastic, and then the load is released, find the residual stress in the central rod.

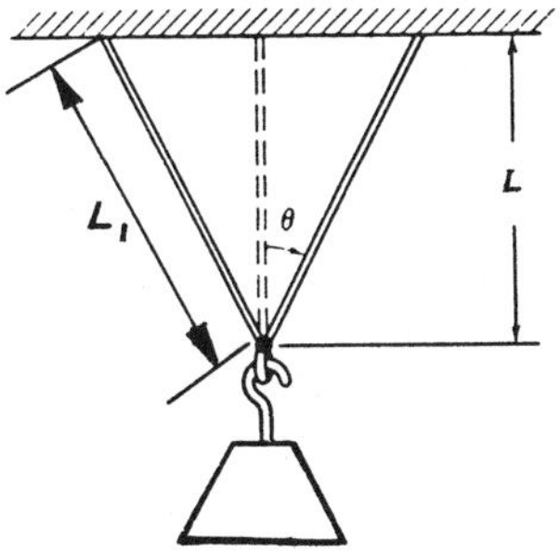

Solution: (a) We begin by finding the bar force, F, in the tie rods in terms of the load, P. Because the rods are made of the same material and have the same area, the bar forces will be the same in each tie rod.

Using trigonometry, the vertical component of the bar force is $F_{vert} = F \cos \theta$.

By equilibrium

$$2F_V = P$$

$$2F \cos \theta = P.$$

If both bars are plasticized, the stress in the bars has reached Y, and the bar force will be the yield stress × area.

$$F = A \times Y.$$

Therefore $$P = 2AY \cos \theta.$$

(b) If a third tie rod is added as shown by the dotted line the equilibrium equation becomes:

$$P = 2F_1 \cos \theta + F_2$$

where F_1 is bar force in inclined ties

F_2 is bar force in vertical bar.

Again, if all the bars are plasticized, they will all have bar force equal to AY. Therefore, the inclined bars contribute the same amount as in part (a). The load will increase by the amount which the vertical bar can contribute, i.e., AY.

(c) To find the load-deflection relation in the elastic region, we are going to find the bar forces F_1 and F_2, which will be different in this case.

By equilibrium

$$P = 2F_1 \cos \theta + F_2.$$

By geometry, we can see that, if the hoist deflects by an amount, δ, then

$$\Delta L_1 = \delta \cos \theta$$

$$\Delta L_2 = \delta$$

Using Hooke's law $\Delta L = \frac{FL}{AE}$ we can derive an expression for each bar force in terms of the deflection, δ

$$F_1 = \frac{\Delta L_1 AE}{L_1}$$

$$F_2 = \frac{\Delta L_2 AE}{L_2}$$

Just as we found ΔL_1 and ΔL_2, by geometry we find

$$L = L_1 \cos\theta$$

or

$$L_1 = \frac{L}{\cos\theta}$$

$$L_2 = L.$$

Therefore, substituting all known values

$$F_1 = \frac{\delta \cos\theta\, AE}{\dfrac{L}{\cos\theta}}$$

$$F_1 = \frac{\delta \cos^2\theta\, AE}{L}$$

$$F_2 = \frac{\delta AE}{L}$$

Substituting these forces into the equilibrium equation we find

$$P = 2\,\frac{\delta \cos^2\theta\, AE}{L} \times \cos\theta + \frac{\delta AE}{L}$$

$$P = \frac{\delta AE}{L}[2\cos^3\theta + 1]$$

or

$$\delta = \frac{PL}{AE(2\cos^3\theta + 1)}$$

• PROBLEM 5-40

A batch of 2024-T4 aluminum alloy yields in uniaxial tension at the stress σ_0 = 48,000 psi. If this material is subjected to the following state of stress, will it yield according to (a) the Mises criterion, and (b) the maximum shear-stress criterion?

σ_x = 20,000 psi $\qquad \tau_{xy}$ = 20,000 psi

σ_y = -10,000 psi $\qquad \tau_{yz}$ = 0

σ_z = 0 $\qquad \tau_{zx}$ = 0

Solution: The Mises criterion is developed by considering the shear stress in the octahedral plane of a material The octahedral plane is one which is inclined to each principal axis equally. The octahedral shear stress, τ_{oct}, can be found by the formula

$$\tau_{oct} = \frac{1}{3}\sqrt{(\tau_1-\tau_2)^2 - (\tau_1-\tau_3)^2 + (\tau_2-\tau_3)^2}$$

where τ_1, τ_2, τ_3 are the principal stresses.

The Mises criterion states that when the octahedral shear stress at a point reaches a value dependent on the material only, yielding will begin. The value of yielding onset is found by considering the conditions of a standard tensile test at yield point.

$$\tau_1 = f_{yield} = f_y$$

$$\tau_2 = \tau_3 = 0$$

and $$[\tau_{oct}]_y = \sqrt{(f_y-0)^2 + (f_y-0)^2 + (0-0)^2}$$

$$= \frac{\sqrt{2}}{3}f_y.$$

Therefore, if $\tau_{oct} > [\tau_{oct}]_y$ we will have yielding. The maximum shear stress criterion is based on the assumption that yielding begins when the maximum shear stress in the material becomes equal to the maximum shear stress at the yield point in a simple tension test.

From Mohr's circle we know that the maximum shear stress is equal to one half the difference between the principal stresses.

$$\tau_{xy_{max}} = \frac{\tau_1 - \tau_2}{2}$$

In a simple tensile test the maximum shear stress is at 45° and using equations of equilibrium we find $[\tau_{xy}] = \frac{\sigma_x}{2}$. So, for the criterion, we compare the maximum shear stress in our material to the yield shear stress in the test sample.

$$\frac{\tau_1 - \tau_2}{2} \overset{?}{\gtrless} \frac{\tau_y}{2}$$

or $$\tau_1 - \tau_2 \overset{?}{\gtrless} \tau_y$$

Having defined the two criteria we now must find the principal stresses, τ_1 and τ_2. (Since stresses in the z-direction are zero, $\tau_3 = 0$)

$$\tau_1 = \frac{\sigma_x + \sigma_y}{2} + \sqrt{\left(\frac{\sigma_x - \sigma_y}{2}\right)^2 + (\tau_{xy})^2}$$

$$= \frac{20k - 10k}{2} + \sqrt{\left(\frac{20k - (-10k)}{2}\right)^2 + (20k)^2}$$

$= 30$ ksi

$$\tau_2 = \frac{\sigma_x + \sigma_y}{2} - \sqrt{\left(\frac{\sigma_x - \sigma_y}{2}\right)^2 + (\tau_{xy})^2}$$

$$= \frac{20k - 10k}{2} - \sqrt{\left(\frac{20k - (-10k)}{2}\right)^2 + (20k)^2}$$

$= -20$ ksi.

$\tau_3 = 0.$

For the Mises criterion:

$$\tau_{oct} = \frac{1}{3}\sqrt{(30k - (-20k))^2 + (30k - 0)^2 + (-20k - 0)^2}$$

$= 20548$ psi

$$[\tau_{oct}]_y = \frac{\sqrt{2}}{3}\tau_y = \frac{\sqrt{2}}{3}(48000) = 22627 \text{ psi}$$

$$20548 < 22627$$

so we do not have yielding.

For the maximum shear stress criterion:

$$\tau_1 = \tau_2 \overset{?}{\gtrless} \tau_y$$

$$30 \text{ ksi} - (-20 \text{ ksi}) = 50 \text{ ksi} > 48 \text{ ksi}.$$

So, we do have yielding.

• PROBLEM 5-41

Determine the creep of a Voigt-Kelvin solid subjected to a constant stress σ_0. Initially the model is unstrained.

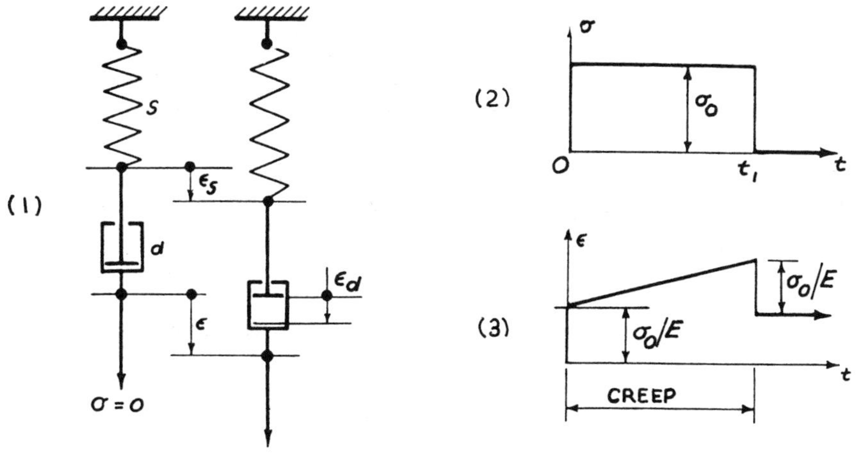

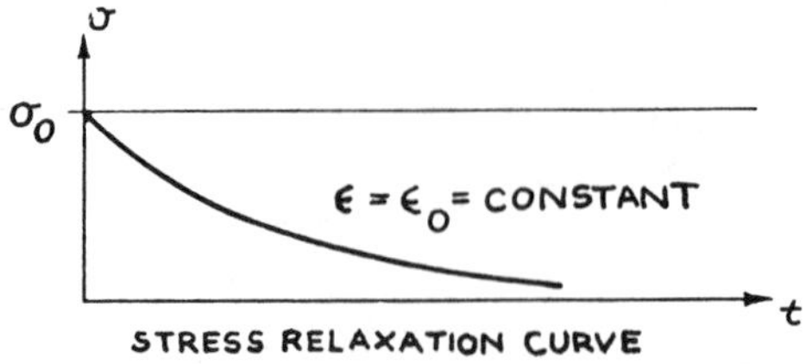

(4)

STRESS RELAXATION CURVE

TWO-ELEMENT MODEL OF A MAXWELL SOLID

<u>Solution</u>: Noting that the stress $\sigma = \sigma_0$ is constant, one can show that the homogeneous and the particular solution to the differential form of strain and stress relationship for the Kelvin-Voight model, a parallel combination of a spring and a dashpot, gives

$$\varepsilon = Ae^{-(E/\eta)t} + \sigma_0/E$$

where A is a constant which can be found from the condition that $\varepsilon(0) = 0 = A + \sigma_0/E$, i.e., $A = -\sigma_0/E$. Therefore,

$$\varepsilon = (1 - e^{-(E/\eta)t})(\sigma_0/E).$$

As time increases, the strain asymptotically approaches the maximum strain associated with the elastic spring until, finally, all the applied stress is carried by the spring, and the dashpot becomes inactive. If the stress is removed at an earlier time as in Fig. 4, an asymptotic recovery of the strain takes place.

The above solution shows that the Voigt-Kelvin material exhibits a delayed elastic response; for this reason it is termed an anelastic material. Based on experimental evidence, it is known that such behavior is not very typical of most materials. Another linear combination of stress, stress rate, and strain rate can be formulated, which is more representative.

By endowing a body with an instantaneous elastic response together with a time-dependent displacement, one can obtain a reasonable approximation of the behavior of many viscoelastic materials. The simplest model having such properties can be visualized as a combination in series of a linear spring and a linear dashpot as in the figure. Material of this type is called a Maxwell solid. In the model in Figure 1, if a stress σ is applied, the stress (force) through the dashpot (d) is the same as that through the spring (S), i.e., $\sigma_d = \sigma_s = \sigma$. However, each element of the model contributes to the total strain, $\varepsilon = \varepsilon_s + \varepsilon_d$, where the subscripts as before designate the spring (S) and the dashpot (d), respectively. The strain relation must be differentiated with respect to time since for viscous materials only the connection between the stress and the strain rate is known. On the other hand, for elastic materials with E constant, on differentiating Hooke's law with respect to time, one has $\dot{\varepsilon} = \dot{\sigma}/E$. Then upon adding the strain rates for the two elements and simplifying, one obtains the basic differential equation for the response of the Maxwell solid:

$\dot{\varepsilon} = \dot{\varepsilon}_s + \varepsilon_d = \dot{\sigma}/E + \sigma/\eta$ where η is the coefficient of viscosity.

or $\dot{\sigma} + (E/\eta)\sigma = E\dot{\varepsilon}$

Figure 3 shows the region in which creep occurs.

For the Maxwell solid in pure shear an analogous expression applies:

$$\dot{\gamma} = \dot{\tau}/G + \tau/\bar{\eta}$$

where, as before, dots over the quantities represent their derivatives with respect to time, and $\bar{\eta}$ is the coefficient of viscosity in shear.

• PROBLEM 5-42

Two bars made of linearly elastic material whose proportions are shown in Figs. 1 and 2 are to absorb the same amount of energy delivered by axial forces. Compare the stresses in the two bars caused by the same input of energy.

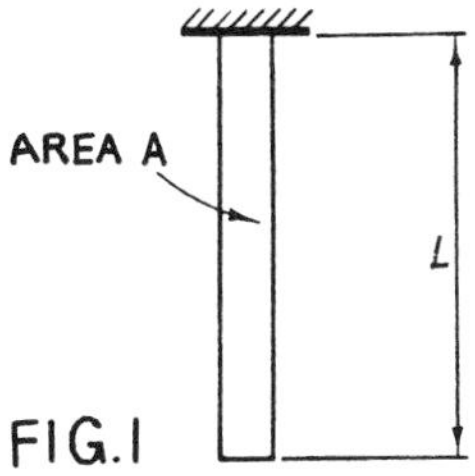

FIG. 1

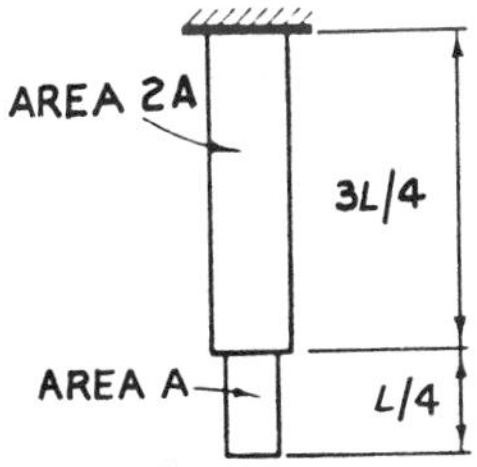

FIG. 2

Solution: The bar shown in Fig. 1 is of uniform cross-sectional area, therefore the normal stress in it σ_1 is constant throughout. By applying the equations for strain-energy in terms of stress

$$U_1 = \frac{(\sigma_1 A)^2}{AE} = \frac{\sigma_1^2 (AL)}{2E} \text{ where } \sigma = \frac{P}{A}$$

A is the cross-sectional area of the bar, and L is its length.

The bar shown in Fig. 2 is of variable cross section. Therefore, if the stress σ_2 acts in the lower part of the bar, the stress in the upper part is $\sigma_2/2$. The strain energy for each part of the bar is computed, and the sum of the two gives the total strain energy applied to the 2nd bar.

$$U_2 = \frac{P^2\left(\frac{L}{4}\right)}{2AE} + \frac{P^2\left(\frac{3L}{4}\right)}{2(2A)E} = \frac{P^2L}{8AE} + \frac{3P^2L}{16AE}$$

$$U_2 = \frac{P^2L}{AE}\left(\frac{1}{8} + \frac{3}{16}\right) = \frac{P^2L}{AE}\left(\frac{5}{16}\right)$$

in terms of stress.

$$U_2 = \frac{5\sigma_2^2(AL)}{16E}$$

But since the same amount of energy is absorbed, by both bars

$$U_1 = U_2$$

$$\frac{\sigma_1^2(AL)}{2E} = \frac{5\sigma_2^2(AL)}{16E}$$

$$\sigma_2 = 1.265\sigma_1$$

The enlargement of the cross-sectional area over a part of the bar in the second case is actually detrimental. For the same energy load, the stress in the "reinforced" bar is 26.5 per cent higher than that in the first bar. This situation is not found in the design of members for static loads.

STRAIN ENERGY

• PROBLEM 5-43

Axial loads are applied to the ends of a long bar. The stress distribution is $\tau_{xx} = F/A$. All other stresses have zero value with respect to the reference coordinates. Find (a) the strain energy in terms of the force F; and (b) the elongation δ.

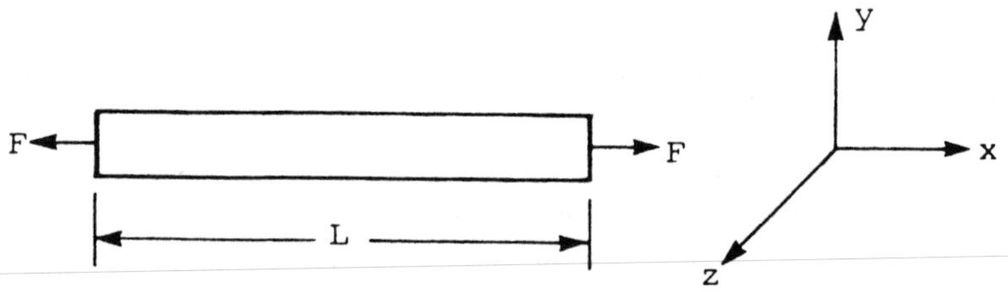

Solution: The strain energy for a body of volume V is given as

$$U = \iiint_V \left\{ \frac{1}{2E}(\tau_{xx}^2 + \tau_{yy}^2 + \tau_{zz}^2) - \frac{\nu}{E}(\tau_{xx}\tau_{yy} + \tau_{yy}\tau_{zz} + \tau_{xx}\tau_{zz}) + \frac{1}{2G}(\tau_{xy}^2 + \tau_{xz}^2 + \tau_{yz}^2) \right\} dv$$

where E is constant for the whole bar and G is the shear modulus $= \frac{E}{2(1 - \nu)}$. Since only τ_{xx} is nonzero, we have

$$U = \iiint_V \frac{1}{2E}\tau_{xx}^2 dv = \frac{1}{2E}\int_0^L \tau_{xx}^2 dx = \frac{1}{2E}\int_0^L \left(\frac{F}{A}\right)^2 dx$$

since F is constant

$$U = \frac{F^2 L}{2AE}$$

If an elongation δ occurs in the rod, the strain energy can be written

$$U = \iiint_V \left\{\frac{E\nu}{2(1 + \nu)(1 - 2\nu)}(\varepsilon_{xx} + \varepsilon_{yy} + \varepsilon_{zz})^2\right.$$

$$\left. + G(\varepsilon_{xx}^2 + \varepsilon_{yy}^2 + \varepsilon_{zz}^2) + \frac{1}{2G}(\gamma_{xy}^2 + \gamma_{yz}^2 + \gamma_{xz}^2)\right\}dv$$

The strains in this case are:

$$\varepsilon_{xx} = \frac{\delta}{L} \quad \varepsilon_{yy} = -\nu\frac{\delta}{L} \quad \varepsilon_{zz} = -\nu\frac{\delta}{LL}$$

The shear strains are all zero so

$$U = \iiint_V \left[\frac{E\nu}{2(1 + \nu)(1 - 2\nu)}\left(\frac{\delta}{L}\right)^2 (1 - 2\nu)^2\right.$$

$$\left. + G\left(\frac{\delta}{L}\right)^2 (1 + 2\nu^2)\right] dv$$

by substituting the given values for the strains. Replacing G by $\frac{E}{2(1 + \nu)}$ and performing the integration

$$U = \iiint_V \left[\frac{E}{2(1 + \nu)}\left(\frac{\delta}{L}\right)^2 (1 - 2\nu) + \frac{E}{2(1 + \nu)}\left(\frac{\delta}{L}\right)^2 (1 + 2\nu^2)\right]$$

$$= \frac{E}{2(1 + \nu)}\left(\frac{\delta}{L}\right)^2 [\nu - 2\nu^2 + 1 + 2\nu^2] \times \text{Volume}$$

$$= \frac{E}{2(1 + \nu)}\left(\frac{\delta}{L}\right)^2 (1 + \nu) \times AL \qquad \begin{aligned} A &= \text{area} \\ L &= \text{length} \end{aligned}$$

$$= \frac{E\delta^2 A}{2L}$$

Two members, A and B, are welded together and are supported by a fixed connection at one end. If there is a tensile force of 1000 lb at end C, as shown in Figure 1, what is the strain-energy density in each of the two members? Compute the total strain energy of the system.

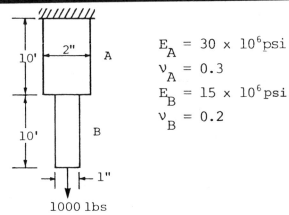

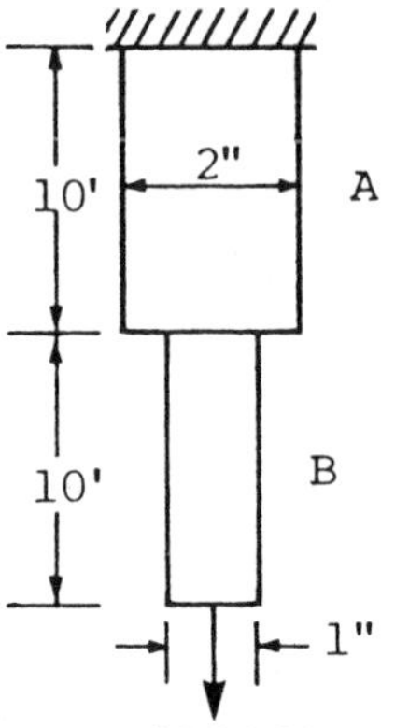

$E_A = 30 \times 10^6$ psi
$\nu_A = 0.3$
$E_B = 15 \times 10^6$ psi
$\nu_B = 0.2$

Solution: The expression for strain-energy, U, in terms of the stress-field is given as

$$U = \iiint_V \left\{ \frac{1}{2E}(\tau_{xx}^2 + \tau_{yy}^2 + \tau_{zz}^2) - \frac{\nu}{E}(\tau_{xx}\tau_{yy} + \tau_{yy}\tau_{zz} + \tau_{xx}\tau_{zz}) + \frac{1}{2\psi}(\tau_{xy}^2 + \tau_{xz}^2 + \tau_{yz}^2) \right\} dv.$$

Therefore, to find the strain energy density, and the total strain energy we need only find the stress-field. Since the only force applied is 1000 lb in the x-direction, the system has only one component of stress, τ_{xx}. Therefore, the expression for strain energy simplifies to

$$U = \iiint \frac{1}{2E}\tau_{xx}^2 dv.$$

Noting that the stress is a constant, we can remove it from the volume integral

$$U = \frac{\tau_{xx}^2}{2E} \iiint_V dv.$$

But $\iiint_V$ dv is just the volume of the bar so

$$U = \frac{\tau_{xx}^2}{2E} \times V.$$

The strain energy density is strain energy/volume or

$$\rho = \frac{\tau_{xx}^2}{2E}.$$

To compute ρ we must first calculate the stress in each bar. The stress is defined as force/area

$$\tau_A = \frac{1000}{\pi(1)^2} = 318.3 \text{ psi}$$

$$\rho_A = \frac{(318.3)^2(\text{psi})^2}{2 \cdot 30 \cdot 10^6 \text{ psi}} \qquad E_A = 30 \times 10^6 \text{ psi}$$

$$= 1.688 \times 10^{-3} \text{ psi}$$

$$\tau_B = \frac{1000}{\pi(.5)^2} = 1273.24 \text{ psi}$$

$$\rho_B = \frac{(1273.24)^2(\text{psi})^2}{2 \times 15 \times 10^6 \text{ psi}} \qquad E_B = 15 \times 10^6 \text{ psi}$$

$$= 54 \times 10^{-3} \text{ psi}.$$

The total strain energy for bars A and B is

$$U = \frac{\tau_A^2}{2E} \times V_A + \frac{\tau_B^2}{2E} \times V_B$$

$$U = \rho_A \times L_A \times A_A + \rho_B \times L_B \times A_B$$

$$L_A = 120 \text{ in}$$

$$L_B = 120 \text{ in}$$

$$A_A = \pi(1)^2 =$$

$$A_B = \pi(.5)^2 = .25\ .$$

$$U = 1.688 \times 10^{-3} \text{ psi} \times 120 \times \pi + 54 \times 10^{-3} \text{ psi} \times 120 \times .25\pi$$

$$= .636 + 5.0929 \text{ lb-in}$$

$$= 5.729 \text{ lb-in}.$$

Three tension members having the dimensions shown in the Figure, each carry the same tensile load P. Compute the amounts of strain energy stored in the three cases. (Assume that the stress is uniformly distributed over each cross-section.)

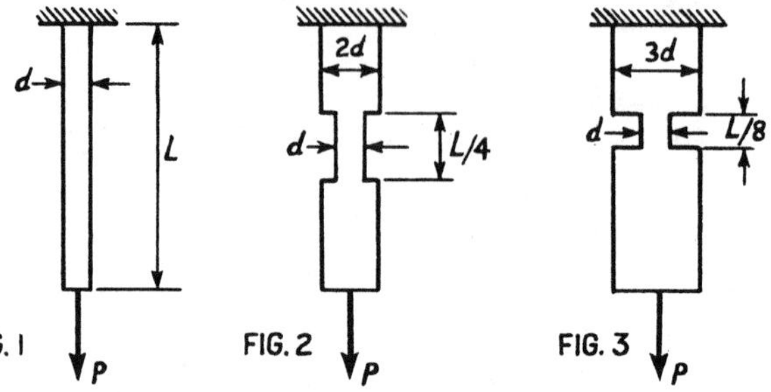

FIG. 1 FIG. 2 FIG. 3

Solution: The strain energy in the bar is

$$U = \frac{P^2 L}{2AE}$$

where $A = \frac{\pi d^2}{4}$. In the first bar, strain energy is

$$U_1 = \frac{P^2 L_1}{2A_1 E}$$

In the second case,

$$U_2 = \frac{P^2 L_2}{2A_2 E}$$

but because the cross section varies, the strain energy for each part is computed and the sum gives the total strain energy for that bar. Expressing all areas and lengths in terms of those for bar 1, for the sake of comparison, let

$$L_2 = \frac{3}{4}L + \frac{L}{4},\ A_2 = \frac{4(\pi d^2)}{4} = 4A_1 \text{ at diameter} = 2d$$

$$\therefore\ U_2 = \frac{P^2(\frac{3}{4}L)}{2(4A_1)E} + \frac{P^2(\frac{L}{4})}{2(A_1)E} = \frac{7}{16}U_1.$$

In the 3rd case, the cross section also varies

$$\therefore\ U_3 = \frac{P^2(\frac{L}{8})}{2A_1 E} + \frac{P^2(7\frac{L}{8})}{2E(9A)} = \frac{2}{9}U_1$$

In diameter = 3d the $A = \frac{\pi(3d)^2}{4} = \frac{9\pi d^2}{4} = 9A_1$.

Comparison of these three expressions show that the strain energy becomes smaller as the cross-sectional area of the bar is increased over more of its length.

• PROBLEM 5-46

A weight W is attached to the lower end of a vertical steel cable that is moving downward with a constant velocity v. What maximum stress is produced in the cable when its upper end is suddenly stopped? Neglect the weight of the cable itself.

Solution: Let us assume that there are no energy losses during impact, so that the total energy of the system (kinetic plus potential energy) before impact is equal to the total energy after impact when the maximum elongation of the cable is δ.

Before impact the kinetic energy of the moving weight is $Wv^2/2g$ and its potential energy with respect to its lowest position is $W(\delta - \delta_{st})$, where δ_{st} is the static elongation of the cable due to the weight

$$\delta = \frac{PL}{AE} \quad \text{or} \quad \delta = \frac{\sigma L}{E} \quad \sigma = \frac{E\delta}{L}$$

so stress is directly proportional to elongation. Note that $\delta_{st} = WL/EA$, where L is the length of the cable and EA is its axial rigidity. The strain energy in the cable before impact is $AE\delta_{st}^2/2L$. After impact, and at the instant the cable has its maximum elongation, the strain energy of the cable is $EA\delta^2/2L$. Equating the energies before and after impact, we obtain

$$\frac{Wv^2}{2g} + W(\delta - \delta_{st}) + \frac{EA\delta_{st}^2}{2L} = \frac{EA\delta^2}{2L}$$

from which, upon introducing the relation $W = EA\ _{st}/L$, we get

$$\frac{Wv^2}{2g} = \frac{EA}{2L}(\delta - \delta_{st})^2$$

Finally, the solution for the total elongation is

$$\delta = \delta_{st} + \sqrt{\frac{Wv^2L}{gEA}}$$

$$(\delta - \delta_{st})^2 = \frac{Wv^2}{2g}\left(\frac{2L}{EA}\right)$$

$$(\delta - \delta_{st})^2 = \frac{Wv^2 L}{gEA} \Rightarrow \delta - \delta_{st} = \sqrt{\frac{Wv^2 L}{gEA}}$$

and the maximum stress in the cable is

$$\sigma = \frac{E\delta}{L} = \frac{E}{L}\left(\frac{WL}{AE} + \sqrt{\frac{Wv^2 L}{gEA}}\right)$$

$$\sigma = \frac{W}{A} + \sqrt{\frac{Wv^2 LE^2}{gEAL^2}} = \frac{W}{A} + \sqrt{\frac{Wv^2 E}{gAL}}$$

$$\therefore \quad \sigma = \frac{E\delta}{L} = \frac{W}{A}\left[1 + \sqrt{\frac{v^2 EA}{gWL}}\right] \qquad \text{(b)}$$

The last term in this expression, which depends upon the properties of the cable and the initial velocity v, may be many times greater than unity. Thus, the dynamic stress in the cable may be much greater than the static stress W/A.

The preceding discussion of elastic impact neglected the mass of the vertical bar or cable in comparison with the mass of the falling body W, and also assumed that the tensile stress was at all times uniform throughout the length of the bar. A more comprehensive solution would take into account the effect of the mass of the bar and longitudinal stress waves.

• PROBLEM 5-47

Determine the strain energy in a vertical prismatic bar hanging under its own weight if L = length of bar, A = cross-sectional area, E = modulus of elasticity, and γ = weight of bar per unit volume.

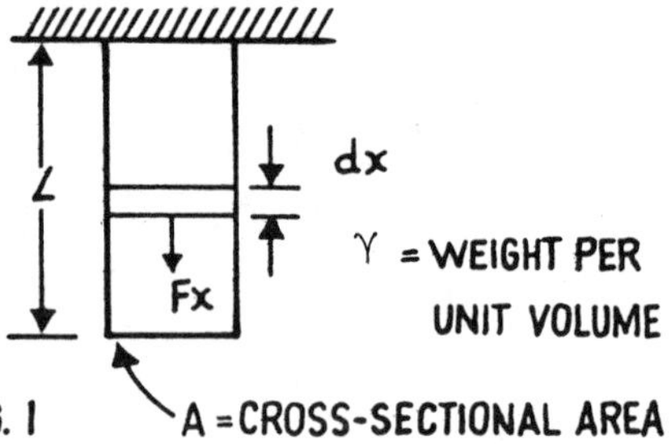

FIG. 1

FIG. 2

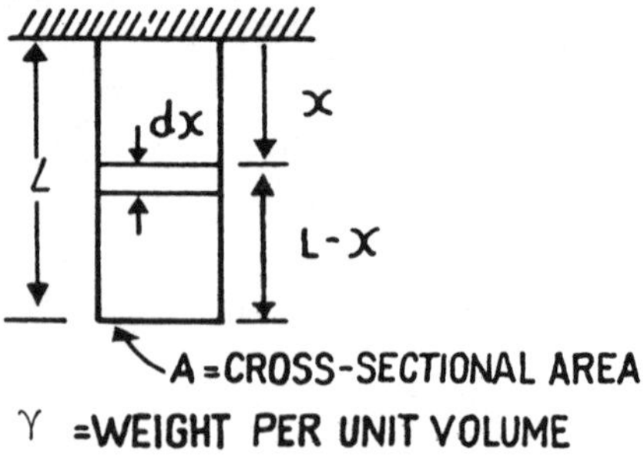

Solution: The expression for strain energy stored in a bar by an arbitrary force F(x), can be acquired by examining the bar as the force F(x) gradually increases from zero to its final value.

In Figure 1 a differential element dx of the bar, which is taken at an arbitrary point between the ends of the bar, is acted on by F_x, whose value is somewhere between 0 and

F(x).

Now, if the force is increased by dF_x, the element changes length by an amount $\Delta(dx)_x$. From Hooke's Law ($\delta = \frac{FL}{AE}$) we get

$$\Delta(dx)_x = \frac{dF_x dx}{AE} \tag{1}$$

The internal work done during the application of dF_x is $\Delta(dx)_x[dF_x + F_x] = \Delta(dx)_x dF_x + \Delta(dx)_x F_x$. We neglect the first term $\Delta(dx)_x dF_x$ since it is a second-order differential and negligible compared to the second term. So, the total internal work, dU, on segment dx during the increase of F(x) from 0 to its final value, will be the sum of the increments of work or

$$dU = \int_0^{F(x)} F_x \Delta(dx)_x \tag{2}$$

By substituting Equation (1) into (2) we obtain

$$dU = \int_0^{F(x)} F_x \frac{dF_x dx}{AE} = \frac{dx}{AE} \int_0^{F(x)} F_x dF_x.$$

Performing the integration:

$$dU = \left.\frac{dxF_x^2}{2AE}\right|_0^{F(x)}$$

$$= \frac{F^2(x)dx}{2AE}.$$

In the particular problem of a bar hanging under its own weight, the force at section dx, Figure 2, will be the weight of the bar below the section.

$$F(x) = \gamma A(L - x)$$

so
$$dU = \frac{\gamma^2 A^2 (L - x)^2}{2AE} dx$$

$$= \frac{\gamma^2 A^2 (L - x)^2}{2AE} dx$$

$$= \frac{\gamma^2 A (L - x)^2 dx}{2E}$$

To find the total strain energy stored we sum dU for all elements dx; in other words, we integrate over the entire length L.

$$U = \int_0^L \frac{\gamma^2 A(L - x)^2}{2E} dx$$

$$= - \frac{\gamma^2 A(L - x)^3}{6E} \Bigg|_0^L$$

$$= - \frac{\gamma^2 A}{6E}(0 - L^3)$$

$$= \frac{\gamma^2 A L^3}{6E}$$

CHAPTER 6

STRESS AND STRAIN PROPERTIES AT A POINT

TRANSFORMATION EQUATIONS FOR STRESS AND STRAIN

• PROBLEM 6-1

Find the magnitudes and directions of the principal stresses, and the maximum shear stress if $\sigma_x = 10$ ksi, $\sigma_y = 8$ ksi, and $\tau_{xy} = -4$ ksi as shown in Figure 1a.

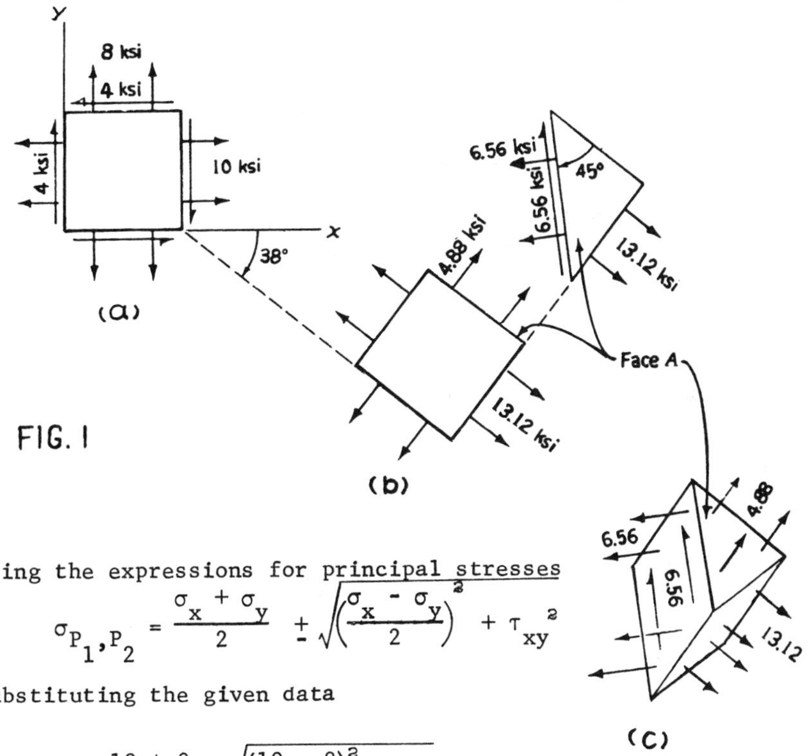

FIG. 1

Solution: Using the expressions for principal stresses

$$\sigma_{P_1,P_2} = \frac{\sigma_x + \sigma_y}{2} \pm \sqrt{\left(\frac{\sigma_x - \sigma_y}{2}\right)^2 + \tau_{xy}^2}$$

we find by substituting the given data

$$\sigma_{p1,p2} = \frac{10 + 8}{2} \pm \sqrt{\left(\frac{10 - 8}{2}\right)^2 + 4^2}$$

$$= 9 \pm 4.123$$

$= 13.12$ ksi T and 4.88 ksi T.

There are no stresses in the z-planes so $\sigma_Z = \sigma_{p3} = 0$. The maximum shear stress in any plane is given by one-half the difference between the principal stresses. In the x-y plane

$$\tau_{xymax} = \frac{\sigma_1 - \sigma_2}{2} = 4.12 \text{ ksi}$$

In the yz plane

$$\tau_{max} = \frac{\sigma_2 - \sigma_3}{2} = \frac{4.88 - 0}{2}$$

$$= 2.44 \text{ ksi} .$$

In the xz plane

$$\tau_{max} = \frac{\sigma_1 - \sigma_3}{2} = \frac{13.12 - 0}{2}$$

$$= 6.56 \text{ ksi} .$$

To find the direction of the first principal stress we use the formula

$$\tan 2\theta_p = \frac{\tau_{xy}}{\sigma_x - \sigma_y}$$

Substituting the given values we have

$$\tan 2\theta_p = \frac{2(-4)}{10 - 8} = \frac{-8}{2} = -4$$

$$2\theta_p = -75.97°$$

$$\theta_p = -37.985° \text{ or } 38°$$

The maximum shear stress occurs on the plane making an angle of $45°$ with the planes of maximum and minimum normal stress -- in this case, the plane inclined $38°$ clockwise from x and the z-plane. The complete sketch in Figure 1b shows the stresses and their orientations. The wedge-shaped block in Figure 1c is the orthographic projection of the lower block in 1b.

• PROBLEM 6-2

In an element, the planar state of stress is given by

$$\sigma_x = 3 \text{ ksi}$$

$$\sigma_y = 1 \text{ ksi}$$

$$\tau_{xy} = 2 \text{ ksi}$$

a) Using the general equations for transformation of stress, find the stresses on a plane inclined by $\theta = -22.5°$.
b) Find the principal stresses and show their sense on a properly oriented element.
c) Find the maximum shearing stresses associated with the principal stresses and show these on a properly oriented element.

Solution: a) We use the transformation equations:

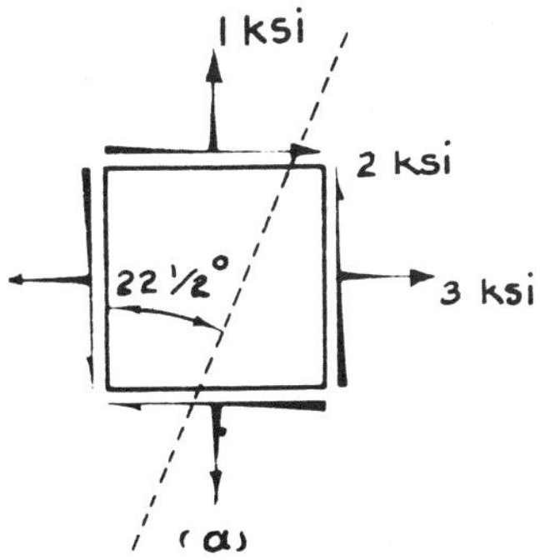

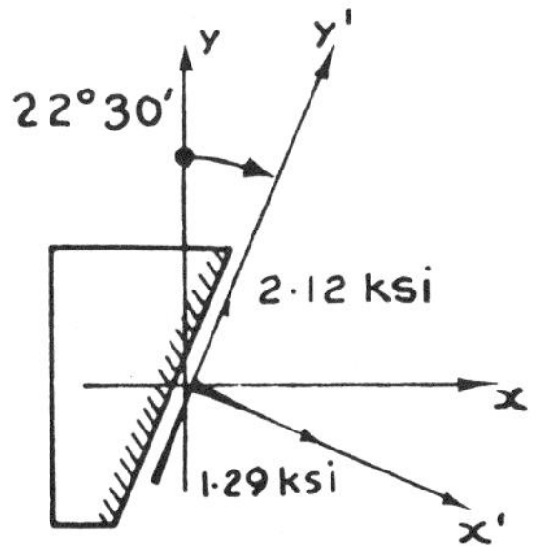

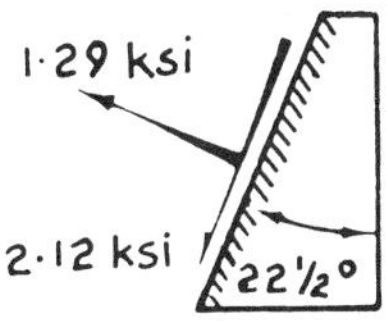

$$\sigma_{x'} = \frac{\sigma_x + \sigma_y}{2} + \frac{\sigma_x - \sigma_y}{2} \cos 2\theta + \tau_{xy} \sin 2\theta$$

$$\tau_{x'y'} = -\frac{\sigma_x - \sigma_y}{2} \sin 2\theta + \tau_{xy} \cos 2\theta$$

Substituting the given values with $2\theta = -45$

$$\sigma_{x'} = \frac{3+1}{2} + \frac{3-1}{2} \cos(-45) + 2 \sin(-45)$$

$$= 2 + .707 - (2)(.707)$$

$$= 1.29 \text{ ksi}$$

$$\tau_{x'y'} = -\frac{3-1}{2} \sin(-45) + 2 \cos(-45)$$

$$= 1\ (.707) + 2(.707)$$

$$= 2.12 \text{ ksi}$$

The positive sign of $\sigma_{x'}$ indicates tension; whereas the positive sign of $\tau_{x'y'}$ indicates that the shearing stress acts in the $+y'$ direction, as shown in Fig. 1(b).

These results are shown in Fig. 1(b) as well as in Fig. 1(c).

b) The principal stresses are given by

$$\sigma_{1,2} = \frac{\sigma_x + \sigma_y}{2} \pm \sqrt{\left(\frac{\sigma_x - \sigma_y}{2}\right)^2 + \tau_{xy}^2}$$

The principal planes are found from the formula

$$\tan 2\theta = \frac{2\tau_{xy}}{\sigma_x - \sigma_y}$$

$$\sigma_{1 \text{ or } 2} = \frac{3+1}{2} \pm \sqrt{\left(\frac{3-1}{2}\right)^2 + 2^2} = 2 \pm 2.24$$

$\sigma_1 + 4.24$ ksi (tension), $\sigma_2 = -0.24$ ksi (compression)

$2\theta_1 = 63°26'$ or $63°26' + 180° = 242°26'$

Hence $\theta'_1 = 31°43'$ and $\theta''_1 = 121°43'$

This locates the two principal planes AB and CD, Figs. 1(d) and (e), on which σ_1 and σ_2 act.

We must find the principal plane on which our principal stresses act. By substituting the first value for θ into the general transforma-

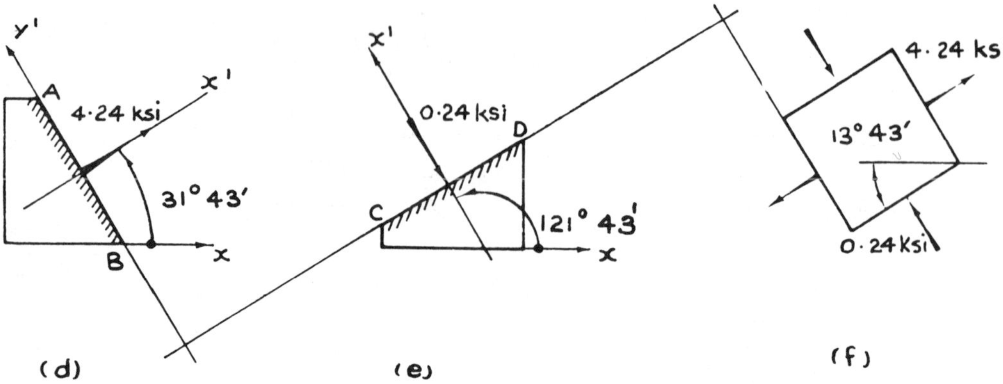

tion equation

$$\sigma_{x'} = \frac{\sigma_x + \sigma_y}{2} + \frac{\sigma_x - \sigma_y}{2} \cos 2\theta + \tau_{xy} \sin 2\theta$$

we find that

$$\sigma_{x'}(\theta = 31°43') = \frac{3 + 1}{2} + \frac{3 - 1}{2} \cos 2\theta + 2 \sin 2\theta$$
$$= 4.24 \text{ ksi}$$

Since this $\sigma_{x'}$ is equal to σ_1, we know that the maximum principal stress acts on AB. The complete state of stress at the given point in terms of the principal stresses is shown in Fig. 1(f).

(c). The maximum shearing stress is found by the formula

$$\tau_{max} = \sqrt{\left(\frac{\sigma_x - \sigma_y}{2}\right)^2 + \tau_{xy}^2}$$

The planes on which these stresses act are given by

$$\tan 2\theta = -\frac{\sigma_x - \sigma_y}{2\tau_{xy}}$$

As before the sense of the shearing stresses is found by substituting one of the calculated angles into the transformation equation. The normal stresses associated with the maximum shearing stresses are given by

$$\sigma' = \frac{\sigma_x + \sigma_y}{2}$$

$$\tau_{max} = \sqrt{[(3 - 1)/2]^2 + 2^2} = \sqrt{5} = 2.24 \text{ ksi}$$

$$\tan 2\theta_2 = -\frac{(3 - 1)/2}{2} = -0.500$$

$$2\theta_2 = 153°26' \quad \text{or} \quad 153°26' + 180° = 333°26'$$

Hence $\theta_2' = 76°43'$ and $\theta_2'' = 166°43'$

These planes are shown in Figs. 1(g) and (h). Then, using $2\theta_2' = 153°26'$

$$\tau_{x'y'} = -\frac{3 - 1}{2} \sin 153°26' + 2 \cos 153°26' = -2.24 \text{ ksi}$$

which means that the shear along the plane EF has an opposite sense to that in Fig. 1(b). The normal stress is

$$\sigma' = \frac{3 + 1}{2} = 2 \text{ ksi}$$

The complete results are shown in Fig. 1(i).

The description of the state of stress now can be exhibited in three alternative forms: as the originally given data, and in terms of the stresses found in parts (b) and (c) of this problem. In matrix repre-

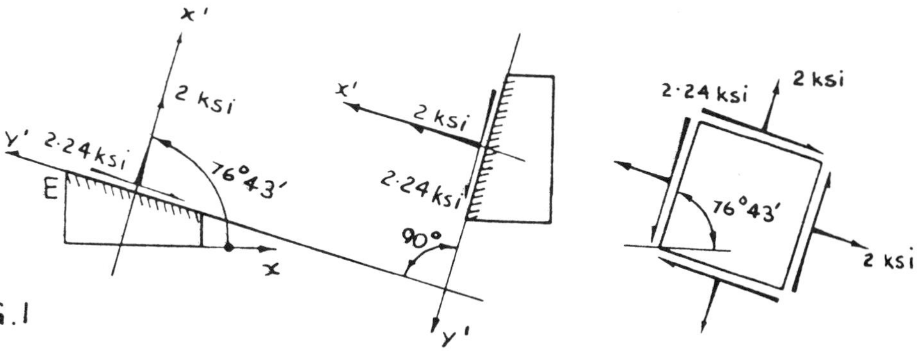

FIG.1

(g) (h) (i)

sentation of the stress tensors this yields

$$\begin{pmatrix} 3 & 2 \\ 2 & 1 \end{pmatrix} \quad \text{or} \quad \begin{pmatrix} 4.24 & 0 \\ 0 & -0.24 \end{pmatrix} \quad \text{or} \quad \begin{pmatrix} 2 & -2.24 \\ -2.24 & 2 \end{pmatrix} \text{ ksi}$$

All these descriptions of the state of stress at the given point are equivalent. Note that in one of the stated forms the matrix is diagonal.

• PROBLEM 6-3

A plate of thickness 1 in. is loaded uniformly by forces F_1 and F_2 having values of 500 and 2000 lb., respectively. What is the normal stress in the direction of the diagonals? What are the shear stresses for a pair of axes rotated 30° counterclockwise from the horizontal and vertical directions?

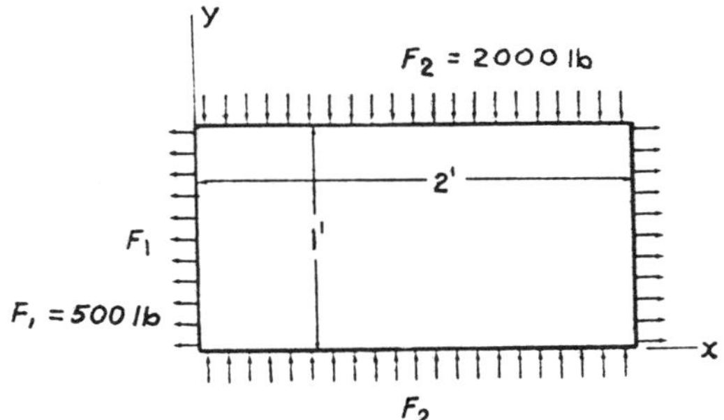

FIG.1

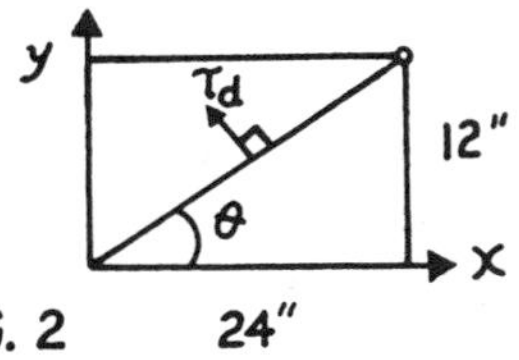

FIG. 2

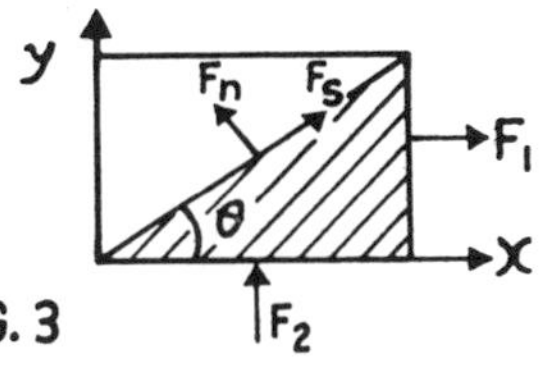

FIG. 3

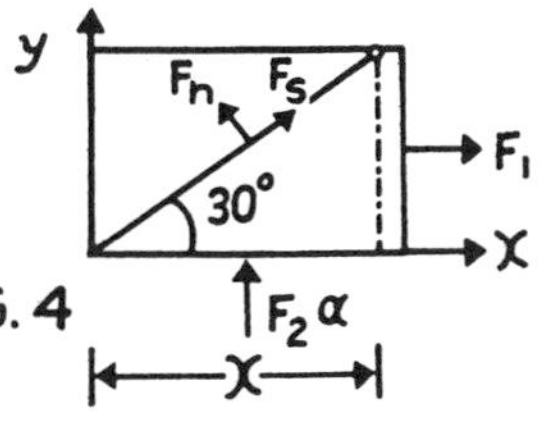

FIG. 4

Solution: There are two methods for solving this problem. The first involves finding the stress field for the applied loads and then using the transformation equations with the given angle to find the inclined stresses. The second method begins by finding the inclined forces, both normal and shear, and dividing by the area of the inclined face to obtain the desired stress.

a) Since $\sigma = F/A$; $\sigma_x = F_1/A_1 = 500/(12)(1) = 41.66$ psi

$$\sigma_y = \frac{-2000}{(24)(1)} = -83.33 \text{ psi}$$

To use the transformation equation we must know the angle between the x-axis and the normal to the diagonal plane. From Fig. 2 we see that

$$\tan\theta = \frac{12}{24}$$

$$\theta = 26.56^\circ$$

Therefore $\theta_d = 90^\circ + \theta = 116.56^\circ$. The transformation equation for normal stress is

$$\tau_{nn} = \frac{\sigma_x + \sigma_y}{2} + \frac{\sigma_x - \sigma_y}{2}\cos 2\theta + \tau_{xy}\sin 2\theta$$

Since $\tau_{xy} = 0$

$$\tau_{nn} = \frac{\sigma_x + \sigma_y}{2} + \frac{\sigma_x - \sigma_y}{2}\cos 2\theta$$

Substituting values we get

$$\tau_d = \frac{41.66 - 83.33}{2} + \frac{41.66 + 83.33}{2}\cos(2 \times 116.56)$$

$$= -58.2 \text{ psi}$$

For axes rotated 30° counterclockwise we will use $\theta = 30^\circ$. The transformation for shear is

$$\tau_{ns} = \frac{\sigma_y - \sigma_x}{2}\sin 2\theta + \tau_{xy}\cos 2\theta$$

so

$$\tau_{ns} = \frac{-83.33 - 41.66}{2}\sin 2(30)$$

$$= -54.12 \text{ psi}$$

The second method uses equilibrium and trigonometric relations to determine the stresses. To find the normal stress on the diagonal, we first find F_n as shown in Figure 3. For equilibrium, this force must be balanced by the components of F_1 and F_2 in this normal direction.

$$F_n + F_2\cos\theta - F_1\sin\theta = 0$$

$$F_n = F_1\sin\theta - F_2\cos\theta$$

The length of the diagonal is given by

$$L = \sqrt{1^2 + 2^2} = \sqrt{5}$$

therefore,

$$\sin\theta = \frac{y}{L} = \frac{1}{\sqrt{5}}$$

$$\cos\theta = \frac{x}{L} = \frac{2}{\sqrt{5}}$$

$$F_n = 500\left(\frac{1}{\sqrt{5}}\right) - 2000\left(\frac{2}{\sqrt{5}}\right)$$

$$= -1565 \text{ lb.}$$

The normal stress is equal to force over area. The area of the diagonal face is the length times thickness.

$$A = (\sqrt{5} \times 12) \text{ in.} \times 1 \text{ in.}$$

$$= 26.83 \text{ in}^2$$

so

$$\tau_d = -\frac{1565}{26.83}$$

$$= -58.32 \text{ psi}$$

To find the shear stress on a 30° inclined plane, we first find the force F_s as in Figure 4. The angle here is greater than that of the diagonal so the equilibrium diagram will include a short section of the top face as shown. Since the vertical forces on the top and bottom of this segment cancel out we can use the triangular section shown in Figure 4, realizing, however, that the vertical force on this segment must be less.

To find the shortened distance we see that

$$\tan 30^\circ = \frac{12}{x}$$

$$x = \frac{12}{\tan 30^\circ}$$

$$= 20.78 \text{ in.}$$

The force is proportionally less so

$$F = F_{2\alpha} = -\frac{20.78}{24} \times 2000$$

$$= -1732 \text{ lb.}$$

We can now use a similar equilibrium equation to find F_s.

$$F_s - F \sin 30^\circ + F_1 \cos 30^\circ = 0$$

$$F_s = -1732(\sin 30^\circ) - 500(\cos 30^\circ)$$

$$= -1300 \text{ lb.}$$

The area of this face is length times thickness. By trigonometry

$$\ell \sin 30 = 12$$

$$\ell = 12/\sin 30 = 24''$$

so

$$A = (24)(1)$$

and

$$\tau_s = -\frac{1300}{24}$$

$$= -54.12 \text{ psi} .$$

• PROBLEM 6-4

Compressive and tensile pressures are applied uniformly to a block as shown. Calculate the normal stress and shear stresses on the diagonal plane indicated.

Solution: It should be apparent that all interfaces parallel to any one face of the reference xyz have constant values of stress. We

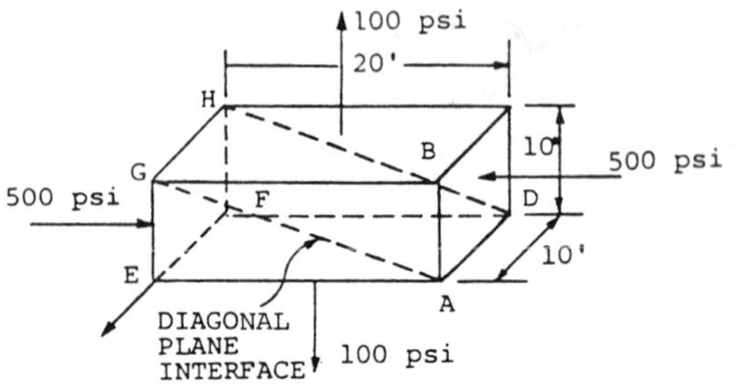

Fig. 1.

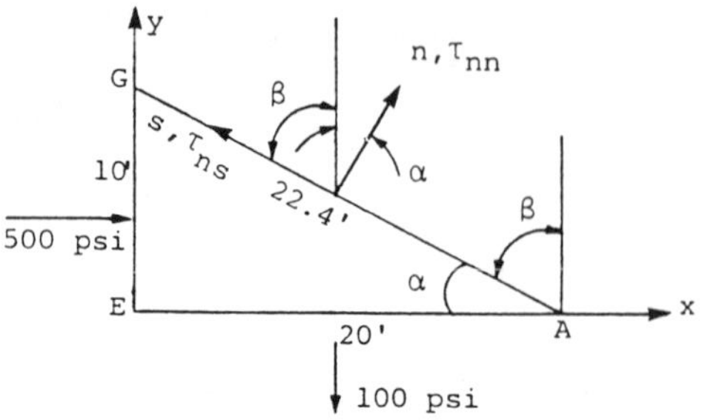

Fig. 2.

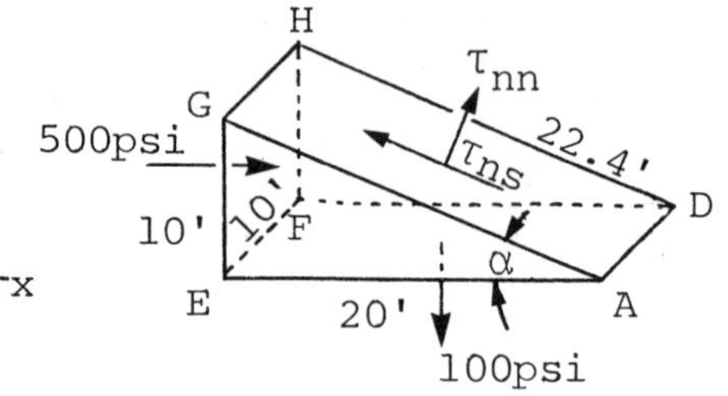

Fig. 3.

thus have here a case where the stresses for a given reference are constant throughout the body - i.e., the stress distribution is uniform. By inspection we can thus say that at all points in the body

$$\tau_{xx} = -500 \text{ psi} \qquad \tau_{xy} = \tau_{yz} = \tau_{yx} = \tau_{zy}$$

$$\tau_{yy} = 100 \text{ psi} \qquad = \tau_{xz} = \tau_{zx} = 0$$

$$\tau_{zz} = 0$$

Hence, at any and all interfaces on surface GHDA we have the same normal and shear stresses. Accordingly, we examine the entire surface shown on edge in Fig. 2. The length of the hypotenuse, GA, is by the Pythagorean Theorem:

$$GA = \sqrt{10^2 + 20^2} = 22.4'$$

We first ascertain the direction cosines of the normal n to this surface.

$$a_{nx} = \cos \beta = \sin \alpha = \frac{10}{22.4} = .446$$

$$a_{ny} = \cos \alpha = \frac{20}{22.4} = .892$$

$$a_{nz} = \cos 90^\circ = 0$$

The normal stress, in any direction, n, at a point where the stresses with respect to x-, y-, and z-coordinates are known, is given by:

$$\begin{aligned} \tau_{nn} = {} & \tau_{xx} a_{nx}^2 + \tau_{xy} a_{nx} a_{ny} + \tau_{xz} a_{nx} a_{nz} \\ & + \tau_{yx} a_{ny} a_{nx} + \tau_{yy} a_{ny}^2 + \tau_{yz} a_{ny} a_{nz} \\ & + \tau_{zx} a_{nz} a_{nx} + \tau_{zy} a_{nz} a_{ny} + \tau_{zz} a_{nz}^2 \end{aligned} \qquad \text{(A)}$$

where a_{ni} is the direction cosine of the axis in question with respect to the direction n.

Substituting, we then have the following result for τ_{nn} at all points on GHDA:

$$\tau_{nn} = \tau_{xx} a^2_{nx} + \tau_{yy} a^2_{ny}$$

$$= (-500)(.446)^2 + (100)(.892)^2$$

$$= -19.89 \text{ psi}$$

As for the shear stress, we choose for s the direction along the inclined surface parallel to side AG (see Fig. 2). The direction cosines for s are then (see Fig. 2)

$$a_{sx} = \cos(\pi - \alpha) = -\cos \alpha = -.892$$

$$a_{sy} = \cos \beta = \sin \alpha = .446$$

$$a_{sz} = \cos 90^\circ = 0$$

The shear stress in a direction s on a face with normal-direction n, is given by

$$\tau_{ns} = \tau_{xx} a_{nx} a_{sx} + \tau_{xy} a_{nx} a_{sy} + \tau_{xz} a_{nx} a_{sz}$$

$$+ \tau_{yx} a_{ny} a_{sx} + \tau_{yy} a_{ny} a_{sy} + \tau_{yz} a_{ny} a_{sz}$$

$$+ \tau_{zx} a_{nz} a_{sx} + \tau_{zy} a_{nz} a_{sy} + \tau_{zz} a_{nz} a_{sz} \quad \text{(B)}$$

Hence, for τ_{ns} at all points on GHDA we get

$$\tau_{ns} = \tau_{xx} a_{nx} a_{sx} + \tau_{yy} a_{ny} a_{sy}$$

$$= (-500)(.446)(-.892) + (100)(.892)(.446)$$

$$= 239 \text{ psi}$$

Equation (B) could be used to solve for the other component of shear stress (at right angles to τ_{ns}) on the interface. However, since no loads whatsoever are applied in the z-direction, force equilibrium automatically dictates that all z-components of stress equal zero.

Because the stresses are uniform, we may easily check the validity of the above results by considering as a free body EFGHDA as shown in Fig. 2. From equilibrium considerations we then have

$\Sigma F_s = 0$:

$$-(500)[(144)(10)(10)]\cos \alpha - (100)[(144)(10)(20)]\sin \alpha$$

$$+ \tau_{ns}(144)(10)(22.4) = 0$$

$$\therefore \tau_{ns} = 239 \text{ psi}$$

$\Sigma F_n = 0$:

$$(500)[(144)(10)(10)]\sin \alpha - (100)[(144)(10)(20)]\cos \alpha$$

$$+ \tau_{nn}(144)(10)(22.4) = 0$$

$$\therefore \tau_{nn} = -19.89 \text{ psi}$$

At a point in a two-dimensional stress field $\sigma_x = 13$ ksi, $\sigma_y = 7$ ksi and $\sigma_{xy} = 2$ ksi. Find (a) the maximum shear stress at this point and (b) the shear stress on the octahedral planes.

FIG. I

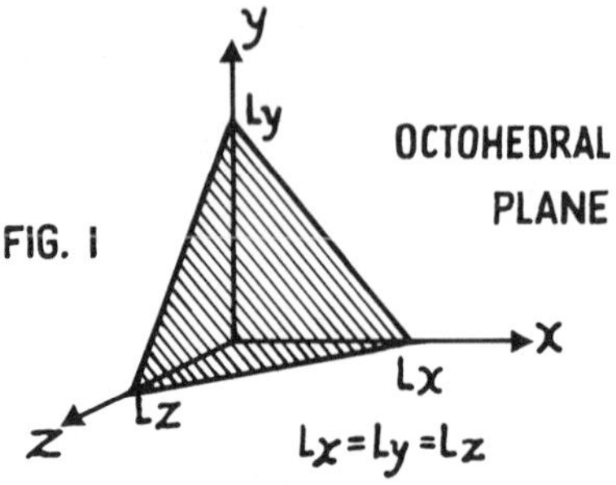

Solution: The maximum shear stress is equal to one-half the difference between the maximum and minimum principal stresses. Therefore, we can find the maximum shear stresses in three orthogonal directions if we know the principal normal stresses.

$$\sigma_1 = \frac{\sigma_x + \sigma_y}{2} + \sqrt{\left(\frac{\sigma_x - \sigma_y}{2}\right)^2 + \tau_{xy}^2}$$

$$= \frac{13K + 7K}{2} + \sqrt{\left(\frac{13K - 7K}{2}\right)^2 + (2K)^2}$$

$$= 13.606 \text{ ksi}$$

$$\sigma_2 = \frac{\sigma_x + \sigma_y}{2} - \sqrt{\left(\frac{\sigma_x - \sigma_y}{2}\right)^2 + \tau_{xy}^2}$$

$$= \frac{13K + 7K}{2} - \sqrt{\left(\frac{13K - 7K}{2}\right)^2 + (2K)^2}$$

$$= 6.394 \text{ ksi.}$$

Since the stress field is two dimensional, there will be no maximum normal stress in the third direction, so $\sigma_3 = 0$.

We can now find the 3 maximum shear stresses.

$$\tau_3 = \frac{\sigma_1 - \sigma_2}{2} = 3.606 \text{ ksi}$$

$$\tau_1 = \frac{\sigma_2 - \sigma_3}{2} = 3.197 \text{ ksi}$$

$$\tau_2 = \frac{\sigma_1 - \sigma_3}{2} = 6.803 \text{ ksi} .$$

Therefore, the maximum shear stress is 6.803 ksi.

The octahedral plane is one that is equally inclined to all three principal axes, as shown in Figure 1. The octahedral shear stress can be found using equlibrium by equating the resultant force due to the shear stresses on the principal planes with the resultant force due to the octahedral shear stress on the octahedral plane.

The force due to each principal shear stress is $F_i = \tau_i \times \text{Area}$ where Area will be equal for each direction since the octahedral plane intersects each normal plane equally.

$$F_R = \sqrt{F_i^2 + F_j^2 + F_K^2}$$

$$= \sqrt{(\tau_1 A)^2 + (\tau_2 A)^2 + (\tau_3 A)^2}$$

$$= A \times \sqrt{\tau_1^2 + \tau_2^2 + \tau_3^2}$$

The resultant due to the octahedral shear stress is

$$F = \frac{3}{2} A \times \tau_{oct}$$

therefore,

$$\frac{3}{2} A \tau_{oct} = A\sqrt{\tau_1^2 + \tau_2^2 + \tau_3^2}$$

$$\tau_{oct} = \frac{2}{3}\sqrt{\tau_1^2 + \tau_2^2 + \tau_3^2}$$

Substituting in the values of the principal shears:

$$\tau_{oct} = \frac{2}{3}\sqrt{(3.197)^2 + (6.803)^2 + (3.606)^2} = 5.56 \text{ ksi.}$$

• PROBLEM 6-6

A circular rod is loaded as shown. Find (a) the maximum normal stress and (b) maximum shear stress.

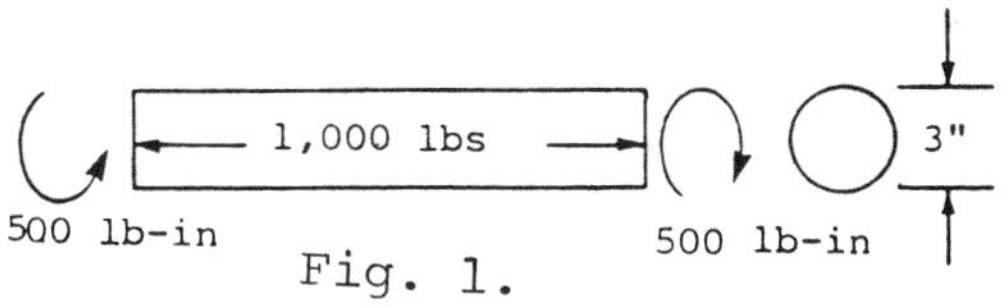

Fig. 1.

Solution: In order to find the maximum normal and maximum shear stresses, we need to know the state of stress for the bar. If we define the longitudinal axis as the x-direction and a tangent to the surface as the φ direction, as in Figure 2 we can calculate the normal and shear stresses in the $x\varphi$ plane due to the loads.

The loads are given then, in terms of our chosen axes by

$$F_x = 1000 \text{ lb.}$$

$$M_x = 500 \text{ in-lb.}$$

We know the normal stress τ_{xx} is force over area so

$$\tau_{xx} = F_x/A$$

$$= \frac{1000 \text{ lb.}}{\pi(3/2)^2}$$

$$= 141.47 \text{ psi .}$$

An applied torque will create a shear stress given by

$$\tau_{x\theta} = M_x r/J$$

where $r \equiv$ radius of bar;

$J \equiv$ polar moment of inertia $= \pi r^4/2$;

M_x = moment about x-axis

$$\tau_{x\theta} = \frac{(500 \text{ in-lb})(1.5 \text{ in})}{\pi(1.5)^4/2}$$

$$= 94.314 \text{ psi} .$$

We can use the coordinate transformation equations to determine both the directions and values for the maximum stresses. For normal stress on a plane inclined by angle θ to the x-axis

$$\tau_{nn} = \frac{\tau_{xx} + \tau_{yy}}{2} + \frac{\tau_{xx} - \tau_{yy}}{2} \cos 2\theta + \tau_{xy} \sin 2\theta$$

The maximum value is attained when the rate of change with respect to φ becomes zero.

$$\frac{\partial \tau_{nn}}{\partial \theta} = 0 = -(\tau_{xx} - \tau_{yy})\sin 2\theta + 2\tau_{xy} \cos 2\theta$$

since $\tau_{yy} = 0$, and we have τ_{xx} and τ_{xy} , we can solve for φ .

$$-\tau_{xx} \sin 2\theta + 2\tau_{xy} \cos 2\theta = 0$$

or

$$\tan 2\theta = 2\tau_{xy}/\tau_{xx}$$

$$= 2(94.314)/141.47$$

$$= 1.33$$

so

$$2\theta = 53.13^\circ .$$

By substituting this value into the expression for normal stress we get:

$$\tau_{nn} = \tau_1 = \frac{141.47}{2} + \frac{141.47}{2} \cos(53.13) + 94.314 \sin(53.13)$$

$$= 188.63 \text{ psi} .$$

There is also a normal stress acting in a direction perpendicular to the first. The angle we must use is $\theta_{original} + 90$ or $2\theta + 180 =$ 233.13 . Substituting this value into the normal stress formula we get:

$$\tau_{nn} = \tau_2 = \frac{141.47}{2} + \frac{141.47}{2} \cos(233.13) + 94.314 \sin(233.13)$$

$$= -47.15 \text{ psi} .$$

Since the maximum normal stress is known as the principal stress, an alternate method of obtaining these values is to substitute the values for τ_{xx} , τ_{yy} , and τ_{xy} into

$$\tau_{1,2} = \frac{\tau_{xx} + \tau_{yy}}{2} \pm \sqrt{\left(\frac{\tau_{xx} - \tau_{yy}}{2}\right)^2 + \tau_{xy}^2}$$

which yields the same result.

The maximum shear stress is found in a similar manner to the normal stress. We differentiate the expression for shear stress on an inclined plane

$$\tau_{ns} = \frac{\tau_{yy} - \tau_{xx}}{2} \sin 2\theta + \tau_{xy} \cos 2\theta$$

$$\frac{\partial \tau_{ns}}{\partial \theta} = (\tau_{yy} - \tau_{xx}) \cos 2\theta - 2\tau_{xy} \sin 2\theta = 0$$

or $$\tan 2\theta = - \frac{\tau_{xx}}{2\tau_{xy}}$$

since $\tau_{yy} = 0$

$$\tan 2\theta = - \frac{141.47}{2(94.314)}$$

$$2\theta = -36.87 \ .$$

Substituting this value into the expression for shear stress

$$\tau_{ns} = - \frac{141.47}{2} \sin(-36.87) + 94.31 \cos(-36.87)$$

$$= 117.89 \text{ psi} \ .$$

An alternate method for obtaining the maximum shear stress is to use the fact that this stress is equal to half the difference between the principal stresses:

$$\tau_{xy\ max} = \frac{\tau_1 - \tau_2}{2}$$

$$= \frac{188.62 - (-47.15)}{2}$$

$$= 117.89 \text{ psi} \quad \text{as before.}$$

• PROBLEM 6-7

A torque is applied to the ends of a thin-walled cylinder. Find the stresses at the two interfaces H and G.

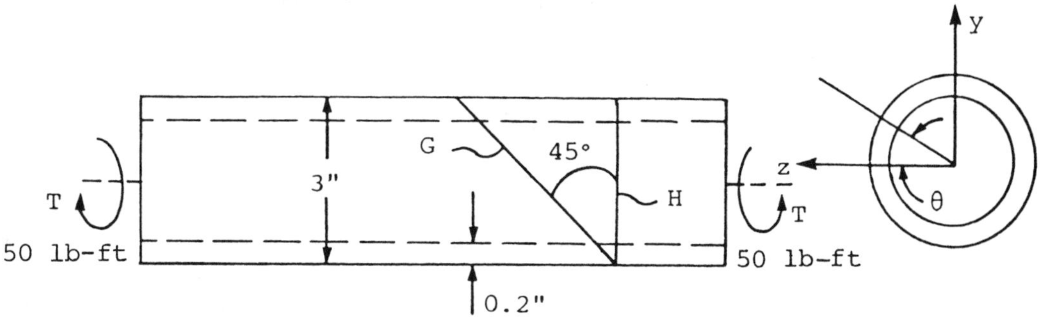

Solution: The stress created by torsion about the x-axis is a shear stress in the $x\theta$ plane.

$$\tau_{x\theta} = \frac{M_x r}{J}$$

where r is the radius of the section ;

J is the polar moment of inertia ;

M_x is the moment about the x-axis.

In this example, by assuming that the stresses do not vary with thickness, we take r to be the radius of the middle surface of the cylinder,

$$r = \frac{r_0 + r_i}{2}$$

$$= \frac{1.5 + (1.5-.2)}{2} = 1.4 \text{ in.}$$

The angle θ is defined as positive clockwise, while the torque applied is counterclockwise. Therefore,

$$M_x = -50(12) \text{ in-lb.}$$

The polar moment of inertia for a hollow circle section is equal to the polar moment of a solid shaft of radius, r_0, minus the polar moment of a solid shaft of radius, r_i.

$$J = \frac{\pi r_0^4}{2} - \frac{\pi r_i^4}{2}$$

$$= \frac{\pi(1.5)^4}{2} - \frac{\pi(1.3)^4}{2} = 3.4658$$

therefore,

$$\tau_{x\theta} = \frac{-(50)(12)(1.4)}{3.4658}$$

$$= -242.37 \text{ psi}$$

The stresses on interface φ are found using the transformation equations

$$\sigma_n = \frac{\sigma_{ii} + \sigma_{jj}}{2} + \frac{\sigma_{ii} - \sigma_{jj}}{2} \cos 2\theta + \tau_{ij} \sin 2\theta$$

$$\tau_{ns} = \frac{\sigma_{jj} - \sigma_{ii}}{2} \sin 2\theta + \tau_{ij} \cos 2\theta$$

Section F is inclined 45° to the xz-plane in a counterclockwise direction so $\theta = 45^\circ$. The normal stresses on the vertical section H, τ_{xx} and τ_{zz}, are both zero. Therefore, the transformation equations become

$$\sigma_n = 0 + 0 + (-242.37) \sin 2.45^\circ$$

$$= -242.37 \times 1$$

$$= -242.37 \text{ psi.}$$

$$\tau_{ns} = 0 + (-242.37) \cos(2 \times 45^\circ)$$

$$= 0 + 0 = 0$$

• PROBLEM 6-8

A compressed air tank with thin walls is under axial torsion. Calculate (a) the maximum normal stress at location A, and (b) the maximum shear stress.

Solution: In order to find the maximum normal (principal) stress and the maximum shear stress at a point A away from the ends we must first

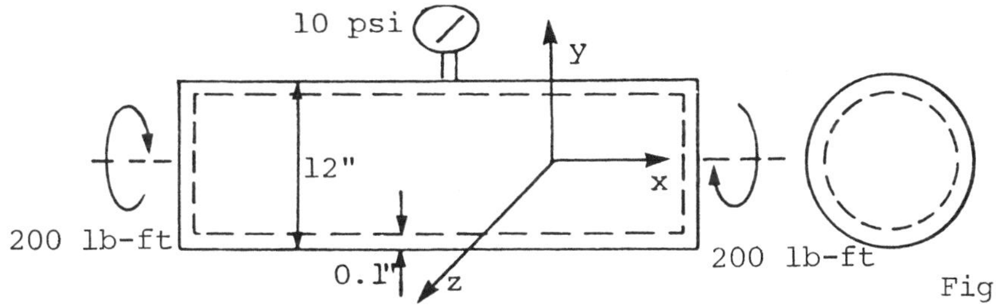

Fig. 1.

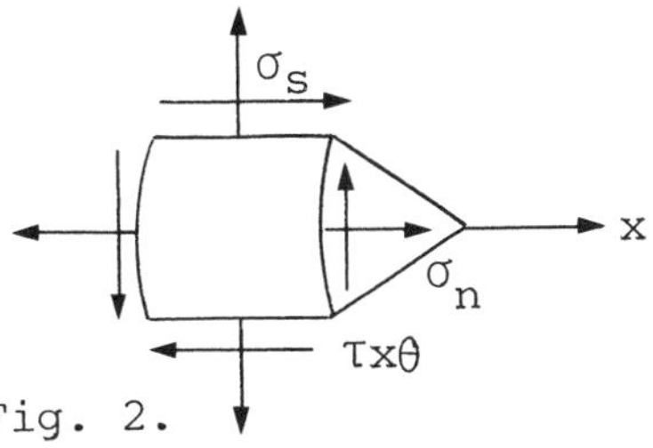

Fig. 2.

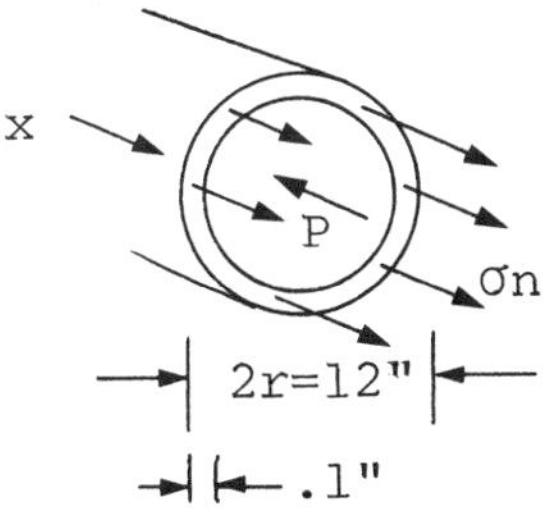

Fig. 3.

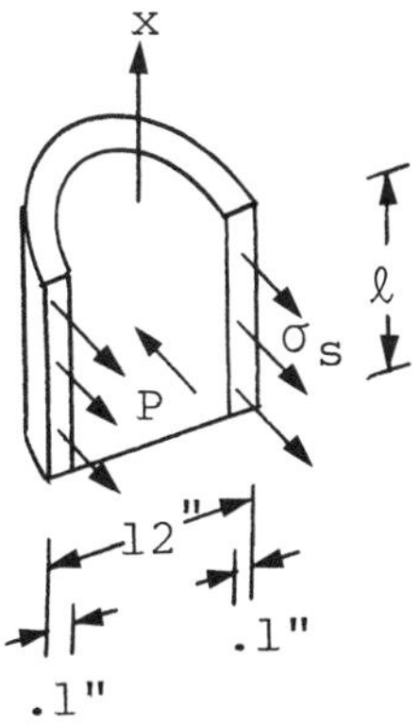

Fig. 4.

find the stress field at that point. We will assume that the direct compressive stress on the cylinder thickness is small compared to the other stresses on the element and can be ignored, which makes the state of stress planar.

The internal pressure causes normal stresses on the element A as shown in Figure 2. We obtain τ_n by considering equilibrium in the x-direction. The force due to the stress in the cylinder wall in the x-direction must equal the force due to the internal pressure on the end plate as in Fig. 3.

$$F = \tau \times A$$

$$A_{wall} = \pi(6)^2 - \pi(5.9)^2$$

$$= 3.73 \text{ in}^2$$

$$A_{end} = \pi \times (5.9)^2$$

$$= 109.35 \text{ in}^2$$

Equating the forces

$$\sigma_n \times A_{wall} = P \times A_{end}$$

$$\sigma_n \times 3.73 \text{ in}^2 = (10 \text{ psi}) \times 109.35 \text{ in}^2$$

$$\sigma_n = 292.5 \text{ psi}$$

In the transverse direction we again use equilibrium to find the hoop stress. The force due to the hoop stress must equal the force due to the pressure on the projected area of the cross-section as shown in Figure 4.

$$\sigma_s \times .2 \times \ell = (10 \text{ psi}) \times (12 - .2) \times \ell$$

$$\sigma_s = \frac{10(11.8)}{.2}$$

$$= 590 \text{ psi}$$

The shear stress is created by the torque on the ends. Using the formula

$$\tau_{x\theta} = \frac{M_x r}{J}$$

where r is the radius of the section; J is the polar moment of inertia; we can find the shear stress on A.

$$M_x = (200)\text{ft-lb}(12 \text{ in/ft})$$

$$= 2400 \text{ in-lb.}$$

We use $r = 6$ in. to get the maximum $\tau_{x\theta}$.

$$J = \frac{\pi r_0^4}{2} - \frac{\pi r_i^4}{2} \quad \text{for a hollow section}$$

$$= \frac{\pi(6)^4}{2} - \frac{\pi(5.9)^4}{2}$$

$$= 132.36 \text{ in}^4$$

$$\tau_{x\theta} = \frac{(2400)(6)}{132.36} \text{ psi}$$

$$= 108.79 \text{ psi}$$

Now we can use the expressions for principal normal and shear stresses.

$$\sigma_{1,2} = \frac{\sigma_x + \sigma_y}{2} \pm \sqrt{\left(\frac{\sigma_x - \sigma_y}{2}\right)^2 + \tau_{xy}^2}$$

$$\tau_{max} = \sqrt{\left(\frac{\sigma_x - \sigma_y}{2}\right)^2 + \tau_{xy}^2}$$

Substituting the calculated values

$$\sigma_n = \sigma_x = 292.5 \text{ psi}$$

$$\sigma_s = \sigma_y = 590 \text{ psi}$$

$$\tau_{x\theta} = \tau_{xy} = 108.79 \text{ psi}$$

we obtain

$$\sigma_{1,2} = \frac{292.5 + 590}{2} \pm \sqrt{\left(\frac{292.5 - 590}{2}\right)^2 + (108.79)^2}$$

$$= 441.25 \pm 184.28$$

$$= 625.5,\ 256.97 \text{ psi}$$

$$\tau_{max} = 184.28 \text{ psi}$$

• PROBLEM 6-9

Compute the principal strains and their corresponding directions for a state of plane strain at a point given as $\varepsilon_{xx} = .002$; $\varepsilon_{yy} = -.001$; and $\varepsilon_{xy} = .003$.

Solution: The following equations are for the case of plane strain:

$$\tan 2\theta = \frac{\epsilon_{xy}}{\left[\frac{\epsilon_{xx} - \epsilon_{yy}}{2}\right]} = \frac{2\epsilon_{xy}}{\epsilon_{xx} - \epsilon_{yy}} \qquad (1)$$

where θ is the clockwise angle that the principal axes must be rotated through so that they correspond with the x-y axes.

$$\tan 2\theta = \frac{2(.003)}{(.002) - (-.001)} = \frac{.006}{.003} = 2$$

$$\arctan 2 = 63.4^\circ \quad \text{or} \quad \theta + 180 = 243.4^\circ$$

We also find the principal strains to be

$$\epsilon_{a,b} = \frac{(\epsilon_{xx} + \epsilon_{yy})}{2} \pm \sqrt{\left[\frac{(\epsilon_{xx} - \epsilon_{yy})}{2}\right]^2 + \epsilon_{xy}^2} \qquad (2)$$

Hence,

$$2\theta = 63.4^\circ, \ 243.4^\circ$$

$$\therefore \quad \theta = 31.7^\circ, \ 121.7^\circ$$

We can compute the principal strains directly from (2). Thus,

$$\epsilon_{a,b} = \frac{(.002) + (-.001)}{2} \pm \sqrt{\left[\frac{(.002) - (-.001)}{2}\right]^2 + .003^2}$$

$$= .0005 \pm .00335 = .00385, \ -.00285 \qquad (c)$$

Since $\epsilon_{xz} = \epsilon_{yz} = 0$, the z-axis is the third principal axis with the third principal strain as zero.

• PROBLEM 6-10

Calculate the principal strains at a point where a rectangular rosette arrangement on a surface provides the following gauge measurements of strain: .002 from element 1; .001 from element 2; -.004 from element 3.

Solution: We can use the transformation equations for strain in the tangent plane of the rosette. Accordingly, we can say for a rotation

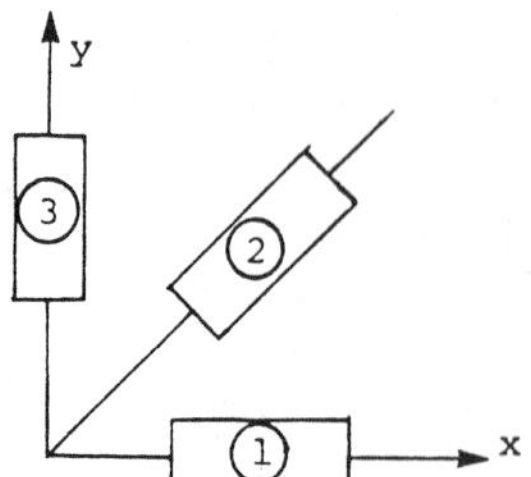

Fig. (a). RECTANGULAR ROSETTE

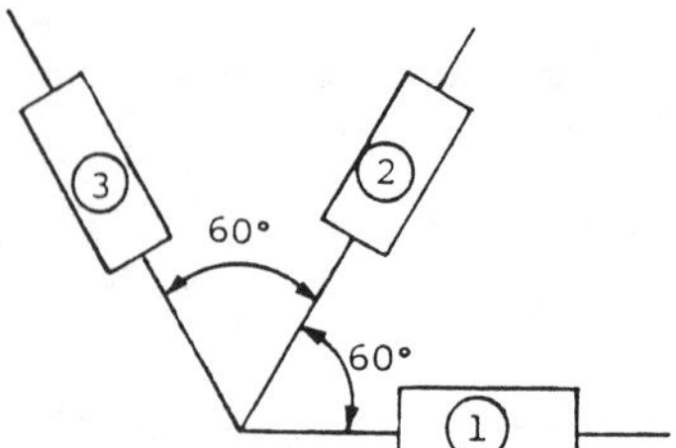

Fig. (b). EQUIANGULAR ROSETTE

β about xy axes in the tangent plane that

$$\epsilon_{x'x'} = \frac{\epsilon_{xx} + \epsilon_{yy}}{2} + \frac{\epsilon_{xx} - \epsilon_{yy}}{2} \cos 2\beta + \epsilon_{xy} \sin 2\beta \qquad \text{(a)}$$

We let x correspond to the direction of gauge 1 and we let y correspond to the direction of gauge 3 (see Fig. (a)). We need ϵ_{xy} in order to get any particular strain in the plane of the rosette. We accordingly use the result for gauge 2 with $\beta = 45^\circ$ in Eq. (a) as follows for this purpose:

$$.001 = \frac{.002 + (-.004)}{2} + \frac{.002 - (.004)}{2} \cos 90^\circ + \epsilon_{xy} \sin 90^\circ$$

$$\therefore \quad \epsilon_{xy} = .002 \qquad \text{(b)}$$

To get the principal strains in the plane of the rosette we may first use Equation (a) to find the direction of the principal axes in the plane of the rosette as per our earlier discussion. We may then employ the relation

$$\tan 2\theta = \frac{\epsilon_{xy}}{\left(\frac{\epsilon_{xx} - \epsilon_{yy}}{2}\right)} = \frac{2\epsilon_{xy}}{\epsilon_{xx} - \epsilon_{yy}}$$

to get the principal strains. Thus, we have

$$\tan 2\theta = \frac{(2)(.002)}{.002 + .004} = .667$$

$$\therefore \quad \theta_{a,b} = 16.8^\circ,\ 106.8^\circ \qquad \text{(c)}$$

where we are using the subscripts a and b to identify the principal axes in the xy plane. The principal strains in the xy plane are these:

$$\epsilon_{a,b} = \frac{\epsilon_{xx} + \epsilon_{yy}}{2} + \frac{\epsilon_{xx} - \epsilon_{yy}}{2} \cos 2\begin{Bmatrix}\theta_a \\ \theta_b\end{Bmatrix} + \epsilon_{xy} \sin 2\begin{Bmatrix}\theta_a \\ \theta_b\end{Bmatrix}$$

$$= \frac{.002 - .004}{2} + \frac{.002 + .004}{2} \cos\begin{Bmatrix}33.6^\circ \\ 213.6^\circ\end{Bmatrix} + .002 \sin\begin{Bmatrix}33.6^\circ \\ 213.6^\circ\end{Bmatrix}$$

$$= .00261,\ -.00461 \qquad \text{(d)}$$

To get the third principal strain, which must be in the z direction, we employ Hooke's law for normal stresses and strains at the point. Remembering that principal axes for stress and strain coincide for a

Hookean material, we may say, employing subscripts a, b, and c to denote the principal stresses and strains, that

$$\epsilon_a = \frac{1}{E}[\tau_a - \nu(\tau_b + \tau_c)]$$

$$\epsilon_b = \frac{1}{E}[\tau_b - \nu(\tau_a + \tau_c)] \qquad \text{(e)}$$

$$\epsilon_c = \frac{1}{E}[\tau_c - \nu(\tau_a + \tau_b)]$$

We know ϵ_a and ϵ_b from the previous calculations, and with no external loading on the surface at the point of interest we can say that $\tau_{zz} = \tau_c = 0$. We have the three equations with three unknowns, If we take $E = 30 \times 10^6$ psi and $\nu = .3$, we can then determine ϵ_c.

Using the equation for ϵ_a and solving for τ_a:

$$\epsilon_a = .00261 = \frac{1}{30 \times 10^6}\left[\tau_a - .3(\tau_b + 0)\right]$$

$$.0783 \times 10^6 = \tau_a - .3\,\tau_b$$

$$\tau_a = .0783 \times 10^6 + .3\,\tau_b$$

Using the equation for ϵ_b and solving for τ_b:

$$\epsilon_b = -.00461 = \frac{1}{30 \times 10^6}[\tau_b - .3(\tau_a)]$$

Multiplying by 30×10^6 and substituting for τ_a:

$$-.1383 \times 10^6 = \tau_b - .3(.0783 \times 10^6 + .3\,\tau_b)$$

$$(-.1383 + .02349) \times 10^6 = \tau_b - .09\,\tau_b$$

$$-.11481 \times 10^6 = .91\,\tau_b$$

$$\tau_b = -.126165 \times 10^6$$

Substituting τ_b into the equation for τ_a:

$$\tau_a = .0783 \times 10^6 + .3(-.126165) \times 10^6$$

$$\tau_a = .04045 \times 10^6$$

These values can now be substituted into the equation for ϵ_c

$$\epsilon_c = \frac{1}{30 \times 10^6}[0 - .3(.04045 - .126165) \times 10^6]$$

$$\epsilon_c = .000857$$

The magnitude of the strain normal to the surface is very small, as is usually the case, and generally need not be considered. Going to our usual notation, which is to label principal strains ϵ_1, ϵ_2, and ϵ_3, with ϵ_1 being the greatest positive strain and ϵ_3 being the least positive (or greatest negative) strain, we can say that

$$\begin{aligned} \epsilon_1 &= .00261 \\ \epsilon_2 &= .000855 \\ \epsilon_3 &= -.00461 \end{aligned} \tag{g}$$

GENERAL VECTOR EQUATIONS FOR STRESS AND STRAIN

• PROBLEM 6-11

A reference system x-y-z is rotated 30° about the z-axis to position x'-y'-z'. If a stress tensor at a point in x-y-z is as shown, find the stress components for the x'-y'-z' reference system.

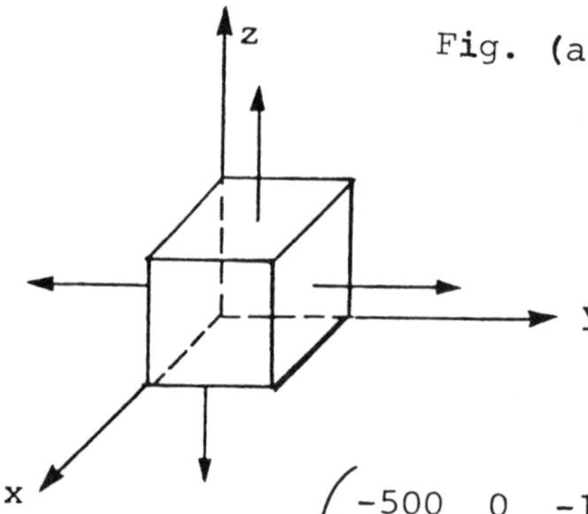

Fig. (a).

$$\tau_{ij} = \begin{pmatrix} -500 & 0 & -100 \\ 0 & 0 & 0 \\ -100 & 0 & 800 \end{pmatrix}$$

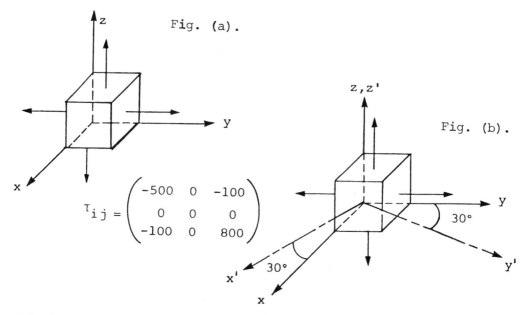

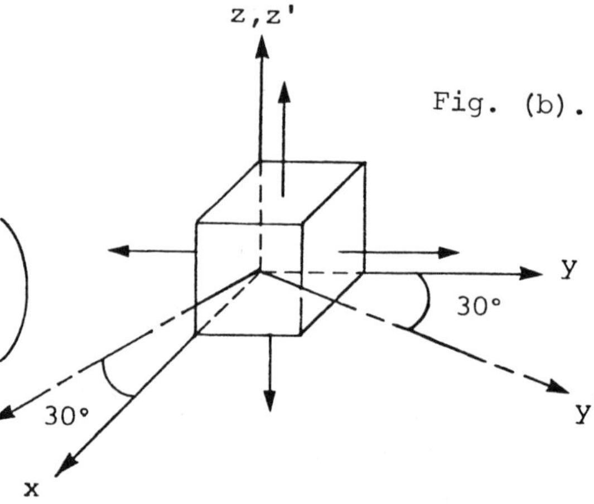

Fig. (b).

Solution: We first need the direction cosines positioning the primed axes relative to the unprimed axes. Thus, we have

$$a_{x'x} = \cos 30° = .866 \qquad a_{y'x} = \cos 120° = -.500$$

$$a_{x'y} = \cos 60° = .500 \qquad a_{y'y} = \cos 30° = .866$$

$$a_{x'z} = \cos 90° = 0 \qquad a_{y'z} = \cos 90° = 0$$

$$a_{z'x} = \cos 90° = 0$$

$$a_{z'y} = \cos 90° = 0$$

$$a_{z'z} = \cos 0^\circ = 1$$

We can now get the stress components in the primed reference by using the transformation equations. The necessary equations are

$$\tau_{x'x'} = \tau_{xx}a^2_{x'x} + \tau_{xy}a_{x'x}a_{x'y} + \tau_{xz}a_{x'x}a_{x'z} + \tau_{yx}a_{x'y}a_{x'x}$$
$$+ \tau_{yy}a^2_{x'y} + \tau_{yz}a_{x'y}a_{x'z} + \tau_{zx}a_{x'z}a_{x'x}$$
$$+ \tau_{zy}a_{x'z}a_{x'y} + \tau_{zz}a^2_{x'z}$$

$$\tau_{y'y'} = \tau_{xx}a^2_{y'x} + \tau_{xy}a_{y'x}a_{y'y} + \tau_{xz}a_{y'x}a_{y'z} + \tau_{yx}a_{y'y}a_{y'x}$$
$$+ \tau_{yy}a^2_{y'y} + \tau_{yz}a_{y'y}a_{y'z} + \tau_{zx}a_{y'z}a_{y'x}$$
$$+ \tau_{zy}a_{y'z}a_{y'y} + \tau_{zz}a^2_{y'z}$$

$$\tau_{z'z'} = \tau_{xx}a^2_{z'x} + \tau_{xy}a_{z'x}a_{z'y} + \tau_{xz}a_{z'x}a_{z'z} + \tau_{yx}a_{z'y}a_{z'x}$$
$$+ \tau_{yy}a^2_{z'y} + \tau_{yz}a_{z'y}a_{z'z} + \tau_{zx}a_{z'z}a_{z'x}$$
$$+ \tau_{zy}a_{z'z}a_{z'y} + \tau_{zz}a^2_{z'z}$$

$$\tau_{z'x'} = \tau_{x'z'} = \tau_{xx}a_{x'x}a_{z'x} + \tau_{xy}a_{x'x}a_{z'y} + \tau_{xz}a_{x'x}a_{z'z}$$
$$+ \tau_{yx}a_{x'y}a_{z'x} + \tau_{yy}a_{x'y}a_{z'y} + \tau_{yz}a_{x'y}a_{z'z}$$
$$+ \tau_{zx}a_{x'z}a_{z'x} + \tau_{zy}a_{x'z}a_{z'y} + \tau_{zz}a_{x'z}a_{z'z}$$

$$\tau_{z'y'} = \tau_{y'z'} = \tau_{xx}a_{y'x}a_{z'x} + \tau_{xy}a_{y'x}a_{z'y} + \tau_{xz}a_{y'x}a_{z'z}$$
$$+ \tau_{yx}a_{y'y}a_{z'x} + \tau_{yy}a_{y'y}a_{z'y} + \tau_{yz}a_{y'y}a_{z'z}$$
$$+ \tau_{zx}a_{y'z}a_{z'x} + \tau_{zy}a_{y'z}a_{z'y} + \tau_{zz}a_{y'z}a_{z'z}$$

$$\tau_{y'x'} = \tau_{x'y'} = \tau_{xx}a_{x'x}a_{y'x} + \tau_{xy}a_{x'x}a_{y'y} + \tau_{xz}a_{x'x}a_{y'z}$$
$$+ \tau_{yx}a_{x'y}a_{y'x} + \tau_{yy}a_{x'y}a_{y'y} + \tau_{yz}a_{x'y}a_{y'z}$$
$$+ \tau_{zx}a_{x'z}a_{y'x} + \tau_{zy}a_{x'z}a_{y'y} + \tau_{zz}a_{x'z}a_{y'z}$$

These are the transformation equations for Cartesian coordinate systems in 3 dimensions. They are used to find the stress components at a point with respect to any set of 3 mutually perpendicular axes, given the stress components with respect to any other set of axes. Substituting the given stresses, and the calculated direction cosines, the stresses are:

$$\tau_{x'x'} = (-500)(.866)^2 + (-100)(0)(.866) + (-100)(.866)(0)$$
$$+ (800)(0)^2 = -375 \text{ psi}$$

$$\tau_{y'y'} = (-500)(-.500)^2 + (-100)(0)(-.500) + (-100)(-.500)(0) + (800)(0)^2 = -125 \text{ psi}$$

$$\tau_{z'z'} = (-500)(0)^2 + (-100)(1)(0) + (-100)(0)(1) + (800)(1)^2 = 800 \text{ psi}$$

$$\tau_{z'x'} = \tau_{x'z'} = (-500)(.866)(0) + (-100)(0)(0) + (-100)(.866)(1) + (800)(0)(1) = -86.6 \text{ psi}$$

$$\tau_{z'y'} = \tau_{y'z'} = (-500)(-.500)(0) + (-100)(0)(0) + (-100)(-.500)(1) + (800)(0)(1) = 50.0 \text{ psi}$$

$$\tau_{y'x'} = \tau_{x'y'} = (-500)(.866)(-.500) + (-100)(0)(-.500) + (-100)(.866)(0) + (800)(0)(0) = 216 \text{ psi}$$

The stress tensor for the primed reference is then given as follows:

$$\tau'_{ij} = \begin{pmatrix} -375 & 216 & -86.6 \\ 216 & -125 & 50 \\ -86.6 & 50 & 800 \end{pmatrix}$$

We have shown in Fig. (b) the nine stresses on three orthogonal interfaces corresponding to reference xyz by using the usual infinitesimal rectangular parallelopiped to generate the desired interfaces at a point. Likewise the nine stresses on three orthogonal interfaces for reference x'y'z' have also been shown in the diagram.

• PROBLEM 6-12

For the following states of stress, determine the principal stresses and axes:

$\tau_{xx} = 200$ psi $\qquad \tau_{xz} = 300$ psi

$\tau_{xy} = 100$ psi $\qquad \tau_{yz} = \tau_{yy} = \tau_{zz} = 0$

Solution: The following cubic equation may be used to find principal stresses in 3 dimensions:

$$\tau^3 - A\tau^2 + B\tau - C = 0 \qquad \text{(A)}$$

where $A \equiv$ first stress invariant $= \tau_{xx} + \tau_{yy} + \tau_{zz}$

$B \equiv$ 2nd stress invariant $= \tau_{xx}\tau_{yy} + \tau_{yy}\tau_{zz} + \tau_{xx}\tau_{zz} - \tau_{xy}^2 - \tau_{yz}^2 - \tau_{xz}^2$

$C \equiv$ 3rd stress invariant $= \tau_{xx}\tau_{yy}\tau_{zz} + 2\tau_{xy}\tau_{yz}\tau_{xz} - \tau_{xx}\tau_{yz}^2 - \tau_{yy}\tau_{xz}^2 - \tau_{zz}\tau_{xy}^2$

$$A = 200$$

$$B = -100{,}000$$

$$C = 0$$

Therefore, from (A)

$$\tau^3 - 200\tau^2 - 100{,}000\tau = 0$$

Factoring we get

$$\tau(\tau^2 - 200\tau - 100{,}000) = 0$$

Applying the Quadratic Formula yields

$$\tau(\tau - 432)(\tau + 232) = 0$$

The roots, arranged in descending order, are

$$\tau_1 = 432$$

$$\tau_2 = 0$$

$$\tau_3 = -232$$

To find the direction of τ_1, substitute 432 for τ in the set of equations

$$(\tau_{xx} - \tau)a_{nx} + \tau_{xy}a_{ny} + \tau_{xz}a_{nz} = 0 \qquad \text{(B)}$$

$$\tau_{yx}a_{nx} + (\tau_{yy} - \tau)a_{ny} + \tau_{yz}a_{nz} = 0 \qquad \text{(C)}$$

$$\tau_{zx}a_{nx} + \tau_{zy}a_{ny} + (\tau_{zz} - \tau)a_{nz} = 0 \qquad \text{(D)}$$

These equations derive from equilibrium considerations. For instance,

$$\tau_{xx}a_{nx} + \tau_{xy}a_{ny} + \tau_{xz}a_{nz} = \bar{X}$$

where $\bar{X}$ is the total surface force on the plane in the x-direction.

$\bar{X} = a_{nx}\tau$, and thus

$$(\tau_{xx} - \tau)a_{nx} + \tau_{xy}a_{ny} + \tau_{xz}a_{nz} = 0\ . \qquad \text{(B)}$$

The other 2 equations, (C) and (D), are derived in the same way, for the y- and z- directions. Thus, from (B), (C), and (D),

$$(200 - 432)a_{nx} + 100a_{ny} + 300a_{nz} = 0$$

$$100a_{nx} + (0 - 432)a_{ny} + 0 = 0$$

$$300a_{nx} + 0 + (0 - 432)a_{nz} = 0$$

We note that these equations are not all independent since -.232 times the second plus -.696 times the third equals the first. Hence, we may solve only for ratios. From the second and third equations,

$$a_{ny} = .232\ a_{nx} \qquad \text{(E)}$$

$$a_{nz} = .695a_{nx} \qquad \text{(F)}$$

As a third relationship we use the fact that the sum of the squares of a set of direction cosines is equal to 1. That is,

$$a_{nx}^2 + a_{ny}^2 + a_{nz}^2 = 1 \qquad \text{(G)}$$

Hence, substituting Eqs. (E) and (F) into Eq. (G) we get

$$a_{nx}^2 + (.232)^2 a_{nx}^2 + (.695)^2 a_{nx}^2 = 1$$

$$\therefore \quad a_{nx} = \frac{1}{\sqrt{1 + .232^2 + .695^2}} = .806$$

Hence,

$$a_{ny} = .1870 \qquad a_{nz} = .560$$

Thus, the principal axis corresponding to the largest principal stress of 432 psi has a direction n_1 given by

$$n_1 = .806i + .1870j + .560k$$

For τ_2, we find the direction n_2 in the same manner:

$$(200 - 0)a_{nx} + 100a_{ny} + 300a_{nz} = 0$$

$$100a_{nx} + 0 + 0 = 0$$

$$300a_{nx} + 0 + 0 = 0$$

So, $a_{nx} = 0$. Also $a_{ny} = 3a_{nz}$. Thus,

$$\sqrt{0^2 + 3^2a_{nz}^2 + a_{nz}^2} = 1$$

$$a_{nz} = .316$$

$$a_{ny} = .949$$

Therefore, the direction n_2 is given by

$$n_2 = 0i + .949j + .316k$$

Likewise, for τ_3, we write the equations

$$-32a_{nx} + 100a_{ny} + 300a_{nz} = 0$$

$$100a_{nx} - 232a_{ny} + 0 = 0$$

$$300a_{nx} + 0 - 232a_{nx} = 0$$

$$a_{nz} = 1.293a_{nx}$$

$$a_{ny} = .431a_{nx}$$

So

$$\sqrt{1.293^2a_{nx}^2 + .431^2a_{nx}^2 + a_{nx}^2} = 1$$

$$a_{nx} = .591$$

$$a_{ny} = .255$$

$$a_{nz} = .764$$

$$n_3 = .591i + .255j + .764k$$

• PROBLEM 6-13

It is not always necessary to solve the general cubic equation for principal stresses in 3 dimensions. Solve for the principal stresses in the following state of stress, without solving the general cubic equation.

$$\tau_{ij} = \begin{pmatrix} 200 & 100 & 0 \\ 100 & 0 & 0 \\ 0 & 0 & 300 \end{pmatrix} \text{ psi}$$

Solution: Here the stresses τ_{zx} and τ_{zy} are zero and so an interface with a normal in the z-direction is devoid of shear. This means that the z-direction must correspond to a principal axis and that one of the principal stresses is known - it is 300 psi. To get the other principal stresses divide $\tau - 300$ into the left-hand side of the cubic equation for principal stress. We then get as a result a quadratic expression in τ, which may be set equal to zero to generate two more roots. We shall illustrate these steps. The cubic equation is

$$\tau^3 - (\tau_{xx} + \tau_{yy} + \tau_{zz})\tau^2 + (\tau_{xx}\tau_{yy} + \tau_{yy}\tau_{zz} + \tau_{xx}\tau_{zz} - \tau_{xy}^2 - \tau_{yz}^2 - \tau_{xz}^2)\tau$$

$$- (\tau_{xx}\tau_{yy}\tau_{zz} + 2\tau_{xy}\tau_{yz}\tau_{xz} - \tau_{xx}\tau_{yz}^2 - \tau_{yy}\tau_{xz}^2 - \tau_{zz}\tau_{xy}^2) = 0$$

For the given state of stress, this becomes

$$\tau^3 - 500\tau^2 + 50 \times 10^3\tau + 30 \times 10^5 = 0 \qquad \text{(a)}$$

Hence,

$$(\tau - 300)\overline{)\tau^3 - 500\tau^2 + 50 \times 10^3\tau + 30 \times 10^5}$$

gives

$$\tau^2 - 200\tau - 10{,}000$$

We can then express Eq. (a) as follows:

$$(\tau - 300)(\tau^2 - 200\tau - 10{,}000) = 0$$

Setting the quadratic expression equal to zero we get

$$\tau^2 - 200\tau - 10{,}000 = 0$$

Using the quadratic formula we then get for roots two additional stresses τ as follows:

$$\tau = \frac{200 \pm \sqrt{200^2 - (4)(1)(-10{,}000)}}{2}$$

$$= 241.5, \ -41.5$$

The principal stresses are then

$$\tau_1 = 300 \text{ psi}$$

$$\tau_2 = 241.5 \text{ psi}$$

$$\tau_3 = -41.5 \text{ psi}$$

A perpendicular to an interface has a direction given by $\varepsilon_1 = .707i + .707j$. (a) Calculate the normal stress for the interface from the values given as $\tau_{xx} = 500$ psi; $\tau_{yy} = -1000$ psi; $\tau_{xy} = 200$ psi (b) Find the unit vector ε_2 at right angles to ε_1 in the x-y plane. (c) On the faces normal to ε_1 and ε_2, find the shear stress.

Solution: To find the normal stress in the given direction we need the directions cosines. These are given by the coefficients of the unit vector so $\varphi\ \vec{\varepsilon} = u\underline{i} + v\underline{j} + w\underline{k}$

$$a_{nx} = u = .707$$

$$a_{ny} = v = .707$$

$$a_{nz} = w = 0$$

The general expression for a normal stress in an inclined direction can be written as a sum

$$\tau_{nn} = \sum_{i=x,y,z} \sum_{j=x,y,z} \tau_{ij} a_{ni} a_{nj}$$

Since we have planar stress, i.e., the stresses on z-planes equal zero, we can sum only over x and y. If we utilize the fact that $a_{nx} = a_{ny} = a$ we can simplify the summation to

$$\tau_{nn} = \sum_{i=x,y} \sum_{j=x,y} \tau_{ij}\ a^2$$

Therefore

$$\tau_{nn} = a^2 \sum_i \sum_j \tau_{ij}$$

$$\tau_{nn} = (.707)^2(500 + 200 + 200 - 1000)$$

$$= (.707)^2(-100)$$

$$= -50 \text{ psi}$$

To find the unit vector at right angles to $\vec{\varepsilon}_1$ we use the properties of the dot product and the fact that a unit vector has unit length. We assume $\vec{\varepsilon}_2 = u\underline{i} + v\underline{j}$ where u and v are unknown. Since the dot product of perpendicular vectors is zero and $\vec{\varepsilon}_2$ is perpendicular to $\vec{\varepsilon}_1$ we have

$$\vec{\varepsilon}_2 \cdot \vec{\varepsilon}_1 = 0$$

$$(u\underline{i} + v\underline{j}) \cdot (.707\underline{i} + .707\underline{j}) = 0$$

$$.707u(1) + .707u(0) + .707v(0) + .707v(1) = 0$$

$$.707u(1) + .707v(1) = 0$$

$$u(1) + v(1) = 0$$

Therefore $u = -v$. Using Pythagoras' theorem

$$1 = u^2 + v^2$$

since u is equal in magnitude to v: $2u^2$; so $u = 1/\sqrt{2}$ and $v = -u = -1/\sqrt{2}$ so

$$\vec{\epsilon_2} = 1/\sqrt{2}\ \underline{i} - 1/\sqrt{2}\ \underline{j} = .707\underline{i} - .707\underline{j}$$

We can get the direction cosines from the coefficients of the vectors, ϵ_1 and ϵ_2, and obtain

$$a_{1x} = .707 \qquad a_{2x} = .707$$

$$a_{1y} = .707 \qquad a_{2y} = -.707$$

We substitute these values into the general equation for shear stress

$$\tau_{12} = \sum_{i=x,y} \sum_{j=x,y} \tau_{ij} a_{1i} a_{2j}$$

Expanding this formula

$$\tau_{12} = 500(.707)(.707) + 200(.707)(-.707)$$

$$+ 200(.707)(.707) + (-1000)(.707)(-.707)$$

$$= -1500(.707)^2 = -750 \text{ psi}$$

• PROBLEM 6-15

Analysis of a particular body indicates that stresses for orthogonal interfaces associated with reference xyz at a given point are, in psi,

$$\tau_{xx} = 3000 \qquad \tau_{xy} = -1000 \qquad \tau_{xz} = 0$$

$$\tau_{yx} = -1000 \qquad \tau_{yy} = 2000 \qquad \tau_{yz} = 2000$$

$$\tau_{zx} = 0 \qquad \tau_{zy} = 2000 \qquad \tau_{zz} = 0$$

Determine the normal stress τ_{nn} on the infinitesimal interface at this point whose unit normal is

$$n = .6j + .80k \qquad \text{(see Figure)}$$

Also determine the shear stress τ_{ns} on the same interface in a direction s, parallel to the x-axis.

The direction cosines for n and s are

$$a_{nx} = 0 \qquad a_{sx} = 1$$

$$a_{ny} = .60 \qquad a_{sy} = 0$$

$$a_{nz} = .80 \qquad a_{sz} = 0$$

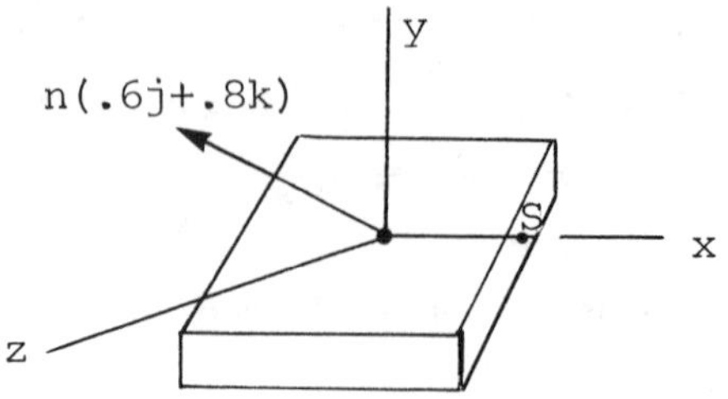

Solution: The normal stress in the n-direction at a point may be written as

$$\tau_{nn} = \tau_{xx}a^2_{nx} + \tau_{xy}a_{nx}a_{ny} + \tau_{xz}a_{nx}a_{nz} + \tau_{yx}a_{ny}a_{nx} + \tau_{zy}a^2_{ny} + \tau_{yz}a_{ny}a_{nz} + \tau_{zx}a_{nz}a_{nx} + \tau_{zy}a_{nz}a_{ny} + \tau_{zz}a^2_{nz}$$

Substituting the given information, we obtain:

$$\tau_{nn} = (3000)(0^2) + (-1000)(0)(.60) + (0)(0)(.80) + (-1000)(.60)(0) + (2000)(.60)^2 + (2000)(.60)(.80) + (0)(.80)(0) + (2000)(.80)(.60) + (0)(.80)^2$$

$$\therefore \tau_{nn} = 2640 \text{ psi}$$

The corresponding equation for shear stress in a direction s, perpendicular to n, is

$$\tau_{ns} = \tau_{xx}a_{nx}a_{sx} + \tau_{xy}a_{nx}a_{sy} + \tau_{xz}a_{nx}a_{sz} + \tau_{yx}a_{ny}a_{sx} + \tau_{yy}a_{ny}a_{sy} + \tau_{yx}a_{ny}a_{sx} + \tau_{zx}a_{nx}a_{sx} + \tau_{zy}a_{nz}a_{sy} + \tau_{zz}a_{nz}a_{sz}$$

Substituting the given values, the shear stress is found to be

$$\tau_{ns} = (3000)(0)(1) + (-1000)(0)(0) + (0)(0)(0) + (-1000)(.60)(1) + (2000)(.60)(0) + (2000)(.60)(0) + (0)(.80)(1) + (2000)(.80)(0) + (0)(.80)(0)$$

$$\therefore \tau_{ns} = -600 \text{ psi}$$

• PROBLEM 6-16

In cylindrical coordinates a set of stresses on orthogonal interface planes is given below:

$$\begin{pmatrix} \tau_{rr} & \tau_{r\theta} & \tau_{rz} \\ \tau_{\theta r} & \tau_{\theta\theta} & \tau_{\theta z} \\ \tau_{zr} & \tau_{z\theta} & \tau_{zz} \end{pmatrix}$$

At a given point where the cylindrical coordinates are $r = 6$, $\theta = 30°$, $z = 10$, compute τ_{xx} for the stress values below:

$$\begin{pmatrix} 5000 & 0 & -3000 \\ 0 & 2000 & 1000 \\ -3000 & 1000 & 0 \end{pmatrix}$$

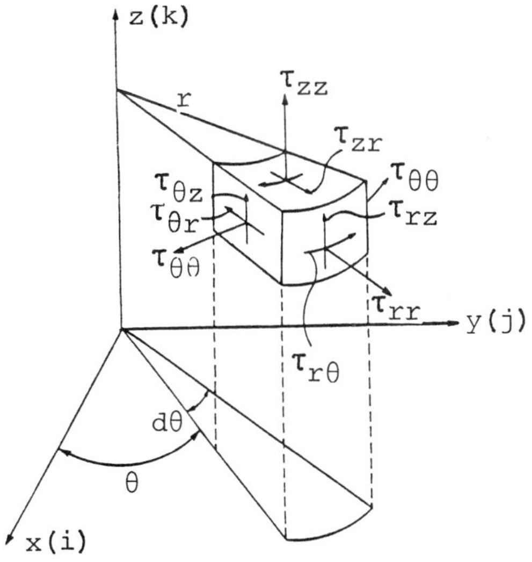

Solution: We can find the normal stress τ_{xx} in terms of the cylindrical stresses by using the direction cosine formula with some subscript modification.

$$\tau_{nn} = \tau_{xx}a^2_{nx} + \tau_{xy}a_{nx}a_{ny} + \tau_{xz}a_{nx}a_{nz} + \tau_{yx}a_{ny}a_{nx} + \tau_{yy}a^2_{ny} + \tau_{yz}a_{ny}a_{nz} + \tau_{zx}a_{nz}a_{nx} + \tau_{zy}a_{nz}a_{ny} + \tau_{zz}a^2_{nz}$$

where a_{nj} is a direction cosine. If we notice that the above formula for τ_{nn} is essentially the stress tensor, only with each term multiplied by the appropriate direction cosines, we can easily convert this to cylindrical coordinates, by multiplying the cylindrical stress tensor by analogous direction cosines. To see this clearly, we write τ_{nn} in the form

$$\sum_{i=x,y,z} \sum_{j=x,y,z} \tau_{ij}a_{ni}a_{nj}$$

Therefore,

$$\tau_{xx} = \sum_{i=r,\theta,z} \sum_{j=r,\theta,z} \tau_{ij}a_{xi}a_{xj}$$

Expanding this once again we have

$$\tau_{xx} = \tau_{rr}a^2_{xr} + \tau_{r\theta}a_{xr}a_{x\theta} + \tau_{rz}a_{xr}a_{xz} + \tau_{r\theta}a_{xr}a_{x\theta} + \tau_{\theta\theta}a^2_{x\theta} + \tau_{\theta z}a_{x\theta}a_{xz} + \tau_{zr}a_{xz}a_{xr} + \tau_{z\theta}a_{xz}a_{x\theta} + \tau_{zz}a^2_{xz}$$

We must now find the direction cosines, the values of the cosine of the angle between the two axes in question.

$$a_{xr} = \cos\theta = \cos 30^\circ = .866$$

Since the θ axis is perpendicular to the r-axis, and the sum of the angles of a triangle must equal 180°, we obtain for $\theta_{x\theta} = 180 - 90 - 30 = 60$, so

$$a_{x\theta} = \cos 60 = .5$$

Since the x-axis is perpendicular to the z axis

$$a_{xz} = \cos 90^\circ = 0$$

So, all terms with a_{xz} will disappear in this example. Therefore,

$$\tau_{xx} = \tau_{rr}a_{xr}^2 + \tau_{r\theta}a_{xr}a_{x\theta} + \tau_{r\theta}a_{xr}a_{x\theta} + \tau_{\theta\theta}a_{x\theta}^2$$

Substituting values,

$$\tau_{xx} = 5000(.866)^2 + 0(.866)(.5) + 0(.866)(.5) + 2000(.5)^2$$
$$= 3150 + 500$$

$$\tau_{xx} = 4250 \text{ psi}$$

• PROBLEM 6-17

Given the second and third tensor invariants for stress. Show (a) that the second tensor is the sum of the minors of the principal diagonal which corresponds to the normal stresses, and (b) that the third tensor is the determinant of the stress tensor.

Solution: The minor of an element τ_{ij} of the stress matrix is defined as the determinant of the matrix formed by omitting the ith row and jth column of the stress matrix.

If the stress matrix is written as

$$\begin{vmatrix} \tau_{xx} & \tau_{xy} & \tau_{xz} \\ \tau_{xy} & \tau_{yy} & \tau_{yz} \\ \tau_{xz} & \tau_{yz} & \tau_{zz} \end{vmatrix}$$

the minor of τ_{xx} is

$$\begin{vmatrix} \tau_{yy} & \tau_{yz} \\ \tau_{yz} & \tau_{zz} \end{vmatrix} = \tau_{yy}\tau_{zz} - \tau_{yz}^2$$

Similarly, the minor of τ_{yy} is given by

$$\begin{vmatrix} \tau_{xx} & \tau_{xy} & \tau_{xz} \\ \tau_{xy} & \tau_{yy} & \tau_{yz} \\ \tau_{xz} & \tau_{yz} & \tau_{zz} \end{vmatrix} = \tau_{xx}\tau_{zz} - \tau_{xz}^2$$

The minor of τ_{zz} is

$$\begin{vmatrix} \tau_{xx} & \tau_{xy} & \tau_{xz} \\ \tau_{xy} & \tau_{yy} & \tau_{yz} \\ \tau_{xz} & \tau_{yz} & \tau_{zz} \end{vmatrix} = \tau_{xx}\tau_{yy} - \tau_{xy}^2$$

The sum of the minors is then

$$\Sigma M_{ii} = \tau_{yy}\tau_{zz} - \tau_{yz}^2 + \tau_{xx}\tau_{zz} - \tau_{xz}^2 + \tau_{xx}\tau_{yy} - \tau_{xy}^2$$

which is equal to the second tensor invariant of stress:

$$\tau_{xx}\tau_{yy} + \tau_{yy}\tau_{zz} + \tau_{xx}\tau_{zz} - \tau^2_{xy} - \tau^2_{yz} - \tau^2_{xz}$$

The third invariant, π_3, is given by

$$\pi_3 = \tau_{xx}\tau_{yy}\tau_{zz} + 2\tau_{xy}\tau_{yz}\tau_{xz} - \tau^2_{xy}\tau_{zz} - \tau^2_{yz}\tau_{xx} - \tau^2_{zx}\tau_{yy}$$

The determinant of the stress tensor is defined as

$$\det A = \sum_{j=x}^{z} a_{xj}(-1)^{i+j} M_{xj}$$

where A is the stress tensor
j is the index notation
a_{xj} is the element in the x row, j column
M_{xj} is the minor of element a_{xj}.

Therefore,

$$\det A = \tau_{xx}(-1)^{1+1}\begin{vmatrix}\tau_{yy} & \tau_{yz}\\ \tau_{yz} & \tau_{zz}\end{vmatrix} + \tau_{xy}(-1)^{1+2}\begin{vmatrix}\tau_{xy} & \tau_{yz}\\ \tau_{xz} & \tau_{zz}\end{vmatrix}$$

$$+ \tau_{xz}(-1)^{1+3}\begin{vmatrix}\tau_{xy} & \tau_{yy}\\ \tau_{xz} & \tau_{yz}\end{vmatrix}$$

$$= \tau_{xx}(\tau_{yy}\tau_{zz} - \tau^2_{yz}) - \tau_{xy}(\tau_{xy}\tau_{zz} - \tau_{xz}\tau_{yz}) + \tau_{xz}(\tau_{xy}\tau_{yz} - \tau_{xz}\tau_{yy})$$

$$= \tau_{xx}\tau_{yy}\tau_{zz} + 2\tau_{xy}\tau_{xz}\tau_{yz} - \tau_{xx}\tau^2_{yz} - \tau_{zz}\tau^2_{xy} - \tau_{yy}\tau^2_{xz}$$

• PROBLEM 6-18

The following displacement field describes the movement of a body under load:

$$\vec{u} = [(x^2 + y^2)\vec{i} + (3 + xz)\vec{j} - .6z^2\vec{k}] \times 10^{-2} \text{ ft} \qquad \text{(a)}$$

Compute the normal strain at (0,1,3) in a direction s given as

$$\vec{s} = .60\vec{i} + .80\vec{j} \quad \text{(see Fig. 1)}$$

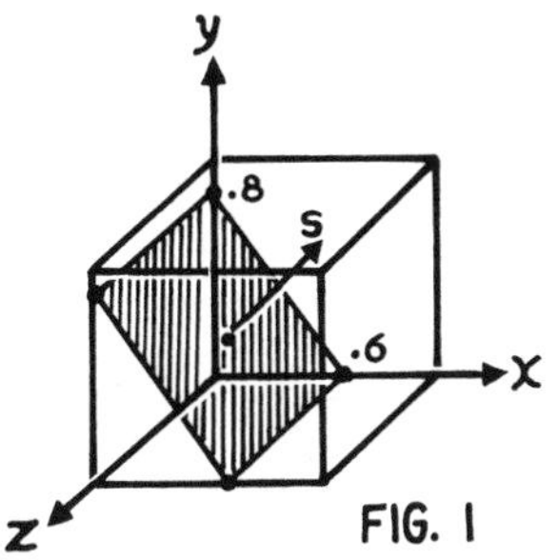

FIG. 1

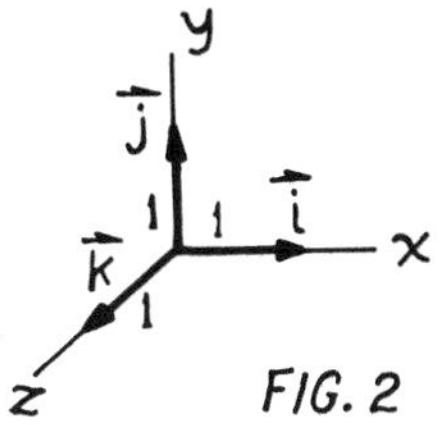

FIG. 2

Solution: We shall do this in two ways. The most direct way is to evaluate $\partial u_s/\partial s$ at (0,1,3). Thus,

$$u_s = \vec{u}\cdot\vec{s} = [(.60)(x^2 + y^2) + (.80)(3 + xz)] \times 10^{-2} \qquad \text{(b)}$$

As shown in the figure, $\vec{i}$, $\vec{j}$, and $\vec{k}$ are vectors pointing in the x, y, and z coordinate directions each with a length of one unit. The dot product $\vec{u}\cdot\vec{s}$ means $(u(s)(\cos\theta)$. Two examples of the dot product are given.

$$\vec{i}\cdot\vec{i} = i^2 \cos(0) = 1 \qquad \vec{i}\cdot\vec{j} = (i)(j)\cos(90^\circ) = 0$$

Noting that $\partial u_s/\partial s$ is both a directional derivative and the desired quantity ϵ_{ss} we have

$$\frac{\partial u_s}{\partial s} = \epsilon_{ss} = \frac{\partial u_s}{\partial x}\frac{dx}{ds} + \frac{\partial u_s}{\partial y}\frac{dy}{ds} + \frac{\partial u_s}{\partial z}\frac{dz}{ds}$$

Noting that

$$\frac{dx}{ds} = a_{sx} = .60$$

$$\frac{dy}{ds} = a_{sy} = .80 \tag{c}$$

$$\frac{dz}{ds} = a_{sz} = 0$$

we get for ϵ_{ss} on taking appropriate partial derivatives of Eq.(b)

$$\epsilon_{ss} = [(1.20x + .80z)(.60) + (1.20y)(.80) + (.80x)(0)] \times 10^{-2}$$

$$= [.72x + .48z + .96y] \times 10^{-2}$$

At the position of interest (0,1,3) we get

$$\epsilon_{ss} = [(.72)(0) + (.48)(3) + (.96)(1)] \times 10^{-2}$$

$$= .0240 \tag{d}$$

We shall now proceed a second way by using the transformation equations. The strain tensor is

$$\epsilon_{ij} = \begin{pmatrix} \epsilon_{xx} & \frac{\gamma_{xy}}{2} & \frac{\gamma_{xz}}{2} \\ \frac{\gamma_{yx}}{2} & \epsilon_{yy} & \frac{\gamma_{yz}}{2} \\ \frac{\gamma_{zx}}{2} & \frac{\gamma_{zy}}{2} & \epsilon_{zz} \end{pmatrix}$$

Note: $\gamma_{ij} = 2\epsilon_{ij}$; where

$$\epsilon_{xx} = \frac{\partial u_x}{\partial x}; \quad \epsilon_{yy} = \frac{\partial u_y}{\partial y}; \quad \epsilon_{zz} = \frac{\partial u_z}{\partial z}$$

$$\gamma_{xy} = \frac{\partial u_x}{\partial y} + \frac{\partial u_y}{\partial x}; \quad \gamma_{yz} = \frac{\partial u_y}{\partial z} + \frac{\partial u_z}{\partial y}; \quad \gamma_{xz} = \frac{\partial u_x}{\partial z} + \frac{\partial u_z}{\partial x}$$

For the situation under consideration, the tensor becomes

$$\epsilon_{ij} = \begin{pmatrix} 2x & (y + \frac{z}{2}) & 0 \\ (y + \frac{z}{2}) & 0 & \frac{x}{2} \\ 0 & \frac{x}{2} & -1.2z \end{pmatrix} \times 10^{-2}$$

At the position of interest we have

$$\epsilon_{ij} = \begin{pmatrix} 0 & 2.5 & 0 \\ 2.5 & 0 & 0 \\ 0 & 0 & -3.6 \end{pmatrix} \times 10^{-2} \qquad \text{(e)}$$

We are now going to make use of the 3-dimensional strain transformation equation:

$$\epsilon_{ss} = \epsilon_{xx}a_{sx}^2 + \epsilon_{xy}a_{sx}a_{sy} + \epsilon_{xz}a_{sx}a_{sz} + \epsilon_{yx}a_{sy}a_{sx}$$
$$+ \epsilon_{yy}a_{sy}^2 + \epsilon_{yz}a_{sy}a_{sz} + \epsilon_{zx}a_{sz}a_{sx}$$
$$+ \epsilon_{zy}a_{sz}a_{sy} + \epsilon_{zz}a_{sz}^2$$

Using the transformation equations in conjunction with the direction cosines (c) we have

$$\epsilon_{ss} = \{(2.5)(.60)(.80) + (2.5)(.80)(.60) + (-3.6)(0^2)\} \times 10^{-2}$$
$$= .0240$$

This is the same answer as before.

• PROBLEM 6-19

Compute the principal strains and directions of principal axes for the following state of strain at a point:

$$\varepsilon_{ij} = \begin{pmatrix} 80 & 0 & 0 \\ 0 & 36.7 & -21.6 \\ 0 & -21.6 & 50 \end{pmatrix} \times 10^{-6}$$

Solution: We are going to make use of the cubic equation for strain in 3 dimensions to find the principal strains. The equation is

$$\epsilon^3 - A\epsilon^2 + B\epsilon - C = 0 ,$$

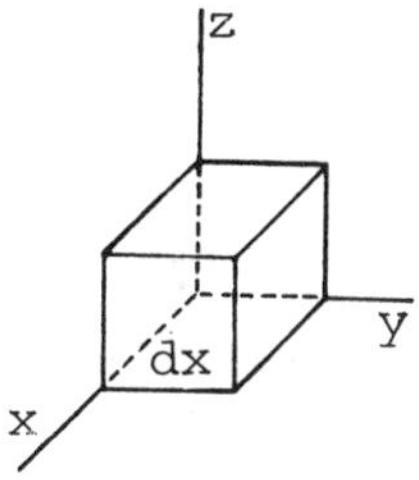

where

$A \equiv$ first strain invariant $= \epsilon_{xx} + \epsilon_{yy} + \epsilon_{zz}$

$B \equiv$ 2nd strain invariant $= \epsilon_{xx}\epsilon_{yy} + \epsilon_{yy}\epsilon_{zz} + \epsilon_{xx}\epsilon_{zz} - (\epsilon_{xy}^2 + \epsilon_{yz}^2 + \epsilon_{xz}^2)$

and $C \equiv$ 3rd strain invariant $= \epsilon_{xx}\epsilon_{yy}\epsilon_{zz} + 2(\epsilon_{xy}\epsilon_{yz}\epsilon_{xz}) - \epsilon_{xx}\epsilon_{yz}^2 - \epsilon_{yy}\epsilon_{xz}^2 - \epsilon_{zz}\epsilon_{xy}^2$

For this purpose we now compute the tensor invariants for strain. We thus get

$$A = (80 + 36.7 + 50) \times 10^{-6} = 166.7 \times 10^{-6}$$

$$B = (80)(36.7) \times 10^{-12} + (80)(50) \times 10^{-12} + (36.7)(50) \times 10^{-12}$$
$$-(-21.6)^2 \times 10^{-12}$$

$$= 8305 \times 10^{-12}$$

$$C = (80)(36.7)(50) \times 10^{-18} - (-21.6)^2(80) \times 10^{-18}$$

$$= 109{,}500 \times 10^{-18}$$

The cubic equation for the principal strain is then

$$\varepsilon^3 - 166.7 \times 10^{-6}\varepsilon^2 + 8305 \times 10^{-12}\varepsilon - 109.5 \times 10^{-15} = 0 \qquad \text{(a)}$$

Now since ε_{xy} and ε_{xz} are zero, it means that the segment dx of the rectangular parallelopiped (see Figure) at the point of interest in the undeformed geometry does not rotate toward the z axis or toward the y axis as a result of deformation. Indeed, other than rigid-body movements it can only stretch or shrink. Accordingly, the x direction must be a principal direction and so one of the principal strains at the point is then $\varepsilon = 80 \times 10^{-6}$. We now divide $\varepsilon - 80 \times 10^{-6}$ into the left-hand side of Eq.(a) to get a quadratic expression

$\varepsilon^2 - 86.7 \times 10^{-6}\varepsilon + 1369 \times 10^{-2}$. We can then express Eq.(a) as follows:

$$(\varepsilon - 80 \times 10^{-6})(\varepsilon^2 - 86.7 \times 10^{-6}\varepsilon + 1369 \times 10^{-12}) = 0$$

To find the remaining principal strains we set the second parenthesized expression equal to zero. Thus,

$$\varepsilon^2 - 86.7 \times 10^{-6}\varepsilon + 1369 \times 10^{-12} = 0$$

Using the quadratic formula we get

$$\varepsilon = \frac{86.7 \times 10^{-6} \pm \sqrt{86.7^2 \times 10^{-12} - (4)(1369) \times 10^{-12}}}{2}$$

$$\therefore \ \varepsilon = 65.9 \times 10^{-6},\ 20.77 \times 10^{-6}$$

We list the principal strains accordingly as follows:

$$\varepsilon_1 = 80 \times 10^{-6}$$

$$\varepsilon_2 = 65.93 \times 10^{-6}$$

$$\varepsilon_3 = 20.77 \times 10^{-6}$$

To find the principal axis for ε_2 we go to the equations analogous to the equilibrium equations for stress, which are a direct result of compatibility requirements:

$$(\varepsilon_{xx} - \varepsilon)a_{nx} + \varepsilon_{xy}a_{ny} + \varepsilon_{xz}a_{nz} = 0$$

$$\varepsilon_{yx}a_{nx} + (\varepsilon_{yy} - \varepsilon)a_{ny} + \varepsilon_{yz}a_{nz} = 0$$

$$\varepsilon_{zx}a_{nx} + \varepsilon_{zy}a_{ny} + (\varepsilon_{zz} - \varepsilon)a_{nz} = 0$$

Remembering that only two of the equations are independent, on substituting $\varepsilon_2 = 65.93$ into the first two equations we get

$$(80 - 65.93) \times 10^{-6}a_{nx} + (0)(a_{ny}) + 0(a_{nz}) = 0 \qquad \text{(b)}$$

$$0(a_{nx}) + (36.7 - 65.93) \times 10^{-6}a_{ny} - 21.6 \times 10^{-6}a_{nz} = 0 \qquad \text{(c)}$$

Also: $$a_{nx}^2 + a_{ny}^2 + a_{nz}^2 = 1 \quad \text{(d)}$$

In Eq.(b) two of the terms are zero leaving:

$$((80 - 65.93) \times 10^{-6})(a_{nx}) = 0$$

Therefore:

$$a_{nx} = 0$$

From Eq.(c) an equation for a_{ny} in terms of a_{nz} can be found:

$$(36.7 - 65.93) \times 10^{-6}(a_{ny}) - 21.6 \times 10^{-6}(a_{nz}) = 0$$

$$-29.23 \times 10^{-6}(a_{ny}) - 21.6 \times 10^{-6}(a_{nz}) = 0$$

$$a_{ny} = \frac{+21.6 \times 10^{-6}(a_{nz})}{-29.23 \times 10^{-6}}$$

$$a_{ny} = -.739\, a_{nz}$$

Substituting into Eq.(d):

$$a_{nx}^2 + a_{ny}^2 + a_{nz}^2 = 1$$

$$0^2 + (-.739a_{nz})^2 + a_{nz}^2 = 1$$

$$(.546)a_{nz}^2 + (1)a_{nz}^2 = 1$$

Adding the a_{nz}^2 terms:

$$1.546a_{nz}^2 = 1$$

$$a_{nz}^2 = 1/1.546$$

$$a_{nz} = 1/\sqrt{1.546} = .804$$

$$a_{ny} = -.739a_{nz} = -.739(.804) = -.594$$

Summarizing the results:

$$a_{nx} = 0$$

$$a_{ny} = -.594$$

$$a_{nz} = .804$$

Using the same method, the following results can be obtained for ϵ_3:

$$a_{nx} = 0$$

$$a_{ny} = .804$$

$$a_{nz} = .594$$

Accordingly, a rectangular parallelopiped having edges originally along the x, ϵ_2, and ϵ_3 directions, respectively, would remain a rectangular parallelopiped after deformation.

Compute the direction of the algebraic minimum normal strain at a point for which there is the following state of strain:

$$\begin{pmatrix} .02 & 0 & -.01 \\ 0 & -.01 & 0 \\ -.01 & 0 & .03 \end{pmatrix}$$

Solution: To find the algebraically minimum normal strain, we must find the principal strains for each pair of orthogonal axes, x-y, x-z, and y-z. The numerically smallest value, i.e., the farthest to the left on the number line, is the algebraic minimum.

The general expression for principal strain is

$$\epsilon_{a,b} = \frac{\epsilon_{ii} + \epsilon_{jj}}{2} \pm \sqrt{\left(\frac{\epsilon_{ii} - \epsilon_{jj}}{2}\right)^2 + (\epsilon_{ij})^2}$$

In the x-y plane we have

$$\epsilon_{xx} = .02$$

$$\epsilon_{yy} = -.01$$

$$\epsilon_{xy} = 0$$

Substituting into the expression for principal strain we obtain

$$\epsilon_{a,b} = \frac{.02 - .01}{2} \pm \sqrt{\left(\frac{.02 + .01}{2}\right)^2 + 0}$$

$$= .02,\ -.01$$

where ϵ_a is in the x-direction ; ϵ_b is in the y-direction .

Now, the y-z plane has strain values

$$\epsilon_{yy} = -.01$$

$$\epsilon_{zz} = .03$$

$$\epsilon_{yz} = 0$$

Substituting in the general expression, we have

$$\epsilon_{a,b} = \frac{-.01 + .03}{2} \pm \sqrt{\left(\frac{-.01 - .03}{2}\right)^2 + 0}$$

$$= .01 \pm .01$$

$$= .02,\ 0$$

ϵ_a is in the y-direction ; ϵ_b is in the z-direction.

Finally, in the x-z plane we have

$$\epsilon_{xx} = .02$$

$$\epsilon_{zz} = .03$$

$$\epsilon_{xz} = -.01$$

$$\varepsilon_{a,b} = \frac{.02 + .03}{2} \pm \sqrt{\left(\frac{.02 - .03}{2}\right)^2 + (-.01)^2}$$

$$= .025 \pm .011$$

$$= .014,\ .036$$

Therefore, the algebraic minimum strain is -.01 , which was in the y-direction.

• PROBLEM 6-21

Calculate (a) the normal strain along a direction at equal angles to the x, y, and z axes, and (b) the shear strain for axes having the directions $\varepsilon_1 = 0.6i + 0.8j$; $\varepsilon_2 = 0.4i - 0.3j + .866k$, using the following state of strain at a point:

$$\varepsilon_{ij} = \begin{pmatrix} .02 & .01 & .0 \\ .01 & -.02 & .03 \\ 0 & .03 & .04 \end{pmatrix}$$

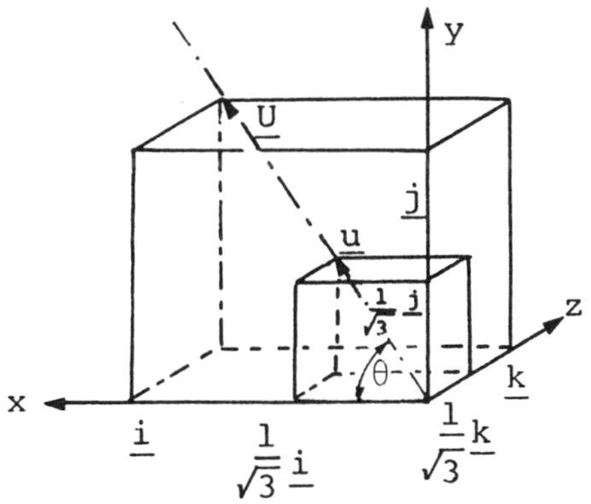

Fig. 1.

Solution: a) The strains for an inclined direction can be found by using the direction cosines and the strains along the original axes.

In Figure 1, $\underline{u}$ is the unit vector along the direction equally inclined to the x, y, and z axes. Thus the angle θ is the same between $\underline{u}$ and each of the three axes. Also the projection of $\underline{u}$ onto each of the three axes has the same magnitude, equal in value to (1) cos θ. In order to find the normal strain in the $\underline{u}$ direction, the magnitude of these direction cosines must be found.

First the direction of $\underline{u}$ will be found. Since all three of the direction cosines are equal, the sum of the unit vectors, $\underline{i}$, $\underline{j}$, and $\underline{k}$ is a vector, $\underline{U}$ in the direction of $\underline{u}$.

$$\underline{U} = \underline{i} + \underline{j} + \underline{k}$$

A vector pointing in the same direction with a magnitude of one is needed. This can be obtained by dividing $\underline{U}$ by its own length, L . The length, L, is found by the Pythagorean Theorem for three dimensions.

$$L = \sqrt{\underline{i}^2 + \underline{j}^2 + \underline{k}^2} = \sqrt{1 + 1 + 1} = \sqrt{3}$$

The unit vector $\underline{u}$ can be obtained by dividing $\underline{U}$ by L.

$$\underline{u} = \underline{U}/L = \frac{\underline{i} + \underline{j} + \underline{k}}{\sqrt{3}}$$

That is:

$$\underline{u} = 1/\sqrt{3}\,\underline{i} + 1/\sqrt{3}\,\underline{j} + 1/\sqrt{3}\,\underline{k}$$

The coefficients of $\underline{u}$ are the direction cosines

$$a_{nx} = 1/\sqrt{3} \qquad a_{ny} = 1/\sqrt{3} \qquad a_{nz} = 1/\sqrt{3}$$

The general expression for a normal strain in an inclined direction can be written as the sum:

$$\epsilon_{nn} = \sum_{i=x,y,z} \sum_{j=x,y,z} \epsilon_{ij} a_{ni} a_{nj}$$

All three direction cosines are equal so this reduces to:

$$\epsilon_{nn} = \sum_{i=x,y,z} \sum_{j=x,y,z} \epsilon_{ij} a^2$$

or

$$\epsilon_{nn} = a^2 \sum_{i=x,y,z} \sum_{j=x,y,z} \epsilon_{ij}$$

Writing out the summations, this becomes:

$$\epsilon_{nn} = (a)^2(\epsilon_{xx} + \epsilon_{xy} + \epsilon_{xz} + \epsilon_{yx} + \epsilon_{yy} + \epsilon_{yz} + \epsilon_{zx} + \epsilon_{zy} + \epsilon_{zz})$$

Substituting in the numbers yields:

$$\epsilon_{nn} = \left(\frac{1}{\sqrt{3}}\right)^2 (.02 + .01 + .0 + .01 - .02 + .03 + 0 + .03 + .04)$$

Adding the strains:

$$\epsilon_{nn} = \left(\frac{1}{\sqrt{3}}\right)^2 (.12)$$

$$\epsilon_{nn} = \frac{1}{3} (.12)$$

$$\epsilon_{nn} = .04$$

b) The second part of the problem is to find the shear strain on the axes in the directions $\underline{\epsilon_1}$, $\underline{\epsilon_2}$. Once the direction cosines are found, the general equation for shear strain can be employed. The general equation is as follows:

$$\epsilon_{ns} = \epsilon_{xx}a_{nx}a_{sx} + \epsilon_{xy}a_{nx}a_{sy} + \epsilon_{xz}a_{nx}a_{sz} + \epsilon_{yx}a_{ny}a_{sx} + \epsilon_{yy}a_{ny}a_{sy}$$
$$+ \epsilon_{yz}a_{ny}a_{sz} + \epsilon_{zx}a_{nz}a_{sx} + \epsilon_{zy}a_{nz}a_{sy} + \epsilon_{zz}a_{nz}a_{sz}$$

The direction cosines are the coefficients of the unit vectors:

$$\underline{\epsilon_1} = .6\underline{i} + .8\underline{j} + 0\underline{k}$$

$$\underline{\epsilon_2} = .4\underline{i} - .3\underline{j} + .866\underline{k}$$

The direction cosines are therefore:

$$a_{nx} = .6 \qquad a_{sx} = .4$$

$a_{ny} = .8 \qquad a_{sy} = -.3$

$a_{nz} = 0 \qquad a_{sz} = .866$

Substituting into the general equation for shear we have:

$$\epsilon_{ns} = (.02)(.6)(.4) + (.01)(.6)(-.3) + (0)(.6)(.866) + (.01)(.8)(.4)$$
$$+ (-.02)(.8)(-.3) + (.03)(.8)(.866) + (0)(0)(.4) + (.03)(0)(-.3)$$
$$+ (.04)(0)(.866)$$
$$= .0318$$

Thus it is seen how convenient unit vectors and direction cosines can be in the solution of three dimensional problems.

MOHR'S REPRESENTATION OF STRESS AND STRAIN

• PROBLEM 6-22

For the stress state shown, using Mohr's circle, find:

(a) The magnitude and direction of the principal stresses.

(b) The stresses on an element whose faces are normal to $\bar{x}$ and $\bar{y}$ where axes $\bar{x}$, $\bar{y}$ are $+45°$ from axes x,y.

(c) The three principal shear stresses at the point.

(d) The maximum shear stress at the point.

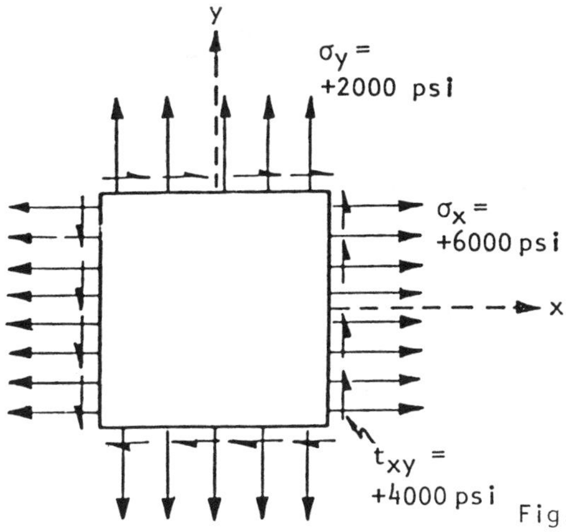

Fig. 1

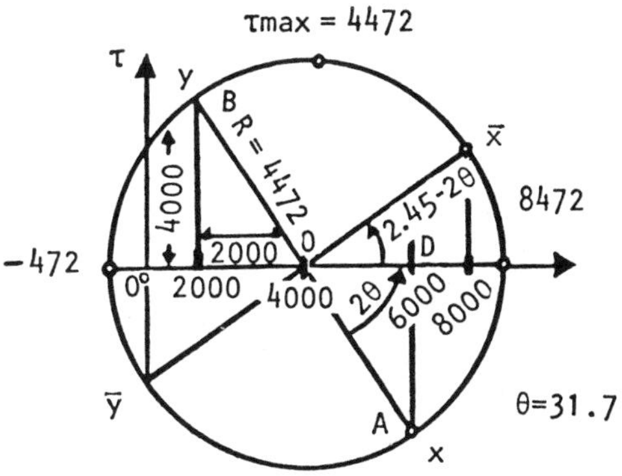

Fig. 2

Solution: We begin the construction of Mohr's circle by locating the center. This point is located on the x (normal stress) axis and is halfway between σ_x and σ_y. It is denoted by 0 in Figure 2.

$$\sigma_0 = \frac{\sigma_x + \sigma_y}{2} = 4000$$

By plotting the values for shear stress we can find the radius of the circle. The point A is marked at a distance τ_{xy} below σ_x; similarly B is a height τ_{xy} above σ_y. We now draw a line connecting A and B which passes through the center 0.

Using Pythagoras' theorem, we find

$$R^2 = \overline{OD}^2 + \overline{DA}^2$$

$$R = \sqrt{\left(\frac{\sigma_x - \sigma_y}{2}\right)^2 + (\tau_{xy})^2}$$

$$= \sqrt{\left(\frac{6000 - 2000}{2}\right)^2 + (4000)^2}$$

$$= 4472$$

The maximum normal stress lies on the normal stress axis and is equal to σ_c plus the radius of Mohr's circle. This is the first principal stress.

$$\sigma_1 = \sigma_c + R$$

$$= 4000 + 4472$$

$$= 8472 \text{ psi}$$

The second principal normal stress is $\sigma_2 = 0$, because there is no applied stress in the z-direction.

The third principal stress, σ_3, is also on the x-axis.

$$\sigma_3 = \sigma_c - R$$

$$= 4000 - 4472$$

$$= -472 \text{ psi}$$

The direction of the principal plane in relation to the original can be found using trigonometry. The angle the original plane makes with the principal plane is one-half the angle between $\overline{OA}$ and $\overline{OD}$ on Mohr's circle. So

$$\cos 2\theta = \frac{\sigma_x - \sigma_y/2}{R}$$

$$\cos 2\theta = \frac{2000}{4472}$$

$$2\theta = 63.43$$

$$\theta = 31.7$$

b) To find the stresses on a plane inclined by 45° to the x-axis, apply trigonometry to Figure 2. By the properties of Mohr's circle we can see that

$$\sigma_x = \sigma_c + R\cos(2.45 - 2\theta)$$

$$\sigma_y = \sigma_c - R\cos(2.45 - 2\theta)$$

$$\tau_{xy} = R\sin(2.45 - 2\theta)$$

Substitute the angles into the general equations.

$$\sigma_x = 4000 + 4472 \times \cos(2.45 - 63.43)$$

$$= 8000 \text{ psi}$$

$$\sigma_y = 4000 - 4472 \times \cos(2.45 - 63.43)$$

$$\approx 0$$

$$\tau_{xy} = 4472 \times \sin(2.45 - 63.43)$$

$$= 2000 \text{ psi}$$

Positive shears on the x face on Mohr's circle correspond to negative shears in reality. Therefore:

$$\tau_{xy} = -2000 \text{ psi}$$

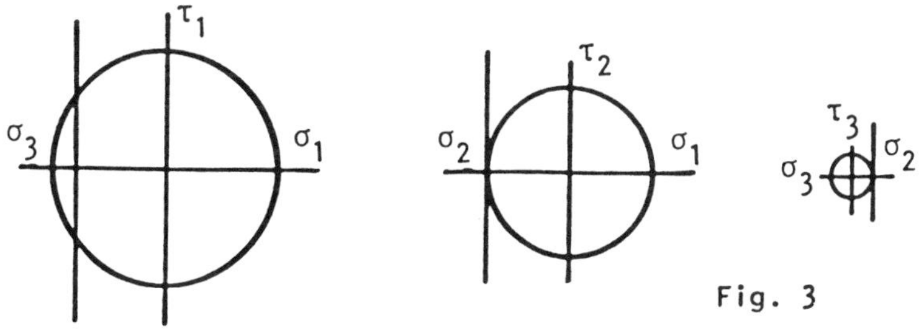

Fig. 3

c) The principal shear stresses are the shear stresses in planes at 45° angles to the principal normal stress planes. Two principal normal stresses have been found above: $\sigma_1 = 8472$, $\sigma_2 = -472$. The third normal stress is $\sigma_3 = 0$ because there is no stress in the z-direction.

The equation for principal shear is:

$$\tau = \left(\sigma_1 - \sigma_2\right)/2$$

Substituting in the values results in:

$$\tau_1 = \frac{\sigma_1 - \sigma_2}{2} = \frac{8472 - (-472)}{2} = 4472$$

$$\tau_2 = \frac{\sigma_1 - \sigma_3}{2} = \frac{8472 - 0}{2} = 4236$$

$$\tau_3 = \frac{\sigma_3 - \sigma_2}{2} = \frac{0 - (-472)}{2} = 236$$

The maximum shear stress is the largest of the principal shears,

$$\tau_1 = 4472$$

This shown in Fig. 3.

• PROBLEM 6-23

At a point in a structural member that is subjected to plane stress there are stresses on horizontal and vertical planes through the point, as shown in Fig. a. Determine, and show on a sketch: (a) The principal stresses and maximum shearing stress at the point. (b) The normal and shearing stresses on plane A-A through the point.

Solution: Mohr's circle is constructed from the given data as follows: On a set of coordinate axes, Fig. b, plot point V (representing the stresses on the vertical plane) at (8, -4) because the stresses on the vertical plane are 8 ksi T and -4 ksi (counterclockwise) shear. Likewise, point H (representing the stresses on the horizontal plane) has the coordinates (-6,4). Draw line HV, which is a diamter of Mohr's circle.

The center of the circle is found by

$$\sigma_c = \frac{\sigma_x + \sigma_y}{2}$$

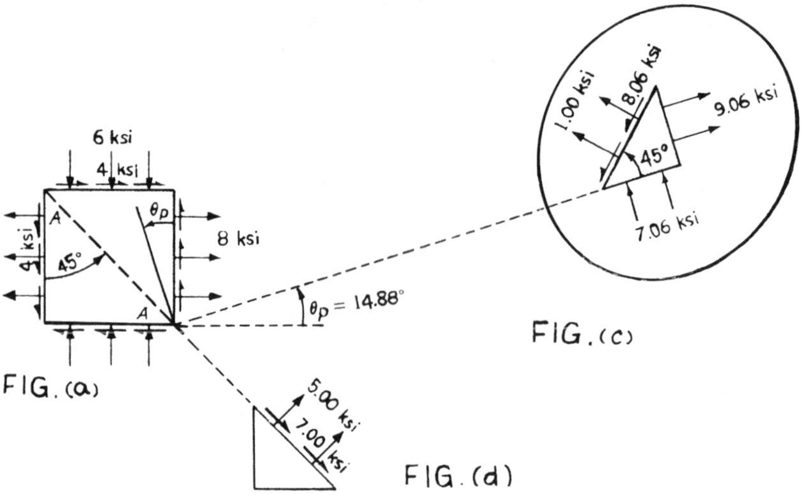

FIG. (a)

FIG. (c)

FIG. (d)

$$= \frac{8 - 6}{2}$$

$$= 1 \text{ ksi}$$

The radius of the circle is

$$CV = \sqrt{7^2 + 4^2} = 8.06 \text{ ksi.}$$

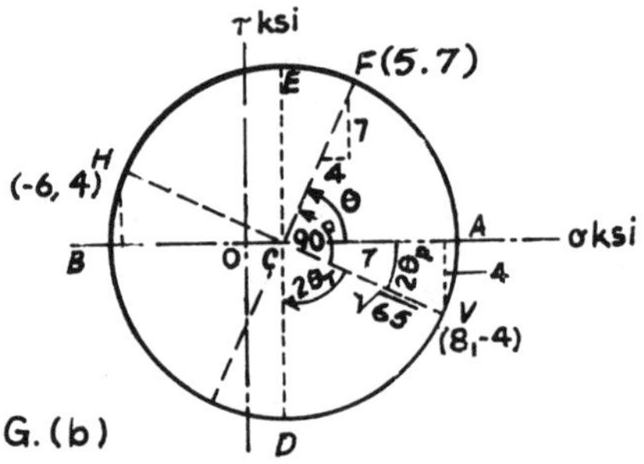

FIG. (b)

(a) The principal stresses and the maximum shearing stress at the point are

$$\sigma_{p1} = OA = 1 + 8.06 = 9.06 \text{ ksi T},$$

$$\sigma_{p2} = OB = 1 - 8.06 = -7.06 = 7.06 \text{ ksi C}.$$

$$\sigma_{p3} = \sigma_z = \underline{0}.$$

The maximum shear stress is given by the radius of the circle.

$$\tau_{max} = R = 8.06 \text{ ksi}$$

The principal planes are represented by lines CA and CB.

By using trigonometry we see that

$$\tan 2\theta_p = \overline{VA}/\overline{AC}$$

$$= 4/7$$

$$2\theta_p = \tan^{-1}(4/7)$$

$$= 29.75° \text{ counterclockwise}$$

Since the angle $2\theta_p$ is counterclockwise, the principal planes are counterclockwise from the vertical and horizontal planes of the stress block, as shown in Fig. c. To determine which principal stress acts on which plane, note that as the radius of the circle rotates counterclockwise, the end of the radius CV moves from V to A, which means that the vertical plane rotates by an angle $\theta = 14.88°$, σ_x changes from 8 ksi to 9.06 ksi and τ_{xy} goes from -4 ksi to 0. Therefore, the stress in the θ_p direction is 9.06 ksi. Similarly, as end H moves to B, the horizontal plane rotates through 14.88° and the normal stress changes to -7.06 ksi; the shear stress to zero therefore, the principal stress on the rotated horizontal plane is -7.06 ksi.

(b) Plane A-A is 45° counterclockwise from the vertical plane; therefore, the corresponding radius of Mohr's circle is 90°, 2θ, counterclockwise from the line CV, and is shown as CF on Fig. b. By trigonometry

$$\sigma = \sigma_c + R\cos\theta$$
$$= 1 + 8.06 \times \cos(90 - 2\theta_p)$$
$$= 1 + 8.06 \cos 60.25$$
$$= 5 \text{ ksi}$$
$$\tau_{xy} = R \sin\theta$$
$$= 8.06 \sin(60.25)$$
$$= 7 \text{ ksi}$$

• PROBLEM 6-24

Find the principal stresses and axes corresponding to the following stress combination:

$\tau_x = -1000$ psi; $\tau_{yy} = 500$ psi; $\tau_{xy} = 800$ psi

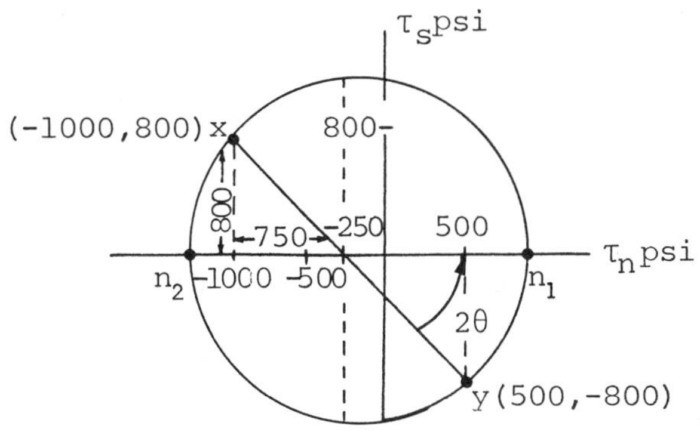

Solution: It will be convenient to use a Mohr's circle analysis in solving this problem. The Mohr's circle for plane stress is shown in the figure, for the stress values given.

The radius is calculated as

$$R = \sqrt{(750)^2 + (800)^2} = 1096.6 \text{ psi}$$

The center is at $\tau_n = .250$ psi. So, the principal stresses are

$$\tau_{n_1} = -.250 + 1096.6 = 846.6 \text{ psi}$$

$$\tau_{n_2} = -250 - 1096.6 = -1346.6 \text{ psi}$$

The location of the principal axes is found from the relation

$$\tan 2\theta = \frac{\tau_{xy}}{(\tau_{xx} - \tau_{yy})/2} = \frac{800}{750}$$

$$\theta = 23.4^\circ$$

Thus the axes n_1 and n_2 are located 23.4° ccw from the y and x axes, respectively (consult Figure).

• PROBLEM 6-25

Draw Mohr's circle and compute (a) the stresses on axes rotated 45° clockwise from x-y axes, when $\tau_{xx} = 2000$ psi; $\tau_{yy} = -1000$ psi ; and $\tau_{xy} = -500$ psi. (b) Calculate the principal stresses.

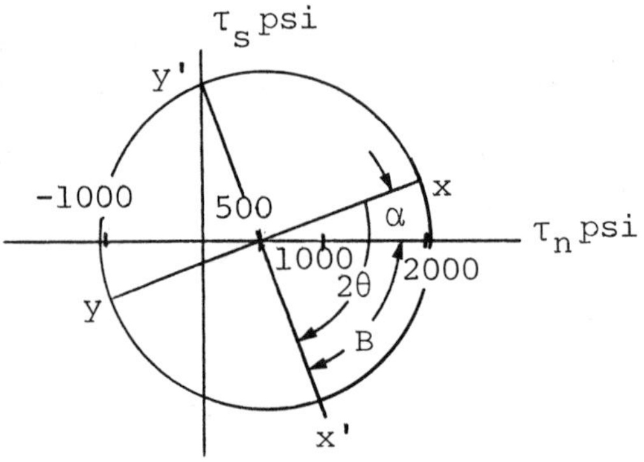

Solution: We are given a set of plane stresses and wish to calculate the state of stress at the same point for different axis orientations. We first plot the points x and y on the circle, at the stress coordinates $(\tau_{xx}, -\tau_{xy})$ and (τ_{yy}, τ_{xy}), respectively. The center is then found. From the geometry, the center of the circle will be halfway between the two normal stresses.

$$c = (\tau_{xx} + \tau_{yy})/2 = (2000 - 1000)/2 = 500$$

The circle drawn as in the Figure.

The radius of the circle is found to be

$$R = \sqrt{(2000 - 500)^2} = 1581 \text{ psi} .$$

The principal stresses are those normal stresses for which no shear stress exists. That is, they are the maximum and minimum normal stresses in the plane. Since the center is at $\tau_n = 500$ psi, the principal stresses are

$$\tau_1 = 500 + R = 500 + 1581 = 2081 \text{ psi.}$$

$$\tau_2 = 500 - R = 500 - 1581 = -1081 \text{ psi.}$$

We also need to find the stresses for x'y' axes, which result from rotating the x-y axes 45° clockwise. The angle on the Mohr's circle is always twice the physical angle, thus the Mohr's circle angle is $2\theta = 90°$ clockwise.

It will be possible to calculate $\tau_{x'x'}$, $\tau_{y'y'}$ and $\tau_{x'y'}$ if we know the value of the angle β (see the Figure). First, calculate the angle α:

$$\alpha = \arctan\left(\frac{500}{1500}\right) = 18.435°$$

So, $\beta = 90° - \alpha = 71.565°$. From the Figure, we can see that

$$\tau_{x'x'} = 500 + 1581 \cos 71.565° = 1000 \text{ psi.}$$

$$\tau_{y'y'} = 500 - 1581 \cos 71.565 = 0 \text{ psi.}$$

$$|\tau_{x'y'}| = 1581 \sin 71.565 = 1500 \text{ psi.}$$

$\tau_{x'y'}$ is positive by the Mohr's circle sign convention, since the point under the greater amount of tension (x') has a negative $\tau_{x'y'}$ value on the circle.

So $\tau_{x'y'} = +1500$ psi.

Of course, it is possible to simply read these values from the Mohr's circle, but usually a trigonometric analysis will be used when a reasonable degree of accuracy is desired.

• PROBLEM 6-26

An element in plane stress Figure (a) is subjected to stresses $\sigma_x = \sigma_y = 0$, $\tau_{xy} = 2000$ psi (pure shear). Find the stresses on all sides of an element rotated ccw through an angle of 15°, and show the results on a sketch of the element.

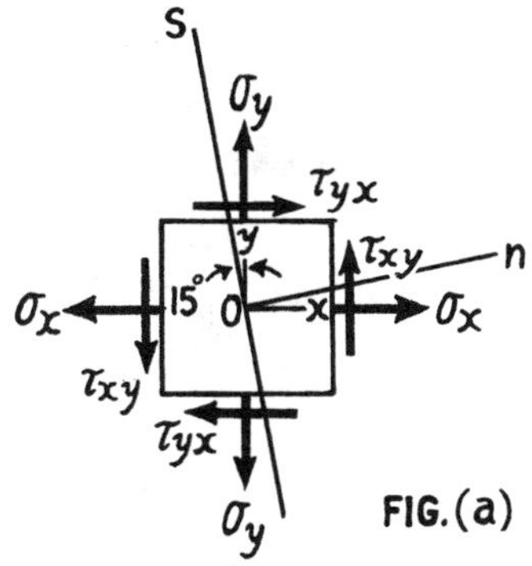

FIG.(a)

Solution: Analysis of a Mohr's circle will provide a solution to this problem. Since the figure is in pure shear, both of the points corresponding to the x and y axes are plotted on the shear (τ) axis. The Mohr's circle for this state of plane stress is shown in Figure (b).

The Mohr's circle in Figure (b) shows the orientations of the new normals to the faces of the element after rotation. Note that a rotation of θ in the physical situation corresponds to a rotation of 2θ on the Mohr's circle. Thus, the new normal n is located 30° counterclockwise from x on the Mohr's circle. The stresses can be

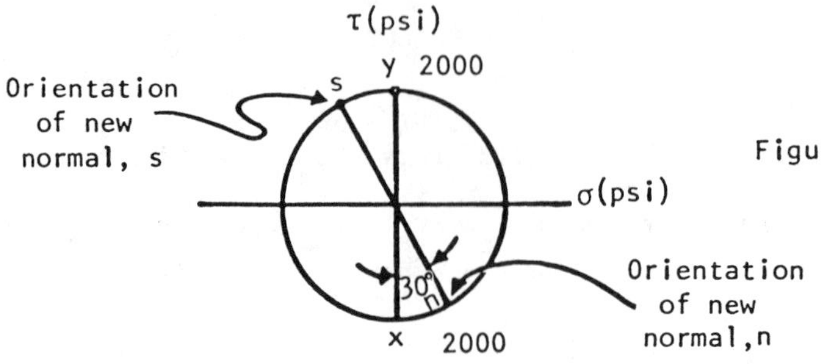

Figure(B)

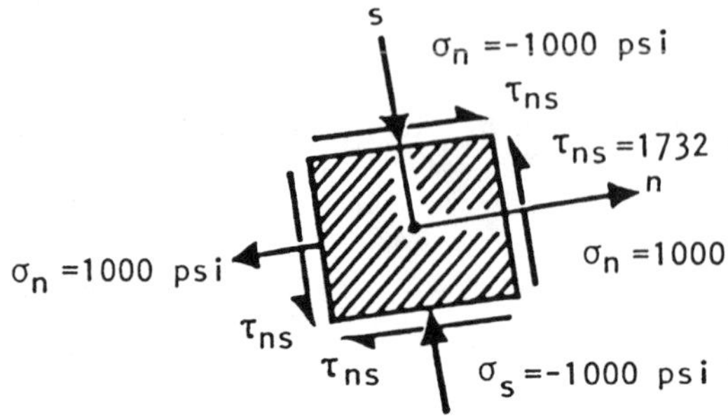

Figure(C)

calculated directly from the Mohr's circle, noting that the radius is 2000 psi.

$$\sigma_n = 2000 \sin 30^\circ = 1000 \text{ psi} \quad (T)$$

$$\sigma_s = -2000 \sin 30^\circ = -1000 \text{ psi} \quad (C)$$

$$\sigma_{ns} = 2000 \cos 30^\circ = 1732 \text{ psi}$$

These stresses are shown on the faces of the rotated element in Figure (c).

• PROBLEM 6-27

Find the principal stresses and their corresponding axes after drawing Mohr's circle for $\tau_{xx} = 0$, $\tau_{yy} = 0$, $\tau_{xy} = 500$ psi.

Solution: The state of stress described is that for which the normal stresses in the plane are both zero. Thus, the Mohr's circle is drawn by plotting $\pm \tau_{xy}$ directly on the τ_{shear} axis, as shown below.

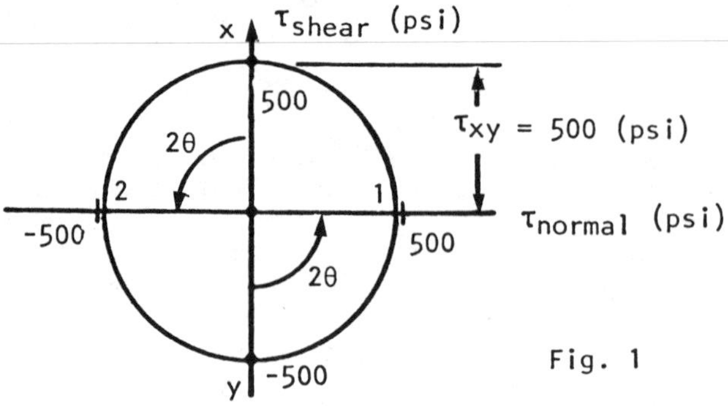

Fig. 1

The circle is then drawn with center at (0,0) and radius 500 psi. The principal stresses may simply be read from the Mohr's circle as

$$\tau_1 = 500 \text{ psi}$$

and

$$\tau_2 = -500 \text{ psi} .$$

Their orientations are $2\theta = 90^\circ$ ccw from the y- and x- axes, respectively. Thus, their physical orientations are 45° ccw from the y- and x-axes, respectively.

• PROBLEM 6-28

A simply supported beam with rectangular cross-section has nonzero stress components at the indicated point. (a) If the x-y axes are rotated 30° clockwise to position x' - y', find the nonzero stresses for x' - y'. (b) Find the maximum normal and shear stresses in the xy plane for point P of the beam.

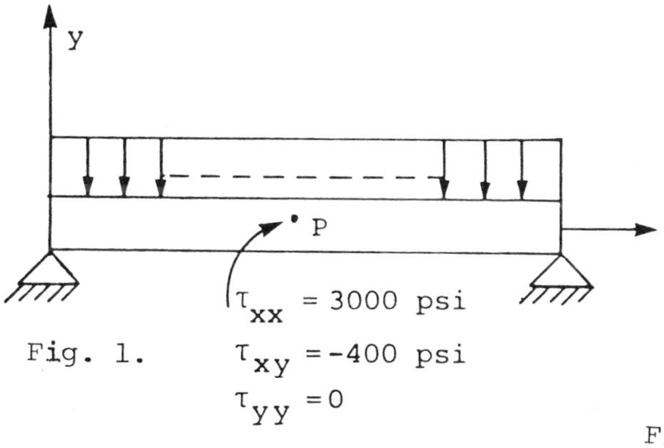

Fig. 1.

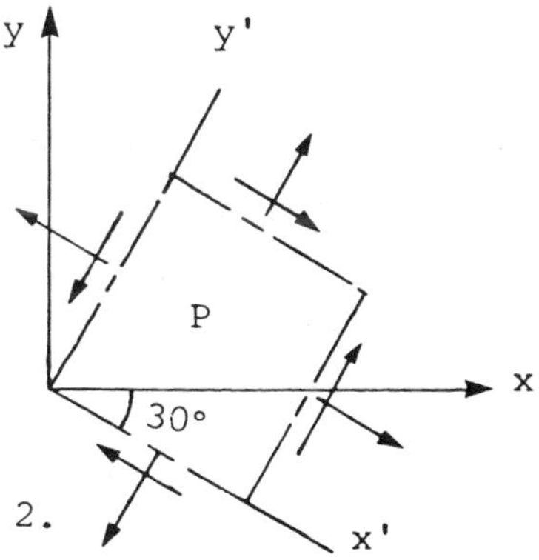

Fig. 2.

Solution: An infinitesimal rectangle depicting interfaces for referency xy in the neighborhood of P is shown in Fig. 2(a) while an infinitesimal rectangle is shown in Fig. 2(b) depicting interfaces for x'y' in the same neighborhood.

Using the given stresses, we can now construct a Mohr's circle for the state of plane stress at P. This is done in Fig. 3.

The radius of the circle is

$$R = \sqrt{1500^2 + 400^2} = 1552 \text{ psi.}$$

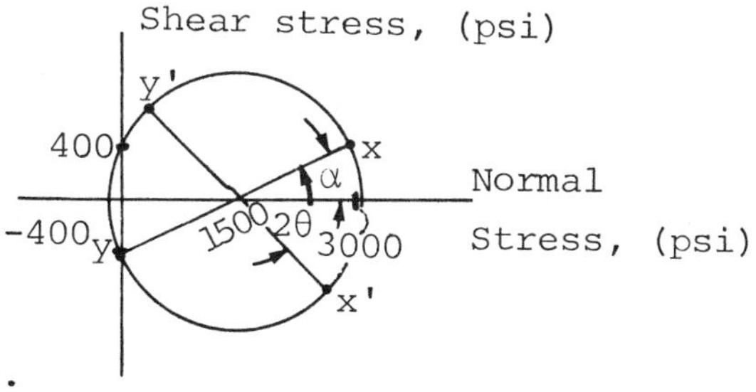

Fig. 3.

α = arctan 4/15 = 14.9°

So,

$$\tau_{x'x'} = 1500 + 1552 \cos(14.9^\circ - 60^\circ)$$

$$\tau_{x'x'} = 2596 \text{ psi}$$

$$\tau_{y'y'} = 1500 - 1552 \cos(14.9^\circ - 60^\circ)$$

$$\tau_{y'y'} = 404 \text{ psi}$$

We can note from Fig. 3, that $\tau_{x'y'}$ is positive by the Mohr's circle sign convention. Thus, $\tau_{x'y'} = 1552 \sin 45.1^\circ = 1100$ psi

Since we are treating this as a case of plane stress all other stress components are zero.

The maximum stresses at P can also be found from the Mohr's circle (Fig. 3).

$$\tau_{max,normal} = 1500 + 1552 = 3052 \text{ psi (tension)}$$

$$\tau_{min.,nornal} = \tau_{max.,compression} = 1500 - 1552 = -52 \text{ psi (compression)}$$

The maximum shearing stress is equal to the radius of the circle. Therefore,

$$\tau_{shear,max} = 1552 \text{ psi} .$$

• PROBLEM 6-29

An open-ended, thin-walled cylinder r = 10 in. and t = 0.1 in., is acted on by an internal pressure p and an axial force F. Find the values of p and F acting in each of the following two situations:

(a) $\sigma_m = 15{,}000$ psi $\sigma_n = 5{,}000$ psi $\tau_{mn} = ?$

(b) $\sigma_m = 15{,}000$ psi $\sigma_n = 15{,}000$ psi $\tau_{mn} = ?$

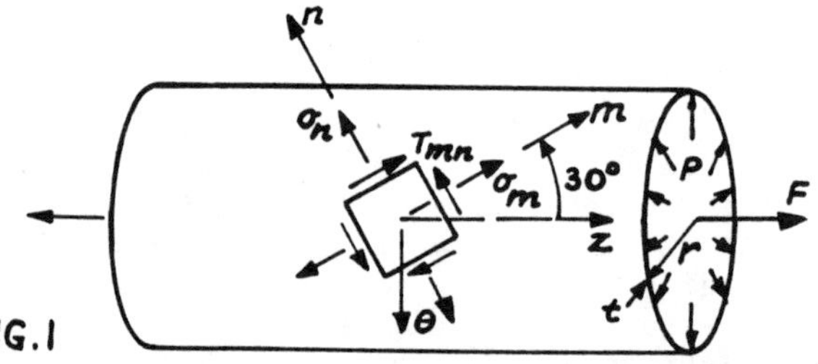

FIG. 1

Solution: The pressure in the cylinder creates stresses

$$\sigma_\theta = pr/t \qquad \text{(a)}$$

and

$$\sigma_r = 0 \qquad \text{(b)}$$

where p is the internal pressure, r is the radius of the cylinder and t is the thickness of the cylinder wall. These equations are the result of a force balance on the cylinder and are good only for thin-walled cylinders. Since the cylinder is open at the ends no axial stress, σ_z, can be created by the internal pressure. (This model would be of use to an engineer considering pipe flow under pressure.) In addition to the internal pressure, there is an axial force F which will create an axial stress given by

$$\sigma_z = \frac{F}{A} = \frac{F}{2\pi r t} \qquad (c)$$

where A is the cross-sectional area of the cylinder.

In this problem, we are given stresses in the m and n directions (see Figure 1). We are asked to find the values of p and F. We will make use of the fact that σ_z and σ_θ are principal stresses (no shearing stresses occur along the z and θ axes) and we will use a Mohr's circle analysis to determine the principal stresses.

(a) $\sigma_m = 15,000$ psi $\quad \sigma_n = 5,000$ psi $\quad \tau_{mn} = ?$

We cannot plot the exact Mohr's circle from this information alone, since τ_{mn} is not given. However, we know that the orientation of the m-n axes is such that the m-axis is 30° counterclockwise from the z-axis. This means that the point m on the Mohr's circle will be twice this angle, or 60°, counterclockwise from the point z, which must lie on the horizontal axis. The Mohr's circle for the state of stress in part (a) is shown in Figure 2.

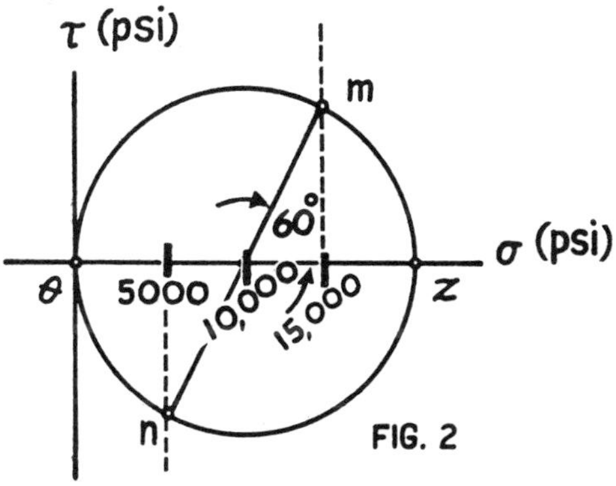

FIG. 2

Figure 2 was drawn in the following order:

(1) Mark off dashed lines at 5000 and 15,000 psi. The points m and n will be along these lines.

(2) Through the center, c = 10,000, (halfway between σ_m and σ_n) draw a line 60° counterclockwise from the σ-axis.

(3) The intersections of this line with the dashed lines are points m and n. The Mohr's circle may now be drawn.

The radius of the circle may be found from the relation

$$R \cos 60^\circ = 5000 \text{ psi.}$$

$$R = 10,000 \text{ psi}$$

Therefore, $\sigma_z = 10,000 + 10,000 = 20,000$ psi

$\sigma_\theta = 10,000 - 10,000 = 0$ psi

We are now in a position to calculate F and p. From equation (a),

$$\sigma_\theta = \frac{pr}{t} = 0 ,$$

therefore,

$$p = 0$$

From equation (c)

$$F = (2\pi r t)(\sigma_z)$$

$$F = 2\pi(10'')(0.1'')(20,000 \text{ psi}) = 126,000 \text{ lb.}$$

(b) We are now given the stresses

$\sigma_m = 15{,}000$ psi $\quad \sigma_n = 15{,}000$ psi $\quad \tau_{mn} = ?$

We will now attempt to draw the Mohr's circle as in part (a). We note that both m and n must be at 15,000 psi. Thus we have the situation in Figure 3(a).

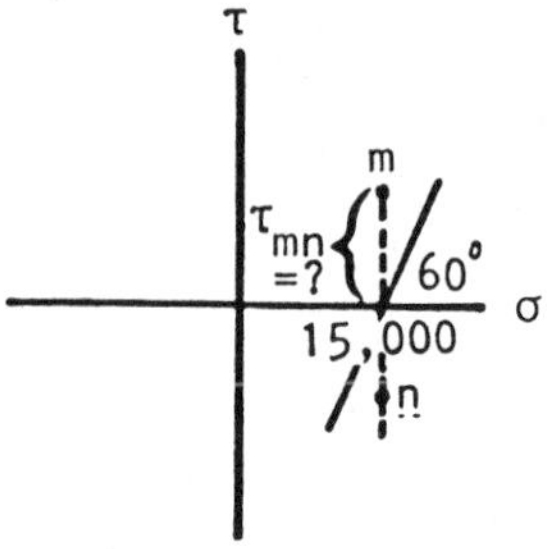

Fig. 3a.

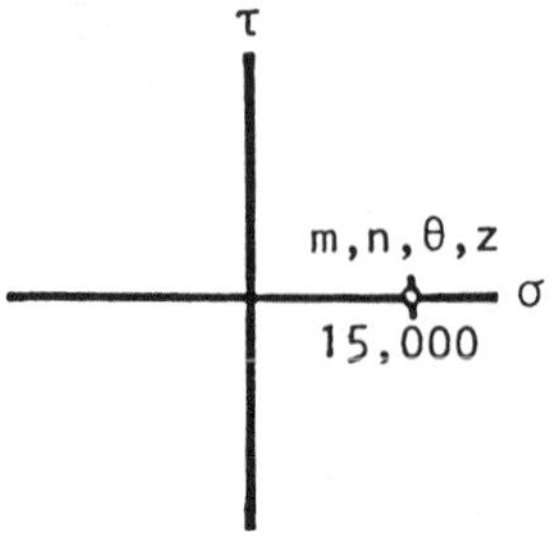

Fig. 3b.

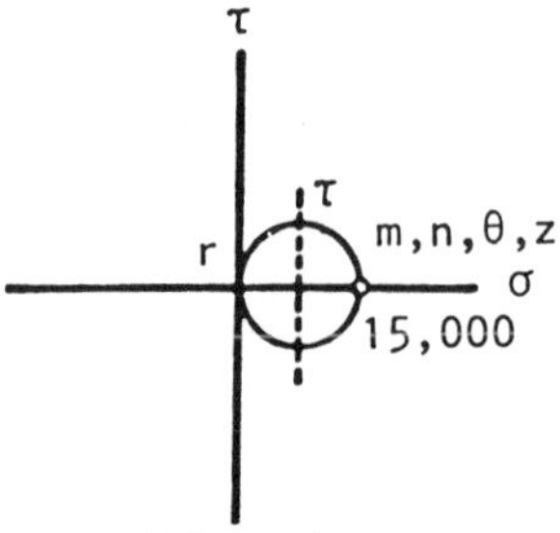

Fig. 4.

The only intersection between the dashed and solid lines is at $\tau_{mn} = 0$, $\sigma = 15{,}000$ psi. This means that the radius of the Mohr's circle is zero, and there are no shears for any axis orientation. The state of stress in this case is shown in Figure 3(b). From this figure,

$$\sigma_z = \sigma_\theta = 15{,}000 \text{ psi}$$

From equation (a)

$$\frac{(\sigma_\theta)t}{r} = p$$

$$p = \frac{(15{,}000 \text{ psi})(.1'')}{10''} = 150 \text{ psi}$$

From equation (b)

$$F = 2\pi(10'')(0.1'')(15{,}000 \text{ psi}) = 94{,}250 \text{ lb.}$$

Recalling (from Figure 3(b)) that there are no shearing stresses present, we see that at 150 psi internal pressure, it would take an axial force of 94,250 lb. to eliminate the shearing stresses in the z-θ plane from the cylinder wall.

Figure 4 is based on Fig. 3(b). There are no shear stresses in the θ-z plane no matter what the angle of rotation. This is because the normal stresses in the θ and z directions are equal. The normal stress in the r direction is not equal to σ_θ and σ_z however. Therefore, there are shear stresses in the r-θ and r-z planes which are zero at a rotation of 0°, and ± 7500 at rotations of 90° on the Mohr's circle, which correspond to 45° rotations in the physical situation.

• PROBLEM 6-30

A tubular member is subjected to the axial forces shown. Compute the shear stress and normal stress at the indicated point A on a plane having the inclination shown.

<u>Solution</u>: Since the cylinder carries only the axial load P, use the

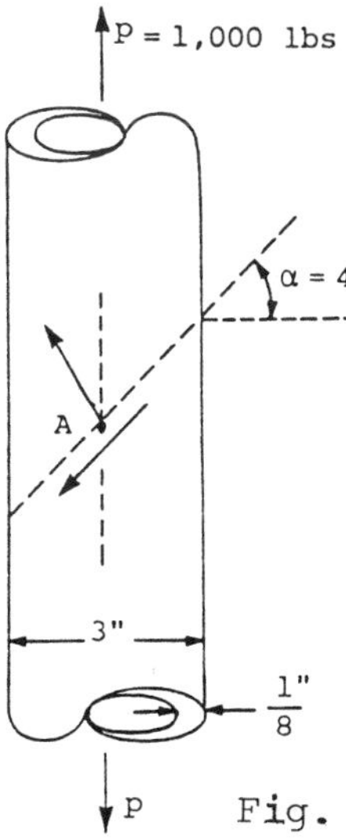

Fig. 1.

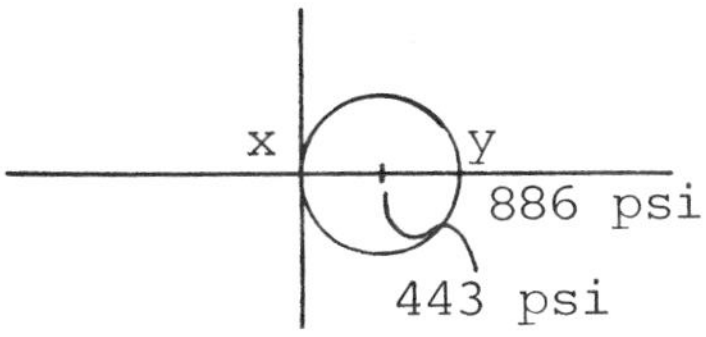

Fig. 2.

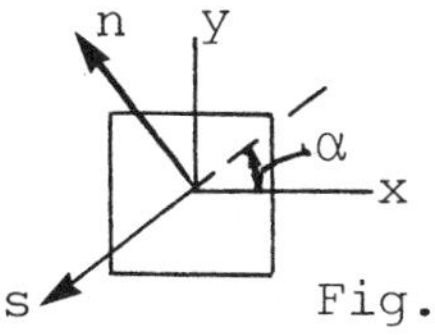

Fig. 3.

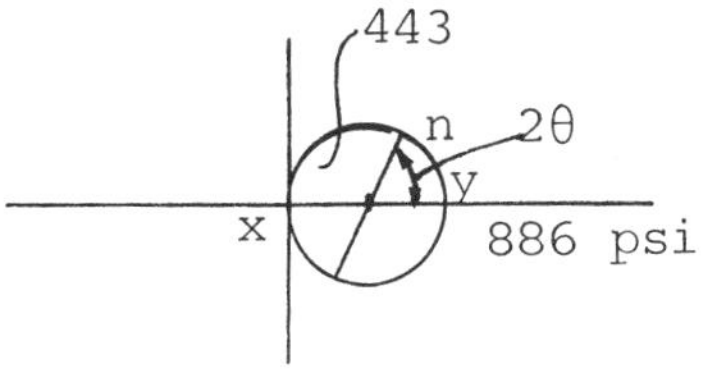

Fig. 4.

Mohr's circle for plane stress to give the desired stresses.

The stress field is

$$\sigma_x = 0$$

$$\sigma_y = \frac{P}{A} = \frac{1000 \text{ lb.}}{\pi\left(\frac{d_0^2 - d_i^2}{4}\right)} = \frac{1000 \text{ lb.}}{\frac{\pi}{4}\left(3''^2 - 2.75''^2\right)}$$

$$= 885.7 \text{ psi}$$

$$\sigma_z = 0$$

In addition, no applied shear stresses are present. Thus, the x-y axes are the principal axes for this state of stress. The Mohr's circle is that of pure tension:

We now want to find the normal and shear stresses on a plane defined by the normal n, shown in Fig. 3.

We must therefore rotate $(90^\circ + \alpha)$ counterclockwise from the x-axis (or α counterclockwise from y-axis) to reach the n-axis, in the physical situation. Recalling that we always rotate through twice the physical angle to reach a new axis on the Mohr's circle, we have

$$2\theta = 2(\alpha) = 80^\circ \text{ ccw from y-axis.}$$

Thus the Mohr's circle becomes as shown in Fig. 4.

The normal stress is simply

$$\tau_{nn} = 443 + 443 \cos 80^\circ = 520 \text{ psi}$$

The magnitude of the shear stress is

$$|\tau_{ns}| = 443 \sin 80^\circ = 436 \text{ psi}$$

We note however that the point n is in the first quadrant of the Mohr's circle (that is, to the right of and above the center). Thus, by convention, τ_{ns} is negative:

$$\tau_{ns} = -436 \text{ psi} .$$

At a certain point in a body the state of stress is two-dimensional. At this point, the principal stresses are 8 ksi tensile and 4 ksi compressive, the first acting at an angle of $+20^\circ$ to the x axis. Find the stresses on the planes normal to x and y at the same point. What is the maximum shear stress at the point and on what plane does it occur? On what planes are the normal stresses zero?

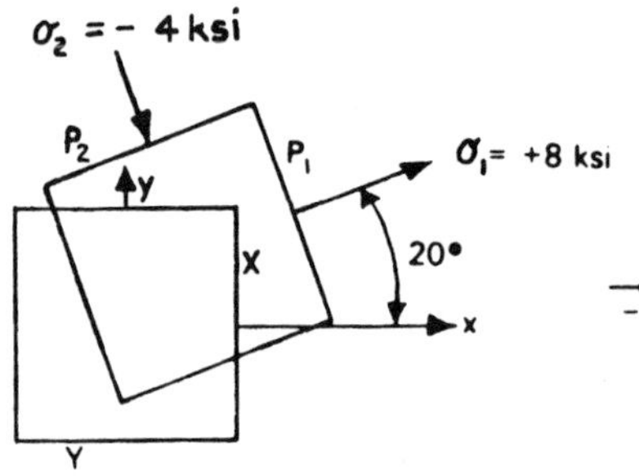

(1)

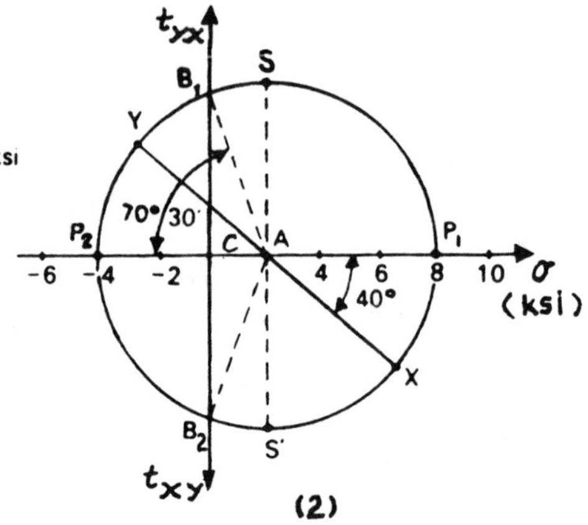

(2)

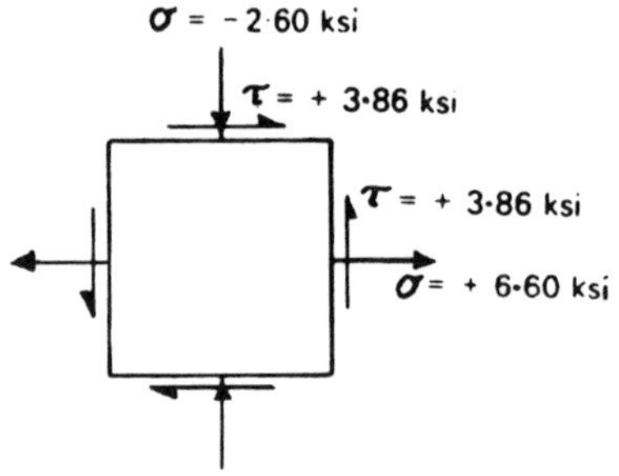

(3)

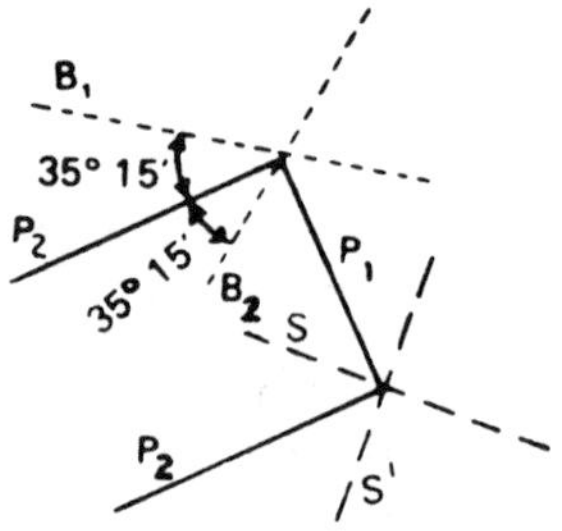

(4)

Solution: To help visualize and simplify the solution we draw both an element of the material and Mohr's circle.

On Mohr's circle, we place the maximum normal stress on the σ axis at 8 ksi, the value of the first principal stress, σ_1 . The minimum normal stress is placed at -4 ksi, on the σ axis, which is σ_2 . We denote the principal planes which correspond to the given principal stresses by P_1 and P_2.

The center of Mohr's circle, C, is found by $(\sigma_x + \sigma_y)/2$ where σ_x and σ_y are the normal stresses on perpendicular planes. Using the principal stresses σ_1, σ_2 we get

$$C = \frac{8K + (-4K)}{2}$$

$$C = 2K$$

The radius is the distance from the center of the circle to a principal stress.

$$R = 8K - 2K$$
$$= 6K$$

To find the stresses normal to the x and y axis, we must first locate these axes on Mohr's circle. The angle from the x-axis to the first principal axis is $+20^\circ$, so on Mohr's circle $2\theta_1 = 40^\circ$. However, because we have the principal axis at $2\theta_1 = 0^\circ$ the x-axis must be at -40°, as shown in Figure 2.

The stresses on this plane are found by trigonometry:

$$\sigma_x = C + R\cos(-40^\circ)$$
$$= 2K + 6K \times (.766)$$
$$= 6.60 \text{ ksi}$$
$$\sigma_y = C - R\cos(-40^\circ)$$
$$= 2K - 6K \times (.766)$$
$$= -2.60$$
$$\tau_{xy} = R\sin(-40^\circ)$$

$\tau_{xy} = -3.86$ ksi

A negative τ_{xy} on the Mohr circle is a positive shear in the physical situation as indicated in Fig. 3. In rality $\tau_{xy} = \tau_{yx}$ so the shear on the y plane is also shown in the positive direction in Fig. 3.

The maximum shears are equal to the value of the radius of Mohr's circle, and are $\tau_{max} = 6$ ksi and occur on planes S and S'. By inspection of Mohr's circle we see that plane S lies halfway between the principal planes and therefore the plane is oriented 45° to the principal plane.

The planes of zero normal stress are represented by points B_1 and B_2 on the vertical axis of the graph. Radius AB_1 is $70^\circ 30'$ clockwise from radius AP_2.

$$2\theta = \text{arc cos}\,\frac{CA}{AB_1} = \text{arc cos}\,\frac{2K}{6K} = \text{arc cos}\,\frac{1}{3} = 70^\circ 30'$$

Therefore plane B_1 is $35^\circ 15'$ clockwise from plane P_2 (as shown in Figure 4). Similarly, B_2 is $35^\circ 15'$ anticlockwise from P_2.

• PROBLEM 6-32

At a certain point the principal stresses are $\sigma_1 = 8000$ psi, $\sigma_2 = 20{,}000$ psi and $\sigma_3 = 12{,}000$ psi. Find the maximum shear stress at this point and the shear stress on the octahedral planes.

Solution: If we consider a general Mohr's circle, as in Figure 1, we see that the radius of the circle is given by

$$R = \frac{\sigma_1 - \sigma_2}{2}$$

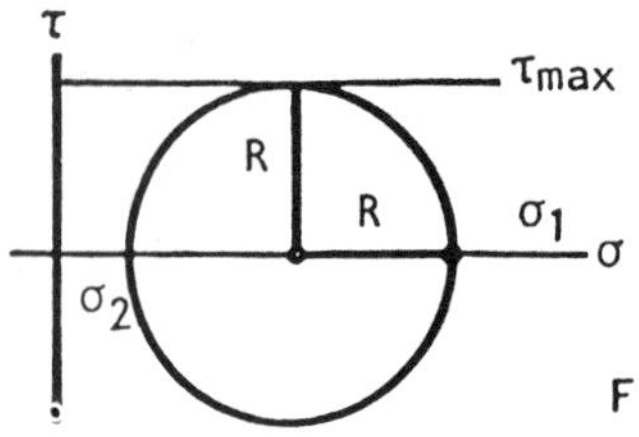

Fig. 1

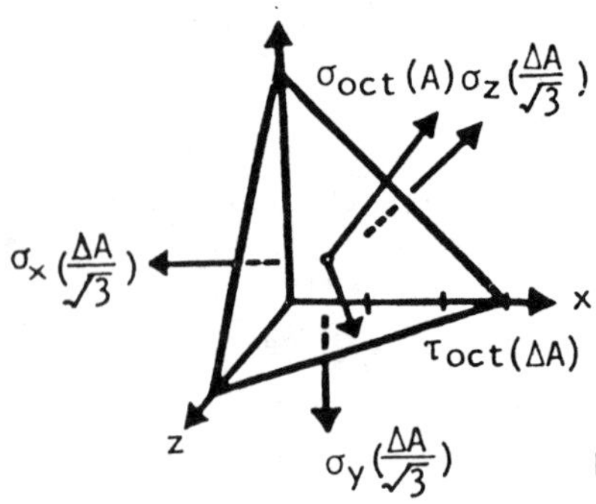

Fig. 2

where σ_1 and σ_2 are the extreme or principal normal stresses. The maximum shear stress is equal to the radius of the circle, so we know that, in general,

$$\tau_1 = \frac{\sigma_1 - \sigma_2}{2}$$

Similarly

$$\tau_2 = \frac{\sigma_2 - \sigma_3}{2}$$

$$\tau_3 = \frac{\sigma_3 - \sigma_1}{2}$$

By substituting the values for σ_1, σ_2, and σ_3 in these expressions, we find

$$\tau_1 = \frac{20K - 8K}{2} = 6 \text{ ksi}$$

$$\tau_2 = \frac{20K - 12K}{2} = 4 \text{ ksi}$$

$$\tau_3 = \frac{12K - 8K}{2} = 2 \text{ ksi}$$

Therefore, the maximum shear stress is 6 ksi. The octahedral plane is one that is equally inclined to the x,y, and z axes. The shear stress on this plane is given by

$$\tau_{oct} = \frac{1}{3}\sqrt{(\sigma_1 - \sigma_2)^2 + (\sigma_1 - \sigma_3)^2 + (\sigma_2 - \sigma_3)^2}$$

$$= \frac{1}{3}\sqrt{(8K - 20K)^2 + (8K - 12K)^2 + (20K - 12K)^2}$$

$$= 4988 \text{ psi} .$$

• PROBLEM 6-33

For interfaces normal to the x-y reference plane, calculate (a) the algebraic maximum stress, and (b) the algebraic minimal normal stress, corresponding to the stress tensor

$$\tau_{ij} = \begin{pmatrix} 2000 & 5000 & -1000 \\ 5000 & -3000 & 3000 \\ -1000 & 3000 & 500 \end{pmatrix}$$

<u>Solution:</u> Interfaces normal to the x-y plane are acted on by normal

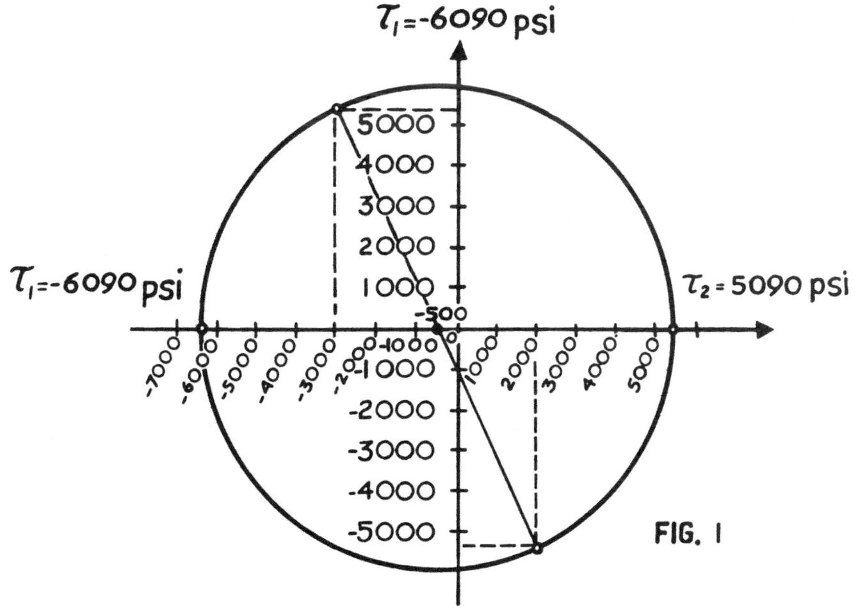

FIG. 1

stresses $\sigma_{x'x'}$ and $\sigma_{y'y'}$ depending on the orientation. Therefore we want to find the principal stresses for the x-y plane. If we construct Mohr's circle for the x-y plane, shown in Figure 1, we see that

$$\sigma_c = \frac{\sigma_{xx} + \sigma_{yy}}{2}$$
$$= \frac{2000 - 3000}{2}$$
$$= -500 \text{ psi}$$

The radius is found using Pythagoras' theorem

$$R^2 = [2000 - (-500)]^2 + (5000)^2$$
$$R = \sqrt{(2500)^2 + (5000)^2}$$
$$= 5590$$

Therefore, the principal stresses are given by moving along the σ-axis from the center a distance R in each direction.

$$\sigma_a = \sigma_c + R$$
$$= -500 + 5590$$
$$= 5090 \text{ psi}$$
$$\sigma_b = \sigma_c - R$$
$$= -500 - 5590$$
$$= -6090 \text{ psi}$$

The algebraic maximum means the number farthest to the right on the number line, and is seen on Mohr's circle as

$$\tau_2 = 5090 \text{ psi}$$

The algebraic minimum is the number farthest to the left and is therefore

$$\tau_1 = -6090 \text{ psi}$$

• PROBLEM 6-34

At a point in a stressed body, there are stresses of 1 ksi T on a vertical plane and 7 ksi C on a horizontal plane. A positive unknown shearing stress acts on the vertical plane and the maximum shearing stress at the point has a magnitude of 5 ksi. Determine the shearing stress on the vertical plane and also the principal stresses. Show the results on an appropriate sketch.

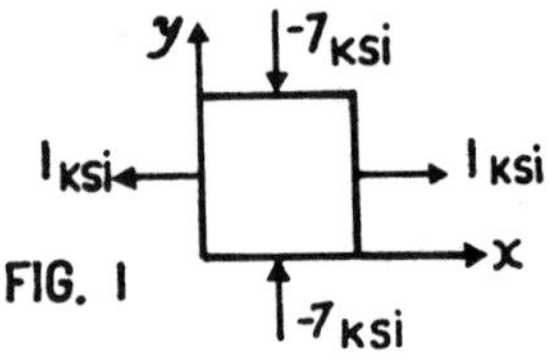

FIG. 1

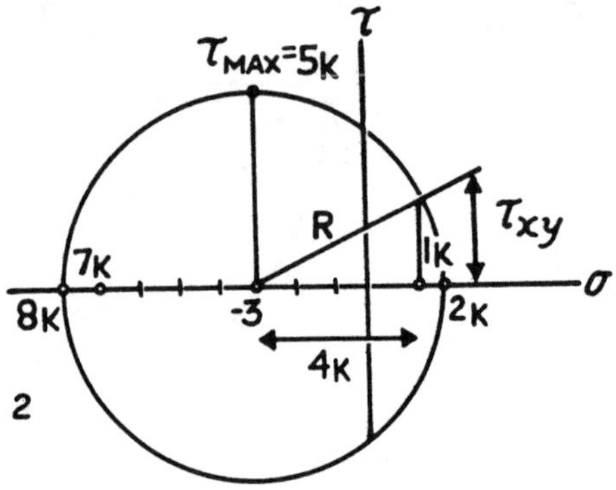

FIG. 2

Solution: With the stress field given, and shown in Figure 1, we can construct Mohr's circle.

We begin by plotting the normal stresses on the horizontal axis. From Figure 1 we see that

$$\sigma_{xx} = 1 \text{ ksi}$$

$$\sigma_{yy} = -7 \text{ ksi}$$

using the standard sign convention of positive-tension.

The center of the circle is given by:

$$\sigma_c = \frac{\sigma_{xx} + \sigma_{yy}}{2}$$

$$= \frac{1K - 7K}{2}$$

$$= -3 \text{ ksi}$$

Because the shear stress is plotted on the vertical axis, the maximum shear stress gives the magnitude of the radius of the circle.

$$R = \tau_{max} = 5 \text{ ksi}$$

We can now draw the circle by using the center -3 ksi and the radius, 5 ksi as shown in Figure 2.

The principal stresses are found at the extremes of the circle on the horizontal axis.

$$\sigma_1 = \sigma_c + R$$

$$= -3 \text{ ksi} + 5 \text{ ksi}$$

$$= 2 \text{ ksi} \quad \text{which is tension}$$

$$\sigma_2 = \sigma_c - R$$

$$= -3 \text{ ksi} - 5 \text{ ksi}$$

$$= -8 \text{ ksi} \quad \text{which is compression.}$$

By using Pythagoras' theorem we can find the shear stress on our original element.

$$R^2 = (\sigma_x - \sigma_c)^2 + \tau_{xy}^2$$

$$\tau_{xy} = \sqrt{R^2 - (\sigma_x - \sigma_c)^2}$$

$$\tau_{xy} = \sqrt{(5K)^2 - (1K - (-3K))^2}$$

$$= \sqrt{25K^2 - 16K^2}$$

$$= \sqrt{9K^2}$$

$$= 3 \text{ ksi}$$

• PROBLEM 6-35

At a point in a stressed member, there exists on the horizontal plane a normal stress of 10 ksi C and an unknown positive shearing stress. One principal stress at the point is 2 ksi C, and the maximum shearing stress has a magnitude of 13 ksi. Determine the unknown stresses on the horizontal and vertical planes and show these stresses as well as the principal stresses on a sketch.

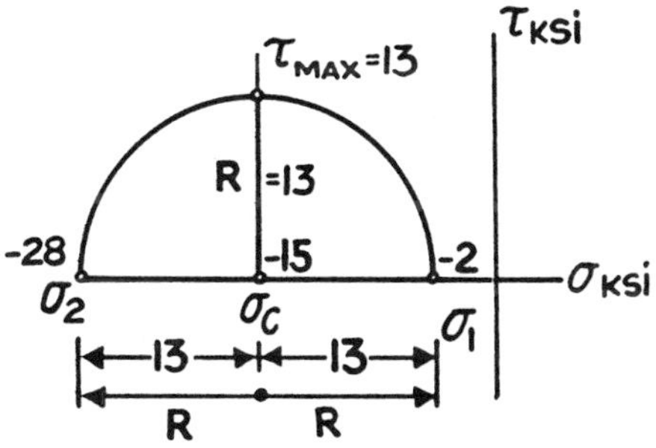

FIG. 1

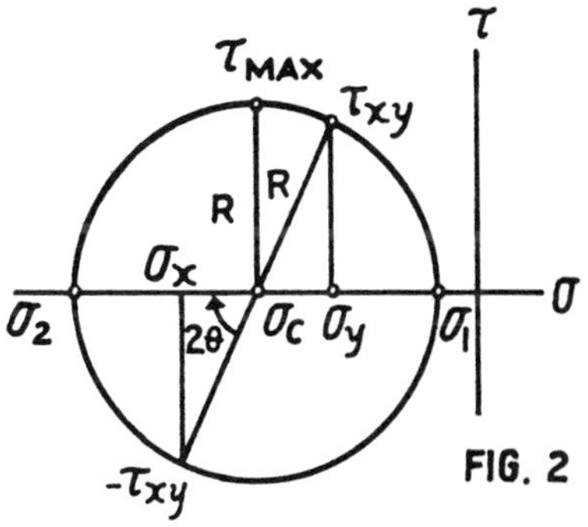

FIG. 2

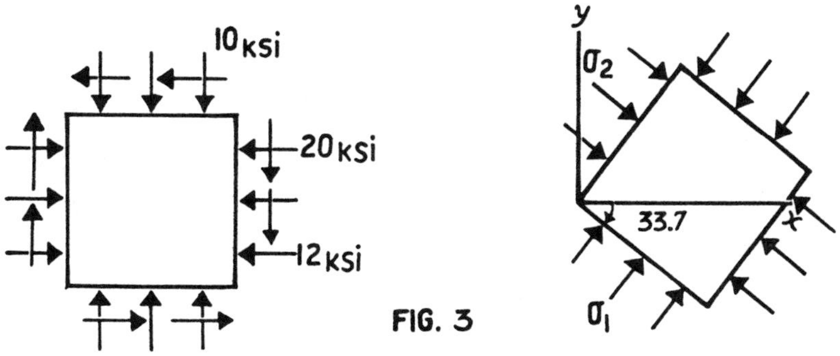

FIG. 3

Solution: We know by the geometry of Mohr's circle that the maximum shear stress is equal to the radius of the circle.

$$\tau_{max} = 13 \text{ ksi}$$

so $$R = 13 \text{ ksi}$$

The principal normal stress farthest to the right on the x axis is σ_1. The principal normal stress farthest to the left on the x-axis is σ_2. The principal stress given is σ_1. This is because the non-principal normal stress given is to the left of the principal stress given, therefore the other principal stress is even farther to the left.

We can also determine the second principal stress by geometry, if we notice that the distance between the two principal stresses is equal to 2R.

$$R = \frac{\sigma_1 - \sigma_2}{2}$$

By substituting for R and σ_1 we have

$$13 \text{ ksi} = \frac{-2 \text{ ksi} - \sigma_2}{2}$$

$$26 \text{ ksi} = -2\text{ksi} - \sigma_2$$

$$\sigma_2 = -28 \text{ ksi}$$

We next locate the center of the circle by using the fact that σ_c is distance R from both principal stresses

$$\sigma_c = \sigma_1 - R$$
$$= -2 - 13 \text{ ksi}$$
$$= -15 \text{ ksi}$$

As a check we calculate σ_2.

$$\sigma_2 = \sigma_c - 13 \text{ ksi}$$
$$= -15 - 13 \text{ ksi}$$
$$= -28 \text{ ksi}$$

Now that we have the radius and the center of the circle, we can use Pythagoras' theorem to find the unknown shear stress.

$$R^2 = \tau_{xy}^2 + (-15 - (-10))^2$$

$$(-13)^2 = \tau_{xy}^2 + (-5)^2$$

$$\tau_{xy} = \sqrt{169 - 25}$$

$$= \sqrt{144}$$

$$= 12 \text{ ksi}$$

Since the normal stress given is on the horizontal plane, it is acting in the y-direction and is therefore σ_y

To find σ_x, we make use of the fact that the center of the circle is equidistant from σ_x and σ_y (just as it is from any pair of perpendicular stresses).

$$\sigma_c = \frac{\sigma_x + \sigma_y}{2}$$

$$-15 \text{ ksi} = \frac{\sigma_x - 10\text{ksi}}{2}$$

$$\sigma_x = -30 - (-10) \text{ ksi}$$
$$= -20 \text{ ksi}$$

Finally, we can find the angle between the normal and principal planes by trigonometry.

$$R \sin 2\theta = \tau_{xy}$$

Solving for θ

$$\sin 2\theta = \frac{\tau_{xy}}{R}$$

$$\theta = \frac{\sin^{-1}(-12/13)}{2}$$

$$= -33.7^{\circ}$$

• PROBLEM 6-36

The stresses shown in Fig. 1 act at a point in a structural member. The tensile principal stress is known to be 1200 psi. Determine:
(a) The maximum shearing stress.
(b) The orientation of the planes on which the stress of part a acts.
(c) The shearing stress on the horizontal plane.

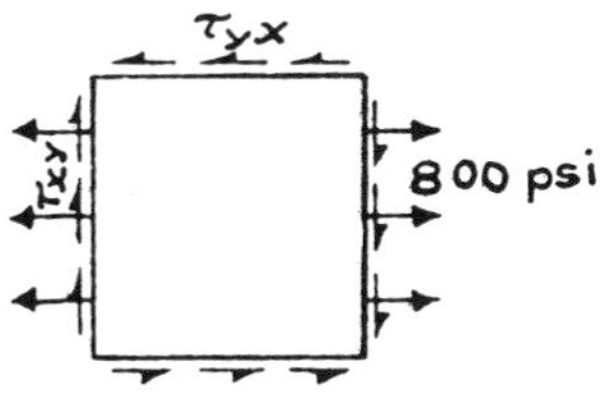

FIG. 1

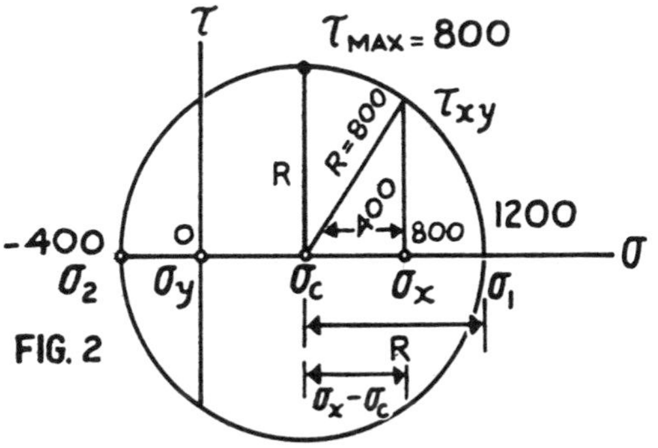

FIG. 2

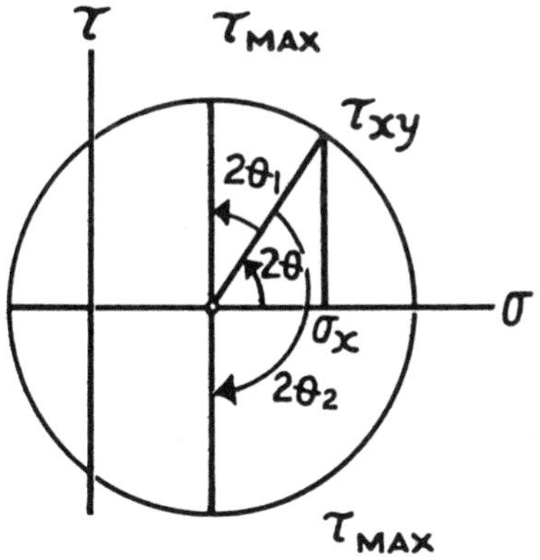

FIG. 3

Solution: We can construct Mohr's circle in this case with τ_{xy} unknown. We know that $\sigma_x = 800$, $\sigma_y = 0$, and the tensile principal stress is 1200 psi. By plotting these values on the σ-axis, as in Figure 2, we see that

$$\sigma_c = \frac{\sigma_x + \sigma_y}{2}$$

$$= \frac{800 + 0}{2}$$

$$= 400 \text{ psi}$$

Since we know one principal stress we can find the radius of the circle

$$R = \sigma_1 - \sigma_c$$
$$= 800$$

The maximum shear stress must equal the radius of the circle since that is the highest point on the τ-axis which can be reached.

$$\therefore \tau_{max} = 800 \text{ psi}$$

From Figure 3 we can find the orientation of the maximum shear planes relative to the x-axis. They are denoted by θ_1 and θ_2. We can also get the relations from Mohr's circle

$$2\theta_1 = 90 - 2\theta$$

$$2\theta_2 = -2\theta_1 - 90,$$

the angles here are negative because we are rotating clockwise.

By trigonometry

$$R \cos 2\theta = 400$$

$$\cos 2\theta = \frac{400}{800}$$

$$2\theta = 60^\circ$$

Therefore

$$2\theta_1 = 90 - 60$$

$$= 30$$

$$\theta_1 = 15^\circ$$

$$2\theta_2 = -60 - 90$$

$$= -150$$

$$\theta_2 = -75^\circ$$

The shearing stress on the horizontal plane can be found by Pythagoras' theorem

$$R^2 = (\sigma_x - \sigma_c)^2 + \tau_{xy}^2$$

$$\tau_{xy}^2 = (800)^2 - (800 - 400)^2$$

$$\tau_{xy} = \sqrt{(800)^2 - (400)^2}$$

$$= 692.8 \text{ psi}$$

• PROBLEM 6-37

Given the state of stress shown in Fig. 1, transform it (a) into the principal stresses, and (b) into the maximum shearing stresses and the associated normal stresses. Show the results for both cases on properly oriented elements.

Solution: To construct Mohr's circle for the given state of stress, we first find the center by geometry.

$$\sigma_c = \frac{\sigma_x + \sigma_y}{2}$$

$$= \frac{-2 + 4}{2}$$

$$= 1 \text{ ksi}$$

We know a point, A, on the circle at (σ_x, τ_{xy})

$$A = (-2, -4)$$

Using Pythagoras' theorem we can find the radius of the circle.

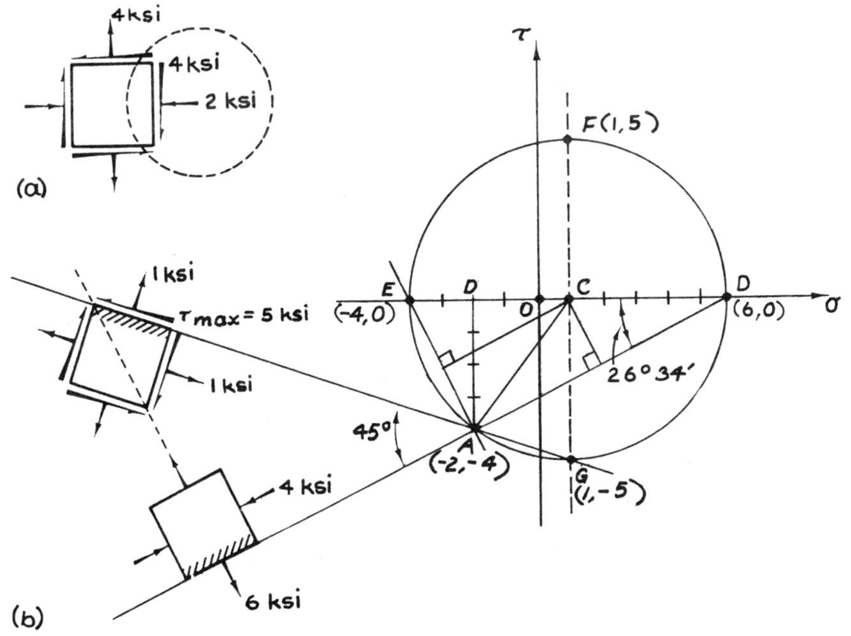

FIG.1

$$R^2 = \tau_{xy}^2 + (\sigma_x - \sigma_c)^2$$
$$= (-4)^2 + (-2-1)^2$$
$$= 16 + 9$$
$$R = 5$$

We can find the principal stresses by using the formulas:

$$\sigma_1 = \sigma_c + R$$
$$= 1 \text{ ksi} + 5 \text{ ksi}$$
$$= 6 \text{ ksi}$$
$$\sigma_2 = \sigma_c - R$$
$$= 1 \text{ ksi} - 5 \text{ ksi}$$
$$= -4 \text{ ksi}$$

The maximum shearing stress is equal to the radius of the circle.

$$\tau_{max} = 5 \text{ ksi}$$

The direction in which σ_1 acts is at one-half the angle between CB and CA on the circle. A line bisecting angle ACB will bisect line AB since AC equals AB. By geometry, this line is perpendicular to AB and since the principal stress is perpendicular to the plane on which it acts, AB must be the direction of the principal plane. By a similar argument line EA is the plane on which σ_2 acts.

Point F gives the values for maximum shear stress and corresponding normal stress.

$$\tau_{max} = 5 \text{ ksi}$$

σ' is read on the σ-axis.

$$\sigma' = 1 \text{ ksi}$$

Using a similar geometrical argument to find the planes for maximum shear stress, we draw a line from A to G, which gives the direction of the maximum shear stress plane.

The complete results are shown on sketches in Fig. 1 on properly oriented elements. The angles shown are determined from suitable trigonometric relations. Thus since tan DBA = AD/DB 4/8 = 0.5, the angle DBA = 26°34'. The plane of maximum shear is located at 45° from the planes of principal stress.

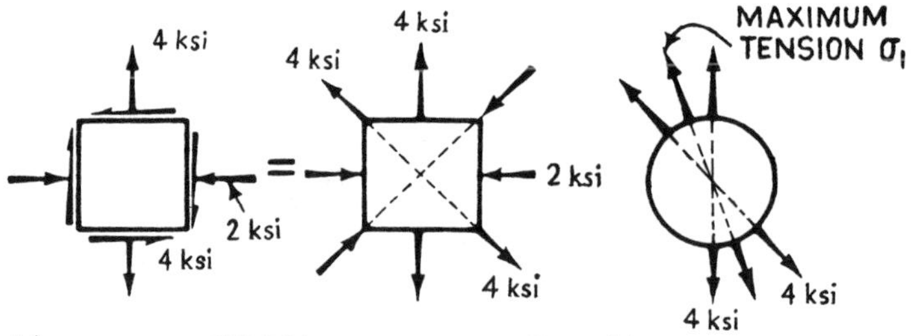

FIG. 2 (a) FIG. 2 (b) FIG. 2 (c)

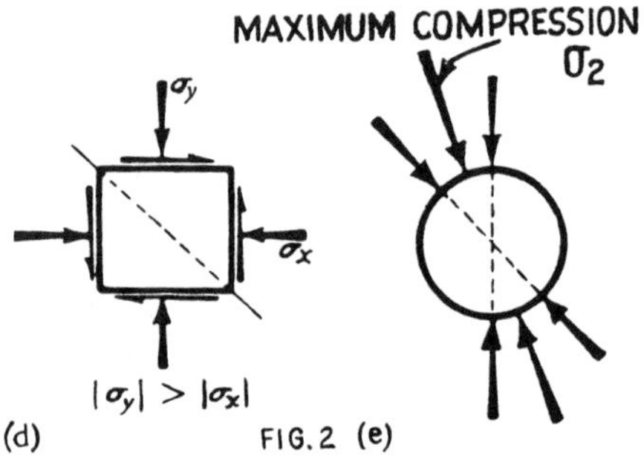

FIG. 2 (d) FIG. 2 (e)

It is significant to note that the approximate direction of the algebraically larger principal stress found in the above example might have been anticipated. Instead of thinking in terms of the normal and the shearing stresses as given in the original data, Fig. 2a, an equivalent problem in Fig. 2b may be considered. Here the shearing stresses have been replaced by the equivalent tension-compression stresses acting along the proper shear diagonals. Then, for qualitative reasoning, the outline of the original element may be obliterated, and the tensile stresses may be singled out as in Fig. 2c. From this new diagram it is apparent that regardless of the magnitudes of the particular stresses involved, the resultant maximum tensile stress must act somewhere between the given tensile stress and the positive shear diagonal. In other words, the line of action of the algebraically larger principal stress is "straddled" by the algebraically larger given normal stress and the positive shear diagonal. The use of the negative shear diagonal, located at 90° to the positive shear diagonal, is helpful in visualizing this effect for cases where both given normal stresses are compressive, Figs. 2(d) and (e). This procedure provides a qualitative check on the orientation of an element for the principal stresses.

Using Mohr's circle, transform the stresses shown in Fig. 1 into stresses acting on the plane at an angle of $22\frac{1}{2}^\circ$ with the vertical axis.

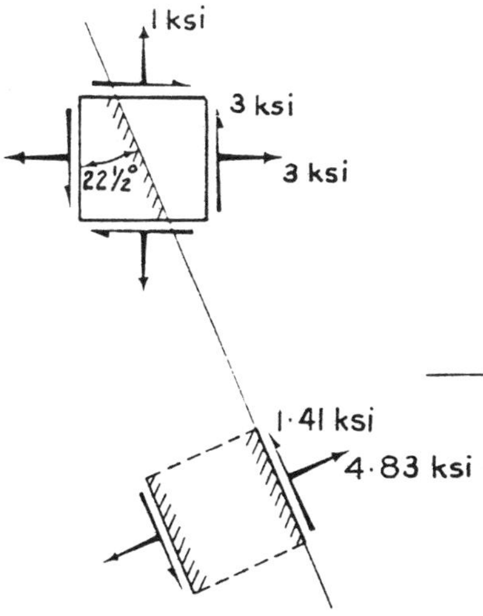

FIG. 1

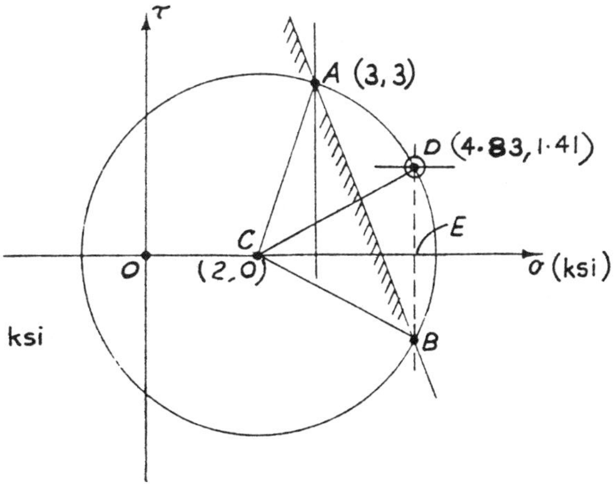

FIG. 3

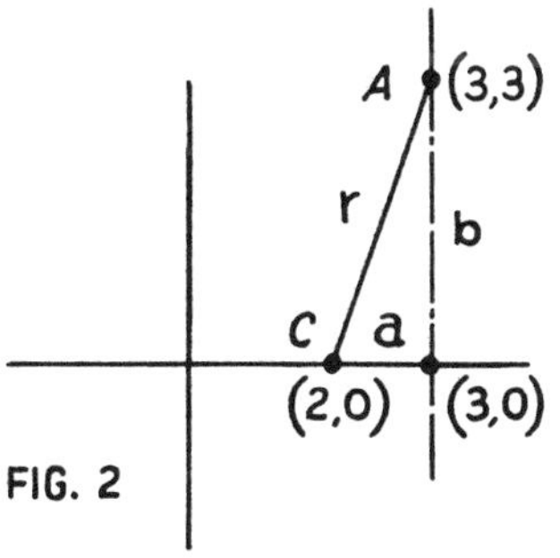

FIG. 2

Solution: This problem will be solved by Mohr's circle analysis. The normal stress coordinate of the center of Mohr's circle is given by

$$\frac{\tau_{xx} + \tau_{yy}}{2} \, .$$

$$\frac{3 \text{ ksi} + 1 \text{ ksi}}{2} = 2 \text{ ksi}$$

so the center is at point (2,0). Since on the verticle face the shear stress is 3 ksi, and the normal stress is also 3 ksi, (3,3) is a point on the circle. The radius of the circle by geometry is:

$$r^2 = a^2 + b^2$$

where a and b are shown in Figure 2.

$$r^2 = (3-2)^2 + (3)^2$$

$$= 1 + 9$$

$$r = 3.16$$

A line drawn parallel to the required inclined plane, $22\frac{1}{2}^\circ$ to the vertical, through point A, will intersect the circle at point B, which is the point for a plane inclined $-22\frac{1}{2}^\circ$ to the vertical since it lies below the σ-axis and the angle is negative. However, a vertical drawn through B, intersects the circle at D, which is the desired plane. This can be seen by noting that point D will be the same height above the σ-axis as B is below, and therefore the angles subtending these distances will be the same, only < DCE is positive since D is above the σ-axis.

• PROBLEM 6-39

For a state of plane strain where $\varepsilon_{xx} = 500 \times 10^{-6}$; $\varepsilon_{yy} = 1000 \times 10^{-6}$; and $\gamma_{xy} = 600 \times 10^{-6}$, (a) draw the Mohr's circle. (b) Then use the Mohr's circle to calculate the strains in a coordinate system 30° counterclockwise from x-y. (c) Also, find the principal strains and axes.

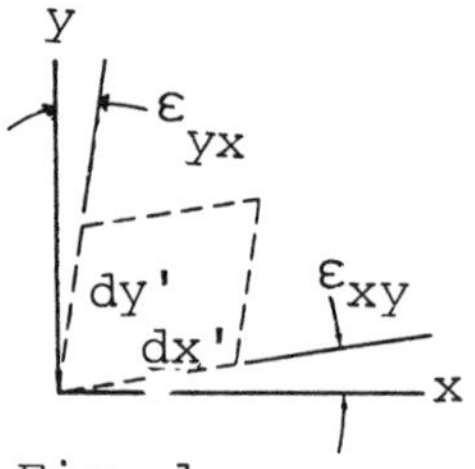

Fig. 1.

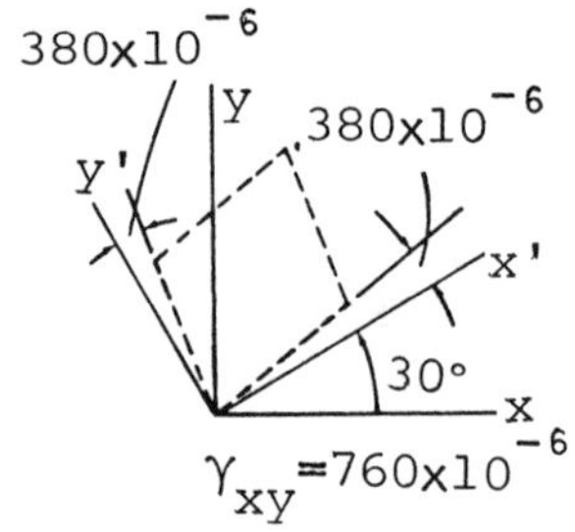

Fig. 3.

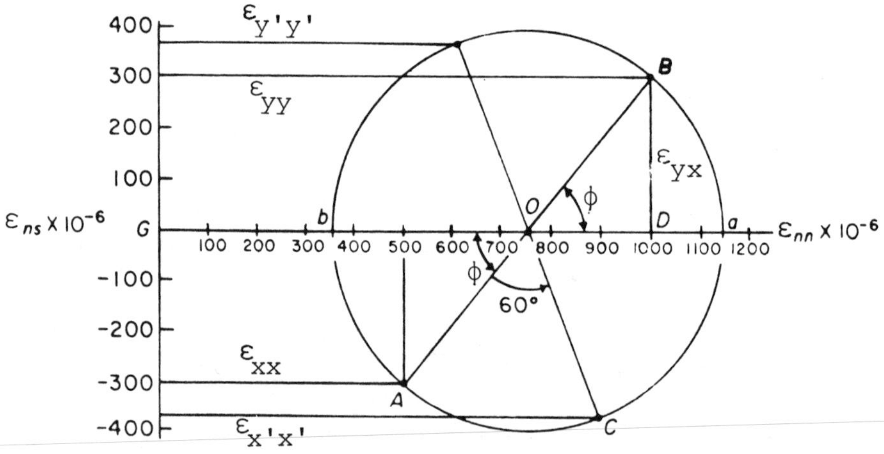

Fig. 2.

Solution: We first examine segment dx at the point. We set off on the normal strain axis the value 500×10^{-6}, while for the shear strain we consider the quantity

$$\varepsilon_{xy} = 300 \times 10^{-6} .$$

This is because:

$$\gamma_{ij} = 2\varepsilon_{ij} .$$

The sign is established by consulting Fig. 1 and noting, for a decreasing angle as a result of the basic sign convention for ε_{xy}, that we have counterclockwise rotation of segment dx. Thus, we plot -300×10^{-6} on the shear strain axis. We thus arrive at point A (see Fig. 2). For the segment dy we plot $\epsilon_{yy} = 1000 \times 10^{-6}$ on the normal strain axis and, consulting Fig. 1 again, we plot ϵ_{xy} as $+300 \times 10^{-6}$ on the shear strain axis, establishing point B. Connecting points A and B we find the center O for Mohr's circle.

$$\frac{(1000 + 500)}{2} = 750 = c$$

To find the normal and shear strains $\epsilon_{x'x'}$ and $\epsilon_{x'y'}$ for segments along axes rotated by an angle of 30° counterclockwise from xy (see Fig. 3), we rotate in the same direction an angle of 60° from OA in the strain plane. We thus establish point C. The strain $\epsilon_{x'x'}$ is seen to be about 880×10^{-6}, while the shear strain $\epsilon_{x'y'}$ is read off as about -380×10^{-6}. The result for shear deformation has been shown in Figure 3 taking into account the shear strain sign convention for Mohr's circle. Thus, from Fig. 3, we can conclude that $\gamma_{x'y'} = +760 \times 10^{-6}$, in accordance with our basic sign convention for shear strain.

We generally use simple trigonometric considerations taken in connection with Mohr's circle to find $\epsilon_{x'x'}$ and $\epsilon_{x'y'}$ rather than depend on reading off these values from the plot. Thus, the radius of the circle is given as

$$r = [\overline{OD}^2 + \overline{DB}^2]^{\frac{1}{2}} = \left[\left(\frac{1000 - 500}{2}\right)^2 + (300)^2\right]^{\frac{1}{2}} \times 10^{-6}$$

$$= 390 \times 10^{-6}$$

Also,

$$\tan\varphi = \frac{\overline{BD}}{\overline{OD}} = \frac{300}{250} = 1.200$$

$$\therefore \quad \varphi = 50.2^\circ$$

Hence,

$$\epsilon_{x'x'} = \overline{OG} + r\cos(\pi - \varphi - 60^\circ)$$

$$= \left[\frac{1000 + 500}{2} + 390\cos(69.8^\circ)\right] \times 10^{-6}$$

$$= 884 \times 10^{-6}$$

$$\epsilon_{y'y'} = \overline{OG} - r\cos(\pi - \varphi - 60^\circ)$$

$$= 615 \times 10^{-6}$$

Also,

$$\epsilon_{x'y'} = -r\sin(\pi - \varphi - 60^\circ)$$

$$= -(390)\sin 69.8^\circ \times 10^{-6} = -366 \times 10^{-6}$$

or,

$$\gamma_{x'y'} = 2\epsilon_{x'y'} = -732 \times 10^{-6}$$

The principal strains are seen from the diagram to be about 1150×10^{-6} and 360×10^{-6}. The third principal strain is $\epsilon_{zz} = 0$. More accurately we can say that

$$\epsilon_a = \overline{OG} + r = \left[\frac{1000 + 500}{2} + 390\right] \times 10^{-6}$$

$$= 1140 \times 10^{-6}$$

$$\epsilon_b = \overline{OG} - r = \left[\frac{1000 + 500}{2} - 390\right] \times 10^{-6}$$

$$= 360 \times 10^{-6}$$

To get to the principal axis for ϵ_a we rotate counterclockwise on Mohr's circle an angle of $\pi - \varphi = 129.8°$ from OA. Hence, in the physical diagram we rotate counterclockwise from the x axis an angle of 64.9°. The other principal axis is 90° from the aforementioned axis.

• PROBLEM 6-40

In a state of plane strain in the xy plane the strain components associated with the xy axes are

$$\epsilon_x = 800 \times 10^{-6}$$

$$\epsilon_y = 100 \times 10^{-6}$$

$$\gamma_{xy} = -800 \times 10^{-6}$$

Find the magnitude of the principal strains and the orientation of the principal strain directions

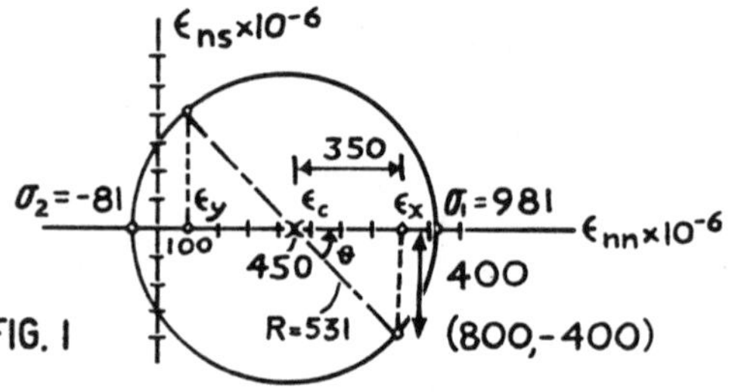

FIG. 1

Solution: By using Mohr's circle with ϵ_x, ϵ_y, and $\epsilon_{xy} (= \frac{1}{2}\gamma_{xy})$ we can determine the magnitude and direction of the principal strains.

The center of the circle is given by

$$\epsilon_c = \frac{\epsilon_x + \epsilon_y}{2}$$

$$= \frac{800 + 100}{2} \times 10^{-6}$$

$$= 450 \times 10^{-6}$$

which is seen from Figure 1. The radius is found by geometry

$$R = \sqrt{(\sigma_x - \sigma_c)^2 + \tau_{xy}^2}$$

$$= \sqrt{(800 - 450)^2 + (400^2)}$$

where $\epsilon_{xy} = \frac{1}{2}\gamma_{xy} = 400 \times 10^{-6} = 531 \times 10^{-6}$

Now, the maximum and minimum strains are located on the normal strain axis and are the distance R in either direction.

$$\epsilon_1 = \epsilon_c + 531 \times 10^{-6}$$

$$= 981 \times 10^{-6}$$

$$\epsilon_2 = \epsilon_c - 531 \times 10^{-6}$$

$$= -81 \times 10^{-6}$$

By trigonometry, the angle between normal strain axis and axis through ϵ_x is found by

$$\tan\theta = \frac{\epsilon_{xy}}{\epsilon_x - \epsilon_c}$$

$$= \frac{-400}{800 - 450}$$

$$= -1.142$$

$$\theta = -48.8^\circ$$

This angle is twice the angle between the x-axis and the principal axis in the element so

$$\theta_p = -24.4^\circ .$$

• PROBLEM 6-41

A sheet of metal is deformed uniformly in its own plane so that the strain components related to a set of axes xy are

$$\epsilon_x = -200 \times 10^{-6}$$

$$\epsilon_y = 1000 \times 10^{-6}$$

$$\gamma_{xy} = 900 \times 10^{-6}$$

Find the strain components associated with a set of axes x'y' inclined at an angle of 30° clockwise to the xy set, as shown in Figure 1. Also, find the principal strains and the direction of the axes on which they exist.

FIG. 1 LOCATION OF x', y' AXES

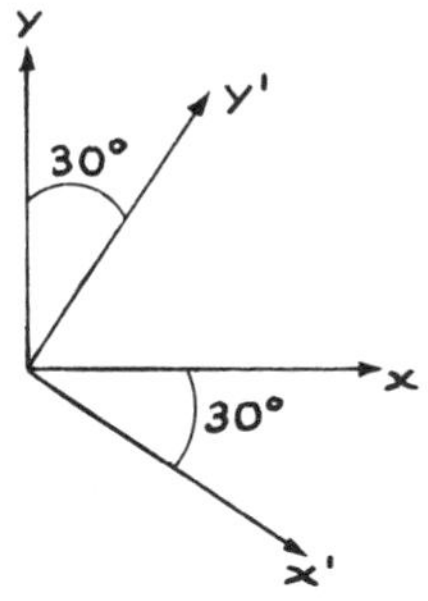

Solution: Figure 2 shows the Mohr's circle laid out on the basis of the given strains ϵ_x, ϵ_y, and γ_{xy}. Note that the diameter x-y has been plotted with the tensile side having a positive $\gamma/2$ and the compressive side, negative $\gamma/2$. This means that at a state of strain where the shear strain is negative on the tensile side, we will have a negative value of shear strain by this sign convention. Point x' lies at a relative angular position twice that existing in the actual body, i.e., at a position 60° clockwise from x on the Mohr's circle.

We find

$$2\varphi_1 = \tan^{-1} 450/600 = 36.9^\circ$$

$$R = \sqrt{600^2 + 450^2} = 750$$

$$\epsilon_{x'} = (400 \times 10^{-6}) - (750 \times 10^{-6})\cos(60^\circ - 36.9^\circ) = -290 \times 10^{-6}$$

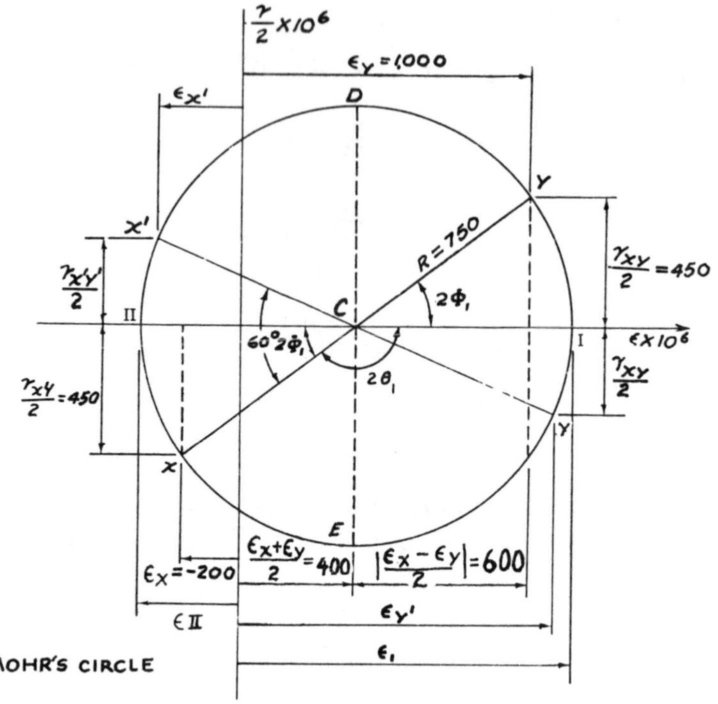

FIG. 2 MOHR'S CIRCLE

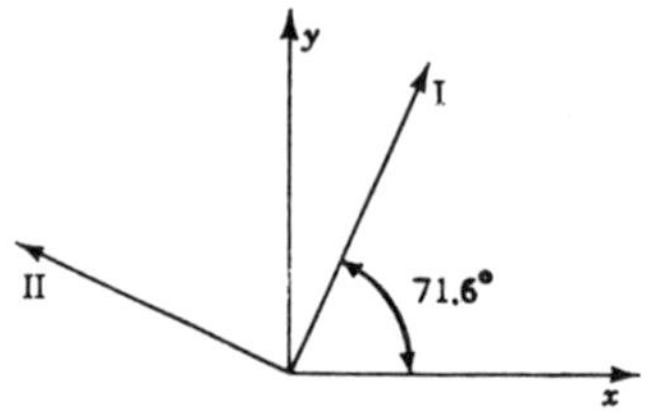

FIG. 3 ORIENTATION OF PRINCIPAL AXES OF STRAIN

$$\epsilon_{y'} = (400 \times 10^{-6}) + (750 \times 10^{-6})\cos(60^\circ - 36.9^\circ) = 1{,}090 \times 10^{-6}$$

Because point x' lies above the ϵ axis (and point y' below), the shear strain $\gamma_{x'y'}$ is negative.

$$\frac{\gamma_{x'y'}}{2} = -(750 \times 10^{-6})\sin(60^\circ - 36.9^\circ) = -295 \times 10^{-6}$$

$$\gamma_{x'y'} = -590 \times 10^{-6}$$

The principal strains are

$$\epsilon_1 = (400 \times 10^{-6}) + (750 \times 10^{-6}) = 1{,}150 \times 10^{-6}$$

$$\epsilon_{11} = (400 \times 10^{-6}) - (750 \times 10^{-6}) = -350 \times 10^{-6}$$

The angle $2\theta_1$ (in Figure 2) is given by

$$2\theta_1 = 180^\circ - 2\Phi_1 = 180^\circ - 36.9^\circ$$
$$\theta_1 = 71.6^\circ$$

The directions of the principal axes of strain are shown in Figure 3.

It is observed that an element of a body contracts 0.00050 in. per inch along the x-axis, elongates 0.00030 in. per inch in the y direction, and distorts through an angle of 0.00060 radian as in Fig. (a). Find the principal strains and determine the directions in which these strains act. Use Mohr's circle of strain to obtain the solution.

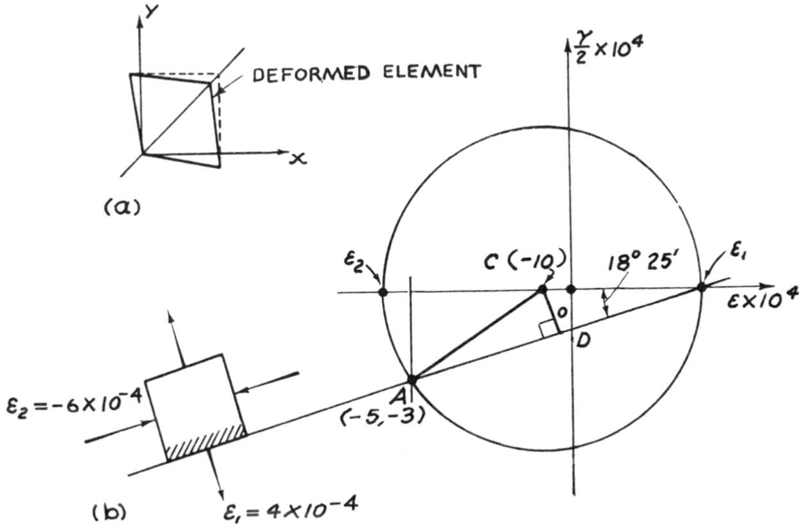

FIG.1

Solution: Mohr's circle of strain is plotted on a set of axes with normal strain on the abscissa and one-half the shear strain, $\varepsilon_{xy} = \frac{1}{2}\gamma_{xy}$, on the ordinate.

The center of the circle is located by

$$\varepsilon_c = \frac{\varepsilon_x + \varepsilon_y}{2}$$

Since the body contracts along the x-axis,

$$\varepsilon_x = -.0005 \ .$$

Due to the elongation in the y-direction

$$\varepsilon_y = .0003 \ .$$

Since the angle of the deformed element is increased we have a negative shear strain

$$\varepsilon_{xy} = \frac{\gamma_{xy}}{2}$$

$$\varepsilon_{xy} = -.0003$$

Therefore,

$$\varepsilon_c = \frac{-.0005 + .0003}{2}$$

$$= -.0001$$

We plot the point A on the circle from our data and can now find the radius of the circle by geometry.

$$R = \sqrt{(-5-(-1))^2 + (-3)^2}$$

$$= 5 \times 10^{-4}$$

The principal strains are at a distance R in each direction from ε_c.

$$\begin{aligned}\epsilon_1 &= \epsilon_c + R\\ &= -.0001 + .0005\\ &= .0004\\ \epsilon_2 &= \epsilon_c - R\\ &= -.0001 - .0005\\ &= .0006\end{aligned}$$

The angle between ϵ_1 and ϵ_x is one-half the angle $AC\epsilon_1$ on Mohr's circle. The direction of action of ϵ_1 is therefore CD on the circle. CD bisects line $A\epsilon_1$ and is therefore perpendicular to line $A\epsilon_1$. The orientations can be drawn graphically as shown.

From the geometry of the figure

$$\theta = \tan^{-1}\left(\frac{.0003}{.0009}\right) = 18^\circ 25'$$

• PROBLEM 6-43

Calculate the strains for axes x'-y' rotated clockwise with respect to an x - y reference by 30°, and draw the corresponding Mohr's circle, when $\varepsilon_{xx} = .002$; $\varepsilon_{yy} = 0$; and $\varepsilon_{xy} = -.003$ are strains for a member under plane strain.

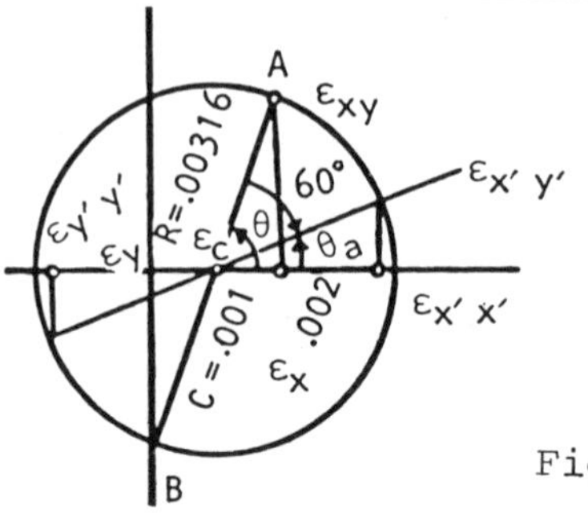

Fig. 1.

Solution: We can find the strains on axes rotated 30° by substituting the given quantities into the transformation equations.

$$\theta = -30^\circ$$

$$\epsilon_{x'x'} = \frac{\epsilon_{xx} + \epsilon_{yy}}{2} + \frac{\epsilon_{xx} - \epsilon_{yy}}{2}\cos 2\theta + \epsilon_{xy}\sin 2\theta$$

$$= \frac{.002 + 0}{2} + \frac{.002 - 0}{2}\cos(-60) + (-.003)\sin(-60)$$

$$= .0041$$

$$\epsilon_{y'y'} = \frac{\epsilon_{xx} + \epsilon_{yy}}{2} - \frac{\epsilon_{xx} - \epsilon_{yy}}{2}\cos 2\theta - \epsilon_{xy}\sin 2\theta$$

$$= \frac{.002}{2} - \frac{.002}{2}\cos(-60) - (-.003)\sin(-60)$$

$$= -.0021$$

$$\epsilon_{x'y'} = \frac{\epsilon_{yy} - \epsilon_{xx}}{2}\sin 2\theta + \epsilon_{xy}\cos 2\theta$$

$$= \frac{-.002}{2}\sin(-60) - .003\cos(-60)$$

$$= -.000634$$

Using Mohr's circle, we plot ϵ_{xx} and ϵ_{yy} on the horizontal axis as in Figure 1. We mark points on the graph with the given normal stress as the abscissa and the shear stress as the ordinate. Therefore, we have point A at (.002,+.003) and point B at (0,-.003).

The center of the circle is given by

$$\epsilon_c = \frac{\epsilon_x + \epsilon_y}{2}$$

$$= \frac{.002 + 0}{2}$$

$$= .001$$

The radius is found by geometry

$$R = \sqrt{(.002 - .001)^2 + (-.003)^2}$$

$$= .00316$$

The strain on an axis rotated 30° clockwise is found by locating the point on the circle which corresponds to a line rotated 60° clockwise from x, as in Figure 1. To find this line we first find the angle which x makes to the normal.

$$\tan\theta = \frac{+.003}{.002 - .001}$$

$$\theta = +71.56$$

Therefore, the line we are interested in is rotated by 71.56 minus 60 from the horizontal

$$\theta_a = 11.56$$

Using trigonometry, we can see from Mohr's circle

$$\epsilon_{x'x'} = \epsilon_c + R\cos\theta_a$$

$$= .001 + .00316\cos(11.56)$$

$$= .0041$$

$$\epsilon_{y'y'} = \epsilon_c - R\cos\theta_a$$

$$= .001 - .00316\cos(11.56)$$

$$= -.0021$$

$$\epsilon_{x'y'} = -R\sin\theta_a$$

$$= -.00316\sin(11.56)$$

$$= -.000633 .$$

STRESS AND STRAIN RELATIONS

• PROBLEM 6-44

A rectangular plate is subjected to uniform stress along all four edges. Due to these stresses the length and width of the plate become elongated by the amounts shown. Compute the strains $\varepsilon_{x'x'}$ and $\varepsilon_{z'x'}$ corresponding to axes x'- y'- z' which are rotated with respect to axes x-y, assuming no change in volume.

Solution: In order to find the strains on an inclined plane, we first have to determine the strain field for the xyz element. There are no shear strains because the faces are only separating; not changing

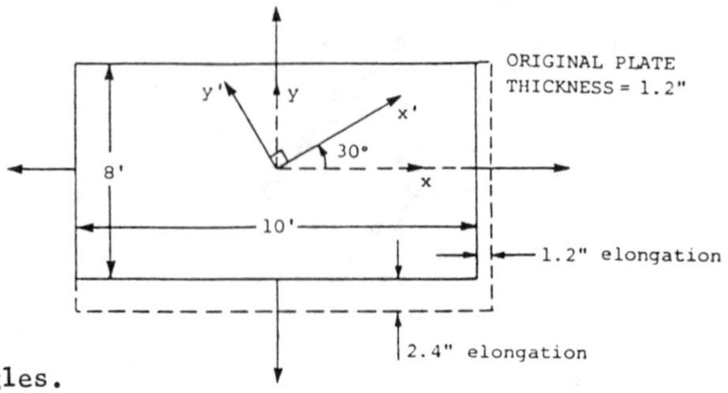

their relative angles.

ϵ_{xx} is, by definition, the change in length over original length

$$\epsilon_{xx} = \frac{.1 \text{ft.}}{10 \text{ ft.}}$$

$$= .01$$

Similarly,

$$\epsilon_{yy} = \frac{.2 \text{ ft.}}{8 \text{ ft.}}$$

$$= .025 \ .$$

To find ϵ_{zz}, we use the fact that the volume of the plate doesn't change. We know all the dimensions except the change in the z-direction, so by equating the volumes before and after the deformation we have

$$(10 \text{ ft.})(8 \text{ ft.})(.1 \text{ ft}) = (10 + .1)\text{ft.}(8 + .2) \text{ ft.}(.1 + \Delta z)\text{ft.}$$

$$8 \text{ ft}^3 = (10.1)(8.2)(.1 + \Delta z)\text{ft}^3$$

$$.09659 \text{ ft.} = .1 + \Delta z \text{ ft.}$$

$$-.0034 \text{ ft.} = \Delta z$$

$$\epsilon_{zz} = \frac{\Delta z}{z} = \frac{-.0034}{.1}$$

$$= -.034$$

Using the transformation equations in the x-y plane, because ϵ_{zz} will not affect the strains due to a rotation about the z-axis, we obtain

$$\epsilon_{x'x'} = \frac{\epsilon_{xx} + \epsilon_{yy}}{2} + \frac{\epsilon_{xx} - \epsilon_{yy}}{2} \cos 2\theta + \epsilon_{xy} \sin 2\theta \ .$$

Substituting the values for ϵ_{xx} and ϵ_{yy} and noting that $\epsilon_{xy} = 0$

$$\epsilon_{x'x'} = \frac{.01 + .025}{2} + \frac{.01 - .025}{2} \cos 60$$

$$= \frac{.035}{2} - \frac{.015}{2} (.5)$$

$$= .01375$$

The rotated shear stress is found using the transformation equation

$$\epsilon_{x'z'} = \frac{\epsilon_{zz} - \epsilon_{xx}}{2} \sin 2\theta + \epsilon_{xz} \cos 2\theta$$

However, θ in this case is the angle of rotation from the xz axes to the x'z' axes. Since the axes are rotated relative to the xy plane, there is no rotation in the z-direction. Therefore the z' axis is the same as the z-axis and the angle between x' and z' is not affected by the 30° rotation in the xy plane. Therefore

$$\theta_{x'z'} = 90^\circ$$

$$\epsilon_{x'z'} = \frac{-.034 - .01}{2} \sin 180^\circ + 0 \times \cos 180$$

Since $\sin 180^\circ = 0$, $\epsilon_{x'z'} = 0 + 0 = 0$. Therefore, although the dimensions change, there is no angular distorsion of the plate.

• PROBLEM 6-45

A cube of material of side 3 in. is subjected to stresses, normal to its faces, of $\sigma_1 = +20{,}000$ psi, $\sigma_2 = 5000$ psi and $\sigma_3 = -4000$ psi. If $E = 30 \times 10^6$ psi and $\mu = 0.3$, find the strains in the three directions and calculate the total change in volume of the block.

Solution: Because the cube is subjected only to normal stresses, there are no shear stresses and therefore no shear strains. We can use the three-dimensional stress-strain equation to find the three normal strains.

$$\epsilon_1 = \frac{1}{E}(\sigma_1 - \nu(\sigma_2 + \sigma_3))$$

$$= \frac{1}{30.10^6} (20k - .3(5k - 4k))$$

$$= 6.567 \cdot 10^{-4}$$

$$\epsilon_2 = \frac{1}{E}(\sigma_2 - \nu(\sigma_1 + \sigma_3))$$

$$= \frac{1}{30.10^6} (5k - .3(20k - 4k))$$

$$= .0667 \times 10^{-4}$$

$$\epsilon_3 = \frac{1}{E}(\sigma_3 - \nu(\sigma_1 + \sigma_2))$$

$$= \frac{1}{30.10^6} (-4k - .3(20k + 5k))$$

$$= -3.833 \times 10^{-4}$$

The find the change in volume we first derive an expression for volume. Since $V = L_1 \times L_2 \times L_3$, the new volume with the loads applied is given by

$$V_{new} = (L_1 + \Delta L_1) \times (L_2 + \Delta L_2) \times (L_3 + \Delta L_3)$$

but $\Delta L = L\epsilon$. So,

$$V_{new} = (L_1 + \epsilon_1 L_1)(L_2 + \epsilon_2 L_2)(L_3 + \epsilon_3 L_3)$$

$$= L_1 \times L_2 \times L_3 \times (1 + \epsilon_1)(1 + \epsilon_2)(1 + \epsilon_3)$$

$$= V(1 + \epsilon_1)(1 + \epsilon_2)(1 + \epsilon_3)$$

Therefore, the change in volume is

$$\Delta V = V_{new} - V$$

$$= V[(1 + \epsilon_1)(1 + \epsilon_2)(1 + \epsilon_3) - 1]$$

The block is a 3" cube so

$$V = 27.\ \text{in.}^3$$

Substituting our values for strain we obtain:

$$\Delta V = 27[(1 + 6.567 \times 10^{-4})(1 + 0.0667 \times 10^{-4})(1 - 3.833 \times 10^{-4}) - 1]$$

$$= 7.56 \times 10^{-3}\ \text{in.}^3$$

Thus the total effect on the block is an increase in volume of 0.00756 in^3.

• PROBLEM 6-46

A cube of material has its faces normal to the x,y and z directions. On the x and y faces the stresses are $\sigma_x = +2000$ psi and $\sigma_y = -6000$ psi. There are no shear stresses on these faces. In the z-direction the material is restrained against any expansion or contraction. If $E = 10 \times 10^6$ psi and $\mu = 0.25$ find the stress in the z-direction and the total strain in the x-direction.

Solution: Because the cube is restrained in the z-direction, and cannot change in length, the strain in the z-direction is zero.

By writing the three-dimensional stress-strain equation for ϵ_2 as

$$0 = \frac{1}{E}(\sigma_z - \mu(\sigma_x + \sigma_y))$$

we can find the stress in the z-direction

$$\sigma_2 = \mu(\sigma_x + \sigma_y)$$

$$= .25(2000 - 6000)$$

$$= -1000 \text{ psi}$$

We now have all the stresses acting on the block, and find the strain in the x-direction simply by substituting these values into the multi-dimensional relation for ϵ_x

$$\epsilon_x = \frac{1}{E}(\sigma_x - \mu(\sigma_y + \sigma_z))$$

$$= \frac{1}{10.10^6}(2000 - .25(-6000 - 1000))$$

$$= \frac{1}{10^7}(2000 + \frac{7000}{4}$$

$$= \frac{15}{4} \times \frac{10^3}{10^7} \text{ psi}$$

$$= 3.75 \cdot 10^{-4} \text{ psi}$$

• PROBLEM 6-47

A cube of material of side 2 in. is acted upon by a compressive force of 12,000 lb. in the y-direction. In the z-direction it is restrained against expansion (see figure) while in the x-direction it is unconfined. If $E = 15 \times 10^6$ psi and $\mu = 0.3$ find the force exerted by the restraining walls upon the block. Also find the strain in the x-direction.

Solution: Since the block is unrestrained in the x-direction and there is no externally applied force in this direction, σ_x is zero.

The stress in the y-direction is, by definition, F/A.

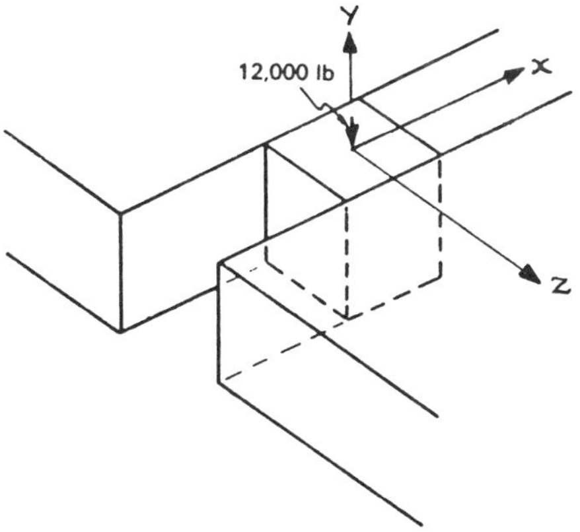

$$\sigma_y = \frac{-12{,}000}{(2\ \text{in})^2}$$

$$= -3000\ \text{psi}$$

The stress in the z-direction is unknown.

In order to compute the total strain in each direction it is convenient to tabulate the three stresses and to write opposite each the three strains to which it gives rise.

Table 1

Stress	ϵ_x	ϵ_y	ϵ_z
$\sigma_x = 0$	0	0	0
$\sigma_y = -3000$	$-0.3\left(\frac{-3000}{15 \times 10^6}\right)$	$\left(\frac{-3000}{15 \times 10^6}\right)$	$-0.3\left(\frac{-3000}{15 \times 10^6}\right)$
σ_z	$-0.3\left(\frac{\sigma_z}{15 \times 10^6}\right)$	$-0.3\left(\frac{\sigma_z}{15 \times 10^6}\right)$	$\left(\frac{\sigma_z}{15 \times 10^6}\right)$

The stress σ_x is zero and causes no strains

The stress σ_y causes a direct strain of $-3000/(15 \times 10^6)$ in the y-direction, and this is noted first under ϵ_y. The lateral strains ϵ_x and ϵ_z are caused by the Poisson effect and equal to Poisson's ratio, ν, times the direct strain ϵ_y.

$$\epsilon_x = \epsilon_z = -.3\,\epsilon_y$$

The stress σ_z causes a direct strain of $\sigma_z/(15 \times 10^6)$ in the z-direction and this is noted under ϵ_z. The lateral strains ϵ_x and ϵ_y are then $-0.3 \times \epsilon_z$.

By summing the values in each column we obtain the value of the total strains ϵ_x, ϵ_y and ϵ_z when all stresses are acting together. Since the block is not allowed to move in the z-direction, ϵ_z must equal zero. From this we can calculate σ_z.

$$\text{Total } \epsilon_z = 0.3\left(\frac{3000}{15 \times 10^6}\right) + \frac{\sigma_z}{15 \times 10^6} = 0$$

$\sigma_z = -900$ psi

Since the area of one face of the cube is 4 in² the force exerted by each of the restraining walls is 3600 lb compression.

The total strain in the x-direction is the sum of the ϵ_x column.

$$\text{Total } \epsilon_x = -0.3\left(\frac{-3000}{15 \times 10^6}\right) - 0.3\left(\frac{-900}{15 \times 10^6}\right)$$

$$= +6.0 \times 10^{-5} + 1.8 \times 10^{-5}$$

$$= 7.8 \times 10^{-5}$$

The total strains of any small element subjected to a general three-dimensional stress system can be found in the same way.

Table 2

Stress	ϵ_x	ϵ_y	ϵ_z
x	σ_x/E	$-\mu\sigma_x/E$	$-\mu\sigma_x/E$
y	$-\mu\sigma_y/E$	σ_y/E	$-\mu\sigma_y/E$
z	$-\mu\sigma_z/E$	$-\mu\sigma_z/E$	σ_z/E

Each line of Table 2 lists the elastic strains due to one of the stresses σ_x, σ_y or σ_z acting alone. Provided the principle of superposition applies, these effects can be added to give:

$$\epsilon_x = \frac{1}{E}[\sigma_x - \mu(\sigma_y + \sigma_z)]$$

$$\epsilon_y = \frac{1}{E}[\sigma_y - \mu(\sigma_z + \sigma_x)]$$

$$\epsilon_z = \frac{1}{E}[\sigma_z - \mu(\sigma_x + \sigma_y)]$$

• PROBLEM 6-48

A copper bar with rectangular cross-section is held between rigid supports (see figure), after which the temperature of the bar is raised 100 °F. Determine the stresses on all sides of the elements A and B, and show your results on sketches of the elements. (Assume $\alpha = 0.00001$ per °F and $E = 16 \times 10^6$ psi.)

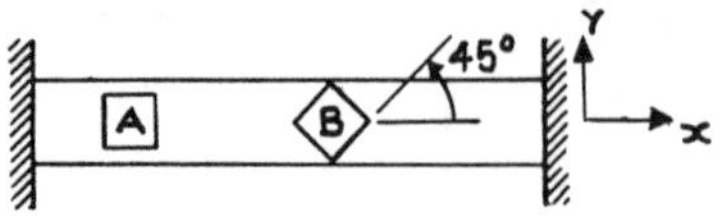

FIG. 1

Solution: The bar is originally free of stresses and strains. When the bar is heated it will try to expand. The supports, in preventing the bar from expanding, exert compressive stresses on the bar.

In this example, there will be strain due to thermal expansion, and strain due to stress.

The contribution due to thermal effects to strain is given by

$$\varepsilon_{th} = \alpha \, \Delta T$$

The strains acting along the x-axis can be added together to get the total strain.

$$\varepsilon_{total} = \alpha \, \Delta T + \frac{\tau}{E}$$

Since the bar is held between rigid supports it cannot expand. Therefore, the total strain is zero.

$$\varepsilon_{total} = 0 = \alpha \, \Delta T + \frac{\tau}{E}$$

From this we can find the stress in the x-direction.

$$\alpha \, \Delta T = - \frac{\sigma_x}{E}$$

$$\begin{aligned} \sigma_x &= -\alpha \, \Delta TE \\ &= -(.00001)(100^\circ) \times (16 \times 10^6) \\ &= -16000 \text{ psi} \end{aligned}$$

The stress in the y-direction is zero because there are no restraints or external forces in that direction.

Since there are no shear stresses on the section A we know that σ_x and σ_y are principal stresses and x and y are the directions of the principal planes. The center of Mohr's circle is at

$$\frac{\sigma_1 - \sigma_2}{2}$$

$$\sigma_c = -8 \text{ ksi}$$

FIG. 2

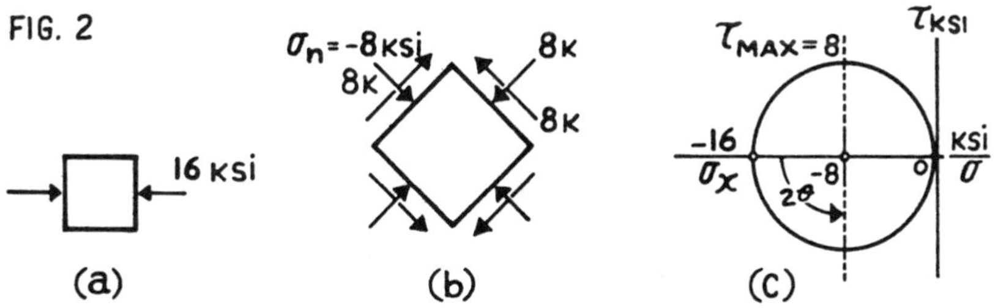

The radius is 8 ksi. For the section inclined by 45° we rotate by $2 \times 45^\circ$ on Mohr's circle, or 90° and this brings us to the maximum shear stress planes.

$$\tau_{max} = 8 \text{ ksi}$$

and the normal stress is the value on the σ-axis below the shear, -8 ksi.

• PROBLEM 6-49

A sheet of material is subjected to a two-dimensional stress system in the xy plane. At a given point, an element with its sides parallel to x and y is found to have a shear strain of 1×10^{-4}, while an element at 45° to the first has a shear strain of 4×10^{-4}. Find the maximum shear strain at this point. If the shear modulus for the material is 10^7 psi find the difference between the two principal stresses.

Solution: To find the maximum shear strain we first set the derivative of the expression for shear strain to zero.

$$\frac{\partial \epsilon_{x'y'}}{\partial \theta} = 0$$

The transformation equation is given by

$$\epsilon_{x'y'} = \frac{\epsilon_{yy} - \epsilon_{xx}}{2} \sin 2\theta + \epsilon_{xy} \cos 2\theta \qquad (1)$$

so

$$\frac{\partial \epsilon_{x'y'}}{\partial \theta} = (\epsilon_{yy} - \epsilon_{xx}) \cos 2\theta - 2\epsilon_{xy} \sin 2\theta$$

$$= 0$$

$$\frac{\epsilon_{yy} - \epsilon_{xx}}{2\epsilon_{xy}} = \frac{\sin 2\theta}{\cos 2\theta} \qquad (2)$$

To find the direction for maximum shear strain, θ, we must determine the value for $\epsilon_{yy} - \epsilon_{xx}$. This can be obtained by using the transformation equation and the value of shear strain on the 45° plane.

$$\epsilon_{x'y'} = .0004 = \frac{\epsilon_{yy} - \epsilon_{xx}}{2} \sin(2 \times 45^\circ)$$

$$+ .0001 \cos(2 \times 45^\circ)$$

$$.0004 = \frac{\epsilon_{yy} - \epsilon_{xx}}{2} \cdot 1 + 0$$

$$\epsilon_{yy} - \epsilon_{xx} = .0008$$

Substituting this in equation 2 we obtain

$$\tan 2\theta = \frac{.0008}{2(.0001)}$$

$$2\theta = \tan^{-1}(4)$$

$$= 75.96^\circ$$

Now substituting this value of θ into equation 2 along with $\epsilon_{yy} - \epsilon_{xx} = .0008$ we find the maximum shear strain

$$\epsilon_{x'y'max} = \frac{.0008}{2} \sin 75.96^\circ + .0001 \cos 75.96^\circ$$

$$= .000412$$

The shear stress is defined as

$$\tau_{xy} = 2G\epsilon_{xy}$$

The maximum shear stress is

$$\tau_{xymax} = 2G\epsilon_{xymax}$$

$$= 2(10^7)(.000412)$$

$$= 8246 \text{ psi}$$

From Mohr's circle we know that the maximum shear stress, equal to the radius of the circle must be equal to the difference between the principal stresses.

An electric 45° strain rosette, which has been applied to a point on a steel machine part, gives the following data:

$$\epsilon_{0°} = -.0005$$

$$\epsilon_{45°} = +.0002$$

$$\epsilon_{90°} = +.0003$$

Given $E = 30 \times 10^6$ psi and $\nu = 0.3$, find the principal stresses at the point investigated.

Solution: There are three major steps in finding the principal stresses. We must find the normal and shear strains, ϵ_{xx}, ϵ_{yy}, ϵ_{xy} for the point from the given data. Then we must find the principal strains at the point using coordinate transformation equations. Once we have the principal strains, we can use the multi-dimensional stress-strain relations to find the principal stresses.

We can simplify the first step by taking the x-axis to coincide with 0° and the y-axis to coincide with the 90°. Therefore, $\epsilon_{xx} = \epsilon_{0°} = -.0005$, $\epsilon_{yy} = \epsilon_{90°} = .0003$. To find ϵ_{xy}, we use the coordinate transformation equation:

$$\epsilon_{x'x'} = \frac{\epsilon_{xx} + \epsilon_{yy}}{2} + \frac{\epsilon_{xx} - \epsilon_{yy}}{2} \cos 2\theta + \epsilon_{xy} \sin 2\theta$$

Since we know $\epsilon_{45°}$, we can find ϵ_{xy} by taking $\epsilon_{x'x'} = \epsilon_{45°}$ and $\theta = 45°$

$$\cos[(2)(45)] = \cos 90 = 0$$
$$\sin[(2)(45)] = \sin 90 = 1$$

so

$$\epsilon_{45°} = \frac{\epsilon_{xx} + \epsilon_{yy}}{2} + 0 + \epsilon_{xy}$$

or

$$\epsilon_{xy} = \epsilon_{45°} - \frac{\epsilon_{xx} + \epsilon_{yy}}{2}$$

$$= .0002 - \frac{-.0005 + .0003}{2}$$

$$= .0003$$

In order to find the principal strains we use the formula

$$\epsilon_{1,2} = \frac{\epsilon_{xx} + \epsilon_{yy}}{2} \pm \sqrt{\left(\frac{\epsilon_{xx} - \epsilon_{yy}}{2}\right)^2 + \epsilon_{xy}^2}$$

$$\epsilon_1 = \frac{-.0005 + .0003}{2} + \sqrt{\left(\frac{-.0005 - .0003}{2}\right)^2 + (.0003)^2}$$

$$= .0004$$

$$\epsilon_2 = \frac{-.0005 + .0003}{2} - \sqrt{\left(\frac{-.0005 - .0003}{2}\right)^2 + (.0003)^2}$$

$$= -.0006$$

We now use the two-dimensional stress-strain formula $\epsilon_{ii} = \frac{1}{E}(\tau_{ii} - \nu\tau_{jj})$

for our principal stresses

$$\epsilon_1 = \frac{1}{E}(\tau_1 - \nu\tau_2)$$

$$\epsilon_2 = \frac{1}{E}(\tau_2 - \nu\tau_1)$$

or

$$\epsilon_1 E = \tau_1 - \nu\tau_2 \qquad (1)$$

$$\epsilon_2 E = -\nu\tau_1 + \tau_2 \qquad (2)$$

We want to find τ_1 so we multiply equation (2) by ν and then add (1) and (2).

The τ_2 terms cancel out and we find

$$\epsilon_1 E + \epsilon_2 E\nu = \tau_1 - \nu^2\tau_1$$

or

$$\tau_1 = \frac{E}{1 - \nu^2}(\epsilon_1 + \nu\epsilon_2)$$

By substituting into (1) with this value for τ_1 we find

$$\tau_2 = \frac{E}{1 - \nu^2}(\epsilon_2 + \nu\epsilon_1)$$

We can now substitute all our data:

$$\tau_1 = \frac{30 \times 10^6}{1 - (.3)^2}[.0004 + (.3)(-.0006)]$$

$$= 7,250 \text{ psi}$$

$$\tau_2 = \frac{30 \times 10^6}{1 - (.3)^2}[-.0006 + .3(.0004)]$$

$$= -15,820 \text{ psi}$$

Thus the principal normal stresses are $\tau_1 = 7,250$ psi, (tension), and $\tau_2 = -15,820$ psi (compression).

CHAPTER 7

STRESSES IN BEAMS

STRESS BY EQUILIBRIUM

• PROBLEM 7-1

The beam of Fig. 1a has a rectangular cross-section 4 in. wide by 12 in. deep and a span of 12 ft. It is subjected to a uniformly distributed load of 100 lb. per ft. and concentrated loads of 600 lb. and 1200 lb. at 2 ft. and 7 ft. respectively from the left support. Determine the maximum fiber stress at the center of the beam.

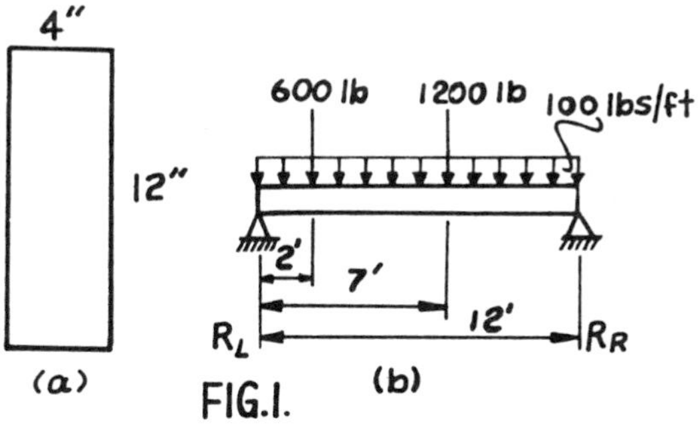

FIG.1.

Solution: The reactions are evaluated from a free-body diagram of the entire beam and moment equations with respect to each of the two reactions. By this method, the reactions are evaluated independently, and summation of forces may be used to check the results. $\Sigma M = 0$ about the right support. Therefore

$$12\ R_L = 100 \times 12 \times \frac{12}{2} + 1200 \times 5 + 600 \times 10$$

$$R_L = 1600 \text{ lbs.}$$

$\Sigma M = 0$ about the left support. Therefore

$$12\ R_R = 100 \times 12 + 600 \times 2 + 1200 \times 7$$

$$R_R = 1400 \text{ lbs.}$$

Check: $\Sigma F_y = 0$

$$600 + 1200 + 100 \times 12 - 1600 - 1400 = 0$$

$$0 = 0$$

The left reaction, R_L is 1600 lb. and the right reaction, R_R, is 1400 lb. both upward. Figure 2a is a free-body diagram of the left

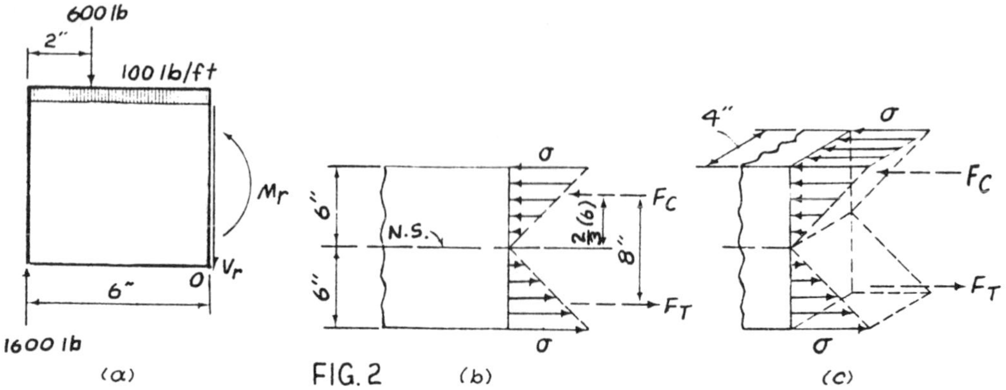

FIG. 2

half of the beam. The equation $\sum M_0 = 0$ gives

$$\circlearrowleft + \; M_r + 600(4) + 100(6)(3) - 1600(6) = 0 \, ,$$

from which

$$M_r = 5400 \text{ ft-lb. or } 5400(12) \text{ in-lb. as shown.}$$

The moment, M_r, is the resultant of the flexural stresses indicated in Fig. 2b and c in which F_c and F_T are the resultants of the compressive and tensile stresses respectively. The resultants F_c and F_T (which act through the centroids of the wedge-shaped stress distribution diagram of Fig. 2c) are located through the centroids of the triangular stress distribution diagrams of Fig. 2b. The magnitude of the couple M_r equals $F_c(8)$ or $F_T(8)$, and $F_c = (1/2)(\sigma)(6)(4) = 12(\sigma)$; therefore

$$M_r = 8(12)\sigma = 5400(12) \text{ in-lb.}$$

from which

$$\sigma_{max} = 675 \text{ psi C at top and T at bottom.}$$

• PROBLEM 7-2

A beam is loaded so that the maximum fiber stress on the section of Fig. 1 is 9000 psi C. Determine the flexural force carried by the flange and its location on the cross-section of the beam.

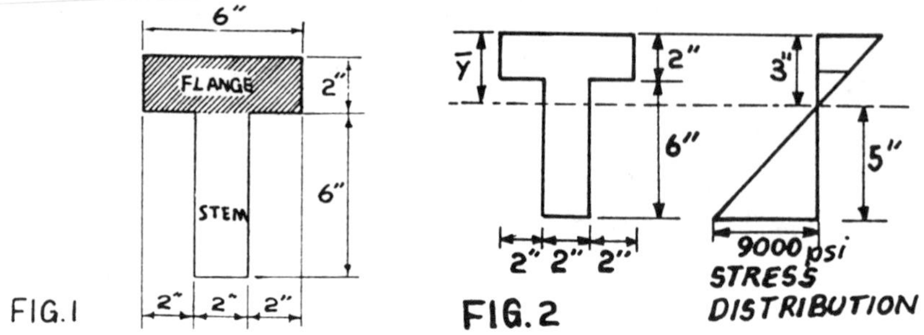

Solution: The neutral axis is located at position $\bar{y}$ such that $\bar{y}(12+12) = 12 \times 1 + 12 \times 5$

$$\bar{y} = 3''$$

From the stress distribution, Fig. 2, it is noticed that the maximum stress occurs at the bottom fibre and its value is given as 9000 psi. The stress at the top fibre is determined using similar triangles

$$\therefore \sigma_{top} = \frac{9000}{5} \times 3$$

$$\sigma_{top} = 5400 \text{ psi} .$$

Also using similar triangles, stress at the bottom of the flange is

$$\sigma_{bot} = \frac{5400}{3} \times 1$$

$$= 1800 \text{ psi} .$$

Flexural force carried by the flange $= 6 \times 2 \times \frac{(1800 + 5400)}{2} = 43,200$ lb.

Its location can be found by finding the centroid of that portion of the stress distribution that acts on the flange, Fig. 3.

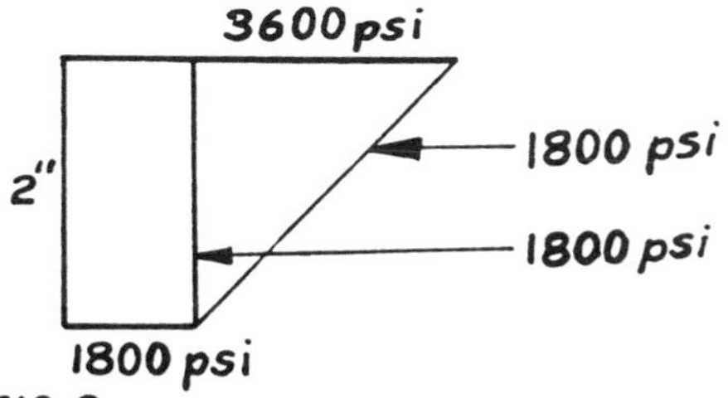

FIG.3

$$y(1800 + 1800) = 1800 \times 1 + 1800 \times 2/3$$

$$y = .833 \text{ in.}$$

The location of the flexural force carried by the flange is .833 in.

• PROBLEM 7-3

Two 2 by 10 in. timbers* are securely fastened together to form a symmetrical T-section with the flange on top. It is subjected to a uniformly distributed load of 100 lb. per ft. and concentrated loads of 600 lbs. and 1200 lbs. at 2 ft. and 7 ft. respectively from the left support Fig. 1. Determine the maximum fiber stress at the center of the beam.

Solution: The horizontal centroidal axis of the cross-section is first determined. $\bar{y}\,\Sigma A = \Sigma Ay$ (y measured from top edge of T)

$$(2 \times 10 + 2 \times 10)\bar{y} = 2 \times 10 \times 1 + 2 \times 10 \times 6$$

$$\therefore \bar{y} = 4 \text{ ins.}$$

Therefore horizontal centroidal axis is 4 ins. from the top. The fiber stress distribution diagrams are shown in Fig. 2. For convenience, the compression diagram is subdivided into three parts composed of two triangular distribution (wedge-shaped) diagrams and one uniform distribution diagram. This is done because the locations of the centroids of these diagrams are known. The values of the force components and their locations are shown in the figure. It will be noted that each component

*Structural timbers specified as rough sawn will be approximately full size. Cross-sectioned dimensions of dressed timbers will be from 3/8 to 1/2 in. smaller than nominal.

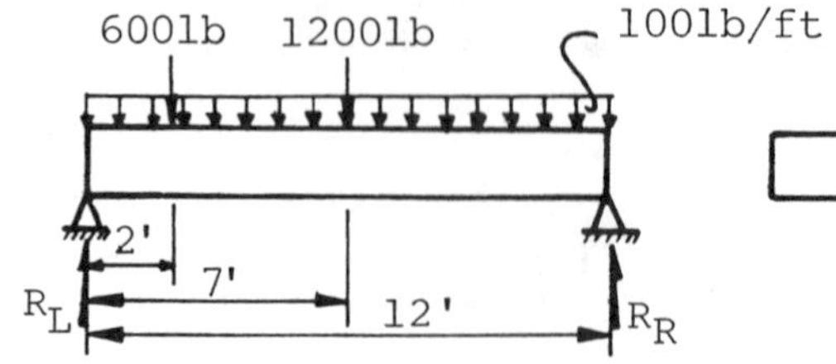

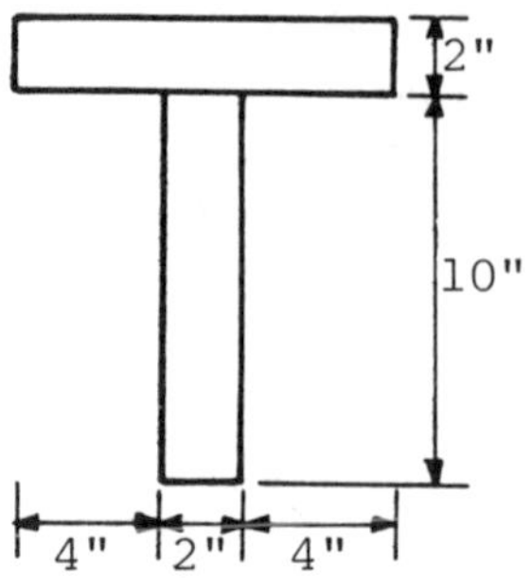

Fig. 1.

$F_1=\frac{1}{2}(\sigma/4)(10)(2)=\frac{5}{2}\sigma$

$F_2=(\sigma/4)(10)(2)=5\sigma$

$F_3=\frac{1}{2}(\sigma/4)(2)(2)=\frac{1}{2}\sigma$.

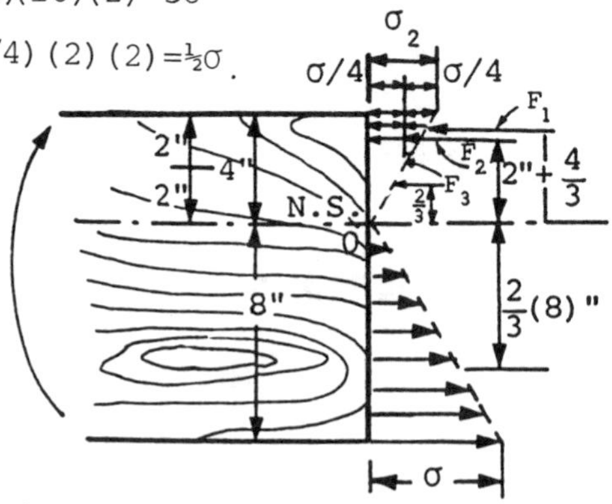

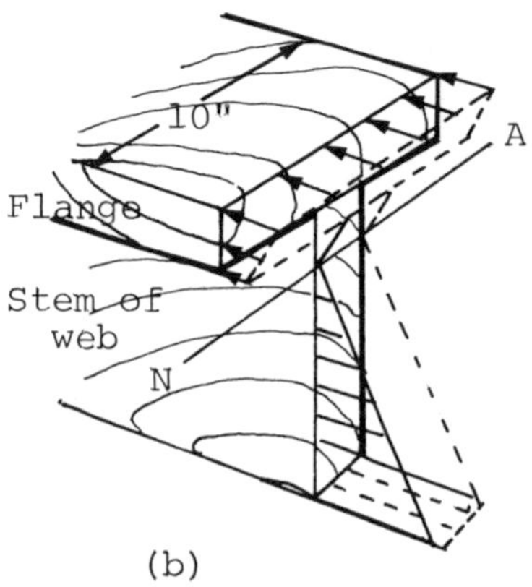

Fig. 2. (a) (b)

F_1, F_2, F_3, being the average stress multiplied by the area on which the stress acts, is equal to the volume of the corresponding part of the three-dimensional diagram of Fig. 2b. The moment of the component forces with respect to O is

$$M_r = F_1\left(\frac{10}{3}\right) + F_2\left(\frac{9}{3}\right) + F_3\left(\frac{4}{3}\right) + F_4\left(\frac{16}{3}\right)$$

In order to find the reaction moment, M_r, at the center of the beam, first the reactions at the supports need to be determined.

$\Sigma M = 0$ about the right support.

$$+\circlearrowright (100 \text{ lb/ft} \times 12 \text{ ft} \times 12 \text{ ft}/2) + (1200 \text{ lb} \times 5 \text{ ft.}) + (600 \text{ lb} \times 10 \text{ ft}) - (R_L \times 12 \text{ ft.}) = 0$$

$$R_L = 1600 \text{ lbs.}$$

$\Sigma M = 0$ about the left support.

$$+\circlearrowleft -600 \text{ lb} \times 2 \text{ ft} - 1200 \text{ lb} \times 7 \text{ ft} - 100 \text{ lb/ft} \times 12 \text{ ft} \times 12 \text{ ft}/2 + R_R \times 12 \text{ ft} = 0$$

$$R_R = 1400$$

Check: $\Sigma F_y = 0$

$$600 + 1200 + 100 \times 12 - 1600 - 1400 = 0$$
$$0 = 0$$

$\Sigma M = 0$ about the center of the beam

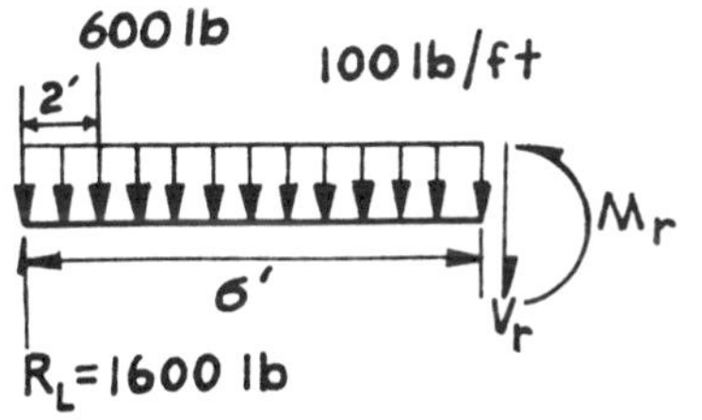

FIG.3

$$\circlearrowleft + \quad M_r + (100 \text{ lb/ft} \times 6 \text{ ft} \times 6 \text{ ft}/2) + 600 \text{ lb} \times 4 \text{ ft} - 1600 \text{ lb} \times 6 \text{ ft} = 0$$

$$M_r = 5400 \text{ ft-lb.} = 5400(12) \text{in-lb.}$$

The moment, M_r, is equal to 5400(12); therefore

$$\left(\frac{5}{2}\right)\sigma\left(\frac{10}{3}\right) + 5\sigma\left(\frac{9}{3}\right) + \left(\frac{1}{2}\right)\sigma\left(\frac{4}{3}\right) + 8\sigma\left(\frac{16}{3}\right) = 5400(12),$$

from which

$$\sigma_{max} = 972 \text{ psi T at bottom.}$$

The second moment of the area can be obtained by integration or by composite areas,

$$I = \Sigma A_i \left(\frac{h_i^2}{12} + c_i^2\right)$$

$$= 2 \times 8\left(\frac{64}{12} + 16\right) + 2 \times 2\left(\frac{4}{12} + 1\right) + 10 \times 2\left(\frac{4}{12} + 9\right)$$

$$= \frac{1600}{3} \text{ in}^4.$$

The maximum fiber stress is

$$\sigma_{max} = \frac{M\bar{y}}{I}$$

$$\sigma_{max} = \frac{5400(12)(8)}{1600/3} = 972 \text{ psi T at bottom.}$$

• PROBLEM 7-4

A 12 in. horizontal segment of a T-shaped wood beam, I = 1600/3 in^4., shown in Figure 1a, is subjected to a moment of +5400 ft-lb. at the left end and a constant shear of 900 lb. Find the average shear stress on a horizontal plane which is located 4 in. from the bottom of the beam.

Solution: A free-body diagram of the segment is shown in Fig. 1a, where AB designates the plane on which the shearing stress is to be evaluated. The moment, M_2, is found by summing moments about the left end,

$$\Sigma M = -M_2 + 900(1') + 5400$$

which must be zero for equilibrium.

$$M_2 = 900 + 5400 \text{ ft-lb.}$$
$$= 6300 \text{ ft-lb.}$$

A free-body diagram of the portion of the beam segment below plane AB is shown in Fig. 1b. The force V_H is the resultant of the shearing

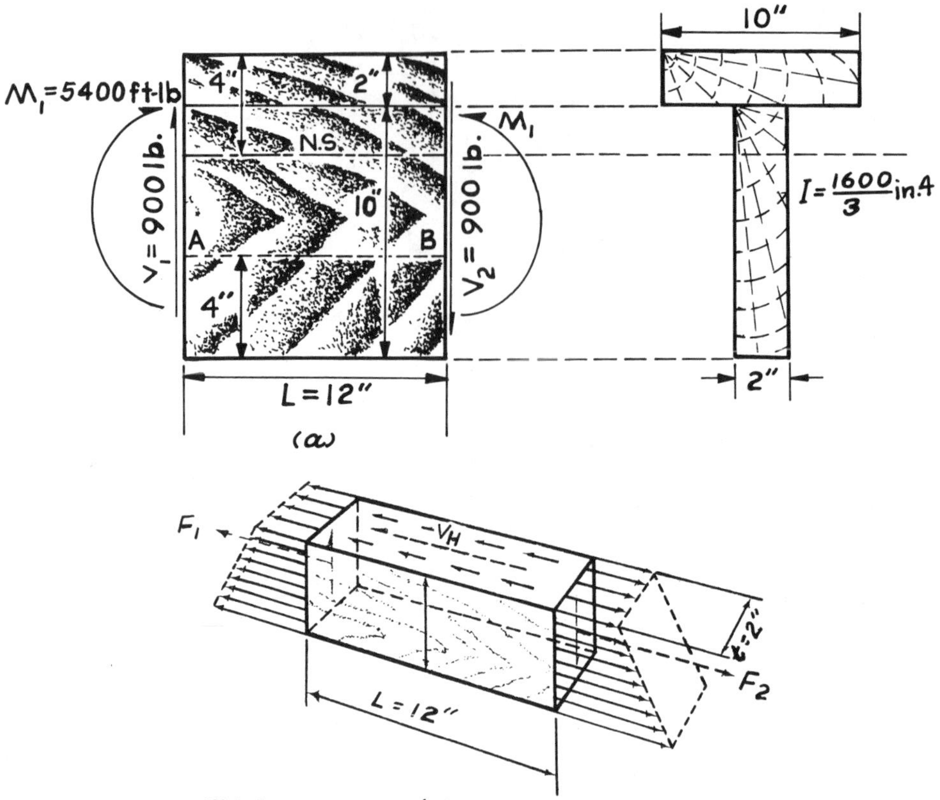

FIG.1 (b)

stresses on plane AB. The forces F_1 and F_2 are the resultants of the normal stresses on the ends of the segment and are equal to the average fiber stress on the end area multiplied by the area.

The normal stress at the neutral axis is zero. The normal stress at the extreme fiber is

$$\sigma = My/I$$

The average fiber stress is found by dividing the volume under the stress distribution by the length over which the stress acts. Since the distribution is triangular, the area is 1/2 bh or $1/2\ y\sigma_{max}$.

The thickness is 2" so the volume under the stress distribution is

$$V = \frac{1}{2} y \times \frac{My/I}{y} \times 2$$

$$= My/I$$

therefore the resultant force F is

$$F_1 = \frac{M_1 y}{I} A$$

$$F_2 = \frac{M_2 y}{I} A$$

The resultant acts at the centroid of the triangular distribution, which is 2y/3, from the neutral axis.

$$d = \frac{2}{3} \times 9$$

$$= 6''$$

$$F_1 = \frac{M_1 y}{I} A = \frac{5400(12)(6)}{1600/3}(2)(4) = 108(54) \text{ lb.}$$

and

$$F_2 = \frac{M_2 y}{I} A = \left(\frac{M_2}{M_1}\right) F_1 = \frac{63}{54}(108)(54) = 108(63) \text{lb.}$$

Summing forces in the horizontal direction on Fig. 1b gives

$$V_H = F_2 - F_1 = 108(63) - 108(54) = 972 \text{ lb.}$$

The average shearing stress on plane AB is equal to the shear force divided by the area of the plane AB.

$$\tau = \frac{V_H}{A_H} = \frac{972}{12(2)} = 40.5 \text{ psi.}$$

In this example, the shearing stress on plane AB does not vary with the length; therefore, because of the complimentary property of shear, the shearing stresses on the vertical planes at A and B are also 40.5 psi in the directions shown.

BENDING STRESS

• PROBLEM 7-5

A rectangular wood beam is to be cut from a circular log of diameter d (see figure). What should be the dimensions b and h in order to have the strongest beam?

Solution: The strongest beam has the greatest section modulus,

$$Z = \frac{bh^2}{6} \tag{1}$$

Consider the Cartesian equation of the log's cross-section - the equation of a circle with b/2 as the horizontal co-ordinate and h/2 as the vertical co-ordinate with the origin at the circle's center as in Figure 2:

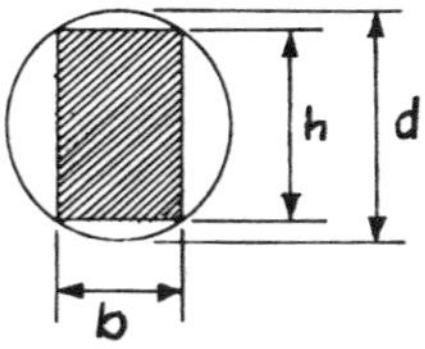

FIG.1

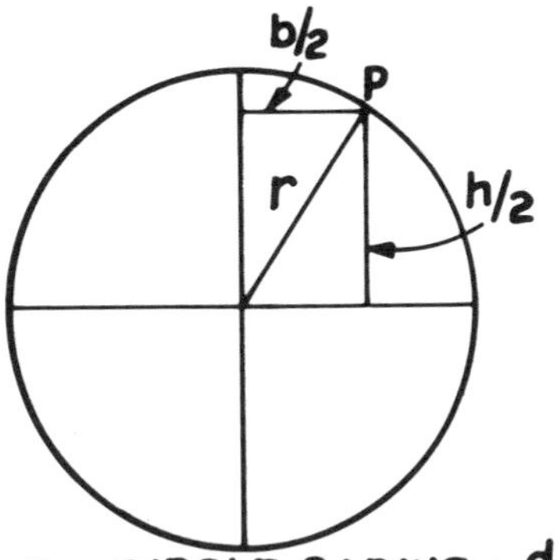

FIG.2. r = CIRCLE RADIUS = d/2

For a point p to lie on this circle (i.e., for the log defined by point p to be cut from the circular log) $(h/2)^2 + (b/2)^2 = (d/2)^2$ or

$$h^2 + b^2 = d^2$$

Therefore $b = (d^2 - h^2)^{1/2}$; $h = (d^2 - b^2)^{1/2}$. (2)

Substituting for h in Eq. (1)

$$Z = \frac{b(d^2 - b^2)}{6} = \frac{bd^2 - b^3}{6}$$

Maximizing:

$$\frac{dz}{db} = 0 = \frac{1}{6}[d^2 - 3b^2]$$

therefore $b = \frac{d}{\sqrt{3}}$.

From $h = (d^2 - b^2)^{1/2}$ in Eq. (2), substitute for b ;

$$h = (d^2 - d^2/3)^{1/2} = d\sqrt{2/3}$$

therefore for the strongest section, $b = d/\sqrt{3}$, $h = d\sqrt{2/3}$.

• PROBLEM 7-6

A 12-in.-by-16-in. (full-sized), wooden cantilever beam weighing 50 lb per foot carries an upward concentrated force of 4,000 lb at the end, as shown in Fig. 1. Determine the maximum bending stresses at a section 6 ft from the free end.

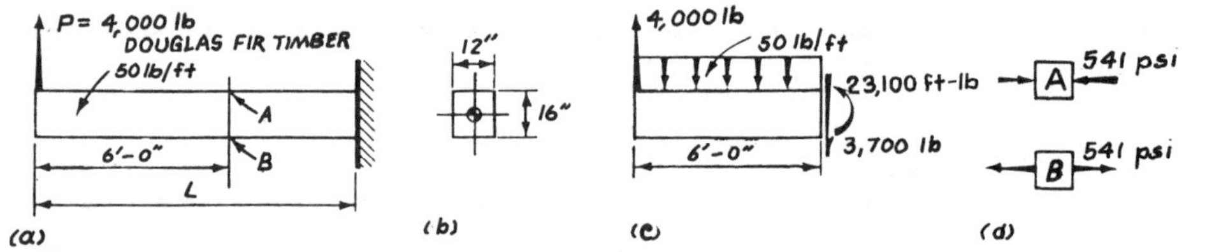

FIG. 1

Solution: A free-body diagram for a 6-ft segment of the beam is shown in Fig. 1c. The weight, 50 lb/ft. is considered as a uniformly distributed external load and the beam is then considered massless. To keep this segment in equilibrium requires a shear of 4,000 - 50(6) = 3,700 lb and a bending moment of 4,000(6) - 50(6)3 = 23,100 ft-lb at the cut section. Both these quantities are shown with their proper sense in Fig. 1. By inspecting the cross-sectional area, the distance from the neutral axis to the extreme fibers is seen to be 8 in., hence c = 8 in. This is applicable to both the tension and the compression fiber.

Therefore,

$$I_{zz} = \frac{bh^3}{12} = \frac{12(6)^3}{12} = 4,095 \text{ in.}^4$$

$$\sigma_{max} = \frac{Mc}{I} = \frac{23,100(12)8}{4,095} = \pm 541 \text{ psi}$$

From the sense of the bending moment shown in Fig. 1c the top fibers of the beam are seen to be in compression, and the bottom ones in tension. In the answer given, the positive sign applies to the tensile stress, the negative sign applies to the compressive stress. Both of these stresses decrease at a linear rate toward the neutral axis where the bending stress is zero. The normal stresses acting on infinitesimal elements at A and B are shown in Fig. 1d.

ALTERNATE SOLUTION

If only the maximum stress is desired, the equation involving the section modulus may be used. The section modulus for a rectangular section in algebraic form is

$$S = \frac{I}{c} = \frac{bh^3}{12}\frac{2}{h} = \frac{bh^2}{6}$$

Therefore $S = 12(16)^2/6 = 512 \text{ in.}^3$, and

$$\sigma_{max} = \frac{M}{S} = \frac{23,100(12)}{512} = 541 \text{ psi} .$$

• PROBLEM 7-7

Find the maximum tensile and compressive bending stresses in the symmetrical T beam of Fig. 1 under the action of a constant bending moment M_b .

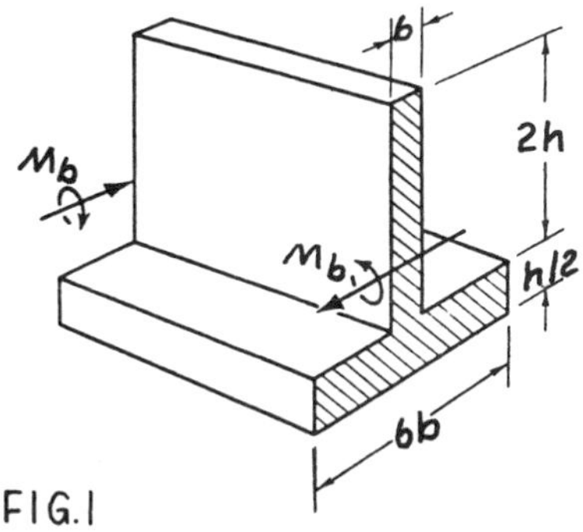

FIG.1

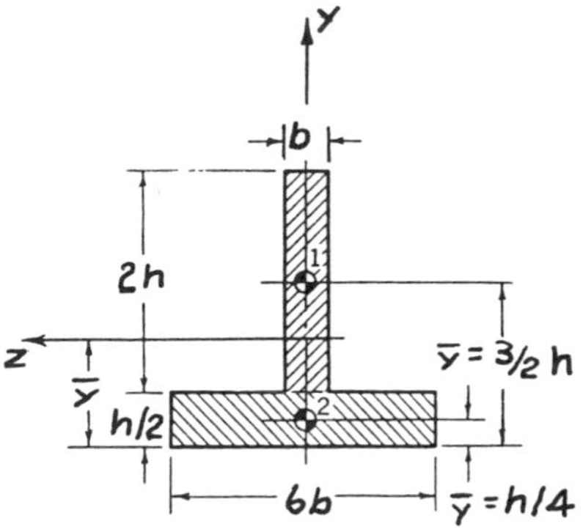

FIG.2

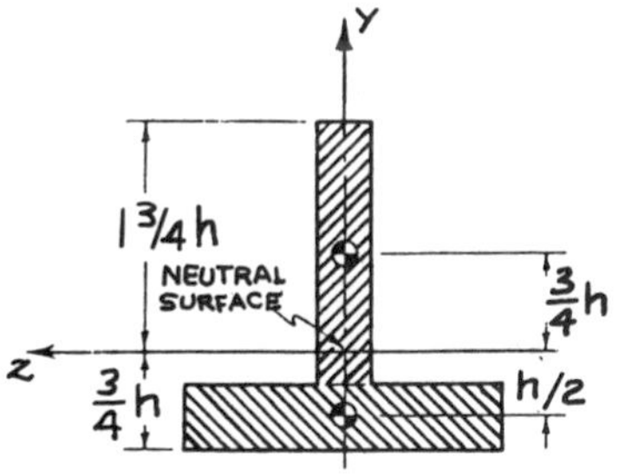

FIG.3

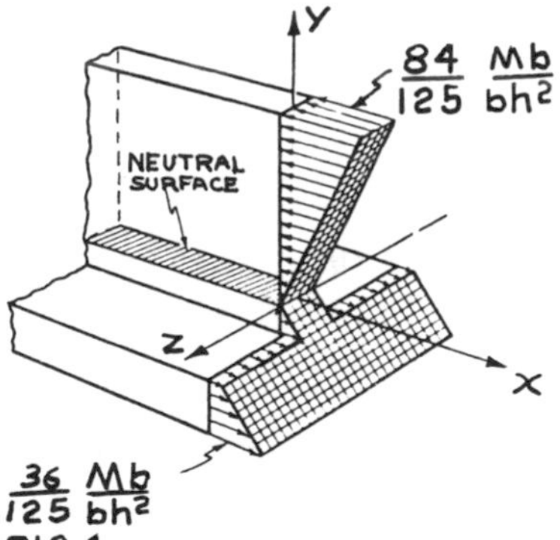

FIG4

Solution: Since we have the relation $\sigma = M_b y/I$ available, our task in this problem centers around the location of the neutral surface and the evaluation of I_{yy} . As a first step we must locate the z-axis in the centroid of the cross section. In Fig. 2 consider the beam to be made up of the rectangle 1 of dimensions b by 2h and the rectangle 2 of dimensions 6h by h/2, and let $\bar{y}$ represent the distance from the base to the centroid of the cross section. Then

$$\bar{y} = \frac{\sum_i \bar{y}_i A_i}{\sum_i A_i} = \frac{3/2\ h(2bh) + (h/4)(3bh)}{2bh + 3bh} = \frac{3}{4} h \tag{a}$$

where $A_i \equiv$ the area of the ith rectangle ;

$\bar{y}_i \equiv$ the distance of the centroid of the ith rectangle to a chosen surface. (Axis which is convenient). In this case, use the outer surface of the flange. The location of the axes in the cross-section is shown in Fig. 3. Now calculate the moment of inertia for the rectangle 1 by use of the parallel-axis theorem, i.e.,

$$I_{yy_1} = I_{yy} + Ah^2$$

where I_{yy} ≡ moment of inertia about the centroidal axis of the section being considered.

A ≡ area of the section;

h ≡ distance from the centroidal axis of the section to the axis about which we desire to find the moment of inertia.

$$(I_{yy})_1 = \frac{b(2h)^3}{12} + 2bh(3/4\ h)^2 = 43/24bh^3 \qquad \text{(b)}$$

Similarly, for the rectangle 2 we obtain

$$(I_{yy})_2 = \frac{6b(h/2)^3}{12} + 3bh(h/2)^2 = 13/16\ bh^3 \qquad \text{(c)}$$

Then, for the entire cross section

$$I_{yy} = (I_{yy})_1 + (I_{yy})_2 = 43/24\ bh^3 + 13/16\ bh^3 = 125/48\ bh^3 \qquad \text{(d)}$$

Now, substituting (d) in the expression relating stress and moment together with $y = -3/4\ h$, we find the maximum tensile bending stress

$$\sigma_x = -\frac{M_b(-3/4\ h)}{125/48\ bh^3} = \frac{36}{125}\ \frac{M_b}{bh^2} \qquad \text{(e)}$$

The maximum compressive bending stress occurs at $y = +1\ 3/4\ h$,

$$\sigma_x = -\frac{M_b(7/4\ h)}{125/48\ bh^3} = -\frac{84}{125}\ \frac{M_b}{bh^2} \qquad \text{(f)}$$

The stress distribution in the beam is illustrated in Fig. 4. We see that the maximum compressive stress is approximately 2.3 times greater than the maximum tensile stress.

• PROBLEM 7-8

The sketch shows the cross section of a T-beam which is transmitting a bending moment. What is the ratio of the maximum bending stress in the stem to that in the flange?

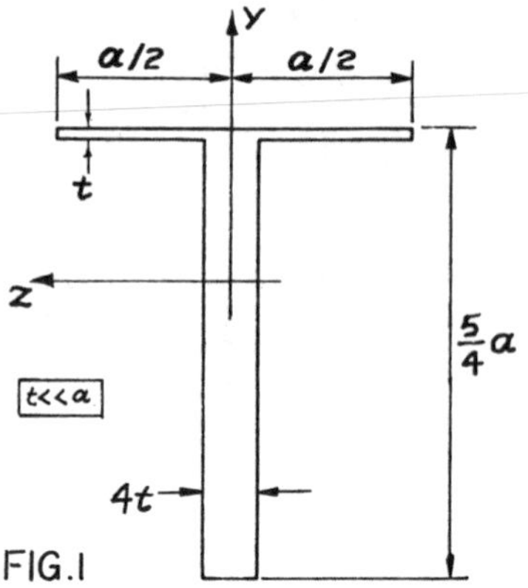

FIG.1

Solution: The expression for bending stress anywhere in the section is

$$\sigma = \frac{My}{I}$$

where $M \equiv$ bending moment acting on the section;
$y \equiv$ distance from the neutral axis to any point on the cross-section;
$I \equiv$ moment of inertia of the whole cross section.
Let the distance to the middle surface from the top of the flange = $\bar{y}$.

$$\bar{y}\,\Sigma A = \Sigma Ay$$

$$\bar{y}(at + (\tfrac{5}{4}a-t)4t) = at \cdot \frac{t}{2} + (\tfrac{5}{4}a-t)4t(\tfrac{5}{4}a-t)/2$$

$$\bar{y}(at + 5at - 4t^2) = \frac{at^2}{2} + 2t\left(\frac{25}{16}a^2 - \frac{5}{2}t + t^2\right)$$

$$\bar{y} = \frac{\frac{at^2}{2} + \frac{25a^2t}{8} - 5t^2 + 2t^3}{at + 5at - 4t^2}$$

Dividing top and bottom by t:

$$\bar{y} = \frac{\frac{at}{2} + \frac{25a^2}{8} - 5t + 2t^2}{a + 5a - 4t}$$

Since $t \ll a$, all the terms with t in them are negligibly small and can be dropped.

$$\bar{y} \approx \frac{\frac{25a^2}{8}}{a + 5a}$$

$$\bar{y} \approx \frac{25}{48}a$$

Since M and I are constant, the ratio of the maximum stresses in the flange and the web will be the ratio of the greatest y's.
For the flange, $y = 25/48\ a$

$$\text{web.}\quad y = \frac{5}{4}a - \frac{25}{48}a = \frac{35}{48}a$$

Therefore ratio of the maximum bending stress in the stem to that in the flange is

$$\frac{35}{48}a \times \frac{48}{25a} = 1.4$$

• PROBLEM 7-9

Find the ratio $K = \frac{M_L}{M_y}$ for the T beam shown. Note:

M_L: limit bending moment

M_y: bending moment at onset of yielding.

Solution: First locate the neutral axis $\bar{y}$

$$\bar{y}\,\Sigma A = \Sigma A \cdot y$$

The vertical and horizontal pieces of the T bar will be treated as

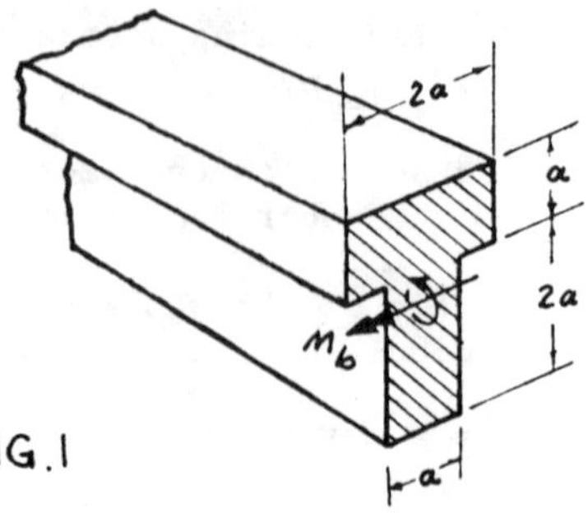

FIG. 1

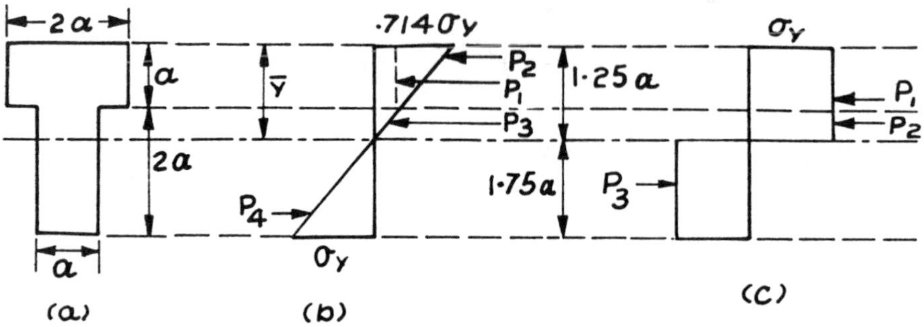

FIG. 2.

separate sections. The area of each section is $\ell \times w = 2a^2$. The distance from the top edge of the T to the center of the horizontal section is a/2, and to the center of the vertical section, $a + \frac{1}{2}(2a) = 2a$.

$$\bar{y}(2a^2 + 2a^2) = 2a^2 \cdot a/2 + 2a^2 \cdot 2a$$

$$\bar{y} = 1.25a$$

When moment M_b is applied, yielding starts first at the lower end. This follows from $\sigma = M_y/I$, since y to the lower fibre is greater than y to the upper fibre. The stress distribution is shown in Fig. 2(b). Stress in the upper fibre,

$$\sigma = \frac{1.25a}{1.75a}\,\sigma_y$$

This means that the stress at the top edge of the T, when the bottom edge just begins to yield, is $.714\sigma_y$, where σ_y is the yield stress. In Fig. 2(b), the stress distribution is divided into sections. Each stress section can be broken down into an area and an equivalent force, P.

The top triangular section of stress distribution is further divided into two smaller triangles and a rectangle. The rectangle and the base of the smallest triangle both have the same width. The height of the smallest triangle is the height of the whole top triangle minus the height of the horizontal of the T bar.

$$h = 1.25a - a = .25a$$

By the geometry of similar triangles, the ratio of the base of the smallest triangle to the base of the whole top triangle is the same as the ratio of their heights.

$$\frac{.25a}{1.25a} = \frac{b}{.714\sigma_y}$$

$$b = .143\sigma_y$$

This distance, b, is the width of the base of the smallest triangle and the width of the rectangle. The width of the base of the other small triangle is:

$$.714\sigma_y - .143\sigma_y = .571\sigma_y$$

For the rectangular stress section, the stress is constant throughout, for the triangular stress sections, the average stress is half the maximum stress which exists at the base.

Using the above facts, the stresses are multiplied by the corresponding areas of the T to find the forces.

$$P_1 = .143 \times 2a^2\sigma_y = .286a^2\sigma_y$$

$$P_2 = \tfrac{1}{2} \times .571 \times 2a^2\sigma_y = .571a^2\sigma_y$$

$$P_3 = \tfrac{1}{2} \times .143\sigma_y \times .25a^2 = .0179a^2\sigma_y$$

$$P_4 = \tfrac{1}{2}\sigma_y \times 1.75a^2 = .875a^2\sigma_y$$

The moment is the sum of the forces multiplied by their distances from the neutral axis. The equivalent force acts at the center of the rectangular stress section and in triangular sections, at distance from the apex of 2/3 the height. Therefore bending moment at the onset of yielding is

$$M_y = .75aP_1 + .917aP_2 + \frac{2}{3} \times .25aP_3 + 1.75a \times \frac{2}{3}aP_4$$

Substituting for P_1, P_2, P_3 and P_4 gives

$$M_y = .75a \times .286a^2\sigma_y + .917a \times .571a^2\sigma_y + \frac{2}{3} \times .25a \times .0179a^2\sigma_y$$

$$+ .875a^2\sigma_y \times 1.75a \times \frac{2}{3}$$

$$= 1.76195a^3\sigma_y$$

When the entire cross section of the beam has yielded, the stress distribution is as shown in Fig. 2(c)

$$P_1 = 2a^2\sigma_y \qquad P_2 = .25a^2\sigma_y \qquad P_3 = 1.75a^2\sigma_y$$

$$M_L = .75aP_1 + .125aP_2 + \frac{1.75a}{2}P_3$$

Substituting for P_1, P_2, P_3 we have

$$M_L = .75a \times 2a^2\sigma_y + .125a \times .25a^2\sigma_y + .875a \times 1.75a^2\sigma_y$$

$$= 3.0625a^3\sigma_y$$

The ratio

$$K = \frac{M_L}{M_y} = \frac{3.0625a^3\sigma_y}{1.76195a^3\sigma_y}$$

$$= 1.72$$

• PROBLEM 7-10

Find the maximum tensile and compressive stresses acting normal to the section A-A of the machine bracket shown in Fig. 1(a) caused by the applied force of 8 kips.

Solution: The shear and bending moment of proper magnitude and sense to maintain the segment of the member in equilibrium are shown in Fig.

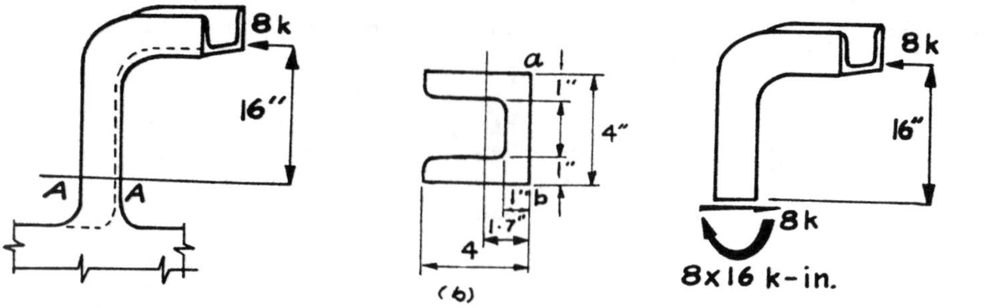

(a) (b) (c)

FIG.1 SECTION A-A

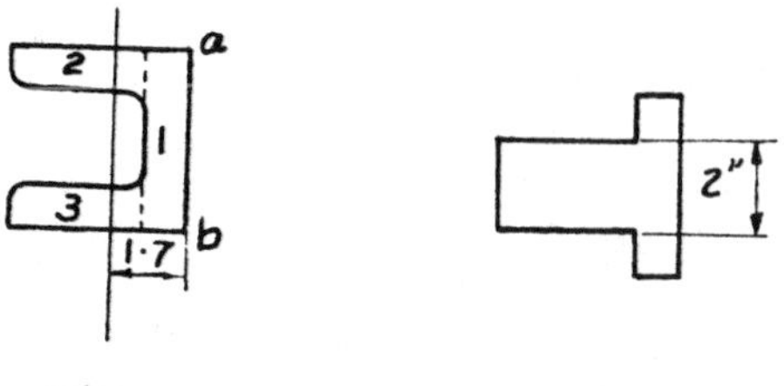

(d) (e)

1(c). Next the neutral axis of the beam must be located. This is done by locating the centroid of the area shown in Fig. 1(b)(also see Fig. 1(d). Then the moment of inertia about the neutral axis is computed. In both these calculations the legs of the cross section are assumed rectangular, neglecting fillets. Then, keeping in mind the sense of the resisting bending moment and applying $\sigma = M_c/I$ one obtains the desired values.

Area Number	A[in.^{2}]	y[in.] (from ab)	Ay
1	4.0	0.5	2.0
2	3.0	2.5	7.5
3	3.0	2.5	7.5
	$\Sigma A = 10.0$ in.^{2}		$\Sigma Ay = 17.0$ in.^{3}

$$\bar{y} = \frac{\Sigma Ay}{\Sigma A} = \frac{17.0}{10.0} = 1.70 \text{ in. from the line ab}$$

$$I = \Sigma(I_0 + Ad^2) = \frac{4(1)^3}{12} + 4(1.2)^2 + \frac{(2)1(3)^3}{12} + 2(3)(0.8)^2$$

$$= 14.43 \text{ in.}^4$$

$$\sigma_{max} = \frac{Mc}{I} = \frac{(8)16(2.3)}{14.43} = 20.4 \text{ ksi} \quad \text{(compression)}$$

$$\sigma_{max} = \frac{Mc}{I} = \frac{(8)16(1.7)}{14.43} = 15.1 \text{ ksi} \quad \text{(tension)}$$

These stresses vary linearly toward the neutral axis and vanish there. If for the same bracket the direction of the force P were reversed, the sense of the above stresses would also reverse. The results obtained would be the same if the cross-sectional area of the bracket were made T-shaped as shown in Fig. 1(e). The properties of this section about the significant axis are the same as those of the channel. Both these sections have an axis of symmetry.

A cantilever beam of width b and length L has a depth which tapers uniformly from d at the tip to 3d at the wall. It is loaded by a force P at the tip, as shown. Find the location and magnitude of the maximum bending stress.

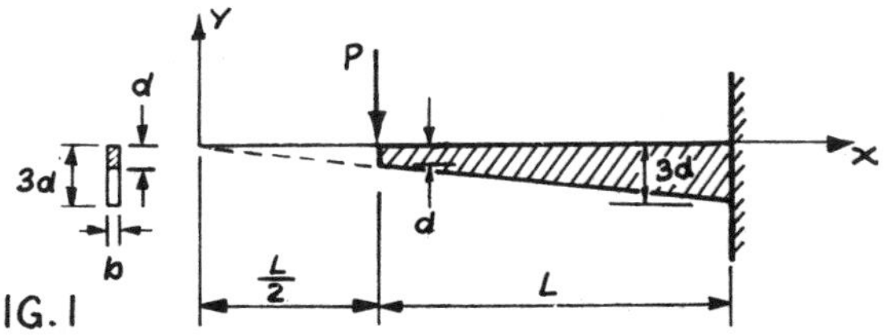

FIG. 1

Solution: Bending stress at any location x, is given by

$$\sigma_x = \frac{M_x y_x}{I_x} \qquad (1)$$

Bending moment at any point, $M_x = P(x - L/2)$

$$y_x = \frac{x}{L}\frac{d}{2}$$

Moment of inertia of the cross-section at any point

$$I_x = 2\int_0^{dx/L} b\bar{y}^2\, dy$$

$$= 2.b\,\frac{1}{3}\left(\frac{dx}{L}\right)^3$$

$$= \frac{2}{3}\, bd^3\, \frac{x^3}{L^3}$$

Substituting Eq. (1) gives

$$\sigma_x = P(x - L/2) \times \frac{dx}{L} \times \frac{L^3}{bd^3x^3} \times \frac{3}{2}$$

$$= \frac{3}{2}\,\frac{L^2}{bd^2}\, P[x - L/2] \cdot \frac{1}{x^2}$$

To get the maximum, maximize the function for σ_x

$$\frac{d\sigma_x}{dx} = 0 = \frac{1}{x^2} - 2[x - L/2] \cdot \frac{1}{x^3}$$

therefore $x = L$.

Therefore maximum stress occurs at a point $x = L$. Substituting for x in the general expression for stress gives the maximum value of stress.

$$\therefore (\sigma_x)_{max} = \frac{3}{2}\frac{L^2}{bd^2}\, P[L - L/2] \cdot \frac{1}{L^2}$$

$$= \frac{3}{4}\frac{PL}{bd^2}$$

• PROBLEM 7-12

A beam having the cross-section shown in Fig. 1 is subjected to a bending moment about the axis zz. The stress distribution is assumed to be linear. Show that the moment fibre stresses can be reduced by cutting off the shaded corners and calculate the optimum value of y_1.

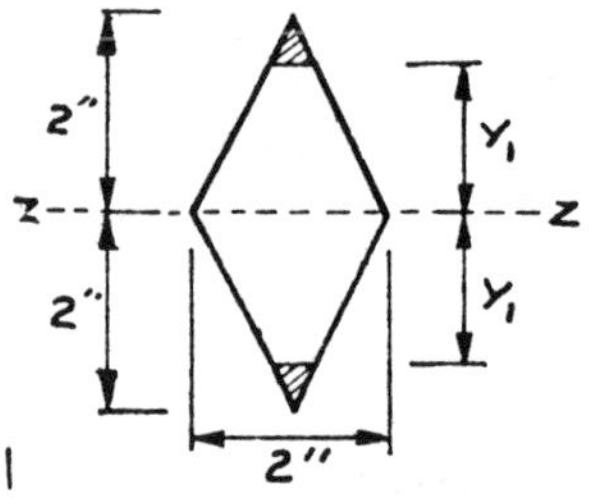

FIG.1

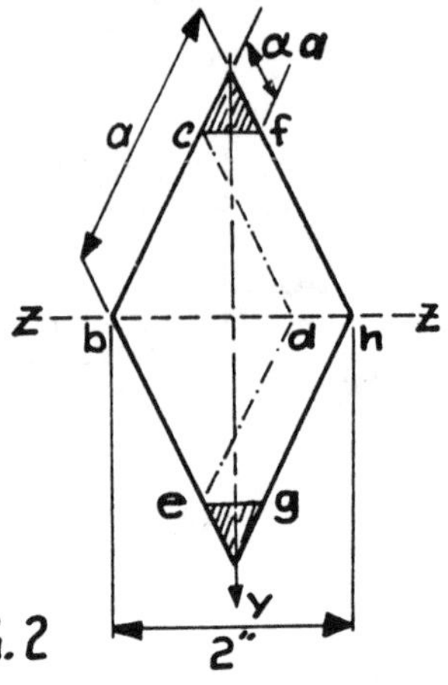

FIG.2

Solution: The moment of inertia of the reduced section will be obtained by adding to the moment of inertia of bcde about its diagonal bd that of the two parallelograms cfdh and gedh about their common bases dh. Thus

$$I = \frac{2a^4(1-\alpha)^4}{12} + 2\cdot\frac{2\alpha a}{3\sqrt{3}}\left[\frac{a(1-\alpha)\sqrt{3}}{2}\right]^3$$

$$= \frac{a^4(1-\alpha^4)}{6} + \frac{a^4\alpha(1-\alpha)^3}{2}$$

$$= \frac{a^4(1-\alpha)^3}{6}(1+3\alpha)$$

The corresponding section modulus is

$$Z = \frac{2I}{\sqrt{3}\,a(1-\alpha)}$$

$$= \frac{2\cdot a^4(1-\alpha)^3(1+3\alpha)}{6\sqrt{3}\,a(1-\alpha)}$$

$$= \frac{a^3(1-\alpha)^2(1+3\alpha)}{3\sqrt{3}}$$

This section modulus is maximum for that value of α which makes $dz/d\alpha = 0$;

$$\frac{dz}{d\alpha} = \frac{a^3}{3\sqrt{3}}\left[(1-\alpha)^2\cdot 3 - 2(1-\alpha)(1+3\alpha)\right] = 0$$

$$\alpha = 1/9$$

$$(Z)_{max} = 1.053 \frac{a^3}{3\sqrt{3}}$$

The moment of inertia of the complete cross-section is $I = a^4/6$ and the corresponding section modulus is

$$Z = \frac{2}{\sqrt{3}} \frac{a^3}{6} = \frac{a^3}{3\sqrt{3}}$$

Thus by cutting off the corners, the section modulus is increased and the maximum bending stress is reduced by a corresponding amount. The optimum value of

$$y_1 = 2 - \frac{1}{9} \cdot 2$$

$$= 16/9 \text{ in.}$$

• PROBLEM 7-13

Compare stresses in a 2-in.by-2-in. rectangular bar subjected to end couples of 13,333 in-lb in the three special cases: (a) straight beam, (b) beam curved to a radius of 10 in. along the centroidal axis, i.e., $\bar{r}$ = 10 in., Fig. 1(a), and (c) beam curved to $\bar{r}$ = 3 in.

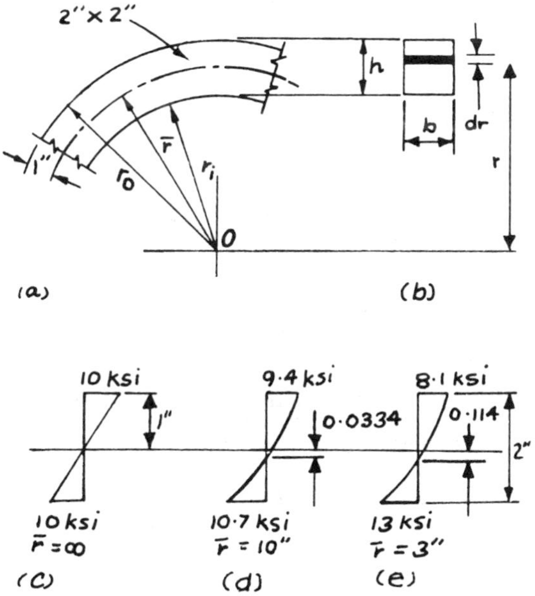

FIG.1

Solution: Case (a) follows directly by applying the equations for the section modulus, S:

$$S = \frac{I}{h/2} = \frac{bh^3/12}{h/2}$$

$$S = \frac{bh^2}{6} = \frac{2(2)^2}{6} = 1.33 \text{ in.}^3$$

$$\sigma_{max} = \frac{M}{S} = \frac{13.333}{1.33} = 10,000 \text{ psi or } 10 \text{ ksi}$$

This result is shown in Fig. 1(c). $\bar{r} = \infty$ since a straight bar has an infinite radius of curvature.

To solve parts (b) and (c) the neutral axis must be located first. This is found in general terms by integrating $RdA = Ar$. For the rectangular section, the elementary area is taken as bdr, Fig. 1(b). The integration is carried out between the limits r_1 and r_0, the inner and outer radii, respectively.

$$R = \frac{A}{\int_A dA/r} = \frac{bh}{\int_{r_i}^{r_0} bdr/r} = \frac{h}{\int_{r_i}^{r_0} dr/r}$$

$$= \frac{h}{\ln r\Big|_{r_i}^{r_0}} = \frac{h}{\ln\left(\frac{r_0}{r_i}\right)} = \frac{h}{2.3026\log\left(\frac{r_0}{r_i}\right)} \qquad \text{(a)}$$

where h is the depth of the section.

For Case (b), $h = 2$ in., $\bar{r} = 10$ in., $r_i = 9$ in., and $r_0 = 11$ in. The solution is obtained by evaluating Eqs. (a) and

$$\sigma = \frac{Mc}{I} = \frac{M(R - r)}{rA(\bar{r} - R)}$$

Subscript i refers to the normal stress σ of the inside fibers; 0 of the outside fibers.

$$R = \frac{2}{2.3026 \log(11/9)} = \frac{2}{2.3026(\log 11 - \log 9)} = 9.9666 \text{ in.}$$

$$e = \bar{r} - R = 10 - 9.9666 = 0.0334 \text{ in.}$$

$$\sigma_i = \frac{M(R - r_i)}{r_i A(\bar{r} - R)} = 13{,}333 \frac{9.9666 - 9}{9(4)(0.0334)} = 10{,}700 \text{ psi}$$

$$\sigma_0 = \frac{M(R - r_0)}{r_0 A(\bar{r} - R)} = 13{,}333 \frac{9.9666 - 11}{11(4)(0.0334)} = -9{,}400 \text{ psi}$$

The negative sign of σ_0 indicates a compressive stress. These quantities and the corresponding stress distribution are shown in Fig. 1(d); $\bar{r} = 10$ in.

Case (c) is computed in the same way. Here $h = 2$ in., $\bar{r} = 3$ in., $r_i = 2$ in., and $r_0 = 4$ in. Results of the computation are shown in Fig. 1(e).

$$R = \frac{2}{\ln(4/2)} = \frac{2}{\ln 2} = \frac{2}{0.6931} = 2.886 \text{ in.}$$

$$e = 3 - 2.886 = 0.114 \text{ in.}$$

$$\sigma_i = 13{,}333 \frac{0.886}{2(0.114)4} = 13{,}000 \text{ psi}$$

$$\sigma_0 = 13{,}333 \frac{-1.114}{4(0.114)4} = -8{,}140 \text{ psi}$$

Calculations of R must be very accurate since differences between R and numerically comparable quantities are used in the stress formula. But the evaluation of the integral for R over the cross-sectional area may become very complex. This difficulty prompted the development of other methods of solution. One such method consists of expanding certain terms of the solution into a series, another of building up a solution on the basis of a special transformed section. Yet another device consists of working "in reverse." Curved beams of various cross-sections, curvatures, and applied moments are analyzed for stress; then these quantities are divided by a flexural stress that would exist for the same beam if it were straight. These ratios are then tabulated. Hence, conversely, if stress in a curved beam is wanted, it is given as

$$\sigma = K(Mc/I)$$

where the coefficient K is obtained from a table or a graph and Mc/I is computed as in the usual flexure formula.

An expression for the distance from the center of curvature to the neutral axis of a curved beam of circular cross-sectional area is given below for future reference:

$$R = (\bar{r} + \sqrt{\bar{r}^2 - c^2})/2$$

where $\bar{r}$ is the distance from the center of curvature to the centroid and c is the radius of the circular cross-sectional area.

• PROBLEM 7-14

A 2-in.by-2-in. elastic bar bent into a U shape as in Fig. 1a is acted upon by two opposing forces P of $1\frac{1}{3}$ kips each. Determine the maximum normal stress occurring at the section A-B.

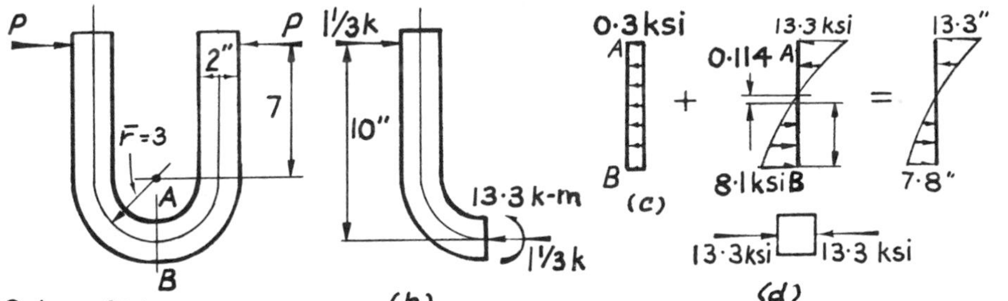

FIG. I (a) (b) (c) (d)

Solution: The section to be investigated is in the curved region of the bar, but this makes no essential difference in the procedure. First a segment of the bar is taken as a free body, as shown in Fig. 1b. At section A-B the axial force, applied at the centroid of the section, and the bending moment necessary to maintain equilibrium are determined. Then, each element of the force system is considered separately. The stress caused by the axial forces is

$$\sigma = \frac{P}{A} = \frac{1.33}{2(2)} = 0.3 \text{ ksi} \quad \text{(compression)}$$

and is shown diagrammatically in the first sketch of Fig. 1c. The normal stresses caused by the bending moment may be obtained by using

$$\sigma = \frac{Mc}{I} = \frac{M(R - r)}{rA(\bar{r} - R)}$$

where R is the radius of the neutral axis, $\bar{r}$ is the radius of the centroidal axis, and r is the radius at which it is desired to know the stress. The equation for R for a curved rectangular beam is

$$R = \frac{h}{\ln\left(\frac{r_0}{r_i}\right)}$$

Substituting in the values:

$$R = \frac{2}{\ln\left(\frac{3+1}{3-1}\right)} = 2.885$$

Thus the stresses on the inner and outer surfaces are:

$$\sigma_i = \frac{M(R - r_i)}{r_i A(\bar{r} - R)} = \frac{(13.3)(2.885 - 2)}{2(4)(3 - 2.885)} = 12.8 \text{ ksi}$$

$$\sigma_0 = \frac{(13.3)(2.885 - 4)}{4(4)(3 - 2.885)} = -8.08 \text{ ksi}$$

The stress distribution corresponding to this case is shown in the second sketch of Fig. 1(c). By superposing the results of these two solutions, the compound stress distribution is obtained. This is shown in the third sketch of Fig. 1(c). The maximum stress occurs at A and is a compressive stress of 13.3 ksi. An isolated element for the point A is shown in Fig. 1(d). Shearing stresses are absent at section A-B as no shearing force is necessary to maintain equilibrium of the segment shown in Fig. 1(b). The relative insignificance of the stress caused by the axial force is striking.

• PROBLEM 7-15

A simple beam carries two wheel loads a distance d = 6 ft. apart (see figure). Each wheel transmits a load P = 3k, and the carriage may occupy any position on the beam. The span length L = 24 ft. Determine the maximum bending stress in the beam if it is an S8 x 23 section.

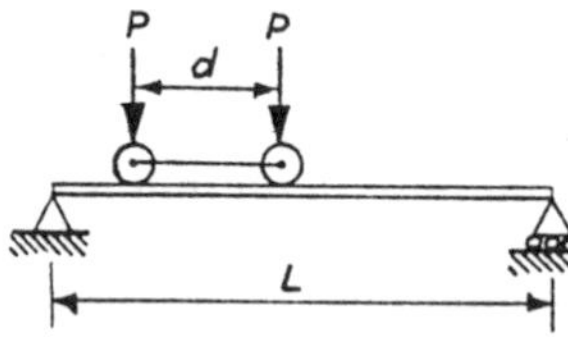

FIG.1

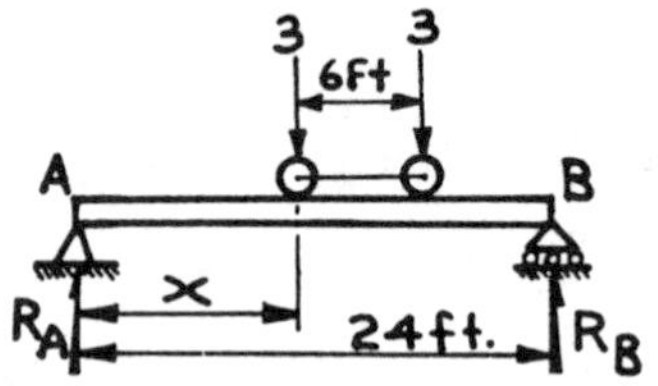

FIG. 2

Solution: Define the position of the wheel on the span by the distance x. At A, $\Sigma M = 0$

$$3x + 3(x + 6) = 24 R_B$$

$$6x + 6(3) = 24 R_B$$

$$R_B = \tfrac{1}{4}(x + 3)$$

$\Sigma F = 0$ vertically

$$R_A = 3 + 3 - \tfrac{1}{4}(x + 3)$$

$$R_A = \tfrac{1}{4}(21 - x)$$

Maximum moment occurs under either of the loads therefore $M = R_A x$. Substituting for R_A gives

$$M = \tfrac{1}{4}(21x - x^2)$$

Maximizing M gives position x where moment is maximum

$$\frac{\partial M}{\partial x} = 0 = \tfrac{1}{4}(21 - 2x)$$

$$\therefore x = 10.5 \text{ ft from A}$$

$$M_{max} = 27.565 \text{ kip ft.}$$

The section properties for an S8 x 23 section are

Depth = 8.00 ins.
Area = 6.71 in^2
Moment of inertia = 64.2 in^4

Recall $\sigma = \frac{My}{I}$

$$\therefore \sigma_{max} = \frac{27.565 \times 12 \times 4}{64.2}$$

$$= 20.6 \text{ ksi.}$$

• PROBLEM 7-16

Compute the normal stress resulting from the couple acting on the cantilever beam shown in the diagram.

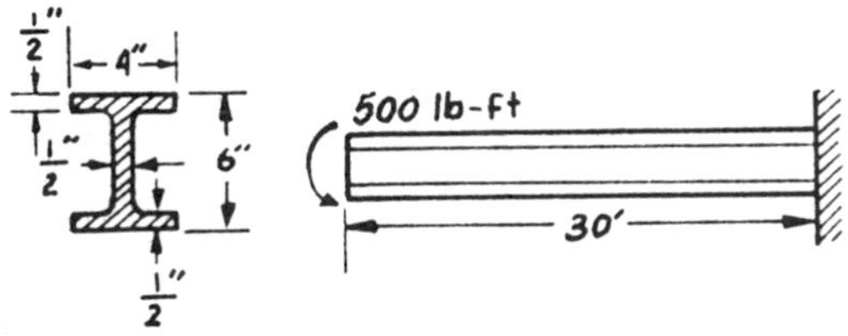

FIG. 1

Solution: The expression relating the moment in a beam and the normal stress in the beam is given by

$$(\sigma_{xx})_{max} = \frac{M_b C}{I_{xx}}$$

where M_b ≡ bending moment in the beam

C ≡ distance from the edge to the neutral axis of the beam

I_{xx} ≡ moment of inertia of the beam about the x-axis

The moment of inertia of the I-shaped section may be most easily found by noting that the I-section is equivalent to two rectangular areas subtracted from a larger rectangular area as shown in Figure 2:

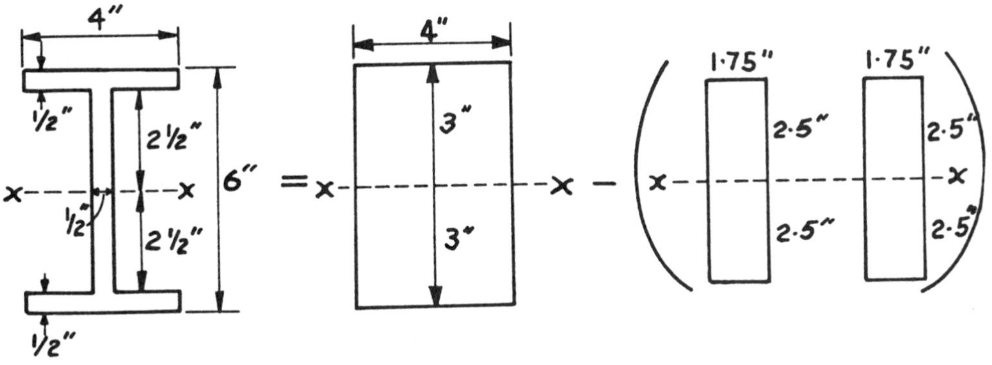

FIG. 2

The moment of inertia of the I-section must equal the moment of inertia of the 4" x 6" rectangle minus twice the moment of inertia of the

1.75" x 5" rectangle. For the 4" x 6" rectangle b = 4", d = 6"

$$I_{xx} = bd^3/12 = 4.6^3/12 = 72 \text{ in.}^4$$

For the two 1.75" x 5" rectangles b = 1.75" and d = 5"

$$I_{xx} = 2 \times 1.75 \times 5^3/12 = 36.46 \text{ in.}^4$$

Therefore for the I-section

$$I_{xx} = \frac{4 \times 6^3}{12} - 2 \times \frac{1.75 \times 5^3}{12}$$

$$= 35.54 \text{ in.}^4$$

Since the I-section is symmetrical about the x-x axis shown in Figure 2,

$$C = 3''$$

$$M_b = 500 \times 12 \text{ in.lb}$$

$$\therefore (\sigma_x)_{max} = \frac{500 \times 12 \times 3}{35.54}$$

$$= 506.45 \text{ lb/in.}^2$$

• PROBLEM 7-17

A beam with overhanging ends (see figure) carries a uniform load of intensity q = 10 kip/ft. on each overhang. Assuming that the beam is a W30 x 172 section with $E = 30 \times 10^6$ psi, determine the maximum normal stress in the beam.

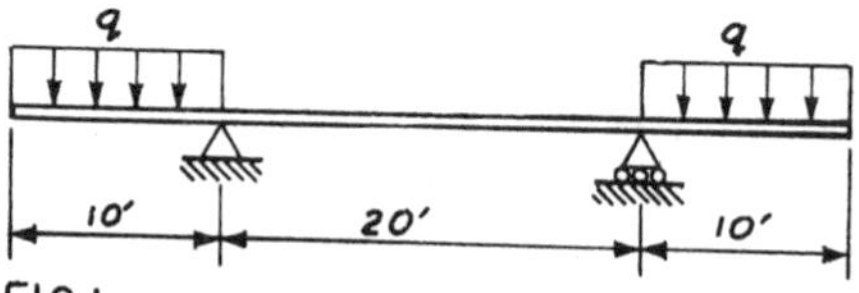

FIG.1

Solution: A W30 x 172 section has the following properties:

nominal size	30" x 15"
depth of section	29.88 ins.
area	50.67 in.^{2}
I	7891.5 in.^{4}

Maximum normal stress occurs at a point where moment is maximum. This is at the midpoint of the beam.

In order to find the moment, the reaction forces need to be determined. The beam is symmetrically loaded, therefore the reactions are equal.

By vertical equilibrium:

$$\Sigma F_y = 0, \; 2 \times 10 \text{ kip/ft} \times 10 \text{ ft} = 2R$$

$$R = 100 \text{ kip}$$

The moment at the midpoint of the beam by moment equilibrium is:

$$\Sigma M = 0 \;\; \circlearrowleft^{+} \;\; M_{max} + 100 \text{ kip} \times 10 \text{ ft} - 10 \text{ kip/ft}$$

$$\times 10 \text{ ft} \times (5 \text{ ft} + 10 \text{ ft}) = 0$$

$$M_{max} = 10 \times 10 \times (5 + 10) - 100 \times 10$$

$$= 6000 \text{ kip-in.}$$

$$\sigma_{max} = \frac{My}{I} = \frac{6000}{7891.5} \times \frac{29.88}{2} = 11.3 \text{ ksi}$$

• PROBLEM 7-18

(a) Determine the required section modulus S for a beam AB to support the distributed load shown in Fig. 1 if $q = 4000$ lb per ft and the allowable bending stress $\sigma_w = 16{,}000$ psi. Neglect the weight of the beam. (b) Choose a wide-flange section from a handbook of structural shapes and beams, taking into account the weight of the beam.

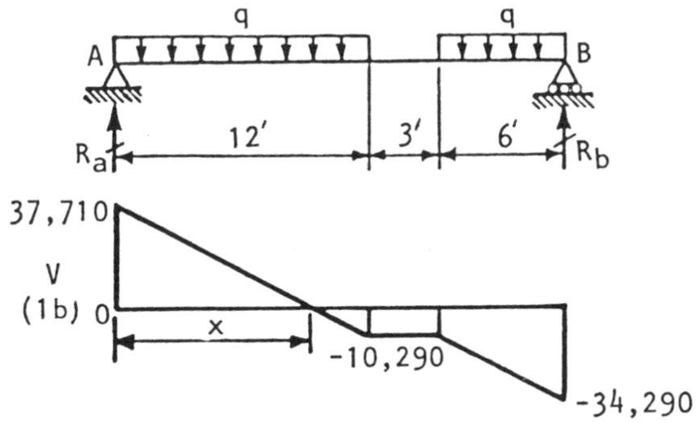

Fig. 1

Solution: (a) To locate the section of maximum bending moment, it is helpful to construct a shear force diagram, shown in Fig. 1. The reactions at the supports are

$$R_a = 37{,}710 \text{ lb} \qquad R_b = 34{,}290 \text{ lb}$$

and the distance x defining the point of zero shear is given by the equation

$$R_a - qx = 0$$

from which $x = R_a/q = 9.43$ ft. At this distance from the left end A, the bending moment is a maximum:

$$M_{max} = R_a x - qx^2/2 = 177{,}800 \text{ ft-lb.}$$

The required section modulus, from $\sigma = M/S$ is

$$S = \frac{177{,}800(12)}{16{,}000} = 133 \text{ in.}^3$$

(b) Referring to the table of wide-flange sections in a handbook of structural shapes and beams, we see that the section listed there, having the required section modulus is W18 $\times$ 85.

If the weight of the beam itself (85 lb per ft) is now added to the other loads on the beam, the maximum moment is found to have increased to 182,400 ft-lb. The required S is then increased to 137 in.^{3}. Inasmuch as the section modulus for the selected section is 157 in.^{3}, it is still satisfactory. If it were not satisfactory, a new beam would be selected and the process repeated using the weight of the new beam when calculating the bending moment.

• PROBLEM 7-19

A steel beam has the cross-section shown in Fig. 1. If the bending moment is +750,000 lb-in. find the stress at the top and bottom surface and at a point 3 in. above the neutral axis.

Solution: By symmetry the neutral axis z-z is at the mid-depth.

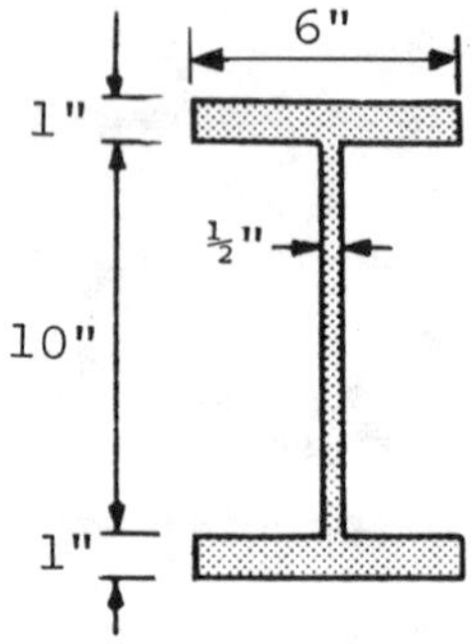

Fig. 1.

The moment of inertia is

$$I = \frac{6 \times 12^3}{12} - \frac{5.5 \times 10^3}{12}$$

$$= 405.67 \text{ in.}^4$$

At the top of the beam, y = +6 in. and

$$\sigma = \frac{-My}{I} = \frac{-750{,}000(+6)}{405.67} = -11{,}100 \text{ psi}$$

At the bottom, y = -6 and

$$\sigma = \frac{-750{,}000(-6)}{405.67} = +11{,}100 \text{ psi}$$

When y = +3

$$\sigma = \frac{-750{,}000(+3)}{405.67} = -5500 \text{ psi}$$

While the stress distribution is linear, the maximum stresses occur at the points farthest from the neutral axis, namely the extreme fibres. If the ordinates of the lower and upper extremities of the section are y_1 and y_2 respectively

$$\sigma_{max} = \frac{My_1}{I} \text{ or } \frac{M y_2}{I}$$

We may put $I/y_1 = Z_1$ and $I/y_2 = Z_2$, where Z_1 and Z_2 are called section moduli. Then the extreme fibre stresses are M/Z_1 and M/Z_2.

• PROBLEM 7-20

When the two boards are tightly clamped together, the maximum stress occurs at section M-M. For the configuration shown, find the depth of the rectangular cross-section if maximum normal stress is 20×10^3 psi.

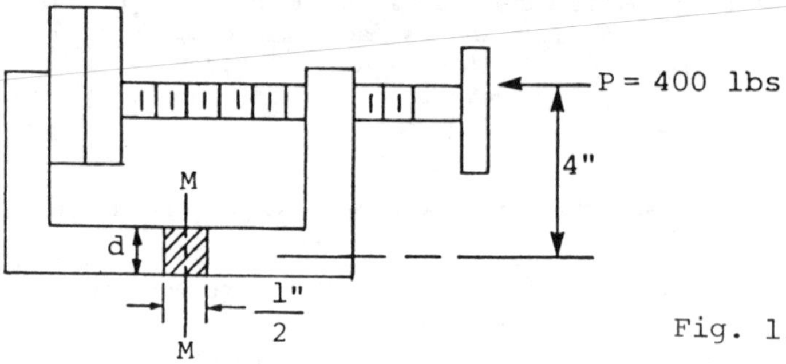

Fig. 1.

Solution: The expression relating moment and stress is

$$\sigma_{xx} = \frac{M_b C}{I_{xx}} \qquad (1)$$

The allowable stress, σ_{xx} = 20,000 psi. Now consider a free body diagram of the clamp with a cut at M-M as seen in Figure 2:

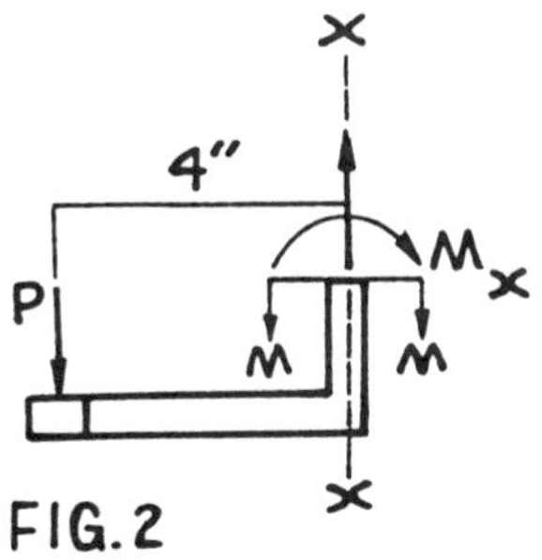

FIG. 2

Moment at M-M; $M_b = M_x = (4")(P)$. But P = 400 lb.

$$\therefore M_b = 1600 \text{ in.lb.}$$

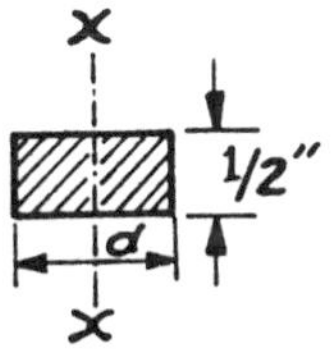

FIG. 3

C ≡ distance from the surface to the midpoint = d/2

$$I_{xx} = \frac{bd^3}{12}, \quad b = \tfrac{1}{2}", \quad d = d$$

$$I_{xx} = \tfrac{1}{2} \cdot \frac{d^3}{12} = \frac{d^3}{24}$$

Substituting in Eq. 1 we have

$$20,000 = 1,600 \times \frac{24}{d^3} \times \frac{d}{2}$$

$$20,000 = \frac{(1600)(12)}{d^2}, \quad d^2 = \frac{19200}{20000}$$

$$\therefore d^2 = \frac{12}{12.5} = 0.96$$

$$d = 0.98 \text{ in.}$$

$$d = 1" \text{ approximately}$$

• PROBLEM 7-21

What is the maximum normal tensile stress τ_{xx} and the minimum radius of curvature for the cantilever beam shown in Fig. 1? Also determine the shear stress at the section 3 ft. from the wall at a position ½ in. from the top surface.

Solution: It is easily seen that the section having the largest moment (and hence the section having the largest τ_{xx}) is at the wall. The bending moment there is

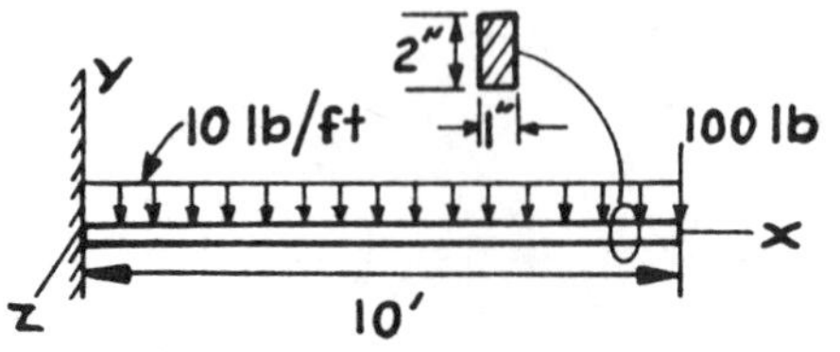

LOADING INCLUDES WEIGHT OF BEAM
E = 30 x 10^6 psi
FIG. 1

$$M_{max} = -(10)(100) - \int_0^{10} 10x\,dx$$

$$= -1500 \text{ lb-ft} = -18{,}000 \text{ in.lb}$$

The maximum tensile stress occurs at the uppermost fibers of the beam. We then get

$$(\tau_{xx})_{max} = \frac{-My}{I} = -\frac{(-18{,}000)(1)}{(1/12)(1)(2^3)}$$

$$= 27{,}000 \text{ psi}$$

The minimum radius of curvature is at this section and is computed as

$$\frac{1}{R} = \frac{M}{EI}$$

$$R = \frac{(30 \times 10^6)(1/12)(1)(2^3)}{(18{,}000)} = 1110 \text{ in.}$$

The shear force V_y at the other section of interest clearly is 170 lb. Hence, we get

$$\bar{\tau}_{xy} = \frac{170[(\frac{1}{2})(1)(\frac{3}{4})]}{[(1/12)(1)(2^3)](1)} = 95.6 \text{ psi}$$

• PROBLEM 7-22

A steel beam 1 in. wide and 3 in. deep is pinned to supports at points A and B, as shown in Fig. 1, where the support B is on rollers and free to move horizontally. The ends of the beam are loaded with 1,000-lb loads. Find the maximum bending stress at the mid-span of the beam and also the angle $\Delta\varphi$ subtended by the cross sections at A and B in the deformed beam.

Solution: First determine the bending moment which is required to satisfy equilibrium at each point along the beam; this is shown in the diagram in Fig. 2 From this diagram we see that the central protion AB is one of constant bending moment, and thus this part of the beam is in a state of pure bending.

To calculate the stress from $\sigma = \frac{M_b C}{I_{yy}}$, we must locate the coordinate axes and calculate I_{yy}. The centroid lies at the mid-height of the cross section, as shown in Fig. 3, and using the integral form of the expression for moment of inertia, i.e.,

$$I_{yy} = \int_{-h/2}^{h/2} y^2 b\,dy$$

Note that this actually is the second moment of area.

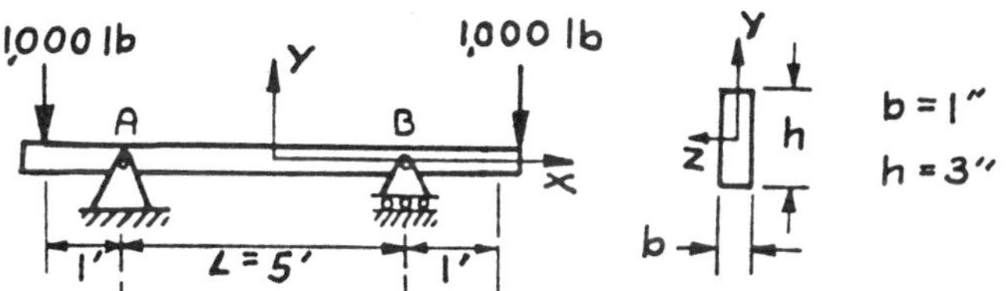

FIG. 1

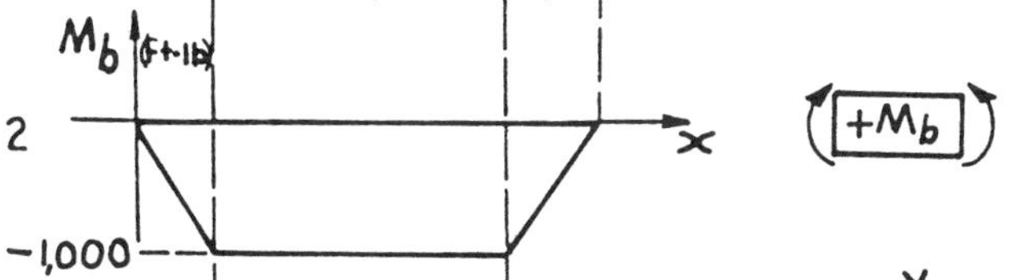

FIG. 2

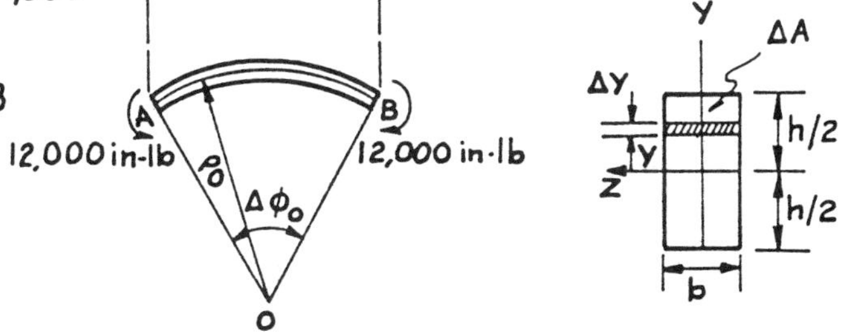

FIG. 3

Consider a strip of thickness dy , see Figure 4.

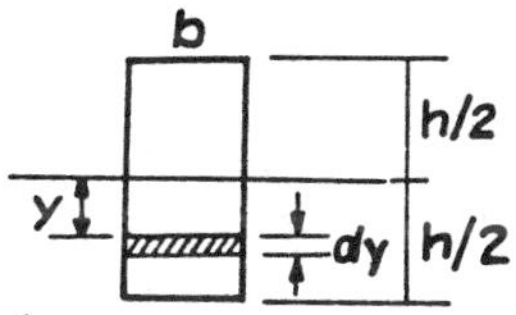

FIG. 4

Area, A = bdy

1st Moment of the element = bydy
2nd Moment of the element = $by^2 dy$

Integrate over the whole cross-section,

$$\int_{-h/2}^{h/2} by^2 \, dy$$

we find

$$I_{yy} = \int_{-h/2}^{h/2} y^2 b \, dy = \frac{bh^3}{12} \tag{a}$$

which on substituting b = 1 in. and h = 3 in. yields

$$I_{yy} = 2.25 \text{ in.}^4 \tag{b}$$

The maximum bending stress occurs at the distance farthest from the neutral surface. At the mid-span the bending stress at the top of the beam is found from

$$\sigma = \frac{M_b C}{I_{yy}}$$

to be

$$\sigma_x = - \frac{(-12{,}000 \text{ in.-lb})(1.5 \text{ in.})}{2.25 \text{ in.}^4} = 8{,}000 \text{ psi} \tag{c}$$

If we use y = -1.5 in., we obtain a numerically equal compressive stress at the bottom of the beam.

To obtain the angle change $\Delta\varphi_0$, we begin by observing that the "force-deformation" relation which is applicable to this situation is the moment-curvature relation

$$\frac{d\varphi}{ds} = \frac{M_b}{EI_{yy}}$$

where $\varphi \equiv$ angle between normals to any two points on the beam
$s \equiv$ distance along the length of the beam
$E \equiv$ modulus of elasticity.

Using $E = 30 \times 10^6$ psi, we find the curvature in the segment AB to be

$$\frac{d\varphi}{ds} = \frac{M_b}{EI_{yy}} = \frac{-12{,}000 \text{ in.-lb}}{(30 \times 10^6 \text{ psi})(2.25 \text{ in.}^4)}$$

$$= -0.000178 \text{ rad/in.}$$
$$= -0.00213 \text{ rad/ft} \qquad \text{(d)}$$

The total angle change between A and B is found by integration of the curvature relation (d).

$$\varphi_B - \varphi_A = \int_A^B d\varphi = \int_{-L/2}^{L/2} \frac{d\varphi}{ds}\, ds$$

$$= -0.00213 \text{ rad/ft} \times 5 \text{ ft.}$$
$$= -0.0106 \text{ rad}$$
$$= -0.61^\circ \qquad \text{(e)}$$

The magnitude of the angle labeled $\Delta\varphi_0$ in Fig. 3 is thus 0.61°.

Note that this angle has been exaggerated in the figure. As a matter of interest, the radius of curvature of the section AB can be obtained from

$$\rho = \frac{1}{d\varphi/ds}$$

where $\rho \equiv$ radius of curvature

$$\rho = \frac{1}{d\varphi/ds} = \frac{1}{-0.00213 \text{ rad/ft}} = -470 \text{ ft.} \qquad \text{(f)}$$

This is indicated in Fig. 4, where $\rho_0 = -\rho$.

• PROBLEM 7-23

An overhanging beam AB is loaded and supported as shown in Fig. 1. Determine the maximum normal stress in the beam and the deflection δ at the center. Assume that the beam has a circular cross section with diameter $d = 10$ in.; also assume $a = 13.5$ in., $L = 59$ in., $P = 26$ k, and $E = 30 \times 10^6$ psi.

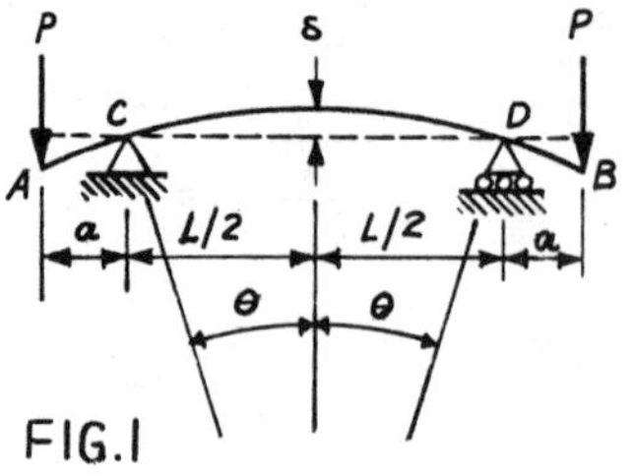

FIG.1

Solution: The part of the beam between the supports is in pure bending with

$$M = Pa = 351,000 \text{ in.-lb}$$

The section modulus of the cross section is $S = \pi d^3/32 = 98.17 \text{ in.}^3$ and, therefore the maximum normal stress is

$$\sigma_{max} = \frac{M}{S} = \frac{351,000}{98.17} = 3580 \text{ psi}$$

From

$$\rho = \frac{EI}{M}$$

where $\rho \equiv$ radius of curvature

$M \equiv$ moment due to bending

$E \equiv$ modulus of elasticity

$I \equiv$ moment of inertia

we obtain the radius of curvature ρ for the circular arc CD (see Fig. 1)

$$\rho = \frac{EI}{M} = \frac{30 \times 10^6 \times 490.9}{351,000} = 41,960 \text{ in.}$$

in which $I = \pi d^4/64 = 490.9 \text{ in.}^4$. From Fig. 1 we see that the deflection δ is

$$\delta = \rho(1 - \cos\theta) \qquad \text{(a)}$$

where θ is a small angle equal to $L/2\rho$, or 0.000703 radian. For small angles $\cos\theta \approx 1 - \theta^2/2$, and hence Eq. (a) becomes

$$\delta = \frac{\rho\theta^2}{2} = \frac{L^2}{8\rho} = 0.0104 \text{ in.}$$

• PROBLEM 7-24

The beam shown is composed of the top element 1 lying freely (not attached) on lower element 2. (a) Calculate the radius of curvature of each element, and (b) the maximum stress.

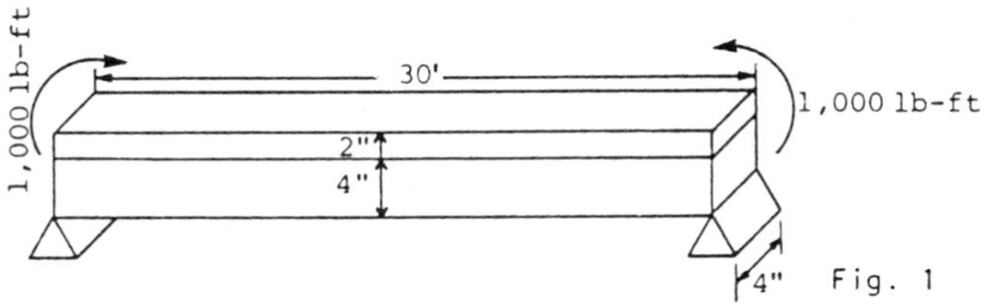

Fig. 1

Solution: The two beams have the same radius of curvature so

$$R = \frac{EI_1}{M_1} = \frac{EI_2}{M_2}$$

$$\therefore \quad \frac{I_1}{I_2} = \frac{M_1}{M_2}$$

The moment resisted by each beam is therefore proportional to its moment of inertia

$$I_1 = \frac{4 \times 2^3}{12} = \frac{8}{3}$$

$$I_2 = \frac{4 \times 4^3}{12} = \frac{64}{3}$$

$$\therefore \frac{I_1}{I_2} = \frac{1}{8} = \frac{M_1}{M_2}$$

$$M_2 = 8M_1$$

but $M_1 + M_2 = 1000 \times 12$ in.-lb. Substituting for M_2 gives

$$9M_1 = 1000 \times 12$$

$$M_1 = 1000 \times \frac{4}{3}$$

$$R = 20 \times 10^6 \times \frac{8}{3} \times \frac{3}{1000 \times 4}$$

$$= 40 \times 10^3 \text{ in.}$$

$$(\sigma_{max})_1 = \frac{M_1 \bar{y}_1}{I_1}$$

$$= 1000 \times \frac{4}{3} \times 1 \times \frac{3}{8}$$

$$= 500 \text{ psi}$$

$$(\sigma_{max})_2 = \frac{M_2 \bar{y}_2}{I_2}$$

$$= 8 \times 1000 \times \frac{4}{3} \times 2 \times \frac{3}{64}$$

$$= 1000 \text{ in.-lb.}$$

• PROBLEM 7-25

A beam is made of two identical metal bars soldered together. What is the ratio of the stiffness

$$K_b = \frac{M_b}{d\varphi/ds}$$

of this beam to the stiffness of a beam in which the two bars are not soldered and act independently? What is the ratio of the maximum bending stresses for the two cases?

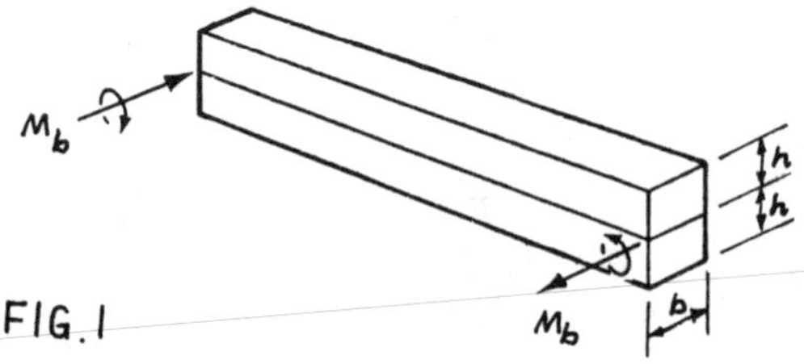

FIG. 1

Solution: First consider the beam when it is soldered together.

$$K_b = \frac{M_b}{d\varphi/ds}$$

but

$$\frac{d\varphi}{ds} = \frac{1}{R} = \frac{M_B}{EI}$$

since beam is soldered, it acts as a unit and $M_b = M_B$ where M_B = maximum bending moment each beam can take and where M_b = maximum bending moment both beams can take

$$K_b = EI$$

$$I = \frac{b(2h)^3}{12} = \frac{8bh^3}{12}$$

$$K_{b_1} = \frac{8bh^3}{12} E$$

Maximum bending stress, $(\sigma_{max})_1 = M_b y/I = M_b \cdot h \cdot \frac{12}{8bh^3}$. Now consider when the beams are free to slide over each other. Since the beams have identical cross sections and are made of the same material, $M_B = \frac{1}{2} M_b$

$$I = \frac{bh^3}{12}$$

$$\frac{1}{R} = \frac{M_b}{2EI}$$

$$K_{b_2} = M_b \cdot \frac{2EI}{M_b}$$

$$= 2 \cdot \frac{bh^3}{12} E$$

Maximum bending stress,

$$(\sigma_{max})_2 = \frac{1}{2} M_b \times \frac{h}{2} \times \frac{12}{bh^3} = M_b h \frac{12}{4bh^3}$$

Ratio of the stiffness,

$$\frac{K_1}{K_2} = \frac{8bh^3 E}{12} \cdot \frac{12}{2bh^3 E} = 4$$

Ratio of the maximum bending stresses,

$$\frac{(\sigma_{max})_1}{(\sigma_{max})_2} = M_b h \cdot \frac{12}{8bh^3} \cdot \frac{4bh^3}{M_b h\, 12} = \frac{1}{2} .$$

• PROBLEM 7-26

A moment M is applied to the end of a cantilever beam. Find the beam deflection at that end.

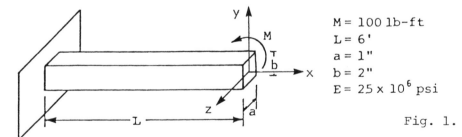

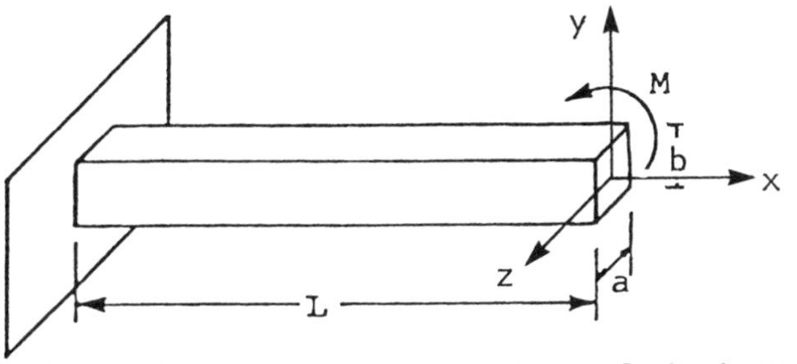

M = 100 lb-ft
L = 6'
a = 1"
b = 2"
E = 25×10^6 psi

Fig. 1.

Solution: The moment at any section of the beam is related to the deflection by

$$M = - EI \frac{\partial^2 \omega}{\partial x^2}$$

where M ≡ bending moment at the section
E ≡ modulus of elasticity
I ≡ moment of inertia about the axis of bending
ω ≡ vertical deflection.

Integrating the above equation and dividing both sides by -EI, we have

$$-M/EI \int dx = \int \frac{\partial^2 \omega}{\partial x^2} dx$$

$$A - (M/EI)x = \frac{\partial \omega}{\partial x}$$

Integrating again we have

$$\int A \, dx - (M/EI)\int x \, dx = \int \frac{\partial \omega}{\partial x} dx$$

$$B + Ax - (M/EI)(x^2/2) = \omega$$

or

$$\omega = -\frac{M}{EI}\frac{x^2}{2} + Ax + B$$

The constants A and B depend on the boundary conditions. At $x = 0$; $\omega = 0$, $\partial\omega/\partial x = 0$, i.e., both deflection ω and slope $\partial\omega/\partial x$ are zero at the fixed end.

$$\therefore \omega\Big|_{x=0} = -M/EI \;\; 0^2/2 + A(0) + B = 0$$

$$\therefore B = 0$$

$$\therefore \frac{\partial \omega}{\partial x}\Big|_{x=0} = -\frac{M}{EI}(0) + A$$

$$\therefore A = 0$$

$$\omega = \frac{-M}{EI}\frac{x^2}{2}$$

E is given as 25×10^6 psi

$$I = \frac{bd^3}{12} = \frac{1 \times 2^3}{12}$$

where d is the transverse dimension in the plane of bending and b the transverse dimension normal to the plane of bending as seen in Figure 2:

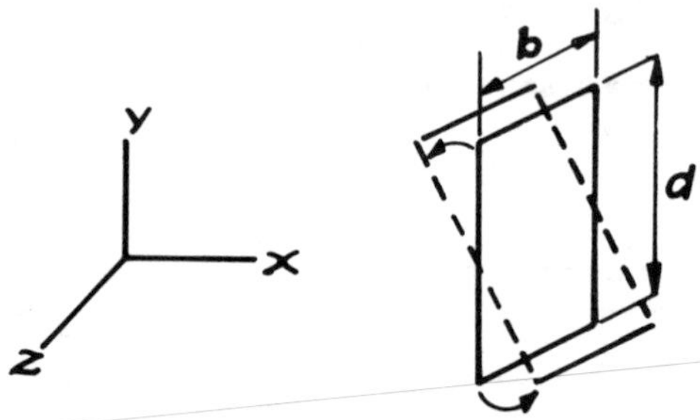

FIG. 2

$$M = -100 \text{ ft-lb}$$

$$= -1200 \text{ in-lb.}$$

at $x = 6' = 72''$

$$\omega = -\left(\frac{-1200 \times 72 \times 72}{25 \times 10^6 \times 2 \times 2^3} \times 12\right)$$

$$= .1867 \text{ in.} \uparrow$$

The positive sign of the numerical answer indicates that the end of the beam deflects upward (in the positive y direction).

• PROBLEM 7-27

A 4-in.by-6-in. (actual size) wooden beam shown in Fig. 1(a) is used to support a uniformly distributed load of 1,000 lb (total) on a simple span of 10 ft. The applied load acts in a plane making an angle of 30 with the vertical as shown in Fig. 1(b) and again in Fig. 1(c). Calculate the maximum bending stress at midspan, and, for the same section, locate the neutral axis. Neglect the weight of the beam.

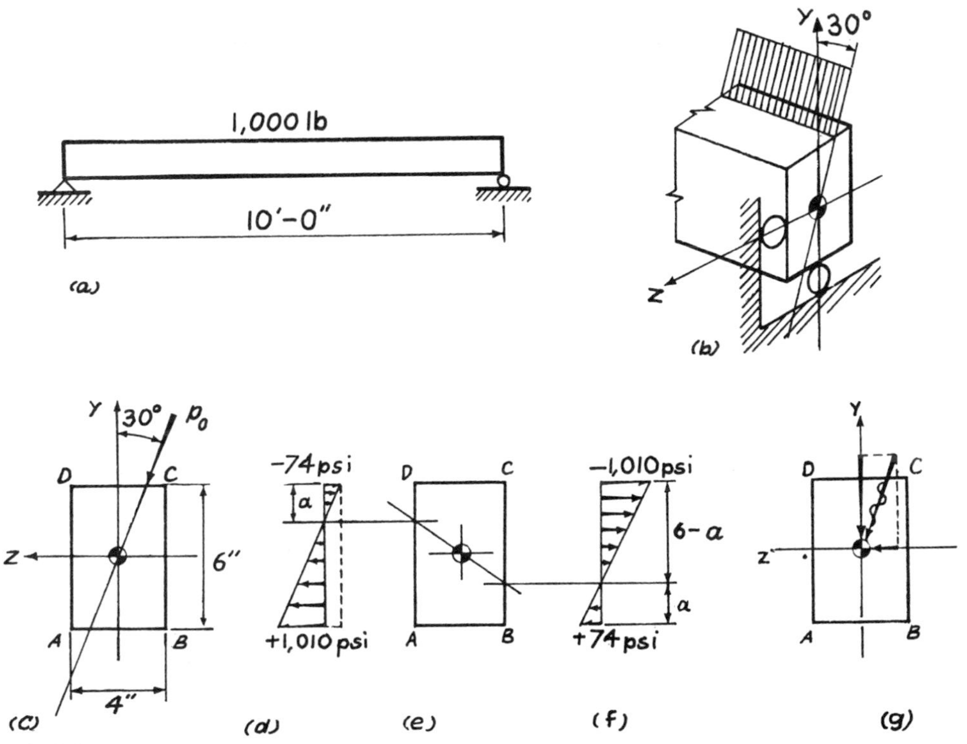

FIG.1

Solution: The maximum bending in the plane of the applied load occurs at the midspan, and it is equal to $P_0L^2/8$ or WL/8, where W is the total load on the span L. Hence

$$M = WL/8 = 1,000(10)/8 = 1,250 \text{ ft-lb}.$$

Here $\alpha = -30^\circ$, and the moment components acting around their respective axes are

$$M_{zz} = M\cos\alpha = 1,250(\sqrt{3}/2)12 = 13,000 \text{ in-lb}$$

$$M_{yy} = -M\sin\alpha = -1,250(-0.5)12 = 7,500 \text{ in-lb}$$

By considering the nature of the flexural stress distribution about both principal axes of the cross section, one may conclude that the maximum tensile stress occurs at A. The value of this stress follows by applying

$$\sigma = \frac{M_{zz}C_z}{I_{zz}} + \frac{M_{yy}C_y}{I_{yy}} + \frac{M_{xx}C_x}{I_{xx}}$$

with $y = c_1 = -3$ in., and $z = c_2 = +2$ in. Stresses at the other corners of the cross section are similarly determined.

$$\sigma_A = -\frac{M_{zz}C_1}{I_{zz}} + \frac{M_{yy}C_2}{I_{yy}} = \frac{13{,}000(3)}{4(6)^3/12} + \frac{7{,}500(2)}{6(4)^3/12}$$

$$= +542 + 468 = +1{,}010 \text{ psi} \quad \text{(tension)}$$

$$\sigma_B = -\frac{M_{zz}C_1}{I_{zz}} - \frac{M_{yy}C_2}{I_{yy}}$$

$$\sigma_B = +542 - 468 = +74 \text{ psi} \quad \text{(tension)}$$

$$\sigma_C = \frac{M_{zz}C_1}{I_{zz}} - \frac{M_{yy}C_2}{I_{yy}}$$

$$\sigma_C = -542 - 468 = -1{,}010 \text{ psi} \quad \text{(compression)}$$

$$\sigma_D = \frac{M_{zz}C_1}{I_{zz}} + \frac{M_{yy}C_2}{I_{yy}}$$

$$\sigma_D = -542 + 468 = -74 \text{ psi} \quad \text{(compression)}$$

To locate the neutral axis the stress distribution diagrams along the sides in Fig. 1(d) or (f) can be used. From similar triangles, $a/(6 - a) = 74/1{,}010$, or $a = 0.41$ in. This locates the neutral axis in Fig. 1(e).

When skew bending of a beam is caused by applied transverse forces, as in the above example, an equivalent procedure is usually more convenient. The applied forces are first resolved into components which act parallel to the principal axes of the cross-sectional area. Then the bending moments caused by these components around the respective axes are computed for use in the flexure formula. For the above example, such components of the applied load are shown in Fig. 1(g).

To avoid torsional stresses the applied transverse forces must act through the shear center. For bilaterally symmetrical sections, e.g. a rectangle, a circle, an I beam, etc., the shear center coincides with the centroid of the cross section. For other cross sections,

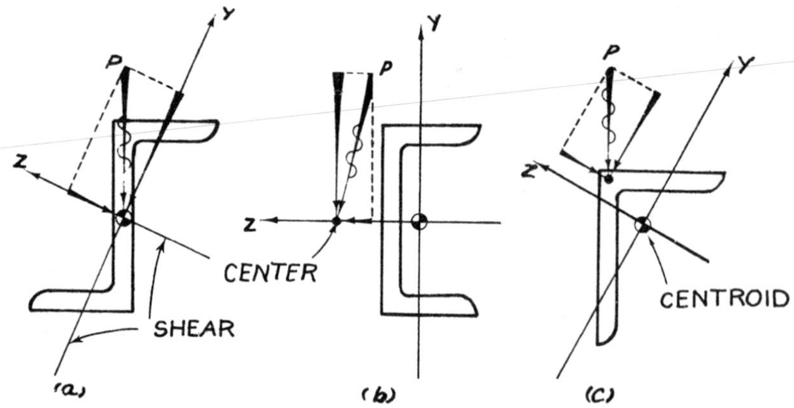

FIG. 2. PRINCIPAL AXES. FORCES APPLIED THROUGH SHEAR CAUSE. NO TORSION.

such as channels, angles, Z sections, etc., the shear center lies elsewhere. In such problems the transverse force must be applied at the shear center to avoid torsional stresses. This approach is illustrated in Fig. 2. Otherwise, in addition to the bending stresses, the torsional stresses must be investigated. In such cases the applied torque equals the applied force multiplied by its moment arm measured from the shear center.

• PROBLEM 7-28

Calculate the maxsimum sterss τ_{xx} in the beam shown, when subjected to the force F.

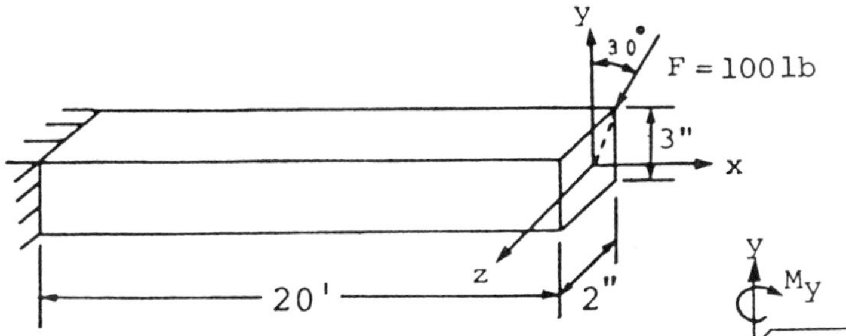

Fig. 1.

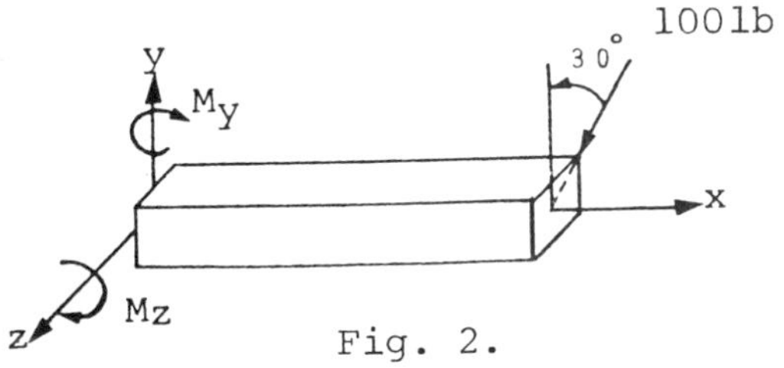

Fig. 2.

<u>Solution</u>: The maximum bending moment occurs at the base of the cantilever beam, and we show a free-body diagram in Fig. 2 exposing this section. Note that positive bending moments conventionwise for M_z and M_y have been shown in the diagram. The algebraic sign from equilibrium equations will then correspond to the convention sign for the bending moments. Hence, from equilibrium we have

$\Sigma M_y = 0$:

$$-M_y - (100)(\sin 30^\circ)(20) = 0$$

$$\therefore M_y = -1000 \text{ ft-lb.}$$

$\Sigma M_z = 0$:

$$-M_z - (100)(\cos 30^\circ)(20) = 0$$

$$\therefore M_z = -1732 \text{ ft-lb.}$$

We can employ

$$\tau_{xx} = \frac{(M_y I_{zz} + M_z I_{zy})z - (M_z I_{yy} + M_y I_{zy})y}{I_{zz} I_{yy} - I_{zy}^2}$$

here as follows:

$$\tau_{xx} = \frac{\begin{pmatrix}[(-1000)(12)(1/12)(2)(3^3) + (-1732)(12)(0)]z \\ -[(-1732)(12)(1/12)(3)(2^3) + (-1000)(12)(0)]y\end{pmatrix}}{(1/12)(2)(3^3)(1/12)(3)(2^3) - (0)^2} \qquad \text{(a)}$$

(Since the axes y-z are principal axes, we could also have used

$$\tau_{xx} = \frac{-(M \cos \alpha)y}{I_{zz}} + \frac{(M \sin \alpha)z}{I_{yy}}$$

directly.) Carrying out the numerical work, we get

$$\tau_{xx} = -(6000z - 4620y) \text{ psi} \qquad \text{(b)}$$

The maximum tensile stress τ_{xx} occurs when $z = -1$ and $y = 1.5$, giving

$$(\tau_{xx})_{max} = 6000 + 6930 = 12{,}930 \text{ psi} \qquad \text{(c)}$$

• PROBLEM 7-29

A standard I Beam, designated S8 x 18.4, is simply supported at the ends and bent by two equal and opposite couples M_0 acting at the ends of the beam. The couples act in the plane mm as shown in the figure. Find the maximum bending stress in the beam and the maximum deflection δ, assuming $M_0 = 50{,}000$ in.-lb., $\alpha = 30°$, $E = 30 \times 10^6$ psi, and the length of the beam is 12 ft.

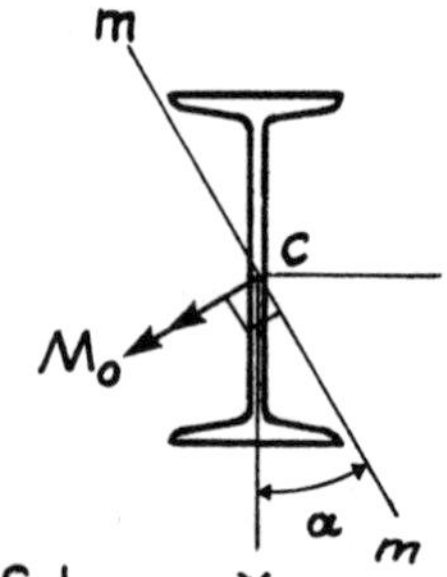

FIG. 1

Solution: The section properties for an S8 x 18.4 beam are

Beam depth , d = 8"

area , A = 5.34"

width of flange, b = 4"

$I_{zz} = 56.9$

$I_{yy} = 3.8$

From Fig. 1, $M_{zz} = 50{,}000 \cos 30$

$M_{yy} = 50{,}000 \sin 30$

but stress

$$\sigma = \frac{M_z(I_y y - I_{yz} z)}{I_z I_y - I_{yz}^2}$$

Since y and z are planes of symmetry, $I_{yz} = 0$. The maximum stress is an algebraic summation of the stresses computed for moments M_{yy}, and M_{zz}

$$\sigma_{max} = \frac{50{,}000 \times .866 \times 4}{56.9} + \frac{50{,}000 \times .5 \times 2}{3.8}$$

$$= 16{,}201.9 \text{ lb/in}^2$$

The radius of curvature in the z direction is given by

$$\frac{1}{R} = \frac{M_z I_y}{E(I_y I_z - I_{yz}^2)}$$

$$\frac{1}{R} = \frac{50,000 \times .866 \times 3.8}{30 \times 10^6 (3.8 \times 56.9)}$$

$$= 25.366 \times 10^{-6} \text{ in.}$$

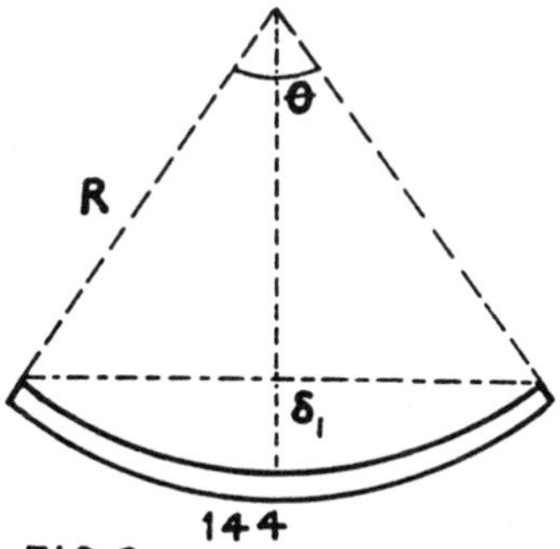

FIG. 2

Fig. 2 shows the deflected shape of the beam. Since R = 39422 ins.

$$\theta = \frac{144}{39422} \times \frac{180}{\pi} = .21^\circ$$

$$\delta_1 = 39422 - 39422 \cos \frac{.21}{2}$$

$$= .06615 \text{ in.}$$

This is the deflection in the z-direction. In the y-direction, the radius of curvature is

$$\frac{1}{R} = \frac{50,000 \times .5}{30 \times 10^6 \times 3.8}$$

$$= 219.3 \times 10^{-6}$$

$$R = 4560$$

$$\therefore \theta = \frac{144}{4560} \times \frac{180}{\pi} = 1.81^\circ$$

$$\delta_2 = 4560(1 - \cos \frac{1.81}{2})$$

$$= .5684 \text{ ins.}$$

Total deflection,

$$\delta = \sqrt{(.06615)^2 + (.5684)^2} = .573 \text{ ins.}$$

• PROBLEM 7-30

A beam of semicircular cross section (see figure) is subjected to a bending moment M_z. Find the maximum permissible value of this moment if the allowable stress is σ_w.

Solution: Recall $\sigma = My/I$ ... Eq. 1. From a table of section properties,

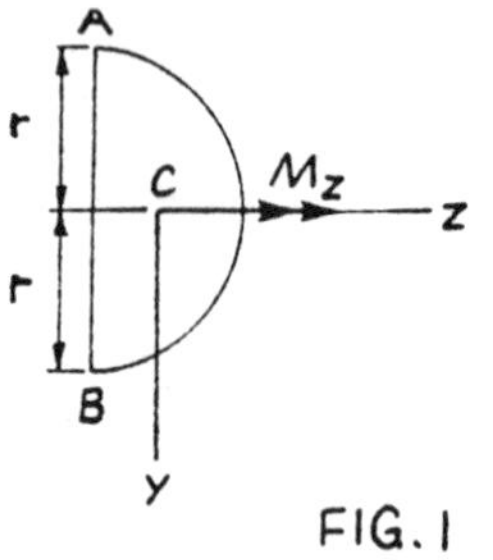

FIG. 1

$$I_z = \pi r^4/8$$

Maximum stress will occur either at point A or point B. ∴ y = r. Substituting in Eq. 1 gives:

$$\sigma_w = M_z r \cdot \frac{8}{\pi r^4}$$

$$M_z = \frac{\pi r^3 \sigma_w}{8} \quad .$$

• PROBLEM 7-31

A rectangular cantilever beam transmits a bending moment whose plane of action is inclined at 30° to the long axis of symmetry, as shown in Fig. 1a. Determine the curvatures in the xy and xz planes and the bending stress in the beam.

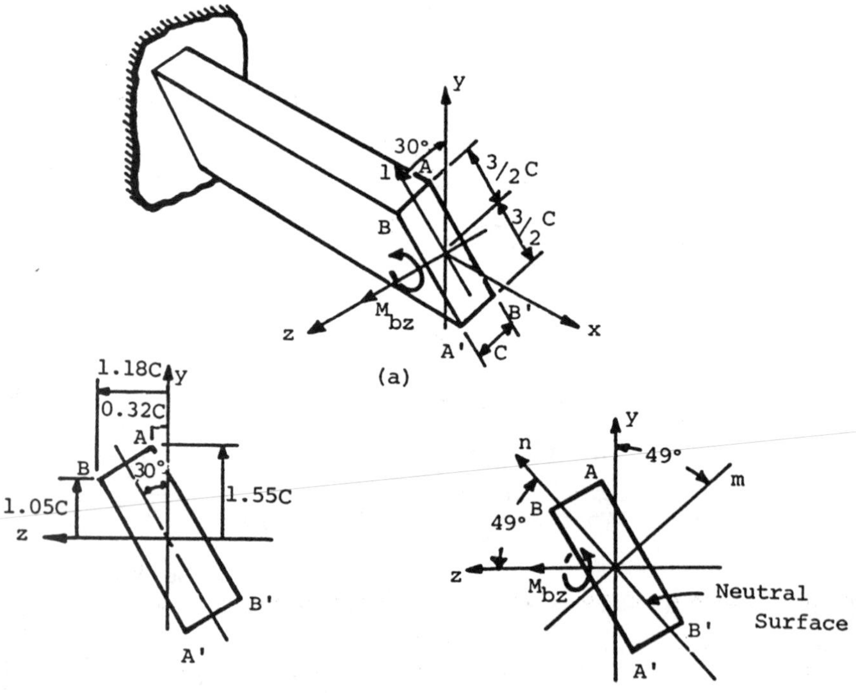

Fig. 1.

Solution: The moments and product of inertia for the beam cross section are

$$I_z = \int y^2 \, dA$$

$$I_y = \int z^i \, dA$$

$$I_{yz} = \int yz \, dA$$

$$\therefore I_{yy} = 1.75c^4 \qquad I_{zz} = 0.75c^4 \qquad I_{yz} = 0.87c^4 \tag{a}$$

Substituting these in

$$\frac{d\alpha}{ds_1} = \frac{I_{zz}}{I_{yy}I_{zz} - (I_{yz})^2} \frac{M_z}{E}$$

we find

$$\frac{d\alpha}{ds_1} = \frac{0.75c^4}{(1.75c^4)(0.75c^4) - (0.87c^4)^2} \frac{M_{bz}}{E}$$

$$= 1.36 \frac{M_{bz}}{Ec^4} \tag{b}$$

From

$$\frac{d\beta}{ds_2} = - \frac{I_{yz}}{I_{zz}} \left(\frac{d\alpha}{ds_1}\right)$$

we obtain

$$\frac{d\beta}{ds_2} = - \frac{.87c^4}{.75c^4} \left(1.36 \frac{M_{bz}}{Ec^4}\right) \tag{c}$$

$$= -1.58 \frac{M_{bz}}{Ec^4}$$

The bending stress will be a maximum at a corner. We shall investigate the corners A and B; the stresses at A' and B' will be reversed in sign. The coordinates of A and B are shown in Fig. 1b. Substituting these in

$$\sigma = \frac{M_z(I_y y - I_{yz} z)}{I_z I_y - I_{yz}^2}$$

we get:

At A,

$$\sigma_x = - \frac{(1.55c)(0.75c^4) - (0.32c)(0.87c^4)}{(1.55c^4)(0.75c^4) - (0.87c^4)^2} M_{bz}$$

$$= -1.60 \frac{M_{bz}}{c^3} \tag{d}$$

At B,

$$\sigma_x = - \frac{(1.05c)(0.75c^4) - (1.18c)(0.87c^4)}{(1.55c^4)(0.75c^4) - (0.87c^4)^2} M_{bz}$$

$$= +0.44 \frac{M_{bz}}{c^3} \tag{e}$$

Since the stresses are of opposite sign at the corners A and B, we conclude that the neutral surface must intersect the side AB. This conclusion is verified when, we find

$$\theta = \tan^{-1}\left(- \frac{I_{yz}}{I_{zz}}\right) = \tan^{-1}\left(- \frac{0.87c^4}{0.75c^4}\right) = -49^\circ \tag{f}$$

which places the neutral surface in the position shown in Fig. 1c .

It is of interest to note how the beam tends to bend in its "weak plane", i.e., how closely the neutral surface coincides with the long axis of symmetry of the cross section.

COMPOSITE BEAMS

• PROBLEM 7-32

Consider a composite beam of the cross-sectional dimensions shown in Fig. 1a. The upper 6-in.-by-10-in. (full-sized) part is wood, $E_w = 1.5 \times 10^6$ psi; the bottom ½-in.by-6-in. strap is steel, $E_s = 30 \times 10^6$ psi. If this beam is subjected to a bending moment of 20,000ft-lb around a horizontal axis, what are the maximum stresses in the steel and wood?

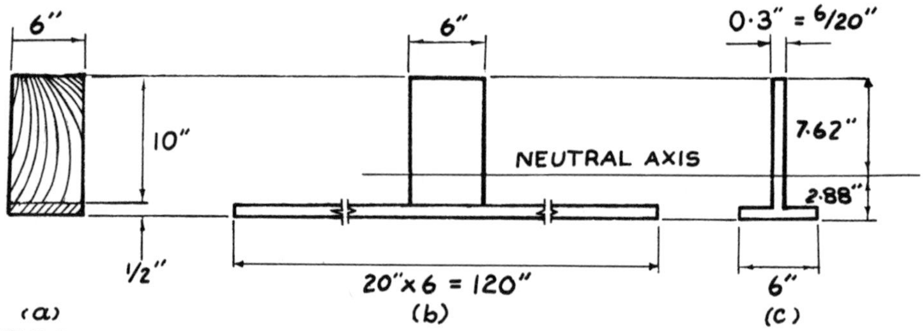

FIG.1

Solution: The ratio of the elastic moduli $E_s/E_w = 20$. Hence, using a transformed section of wood, the width of the bottom strip is $6(20) = 120$ in. The transformed area is shown in Fig. 1b. Its centroid and moment of inertia around the centroidal axis are the centroid, $\bar{y}$, measured down from the top edge:

$$\bar{y} = \frac{\Sigma A_y}{\Sigma A}$$

$$\bar{y} = \frac{6(10)5 - (0.5)120(10.25)}{6(10) + (0.5)120} = 7.62 \text{ in. from the top}$$

The equivalent moment of inertia about the centroidal axis is the moment of inertia about the centroidal axis of each area, plus the parallel axis theorom term to transfer the moment of inertia to the centroid of the whole cross section,

$$I = \Sigma(I_0 + Ad^2)$$

$$I_{zz} = \frac{6(10)^3}{12} + (6)10(2.62)^2 + \frac{120(0.5)^3}{12} + (0.5)120(2.63)^2$$

$$= 1,328 \text{ in.}^4$$

The maximum stress in the wood is

$$(\sigma_w)_{max} = \frac{Mc}{I} = \frac{(20,000)12(7.62)}{1,328} = 1,380 \text{ psi}$$

The maximum stress in the steel is

$$(\sigma_s)_{max} = n\sigma_w = 20\frac{(20,000)12(2.88)}{1,328} = 10,400 \text{ psi}$$

ALTERNATE SOLUTION:

A transformed area in terms of steel may be used instead. Then the equivalent width of wood is $b/n = 6/20$, or 0.3 in. This transformed area is shown in Fig. 1c.

$$\bar{y} = \frac{(0.3)10(5.5) + 6(0.5)(0.25)}{(0.3)10 + 6(0.5)} = 2.88 \text{ in. from the bottom}$$

$$I_{zz} = \frac{(0.3)10^3}{12} + (0.3)10(2.62)^2 + \frac{6(0.5)^3}{12} + (0.5)6(2.63)^2$$

$$= 66.5 \text{ in.}^4$$

$$(\sigma_s)_{max} = \frac{(20,000)12(2.88)}{66.5} = 10,400 \text{ psi}$$

$$(\sigma_w)_{max} = \frac{\sigma_s}{n} \left(\frac{1}{20}\right) \frac{(20,000)12(7.62)}{66.5} = 1,380 \text{ psi}$$

The stress in a material stiffer than the material of the transformed section is greater since to cause the same unit strain a higher stress is required.

• PROBLEM 7-33

The cross section of a bimetallic strip is shown in the figure. Assuming $E_a = 42 \times 10^6$ psi and $E_b = 21 \times 10^6$ psi, determine the smaller section modulus for the beam, that is, the ratio of bending moment to maximum bending stress.

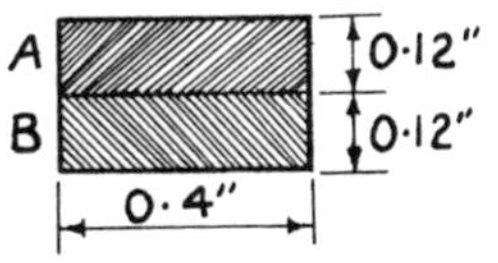

FIG.1

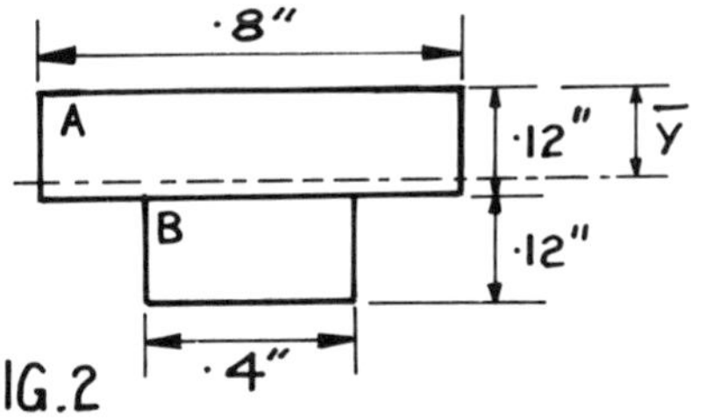

FIG.2

Solution: In solving this problem, metalic strip a, is converted into an equivalent section consisting of material b, Fig. 2.
First determine the neutral axis $\bar{y}$;

$$(.12 \times .8 + .4 \times .12)\bar{y} = .8 \times .12 \times .06 + .4 \times 12 \times .18$$

$$\bar{y} = .10 \text{ in.}$$

The moment of inertia of the equivalent cross-section is determined from

$$I = \Sigma A_i \left(\frac{h_i^2}{12} + c_i^2\right)$$

The cross-section in Fig. 2 is divided into three areas. The first is the area of strip A above the neutral axis. The second is the area of strip A below the neutral axis. The third is the area of strip B. To avoid having to deal with long strings of zeros to the right of decimal points, all dimensions are multiplied by 100, and the whole expression is divided by 10^8 .

$$I_{eq} = \left[80 \times 10\left(\frac{10^2}{12} + 5^2\right) + 80 \times 2\left(\frac{2^2}{12} + 1^2\right) + 40 \times 12\left(\frac{12^2}{12} + 8^2\right)\right] \times 10^{-8}$$

$$= 63360 \times 10^{-8} \text{in}^4.$$

Recall
$$\sigma = \frac{M\bar{y}}{I} = \frac{M}{S}$$

In element A maximum stress is

$$\sigma_a = \frac{M \times .10 \times 2}{.0006336}$$

where the expression is multiplied by 2 to account for E_a being twice as large as E_b.

$$\frac{M}{\sigma_a} = S = \frac{.0006336}{.10 \times 2}$$

$$= .003168 \text{ in.}^3$$

In element B maximum stress is

$$\sigma_b = \frac{M \times .14}{.0006336}$$

$$\frac{M}{\sigma_b} = S = .004526 \text{ in.}^3$$

The smaller section modulus, is $S = .003168 \text{ in.}^3$

• PROBLEM 7-34

A beam consisting of two different materials has the cross-sectional dimensions shown in Fig. 1 and is subjected to a positive bending moment of 30,000 in.-lb. a) Find the maximum and minimum stresses in both materials of the beam assuming that $E_1 = 1{,}000{,}000$ psi and $E_2 = 20{,}000{,}000$ psi.

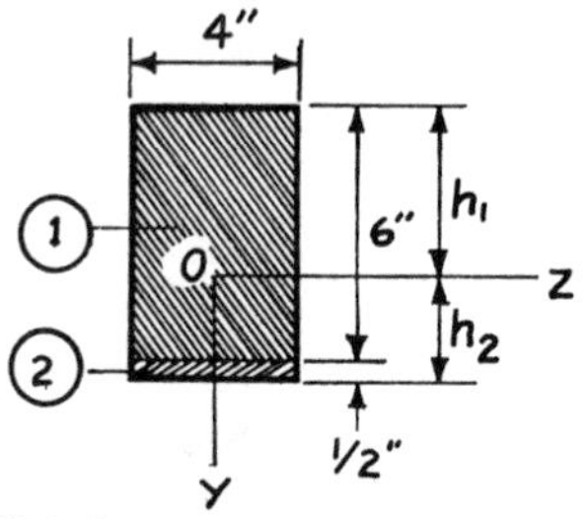

FIG. 1.

Solution: a) The first step is to locate the neutral axis of the cross-section. Let us assume that the neutral axis lies within material 1, as shown in the figure. Then we denote the distances from this axis to the top and bottom of the beam as h_1 and h_2, respectively. Using units of pounds and inches, we see that

$$E_1 \int_1 y \, dA = (1 \times 10^6)\left[\left(-\frac{h_1}{2}\right)(h_1)(4) + \left(\frac{6 - h_1}{2}\right)(6 - h_1)(4)\right]$$

$$= 24 \times 10^6(3 - h_1)$$

$$E_2 \int_2 y \, dA = (20 \times 10^6)[(6 - h_1 + \tfrac{1}{4})(\tfrac{1}{2})(4)] = 10 \times 10^6(25 - 4h_1)$$

where $E \equiv$ modulus of elasticity
$A \equiv$ cross-sectional area.

Now substituting into

$$E_1 \int_1 y\, dA + E_2 \int_2 y\, dA = 0$$

$$\therefore 24 \times 10^6 (3-h_1) + 10 \times 10^6 (25 - 4h_1) = 0$$

$$h_1 = \frac{322}{64} = 5.03$$

That is, $h_1 = 5.03$ in., thus locating the neutral axis.

The moments of inertia I_1 and I_2 about the neutral axis can be found using the parallel-axis theorem:

$$I_{x'} = I_x + Ay^2$$

$$I_1 = (1/12)(4)(6)^3 + 4(6)(5.03 - 3.00)^2 = 171 \text{ in.}^4$$

$$I_2 = (1/12)(4)(\tfrac{1}{2})^3 + (\tfrac{1}{2})(4)(6.25 - 5.03)^2 = 3.02 \text{ in.}^4$$

As a check, we observe by direct calculation that $I = (\frac{1}{3})(4)(5.03)^3 + (\frac{1}{3})(4)(1.47)^3 = 174 \text{ in.}^4$, which is equal to the sum of I_1 and I_2.

The maximum compressive stress in material 1 occurs at the top of the beam where $y = -5.03$ in. This stress is

$$\sigma_1 = \frac{My}{I_{Eq}}$$

$$I_{Eq} = 171 + \frac{3.02 \times 20 \times 10^6}{10 \times 10^5} = 231.4$$

$$\therefore \sigma_1 = -\frac{30,000 \times 5.03}{231.4} = -653 \text{ psi} .$$

At the juncture of the two materials the stress in material 1 (obtained from

$$\sigma = \frac{My}{I_{Eq}} = \frac{30,000 \times 0.97}{231.4}$$

with $y = 0.97$ in.) is 126 psi and the stress in material 2 (obtained from

$$\sigma_{eq} = \frac{My}{I_{Eq}} = \frac{30,000 \times 0.97}{231.4}$$

$$= 126$$

$$\sigma = \frac{E_2}{E_1} \sigma_{eq} = 20 \times 126$$

with the same value of y) is 2520 psi. At the lower edge of the beam ($y = 1.47$ in.) the stress in material 2 is

$$\sigma = \frac{E_2}{E_1} \cdot \frac{My}{I}$$

$$= 20 \times \frac{30,000 \times 1.47}{231.4}$$

$$= 3812 \text{ psi}$$

(b) Analyze above beam by the transformed section method using a section consisting entirely of material 1.

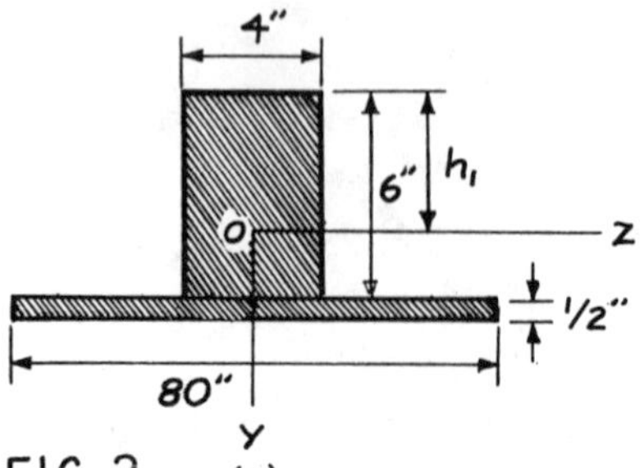

FIG. 2 (a)

Let the upper part of the beam remain unchanged in the transformed section (see Fig. 2a), but the lower part will have its width multiplied by $n = E_2/E_1$, which is 20 in this example.

To locate the neutral axis, we must find the centroid of the transformed section. Calculating the first moments of the areas about the top of the beam, and dividing by the total area, we find the calculation for h_1 to be as follows:

$$h_1 = \frac{4(6)(3) + (80)(6.25)/2}{4(6) + 80/2} = \frac{322}{64} = 5.03 \text{ in.}$$

The moment of inertia of the transformed section is

$$I_t = (1/12)(4)(6)^3 + 4(6)(2.03)^2 + (1/12)(80)(\tfrac{1}{2})^3 + (\tfrac{1}{2})(80)(1.22)^2 = 231 \text{ in.}^4$$

The stresses in the transformed beam at the top, at the juncture, and at the bottom, are, respectively,

$$\sigma = \frac{My}{I_t} = \frac{30{,}000(-5.03)}{231} = -653 \text{ psi}$$

$$\sigma = \frac{My}{I_t} = \frac{30{,}000(0.97)}{231} = 126 \text{ psi}$$

$$\sigma = \frac{My}{I_t} = \frac{30{,}000(1.47)}{231} = 191 \text{ psi}$$

The stresses in the original beam will be the same as in the transformed beam for material 1 but not for material 2. Therefore, the first two stresses calculated above will give the stresses at the corresponding locations in the original beam for material 1. For material 2, the stresses at the juncture and at the lower edge of the beam are obtained by multiplying by n (equal to 20); thus,

$$\sigma = 20(126) = 2520 \text{ psi} \quad \text{and} \quad \sigma = 20(191) = 3820 \text{ psi}$$

respectively. All these results agree with those found in Part a).

(c) In order to illustrate further the transformed section method, solve the preceding problem b) by transforming the beam to material 2.

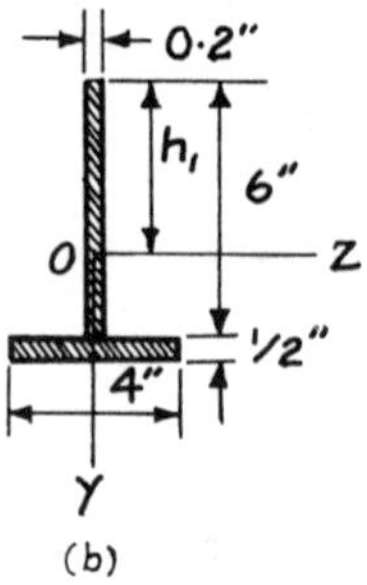

(b)

In this event, n will have the value 1/20. In obtaining the transformed section, we note that the part of the beam consisting of material 2 will not change, whereas the part consisting of material 1 will have its width decreased by the factor n (see Fig. 2b.) We now follow the same steps as in part b.

$$h_1 = \frac{0.2(6)(3) + (0.5)(4)(6.25)}{0.2(6) + (0.5)(4)} = \frac{16.1}{3.2} = 5.03 \text{ in.}$$

$$I_t = (1/12)(0.2)(6)^3 + 0.2(6)(2.03)^2 + (1/12)(4)(\tfrac{1}{2})^3 + \tfrac{1}{2}(4)(1.22)^2 = 11.5 \text{ in.}^4$$

The stresses in the transformed section at the top, juncture, and bottom are, respectively,

$$\sigma = \frac{My}{I_t} = \frac{30,000(-5.03)}{11.5} = -13,100 \text{ psi}$$

$$\sigma = \frac{My}{I_t} = \frac{30,000(0.97)}{11.5} = 2530 \text{ psi}$$

$$\sigma = \frac{My}{I_t} = \frac{30,000(1.47)}{11.5} = 3830 \text{ psi}$$

To obtain the stresses in the original beam, the stresses in material 1 must be transformed by multiplying by n; thus, at the top and at the juncture we have

$$\sigma = -\frac{1}{20}(13,100) = -655 \text{ psi} \quad \text{and} \quad \sigma = \frac{1}{20}(2530) = 126 \text{ psi}$$

The stresses in material 2 are valid for the original beam.

• PROBLEM 7-35

Find the maximum tensile bending stress and its location in the beam arrangement shown.

Fig. 1.

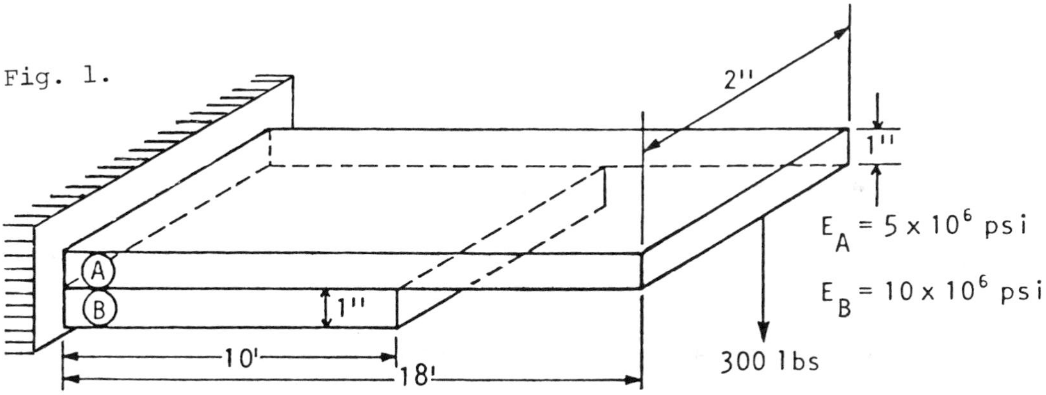

Solution: There are two possible locations of maximum tensile stress. These are at the fixed end, 1, and at the point where there is a change in the cross-section, 2.

First consider the point where there is a change in the cross-section.

$$\text{Stress, } \sigma = \frac{My}{I}$$

$$M = 300 \times 8 \times 12 \text{ in-lb}$$

$$y = \tfrac{1}{2} \text{ in.}$$

$$I = \frac{2 \times 1^3}{12} = \frac{1}{6} \text{ in.}^4$$

$\therefore$ max tensile stress, $\sigma = 300 \times 8 \times 12 \times \frac{1}{2} \times \frac{6}{1} = 86400$ psi

Now consider the fixed end. The equivalent cross-section of the beam at the fixed end if material B was converted to A is shown in Fig. 2.

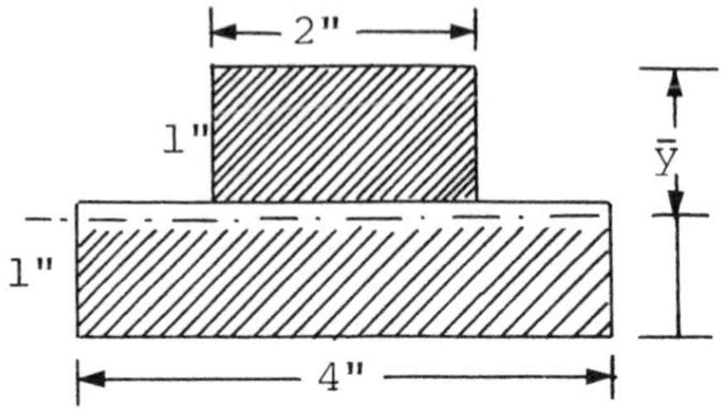

Fig. 2.

The neutral axis, $\bar{y} = \frac{2 \times .5 + 4 \times 1.5}{2 + 4} = 7/6$ in.

$$I_{eq} = 2\left(\frac{1}{12} + .333^2\right) + 4 \times .1667\left(\frac{.1667^2}{12} + .08333^2\right)$$

$$+ 4 \times .8333\left(\frac{.8333^2}{12} + .4167^2\right)$$

$$= 1.1667$$

Maximum tensile stress occurs at the top fiber

$$\therefore \sigma_{max} = \frac{64800 \times 1.1667}{1.1667}$$

$$= 64800 \text{ lb/in.}^2$$

Maximum tensile stress occurs at the point where there is a change in cross-section and its value is

$$\sigma_{max} = 86400 \text{ psi} .$$

• PROBLEM 7-36

A structural beam is formed from 3 elements bolted together. Compute the maximum tensile bending stress in each material for an applied positive bending moment of 8.00×10^5 lb-in.

Solution: The first task is to make an equivalent cross-section. We shall use the modulus of the wood for that purpose. The modulus of elasticity of aluminum is seven times greater than that of wood, so the wood strips to be equivalent to the aluminum must be seven times as wide. The equivalent cross-section is shown in Fig. 2.
The position of the neutral axis is then computed. Do this by equating the first moment of the total area A of the equivalent section about a convenient axis with the sum of the first moments of the three areas representing the two aluminum strips and the wooden beam.

Choose as the axis about which to take moments the center axis D-D of the wooden section (Fig. 2). Thus we have

$$Ay' = [(56)(\tfrac{1}{2}) + (42)(\tfrac{3}{4}) + (12)(8)]y'$$
$$= -(56)(\tfrac{1}{2})(6.25) + (42)(\tfrac{3}{4})(6.375)$$
$$\therefore\ y' = .1670 \text{ in.}$$

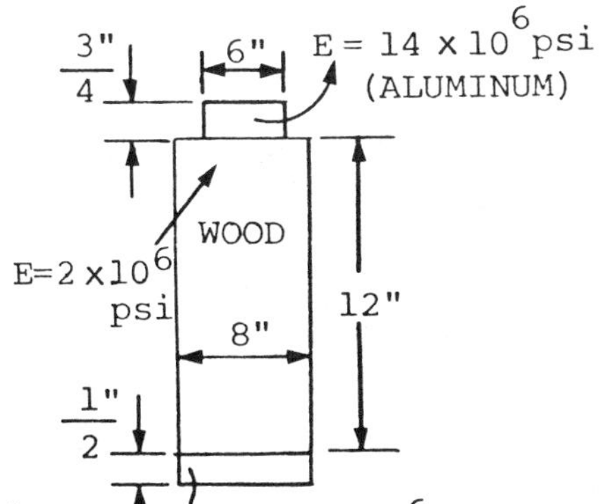

Fig. 1.

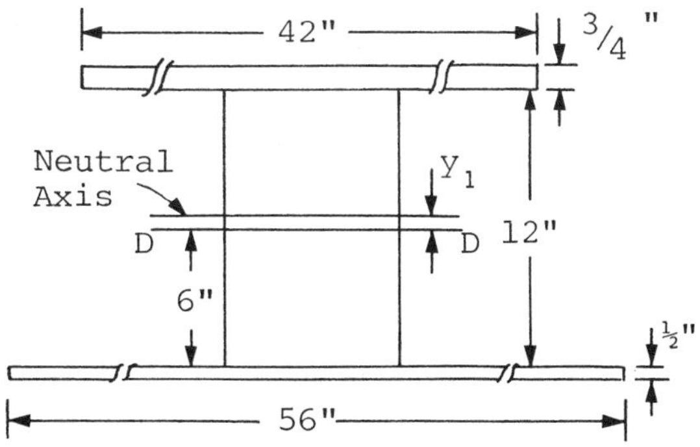

Fig. 2.

Thus, the neutral axis is a distance .1670 in. above the axis D-D. Next we shall need I_{Eq} about the neutral axis. Accordingly,

$$I_{Eq} = (1/12)(42)(\tfrac{3}{4})^3 + (42)(\tfrac{3}{4})(.375 + 6.00 - .1670)^2$$
$$+ (1/12)(8)(12)^3 + (8)(12)(.1670)^2$$
$$+ (1/12)(56)(\tfrac{1}{2})^3 + (56)(\tfrac{1}{2})(.250 + 6.00 + .1670)^2$$
$$= 3520 \text{ in.}^4$$

Now compute the normal stresses in the equivalent section. For the wood we have for the maximum normal stress

$$[(\tau_{xx})_{Eq}]_{max} = -\frac{M(-6.167)}{3520} = \frac{(8 \times 10^5)(6.167)}{3520} = 1400 \text{ psi}$$

This is the same stress at the corresponding value of y in the actual section so that for the wooden portion of the composite member we have

$$[(\tau_{xx})_{wood}]_{max} = 1400 \text{ psi} \qquad \text{(a)}$$

As for the aluminum strips it is easily seen that the bottom member will be in tension and that the maximum stress occurs at the lowest fibers. Accordingly, for the maximum equivalent tensile stress we have

$$[(\tau_{xx})_{Eq}]_{max} = -\frac{M(-6.67)}{3520} = \frac{(8 \times 10^5)(6.67)}{3520} = 1515 \text{ psi}$$

The corresponding stress for the actual section is then computed as

$$[(\tau_{xx})_{Al}]_{max} = \frac{E_{Al}}{E_{wood}}(1515) = (7)(1515) = 10{,}608 \text{ psi} \qquad \text{(b)}$$

• PROBLEM 7-37

A beam has a rectangular cross-section 4 in. wide and 12 in. deep. For a depth of 1 in. at the top and bottom of the beam, the material has an elastic modulus of 30×10^6 psi. For the remainder of the depth the material has an elastic modulus of 15×10^6 psi. At a certain cross-section, the bending moment causes a stress of 12,000 psi at the top surface A (Fig. 1.)

(a) Find the strain at level A.
(b) Find the strain at level B.
(c) Sketch the distribution of stress on the cross-section.
(d) Find the bending moment.

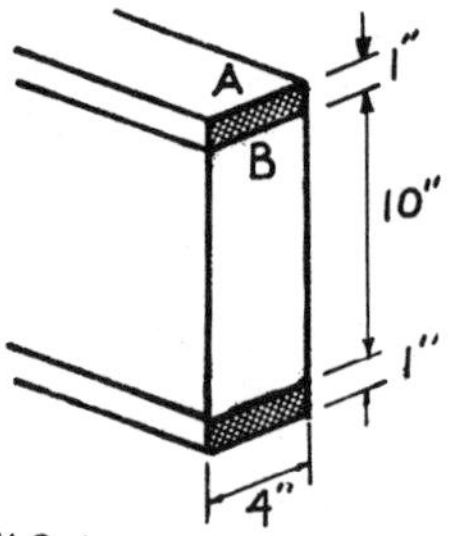

FIG.1

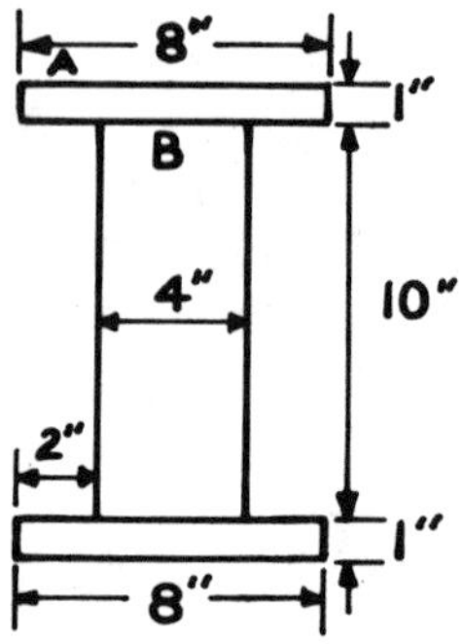

FIG.2

Solution: The equivalent section method is used in solving this problem. Convert the top and bottom sections of the beam to an equivalent section of the middle piece (Fig. 2).

Stress at level A, $\sigma = 12,000$ psi ; but $\sigma = E\epsilon$ where

$E \equiv$ modulus of elasticity
$\epsilon \equiv$ strain

a) $$\text{strain, } \epsilon = \frac{12,000}{30 \times 10^6} = 4 \times 10^{-4}$$

It is more convenient to first calculate the moment in the beam from $\sigma = My/I$. Moment of inertia of the equivalent section is the I of a solid 12" x 8" beam, minus the I's of the two 10" x 2" empty spaces.

$$I_{eq} = \frac{8 \times 12^3}{12} - 2\left(\frac{2 \times 10^3}{12}\right) = 818.667$$

Substituting in Eq.(1) we have

$$12000 = \frac{M \times 6}{818.667} \times 2$$

where the formula for the stress is multiplied by 2 because the elastic modulus of the actual material is twice that of the equivalent material.

$$M = 818.667 \times 10^3 \text{ in.-lb.}$$

At level B in top material, y = 5"

$$\text{stress } \sigma = \frac{818.667 \times 5}{818.667} \times 2 \times 10^3 \text{ lb/in.}^2$$

$$= 10,000 \text{ psi}$$

$$\text{strain, } \epsilon = \frac{\sigma}{E} = \frac{10{,}000}{30 \times 10^6}$$

$$= 3.33 \times 10^{-4}$$

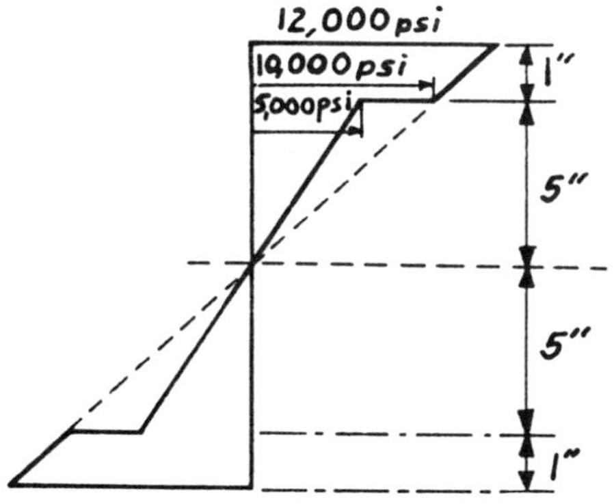

FIG. 3 DISTRIBUTION OF STRESS ON THE CROSS-SECTION

Check: At level B in middle material, y = 5"

$$\sigma = \frac{My}{I} = \frac{(818.667 \times 10^3)(5)}{818.667}$$

$$\sigma = 5{,}000 \text{ psi}$$

$$\epsilon = \frac{\sigma}{E} = \frac{5000}{15 \times 10^6}$$

$$\text{strain, } \epsilon = 3.33 \times 10^{-4} .$$

• PROBLEM 7-38

Calculate the bending stresses in a beam having the cross-section of Fig. 1 if the bending moment is 500 kip-in. $E_A = 20 \times 10^3$ ksi and $E_B = 5 \times 10^3$ ksi.

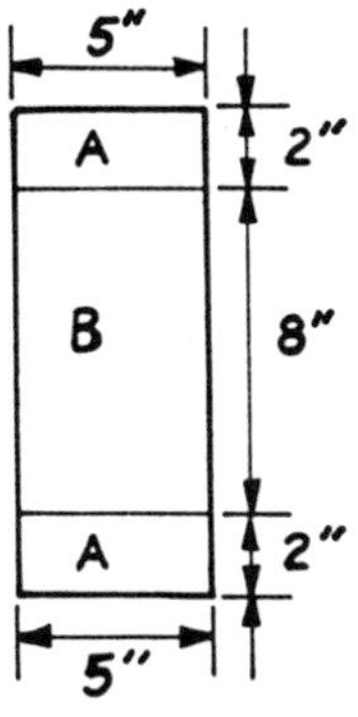

FIG. 1

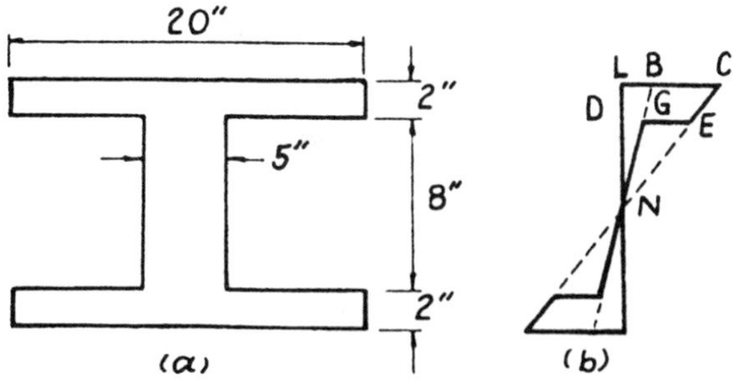

FIG. 2

Solution: Transform the section to an equivalent one of material B alone.

$$n = E_A/E_B = 4$$

The areas A are extended to 4 times their real width, giving the transformed section of Fig. 2a. The total moment of inertia, I, of the section is:

$$I = \Sigma I_0 + Ay^2$$

I_0 will be found for the web and the flanges.

$$I_w = \frac{bh^3}{12} = \frac{(5)(8)^3}{12} = 213.33$$

$$I_f = \frac{bh^3}{12} = \frac{20(2)^3}{12} = 13.33$$

$$A_f y^2 = (20)(2)(8/2 + 2/2)^2 = 1000$$

$$I = 213.33 + 2(13.33 + 1000) = 2239.99$$

This section has a moment of inertia of 2240 in.^{4} A homogeneous beam of material B with this section can now be analyzed in the usual way. Stresses within the web will be correct, but stresses within the flanges are fictitious and must be multiplied by n to give the true stresses in A.

With M = 500 kip-in. the (fictitious) extreme fibre stresses are

$$\sigma' = \frac{My}{I} = \frac{500 \times 6}{2240} = 1.34 \text{ ksi}$$

This is the ordinate LB (Fig. 2(b)). The true stress:

$$\sigma = n\sigma' = 4 \times 1.34 = 5.36 \text{ ksi}$$

The stress in material B at the junction of A and B is

$$\sigma = \frac{My}{I} = \frac{500 \times 4}{2240} = 0.893 \text{ ksi}$$

This is the ordinate DC (Fig. 2 (b)).

It is equally valid to transform the section to an equivalent one of material A. This will simply be an I section one-quarter of the width of that in Fig. 2 (a). For the same bending moment, stresses will be 4 times as great. They will be true for A and must be multiplied by ¼ for B.

• PROBLEM 7-39

A box beam is constructed with webs of Douglas fir plywood and with flanges of redwood, as shown in the figure. The plywood is 1 in. thick and 12 in. wide. The redwood flanges are 2 in. x 4 in. (actual size). The modulus of elasticity for the plywood is 1,600,000 psi and for the redwood is 1,200,000 psi. If the allowable stresses are 2000 psi for the plywood and 1700 psi for the redwood, find the allowable bending moment for the beam.

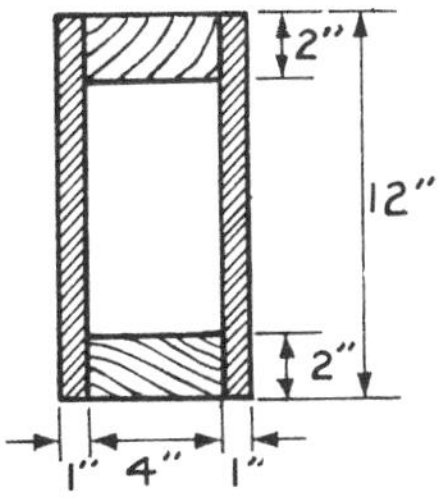

FIG.1

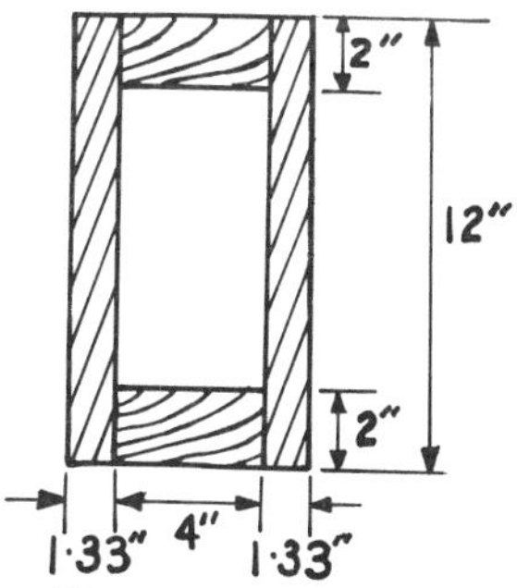

FIG.2

Solution: In solving this problem, use the equivalent section method. Convert the plywood to the redwood equivalent by multiplying the width by

$$n = \frac{E_{plywood}}{E_{redwood}} = \frac{1600000}{1200000} = 1.333 .$$

The resulting section is shown in Fig. 2. The moment of inertia of the equivalent section is the moment of inertia of a solid beam minus the moment of inertia of the hollow inside.

$$I_{eq} = \frac{b_1h_1^3}{12} - \frac{b_2h_2^3}{12}$$

$$I_{eq} = \frac{1}{12} \times 6.667 \times 12^3 - \frac{1}{12} \times 4 \times 8^3$$

$$= 789.33 \text{ in.}^4$$

The expression relating stress with moment is

$$\sigma = \frac{My}{I}$$

The beam will fail first at the external fibres, but which of the woods will fail first is not obvious.
Assuming the redwood fails first,

$$\therefore\ 1700 = \frac{M \times 6}{789.33}$$

Bending moment, M = 223,643.5 in.lb. Assuming the plywood fails first,

$$\therefore\ 2000 = \frac{M \times 6}{789.33} \times 1.33$$

Bending moment, M = 197,827.07 in-lb.
The assumption that the plywood fails first is the correct one because the maximum moment it can sustain is lower. The allowable bending moment is 197,827.07 in-lb.

• PROBLEM 7-40

A composite beam $4\frac{1}{2}$ in. wide by 12 in. deep and 14 ft. long is made by fastening two timber planks, 2 in. by 12 in., to the sides of a steel plate, $\frac{1}{2}$ in. by 12 in., as shown in Fig. 1. E_{wood} = 1200 ksi.
The composite beam, simply supported at the ends, acts as a single unit in supporting a uniformly distributed load of 1080 lb. per ft. Determine the maximum fiber stresses in the steel and wood.

Solution: For the simply supported beam, maximum moment occurs at the center and its value is

$$M_{max} = \frac{w\ell^2}{8}$$

$$= \frac{1080 \times 14 \times 14}{8} \times 12 \text{ lb-in.}$$

$$= 317520 \text{ lb.-in.}$$

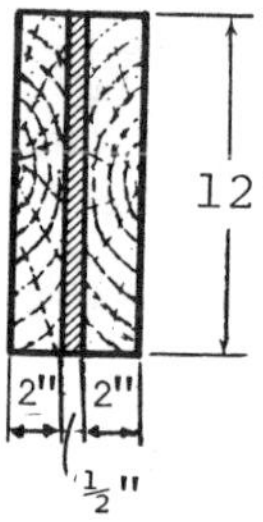

Fig. 1

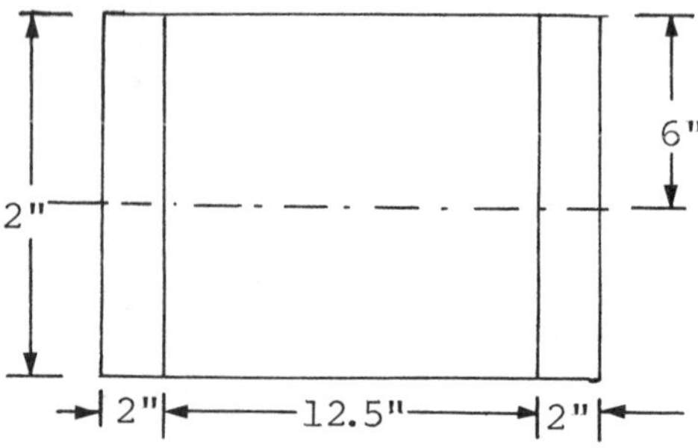

Fig. 2.

Let

$$E_{steel} = 30 \times 10^6$$

Transform the steel section into an equivalent wood section, Fig. 2. Since the cross-section is symmetric, the neutral axis is at the middle.

Moment of inertia of the equivalent section is

$$I_{eq} = \frac{16.5 \times 12^3}{12} = 2376 \text{ in.}^3$$

Recall

$$\sigma = \frac{My}{I}$$

Maximum stress occurs at the extreme fibre for both steel and wood. It is compressive at the top and tensile at the bottom.

$$(\sigma_{max})_{wood} = \frac{317520 \times 6}{2376} \text{ lb.-in.}$$

$$= 801.8 \text{ lb.-in.}$$

$$(\sigma_{max})_{steel} = \frac{317520 \times 6}{2376} \times \frac{30 \times 10^6}{1.20 \times 10^6}$$

$$= 20045.45 \text{ lb.-in.}$$

• PROBLEM 7-41

A concrete beam has three steel reinforcing rods in the bottom portion. Compute the maximum stress in the concrete and steel for an applied bending moment of 80×10^3 lb-ft, assuming the rods are under tension.

Solution: Since the concrete cannot be depended on to offer much resistance in tension, we shall assume that in the tensile zone the con-

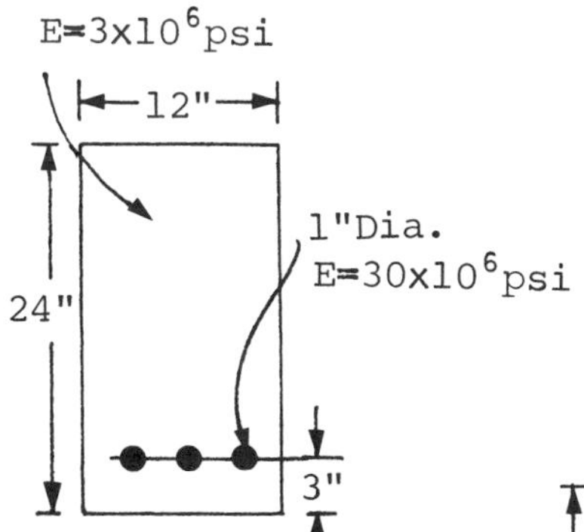

Fig. 1.

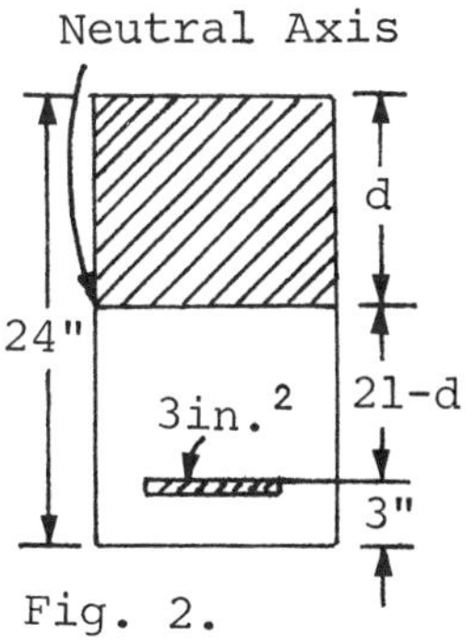

Fig. 2.

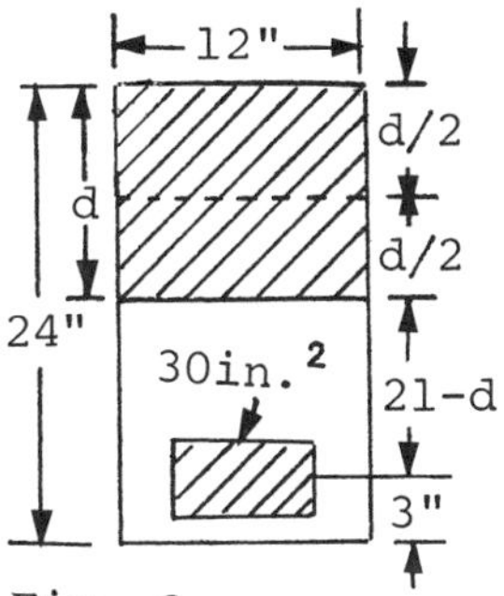

Fig. 3.

crete merely holds the reinforcing rods in place. Accordingly, we shall employ only that part of the concrete above the neutral axis where we have compression for computation of I_{Eq}. Also we shall simplify the cross section of the reinforcing bars into that of a narrow rectangle having an area of 3 in.^{2}. This shown in Fig. 2, where we consider for determining I_{eq} just the crosshatched areas. Note that the neutral axis is at the bottom of the compression zone at some yet unknown distance d below the top surface. For the equivalent section we shall change the thin rectangular section of area 3 in.^{2} to one of 30 in^2, thereby assigning a modulus E of 3×10^6 psi for the equivalent section. We can get the neutral axis and thus determine d now by finding the centroid of the equivalent section. Thus, taking moments about the neutral axis we have

$$\text{Area} \times \text{Length} = \text{Area} \times \text{Length}$$

$$[(12)(d)]\,\frac{d}{2} - (30)(21 - d) = 0$$

$$6d^2 - 630 + 30d = 0$$

Using the quadratic formula

$$x = \frac{-b \pm \sqrt{b^2 - 4ac}}{2a}$$

$$d = \frac{-30 \pm \sqrt{30^2 - 4(6)(-630)}}{2(6)}$$

$$d = 8.05,\ -13.05$$

Since d is a positive length, discard the negative solution.

$$\therefore\ d = 8.05 \text{ in.}$$

The moment of inertia of the equivalent section about the neutral axis is then

$$I_{eq} = \frac{1}{12}(12)(8.05)^3 + (12)(8.05)\left(\frac{8.05}{2}\right)^2 + (30)(21 - 8.05)^2$$

$$= 7118 \text{ in.}^4$$

The equivalent maximum compressive stress in the concrete and the equivalent stress in the steel may be, respectively, given as follows:

$$\sigma = \frac{My}{I}$$

$$[(\sigma_{xx})_{eq}]_{conc} = -\frac{[(80 \times 10^3) \times 12]8.05}{7118} = -1086 \text{ psi}$$

$$[(\sigma_{xx})_{eq}]_{stl} = \frac{[(80 \times 10^3) \times 12] \times (21 - 8.05)}{7118} = 1746 \text{ psi}$$

The corresponding actual stresses are then

$$[(\sigma_{xx})_{act}]_{conc} = -1086 \text{ psi}$$

$$[(\sigma_{xx})_{act}]_{stl} = \frac{30 \times 10^6}{3 \times 10^6}(1746) = 17{,}460 \text{ psi}$$

Notice that we have been somewhat approximate in the calculations in the way we handled the geometrical aspects of the reinforcing rods. Since these rods are positioned in the concrete in actual construction in a manner only approximating the specifications, such simplifications that we have made are reasonable.

• PROBLEM 7-42

Determine the maximum stress in the concrete and the steel for a reinforced-concrete beam with the section shown in Fig. 1a if it is subjected to a positive bending moment of 50,000 ft-lb. The reinforcement consists of two #9 steel bars. (These bars are 1 1/8 in. in diameter and have a cross-sectional area of 1 in.^{2}). Assume the ratio of E for steel to that of concrete to be 15, i.e., n = 15.

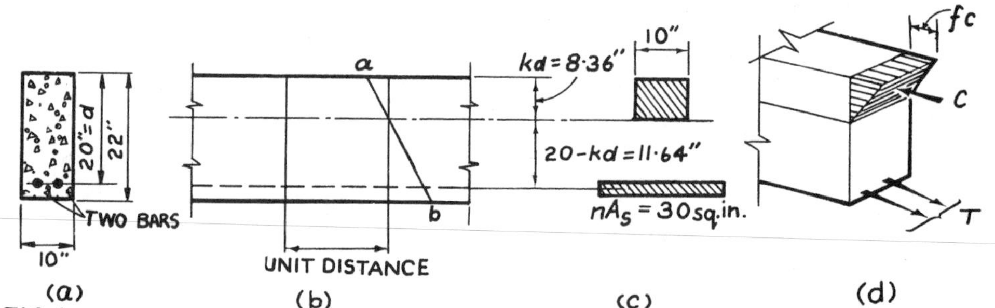

FIG. I

Solution: Plane sections are assumed to remain plane in a reinforced-concrete beam. Strains vary linearly from the neutral axis as shown in Fig. 1(b) by the line ab. A transformed section in terms of concrete is used to solve this problem. However, concrete is so weak in tension that there is no assurance that minute cracks will not occur in the tension zone of the beam. For this reason no credit is given to concrete for resisting tension. On the basis of this assumption, concrete in the tension zone of a beam only holds the reinforcing steel in place. Hence in this analysis it virtually does not exist at all, and the transformed section assumes the form shown in Fig. 1(c). The cross-section of concrete has its own shape above the neutral axis; below it no concrete is shown,
Steel, of course, can resist tension, so it is shown as the transformed

concrete area. For computation purposes, the steel is located by a single dimension from the neutral axis to its centroid. There is a negligible difference between this distance and the true distances to the various steel fibers.

So far the idea of the neutral axis has been used, but its location is unknown. However, it is known that this axis coincides with the axis through the centroid of the transformed section. It is further known that the first (or statical) moment of the area on one side of a centroidal axis is equal to the first moment of the area on the other side. Thus, let kd be the distance from the top of the beam to the centroidal axis as shown in Fig. 1(c), where k is an unknown ratio and d is the distance from the top of the beam to the center of the steel. An algebraic restatement of the foregoing locates the neutral axis, about which I is computed and stresses are determined.

$$\underbrace{10(kd)}_{\text{concrete area}} \times \underbrace{(kd/2)}_{\text{arm}} = \underbrace{30}_{\text{transformed steel area}} \times \underbrace{(20 - kd)}_{\text{arm}}$$

$$5(kd)^2 = 600 - 30(kd)$$

$$(kd)^2 + 6(kd) - 120 = 0$$

$$kd = \frac{-6 \pm \sqrt{36 + 480}}{2}$$

Hence $kd = 8.36$ in. and $20 - kd = 11.64$ in.

$$I = \Sigma(I_0 + Ay^2)$$

where I is the total moment of inertia of the cross section, I_0 is the moment of inertia of one section of the total about its own centroid and Ay^2 is the transfer term from the parallel axis theorem which when added to I_0 gives the moment of inertia about the centroidal axis of the total cross section.

$$I = \frac{10(8.36)^3}{12} + 10(8.36)\left(\frac{8.36}{2}\right)^2 + 0 + 30(11.64)^2 = 6{,}020 \text{ in.}^4$$

$$(\sigma_c)_{max} = \frac{Mc}{I} = \frac{(50{,}000)12(8.36)}{6{,}020} = 833 \text{ psi}$$

$$\sigma_s = n\frac{Mc}{I} = \frac{15(50{,}000)12(11.64)}{6{,}020} = 17{,}400 \text{ psi}$$

ALTERNATE SOLUTION:

After kd is determined, instead of computing I, a procedure evident from Fig. 1(d) may be used. The resultant force developed by the stresses acting in a "hydrostatic" manner on the compression side of the beam must be located kd/3 below the top of the beam. Moreover, if b is the width of the beam, this resultant force $C = \frac{1}{2}(\sigma_c)_{max}b(kd)$ (average stress times area). The resultant tensile force T acts at the center of the steel and is equal to $A_s\sigma_s$, where A_s is the cross-sectional area of the steel. Then if jd is the distance between T and C, and since T = C, the applied moment M is resisted by a couple equal to Tjd or Cjd.

$$jd = d - kd/3 = 20 - (8.36/3) = 17.21 \text{ in.}$$

$$M = Cjd = \tfrac{1}{2}\, b(kd)(\sigma_c)_{max}(jd)$$

$$(\sigma_c)_{max} = \frac{2M}{b(kd)(jd)} = \frac{2(50{,}000)12}{10(8.36)(17.21)} = 833 \text{ psi}$$

$$M = T(jd) = A_s\sigma_s jd$$

$$\sigma_s = \frac{M}{A_s(jd)} = \frac{(50{,}000)12}{2(17.21)} = 17{,}400 \text{ psi}$$

Both methods naturally give the same answer. The second method is more convenient in practical applications. Since steel and concrete have different allowable stresses, the beam is said to have balanced reinforcement when it is designed so that the respective stresses are at their allowable level simultaneously. Note that the beam shown would become virtually worthless if the bending moments were applied in the opposite direction.

• PROBLEM 7-43

Determine the ultimate moment carrying capacity for the reinforced-concrete beam shown in Fig. 1. The reinforcement consists of two #9 steel bars (i.e., 1 1/8" φ bars with cross-sectional area of 1 in.^{2}). Assume that the steel reinforcement yields at 40,000 psi and that the ultimate strength of concrete $f'_c = 2{,}500$ psi.

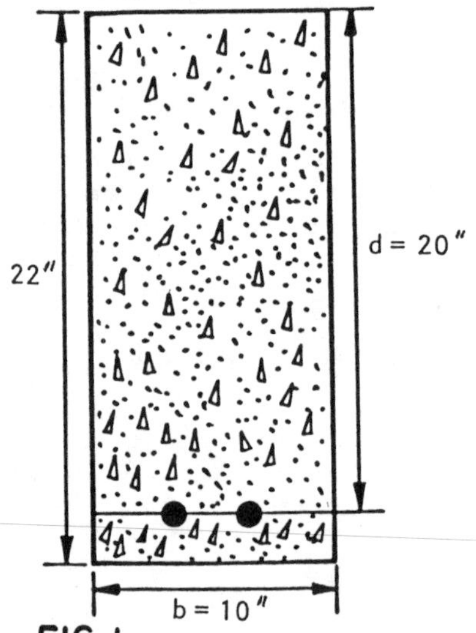

FIG. 1

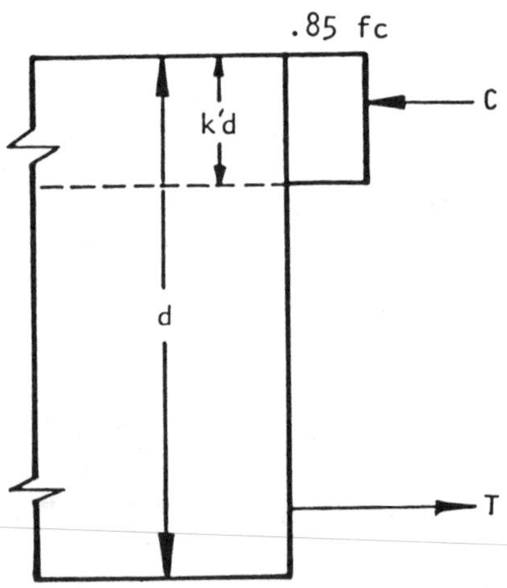

FIG. 2

Solution: When the reinforcing steel begins to yield, large deformations commence. This is taken to be the ultimate capacity of steel; hence $T_{ult} = A_s\sigma_{yp}$.

At the ultimate moment, experimental evidence indicates that the compressive stresses can be approximated by the rectangular stress block shown in Fig. 2. It is customary to assume the average stress in this compressive stress block to be $0.85\, f'_c$. On this basis, keeping in mind that $T_{ult} = C_{ult}$, one has

$$T_{ult} = \sigma_{yp}A_s = 40{,}000 \times 2 = 80{,}000 \text{ lb.} = C_{ult}$$

σ = F/A. The area A is (k'd)b. See Fig. 2. $0.85f'_c b = \dfrac{C_{ult}}{(k'd)b}$

$$k'd = \frac{C_{ult}}{0.85f'_c b} = \frac{80,000}{0.85 \times 2,500 \times 10} = 3.77 \text{ in.}$$

The moment is the moment arm of the couple times the force.

$$M_{ult} = T_{ult}\left(d - \frac{k'd}{2}\right) = 80,000\left(20 - \frac{3.77}{2}\right)\frac{1}{12} = 121,000 \text{ ft.-lb.}$$

• PROBLEM 7-44

The reinforced-concrete beam shown in the sketch contains five $\frac{3}{4}$-in-diameter steel bars. If the tensile stress in the steel is not to exceed 20,000 psi and the compressive stress in the concrete is not to exceed 1,350 psi, what is the maximum bending moment which the beam can transmit? Take $E_c = 1.5 \times 10^6$ psi., $E_s = 30 \times 10^6$ psi.

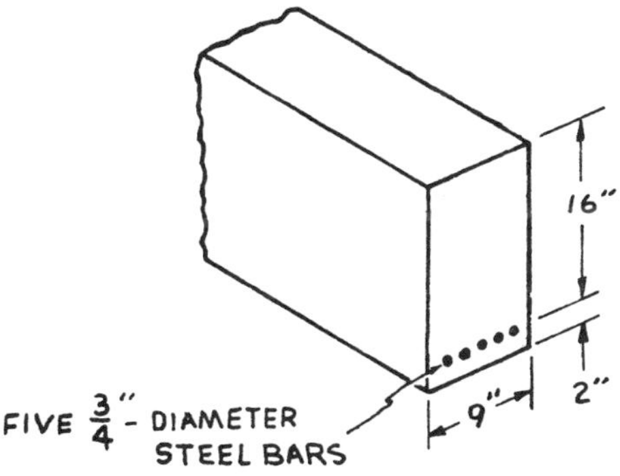

FIG. 1

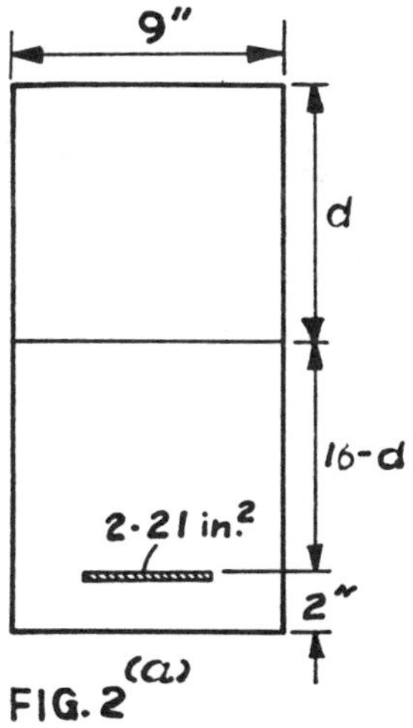

FIG. 2 (a)

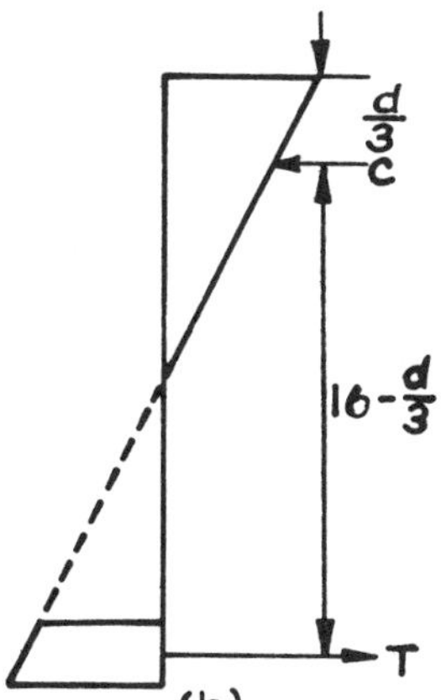

FIG. 2 (b)

Solution: This problem will be solved by finding the equivalent bending moment of the steel and concrete. Total steel area,

$$A_s = 5 \times \frac{\pi}{4}(.75)^2 = 2.21 \text{ in.}^2$$

Assume that the concrete only takes compressive stress and all the tensile stress is carried by the steel. The neutral axis is a distance, d, from the top edge of the beam. The neutral axis is that axis about which the sum of the moments is zero. The moment is the area multiplied by the length from the center of the area to the axis about which the moment is being found. Young's modulus for the steel is $E_s = 30 \times 10^6$ psi, whereas for the concrete it is only $E_c = 1.5 \times 10^6$ psi, so the area of the steel is multiplied by a compensating factor. Thus taking moment about the neutral axis we have

$$(9 \times d) \times \frac{d}{2} - (2.21) \times \frac{30}{1.5}(16 - d) = 0$$

$$4.5d^2 + 44.2d - 707.2 = 0$$

$$d = \frac{-9.8 \pm \sqrt{96.48 + 628.64}}{2}$$

$$= 8.56 \quad \text{(disregard the negative answer)}$$

Maximum force the steel can take is

$$F = A\sigma = 2.21 \times 20{,}000 = 44200 \text{ lb.}$$

Maximum force concrete can take is

$$8.56 \times 9 \times 1350 = 104004 \text{ lb.}$$

Steel fails before concrete.

In Fig. 2(b), the compression force, C, is the concentrated force equivalent to the triangular force distribution. Therefore the point of application of the equivalent force is one-third of the way from the base to the apex of the triangle. The length of the moment arm of the couple is then (16" - d/3). So the maximum bending moment the beam can transmit is

$$M = F \times \ell = 44200 \times \left(16 - \frac{8.56}{3}\right) = 581082 \text{ lb-in.}$$

This design doesn't make maximum use of the concrete. A design using steel bars of larger diameter would be better.

• PROBLEM 7-45

When the beam in Fig. 1 is transmitting its maximum allowable bending moment, the tensile stress in the steel is 20,000 psi and the maximum compressive stress in the concrete is 1,350 psi. What is the diameter of the bars and what is the maximum allowable bending moment?

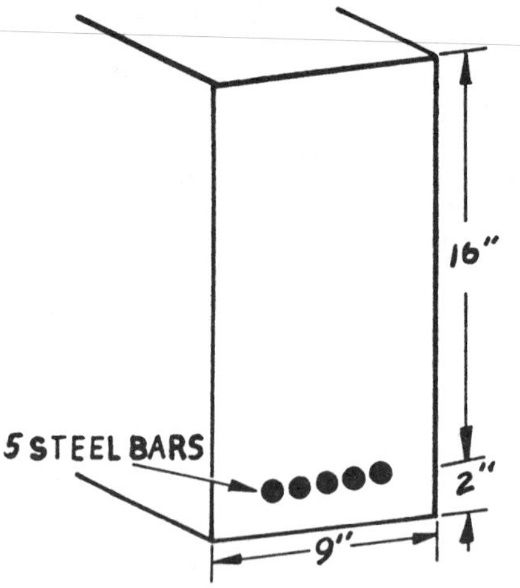

FIG.1.

Solution: Since the stresses are proportional to their distances from the neutral axis, then allowing for the ratio of the Young's Moduli:

$$\frac{\sigma_c}{16k} = \frac{\sigma_s}{16 - 16k}\left(\frac{1.5}{30}\right)$$

$$\frac{16 - 16k}{16k} = \frac{\sigma_s}{\sigma_c}\frac{1.5}{30}$$

$$\frac{1}{k} - 1 = \frac{20000 \times 1.5}{1350 \times 30} = .7407$$

$$k = \frac{1}{1 + .7407} = .574$$

$$k = .574$$

The compression force, c, is the equivalent concentrated force of the triangular force distribution. Therefore the point of application of the equivalent force is one-third of the way from the base to the apex.

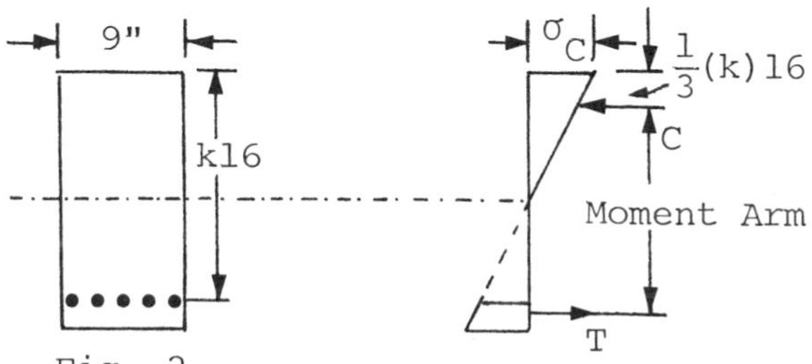

Fig. 2.

$$\text{Moment arm of couple} = 16 - \frac{16 \times .574}{3}$$

$$= (1 - .574/3)16$$

$$= .81 \times 16$$

but $T = C$; $C = \frac{1}{2}\sigma_c A_c$, $T = \sigma_s A_s$

$$20{,}000\, A_s = \tfrac{1}{2} \times 1350 \times (.574 \times 16) \times 9$$

$\therefore$ Total steel area, $A_s = 2.79$ in.^{2}

$$= 5 \times \pi \frac{d^2}{4}$$

$\therefore$ diameter of steel, $d = .843$ in.

The maximum allowable bending moment,

$$M = (\text{Force}) \times (\text{Moment arm})$$

$$M = \tfrac{1}{2} \times 1350 \times 9 \times .574 \times 16 \times .81 \times 16$$

$$= 7.23 \times 10^5 \text{ in.-lb.}$$

In this design the steel and the concrete are stressed equally.

• PROBLEM 7-46

A compound cantilever is composed of two prismatic members of equal cross-sections, but of different materials which are not attached. Compute the maximum stress σ_{xx} in the members.

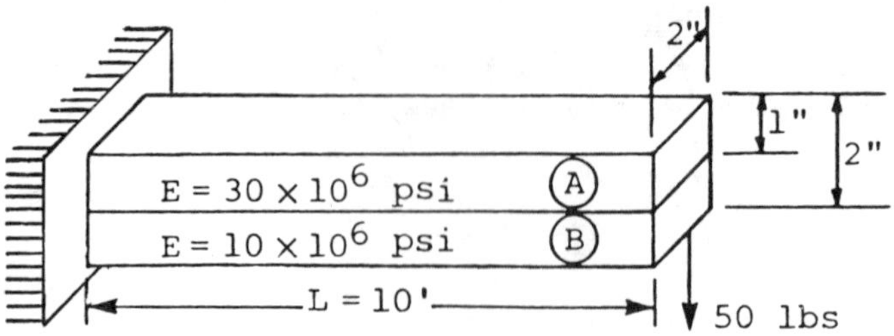

Fig. 1.

Solution: Since the two beams are free to slide over each other with negligible resistance, the equivalent section method cannot be used. An important fact to note, however, is that the radii of curvature of the two beams are the same. Recall $R = EI/M$ where

R = radius of curvature
I = moment of inertia
M = maximum moment in the section

For both beams, $M = P \times L$

$$M = 50 \text{ lb} \times 10 \text{ ft.} \times 12 \text{ in./ft.}$$

$$= 6000 \text{ lb.-in.} = M_A + M_B$$

$$I_A = I_B = I = \frac{bd^3}{12}, \; b = 2", \; d = 1", \; I = \frac{2 \times 1^3}{12}$$

$$= \frac{1}{6} \text{ in.}^4$$

$$R = \frac{E_A I_A}{M_A} = \frac{E_B I_B}{M_B}$$

$$I_A = I_B$$

$$\therefore \; \frac{E_A}{E_B} = \frac{M_A}{M_B} = \frac{30 \times 10^6}{10 \times 10^6} = \frac{1}{3}$$

$$M_A = 3M_B$$

but $M_A + M_B = 6000$ in.-lb. $M_A = 4500$ in.-lb., $M_B = 1500$ in.-lb.

Stress $\sigma = My/I$; $y = \frac{1}{2}"$ for both beams. $\sigma_A = \frac{4500 \times \frac{1}{2}}{1/6} = 13{,}500$ psi

$\sigma_B = \frac{1500 \times \frac{1}{2}}{1/6} = 4{,}500$ psi

INELASTIC BENDING

• PROBLEM 7-47

Determine the plastic or the ultimate capacity in flexure of a mild steel beam of rectangular cross section. Consider the material to be ideally elastic-plastic.

Solution: The idealized stress-strain diagram is in Fig. 1(a). It is assumed that the material has the same properties in tension and compression. The strains that can take place during yielding are much greater than the maximum elastic strain (15 to 20 times the latter quantity). Therefore, since unacceptably large deformations of the beam occur along with very large strains, the plastic moment may be taken as the ultimate moment.

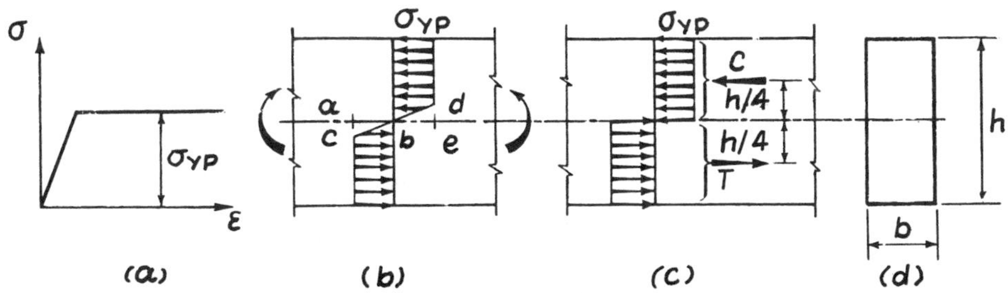

FIG.1

The stress distribution shown in Fig. 1(b) applies after a large amount of deformation takes place. In computing the resisting moment the stresses corresponding to the triangular areas abc and bde may be neglected without unduly impairing the accuracy. They contribute little resistance to the applied bending moment because of their short moment arms. Hence the idealization of the stress distribution to that shown in Fig. 1(c) is permissible and has a simple physical meaning. The whole upper half of the beam is subjected to a uniform compressive stress σ_{yp}, while the lower half is all under a uniform tension σ_{yp}. That the beam is divided evenly into a tension and a compression zone follows from symmetry. Numerically

$$C = T = \sigma_{yp}(bh/2), \quad \text{i.e., (stress)} \times \text{(area)}$$

Each one of these forces acts at a distance $h/4$ from the neutral axis. Hence the plastic or ultimate resisting moment of the beam is

$$M_p = M_{ult} = C\left(\frac{h}{4} + \frac{h}{4}\right) = \sigma_{yp}\frac{bh^2}{4}$$

where b is the breadth of the beam and h is its height.
The resisting bending moment of a beam of rectangular section when the outer fibers just reach σ_{yp}, as given by the elastic flexure formula, is

$$M_{yp} = \sigma_{yp}I/c = \sigma_{yp}(bh^2/6) \quad \text{therefore} \quad M_p/M_{yp} = 1.50$$

The ratio M_p/M_{yp} depends only on the cross-sectional properties of a member and is called the shape factor. The shape factor above for the rectangular beam shows that M_{yp} may be exceeded by 50 percent before the ultimate capacity of a rectangular beam is reached.
For static loads such as occur in buildings, ultimate capacities can be determined using plastic moments. The procedures based on such concepts are referred to as the plastic method of analysis or design. For such work plastic section modulus Z is defined as follows:

$$M_p = \sigma_{yp}Z \tag{1}$$

For the rectangular beam analyzed above $Z = bh^2/4$.
The Steel Construction Manual provides a table of plastic section moduli for many common steel shapes. For a given M_p and σ_{yp} the solution of Eq. (1) for Z is very simple.
The method of limit or plastic analysis is unacceptable in machine design in situations where fatigue properties of the material are important.

• PROBLEM 7-48

Find the residual stresses in a rectangular beam upon removal of the ultimate bending moment.

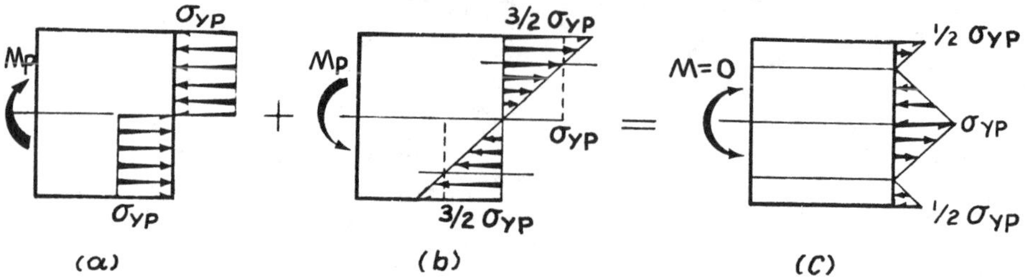

FIG. I

Solution: The stress distribution associated with an ultimate moment is shown in Fig. 1(a). The magnitude of this moment is

$$M_p = \sigma_{yp} bh^2/4.$$

Upon release of this plastic moment M_p every fiber in the beam can rebound elastically. Neglecting Bauschinger's effect, one sees that the elastic range during the unloading is double that which could take place initially. Therefore, since $M_{yp} = \sigma_{yp} bh^2/6$ and the moment being released is $\sigma_{yp}(bh^2/4)$ or $1.5M_{yp}$, the maximum stress calculated on the basis of elastic action is $3/2\ \sigma_{yp}$ as shown in Fig. 1(b). Superimposing the initial stresses at M_p with the elastic rebound stresses due to the release of M_p, one finds the residual stresses, Fig. 1(c). Note that both tensile and compressive longitudinal micro-residual stresses remain in the beam. The tensile zones are shaded in the figure. If such a beam were machined by gradually reducing its depth, the release of the residual stresses would cause undesirable deformations of the bar.

• PROBLEM 7-49

A cantilever beam AB supporting a concentrated load P at the free end (see Fig. 1(a) is constructed of an elastic-plastic material. Determine the angle of rotation θ and the deflection δ at the free end of the beam from the onset of loading up to failure, assuming that the beam is of rectangular cross section.

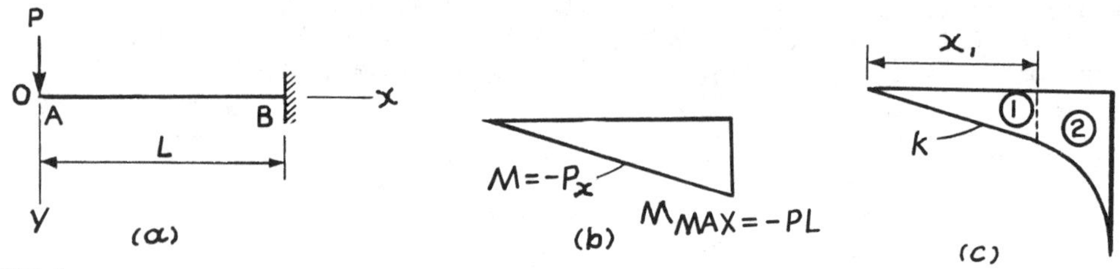

FIG. I

Solution: Let us begin by sketching the bending moment diagram for the beam (Fig. 1(b)). We see that the maximum moment is equal to PL, and as long as this value is less than the yield moment M_y, the beam is fully elastic. For the elastic range we have

$$\theta = \frac{PL^2}{2EI} \qquad \delta = \frac{PL^3}{3EI}$$

The yield load P_y which first produces yielding of the beam is given by the equation

$$P_y = \frac{M_y}{L} \tag{a}$$

The angle θ_y and deflection δ_y caused by the yield load are

$$\theta_y = \frac{P_y L^2}{2EI} \qquad \delta_y = \frac{P_y L^3}{3EI} \tag{b}$$

These are the maximum values of angle of rotation and deflection for the elastic range. In nondimensional form we can express the angle of rotation and the deflection for the entire elastic range by the following simplified equations:

$$\frac{\theta}{\theta_y} = \frac{P}{P_y} \qquad \frac{\delta}{\delta_y} = \frac{P}{P_y} \qquad \left(0 \le \frac{P}{P_y} \le 1\right) \tag{c}$$

When the maximum moment in the beam exceeds M_y, the beam will have two regions: (1) a region of fully elastic behavior, and (2) a region of elastic-plastic behavior, as shown in the curvature diagram of Fig. 1(c). In region (1) the curvature is

$$K = \frac{Px}{EI} \tag{d}$$

and in the region (2) it is

$$K = \frac{K_y}{\sqrt{3 - 2Px/M_y}} \tag{e}$$

where $K_y = M_y/EI$. The length x_1 of the elastic region is found from the equation $Px_1 = M_y$, so that

$$x_1 = \frac{M_y}{P} \tag{f}$$

The angle at the end of the beam, from the first curvature-area theorem, is equal to the area of the curvature diagram:

$$\theta = \int_0^{x_1} \frac{Px\,dx}{EI} + \int_{x_1}^{L} \frac{K_y\,dx}{\sqrt{3 - 2Px/M_y}}$$

$$= \frac{Px_1^2}{2EI} + \frac{K_y M_y}{P}\left[\sqrt{3 - 2Px/M_y} - \sqrt{3 - 2PL/M_y}\right]$$

If we substitute M_y/EI for K_y, M_y/P for x_1, and P_yL for M_y, the preceding equation becomes

$$\frac{\theta}{\theta_y} = \frac{P_y}{P}\left[3 - 2\sqrt{3 - 2P/P_y}\right] \qquad \left(1 \le \frac{P}{P_y} \le \frac{3}{2}\right) \tag{g}$$

in which θ_y is given by Eq. (b). This equation is valid until the maximum moment in the beam becomes equal to the plastic moment M_p, which corresponds to $P/P_y = 3/2$. At the instant when P/P_y reaches this value, the angle of rotation is $\theta/\theta_y = 2$. Subsequently, this angle increases indefinitely. A graph of load P/P_y versus angle of rotation θ/θ_y is shown in Fig. 2.

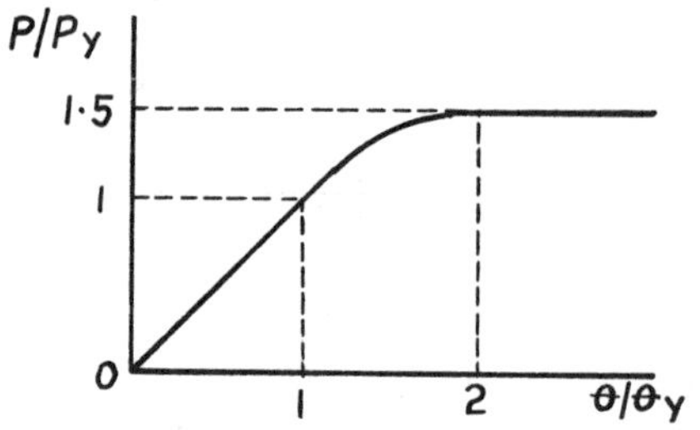

FIG. 2

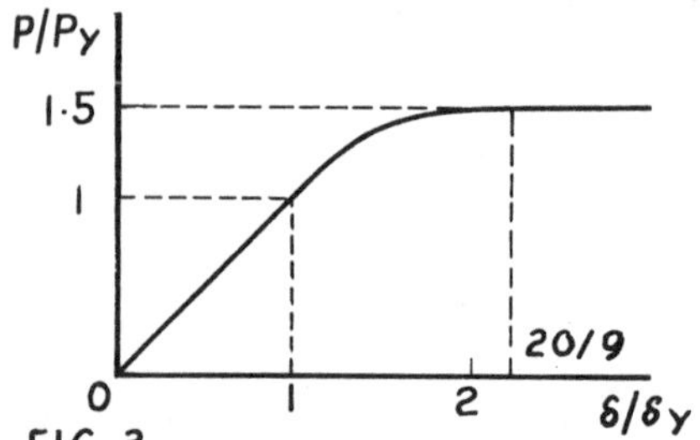

FIG. 3

The deflection at the end of the beam is calculated from the second curvature-area theorem as follows:

$$\delta = \int_0^{x_1} \frac{Px^2\,dx}{EI} + \int_{x_1}^{L} \frac{K_y x\,dx}{\sqrt{3 - 2Px/M_y}}$$

By evaluating these integrals and making the same substitutions as for Eq. (g), we get

$$\frac{\delta}{\delta_y} = \left(\frac{P_y}{P}\right)^2 \left[5 - \left(3 + \frac{P}{P_y}\right)\sqrt{3 - \frac{2P}{P_y}}\right] \quad \left(1 \le \frac{P}{P_y} \le \frac{3}{2}\right) \qquad \text{(h)}$$

in which δ_y is given by Eq. (b). When P/P_y equals 3/2, the deflection is $\delta/\delta_y = 20/9$. The load-deflection diagram is plotted in Fig. 3.

• PROBLEM 7-50

Determine the moment resisting capacity of an elastic-plastic rectangular beam.

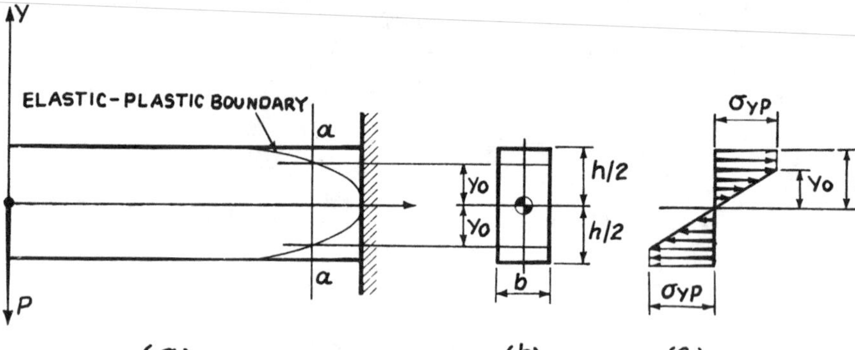

FIG. I. ELASTIC-PLASTIC CANTILEVER

Solution: To make the problem more definite consider a cantilever loaded as in Fig. 1(a). If the beam is made of ideal elastic-plastic material and the applied force P is large enough to cause yielding, plastic zones will be formed (shown shaded in the figure). At an arbitrary section a-a the corresponding stress distribution will be as shown in Fig. 1(c). The elastic zone extends over the depth of $2y_0$. Noting that within the elastic zone the stresses vary linearly and that everywhere in the plastic zone the axial stress is σ_{yp}, one finds that the resisting moment M is

$$M = -2\int_0^{y_0}\left(-\frac{y}{y_0}\sigma_{yp}\right)(b\ dy)y - 2\int_{y_0}^{h/2}(-\sigma_{yp})(b\ dy)y$$

$$= \sigma_{yp}\frac{bh^2}{4} - \sigma_{yp}\frac{by_0^2}{3} = M_p - \sigma_{yp}\frac{by_0^2}{3} \qquad (1)$$

where the last simplification is done in accordance with equation

$$M_p = \sigma_{yp}\frac{bh^2}{4}.$$

It is interesting to note that, in this general equation, if $y_0 = 0$, the moment capacity becomes equal to the plastic or ultimate moment. On the other hand, if $y_0 = h/2$, the moment reverts back to the limiting elastic case where $M = \sigma_{yp} bh^2/6$. When the applied bending moment along the span is known, the elastic-plastic boundary can be determined by solving Eq. (1) for y_0. As long as an elastic zone or core remains, the plastic deformations cannot progress without a limit. This is a case of contained plastic flow.

• PROBLEM 7-51

Figure 2 shows a beam built-in at C, simply supported at A, and subjected to a concentrated load P at B. Find the magnitude of the limit load P_L which corresponds to the condition of plastic collapse. Let the bending moment corresponding to the onset of yielding for the beam section be M_y, and let the limiting or fully plastic bending moment be M_L.

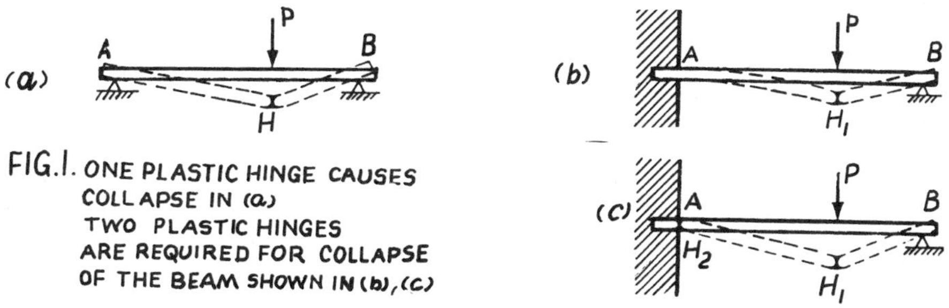

FIG.1. ONE PLASTIC HINGE CAUSES COLLAPSE IN (a) TWO PLASTIC HINGES ARE REQUIRED FOR COLLAPSE OF THE BEAM SHOWN IN (b),(c)

Solution: In Fig. 2a the reactions are calculated according to the equilibrium requirements in terms of the statically indeterminate quantity M_C. The equilibrium analysis is extended in Fig. 2b where free bodies of the segments AB and BC are shown. Note that all shear forces and bending moments depend on the statically indeterminate quantity M_C. It should be emphasized again that this equilibrium

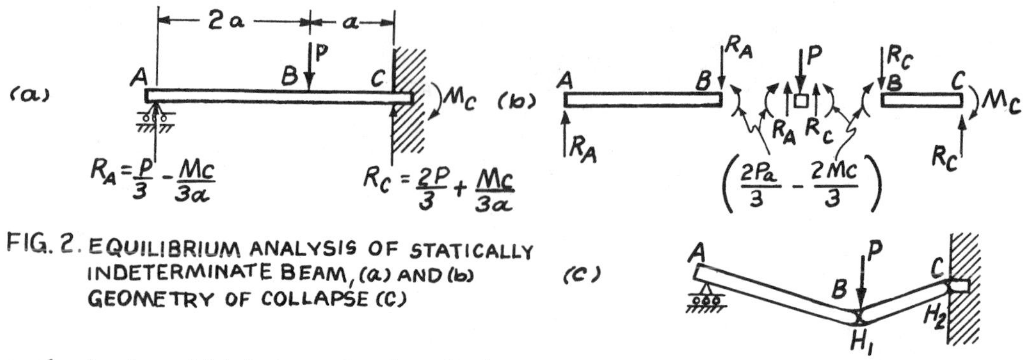

FIG. 2. EQUILIBRIUM ANALYSIS OF STATICALLY INDETERMINATE BEAM, (a) AND (b) GEOMETRY OF COLLAPSE (c)

analysis is valid independently of the stress-strain law. The stress-strain law and the conditions of geometric compatibility enter only in fixing the magnitude of M_C. The only condition for the determination of M_C is the requirement that sufficient hinges have formed so that P causes collapse.

In Fig. 2c we show the collapse geometry with plastic hinges at B and C. We obtain our quantitative result by observing that the magnitudes of the bending moments at B and C must both be M_L. Referring to Fig. 2b, we have

$$\frac{2Pa}{3} - \frac{2M_C}{3} = M_L \qquad\qquad M_C = M_L \tag{a}$$

Eliminating M_C gives $P_L = 2.5\,\frac{M_L}{a}$

• PROBLEM 7-52

The structure shown in Fig. 1 consists of two equal cantilever beams AC and CD with roller contact at C. Given the limiting bending moment M_L for the beams, find the limiting value of the load P which corresponds to plastic collapse of the structure.

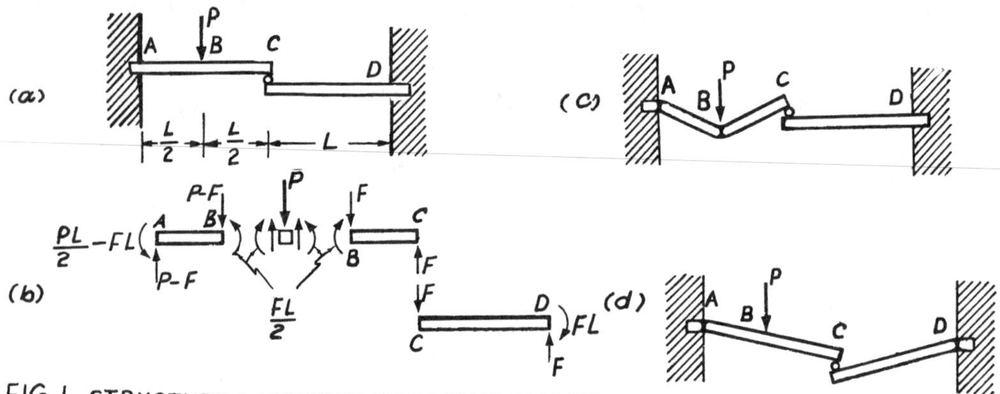

FIG. 1. STRUCTURE WITH TWO POSSIBLE MODES OF COLLAPSE.

Solution: The forces and equilibrium requirements are analyzed in Fig. 1b which shows free-body diagrams of the various beam segments. The structure is statically indeterminate, but all forces and moments can be expressed in terms of the single unknown F, which is the magnitude of the interaction at C.

Turning next to the geometry of collapse, we find that there are two different geometrically admissible modes of collapse, as shown in Fig. 1c and d. In Fig. 1c plastic hinges form at A and B, causing collapse under the load but without incurring large deformations in the cantilever CD. In Fig. 1d plastic hinges form at A and D, causing large deformations of both beams. To decide which collapse mechanism would actually occur, we obtain the value of P corresponding to each mode of collapse. The mode with the smaller value of P is the actual collapse mechanism.

For the mechanism of Fig. 1c we set the bending moments at A and B equal to the limiting bending moments M_L.

$$\frac{PL}{2} - FL = M_L$$

$$\frac{FL}{2} = M_L \tag{a}$$

Eliminating F, we obtain

$$P = 6\frac{M_L}{L} \tag{b}$$

as the load corresponding to Fig. 1c.

Similarly, for the mechanism of Fig. 1d, we set the bending moments at A and D equal to the limiting bending moment M_L.

$$\frac{PL}{2} - FL = M_L \tag{c}$$

$$FL = M_L$$

Eliminating F, we obtain

$$P = 4\frac{M_L}{L} \tag{d}$$

as the load corresponding to Fig. 1d. Since (d) is smaller than (b), the structure collapses in the mechanism of Fig. 1d under the limit load

$$P_L = 4\frac{M_L}{L} \tag{e}$$

• PROBLEM 7-53

A beam of rectangular cross section is constructed of material having a stress-strain diagram consisting of two lines, as shown in Fig. 1. The modulus of elasticity in tension is E_1 and in compression is E_2, so that

$$\sigma = E_1\epsilon \qquad \epsilon \geq 0$$

$$\sigma = E_2\epsilon \qquad \epsilon \leq 0$$

The beam is assumed to be subjected to a positive bending moment M. Obtain the moment-curvature expression, and find the maximum stresses and strains in the beam.

Solution: Let us denote the strains at the bottom and top of the beam as ϵ_1 and ϵ_2, respectively. The corresponding maximum stresses are σ_1 and σ_2. These stresses and strains are indicated in Fig. 1. To locate the neutral axis, we observe that the two shaded areas under the stress-strain curve must be equal, so that

$$\frac{\sigma_1\epsilon_1}{2} = \frac{\sigma_2\epsilon_2}{2} \tag{1}$$

We know that

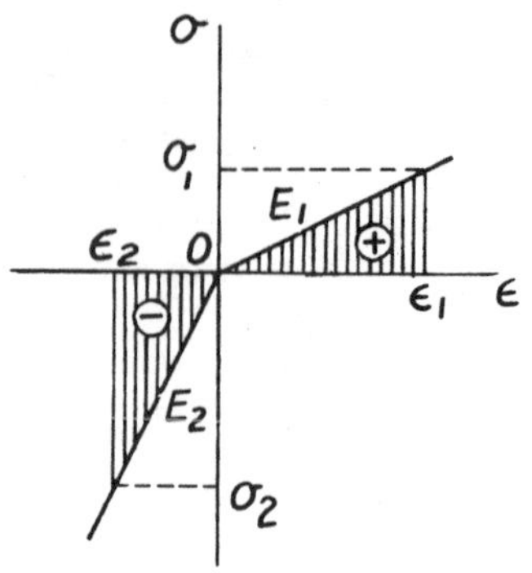

FIG.1

$$\sigma_1 = E_1\epsilon_1 \qquad \sigma_2 = E_2\epsilon_2 \tag{2}$$

Also, we have the relations

$$\epsilon_1 = kh_1 \qquad \epsilon_2 = -kh_2 \tag{3}$$

Substituting the preceding four equations into Eq. (1) we get

$$\frac{E_1(kh_1)(kh_1)}{2} = \frac{E_2(-kh_2)(-kh_2)}{2}$$

or

$$E_1h_1^2 = E_2h_2^2 \tag{4}$$

as the first equation relating h_1 and h_2. In addition, we have the equation

$$h = h_1 + h_2 \tag{5}$$

The distances h_1 and h_2 can now be found by simultaneous solution of Eqs. (4) and (5), yielding

$$h_1 = \frac{h\sqrt{E_2}}{\sqrt{E_1}+\sqrt{E_2}} \qquad h_2 = \frac{h\sqrt{E_1}}{\sqrt{E_1}+\sqrt{E_2}} \tag{6}$$

Thus the position of the neutral axis is determined. The bending moment is given by

$$M = \frac{bh^2}{\epsilon_t^2}\left[\int_{\epsilon_2}^{0} E_2\epsilon^2\, d\epsilon + \int_0^{\epsilon_1} E_1\epsilon^2\, d\epsilon\right]$$

Integrating one obtains,

$$M = \frac{bh^2}{3\epsilon_t^2}\left[-E_2\epsilon_2^3 + E_1\epsilon_1^3\right] \tag{7}$$

The strains ϵ_1 and ϵ_2 are related to the curvature by Eqs. (3); substituting Eq. (6) into Eq. (3), gives

$$\epsilon_1 = kh\frac{\sqrt{E_2}}{\sqrt{E_1}+\sqrt{E_2}} \qquad \epsilon_2 = -kh\frac{\sqrt{E_1}}{\sqrt{E_1}+\sqrt{E_2}}$$

Also, the strain ϵ_t is equal to kh. We can now substitute these expressions for ϵ_1, ϵ_2, and ϵ_t into Eq. (7), obtaining

$$M = \frac{bh^2}{3(kh)^2}\left[-E_2\left\{-kh\frac{\sqrt{E_1}}{\sqrt{E_1}+\sqrt{E_2}}\right\}^3 + E_1\left\{kh\frac{\sqrt{E_2}}{\sqrt{E_1}+\sqrt{E_2}}\right\}^3\right]$$

$$= \frac{bh^2(kh)^3 E_1 E_2}{3(kh)^2[\sqrt{E_1} + \sqrt{E_2}]^3} \left[\sqrt{E_1} + \sqrt{E_2}\right]$$

or

$$M = \frac{4bh^3 k E_1 E_2}{12[\sqrt{E_1} + \sqrt{E_2}]^3}$$

Since $I = bh^3/12$, the above equation can be written as

$$M = \frac{4E_1 E_2 I\ k}{[\sqrt{E_1} + \sqrt{E_2}]^3} \tag{8}$$

Finally, let us introduce the notation

$$E_r = \frac{4E_1 E_2}{(\sqrt{E_1} + \sqrt{E_2})^2} \tag{9}$$

so that Eq. (8) becomes $M = E_r Ik$, and hence the curvature becomes

$$k = \frac{M}{E_r I} \tag{10}$$

The quantity E_r is called the reduced modulus of elasticity and always has a value between E_1 and E_2. In the special case when both moduli are the same and equal to E, then E_r equals E also.

The stresses and strains at the extreme fibers of the beam are now readily found in terms of the bending moment. We take Eqs. (3) for ϵ_1 and ϵ_2 and substitute Eq. (10) for the curvature, obtaining

$$\epsilon_1 = \frac{Mh_1}{E_r I} \qquad \epsilon_2 = -\frac{Mh_2}{E_r I} \tag{11}$$

Next, the stress-strain equations (Eq. 2) yield

$$\sigma_1 = \frac{Mh_1}{I}\frac{E_1}{E_r} \qquad \sigma_2 = -\frac{Mh_2}{I}\frac{E_2}{E_r} \tag{12}$$

and the analysis of the beam is completed.

• PROBLEM 7-54

Determine and plot the moment-curvature relationship for an elastic-ideally-plastic rectangular beam.

Solution: In a rectangular elastic-plastic beam at y_0, where the juncture of the elastic and plastic zones occurs, the linear strain $\epsilon_x = \pm \epsilon_{yp}$. Therefore, with the curvature $1/\rho = k$,

$$\frac{1}{\rho} = k = -\frac{\epsilon_{yp}}{y_0} \quad \text{and} \quad k_{yp} = -\frac{\epsilon_{yp}}{h/2}$$

where the last expression gives the curvature of the member at impending yielding when $y_0 = h/2$. From the above relations

$$\frac{y_0}{h/2} = \frac{k_{yp}}{k}$$

On substituting this expression into the plastic moment equation one obtains the required moment-curvature relationship:

$$M = M_p\left[1 - \tfrac{1}{3}\left(\frac{y_0}{h/2}\right)^2\right] = \frac{3}{2} M_{yp}\left[1 - \tfrac{1}{3}\left(\frac{k_{yp}}{k}\right)^2\right] \qquad \text{(a)}$$

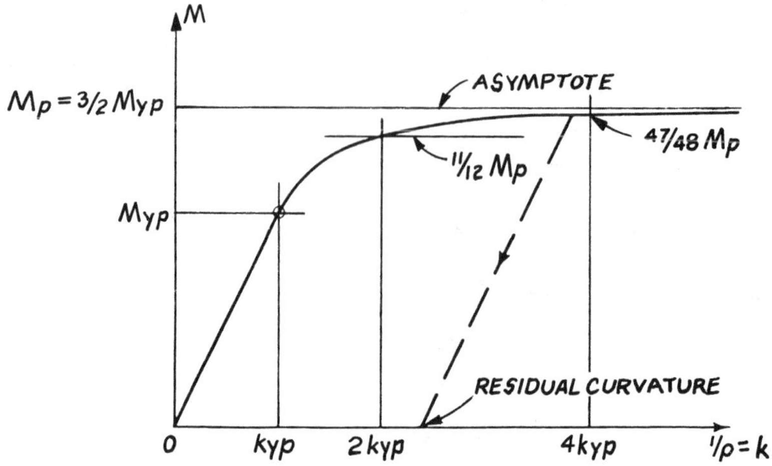

FIG.1. MOMENT - CURVATURE - RELATION FOR A RECTANGULAR BEAM

This function is plotted in Fig. 1. Note how rapidly it approaches the asymptote. At curvature just double that of the impending yielding, eleven-twelfths or 91.6 percent of the ultimate plastic moment M_p is already reached. At this point the middle half of the beam remains elastic.
On releasing an applied moment the beam rebounds elastically as shown in the figure. On this basis residual curvature can be determined.

• PROBLEM 7-55

A 3-in.-wide mild-steel cantilever beam has the other dimensions as shown in Fig. 1. Determine the tip deflection caused by applying the two loads of 5 kips each. Assume $E = 30 \times 10^3$ ksi, and $\sigma_{yp} = \pm 40$ ksi.

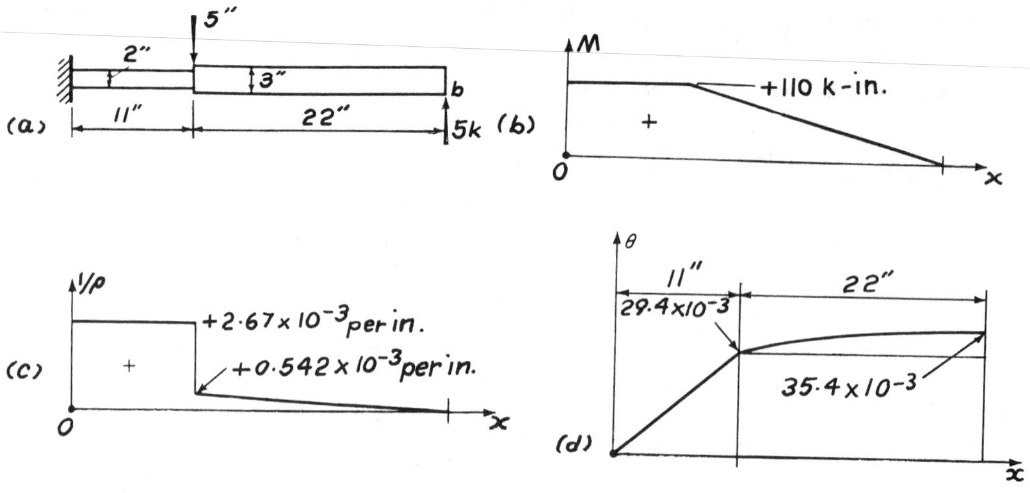

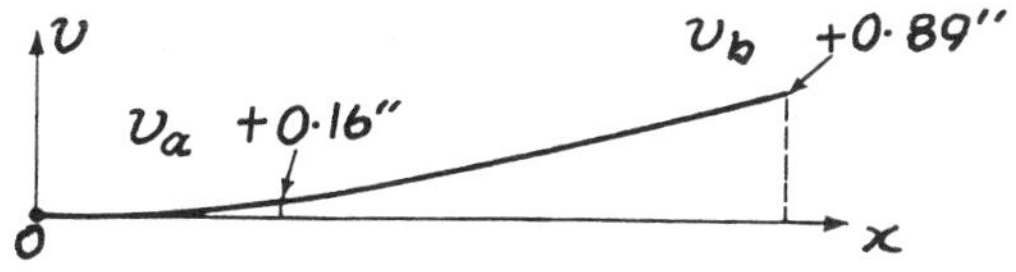

FIG. 1 (e)

Solution: Start by determining the bending moment in the beam, then plot the bending moment diagram, Fig. 1b. From $\sigma_{max} = Mc/I$ it is found that the largest stress in the beam segment ab is, $\sigma = 110c/I$ but $c = 1.5''$

$$I = \frac{3 \times 3^3}{12} = \frac{27}{4} \text{ in.}^4$$

$$\therefore \sigma_{max} = 110 \times \frac{3}{2} \times \frac{4}{27} = \frac{220}{9} = 24.4 \text{ ksi}$$

which indicates elastic behavior. An analogous calculation for the shallow section of the beam gives a stress of

$$\sigma = \frac{110c}{I}$$

$$c = 1''$$

$$I = \frac{3 \times 2^3}{12} = 2 \text{ in.}^4$$

$$\therefore \sigma_{max} = \frac{110 \times 1}{2} = 55 \text{ ksi}$$

which is not possible as the material yields at 40 ksi.
A check of the ultimate capacity for the 2-in.-deep section based on

$$M_{ult} = \sigma_{yp} \frac{bh^2}{4}$$

gives

$$M_p = M_{ult} = \sigma_{yp} \frac{bh^2}{4} = \frac{40 \times 3 \times 2^2}{4} = 120 \text{ k-in.}$$

This calculation shows that although the beam yields partially, it can carry the applied moment. The applied moment is $11/12\ M_p$. From

$$M = M_p\left[1 - \frac{1}{3}\left(\frac{k_{yp}}{k}\right)^2\right]$$

$$\frac{11}{12} M_p = M_p\left[1 - \frac{1}{3}\left(\frac{k_{yp}}{k}\right)^2\right]$$

$$\frac{k_{yp}}{k} = \frac{1}{2}$$

$$k = 2\, k_{yp}$$

This means that the curvature in the 2-in.-deep section of the beam is twice that at the beginning of yielding. Therefore the curvature in the 11-in. segment of the beam adjoining the support is

$$\frac{1}{\rho} = 2k_{yp} = 2\,\frac{\epsilon_{yp}}{h/2} = 2\,\frac{\sigma_{yp}}{Eh/2} = \frac{2 \times 40}{30 \times 10^3 \times 1} = 2.67 \times 10^{-3} \text{ per in.}$$

The maximum curvature for segment ab is

$$\frac{1}{\rho} = \frac{M_{max}}{EI} = \frac{\sigma_{max}}{Ec} = \frac{24.4}{30 \times 10^3 \times 1.5} = 0.542 \times 10^{-3} \text{ per in.}$$

These data on curvatures are plotted in Fig. 1c. On integrating this twice with $\theta(0) = 0$ and $v(0) = 0$, the deflected curve, Fig. 1e is

obtained. The tip deflection is 0.89 in. upward.
If the applied loads were released, the beam would rebound elastically. This amounts to 0.64 in. at the tip and a residual tip deflection of 0.25 in. would remain. The residual curvature would be confined to the 2-in.-deep segment of the beam.
If the end load were applied alone, the beam would collapse. Superposition cannot be used to solve this problem because it is non-linear.

CHAPTER 8

SHEAR

SHEAR STRESS

• **PROBLEM 8-1**

Determine the maximum shear stress in the web of a beam having the T-shaped cross section shown in Fig. 1 if b = 4 in., t = 1 in., h = 8 in., h_1 = 7 in., and V = 10,000 lb.

FIG.1

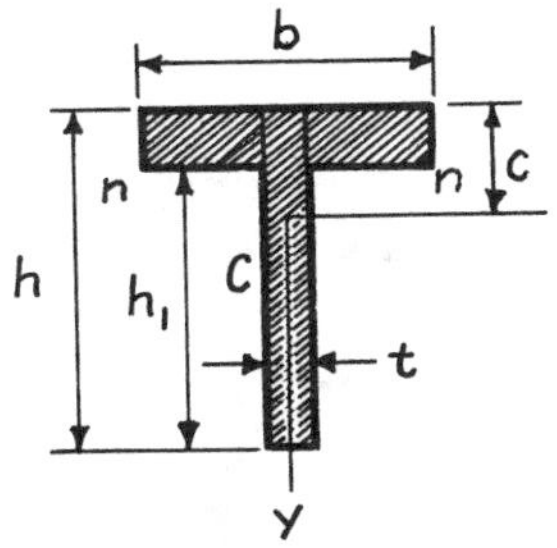

Solution: The maximum shear stress in the web of a beam occurs at the neutral axis and is given by the formula

$$\tau = \frac{VQ}{Ib}$$

To find this stress we must first find the location of the neutral axis, given with respect to the top of the section by

$$c = \frac{\Sigma yA}{\Sigma A}$$

where y is the distance from the top of the section to the centroid of the area. Considering the T section to be an 8" web with two 1.5" flanges we have

$$c = \frac{2(1.5)(1)(.5) + 8(1)(4)}{2(1.5)(1) + 8(1)} = 3.05 \text{ in.}$$

The moment of inertia I of the cross section about the neutral axis can be found by first obtaining the moment of inertia about axis nn and then using the parallel axis theorem.

Again considering an 8" web with no 1.5" flange on either side we calculate

$$I = \frac{1(8)^3}{12} + (1)(8)(4-3.05)^2 + \frac{(3)(1)^3}{12} + (3)(1)(3.05-.5)^2 = 69.64 \text{ in.}^4$$

The maximum shear stress occurs at the neutral axis; the first moment Q of the area below the neutral axis is

$$Q = \frac{(8-3.05)^2}{2} = 12.3 \text{ in.}^3$$

Now substituting into the shear formula, we get

$$\tau = \frac{VQ}{It} = \frac{10,000(12.3)}{69.7(1)} = 1760 \text{ psi}$$

which is the maximum shear stress.

• PROBLEM 8-2

A laminated wood beam is built up by gluing together three 2 in. x 4 in. boards to form a solid beam 4 in. x 6 in. in cross section as shown in the figure. The allowable shear stress in the glued joints is 50 psi. If the beam is a 3-ft. long cantilever, what is the allowable load P at the free end? What is the corresponding maximum bending stress?

FIG. 1

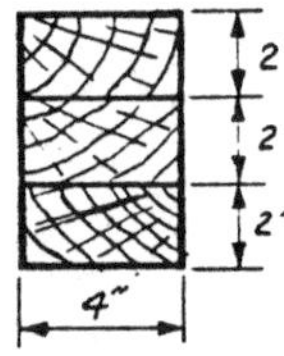

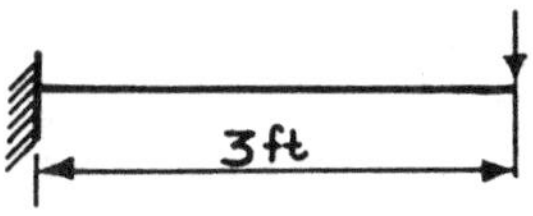

FIG. 2.

Solution: Allowable shear stress, $\tau_{all} = 50$ psi. Recall

$$\tau = \frac{V}{2I}\left(\frac{h^2}{4} - y_1^2\right) \tag{1}$$

where

V = shear at a section
I = moment of inertia of the cross-sectional area at that section
h = height of section
y_1 = distance from middle surface to a point where the stress is desired

For this particular problem,

$$V = P;\ h = 6";\ y_1 = 1$$

$$I = \frac{4 \times 6^3}{12} = 72 \text{ in.}^4$$

Substituting in Eq. 1 we have

$$\tau_{all} = 50 = \frac{P}{144}\left(\frac{36}{4} - 1\right)$$

$$\therefore P = 900 \text{ lbs.}$$

Maximum moment:

$$M_{max} = P \times 36 \text{ in.-lb.}$$

$$\text{but} \quad \sigma = \frac{My}{I} = \frac{36P \times 3}{72}$$

Substituting for P gives

$$\sigma = \frac{900 \text{x} 36 \text{x} 3}{72} = 1350 \text{ psi.}$$

• PROBLEM 8-3

Four identical bars of the same material, each 3 in. x 4 in. in cross-section are placed one above the other and glued together with epoxy jointing material to form a beam of section 12 in. x 4 in. (Fig. 1). At a cross-section where the total shear force is 5000 lb. find the shear force per inch run of beam resisted by the epoxy glue at joint A. Also find the shear force per inch run resisted at joint B.

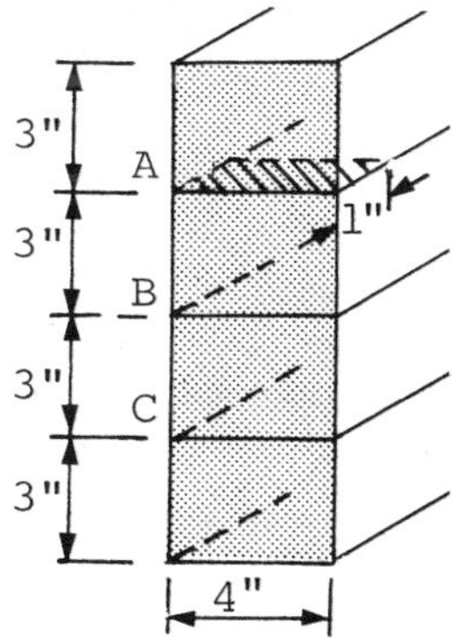

Fig. 1.

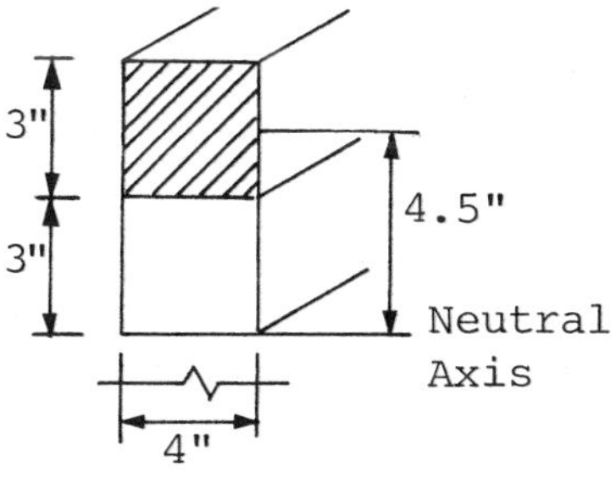

Fig. 2.

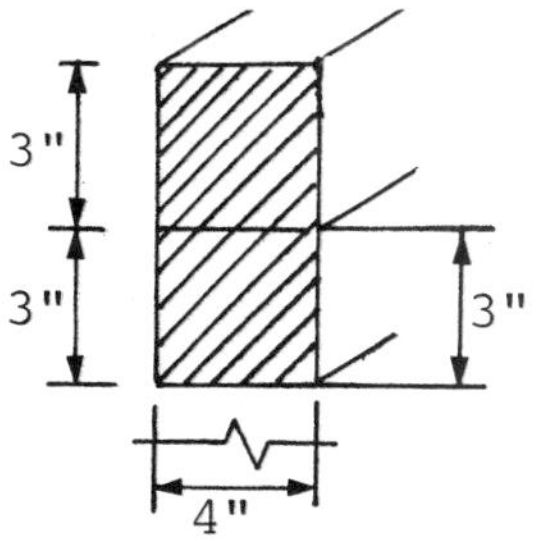

Fig. 3.

Solution: First compute the moment of inertia of the whole cross-section.

$$\text{i.e.} \quad I = \frac{4 \times 12^3}{12} = 576 \text{ in.}^4$$

The shear force at the cross-section being considered,

$$V = 5000 \text{ lbs.}$$

The shear force per inch run of beam at joint A is the shear flow at joint A.

Recall $q = \frac{VQ}{I}$ (1)

where Q is the first moment of area of the shaded part about the neutral axis (Fig. 2).

$$Q = 3 \times 4 \times 4.5 = 54 \text{ in.}^3$$

Substituting in Eq. (1) we have

$$q = \frac{5000 \times 54}{576} = 468.75 \text{ lb./in.}$$

∴ Shear force per inch run resisted by the epoxy glue at joint A = 468.75 lb./in.

To find the shear force per inch run resisted at joint B, we notice that all the parameters in Eq. (1) are the same except Q. In this case, Q is the first moment of area of the shaded portion in Fig. 3.

$$Q = 6 \times 4 \times 3 = 72 \text{ in}^3$$

$$\therefore q = \frac{5000 \times 72}{576}$$

$$= 625 \text{ lb/in}$$

∴ Shear force per inch run resisted by the epoxy glue at joint B = 625 lb./in.

• PROBLEM 8-4

A composite beam has the cross-section shown in Fig. 1. Materials A and B are both elastic, the elastic modulus of A being twice that of B. If the joints between A and B are glued, find the shear resisted by each joint per inch run of beam if the total shear force is 4000 lbs.

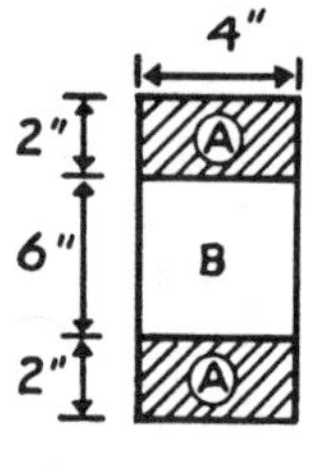

FIG. 1

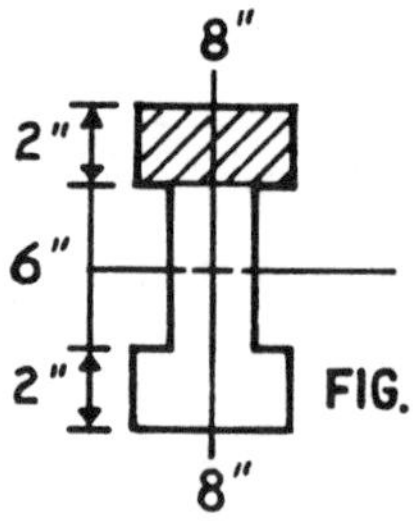

FIG. 2

Solution: First transform the beam cross-section into an equivalent section made of material B (Fig. 2).

The moment of inertia for the equivalent cross-section is

$$I = \frac{4 \times 6^3}{12} + 2 \times 8 \times 2 \left(\frac{2^2}{12} + 4^2\right)$$

$$= 72 + 522.667 = 594.667 \text{ in.}^4$$

The first moment of area of the shaded portion about the neutral axis is

$$Q = 8 \times 2 \times 4 = 64$$

Shear resisted by each joint per inch run or shear flow at the joint, $q = \frac{VQ}{I}$

$$= \frac{4000 \times 64}{594.667} = 429.05 \text{ lb./in.}$$

• PROBLEM 8-5

An I-shaped beam is formed by attaching the flanges to the web by screws spaced along the beam. Calculate the maximum permissible distance between screws for a maximum shear force of 200 lbs in any screw.

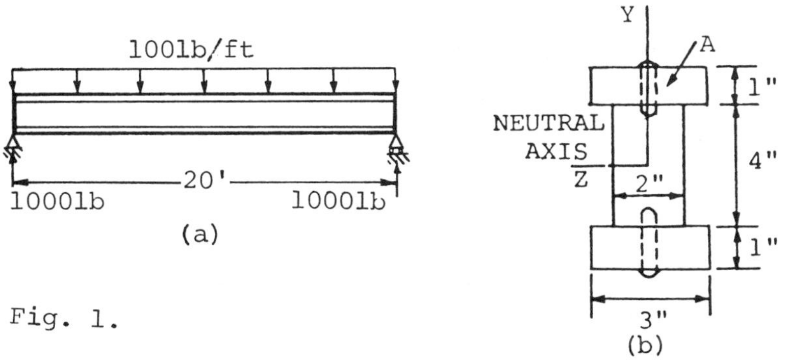

Fig. 1.

Solution: Consider a free body of a portion of the upper member as shown in Fig. 2.

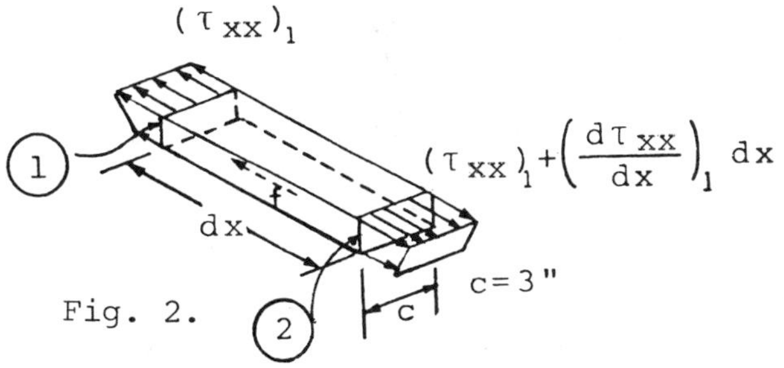

Fig. 2.

We have shown only stresses τ_{xx} and forces from the screws in the x direction. Note that it is the forces from the screws rather than shear stress over the bottom face that resists the force in the x direction stemming from non-uniform normal stress τ_{xx} in that direction. Were this a single-member we would need a force on the bottom face:

$$dF_s = \left(\bar{\tau}_{yx} b\ dx\right)$$

where b is the width of the contact surface (2 in.). Based

per unit length, we would need a force intensity D_s along the beam given as

$$D_s = \frac{dF_s}{dx} = \bar{\tau}_{yx} b \tag{1}$$

This force intensity can be given as

$$D_s = \frac{V_y Q_z}{I_{zz}} \tag{2}$$

where Q is the first moment of cross section of the top member about the neutral axis. Now in the problem at hand, the force D_s is developed by the shear forces from the screws. If f is the force from one screw and there are n screws per unit length of beam at the region of interest, we can then imagine a force intensity (based on per unit length) arising from the screws and given as nf. Equating this force intensity with that given by Eq. (2) we get

$$nf = \frac{V_y Q_z}{I_{zz}} \tag{3}$$

Using the largest value of V_y over the beam and the allowable value of f, we can then solve for n, the minimum number of screws per unit length of beam. For the problem at hand we have

$$\left(V_y\right)_{max} = 1000 \text{ lb.}$$

$$Q = (1)(3)(2.5) = 7.5 \text{ in.}^3$$

$$I_{zz} = \left(\frac{1}{12}\right)(2)(4)^3 + 2\left[\frac{1}{12}(3)(1)^3 + (3)(1)(2.5)^2\right] = 10.67 + 2\left[\frac{1}{4} + 18.75\right]$$

$$= 48.7 \text{ in.}^4$$

Hence,

$$n = \frac{1}{200}\frac{(1000)(7.5)}{(48.7)} = .77$$

We thus require .77 screw/in., or, in other words, the screws should be spaced 1/n = 1.300 in. apart at sections where the shear force is greatest. This is true also for the bottom member.

• PROBLEM 8-6

A simple beam on a 20-ft. span carries a load of 200 lb. per foot including its own weight. The beam cross section is to be made from several full-sized wooden pieces as in Fig. 1(a). Specify the spacing of the 1/2-in. lag screws shown which is necessary to fasten this beam together. Assume that one 1/2-in. lag screw, as determined by laboratory tests, is good for 500 lb. when transmitting a lateral load parallel to the grain of the wood. For the entire section I is equal to 6,060 in.^{4}.

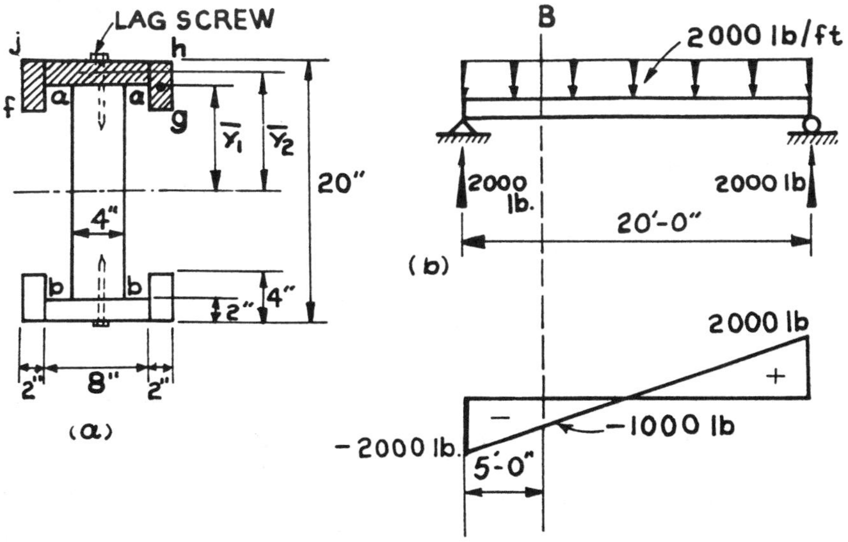

FIG.1. (c)

Solution: To find the spacing of the lag screws, the shear flow at section a-a must be determined. The loading on the given beam is shown in Fig. 1(b); to show the variation of the shear along the beam, the shear diagram is constructed in Fig. 1(c). Then, to apply the shear flow formula, Q must be determined. This is done by considering the shaded area to one side of the cut a-a in Fig. 1(a). The statical moment of this area is most conveniently computed by multiplying the area of the two 2-in.-by-4-in. pieces by the distance from their centroid to the neutral axis of the beam and adding to this product a similar quantity for the 2-in.-by-8-in. piece. The largest shear flow occurs at the supports, as the largest vertical shears V of 2,000 lb. act there:

$$Q = A_{fghj}\bar{y} = \sum A_i\bar{y}_i = 2A_1\bar{y}_1 + A_2\bar{y}_2 = 2(2)4(8) + 2(8)9$$

$$= 272 \text{ in.}^3$$

$$q = \frac{VQ}{I} = \frac{2{,}000(272)}{6{,}060} = 90 \text{ lb. per in.}$$

At the supports the spacing of the lag screws must be 500/90 = 5.56 in. apart. This spacing of the lag screws applies only at a section where the shear V is equal to 2,000 lb. Similar calculations for a section where V = 1,000 lb. gives q = 45 lb. per inch, and the spacing of the lag screws becomes 500/45 = 11.12 in. Thus it is proper to specify the use of 1/2-in. lag screws at 5-1/2 in. on centers for a distance of 5 ft. nearest both the supports and at 11 in. for the middle half of the beam.

A greater refinement in making the transition from one spacing of fastenings to another may be desirable in some problems. The same spacing of lag screws should be used at the section b-b as at the section a-a.

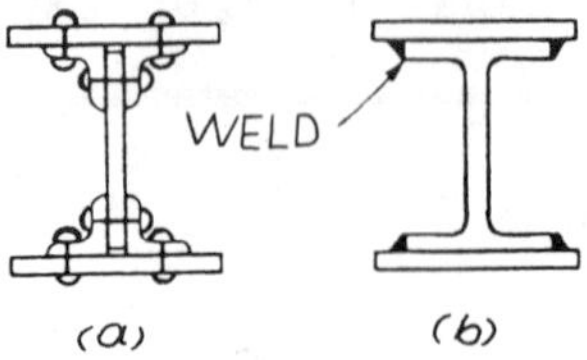

FIG. 2

In a manner analogous to the above, the spacing of rivets or bolts in fabricated beams made from continuous angles and plates, Fig. 2, may be determined. Welding requirements are established similarly. The nominal shearing stress in a rivet is determined by dividing the total shearing force transmitted by the rivet (shear flow times spacing of the rivets) by the cross-sectional area of the rivet.

• PROBLEM 8-7

> A beam has a rectangular cross-section, 3 in. wide and 8 in. deep. At a certain cross-section the bending moment is 200,000 lb-in while at a section 1.5 in. further along, the bending moment is 224,000 lb-in. Find the vertical shear flow on a cross-section between CC_1 and DD_1 at a depth of 2.8 in. from the top of the beam. Assume that the bending stresses are distributed linearly.

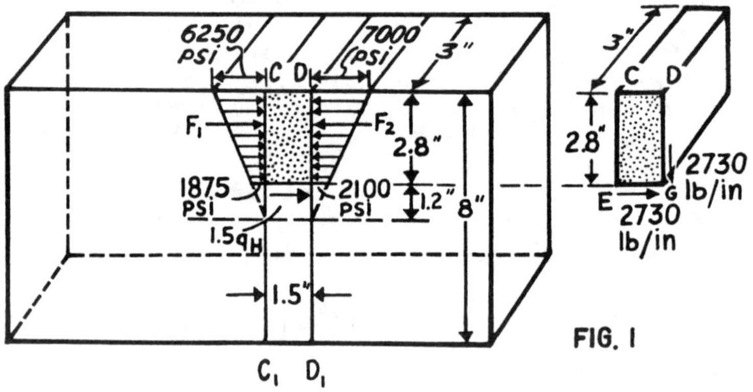

FIG. 1

Solution: We first calculate the bending stresses on the sections CC_1 and DD_1 (Fig. 1).

$$I = \frac{bd^3}{12} = \frac{3 \times 8^3}{12} = 128 \text{ in.}^4$$

On section CC_1:
At the top,

$$\sigma = \frac{My}{I} = \frac{200{,}000 \times 4}{128} = 6250 \text{ psi}$$

2.8 in. below the top,

$$\sigma = \frac{200{,}000 \times 1.2}{128} = 1875 \text{ psi}$$

On section DD_1:
At the top,

$$\sigma = \frac{224{,}000 \times 4}{128} = 7000 \text{ psi}$$

2.8 in. below the top,

$$\sigma = \frac{224{,}000 \times 1.2}{128} = 2100 \text{ psi}$$

We now consider the equilibrium of the block of material whose side elevation is CEGD (Fig. 1) and which runs the full width of the beam. The forces on the ends of this block are:

$$F_1 = \left(\frac{6250 + 1875}{2}\right) \times 3 \times 2.8 = 34{,}125 \text{ lb.}$$

and

$$F_2 = \left(\frac{7000 + 2100}{2}\right) \times 3 \times 2.8 = 38{,}220 \text{ lb.}$$

For horizontal equilibrium, the difference between these two forces is balanced by the total shear on the face EG, which is $q_H \times 1.5$

$$\therefore \quad 1.5q_H = 38{,}220 - 34{,}125 = 4095 \text{ lb.}$$

and

$$q_H = 2730 \text{ lb/in}$$

The shear flow q_V on the vertical cross-section is also 2730 lb/in at a depth of 2.8 in. below the top of the beam.

• PROBLEM 8-8

A T-beam to serve as a temporary support is to be built of two equal wood members nailed together. If the expected loading is as shown, compute the minimum distance between nails if maximum shear load on a nail is to be 200 lbs.

Solution: This problem will be solved using the concept of shear flow, or force intensity, the name by which it is also known. To compute the force intensity, the value of the maximum shear is needed. The shear is related to the moment by the following equation:

$$V = \frac{dM}{dx}$$

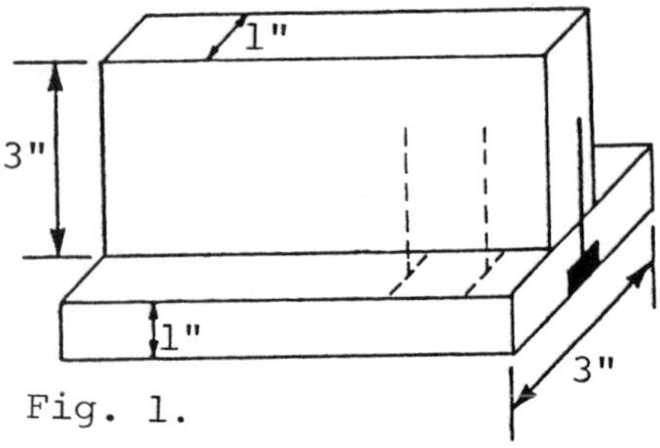

Fig. 1.

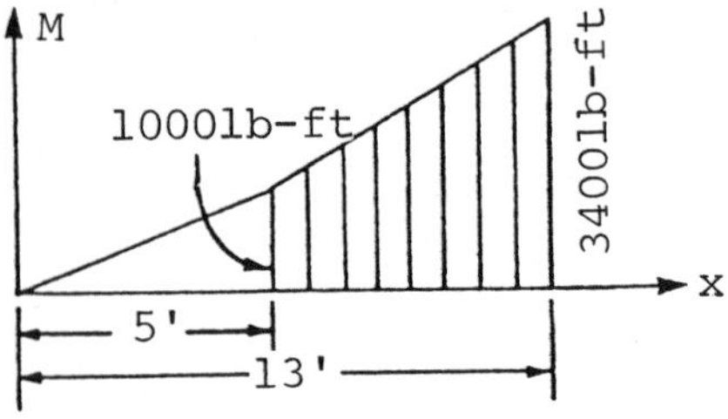

Fig. 2.

This means the shear is equal to the slope of the moment diagram. The slope of the right hand section of the moment diagram in Fig. 2 is largest. The slope is

$$\text{slope} = \frac{\Delta y}{\Delta x} = \frac{(3400-1000)}{8} = 300 \text{ lb.}$$

∴ Maximum shear, V = 300 lbs.

Recall that the force intensity at any section of the beam is given by $F = \frac{VQ}{I_{zz}}$.

To compute Q and I_{zz}, first locate the neutral axis

$$\bar{y}(3+3) = 3 \times \frac{1}{2} + 3 \times \frac{5}{2}$$

$$\therefore \bar{y} = 1.5$$

where $\bar{y}$ is the distance of the neutral axis from the bottom fibre.

$$I = 2.5\left[\frac{2.5^2}{12} + \left(\frac{2.5}{2}\right)^2\right] + .5\left(\frac{.5^2}{12} + .25^2\right)$$

$$+ 3\left(\frac{1}{12} + 1\right) = 5.21 + .042 + 3.25 = 8.502 \text{ in.}^4$$

$$Q = 3 \times 1.5 = 4.5 \text{ in.}^3$$

but force intensity, F = nf

where n = the minimum number of nails per unit length
f = allowable force on one nail

$$\therefore nf = \frac{VQ}{I_{zz}}$$

Substituting for f, V, Q and I_{zz} from above we have

$$n \times 200 = \frac{300 \times 4.5}{8.502}$$

$$\therefore n = .7939$$

The nails should be spaced 1/n = 1.259" apart. In practice the nails would be spaced 1.25" on center.

• PROBLEM 8-9

Two long wooden planks form a T section of a beam as shown in Fig. 1(a). If this beam transmits a constant vertical shear of 690 lb, find the necessary spacing of the nails between the two planks to make the beam act as a unit. Assume that the allowable shearing force per nail is 150 lb.

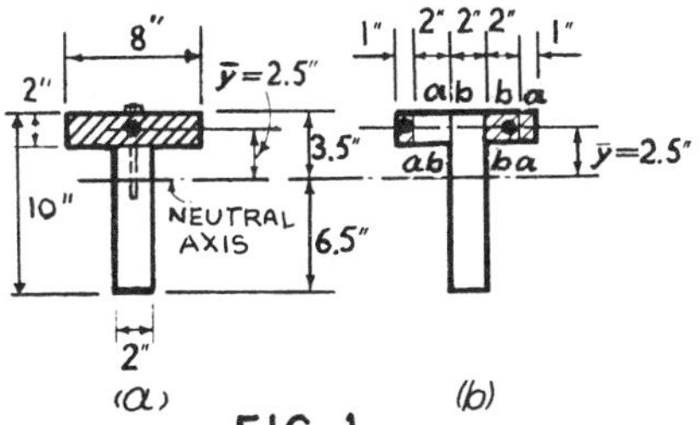

FIG. 1

Solution: When a load is applied to the beam, the two planks are going to try to slide longitudinally. To determine the nail spacing we first find the shear flow in this plane. To do this the neutral axis of the whole section and its moment of inertia around the neutral axis must be found. Then as V is known and Q is defined as the statical moment of the area of the upper plank around the neutral axis, the shear flow, $\frac{VQ}{I}$ may be determined. The distance y_c from the top to the neutral axis is

$$y_c = \frac{\Sigma Ay}{\Sigma A}$$

where y is the distance from the top of the section to the centroid of the area.

$$y_c = \frac{2(8)1 + 2(8)6}{2(8) + 2(8)} = 3.5 \text{ in.}$$

Using the parallel axis theorem:

$$I = \Sigma I_g + y^2 A$$

where I_g is the moment of inertia of an area about its centroid. y is the vertical distance from the centroid.

$$I = \frac{8(2)^3}{12} + (2)8(2.5)^2 + \frac{2(8)^3}{12} + (2)8(2.5)^2$$

$$= 291 \text{ in.}^4$$

Since the area above the plane of interest is a rectangle, Q is computed as follows:

$$Q = Ay = 2(8)(2.5) = 40 \text{ in.}^3$$

$$q = \frac{VQ}{I} = \frac{690(40)}{291} = 95 \text{ lb. per in.}$$

Thus, a force of 95 lb. must be transferred from one plank to the other in every linear inch along the length of the beam. However, from the data given, each nail is capable of resisting a force of 150 lb., hence one nail can take care of 150/95 = 1.59 linear inches along the length of the beam. As shear remains constant at the consecutive sections of the beam, the nails should be spaced throughout at 1.59-in. intervals. In a practical problem a 1.5-in. spacing would probably be used.

Solution for an alternate arrangement of planks:
If, instead of using the two planks as above, a beam of the same cross section were made from five pieces, Fig. 1(b), a different nailing schedule would be required.

To begin, the shear flow between one of the 1-in.-by-2-in. pieces and the remainder of the beam is found, and although the contact surface a-a is vertical, the procedure is the same as before. The push or pull on an element is built up in the same manner as formerly:

$$Q = A\bar{y} = (1)2(2.5) = 5 \text{ in.}^3$$

$$q = \frac{VQ}{I} = \frac{690(5)}{291} = 11.8 \text{ lb. per in.}$$

If the same nails as before are used to join the 1-in.-by-2-in. piece to the 2-in.-by-2-in. piece, they may be 150/11.8 = 12.7 in. apart. This nailing applies to both sections a-a.

To determine the shear flow between the 2-in.-by-10-in. vertical piece and either one of the 2-in.-by-2-in. pieces, the entire area to the right or left of the 2 x 10 in. web must be used to determine Q. It is the difference of pushes (or pulls) on this whole area that causes the unbalanced force which must be transferred at the surface b-b:

$$Q = A\bar{y} = (3)2(2.5) = 15 \text{ in.}^3$$

$$q = \frac{VQ}{I} = \frac{690(15)}{291} = 35.6 \text{ lb. per in.}$$

Space nails at 150/35.6 = 4.2 in. or, in practice, 4-in. intervals along the length of the beam in both sections b-b. These nails could be driven in first and then the 1-in.-by-2-in. pieces put on.

• PROBLEM 8-10

Two W10x25 steel beam sections are bolted together to form a single beam as shown in the figure. What is the maximum permissible bolt spacing if the shear force applied is 20 kips and the allowable load in shear on each bolt is 3.1 kips?

The section properties for W10x25 are:

$d = 10.08"$

$A = 7.35"$

$I_{xx} = 133.2 \text{ in.}^4$

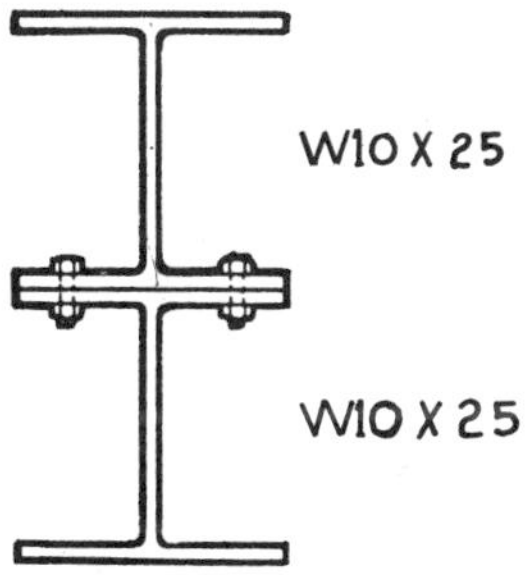

FIG. 1

Solution: When the beam section shown is subjected to a shear force, the beam will bend and the two W10x25 sections will try to slide over each other. If the section loaded were solid, this sliding tendency is counteracted by internal shear stresses in the section. However, this section is made up of two separate sections so the shear stresses resisting the sliding are those in the bolts.

The shear flow in the section at the line of bolts is the force per inch that is trying to cause sliding between the two wide flange beams.

$$\tau t = \frac{VQ}{I}$$

where Q is the moment of area above the neutral axis and I is the moment of inertia of the entire section. Q is the area times the distance to the centroid of the area, the neutral axis is at the interface of the two W10x25's so the area is the area of one W10x25 and the distance is that of half the depth of the W10x25.

$$Q = A \times \frac{d}{2} = (7.35)\left(\frac{10.08}{2}\right) = 37.044 \text{ in.}^3$$

The moment of inertia is found using the parallel axis theorem:

$$I_{total} = 2\left[I_{xx} + A \times \left(\frac{d}{2}\right)^2\right]$$

$$= 2\left[133.2 + 7.35(5.04)^2\right] = 639.8 \text{ in.}^4$$

Substituting these values into the expression for shear flow we have

$$\tau t = \frac{20k(37.044)}{639.8} \text{ k/in.} = 1.158 \text{ k/in.}$$

The shear capacity over the spacing s is going to be the allowable load in shear of two bolts, since the bolts come in pairs, one on each side of the web (see Fig.). Therefore the force per inch due to the bolts is

$$\frac{2F}{s}$$

This shear capacity per inch must equilibrate the shear flow, so we have

$$\frac{2F}{s} = 1.158 \text{ k/in.}$$

The allowable load in shear of one bolt is 3.1 kips so we can solve for the spacing s.

$$s = \frac{2(3.1k)}{1.158k} = 5.35 \text{ in.}$$

• PROBLEM 8-11

A beam (Fig. 1) is built up by welding a 10 in. x 1/2 in. steel plate to each flange of a 12 in. x 5 in. R.S.J. The moment of inertia of the combined section is 598 in^4. Each plate is attached by two welds as shown. At a section where the shear force is 20,000 lb: (a) Find the shear force per inch run resisted by each weld. (b) Find the shear flow at the mid-height of the web. (The first moment of half of the unplated R.S.J. about the neutral axis is 19.90 in^3.) (c) Find the shear stress at this point if the stress is assumed to be uniformly distributed across the thickness of the web.

Solution: Moment of inertia of the combined section, I = 598 in.^{4}. At the section being considered, shear force, S = 20,000 lbs. A length of 1 in. of weld at B and C together have to resist the shear on the horizontal plane HH for a length of 1 in. along the beam. This force is the shear flow at level HH and is given by

$$q = S \times \frac{Q}{I}$$

where Q is the first moment of the shaded area about the neutral axis.

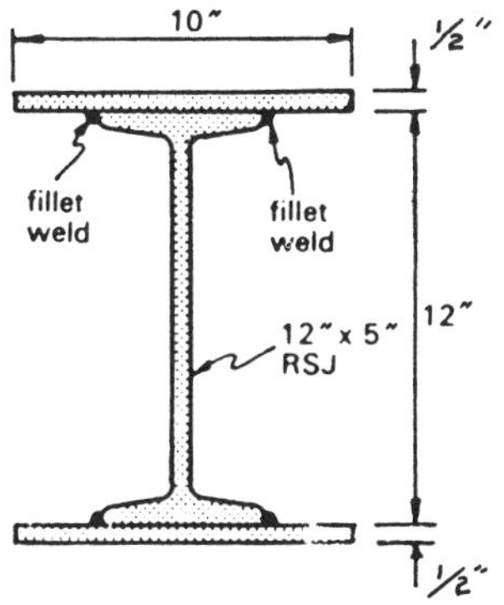

FIG.1

FIG. 2

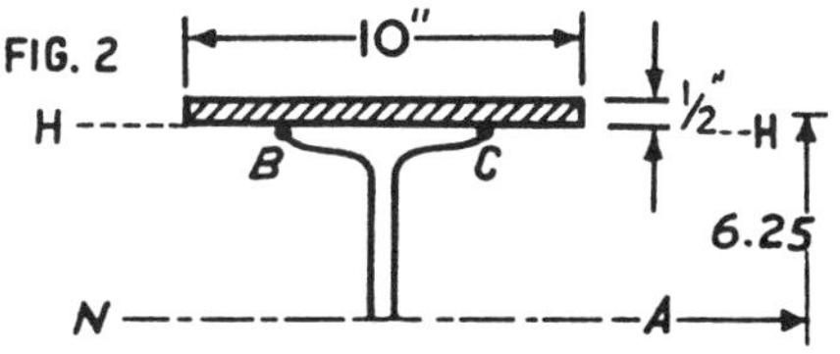

$$Q = (10 \times .5) \times 6.25 = 31.25$$

$$q = 20{,}000 \times \frac{31.25}{598} = 1045.15 \text{ lb/in}$$

Force resisted by one weld = 522.5 lb/in.

(b) Recall shear flow, $q = S \times \frac{Q}{I}$. S and I are the same as above but Q now becomes 19.9 + 31.25 = 51.15 in.^3

$\therefore$ Shear flow $q = 20{,}000 \times \frac{51.15}{598} = 1710.7$ lb/in.

(c) For a 12 in. x 5 in. RSJ, the breadth of the web is .33" (see steel handbook).

$\therefore$ Shear stress at mid-point, $\tau = \frac{q}{b} = \frac{1710.7}{.33} = 5184$ psi.

• PROBLEM 8-12

A beam (Fig. 1) is built up by riveting a 10 in. x 1/2 in. steel plate to each flange of a 12 in. x 5 in. RSJ by 3/4" rivets. If each rivet is capable of safely transmitting 10 kips in shear, how many rivets per foot are required in each flange where the shear force in the beam is 20,000 lb.? The moment of inertia of the combined section is 598 in.^4.

Solution: Recall that shear flow, $q = \frac{SQ}{I}$

but $q = nf$

where n = number of rivets per foot
f = safe load rivet can transmit
S = 20,000 lbs.
I = 598 $in.^4$
f = 10,000 lbs.
$Q = 10 \times .5 \times 6.25 = 31.25$

Fig. 1.

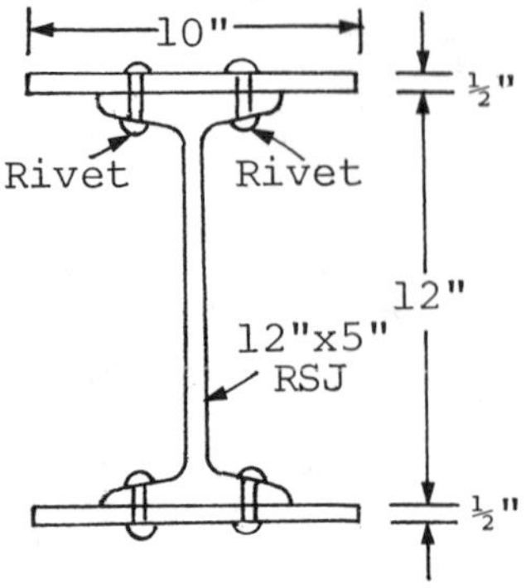

Substituting we have

$$10,000n = 20,000 \times \frac{31.25}{598} \times 12$$

$$\therefore n = 1.254 \text{ rivets/ft.}$$

• PROBLEM 8-13

Wide-flange beams are often reinforced with plates riveted to their flanges. For the loading shown, compute the number of rivets if they are to be equally spaced and have a maximum shear stress S_m.

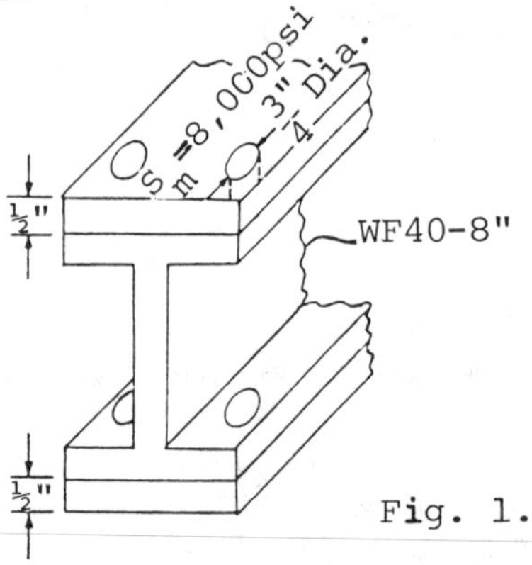

Fig. 1.

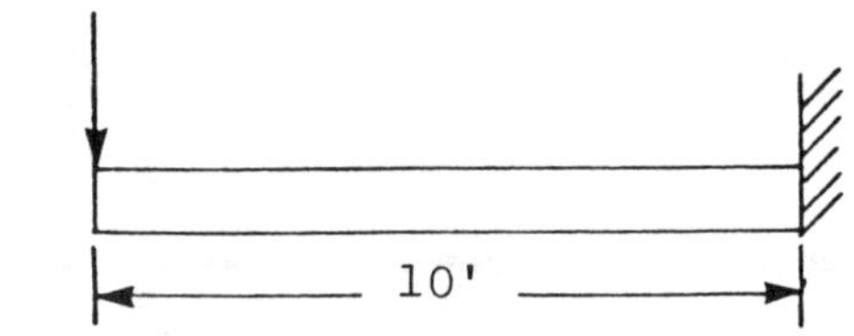

Fig. 2.

Solution: An 8WF40 has section properties as follows:

depth, d = 8.25"; flange thickness, f = .558"
breadth, b = 8.08"; web thickness, t = .365"

Moment of Inertia, I = 146.3 $in.^4$

$\therefore$ Moment of inertia for the whole cross section of the beam is

$$I = 146.3 + 2 \times 8.08 \times \frac{1}{2}\left(\frac{.5^2}{12} + 4.375^2\right)$$

$$= 301.1 \text{ in.}^4$$

The maximum shear force in the beam is

$$V = 100{,}000 \text{ lbs.}$$

To find the shear force per inch, F, that is being resisted by the top rivets, the first moment, Q, of the top plate about the neutral axis of the beam is needed.

$$Q = 8.08 \times \frac{1}{2} \times 4.375 = 17.675 \text{ in.}^3$$

But $$F = nf = \frac{VQ}{I} \qquad (1)$$

where $n \equiv$ number of rivets per inch

$f \equiv$ shearing force rivets can stand

$$\tau \approx \frac{f}{A} \qquad \therefore f = A\tau = \frac{\pi d^2}{4} \cdot \tau$$

$$= \pi \cdot \frac{9}{16} \cdot \frac{1}{4} \cdot 8000 = 3534.29 \text{ lbs.}$$

The rivets come in pairs, one to the left and one to the right of the web. The force per inch that can be withstood is thus twice as great.

$$f = 2 \times 3534.29 \text{ lbs.}$$

Substituting in Eq.(1) gives

$$2 \times 3534.29n = \frac{100{,}000 \times 17.675}{301.1}$$

$$\therefore n = .83 \text{ rivets/in.}$$

The beam is 10 feet long, which is 120 inches.

$$(.83 \text{ rivets/in.})(120 \text{ in.}) = 99.6 \text{ rivets}$$

The beam is symmetrical, so the stress on the bottom needs the same number of rivets to resist it.

Altogether there are four rows of rivets, two on the top flange and two on the bottom. Each row should have 100 equally spaced rivets.

This answer can be checked by finding the thickness, t, in the shearing stress formula

$$\tau = \frac{VQ}{It}$$

equivalent to the rows of rivets. The area of each rivet is:

$$A = \pi \frac{d^2}{4} = \frac{3.14159 \times (3/4)^2}{4} = .4418 \text{ in.}^2$$

Since there are two rows of rivets resisting the shear between the top plate and the top flange, the area is double the area of one rivet

$$A = 2 \times .4418 = .8836 \text{ in.}^2$$

The spacing of the rivets is

$$\frac{100 \text{ rivets}}{120 \text{ inches}} = .833 \text{ rivets/in.}$$

The equivalent thickness is then

$$t = (.8836 \text{ in.}^2)(.833 \text{ rivets/in.}) = .736 \text{ in.}$$

Now everything in the shear stress equation is known and τ can be calculated

$$\tau = \frac{VQ}{It} = \frac{(100{,}000)(17.675)}{(301.1)(.736)} = 7980 \text{ psi}$$

This is just under the maximum allowable shear of 8000 psi and thus confirms the result arrived at above.

• PROBLEM 8-14

A box beam (Fig. 1) is constructed of wood boards (1 in. x 6 in.) joined by screws. The shear force V acting on the cross section is 920 lb., and the allowable load in shear on each screw is F = 250 lb. Determine the required spacing s of the screws.

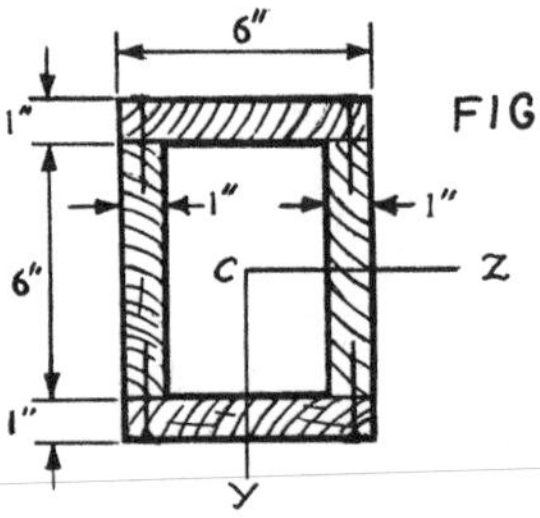

FIG. 1

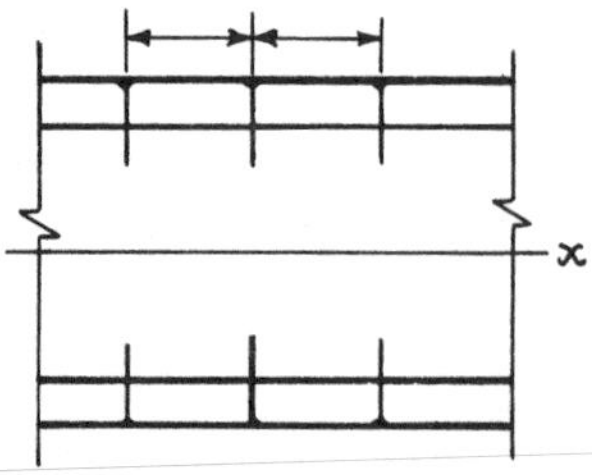

NUMERICAL EXAMPLE

Solution: The shear flow in a section is equal to the shear stress times the distance over which it acts. Since shear stress is given by $\tau = \frac{VQ}{Ib}$ and b is the distance over which τ acts, the shear flow, f, is

$$f = \frac{VQ}{I}$$

Q in this case is the first moment of area above the point where the shear flow is desired, so it will be for the area of the top board, about the neutral axis.

$$Q = 6(1)(3.5) = 21 \text{ in.}^3$$

The moment of inertia of the entire cross section about the neutral axis is

$$I = \frac{6(8)^3}{12} - \frac{4(6)^3}{12} = 184 \text{ in.}^4$$

Substituting into the expression for shear flow, we find

$$f = \frac{920(21)}{184} = 105 \text{ lb/in.}$$

Since the forces from the screws rather than shear stress over the bottom face resist the force in the x-direction due to the applied shear force, we must find the capacity of the screws per unit length. There are two rows of screws so that the force due to screws is 2F for the distance s. The total capacity per inch is therefore $\frac{2F}{s}$, and this quantity must equilibrate the shear flow.

$$f = \frac{2F}{s}$$

Since we know the shear flow and the capacity of one screw we can solve for the required spacing, s.

$$s = \frac{2F}{f} = \frac{2(250)}{105} = 4.76 \text{ in.}$$

This spacing, or a lesser one, must be used for the screws in order to have a safe design.

• PROBLEM 8-15

The total vertical shear at a certain section of a beam is 3200 lb. The beam has the cross section shown in Fig. 1. Determine:
(a) The maximum horizontal shearing stress, and indicate where it occurs within the cross section.
(b) The vertical shearing stress 3 in. below the top.

Solution: A beam which is subjected to a vertical shear force will deflect, as shown in Fig. 2. As the beam deflects the horizontal layers try to slide on each other and this tendency is resisted by horizontal shearing stresses in the direction of the longitudinal axis. The magnitude of these stresses is given by

$$\tau = \frac{VQ}{Ib}$$

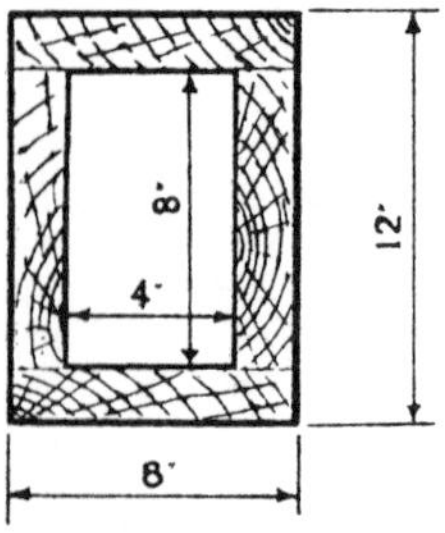

FIG. 1

which is calculated about the neutral axis. Since at any point the vertical and horizontal shear stresses are equal, this equation applies to both. The maximum shear stress is at the neutral axis ($y_h = 0$). Therefore Q must be found for the entire section above the neutral axis.

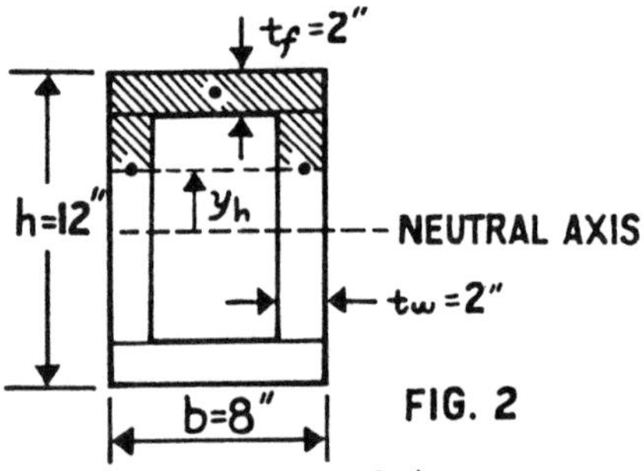

FIG. 2

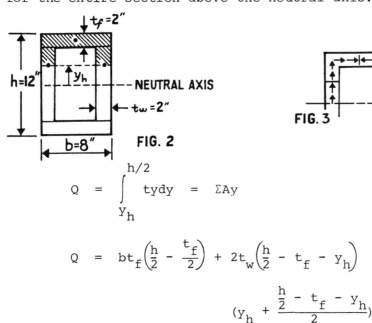

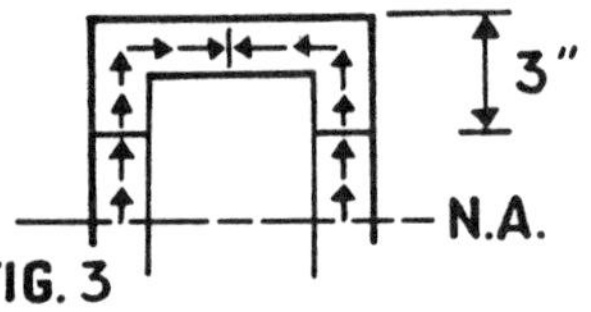

FIG. 3

$$Q = \int_{y_h}^{h/2} tydy = \Sigma Ay$$

$$Q = bt_f\left(\frac{h}{2} - \frac{t_f}{2}\right) + 2t_w\left(\frac{h}{2} - t_f - y_h\right)$$

$$\left(y_h + \frac{\frac{h}{2} - t_f - y_h}{2}\right)$$

$$Q = 2(8)(5) + 4(4)(2) = 112 \text{ in.}^3$$

The moment of inertia of the section is

$$I = \left[\frac{bt_f^3}{12} + bt_f\left(\frac{h-t_f}{2}\right)^2\right] \times 2 + \left[\frac{2t_w \times (h-2t_f)^3}{12}\right]$$

$$= \left[\frac{8(2)^3}{12} + (8)(2)(5)^2\right] \times 2 + \left[\frac{2(2)(8)^3}{12}\right]$$

$$= 982 \text{ in.}^4$$

Since the shear is resisted by both webs the thickness b is equal to the sum of the web thickness

$$b = 4 \text{ in.}$$

Substituting these values into the formula we have

$$\tau_{max} = \frac{(3200)(112)}{(982)(4)} \frac{(\text{lb})(\text{in.}^3)}{(\text{in.}^4)(\text{in.})}$$

$$= 91.4 \text{ psi at the neutral axis.}$$

The vertical shearing stress in the section must equilibrate the vertical shear force by equilibrium as shown in Fig. 3. If we cut the section 3 in. below the top, the thickness of the section which resists shear is equal to the thickness of the webs.

$$b = 4''$$

We calculate Q for the section of beam above the line 3" below the top (y = 3" above the neutral axis).

$$Q = (2)(8)(5) + 2\left[(1)(2)(3.5)\right] = 108 \text{ in.}^3$$

We know the shear force and moment of inertia, so by substituting these results into the expression for shear we get

$$\tau = \frac{(3200 \text{ lb.})(108 \text{ in.}^3)}{(982 \text{ in.}^4)(4 \text{ in.})} = 76.5 \text{ psi}$$

• PROBLEM 8-16

The beam illustrated is clamped together with 1/4-in. bolts with a spacing as shown. If each bolt can safely resist a shear force across it of 400 lb., what is the bolt spacing required when the shear force V is 10,000 lb.?

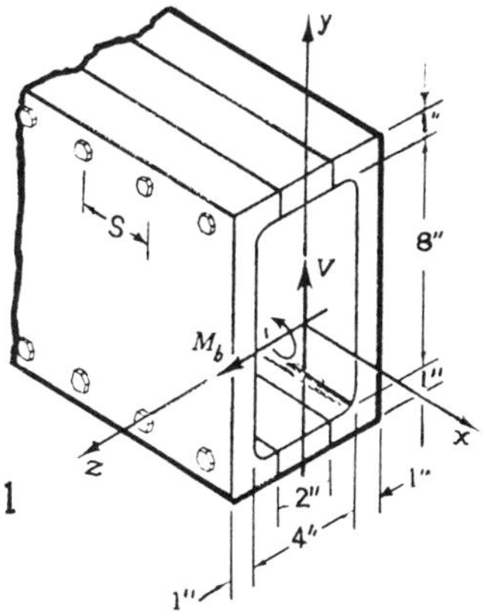

FIG .1

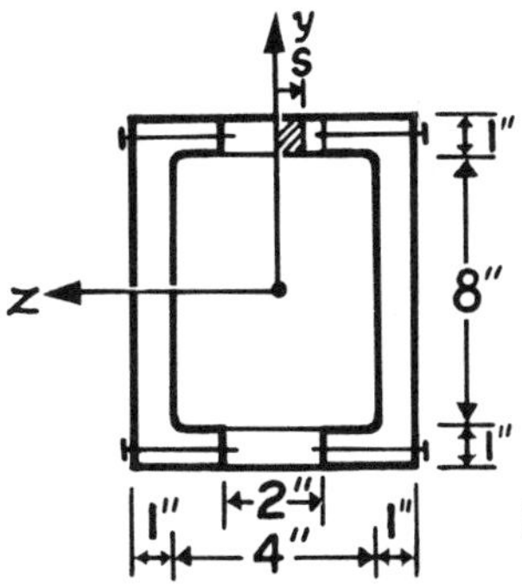

FIG. 2

Solution: Moment of inertia for the whole cross-section,

$$I = \frac{6 \times 10^3}{12} - \frac{4 \times 8^3}{12} = 329.33 \text{ in.}^4$$

Let s be a distance along the contour starting from y.

∴ The first moment of area of the shaded section about the z-axis is

$$Q = 4.5(s \times 1)$$

At the cut which is 2 in. from the y-axis, Q = 4.5 x 2. Let n be the number of bolts required per unit length of beam and f the force from one bolt.

$$\therefore nf = q = \frac{VQ}{I}$$

Substituting for f, V, Q and I from above we have

$$400n = \frac{4.5 \times 10{,}000}{329.33}$$

$$\therefore n = .34 \text{ bolts/in.}$$

∴ Bolt spacing required is 1/n = 2.93 in.

• PROBLEM 8-17

A beam has a channel section (Fig. 1) built up of two vertical plates 6 in. x 1/2 in. welded to a horizontal plate 10 in. x 1/2 in. The beam is loaded vertically and the bending stresses are linearly distributed. At a section where the shear force is 2000 lb., find the shear flow at point A.

Find the shear flow at point B, y in. below the top and hence find the total shear resisted by each vertical plate, and the vertical shear resisted by the 10 in. plate.

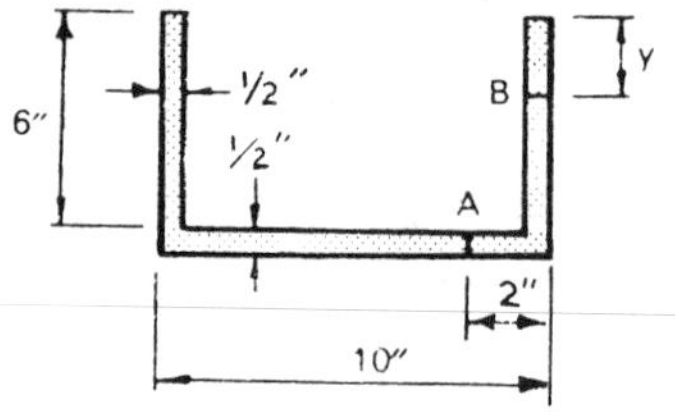

FIG. 1

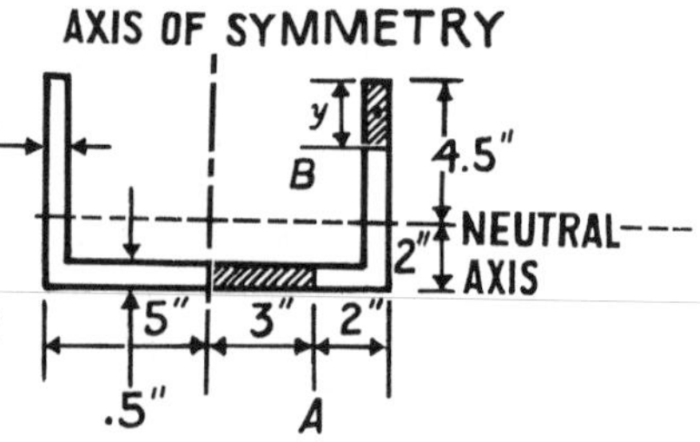

FIG. 2

Solution: First determine the neutral axis:

$$\bar{y}\left(2 \times 6 \times \frac{1}{2} + 10 \times \frac{1}{2}\right) = 10 \times \frac{1}{2} \times \frac{1}{4} + 2 \times 6 \times \frac{1}{2} \times \frac{7}{2}$$

$$\bar{y} = 2.0 \text{ in.}$$

where $\bar{y}$ is the distance of the neutral axis from the bottom fibre.

The moment of inertia for the whole cross-section is then determined from

$$I = \Sigma A_i \left(\frac{h_i^{\,2}}{12} + c_i^{\,2}\right)$$

where
A ≡ area of each element
h ≡ height of each element
C ≡ distance of the centroid of each element from the neutral axis

Each 6" plate is divided at the neutral axis into two regions.

$$\therefore I = 2 \times 4.5 \times \frac{1}{2}\left[\frac{4.5^2}{12} + \left(\frac{4.5}{2}\right)^2\right]$$

$$+ 2 \times 1.5 \times \frac{1}{2}\left[\frac{1.5^2}{12} + \left(\frac{1.5}{2}\right)^2\right] + 10 \times \frac{1}{2}\left[\frac{.5^2}{12} + 1.75^2\right]$$

$$= 46.92 \text{ in.}^4$$

Recall $q = \dfrac{VQ}{I}$

At point A, $Q = 1.75 \times \frac{1}{2} \times 3 = 2.63 \text{ in.}^3$

Substituting in equation for shear flow above gives

$$q = \frac{2000 \times 2.3}{46.92} = 112 \text{ lb/in.}$$

At point B;

V and I are the same as above
$Q = .5y(4.5 - .5y) = 2.25y - .25y^2$

$$\therefore q = \frac{2000(2.25y - .25y^2)}{46.9167}$$

$$= \left(95.9y - 10.67y^2\right) \text{ lb/in.} \qquad (1)$$

The total shear resisted by each vertical plate is the integral of Eq.(1).

$$\therefore V = \int_0^6 \left(95.9y - 10.67y^2\right)dy$$

$$= \frac{95.9}{2} \cdot 6^2 - \frac{10.67}{3} \cdot 6^3 = 957.96 \text{ lb.}$$

To compute the vertical shear resisted by the 10 in. plate, first compute a new Q, i.e. the first moment of area of the 10 in. plate about the neutral axis.

$$\therefore Q = 10 x \left[2 - \frac{x}{2}\right] = 20x - 5x^2$$

$$q = \frac{2000}{46.9167}\left(20x - 5x^2\right)$$

$$V = \int_0^{.5} 42.63\left(20x - 5x^2\right)dx$$

$$= 42.63\left(10x^2 - \frac{5}{3} x 3\right)\Big|_0^{.5} = 97.7 \text{ lb.}$$

• PROBLEM 8-18

In the I-beam shown, compute the maximum shear stress and the total shear stress at the indicated point.

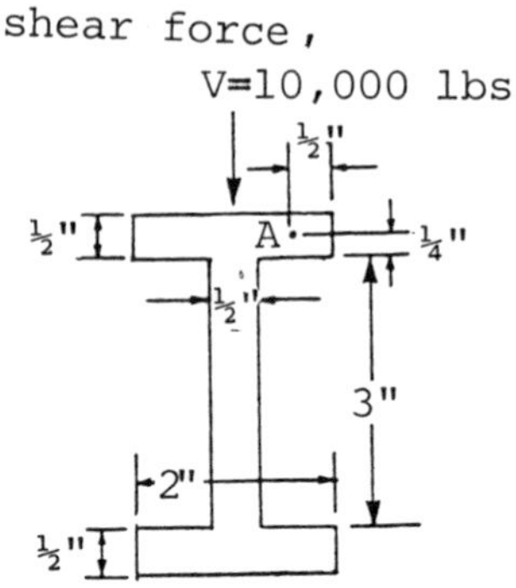

Fig. 1.

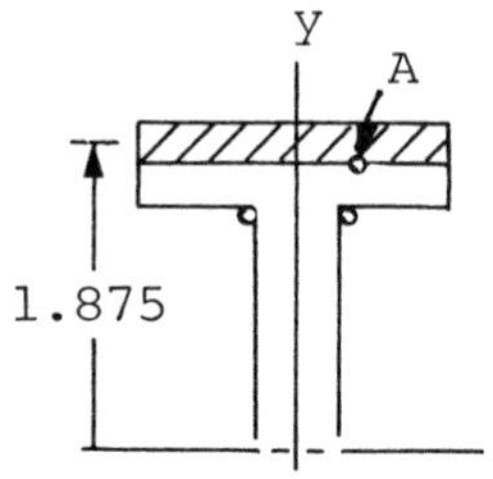

Fig. 2.

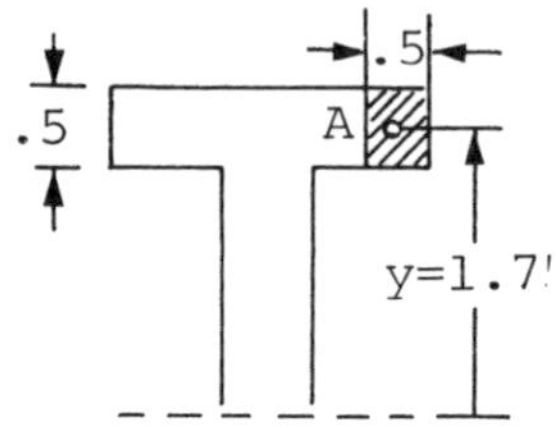

Fig. 3.

Solution: Maximum shear stress, τ_{xy}, occurs at the mid-point of the beam.

$$\therefore Q = 1.5 \times \frac{1}{2} \times \frac{1.5}{2} + 2 \times \frac{1}{2} \times 1.75 = 2.3125 \text{ in.}^3$$

Moment of inertia for the whole cross-section,

$$I = \frac{.5 \times 3^3}{12} + 2 \times 2 \times \frac{1}{2}\left(\frac{.5^2}{12} + 1.75^2\right) = 7.29$$

But $\tau_{xy} = \frac{VQ}{It}$

and $V = 10{,}000$ lbs.

$t = .5$ in.

Substituting we have

$$\tau_{max} = \frac{10{,}000 \times 2.3125}{7.29 \times .5} = 6344.3 \text{ psi}$$

To get the approximate vertical shear at point A, first compute Q for the shaded area in Fig. 2.

$$Q = 2 \times \frac{1}{4} \times 1.875 = .9375$$

$\therefore$ Shear at point A: $\tau = \frac{QV}{It}$

V and I are constant and t = 2".

Therefore substituting gives

$$\tau = \frac{10{,}000 \times .9375}{7.29 \times 2} = 643 \text{ psi}$$

Now compute Q for the shaded area in Fig. 3 to get the approximate horizontal shear at point A.

$$Q = Ay = (.5)(.5)(1.75) = .4375 \text{ in.}^3$$

Substituting into the shearing stress formula (t = .5"):

$$\tau = \frac{10{,}000 \times .4375}{7.29 \times .5} = 1200.3 \text{ psi}$$

The resultant of the two shears is the total shear.

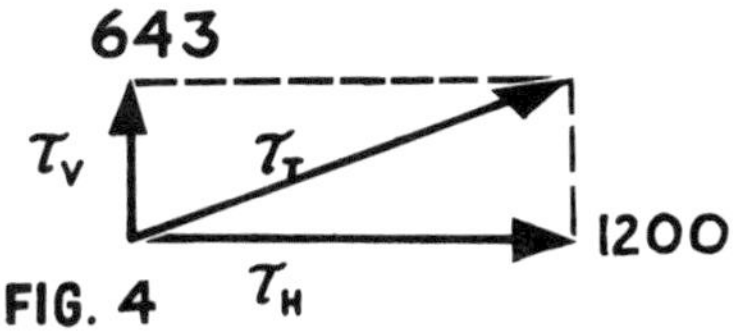

FIG. 4

The total shear $\tau_T = \sqrt{(643)^2 + (1200)^2} = 1360$ psi.

The total shear at point A is approximately 1360 psi.

A beam has the cross-section shown in Fig. 1. Calculate both the horizontal and vertical shear force resisted by each of the elements of the cross-section if the total shear force is 20,000 lb. and acts in the plane of symmetry.

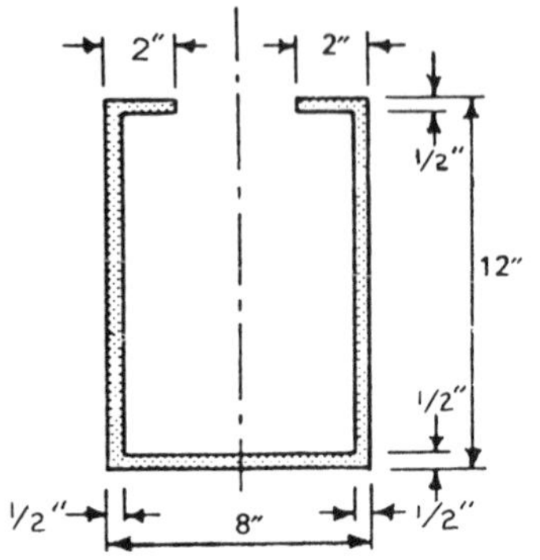

FIG. 1

Solution: The position of the centroid and the moment of inertia of the section about the neutral axis are first determined. Use a handbook of structural shapes or a steel manual. The centroid is 5.323 in above the base and 6.677 in below the top. The moment of inertia is 301.606 in^4.

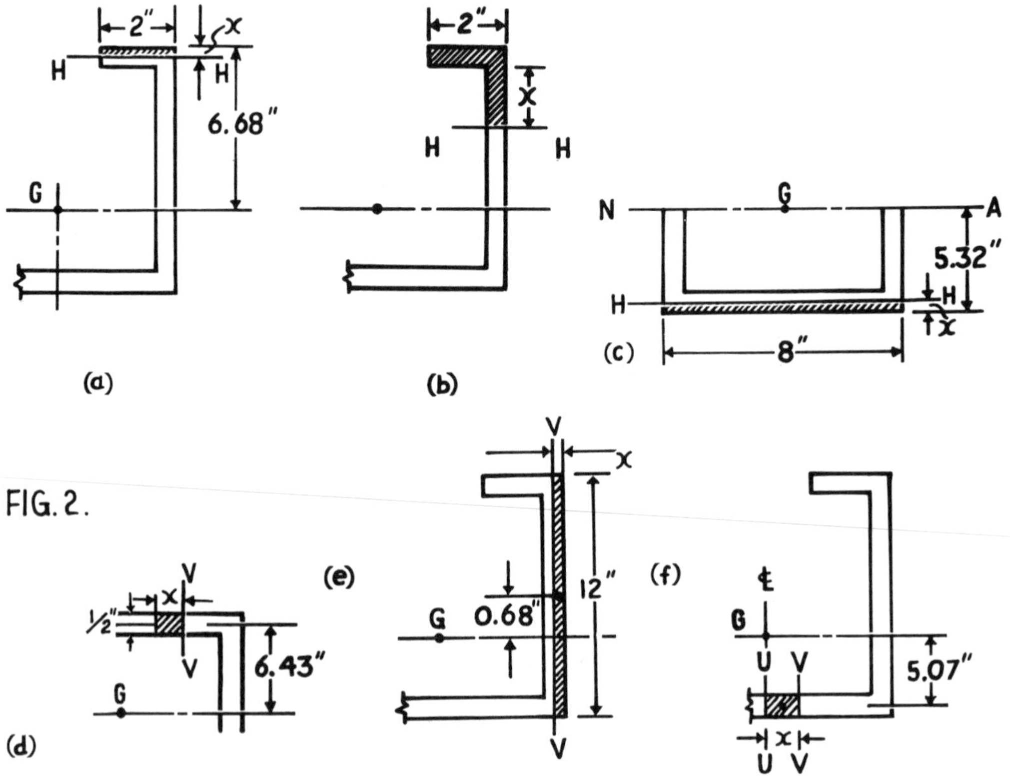

FIG. 2.

(a) Vertical shear force in the top flange.
Consider a cutting plane such as H-H (Fig. 2a) at x inches from the top. For the area above H-H,

$$Q = 2 x \left(6.667 - \frac{x}{2}\right)$$

$$q = \frac{S}{I} Q = \frac{20,000}{301.606} \left(13.352x - x^2\right)$$

$$V_1 = \int_0^{0.5} q \cdot dx = 66.311 \times 1.628 = 108 \text{ lb.}$$

(b) Vertical shear force in the web.
Consider the plane H-H (Fig. 2b) to cut the web.

$$Q = \left(2 \times \frac{1}{2}\right) 6.426 + \frac{x}{2}\left(6.177 - \frac{x}{2}\right)$$

$$q = \frac{S}{I} Q = 66.311\left(6.427 + 3.088x - \frac{x^2}{4}\right)$$

$$V_2 = \int_0^{11} q \cdot dx = 9721 \text{ lb.}$$

(c) Vertical shear force in bottom flange.
For the lower flange it is convenient to consider the area below, rather than above, a plane such as H-H (Fig. 2c).

$$Q = 8x\left(5.323 - \frac{x}{2}\right)$$

$$q = \frac{S}{I} Q = 66.311\left(42.584x - 4x^2\right)$$

$$V_3 = \int_0^{0.5} q \cdot dx = 342 \text{ lb.}$$

(d) Horizontal shear force in top flange.
To find the horizontal shear flow, a cutting plane such as V-V is considered. For the shaded area (Fig. 2d),

$$Q = \frac{x}{2} 6.427$$

$$q = \frac{S}{I} Q = 66.311(3.213x)$$

$$H_1 = \int_0^{1.5} q \cdot dx = 240 \text{ lb.}$$

(The integration can only be taken as far as x = 1.5 otherwise the plane V-V will enter the vertical web.)

(e) Horizontal shear force in web.
For the shaded area in Fig. 2e,

$$Q = 12x \times 0.677$$

$$q = \frac{S}{I} Q = 66.311(8.124x)$$

$$H_2 = \int_0^{0.5} q \cdot dx = 67 \text{ lb.}$$

(f) Horizontal shear force in bottom flange.
Cutting the bottom flange with a plane V-V (Fig. 2f), we can consider the area to the right of this plane. However, it is more convenient to consider the area between the planes V-V and U-U. Since the horizontal shear flow on U-U (the centreline) is zero by symmetry,

$$q = \frac{dM}{dx} \times \frac{Q}{I} = \frac{SQ}{I}$$

This gives the shear flow on plane V-V

$$Q = \frac{x}{2}\, 5.073$$

$$q = \frac{S}{I} Q = 66.311(2.536x)$$

Since the stresses on the section are symmetrical, the total horizontal shear in the bottom flange is zero. The shear on each half separately will be found

$$H_3 = \int_0^{3.5} q \cdot dx = 1030 \text{ lb.}$$

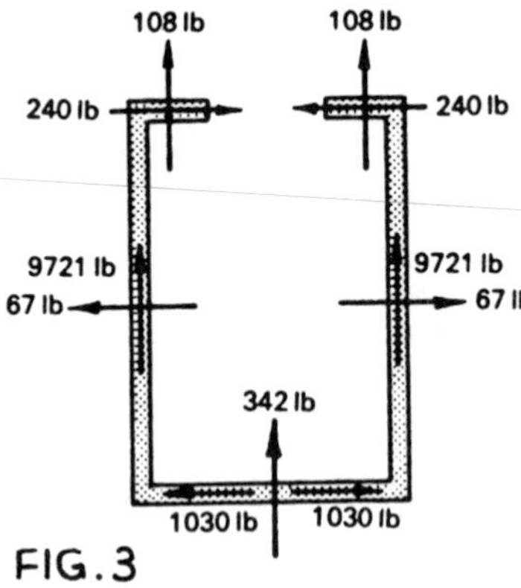

FIG.3

The total shear forces carried by the various portions of the cross-section are summarized in Fig. 3. It should be noted that every portion sustains both horizontal and vertical shear components. The total of the vertical components is 20,000 lbs. which is the shear force on the cross-section.

• PROBLEM 8-20

Investigate the shear stresses in a wide-flange beam loaded by a force P acting perpendicular to the web (see figure). Determine the magnitude and direction of all shear stresses, and the maximum shear stress. Use centerline dimensions for making the calculations for I_z and Q_z.

VERTICAL SHEAR IN THE WEBS

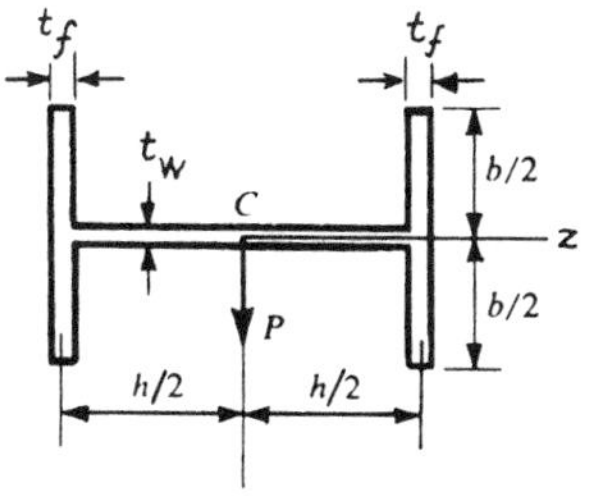

FIG. 1

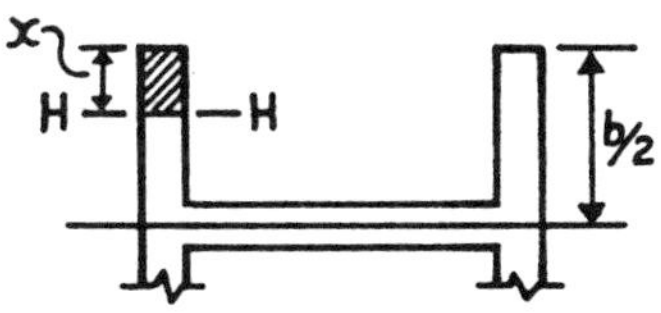

FIG. 2

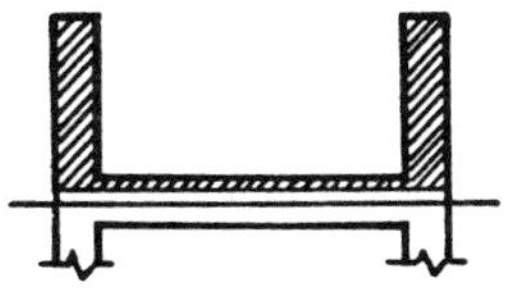

FIG. 3

Solution: First compute the moment of inertia for the whole cross section,

$$I_{zz} = \frac{2t_f b^3}{12} + \frac{ht_w^3}{12}$$

Recall that shear flow for any cross-section is given by

$$q = \frac{VQ}{I} \tag{1}$$

where V ≡ Shear at the cross-section being considered
Q ≡ First moment of area
I ≡ Moment of inertia for the whole cross-section

∴ For section H-H

$$Q = xt_f\left(\frac{b}{2} - \frac{x}{2}\right) = \frac{x}{2}\, t_f(b-x)$$

$$V = P$$

Substituting for V, Q and I in Eq. (1) gives

$$q = P \cdot \frac{x}{2}\, t_f(b-x) \cdot \frac{12}{ht_w^3 + 2t_f b^3}$$

$$\text{Shear stress} = \frac{q}{t_f} = \frac{6Px(b-x)}{ht_w^3 + 2t_f b^3} \qquad 0 \le x \le b/2$$

Vertical shear force in the middle flange.
In this case, everything is the same as above except Q.

$$\therefore Q = 2\cdot x\cdot t_f\left(\frac{x}{2} + \frac{b}{2} - x\right) + h\left[t_w - \left(\frac{b}{2} - x\right)\right]$$

$$\cdot \frac{1}{2}\left[t_w - \left(\frac{b}{2} - x\right)\right] = xt_f(b-x) + \frac{h}{2}\left(t_w + x - \frac{b}{2}\right)^2$$

$$\text{Shear flow, } q = \frac{VQ}{I} = \frac{12P}{ht_w^3 + 2t_f b^3}\left[xt_f(b-x) + \frac{h}{2}\left(t_w + x - \frac{b}{2}\right)^2\right]$$

$$\therefore \text{Shear stress} = \frac{q}{t_w} = \frac{12P}{t_w\left(ht_w^3 + 2t_f b^3\right)}\left[xt_f(b - x) + \frac{h}{2}\left(t_w + x - \frac{b}{2}\right)^2\right]$$

$$\frac{b}{2} - t_w \le x \le \frac{b}{2}$$

Maximum shear stress occurs at mid section.

$$\therefore Q = 2 \cdot \frac{b}{2} \cdot t_f \cdot \frac{b}{4} + h \cdot \frac{t_w}{2} \cdot \frac{t_w}{4}$$

$$= \frac{b^2 t_f}{4} + \frac{h\cdot t_w^2}{8}$$

$$\text{Shear flow } q = \frac{P\left(\frac{b^2 t_f}{4} + \frac{ht_w^2}{8}\right)\cdot 12}{ht_w^3 + 2t_f b^3}$$

Neglecting higher order terms of t_f and t_w gives

$$q = \frac{P\left(\frac{b^2 t_f}{4}\right)}{2t_f b^3}\cdot 12$$

$$\text{Shear stress, } \tau_{max} = \frac{q}{2t_f} = \frac{3P}{4bt_f}$$

SHEAR STRESS DISTRIBUTION

• PROBLEM 8-21

Derive an expression for the shearing stress distribution in a beam of solid rectangular cross section transmitting a vertical shear V.

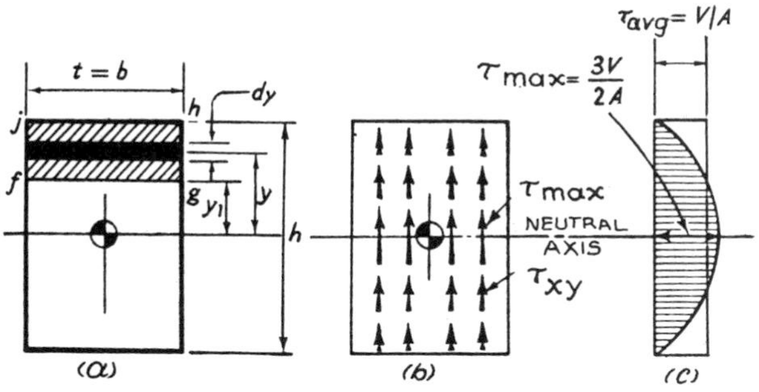

FIG. 1

Solution: The cross-sectional area of the beam is in Fig. 1(a). A longitudinal cut through the beam at a distance y_1 from the neutral axis isolates the partial area fghj of the cross section. Here t = b and the infinitesimal area of the cross section may be conveniently expressed as b dy. By applying the shear formula, $\tau = \frac{VQ}{Ib}$ the horizontal shearing stress is found at the level y_1 of the beam. At the same cut, numerically equal vertical shearing stresses act in the plane of the cross section.

$$\tau_{xy} = \tau_{yx} = \frac{VQ}{It}$$

The statical moment of area, Q, is defined as $\int_A y dA$, but we have dA = bdy here because the width is constant, so

$$Q = \int_A yda = \int_y bydy = \int_{y_1}^{h/2} bydy = b \left. \frac{y^2}{2} \right|_{y_1}^{h/2}$$

$$= \frac{b}{2}\left[\left(\frac{h}{2}\right)^2 - y_1^2\right]$$

Therefore $\tau_{xy} = \tau_{yx} = \frac{VQ}{Ib} = \frac{Vb}{2Ib}\left[\left(\frac{h}{2}\right)^2 - y_1{}^2\right]$

$$= \frac{V}{2I}\left[\left(\frac{h}{2}\right)^2 - y_1{}^2\right]$$

Thus, in a beam of rectangular cross section both the horizontal and the vertical shearing stresses vary parabolically. The maximum value of the shearing stress is obtained when y_1 is equal to zero. In the plane of the cross section, Fig. 1(b), this is diagrammatically represented by τ_{max} at the neutral axis of the beam. At increasing distances from the neutral axis, the shearing stresses gradually diminish. At the upper and lower boundaries of the beam, the shearing stresses cease to exist as $y_1 = \pm h/2$. These values of the shearing stresses at the various levels of the beam may be represented by the parabola shown in Fig. 1(c).

To satisfy the condition of statics $\Sigma F_y = 0$, at a section of the beam the sum of all the vertical shearing stresses τ_{xy} times their respective areas dA must be equal to the vertical shear V. That this is the case may be shown by integrating τ_{xy}dA over the whole cross-sectional area A of the beam, using the general expression for τ_{xy} found above.

$$\int_A \tau_{xy} dA = \frac{V}{2I} \int_{-h/2}^{+h/2} \left[\left(\frac{h}{2}\right)^2 - y_1^2\right] b\, dy_1 = \frac{Vb}{2I}\left[\left(\frac{h}{2}\right)^2 y_1\right.$$

$$\left. - \left(\frac{y_1^3}{3}\right)\right]_{-h/2}^{+h/2} = \frac{Vb}{(2bh^3/12)} \left[\left(\frac{h}{2}\right)^2 h - \frac{2}{3}\left(\frac{h}{2}\right)^3\right]$$

$$= \frac{Vb}{\left(\frac{2bh^3}{12}\right)} \left[\frac{h^3}{4} - \frac{h^3}{12}\right] = \frac{Vb}{\frac{2bh^3}{12}} \left[\frac{3h^3 - h^3}{12}\right]$$

$$= V \left(\frac{\frac{2bh^3}{12}}{\frac{2bh^3}{12}}\right) = V$$

Since an agreement in signs is found, this result indicates that the direction of the shearing stresses at the section through a beam is the same as that of the shearing force V. This fact may be used to determine the sense of the shearing stresses.

As noted above, the maximum shearing stress in a rectangular beam occurs at the neutral axis, and for this case the general expression for τ_{max} may be simplified since y_1 0.

$$\frac{Vh^2}{8I} = \frac{Vh^2}{8bh^3/12} = \frac{3}{2}\frac{V}{bh} = \frac{3}{2}\frac{V}{A}$$

where V is the total shear and A is the entire cross-sectional area. The same result may be obtained more directly if it is noted that to make VQ/(It) a maximum, Q must attain its largest value since in this case V, I and t are constants. From the property of the statical moments of areas around a centroidal axis, the maximum value of Q is obtained by considering one-half the cross-sectional area around the neutral axis of the beam. Hence, alternately,

$$\tau_{max} = \frac{VQ}{It} = \frac{V(bh/2)(h/4)}{(bh^3/12)b} = \frac{3}{2}\frac{V}{A} \qquad (1)$$

Since beams of rectangular cross-sectional area are used frequently in practice, Eq.(1) is very useful. It is widely used in the design of wooden beams as the shearing strength of wood on planes parallel to the grain is small. Thus, although equal shearing stresses exist on mutually perpendicular planes, wooden beams have a tendency to split longitudinally along the neutral axis. Note that the maximum shearing stress is 1 1/2 times as great as the average shearing stress V/A.

• PROBLEM 8-22

Determine the distribution of shear flow for a beam of rectangular cross-section.

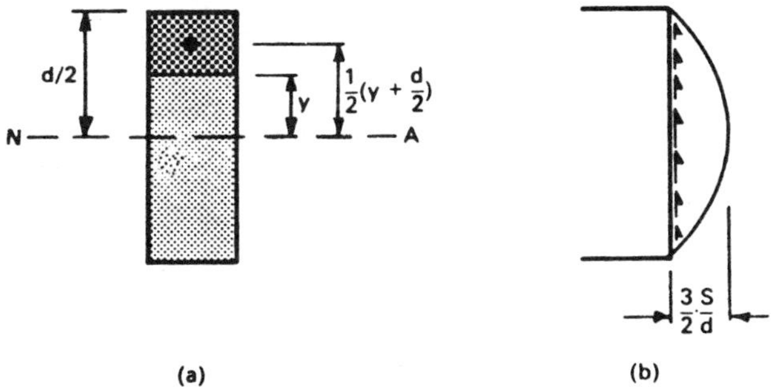

FIG. 1

Solution: We find the shear flow at y from the neutral axis. The area above y (Fig. 1a) is b(d/2 - y). Its centroid is $\frac{1}{2}$(y + d/2) from the neutral axis.

$$\therefore Q = b\left(\frac{d}{2} - y\right)\frac{1}{2}\left(\frac{d}{2} + y\right) = \frac{b}{2}\left(\frac{d^2}{4} - y^2\right)$$

$$I = \frac{bd^3}{12}$$

$$\frac{Q}{I} = \frac{12}{bd^3}\,\frac{b}{2}\left(\frac{d^2}{4} - y^2\right) = \frac{6}{d}\left(\frac{1}{4} - \left(\frac{y}{d}\right)^2\right)$$

∴ at y from N.A.

$$q = \frac{dM}{dx}\frac{6}{d}\left(\frac{1}{4} - \left(\frac{y}{d}\right)^2\right) \qquad (1)$$

from $q = \frac{VQ}{I}$,

since $\frac{dM}{dx} \equiv$ shear force on the cross-section.

This indicates a parabolic variation of q.
When $y = +d/2$,

$$q = 0$$

and at the centre, $y = 0$ and

$$q = \frac{dM}{dx}\frac{6}{4d}$$

S is the shear force $\frac{dM}{dx}$.

Therefore:

$$q = \frac{3}{2} \cdot \frac{S}{d}$$

The variation is often represented graphically as in Fig. 1b. It should be noted that although the ordinates as plotted are normal to the section they represent stresses parallel to the section. The area of this graph must represent the total shear force, and this result satisfies this requirement.

For a rectangular beam it is reasonable to assume that the stress is uniform across the width. The maximum shear stress is then obtained by dividing the shear flow at mid-depth by b.

$$\tau_{max} = \frac{q_{max}}{b} = \frac{3S}{2bd} \qquad (2)$$

The expression S/bd is the average vertical shear stress on the cross-section.

• PROBLEM 8-23

What is the average shear-stress distribution $\bar{\tau}_{xy}$, as a function of y for the rectangular cross section shown in Fig. 1 in terms of V_y and the dimensions of the cross section?

Solution: At any position y above the neutral surface, for Q_z we have

$$Q_z = Ay_1$$

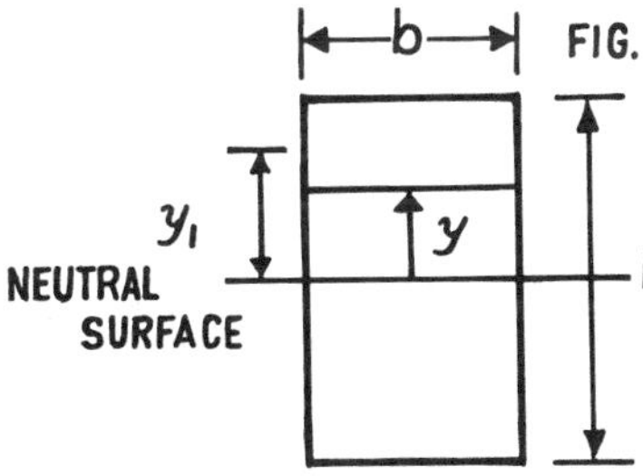

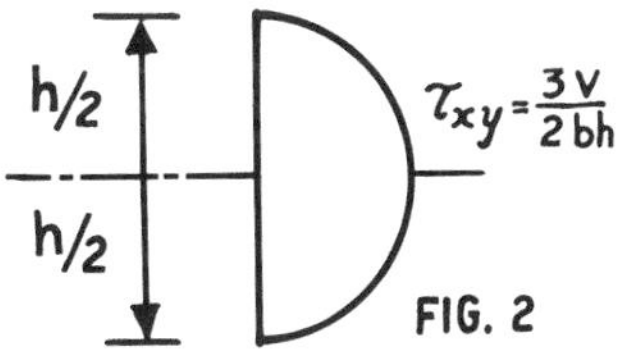

where y_1 is the distance to the centroid of the area.

$$A = b\left(\frac{h}{2} - y\right)$$

and

$$y_1 = y + \frac{(\frac{h}{2} - y)}{2}$$

so

$$Q_z = b\left(\frac{h}{2} - y\right)\left(y + \frac{\frac{h}{2} - y}{2}\right) = b\left(\frac{h}{2} - y\right)\left(\frac{y}{2} + \frac{h}{4}\right)$$

$$= b\left(\frac{hy}{4} - \frac{hy}{4} - \frac{y^2}{2} + \frac{h^2}{8}\right) = \frac{b}{2}\left[\left(\frac{h}{2}\right)^2 - y^2\right]$$

The moment of inertia for a rectangular section is

$$I = \frac{bh^3}{12}$$

By substituting these expressions into the shear formula

$$\bar{\tau}_{xy} = \frac{VQ}{Ib}$$

we get

$$\bar{\tau}_{xy} = \frac{V_y}{\left(\frac{1}{12}\right)\left(bh^3\right)b}\left(\frac{b}{2}\right)\left[\left(\frac{h}{2}\right)^2 - y^2\right]$$

$$= \frac{6V_y}{bh^3}\left[\left(\frac{h}{2}\right)^2 - y^2\right]$$

The stress therefore has a parabolic distribution, with a maximum value of $\frac{3}{2}\frac{V_y}{bh}$ at the neutral axis and goes to zero at the extreme fibers as shown in Fig. 2.

• PROBLEM 8-24

Derive an expression for the shearing stress distribution in a beam of solid rectangular cross-section transmitting a vertical shear V using differential equations of equilibrium. For convenience assume the beam to be 1 in. wide.

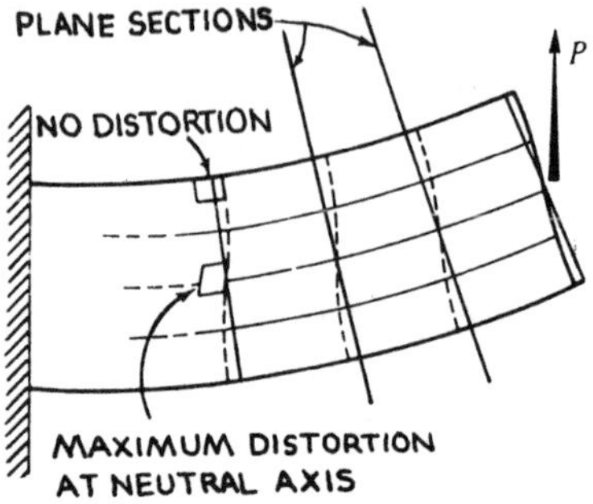

SHEARING DISTORTIONS OF A BEAM

FIG.1

Solution: From the point of view of elasticity, internal stresses and strains in beams are statically indeterminate. However, in the technical theory discussed here, the introduction of a kinematic hypothesis that plane sections remain plane after bending changes this situation. Here it is asserted that in a beam $\sigma_x = -My/I$. Therefore, the differential equation of equilibrium for a two-dimensional problem with a body force X = 0--suffices to solve for the unknown shearing stress. From the conditions of no shearing stress at the top and the bottom boundaries, $\tau_{yx} = 0$ at $y = \pm h/2$, the constant of integration is found.

$$\frac{\partial \sigma_x}{\partial x} + \frac{\partial \tau_{xy}}{\partial y} = 0 \tag{1}$$

But $\sigma_x = -\frac{My}{I}$, hence $\frac{\partial \sigma_x}{\partial x} = -\frac{\partial My}{\partial x I} = \frac{Vy}{I}$

and Eq.(1) becomes $\frac{Vy}{I} + \frac{d\tau_{xy}}{dy} = 0$

Upon integrating $\tau_{xy} = -\frac{Vy^2}{2I} + C_1$

Since $\tau_{xy}(\pm h/2) = 0$, we have $C_1 = +\frac{Vh^2}{8I}$

and $\tau_{xy} = \tau_{yx} = +\frac{V}{2I}\left[\left(\frac{h}{2}\right)^2 - y^2\right]$

According to Hooke's law, shearing deformations must be associated with shearing stresses. Therefore the shearing stresses given by the above relation must cause shearing deformations. As shown in Fig. 1, maximum shearing distortions occur at $y = 0$, and no distortions take place at $y = \pm h/2$. This warps the initially plane section through the beam and contradicts the basic assumption of the technical bending theory. However, by the methods of elasticity it can be shown that these shearing distortions of the plane sections are negligibly small for slender members; the technical theory is completely adequate if the length of a member is at least two to three times greater than its total depth. This conclusion is of far-reaching importance since it means that the existence of a shear at a section does not invalidate the expressions for bending stresses derived earlier. Note that at the point of load application as well as at a rigidly built-in end, additional local disturbances of stresses occur.

• PROBLEM 8-25

A 14WF202 I beam has the dimensions shown. Find $\bar{\tau}_{xy}$ as a function of y.

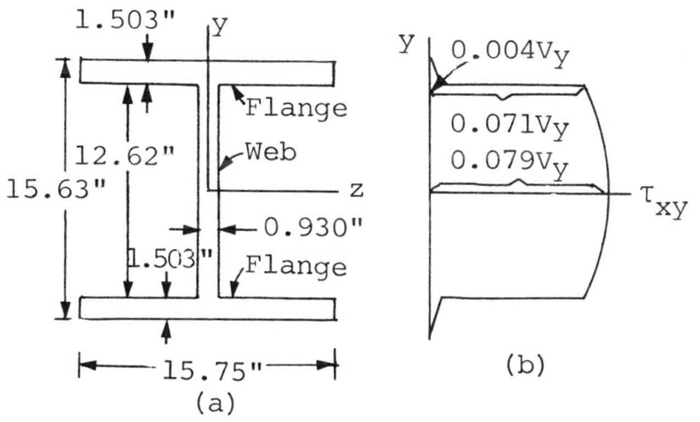

Fig. 1.

Solution: The dimensions of structural shapes can be found in handbooks, such as the Manual of Steel Construction, American Institute of Steel Construction.

Find $\bar{\tau}_{xy}$ as a function of y.

Using the shear formula

$$\tau_{xy} = \frac{VQ}{Ib}$$

$V \equiv$ shear force in section

$Q \equiv$ first moment of area $= \int_A y dA$

$I \equiv$ moment of inertia of section

$b \equiv$ width of section

we must calculate the shear stress in the web and flange separately because the widths are different.

For the upper flange region we have the properties of the section:

$$b_f = 15.75''$$

$$I = 2540 \text{ in.}^4$$

We must also obtain Q, the first moment of area, as a function of y.

$$Q = \int_A y\,dA$$

However, the flange width is constant so

$$dA = b\,dy$$

$$Q = \int_y^{y_{max}} by\,dy$$

which can also be expressed as the area of a section which extends from y to the extreme fiber of the flange times the distance to the centroid of this section. By referring to Figure 1a we can write the area

$$A = b \times \left(\frac{15.63}{2} - y\right)$$

The distance to the centroid of this section is equal to y plus one-half the thickness of the section

$$d = y + \left(\frac{\frac{15.63}{2} - y}{2}\right)$$

so

$$Q = b\left(\frac{15.63}{2} - y\right)\left[y + \frac{1}{2}\left(\frac{15.63}{2} - y\right)\right]$$

Substituting these values into the expression for shear, we get

$$\bar{\tau}_{xy} = \frac{V_y}{2540(15.75)}\left[15.75\left(\frac{15.63}{2} - y\right)\left\{y + \frac{1}{2}\left(\frac{15.63}{2} - y\right)\right\}\right]$$

$$= \frac{V_y}{2540}\left[\left(\frac{15.63}{2} - y\right)\left(\frac{y}{2} + \frac{15.63}{4}\right)\right]$$

$$= \frac{V_y}{2540}\left[\frac{15.63y}{4} - \frac{15.63y}{4} - \frac{y^2}{2} + \frac{15.63^2}{8}\right]$$

$$= \frac{V_y}{2540}\left[\frac{(7.81)^2}{2} - \frac{y^2}{2}\right]$$

$$= \frac{V_y}{5080}\left(7.81^2 - y^2\right) \qquad (1)$$

For the web region we proceed in the same manner. From the handbooks, we have

$$b_w = .930 \text{ in.}$$

$$I = 2540 \text{ in.}^4$$

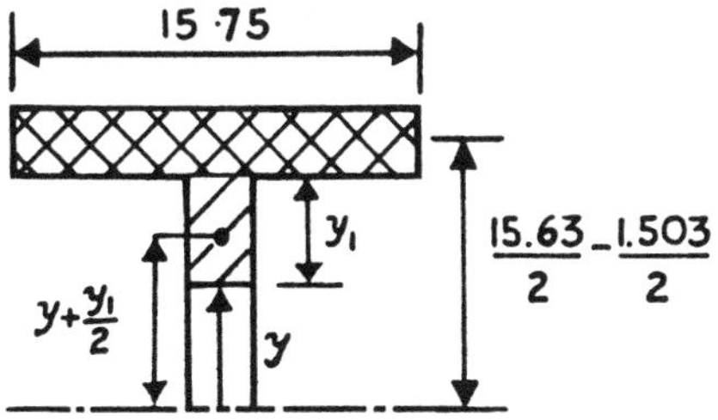

FIG. 2

The first moment of area for a distance y above the axis in the web region is a summation due to the flange area and the web area between y and the bottom of the flange as shown in Fig. 2. For the flange we have

$$Q_f = \left(15.75\right)\left(1.503\right)\left(\frac{15.63}{2} - \frac{1.503}{2}\right)$$

For the web area

$$Q_w = \left(.930\right)\left(\frac{12.62}{2} - y\right)\left[y + \frac{1}{2}\left(\frac{12.62}{2} - y\right)\right]$$

Therefore,

$$Q = \left(15.75\right)\left(1.503\right)\left(\frac{15.63}{2} - \frac{1.503}{2}\right) + \left(.930\right)\left(\frac{12.62}{2} - y\right)\left[y + \frac{1}{2}\left(\frac{12.62}{2} - y\right)\right]$$

Substituting in the shear formula we get

$$\bar{\tau}_{xy} = \frac{V_y}{(2540)(.930)}\left[(15.75)(1.503)\left(\frac{15.63}{2} - \frac{1.503}{2}\right) + \left(.930\right)\left(\frac{12.62}{2} - y\right)\left\{y + \frac{1}{2}\left(\frac{12.62}{2} - y\right)\right\}\right]$$

$$= \frac{V_y}{(2540)(.930)}\left[167.21 + .930\left(\frac{12.62}{2} - y\right)\left(\frac{y}{2} + \frac{12.62}{4}\right)\right]$$

$$= \frac{V_y}{2540}\left[180 + \left(\frac{12.62y}{4} - \frac{12.62y}{4} - \frac{y^2}{2} + \frac{(12.62)^2}{8}\right)\right]$$

$$= \frac{V_y}{2540}\left[180 - \frac{y^2}{2} + \frac{1}{2}\,\frac{(12.62)^2}{4}\right]$$

$$= \frac{V_y}{2540}\; 180 + \frac{1}{2}\; 6.31^2 - y^2 \qquad (2)$$

A plot of τ_{xy} for the section is shown in Fig. 1(b) which represents the case where fillets between flanges and web are assumed to have zero radius, thus giving a curve with discontinuities.

Note from this curve that the shear stress $\bar{\tau}_{xy}$ in the flange is very small compared to the shear stress of $\bar{\tau}_{xy}$ in the web. Furthermore, the shear stress in the web is approximately uniform in value over the entire web. For such problems, it is often assumed for simplicity that the web carries the shear load with a uniform shear stress given by

$$\bar{\tau}_{xy} = \frac{V_y}{A} = \frac{V_y}{(.930)(12.62)} = .085V_y$$

This result is about 7.6% in error on the conservative side, making this formulation acceptable in many applications.

• PROBLEM 8-26

A beam has a rectangular section 4 in. wide and 10 in. deep. The material has a tangent modulus of 10×10^6 psi up to a stress of 8000 psi and a tangent modulus of 6×10^6 psi thereafter. At cross-section A the bending moment is 400 kip-in. and at section B the bending moment is 1100 kip-in. At each of these sections the shear force is 24 kips. Compare the distribution of shear stress and the maximum shear stress at the two sections. Assume that the shear stress is uniform across the width of the beam.

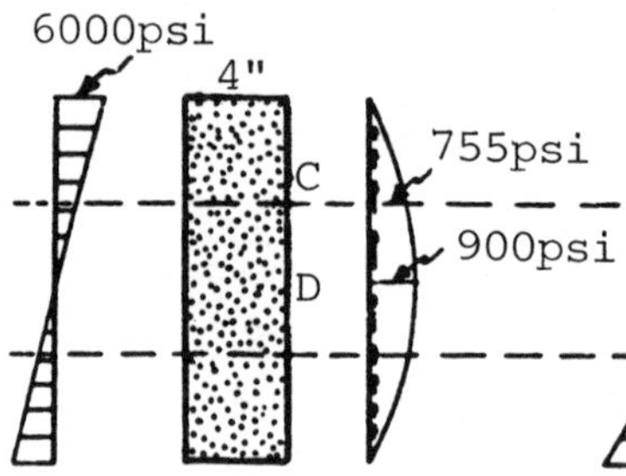

Bending Stresses (a) | **Effective Section** (b) | **Shear Stresses** (c)

Fig. 1

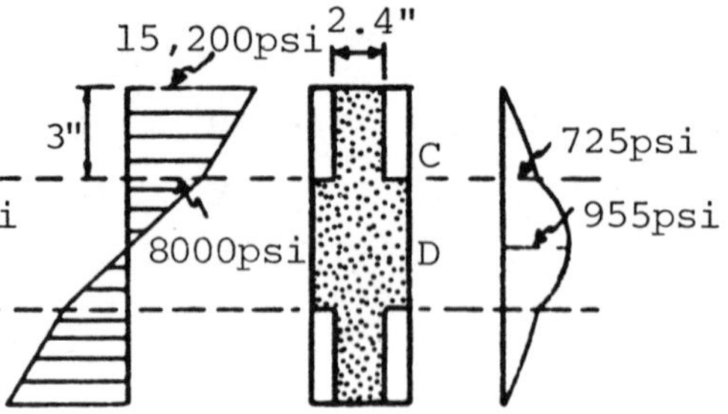

Bending Stresses (a) | **Transformed Section** (b) | **Shear Stresses** (c)

Fig. 2

Solution: At section A, we find that the extreme fibre stress due to bending is

$$\tau = \frac{My}{I}$$

where $I = \frac{4 \times 10^3}{12} = 333.3 \text{ in.}^4$

$$y = 5 \text{ in.}$$

$$M = 400{,}000 \text{ lb-in.}$$

$$\therefore \tau = \frac{400{,}000 \times 5 \times 12}{4 \times 10^3} = 6000 \text{ psi}$$

so that the bending stress distribution is linear (Fig. 1a). The distribution of shear flow is therefore computed from the whole cross-section (Fig. 1b).

Recall $I = 333.33 \text{ in.}^4$

At level C, 3 in. below the top

$$Q_c = 4 \times 3 \times 3.5 = 42 \text{ in.}^3$$

$$q_c = \frac{SQ_c}{I} = \frac{24{,}000 \times 42}{333.3} = 3020 \text{ lb/in.}$$

and, assuming a uniform stress distribution across the width,

$$\tau_c = \frac{3020}{4} = 755 \text{ psi}$$

Similarly, at the mid-depth, D

$$q_D = \frac{24{,}000 \times 50}{333.3}$$

$$\therefore \tau_D = \frac{24{,}000 \times 50}{3.333 \times 4} = 900 \text{ psi}$$

The shear stress distribution is parabolic (Fig. 1c).

At section B we find that the extreme fibre stress exceeds 8000 psi so that the bending stresses are not linear. The maximum bending stress is 15,200 psi. The stress of 8000 psi occurs at C, 3 in. below the top (Fig. 2a). Above C the tangent modulus is constant and equal to 0.6 times the initial tangent modulus. The effective section is therefore as shown dotted in Fig. 2b. For this section

$$I' = \frac{2.4 \times 10^3}{12} + \frac{1.6 \times 4^3}{12} = 208.5 \text{ in.}^4$$

At level C,

$$Q'_C = 2.4 \times 3 \times 3.5 = 25.2 \text{ in.}^3$$

$$q_C = \frac{24{,}000 \times 25.2}{208.5} = 2900 \text{ lb/in.}$$

This is the shear flow in the real beam and must therefore be divided by 4 in. (not 2.4 in.) to obtain the shear stress.

$$\tau_C = \frac{2900}{4} = 725 \text{ psi}$$

The distribution of stress down to C is parabolic since the width of the effective section is uniform.

Similarly, at D

$$Q'_D = 33.2 \text{ in.}^3$$

and

$$\tau_D = \frac{24{,}000 \times 33.2}{4 \times 208.5} = 955 \text{ psi}$$

The shear stress distribution at section B is shown in Fig. 2c.

• PROBLEM 8-27

Investigate the shear stresses in a wide-flange beam loaded by a force P acting in the vertical direction in the plane of the web (Fig. 1a).

Solution: Let us begin by taking an intermediate cross section of the beam (Fig. 1b) and considering the stresses in the right-hand part of the top flange. The distance s for this part of the beam will be measured from point a, where the shear stress is zero, leftward toward section bb. The area between point a and section bb is st_f, where t_f is the thickness of the flange, and the distance of the centroid of this area from the neutral axis is h/2 (note that h is the height of the beam between the centerlines of the flanges). Thus, for section bb, we have $Q_z = st_f h/2$; therefore, the shear stress at bb is

$$\tau = \frac{shP}{2I_z} \tag{1}$$

as obtained from

$$\tau = \frac{V_y Q_z}{I_{zz} t} .$$

The direction of this stress can be found by considering

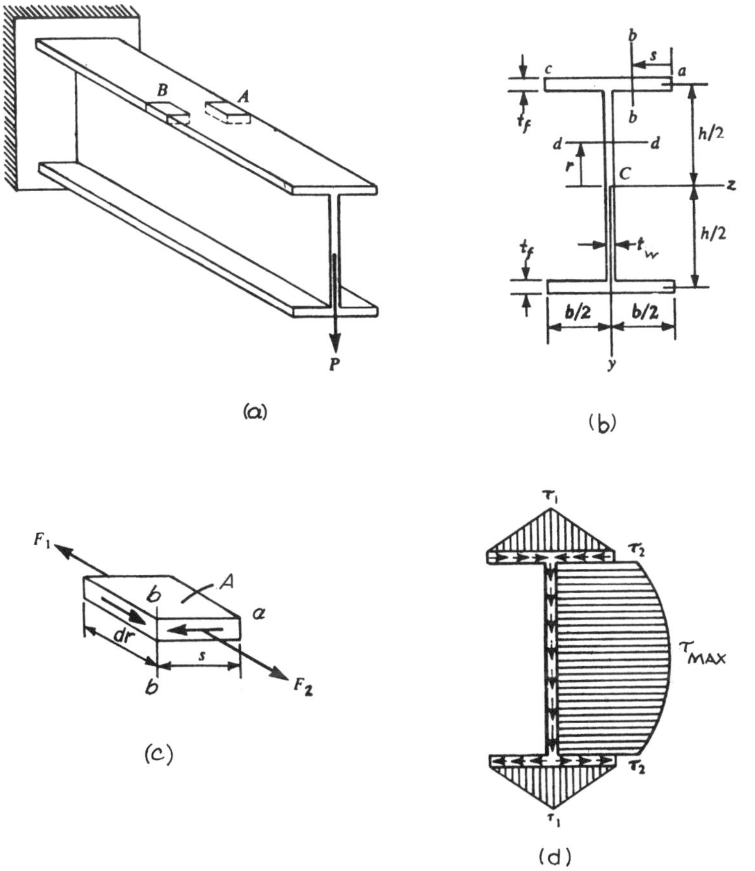

FIG. 1 SHEAR STRESSES IN A WIDE-FLANGE BEAM

the forces acting on an element cut out of the flange between point a and section bb (see element A in Fig. 1a). This element is drawn to a larger scale in Fig. 1c, in order to show clearly the forces acting on it. We can see immediately that the tensile force F_1 is larger than the force F_2, because the bending moment is larger on the rear face of the element than it is on the front face. Hence, it follows that, for equilibrium, the shear stress τ on the left face of element A must act toward the reader. This conclusion then dictates the direction of the shear stresses on the cross section, namely, they must act toward the left. Returning now to Fig. 1b, we see that we have completely determined the magnitude and direction of the shear stress at section bb. This section may be taken anywhere between point a and the juncture of the flange and web; hence, throughout this region the shear stress is horizontal and to the left, and its magnitude is given by Eq. (1). We see also from Eq. (1) that the stress increases linearly with the distance s, as shown graphically in Fig. 1d. The maximum value τ_1 is reached when s = b/2, where b is the flange width; thus,

$$\tau_1 = \frac{bhP}{4I_z} \tag{2}$$

and the corresponding shear flow is

$$f_1 = \tau_1 t_f = \frac{bht_f P}{4I_z} \tag{3}$$

Note that, in this approximate analysis, we have calculated the shear stress at the centerline juncture of the flange and web, without taking into account the thickness of the cross section. This procedure is satisfactory for thin walled sections.

By beginning at point c on the left part of the top flange (Fig. 1b) and measuring s toward the right, we can make the same kind of analysis over again. We will find that the magnitude of the shear stresses is again given by Eqs. (1) and (2). However, by cutting out an element B (Fig. 1a) and considering its equilibrium, we will find that the shear stresses on the cross section now act toward the right, as shown in Fig. 1d.

The next step is to determine the shear stresses in the web. Considering a horizontal cut at the top of the web, just below the flange, we find the first moment to be

$$Q_z = \frac{bt_f h}{2}$$

and the corresponding shear stress is

$$\tau_2 = \frac{bht_f P}{2I_z t_w} \tag{4}$$

where t_w is the thickness of the web. The associated shear flow is

$$f_2 = \tau_2 t_w = \frac{bht_f P}{2I_z} \tag{5}$$

which is equal to twice the shear flow f_1, as expected. The shear stresses in the web act vertically downward and increase in magnitude until the neutral axis is reached. At section dd, located distance r from the neutral axis, the shear stress is calculated as follows:

$$\begin{aligned} Q_z &= \frac{bt_f h}{2} + \left(\frac{h}{2} - r\right)\left(t_w\right)\left(\frac{h/2 + r}{2}\right) \\ &= \frac{bt_f h}{2} + \frac{t_w}{2}\left(\frac{h^2}{4} - r^2\right) \end{aligned}$$

and

$$\tau = \left(\frac{bt_f h}{t_w} + \frac{h^2}{4} - r^2\right)\frac{P}{2I_z} \tag{6}$$

When r = h/2, this equation reduces to Eq. (4), and when r = 0, it gives the maximum shear stress:

$$\tau_{max} = \left(\frac{bt_f}{t_w} + \frac{h}{4}\right)\frac{Ph}{2I_z} \qquad (7)$$

Again it should be pointed out that we have made all calculations on the basis of the centerline dimensions of the cross section, which gives reasonably accurate results for thin sections.

The shear stresses in the web vary parabolically, as shown in Fig. 1d, although the variation is not great. This fact can be seen from the ratio of τ_{max} to τ_2, which is

$$\frac{\tau_{max}}{\tau_2} = 1 + \frac{ht_w}{4bt_f} \qquad (8)$$

The second term is usually small; for example, if we take typical values such as h = 2b and $t_f = 2t_w$, the ratio is $\tau_{max}/\tau_2 = 1.25$.

Lastly, we may investigate the shear stresses in the lower flange by the same methods used for the top flange. We will find that the stresses are the same as in the top flange, except that they have the directions shown in Fig. 1d.

From Fig. 1d, we see that the shear stresses on the cross section "flow" inward from the outermost edges of the top flange, then down through the web, and finally outward to the edges of the bottom flange. This flow is always continuous in any structural section, and therefore it serves as a convenient way to determine the directions of the stresses. Because the shear force acts downward on the beam, we know that the shear flow in the web must be downward. Then, knowing the direction of the shear flow in the web, we immediately know the directions in the flanges also, because of the required continuity in the shear flow. Using this simple technique to get the directions of the stresses is easier than visualizing elements such as A (Fig. 1c) cut out from the beam.

The resultant of all shear stresses on the cross section is clearly a vertical force, because the horizontal stresses in the flanges cancel one another and produce no resultant. The shear stresses in the web have a resultant R which can be found by integrating the shear stresses over the height of the web, as follows:

$$R = \int \tau \, dA = 2\int_0^{h/2} \tau t_w dr$$

Now substituting from Eq. (6), we get

$$R = 2t_w \int_0^{h/2} \left(\frac{bt_f h}{t_w} + \frac{h^2}{4} - r^2 \right) \left(\frac{P}{2I_z} \right) dr$$

$$= \left(\frac{bt_f}{t_w} + \frac{h}{6} \right) \frac{h^2 t_w P}{2I_z} \qquad (9)$$

The term I_z can be expanded as follows:

$$I_z = \frac{t_w h^3}{12} + \frac{bt_f h^2}{2} \qquad (10)$$

where the first term is the moment of inertia of the web and the second term is the moment of inertia of the flanges, again calculated by using centerline dimensions. When this expression for I_z is substituted into Eq.(9) we get $R = P$, which establishes the fact that the resultant of the shear stresses acting on the cross section is equal to the vertical load P. The resultant passes through the centroid C, which is also the shear center for a wide-flange beam.

• PROBLEM 8-28

We wish to determine the distribution of shear flows in the angle section of Fig. 1a .

Assume $I_{yy} = \frac{4}{3} a^3 t$

$$I_{zz} = \frac{1}{4} a^3 t \qquad (1)$$

$$I_{yz} = - \frac{1}{3} a^3 t$$

and the centroid is $\frac{2}{3}$ a from the top and $\frac{a}{6}$ from the left edge.

Solution: We begin by considering loading in a plane parallel to the xy plane. The shear flow q_{xz} in the horizontal leg can be obtained from

$$q_{xs} = \frac{-V_y}{I_{yy}I_{zz} - I_{yz}^2} \left(I_{zz} \int_{A_1} y dA - I_{yz} \int_{A_1} z dA \right)$$

In developing the relation for q_{xs}, the coordinate s in Fig. 1 increased as we moved around the section in a counterclockwise manner. In the horizontal leg the coordinate z increases as we move in a counterclockwise manner, and hence z corresponds to s.

$$q_{xz} = q_{xs} = \frac{-V_y}{I_{yy}I_{zz} - I_{yz}^2}$$

$$\left(I_{zz} \int_{A_1} y \, dA - I_{yz} \int_{A_1} z \, dA \right) \qquad (2)$$

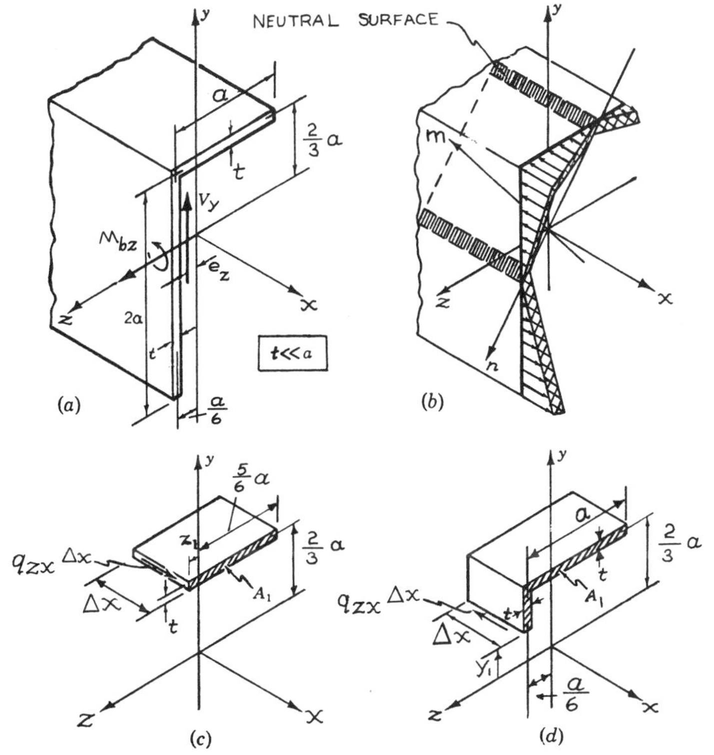

FIG. 1

We evaluate the integrals from the sketch in Fig. 1c

$$\int_{A_1} y \, dA = \left[t\left(z_1 + \frac{5}{6}a\right)\right]\frac{2}{3}a$$
$$\int_{A_1} z \, dA = \left[t\left(z_1 + \frac{5}{6}a\right)\right]\frac{1}{2}\left(z_1 - \frac{5}{6}a\right) \qquad (3)$$

Substituting (1) and (3) in (2) we find

$$q_{xz} = \frac{-V_y}{I_{yy}I_{zz} - I_{yz}^2}\left\{ I_{zz}\,\frac{2}{3a}\left[t\left(z_1 + \frac{5}{6a}\right)\right] - I_{yz} \cdot \frac{t}{2}\left(z_1 - \frac{5}{6a}\right)\left(z_1 + \frac{5}{6a}\right)\right\}$$

Substituting for I_{yy}, I_{zz}, and I_{yz} and simplifying gives

$$q_{xz} = -\frac{1}{48}\frac{V_y}{a^3}\left(36z_1^{\,2} + 36az_1 + 5a^2\right) \qquad (4)$$

As we move in a counterclockwise manner in the vertical leg, the coordinate y decreases and hence y corresponds to -s. Thus the shear flow q_{xy} in the vertical leg can be obtained from

$$q_{xy} = -q_{xs} = \frac{V_y}{I_{yy}I_{zz} - I_{yz}^{\,2}}\left(I_{zz}\int_{A_1} y\, dA - I_{yz}\int_{A_1} z\, dA\right) \qquad (5)$$

From Fig. 1d we obtain

$$\int_{A_1} y\, dA = (at)\tfrac{2}{3}a + \left[t\left(\tfrac{2}{3}a - y_1\right)\right]\tfrac{1}{2}\left(\tfrac{2}{3}a + y_1\right)$$

$$\int_{A_1} z\, dA = (at)\left(-\tfrac{1}{3}a\right) + \left[t\left(\tfrac{2}{3}a - y_1\right)\right]\left(\tfrac{1}{6}a\right) \qquad (6)$$

Combining (1), (6), and (5), we find,

$$q_{xy} = -q_{xs} = \frac{V_y}{\frac{1}{3}a^6t^2 - \frac{1}{9}a^6t^2}\left\{\frac{4}{3}a^3t\left[(at)\frac{2}{3a} + \left[t\left(\frac{2}{3a} - y_1\right)\right]\frac{1}{2}\left(\frac{2}{3a} + y_1\right)\right] + \frac{1}{3}a^3t\left[(at)\left(-\frac{1}{3}a\right) + \left[t\left(\frac{2}{3a} - y_1\right)\right]\left(\frac{1}{6}a\right)\right]\right\}$$

Simplifying gives

$$q_{xy} = \frac{1}{48}\frac{V_y}{a^3}\left(32a^2 - 12ay_1 - 27y_1^{\,2}\right) \qquad (7)$$

FIG. 2

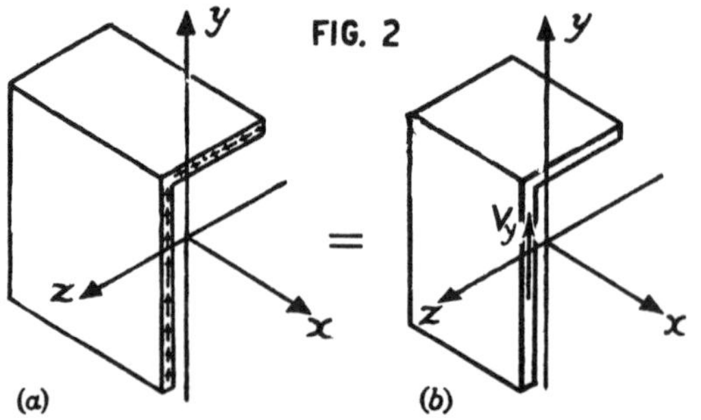

(a) (b)

The distributions (4) and (7) are indicated in Fig. 2a. The maximum value of q_{xy} (which is positive throughout the vertical leg) and the maximum positive value of q_{xz} coincide with the points where the neutral surface cuts the vertical and horizontal legs in Fig. 1b.

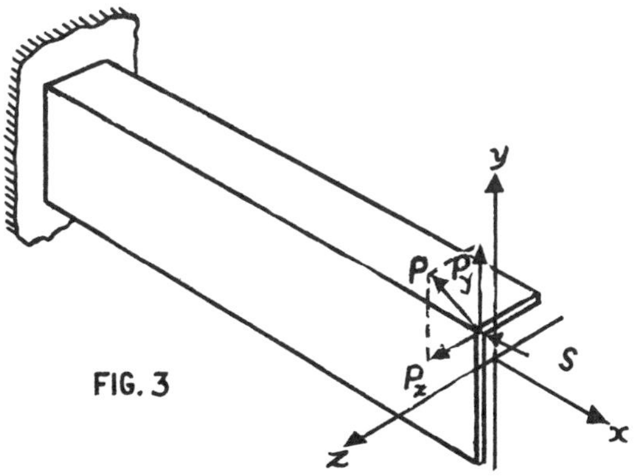

FIG. 3

A similar analysis applies to loadings in a plane parallel to the xz plane. It is clear that for this loading the resultant of the shear-flow distribution will be a force in the horizontal leg. The intersection of these two shear-flow resultants is at the intersection of the two legs, and this point is, therefore, the shear center for the angle. For any thin-walled angle section the horizontal shear flow is confined to the horizontal leg and the vertical shear flow is confined to the vertical leg. Their resultant must always pass through the intersection of the legs. Thus without further calculation we see that the shear center S of any thin-walled angle section must be at the intersection of the legs, as illustrated in Fig. 3.

SHEAR CENTER

• PROBLEM 8-29

Find the approximate location of the shear center for the cross section of the I beam in Fig. 1. Note that the flanges are unequal.

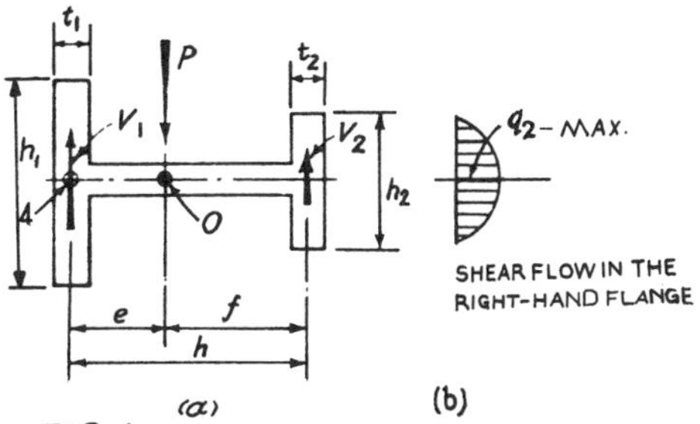

FIG.1

Solution: This cross section has a horizontal axis of symmetry, and the shear center is located on it; where remains to be answered. The applied force P causes significant bending and shearing stresses only in the flanges, and the contribution of the web to the resistance of the applied force P is negligible.

Let the shearing force resisted by the left flange of the beam be V_1, and that by the right flange, V_2. For equilibrium, $V_1 + V_2 = P$. Likewise, for no twist of the section, from $\Sigma M_A = 0$, $Pe = V_2 h$ (or $Pf = V_1 h$). Thus only V_2 remains to be determined to solve the problem. This may be done by noting that the right flange is actually an ordinary rectangular beam. The shearing stress (or shear flow) in such a beam is distributed parabolically, Fig. 1b, and since the area of a parabola is two-thirds of the base times the maximum altitude, $V_2 = 2/3\, b_2 (q_2)_{max}$. However, since the total shear $V = P$, $(q_2)_{max} = VQ/I = PQ/I$, where Q is the statical moment of the upper half of the right flange and I is the moment of inertia of the whole section. Hence

$$Pe = V_2 h = \frac{2}{3} b_2 (q_2)_{max} h = \frac{2/3 h b_2 PQ}{I}$$

$$e = \frac{2hb_2}{3I} Q = \frac{2hb_2}{3I} \frac{b_2 t_2}{2} \frac{b_2}{4} = \frac{h}{I} \frac{t_2 b_2^3}{12} \qquad (1)$$

$$= \frac{hI_2}{I}$$

where I_2 is the moment of inertia of the right flange around the neutral axis. Similarly, if the web of the beam is thin, as originally assumed, $I \approx I_1 + I_2$, and $e + f = h$ as is to be expected.

$$V_1 = \frac{2}{3} b_1 (q_1)_{max}$$

$$q_{1max} = \frac{VQ}{I} = \frac{PQ}{I}$$

where q in this case is the static moment of the upper half of the left flange.

$$Pf = V_1 h = \frac{2}{3} b_1 \left(q_{1max}\right) h = \frac{2}{3} b_1 \frac{PQ}{I} h$$

$$\therefore\ f = \frac{2hb_1}{3I} Q = \frac{2hb_1}{3I} \cdot \frac{b_1 t_1}{2} \cdot \frac{b_1}{4}$$

$$= \frac{h}{I} \cdot \frac{t_1 b_1^3}{12} = h \frac{I_1}{I}$$

Find the shear center for the pipe cross-section and show that it is equal to e = 4R/π.

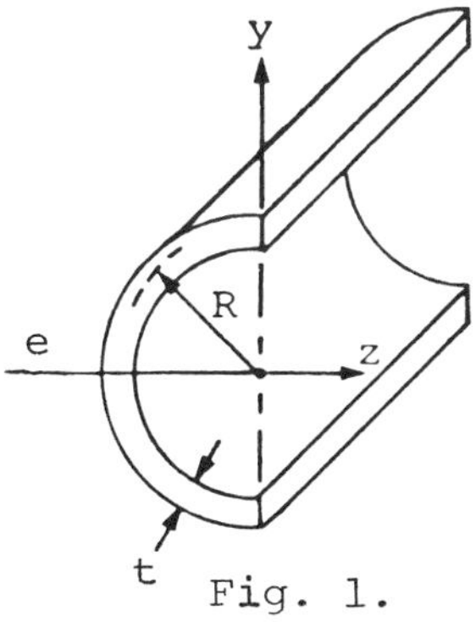

Fig. 1.

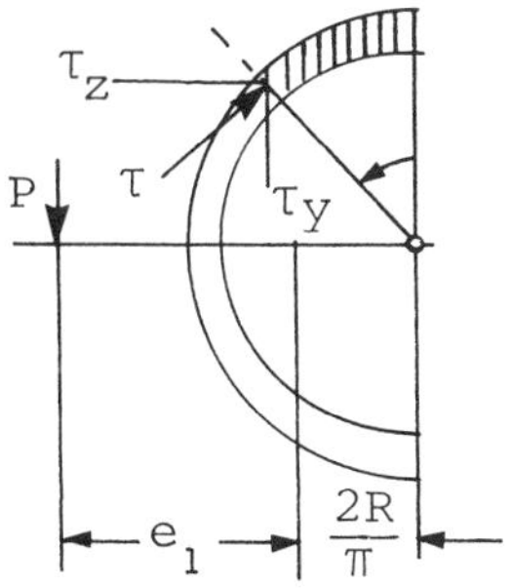

Fig. 2.

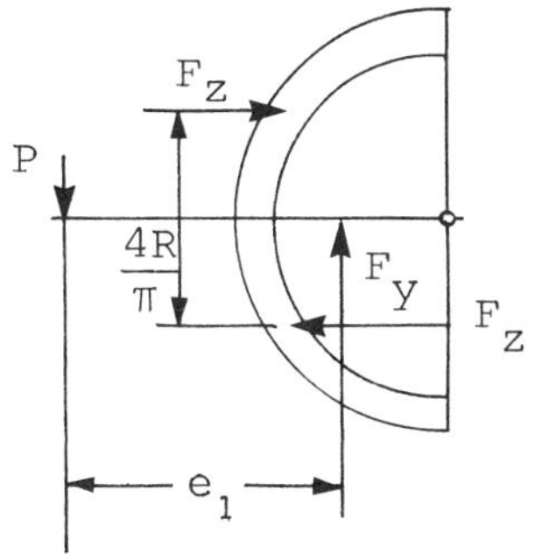

Fig. 3.

Solution: The shear center is defined as the point in the plane of the cross-section through which the resultant of the transverse shearing stresses due to flexure (no torsion) will pass for any orientation of transverse loads. Assume there is a shear force, V in the cross-section. The shearing stress distribution, τ can be obtained from

$$\tau = \frac{V}{It}\int_0^s y(tds)$$

where
I ≡ moment of inertia of the cross-section
t ≡ thickness of the cross-section
y ≡ distance of the fibres from the neutral axis
s ≡ distance along the contour

The resultant of the shearing stress distribution in the y and z directions are τ_y and τ_z

$$\tau_z = \tau\cos\theta \quad ; \quad \tau_y = \tau\sin\theta$$

In the z direction, the resultant shear forces, F_z in each half are equal and opposite and form a couple

$$\frac{4R}{\pi} F_z$$

In the y-direction, the resultant shear force F_y must be equal and opposite to P, for equilibrium and form a couple $F_y e_1$

$$\therefore \frac{4R}{\pi} F_z = F_y e_1 \qquad (1)$$

$$F_z = (\tau_z \text{ avg})(\text{area}) = \frac{\pi Rt}{2}\tau_z$$

$$\tau_z = \int_0^{\pi/2} \tau\cos\theta d\theta = \tau$$

$$\therefore\ F_z = \frac{\pi R t}{2}\tau$$

$$F_y = (\tau_y\ \text{avg})(\text{area}) = \pi R t \tau_y$$

but $$\tau_y = \int_0^{\pi} \tau \sin d\theta = \tau$$

$$\therefore\ F_y = \pi R t \tau$$

Substituting in Eq.(1) gives

$$\frac{4R}{\pi} \cdot \frac{\pi R t}{2}\tau = \pi R t \tau e_1$$

$$\therefore\ e_1 = \frac{2R}{\pi}$$

but $$e = e_1 + \frac{2R}{\pi} = \frac{4R}{\pi}$$

$$\therefore\ \text{Shear Center} = \frac{4R}{\pi}$$

• PROBLEM 8-31

Locate the shear center S of the thin-walled, semicircular cross section shown in Fig. 1.

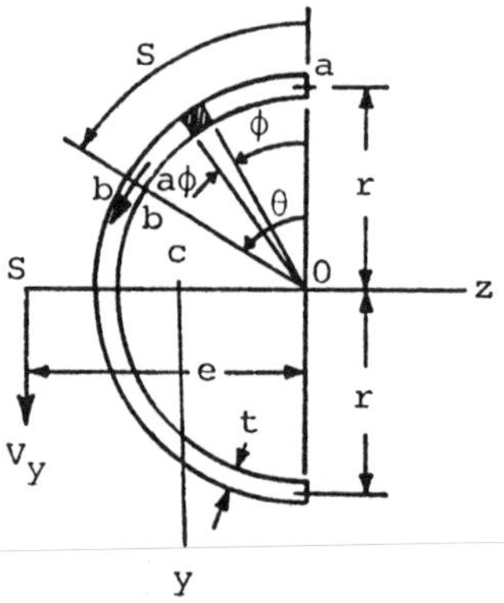

Fig. 1 SHEAR CENTER FOR A THIN-WALLED SEMI-CIRCULAR SECTION.

Solution: Let us consider a section bb defined by the distance s measured along the middle line of the cross section. The central angle subtended between point a, which is at the edge of the section, and section bb is denoted by θ. Therefore, we have $s = r\theta$, where r is the radius of the middle line. The first moment of the area between a and bb is

$$Q_z = \int y dA = \int_0^{\theta} (r \cos\phi)(rt)d\phi = r^2 t \sin\theta$$

where t is the thickness of the section. Thus, the shear stress τ at section bb is

$$\tau = \frac{V_y Q_z}{I_z t} = \frac{V_y r^2 \sin\theta}{I_z}$$

Substituting $I_z = \pi r^3 t/2$, we get

$$\tau = \frac{2V_y \sin\theta}{\pi r t} \qquad (1)$$

When $\theta = 0$ and $\theta = \pi$, this expression gives $\tau = 0$, and when $\theta = \pi/2$, we get the maximum shear stress.

The moment about point O due to the shear stresses τ is

$$T = \int \tau r dA = \int_0^{\pi} \frac{2V_y r \sin\theta \, d\theta}{\pi} = \frac{4rV_y}{\pi}$$

which must be the same as the moment due to the force V_y acting at the shear center; hence,

$$V_y e = \frac{4rV_y}{\pi}$$

Thus, the distance e from point O to the shear center is

$$e = \frac{4r}{\pi}$$

• PROBLEM 8-32

A channel is 15 in. deep overall, and has flanges which are 3.4 in. wide and 0.650 in. thick. The web is 0.400 in. thick as shown in Fig. 1. Locate the shear center with respect to the outside edge of the web.

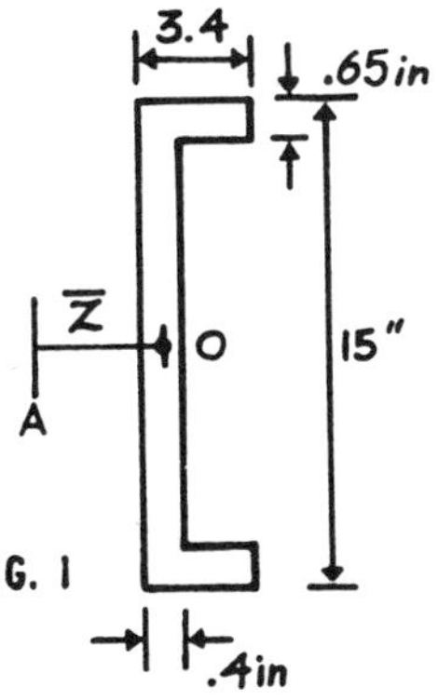

FIG. 1

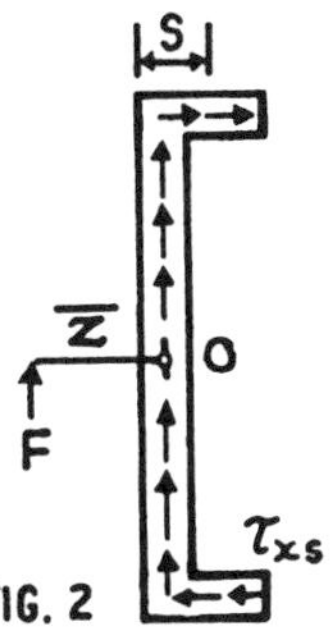

FIG. 2

Solution: The shear center of a section is the point where an applied shear force causes no twisting in the section. The coordinates $\bar{y}$ and $\bar{z}$ of the shear center are found by equating the twisting moment about the center of gravity due to the shear force and the stress distribution. Because of the symmetry of this section a force applied at the middle of the web in the z direction causes no twisting so $\bar{y} = 0$.

By taking moments about the point O, which must be zero, as we require no twisting, we can find the distance $\bar{z}$.

The moment due to a force F, applied at point A, about point O is

$$M = -F(\bar{z})$$

Because O is at the midplane of the web, the shear stress in the web has a line of action through point O and therefore causes no moment.

The moment due to the shear stress at a section in the flange, a distance s from the web is

$$M_s = -\left(\frac{h}{2} - \frac{t_f}{2}\right)\tau_{xs} t_f ds$$

where $(\frac{h}{2} - \frac{t_f}{2})$ is the moment arm and $\tau_{xs} t_f ds$ gives the force.

To find the total moment due to the shear stress in one flange we integrate over the length of the flange. The moment due to both flanges is twice the moment due to one flange due to the symmetry of the section so

$$M_{total} = 2\int_0^b -\left(\frac{h}{2} - \frac{t_f}{2}\right)\tau_{xs} t_f ds$$

We now need to express τ_{xs} as a function of position and shear force V_y.

Using the shear force formula we have

$$\bar{\tau}_{xs} = \frac{VQ}{It_f}$$

Q is moment of area for flange

I is moment of inertia of section

t_f is thickness of flange

The moment of area for the stress which is a distance s along the flange is given by

$$Q = S \times t_f\left(\frac{h}{2} - \frac{t_f}{2}\right)$$

so that

$$\bar{\tau}_{xs} = \frac{Vst_f\left(\frac{h}{2} - \frac{t_f}{2}\right)}{It_f}$$

Substituting this expression into that for moment we get:

$$M_{total} = 2\int_0^b -\left(\frac{h}{2} - \frac{t_f}{2}\right) \frac{Vst_f\left(\frac{h}{2} - \frac{t_f}{2}\right)}{It_f} \left|t_f ds\right|$$

$$= -2\int_0^b \frac{Vst_f\left(h-t_f\right)^2}{4I} ds$$

$$= -\int_0^b \frac{Vt_f\left(h-t_f\right)^2}{2I} sds$$

We now sum these moments

$$-F(\bar{z}) - M_{total} = 0$$

so

$$-F(\bar{z}) = \int_0^b \frac{Vt_f\left(h-t_f\right)^2}{2I} sds$$

We substitute F = -V in order to solve for $\bar{z}$.

$$V(\bar{z}) = \int_0^b \frac{Vt_f\left(h-t_f\right)^2}{2I} sds = \frac{Vt_f\left(h-t_f\right)^2}{4I} s^2\Big|_0^b$$

$$= \frac{Vt_f\left(h-t_f\right)^2}{4I} b^2$$

$$\bar{z} = \frac{t_f\left(h-t_f\right)^2}{4I} \times (b)^2$$

The last quantity to be calculated is the moment of inertia of the section.

$$I = \left[\frac{bt_f^3}{12} + \left(bt_f\right)\left(\frac{h}{2} - \frac{t_f}{2}\right)^2\right]2 + \frac{t_w\left(h-2t_f\right)^3}{12}$$

$$= \left[\frac{(3.4)(.65)^3}{12} + (3.4)(.65)(7.5-.325)^2\right]2$$

$$+ \frac{.4(15-1.3)^3}{12} = 313.411 \text{ in.}^3$$

Substituting the values for all quantities we have

$$\bar{z} = \frac{(.65)(15-.65)^2}{4(313.411)} (3.4)^2 = 1.234''$$

which is the distance from the midplane of the web. The distance from the outside of the web is

$$e = \bar{z} - \frac{t_w}{2} = 1.234 - \frac{.4}{2} = 1.034"$$

• **PROBLEM 8-33**

Find the approximate location of the shear center for a beam with the cross section of the channel shown in Fig. 1.

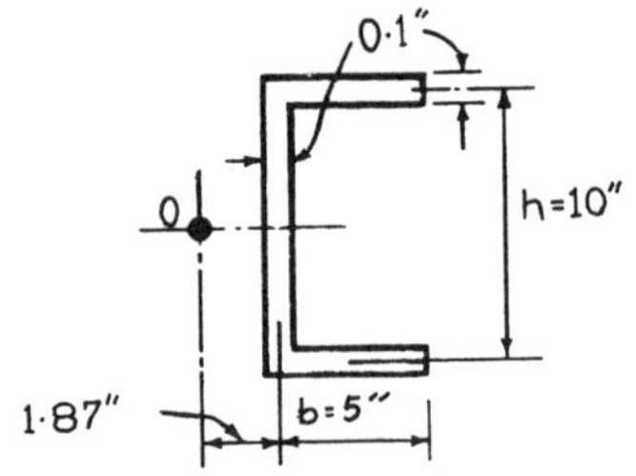

FIG. 1

Solution: Instead of using

$$e = \frac{t(h-t)^2 b^2}{4I_{zz}} \tag{1}$$

directly, some further simplifications may be made. The moment of inertia of a thin-walled channel around the neutral axis may be found with sufficient accuracy by neglecting the moment of inertia of the flanges around their own axes (only!). This expression for I may then be substituted into Eq.(1) and, after simplifications, a formula for e of channels is obtained.

$$I \approx I_{web} + \left(Ad^2\right)_{flanges} = \frac{th^3}{12} + 2bt\left(\frac{h}{2}\right)^2$$

$$= \frac{th^3}{12} + \frac{bth^2}{2}$$

$$e = \frac{b^2h^2t}{4I} = \frac{b^2h^2t}{4\left(\frac{bth^2}{2} + \frac{th^3}{12}\right)} = \frac{b}{2 + h/(3b)} \tag{a}$$

Equation (a) shows that when the width of flanges b is very large, e approaches its maximum value of b/2. When h is very large, e approaches its minimum value of zero. Otherwise, e assumes an intermediate value between these two limits. For the numerical data given in Fig. 1

$$e = \frac{5}{2 + 10/(3 \times 5)} = 1.87 \text{ in.}$$

Hence the shear center O is 1.87 - 0.05 = 1.82 in. from the outside vertical face of the channel. The answer would not be improved if Eq.(1) were used in the calculations.

• PROBLEM 8-34

We are to determine the shear stresses in the channel cantilever beam shown in Fig. 1 loaded by a single force F for the condition of no twisting in the beam.

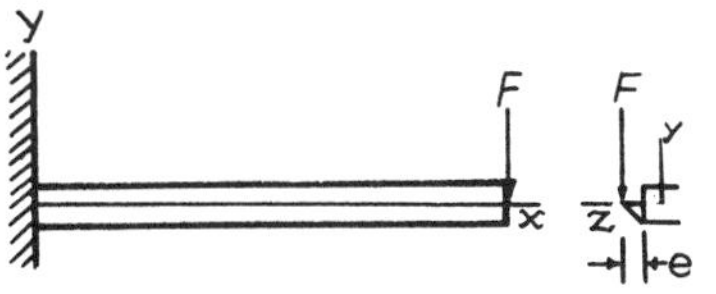

FIG. 1

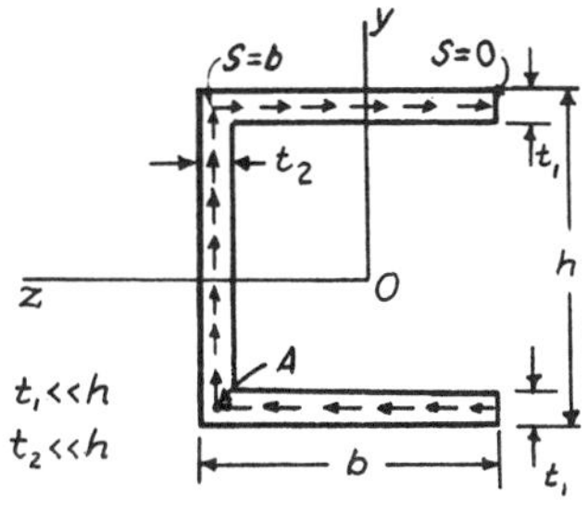

FIG. 2

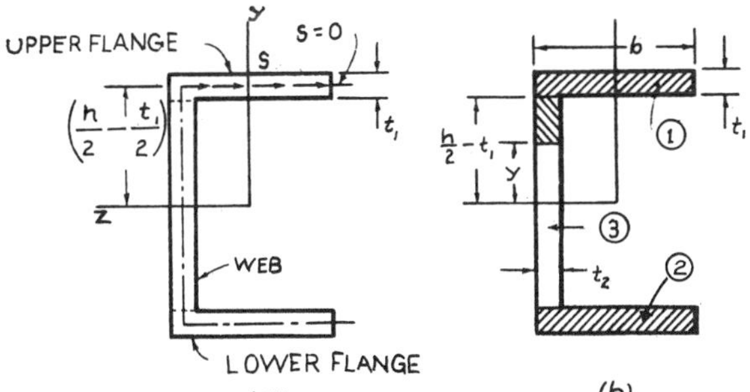

(a) (b)

FIG. 3

Solution: We have shown an enlargement of the cross section having its normal in the plus x direction of the channel in Fig. 2. The zy axes are centroidal axes drawn parallel to the sides of the channel. These axes also happen to be principal axes of the section. In accordance with recommended procedure the shear stress τ_{xy} is shown corresponding to a positive shear force V_y. It must be pointed out that the thicknesses t_1 and t_2 are small compared to h, the height of the channel, making the thin-walled beam theory applicable.

Accordingly,

$$\tau_{sx} = \frac{V_y}{t_c\left(I_{zz}I_{yy} - I_{zy}^2\right)}\left[I_{yy}\int_0^s yt\,d\tau - I_{zy}\int_0^s zt\,d\tau\right]$$

becomes for this case, remembering that y and z are principal axes,

$$\tau_{xs} = \frac{V_y}{t_c I_{zz} I_{yy}} \left[I_{yy} \int_0^s ytds \right] = \frac{V_y Q_z}{I_{zz} t_c} \qquad \text{(a)}$$

Considering the upper flange to include the left top corner, as has been shown in Fig. 3a, we compute τ_{xs} at position s in the upper flange in the following manner:

$$(\tau_{xs})_{flange} = \frac{V_y s \frac{h - t_1}{2}}{I_{zz}} \qquad \text{(b)}$$

The term I_{zz} is most easily computed by decomposing the cross section into two flanges, shown as 1 and 2 in Fig. 3b, with the web shown as 3. Thus,

$$I_{zz} = \frac{1}{12} t_2 \left(h - 2t_1\right)^3 + 2\left[\frac{1}{12} bt_1^3 + bt_1\left(\frac{h}{2} - \frac{t_1}{2}\right)^2\right] \qquad \text{(c)}$$

As for the shear force we must use the proper sign conventionwise. In this case we have $V_y = -F$, as can be seen by inspection of Fig. 1. Accordingly, $(\tau_{xs})_{flange}$ is negative and hence must be directed oppositely to what is shown in Fig. 2. Clearly, the lower flange will have an equal but oppositely directed shear-stress distribution as that of the upper flange.

The shear stress in the web is taken so as not to include the inside fillets of the channel. Observing Fig. 3b, the term Q_z is computed as

$$Q_z = bt_1 \frac{\left(h - t_1\right)}{2} + t_2\left(\frac{h}{2} - t_1 - y\right) \left\{ y + \frac{\left(\frac{h}{2} - t_1\right) - y}{2} \right\} \qquad \text{(d)}$$

The shear stress can then be given as

$$\left(\tau_{xs}\right)_{web} = \frac{V_y}{I_{zz} t_2} \left\{ \frac{bt_1}{2}\left(h - t_1\right) + \frac{t_2}{2}\left[\left(\frac{h}{2} - t_1\right)^2 - y^2\right] \right\} \qquad \text{(e)}$$

where I_{zz} is given by Eq.(c) and $V_y = -F$.

It must be pointed out that at the corners, where the direction of the cross-section center line is rapidly changing from horizontal to vertical, we have not really evaluated the shear stress. It should be apparent that our simple theory cannot give a good account of shear stress at this region where the geometry is comparatively complex. Unfortunately, large stress concentrations arise at such corners. Such regions must be examined by more powerful theories or by methods of experimental stress analysis. Also, despite the inadequacy of the theory at the corners, we shall still be able to formulate a reasonably accurate value of e (see Fig. 2) for no twisting.

Let us now as a check compute the shear force V_y from the shear stress distribution. Since the forces in the flanges are equal and opposite, we need consider only the web for computing V_y. Thus,

$$V_y = \int_{-[(h/2)-t_1]}^{[(h/2)-t_1]} \frac{V_y}{I_{zz}t_2}\left\{\frac{bt_1}{2}\left(h - t_1\right) + \frac{t_2}{2}\left[\left(\frac{h}{2} - t_1\right)^2 - y^2\right]\right\} t_2 dy \qquad \text{(f)}$$

Integrating and putting in limits, we get

$$V_y = \frac{V_y}{I_{zz}}\left[\left(bt_1\right)\left(h - t_1\right)\left(\frac{h}{2} - t_1\right) + \frac{1}{12}t_2\left(h - 2t_1\right)^3\right] \qquad \text{(g)}$$

The bracketed expression on the right-hand side of Eq. (g) has a value close but not quite equal to I_{zz} , as can be readily seen when we express I_{zz}--see Eq. (c)--in the following way:

$$I_{zz} = bt_1\left(h - t_1\right)\left(\frac{h}{2} - \frac{t_1}{2}\right) + \frac{1}{12}t_2\left(h - t_1\right)^3 + \frac{1}{6}bt_1^3 \qquad \text{(h)}$$

If the right-hand side of the preceding equation were the same as the bracketed quantity on the right-hand side of Eq. (g), we would satisfy Eq. (g). The discrepancy arises in the uncertainty in the upper and lower corners of the channel. In this analysis, they have arbitrarily been included as part of the flanges, but they could just as well have been made part of the web, which would have resulted in a different formulation of shear stress there. If t_1 and t_2 are much smaller than h and b, we can drop t_1 and t_2 when added or subtracted to h or h/2 and we can delete the expression $\frac{1}{6}bt_1^3$ as small compared to the remaining terms in Eqs. (g) and (h). We see that the proper requirement of $V_y = V_y$ in Eq. (g) is then reached.

Given a cantilever beam with a channel cross-section and a force applied as shown. Compute e so that there is bending only (no twisting).

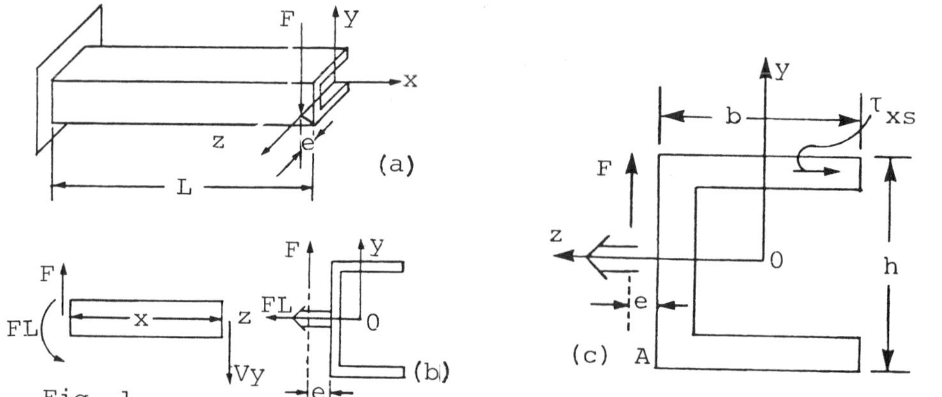

Fig. 1.

Solution: We have drawn the figure for this example in Fig. 1a. Furthermore, in Fig. 1b we have shown a free body exposing a section at x having a normal in the plus x coordinate direction. Finally, in Fig. 1c is shown this section with a shear-stress distribution corresponding to a positive shear force V_y. For the free body shown in Fig. 1b the applied shear loading system is the force F and the couple FL. To determine e, we set the twisting moment of the applied shear-force system about an axis parallel to the x axis and going through point A (see Fig. 1(c)) equal and opposite to the moment about this axis of the shear-stress distribution of the section at position x. For such an axis only the stresses in the upper flange contribute moment, because the other stresses have no moment arm with respect to A. Accordingly, we can say, using the proper directional signs, for the moments that

$$[-(Fe)] = -\left[\int_0^b \left\{[-\left(h - t_1\right)\tau_{xs}\right\} t_1 ds\right] \qquad (a)$$

Note that the couple FL has no moment about the axis at A since it is orthogonal to this axis. Employing

$$\left(\tau_{xs}\right)_{flange} = \frac{V_y s \dfrac{h - t_1}{2}}{I_{zz}}$$

for τ_{xs} we get

$$-[Fe] = \int_0^b t_1 \frac{V_y\left(h - t_1\right)^2}{2I_{zz}} s\, ds$$

$$= \frac{t_1 V_y \left(h - t_1\right)^2}{2I_{zz}} \left. \frac{s^2}{2} \right|_0^b = \frac{t_1 V_y \left(h - t_1\right)^2 b^2}{4I_{zz}} \qquad \text{(b)}$$

Since $V_y = -F$, for e we get

$$e = \frac{t_1\left(h - t_1\right)^2 b^2}{4I_{zz}} \qquad \text{(c)}$$

Since t_1 and t_2 are small compared to b, we shall approximate I_{zz} employing

$$I_{zz} = bt_1\left(h - t_1\right)\left(\frac{h}{2} - \frac{t_1}{2}\right) + \frac{1}{12}t_2\left(h - t_1\right)^3 + \frac{1}{6}bt_1^3$$

for this purpose. We may thus say for $t \ll h$ that

$$I_{zz} \approx \frac{bt_1h^2}{2} + \frac{1}{12}t_2h^3 \qquad \text{(d)}$$

$$\therefore e = \frac{t_1\left(h - t_1\right)^2 b^2}{4} \cdot \frac{12}{6bt_1h^2 + t_2h^3}$$

dropping t_1 in the squared bracket

$$e = \frac{t_1h^2b^2}{1} \times \frac{3}{6bt_1h^2 + t_2h^3} = \frac{t_1b^2}{2bt_1 + \frac{t_2h}{3}} \qquad \text{(e)}$$

• PROBLEM 8-36

Locate the shear center S of the unsymmetrical channel section shown in Fig. 1.

Solution: We begin by noting that the flange widths are b_1 and b_2 for the upper and lower flanges, respectively, and the height of the section is h. The thickness is constant and equal to t. The y and z axes are through the centroid C and are parallel to the web and flanges. The centroid is located by the dimensions c and d.

$$c\left(b_1 + h + b_2\right)t = b_2\frac{t^2}{2} + ht\cdot\frac{h}{2} + b_1t\cdot h$$

Neglecting second order terms of t and solving gives

$$c = \frac{h^2 + 2b_1h}{2\left(h + b_1 + b_2\right)}$$

$$d\left(b_1 + h + b_2\right)t = h\frac{t^2}{2} + b_1 t\cdot\frac{b_1}{2} + b_2 t\cdot\frac{b_2}{2}$$

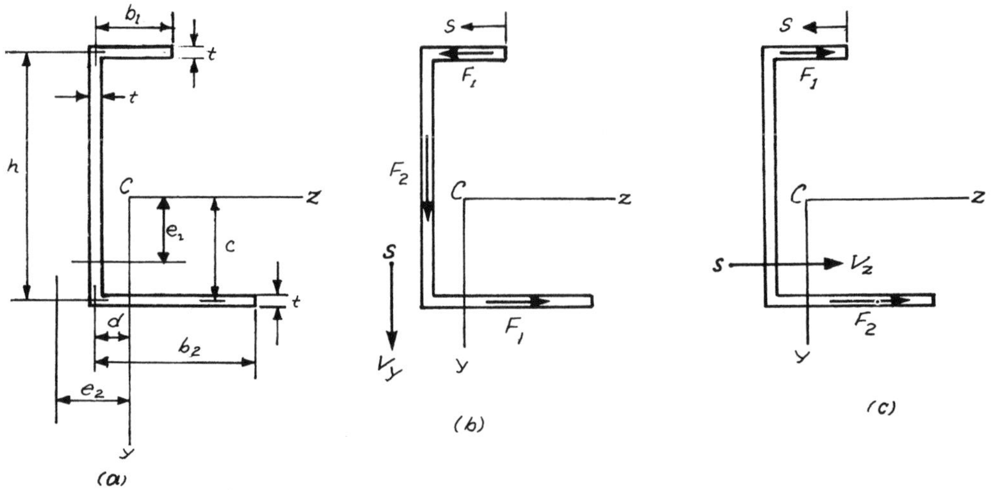

FIG.1 SHEAR CENTER FOR AN UNSYMMETRICAL CHANNEL SECTION

Also neglecting second order terms of t and solving gives

$$d = \frac{b_1^2 + b_2^2}{2\left(h + b_1 + b_2\right)}$$

The shear center S is located by the distances e_1 and e_2 from the centroidal axes, which must be determined next.

Now let us assume that a shear force V_y acts through the shear center (Fig. 1b). The shear stresses in the top flange are

$$\tau = \frac{V_y}{t\left(I_y I_z - I_{yz}^2\right)}\left[I_{yz}\int_0^s \left(b_1 - d - s\right)t\,ds + I_y\int_0^s (h - c)t\,ds\right]$$

$$= \frac{V_y}{I_y I_z - I_{yz}^2}\left[I_{yz}\left(b_1 - d\right)s + I_y(h-c)s - \frac{I_{yz}s^2}{2}\right] \qquad (g)$$

where s is measured as shown in the figure. The total force F_1 in the flange is

$$F_1 = \int_0^{b_1} \tau t\,ds = \frac{b_1^2 t V_y}{6\left(I_y I_z - I_{yz}^2\right)}\left[I_{yz}\left(2b_1 - 3d\right) + 3I_y(h-c)\right] \qquad (h)$$

Because there is no external horizontal force acting on the beam, the shear force in the lower flange must also equal F_1; also, the force F_2 in the web must equal V_y. Because the moment about C of the force V_y acting through the shear center must equal the moment about C of the three forces in the flanges and web, we get

$$V_y e_2 = F_2 d + F_1 h$$

or

$$e_2 = d + \frac{F_1 h}{V_y}$$

Substituting for F_1 from Eq.(h), we obtain the following equation for e_2:

$$e_2 = d + \frac{b_1^2 ht}{6\left(I_y I_z - I_{tz}^2\right)}\left[I_{yz}\left(2b_1 - 3d\right) + 3I_y(h-c)\right] \quad (1)$$

In the special case when the flanges are equal, the y and z axes become principal axes, and we have $I_{yz} = 0$, $c = h/2$, and $b_1 = b_2 = b$; then, from above, we obtain

$$e_2 = d + \frac{b^2 h^2 t}{4I_z}$$

Now let us assume that a shear force V_z acts on the beam (Fig. 1c). In this event we can use

$$\tau = \frac{V_z}{t\left(I_y I_z - I_{yz}^2\right)}\left[I_{yz}\int_0^s (c-h)tds - I_z\int_0^s \left(b_1 - d - s\right)tds\right]$$

to calculate the shear stresses in the top flange.

$$\therefore \tau = \frac{V_z}{I_y I_z - I_{yz}^2}\left[I_{yz}(c-h)s + I_z\left(d-b_1\right)s + \frac{I_z s^2}{2}\right] \quad (i)$$

The total force F_1 in the flange is

$$F_1 = -\int_0^{b_1} \tau tds = \frac{b_1^2 tV_z}{6\left(I_y I_z - I_{yz}^2\right)}\left[3I_{yz}(h-c) + I_z\left(2b_1 - 3d\right)\right] \quad (j)$$

where we have introduced the minus sign in front of the equation because τ is positive to the left in Eq.(i) and we prefer to take F_1 positive to the right, as shown in Fig. 1c. The resultant force in the web must equal zero because there is no external force in the y direction. The force in the lower flange is denoted F_2, as shown in the figure. Taking moments about the lower flange gives the equation

$$V_z\left(c-e_1\right) = F_1 h$$

from which

$$e_1 = c - \frac{F_1 h}{V_z}$$

Substituting for F_1 from Eq.(j), we get the following equation for e_1:

$$e_1 = c - \frac{b_1^2 ht}{6\left(I_y I_z - I_{yz}^2\right)}\left[3I_{yz}(h-c) + I_z\left(2b_1 - 3d\right)\right] \quad (2)$$

Again considering the special case of equal flanges, we have $I_{yz} = 0$, $c = h/2$, $b_1 = b_2 = b$, and $d = b^2/(h+2b)$; whence,

$$e_1 = \frac{h}{2} - \frac{b^3 ht(b+2h)}{6I_y(h+2b)}$$

Now substituting

$$I_y = \frac{b^3 t(b+2h)}{3(h+2b)}$$

which is the moment of inertia for a symmetric channel, we get $e_1 = 0$, as anticipated.

Thus, in any particular case of an unsymmetrical channel, we can substitute the dimensions and properties of the cross section into Eqs.(1) and (2) and thereby obtain the location of the shear center. As a numerical example, let us take the following dimensions:

$$b_1 = b \qquad b_2 = 2b \qquad h = 3b$$

Then we find

$$c = \frac{5b}{4} \qquad d = \frac{5b}{12}$$

$$I_y = \frac{47}{24}b^3 t \qquad I_z = \frac{69}{8}b^3 t \qquad I_{yz} = \frac{13}{8}b^3 t$$

Substituting into Eqs.(1) and (2), we obtain

$$e_1 = \frac{55b}{76} \qquad e_2 = \frac{187b}{228}$$

as the distances from the centroidal axes to the shear center.

• PROBLEM 8-37

Determine the shear stresses in a Z section (Fig. 1a) due to shear forces V_y and V_z.

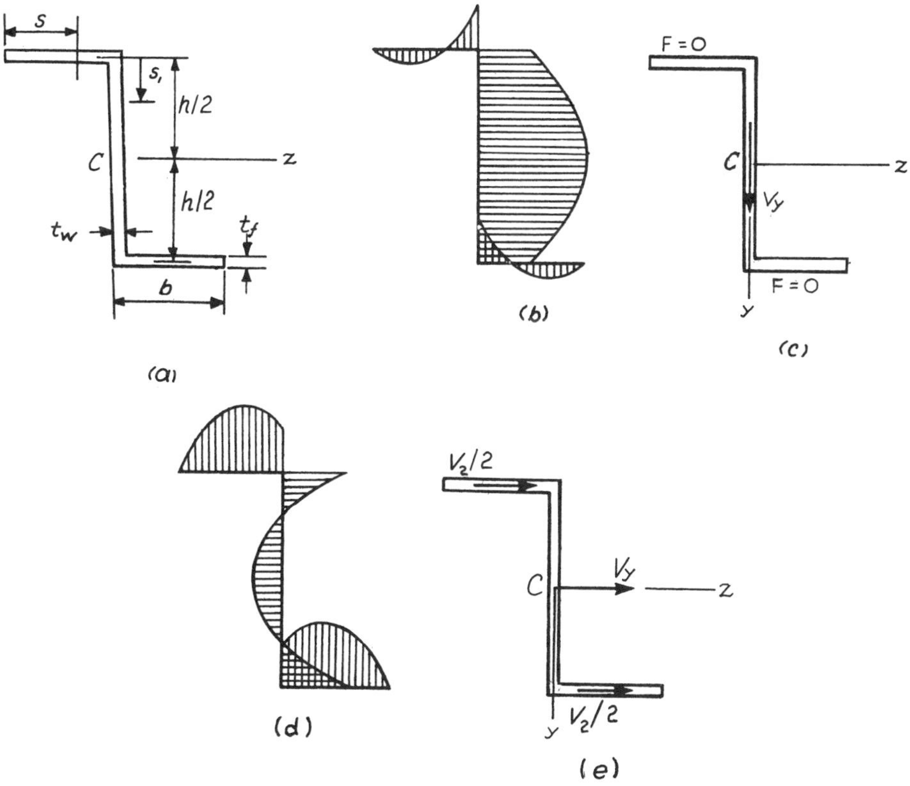

FIG. 1 SHEAR STRESSES IN A Z SECTION

Solution: Begin by calculating the properties of the section as follows:

$$I_z = \frac{h^3 t_w}{12} + \frac{bh^2 t_f}{2} \qquad I_y = \frac{2b^3 t_f}{3} \quad I_{yz} = \frac{b^2 h t_f}{2} \qquad \text{(a)}$$

in which the dimensions h, b, t_w, and t_f are defined as shown in the figure. Because of the shear force V_y, the shear stresses in the upper flange are

$$\tau = \frac{V_y}{t_f\left(I_y I_z - I_{yz}^2\right)}\left[I_{yz}\int_0^s (s-b)\,t_f\,ds + I_y\int_0^s \frac{h}{2} t_f\,ds\right]$$

where s is measured from left to right along the flange. Carrying out the integrations for the terms in the bracket,

$$I_{yz}\int_0^s (s-b)t_f ds + I_y\int_0^s \frac{h}{2}t_f ds$$

$$= I_{yz}\left[\frac{1}{2}s^2 - bs\right]t_f + I_y\frac{h}{2}t_f ds$$

Substituting for I_{yz} and I_y from above we have

$$\frac{b^2ht_f}{2}\left[\frac{1}{2}s^2 - bs\right]t_f + \frac{2b^3t_f}{3} \cdot \frac{ht_f}{2} s$$

$$= b^2ht_f^2\left[\frac{1}{4}s^2 - \frac{bs}{6}\right] = \frac{b^2ht_f^2}{12}\left[3s^2 - 2bs\right]$$

Substituting this expression, in addition to the expressions for I_y , I_z , and I_{yz} , into the equation for τ,

$$\tau = \frac{V_y}{t_f\left[\frac{2b^3t_f}{3}\left(\frac{h^3t_w}{12} + \frac{bh^2t_f}{2}\right) - \left(\frac{b^2ht_f}{2}\right)^2\right]} \cdot \frac{b^2ht_f^2}{12}(3s^2 - 2bs)$$

$$= \frac{V_y}{t_f\left[\frac{h^3b^3t_ft_w}{18} + \frac{b^4h^2t_f^2}{3} - \frac{b^4h^2t_f^2}{4}\right]} \cdot \frac{b^2ht_f^2}{12}(3s^2 - 2bs)$$

$$= \frac{2 \times s4\ V_y}{t_f^2b^3h^2\left(6ht_w + 9bt_f\right)} \cdot \frac{b^2ht_f^2}{12}(3s^2 - 2bs)$$

$$\therefore \tau = \frac{3V_y(3s^2-2bs)}{bh(2ht_w-3bt_f)} \qquad 0 \le s \le b \qquad \text{(b)}$$

This is the formula for the stresses in the flange.

These shear stresses in the upper flange act toward the left when s is less than 2b/3; then they reverse in direction and act toward the right when s is between 2b/3 and b. The total resultant shear force in the flange is

$$F = \int_0^b \tau t_f ds = 0$$

An analogous condition exists in the lower flange.

The shear stresses in the web can also be found from

$$\tau = \frac{V_y}{t_f\left(I_y I_z - I_{yz}^2\right)}\left[I_{yz}\int_0^s (s-b)t_f ds + I_y\int_0^s \frac{h}{2}t_f ds\right]$$

and it can be shown that the total resultant force in the web is equal to V_y. At the neutral axis, the stress is

$$\tau_{max} = \frac{3V_y(ht_w+bt_f)}{ht_w(2ht_w+3bt_f)} \qquad \text{(c)}$$

The distribution of the shear stresses due to V_y is shown in Fig. 1b, and the resultant forces in the flanges and web are shown in Fig. 1c.

Now let us consider a horizontal shear force V_z acting on the cross section. For the upper flange, we make use of

$$\tau = \frac{V_z}{t_f\left(I_y I_z - I_{yz}^2\right)}\left[-I_{yz}\int_0^s \frac{h}{2}t_f ds + I_z\int_0^s (b-s)t_f ds\right]$$

Evaluating the term in brackets, we get

$$I_z[bs - \frac{s^2}{2}]t_f - I_{yz}\frac{h}{2}t_f s$$

$$= \left(\frac{h^3 t_w}{12} + \frac{bh^2 t_f}{2}\right)\left(bs - \frac{s^2}{2}\right)t_f - \frac{b^2 h t_f}{2} \cdot \frac{h}{2}t_f s$$

$$= \frac{h^2 t_f}{24}\left[[2hbst_w + 12b^2 st_f - ht_w s^2 - 6bs^2 t_s\right.$$

$$\left. - 6b^2 t_f s\right]$$

$$= \frac{h^2 t_f}{24}\left[bs\left(2ht_w + 6bt_f\right) - s^2\left(ht_w + 6bt_f\right)\right]$$

and then the final expression for τ becomes

$$\tau = \frac{3V_z}{2b^3 t_f\left(2ht_w+3bt_f\right)}\left[bs\left(\left(2ht_w+6bt_f\right)\right.\right.$$

$$\left. - s^2\left(ht_w+6bt_f\right)\right] \qquad \text{(d)}$$

These stresses act toward the right in the upper flange and have the distribution shown in Fig. 1d. The total resultant force F in the flange is

$$F = \int_0^b \tau t_f ds = \frac{V_z}{2}$$

as shown in Fig. 1e.

The shear stresses in the web due to V_z, as found are

$$\tau = \frac{3V_z\left(h^2+6s_1^2-6hs_1\right)}{2bh\left(2ht_w+3bt_f\right)} \qquad \text{(e)}$$

where s_1 is measured from the juncture of the flange and web (Fig. 1a). This shear stress reverses its direction in the middle region of the web (see Fig. 1d), with the result that the total resultant shear force in the web is zero.

• PROBLEM 8-38

A simple beam of wide-flange section supports a uniform load q = 300 lb/ft, as shown in the figure. The dimensions of the cross section are h = 11.5 in., b = 8 in., $t_f = t_w$ = 0.5 in. (a) What is the maximum shear stress on the cross section at section A-A? (b) What is the shear stress (magnitude and direction) at point B in section A-A? Point B is located at a distance a = 1 in. from the edge of the lower flange. Note: Use centerline dimensions of the cross section when making the calculations for moment of inertia I_z and first moments Q_z.

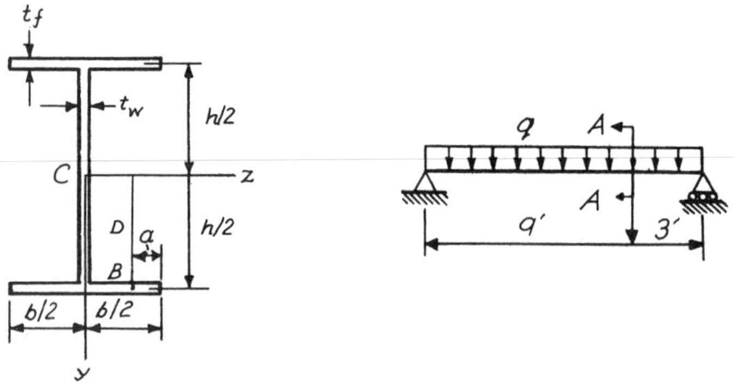

SECTION A-A

FIG.1

Solution: The moment of inertia for the whole cross-section,

$$I = \frac{.5 \times 11.5^3}{12} + 2 \times 8 \times .5\left[\frac{.5^2}{12} + \left(\frac{11.5}{2}\right)^2\right]$$

$$= 328.04 \text{ in.}^4$$

Shear force, V at point A-A is

$$V = \frac{300 \times 12}{2} - 300 \times 3 = 900 \text{ lbs.}$$

Maximum shear stress occurs at the neutral axis. Therefore, at the neutral axis,

$$Q = 8 \times .5 \times 5.75 + .5 \times 5.75 \times \frac{5.75}{2} = 31.26 \text{ in.}^3$$

But shear stress $\tau = \frac{VQ}{It} = \frac{900 \times 31.26}{328.04 \times .5} = 171.5$ psi

At point B in section A-A, the shear stress can be calculated from

$$\tau = \frac{VQ}{It} = \frac{V}{It}(qtD) = 900 \times 1 \times \frac{11.5}{2} \times \frac{1}{328.04}$$

$$= 15.78 \text{ psi}$$

• PROBLEM 8-39

A beam of hollow box section is 1.2 in. deep and 2.4 in. wide overall. The wall thickness is 0.04 in. If the shear force is 500 lb. and the torsional moment is 2000 lb-in. at a certain cross-section, find the shear stress at the mid-points A and B of the vertical portions and also at C which is 0.8 in. from the centre of the top face.

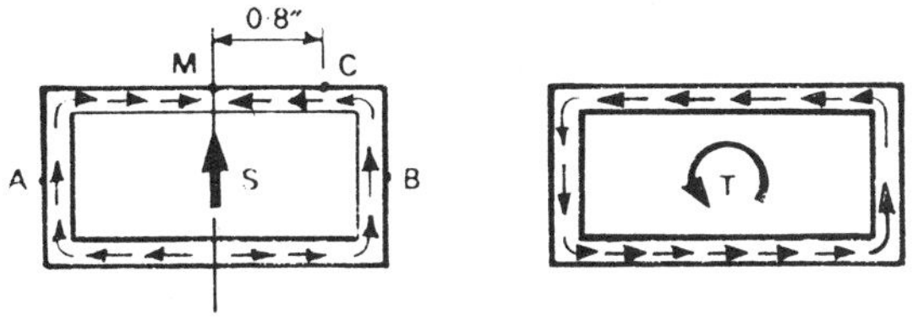

(a) (b)

FIG 1

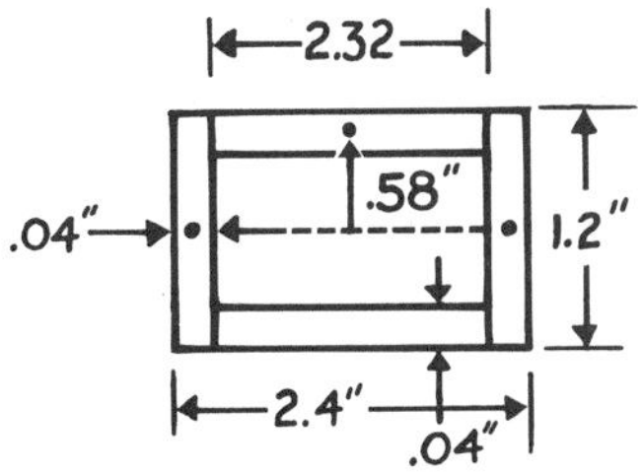

FIG. 2

Solution: The stresses due to shear force and to torsion are distributed as indicated in Figs. 1(a) and 1(b) respectively.

(a) Shear force
To find the shear stresses due to the applied shear force, S, we use the expression

$$\tau = \frac{VQ}{Ib}$$

We are given the shear force, V, which is S = 500 lb. in this case. We must find the moment of inertia, I, for the entire section, and the first moment of area about the points of interest, line AB here.

The beam is divided into two vertical pieces, 1.2" x .04", and two horizontals, (2.4" - 2 x .04") x .04", as shown in Fig. 2. The moment of inertia of the whole section is then:

$$I = 2 \times \frac{bh^3}{12} + 2A\bar{y}^2$$

Substituting in the numbers:

$$I = 2 \times \frac{0.04 \times 1.2^3}{12} + 2(2.4 - 2 \times .04)(.04)\left(\frac{1.2}{2} - \frac{.04}{2}\right)^2$$

$$I = \frac{0.08 \times 1.2^3}{12} + 2(2.32 \times 0.04 \times 0.58^2)$$

$$= 0.0740 \text{ in.}^4$$

Since we want to find the shear stresses at A and B, we calculate the first moment of area, Q, for the beam section above line AB.

$$Q - Ay$$

where y is the distance to the centroid of the area. The area of the web sections can be taken as one web of thickness 2(.04) so we obtain

$$Q = (.6)(.08)(.3) + (2.4-.08)(.04)(.6-.02)$$

$$= 0.0683 \text{ in.}^3$$

Since Q was calculated for the half of the beam above line AB, the web thickness which is resisting shear is equal to the thickness of both webs. Therefore b = .08.

At A and B, the shear stress is

$$\tau_s = \frac{SQ}{Ib} = \frac{500 \times 0.0683}{0.0740 \times 0.08} = 5770 \text{ psi}$$

Since we know the shear force and the moment of inertia, we must find the first moment of area and the thickness for section MC.

We find Q about the center of gravity, which is line AB.

$$Q = Ay = (.8)(.04) \times (.6-.02) = .0186 \text{ in.}^3$$

From the Figure we can see that the shear stress in MC is acting over the thickness of the top piece, so that b = .04.

At C, $\tau_s = \frac{SQ}{Ib} = \frac{500 \times 0.0186}{0.0740 \times 0.04} = 1570$ psi

(b) Torsion

The shear stress due to simple torsion is given by

$$\tau_T = \frac{M_x}{2tA}$$

where A is the area enclosed by the centerline of the section. The area A is,

$$A = (2.4 - 2(.02)) \times (1.2 - 2(.02)) = 2.74 \text{ in.}^2$$

∴ At every section

$$\tau_T = \frac{T}{2A_0 t} = \frac{2000}{2 \times 2.74 \times 0.04} = 9130 \text{ psi}$$

(c) Combined shear stress

By referring to Figs. la and b we see that, at point A, the shear stress due to shear is directed opposite to that due to torsion, while at B and C they are in the same direction so we have

$$\text{At A, } \tau = \tau_T - \tau_s = 9130 - 5770 = 3360 \text{ psi}$$

$$\text{At B, } \tau = \tau_T + \tau_s = 9130 + 5770 = 14,900 \text{ psi}$$

$$\text{At C, } \tau = \tau_T + \tau_s = 9130 + 1570 + 10,700 \text{ psi}$$

• PROBLEM 8-40

Find the maximum shearing stress due to the applied forces in the plane A-B of the 1/2 in. diameter, high-strength shaft in Fig. 1.

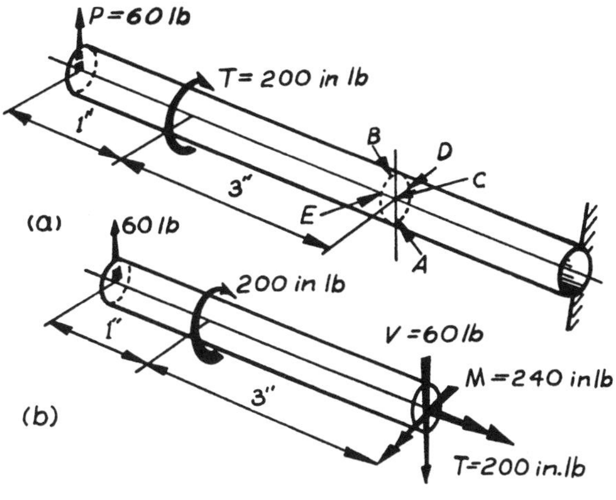

FIG. 1

Solution: The free body of a segment of the shaft is shown in Fig. 1b. The system of forces at the cut necessary to keep this segment in equilibrium consists of a torque $T = 200$ in-lb, a shear $|V| = 60$ lb, and a bending moment $M = 240$ in-lb.

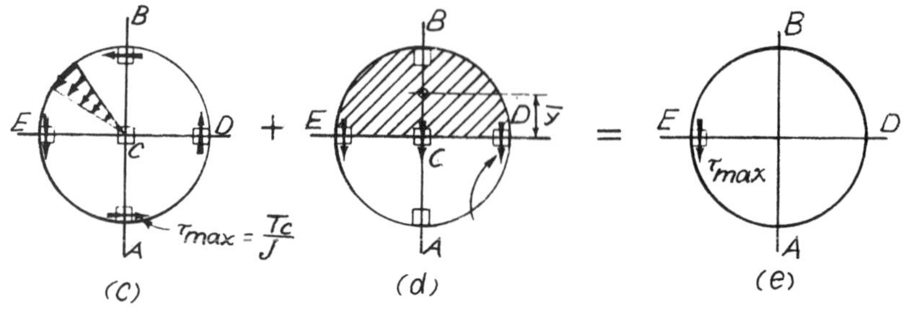

FIG. 1

Because of the torque T, the shearing stresses in the cut A-B vary linearly from the axis of the shaft and reach the maximum value given by $\tau_{max} = Tc/J$. These maximum shearing stresses, agreeing in sense with the resisting torque T, are shown at points A, B, D, and E in Fig. 1c.

The "direct" shearing stresses caused by the shearing force V may be obtained by using $\tau = VQ/(It)$. For the elements A and B, Fig. 1d, $Q = 0$, hence $\tau = 0$. The shearing stress reaches a maximum value at the level ED. To determine this, consider Q equal to the shaded area in Fig. 1d multiplied by the distance from its centroid to the neutral axis. The latter quantity is $\bar{y} = 4c/(3\pi)$, where c is the radius of the cross-sectional area. Hence $Q = (\pi c^2/2)[4c/(3\pi)] = 2c^3/3$. Moreover, since $t = 2c$, and $I = J/2 = \pi c^4/4$, the maximum direct shearing stress is

$$\tau_{max} = \frac{VQ}{It} = \frac{V}{2c}\,\frac{2c^3}{3}\,\frac{4}{\pi c^4} = \frac{4V}{3\pi c^2} = \frac{4V}{3A}$$

where A is the entire cross-sectional area of the rod. In Fig. 1d this shearing stress is shown acting downward on the elementary areas at E, C, and D. This direction agrees with the direction of the shear V.

To find the maximum compound shearing stress in the plane A-B, the stresses shown in Figs. 1c and 1d are superposed. Inspection shows that the maximum shearing stress is at E since in the two diagrams the shearing stresses at E have the same direction and sense. There are no direct shearing stresses at A and B, and at C there is no torsional shearing stress. The two shearing stresses have an opposite sense at D. The five points A, B, C, D, and E thus considered for the compound shearing stress are all that may be adequately treated by the methods developed in this text. However, this procedure selects the elements where the maximum shearing stresses occur.

$$J = \frac{\pi d^4}{32} = \frac{\pi(0.5)^4}{32} = 0.00614 \text{ in.}^4$$

and

$$I = \frac{J}{2} = 0.00307 \text{ in.}^4$$

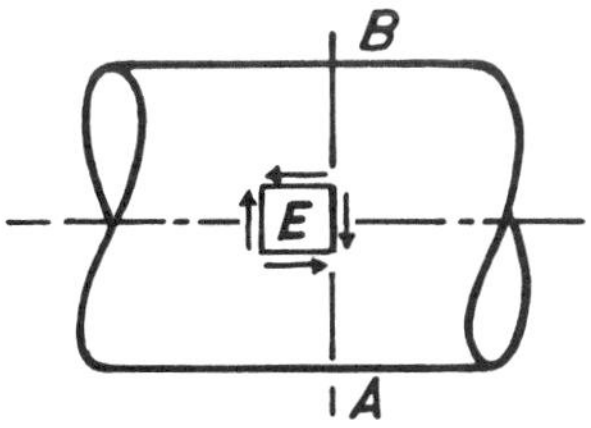

(f)

$$A = \pi d^2/4 = 0.196 \text{ in.}^2$$

$$\left(\tau_{max}\right)_{torsion} = \frac{Tc}{J} = \frac{200(0.25)}{0.00614} = 8{,}150 \text{ psi}$$

$$\left(\tau_{max}\right)_{direct} = \frac{VQ}{It} = \frac{4V}{3A} = \frac{4(60)}{3(0.196)} = 408 \text{ psi}$$

$$\tau_E = 8{,}150 + 408 = 8{,}560 \text{ psi}$$

A planar representation of the shearing stress at E with the matching stresses on the longitudinal planes is shown in Fig. 1f. No normal stress acts on this element as it is located on the neutral axis.

• PROBLEM 8-41

A beam of homogeneous material has a rectangular section 12 in x 20 in with the longer side vertical. At a section where the twisting moment is 60,000 lb-ft and the shear force (vertical) is 80,000 lb, find the shear stress at the mid-point of each face.

Solution: Consider first the stresses arising due to the shear force. At the top and bottom faces the stress is zero.

For the whole section,

$$I = \frac{bd^3}{12} = 8000 \text{ in.}^4$$

At the mid-height,

$$Q = \left(\frac{bd}{2}\right)\frac{d}{4} = 600 \text{ in.}^3$$

so that

$$\tau_s = \frac{SQ}{Ib} = \frac{80{,}000 \times 600}{8000 \times 12} = 500 \text{ psi}$$

Now consider the torsion stresses. With $d/b = 1.67$, we find from a table of Data for the Twist of a Shaft of Rectangular cross-section that $\beta = 0.208$, $\lambda_1 = 0.88$ and $\lambda_2 = 0.44$.

$\therefore$ The torsion constant, $J = 20 \times 12^3 \times 0.208 = 7260 \text{ in.}^4$

At the mid-points of the vertical faces

$$\tau_T = \frac{T(\lambda_1 b)}{J} = \frac{(60{,}000 \times 12)(0.88 \times 12)}{7260} = 1055 \text{ psi}$$

and at the mid-points of the horizontal faces

$$\tau_T = \frac{T(\lambda_2 b)}{J} = \frac{(60{,}000 \times 12)(0.44 \times 12)}{7260} = 520 \text{ psi}$$

Hence the resultant shear stresses are as follows:
At the mid-points of the horizontal faces

$$\tau = \tau_T = 520 \text{ psi}$$

At the mid-points of the vertical faces,

$$\tau = \tau_T \pm \tau_s = 1055 \pm 500 = 1555 \text{ psi or } 555 \text{ psi}$$

NORMAL STRESS AND SHEAR STRESS

• PROBLEM 8-42

The beam of Fig. 1 has a cross-section 12 in x 6 in.
(a) Find the principal stresses at the mid-points of the vertical sides at the quarter point (section D).
(b) Also find the maximum shear stress in the beam.

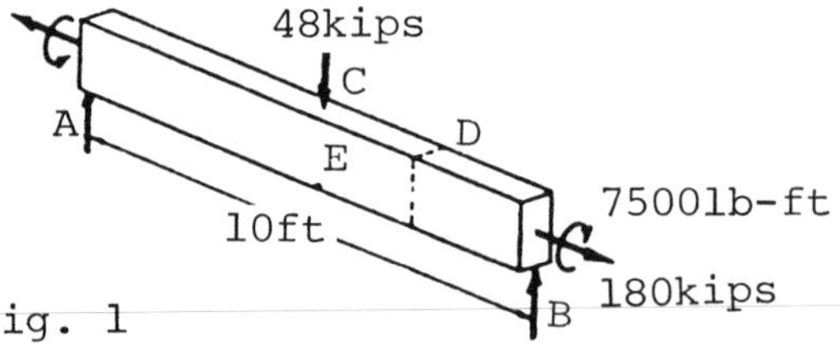

Fig. 1

Solution: (a) Stresses at Section D
(i) Normal stress σ_x

At the mid-height the bending stress is zero. Thus σ_x is due to axial force alone.

$$\sigma_x = \frac{N}{A} = \frac{180{,}000}{72} = 2500 \text{ psi}$$

(ii) Shear stress
At D, S = 24,000 lb. and T = 7500 lb-ft
For a rectangular section, the shear stress at mid-height is $\frac{3}{2}\frac{S}{bd}$. Hence

$$\tau_s = \frac{3}{2} \times \frac{24,000}{72} = 500 \text{ psi}$$

At the same points, due to torsion where λ can be obtained from a table of Data for the Twist of a Shaft of Rectangular cross-section,

$$\tau_T = \frac{T\left(\lambda_1 b\right)}{\beta d b^3} = \frac{\lambda_1}{\beta}\,\frac{T}{db^2} = 4.07\left(\frac{7500 \times 12}{12 \times 6^2}\right) = 845 \text{ psi}$$

On one side

$$\tau = \tau_T - \tau_s = 345 \text{ psi}$$

On the other side

$$\tau = \tau_T + \tau_s = 1345 \text{ psi}$$

(iii) Principal stresses
It is assumed that $\sigma_y = \sigma_z = 0$
On one side,

$$\left.\begin{matrix}\sigma_1\\ \sigma_2\end{matrix}\right\} = \frac{2500}{2} \pm \sqrt{\left(\frac{2500}{2}\right)^2 + 345^2} = \left.\begin{matrix}+2547\\ -\ \ 47\end{matrix}\right\}$$

On the other side,

$$\left.\begin{matrix}\sigma_1\\ \sigma_2\end{matrix}\right\} = \frac{2500}{2} \pm \sqrt{\left(\frac{2500}{2}\right)^2 + 1345^2} = \left.\begin{matrix}+3086\\ -\ 586\end{matrix}\right\}$$

(b) In this beam high values of σ_x do not coincide with high values of τ on the cross-section. The maximum principal shear stress is then likely to be governed by the maximum value of σ_x which in this problem is at the bottom fibre of the central section (E in Fig. 1).

At E, $M = \dfrac{48,000 \times 120}{4} = 1,440,000 \text{ lb-in};$

$$I = \frac{6 \times 12^3}{12} = 864 \text{ in}^4$$

$$\sigma_x = \frac{My}{I} + \frac{N}{A} = \frac{1,440,000 \times 6}{864} + \frac{180,000}{72}$$

$$= 10,000 + 2,500 = 12,500 \text{ psi}$$

At this point,

$$\tau_s = 0 \text{ (bottom of section).}$$

At the mid-point of the lower face,

$$\tau_s = \frac{T(\lambda_2 b)}{\beta d b^3} = 1.62 \left(\frac{7500 \times 12}{12 \times 6^2}\right) = 337 \text{ psi}$$

$$\left.\begin{matrix}\sigma_1\\ \sigma_2\end{matrix}\right\} = \frac{12,500}{2} \pm \sqrt{\left(\frac{12,500}{2}\right)^2 + 337^2} = \left\{\begin{matrix}+12,510\\ -\quad 10\end{matrix}\right\}$$

$$\sigma_3 = 0,$$

being the stress normal to the lower face of the beam (since this is an external surface it is a principal plane).

Hence the maximum shear stress at this point is

$$\tau_3 = \frac{\sigma_1 - \sigma_2}{2} = 6260 \text{ psi}$$

The shear force and torsion are the same at every section of the beam. Hence the maximum shear stress on a cross-section is 1345 psi (calculated in part (a)). So we see that the maximum shear stress in the beam is much greater than any shear stress which occurs on a normal cross-section. This is a matter which must be carefully considered in the case of members made of a material which is liable to shear failure.

• PROBLEM 8-43

For the compound beam loadings shown, find the maximum normal stress and the maximum shear stress.

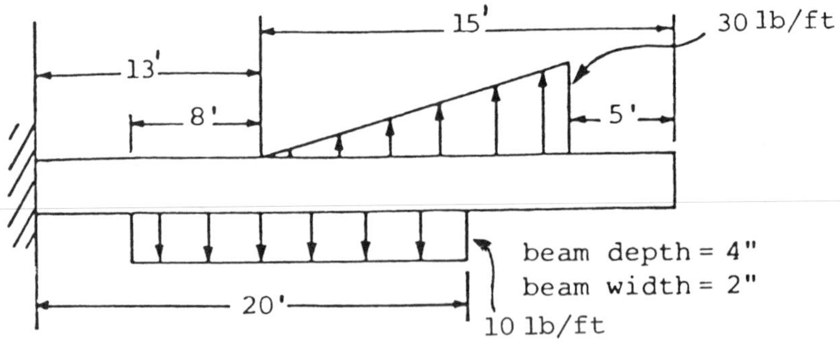

Fig. 1.

Solution: The maximum normal stress σ_{xx} defined as the stress on an x-normal face in the x-direction can be determined from

$$\sigma_{xx} = \frac{M_b \bar{y}}{I_{zz}}$$

where M_b ≡ maximum bending moment

$\bar{y}$ ≡ distance from the neutral axis to the surface of the beam

I_{zz} ≡ moment of inertia about the z axis

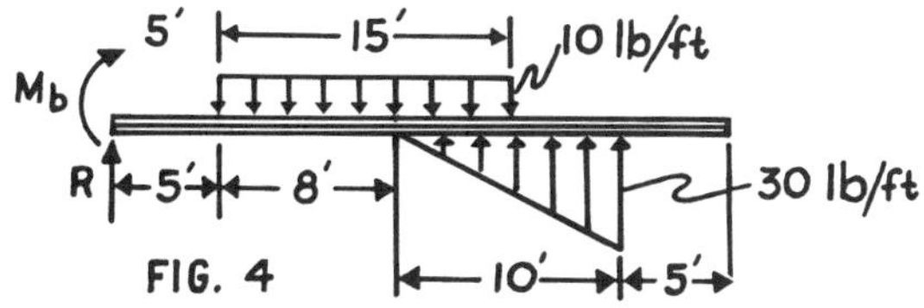

FIG. 4

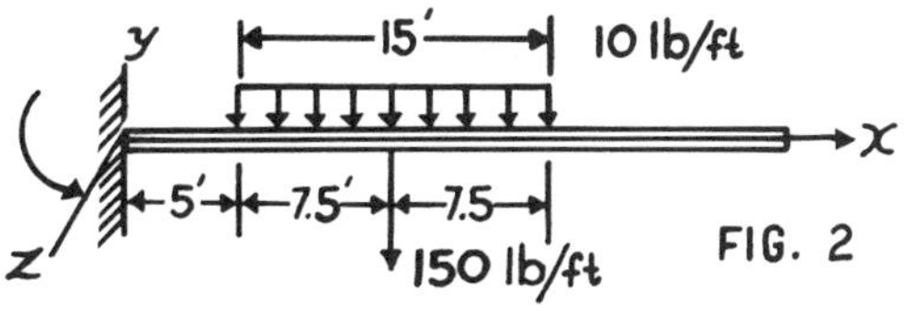

FIG. 2

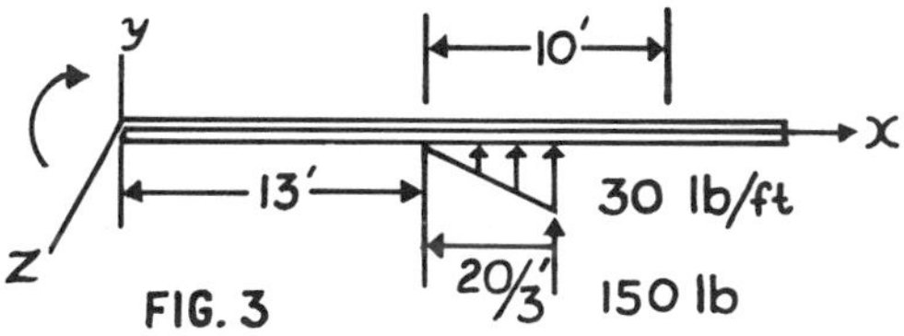

FIG. 3

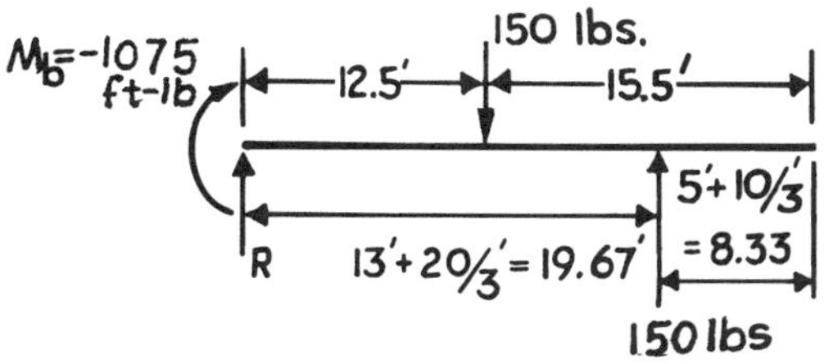

FIG. 5

The maximum moment occurs at the fixed end. Consider the effect of the uniformly distributed downward load as shown in Figure 2. The load diagram of this load is a rectangle, and the magnitude of the resultant of this load is the rectangle's area, or 10 lb/ft x 15 ft = 150 lbs. The resultant acts midway between the ends of the load at the centroid of this rectangle 12.5 ft. from the fixed end as seen in Fig. 2. The moment needed at the fixed end to counteract the moment caused by the uniform load = 150 lbs. x 12.5 ft = 1875 ft-lbs counterclockwise. Next consider the effect of the triangular load distribution as seen in Figure 3. The magnitude of the resultant = 1/2(10' x 30 lb/ft) = 150 lbs. acting upward where the load = 20 lb/ft. (centroid of the triangle) 13' + 20/3' from the fixed end. Moment required at the fixed end = $\left(\frac{39+20'}{3}\right)$(150 lbs.) = 2950 ft-lbs. clockwise. Total moment at fixed end = (2950-1875) ft-lbs clockwise = -1075 ft-lbs using the appropriate sign convention.

$$I = \frac{bd^3}{12} \qquad b = 2" \qquad d = 4"$$

$$= \frac{2 \times 4^3}{12} = 10.667 \text{ in}^4$$

$$\therefore \sigma_{xx} = \frac{1075 \times 12 \times 2}{10.667} = 2418.67 \text{ lb/in}^2 \text{ (psi)}$$

To evaluate maximum shear stress τ_{xy}, first find the maximum value of shear. Fig. 4 shows the beam with all the forces acting. To determine the reaction, R, $\Sigma M = 0$ about the free end, taking counterclockwise as positive. Using values for M_b (moment at the fixed end) and locations and magnitudes of resultants of distributed loads as shown in Figure 5:

$$-1075 - 28R - 150(8.33) + 150(15.5) = 0$$

$$-28R = 1075 + 150(8.33) - 150(15.5)$$

$$-28R = 2325 - 2325 = 0$$

$$R = 0$$

Using duplet functions to define the loading, w(x) we have

$$w(x) = -10\{u(x-5)\} + 10\{u(x-20)\} + 3x\{u(x-13)\}$$

$$- 30\{u(x-23)\} - 3x\{u(x-23)\}$$

but $V = -\int w dx$

The maximum value of shear occurs where

$$\frac{\partial V}{\partial x} = 0 = w$$

$$\therefore 0 = -10+3(x-13)$$

$$x = 10.67 \text{ from right free end}$$

$$\therefore V_{max} = 10 \times 10.67 - \frac{2.67}{10} \times 30 \times \frac{1}{2} \times 2.67$$

$$= 96.1 \text{ lbs}$$

$$\tau_{xy} = \frac{V_{max}}{2I}\left(\bar{y}^2 - y_1^2\right) = \frac{96.1}{2 \times 10.667} \times (4-0)$$

$$= 18.02 \text{ psi}$$

• PROBLEM 8-44

A horizontal beam having the cross section of Fig. 1 is subjected to vertical loads which produce the following maximum values: positive moment, 12,000 ft-lb; negative moment, 10,000 ft-lb; and shear, -2000 lb.
(a) Determine the maximum compressive fiber stress.
(b) Determine the maximum horizontal shearing stress.

(c) Determine the fiber stress at a point 2 in. above the bottom of the beam at a section where the bending moment is +6000 ft-lb.

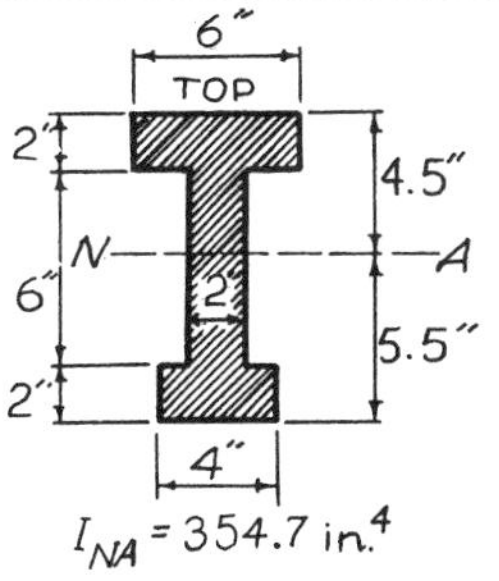

FIG. 1

Solution: Because the beam is subjected to both positive and negative moment, the maximum compressive fiber stress may occur in either the top or bottom flange. When the positive moment is applied the beam is bending downward so the top flange will be in compression.

$$f = \frac{My}{I}$$

Using the positive moment M = 12K ft-lb, the extreme fiber, y = 4.5", and the I given we obtain

$$f = \frac{12(12000)\text{in} - K(4.5)\text{in}}{354.7\ \text{in}^4} = 1826.9 \text{ psi compression}$$

The negative bending moment deflects the beam upward, putting the bottom flange in compression. Therefore,

$$f = \frac{(10K)(12)\text{in} - K(5.5)\text{in}}{354.7\ \text{in}^4} = 1860 \text{ psi compression}$$

which is the maximum.

The maximum horizontal shear stress occurs at the neutral axis of the section, where Q is the greatest.

To use the formula for shear, $\tau = \frac{VQ}{Ib}$, we must find Q, for the neutral axis.

$$Q = 2(6)(4.5-1) + (4.5-2)(2)\left(\frac{4.5-2}{2}\right) = 48.25 \text{ in}^3$$

Substituting the given values for the other terms we have

$$\tau = \frac{2000(48.25)}{(354.7)(2)} = 136 \text{ psi}$$

To find the fiber stress at a point 2 in above the bottom of the section, we must express this point as a distance from the neutral axis.

$$y = 5.5 - 2\text{in} = 3.5 \text{ in}$$

Substituting this value into the expression

$$f = \frac{My}{I}$$

with M and I as given, we get

$$f = \frac{(6000)(12')\text{in} - K(3.5)\text{in}}{354.7\ \text{in}^4} = 710\ \text{psi tension}$$

• PROBLEM 8-45

A 5-ft steel beam with the cross section shown in Fig. 1a is loaded and supported as shown in Fig. 1b. At point A, which is just to the right of the 15,000-lb load and just above the flange, determine and show on a sketch the principal stresses and the maximum shearing stress.

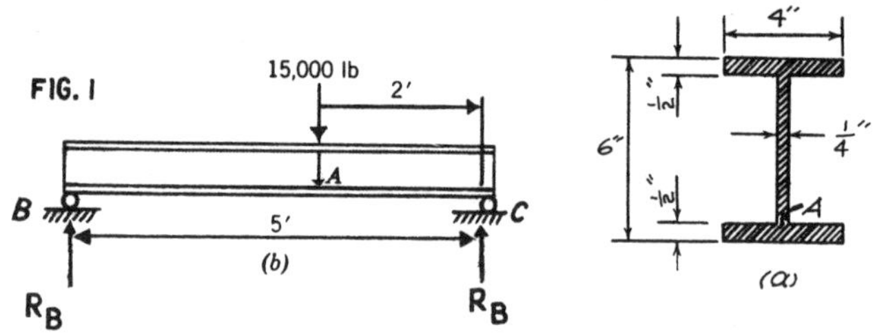

Solution: For the whole section,

$$I = \frac{b_1h_1^3}{12} - \frac{b_2h_2^3}{12} = \frac{4 \times 6^3}{12} - \frac{3.75 \times 5^3}{12} = 32.9375\ \text{in}^4$$

At point B, $\Sigma M = 0$

$$\therefore\ 5R_c = 3 \times 15000$$

$$R_c = 9000\ \text{lb}$$

At point A,

$$M = 9000 \times 2 = 18{,}000\ \text{ft-lb}$$

Recall

$$\sigma_x = \frac{My}{I} = \frac{18{,}000 \times 2.5 \times 12}{32.9375} = 16394.687$$

For an I section,

$$\tau_{xy} = \frac{V}{It}\left[\frac{b}{2}\left(\frac{h^2}{4} - \frac{h_1^2}{4}\right)^2 + \frac{t}{2}\left(\frac{h_1^2}{4} - y_1^2\right)\right]$$

$$= \frac{9000}{32.9375 \times .25}\left[\frac{4}{2}\left(\frac{6^2}{4} - \frac{5^2}{4}\right) + \frac{.25}{2}\left(\frac{5^2}{4} - 2\cdot5^2\right)\right]$$

$$= 6011.385\ \text{psi}$$

The expression for the principal stresses is

$$\sigma_{1,2} = \frac{\sigma_x}{2} \pm \sqrt{\left(\frac{\sigma_x}{2}\right)^2 + \tau_{xy}^2}$$

$$= \frac{16394.687}{2} \pm \sqrt{\left(\frac{16394.687}{2}\right)^2 + 6011.385^2}$$

$$= 8197.344 \pm 10165.293$$

$$\sigma_{1,2} = 18362.637,\ -1967.95$$

The angle between the long axis of the beam and the axis of principal normal stress is:

$$\tan 2\theta = \frac{\tau_{xy}}{\left(\sigma_x - \sigma_y\right)/2}$$

$$\tan 2\theta = \frac{6011.385}{(16394.687-0)/2}$$

$$\tan 2\theta = .7333$$

$$\theta = 18.1°$$

$$\tau_{max} = \frac{\sigma_1 - \sigma_2}{2} = 10,165.3 \text{ psi}$$

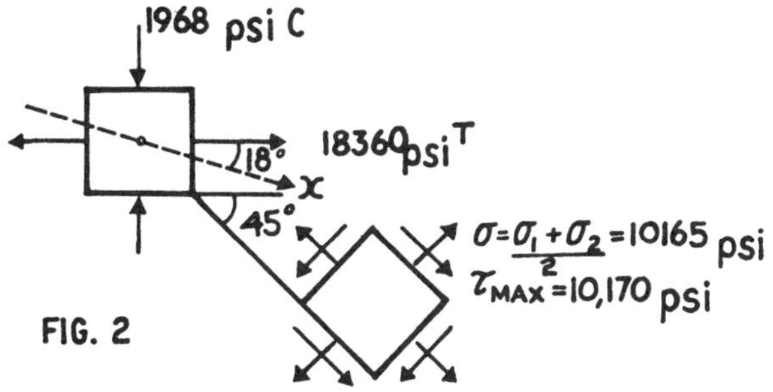

FIG. 2

The normal stress on the plane of maximum shear (θ=45°) is

$$\sigma = \frac{\sigma_1 - \sigma_2}{2} + \frac{\sigma_1 + \sigma_2}{2} \cos 2\theta + \tau \sin 2\theta$$

$$\sigma = \frac{(18362.6) - (-1967.95)}{2} + 0 + 0$$

$$\sigma = 10165 \text{ psi}$$

• PROBLEM 8-46

A 24 WF 100 cantilever beam, supported at the left end, carries a uniformly distributed load of 11.60 kips per ft on a span of 8.00 ft. Determine the maximum normal and shearing stresses in the beam.

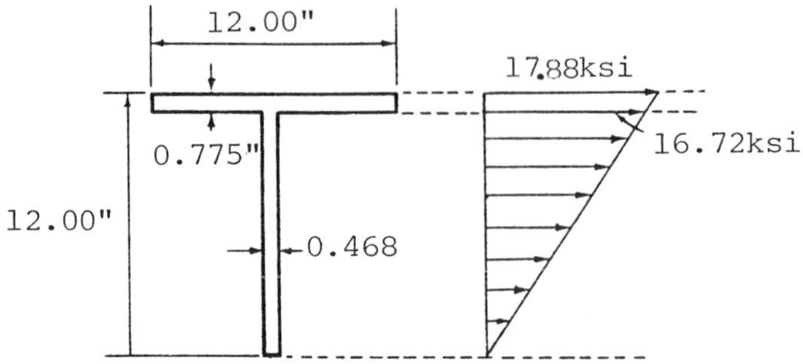

Fig. 1. (a) (b)

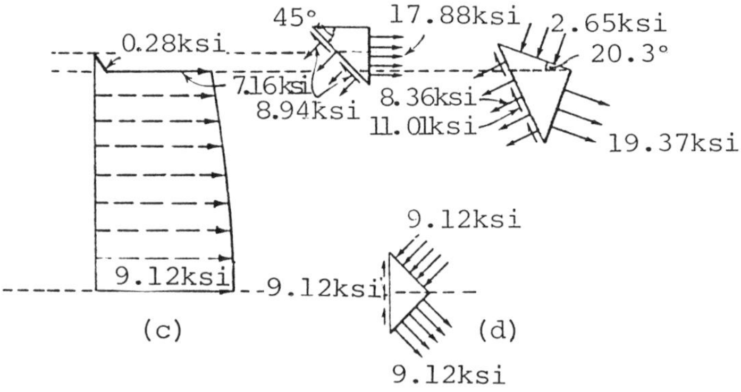

Fig. 1. (c) (d)

Solution: For a cantilever beam with a uniformly distributed load, both the maximum bending moment and the maximum transverse shear occur on the section at the support. In this case they are

$$M = \frac{wL^2}{2} = \frac{(11.6\ \text{kips/ft})(8\text{ft})^2(12\text{in/ft})}{2} = 4454\ \text{in-kips}$$

and $V = wL = (11.6)(8) = 92.8$ kips.

The upper half of the cross section of the beam at the wall is shown in Fig. 1a. The distribution of fiber stress for this half of the section is shown in Fig. 1b, and the distribution of the average transverse shearing stress is as shown in Fig. 1c. The vertical stresses, σ_y, due to the pressure of the load on the top of the beam are considered negligible.

Values will be calculated for three points, namely, at the neutral axis, in the web at the junction of the web and the top flange, and at the top surface. Both the fillets and the stress concentrations at the junction of the web and flange will be neglected. At the neutral axis, the fiber stress is zero, and the transverse shearing stress is

$$\tau = \frac{VQ}{It}$$

where V is the shear force

$$V = (11.6 \text{ kips/ft})(8\text{ft}) = 92.8 \text{ kips}$$

Q is the first moment of the region of the cross section beyond the line at which the shear stress is being determined, that is,

$$Q = \int_h^c ty\,dy$$

$$Q = \Sigma Ay$$

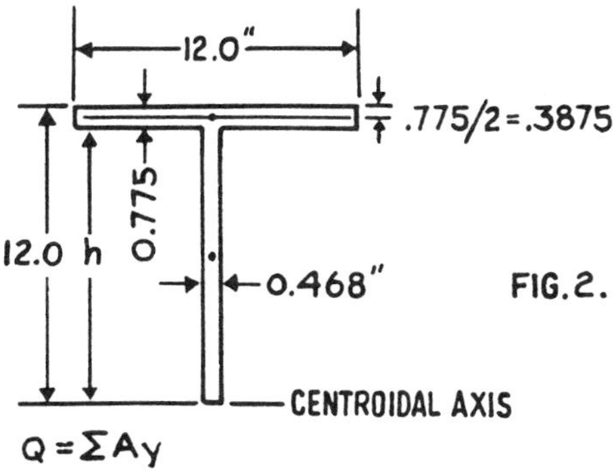

FIG. 2.

The shear stress is being determined at the neutral axis therefore Q is the first moment of the region beyond the axis. This region which is half the wide flange I beam, is "T" shaped. The T will be divided into two areas and the moment of each calculated. The cross bar has an area of 12" x .775". The centroid is at half the thickness or .775/2 = .3875. The distance from the centroid of the whole beam to the top edge is 12". The distance from centroid to centroid is then 12 - .3875 = 11.61". The area of the stem of the T is h x .468. The centroid of the stem is at a distance of 1/2h from the centroid of the whole beam. The height of the stem, h, is 12 - .775 = 11.225". One-half h is then 11.225/2 = 5.61".

Q is then 12 x .775 (11.61) + 11.225 x .468 (5.61). I is the moment of inertia which can be found in a beam table or calculated and t is the thickness.

Substituting into the equation yields:

$$\tau = \frac{VQ}{It} = \frac{92.8[12(0.775)(11.61) + 11.225(0.468)(5.61)]}{2987(0.468)}$$

$$= 9.12 \text{ ksi.}$$

In the web at the junction with the top flange, the fiber stress is

$$\sigma = \frac{My}{I} = \frac{4454(11.225)}{2987} = 16.72 \text{ ksi T,}$$

and the transverse shearing stress is

$$\tau = \frac{VQ}{It} = \frac{92.8(12)(0.775)(11.61)}{2987(0.468)} = 7.16 \text{ ksi.}$$

At the junction of the web and the top flange the only region beyond is the top flange which is the cross bar of the T. Q for the cross bar is already known.

At the top surface, the transverse shearing stress is zero, and the fiber stress is

$$\sigma = \frac{My}{I} = \frac{M}{Z} = \frac{4454}{248.9} = 17.88 \text{ ksi T.}$$

The principal stresses and maximum shearing stresses for each of the three selected points are shown in Fig. 1d.

The other stresses of Fig. 1d are obtained by inspection. It should be noted that the maximum tensile stress of 19.37 ksi is 8.32 percent above the maximum tensile fiber stress of 17.88 ksi and that the maximum shearing stress of 11.01 ksi is 20.7 percent above the maximum transverse shearing stress of 9.12 ksi.

• PROBLEM 8-47

A hollow rectangular timber beam with the cross section in Fig. 1a is loaded as shown in Fig. 1b. Determine the principal and maximum shearing stresses at point A.

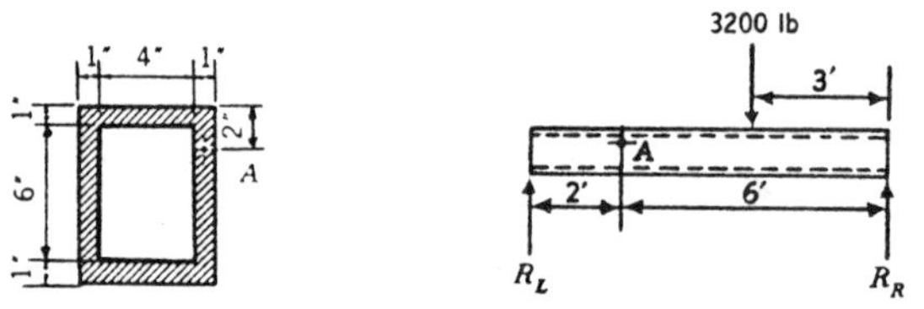

(a)

(b)

FIG. 1

Solution: From equilibrium consideration, $\Sigma M = 0$ about the right support

$$\therefore \; 8R_L = 3 \times 3200$$

$$R_L = 1200$$

$\therefore$ Moment at A, M_A = 1200lb x 2 ft x 12 in/ft = 28,800 in-lb

The moment of inertia of the cross section,

$$I = \frac{b_1h_1^3}{12} - \frac{b_2h_2^3}{12} = \frac{6 \times 8^3}{12} - \frac{4 \times 6^3}{12} = 184 \text{ in}^4$$

but stress, $\sigma = \frac{My}{I}$

Point A is 2" above the neutral axis.

$\therefore$ Stress at point A, $\sigma = \dfrac{28,880 \times 2}{184} = 313\ \text{lb/in}^2$

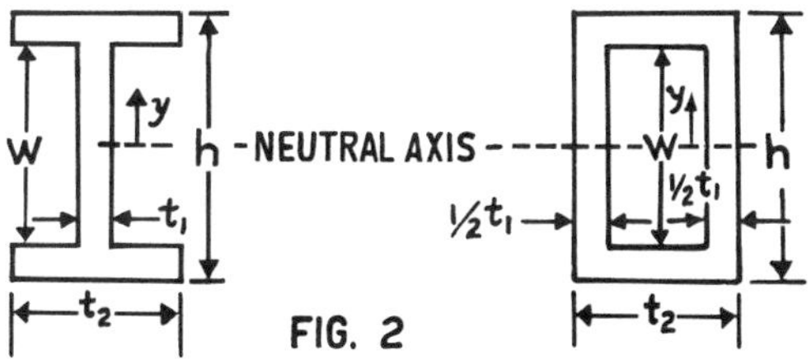

FIG. 2

Also at point A, shear force, V = 1200 lbs. The formula for the shear stress for I beams and tubular rectangular beams is as follows:

$$\tau = \frac{V}{It}\left[\frac{t_2}{2}\left(\frac{h^2}{4} - \frac{w^2}{4}\right) + \frac{t_1}{2}\left(\frac{w^2}{4} - y^2\right)\right]$$

where y is the distance from the neutral axis at which it is desired to find the shear stress.

$$\therefore \text{ Shear Stress, } \tau = \frac{1200}{184 \text{x} 2}\left[\frac{6}{2}\left(\frac{8^2}{4} - \frac{6^2}{4}\right) + \frac{2}{2}\left(\frac{6^2}{4} - 2^2\right)\right]$$

$$= 84.78$$

$$\text{Principal stresses, } \sigma_{1,2} = -\frac{\sigma_x}{2} \pm \sqrt{\left(\frac{\sigma_x}{2}\right)^2 + \tau_{xy}^2}$$

$$= -156.5 \pm \sqrt{(156.5)^2 + 84.78^2}$$

$$= -344.5 \text{ psi, } 21.5 \text{ psi}$$

$$\text{maximum shearing stress at point A} = \frac{21.5 - (-344.5)}{2}$$

$$= 183 \text{ psi.}$$

• PROBLEM 8-48

A round bar 2 in diameter and 6 in long is cantilevered from one end (Fig. 1). Attached to the free end is a bracket which supports a load of 1500 lb at 4 in from the axis of the bar.

Find the principal stresses and the principal shear stresses at the points A, B, C and D of the section close to the support.

Solution: D = 2in; I = 0.785 in^4; J = 1.57 in^4

(a) Normal stress σ_x

The axial force is zero, and σ_x arises due to bending alone.

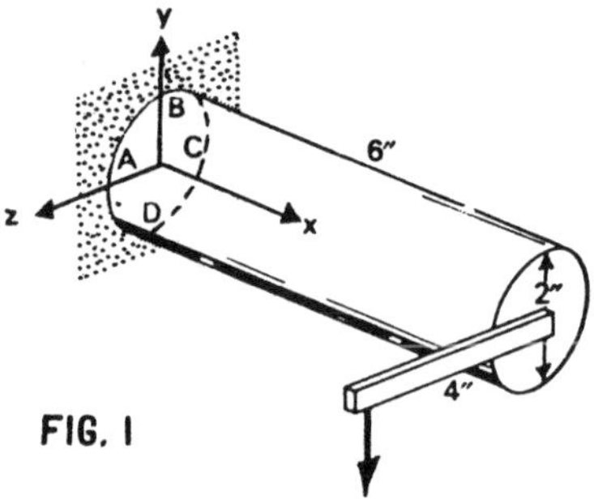

FIG. 1

At A and C, $\sigma_x = 0$

At B and D, $\sigma_x = \frac{My}{I} = \frac{(1500 \times 6) \times 1}{0.785} = 11{,}450$ psi

(+ at B, - at D)

This is because y = 1 at B and y = -1 at D.

(b) Shear stress

At A, B, C and D, $\tau_T = \frac{Tr}{J} = \frac{(1500 \times 4) \times 1}{1.57} = 3820$ psi

At B and D, $\tau_s = 0$

At A and C, $\tau_s = \frac{SQ}{ID} = \frac{1500}{0.785}\frac{0.67}{2} = 636$ psi

(for a semicircle, Q about the diameter = $2r^3/3$).

The resultant shear stresses on the cross-section are:

At A, $\tau = \tau_T + \tau_s = 3820 + 636 = 4456$ psi

At B, $\tau = \tau_T$ = 3820 psi

At C, $\tau = \tau_T - \tau_s = 3820 - 636 = 3184$ psi

At D, $\tau = \tau_T$ = 3820 psi

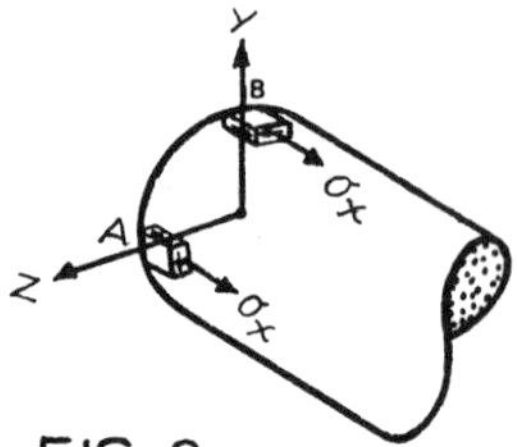

FIG. 2

(c) Principal stresses
At each of the points A, B, C and D we consider the equilibrium of a small element of material with its faces normal to the x, y and z directions. The elements at A

and B are indicated in Fig. 2. The elements are shown as free-bodies in Fig. 3(a),(b),(c) and (d).

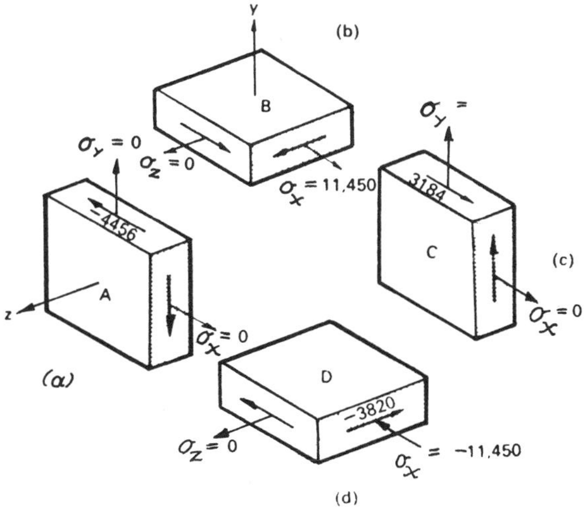

FIG. 3

For each element, the face which lies in the surface of the bar is free of shear. Hence it is a principal plane. This plane also happens to be free of normal stress. The other two principal stresses lie in planes perpendicular to the bar surface. Since the transverse normal stress is zero in each case, the principal stress will be given by

$$\left.\begin{matrix}\sigma_1\\ \sigma_2\end{matrix}\right\} = \frac{\sigma_x}{2} \pm \sqrt{\left(\frac{\sigma_x}{2}\right)^2 + \tau^2}$$

and the principal shear stress $\tau_3 = \dfrac{\sigma_1 - \sigma_2}{2}$

Hence using these formulas and the values of σ_x and τ as shown in Fig. 3 we have

At A, $\sigma_1 = +4456$; $\sigma_2 = -4456$; $\tau_3 = 4456$

At B, $\sigma_1 = +12,600$; $\sigma_2 = -1160$; $\tau_3 = 6882$

At C, $\sigma_1 = +3184$; $\sigma_2 = -3184$; $\tau_3 = 3184$

At D, $\sigma_1 = -12,600$; $\sigma_2 = +1160$; $\tau_3 = 6882$

It can be noted that the maximum tensile and compressive stresses in this bar are each 12,600 psi. The maximum shear stress is 6882 psi.

SHEAR FORCE AND BENDING MOMENT

• PROBLEM 8-49

A rectangular beam is carried on simple supports and subjected to a central load, as illustrated in Fig. 1. Find the ratio of the maximum shear stress $\left(\tau_{xy}\right)_{max}$ to the maximum bending stress $\left(\sigma_x\right)_{max}$.

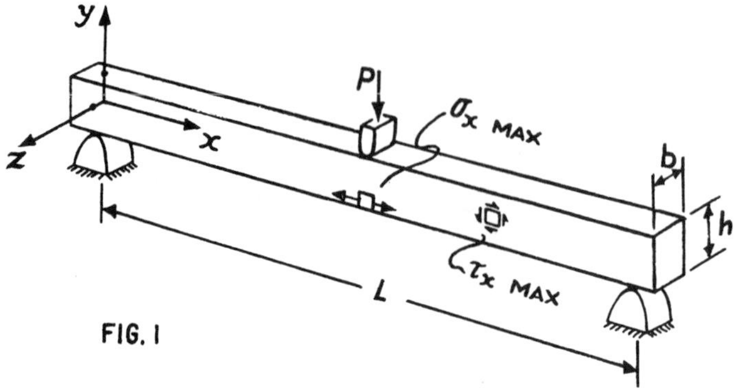

FIG. 1

Solution: The maximum bending stress occurs at mid-span where the bending moment has its maximum value of

$$\frac{P}{2}\left(\frac{L}{2}\right) = M_b \quad \text{or}$$

$$M_b = \frac{PL}{4} \qquad \text{(a)}$$

knowing that the reactions are equal due to the symmetry.

$$R_L = R_R = \frac{P}{2}$$

The bending stresses are of equal magnitude on the top and the bottom of the beam (compression on the top and tension on the bottom).

Second moment of area or moment of inertia about the z-axis is

$$I_{zz} = \frac{bh^3}{12} \qquad \text{(b)}$$

The bending stress at the bottom (y = -h/2) is

$$\left(\sigma_x\right)_{max} = \frac{\left(M_b\right)_{max} C}{I_{zz}}$$

or $$\left(\sigma_x\right)_{max} = \frac{\left(M_b\right)_{max}}{S}$$

where S (section modulus) $= \frac{I}{C}$

$$\left(\sigma_x\right)_{max} = \frac{-(PL/4)(-h/2)}{bh^3/12} \qquad \text{(c)}$$

$$\frac{+PLh/8}{bh^3/12} = \frac{12PLh}{8bh^3} = \frac{3}{2}\frac{PL}{bh^2}$$

The shear force has the constant magnitude P/2 between the load and each support. The shear stress is a maximum at the neutral surface, i.e. at the mid-height of the beam, as illustrated in Fig. 1. Substituting $y_1 = 0$ in

$$\tau_{xy} = \frac{V}{2I_{yy}}\left[y^2 - y_1^2\right]$$

or

$$\left(\tau_{xy}\right)_{max} = \frac{V_{max}}{2I_{yy}}\left[c^2 - y_1^2\right]$$

$$\left(\tau_{xy}\right)_{max} = \frac{P/2}{2(bh^3/12)}\left[\left(\frac{h}{2}\right)^2 - 0^2\right]$$

$$= \frac{3}{2}\frac{P/2}{bh} = \frac{3}{4}\frac{P}{bh} \qquad \text{(d)}$$

We note that (d) states that the maximum shear stress in a rectangular beam is one and one-half times the average shear stress.

Combining (c) and (d), we get the ratio of the maximum shear stress to the maximum bending stress in the beam.

$$\frac{\left(\tau_{xy}\right)_{max}}{\left(\sigma_x\right)_{max}} = \frac{1}{2}\frac{h}{L} \qquad \text{(e)}$$

Thus the bending and shear stresses are of comparable magnitude only when L and h are of the same magnitude. Since L is much greater than h in most beams (say, $L > 10h$), it may be seen from (e) that the shear stresses τ_{xy} will usually be an order of magnitude smaller than the bending stresses σ_x.

If a different loading is put on the beam in Fig. 1, the ratio of the maximum stresses will again be found to depend upon the ratio of the depth to the length of the beam, although, of course, the factor of proportionality will differ from that just found. If beams of other cross-sectional shape are investigated, similar results are obtained. The factor of proportionality does, however, depend importantly on the shape of the section; e.g., the factor of 1/2 in (e) can be as large as 3 or 4 for I beams with thin webs.

• PROBLEM 8-50

The beam of Fig. 1 is composed of 3 pieces of timber glued together as shown. The maximum horizontal shearing stresses are not to exceed 100 psi and 120 psi in the glue joint and the wood respectively. The tensile and compressive fiber stresses are not to exceed 1800 psi anywhere in the beam. What is the maximum permissible value of P?

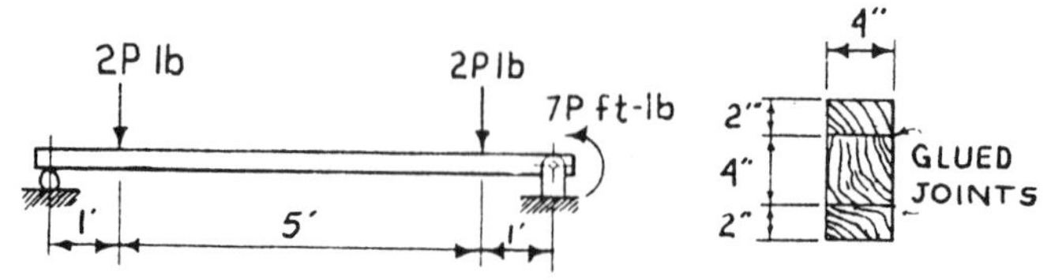

FIG. 1

Solution: There are three limitations applied to this beam, all of which must be satisfied by the choice of the load parameter, P. To insure that these restrictions are not exceeded we must check the shear stress limitations in the section of the beam that has the maximum shear force and the bending stress limitations where the bending moment is maximum. We must also check the stresses at these points in the beam at the position in the section which gives the maximum stress for a given loading.

To begin we calculate the shear and moment in terms of P. By taking sum of moments about A we find the reaction at B.

$$\Sigma M_A = 0 = -2P(12") - 2P(72") + 7P(12) + 7(12)R_B$$

$$R_B = P$$

By vertical equilibrium we find R_A

$$R_A + R_B - 2P - 2P = 0$$

$$R_A = 3P$$

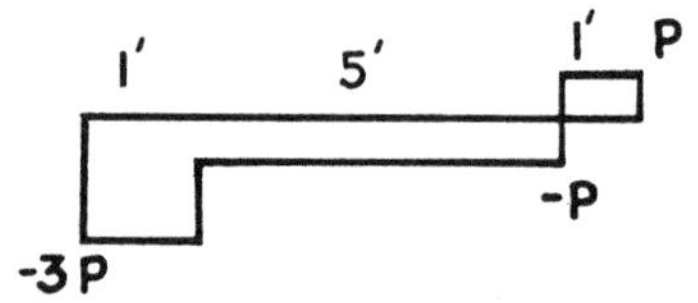

We now draw the shear diagram for the beam. The value of the moment at a section is equal to the area under the shear diagram up to that section, since $\frac{dM}{dx} = -V$

$$\text{or} \qquad M = -\int_x V dx$$

so we can draw the moment diagram by inspection.

The area under shear at x = 1" is

$$A(1) = 3P \times 12\text{in} = 36P$$

At section x = 6"

$$A(6) = 36P + P \times 5(12) = 96P$$

At x = 7"

$$A(7) = 96P - 12 \times P = 84P$$

By connecting these points on a diagram we have

M (in-K)

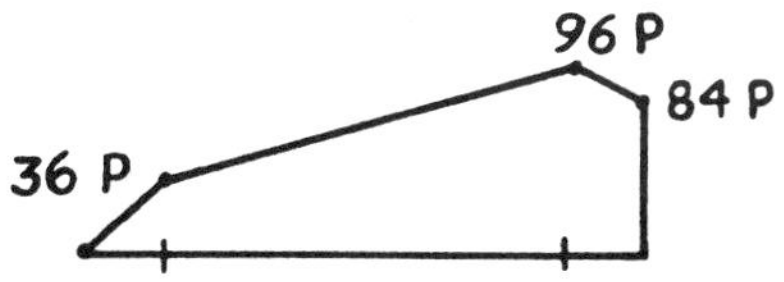

From these diagrams we see that we must check the shear stresses in the section subjected to a shear force of 3P. The bending stresses are checked at x = 6" where M = 96P in-k.

The first restriction is the shear stress in the glue joint, which must be less than 100 psi. Using the formula

$$\tau = \frac{VQ}{Ib}$$

we must find Q, I, and b.

The moment of inertia for a rectangular section is

$$I = \frac{bh^3}{12}$$

so $$I = \frac{4(8)^3}{12} = 170.66 \text{ in}^4$$

The first moment of area for the section above the glue joint is

$$Q = Ay = (2)(4) \times (3) = 24 \text{ in}^3$$

The thickness in this case is the width of the section.

$$b = 4"$$

Substituting these values we get

$$\tau_{max} = \frac{3P(24)}{(170.66)(4)}$$

$$100 = .1055P$$

so $P < 948$ lb to satisfy the limitation on the glue joint.

The maximum shear stress in a section occurs at the neutral axis so we must check the maximum wood shear stress there. We still check at the section with shear force 3P. The only thing that has changed is the position in the section so we only recalculate Q.

$$Q = 4(4)(2) = 32 \text{ in}^3$$

Therefore $\tau_{max} = 120 \text{ psi} > \frac{(3P)(32)}{(170.66)(4)}$

$$P < 853.3 \text{ lb}$$

to satisfy the wood shear stress restriction.

The maximum bending stresses occur at the extreme fibers of the section. Since the neutral axis is at the center of the beam, the distances to the extreme fibers are equal. Therefore $y_T = y_C$

$$\tau_T = \frac{My_T}{I} = \frac{My_C}{I} = \tau_C$$

so the tensile and compressive stresses will be of the same magnitude.

At the section at x = 6'

$$M = 96P \text{ in-k}$$

so $\tau_{max} = 1800 \text{ psi} > \frac{(96P)(4")}{170.66}$

$$P = 800 \text{ lb}$$

Since 800 lb is the smallest permissible value of all the limitations, the bending stress condition controls. P = 800 lb is the maximum permissible

• PROBLEM 8-51

A simple beam carrying two concentrated loads P (Fig. 1) has a rectangular cross section of width b = 4 in. and height h = 6 in. The distance a from the end of the beam to one of the loads is 18 in. Determine the allowable value of P if the beam is constructed of wood having σ_w = 1600 psi and τ_w = 200 psi.

FIG. 1

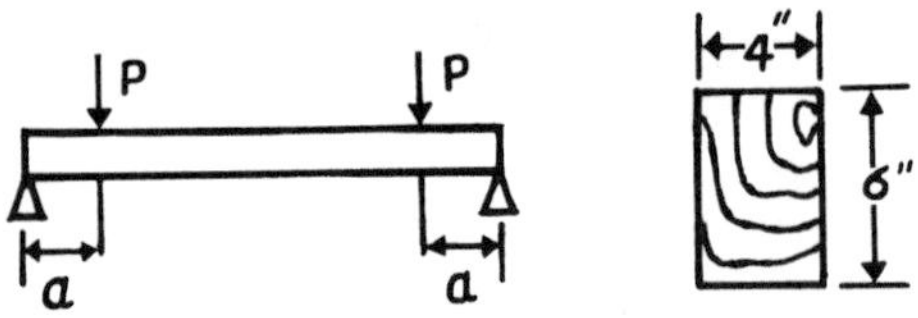

Solution: Because of the symmetry of the loading, both reactions must be equal to P to satisfy equilibrium. The shear diagram is below. Therefore, the maximum shear

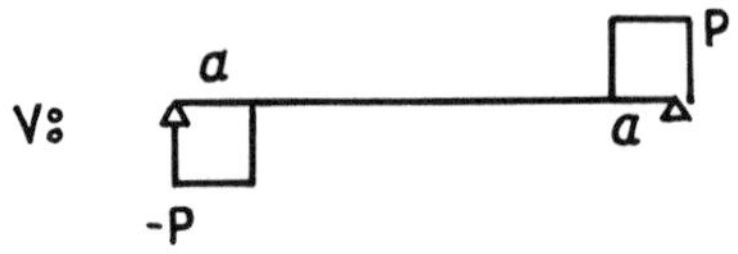

force is P. The moment diagram is found by integrating the shear, sc the maximum moment is Pa.

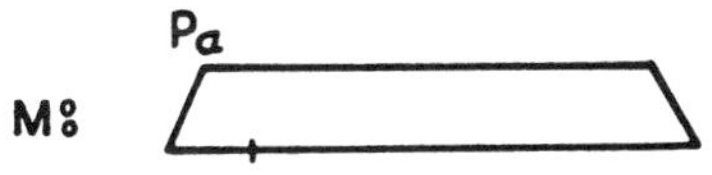

Also, the section modulus S which is equal to $\frac{I}{C}$ (C is the distance to the extreme fiber) and cross-sectional area A are

$$S = \frac{\frac{bh^3}{12}}{\frac{h}{2}} \qquad \text{for a rectangular section}$$

$$= \frac{bh^2}{6}$$

$$A = bh$$

The maximum bending stress is given by $\sigma = \frac{M}{S}$ while the maximum shear stress is located at the neutral axis and is equal to

$$\tau = \frac{VQ}{Ib} = \frac{V\frac{bh^2}{8}}{\frac{bh^3}{12}\,b} = \frac{V}{\frac{2}{3}hb} = \frac{3V}{2A}$$

$$\sigma = \frac{M}{S} = \frac{6Pa}{bh^2} \qquad \tau = \frac{3V}{2A} = \frac{3P}{2bh}$$

By solving these equations for P and using the allowable shear and bending stress values we can obtain the maximum values for P.

$$P = \frac{\sigma_w bh^2}{6a} \qquad \text{and } P = \frac{2\tau_w bh}{3}$$

Substituting numerical values into these formulas, we get

P = 2133 lb and P = 3200 lb

Thus, the bending stress governs the design, and the allowable load is P = 2133 lb.

• PROBLEM 8-52

Select a Douglas Fir beam of rectangular cross section to carry two concentrated forces as shown in Fig. la. The allowable stress in bending is 1,200 psi, in shear 100 psi, and in bearing perpendicular to the grain of the wood 200 psi.

Solution: Shear and moment diagrams for the applied forces are prepared first and are shown, respectively, in Figs.

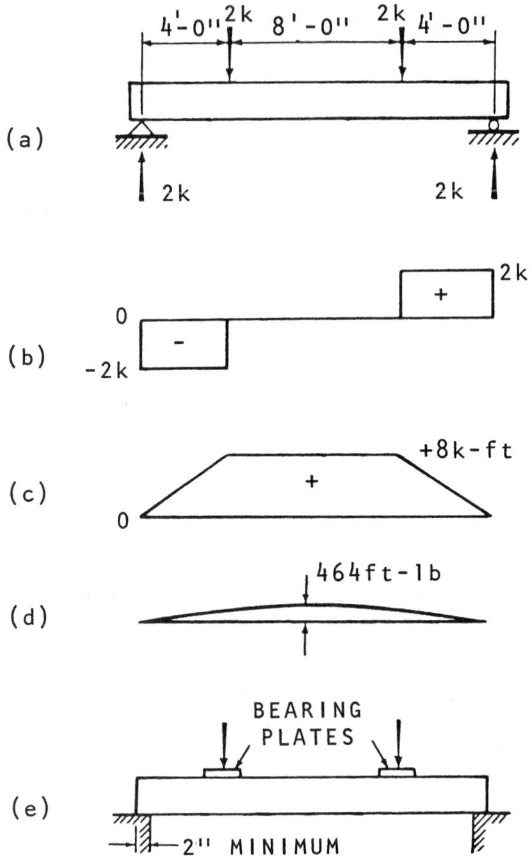

FIG. 1

1(b) and (c). From Fig. 1(c) it is seen that $M_{max} = 8$ kip-ft.

$$\text{Section Modulus, } S = \frac{M}{\sigma_{allowable}} = \frac{bh^2}{6}$$

$$S = \frac{M}{\sigma_{allow}} = \frac{8,000(12)}{1,200} = 80 \text{ in.}^3$$

By arbitrarily assuming that the depth h of the beam is to be two times greater than its width b,

$$S = \frac{bh^2}{6} = \frac{h^3}{12} = 80 \quad \text{hence} \quad h = 9.86 \text{ in. and}$$

$$b = 4.93 \text{ in.}$$

From a handbook of structural shapes and beams it may be found that a surfaced 6-in.-by-10-in. beam is seen to fulfill this requirement. The actual size of this beam is 5-1/2 in. by 9-1/2 in., and its section modulus is S = 82.7 in.^{3} For this beam, from

$$\tau_{max} = \frac{3V}{2A}$$

where $V \equiv$ maximum shear force
$A \equiv$ cross-sectional area

$$\tau_{max} = \frac{3V}{2A} = \frac{3(2,000)}{2(5.5)(9.5)} = 57.3 \text{ psi}$$

This stress is within the allowable limit. Hence the beam is satisfactory. Note that other proportions of the beam can be used; a more direct method of design is to find a beam of size corresponding to that of the wanted section modulus directly from the handbook.

The above analysis was made without regard for the weight of the beam, which initially was unknown. (Experienced designers usually make an allowance for the weight of the beam at the outset.) However, this may be accounted for now. Assuming that wood weighs 40 lb per cubic foot the beam selected weighs 14.5 lb per lineal foot. This uniformly distributed load causes a parabolic bending-moment diagram, shown in Fig. 1d, where the maximum ordinate, i.e. the maximum value of the bending moment, is $P_oL^2/8 = 14.5(16)^2/8 = 464$ ft-lb. This bending-moment diagram should be added to the moment diagram caused by the applied forces. Inspection of these diagrams shows that the maximum bending moment due to both causes is $464 + 8,000 = 8,464$ ft-lb. Hence the required section modulus actually is $S = M/\sigma_{allow} = 8,464(12)/(1,200) = 84.64$ in.^{3} The surfaced 6-in-by-10-in. beam originally selected provides an S of 82.7 in.^{3}, which is about 2-1/2 percent below the required value. Under most circumstances this would be considered satisfactory.

In actual construction, beams are not supported as in Fig. 1a. Wood may be crushed by the supports or the applied concentrated forces. For this reason an adequate bearing area must be provided at the supports and at the applied forces. Assuming that both reactions and the applied forces are 2 kips each, i.e. by neglecting the weight of the beam, it is found that the required bearing area at each concentrated force is

$$A = \frac{P}{\sigma_{allow}} = \frac{2,000}{200} = 10 \text{ in.}^2$$

These areas may be provided by specifying that the ends of the beam rest on at least 2-in.-by-5.5-in. (11-in.^{2}) pads; and at the concentrated forces 3.5-in-by-3.5-in.(12.2-in.^{2}) steel washers can be used.

• PROBLEM 8-53

Select an I beam or a wide-flange steel beam to support the load in Fig. 1a. Given, $\sigma_{allow} = 24,000$ psi, $\tau_{allow} = 14,500$ psi.

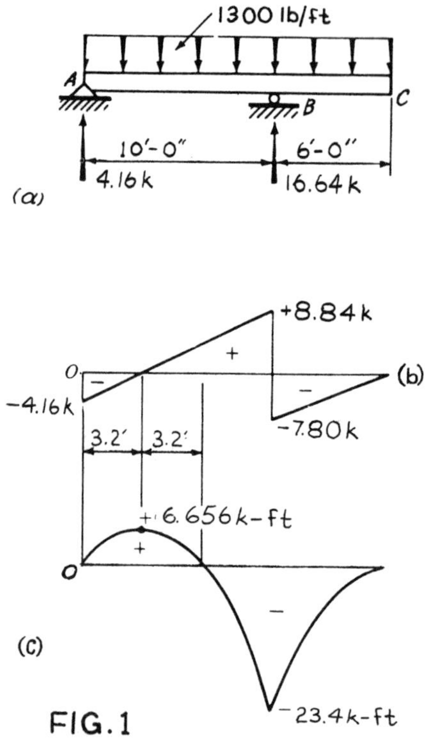

FIG. 1

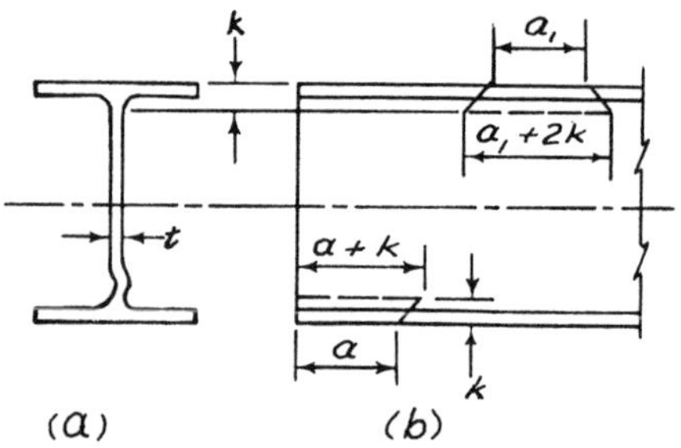

FIG. 2

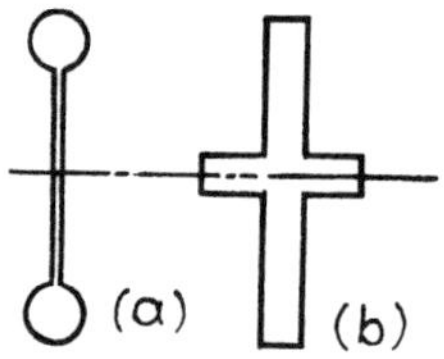

FIG. 3

Solution: The shear and the bending-moment diagrams for the loaded beam are shown in Fig. 1(b) and (c), respectively. The maximum moment is 23.4 kip-ft.

$$\text{Section Modulus,} \quad S = \frac{bh^2}{6} = \frac{M}{\sigma_{allowable}}$$

$$S = \frac{(23.4)12}{24} = 11.6 \text{ in.}^3$$

Examination of a handbook of structural shapes and beams shows that this requirement for the section modulus is met by a 7-in. I beam weighing 20.0 lb per foot. ($S = 12.0$ in.^{3}) However, lighter members, such as an 8-in. I beam weighing 18.4 lb per foot ($S = 14.2$ in.^{3}) and an 8-in. wide-flange section weighing 17 lb per foot ($S = 14.1$ in.^{3}) can also be used. For weight economy the 8 WF 17 section will be used. The weight of this beam is very small in comparison with the applied load and so is neglected.

From Fig. 1b, $V_{max} = 8.84$ kips. Hence,

$$(\tau_{max})_{approx} = \frac{V}{A_{web}} = \frac{8.840}{(0.23)8} = 4{,}800 \text{ psi}$$

This stress is within the allowable value, and the beam selected is satisfactory.

At the supports or at concentrated loads, I and wide-flange beams should be checked for crippling of the webs. This phenomenon is illustrated at the bottom of Fig. 2a. Crippling of the webs is more critical for members with thin webs than direct bearing of the flanges. To preclude crippling, a design rule is specified by the AISC. It states that the direct stress on area, $(a + k)t$ at the ends or $(a_1 + 2k)t$ at the interior points, must not exceed $0.75\sigma_{yp}$. In these expressions, a and a_1 are the respective lengths of bearing of the applied forces at exterior or interior portions of a beam. Fig. 2b; t is the thickness of the web; and k is the distance from the outer face of the flange to the toe of the web fillet. The values of k and t are tabulated in manufacturers' catalogues.

For the above problem assuming $\sigma_{yp} = 36$ ksi, the minimum widths of the supports, according to the above rule, are as follows: $.75(36) = 27$ ksi

At support A:

$$27(a + k)t = 4.16 \quad \text{or} \quad 27(a + 5/8)(0.23) = 4.16$$

$$a = 0.05 \text{ in.}$$

At support B:

$$27\left(a_1 + 2k\right)t = 16.64 \quad \text{or} \quad 27\left(a_1 + 5/4\right)\left(0.23\right) = 16.64$$

$$a_1 = 1.43 \text{ in.}$$

The preceding two examples illustrate the design of beams whose cross sections have two axes of symmetry. In both cases the bending moments controlled the design, and, since this is usually true, it is significant to note which members are efficient in flexure. A concentration of as much material as possible away from the neutral axis results in the best sections for resisting flexure, Fig. 3a. Material concentrated near the outside fibers works at a high stress. For this reason, I sections, which approximate this requirement, are widely used in practice.

The above statements apply for materials which have nearly equal properties in tension and compression. If this is not the case, a deliberate shift of the neutral axis from the mid-height position is desirable. This accounts for the wide use of T and channel sections for cast iron beams.

CHAPTER 9

DEFLECTIONS OF BEAMS

INTEGRATION METHOD

• PROBLEM 9-1

A bending moment M_1 is applied at the free end of a cantilever of length L and of constant flexural rigidity EI, Fig. 1a. Find the equation of the elastic curve.

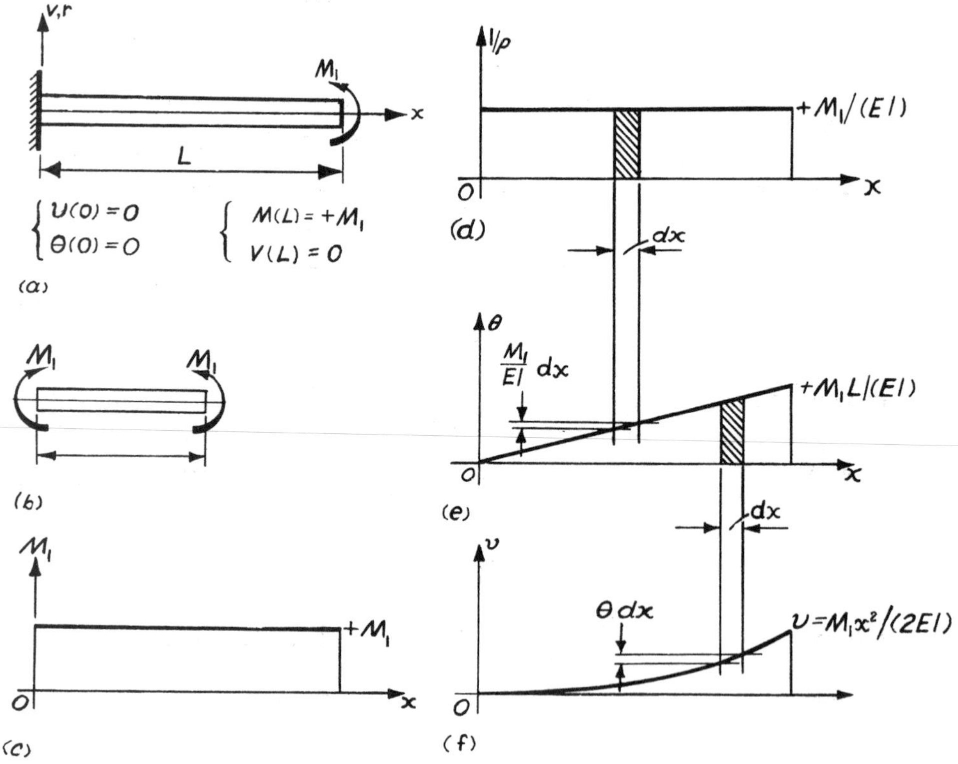

FIG. 1

Solution: This problem will be solved by successive integrations of the differential beam curvature equation. The boundary conditions are recorded near the figure from inspection of the conditions at the ends.

At $x = L$, $M(L) = + M_1$, a nonhomogeneous condition.

From a free-body diagram of Fig. 1b it can be observed that throughout the beam the bending moment is $+M_1$. By applying

$$M = \frac{EId^2 v}{dx^2}$$

integrating successively, and making use of the boundary conditions, one obtains the solution for v :

$$EI \frac{d^2 v}{dc^2} = M = M_1$$

$$EI \frac{dv}{dx} = M_1 x + C_3$$

But $O(0) = 0$; hence at $x = 0$ one has $EIv'(0) = C_3 = 0$ and

$$EI \frac{dv}{dx} = M_1 x$$

$$EIv = 1/2\ M_1 x^2 + C_4$$

But $v(0) = 0$; hence $EIv(0) = C_4 = 0$ and

$$v = M_1 x^2/(2EI) \qquad \text{(a)}$$

The positive sign of the result indicates that the deflection due to M_1 is upward. The largest value of v occurs at $x = L$. The slope of the elastic curve at the free end is $+M_1 L/(EI)$ radians.

Equation (a) shows that the elastic curve is a parabola. However, every element of the beam experiences equal moments and deforms alike. Therefore the elastic curve should be a part of a circle. The inconsistency results from the use of an approximate relation for the curvature $1/\rho^3$. It can be shown that the error committed is in the ratio of $(\rho - v)^3$ to ρ^3. As the deflection v is much smaller than ρ, the error is not serious.

• PROBLEM 9-2

For the beam loaded and supported as shown in Fig. 1, determine the maximum deflection between the supports in terms of P,L,E, and I.

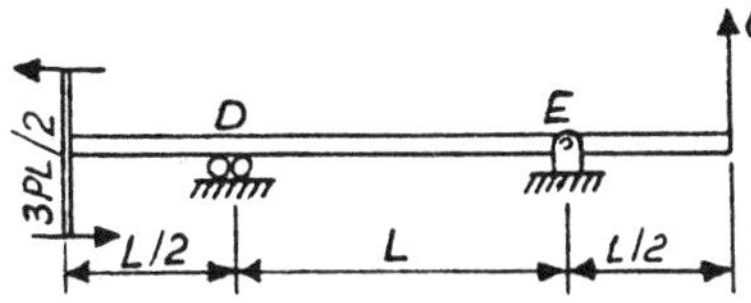

FIG.1

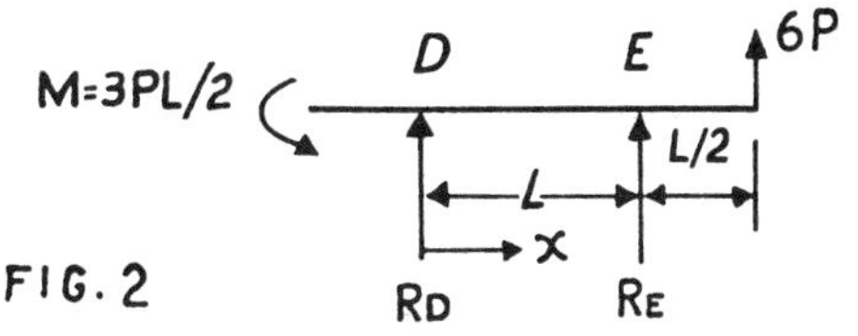

FIG. 2

Solution: This problem will be solved using the moment curvature equation,

$$EI \frac{d^2 y}{dx^2} = M_x .$$

In order to write the expression for the moment the reaction forces at the supports are needed (see Fig. 2). The reactions are found by moment equilibrium.

$$\Sigma M_D = 0 = \frac{3PL}{2} + R_E L + 6P(3L/2)$$

$$R_E = -\frac{3P}{2} - \frac{18P}{2} = -21P/2$$

$$\Sigma M_E = 0 = \frac{3PL}{2} - R_D L + 6PL/2$$

$$R_D = 9P/2$$

The moment at x is then

$$\Sigma M = 0 = \frac{3PL}{2} - \frac{9Px}{2} + M_x$$

$$M_x = \frac{9Px}{2} - \frac{3PL}{2}$$

Substituting into the curvature equation yields

$$EI \frac{d^2y}{dx^2} = M_x = \frac{9Px}{2} - 3PL/2$$

Integrating twice gives the deflection

$$EIy = \frac{9Px^3}{12} - \frac{3PLx^2}{4} + C_1 x + C_2$$

Since the deflection at D is zero, C_2 is zero. At $x = L$, y is also zero. Substituting

$$0 = \frac{9PL^3}{12} - \frac{3PL^3}{4} + C_1 L$$

$$C_1 = PL^2(-9 + 3(3))12 = 0$$

The deflection equation is thus

$$EIy = \frac{3Px^3}{4} - 3PLx^2/4$$

Setting the first derivative equal to zero locates the point of maximum deflection.

$$EI \frac{dy}{dx} = \frac{9Px^2}{4} - 3PLx/2 = 0$$

$$9Px^2/4 = 3PLx/2$$

$$x = 2L/3 \quad .$$

The maximum deflection occurs at the point $x = 2L/3$. Substituting this value into the deflection equation will give the maximum deflection.

$$EIy = \frac{3P(2L/3)^3}{4} - 3PL(2L/3)^2/4$$

$$EIy = \frac{2PL^3}{9} - 3PL^3/9$$

$$EIy = -PL^3/9$$

The maximum deflection between the supports is thus $PL^3/9\,EI$ downwards.

• PROBLEM 9-3

Find the central deflection of the uniform, simply supported beam due to the uniformly distributed load over the right half of the beam.

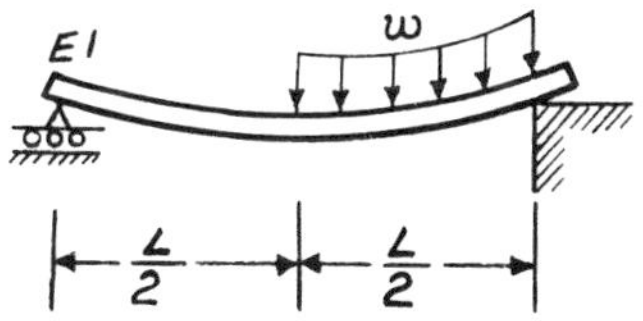

FIG. 1

FIG. 2

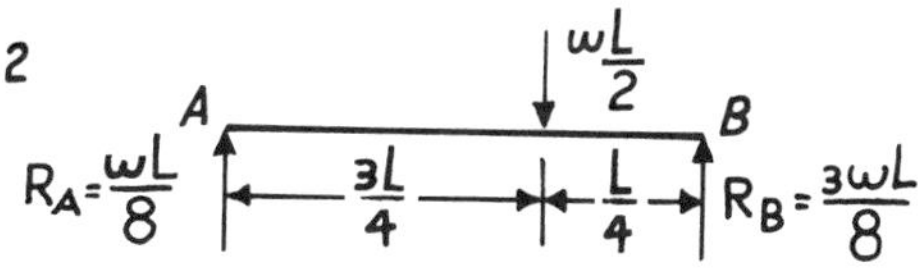

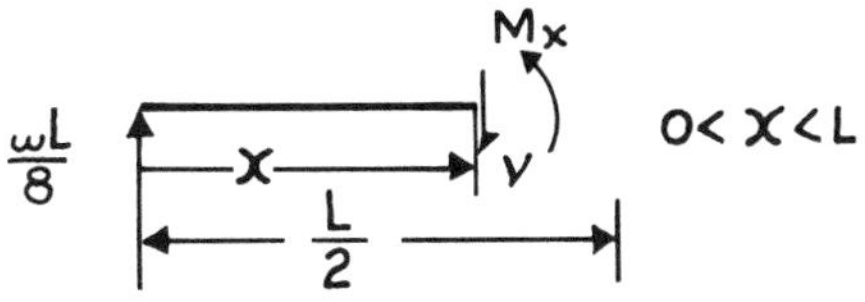

FIG. 3

FIG. 4

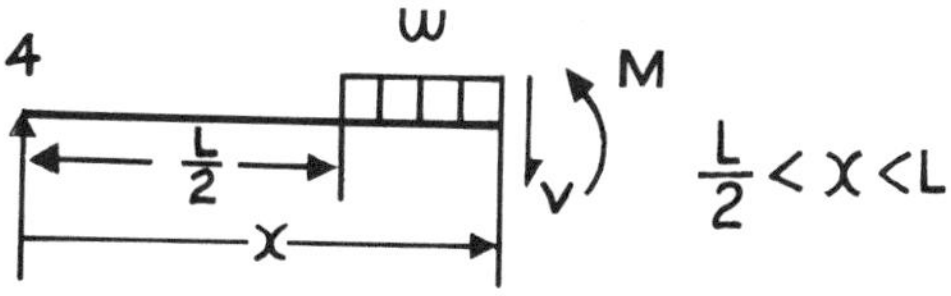

Solution: This problem will be solved by integrating the curvature due to moment equation,

$$EI \frac{d^2y}{dx^2} = M_x \ .$$

In order to write the moment equation, the end reactions need to be determined. For this purpose the distributed load can be replaced by the equivalent concentrated force as shown in Fig. 2.

$$\Sigma M_B = 0 = R_A L - w \frac{L}{2} \times \frac{L}{4} , \quad R_A = \frac{wL}{8}$$

$$\Sigma M_A = 0 = R_B L - w \frac{L}{2} \times \frac{3L}{4} , \quad R_B = \frac{3wL}{8}$$

The moment equation for the left half of the beam is from Fig. 3 , $0 < x < L$, ΣM about x is zero,

$$0 = - \frac{wL}{8} x + M_x$$

$$M_x = \frac{wL}{8} x \ .$$

Substituting for the moment in the curvature equation yields

$$EI \frac{d^2y}{dx^2} = \frac{wL}{8} x$$

Integrating once gives the slope equation

$$EI \frac{dy}{dx} = \frac{wL}{16} x^2 + C_1$$

Integrating a second time gives the deflection

$$EIy = \frac{wL}{48} x^3 + C_1 x + C_2$$

The deflection is zero at the left end. Since y is zero when x is zero, C_2 is zero. The deflection equation is therefore

$$RIy = \frac{wL}{48} x^3 + C_1 x$$

To find C_1, the deflection equation for the right hand side of the beam is needed. The moment equation for the right hand side is from Fig. 4

$$\frac{L}{2} < x < L \qquad \Sigma M \ \text{about} \ x \ \text{is zero}$$

$$0 = \frac{-wLx}{8} + w(x - \frac{L}{2}) \frac{(x - L/2)}{2} + M_x$$

$$M_x = \frac{wL}{8} x - \frac{w}{2}(x - L/2)^2$$

Substituting M_x into the curvature equation

$$EI \frac{d^2y}{dx^2} = \frac{wL}{8} x - \frac{w}{2} (x - L/2)^2$$

Integrating once gives the slope.

$$EI \frac{dy}{dx} = \frac{wL}{16} x^2 - \frac{w}{6}(x - L/2)^3 + C_3$$

Integrating a second time gives the deflection.

$$EIy = \frac{wL}{48} x^3 - \frac{w}{24}(x - L/2)^4 + C_3x + C_4$$

At the right end of the beam the deflection is zero. Substituting L for x, zero for y, and solving for C_4 yields

$$0 = \frac{wL}{48} L^3 - \frac{w}{24}(L - L/2)^4 + C_3L + C_4$$

$$C_4 = - \frac{w}{48} L^4 + \frac{w}{24}(\frac{L^4}{16}) - C_3L$$

$$C_4 = - \frac{7w}{384} L^4 - C_3L$$

The equation for the deflection is thus

$$EIy = \frac{wL}{48} x^3 - \frac{w}{24} (x - L/2)^4 + C_3x - \frac{7w}{384} L^4 - C_3L$$

At the midpoint $(x = L/2)$ the slope has a single value and the deflection has a single value. The equation for the left half of the beam will give the same result as the equation for the right half. For this reason, they can be set equal to one another and the remaining integration constants solved for.

The equations for the slope at L/2 set equal to each other become

$$\frac{wL}{16}(L/2)^2 + C_1 = \frac{wL}{16} (L/2)^2 - \frac{w}{6} (L/2 - L/2)^3 + C_3$$

Cancelling yields

$$C_1 = C_3 .$$

The equations for the deflection at L/2 set equal to each other become

$$\frac{wL}{48} (L/2)^3 + C_1 \frac{L}{2} = \frac{wL}{48} (L/2)^3 - \frac{w}{24} (L/2 - L/2)^4 + C_3 \frac{L}{2} - \frac{7w}{384} L^4 = C_3L$$

Substituting C_1 for C_3 and cancelling yields

$$0 = - \frac{7w}{384} L^4 - C_1L$$

Solving for C_1

$$C_1 = - \frac{7w}{384} L^3$$

Substituting the quantity just determined for C_1 and L/2 for x in the deflection equation for the left half of the beam yields

$$EIy = \frac{wL}{48}(L/2)^3 - \frac{7w}{384} L^3(L/2) = \frac{w}{384} L^4 - (7/2) \frac{w}{384} L^4$$

$$EIy = \frac{2}{768} wL^4 - \frac{7}{768} wL^4 = -\frac{5wL^4}{768}$$

The deflection of the midpoint of the beam is thus

$$y = -\frac{5wL^4}{768EI}$$

• PROBLEM 9-4

For the continuous beam in Fig. 1 the bending moment at the second support is $-wL^2/6$ and the vertical shear just to the right of the second support is $+7wL/12$. Determine the equation of the elastic curve for the portion of the beam between the second and third supports.

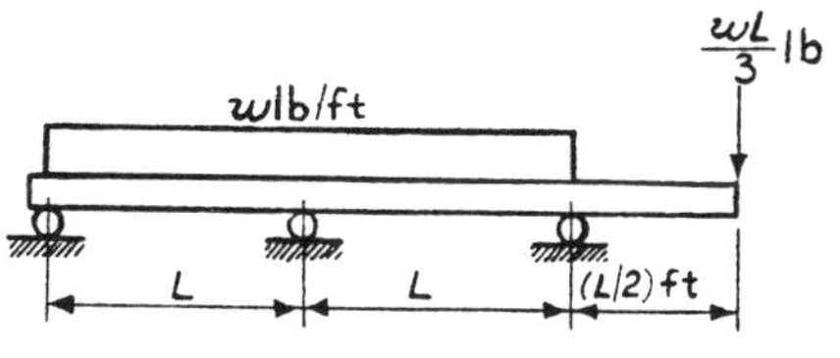

FIG. 1

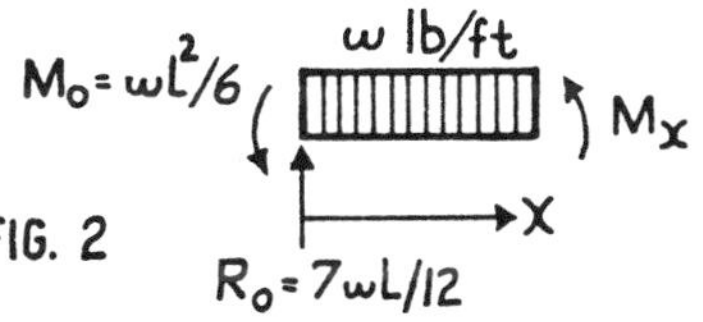

FIG. 2

Solution: This problem will be solved by integration of the curvature equation.
The moment equation can be written using the information given in the statement of the problem (see Fig. 2).
Figure 2 is a free body diagram of that part of the beam that extends from the second support to some point x which is between the second support and the third support. The moment equation is found by moment equilibrium about point x.

$$\Sigma M = 0 = (wL^2/6) - (7wLx/12) + (wx^2/2) + M_x$$

$$M_x = -(wx^2/2) + (7wLx/12) - wL^2/6$$

This expression for the moment is substituted into the curvature equation.

$$EI\frac{d^2y}{dx^2} = M_x = \frac{-wx^2}{2} + \frac{7wLx}{12} - \frac{wL^2}{6}$$

Integrating twice results in the deflection curve equation.

$$EIy = -(wx^4/24) + (7wLx^3/72) - (wL^2x^2/12) + C_1x + C_2$$

The deflection at the origin is zero therefore $C_2 = 0$. At $x = L$, y is also zero. Substituting

$$0 = -(wL^4/24) + (7wL^4/72) - (wL^4/12) + C_1L$$

$$C_1 = wL^3(3 - 7 + 6)/72 = wL^3/36$$

Thus the equation of the elastic curve for the portion of the beam between the second and third supports is

$$EIy = -(wx^4/24) + (7wLx^3/72) - (wL^2x^2/12) + (wL^3x/36).$$

Find the deflection curve for the beam shown.

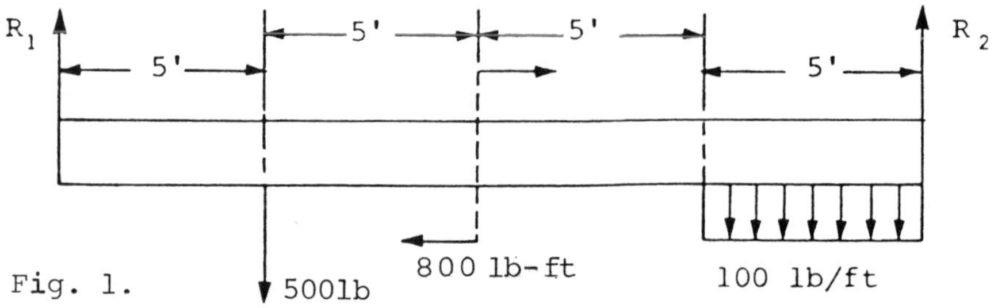

Fig. 1.

Solution: To find R_1 and R_2

$$\Sigma M_2 = 0$$

$$-R_1(20) + (500)(15) - 800 + (500)(2.5) = 0$$

$$\therefore R_1 = 397.5 \text{ lb}$$

$$\Sigma M_1 = 0$$

$$20R_2 - (500)(5) - 800 - (500)(17.5) = 0$$

$$\therefore R_2 = 602.5 \text{ lb} .$$

Analyze separately the four sections of the beam.

$0 \le x \le 5$

$$M = 397.5x$$

$$\therefore \frac{d^2Y}{dx^2} = \frac{1}{EI}(397.5x)$$

$$\frac{dY}{dx} = \frac{1}{EI}\left(397.5\frac{x^2}{2} + C_1\right) \qquad \text{(a)}$$

$$Y = \frac{1}{EI}\left(397.5\frac{x^3}{6} + C_1x + C_2\right) \qquad \text{(b)}$$

$5 \le x < 10$

$$M = 397.5x - 500(x - 5)$$

$$\therefore \frac{d^2Y}{dx^2} = \frac{1}{EI}[397.5x - 500(x - 5)]$$

Integrating yields

$$\frac{dY}{dx} = \frac{1}{EI}\left[397.5\frac{x^2}{2} - 500\frac{(x-5)^2}{2} + C_3\right] \qquad \text{(c)}$$

$$Y = \frac{1}{EI}\left[397.5\frac{x^3}{6} - 500\frac{(x-5)^3}{6} + C_3x + C_4\right] \qquad \text{(d)}$$

$10 < x \le 15$

$$M = 397.5x - 500(x - 5) + 800$$

$$\therefore \frac{d^2Y}{dx^2} = \frac{1}{EI}[397.5x - 500(x - 5) + 800]$$

$$\frac{dY}{dx} = \frac{1}{EI}\left[397.5\frac{x^2}{2} - 500\frac{(x-5)^2}{2} + 800x + C_5\right] \quad \text{(e)}$$

$$Y = \frac{1}{EI}\left[397.5\frac{x^3}{6} - 500\frac{(x-5)^3}{6} + 800\frac{x^2}{2} + C_5x + C_6\right] \quad \text{(f)}$$

$15 \le x \le 20$

$$M = 397.5x - 500(x-5) + 800 - 100\frac{(x-15)^2}{2}$$

$$\therefore \frac{d^2Y}{dx^2} = \frac{1}{EI}\left[397.5x - 500(x-5) + 800 - 100\frac{(x-15)^2}{2}\right]$$

$$\frac{dY}{dx} = \frac{1}{EI}\left[397.5\frac{x^2}{2} - 500\frac{(x-5)^2}{2} + 800x - 100\frac{(x-15)^3}{6} + C_7\right] \quad \text{(g)}$$

$$Y = \frac{1}{EI}\left[397.5\frac{x^3}{6} - 500\frac{(x-5)^3}{6} + 800\frac{x^2}{2} - 100\frac{(x-15)^4}{24} + C_7x + C_8\right] \quad \text{(h)}$$

Applying boundary conditions,

1. When $x = 0$, $Y = 0$.
From Eq. (b), $C_2 = 0$. Also:
2. When $x = 20$, $Y = 0$.
From Eq. (h),

$$0 = \frac{397.5(20^3)}{6} - \frac{500(15^3)}{6} + \frac{800(20^2)}{2} - \frac{100(5^4)}{24} + 20C_7 + C_8$$

$$\therefore 20C_7 + C_8 = 406{,}145 \quad \text{(i)}$$

The slope and the deflection at the end of one domain must, respectively, equal the slope and deflection at the beginning of the next domain. Thus between the first and second domain. Thus between the first and second sections

$$\left[\frac{dY(5)}{dx}\right]_{eq.(a)} = \left[\frac{dY(5)}{dx}\right]_{eq.(c)}$$

$$\therefore \frac{1}{EI}\left(397.5\frac{5^2}{2} + C_1\right) = \frac{1}{EI}\left(397.5\frac{5^2}{2} + 0 + C_3\right)$$

Hence, $$C_1 = C_3 \quad \text{(j)}$$

Also,

$$[Y(5)]_{eq.(b)} = [Y(5)]_{eq.(d)}$$

$$\frac{1}{EI}\left(397.5\frac{5^3}{6} + 5C_1\right) = \frac{1}{EI}\left(397.5\frac{5^3}{6} - 0 + 5C_3 + C_4\right)$$

$$\therefore 5C_1 - 5C_3 - C_4 = 0 \quad \text{(k)}$$

For the next two sections, just to the left of $x = 10$ - i.e., $x = 10^-$, and just to the right of $x = 10$, - ie., $x = 10^+$.

$$\left[\frac{dY(10^-)}{dx}\right]_{eq.(c)} = \left[\frac{dY(10^+)}{dx}\right]_{eq.(e)}$$

$$\therefore \frac{1}{EI}\left[397.5\frac{(10^2)}{2} - \frac{500(5^2)}{2} + C_3\right] = \frac{1}{EI}\left[397.5\frac{(10^2)}{2} - \frac{500(5^2)}{2} + (800)(10) + C_5\right]$$

$$C_3 - C_5 = 8000 \qquad (l)$$

$$[Y(10^-)]_{Eq.(d)} = [Y(10^+)]_{Eq.(f)}$$

$$\therefore \frac{1}{EI}\left[397.5\frac{(10^3)}{6} - 500\frac{(5^3)}{6} + 10C_3 + C_4\right] = \frac{1}{EI}\left[397.5\frac{(10^3)}{6} - 500\frac{(5^3)}{6} + 800\frac{(10^2)}{2} + 10C_5 + C_6\right]$$

$$10C_3 + C_4 - 10C_5 - C_6 = 40{,}000 \qquad (m)$$

Now,

$$\left[\frac{dY(15)}{dx}\right]_{eq.(e)} = \left[\frac{dY(15)}{dx}\right]_{eq.(g)}$$

$$\frac{1}{EI}\left[397.5\frac{(15^2)}{2} - 500\frac{(10^2)}{2} + (800)(15) + C_5\right] = \frac{1}{EI}\left[397.5\frac{(15^2)}{2} - 500\frac{(10^2)}{2} + (800)(15) + 0 + C_7\right]$$

$$C_5 = C_7 \qquad (n)$$

$$[Y(15)]_{eq.(f)} = [Y(15)]_{eq.(h)}$$

$$\frac{1}{EI}\left[397.5\frac{(15^3)}{6} - 500\frac{(10^3)}{6} + 800\frac{(15^2)}{2} + 15C_5 + C_6\right] =$$

$$\frac{1}{EI}\left[397.5\frac{(15^3)}{6} - 500\frac{(10^3)}{6} + 800\frac{(15^2)}{2} + 0 + 15C_7 + C_8\right]$$

$$15C_5 + C_6 - 15C_7 - C_8 = 0 \qquad (o)$$

Now rewrite the equations involving the constants.

$$C_2 = 0$$

$$20C_7 + C_8 = -406{,}145 \qquad (i)$$

$$C_1 = C_3 \qquad (j)$$

$$5C_1 - 5C_3 - C_4 = 0 \qquad (k)$$

$$C_3 - C_5 = 8000 \qquad (l)$$

$$10C_3 + C_4 - 10C_5 - C_6 = 40{,}000 \qquad (m)$$

$$C_5 = C_7 \qquad (n)$$

$$15C_5 + C_6 - 15C_7 - C_8 = 0 \qquad (o)$$

Substituting for C_3 in Eq.(k), using Eq.(j), results in

$$5C_1 - 5C_1 - C_4 = 0$$

$$\therefore C_4 = 0 \qquad (p)$$

From Eq.(m),

$$10(C_3 - C_5) - C_6 = 40{,}000 \qquad (q)$$

since $(C_3 - C_5) = 8000$, from Eq.(l), solve for C_6.

$$C_6 = 40{,}000 \qquad (r)$$

From Eq.(0), and replacing C_5, using Eq.(n), yields

$$15C_7 + C_6 - 15C_7 - C_8 = 0$$

$$\therefore C_8 = C_6 = 40,000 \qquad \text{(s)}$$

Find C_7 from equation (i)

$$20C_7 + 40,000 = -406,145$$

$$\therefore C_7 = -22,307 \qquad \text{(t)}$$

From Eq.(n),

$$C_5 = -22,307 \qquad \text{(u)}$$

From Eq.(l),

$$C_3 = 8000 - 22,307 = -14,307$$

From Eq.(j),

$$C_1 = -14,307 \qquad \text{(v)}$$

The constants of integration are all now known. Substituting in the values:

$0 \le x \le 5$

$$Y = \frac{1}{EI}\left(397.5\frac{x^3}{6} - 14,307x\right)$$

$5 \le x < 10$

$$Y = \frac{1}{EI}\left(397.5\frac{x^3}{6} - 500\frac{(x-5)^3}{6} - 14,307\right)$$

$10 < x \le 15$

$$Y = \frac{1}{EI}\left(397.5\frac{x^3}{6} - 500\frac{(x-5)^3}{6} + 800\frac{x^2}{2} - 22,307x + 40,000\right)$$

$15 \le x \le 20$

$$Y = \frac{1}{EI}\left(397.5\frac{x^3}{6} - 500\frac{(x-5)^3}{6} + 800\frac{x^2}{2} - 100\frac{(x-15)^4}{24} - 22,307x + 40,000\right)$$

• PROBLEM 9-6

The simply supported beam of uniform cross section shown in Fig. 1, is subjected to a concentrated load W. Obtain the deflection curve of the deformed neutral axis.

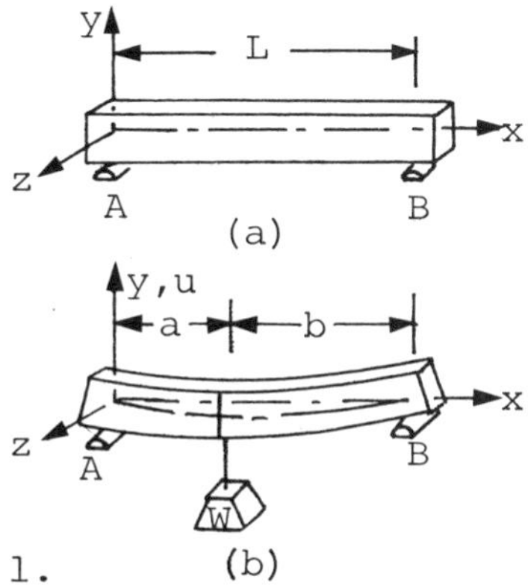

Fig. 1.

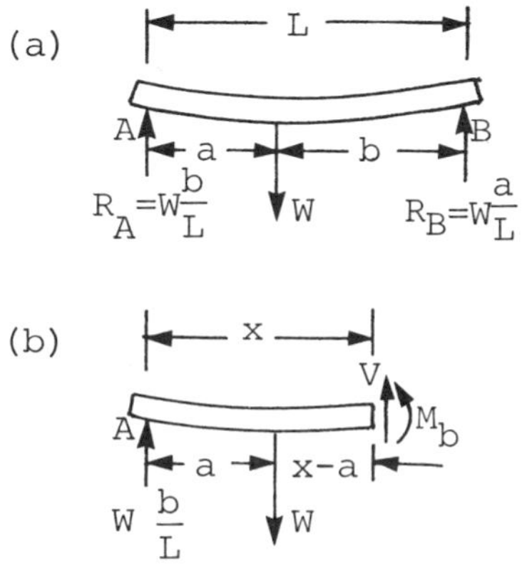

Fig. 2.

Solution: This problem is solved by integration of the curvature equation. Begin the analysis by drawing a free-body diagram of the beam, as shown in Fig. 2a. The reactions R_A and R_B are obtained from the overall force and moment balance conditions, i.e.,

$$\Sigma M = 0 \quad \text{at} \quad A$$

$$W_a = R_b L$$

$$R_b = \frac{W_a}{L}$$

$$\Sigma M = 0 \quad \text{at} \quad B$$

$$W_b = R_a L$$

$$R_a = \frac{Wb}{L} .$$

Using the singularity functions and bracket notation, we can write a single expression for the bending moment M_b directly from the free-body of Fig. 2b.

$$M_b = \frac{Wb}{L} x - W \langle x - a \rangle^1 \qquad \text{(a)}$$

Which is valid for $0 \leq x \leq L$. The moment-curvature relation

$$M = EI\frac{d^2v}{dx^2}$$

combined with (a) leads to

$$EI\frac{d^2v}{dx^2} = M_b = \frac{Wb}{L} x - W \langle x - a \rangle^1 \qquad \text{(b)}$$

Since the bending modulus EI is constant along the beam, integration of (b) yields

$$EI \frac{dv}{dx} = \frac{Wb}{L}\frac{x^2}{2} - W \frac{\langle x - a \rangle^2}{2} + c_1 \qquad \text{(c)}$$

$$EIv = \frac{Wb}{L}\frac{x^3}{6} - W \frac{\langle x - a \rangle^3}{6} + c_1 x + c_2 \qquad \text{(d)}$$

where c_1 and c_2 are constants of integration.

The geometric boundary conditions for this problem are that there should be no transverse displacement over the supports; i.e.,

$$v = 0 \quad \text{at} \quad x = 0 \quad \text{and at} \quad x = L \qquad \text{(e)}$$

These conditions together with (d) give us the following relations for the determination of c_1 and c_2:

$$0 = c_2$$

$$0 = \frac{Wb}{6L} L^3 - \frac{Wb^3}{6} + c_1 L \qquad \text{(f)}$$

$$\therefore c_1 = \frac{Wb^3}{6L} - \frac{WbL}{6}$$

If we insert the values for c_1 and c_2 determined from (f) into (d), we obtain the following deflection curve for the neutral axis of the beam:

$$v = -\frac{W}{6EI}\left[\frac{bx}{L}(L^2 - b^2 - x^2) + \langle x - a \rangle^3\right] \qquad \text{(g)}$$

To give some idea of order of magnitudes, let us consider the following particular case:

$$L = 12 \text{ ft}$$
$$a = b = 6 \text{ ft}$$
$$W = 400 \text{ lb}$$
$$E = 1.6 \times 10^6 \text{psi}$$
$$I = 57.1 \text{ in}^4 . \qquad (h)$$

These values correspond to a very common case in small-house construction. The beam is a nominal 2 x 8 in. (actually 1 5/8 x 7 1/2 in.) floor joist spanning 12 ft with a central load close to the maximum which would be considered for a single joist of this span in small-house design. If we insert the particular values (h) into (g), the greatest deflection occurs at the center and has the value

$$(v)_{x=L/2} = - \frac{400 \frac{72 \times 72}{144} [(144)^2 - (72)^2 - (72)^2]}{6 \times 1.6 \times 10^6 \times 57.1}$$

$$= -0.27 \text{ in.} \qquad (i)$$

Another magnitude of interest is the greatest slope of the deformed neutral surface. For the particular case (h) the greatest slope magnitude occurs simultaneously at the two ends. To evaluate the slope, we can either substitute (f) back into (c) or differentiate (g). Inserting the values (h) and setting $x = 0$ yields

$$\left(\frac{dv}{dx}\right)_{x=0} = -0.0057 \qquad (j)$$

which may be taken as the value of the slope angle φ, in radians. Converted to degrees, this is $0.33°$.

• PROBLEM 9-7

For the beam in Fig. 1 determine the equation of the elastic curve for the portion of the beam between the supports in terms of E, I, w, and L.

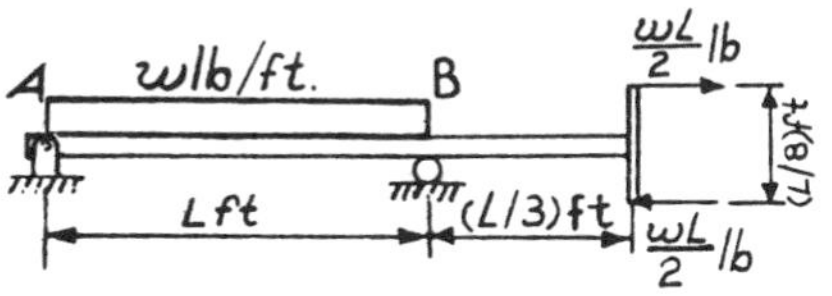

FIG.1

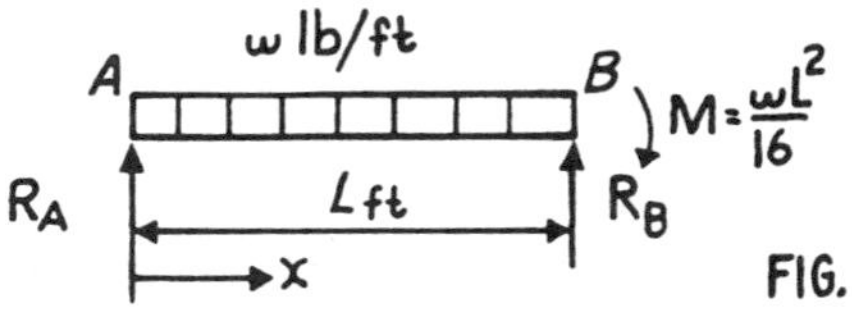

FIG. 2

Solution: This beam can be analyzed using the curvature equation

$$EI\frac{d^2y}{dx^2} = M .$$

In order to write the moment the reactions at the supports are needed (see Fig. 2)

$$\Sigma M_A = 0 = wL^2/2 + wL^2/16 - R_B L, \; R_B = 9wL/16$$

$$\Sigma M_B = 0 = R_A L + wL^2/16 - wL^2/2 , \; R_A = 7wL/16$$

The moment about x is then

$$M_x = 0 = 7wLx/16 - wx^2/2 + M$$

$$M = wx^2/2 - 7wLx/16$$

The expression for the moment can now be substituted into the curvature equation

$$EI\frac{d^2y}{dx^2} = wx^2/2 - 7wLx/16$$

The first integration gives the slope

$$EI\frac{dy}{dx} = wx^3/6 - 7wLx^2/32 + C_1$$

The second integration gives the deflection

$$EIy = wx^4/24 - 7wLx^3/96 + C_1x + C_2$$

The integration constants are found by applying the boundary conditions. Since the deflection at $x = 0$ is zero, $C_2 = 0$. The other boundary condition is $y = 0$ when $x = L$. Substituting these values into the deflection equation yields

$$0 = wL^4/24 - 7wL^4/96 + C_1L$$

Solving for C_1

$$C_1 = 7wL^3/96 - wL^3/24 = -wL^3/32$$

The equation of the elastic curve for the portion of the beam between the supports is

$$EIy = wx^4/24 - 7wLx^3/96 - wL^3x/32 .$$

• PROBLEM 9-8

Develop, in terms of w, L, E, I, x, and y, the elastic curve equation for span BC of the beam in Fig. 1. Use the indicated origin.

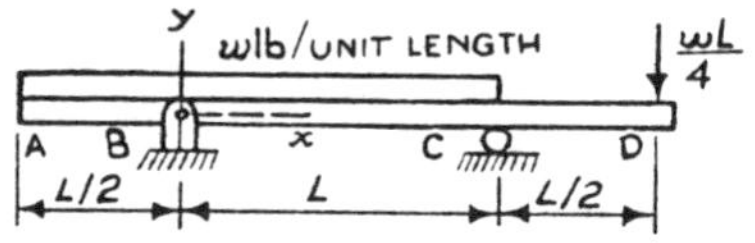

FIG. 1

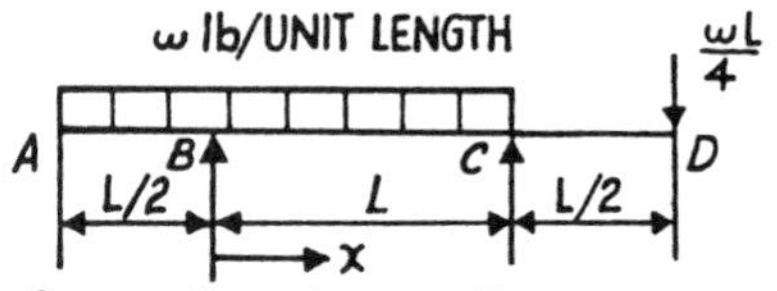

FIG. 2 $R_B = wL$ $R_C = 3wL/4$

Solution: Integrating the curvature equation twice will give the deflection curve equation.

In order to use the curvature equation the moment equation is needed and in order to write the moment equation the reactions at the supports R_B and R_C are needed (see Fig. 2). The reaction forces are found by moment equilibrium.

$$\Sigma M_B = 0 = wL^2/8 - wL^2/2 + R_CL - 3wL^2/8$$

$$R_C = 3wL/4$$

$$\Sigma M_C = 0 = R_BL - 9wL^2/8 + wL^2/8$$

$$R_B = wL .$$

The moment equation at any x is from moment equilibrium

$$\Sigma M_x = 0 = w(L/2 + x)^2/2 - wLx + M$$

$$M = -wx^2/2 + wLx/2 - wL^2/8$$

This expression is substituted into the curvature equation

$$EI\frac{d^2y}{dx^2} = M = -wx^2/2 + wLx/2 - wL^2/8$$

Integrating twice gives the deflection curve equation

$$EIy = -wx^4/24 + wLx^3/12 - wL^2x^2/16 + C_1x + C_2$$

At $x = 0$, $y = 0$, therefore $C_2 = 0$. Also at $x = L$, $y = 0$. Substituting

$$0 = -wL^4/24 + wL^4/12 - wL^4/16 + C_1L$$

$$C_1 = wL^3(2 - 4 + 3)/48 = wL^3/48$$

Thus the elastic curve equation for span BC of the beam is

$$EI\bar{y} = -wx^4/24 + wLx^3/12 - wL^2x^2/16 + wL^3x/48 \quad .$$

• PROBLEM 9-9

Figure 1a shows a cantilever beam built-in at A and subjected to a uniformly distributed load of intensity w per unit length acting on the segment BC. It is desired to obtain the deflection δ of the neutral axis at C due to the distributed load in terms of the constant bending modulus EI and the dimensions shown.

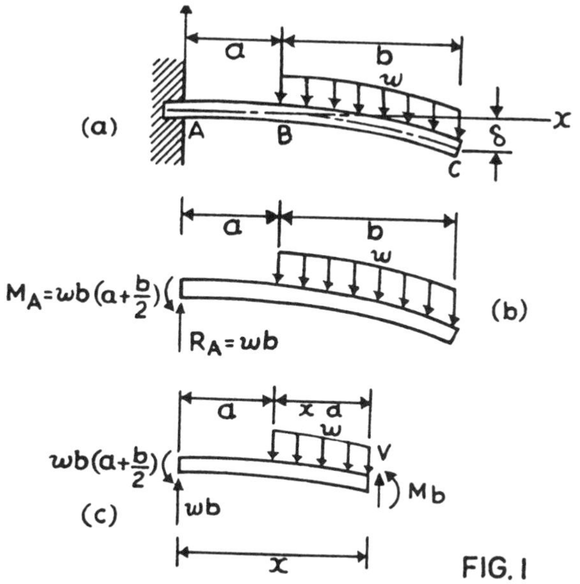

FIG. 1

Solution: This problem is solved by integrating the moment curvature equation. The analysis begins with a study of the forces and equilibrium requirements in Fig. 1b and c. A free-body diagram of the entire beam, from which we compute the reactions,

$$\Sigma F_x = 0$$

$$\therefore \quad R_A - wb = 0$$

$$\therefore \quad R_A = wb$$

is shown in Fig. 1b. In Fig. 1c a free-body diagram of a segment of length x is shown, from which we obtain the bending moment using duplet function;

$$M_b = wbx - wb(a + b/2) - \frac{w\langle x - a\rangle^2}{6}$$

This is then inserted into

$$M = EI\frac{d^2 v}{dx^2} .$$

$$EI\frac{d^2 v}{dx^2} = M_b = wbx - wb(a + b/2) - \frac{w\langle x - a\rangle^2}{2} \tag{a}$$

One integration of (a) leads to

$$EI\frac{dv}{dx} = wb\,\frac{x^2}{2} - wb(a + b/2)x - \frac{w\langle x - a\rangle^3}{6} + c_1 \tag{b}$$

where c_1 is a constant of integration. We can evaluate c_1 at this time because one of the conditions of geometric constraint is that at the built-in end A the slope of the neutral axis should remain zero.

$$\left(\frac{dv}{dx}\right)_{x=0} = 0 \tag{c}$$

In order for (b) to satisfy (c) we must have $c_1 = 0$. One more integration of (b) then yields

$$EIv = wb\,\frac{x^3}{6} - wb(a + b/2)\,\frac{x^2}{2} - \frac{w\langle x - a\rangle^4}{24} + c_2 \tag{d}$$

The constant of integration c_2 is evaluated by applying the geometric requirement that the displacement of the neutral axis at the built-in end A should remain zero.

$$(v)_{x=0} = 0 \tag{e}$$

In order for (d) to satisfy (e) we must have $c_2 = 0$. We thus obtain from (d) an equation for the locus of the deformed neutral axis. The displacement labeled δ in Fig. 1a is the negative of the value of v at $x = a + b$. Substituting $x = a + b$ in (d) and simplifying, we obtain

$$\delta = -(v)_{x=a+b} = \frac{wb}{EI}\left(\frac{a^3}{3} + \frac{3a^2 b}{4} + \frac{ab^2}{2} + \frac{b^3}{8}\right) \tag{f}$$

Two special cases of (f) are of interest. When $b = 0$, there is no loaded portion of the beam and according to (f) there is no deflection. When $a = 0$, the entire beam is loaded uniformly, and the deflection at the end is

$$\delta = \frac{wb^4}{8EI} \tag{g}$$

where now b is the entire length of the beam.

• PROBLEM 9-10

Find the slope angle φ at the point A due to the applied couple M_0 in terms of the dimensions shown, and the bending modulus EI of the uniform beam.

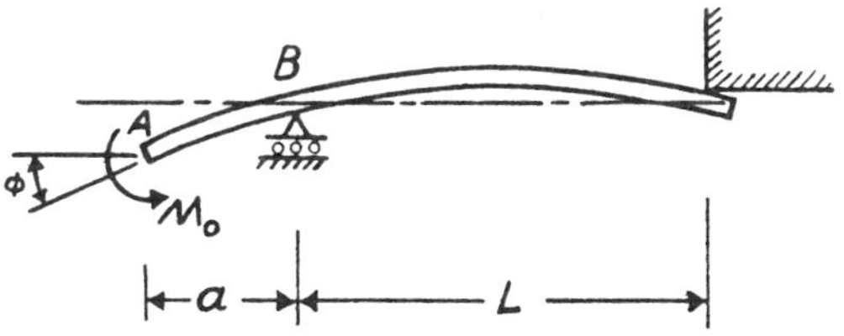

FIG. 1

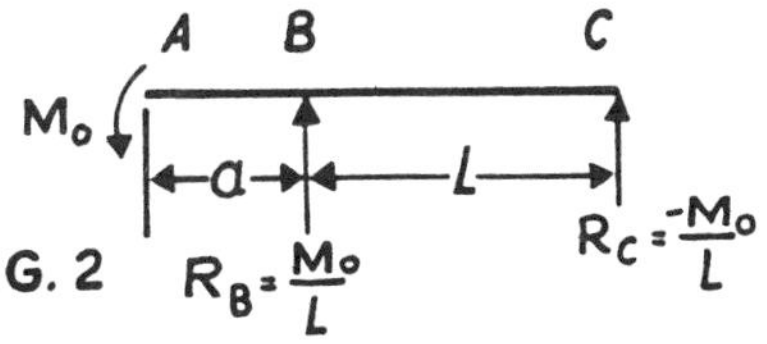

FIG. 2

Solution: This problem will be solved by integrating the curvature equation. The reactions are from Fig. 2.

$$\Sigma M_C = 0 = R_B L - M_0 \text{ , } R_B = M_0/L$$

$$\Sigma M_B = 0 = M_0 + R_C L \text{ , } R_C = -M_0/L$$

The moment equations are for the segments

$0 \le x \le a$

$$M_x = -M_0$$

$a \le x \le (L + a)$

$$M_x = -M_0 + \frac{M_0}{L}(x - a)$$

Substituting the expressions for the moments into the curvature equation yields

$$EI\frac{d^2y}{dx^2} = -M_0$$

$$EI\frac{d^2y}{dx^2} = -M_0 + \frac{M_0}{L}(x - a)$$

Integration results in the slope equations

$$EI\frac{dy}{dx} = -M_0 x + C_1$$

$$EI\frac{dy}{dx} = -M_0 x + \frac{M_0 x^2}{2L} - \frac{M_0 ax}{L} + C_3$$

Integrate again to get the deflection equations

$$EIy = -\tfrac{1}{2} M_0 x^2 + C_1 x + C_2$$

$$EIy = -\frac{M_0 x^2}{2} + \frac{M_0 x^3}{6L} - \frac{M_0 ax^2}{2L} + C_3 x + C_4$$

The deflection at a is zero. Substituting zero for y and a for x yields

$$0 = -\tfrac{1}{2} M_0 a^2 + C_1 a + C_2$$

$$C_2 = \tfrac{1}{2} M_0 a^2 - C_1 a$$

$$0 = -\frac{M_0 a^2}{2} + \frac{M_0 a^3}{6L} - \frac{M_0 a^3}{2L} + C_3 a + C_4$$

$$0 = -\frac{M_0 a^2}{2} - \frac{M_0 a^3}{3L} + C_3 a + C_4$$

$$C_4 = \frac{M_0 a^2}{2} + \frac{M_0 a^3}{3L} - C_3 a$$

The deflection is also zero at $x = a + L$. Substituting yields

$$0 = -\frac{M_0(a+L)^2}{2} + \frac{M_0(a+L)^3}{6L} - \frac{M_0 a(a+L)^2}{2L} + C_3(a+L) + \frac{M_0 a^2}{2} + \frac{M_0 a^3}{3L} - C_3 a$$

$$C_3 L = \frac{M_0(a+L)^2}{2} - \frac{M_0(a+L)^3}{6L} + \frac{M_0 a(a+L)^2}{2L} - \frac{M_0 a^2}{2} - \frac{M_0 a^3}{3L}$$

$$C_3 = \frac{M_0(a+L)^2}{2L} - \frac{M_0(a+L)^3}{6L^2} + \frac{M_0 a(a+L)^2}{2L^2} - \frac{M_0 a^2}{2L} - \frac{M_0 a^3}{3L^2}$$

As these operations are being performed the results can be checked by verifying that each term has the correct units. The units of C_3

are moments times distance. Substitute M for moments and d for distances in the equation for C_3.

$$C_3 = \frac{Md^2}{d} + \frac{Md^3}{d^2} + \frac{Md(d)^2}{d^2} + \frac{Md^2}{d} + \frac{Md^3}{d^2}$$

Reducing yields $C_3 = Md + Md + Md + Md + Md$. All the terms have units of moment times distance. Thus the units of each term of the equation are correct. However this test cannot detect errors in the numerical part of a term.

Now C_1 will be solved for. At point B, there is only one value for the slope. Using the slope equation for the region to the left of B will give the same result for the slope at B as the equation for the region to the right of B. Therefore they can be set equal to one another. At point B, x is equal to a. Substituting this value and the constants that have been solved for into the equations yields

$0 \le x \le a$

$$EI\frac{dy}{dx} = -M_0 a + C_1$$

$a \le x \le a + L$

$$EI\frac{dy}{dx} = -M_0 a + \frac{M_0 a^2}{2L} - \frac{M_0 a^2}{L} + \frac{M_0(a+L)^2}{2L} - \frac{M_0(a+L)^3}{6L^2} + \frac{M_0 a(a+L)^2}{2L^2} - \frac{M_0 a^2}{2L} - \frac{M_0 a^3}{3L^2}$$

$$= -M_0 a - \frac{M_0 a^2}{2L} + \frac{M_0(a^2+2aL+L^2)}{2L} - \frac{M_0(a^3+3a^2L+3aL^2+L^3)}{6L^2}$$

$$+ \frac{M_0(a^3+2a^2L+aL^2)}{2L^2} - \frac{M_0 a^2}{2L} - \frac{M_0 a^3}{3L^2}$$

$$= -\frac{M_0 L}{6} + \frac{M_0 L}{2}$$

$$EI\frac{dy}{dx} = \frac{M_0 L}{3}$$

Setting the two slope equations equal to one another and solving for C_1 yields

$$-M_0 a + C_1 = \frac{M_0 L}{3}$$

$$C_1 = M_0(a + L/3)$$

Now all the integration constants are known. The slope at A which is the result asked for in the statement of the problem can now be calculated. At A, x is equal to zero. Substituting this into the slope equation for the region $0 \le x \le a$ yields

$$EI\frac{dy}{dx} = -M_0(0) + M_0(a + L/3)$$

$$EI\frac{dy}{dx} = M_0(a + L/3)$$

$$\frac{dy}{dx} = \frac{M_0}{EI}(a + L/3)$$

Thus the slope at the left end of the beam is positive and has a value of $(M_0/EI)(a + L/3)$.

A uniform cantilever beam carries a total load of W, which is distributed in the linearly varying fashion shown. Find the deflection at the right end.

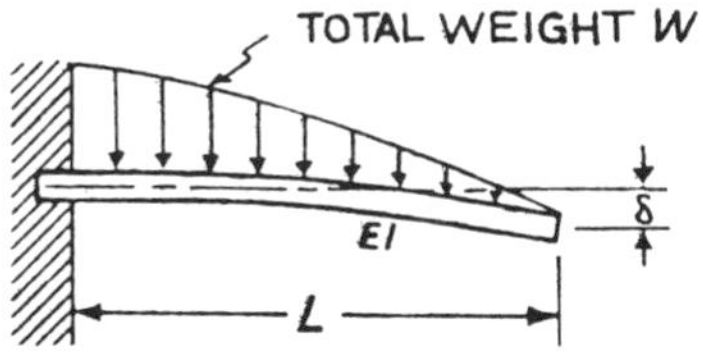

FIG. 1

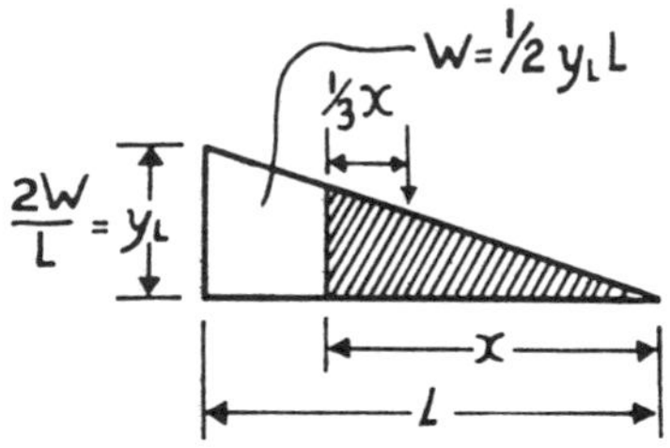

FIG. 2

Solution: This problem will be solved by integrating the curvature equation. The moment equation is determined from Fig. 2. The total load is W. Therefore the total area of the triangular loading is W

$$W = \tfrac{1}{2}\, y_L\, L$$

where L is the length of the beam and y_L is the magnitude of the loading at $x = L$.

$$y_L = \frac{2W}{L}$$

The magnitude of the loading at x is

$$y = \frac{2Wx}{L^2}$$

The average loading between 0 and x is $\bar{y} = \frac{Wx}{L^2}$. The total force applied between 0 and x is the average loading times the distance.

$$F = \frac{Wx^2}{L^2}$$

The moment is the force times the moment arm. The moment arm of the force about point x is $\frac{1}{3}$ x.

$$M = \frac{Wx^3}{3L^2}$$

This expression for the moment is substituted into the curvature equation.

$$EI\frac{d^2y}{dx^2} = \frac{Wx^3}{3L^2}$$

Integrating the first time gives the slope

$$EI\frac{dy}{dx} = \frac{Wx^4}{12L^2} + c_1$$

Integrating the second time gives the deflection

$$EIy = \frac{Wx^5}{60L^2} + c_1x + c_2$$

At $x = L$ the slope is 0. Substituting into the slope equation and solving for c_1 yields

$$0 = \frac{WL^4}{12L^2} + c_1$$

$$c_1 = -\frac{WL^2}{12}$$

At $x = L$ the deflection is also zero. Substituting into the deflection equation yields

$$0 = \frac{WL^5}{60L^2} - \frac{WL^2(L)}{12} + c_2$$

$$c_2 = \frac{4WL^3}{60} = \frac{WL^3}{15}$$

The deflection equation has become

$$EIy = \frac{Wx^5}{60L^2} - \frac{WL^2x}{12} + \frac{WL^3}{15}$$

Substitute $x = 0$ into the equation

$$EIy = \frac{WL^3}{15}$$

$$y = \frac{WL^3}{15EI}$$

The deflection at the tip of the cantilever is $\frac{WL^3}{15EI}$ downwards.

• PROBLEM 9-12

What must be the equation of the axis of the curved bar AB (see figure) before the load is applied in order that the load P, moving along the bar, remains always on the same level?

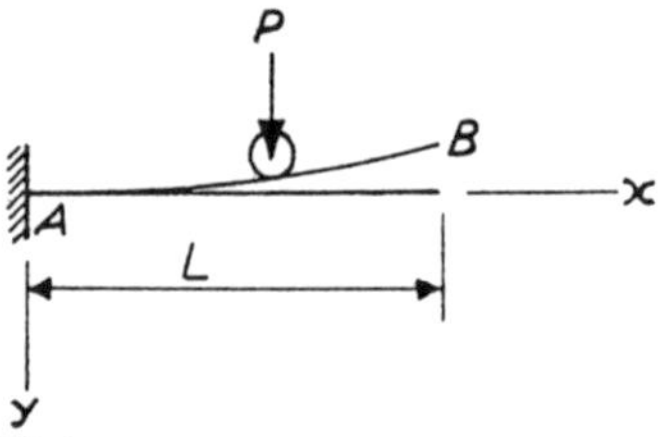

FIG.1

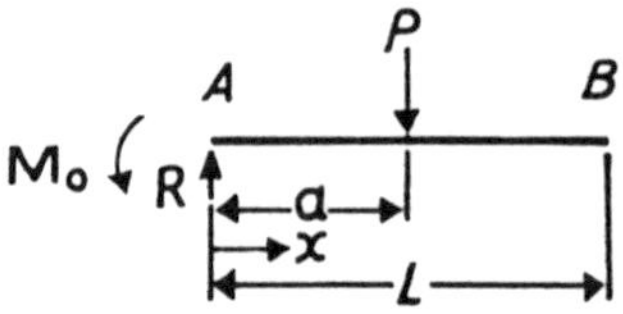

FIG. 2

Solution: In order to satisfy the conditions of this problem the height above the horizontal of any point along the beam must be equal and opposite to the deflection due to the application of the concentrated load at that point. Thus the equation of the axis of the curved bar will be the negative of the deflection equation of a straight bar.

The reactions at the built in end are $R = P$, $M_0 = Pa$.

The moment about x is $\Sigma M_x = 0 = M + Px - Pa$, $M = -Px + Pa$.

Substituting into the curvature equation

$$EI\frac{d^2y}{dx^2} = -Px + Pa$$

The slope is

$$EI\frac{dy}{dx} = -Px^2/2 + Pax$$

(The integration constant is zero because the slope is zero when x equals zero). The deflection is

$$EIy = -Px^3/6 + pax^2/2$$

(The integration constant is again zero because the deflection is zero when x is zero.) The value of a is not fixed. The point a takes on all values from zero to L as the load moves along the bar. That is a is equal to x. Substituting into the deflection equation yields

$$EIy = -Px^3/6 + Px^3/2 = Px^3/3$$

This is the equation of deflection of a straight bar. What is needed is the negative of this.
The equation of the axis of a curved bar such that a moving load remains always on the same level is

$$y = \frac{-Px^3}{3EI} \ .$$

• PROBLEM 9-13

Shown in the figure is a simply supported beam with a triangular loading. What is the deflection curve of this beam.

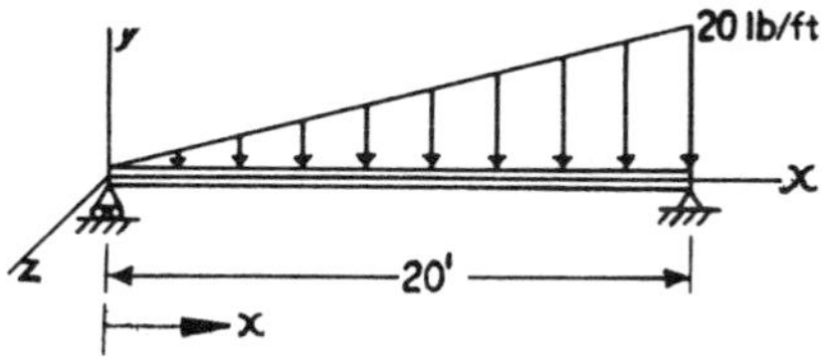

Solution: This problem will be solved by integrating the fourth order differential equation of the curvature due to loading

$$EI\frac{d^4y}{dx^4} = w$$

The equation for the loading is

$$w = \frac{20 \text{ lb/ft}(x)}{20 \text{ ft}} = x \text{ lb/ft}^2$$

Integrating the loading gives the shear

$$EI\frac{d^3y}{dx^3} = x^2/2 + c_1$$

Integrating the shear gives the moment

$$EI\frac{d^2y}{dx^2} = x^3/6 + c_1x + c_2$$

The moments at the ends of the beam are both zero. At $x = 0$

$$EI(0) = (0)^3/6 + c_1(0) + c_2$$

$$c_2 = 0$$

At $x = 20$

$$EI(0) = (20)^3/6 + c_1(20)$$

$$c_1 = -400/6$$

Substituting the moment equation becomes

$$EI\frac{d^2y}{dx^2} = x^3/6 - 400x/6$$

Integrating the moment gives the slope

$$EI\frac{dy}{dx} = x^4/24 - 400x^2/12 + c_3$$

Integrating the slope gives the deflection

$$EIy = x^5/120 - 400x^3/36 + c_3x + c_4$$

The deflections at the ends of the beam are both zero. At $x = 0$

$$EI(0) = (0)^5/120 - 400(0)^3/36 + c_3(0) + c_4$$

$$c_4 = 0$$

At $x = 20$

$$EI(0) = (20)^5/120 - 400(20)^3/36 + c_3(20)$$

$$c_3 = \frac{88,888.9 - 26,666.7}{20} = 3110$$

Substituting yields

$$EIy = x^5/120 - 400x^3/36 + 3110x$$

Thus the equation of the deflection curve of the beam is

$$y = \frac{1}{EI}(x^5/120 - 400x^3/36 + 3110x) .$$

• PROBLEM 9-14

Compute the deflection curve for the cantilever beam supporting a sinusoidal distribution of loading.

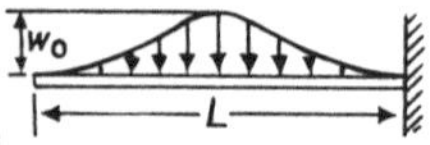

FIG.1

Solution: This problem will be solved by integrating the loading curvature equation

$$EI\frac{d^4y}{dx^4} = w \qquad \text{Eq.(1)}$$

The loading equation is

$$w = w_0 \sin(\pi x/L)$$

Substituting into Eq.(1) yields

$$EI\frac{d^4y}{dx^4} = w_0 \sin(\pi x/L)$$

Integrating the loading gives the shear

$$EI\frac{d^3y}{dx^3} = -(w_0L/\pi) \cos(\pi x/L) + c_1$$

The shear at the free end is zero. Substituting yields

$$0 = -(w_0L/\pi) \cos(0) + c_1$$

Solving for c_1

$$c_1 = w_0L/\pi$$

Integrating the shear gives the moment

$$EI\frac{d^2y}{dx^2} = -(w_0L^2/\pi^2)\sin(\pi x/L) + (w_0L/\pi)x + c_2$$

The moment at the free end is zero, therefore c_2 is zero. Integrating the moment gives the slope

$$EI\frac{dy}{dx} = (w_0L^3/\pi^3)\cos(\pi x/L) + (w_0L/\pi)x^2/2 + c_3$$

The slope at the wall is zero. Substituting L for x yields

$$0 = (w_0L^3/\pi^3)\cos(\pi) + (w_0L^3/2\pi) + c_3$$

$$c_3 = (w_0L^3/\pi^3) - (w_0L^3/2\pi)$$

The integral of the slope is the deflection

$$EIy = (w_0L^4/\pi^4)\sin(\pi x/L) + (w_0L/\pi)x^3/6 + ((w_0L^3/\pi^3) - (w_0L^3/2\pi))x + c_4$$

The deflection is zero at the wall.
Substituting L for x yields

$$0 = 0 + (w_0L^4/6\pi) + (w_0L^4/\pi^3) - (w_0L^4/2\pi) + c_4$$

$$c_4 = (w_0L^4/3\pi) - (w_0L^4/\pi^3)$$

Substituting back into the deflection equation gives

$$EIy = (w_0L^4/\pi^4)\sin(\pi x/L) + (w_0L/\pi)(x^3/6) + (w_0L^3x/\pi^3)$$

$$- (w_0L^3x/2\pi) + (w_0L^4/3\pi) - (w_0L^4/\pi^3)$$

Simplifying yields

$$y = w_0L/\pi EI\ [(L^3/\pi^3)\ \sin(\pi x/L) + x^3/6 + L^2x(1/\pi^2 - \tfrac{1}{2}) + L^3(\tfrac{1}{3} - 1/\pi^2)]$$

• PROBLEM 9-15

A cantilever beam supporting a triangularly distributed load of maximum intensity q_0 is shown in the figure. Obtain formulas for the deflection δ and slope at the free end.

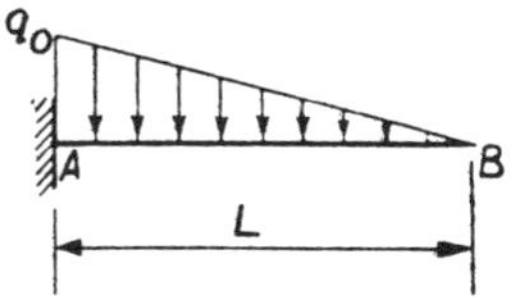

FIG. 1

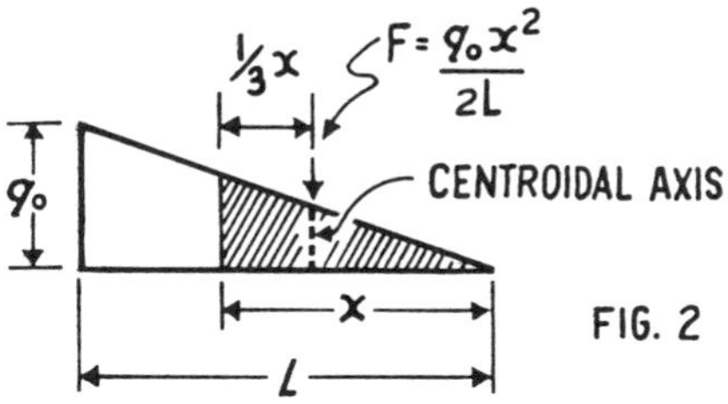

FIG. 2

Solution: This problem will be solved using the differential equation of curvature for elastic beams. To use this equation, the moment as a function of x is needed.
To find the moment an imaginary section cut is made at x (see Fig.2). The internal moment acting in the beam at the cut is found by moment equilibrium. The intensity of the distributed load at x is $q_0\ x/L$.

The average magnitude of the distributed load in the shaded section is $q_0x/2L$. The weight of the shaded portion of the distributed loading is the average intensity times the length.

$$F = \frac{q_0x^2}{2L}$$

The moment about point x is the force times the distance to the centroidal axis of the distributed loading from x. For a triangle the centroidal axis is one-third of the way from the base to the apex. The moment is thus

$$\Sigma M_x = 0 = M - \frac{q_0 x^2}{2L}\left(\frac{x}{3}\right)$$

$$M = \frac{q_0 x^3}{6L}$$

The curvature equation can now be employed.

$$EI\frac{d^2y}{dx^2} = M = \frac{q_0 x^3}{6L}$$

Integrating gives the slope.

$$EI\frac{dy}{dx} = \frac{q_0 x^4}{24L} + c_1$$

The integration constant can be found using a boundary condition. At the wall, the slope is zero. Therefore at $x = L$, $dy/dx = 0$. Substituting into the slope equation

$$0 = \frac{q_0 L^4}{24L} + c_1$$

Solving for c_1

$$c_1 = -\frac{q_0 L^3}{24}$$

The equation of the slope is thus

$$EI\frac{dy}{dx} = \frac{q_0 x^4}{24L} - \frac{q_0 L^3}{24}$$

Integrating the slope gives the deflection

$$EIy = \frac{q_0 x^5}{120L} - \frac{q_0 L^3 x}{24} + c_2$$

The integration constant, c_2, can also be found using boundary conditions. At the wall the deflection is zero. Therefore at $x = L$, $y = 0$. Substituting

$$0 = \frac{q_0 L^5}{120L} - \frac{q_0 L^3 (L)}{24} + c_2$$

$$c_2 = \frac{4q_0 L^4}{120} = \frac{q_0 L^4}{30}$$

The deflection equation is thus

$$EIy = \frac{q_0 x^5}{120L} - \frac{q_0 L^3 x}{24} + \frac{q_0 L^4}{30}$$

The statement of the problem asks for formulas for the slope and the deflection at the free end. At the free end $x = 0$. Substituting into the equations for slope

$$EI\frac{dy}{dx} = -\frac{q_0 L^3}{24}$$

$$\frac{dy}{dx} = -\frac{q_0 L^3}{24EI} \qquad \text{(slope)}$$

and for the deflection

$$EIy = \frac{q_0 L^4}{30}$$

$$y = \frac{q_0 L^4}{30EI} \qquad \text{(deflection)}$$

The beam shown in Fig. 1a is built-in at A and D and has an offset arm welded to the beam at the point B with a load W attached to the arm at C. Find the deflection of the beam at the point B.

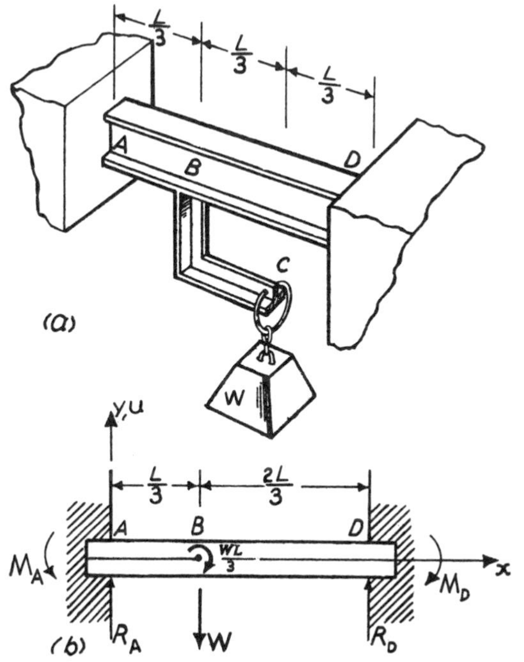

FIG. 1 OFFSET LOADING IS EQUIVALENT TO A FORCE AND A COUPLE AT B

Solution: The load-deflection equation

$$EI\frac{d^4v}{dx^4} = q$$

is employed in the solution of this problem. The effect of the arm on the beam is to supply a vertical force W and a couple WL/3 at B, as shown in Fig. 1b. With this replacement, the load-intensity function q for $0 < x < L$ is

$$q = \frac{WL}{3}\langle x - L/3\rangle_{-2} - W\langle x - L/3\rangle_{-1} \qquad \text{(a)}$$

Because of the built-in support the boundary conditions are $v = 0$ and $dv/dx = 0$ at $x = 0$ and L. (b)

Insertion of (a) into the load-deflection differential equation

$$M = EI\frac{d^2v}{dx^2}$$

but

$$M = \int vdx \quad \text{and} \quad v = \int qdx$$

$$\therefore \quad q = EI\frac{d^4v}{dx^4}$$

yields

$$EI\frac{d^4v}{dx^4} = W\left[\frac{L}{3}\langle x - L/3\rangle_{-2} - \langle x - L/3\rangle_{-1}\right] \qquad \text{(c)}$$

Expressions for dv/dx and v are obtained by integrating (c).

After three integrations

$$\frac{dv}{dx} = \frac{W}{EI}\left[\frac{L}{3}<x - L/3>^1 - \frac{<x - L/3>^2}{2} + c_1\frac{x^2}{2} + c_2x + c_3\right] \quad (d)$$

$$v = \frac{W}{EI}\left[\frac{L}{6}<x - L/3>^2 - \frac{<x - L/3>^3}{6} + c_1\frac{x^3}{6} + c_2\frac{x^2}{2} + c_3x + c_4\right] \quad (e)$$

Substitution of (d) and (c) into the boundary conditions (b) gives four simultaneous equations for the constants of integration.

At $x = 0$

$$v = 0 = \frac{W}{EI}[c_4]$$

$$\therefore c_4 = 0$$

$$\frac{dv}{dx} = 0 = \frac{W}{EI}[c_3]$$

$$\therefore c_3 = 0$$

At $x = L$

$$\frac{dv}{dx} = 0 = \frac{W}{EI}\left[\frac{L}{3}\cdot\frac{2L}{3} - \frac{1}{2}\cdot\frac{4L^2}{9} + c_1\frac{L^2}{2} + c_2L\right]$$

$$\therefore c_2 = -\frac{c_1L}{2}$$

$$v = 0 = \frac{W}{EI}\left[\frac{L}{6}\cdot\frac{4L^2}{9} - \frac{8L^3}{6\times27} + \frac{c_1L^3}{6} + \frac{c_2L^2}{2}\right]$$

Substituting for c_2 gives

$$\frac{4L^3}{6\times27} + \frac{c_1L^3}{6} - \frac{c_1L}{2}\cdot\frac{L^2}{2} = 0$$

$$\therefore c_1 = 8/27$$

$$c_2 = \frac{-4}{27}L$$

Inserting these in (e) we find

$$v = \frac{W}{27EI}\left[\frac{9}{2}L<x - L/3>^2 - \frac{9}{2}<x - L/3>^3 + \frac{4}{3}x^3 - 2Lx^2\right]$$

We obtain the desired deflection by setting $x = L/3$.

$$\delta_B = -(v)_{x=L/3} = \frac{14WL^3}{2,187EI}$$

• PROBLEM 9-17

A long uniform rod of length L, weight w per unit length, and bending modulus EI is placed on a rigid horizontal table such that a short segment CD of length a overhangs the table, as shown in Fig. 1a. It is required to find the length b of the segment BC which lifts up from the table.

Solution: The equation of curvature due to moment

$$EI\frac{d^2v}{dx^2} = M$$

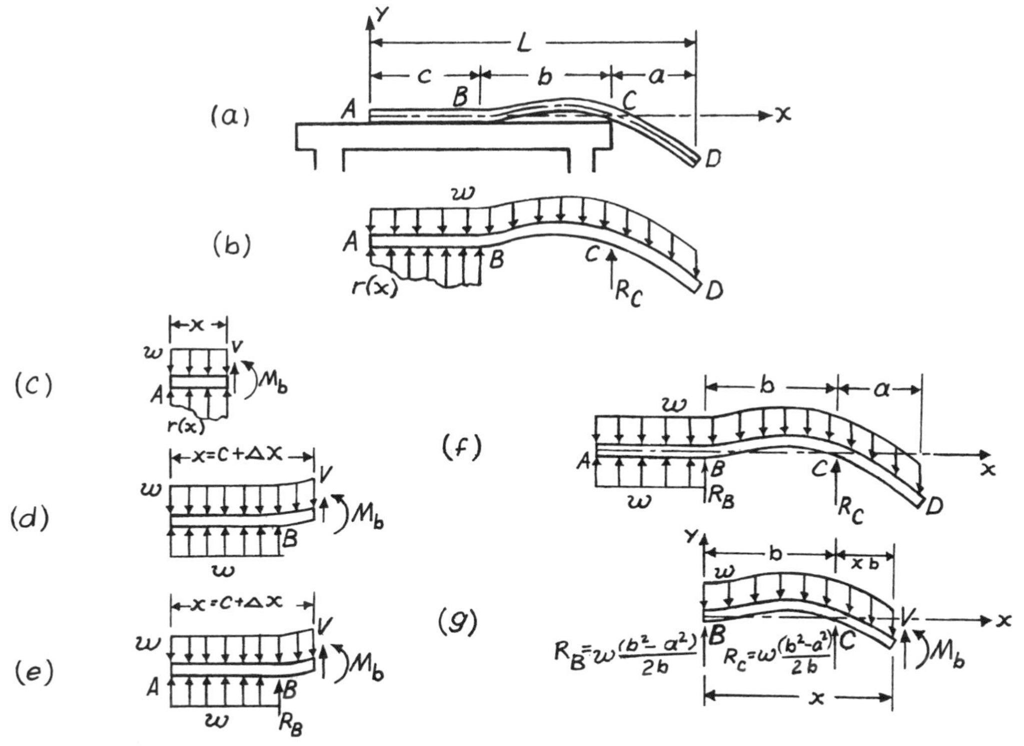

FIG.1 BEAM OVERHANGING EDGE OF THE TABLE CAUSES SEGMENT BC TO LIFT FROM TABLE.

will be used in the analysis of this problem. The difficult part of this example is the determination of the reactions with the table. There is a concentrated vertical reaction at the edge of the table at C, but the nature of the reaction between the table and the segment AB is not at all clear, as is indicated in Fig. 1b by the arbitrary shape shown for the reaction distribution $r(x)$. It is possible, however, to deduce the nature of this reaction distribution by considering the equilibrium, geometric compatibility, and moment-curvature requirements for the beam segment AB.

We begin by observing that, since the table is flat, the beam must have zero curvature in the region AB. Then from the moment-curvature relation we conclude that the bending moment must be zero throughout the segment of the beam from A to B. Also, since the bending moment is constant (zero) along the beam, we reason that the shear force must also be zero in this region. Pursuing our reasoning one step further, we conclude that the net intensity of loading must be zero in the region AB because of the constant (zero) shear force. Thus for the free body of Fig. 1c we must have

$$M_b = V = 0$$
$$r(x) = w \qquad \text{(a)}$$

In the free body of Fig. 1d we have included the results (a); that is, we show the reaction in the region between A and B to be of magnitude w per unit length. If we now satisfy the requirement of moment equilibrium for this free body, we shall obtain a negative value for the bending moment M_b. A negative bending moment at this point (a distance Δx to the right of B) is not compatible with the requirement that the beam must have a positive curvature in order to leave the surface, since a positive curvature implies a positive bending moment. A positive bending moment a distance Δx to the right of B requires the existence of a preponderantly upward external force in this interval, and therefore we conclude that there must be a concentrated upward reaction force at point B, as indicated in Fig. 1e. It is to be noted that the presence of R_B is not in conflict with any of our previous arguments which led to the uniformly distributed reaction in the region between A and B. Thus, after a rather lengthy series of arguments, we have determined that the reaction with the table must be as shown in Fig. 1f. By applying the equilibrium requirements to this free body, we obtain the magnitudes of the reactions shown in Fig. 1g.

To proceed further, it is convenient to deal only with the segment of the beam between B and D. Relocating our coordinate system to measure x from point B, we obtain M_b from the free body of Fig. 1g and insert in

$$EI\frac{d^2v}{dx^2} = M_b = \frac{w(b^2 - a^2)}{2b} x + \frac{w(b + a)^2}{2b} <x - b>^1 - \frac{wx^2}{2} \tag{b}$$

Integrating (b), we find

$$EI\frac{dv}{dx} = \frac{w(b^2 - a^2)}{4b} x^2 + \frac{w(b + a)^2}{4b} <x - b>^2 - \frac{wx^3}{6} + c_1 \tag{c}$$

Since the beam is tangent to the table at $x = 0$, we conclude that $c_1 = 0$. Integrating once more, we then obtain

$$EIv = \frac{w(b^2 - a^2)}{12b} x^3 + \frac{w(b + a)^2}{12b} <x - b>^3 - \frac{wx^4}{24} + c_2 \tag{d}$$

The constant of integration c_2 is zero since $v = 0$ at $x = 0$.

Finally, we can evaluate b from Eq. (d) by requiring the condition that $v = 0$ at $x = b$.

$$0 = \frac{w(b^2 - a^2)}{12b} b^3 + 0 - \frac{wb^4}{24} \tag{e}$$

Solving (e) for b, we find

$$b = \sqrt{2}a \tag{f}$$

Thus when a long, uniform, flexible rod overhangs a rigid table by a distance a, the rod is not in continuous contact with the table until a distance $\sqrt{2}a$ back from the edge. It is instructive to review again the conditions at point B in Fig. 1 where the rod separates from the table. The deflection and slope are both zero since the curved segment BC must join smoothly with the uncurved segment AB. The bending moment is zero since there is no bending moment in the segment AB and there is no mechanism for introducing a sudden change in bending moment at B. There is, however, a sudden appearance of shear force at B since the table can exert a concentrated upward reaction force.

• PROBLEM 9-18

A strip of mirror glass in a precision optical instrument is to be simply supported by a pair of symmetrically placed supports, as shown in Fig. 1. During operation the angle θ will vary from 0 to 90° so that the bending due to gravity will vary. For what position of the supports will the deviations from flatness be minimized; i.e., at any fixed θ for what value of a will the greatest deflection in the mirror be minimized?

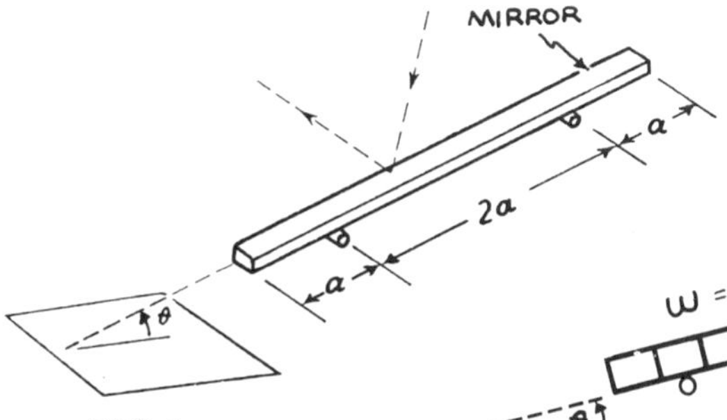

FIG. 1

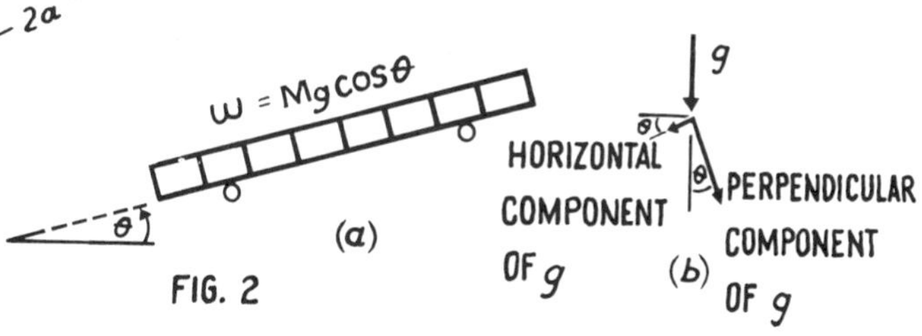

FIG. 2

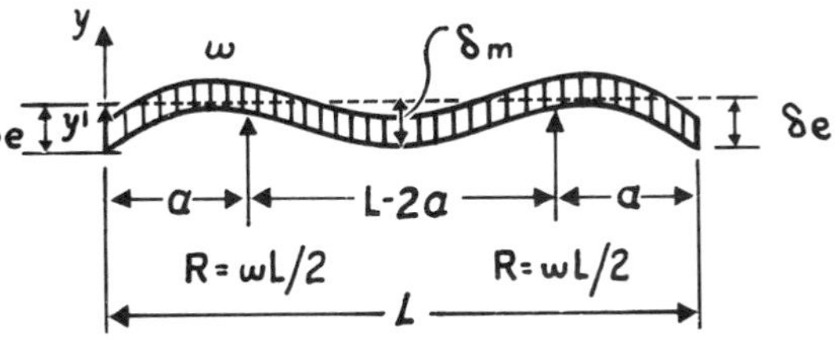

FIG. 3

Solution: The strip of mirror glass can be considered to be a uniformly loaded, simply supported beam with overhanging ends. The perpendicular component of the gravitational force on the glass is the uniformly distributed loading (see Fig. 2a). The magnitude of the perpendicular component varies with the angle (see Fig. 2b). However in seeking to minimize the maximum deflection, the magnitude of the loading is not needed, only the fact that the loading is uniform. Thus the problem has the same solution as the case of the uniformly loaded horizontal beam shown in Fig. 3.

The maximum deflection can occur either at the ends or at the midpoint of the beam. The deflection is minimized when the deflection at the mid point equals the deflection at the ends.

This problem will be solved by integrating the moment curvature equation

$$EI\frac{d^2y}{dx^2} = M \qquad \text{Eq. 1}$$

The relation for the moment is from Fig. 3.

$$M = wx^2/2 - (w_0L/2)\langle x - a\rangle - (w_0L/2)\langle x - L + a\rangle$$

Substituting into Eq. 1 yields

$$EI\frac{d^2y}{dx^2} = M = wx^2/2 - (w_0L/2)\langle x - a\rangle - (w_0L/2)\langle x - L + a\rangle$$

Integrating the moment gives the slope

$$EI\frac{dy}{dx} = wx^3/6 - (w_0L/4)\langle x - a\rangle^2 - (w_0L/4)\langle x - L + a\rangle^2 + c_1$$

Integrating the slope gives the deflection

$$EIy = wx^4/24 - (w_0L/12)\langle x - a\rangle^3 - (w_0L/12)\langle x - L - a\rangle^3 + c_1x + c_2$$

To simplify calculations, the y coordinate axis will be replaced with a new vertical coordinate axis $y' = y - \delta$. In this new coordinate system the deflection at the middle and at the ends is zero. The deflection at the middle will be made zero by giving the ratio a/L the proper value. First however the constants of integration must be found using the fact that the deflection is zero at the end points. Substituting $y' = 0$ and $x = 0$

$$0 = c_4$$

Substituting $y' = 0$ and $x = L$

$$0 = wL^4/24 - (wL/12)(L - a)^3 - (wL/12)(a)^3 + c_3 L$$

$$c_3 = - wL^4/24 + wL^3/12 - 3waL^2/12 + 3wa^2 L/12$$

$$c_3 = (wL/24)(L^2 - 6aL + 6a^2)$$

The deflection equation is thus

$$EIy' = \frac{wx^4}{24} - \frac{wL}{12}\langle x - a\rangle^3 - \frac{wL}{12}\langle x - L + a\rangle^3$$

$$+ \frac{wLx}{24}(L^2 - 6aL + 6a^2)$$

In order to find the ratio between a and L, define a new constant n where $a = nL$. When x is equal to $L/2$, y' is equal to zero. Making these substitutions into the deflection equation yields

$$0 = \frac{wL^4}{24.16} - \frac{wL}{12}\left(\frac{1}{2} - nL\right)^3 + \frac{wL^2}{24.2}(L^2 - 6nL^2 + 6n^2 L^2)$$

Simplifying

$$0 = \frac{wL^4}{384}(32n^3 - 24n + 5)$$

Since none of the constants are zero, the only way this equation can be equal to zero is if the term inside the parentheses is equal to zero.

$$0 = (32n^3 - 24n + 5)$$

This cubic equation can be solved by trial and error. Since the extreme values for n are zero and .5 a good first guess is the point halfway between the two, n = .25.

The results are recorded in tabular form

n	f(n)
.25	-.5
.2	.456
.23	-.131
.22	.061
.225	-.036
.222	.022
.224	-.016
.223	.0027

If a = .223L, the greatest deflection will be minimized.

• PROBLEM 9-19

A simply supported beam is constructed by welding a very stiff beam to a beam which is relatively much less stiff in bending. What is the deflection at B under a load P applied in the middle of the stiff part if it is assumed that this part carries a bending moment without any resulting curvature and the flexural rigidity of the other part is EI ?

Solution: This problem will be solved by applying the curvature equation to the flexible beam and geometry to the stiff beam.

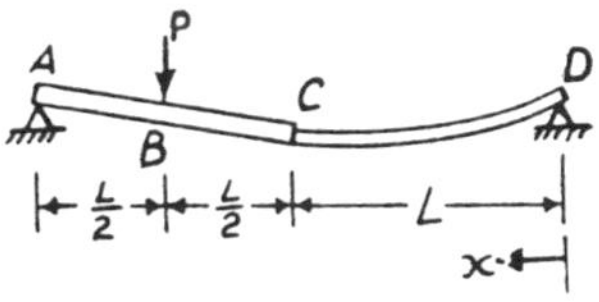

FIG. 1

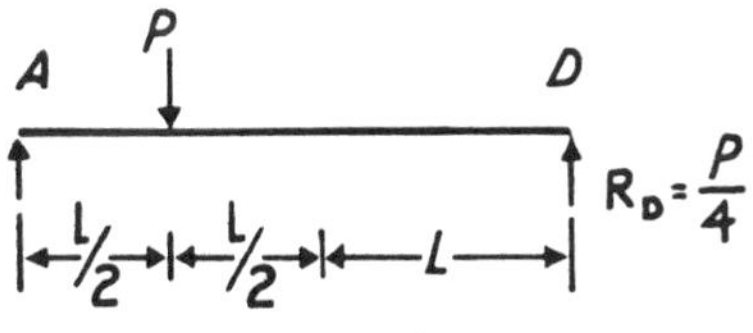

FIG. 2

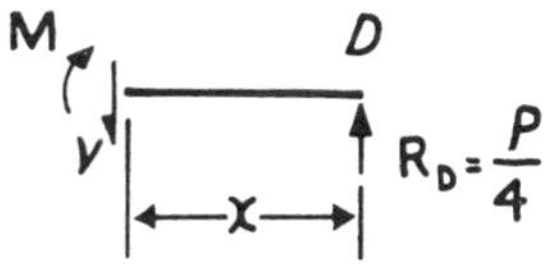

FIG. 3

The reaction force R_D is, from Fig. 2

$$\Sigma M_A = 0 = -P(L/2) + R_D(2L),\ R_D = P/4$$

From Fig. 3, the moment equation is

$$\Sigma M_x = 0 = M - P/4(x)\ ,\ M = Px/4$$

Substituting this result into the curvature equation yields

$$EI\frac{d^2y}{dx^2} = Px/4$$

Integrating once gives the slope

$$EI\frac{dy}{dx} = Px^2/8 + c_1$$

Integrating the slope gives the displacement

$$EIy = Px^3/24 + c_1x + c_2$$

At point D there is no displacement. Substituting zero for x and y

$$0 = \frac{P(0)^3}{24} + c_1(0) + c_2$$

Therefore dropping the zero terms

$$c_2 = 0$$

The displacement has become

$$EIy = \frac{Px^3}{24} + c_1x$$

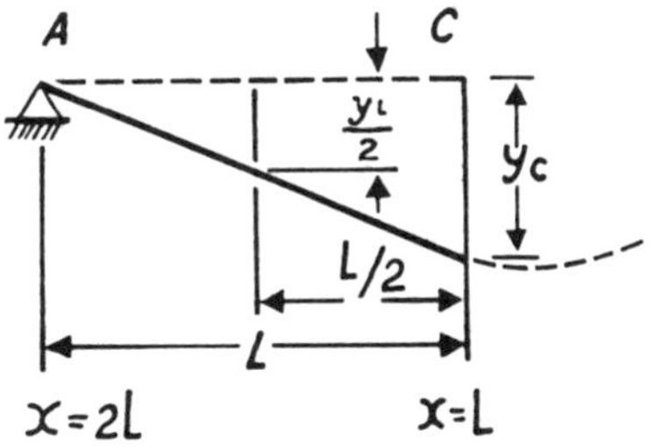

FIG. 4

Now the stiff bar will be analyzed as shown in Fig. 4.

The displacement of the stiff beam changes linearly from zero at A to $-y_C$ at C. The displacement of the stiff beam at C is the same as the displacement of the flexible beam at C because they are welded together at that point.

The slope of the stiff beam is constant. The slope is the change in y divided by the change in x.

$$\frac{dy}{dx} = \frac{-y_L}{L}$$

Since the two beams are welded together, the slope of the flexible beam at C is also $-y_C/L$.

The equations for the slope and deflection of the flexible beam at $x = L$ can be substituted into the relation just determined.

$$\frac{PL^2}{8} + c_1 = \frac{\frac{-PL^3}{24} - c_1L}{L}$$

Solving for c_1

$$2c_1 = \frac{-PL^2}{24} - \frac{PL^2}{8} = \frac{-PL^2}{6}$$

$$c_1 = \frac{-PL^2}{12}$$

The deflection at C is then

$$EIy = \frac{PL^3}{24} - \frac{PL^2}{12}(L)$$

$$y_C = \frac{-PL^3}{24EI}$$

From the geometry of similar triangles (see Fig. 4), the displacement at B is half the displacement at C.

$$y_B = \frac{1}{2} y_C$$

Substituting for y_C

$$y_B = \frac{1}{2}\left(\frac{-PL^3}{24EI}\right)$$

$$y_B = \frac{-PL^3}{48EI}$$

Thus the deflection at point B under the applied load P is $\frac{PL^3}{48EI}$ downwards.

SINGULARITY FUNCTIONS

• PROBLEM 9-20

A simple beam supports a concentrated downward force P at a distance a from the left support, Fig. 1a. The flexural rigidity EI is constant.
(a) Find the equation of the elastic curve without the use of operational notation.
(b) Rework the problem using singularity functions.

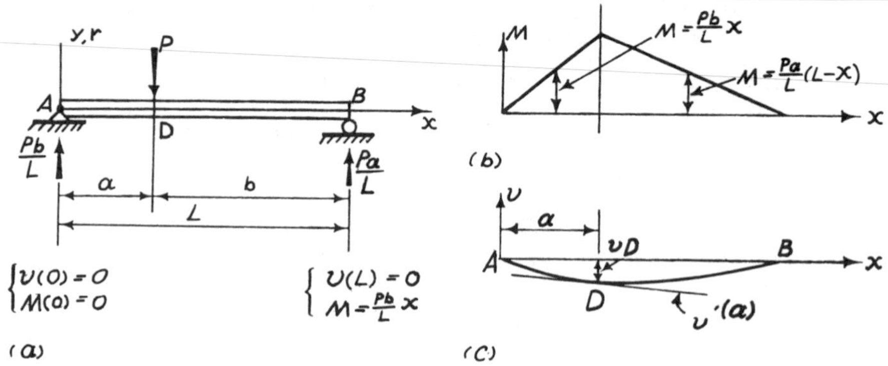

FIG. 1

Solution: Case (a). The solution will be made by using the second-order differential equation. The reactions and boundary conditions are noted in Fig. 1a. The moment diagram plotted in Fig. 1b clearly shows that a discontinuity at $x = a$ exists in $M(x)$, requiring two different functions for it. At first the solution proceeds independently for each segment of the beam.

For segment AD:

$$\frac{d^2v}{dx^2} = \frac{M}{EI} = \frac{Pb}{EIL} x$$

$$\frac{dv}{dx} = \frac{Pb}{EIL}\frac{x^2}{2} + A_1$$

$$v = \frac{Pb}{EIL}\frac{x^3}{6} + A_1 x + A_2$$

For segment DB:

$$\frac{d^2v}{dx^2} = \frac{M}{EI} = \frac{Pa}{EI} - \frac{Pa}{EIL} x$$

$$\frac{dv}{dx} = \frac{Pa}{EI} x - \frac{Pa}{EIL}\frac{x^2}{2} + B_1$$

$$v = \frac{Pa}{EI}\frac{x^2}{2} - \frac{Pa}{EIL}\frac{x^3}{6} + B_1 x + B_2$$

To determine the four constants A_1, A_2, B_1, and B_2, two boundary and two continuity conditions must be used.

For segment AD: $v(0) = 0 = A_2$

For segment DB: $v(L) = 0 = \frac{PaL^2}{3EI} + B_1 L + B_2$

Equating deflections for both segments at $x = a$:

$$v_D = v(a) = \frac{Pa^3 b}{6EIL} + A_1 a = \frac{Pa^3}{2EI} - \frac{Pa^4}{6EIL} + B_1 a + B_2$$

Equating slopes for both segments at $x = a$:

$$\theta_D = v'(a) = \frac{Pa^2 b}{2EIL} + A_1 = \frac{Pa^2}{EI} - \frac{Pa^3}{2EIL} + B_1$$

Upon solving the above four equations simultaneously, one finds

$$A_1 = -\frac{Pb}{6EIL}(L^2 - b^2) \qquad A_2 = 0$$

$$B_1 = -\frac{Pa}{6EIL}(2L^2 + a^2) \qquad B_2 = \frac{Pa^3}{6EI}$$

With these constants, for example, the elastic curve for the left segment AD of the beam becomes

$$v = [(Pb/(6EIL)][x^3 - (L^2 - b^2)x] \tag{a}$$

The largest deflection occurs in the longer segment of the beam if $a > b$, the point of maximum deflection is at $x = \sqrt{a(a + 2b)/3}$, which follows from setting the expression for the slope equal to zero. The deflection at this point is

$$|v|_{max} = \frac{Pb(L^2 - b^2)^{3/2}}{9\sqrt{3}EIL} \tag{b}$$

Usually the deflection at the center of the span is very nearly equal to the numerically largest deflection. Such a deflection is much simpler to determine, recommending its use in practice. If the force P is applied at the middle of the span, i.e., $a = b = L/2$, it can be shown by direct substitution into Eq. (a) or (b) that $x = L/2$

$$|v|_{max} = PL^3/(48EI) \tag{c}$$

Case (b). The solution of the same problem using singularity functions is very direct.

$$EI\frac{d^4v}{dx^4} = P = -P\langle x - a\rangle^{-1}$$

$$EI\frac{d^3v}{dx^3} = -P\langle x - a\rangle^{0} + C_1$$

$$EI\frac{d^2v}{dx^2} = -P\langle x - a\rangle^{1} + C_1x + C_2$$

But (M(0) = 0; hence $EIv''(0) = 0 = C_2$; and, since also $M(L) = 0$,

$$EIv''(L) = -Pb + C_1L = 0 \quad \text{or} \quad C_1 = Pb/L$$

$$EI\frac{dv}{dx} = -\frac{P}{2}\langle x - a\rangle^2 + \frac{Pb}{2L}x^2 + C_3$$

$$EIv = -\frac{P}{6}\langle x - a\rangle^3 + \frac{Pb}{6L}x^3 + C_3x + C_4$$

But $v(0) = 0$; hence $EIv(0) = 0 = C_4$. Similarly, from $v(L) = 0$,

$$EIv(L) = 0 = -\frac{Pb^3}{6} + \frac{PbL^2}{6} - C_3L \quad \text{or} \quad C_3 = -\frac{Pb}{6L}(L^2 - b^2)$$

$$v = \frac{Pb}{6EIL}\left[x^3 - (L^2 - b^2)x - \frac{L}{b}\langle x - a\rangle^3\right] \qquad \text{(d)}$$

For segment AD this general equation is the same as Eq. (c).

• PROBLEM 9-21

Find the deflection curve for a beam loaded as shown.

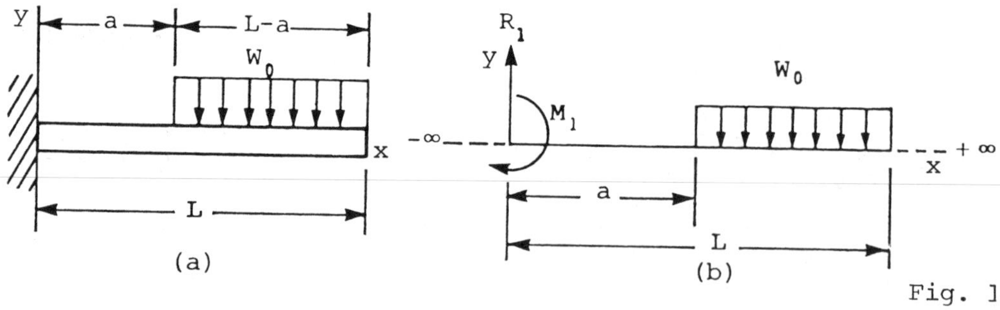

Fig. 1

Solution: From an infinite beam, the loading is

$$w_y(x) = M_1[\eta(x)] + R_1[\delta(x)] - w_0[u(x - a)] + w_0[u(x - L)] \qquad \text{(a)}$$

From which

$$\frac{d^4Y}{dx^4} = \frac{1}{EI}\{M_1[\eta(x)] + R_1[\delta(x)] - w_0[u(x - a)] + w_0[u(x - L)] \qquad \text{(b)}$$

Performing four quadratures from $-\infty$ to x,

$$\frac{d^3Y}{dx^3} = \frac{1}{EI}\{M_1[\delta(x)] + R_1[u(x)] - w_0(x - a)[u(x - a)] + w_0(x - L)[u(x - L)]\} \tag{c}$$

$$\frac{d^2Y}{dx^2} = \frac{1}{EI}\left\{M_1[u(x)] + R_1x[u(x)] - w_0\frac{(x - a)^2}{2}[u(x - a)] + w_0\frac{(x - L)^2}{2}[u(x - L)]\right\} \tag{d}$$

$$\frac{dY}{dx} = \frac{1}{EI}\left\{M_1x[u(x)] + R_1\frac{x^2}{2}[u(x)] - \frac{w_0(x - a)^3}{6}[u(x - a)] + \frac{w_0(x - L)^3}{6}[u(x - L)] + C_3\right\} \tag{e}$$

$$Y = \frac{1}{EI}\left\{\frac{M_1x^2}{2}[u(x)] + \frac{R_1x^3}{6}[u(x)] - \frac{w_0(x - a)^4}{24}[u(x - a)] + \frac{w_0(x - L)^4}{24}[u(x - L)] + C_3x + C_4\right\} \tag{f}$$

At $x = L^+$, $d^3Y/dx^3 = d^2Y/dx^2 = 0$. Therefore,

$$\frac{1}{EI}[R_1 - w_0(L - a)] = 0 \tag{g}$$

and

$$\frac{1}{EI}\left[M_1 + R_1L - \frac{w_0(L - a)^2}{2}\right] = 0 \tag{h}$$

Solving for R_1 and M_1,

$$R_1 = w_0(L - a) \tag{i}$$

$$M_1 = -w_0L(L - a) + \frac{w_0(L - a)^2}{2} = \frac{w_0}{2}(a^2 - L^2) \tag{j}$$

Applying the boundary conditions at the support, $Y = dY/dx = 0$ at $x = 0$ yields $C_3 = C_4 = 0$. Substituting into Eq. (f), gives the deflection curve as,

$$Y = \frac{1}{EI}\left\{\frac{w_0(a^2 - L^2)}{4}x^2[u(x)] + \frac{w_0(L - a)}{6}x^3[u(x)] - \frac{w_0(x - a)^4}{24}[u(x - a)] + \frac{w_0(x - L)^4}{24}[u(x - L)]\right\} \tag{k}$$

• PROBLEM 9-22

Find the deflection curve using singularity functions and the deflection at location A for the beam shown.

Solution: The equation for the loading will be written in singularity function form and integrated four times to get the deflection.

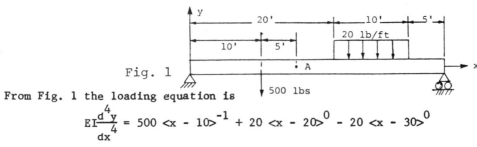

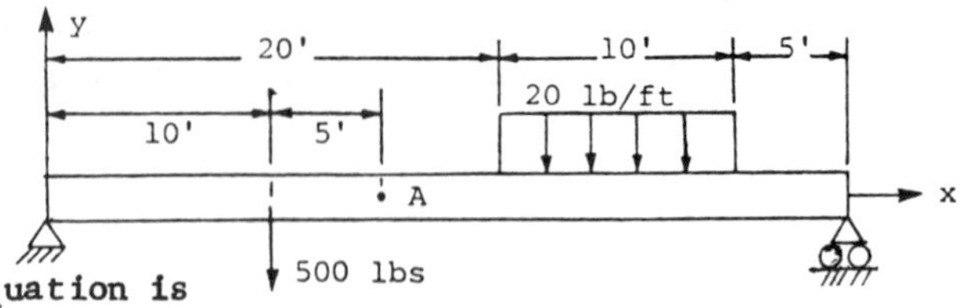

Fig. 1

From Fig. 1 the loading equation is

$$EI\frac{d^4y}{dx^4} = 500 <x - 10>^{-1} + 20 <x - 20>^0 - 20 <x - 30>^0$$

Integrating gives the shear

$$EI\frac{d^3y}{dx^3} = 500 <x - 10>^0 + 20 <x - 20>^1 - 20 <x - 30>^1 + c_1$$

Integrating the shear gives the moment

$$EI\frac{d^2y}{dx^2} = 500 <x - 10>^1 + 20 <x - 20>^2/2 - 20 <x - 30>^2/2 + c_1x + c_2$$

Since the moment at the left end is zero, c_2 is zero. The moment at the right end is also zero. Substituting in 35', the value of x at the right end, yields

$$0 = 500(35-10) + 20(35-20)^2/2 - 20(35-30)^2/2 + c_1(35)$$

Solving for c_1

$$c_1(35) = -14500$$

$$c_1 = -414.3$$

Integrating the moment gives the slope

$$EI\frac{dy}{dx} = 500<x - 10>^2/2 + 20<x - 20>^3/6 - 20<x - 30>^3/6 - 414.3x^2/2 + c_3$$

Integrating the slope gives the deflection

$$EIy = 500<x - 10>^3/6 + 20<x - 20>^4/24 - 20<x - 30>^4/24 - 414.3x^3/6 + c_3x + c_4$$

The deflection at $x = 0$ is zero so $c_4 = 0$. The deflection at the right end $(x = 35)$ is also zero. Substituting yields

$$0 = 500(25)^3/6 + 20(15)^4/24 - 20(5)^4/24 - 414.3(35)^3/6 + c_3(35)$$

Solving for c_3

$$c_3(35) = 1617000$$

$$c_3 = 46200$$

The deflection equation is thus

$$EIy = 500<x - 10>^3/6 + 20<x - 20>^4/24 - 20<x - 30>^4/24 - 414.3x^3/6 + 46200x$$

It is desired to find the deflection at $x = 15$. Substituting yields

$$EIy = 500(15-10)^3/6 - 414.3(15)^3/6 + 46200(15)$$

$$EIy = 470000$$

$$y = 470000/EI$$

The deflection at $x = 15$ is $470000/EI$.

A simple beam supports a uniformly distributed downward load P_0. The flexural rigidity EI is constant. Find the elastic curve by the following three methods: (a) Use the second-order differential equation to obtain the deflection of the beam. (b) Use the fourth-order equation instead of the one in (a). (c) Illustrate a graphical solution of the problem.

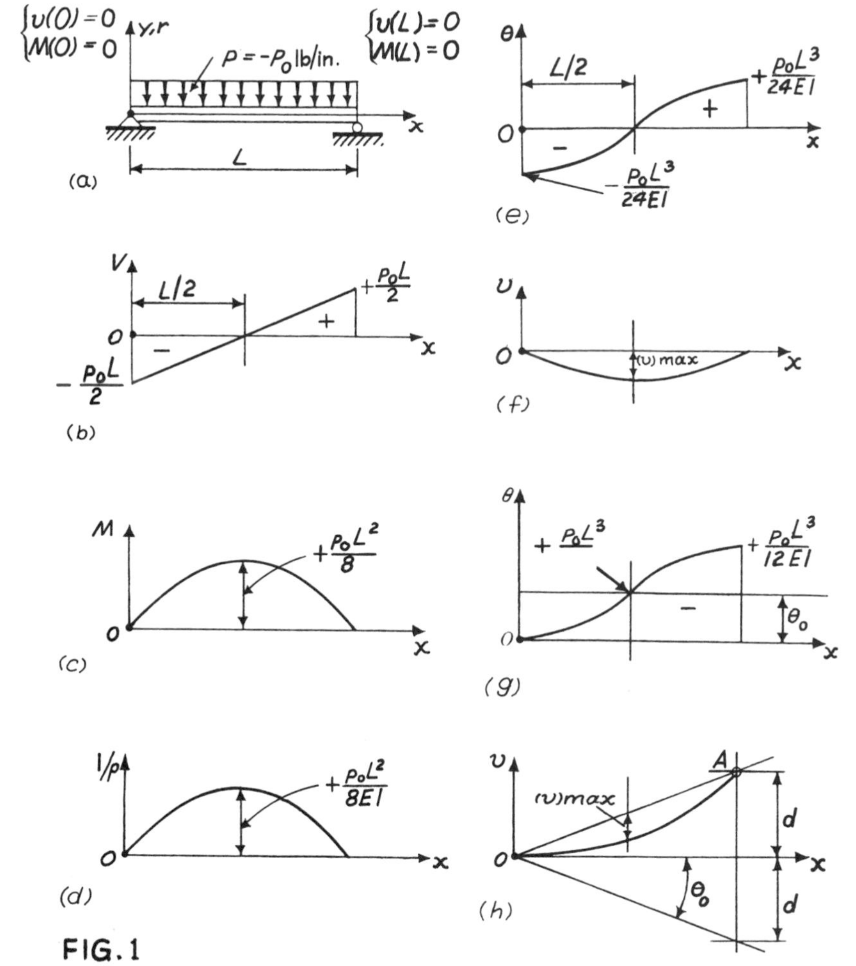

FIG. 1

Solution: Case (a). A diagram of the beam together with the implied boundary conditions is in Fig. 1a. The expression for M for use in the second order differential equation is

$$M = \frac{P_0 Lx}{2} - \frac{P_0 x^2}{2}$$

Substituting this relation into

$$M = EI \frac{d^2 v}{dx^2}$$

integrating it twice in succession, and making use of the boundary conditions, one finds the equation of the elastic curve:

$$EI\frac{d^2v}{dx^2} = M = \frac{P_0 Lx}{2} - \frac{P_0 x^2}{2}$$

$$EI\frac{dv}{dx} = \frac{P_0 Lx^2}{4} - \frac{P_0 x^3}{6} + C_3$$

$$EIv = \frac{P_0 Lx^3}{12} - \frac{P_0 x^4}{24} + C_3 x + C_4$$

But $v(0) = 0$; hence $EIv(0) = 0 = C_4$; and, since also $v(L) = 0$,

$$EIv(L) = 0 = \frac{P_0 L^4}{24} + C_3 L \quad \text{and} \quad C_3 = \frac{P_0 L^3}{24}$$

$$v = -\frac{P_0}{24EI}(L^3 x - 2Lx^3 + x^4) \qquad \text{(a)}$$

By virtue of symmetry, the largest deflection occurs at $x = L/2$. On substituting this value of x into Eq. a one obtains

$$|v|_{max} = 5P_0 L^4/(384EI) \qquad \text{(b)}$$

The condition of symmetry could also have been used to determine the constant C_3. As it is known that $v'(L/2) = 0$, one has

$$EIv'(L/2) = \frac{P_0 L(L/2)^2}{4} - \frac{P_0 (L/2)^3}{6} + C_3 = 0$$

and, as before, $C_3 = -(1/24)P_0 L^3$.

Case (b). Application of $-P_0 = EI\frac{d^4v}{dx^4}$ to the solution of this problem is direct. The constants are found from the boundary conditions.

$$EI\,\frac{d^4v}{dx^4} = P = -P_0$$

$$EI\,\frac{d^3v}{dx^3} = -P_0 x + C_1$$

$$EI\,\frac{d^2v}{dx^2} = \frac{P_0 x^2}{2} + C_1 x + C_2$$

But $M(0) = 0$; hence $EIv''(0) = 0 = C_2$; and, since also $M(L) = 0$,

$$EIv''(L) = 0 = -\frac{P_0 L^2}{2} + C_1 L \quad \text{or} \quad C_1 = \frac{P_0 L}{2}$$

hence

$$EI\frac{d^2v}{dx^2} = \frac{P_0 Lx}{2} - \frac{P_0 x^2}{2}$$

The remainder of the problem is the same as in Case (a). In this approach no preliminary calculation of reactions is required. As will be shown later, this is advantageous in some statically indeterminate problems.

Case (c). The steps needed for a graphical solution of the complete problem are in Figs 1(b) through (f). In Figs 1(b) and (c) the conventional shear and moment diagrams are shown. The curvature diagram is obtained by plotting $M/(EI)$, as in Fig. 1d.

Since by virtue of symmetry the slope to the elastic curve at $x = L/2$ is horizontal, $\theta(L/2) = 0$. Therefore, the construction of the θ diagram can be started from the center. In this procedure, the right ordinate in Fig.1(e) must equal the shaded area of Fig.1(d), and vice versa. By summing the θ diagram, one finds the elastic deflection v. The shaded area of Fig.1(e) is equal numerically to the maximum deflection. In the above, the condition of symmetry was employed. A generally applicable procedure follows.

After the curvature diagram is established as in Fig.1(d), the θ diagram can be constructed with an assumed initial value of θ at the origin. For example, let $\theta(0) = 0$ and sum the curvature diagram to obtain the θ diagram, Fig.1(g). Note that the shape of the curve so found is identical to that of Fig.1(e). Summing the area of the θ diagram gives the elastic curve. In Fig.1(h) this curve extends from 0 to A. This violates the boundary condition at A, where the deflection must be zero. Correct deflections are given, however, by measuring them vertically from a straight line passing through 0 and A. This inclined line corrects the deflection ordinates caused by the incorrectly assumed $\theta(0)$. In fact, after constructing Fig.1(h), one knows that $\theta(0) = -d/L = P_0L^3/(24EI)$. When this value of $\theta(0)$ is used, the problem reverts to the preceding solution (Fig.1(e) and (f)). In Fig.1(h) inclined measurements have no meaning. The procedure described is applicable for beams with overhangs. In such cases the base line for measuring deflections must pass through the support points.

• PROBLEM 9-24

Determine the deflection at the left end of the beam of Fig. 1a.

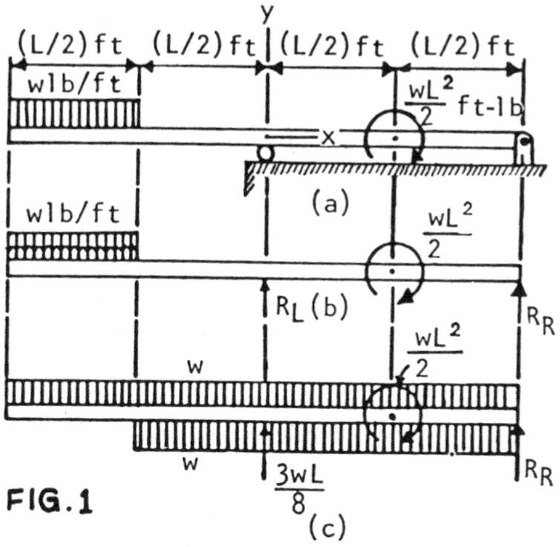

FIG.1

Solution: The equations of equilibrium, applied to the free-body diagram of Fig. 1b, give the reaction R_L as 3wL/8 upward. By use of singularity functions and the superposed loads of Fig. 1c, the bending-moment equation becomes

$$EI\,\frac{d^2y}{dx^2} = -\frac{w}{2}(x+L)^2 + \frac{w}{2}\left\langle x+\frac{L}{2}\right\rangle^2 + \frac{3wL}{8}(x)^1 + \frac{wL^2}{2}\left\langle x-\frac{L}{2}\right\rangle^0$$

The boundary conditions are $y = 0$ when $x = 0$, and $y = 0$ when $x = L$. Two integrations of the moment equation give

$$EI\,\frac{dy}{dx} = -\frac{w}{6}(x+L)^3 + \frac{w}{6}\left\langle x+\frac{L}{2}\right\rangle^3 + \frac{3wL}{16}(x)^2 + \frac{wL^2}{2}\left\langle x-\frac{L}{2}\right\rangle^1 + C_1$$

and

$$EIy = -\frac{w}{24}(x + L)^4 + \frac{w}{24}\left(x + \frac{L}{2}\right)^4 + \frac{wL}{16}(x)^3 + \frac{wL^2}{4}\left(x - \frac{L}{2}\right)^2 + C_1x + c_2 .$$

The first boundary condition, $y = 0$ when $x = 0$, gives

$$0 = -\frac{wL^4}{24} + \frac{wL^4}{384} + 0 + 0 + 0 + C_2 ,$$

from which

$$C_2 = + \frac{5}{128} wL^4 .$$

The second boundary condition, $y = 0$ when $x = L$, gives

$$0 = -\frac{16wL^4}{24} + \frac{81wL^4}{384} + \frac{wL^4}{16} + \frac{wL^4}{16} + C_1L + \frac{5wL^4}{128} ,$$

from which

$$C_1 = + \frac{7}{24} wL^3 .$$

The deflection at $x = -L$ is found, by substitution, to be

$$y = -\frac{97}{384}\frac{wL^4}{EI} = \frac{97}{384}\frac{wL^4}{EI} \text{ downward.}$$

• PROBLEM 9-25

Use singularity functions to write a single equation for the bending moment at any section of the beam of Fig. 1a.

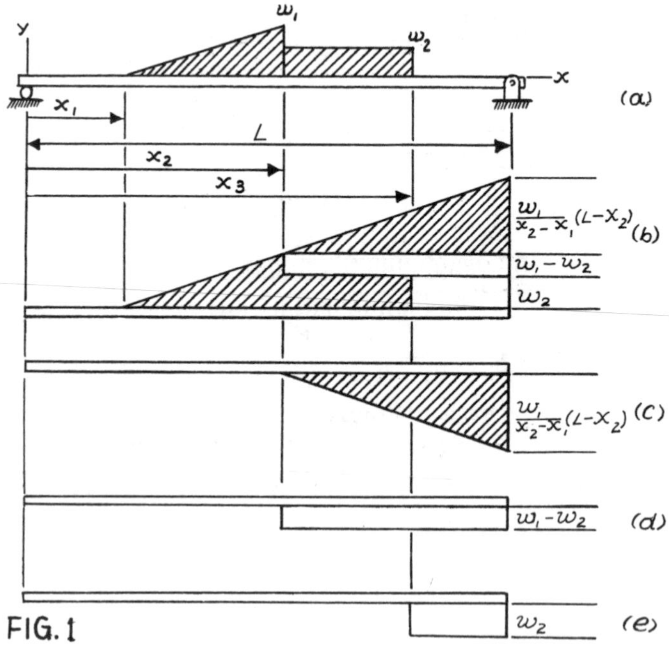

FIG. 1

Solution: The loading on the beam of Fig. 1a can be considered as a combination of the loadings shown in Fig. 1b, c, d, and e; where downward-acting loads are shown on top of the beam and upward-acting loads

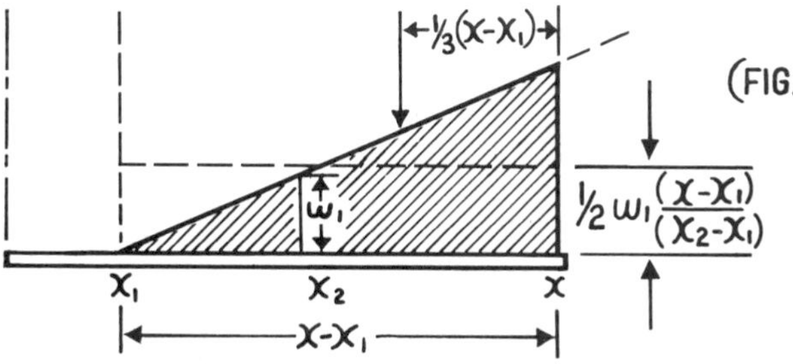

on the bottom. The moment of the linearly varying load can be obtained from the geometry of the load diagram. The moment due to the triangular load for any x to the right of x_1 is

$$M = F \times L = \frac{1}{2} w_1 \frac{(x - x_1)}{(x_2 - x_1)} (x - x_1) \times \frac{1}{3}(x - x_1)$$

Using the singularity function, the moment at any x is

$$M = \frac{w_1}{6(x_2 - x_1)} \langle x - x_1 \rangle^3$$

The total moment equation due to both the loadings is therefore

$$M_x = R_L x - \frac{w_1}{6(x_2 - x_1)} \langle x - x_1 \rangle^3 + \frac{w_1}{6(x_2 - x_1)} \langle x - x_2 \rangle^3$$

$$+ \frac{w_1 - w_2}{2} \langle x - x_2 \rangle^2 + \frac{w_2}{2} \langle x - x_3 \rangle^2 .$$

• PROBLEM 9-26

A simply supported beam 10 in. long is loaded with a 10-lb downward force 8 in. from the left support, Fig. 1a. The cross section of the beam is such that in the segment AB the moment of inertia is $4I_1$, in the remainder of the beam it is I_1. Determine the elastic curve.

Solution: This problem will be solved two ways. First using singularity functions and the equation

$$\frac{d^4 v}{dx^4} = P/EI$$

and secondly using the graphical procedure.

The beam is separated at the point of discontinuity in I and the forces necessary for the equilibrium of segments are computed, Fig. 1b. Then the solution is commenced independently for each segment of the beam with the same location of the origin at A. The successive integrations are carried out until the moment-curvature equations are found. No constants of integration appear in the first two integrations as the reactive forces are computed beforehand. For segment AB:

$$\frac{d^4 v}{dx^4} = \frac{P}{EI} = \frac{1}{4EI_1}[+2(x)^{-1} - 2(x - 8)^{-1} - 16(x - 8)^{-2}]$$

$$\frac{d^3 v}{dx^3} = -\frac{V}{LI} = \frac{1}{2EI_1} \langle x \rangle^0 - \frac{1}{2EI_1} \langle x - 8 \rangle^0 - \frac{4}{EI_1} \langle x - 8 \rangle^{-1}$$

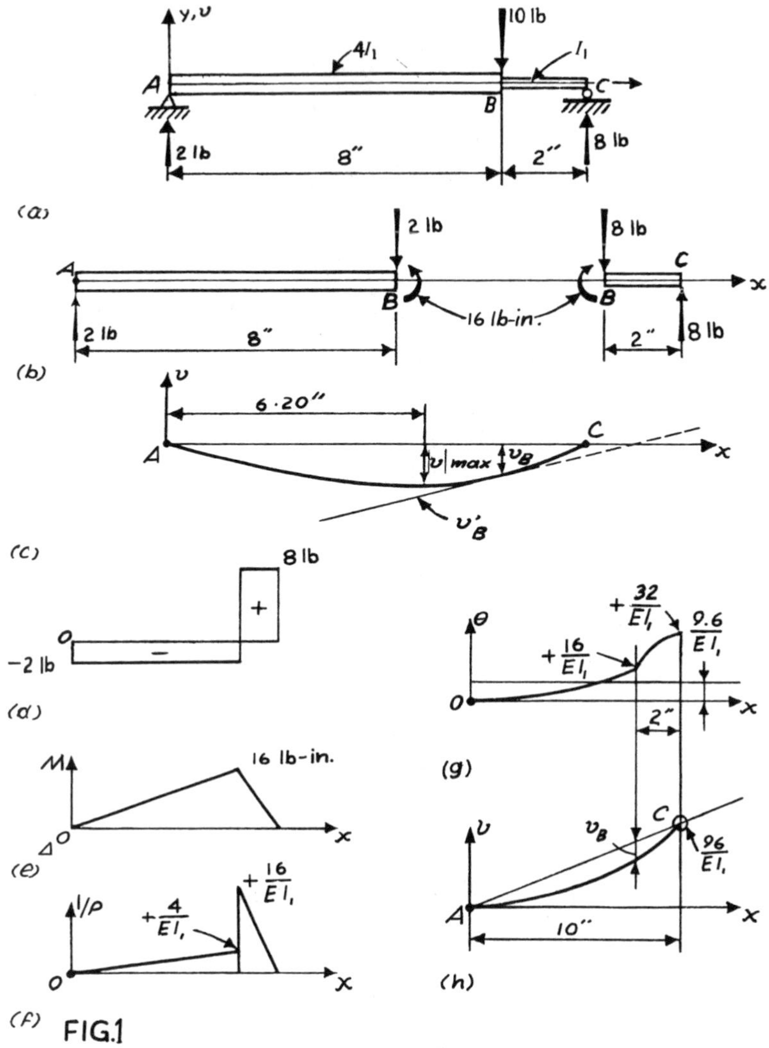

FIG.1

$$\frac{d^2v}{dx^2} = \frac{M}{EI} - \frac{1}{2EI_1}\langle x\rangle^1 - \frac{1}{2EI_1}\langle x - 8\rangle^1 - \frac{4}{EI_1}\langle x - 8\rangle^0$$

$$\frac{dv}{dx} = 0 - \frac{1}{4EI_1}\langle x\rangle^2 - \frac{1}{4EI_1}\langle x - 8\rangle^2 - \frac{4}{EI_1}\langle x - 8\rangle^1 + \theta_0$$

where θ_0 is an unknown constant of integration. For segment BC:

$$\frac{d^4v}{dx^4} = \frac{P}{EI} = \frac{1}{EI_1}\left[+16\langle x - 8\rangle^{-2} - 8\langle x - 8\rangle^{-1} + 8\langle x - 10\rangle^{-1}\right]$$

$$\frac{d^3v}{dx^3} = -\frac{V}{EI} = \frac{16}{EI_1}\langle x - 8\rangle^{-1} - \frac{8}{EI_1}\langle x - 8\rangle^0 + \frac{8}{EI_1}\langle x - 10\rangle^0$$

$$\frac{d^2v}{dx^2} = \frac{M}{EI} = \frac{16}{EI_1}\langle x - 8\rangle^0 - \frac{8}{EI_1}\langle x - 8\rangle^1 + \frac{8}{EI_1}\langle x - 10\rangle^1$$

At this stage of integration it must be recognized that by virtue of the continuity requirements, the terminal value of θ for the segment AB is the initial one for the segment BC. Moreover, this expression of θ for the segment AB for $x = 8$ remains constant. Therefore it is possible to integrate the last expression above for the segment BC and add to it the θ for segment AB. This yields a complete continuous function of θ for the whole beam AC. On subsequent integrations the boundary conditions can be used for determining the constants. For segment BC:

$$\frac{dv}{dx} = \theta = \frac{16}{EI_1} \langle x - 8 \rangle^1 - \frac{4}{EI_1} \langle x - 8 \rangle^2$$

Here the last term of the earlier expression, having no relevance, has been dropped. Adding this expression to the one found earlier for the segment AB, one has for the entire beam AC:

$$\frac{dv}{dx} = \theta = \frac{1}{4EI_1} \langle x \rangle^2 - \frac{4.25}{EI_1} \langle x - 8 \rangle^2 + \frac{12}{EI_1} \langle x - 8 \rangle^1 + \theta_0$$

and

$$v = \frac{1}{12EI_1} \langle x \rangle^3 - \frac{4.25}{3EI_1} \langle x - 8 \rangle^3 + \frac{6}{EI_1} \langle x - 8 \rangle^2 + \theta_0 x + v_0$$

But since $v(0) = 0$, one has $v_0 = 0$. The condition that $v(10) = 0$ yields

$\theta_0 = -9.6/(EI_1)$. This completes the solution of the problem.

The equation for the slope in segment AB is $\theta = x^2/(4EI_1) - 48/(5EI_1)$. Upon setting this quantity equal to zero, x is found to be 6.20 in. The largest deflection occurs at this value of x, and $|v|_{max} = 39.7/(EI_1)$. Characteristically, the deflection at the center of the span - i.e., at x = 5 in. - is nearly the same, being $37.6/(EI_1)$.

A self-explanatory graphical procedure is in Figs. 1(d) through (h). Variation in I causes virtually no complications in the graphical solution, a great advantage in complex problems.

MOMENT-AREA METHOD

• PROBLEM 9-27

An 8-in. wide by 12-in. deep timber beam is simply supported on a span of 21 ft. A 3.50-kip load is applied 6 ft from the right support. Determine:

(a) The maximum deflection for a modulus of elasticity of 10^6 psi.
(b) The maximum fiber stress.
(c) The maximum horizontal shearing stress.

Solution: This problem will be solved using the area moment method. The loading, shear, moment and curvature diagrams are shown in Figs. 1(a), (b), (c), and (d) respectively.

Part (a) will be solved as follows: the vertical distance, $t_{C/A}$, from C to the tangent of A will be found by the second area moment theorem; the angle θ will be found by trigonometry; an equation for θ in terms of x will be found by applying the first area moment theorem between A and B (since B is the point of maximum deflection, the slope is zero and the tangent is parallel to the x axis);

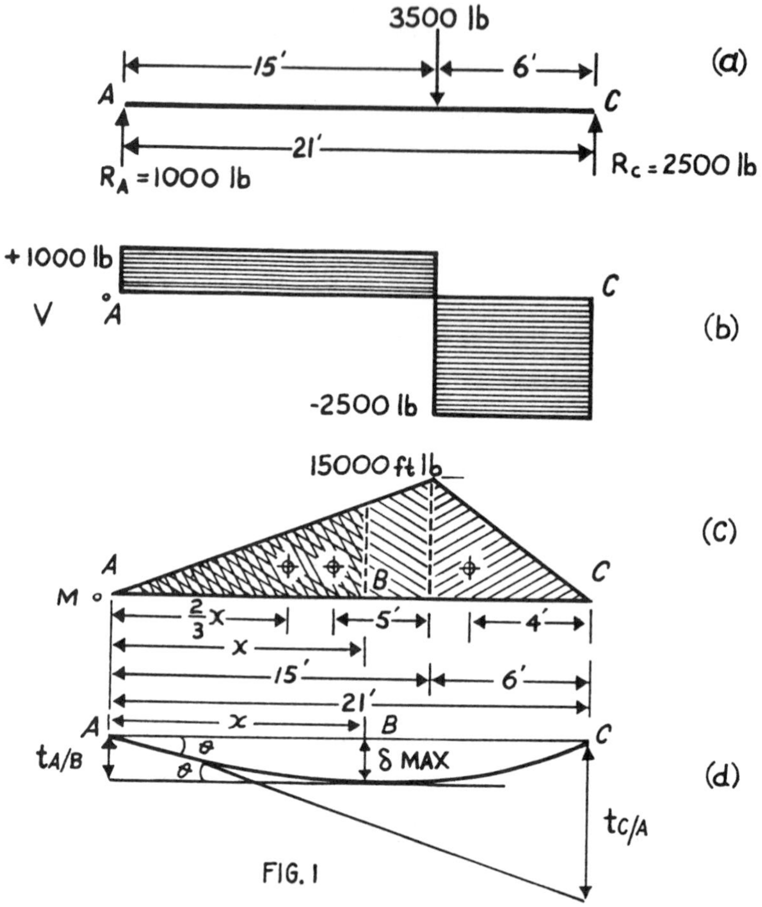

FIG. 1

the equation will be solved for x; with x known, the second area moment theorem will be applied between A and B to get the value of the maximum deflection.

By the second area moment theorem, the vertical distance $t_{C/A}$ is equal to the area of the moment diagram, times the distance from the centroid of the area divided by EI. The moment diagram is conveniently divided into two areas

$$t_{C/A} = (\bar{x}_1 A_1 + \bar{x}_2 A_2)/EI$$

$$= ((6+5)(\tfrac{1}{2}(15)(15000)) + (4)(\tfrac{1}{2}(6)(15000)))/EI$$

$$t_{C/A} = 1417500/EI$$

By trigonometry

$$\tan\theta = \frac{t_{C/A}}{L}$$

For small angles, $\tan\theta \approx \theta$, $\theta = \dfrac{t_{C/A}}{L} = \dfrac{1417500/EI}{21} = 67500/EI$.

By the first area moment theorem, the angle between the tangent at A and the tangent at B which is also equal to θ, is the area of the moment diagram divided by EI between A and B.

$$\theta = \tfrac{1}{2}x((x/15)(15000))/EI$$

$$\theta = 500x^2/EI$$

Solving for x

$$x = \sqrt{\frac{\theta\ EI}{500}}$$

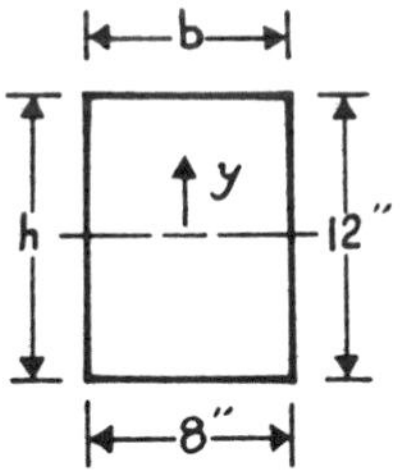

FIG. 2

Substituting in the value of θ yields

$$x = \sqrt{\frac{(67500/EI)EI}{500}}$$

$$x = \sqrt{135}$$

By the second area moment theorem the vertical distance $t_{A/B}$ is equal to the area of the moment diagram between A and B times the distance from A to the centroid of the area divided by EI

$$t_{A/B} = (\tfrac{2}{3}\ x)(\tfrac{1}{2}x(x/15)(15000))/EI$$

The moment of inertia, I, of the beam is from Fig. 2

$$I = bh^3/12 = 8(12)^3/12 = 1152\ in^4$$

Substituting for x, E, and I and employing the conversion factor ($1728\ in^3/ft^3$) yields

$$t_{A/B} = (\tfrac{2}{3}\sqrt{135})(\tfrac{1}{2}\sqrt{135}(\sqrt{135}/15)(15000))(1728)/1152 \times 10^6$$

The maximum deflection is thus $t_{A/B}$ = .784 inches downwards.

For part (b) the equation for the fiber stress is

$$\sigma = My/I$$

The fiber stress will be maximum when the moment, M, and distance from the neutral axis y are both maximum since the moment of inertia I is constant.

From Fig. 1(c) the maximum moment is M = 15000 ft lb. From Fig. 2, y_{max} = 6 in. and I = 1152 in^4 . Substituting these values into the equation for the fiber stress and employing the conversion factor (12 in/ft) yields

$$\sigma_{max} = \frac{(M_{max})(y_{max})}{I} = \frac{(15000)(12)(6)}{1152}$$

Thus the maximum fiber stress is σ_{max} = 937.5 psi tension and compression.

For part (c) the equation for the horizontal shearing stress is

$$\tau = \frac{VQ}{Ib}$$

From Fig. 1(b) the maximum shear, V_{max} = 2500 lb. The maximum shearing stress occurs at the neutral axis so

$$Q_{max} = \int_0^{h/2} by\ dy$$

From Fig. 2 this is

$$Q_{max} = \int_0^6 8ydy = 8y^2/2\Big|_0^6 = 144\ in^3$$

Again from Fig. 2, b = 8 in and I = 1152 in^4. Substituting into the shear equation

$$\tau_{max} = \frac{(V_{max})(Q_{max})}{(I)\ (b)} = \frac{(2500)(144)}{(1152)(8)}$$

The maximum horizontal shear stress is thus

$$\tau_{max} = 39.06 \text{ psi}$$

• PROBLEM 9-28

Find the deflection due to the concentrated force P applied as shown in Fig. 1a at the center of a simply supported beam. The flexural rigidity EI is constant.

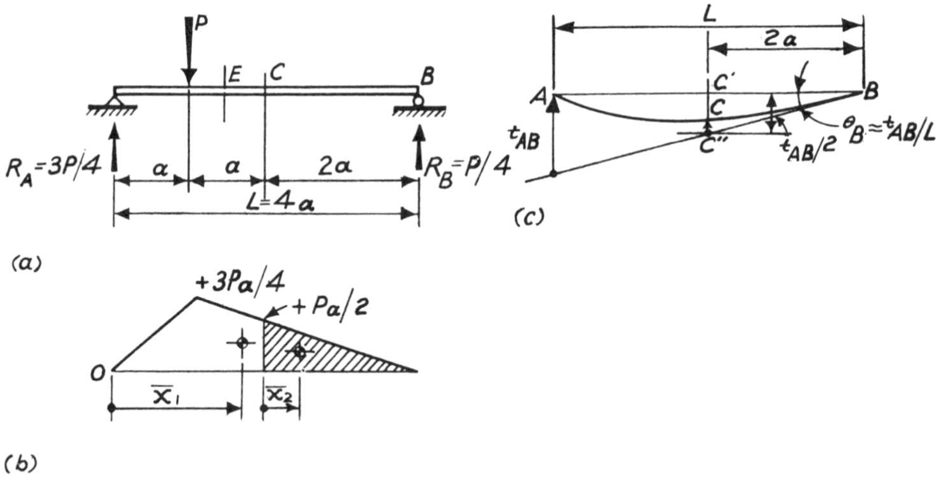

FIG. 1

Solution: The bending-moment diagram is in Fig. 1b. Since EI is constant, the M/(EI) diagram need not be made, as the areas of the bending-moment diagram divided by EI give the necessary quantities for use in the moment-area theorems. The elastic curve is in Fig. 1c. It is concave upward throughout its length as the bending moments are positive. This curve must pass through the points of the support at A and B.

It is apparent from the sketch of the elastic curve that the desired quantity is represented by the distance CC'. Moreover, from purely geometrical or kinematic considerations, CC' = C'C'' - C''C, where the distance C''C is measured from a tangent to the elastic curve passing through the point of support B. However, since the deviation of a support point from a tangent to the elastic curve at the other support may always be computed by the second moment-area theorem, a distance such as C'C'' may be found by proportion from the geometry of the figure. In this case, t_{AB} follows by taking the whole M/(EI) area between A and B and multiplying it by its $\bar{x}$ measured from a vertical through A, whence C'C'' = 1/2 t_{AB}. By another application of the second theorem, t_{CB}, which is equal to C''C, is determined. For this case, the M/(EI) area is shaded in Fig. 1b, and, for it, the $\bar{x}$ is measured from C. Since the right reaction is P/4 and the distance

CB = 2a, the maximum ordinate for the shaded triangle is $+Pa/2$.

$$v_C = C'C'' - C''C = (t_{AB}/2) - t_{CB}$$

$$t_{AB} = \Phi_1\bar{x}_1 = \frac{1}{EI}\left(\frac{4a}{2}\ \frac{3Pa}{4}\right)\frac{(a + 4a)}{3} = + \frac{5Pa^3}{2EI}$$

$$t_{CB} = \Phi_2\bar{x}_2 = \frac{1}{EI}\left(\frac{2a}{2}\ \frac{Pa}{2}\right)\frac{(2a)}{3} = + \frac{Pa^3}{3EI}$$

$$v_C = \frac{t_{AB}}{2} - t_{CB} = \frac{5Pa^3}{4EI} - \frac{Pa^3}{3EI} = \frac{11Pa^3}{12EI}$$

The positive signs of t_{AB} and t_{CB} indicate that points A and C lie above the tangent through B. As may be seen from Fig. 1c, the deflection at the center of the beam is in a downward direction.

The slope of the elastic curve at C can be found from the slope at one of the ends. For point B on the right

$$\theta_B = \theta_C + \Delta\theta_{BC} \quad \text{or} \quad \theta_C = \theta_B - \Delta\theta_{BC}$$

$$\theta_C = \frac{t_{AB}}{L} - \Phi_2 = \frac{5Pa^2}{8EI} - \frac{Pa^2}{2EI} = \frac{Pa^2}{8EI}$$

radians counterclockwise.

• PROBLEM 9-29

A simple beam is acted upon by couples M_0 at the ends (see Fig. 1). Obtain expressions for the angles of rotation θ_a and θ_b at the ends of the beam and the deflection δ at the middle.

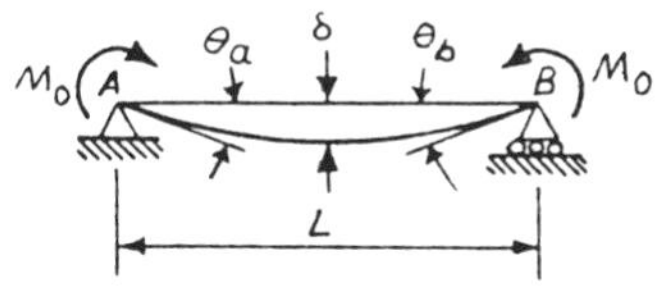

FIG.1 SIMPLE BEAM WITH COUPLES ACTING AT THE ENDS.

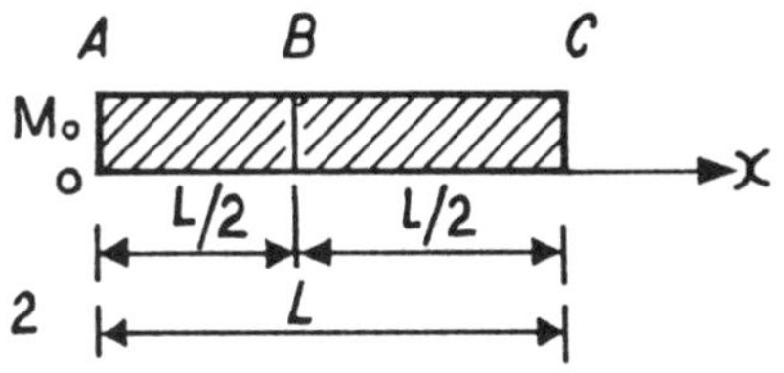

FIG. 2

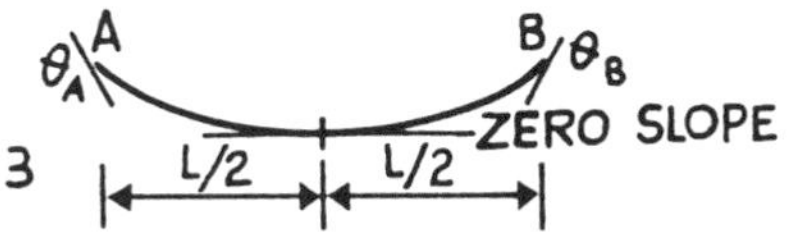

FIG. 3

Solution: This problem will be solved using the first and second moment area theorems.

The moment diagram is given in Fig. 2. The slope at the mid-point of the beam, x = L/2, is zero (see Fig. 3)

By the first moment-area theorem, the difference in slope between points A and B is

$$\theta_B - \theta_A = \int_A^B \frac{M}{EI}\,dx$$

Since θ_B is zero and the value of the integral is the area of the moment diagram (Fig. 2) between A and B ($M_0L/2$) divided by EI the

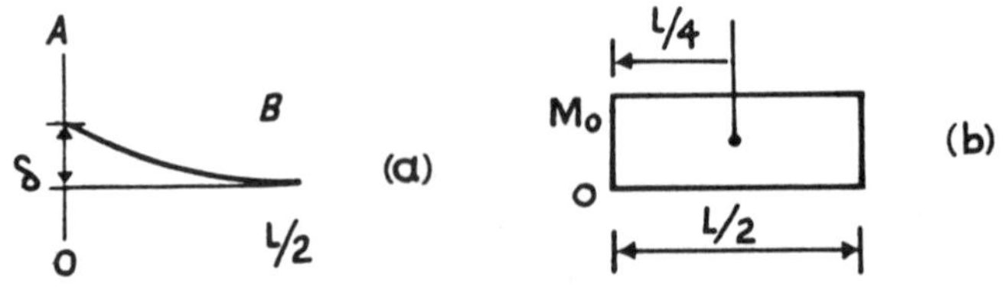

FIG. 4

slope at A is

$$\theta_A = \frac{-M_0L}{2EI}$$

Again by the first moment-area theorem the difference in slope between points B and C is

$$\theta_C - \theta_B = \int_B^C \frac{M}{EI}\,dx$$

The area of the moment diagram Mx from B to C is $M_0L/2$ and θ_B is zero. Substituting yields

$$\theta_C = \frac{M_0L}{2EI}$$

By the second moment-area theorem, the deflection is from Fig. 4.

$$\delta = A\bar{x}/EI = M_0L/2(L/4)/EI = M_0L^2/8EI$$

The deflection at the middle of the beam is $M_0L^2/8EI$ downwards.

The results obtained can be checked by referring to a table of beam deflections and slopes. If the case of a simply supported beam with couples acting at both ends is not listed, the formulas for a beam with a couple acting at only one end can be modified using superposition. This results in

$$-\theta_a = \theta_b = \frac{M_0L}{3EI} + \frac{M_0L}{6EI} = \frac{M_0L}{2EI}$$

$$\delta = (2)\,\frac{M_0L^2}{16EI} = \frac{M_0L^2}{8EI}$$

This agrees with the results obtained using the moment-area theorems.

• PROBLEM 9-30

A concentrated load P acts on a simple beam AB (Fig. 1). Find the angle of rotation θ_a of the deflection curve at point A, the deflection δ under the load P, and the maximum deflection of the beam.

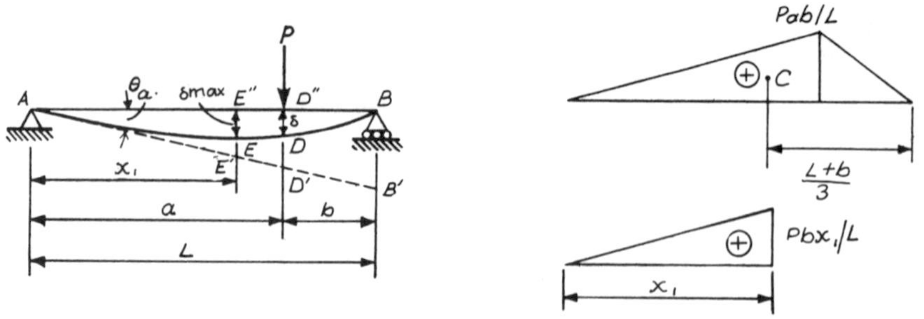

FIG.1 SINGLE BEAM WITH A CONCENTRATED LOAD

Solution: To find the angle at A we note first that θ_a is equal to the distance BB' divided by the length L. The distance BB' is the deflection of point B from the tangent at A, and therefore it can be calculated by taking the first moment about B of the bending moment area divided by EI. The area of the moment diagram is Pab/2 and the distance of its centroid C from B is (L + b)/3, as obtained from a handbook on mathematical formulas and shapes. Therefore,

$$BB' = \frac{Pab}{2EI}\left(\frac{L+b}{3}\right) = \frac{Pab}{6EI}(L+b)$$

The bending moment area is positive, which means that B is above the tangent, as expected. Finally, we have

$$\theta_a = \frac{Pab}{6LEI}(L+b)$$

The deflection δ under the load P can be found as the distance D"D' minus the distance DD' (see figure). The distance D"D' is equal to $a\theta$. The distance DD' is equal to the deflection of point D from the tangent at A and can be found by the second moment-area theorem:

$$DD' = \frac{Pab}{LEI}\left(\frac{a}{2}\right)\left(\frac{a}{3}\right) = \frac{Pa^3b}{6LEI}$$

Thus, for δ we get

$$\delta = a\theta_a - \frac{Pa^3b}{6LEI} = \frac{Pa^2b^2}{3LEI}$$

The maximum deflection of the beam occurs at point E, where the deflection curve has a horizontal tangent. The angle θ between the tangents at A and E is equal to the area of the moment diagram between A and E (shown in the last part of the figure) divided by EI. This angle must be the same as θ_a because the slope at E is zero. Hence, we obtain

$$\theta_a = \frac{x_1}{2}\left(\frac{Pbx_1}{LEI}\right) = \frac{Pbx_1^2}{2LEI}$$

where x_1 is the distance from A to the point of maximum deflection. Substituting the expression for θ_a into this equation and solving for x_1 gives

$$x_1 = \sqrt{\frac{a(L+b)}{3}} = \sqrt{\frac{L^2 - b^2}{3}}$$

The maximum deflection δ_{max} may be found as follows:

$$\delta_{max} = E''E' - EE' = x_1\theta_a - \frac{Pbx_1}{LEI}\left(\frac{x_1}{2}\right)\left(\frac{x_1}{3}\right) = \frac{Pb}{9\sqrt{3}LEI}(L^2 - b^2)^{3/2}$$

Alternatively, we can find δ_{max} somewhat easier by observing that it is equal to the deflection of point A above the tangent to the elastic curve at E. This deflection is the first moment of the bending-moment area between points A and E taken about point A, divided by EI; hence,

$$\delta_{max} = \frac{x_1}{2}\left(\frac{Pbx_1}{LEI}\right)\left(\frac{2x_1}{3}\right) = \frac{Pb}{9\sqrt{3}LEI}(L^2 - b^2)^{3/2}$$

as before. The preceding results are for the case where $a \geq b$.

• PROBLEM 9-31

In a simply supported beam, find the maximum deflection and rotation of the elastic curve at the ends caused by the application of a uniformly distributed load of P_0 lb per foot, Fig. 1a. The flexural rigidity EI is constant.

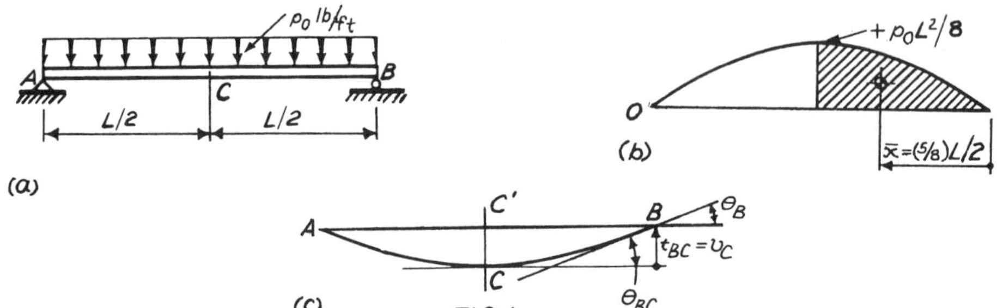

FIG. 1

Solution: The bending-moment diagram is in Fig. 1b. It is a second-degree parabola with a maximum value at the vertex of $P_0L^2/8$. The elastic curve passing through the points of the support A and B is shown in Fig. 1c.

In this case, the M/(EI) diagram is symmetrical about a vertical line passing through the center. Therefore the elastic curve must be symmetrical, and the tangent to this curve at the center of the beam is horizontal. From the figure, it is seen that $\Delta\theta_{BC}$ is equal to θ_B, and the rotation of the end B is equal to one-half the area of the whole M/(EI) diagram. The distance CC' is the desired deflection, and from the geometry of the figure it is seen to be equal to t_{BC}.

$$\Phi = \frac{1}{EI}\left(\frac{2}{3}\,\frac{L}{2}\,\frac{P_0L^2}{8}\right) = \frac{P_0L^3}{24EI}$$

$$\theta_B = \Delta\theta_{BC} = \Phi = +\frac{P_0L^3}{24EI}$$

$$v_C = v_{max} = t_{BC} = \Phi\bar{x} = \frac{P_0L^3}{24EI}\,\frac{5L}{16} = \frac{5P_0L^4}{384EI}$$

Since the point B is above the tangent through C, the sign of v_C is positive.

• PROBLEM 9-32

Determine the angle of rotation θ_b and deflection δ at the free end of a cantilever beam with a concentrated load P (see Fig. 1). The bending moment diagram is triangular in shape and is shown in the lower part of the figure.

Solution: This problem will be solved using the first and second moment-area theorems.

First Moment-Area Theorem: The difference of slope between any two points is equal to the area under the graph of curvature taken between these two points.

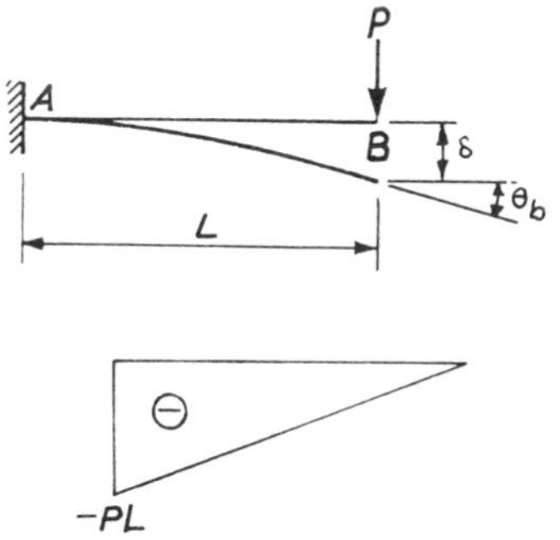

FIG.1 CANTILEVER BEAM WITH A CONCENTRATED LOAD

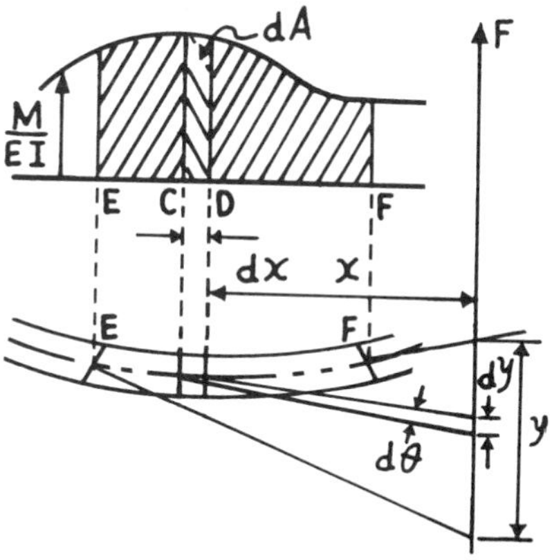

Second Moment-Area Theorem: On any vertical line, the distance y, between the intersections made by the tangents at points E and F is equal to the first moment about that line of the area of the M/EI graph between the points E and F.

From the first moment-area theorem we observe that the difference in angles between points A and B is equal to the area of the bending moment diagram divided by EI; this is $-PL^2/2EI$. The minus sign means that the tangent at B is rotated clockwise from the tangent at A, which is horizontal. Therefore, the angle θ_b, positive as shown in the figure, is

$$\theta_b = \frac{PL^2}{2EI}$$

The deflection δ at the end of the beam can be obtained by applying the second theorem. The distance Δ of point B on the deflection curve from the tangent at A is equal to the first moment of the bending moment area about B divided by EI:

$$\Delta = -\frac{PL^2}{2EI}\left(\frac{2L}{3}\right) = -\frac{PL^3}{3EI}$$

The minus sign means that point B on the deflection curve is below the tangent at A. The deflection δ, therefore, is

$$\delta = \frac{PL^3}{3EI}$$

• PROBLEM 9-33

Determine the deflection of the free end of the cantilever beam of Fig. 1a in terms of w, L, E, and I.

Solution: Since E and I are constant, a bending moment diagram is used instead of an M/(EI) diagram. The moment diagram is shown in Fig. 1b, and the area under it has been divided into rectangular, triangular, and parabolic parts for ease in calculating areas and moments. The elastic curve is shown in Fig. 1c with the deflection greatly exaggerated. Points A and B are selected at the ends of the beam because the beam has a horizontal tangent at B and the deflection at A is required. The vertical distance to A from the tangent at B, $t_{A/B}$ in Fig. 1c, equals the deflection of the free end of the beam, y_A. For this reason, the second area-moment theorem can be used directly to obtain the required deflection. The area of each of the three portions of the area under the moment diagram is shown in Fig. 1b along with the distance from the centroid of each part to the moment axis at

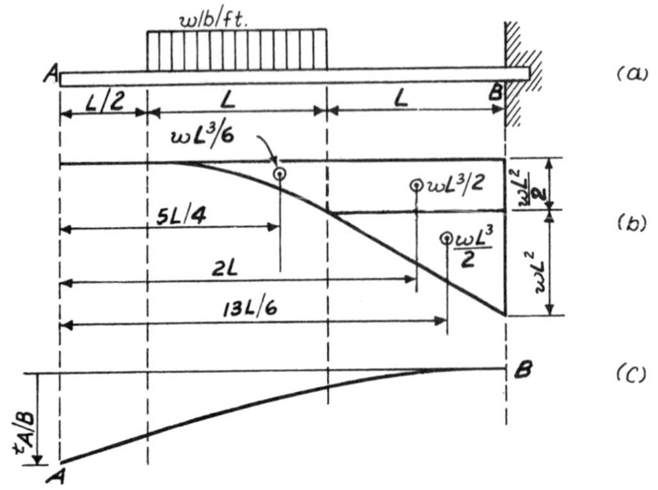

FIG.1

the free end A. The second area-moment theorem gives

$$EIt_{A/B} = -\frac{wL^3}{6}\left(\frac{5L}{4}\right) - \frac{wL^3}{2}(2L) - \frac{wL^3}{2}\left(\frac{13L}{6}\right),$$

from which

$$y_A = t_{A/B} = -\frac{55wL^4}{24EI} = \frac{55wL^4}{24EI} \text{ downward.}$$

• PROBLEM 9-34

Find the deflection of the free end A of the beam shown in Fig. 1a caused by the applied forces. The EI is constant.

Solution: The bending-moment diagram for the applied forces is in Fig. 1b. The bending moment changes sign at a/2 from the left support. At this point an inflection in the elastic curve takes place. Corresponding to the positive moment, the curve is concave up, and vice versa. The elastic curve is so drawn and passes over the supports at B and C, Fig. 1c. To begin, the inclination of the tangent to the elastic curve at the support B is determined by finding t_{CB} as the statical moment of the areas with the proper signs of the M/(EI) diagram between the verticals through C and B about C.

$$t_{CB} = \Phi_1\bar{x}_1 + \Phi_2\bar{x}_2 + \Phi_3\bar{x}_3$$

$$= \frac{1}{EI}\left[\frac{a}{2}(+Pa)\frac{2a}{3} + \frac{1}{2}\frac{a}{2}(+Pa)\left(a + \frac{1}{3}\frac{a}{2}\right) + \frac{1}{2}\frac{a}{2}(-Pa)\left(\frac{3a}{2} + \frac{2}{3}\frac{a}{2}\right)\right]$$

$$= +\frac{Pa^3}{6EI}$$

The positive sign of t_{CB} indicates that the point C is above the tangent through B. Hence a corrected sketch of the elastic curve is made, Fig. 1d, where it is seen that the deflection sought is given by the distance AA' and is equal to AA" - A'A". Further, since the triangles A'A"B and CC'B are similar, the distance A'A" = $t_{CB}/2$.

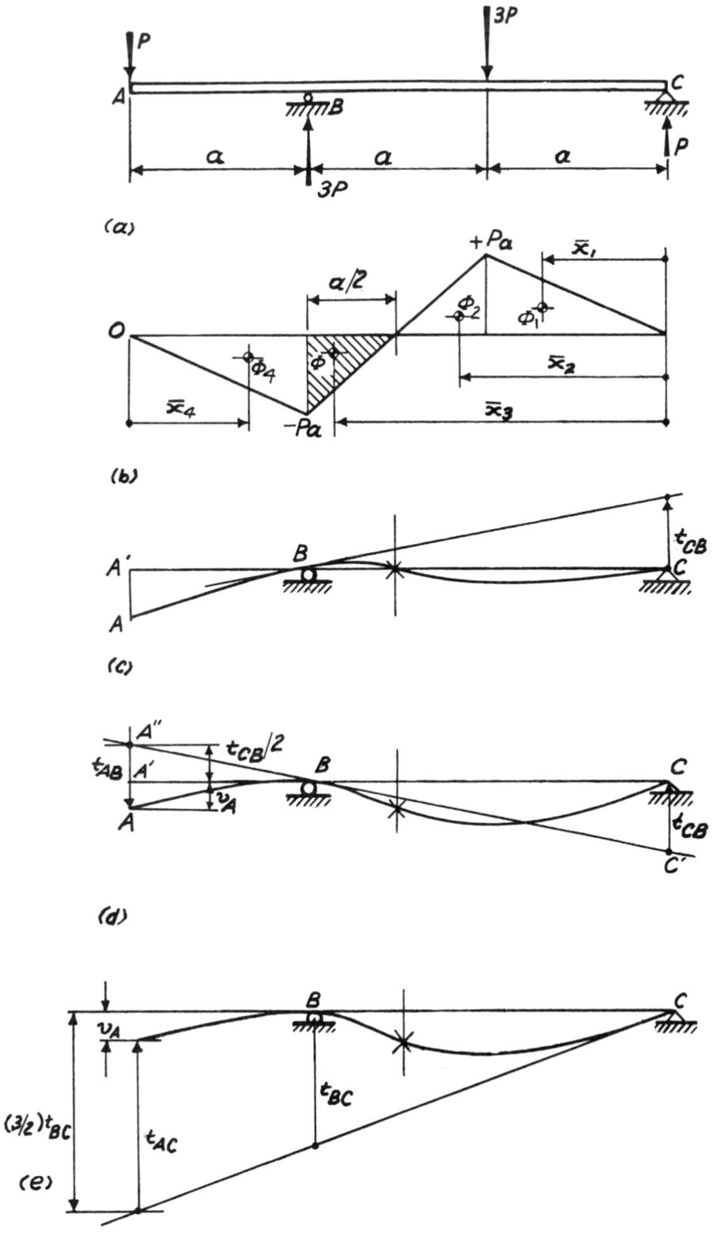

FIG.1

On the other hand, the distance AA'' is the deviation of the point A from the tangent to the elastic curve at the support B. Hence

$$v_A = AA' = AA'' - A'A'' = t_{AB} - (t_{CB}/2)$$

$$t_{AB} = \frac{1}{EI}(\Phi_4 \bar{x}_4) = \frac{1}{EI}\left[\frac{a}{2}(-Pa)\ \frac{2a}{3}\right] = -\frac{Pa^3}{3EI}$$

where the negative sign means that point A is below the tangent through B. This sign is not used henceforth as the geometry of the elastic curve indicates the direction of the actual displacements. Thus the deflection of point A below the line passing through the supports is

$$v_A = \frac{Pa^3}{3EI} - \frac{1}{2}\frac{Pa^3}{6EI} = \frac{Pa^3}{4EI}$$

This example illustrates the necessity of watching the signs of the quantities computed in the applications of the moment-area method, although usually less difficulty is encountered than in the above example. For instance, if the deflection of the end A is established by first finding the rotation of the elastic curve at C, no ambiguity in the direction of tangents occurs. This scheme of analysis is shown in Fig. 1c, where $v_A = 3/2\ t_{BC} - t_{AC}$.

The foregoing examples illustrate the manner in which the moment-area method may be used to obtain the deflection of any statically determinate beam. No matter how complex the M/(EI) diagrams may become, the above procedures are applicable. In practice, any M/(EI) diagram whatsoever may be approximated by a number of rectangles and triangles. It is also possible to introduce concentrated angle changes at hinges to account for discontinuities in the directions of the tangents at such points. The magnitudes of the concentrations can be found from kinematic requirements.

For complicated loading conditions, deflections of elastic beams determined by the moment-area method are often best found by superposition. In this manner the areas of the separate M/(EI) diagrams may become simple geometrical shapes.

The method described here can be used very effectively in determining the inelastic deflection of beams, providing the M/(EI) diagrams are replaced by the appropriate curvature diagrams.

• PROBLEM 9-35

Consider an aluminum cantilever beam 16 in. long with a 1,000-lb force applied 4 in. from the free end, as shown in Fig. 1a. For a distance of 6 in. from the fixed end, the beam is of greater depth than it is beyond, having $I_1 = 5$ in.^{4}. For the remaining 10 in. of the beam, $I_2 = 1$ in.^{4}. Find the deflection and the angular rotation of the free end. Neglect the weight of the beam, and assume E for aluminum at 10^7 psi.

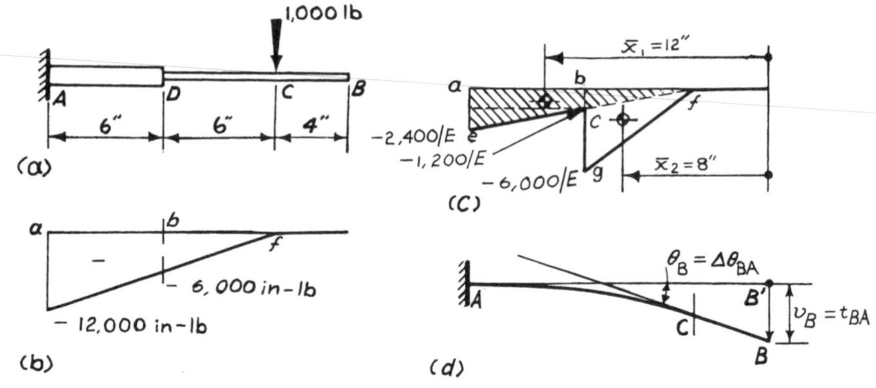

FIG. 1

Solution: The bending-moment diagram is in Fig. 1b. By dividing all ordinates of the M diagrams by EI, the M/(EI) diagram in Fig. 1c is obtained. Two ordinates appear at point D. One, -1,200/E, is applicable just to the left of D, the other, -6,000/E, applies just to the right of D. Since the bending moment is negative from A to C, the elastic curve throughout this distance is concave down, Fig. 1d. At the fixed support A, the elastic curve must start out tangent to the initial direction AB' of the unloaded beam. The unloaded straight segment CB of the beam is tangent to the elastic curve at C.

After the foregoing preparatory steps, from the geometry of the sketch of the elastic curve it may be seen that the distance BB' represents the desired deflection of the free end. However, BB' is also the tangential deviation of the point B from the tangent at A. Therefore the second moment-area theorem may be used to obtain t_{BA}, which in this special case represents the deflection of the free end. Also, from the geometry of the elastic curve it is seen that the angle included between the lines BC and AB' is the angular rotation of the segment CB. This angle is the same as the one included between the tangents to the elastic curve at the points A and B, and the first moment-area theorem may be used to compute this quantity.

It is convenient to extend the line ec in Fig. 1c to the point f for computing the area of the M/(EI) diagram. This gives two triangles, the areas of which can be calculated.

The area of triangle afe:

$$\Phi_1 = -1/2(12)(2,400)/E = -14,400/E$$

The area of triangle fcg:

$$\Phi_2 = -1/2(6)(4,800)/E = -14,400/E$$

$$\theta_B = \Delta\theta_{BA} = \int_A^B \frac{M}{EI}dx = \Phi_1 + \Phi_2 = -\frac{28,800}{10^7} = -0.00288 \text{ radian}$$

$$v_B = t_{BA} = \Phi_1\bar{x}_1 + \Phi_2\bar{x}_2 = (-14,400/E)(12) + (-14,400/E)(8)$$

$$= -0.0288 \text{ in.}$$

Note the numerical smallness of both the above values. The negative sign of $\Delta\theta$ indicates clockwise rotation of the tangent at B in relation to the tangent at A. The negative sign of t_{BA} means that point B is below a tangent through A.

• PROBLEM 9-36

Find the maximum deflection caused by the applied force P on a prismatic beam, Fig. 1a.

Solution: The bending-moment diagram and the elastic curve are in Figs.1 (b) and (c) respectively. The elastic curve is concave up throughout its length, and the maximum deflection occurs where the tangent to the elastic curve is horizontal. This point of tangency is designated in the figure by D and is located by the unknown horizontal distance d measured from the right support B. Then, by drawing a tangent to the elastic curve through point B at the support, one sees that $\Delta\theta_{BD} = \theta_B$ since the line passing through the supports is horizontal. However, the slope θ_B of the elastic curve at B may be determined by obtaining t_{AB} and dividing it by the length of the span. On the other hand, by using the first moment-area theorem, $\Delta\theta_{BD}$ may be expressed in terms of the shaded

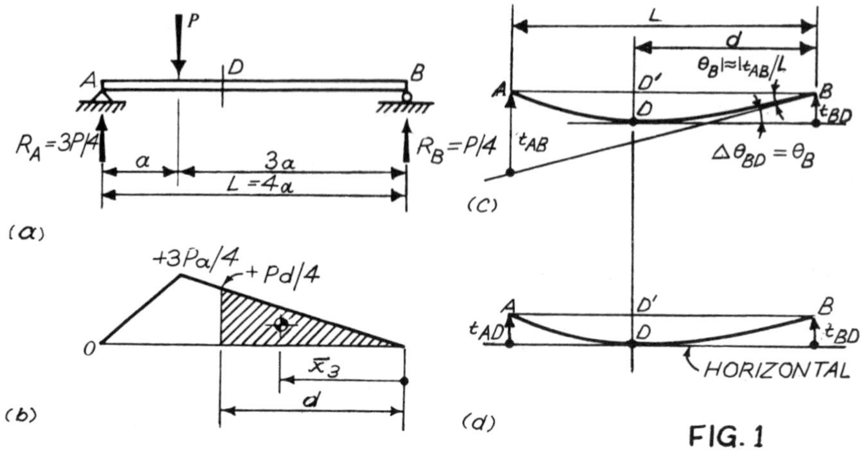

FIG. 1

area in Fig. 1b. Equating $\Delta\theta_{BD}$ to θ_B and solving for d locates the horizontal tangent at D. Then, again from geometrical considerations, it is seen that the maximum deflection represented by DD is equal to the tangential deviation of B from a horizontal tangent through D, i.e., t_{BD} .

$$t_{AB} = \Phi_1 \bar{x}_1 = + \frac{5Pa^3}{2EI}$$

$$\theta_B = \frac{t_{AB}}{L} = \frac{t_{AB}}{4a} = \frac{5Pa^2}{8EI}$$

$$\Delta\theta_{BD} = \frac{1}{EI}\left(\frac{d}{2}\,\frac{Pd}{4}\right) = \frac{Pd^2}{8EI} \quad \text{(area between D and B)}$$

Since $\theta_B = \theta_D + \Delta\theta_{BD}$ and it is required that $\theta_D = 0$,

$$\Delta\theta_{BD} = \theta_B\,, \quad \frac{Pd^2}{8EI} = \frac{5Pa^2}{8EI} \quad \text{hence} \quad d = \sqrt{5}a$$

$$v_{max} = v_D = DD' = t_{BD} = \Phi_3 \bar{x}_3$$

$$= \frac{1}{EI}\left(\frac{d}{2}\,\frac{Pd}{4}\right)\frac{2d}{3} = \frac{5\sqrt{5}\,Pa^2}{12EI} = \frac{11.2Pa^3}{12EI}$$

After the distance d is found, the maximum deflection may also be obtained, as $v_{max} = t_{AD}$, or $v_{max} = (d/L)t_{AB} - t_{DB}$ (not shown). Also note that using the condition $t_{AD} = t_{BD}$, Fig. 1d, an equation may be set up for d.

It should be apparent from the above solution that it is easier to calculate the deflection at the center of the beam, than to determine the maximum deflection. Yet, by examining the end results, one sees that numerically the two deflections differ little.

SUPERPOSITION METHODS

• PROBLEM 9-37

Determine the deflection δ_b at the hinge B for the structure shown in Fig. 1. Note that the structure is composed of two parts: (1) beam AB, simply supported at A, and (2) cantilever beam BC, fixed at C. The two beams are linked together at B by a pin connection.

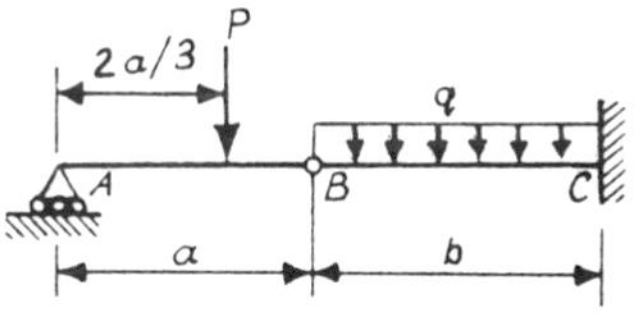

FIG. 1 BEAM WITH A HINGE

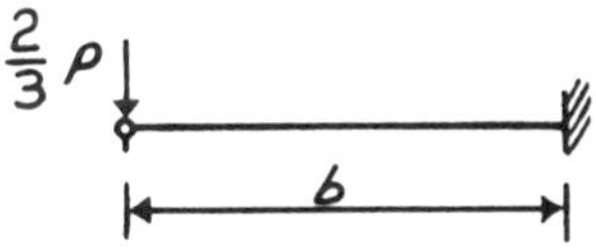

FIG. 2

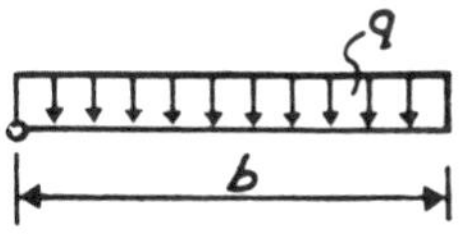

FIG. 3

Solution: Considering beam AB as a free body, we see that it has vertical reactions P/3 and 2P/3 at ends A and B, respectively. Therefore, beam BC is in the condition of a cantilever beam subjected to a uniform load of intensity q and a concentrated load at the end equal to 2P/3. The deflection of the end of this cantilever which is the same as the deflection of the hinge, can be obtained by superposing Figs. 2 and 3. Deflection of a cantilever due to the loading in Fig. 2 can be obtained from

$$\delta = \frac{Q\ell^3}{3EI}$$

where Q = applied load ; $\ell \equiv$ length of cantilever ;

$$\therefore \delta_2 = \frac{2Pb^3}{9EI}$$

For the loading in Fig. 3;

$$\delta = \frac{w\ell^4}{8EI}$$

where w $\equiv$ uniformly distributed load.

$$\therefore \delta_3 = \frac{qb^4}{8EI}$$

Superposition of these two cases will give the desired deflection. Therefore the deflection of the hinge is

$$\delta_b = \delta_2 + \delta_3$$

$$= \frac{qb^4}{8EI} + \frac{2Pb^3}{9EI}$$

• PROBLEM 9-38

A simple beam with an overhang is loaded as shown in Fig. 1. Find the deflection δ_c at the end of the overhang.

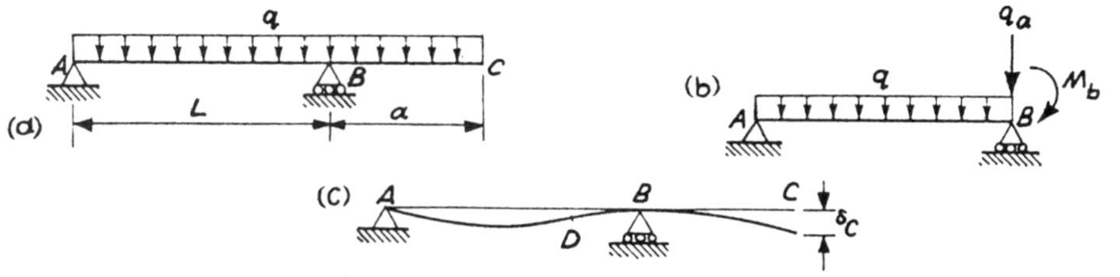

FIG. 1 SINGLE BEAM WITH AN OVERHANG

Solution: The deflection of point C is made up of two parts: (1) a deflection δ_1 caused by the rotation of the beam axis at support B, and (2) a deflection δ_2 caused by the bending of part BC acting as a cantilever beam. To obtain the first part of the deflection, we observe that portion AB of the beam is in the same condition as a simple beam carrying a uniform load and subjected to a couple M_b (equal to $qa^2/2$) and a vertical load (equal to qa) acting at the right-hand end as shown in Fig. 1b. The angle θ_b at end B is from a table of beam deflections and slopes:

$$\theta_b = \frac{qL^3}{24EI} - \frac{M_b L}{3EI} = \frac{qL(L^2 - 4a^2)}{24EI}$$

The deflection δ_1 of point C, due to the rotation at B, is equal to $a\theta_b$, or

$$\delta_1 = \frac{qaL(L^2 - 4a^2)}{24EI}$$

This deflection is positive when in the upward direction because θ_b is assumed to be positive when the rotation is counterclockwise.

The bending of the overhang itself produces the deflection δ_2 in the downward direction at C. This downward deflection is the same as for a cantilever beam of length a from a table of beam deflections and slopes:

$$\delta_2 = \frac{qa^4}{8EI}$$

The total deflection of point C, assumed positive when downward, is

$$\delta_c = \delta_2 - \delta_1 = \frac{qa}{24EI}(3a^3 + 4a^2L - L^3) \qquad \text{(a)}$$

From this result, we see that, when a is small compared to L, the deflection δ_c becomes negative and point C deflects upward.

The shape of the deflection curve for the beam in this example is shown in Fig. 1c for the case where a is large enough ($a > 0.43L$, approximately) to produce a downward deflection at C and small enough to insure that the reaction at A is upward ($a < L$). Under these conditions the beam has positive bending moment from A to a point such as D, and hence the deflection curve is convex downward in this part of the beam. From D to C the bending moment is negative, and the deflection curve is convex upward. Point D, where the curvature of the axis of the beam is zero (because the bending moment is zero), is called a point of inflection or point of contraflexure. The curvature of the deflection curve changes sign at a point of inflection.

• PROBLEM 9-39

Determine the deflection at mid-span for the steel beam ($I = 180$ in.^{4}) of Fig. 1a.

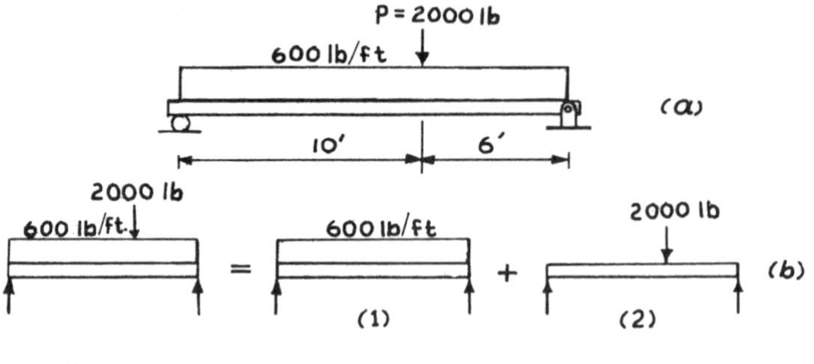

FIG. 1

Solution: The given loading is equivalent to the two loads, parts 1 and 2, shown in Fig. 1b. For part 1, the deflection at the center of the span is from a table of beam deflections:

$$y = -\frac{5wL^4}{384EI}$$

Substituting in the values:

$$(y_c)_1 = -\frac{5(600)(16^4)(12^3)}{384(30)(10^6)(180)} = -0.1638 \text{ in.}$$

For part 2, the deflection at the center is from a table of beam deflections:

$$y = -\frac{Pb(3L^2 - 4b^2)}{48EI}$$

where b is the distance from the load to the closer end of the beam. Substituting gives:

$$(yc)_2 = -\frac{2000(6)[3(16^2) - 4(6^2)]12^3}{48(30)(10^6)(180)} = -0.0499 \text{ in.}$$

The algebraic sum of the deflections for mid-span is

$$y_c = -0.1638 + (-0.0499) = -0.2137 \text{ in.} = 0.214 \text{ in. downward.}$$

• PROBLEM 9-40

Shown in Fig. 1 is a simply supported beam carrying a uniform loading of 50 lb/ft and a 5000-lb concentrated load. What is the deflection at the midpoint of the beam?

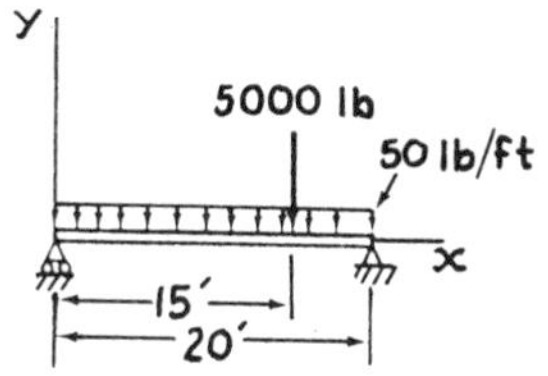

FIG.1

Solution: This problem will be solved using the superposition principle. The superposition principle says that when there is a linear relationship between load and deflection (as long as the elastic limit is not exceeded), the total deflection is equal to the sum of the deflections due to each of the loads considered separately. For a beam subjected to combined loading, the loading can be broken down into simple cases that are listed in tables, and the resulting deflections added together. Noting that the value of x to be used is less than a = 15, from a table of beam deflection equations it is found that for the concentrated load:

$$Y_c = \frac{-Pb}{6LEI}(-x^3 + (L^2 - b^2)x)$$

where b is the distance from the load to the closer end of the beam. The equation for a distributed load from the same table is:

$$Y_d = \frac{-wx}{24EI}(L^3 - 2Lx^2 + x^3) .$$

The total deflection is the sum of the deflections due to the concentrated load and the distributed load. Substituting in the values of L and b and adding the equations to get the total deflection yields

$$Y = \frac{(-5000)(5)}{(6)(20)(EI)}[-x^3 + (20^2 - 5^2)x] + \frac{(-50)x}{24EI}[20^3 - (2)(20)x^2 + x^3]$$

At x = 10

$$Y(10) = \frac{1}{EI}\left\{-\frac{(5000)(5)}{(6)(20)}[-1000 + (400 - 25)(10)] - \frac{(50)(10)}{24}[8000 - (2)(20)(100) + 1000]\right\}$$

$$Y(10) = -\frac{6.77 \times 10^5}{EI} \text{ ft}$$

If E and I are given in terms of inches, multiply by 144 to get Y(10) in terms of feet.

• PROBLEM 9-41

Find the deflection δ at the middle of the simple beam shown in the figure.

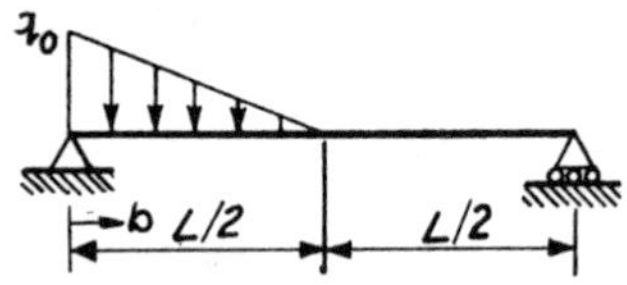

Solution: This problem will be solved by integrating the formula for a simply supported beam subject to a concentrated load.

From a table of beam deflection formulas the deflection y is

$$y = \frac{Pbx}{6\ell EI}(\ell^2 - b^2 - x^2)$$

In this problem b is the distance from the left hand support. The differential force dP is

$$dP = q_0(1 - 2b/L)\, db$$

The other values are $\ell = L$ and $x = L/2$. Substituting yields

$$dy = \frac{q_0(1 - 2b/L)db(b)(L/2)}{6LEI}(L^2 - b^2 - L^2/4)$$

Simplifying this becomes

$$dy = \frac{q_0(1 - 2b/L)b(3L^2 - 4b^2)\, db}{48EI}.$$

The total deflection is the integral of all the differential deflections due to the differential concentrated forces.

$$y = \int_0^{L/2} \frac{q_0(1 - 2b/L)}{48EI} b(3L^2 - 4b^2)\, db$$

Expanding

$$y = \int_0^{L/2} \frac{q_0}{48EI} (3bL^2 - 4b^3 - 6b^2L + 8b^4/L)db$$

Performing the integration.

$$y = \frac{q_0}{48EI}\left(\frac{3}{2} L^2b^2 - b^4 - 2Lb^3 + \frac{8b^5}{5L}\right)\Bigg|_0^{L/2}$$

Substituting in the limits of integration

$$y = \frac{q_0}{48EI}\left(\frac{3L^4}{8} - \frac{L^4}{16} - \frac{2L^4}{8} + \frac{L^4}{20}\right)$$

The lowest common denominator is 80

$$y = \frac{q_0L^4}{48EI}\left(\frac{30}{80} - \frac{5}{80} - \frac{20}{80} + \frac{4}{80}\right)$$

Simplifying

$$y = \frac{q_0L^4}{48EI}\left(\frac{9}{80}\right)$$

Factoring out a 3 top and bottom

$$y = \frac{q_0L^4(3)}{(16)EI80}$$

The final result is

$$y = \frac{3q_0L^4}{1280EI}$$

Thus the deflection at the middle of the beam is $\frac{3q_0L^4}{1280EI}$ downwards.

• PROBLEM 9-42

Find the supporting force system for the beam shown.

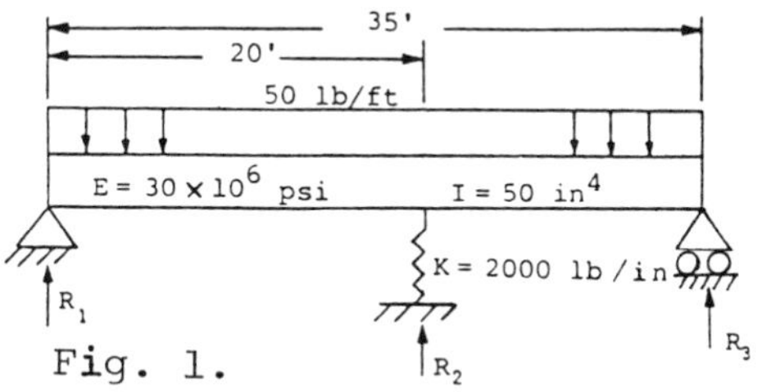

Fig. 1.

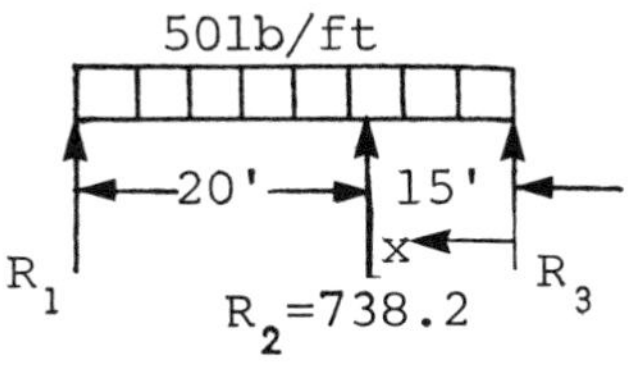

Fig. 2.

Solution: Superposition will be employed in the solution of this problem.

From a table of beam deflection equations, the deflection of the beam due to R_2 considered as an applied force is

$$Y = \frac{Pa}{6LEI} (-x^3 + (L^2 - a^2)x)$$

The deflection of the beam due to the distributed load is

$$Y = \frac{wx}{24EI} (L^3 - 2Lx^2 + x^3)$$

The superposition principle says that the total deflection is the sum of the deflections due to each of the loadings.

The deflection at R_2 is found by substituting in the appropriate values and adding together the two equations. Remember to include the term $(1728\ in^3/ft^3)$ to convert from feet to inches.

$$Y = \frac{1728(R_2)(20)(-15^3 + (35^2 - 20^2)15)}{6(35)(30 \times 10^6)(50)} + \frac{(50)(15)(35^3 - 2(35)(15^2) + 15^3)(1728)}{24(30 \times 10^6)(50)}$$

$$Y = R_2\ (9.874 \times 10^{-4}) + 1.098 .$$

The force the compressed spring exerts on the beam is $F = -kY$.

In this case F is equal to R_2 . Substituting and solving for Y yields

$$Y = -R_2/k = -R_2/2000 .$$

There are now two equations for the two unknowns Y and R_2 . Eliminating Y and solving for R_2 results in

$$\frac{-R_2}{2000} = R_2(9.874 \times 10^{-4}) + 1.098 .$$

Dividing both sides by 9.874×10^{-4}

$$\frac{-R_2}{1.9748} = R_2 + 1112$$

Subtracting R_2 from both sides

$$R_2\left(\frac{-1}{1.9748} - 1\right) = 1112$$

$$R_2(-1.5064) = 1112$$

$$R_2 = -738.2$$

The convention for applied forces is positive downwards. Since R_2 was temporarily considered an applied force in order to apply superposition, R_2 is equal to 738.2 lbs upwards. In Fig. 2 the other reactions by moment equilibrium are

$$\Sigma M_1 = (50)(35)^2/2 - 738.2(20) - R_3(35)$$

$$R_3 = 453.2$$

$$\Sigma M_3 = -50(35)^2/2 + 738.2(15) + R_1(35)$$

$$R_1 = 558.6$$

The supporting force system for the beam is from the left, R_1 is 558.6 lb, R_2 is 738.2 lb, and R_3 is 453.2 lb, all upwards.

• PROBLEM 9-43

Fig. 1 shows a cantilever beam supporting two concentrated loads and a uniform loading. Establish the deflection curve.

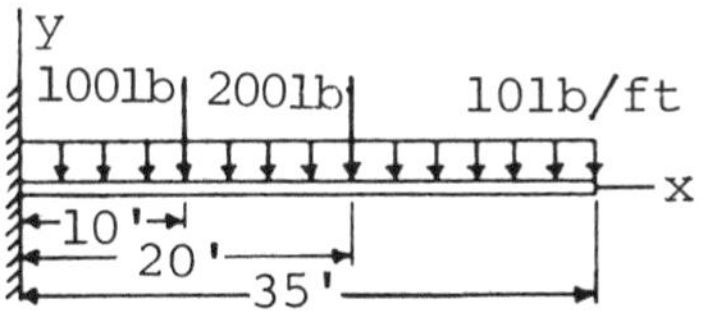

Fig. 1.

Solution: This problem will be solved by superposition. From a table of beam deflections, the formula for a concentrated load is

$$Y = \frac{-P}{6EI}([u(x - a)](x - a)^3 - x^3 + 3ax^2)$$

where a is the distance from the origin to the load.

From the same table, the formula for a distributed load is

$$Y = \frac{-wx^2}{24EI}(x^2 + 6L^2 - 4Lx)$$

Substituting the given values into the equations, the deflection due to the 100 lb load is

$$Y = \frac{-100}{6EI}([u(x - 10)](x - 10)^3 - x^3 + 30x^2)$$

The deflection due to the 200 lb load is

$$Y = \frac{-200}{6EI}([u(x - 20)](x - 20)^3 - x^3 - 60x^2)$$

The deflection due to the 10 lb/ft distributed loading is

$$Y = \frac{-10x^2}{24EI}(x^2 + 6(35)^2 - 4(35)x)$$

Superpose the contributions of each load as follows:

$$Y = \frac{(-100)}{6EI}\{[u(x - 10)](x - 10)^3 - x^3 + 30x^2\} + \frac{(-200)}{6EI}$$

$$\times \{[u(x - 20)](x - 20)^3 - x^3 + 60x^2\} \qquad \text{(a)}$$

$$+ \frac{(-10x^2)}{24EI}\{x^2 + 6(35)^2 - (4)(35)x\}$$

Collecting terms, we then have

$$Y = -\frac{1}{6EI}\{100(x - 10)^3[u(x - 10)] + 200(x - 20)^3[u(x - 20)]$$

$$+ 2.5x^4 - 650x^3 + 33,400x^2\} \qquad \text{(b)}$$

• PROBLEM 9-44

Find the deflection of the beam at the location A.

Solution: This problem will be solved by superposition. The deflection at x = 15 is the sum of the deflections due to the applied end moment

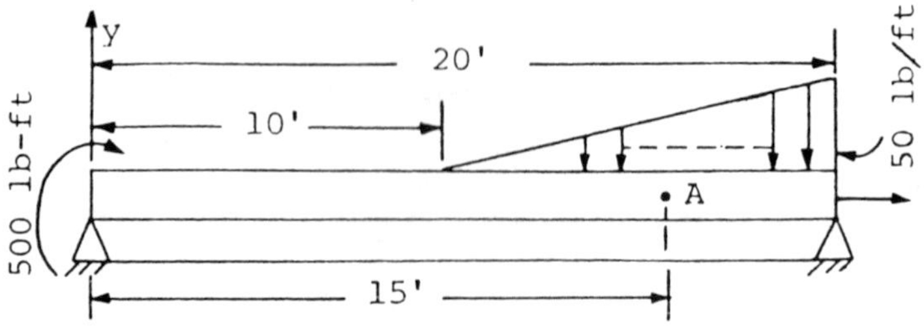

Fig. 1.

and the triangular loading. The deflection due to the triangular loading is the integral of the deflections due to the differential concentrated forces that make up the triangular load.

From a table of beam deflections the formula for the deflection due to the end moment is

$$y = \frac{M}{6\ell EI}(2\ell^2 x - 3\ell x^2 + x^3) \quad \text{Eq. (1)}$$

From the same table, the formula for the deflection due to a concentrated force is for the case where the desired deflection is to the left of the force (see Fig. 2a)

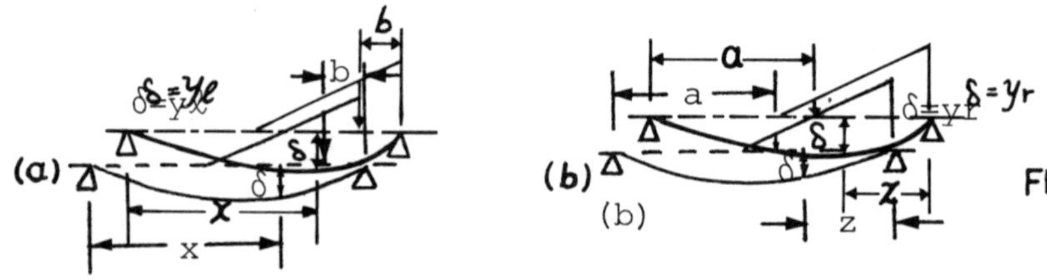

FIG. 2

Fig. 2.

$$y_\ell = \frac{Pbx}{6\ell EI}(\ell^2 - b^2 - x^2) \quad \text{Eq. (2)}$$

and for the case where the desired deflection is to the right of the force (see Fig. 2b)

$$y_r = \frac{Paz}{6\ell EI}(\ell^2 - a^2 - z^2) \quad \text{Eq. (3)}$$

Putting Eqs. (2) and (3) in integral form and substituting in the appropriate values yields

$$y = \int_0^5 \frac{(50 - 5b)(b)(15)(20^2 - b^2 - 15^2)db}{6(20)EI} + \int_{10}^{15} \frac{(5a - 50)a(5)(20^2 - a^2 - 5^2)da}{6(20)EI}$$

Integrating gives a value for the deflection due to the triangular load of

$$y = 15230/EI.$$

The deflection due to the end moment is from Eq. (1).

$$y = \frac{500}{6(20)EI}(2(20)^2 15 - 3(20)15^2 + 15^3)$$

Evaluating gives a value for the deflection due to the end moment of

$$y = 7812.5/EI$$

Superpositioning the two deflections gives a total deflection of

$$\delta = 15230/EI + 7812.5/EI = 23040/EI$$

Thus the deflection of the beam at $x = 15$ is $23040/EI$ downwards.

• PROBLEM 9-45

A vertically supported beam has two pin-connected links attached to it. Find the horizontal deflection of the beam at its center.

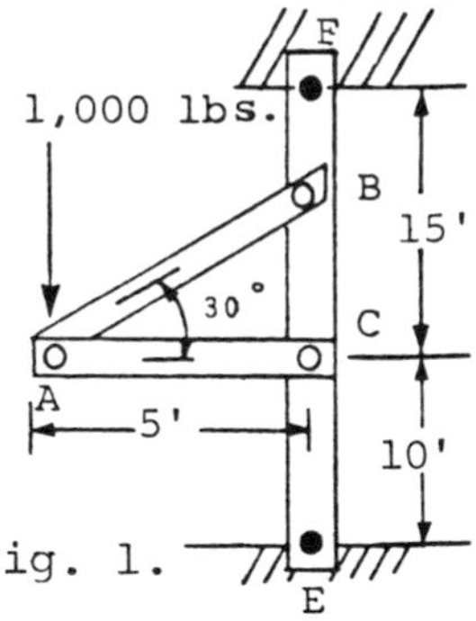

Fig. 1.

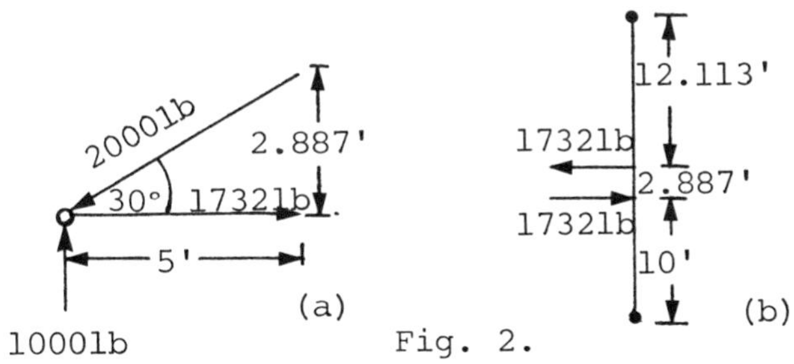

Fig. 2.

Solution: This problem will be solved using superposition.

First the loads that members AB and AC exert on the beam EF are determined (see Fig. 2).

Then a table of beam deflections is referred to, to find the appropriate deflection formula. This formula is

$$y = \frac{Pb(3L^2 - 4b^2)}{48\ EI}$$

Substitute in the values for the leftwardly pointing force

$$y_L = \frac{(1732)(12.113)(3(25)^2 - 4(12.113)^2)}{48\ EI}$$

Substitute in the values for the rightwardly pointing force

$$y_R = \frac{(-1732)(10)(3(25)^2 - 4(10)^2)}{48\ EI}$$

The total deflection is the sum of these two

$$y = \frac{(1732)}{48\ EI}[(12.113)(3(25)^2 - 4(12.113)^2) - (10)(3(25)^2 - 4(10)^2)]$$

Evaluating, the deflection is found to be 30,800/EI .

Thus the deflection at the middle of the beam is 30,800/EI to the left.

• PROBLEM 9-46

In the beam shown, find the deflection at location A, using superposition method.

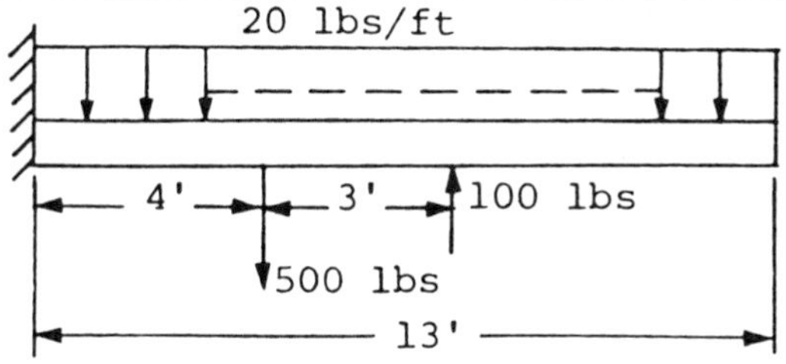

Solution: The deflections due to each of the loadings will be found separately and then added together to get the total deflection.

From a table of beam deflection equations, the equation for the deflection due to a uniformly distributed load is

$$EIy = -wx^4/24 + wLx^3/6 - wL^2x^2/4$$

The equation for the deflection due to a concentrated load is

$$EIy = -Pax^2/2 + Px^3/6 - P\langle x - a\rangle^3/6$$

Substituting, the deflection due to the distributed load is

$$EIy = -20(9)^4/24 + 20(13)(9)^3/6 - 20(13)^2(9)^2/4$$

Evaluating

$$EIy = -42322.5 \ .$$

The deflection due to the 500 lb. concentrated load is

$$EIy = -500(4)(9)^2/2 + 500(9^3)/6 - 500(9 - 4)^3/6$$

Evaluating

$$EIy = -30667 \ .$$

The deflection due to the 100 lb. concentrated load is

$$EIy = 100(7)(9)^2/2 - 100(9)^3/6 + 100(9 - 7)^3/6$$

$$EIy = 16333.$$

The total deflection at a position 4 ft. from the end of the beam is thus 56660/EI downwards.

• PROBLEM 9-47

The uniform beam shown has pinned supports at A, B and C. Find the slope angle φ at C due to the applied couple M_0 .

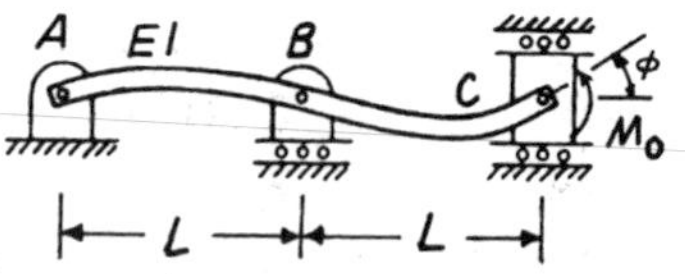

FIG.1

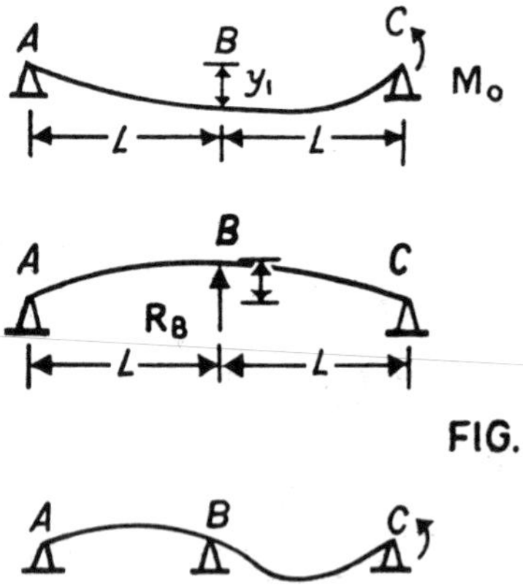

FIG. 2

Solution: This problem will be solved by the superposition of the deflections in a simply supported beam due to an applied end moment at point C and a concentrated force at B (see Fig. 2).

From a table of beam deflections and slopes the deflection due to moment is

$$y = \frac{m\ell^2}{16EI}$$

Substituting in the values yields

$$y_1 = \frac{M_0 L^2}{4EI}$$

From the same table, the deflection due to a concentrated load at midspan is

$$y = \frac{P\ell^3}{48EI}$$

Substituting

$$y_2 = \frac{R_B L^3}{6EI}$$

The sum of the deflections has to be zero because the deflection at B is zero.

$$0 = \frac{M_0 L^2}{4EI} + \frac{R_B L^3}{6EI}$$

Solving for R_B

$$R_B = -\frac{3M_0}{2L}$$

Now that the force is known the slope angle can be found. The total slope is the slope due to the moment plus the slope due to the force.

From the table, slope due to moment is

$$\varphi = \frac{M\ell}{3EI}$$

Substituting

$$\varphi_1 = \frac{2M_0 L}{3EI}$$

The slope due to a concentrated force at midspan is

$$\varphi = \frac{P\ell^2}{16EI}$$

Substituting

$$\varphi_2 = \frac{(-3M_0/2L)(2L)^2}{16EI} = \frac{-3M_0 L}{8EI}$$

The total slope is

$$\varphi_T = \varphi_1 + \varphi_2 = \frac{2M_0 L}{3EI} + \frac{-3M_0 L}{8EI} = \frac{7M_0 L}{24EI}$$

Thus the slope angle φ at point C is

$$\frac{7M_0 L}{24EI} \text{ counterclockwise.}$$

• PROBLEM 9-48

Determine the deflection of the free end of the beam in Fig. 1 in terms of w, L, E, and I.

FIG.1

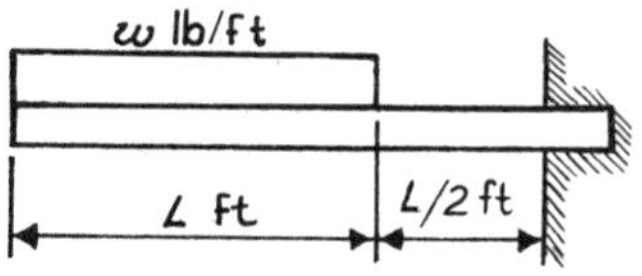

Solution: The total deflection will be found by breaking down the loading into three simpler cases, finding the deflections and superimposing

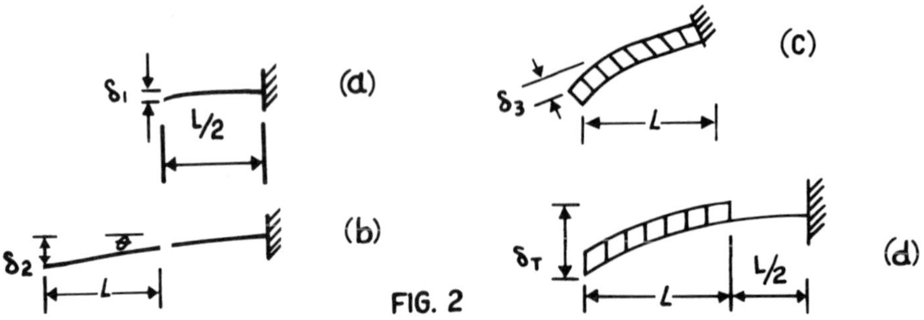

FIG. 2

them (see Fig. 2).

The first case is a cantilever of length L/2 subjected to a force wL and moment $-wL^2/2$ (see Fig. 2(a)). Substituting these values into the formula from a table of beam deflections and slopes yields a deflection of

$$\delta_1 = -\frac{(wL)(L/2)^3}{3EI} + \frac{(-wL^2/2)(L/2)^2}{2EI} = -\frac{5wL^4}{48EI}$$

The second case is the deflection of the end due to the rotation (see Fig. 2(b)). The rotation is from the table

$$\theta = \frac{(-wL^2/2)(L/2)}{EI} = \frac{-wL^3}{4EI}$$

The deflection at the end is the angle times the distance to the end

$$\delta_2 = \theta L = \frac{-wL^4}{4EI}$$

The third case is that of a cantilever of length L with a load of w lb/ft distributed over it (see Fig. 2(c)). From the table the deflection is

$$\delta_3 = \frac{-wL^4}{8EI}$$

Superpositioning the three partial deflections gives the total deflection.

$$\delta_T = \delta_1 + \delta_2 + \delta_3$$

$$\delta_T = \frac{-5wL^4}{48EI} + \frac{-wL^4}{4EI} + \frac{-wL^4}{8EI}$$

$$\delta_T = -wL^4(5 + 12 + 6)/48EI$$

$$\delta_T = -23wL^4/48EI$$

The total deflection of the end of the beam is $23wL^4/48EI$ downward.

• PROBLEM 9-49

For the beam of Fig. 1, determine the deflection at point D, the right end, in terms of w, L, E, and I.

FIG.1

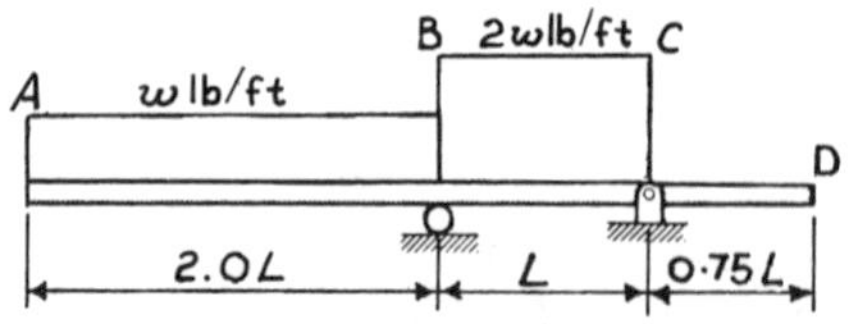

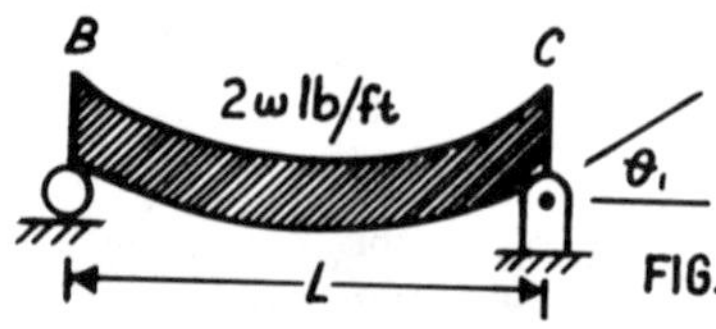

FIG. 2

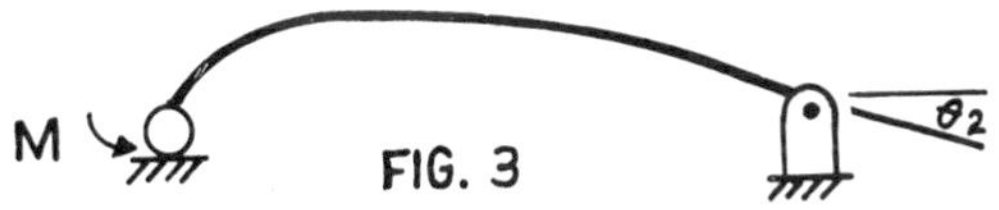

FIG. 3

Solution: This problem will be solved by superposition. The deflection at the right hand end, D, is equal to the total angle of rotation at C times the distance from C to D. The contributions of the two distributed loads to the angle of rotation at C will be determined separately and then added together.

Consider first the 2w lb/ft load distributed over segment BC (see Fig. 2). The angle of rotation at C due to this loading is from a table of beam deflections and slopes

$$\theta_1 = \frac{(2w)L^3}{24EI} \quad \text{(counterclockwise)}$$

Consider now the angle of rotation at C due to the w lb/ft load distributed over the cantilevered segment AB. This distributed load is equivalent to a moment of magnitude $-2wL^2$ acting at point B (see Fig. 3). The angle of rotation due to this loading is from the table

$$\theta_2 = \frac{(-2wL^2)L}{6EI} \quad \text{(clockwise)}$$

The total angle of rotation at C is by superposition the sum of angles due to each of the loadings.

$$\theta_T = \theta_1 + \theta_2$$

Substituting in the values yields

$$\theta_T = \frac{2wL^3}{24EI} + \frac{(-2wL^2)L}{6EI}$$

Simplifying results in

$$\theta_T = \frac{-wL^3}{4EI} \quad \text{(clockwise)}$$

The deflection at D is equal to the total angle of rotation at C times the length of the segment CD.

$$\delta = (\theta_T)(\ell_{CD})$$

Substituting in the values yields

$$\delta = \left(\frac{-wL^3}{4EI}\right)\left(\frac{3}{4}L\right) = \frac{-3wL^4}{16EI} \quad \text{(downward)}$$

The deflection at point D, the right end of the beam is $3wL^4/16EI$ downward.

• PROBLEM 9-50

The beam shown in the figure has fixed supports at A and D and is composed of three members that are pinned together at B and C. Find the deflection δ under the load P.

FIG.1

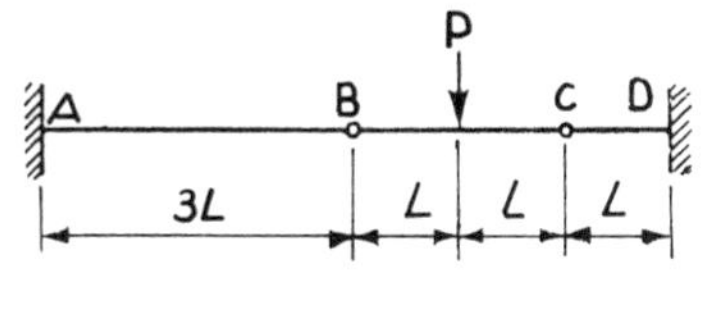

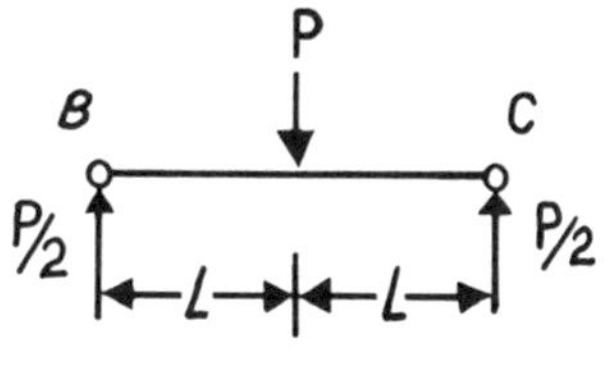

FIG. 2

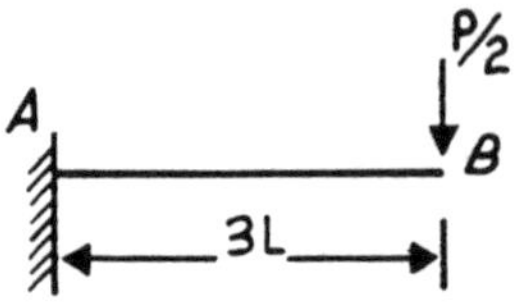

FIG. 3

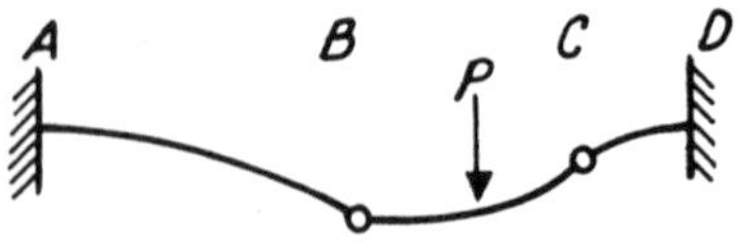

FIG. 5

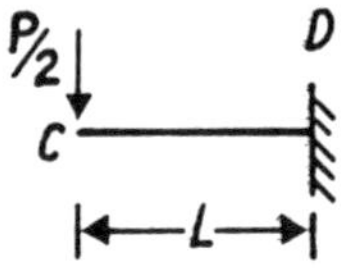

FIG. 4

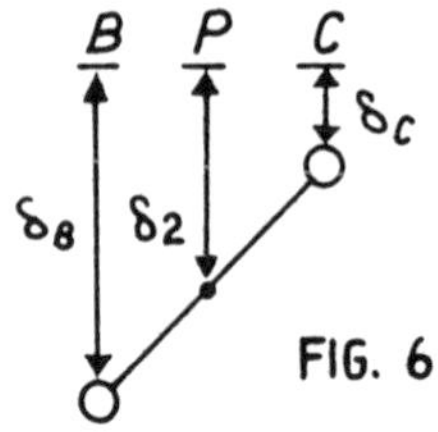

FIG. 6

Solution: The deflection of each of the three members will be found separately and then the total deflection determined.

First member BC will be analyzed. The joints at B and C are pin connected so member BC can be considered to be simply supported (see Fig. 2). From a table of beam deflections the formula for this case is

$$\delta_1 = \frac{Fd^3}{48EI}$$

Substituting the load and the length yields

$$\delta_1 = \frac{P(2L)^3}{48EI} = \frac{PL^3}{6EI}$$

Member AB is a cantilever sustaining an applied end load (see Fig. 3). From the table the formula for this case is

$$\delta = \frac{Fd^3}{3EI}$$

Substituting in the length and the load yields

$$\delta_B = \frac{(P/2)(3L)^3}{3EI} = \frac{9PL^3}{2EI}$$

Member CD is also a cantilever (see Fig. 4). Substituting into the formula yields

$$\delta_C = \frac{(P/2)L^3}{3EI} = \frac{PL^3}{6EI}$$

The deflection curve of the beam is shown in Fig. 5. A close up of the deflections at B and C, greatly exaggerated, is shown in Fig. 6. The deflection under P due to the deflections at B and C alone is

$$\delta_2 = (\delta_B + \delta_C)/2$$

Substituting in the values yields

$$\delta_2 = \frac{9PL^3/2EI + PL^3/6EI}{2} = \frac{(27+1)PL^3/12EI}{12EI} = \frac{7PL^3}{3EI}$$

The total deflection, δ_T, is equal to the simply supported beam deflection, δ_1, plus the cantilever deflection, δ_2.

$$\delta_T = \delta_1 + \delta_2 .$$

Substituting in the values and simplifying

$$\delta_T = \frac{PL^3}{6EI} + \frac{7PL^3}{3EI} = \frac{(1+14)PL^3}{6EI} = \frac{5PL^3}{2EI}$$

The total deflection under the load P is

$$\frac{5PL^3}{2EI} \quad \text{(downwards)}$$

• PROBLEM 9-51

A beam with an overhang supports two concentrated loads as shown in the figure. Find the deflections at points C and D when Q = 0. Find the angle of rotation θ_a at support A of the overhanging beam shown in the figure if Q = 2P and a = L/2.

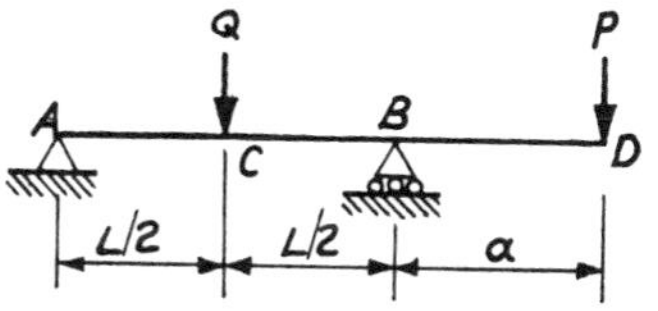

FIG.1

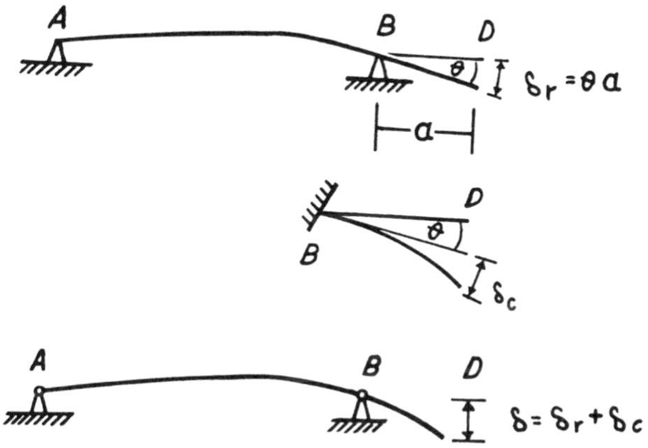

FIG. 2

Solution: This problem will be solved by superposition.

The deflection at point C is found by substituting the moment Pa into the equation for a simply supported beam with an end moment. From a table of beam deflections and slopes this equation is

$$\delta = \frac{ML^2}{16EI}$$

Substituting in the moment

$$\delta = \frac{P_a L^2}{16EI} \quad \text{(upward)}$$

The deflection at D is found by adding the deflection due to the rotation at B to the cantilever deflection of segment BD (see Fig. 2).

From the table, the rotation at B is

$$\theta = \frac{ML}{3EI}$$

Substituting Pa for the moment

$$\theta = \frac{PaL}{3EI}$$

The deflection at the end is the distance, a, times the rotation, θ. The deflection due to rotation, δ_r, is thus

$$\delta_r = a\theta = \frac{aPaL}{3EI}$$

The formula for cantilever deflection is from the table

$$\delta_c = \frac{Pa^3}{3EI}$$

Adding the two deflections yields

$$\delta = \delta_r + \delta_c = \frac{aPaL}{3EI} + \frac{Pa^3}{3EI} = \frac{Pa^2(L + a)}{3EI}$$

The deflection at D is

$$\frac{Pa^2(L + a)}{3EI} \quad \text{(downward)}$$

The angle of rotation at A when Q is 2P and a is L/2 is the rotation due to the moment PL/2 minus the rotation due to the load Q. The formula for the rotation due to moment is from the table

$$\theta_M = \frac{ML}{6EI}$$

Substituting for PL/2 for the moment yields

$$\theta_M = \frac{PL^2}{12EI}$$

The formula for the rotation due to the load Q is from the table

$$\theta_a = \frac{-FL^2}{16EI}$$

Substituting 2P for the load yields

$$\theta_Q = \frac{-PL^2}{8EI}$$

The total rotation at A is thus

$$\theta = \frac{PL^2}{12EI} - \frac{PL^3}{8EI} = \frac{2PL^2}{24EI} - \frac{3PL^2}{24EI} = \frac{-PL^2}{24EI}$$

The total rotation at A is

$$\frac{PL^2}{24EI} \quad \text{radians clockwise.}$$

• PROBLEM 9-52

Two equal wheel loads, distance L/4 apart, move slowly across a simple beam of length L (see figure). Determine the maximum value of the deflection at the middle of the beam.

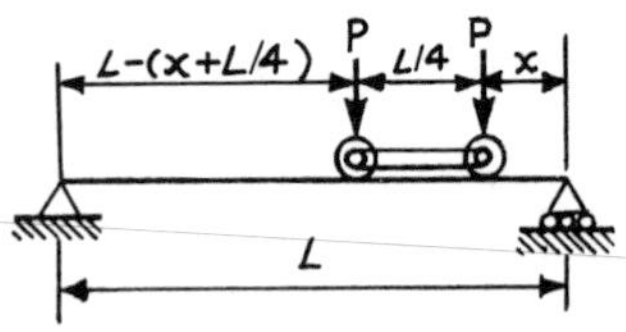

FIG. I

Solution: This problem will be solved by superposition. The deflections due to the loads will be calculated separately and then added together to get the total load.

The equation for the deflection from a table of beam deflections is

$$y = \frac{-Pb(3L^2 - 4b^2)}{48EI}$$

where b is the distance from the load to the closer end of the beam.

There are two different cases. In one case b for both loads are measured from the same end of the beam. In the other case, b for one load is measured from the left end of the beam and b for the other load is measured from the right end of the beam.

The case where both b's are measured from the same end of the beam will be considered first. Substituting the values x and (x + L/4), for b and summing yields for the region $0 \le x \le L/4$

$$y = \frac{-Px(3L^2 - 4x^2)}{48EI} - \frac{P(x+L/4)(3L^2-4(x+L/4)^2)}{48EI}$$

$$y = (8Px^3+3Px^2L - 21PxL^2/4 - 11PL^3/16)/48EI$$

This equation is differentiated and the result set equal to zero to find the maximum

$$0 = (24Px^2 + 6PxL - 21PL^2/4)/48EI$$

Using the quadratic equation the roots are found to be $x = -.61L$ and $x = .36L$. Both of these values for x are outside of the region $0 \le x \le L/4$ where the equation holds. Therefore there is no maximum due to applied loads in that region.

Now the case where the b's are measured from opposite ends of the beam is considered. Substituting the values x and (L - (x + L/4)) for b and summing yields for the region $L/4 \le x \le L/2$

$$y = \frac{-Px(3L^2 - 4x^2)}{48EI} - \frac{P(L - (x + L/4))(3L^2 - 4(L - (x+L/4))^2)}{48EI}$$

$$y = (9PLx^2 - 27PL^2x/4 - 9PL^3/16)/(48EI)$$

Maximize by setting the derivative equal to zero.

$$0 = (18PLx - 27PL^2/4)/(48EI)$$

Solving for x yields

$$x = .375L$$

Substituting this value for x in the deflection equation will give the maximum deflection, y, at the midpoint of the beam.

$$y = (9PL(.375L)^2 - 27PL^2(.375L)/4 - 9PL^3/16)/(48EI)$$

$$y = \frac{-39PL^3}{1024EI}$$

The maximum deflection at the middle of the beam due to two equal wheel loads a distance L/4 apart as they move slowly across is

$$\frac{39PL^3}{1024EI} \text{ downwards.}$$

• PROBLEM 9-53

The cantilever beam AB shown in the figure has a bracket BC attached to its free end. A force P acts at the end of the bracket. Find the ratio a/L in order that the vertical deflection of point B will be zero.

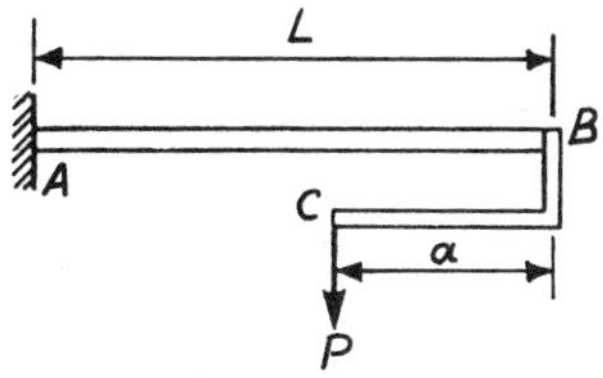

FIG.1

Solution: This problem will be solved by superposition. The force P acting on the bracket can be represented by a moment Pa and a force P both applied at B. The upward deflection due to the moment must just cancell the downward deflection due to the force.

The equation for the deflection due to the moment from a table of beam deflections is

$$y = \frac{ML^2}{2EI}$$

From the same table, the deflection due to the force is

$$y = \frac{-PL^3}{3EI}$$

The superposition principle says that the total deflection is equal to the sum of the deflections due to the forces and moments. Substituting in the values and summing the deflections yields

$$0 = \frac{PaL^2}{2EI} - \frac{PL^3}{3EI}$$

Solving for a in terms of L

$$a = 2/3\ L\ .$$

The ratio of the two is thus

$$a/L = 2/3\ .$$

CONJUGATE BEAM METHOD

• PROBLEM 9-54

Find the maximum deflection of the beam of Fig. 1a. For the segment AC, EI = 12×10^4 kip-ft^2, and for CB, EI = 3×10^4 kip-ft^2.

$$M' = (90 \times \frac{10.4}{3} - 90 \times 10.4)10^{-4}$$
$$= -0.0624 \text{ ft}$$
$$= -0.75 \text{ in.}$$

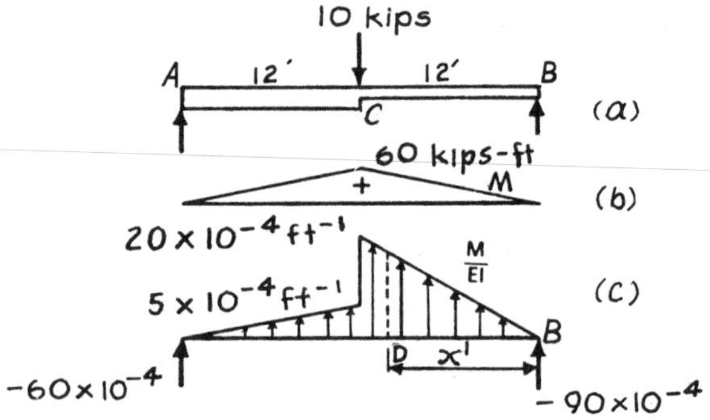

FIG.1

Solution: The conjugate beam method is used to find the desired deflection.

First compute the bending moment, then plot the bending moment diagram;

Reaction at A, R_A = 5 kips

Reaction at B, R_B = 5 kips

On section AC; shear $v = -5$.
But

$$M = -\int v\,dx$$

$$\therefore M = \int 5\,dx$$

$$= 5x$$

$\therefore$ Moment varies linearly from 0 at A to 60 kip-ft. at C and back to zero at B as shown in Fig. 1b. To plot the M/EI diagram, divide section AC by 12×10^4 kip-ft^2 and section CB by 3×10^4 kip-ft. The result is plotted in Fig. 1c. Now use the M/EI diagram as the conjugate load and compute the reactions thus; taking moments about A;

$$\left[\tfrac{1}{2} \times 5 \times 12 \times 2 \times \frac{12}{3} + \tfrac{1}{2} \times 20 \times 12\left(12 + \frac{12}{3}\right)\right] \times 10^{-4} + R_B \times 24 = 0$$

$$\therefore R_B = -90 \times 10^{-4}\ \text{ft}^{-1}.$$

Taking moment about B;

$$\left[\tfrac{1}{2} \times 20 \times 12 \times 2 \times \frac{12}{3} + \tfrac{1}{2} \times 5 \times 12\left(12 + \frac{12}{3}\right)\right] \times 10^{-4} + R_A \times 24 = 0$$

$$\therefore R_A = -60 \times 10^{-4}\ \text{ft}^{-1}.$$

The maximum M' occurs when S' = 0. This will be at a point D such that the load above DB is equal to the reaction R_B'. Thus

$$\left(20 \times 10^{-4}\,\frac{x}{12}\right)\frac{x}{2} = 90 \times 10^{-4}$$

$$x = 10.4 \text{ ft.}$$

Then at D,

$$M' = \left(90 \times \frac{10.4}{3} - 90 \times 10.4\right)10^{-4}$$

$$= -0.0624 \text{ ft}$$

$$= -0.75 \text{ in.}$$

• PROBLEM 9-55

For the beam of constant EI supported and loaded as shown in Fig. 1a find the slope over the support B and the slope and deflection at D.

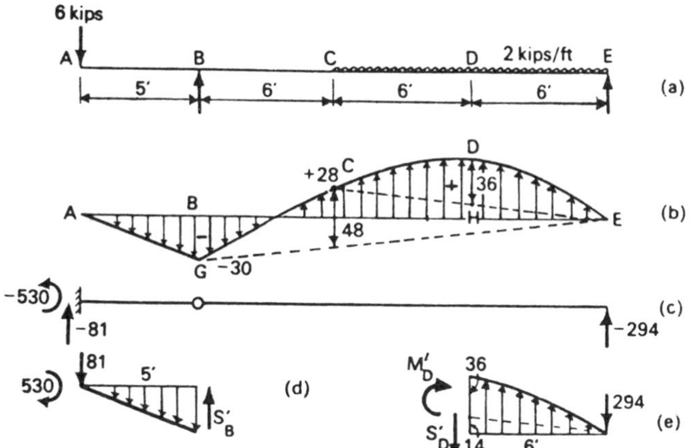

FIG. 1

Solution: This problem will be solved by the conjugate beam method. The bending moment diagram with the real beam is first drawn (Fig. 1b) To use this as a conjugate load diagram we draw upward arrows where the bending moment is positive and downward arrows where the bending moment is negative. If we draw the chord CE on this diagram (CE is the segment carrying the uniformly distributed load), then the mid-ordinate of the parabola measured from this chord is $wa^2/8 = 2 \times 12^2/8 =$ 36 kip-ft, where a is the length of the loaded segment.

The support conditions of the conjugate beam (Fig. 1c) are determined from the table.

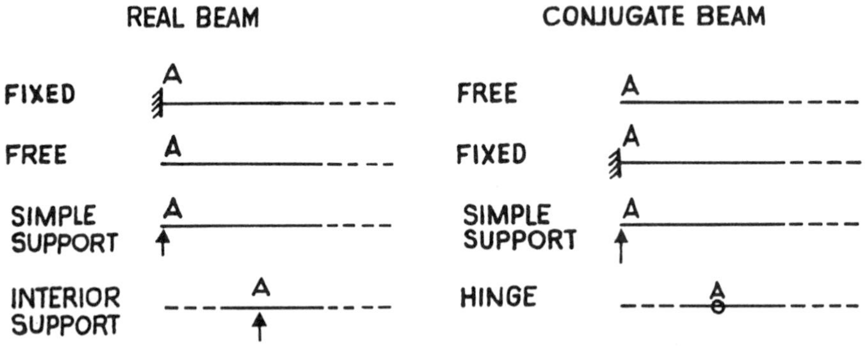

Now regarding the diagram of Fig. 1b as the conjugate load on the beam of Fig. 1c we can determine the conjugate reactions by statics. The load can be broken up into triangles ABG(-), BGE(-), GCE(+) and the parabolic section CDEHC(+). The resultants of these areas are

	Area	Centroid	
ABG	-75	-1.67'	from B
BGE	-270	+6'	from B
GCE	+432	+8'	from B
CDEHC	+288	+12'	from B

From these values the reactions are found. They are shown on Fig. 1c. The constant EI is omitted for the time being.

The real slope at B corresponds to the conjugate shear force with the sign changed. From the free-body of Fig. 1d we see that

$$EIS'_B = +81 + \frac{30 \times 5}{2} = +156$$

The real slope at B is thus -156/EI ft.

The real slope and deflection at D correspond to the conjugate shear force (with the sign changed) and bending moment at D. From Fig. 1c we see that

$$EIS'_D - \left(\frac{14 \times 6}{2}\right) - \left(\tfrac{2}{3} \times 36 \times 6\right) + 294 = 0$$

or

$$S'_D = -108/EI$$

$$-EIM'_D + (42 \times 2) + (144 \times 2.25) - (294 \times 6) = 0$$

or

$$M'_D = 1356/EI$$

The real slope at D is 108/EI radian and the deflection is 1356 /EI ft.

NOTE: When the curvature is expressed by M/EI, then M/EI of the real beam becomes W in the conjugate beam, dv/dx of the real beam becomes -S in the conjugate beam and v of the real beam becomes M in the conjugate beam.

• PROBLEM 9-56

Using the finite difference method, calculate the deflections of a simple beam carrying a uniform load (Fig. 1a).

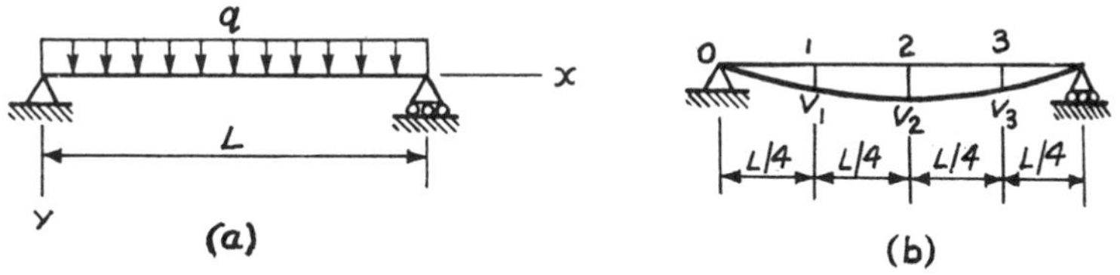

FIG. 1

Solution: This problem will be solved using the finite difference equation:

$$v_{i-1} - 2v_i + v_{i+1} = -(h)^2(M_i/EI)$$

To use the equation, the beam is divided into equal intervals each of length h. The left hand end of the beam is labeled 0, the right-hand end of the first interval is labeled 1, the right-hand end of the second interval is labeled 2 and so on until the right-hand end of the beam is reached (see Fig. 1(b)). M_i is the moment at point i and v_i is the deflection at that point.

The beam is assumed to have constant flexural rigidity EI and length L. The beam is divided into four equal intervals (Fig. 1b) and, the deflections at the three points 1, 2, and 3 must be determined. However, because of symmetry, it is known that two of the deflections are the same ($v_1 = v_3$), so that only two of the deflections will be considered as unknown quantities in the equations.

The finite difference equation at point 1 becomes

$$v_0 - 2v_1 + v_2 = -\left(\frac{L}{4}\right)^2 \left(\frac{3qL^2}{32EI}\right)$$

inasmuch as $h = L/4$ and $M_1 = 3qL^2/32$. Furthermore, because the deflection at the end of the beam is zero ($v_0 = 0$), the foregoing equation simplifies to

$$2v_1 - v_2 = \frac{3qL^4}{512EI} \qquad \text{(a)}$$

At point 2 the bending moment M_2 is $qL^2/8$, and the difference equation becomes

$$v_1 - 2v_2 + v_3 = -\left(\frac{L}{4}\right)^2 \left(\frac{qL^2}{8EI}\right)$$

or, since $v_1 = v_3$,

$$v_1 - v_2 = -\frac{qL^4}{256EI} \qquad \text{(b)}$$

Now solve Eqs. (a) and (b) for the deflections:

$$v_1 = v_3 = \frac{5qL^4}{512EI} = 0.00977\,\frac{qL^4}{EI}$$

$$v_2 = \frac{7qL^4}{512EI} = 0.01367\,\frac{qL^4}{EI}$$

The exact results for these deflections are

$$v_1 = v_3 = \frac{19qL^4}{2048EI} = 0.00928\ \frac{qL^4}{EI}$$

$$v_2 = \frac{5qL^4}{384EI} = 0.01302\ \frac{qL^4}{EI}$$

Comparing the values given above, it is seen that the finite difference results are about percent higher than the exact results, which is reasonable accuracy considering that only four segments were used along the beam. Increased accuracy can be obtained by dividing the beam into more segments and solving the correspondingly larger number of equations.

• PROBLEM 9-57

This example pertains to the nonprismatic cantilever beam shown in Fig. (a). Note that region AB of the beam has a moment of inertia twice that of region BC. The deflection at the free end of the beam is to be determined.

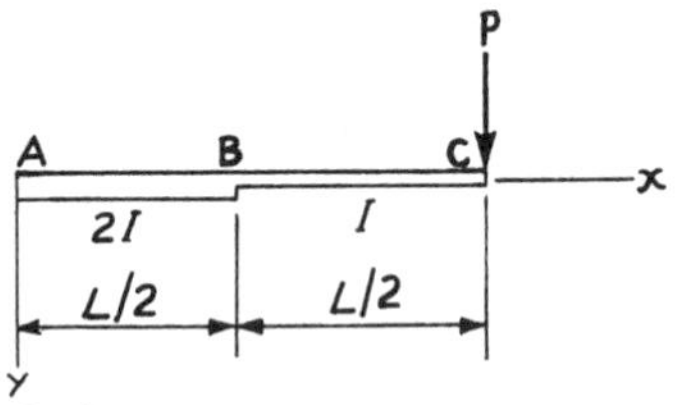

FIG.(a)

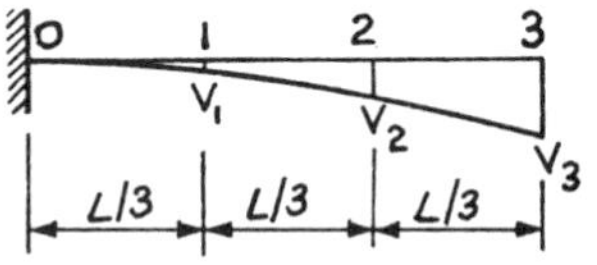

FIG.(b)

Solution: When the beam is divided into three equal intervals, there will be three unknown deflections to be obtained (see Fig. (b).) The bending moments at points 0, 1, and 2 are

$$M_0 = -PL \qquad M_1 = -\frac{2PL}{3} \qquad M_2 = -\frac{PL}{3}$$

Thus, the finite difference equations at points 0, 1, and 2 become

$$v_{-1} - 2v_0 + v_1 = -\left(\frac{L}{3}\right)^2 \left(-\frac{PL}{2EI}\right) \tag{c}$$

$$v_0 - 2v_1 + v_2 = -\left(\frac{L}{3}\right)^2 \left(-\frac{2PL}{3 \times 2EI}\right) = -\left(\frac{L}{3}\right)^2 \left(-\frac{PL}{3EI}\right) \tag{d}$$

$$v_1 - 2v_2 + v_3 = -\left(\frac{L}{3}\right)^2 \left(-\frac{PL}{3EI}\right) \tag{e}$$

In the first of these equations, there appears a fictitious deflection v_{-1} located at an imaginary point to the left of the fixed support. This fictitious deflection can be expressed in terms of the real deflections by using one of the boundary conditions for a fixed support, namely, that the slope is zero. When the first derivative equation is applied at point 0 to obtain the slope of the beam, the result is

$$v_1 - v_{-1} = 0 \quad \text{or} \quad v_{-1} = v_1 \tag{f}$$

Thus, the deflection v_{-1} has been expressed in terms of the actual deflection of the beam.

The second boundary condition for the fixed support is $v_0 = 0$. When the two boundary conditions are used, Eq. (c) simplifies to

$$v_1 = \frac{PL^3}{36EI}$$

Solve the remaining finite difference equations (d) and (e), obtaining

$$v_2 = \frac{5PL^3}{54EI} \qquad v_3 = \frac{7PL^3}{36EI} = 0.1944\,\frac{PL^3}{EI}$$

By comparison with the value obtained above for v_3, the exact deflection at the free end of the beam is

$$v_3 = \frac{3PL^3}{16EI} = 0.1875\,\frac{PL^3}{EI}$$

Thus, using only three segments along the beam gives a result that is only 4 percent higher than the exact value.

• PROBLEM 9-58

For the beam in Fig. 1a, determine the maximum deflection when E is $12(10^6)$ psi and I is 81 in.^{4} .

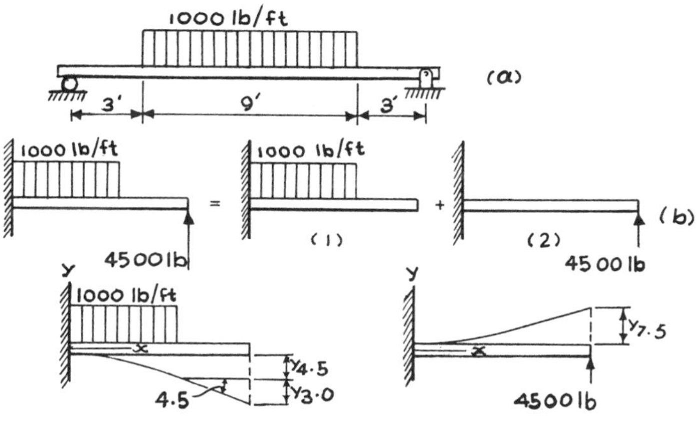

FIG. 1

Solution: From symmetry and $\Sigma F_y = 0$, the reactions are each 4500 lb upward. Because of the symmetrical loading the slope of the beam is zero at the center of the span and the right (or left) half of the beam can be considered as a cantilever beam with two loads. As shown in Fig. 1b, the cantilever with two loads can be replaced by two beams (designated 1 and 2), each carrying one of the two loads.

The elastic curve (exaggerated) for part 1, as shown in Fig. 1c, gives the deflection at the right end as $y_{4.5} + y_3$, where $y_{4,5}$ is the deflection at the end of the uniformly distributed load and y_3 is the additional deflection of the unloaded 3ft. From a table of beam deflections and slopes:

$$y = -\frac{wL^4}{8EI}$$

Substituting in the numbers:

$$y_{4.5} = -\frac{1000(4.5^4)(12^3)}{8(12)(10^6)(81)} = -\frac{9^3}{8(10^3)} = -0.0911 \text{ in.},$$

Again from a table:

$$\theta = -\frac{wL^3}{6EI}$$

Substituting in the numbers:

$$\theta_{4.5} = -\frac{1000(4.5^3)(12^2)}{6(12)(10^6)(81)} - \frac{9}{4(10^3)} = -0.00225 \text{ rad.,}$$

from which

$$y_3 = 3(12)(0.00225) = -0.0810 \text{ in.,}$$

consequently the total deflection of the right end is 0.1721 in. downward.

The elastic curve (exaggerated) for part 2 is shown in Fig. 1d. From a table of beam deflections and slopes:

$$y = -\frac{PL^3}{3EI}$$

Substituting in the numbers:

$$y_{7.5} = +\frac{4500(7.5^3)(12^3)}{3(12)(10^6)(81)} = 1.125 \text{ in. upward.}$$

The algebraic sum of the deflections for parts 1 and 2 is +0.953 in., which means that the right end of the beam is 0.953 in. above the center. The right end does not move, so the maximum deflection is at the center and is

$$y_{max} = 0.953 \text{ in. downward.}$$

CHAPTER 10

STATICALLY INDETERMINATE SYSTEMS

INTEGRATION METHOD

• PROBLEM 10-1

For the beam loaded and supported as shown in Fig. 1a, determine the reactions in terms of w and L.

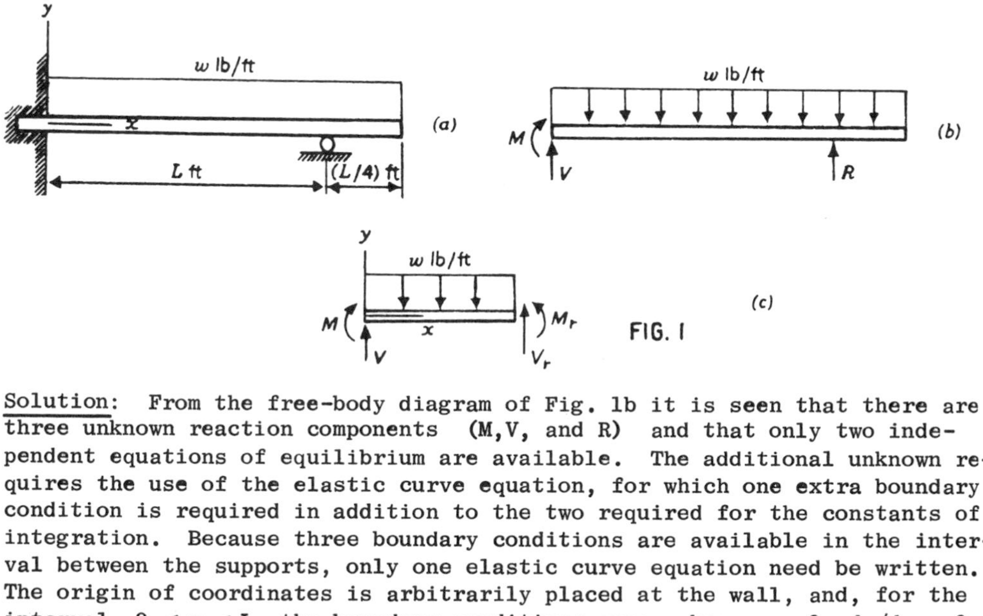

FIG. 1

Solution: From the free-body diagram of Fig. 1b it is seen that there are three unknown reaction components (M,V, and R) and that only two independent equations of equilibrium are available. The additional unknown requires the use of the elastic curve equation, for which one extra boundary condition is required in addition to the two required for the constants of integration. Because three boundary conditions are available in the interval between the supports, only one elastic curve equation need be written. The origin of coordinates is arbitrarily placed at the wall, and, for the interval $0 \le x \le L$, the boundary conditions are: when $x = 0$, $dy/dx = 0$; when $x = 0$, $y = 0$; and when $x = L$, $y = 0$. From Fig. 1c the bending moment equation is

$$EI \frac{d^2y}{dx^2} = M_x = Vx + M - \frac{wx^2}{2} .$$

Integration gives

$$EI \frac{dy}{dx} = \frac{Vx^2}{2} + Mx - \frac{wx^3}{6} + C_1 .$$

Applying the first boundary condition $x = 0$; $dy/dx = 0$, one obtains $C_1 = 0$. A second integration yields

$$EIy = \frac{Vx^3}{6} + \frac{Mx^2}{2} - \frac{wx^4}{24} + C_2$$

The second boundary condition gives $C_2 = 0$, and the last boundary condition gives

$$0 = \frac{VL^3}{6} + \frac{ML^2}{2} - \frac{wL^4}{24}$$

or

$$4VL + 12M = wL^2 \qquad (1)$$

The equation of equilibrium $\Sigma M_R = 0$ for the free-body diagram of Fig. 1b gives

$$VL + M = w\left(\frac{5L}{4}\right)\left(\frac{5L}{8} - \frac{L}{4}\right) = \frac{15wL^2}{32} \qquad (2)$$

Solving equations (1) and (2) yields

$$M = -\frac{7wL^2}{64} = \frac{7wL^2}{64} \text{ lb.-ft counterclockwise}$$

and

$$V = \frac{37wL}{64} \text{ lb. upward}$$

Finally, the equation $\Sigma Fy = 0$ for Fig. 1b gives

$$R + V = \frac{5wL}{4}.$$

Hence

$$R = \frac{5wL}{4} - \frac{37wL}{64}$$

$$= \frac{43wL}{64} \text{ lb.}$$

• PROBLEM 10-2

Figure 1a shows a beam whose neutral axis coincided with the x axis before the load P was applied. The beam has a simple support at A and a clamped or built-in support at C. The bending modulus EI is constant along the length of the beam. Sketch the bending-moment diagram for the bending moments due to the load P.

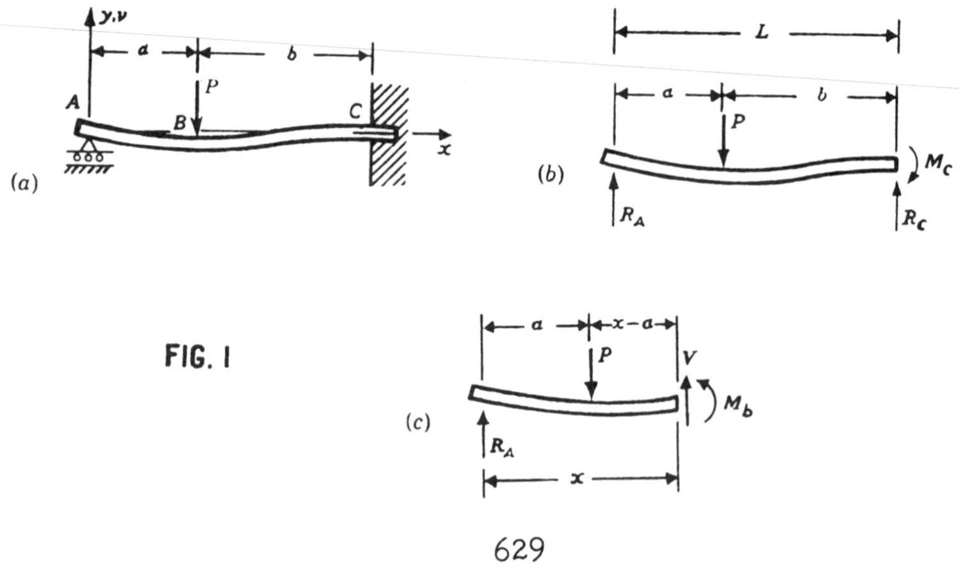

FIG. 1

Solution: The moment curvature relation will be used to analyze this statically indeterminate beam. Figure 1b shows a free-body diagram of the entire beam. Since P is given as vertical and R_A because of the rollers, can only be vertical, the reaction at C can only consist of a vertical force R_C and a clamping moment M_C. There are no horizontal forces, and hence there are only two independent equilibrium requirements, but there are three unknowns: R_A, R_C, and M_C. The equilibrium conditions furnish only two relations between three quantities. The best we can do by considering only equilibrium is to take one of the reactions as an unknown and express the other two in terms of this unknown. For example, taking R_A as unknown, the conditions of equilibrium applied to Fig. 1b yield

$$\begin{aligned} R_C &= P - R_A \\ M_C &= Pb - R_A L \end{aligned} \tag{a}$$

Similarly, applying the conditions of equilibrium to the segment of length x in Fig. 1c gives the following expression for the bending moment:

$$M_b = R_A x - P\langle x - a\rangle^1 \tag{b}$$

which is valid for $0 < x < L$.

Turning to the geometrical requirements for the deformed beam, we see that now we have three compatibility conditions

$$\begin{aligned} v &= 0 \quad \text{at} \quad x = 0 \\ v &= 0 \quad \text{at} \quad x = L \\ \frac{dv}{dx} &= 0 \quad \text{at} \quad x = L \end{aligned} \tag{c}$$

Thus, if we integrate the moment-curvature relation, we have enough conditions not only to evaluate the two constants of integration but also to evaluate the unknown reaction R_A which appears in (b). Setting up the moment-curvature relation and carrying out one integration gives

$$\begin{aligned} EI\frac{d^2v}{dx^2} &= M_b = R_A x - P\langle x - a\rangle^1 \\ EI\frac{dv}{dx} &= R_A \frac{x^2}{2} - P\,\frac{\langle x - a\rangle^2}{2} + c_1 \end{aligned} \tag{d}$$

In order for the third of (c) to be satisfied, we must have

$$c_1 = \frac{Pb^2}{2} - \frac{R_A L^2}{2} \tag{e}$$

Inserting (e) in (d) and carrying out one more integration gives

$$EIv = R_A \frac{x^3}{6} - P\,\frac{\langle x - a\rangle^3}{6} + \frac{Pb^2 x}{2} - \frac{R_A L^2 x}{2} + c_2 \tag{f}$$

In order for the first of (c) to be satisfied we must have $c_2 = 0$. Finally, to satisfy the second of (c) we must have

$$0 = R_A \frac{L^3}{6} - P\,\frac{b^3}{6} + \frac{Pb^2 L}{2} - \frac{R_A L^3}{2} \tag{g}$$

from which we find

$$R_A = \frac{Pb^2}{2L^3}(3L - b) \tag{h}$$

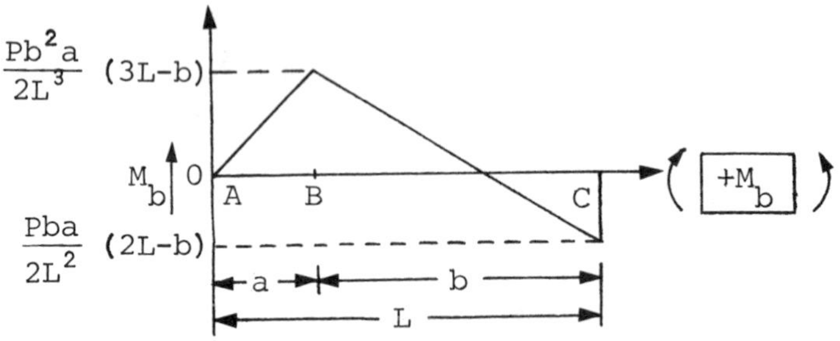

Fig. 2.

Thus, to complete the force analysis, we had to bring in the geometric restrictions and the moment-curvature relation. Now we can return to (a) with the value (h) to obtain explicit results for the reactions. With these values it is an easy matter to sketch the bending-moment diagram shown in Fig. 2.

• PROBLEM 10-3

Find the deflection curve for the beam shown.

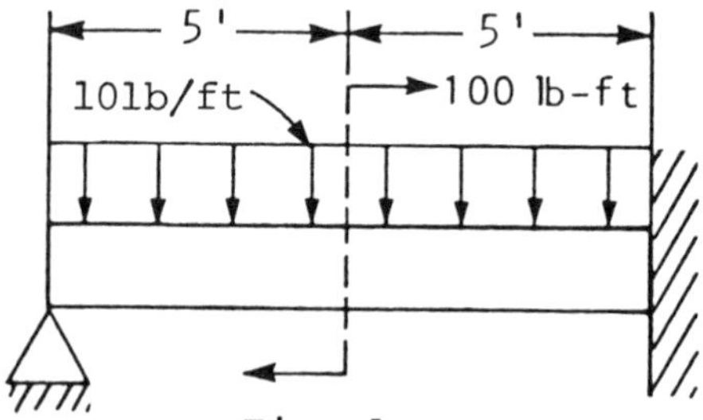

Fig. 1.

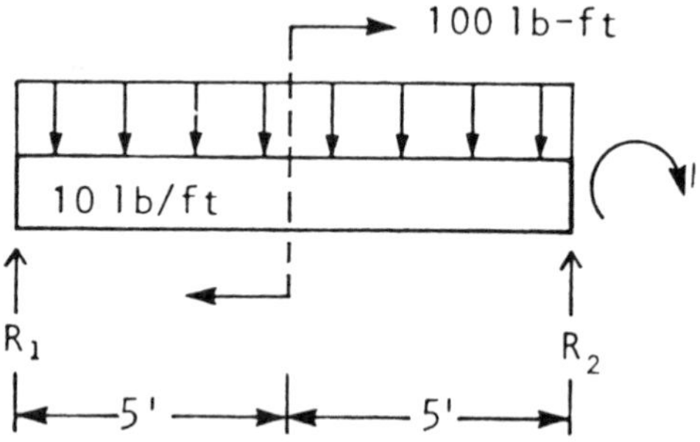

Fig. 2.

Solution: The curvature of this statically inderterminate beam will be found by integrating the differential equation of elastic curvature due to moment

$$EI \frac{d^2Y}{dx^2} = Mx \quad .$$

In free-body diagram shown in Fig. 2, R_1 is the redundant constraint. Find M in terms of R_1 without determining other supporting forces or torques in terms of R_1. Substituting for two spans of the beam, the moments into the curvature equation,

for $0 \leq x < 5$: $$EI \frac{d^2Y}{dx^2} = R_1x - \frac{10x^2}{2} \qquad (a)$$

for $5 < x < 10$: $$EI \frac{d^2Y}{dx^2} = R_1x - 10\frac{x^2}{2} + 100 \qquad (b)$$

Integrating yields

for $0 \le x < 5$:

$$EI\frac{dY}{dx} = R_1\frac{x^2}{2} - \frac{10x^3}{6} + C_1 \qquad (c)$$

$$EIY = R_1\frac{x^3}{6} - \frac{10x^4}{24} + C_1x + C_2 \qquad (d)$$

for $5 < x < 10$:

$$EI\frac{dY}{dx} = R_1\frac{x^2}{2} - 10\frac{x^3}{6} + 100x + C_3 \qquad (e)$$

$$EIY = R_1\frac{x^3}{6} - \frac{10x^4}{24} + 100\frac{x^2}{2} + C_3x + C_4 \qquad (f)$$

Since four constants of integration and R_1 need to be determined,

$$\text{at } x = 0\ ,\quad Y = 0$$

$$\text{at } x = L\ ,\quad \frac{dY}{dx} = Y = 0\ .$$

Hence,

$$C_2 = 0 \qquad (g)$$

$$C_3 = -\frac{R_1(10)^2}{2} + \frac{(10)(10)^3}{6} - (100)(10) = -50R_1 + 667 \qquad (h)$$

$$C_4 = -\frac{R_1(10)^3}{6} + \frac{(10)(10)^4}{24} - (100)\frac{(10^2)}{2} - (-50R_1 + 667)(10)$$

$$= 333R_1 - 7.51 \times 10^3 \qquad (i)$$

Find C_1 and R_1, equating solutions for the spans at $x = 5$:

$$\left\{\left(\frac{dY}{dx}\right)_{x=5}\right\}_{\text{span 1}} = \left\{\left(\frac{dY}{dx}\right)_{x=5}\right\}_{\text{span 2}}$$

$$R_1\left(\frac{5^2}{2}\right) - 10\frac{(5^3)}{6} + C_1 = R_1\left(\frac{5^2}{2}\right) - \frac{10(5^3)}{6} + 100(5) + C_3$$

$$\therefore C_1 = 500 + C_3 \qquad (j)$$

and

$$\{(Y)_{x=5}\}_{\text{span 1}} = \{(Y)_{x=5}\}_{\text{span 2}}$$

$$R_1\left(\frac{5^3}{6}\right) - \frac{10(5^4)}{24} + C_1(5) = R_1\left(\frac{5^3}{6}\right) - \frac{10(5^4)}{24} + 100\frac{(5)^2}{2} + C_3(5) + C_4$$

$$\therefore 5C_1 = 1250 + 5C_3 + C_4 \qquad (k)$$

Replacing C_3 and C_4 with Eqs. (h), (i), (j), and (k) yields:

$$C_1 = 1167 - 50R_1$$

$$5C_1 = 83R_1 - 2.92 \times 10^3$$

Solving,

$$R_1 = 26.3 \text{ lb}$$

$$C_1 = -148$$

The deflection curves for the two spans of the beam are therefore

$0 \le x < 5$:

$$EIY = 26.3 \frac{x^3}{6} - \frac{10x^4}{24} - 148x$$

$5 < x < 10$:

$$EIY = 26.3 \frac{x^3}{6} - \frac{10x^4}{24} + 100 \frac{x^2}{2} - 648x + 1250 \ .$$

The other supporting forces are now readily available from rigid-body mechanics. Thus,

$\Sigma F_y = 0$:

$$R_1 - (10)(10) + R_2 = 0$$

$$\therefore R_2 = 73.7 \text{ lb.}$$

$\Sigma M_0 = 0$:

$$-(100)(5) - 100 + R_2(10) - M_2 = 0$$

$$\therefore M_2 = 137 \text{ ft-lb.}$$

• PROBLEM 10-4

Find the equation of the elastic curve for the uniformly loaded, two-span continuous beam shown in Fig. 1a. The EI is constant.

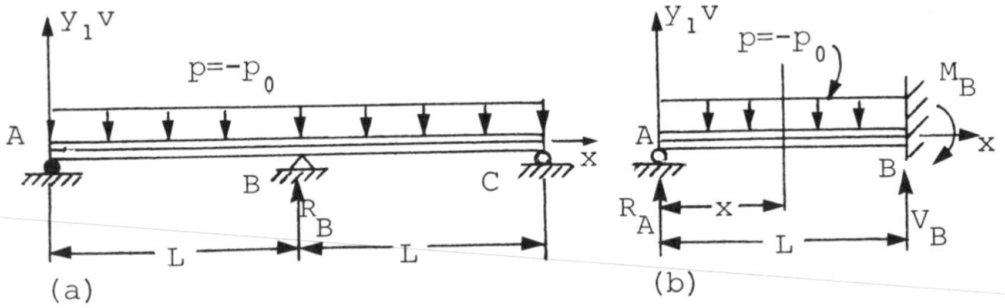

Fig. 1.

Solution: The equation, $EIv^{iv} = p$, can be used here. In addition to the boundary conditions of zero moment and zero deflection at the ends A and C, the deflection at B is also zero. The reaction R_B at B must be treated as an unknown force. On this basis

$$EI \frac{d^4v}{dx^4} = p = -p_0 + R_B\langle x - L\rangle^{-1}$$

$$EI \frac{d^3v}{dx^3} = -p_0x + R_B\langle x - L\rangle^0 + C_1$$

$$EI\frac{d^2v}{dx^2} = -\frac{p_0x^2}{2} + R_B\langle x - L\rangle^1 + C_1x + C_2$$

$$EI\frac{dv}{dx} = -\frac{p_0x^3}{6} + \frac{R_B}{2}\langle x - L\rangle^2 + \frac{C_1x^2}{2} + C_2x + C_3$$

$$EIv = -\frac{p_0x^4}{24} + \frac{R_B}{6}\langle x - L\rangle^3 + \frac{C_1x^3}{6} + \frac{C_2x^2}{2} + C_3x + C_4$$

The five constants R_B, C_1, C_2, C_3, and C_4 are found from three deflection and two moment conditions:

$$v_A = v(0) = 0,\ v_B = v(L) = 0,\ v_C = v(2L) = 0$$

$$M_A = EIv''(0) = 0 \text{ and } M_C = EIv''(2L) = 0$$

The boundary conditions at $x = 0$ yield directly $C_4 = 0$ and $C_2 = 0$. The remaining three conditions $v_B = v_C = M_C = 0$ give the following three simultaneous equations:

$$+(1/6)L^3C_1 + LC_3 = (1/24)p_0L^4$$

$$+(1/6)L^3R_B + (4/3)L^3C_1 + 2LC_3 = (2/3)p_0L^4$$

$$+ LR_B + 2LC_1 = 2p_0L^2$$

from which $R_B = (5/4)p_0L$, $C_1 = -(3/8)p_0L$, and $C_3 = -(1/48)p_0L^3$. Therefore

$$v = -[p_0/(48EI)][2x^4 - 3Lx^3 + L^3x - 10L\langle x - L\rangle^3] \qquad \text{(a)}$$

APPLICATION OF MOMENT-AREA PRINCIPLES

• PROBLEM 10-5

A steel beam 20 ft long is simply supported at the ends and at the mid-point. Under a load of 400 lb per ft uniformly distributed over the entire beam, the center support is 0.12 in above the end supports. Determine the reactions. The moment of inertia of the cross section with respect to the neutral axis is 100 in^4.

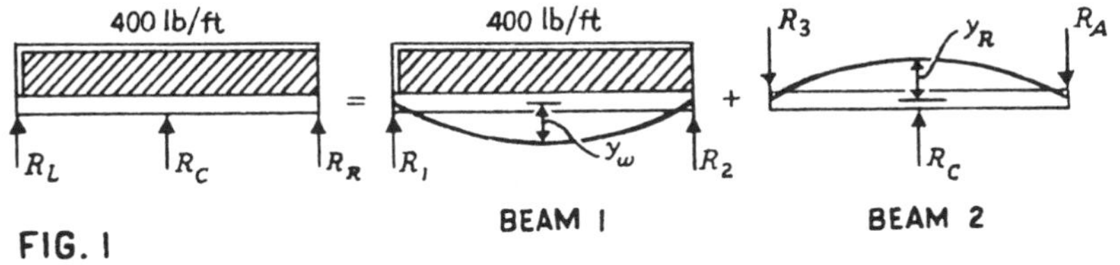

FIG. 1

Solution: With three unknown reactions and only two equations of equilibrium available, the beam is statically indeterminate. Replace the center support with an unknown applied load. The resulting simply supported beam is equivalent to two beams with individual loads as shown in Fig. 1. The resulting deflection at the mid-point of the beam is the upward deflection, y_R, due to R_C minus the downward deflection, y_w, due to the uniform load; that is,

$$y = y_R - y_w = 0.12 \text{ in.} \qquad \text{(a)}$$

For a uniformly loaded simply supported beam of length L, its maximum deflection which occurs at its midpoint, is given by

$$y_w = \frac{5wL^4}{384\ EI}$$

For the second beam, the concentrated load R_C is acting upwards at the midpoint of the beam. We know that such a load produces a maximum displacement of

$$\frac{R_C L^3}{48EI}\ .$$

Hence,

$$y_R = \frac{R_C L^3}{48EI}$$

Substituting the values of y_w and y_R into equation (a), we have,

$$\frac{R_C L^3}{48EI} - \frac{5wL^4}{384EI} = 0.12$$

Multiply this equation by $48EI/L^3$ to obtain

$$R_C - \frac{5wL}{8} = \frac{0.12(48EI)}{(L)^3}$$

or

$$R_C = \frac{5wL}{8} + \frac{0.12(48EI)}{L^3}$$

or

$$R_C = \frac{5(400 \times 20)}{8} + \frac{0.12(48)(30)(10^6)100}{(20 \times 12)^3}$$

$$= 6250 \text{ lb. upwards}$$

The equilibrium equation $\Sigma F_y = 0$, gives

$$R_R + R_L + R_C - w\ell = 0\ .$$

Since $R_L = R_R$ (by symmetry), we have

$$2R_L = w\ell - R_C = 400 \times 20 - 6250$$

or

$$R_L = 875 \text{ lbs.}$$

and

$$R_R = 875 \text{ lbs.}$$

• PROBLEM 10-6

Find the moments at the supports for a fixed-ended beam loaded with a uniformly distributed load of p_0 lb per unit length, Fig. 1 (a).

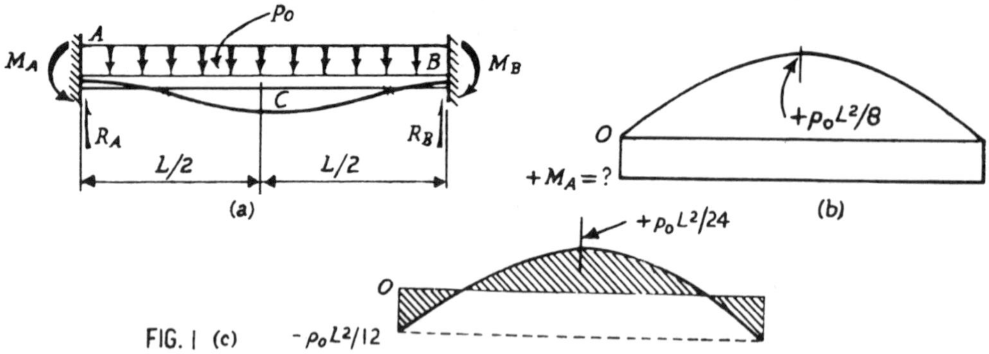

FIG. 1 (c)

Solution: The moments at the supports are called fixed-end moments, and their determination is of great importance in structural theory. Due to symmetry in this problem, the fixed-end moments are equal, as are the vertical reactions, which are $p_0L/2$ each. The moment diagram for this beam considered simply supported is a parabola, Fig. 1 (b), while the fixed-end moments give the rectangular diagram in the same figure.

Although this beam is indeterminate to the second degree because of symmetry a single equation based on a geometrical condition is sufficient to yield the redundant moments. From the geometry of the elastic curve, several conditions may be used such as, $\Delta\theta_{AB} = 0$, $t_{BA} = 0$, or $t_{AB} = 0$. From the condition $\Delta\theta_{AB} = 0$,

$$\frac{1}{EI}\left[\frac{2L}{3}\left(+ \frac{p_0L^2}{8}\right) + L(+ M_A)\right] = 0$$

then

$$M_A = M_B = -p_0L^2/12 \quad .$$

The composite moment diagram is in Fig. 1 (c). In comparison with the maximum bending moment of a simple beam, a considerable reduction in the magnitude of the critical moments occurs.

• PROBLEM 10-7

For the beam of Fig. 1a determine the reactions in terms of w and L.

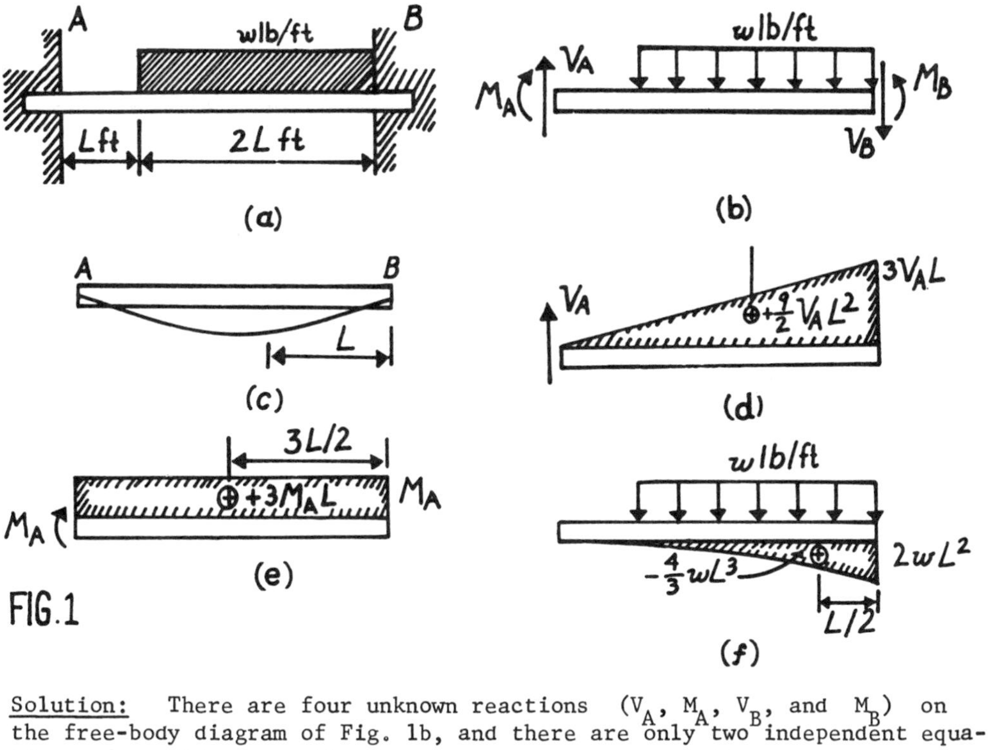

FIG.1

Solution: There are four unknown reactions (V_A, M_A, V_B, and M_B) on the free-body diagram of Fig. 1b, and there are only two independent equations of equilibrium. Therefore two area-moment relations are necessary to supplement the equations of equilibrium.

Inspection of the elastic curve (very much exaggerated) of Fig. 1c reveals that the angle between tangents drawn at A and B is zero. Also the distance from a tangent drawn at A to point B is zero.

These geometrical statements can be expressed mathematically by the area-moment theorems. Thus, since the angle between the tangents at A and B is zero, the area under the moment diagram between A and B must be zero. Also, since the distance from the tangent drawn at A to point B is zero, the moment of the area under the M/(EI) diagram between A and B, with respect to an axis at B, is zero. (In this particular problem the moment axis could also have been selected at A since the deflection of A from a tangent drawn at B is also zero.) These two area-moment relations give

$$EI\theta_{AB} = 0 = \frac{9}{2} V_A L^2 + 3M_A L - \frac{4}{3} wL^3 ,$$

from which

$$27V_A L + 18M_A = 8wL^2 ,$$

and

$$EIt_{B/A} = 0 = \frac{9}{2} V_A L^2 (L) + 3M_A L\left(\frac{3L}{2}\right) - \frac{4wL^3}{3}\left(\frac{L}{2}\right) ,$$

from which

$$27V_A L + 27M_A = 4wL^2 .$$

The simultaneous solution of these equations yields

$$M_A = -\frac{4wL^2}{9} = \frac{4wL^2}{9} \text{ ft-lb counterclockwise}$$

and

$$V_A = \frac{16wL}{27} \text{ lb upward.}$$

With two reactions known, the equations of equilibrium give the other two as

$$M_B = -\frac{2wL^2}{3} = \frac{2wL^2}{3} \text{ ft-lb clockwise}$$

and

$$V_B = -\frac{38wL}{27} = \frac{38wL}{27} \text{ lb upward.}$$

• PROBLEM 10-8

Determine the reactions for the fixed-end beam loaded by a couple M_0 (Fig. 1a). Also, find the deflection of the beam at point C where the couple acts.

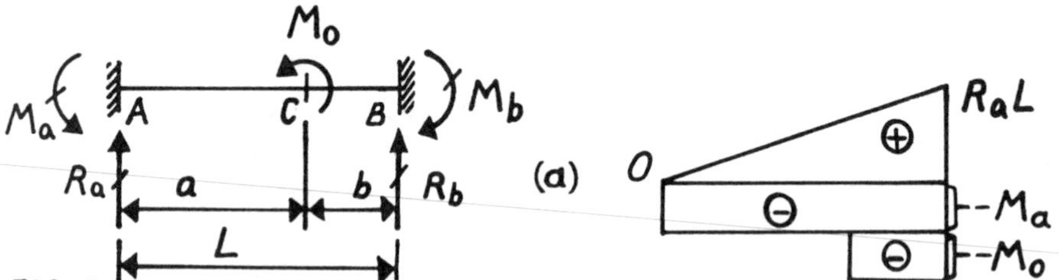

FIG. 1

Solution: The choice of redundants must be made first; the possibilities are R_a and M_a, or R_b and M_b, or M_a and M_b. Let us make the first choice and take the reactions at support A as the redundants. Then we have a cantilever beam fixed at B as the released structure, and we can easily draw the bending moment diagrams produced by R_a, M_a, and the load M_0 (see Fig. 1b).

Two conditions concerning the deflections of the beam are required for finding the two redundants. As a first condition, we note that both ends of the beam have zero slopes; hence the change in slope between A and B is zero. It follows from the first moment-area theorem that the area of the M/EI diagram between A and B must be zero; thus,

$$\frac{1}{2}\left(\frac{R_aL}{EI}\right)(L) - \frac{M_a}{EI}(L) - \frac{M_0}{EI}(b) = 0$$

or

$$R_aL^2 - 2M_aL = 2M_0b \qquad (a)$$

The second condition is obtained from the fact that the tangent to the deflection curve at A passes through point **B**, which means that the first moment of the area of the M/EI diagram between A and B, taken about B, is zero. The resulting equation is

$$\frac{1}{2}\left(\frac{R_aL}{EI}\right)(L)\left(\frac{L}{3}\right) - \frac{M_a}{EI}(L)\left(\frac{L}{2}\right) - \frac{M_0}{EI}(b)\left(\frac{b}{2}\right) = 0$$

or

$$R_aL^3 - 3M_aL^2 = 3M_0b^2 \quad . \qquad (b)$$

Now we can solve simultaneously Eqs. (a) and (b) for the redundants:

$$R_a = \frac{6M_0ab}{L^3} \qquad M_a = \frac{M_0b}{L^2}(2a - b) \qquad (1)$$

The other two reactions are

$$R_b = -R_a \qquad M_b = \frac{M_0a}{L^2}(a - 2b)$$

as found from static equilibrium considerations.

The deflection δ_c at the point where the load is applied can be found from the second moment-area theorem. This deflection is equal to the first moment of the area of the M/EI diagram between A and C, taken about point C. Referring to Fig. 1b, we see that this deflection is

$$\delta_c = \frac{1}{2}\left(\frac{a}{L}\right)\left(\frac{R_aL}{EI}\right)(a)\left(\frac{a}{3}\right) - \frac{M_a}{EI}(a)\left(\frac{a}{2}\right) = \frac{R_aa^3}{6EI} - \frac{M_aa^2}{2EI}$$

Substituting the expressions for R_a and M_a (see Eqs. (1), we get

$$\delta_c = \frac{M_0a^2b^2(b - a)}{2L^3EI} \qquad (2)$$

for the deflection under the load.

When the couple M_0 acts at the midpoint of the span, the reactions for the beam are

$$M_a = -M_b = \frac{M_0}{4} \qquad R_a = -R_b = \frac{3M_0}{2L}$$

and the deflection at the middle (Eq. (2)) becomes zero.

• PROBLEM 10-9

Using the moment-area method, find the reactions for the fixed simple beam shown in Fig. 1a.

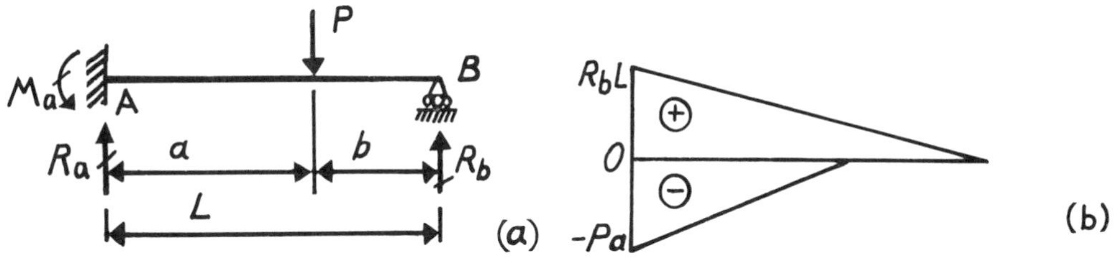

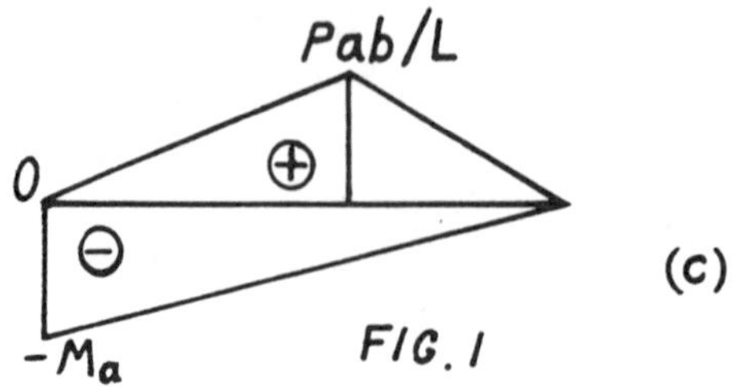

FIG. 1

Solution: If R_b is selected as the redundant, the released structure is a cantilever beam for which the bending moment diagrams produced by P and R_b are shown in Fig. 1b. Because the slope of the beam at support A is zero, we see that the tangent to the deflection curve at A will pass through point B. Hence, it follows from the second moment-area theorem that the first moment of the M/EI diagram between A and B, taken about point B, must equal zero. This relation gives the equation

$$\frac{1}{2}\left(\frac{R_b L}{EI}\right)(L)\left(\frac{2L}{3}\right) - \frac{1}{2}\left(\frac{Pa}{EI}\right)(a)\left(L - \frac{a}{3}\right) = 0$$

from which

$$R_b = \frac{Pa^2}{2L^3}(3L - a) .$$

Knowing this redundant reaction, we can find from static equilibrium the other reactions; the results are

$$R_a = \frac{Pb}{2L^3}(3L^2 - b^2) \qquad M_a = \frac{Pab}{2L^2}(L + b) \tag{1}$$

As an alternative procedure, we can solve the same beam problem by considering the reactive moment M_a as the redundant. In that event the released structure is a simple beam and the corresponding bending moment diagrams due to P and M_a are shown in Fig. 1c. Again using the second moment-area theorem and taking the first moment of the M/EI diagrams about point B, we get

$$\frac{1}{2}\left(\frac{Pab}{LEI}\right)(L)\left(\frac{L + b}{3}\right) - \frac{1}{2}\left(\frac{M_a}{EI}\right)(L)\left(\frac{2L}{3}\right) = 0 .$$

Solving this equation, we obtain for M_a the same result as before (see Eq. 1). From the foregoing results, we can easily get the reactions for a beam with a concentrated load at the middle by substituting $a = b = L/2$; thus,

$$R_a = \frac{11P}{16} \qquad R_b = \frac{5P}{16} \qquad M_a = \frac{3PL}{16} .$$

• PROBLEM 10-10

Find the maximum downward deflection due to an applied force P = 100 lb for the small aluminum beam shown in Fig. 1(a). The beam's constant flexural rigidity $EI=25,000$ lb-in^2.

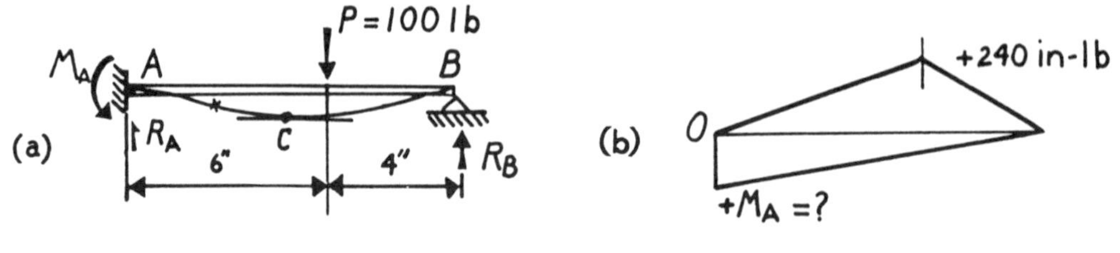

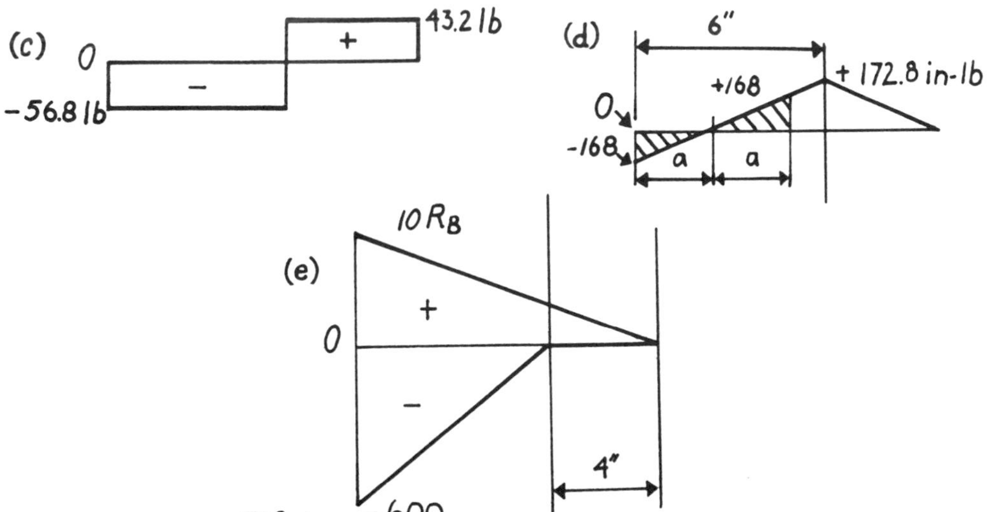

FIG. 1

Solution: The solution of this problem consists of two parts. First, a redundant reaction is determined to establish the numerical values for the bending-moment diagram; then the usual moment area procedure is applied to find the deflection.

Imagining the beam released from the redundant end moment, one can construct the simple beam moment diagram above the baseline in Fig. 1(b). The moment diagram of known shape due to the unknown redundant moment M_A is shown on the same diagram below the base line. One assumes M_A to be positive since in this manner its correct sign according to the beam convention is automatically obtained. The composite diagram represents a complete bending-moment diagram.

The tangent at the built-in end remains horizontal after the application of the force P. Hence the geometrical condition is $t_{BA} = 0$. An equation formulated on this basis yields a solution for M_A. The equations of static equilibrium are used to compute the reactions. The final bending-moment diagram, Fig. 1(d), is obtained in the usual manner after the reactions are known.

Thus, since $t_{BA} = 0$

$$\frac{1}{EI}\left[\frac{(10)(+240)}{2}\,\frac{(10+4)}{3} + \frac{(10)(+M_A)}{2}\,2/3(10)\right] = 0 .$$

A solution of this equation yields $M_A = -168$ in-lb.

$$\Sigma M_A = 0 \circlearrowright +,\quad 100(6) - R_B(10) - 168 = 0 ,\quad R_B = 43.2 \text{ lb.}$$

$$\Sigma M_B = 0 \circlearrowleft +,\quad 100(4) + 168 - R_A(10) = 0,\quad R_A = 56.8 \text{ lb.}$$

Check: $\Sigma F_y = 0 \uparrow +,\quad 43.2 + 65.8 - 100 = 0$.

The maximum deflection occurs where the tangent to the elastic curve is horizontal, point C in Fig. 1(a). Hence, by noting that the tangent at A is also horizontal and using the first moment-area theorem, one locates point C. This occurs when the shaded areas in Fig. 1(d) having opposite signs are equal, i.e., at a distance $2a = 2(168/56.8) = 5.92$ in. from A. The tangential deviation t_{AC} (or t_{CA}) gives the deflection of point C.

$v_{max} = v_C = t_{AC}$

$$= \frac{1}{EI}\left\{\frac{(2.96)}{2}(+168)\left[2.96 + \frac{2(2.96)}{3}\right] + \frac{(2.96)}{2}(-168)\frac{(2.96)}{3}\right\}$$

$$= (982/EI) = 0.0393 \text{ in. down.}$$

Alternate Solution:

A rapid solution may also be obtained by plotting the moment diagram as for a cantilever. This is shown in Fig. 1(e). Note that one of the ordinates is in terms of the redundant reaction R_B. Again using the geometrical condition $t_{BA} = 0$, one obtains an equation yielding R_B. Other reactions follow by statics.

From the condition $t_{BA} = 0$, one has

$$(1/EI)\{(1/2(10)(+10R_B)\ 2/3(10) + 1/2(6)(-600)[4 + 2/3(6)]\} = 0 .$$

Hence, $R_B = 43.2$ lb, up as assumed.

$$\Sigma M_A = 0 \circlearrowleft +, \quad M_A + 43.2(10) - 100(6) = 0,$$

$$M_A = 168 \text{ in-lb} \circlearrowleft .$$

The remainder of the work is the same as in the preceding solution.

• PROBLEM 10-11

Find the fixed-end moments for a fixed-ended beam loaded with a concentrated load P as shown in Fig. 1.

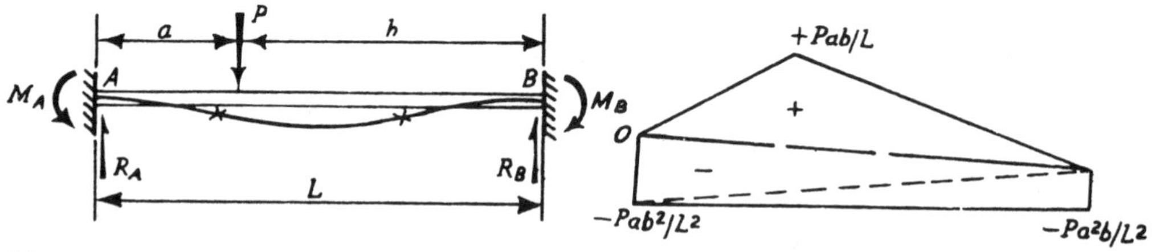

(a) (b) FIG. 1

Solution: Treating the beam AB as a simple beam gives the moment diagram due to P as shown above the baseline in Fig. 1(b). The fixed-end moments are not equal and result in the trapezoidal diagram. Three geometrical conditions for the elastic curve are available to solve this problem, indeterminate to the second degree: (a) $\Delta\theta_{AB} = 0$ since the tangents at A and B are parallel, (b) $t_{BA} = 0$ since the support B does not deviate from a fixed tangent at A. (c) Similarly, $t_{AB} = 0$.

Any two of the above conditions may be used; arithmetical simplicity of the resulting equations governs the choice. Thus, using condition (a), which is always the simplest, and condition (b) two equations are

$$\Delta\theta_{AB} = \frac{1}{EI}\left(\frac{L}{2}\frac{Pab}{L} + \frac{LM_A}{2} + \frac{LM_B}{2}\right) = 0$$

or

$$M_A + M_B = -Pab/L$$

$$t_{BA} = \frac{1}{EI}\left[\frac{L}{2}\frac{Pab}{L}\frac{(L+b)}{3} + \frac{L}{2}M_A\frac{2L}{3} + \frac{LM_B}{2}\frac{L}{3}\right] = 0$$

or

$$2M_A + M_B = -(Pab/L^2)(L + b)$$

Solving the two reduced equations simultaneously

$$M_A = -\frac{Pab^2}{L^2} \quad \text{and} \quad M_B = -\frac{Pa^2b}{L^2}$$

• PROBLEM 10-12

Plot moment and shear diagrams for the continuous beam loaded as shown in Fig. 1(a). The EI is constant for the whole beam.

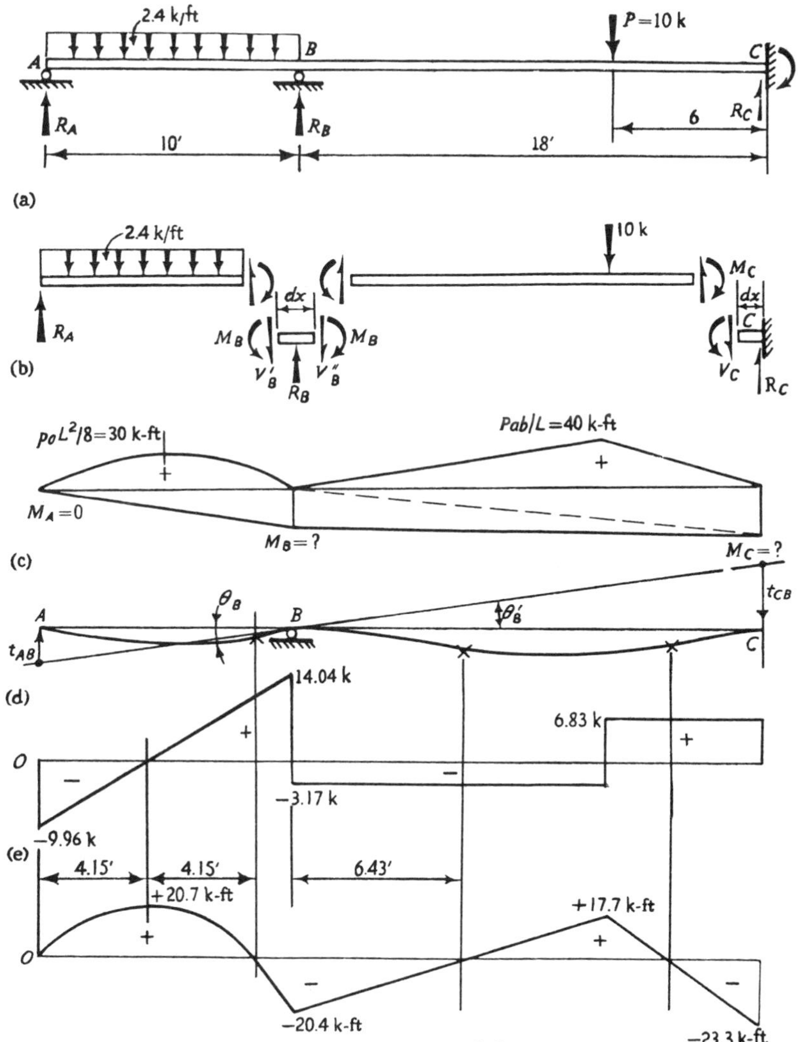

FIG. 1

Solution: This beam is indeterminate to the second degree. By treating each span as a simple beam with the redundant moments, Fig. 1(b), one obtains the moment diagram in Fig. 1(c). No end moments exist at A as this end is on a roller. The clue to the solution is contained in two geometrical conditions for the elastic curve for the whole beam, Fig. 1(d):

(a) $\theta_B = \theta'_B$. Since the beam is physically continuous, there is a line at the support B which is tangent to the elastic curve in either span.

(b) $t_{BC} = 0$ since the support B does not deviate from a fixed tangent at C.

To apply condition (a), t_{AB} and t_{CB} are determined, and, by dividing these quantities by the respective span lengths, the two angles θ_B and θ_B' are obtained. These angles are equal. However, although t_{CB} is algebraically expressed as a positive quantity, the tangent through point B is above point C. Therefore this deviation must be considered negative. Whence, by using condition (a), one equation with the redundant moments is obtained:

$$t_{AB} = \frac{1}{EI}\left[\frac{2(10)}{3}(+\ 30)\ \frac{(10)}{2} + \frac{(10)}{2}(+\ M_B)\ \frac{2(10)}{3}\right]$$

$$= \frac{1}{EI}\left[1{,}000 + \frac{(100)M_B}{3}\right]$$

$$t_{CB} = \frac{1}{EI}\left[\frac{(18)}{2}(\ +\ 40)\frac{(18\ +\ 6)}{3} + \frac{(18)(+\ M_B)}{2}\frac{2(18)}{3} + \frac{(18)(+M_C)}{2}\ \frac{(18)}{3}\right]$$

$$= (1/EI)(2{,}880 + 108M_B + 54M_C)$$

Since $\theta_B = \theta_B'$ or $(t_{AB}/L_{AB}) = -(t_{CB}/L_{CB})$.

$$\frac{1}{EI}\left(\frac{1{,}000 + 1/3(100)M_B}{10}\right) = -\ \frac{1}{EI}\left(\frac{2{,}880 + 108M_B + 54M_C}{18}\right)$$

or

$$(28/3)M_B + 3M_C = -260 \qquad (1)$$

Using condition (b) for the span BC provides another equation, t_{BC} = 0, or

$$\frac{1}{EI}\left[\frac{(18)}{2}(+\ 40)\ \frac{(18\ +\ 12)}{3} + \frac{(18)(+M_B)}{2}\frac{(18)}{3} + \frac{(18)(+M_C)}{2}\ \frac{2(18)}{3}\right] = 0$$

or

$$3M_B + 6M_C = -200 \qquad (2)$$

Solving the equations (1) and (2), yields,

$$M_B = -20.4 \text{ ft-lb} \quad \text{and} \quad M_C = -23.3 \text{ ft-lb}$$

where the signs agree with the convention of signs used for beams. These moments with their proper sense are shown in Fig. 1(b).

After the redundant moments M_A and M_C are found, no new techniques are necessary to construct the moment and shear diagrams. However, particular care must be exercised to include the moments at the supports while computing shears and reactions. Usually, isolated beams as shown in Fig. 1(b) are the most convenient free bodies for determining shears. Reactions follow by adding the shears on the adjoining beams. In units of kips and feet, for free body AB:

$$\Sigma M_B = 0 \circlearrowleft +,\quad 2.4(10)5 - 20.4 - 10R_A = 0,\ R_A = 9.96 \text{ kips}\uparrow$$

$$\Sigma M_A = 0 \circlearrowright +,\quad 2.4(10)5 + 20.4 - 10V_B' = 0,\ V_B' = 14.04 \text{ kips}\uparrow$$

For free body BC:

$$\Sigma M_C = 0 \circlearrowleft +,\ 10(6) + 20.4 - 23.3 - 18V_B'' = 0,\ V_B'' = 3.17 \text{ kips}\uparrow$$

$$\Sigma M_B = 0 \circlearrowright +,\ 10(12) - 20.4 + 23.3 - 18V_C = 0,\ V_C = R_C = 6.83 \text{ kips}\uparrow$$

Check: $R_A + V_B' = 24$ kips↑ and $V_B'' + R_C = 10$ kips↑

From above, $R_B = V_B' + V_B'' = 17.21$ kips ↑.

The complete shear and moment diagrams are in Figs. 1(e) and (f), respectively.

SUPERPOSITION METHOD

• PROBLEM 10-13

Determine the supporting forces for the statically indeterminate beam shown.

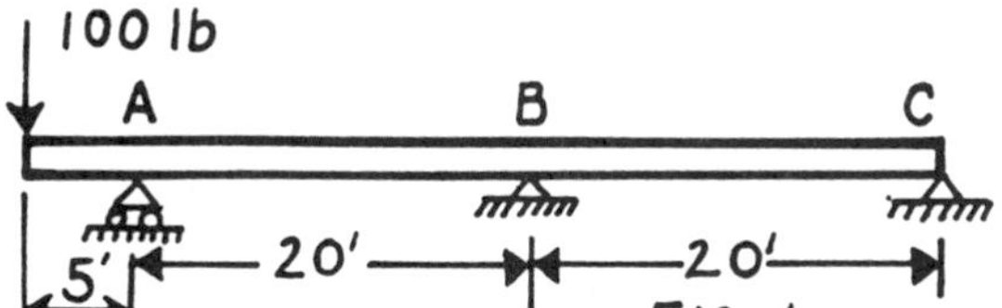

FIG. 1

Solution: The superposition principle will be employed in solving this problem. Two cases of partial loading will be considered and then added together to get the total forces.

In the first case the reaction force at B will be left out. This part of the problem then reduces to a simply supported beam with a moment of -500 ft-lb applied to one end (see Fig. 2).

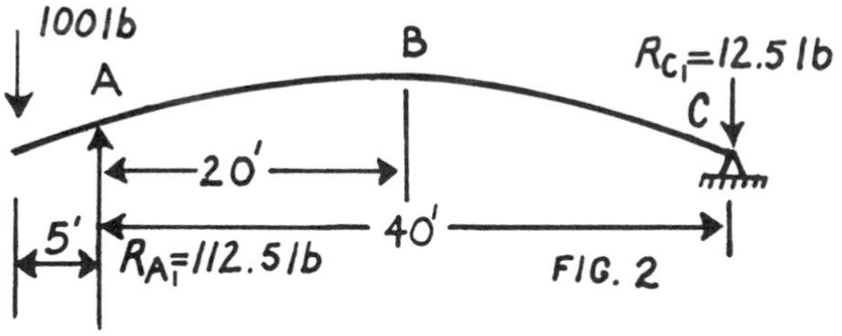

FIG. 2

By moment equilibrium about A the partial reaction force at C, R_{C_1} is

$$\Sigma M_A = 0 = 500 \text{ ft-lb} - 40' R_{C_1}, \quad R_{C_1} = 12.5 \text{ lb. downwards.}$$

The partial reaction at A, R_{A_1}, is by vertical force equilibrium

$$\Sigma F_y = 0 = 100 \text{ lb} - R_{A_1} + 12.5 \text{ lb}, \quad R_{A_1} = 112.5 \text{ lb upwards.}$$

The formula for the deflection at B, the midpoint of a simple supported beam with an applied moment is

$$\delta_1 = \frac{-ML^2}{16EI} .$$

Substituting in the numbers gives

$$\delta_1 = \frac{-(-500 \text{ ft-lb})(40 \text{ ft})^2}{16EI} = \frac{50000}{EI} \text{ ft (upwards)}$$

In the actual situation there is no deflection at B. Therefore a second case will be considered of a simply supported beam this time with a load at B of the force necessary to cancell out the deflection found in the first case. Leaving out the moment due to the 100 lb load and considering the reaction force at B to be an applied load results in the situation shown in Fig. 3.

The formula for the deflection at the center of a simply supported beam with a concentrated load applied at the midpoint is

$$\delta_2 = \frac{-PL^3}{48EI}$$

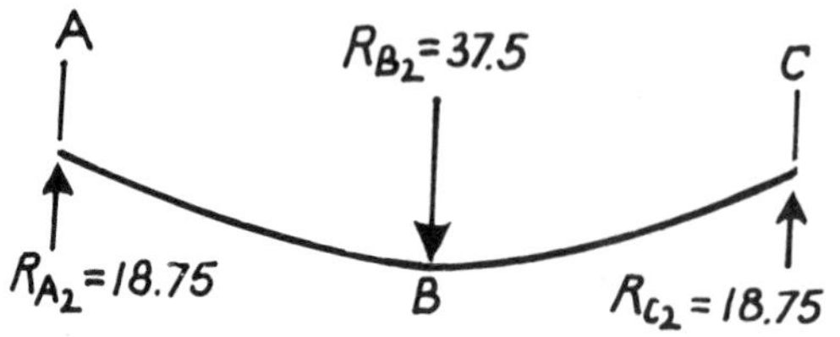

FIG.3

It is desired that this deflection be of the same magnitude as the deflection in case 1, but in the opposite direction. Then the total deflection at B will be zero.

$$\delta_2 = -\delta_1 = -50000/EI \text{ ft downwards.}$$

Substituting for δ_2 gives

$$\frac{PL^3}{48EI} = \frac{50000}{EI} \quad \text{downwards.}$$

Inserting the values for P and L yields

$$R_{B_2} \frac{(40 \text{ ft})^3}{48 \text{ EI}} = \frac{50000}{EI} \text{ downwards.}$$

Solving for R_{B_2} results in

$$R_{B_2} = 37.5 \text{ lb} \quad \text{downwards.}$$

By vertical force equilibrium and symmetry

$$R_{A_2} = 18.75 \text{ lb upwards and } R_{C_2} = 18.75 \text{ lb upwards.}$$

The total loading will now be found by adding together the partial loadings. At point A the total force is

$$R_A = R_{A_1} + R_{A_2}$$

$$R_A = 112.5 \text{ lb upwards} + 18.75 \text{ lb upwards} = 131.25 \text{ lb upwards.}$$

At point B

$$R_B = R_{B_1} + R_{B_2}$$

$$R_B = 0 + 37.5 \text{ lb downwards} = 37.5 \text{ lb downwards.}$$

And at point C

$$R_C = R_{C_1} + R_{C_2}$$

$$R_C = 12.5 \text{ lb downwards} + 18.75 \text{ lb upwards} = 6.25 \text{ lb upwards.}$$

In summary the reaction force at A is 131.25 lb upwards, the reaction force at B is 37.5 lb downwards, and the reaction force at C is 6.25 lb upwards.

• PROBLEM 10-14

Determine all reactions for the beam in Fig. 1a in terms of P, L, and a.

Solution: There are four unknown reactions (a shear and moment at each end), and only two equations of equilibrium are available; therefore the beam is statically indeterminate, and two deformation equations are necessary. Replace the constraint at the right end with an unknown force and couple. The resulting cantilever beam is equivalent to three beams with individual loads as shown in Fig. 1b. Note that the unknown shear and moment at the right end are both shown as positive values so that the algebraic sign of the result will be correct. From the geometry of the constrained beam, the resultant slope and the resultant deflection at the right end are both zero. The first beam with load P has a constant slope from P to the end of the beam which is

$$\theta_P = -\frac{Pa^2}{2EI} .$$

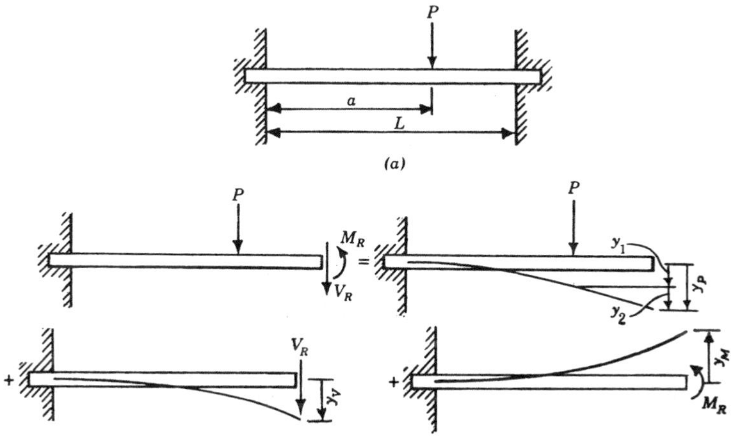

FIG. 1

The deflection, y_P, at the end is made up of two parts: y_1 for a beam of length a, and y_2 the added deflection of the tangent segment (straight line) from P to the end of the beam. This deflection is

$$y_P = -y_1 - y_2$$

Since $y_1 = \frac{Pa^3}{3EI}$, and $y_2 = (L-a)\theta_P$, the above equation becomes

$$y_P = \frac{-Pa^3}{3EI} - (L-a)\theta_P$$

or,

$$y_P = -\frac{Pa^3}{3EI} - (L-a)\frac{Pa^2}{2EI} = \frac{Pa^3}{6EI} - \frac{Pa^2L}{2EI} .$$

The slope and deflection at the end of the beam due to the shear V_R are (from table of beam deflections and slopes)

$$\theta_V = -\frac{V_RL^2}{2EI} \quad \text{and} \quad y_V = -\frac{V_RL^3}{3EI}$$

Finally the slope and deflection at the right end of the beam due to M_R are

$$\theta_M = \frac{M_RL}{EI} \quad \text{and} \quad y_M = \frac{M_RL^2}{2EI} .$$

Since the resultant slope is zero,

$$\theta_P + \theta_V + \theta_M = -\frac{Pa^2}{2EI} - \frac{V_RL^2}{2EI} + \frac{M_RL}{EI} = 0 . \qquad (1)$$

Similarly

$$y_P + y_V + y_M = \frac{Pa^3}{6EI} - \frac{Pa^2L}{2EI} - \frac{V_RL^3}{3EI} + \frac{M_RL^2}{2EI} = 0 . \qquad (2)$$

The equations (1) and (2) can be written as

$$\frac{M_R L}{EI} - \frac{V_R L^2}{2EI} = \frac{Pa^2}{2EI}$$

$$\frac{M_R L^2}{2EI} - \frac{V_R L^3}{3EI} = \frac{Pa^2 L}{2EI} - \frac{Pa^3}{6EI}$$

or

$$M_R - V_R \frac{L}{2} = \frac{Pa^2}{2L}$$

$$M_R - \frac{2}{3} V_R L = \frac{Pa^2}{L} - \frac{Pa^2}{3L^2}$$

Solving these two equations, we obtain

$$M_R = \frac{-Pa^2 (L - a)}{L^2} \quad \text{and} \quad V_R = \frac{-Pa^2 (3L - 2a)}{L^3} .$$

When the equations of equilibrium are applied to a free-body diagram of the beam, the shear and moment at the left end are found to be

$$M_L = \frac{-Pa(L - a)^2}{L^2} \quad \text{and} \quad V_L = \frac{+P(L^3 - 3a^2 L + 2a^3)}{L^3} .$$

• PROBLEM 10-15

Plot shear and moment diagrams for a uniformly loaded beam fixed at one end and simply supported at the other, Fig. 1(a). The EI is constant.

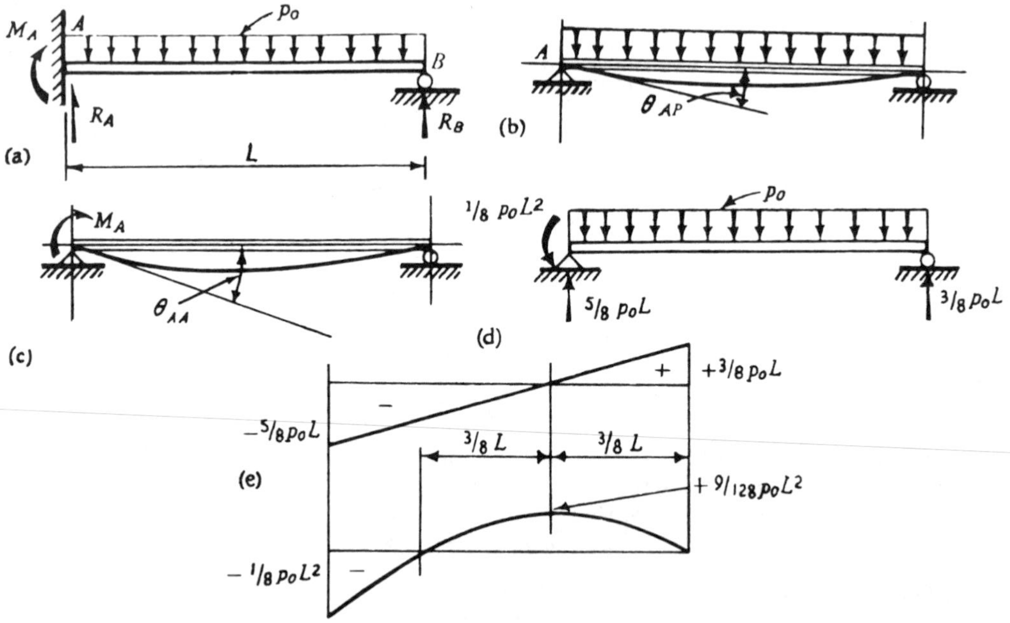

FIG. 1

Solution: This beam is indeterminate to the first degree, but it can be reduced to determinacy by removing M_A as in Fig. 1(b). A positive moment M_A acting at A on the same structure is shown in Fig. 1(c). The rotations at A for the two determinate cases can be found from Table of beam deflection and slopes. The requirement of zero rotation at A in the original structure provides the necessary equation for determining M_A.

$$\theta_{AP} = p_0 L^3/(24EI) \qquad \text{(clockwise)}$$

and

$$\theta_{AA} = M_A L/(3EI) \qquad \text{(clockwise)}$$

$$\theta_A = \theta_{AP} + \theta_{AA} = 0$$

Taking clockwise rotations as positive,

$$\frac{p_0 L^3}{24EI} + \frac{M_A L}{3EI} = 0 \quad \text{and} \quad M_A = -\frac{p_0 L^2}{8}$$

The negative sign of the result indicates that M_A acts in the direction opposite to that assumed. Its correct sense is shown in Fig. 1(d).

The remainder of the problem may be solved with the aid of statics. Now,

$$\Sigma M_B = 0 = \frac{1}{8} p_0 L^2 + p_0 L \frac{L}{2} - R_A L$$

from which

$$R_A = \frac{5}{8} p_0 L \quad .$$

Applying equation $\Sigma F_y = 0$, one obtains,

$$p_0 L - R_A - R_B = 0$$

or

$$R_B = p_0 L - \frac{5}{8} p_0 L = \frac{3}{8} p_0 L \ .$$

Reactions, shear diagram, and moment diagram are in Figs. 1(d), (e), and (f) respectively.

This problem may also be analyzed by treating R_B as the redundant.

• PROBLEM 10-16

Find the reactions for a fixed-end beam with a uniform load over part of the span (Fig. 1).

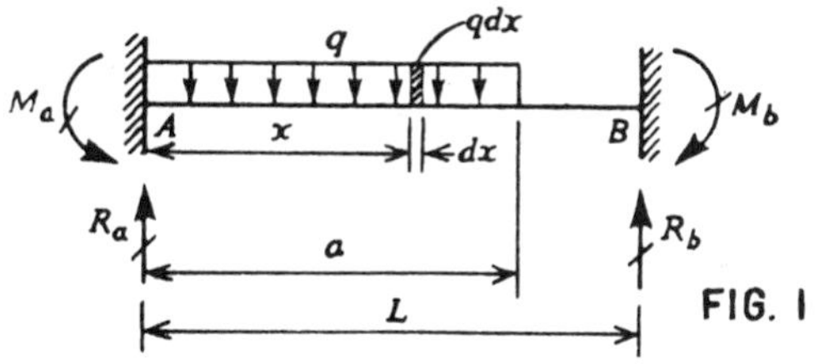

FIG. 1

Solution: Let us isolate an element qdx of the load at distance x from the left-hand end of the beam. By treating this element as a concentrated force, we can utilize the formulas for the fixed-end beam with concentrated load P at a distance a from the left end. Thus fixed end moments are

$$M_a = \frac{Pab^2}{L^2}$$

and

$$M_b = \frac{Pa^2 b}{L^2}$$

Beginning with the above formulas for the moments M_a and M_b, we can replace P by qdx, a by x, and b by L - x; hence, the fixed-end moments due to the element of load are

$$dM_a = \frac{qx(L-x)^2 dx}{L^2} \qquad dM_b = \frac{qx^2(L-x)dx}{L^2}$$

Integration over the loaded length of the beam yields

$$\int dM_a = \int_0^a \frac{q}{L^2} x(L - x)^2 dx$$

$$M_a = \frac{q}{L^2}\int_0^a (xL - 2Lx^2 + x^3)dx$$

$$= \frac{q}{L^2}\left[\frac{x^2L}{2} - \frac{2Lx^3}{3} + \frac{x^4}{4}\right]_0^a$$

$$= \frac{q}{L^2}\left[\frac{a^2L}{2} - \frac{2La^3}{3} + \frac{a^4}{4}\right]$$

$$= \frac{qa^2}{12L^2}[6L - 8aL + 3a^2]$$

and

$$\int dM_b = \frac{q}{L^2}\int_0^a x^2(L - x)dx$$

$$M_b = \frac{q}{L^2}\int_0^a (Lx^2 - x^3)dx$$

$$= \frac{q}{L^2}\left[\frac{Lx^3}{3} - \frac{x^4}{4}\right]_0^a$$

$$= \frac{q}{L^2}\left[\frac{La^3}{3} - \frac{a^4}{4}\right]$$

$$= \frac{qa^3}{12L^2}[4L - 3a] .$$

Now the vertical reactions at the ends for fixed-end beam with a concentrated load P at a distance a from the left-end are

$$R_a = \frac{Pb^2}{L^3}(3a + b) \tag{1}$$

and

$$R_b = \frac{Pa^2}{L^3}(3b + a) \tag{2}$$

Hence, for the given problem, the vertical reactions at the ends can be found with the aid of equations (1) and (2). Thus,

$$R_a = \frac{q}{L^3}\int (L - x)^2(L + 2x)dx$$

$$R_a = \frac{q}{L^3}\int_0^a (L^3 - 3Lx^2 + 2x^3)dx$$

$$= \frac{q}{L^3}\left[L^3x - \frac{3Lx^3}{3} + \frac{2x^4}{4}\right]_0^a$$

$$= \frac{q}{L^3}\left[L^3a - La^3 + \frac{a^4}{2}\right]$$

$$= \frac{qa}{2L^3}[2L^3 - 2La^2 + a^3]$$

and

$$R_b = \frac{q}{L^3}\int_0^a x^2(3L - 2x)dx$$

$$= \frac{q}{L^3}\left[\frac{3Lx^3}{3} - \frac{2x^4}{4}\right]_0^a$$

$$= \frac{q}{L^3}\left[La^3 - \frac{a^4}{2}\right]$$

$$= \frac{qa^3}{2L^3}\left[2L - a\right]$$

Thus, the desired results have been found.

• PROBLEM 10-17

Determine the reactions for the two-span continuous beam shown in Fig. 1 by the method of superposition. Note that the beam supports uniform load of intensity q.

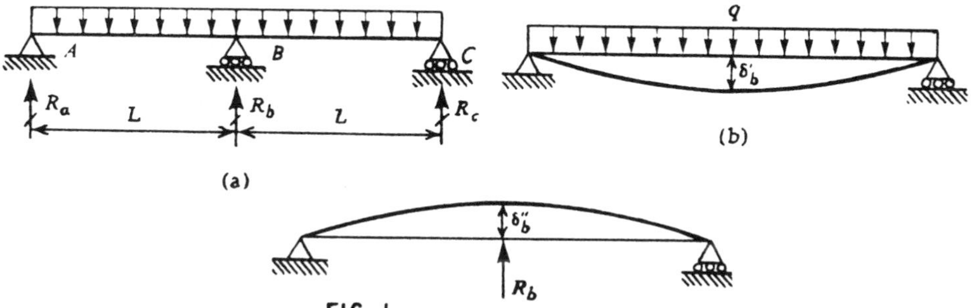

FIG. I

(c)

Solution: Selecting the middle reaction R_b as the redundant, we see that the released structure is a simple beam (Fig. 1(b)). Under the action of the uniform load, the deflection at point B in the released structure (from a beam deflection table) is

$$\delta''_b = \frac{5q(2L)^4}{384EI} = \frac{5qL^4}{24EI}$$

where L is the length of each span. The deflection in the upward direction produced by the redundant (see Fig. 1(c)) is

$$\delta''_b = \frac{R_b(2L)^3}{48EI} = \frac{R_bL^3}{6EI}$$

as obtained from beam deflection table. The equation of compatibility pertaining to the vertical deflection at point B is

$$\delta_b = \delta'_b - \delta''_b = \frac{5qL^4}{24EI} - \frac{R_bL^3}{6EI} = 0$$

from which

$$R_b = \frac{5qL}{4} .$$

The other two reactions have the values $R_a = R_c = 3qL/8$, as found from static equilibrium.

• PROBLEM 10-18

A beam ABC (Fig. 1a) is simply supported at A and B and from a cable CD at point C. Prior to the application of the uniform load q, the force in the cable is T. There is no slack in the cable. When the load q is applied the beam deflects downward at C and a tensile force T develops in the cable. Find the magnitude of this force.

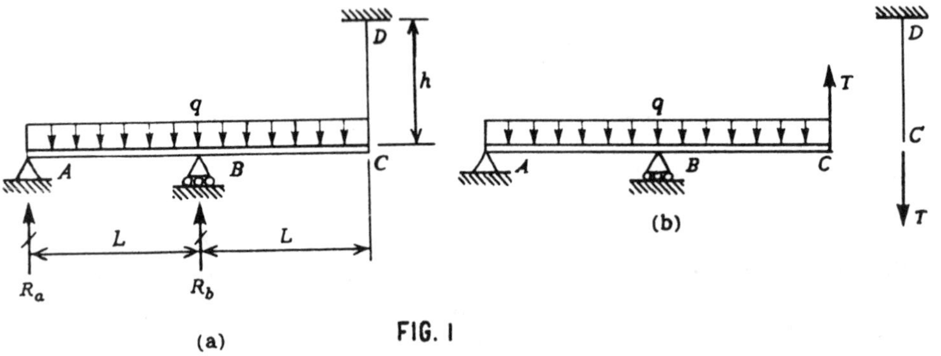

FIG. 1

Solution: It is convenient in this analysis to select the unknown force T in the cable as the redundant and to cut the structure into two parts (Fig. 1b). The released structure then consists of the beam ABC and the cable CD as independent structures, with the force T acting upward on the beam and downward on the cable. The deflection at point C on the beam will consist of two parts, a downward deflection δ_c' due to the uniform load and an upward deflection δ_c'' due to the force T. At the same time, the end of the cable (point C) will deflect downward by an amount δ_c''', equal to the elongation of the cable. Therefore, the equation of compatibility, expressing the fact that the downward displacement of the end of the beam is equal to the displacement of the end of the cable, is

$$\delta_c' - \delta_c'' = \delta_c''' .$$

Having formulated this equation, we now turn to the task of evaluating the three deflection terms.

The deflection at the end of the overhang produced by the uniform load can be found from a table of beam deflection. Thus

$$\delta_c' = \frac{qL^4}{4EI}$$

where EI is the flexural rigidity of the beam. The deflection of the beam at C due to the force T is given by

$$\delta''_c = \frac{2TL^3}{3EI} .$$

Finally, the stretch of the cable is

$$\delta_c''' = \frac{Th}{EA}$$

where h is the length of the cable and EA is its axial rigidity.

By substituting the preceding deflection formulas into the equation of compatibility we get

$$\frac{qL^4}{4EI} - \frac{2TL^3}{3EI} = \frac{Th}{EA}$$

or

$$T[\frac{h}{A} + \frac{2L^3}{3I}] = \frac{qL^4}{4EI}$$

or

$$T\ [\frac{3hI + 2L^3A}{3AI}] = \frac{qL^4}{4EI}$$

from which

$$T = \frac{3qAL^4}{8AL^3 + 12Ih}$$

Note that in this example the redundant was selected as an internal force quantity instead of an external reaction. The choice of redundant is usually based upon convenience in the solution.

• PROBLEM 10-19

A simply supported beam is bolted to the end of the cantilever beam of same material and cross-section. Find the deflection of this bolted end.

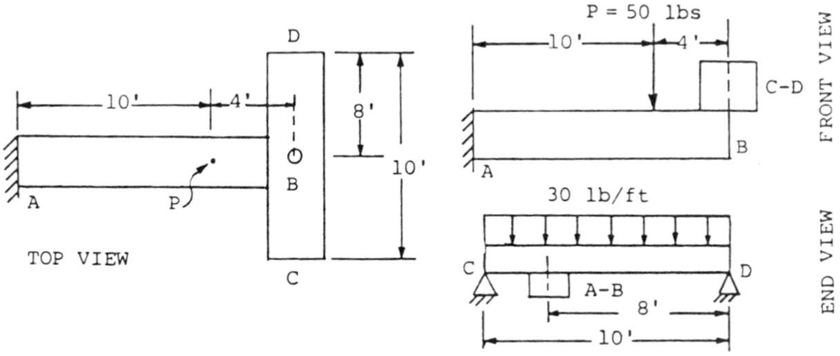

Solution: This problem lends itself to be solved by the superposition method, using a table of formulas of beam deflections.

Consider the cantilever beam first using R as the reactive force from the simply supported beam. The redundant force is R. From a table of beam deflections, the formula for a concentrated load applied to a cantilever beam is

$$Y = \frac{-P}{6EI}((x - a)^3 - x^3 + 3x^2a) .$$

The deflection due to the 50 lb load is

$$Y = \frac{-50}{6EI}((x - 10)^3 - x^3 + 3x^2 10) .$$

The deflection due to R is

$$Y = \frac{-R}{6EI}((x - 14)^3 - x^3 + 3x^2 14) .$$

Adding the two equations, the total deflection of the cantilever is

$$Y = \frac{(-50)}{6EI}\{(x - 10)^3 - x^3 + (3)(x^2)(10)\}$$

$$+ \frac{(-R)}{6EI}\{(x - 14)^3 - x^3 + (3)(x^2)((14)\}$$

Next use the boundary condition at the redundant constraint. Thus, setting x = 14, for δ, the deflection at the tip of the cantilever beam:

$$\delta = \frac{(-50)}{6EI}\{(14 - 10)^3 - 14^3 + (3)(14^2)(10)\} + \frac{(-R)}{6EI}\{0 - 14^3 + 3(14)^3\}$$

$$= -\frac{1}{EI}[26.7 \times 10^3 + .914 \times 10^3 R] \qquad \text{(a)}$$

From a beam deflection table the formula for a uniformly loaded simply supported beam is

$$Y = \frac{-wx}{24EI}(L^3 - 2Lx^2 + x^3) .$$

The formula for a concentrated load applied to a simply supported beam is

$$Y = \frac{-Pb}{6LEI}\left(-x^3 + \frac{L}{b}(x - a) + (L^2 - b^2)x\right)$$

Substituting in the values for $x = 2$ and adding the equations together gives the total deflection, δ .

$$\delta = \frac{(-30)(2)}{24EI}[10^3 - (2)(10)(4) + 8]$$
$$+ \frac{R(8)}{(6)(10)(EI)}\left[-2^3 + \frac{10}{8}(0) + (10^2 - 8^2)(2)\right]$$
$$- \frac{1}{EI}[2.32 \times 10^3 - 8.54R] \qquad \text{(b)}$$

To satisfy the boundary condition at the constraint R, equate δ from Eqs. (a) and (b) to get

$$-26.7 \times 10^3 - .914 \times 10^3 R = -2.32 \times 10^3 + 8.54R$$

therefore

$$R = -26.4 \text{ lb}$$

Now get δ from Eq.(a). Thus,

$$\delta = \frac{-1}{EI}[26.7 \times 10^3 + (.914)(-26.4) \times 10^3] = \frac{-2.3 \times 10^3}{EI} \text{ ft.}$$

THREE MOMENT EQUATION

• PROBLEM 10-20

Find the moments at all supports for the continuous beam loaded as shown in Fig. 1. The EI is constant for the whole beam.

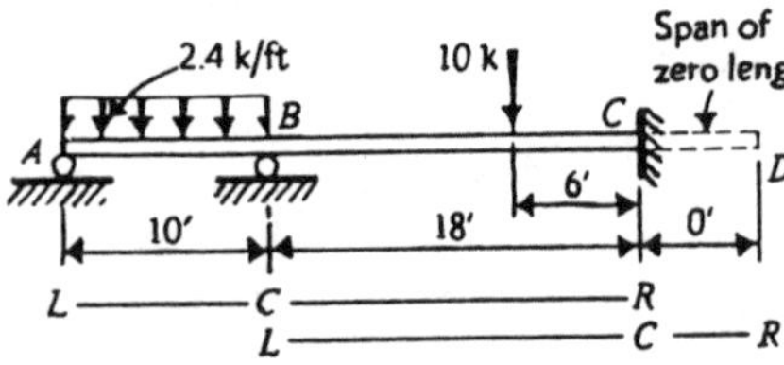

FIG. 1

Solution: No difficulty is encountered in setting up a three-moment equation for the spans AB and BC. Note that an unknown moment does exist at the built-in end, and, since the end A is on a roller, $M_A = 0$. By using three-moment equation, one obtains,

$$10M_A + 2(10 + 18)M_B + 18M_C$$

$$= -\frac{2.4(10)^3}{4} - 10(6)12\left(1 + \frac{6}{18}\right)$$

$$56M_B + 18M_C = -1,560 \ .$$

To set up the next equation, an artifice is introduced. An imaginary span of zero length is added at the fixed end, and the three-moment equation can be used for the spans BC and CD. Thus,

$$18M_B + 2(18 + 0)M_C + 0(M_D) = -10(12)6\left(1 + \frac{12}{18}\right)$$

$$18M_B + 36M_C = -1,200$$

Solving the reduced equations simultaneously

$$M_B = -20.4 \text{ kip-ft} \quad \text{and} \quad M_C = -23.3 \text{ kip-ft}$$

The use of a zero-length span at the fixed ends of beams is justified by the moment-area procedure. This expedient is equivalent to the requirement of a zero deviation of a support nearest the fixed end from the tangent at the fixed end.

• PROBLEM 10-21

Find the moments at all supports and the reactions at C and D for the continuous beam loaded as shown in Fig. 1(a). The flexural rigidity EI is constant.

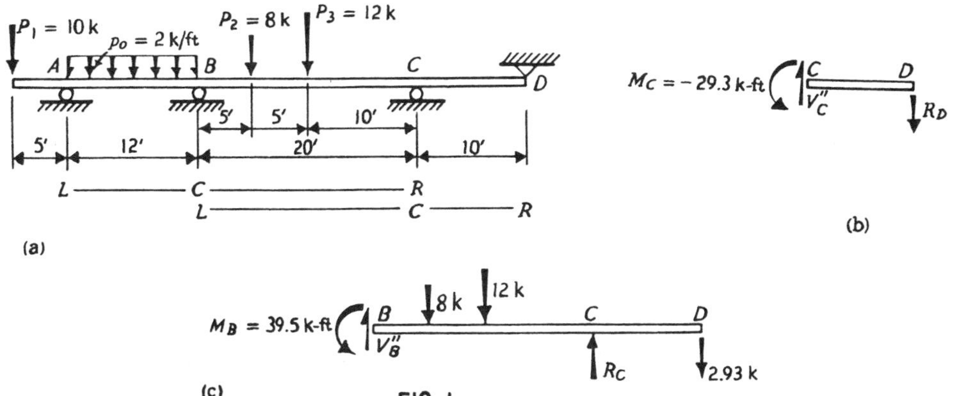

FIG. 1

Solution: By using three-moment equation for the spans AB and BC, one equation is written. From statics, the beam convention being used for signs, $M_A = -10(5) = -50$ kip-ft. The moments of inertia I_L and I_R are equal.

$$12M_A + 2(12 + 20)M_B + 20M_C$$

$$= -\frac{2(12)^3}{4} - 8(15)5\left(1 + \frac{15}{20}\right) - 12(10)10\left(1 + \frac{10}{20}\right)$$

Substituting $M_A = -50$ kip-ft and simplifying gives

$$64M_B + 20M_C = -3,114 \qquad (1)$$

Next, three-moment equation is again applied for the spans BC and CD. No constant terms are contributed to the right side of the three-moment equation by the unloaded span CD. At the pinned end, $M_D = 0$.

$$20M_B + 2(20 + 10)M_C + 10M_D$$

$$= -8(5)15\left(1 + \frac{5}{20}\right) -12(10)10\left(1 + \frac{10}{20}\right)$$

or

$$20M_B + 60M_C = -2{,}550 \qquad (2)$$

Solving the equations (1) and (2) simultaneously gives

$$M_B = -39.5 \text{ kip-ft} \quad \text{and} \quad M_C = -29.3 \text{ kip-ft}$$

Isolating the span CD as in Fig. 1(b), one obtains the reaction R_D from statics. Instead of isolating the span BC and computing V_C' to add to V_C'' to find R_C, the free body shown in Fig. 1(c) is used. For free body CD:

$$\Sigma M_C = 0 \circlearrowleft +, \quad 29.3 - 10R_D = 0, \quad R_D = 2.93 \text{ kips}\downarrow$$

For free body BD :

$$\Sigma M_B = 0, \circlearrowright +, \quad 8(5) + 12(10) - R_C(20) + 2.93(30) - 39.5 = 0,$$

$$R_C = 10.42 \text{ kips}\uparrow$$

• PROBLEM 10-22

As shown in Fig. 1, the beam has three spans of equal length and constant moment of inertia and is loaded in the first and third spans. The concentrated load P is assumed to be equal to qL . Find the moments at all supports and the reactions.

Solution: The three-moment equation is applied for the spans 1-2 and 2-3. Note that no constant terms are contributed to the right side of the three-moment equation by the unloaded span 2-3, and since the end 1 is on a roller, $M_1 = 0$. Then,

$$LM_1 + 2M_2(L + L) + M_3L = -\frac{qL^3}{4}$$

or

$$4M_2L + M_3L = -\frac{qL^3}{4}$$

or

$$4M_2 + M_3 = -\frac{qL^3}{4} \qquad (1)$$

Similarly, the three-moment equation for the span 2-3 and 3-4 is

$$M_2L + 2M_3(L + L) = -\frac{P(L/4)}{L}\left[L^2 - (L/4)^2\right]$$

since, P = 2L, we have,

$$M_2L + 4M_3L = -\frac{qL}{4}\left[L^2 - \frac{L^2}{16}\right]$$

or

$$M_2 + 4M_3 = -\frac{15qL^2}{64} \qquad (2)$$

Solving Eqs. (1) and (2) gives the bending moments:

$$M_2 = -\frac{49qL^2}{960} \quad M_3 = -\frac{11qL^2}{240} .$$

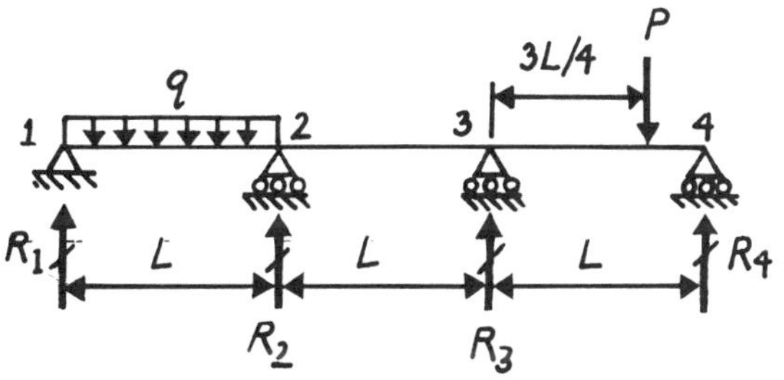

FIG.1 (a)

By drawing free-body diagrams of each of the three parts of the beam and then writing equations of static equilibrium, we obtain the reactions:

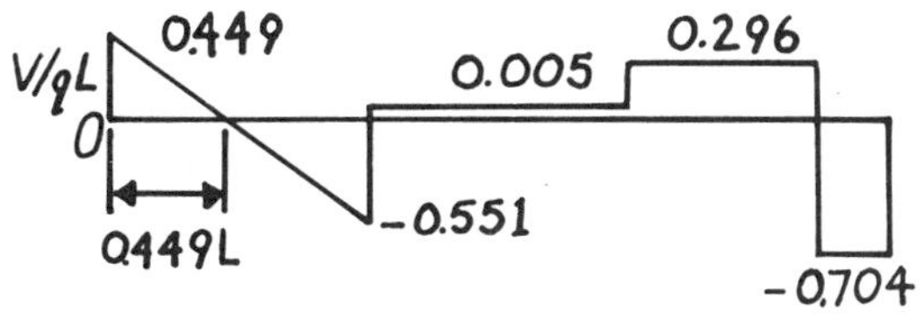

(b)

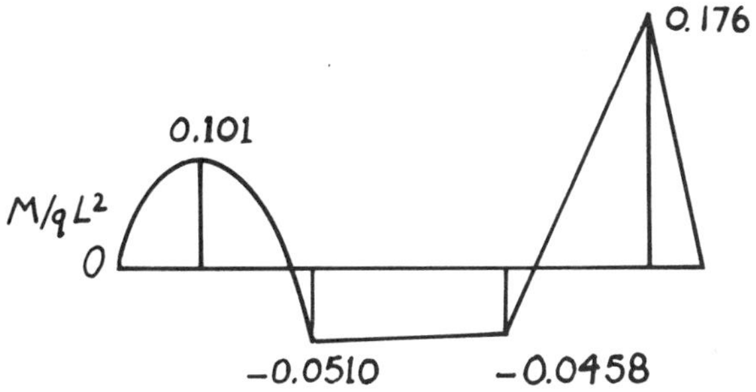

FIG.1 (c)

$$R_1 = \frac{431qL}{960} \quad R_2 = \frac{89qL}{160} \quad R_3 = \frac{93qL}{320} \quad R_4 = \frac{169qL}{240}$$

With this information we can construct the shear force and bending moment diagrams for the entire beam, shown in Fig. 1 b and c.

• PROBLEM 10-23

A restrained beam of ductile material is loaded as shown in Fig. 1(a). Find the limit load P_{ult}. Neglect the weight of the beam.

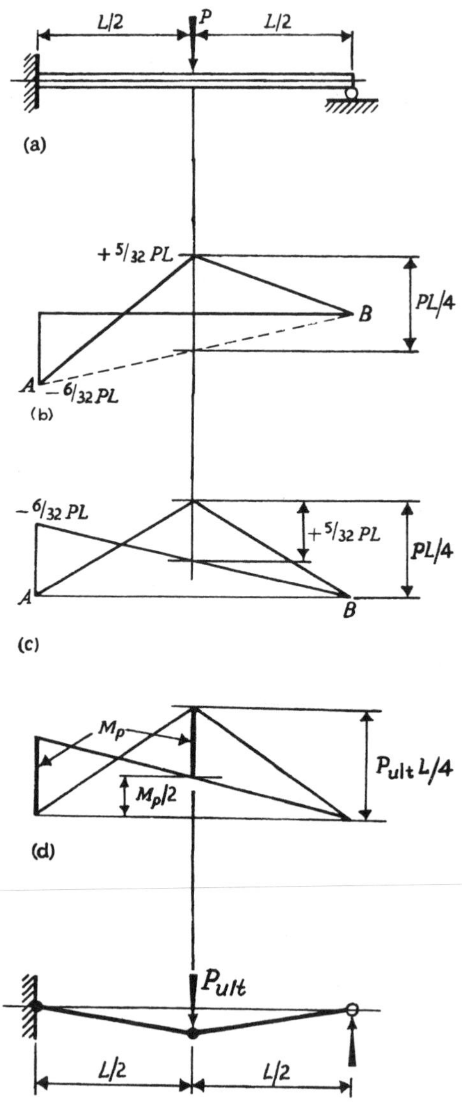

FIG. 1

Solution: The results of an elastic analysis are shown in Fig. 1(b) in the usual manner. The same results are replotted in Fig. 1(c) from a horizontal baseline AB. In both diagrams the values of the moment ordinates are the same, and the shaded portions of the diagrams represent the final results. Note that the auxiliary ordinate PL/4 has precisely the value of the maximum moment in a simple beam with a concentrated force in the middle.

By setting the maximum elastic moment equal to M_{yp}, one obtains the load P_{yp} at impending yield:

$$P_{yp} = (16/3)M_{yp}/L .$$

When the load is increased above P_{yp}, the moment at the built-in end can reach but cannot exceed M_p. This is also true of the moment at the middle of the span. These limiting conditions are shown in Fig. 1(d). The sequence in which M_p's occur is unimportant. In determining the limit load it is necessary to have only a kinematically admissible mechanism. With the two plastic hinges and a roller on the right this condition is assured, Fig. 1(e).

From Fig. 1(d) it can be seen that by proportions the end moment M_p gives an ordinate of $M_p/2$ at the middle of the span. Therefore, the simple beam ordinate $P_{ult}L/4$ in the middle of the span must be equated to $3M_p/2$ to obtain the limit load. This gives

$$P_{ult} = 6M_p/L .$$

Comparing this result with P_{yp}, one has

$$P_{ult} = \frac{9M_p}{8M_{yp}} P_{yp} = 9/8\ kP_{yp}$$

which shows that the increase in P_{ult} over P_{yp} is due to two causes: $M_p > M_{yp}$, and the maximum moments are distributed more advantageously in the plastic case. (Compare the moment diagram in Figs. 1(c) and (d).)

• PROBLEM 10-24

A fixed beam of ductile material supports a uniformly distributed load, Fig. 1(a). Determine the limit load P_{ult}.

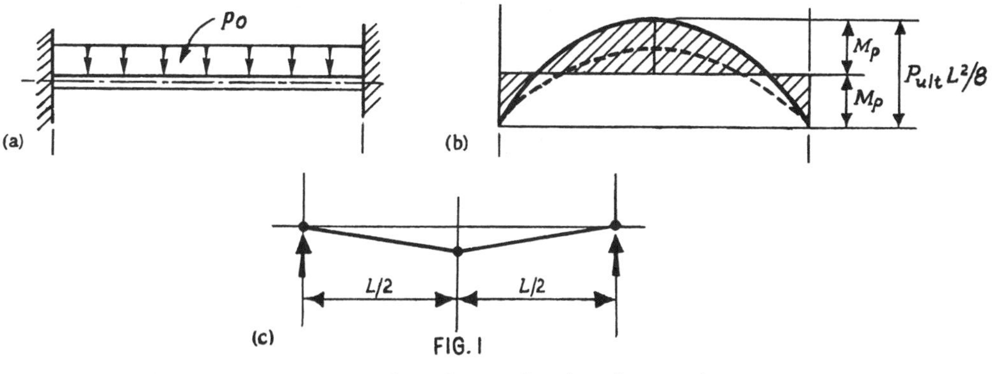

FIG. 1

Solution: According to the elastic analysis the maximum moments occur at the built-in ends and are equal to $P_0L^2/12$. Therefore

$$M_{yp} = P_{yp}L^2/12 \quad \text{or} \quad P_{yp} = 12M_{yp}/L^2 .$$

On increasing the load, plastic hinges develop at the supports. The collapse mechanism is not formed, however, until a plastic hinge also occurs in the middle of the span, Figs. 1(b) and (c).

The maximum moment for a simply supported, uniformly loaded beam is $P_0L^2/8$. Therefore, as can be seen from Fig. 1(b), to obtain the limit load in a clamped beam, this quantity must be equated to $2M_p$ with $P_0 = P_{ult}$. Hence,

$$P_{ult}L^2/8 = 2M_p \quad \text{or} \quad P_{ult} = 16M_p/L^2$$

Comparing this result with P_{yp}, one has

$$P_{ult} = \frac{4M_p}{3M_{yp}} P_{yp} = 4/3\ kP_{yp} .$$

The increase of P_{ult} over P_{yp} depends on the shape factor k and the equalization of the maximum moments.

• PROBLEM 10-25

The continuous beam of Fig. 1a is a steel 36 WF 160 section. Consider the steel to be elastoplastic with a yield point of 36 ksi, and determine the ultimate load, w, (which for span BC includes the weight of the beam) for the beam.

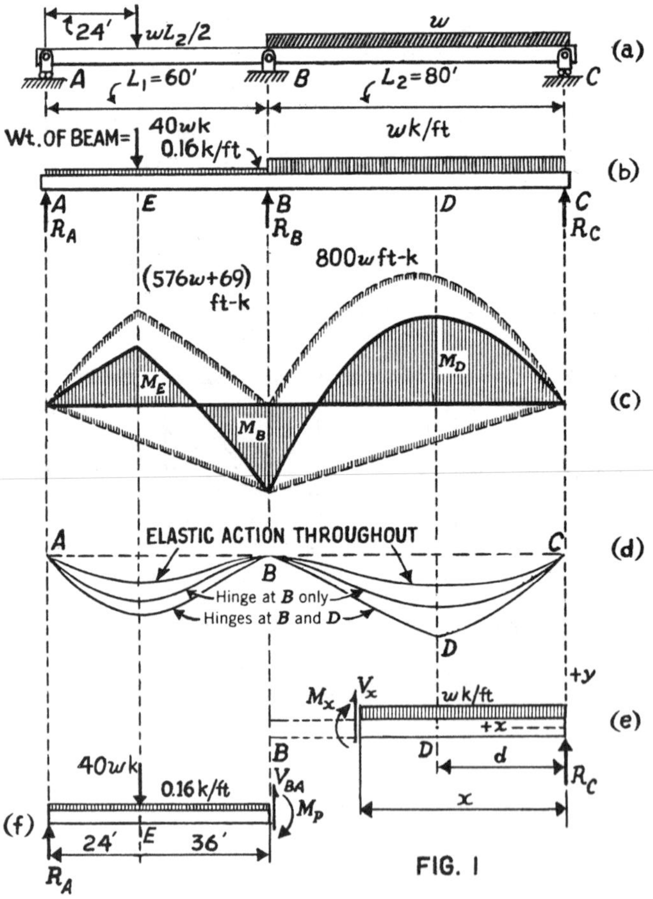

FIG. 1

Solution: The free-body diagram of Fig. 1b indicates three unknown reactions, and for this force system there are only two independent equations of equilibrium; hence, there is one redundant quantity. If one moment, shear, or reaction is determined, the beam becomes statically determinate. However, the ultimate load is not attained until a mechanism forms; therefore it becomes necessary to assume more than one possible hinge location. To assist in estimating the location of possible hinges, the shape of the moment diagram by parts and the composite moment diagram are shown in Fig. 1c, where the solid line indicates the composite diagram and the dashed lines represent the diagrams for two simple beams with a moment at B. This diagram indicates that hinges may possibly form at B, D, and E. Possible deformations are indicated (greatly exaggerated) in Fig. 1d, the top curve indicating the shape of the elastic curve when the action is entirely elastic. As the magnitude of the loading is increased beyond that necessary to produce the yield point stress in the outer fibers, a hinge will form at the section where the flexural stress is the highest. The first hinge is assumed to form at B, and under this condition the beam would assume the shape indicated by the middle curve of Fig. 1d. Since a mechanism has not yet formed, the loading is increased until a second hinge forms. This hinge is assumed to form at D, and from the lower curve of Fig. 1d it is apparent that a mechanism has developed since, with hinges at B and D and with end C supported on rollers, deflection can continue in the span BC without an increase in the load. The second hinge may have formed at E instead of at D; hence, the moment at E must be evaluated as a check on the hinge assumptions.

The magnitude of the load necessary to produce hinges at B and D will first be determined, after which the moment at E will be checked. It should be noted that, when the plastic moment, M_p, is used in either an equilibrium or a moment equation, it must have the correct sense or sign. With reference to the free-body diagram of Fig. 1e, which represents the right portion of span BC, the equation for the moment in span BC is

$$M_x = R_c x - wx^2/2 \quad . \tag{a}$$

When x is 80 ft, $M_B = -M_p = R_c(80) - w(80)^2/2$,

from which

$$R_c = 40w - M_p/80. \tag{b}$$

The negative sign on M_B is obtained from Fig. 1c. The section of maximum positive moment in span BC is at D where the shear is zero and is located from the shear equation

$$V_x = -R_c + wx.$$

When x is equal to d,

$$V_x = 0 = -R_c + wd,$$

from which

$$d = R_c/w. \tag{c}$$

From Eq. (a) the moment at D (the plastic moment) is

$$M_D = + M_p = R_c d - wd^2/2.$$

Since R_c is equal to wd from Eq. (c), the plastic moment becomes

$$M_p = wd^2 - \frac{wd^2}{2} = \frac{w}{2}\left(40 - \frac{M_p}{80w}\right)^2 \quad , \tag{d}$$

where the plus sign on M_D is obtained from Fig. 1c and R_c is obtained from Eq. (b). Solving Eq. (d) for w gives

$$w = \frac{5.8284M_p}{3200} \quad \text{or} \quad \frac{0.1716M_p}{3200} \quad .$$

When these expressions are substituted into Eq. (b), only the larger value yields a positive result for d; therefore this expression will give the correct magnitude for w unless the bending moment at E exceeds M_p.

The plastic moment for the specified section is equal to 616_{σ}, which amounts to 616(36)/12, or 1848 ft-kips, for this problem. Substituting this value for M_p in the expression for w yields

$$w = 5.828(616)(3)/3200 = 3.366 \text{ kips per ft.}$$

To check the bending moment at E, the reaction at A will first be obtained by summing moments with respect to B on the free-body diagram of Fig. 1f. The equation

$$60R_A - 40w(36) - 0.16(60)(30) + M_p = 0$$

gives

$$R_A = 24(3.366) + 4.80 - 616(3)/60 = 54.8 \text{ kips.}$$

The bending moment at E is

$$M_E = 54.8(24) - 0.16(24)(12) = 1269 \text{ ft-kips,}$$

which is less than 1848; therefore a hinge does not form at E, the moment in the beam is nowhere greater than M_p, and the ultimate load is

$$w = 3.37 \text{ kips per ft.}$$

CHAPTER 11

TORSION

CIRCULAR SHAFT

• PROBLEM 11-1

A circular rod is fixed at one end and simply supported at the other end in a bearing. After applying a torque T, determine the maximum shear stress and angle of twist at B. If the diameter of the shaft were halved, what would be the maximum torsional shear stress?

Solution: The maximum shear stress resulting from torsion at a section (away possibly from the ends) can be computed in the following way using the formula

$$J = \frac{\pi r^4}{2} \quad :$$

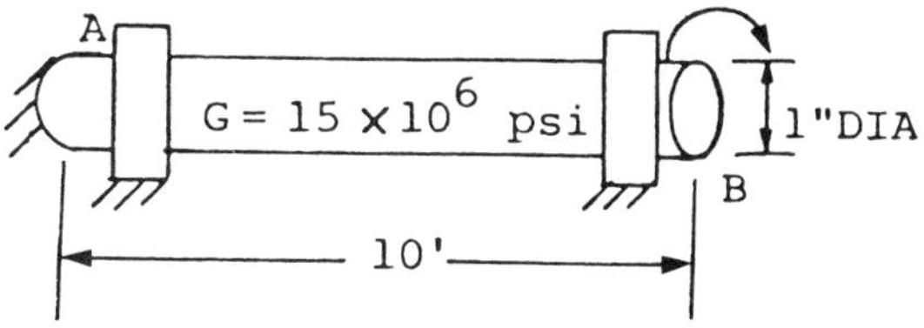

$$\tau_{max} = \frac{T\frac{D}{2}}{J}$$

$$= \frac{(200 \text{ in-lb})(\frac{1}{2}\text{ in})}{\frac{\pi}{2}(\frac{1}{2})^4 \text{ in}^4}$$

$$= 1019 \text{ psi} \qquad (1)$$

The angle of twist at B is given by

$$\phi = \frac{TL}{GJ}$$

$$= \frac{200 \times 10 \times 12}{15 \times 10^6 \times \frac{\pi}{2}(\frac{1}{2})^4}$$

$$= .01630 \text{ rad.} \qquad (2)$$

If the diameter of the shaft were halved, the maximum torsional shear stress would be

$$\tau_{max} = \frac{200\ (\frac{1}{4})}{\frac{\pi}{2}\ (\frac{1}{4})^2}$$

$$= 8150 \text{ psi.}$$

• PROBLEM 11-2

Two small lathes are driven by the same motor through a 1/2 inch diameter steel shaft, as shown in Fig. 1(a). Determine the maximum shear stress in the shaft due to twisting, and the angle of twist between the two ends of the shaft. (Take $G = 11.5 \times 10^6$ psi).

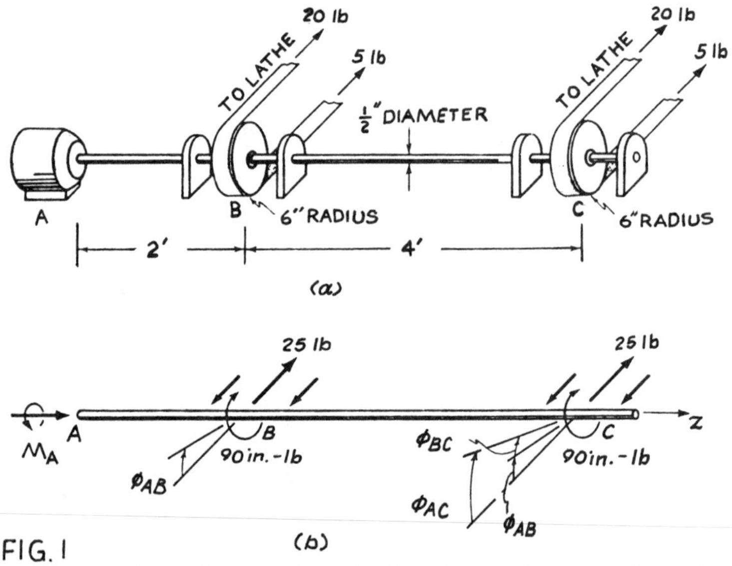

FIG. 1

Solution: We begin the analysis by idealizing the situation, as shown in Fig. 1(b). Here we represent each pulley loading by its static equivalent of a force of 25 lb through the axis of the shaft and a couple about the z axis of 6(20 - 5) = 90 in.-lb. Because each pulley is supported by a pair of immediately adjacent bearings, we make the idealization that the 25-lb transverse forces are balanced by the bearing reactions in such a way that there is negligible shear force and bending moment transmitted beyond the bearings. In this case it is only necessary for the motor to supply a torque M_A, as shown.

Establishing moment equilibrium, we have, since all moment vectors are parallel to z, $\Sigma M_A = 0$ if

$$M_A - 90 - 90 = 0$$

$$M_A = 180 \text{ in.-lb} \tag{a}$$

The twisting moments in sections AB and BC of the shaft are then clearly

$$M_{AB} = 180 \text{ in.-lb} \qquad M_{BC} = 90 \text{ in.-lb} \tag{b}$$

We next find the angle ϕ_{AC} which describes the rotation of the end C with respect to the end A. From the sketch in Fig. 1(b) we see that

$$\phi_{AC} = \phi_{AB} + \phi_{BC} \tag{c}$$

Using equation $\phi = \dfrac{M_t L}{GI_z}$,

$$\phi_{AB} = \frac{M_{AB}L_{AB}}{GI_z} \qquad \phi_{BC} = \frac{M_{BC}L_{BC}}{GI_z} \tag{d}$$

where $I_z = \dfrac{\pi d^4}{32}$.

Combining Eqs. (b), (c), and (d), and having proper regard for units, we find

$$\phi_{AC} = \frac{180 \times 2 \times 12}{11.5 \times 10^6 \times 6135.9 \times 10^{-6}} + \frac{90 \times 4 \times 12}{11.5 \times 10^6 \times 6135.9 \times 10^{-6}}$$

$$= 0.123 \text{ rad} = 7.0° \ .$$

The maximum shear stress occurs at the outside of the shaft in section AB. Using equation

τ_{max} $\dfrac{Mr}{I_z}$, we find

$$(\tau_{\phi z})_{max} = \frac{M_{AB}r_o}{I_z} = 7{,}300 \text{ psi}$$

• PROBLEM 11-3

A shaft 2 in in diameter is made of material whose stress-strain graph is given in Fig. 1(a). Find the stress distribution and maximum stress in the shaft when the twisting moment is 50 kip-in. Find also the angle of twist per unit length. (The stress at the surface exceeds 24 ksi.)

Solution: The problem is completely solved as soon as we know the stress corresponding to some radius. We could express the total torque in terms of the maximum stress. It is easier to express it in terms of the radius at which

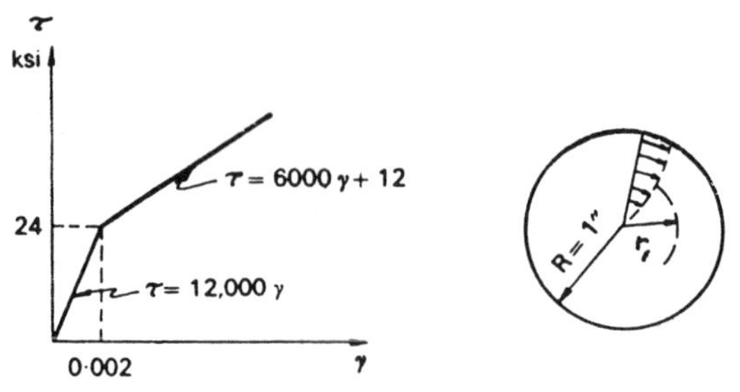

FIG. I (a) (b)

the stress 24 ksi occurs.

Suppose that $\tau = 24$ ksi at radius r_1 (Fig. 1(b)). The total torque is the sum of that part, T_1, resisted within r_1 and the part, T_2, resisted outside r_1.

For $r < r_1$

$$\tau = \frac{r}{r_1} \times 24 \text{ ksi}$$

$$T_1 = \int_0^{r_1} 2\pi r^2 \left(\frac{r}{r_1} \times 24\right) dr = 12\pi r_1^3$$

For $r > r_1$

$$\gamma = 0.002 \times \frac{r}{r_1}$$

and

$$\tau = 6000\gamma + 12 = 12\frac{r}{r_1} + 12$$

$$T_2 = \int_{r_1}^{R} 2\pi r^2 \left(12\frac{r}{r_1} + 12\right) dr$$

$$= \frac{6\pi R^4}{r_1} + 8\pi R^3 - 14\pi r^3$$

Since R = 1, the total torque is

$$T = 8\pi + \frac{6\pi}{r_1} - 2\pi r_1^3 \quad .$$

When T = 50, this equation becomes,

$$50 = 8\pi + \frac{6\pi}{r_1} - 2\pi r_1^3$$

from which

$$r_1^4 + 4r_1 - 3 = 0.$$

By trial and error method, one finds

$$r_1 = 0.7 \text{ in.}$$

At outer surface,

$$\tau = 12 \frac{R}{r_1} + 12$$

$$= \frac{12}{.7} + 12 = 29.1 \text{ ksi.}$$

We can find the deformation since we know that the strain $\gamma = 0.002$ occurs at a radius of 0.70 in.

Then

$$\frac{d\phi}{dx} = \frac{\gamma}{r} = \frac{0.002}{0.7}$$

$$= 0.0029 \text{ radian/in.}$$

• PROBLEM 11-4

The steel shaft of Fig. 1(a) is in equilibrium under the torques shown. Determine:

(a) The maximum shearing stress in the shaft.
(b) The angle of twist of end B of the 6-in. segment with respect to end A.
(c) The angle of twist of the end C with respect to end A.

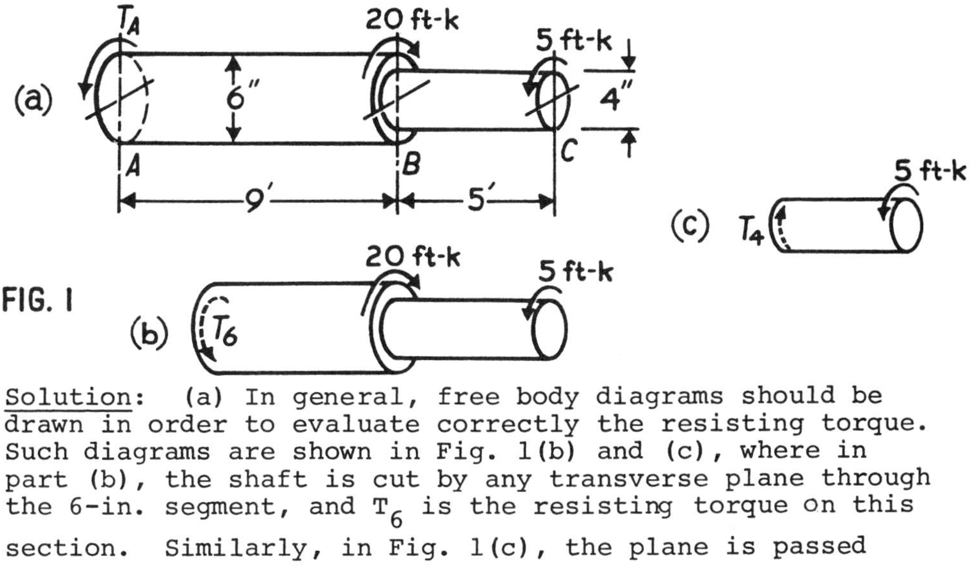

FIG. 1

Solution: (a) In general, free body diagrams should be drawn in order to evaluate correctly the resisting torque. Such diagrams are shown in Fig. 1(b) and (c), where in part (b), the shaft is cut by any transverse plane through the 6-in. segment, and T_6 is the resisting torque on this section. Similarly, in Fig. 1(c), the plane is passed through the 4-in. section, and T_4, is the resisting torque on this section. The location of the maximum shearing stress is not apparent; hence, the stress must be checked at both sections. Thus, from Fig. 1(b),

$$\Sigma M = 0,\ T_6 = 20 - 5 = 15 \text{ ft-kips} = 15{,}000(12) \text{ in-lb},$$

and $$\tau_{max} = \frac{Tc}{J} = \frac{15{,}000(12)(3)}{(\pi/2)(3^4)} = \frac{40{,}000}{3\pi}.$$

From Fig. 1(c), $\Sigma M = 0,\ T_4 = 5 \text{ ft-kips} = 5000(12) \text{ in-lb}$,

and $$\tau_{max} = \frac{5000(12)(2)}{(\pi/2)(2^4)} = \frac{15{,}000}{\pi}\ ;\ > \frac{40{,}000}{3\pi}\ ;$$

therefore, the maximum shearing stress is

$$15{,}000/\pi = 4770 \text{ psi}.$$

This stress is less than the shearing proportional limit of any steel; hence, the torsion formula applies. Note that had the larger torque been carried by the smaller section, the maximum stress would obviously occur in the small section and only one stress determination would have been required.

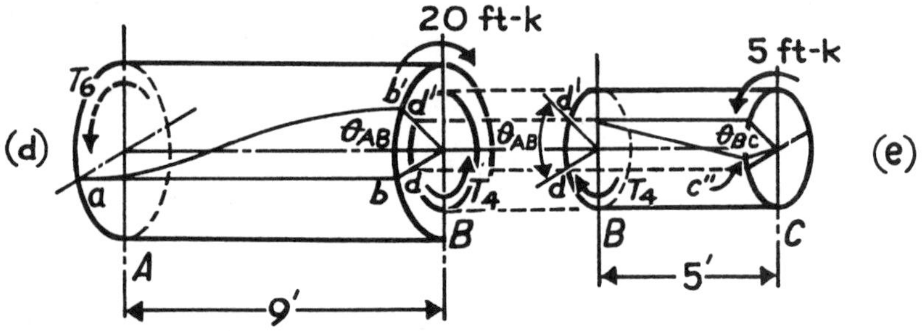

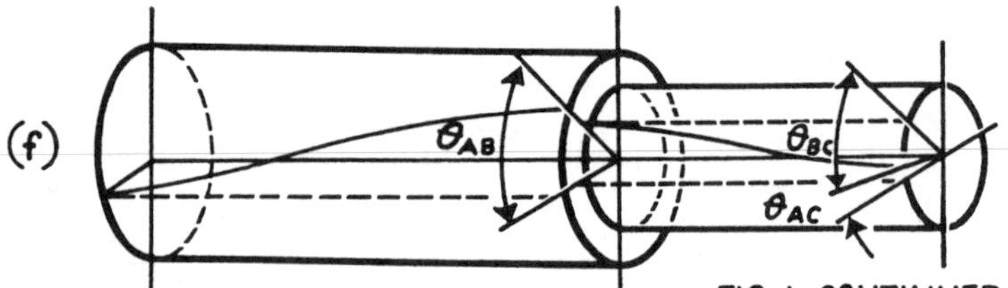

FIG. 1 CONTINUED

(b,c) As an aid to visualizing the distortion of the shaft, the segments AB and BC and the torques acting on them are drawn separately in Fig. 1(d) and (e) with the distortions greatly exaggerated. As the resultant torque of 15 ft-kips twists segment AB through the angle θ_{AB}, points b and d move to b' and d' respectively, and segment BC may be considered as a rigid body rotating through the same angle, point c moving to c', after which the torque of 5 ft-kips acting on BC twists this part of the shaft back through the angle θ_{BC}, point c' moving back to c". The resultant distortion for the entire shaft is shown in Fig. 1(f).

Now

$$\gamma = \frac{c\theta}{L} = \frac{\tau}{G} = \frac{Tc}{JG} .$$

When this expression is applied to Fig. 1(d), the twist in segment AB is obtained as,

$$\theta_{AB} = \frac{(20 - 5)(12)(9)(12)}{(\pi/2)(3^4)(12)(10^3)} = \frac{40}{\pi(10^3)} = 0.012,73 \text{ rad} .$$

From Fig. 1(e) and (f),

$$\theta_{AC} = \theta_{AB} - \theta_{BC} = \frac{40}{\pi(10^3)} - \frac{5(12)(5)(12)}{(\pi/2)(2^4)(12)(10^3)}$$

$$= \frac{40 - 37.5}{\pi(10^3)} = 0.000,796 \text{ rad.}$$

HOLLOW CIRCULAR SHAFT

• PROBLEM 11-5

A circular tube is fixed at one end and subjected to a torque at the other (free) end. Find the maximum and minimum torsional shear stresses at any cross-section, and the angle of deflection at the free end.

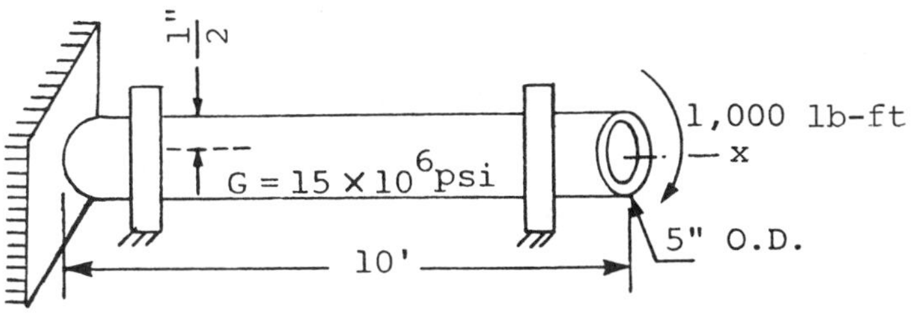

Solution: Because of the symmetry of this shaft about the x axis we can conclude that the deformation prescribed for the solid circular shaft holds for the hollow circular shaft. Therefore, we can use formulas for solid circular shafts provided that we insert the proper evaluation of J.

It is then clear that minimum torsional shear stress occurs at the inner radius of the shaft and is given as

$$\tau_{min} = \frac{M_x r_{min}}{J} \tag{a}$$

For hollow shaft of inner radius r_i and outer radius r_0

$$J = \frac{\pi}{2}(r_0^4 - r_i^4)$$

Substituting numerical data into equation (a),

$$\tau_{min} = \frac{1000(12)(2)}{\frac{\pi}{2}\,[(2\cdot 5)^4 - (2)^4]} \qquad (a)$$

$$= 662 \text{ psi}.$$

The maximum shear stress is

$$\tau_{max} = \frac{2.5}{2}(662) = 828 \text{ psi} \qquad (b)$$

Finally, the angle of twist for the right-end section becomes

$$\phi = \frac{M_x L}{GJ} = \frac{(1000)(12)(10)(12)}{(15 \times 10^6)(\frac{\pi}{2})(2.5^4 - 2^4)} = .00265 \text{ rad} \qquad (c)$$

• PROBLEM 11-6

A hollow circular shaft of outer diameter 4 in. and inner diameter 2 in. is loaded (as shown) in Fig. 1a.

(a) Determine the principal stresses and the maximum shearing stress at the point (or points) where the stress situation is most severe.

(b) On a sketch show the approximate directions of these stresses.

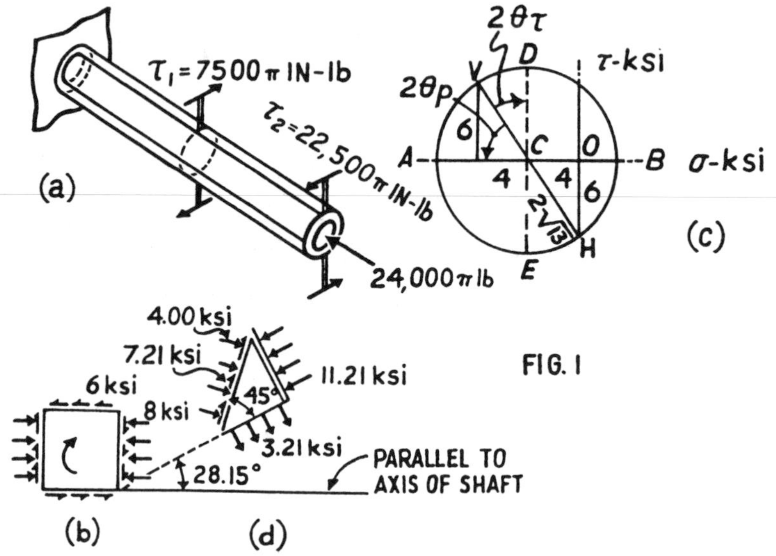

FIG. 1

Solution: The axial stress is constant throughout the shaft and is equal to

$$\sigma = \frac{P}{A} = \frac{24,000\pi}{\pi(2^2 - 1^2)} = 8000 \text{ psi C.}$$

The torsional load is highest to the right of the torque T_1 and the torsional stress is maximum on the outer surface of the shaft; therefore, the maximum torsional shearing stress is

$$\tau = \frac{Tc}{J} = \frac{22,500\pi(2)}{\pi(2^4 - 1^4)/2} = 6000 \text{ psi.}$$

These stresses are shown acting on mutually perpendicular planes through a point on the surface of the right portion of the shaft in Fig. 1b. Mohr's circle for the stresses at any point on the surface of the right portion of the shaft is shown in Fig. 1c.

(a) The principal stresses OA and OB from Mohr's circle are

$$\sigma_{p1} = OA = -4.00 - 2\sqrt{13} = -11.21 = 11.21 \text{ ksi C}$$

and

$$\sigma_{p2} = OB = -4.00 + 2\sqrt{13} = 3.21 \text{ ksi T.}$$

The maximum shearing stress CD or CE from Mohr's circle is

$$\tau_{max} = CD = 2\sqrt{13} = 7.21 \text{ ksi}$$

(b) From the Mohr's circle,

$$\tan 2\theta_p = 6/4 = 1.5,$$

which gives

$$2\theta_p = 56.30°\circlearrowright$$

and

$$\theta_p = 28.15°\circlearrowright.$$

The stresses are shown in their proper directions in Fig. 1d.

• PROBLEM 11-7

Consider a long tube of 1-in. outside diameter d_o and of 0.9-in. inside diameter d_i twisted about its longitudinal axis with a torque T of 400 in-lb. Determine the shearing stresses at the outside and the inside of the tube, Fig. 1.

FIG. 1

Solution: The maximum shearing stress occurs at the outside of the shaft and is given by

$$\tau_{max} = \frac{Tr_o}{J}$$

and

$$J = \frac{\pi(d_o{}^4 - d_i{}^4)}{32}$$

$$= \frac{\pi(1^4 - 0.9^4)}{32} = 0.0337 \text{ in}^4.$$

Thus,

$$\tau_{max} = \frac{(400)(\frac{1}{2})}{0.0337} = 5{,}930 \text{ psi.}$$

Now, $$\tau_{inside} = \frac{T\rho}{J} = \frac{400\ (\frac{0.9}{2})}{0.0337} = 5{,}340 \text{ psi.}$$

Since no material works at a low stress, it is important to note that a tube requires less material than a solid shaft to transmit a given torque at the same stress. By making the wall thickness small and the diameter large, nearly uniform shearing stress τ is obtained in the wall. This fact makes thin tubes suitable for experiments where a uniform "field" of pure shearing stress is wanted. To avoid local crimping or buckling, the wall thickness, however, cannot be excessively thin.

• PROBLEM 11-8

A steel rod ($G = 12 \times 10^3$ ksi) $1\frac{1}{2}$ in diameter and 50 in long fits inside a brass tube ($G = 6 \times 10^3$ ksi) of the same length. The tube has inside and outside diameters of $1\frac{1}{2}$ and 2 in respectively. The bar and the tube are fixed to rigid end plates so that they twist together. If the assembly is subjected to twisting couples of 4 kip-in at its ends, find the total angular twist and the maximum stress in each material.

Solution: The total torque is shared between the bars in proportion to their stiffnesses. For the steel rod:

$$I_p = \frac{\pi \times 1.5^4}{32} = 0.497 \text{ in}^4$$

Then the torsional stiffness coefficient for the steel rod is given by

$$k_s = \frac{G\ I_p}{L}$$

$$\therefore \quad k_s = \frac{12 \times 10^3 \times 0.497}{50} = 119.2 \text{ kip-in/radian}$$

For hollow section,

$$I_p = \frac{\pi}{32}\ (D_o^{\ 4} - D_i^{\ 4})$$

Hence, polar moment of inertia I_p for the brass tube is,

$$I_p = \frac{\pi(2^4 - 1.5^4)}{32} = 1.074 \text{ in}^4$$

$$\therefore \quad k_B = \frac{6 \times 10^3 \times 1.074}{50} = 128.7 \text{ kip-in/radian}$$

Thus the torque carried by the steel is

$$T_s = 4\left(\frac{119.2}{119.2 + 128.7}\right) = 1.92 \text{ kip-in}$$

Similarly, the torque carried by the brass is

$$T_B = 4\left(\frac{128.7}{119.2 + 128.7}\right) = 2.08 \text{ kip-in}$$

The two bars may now be analyzed separately.

Steel:

$$\tau_s = \frac{T_s r}{I_p}$$

$$T_s = \frac{1.92 \times 0.75}{0.497} = 2.90 \text{ ksi}$$

The angle of twist is

$$\phi = \frac{T_s}{k_s} = \frac{1.92}{119.2} = 0.016 \text{ radian}$$

Brass: $$T_B = \frac{2.08 \times 1.0}{1.074} = 1.93 \text{ ksi}$$

The angle of twist can be re-calculated as a check

$$\phi = \frac{T_B}{K_B} = \frac{2.08}{128.7} = 0.016 \text{ radian}$$

(a) What twisting moment (torque) could safely be transmitted by a solid shaft of 4 in diameter if the maximum shear stress is not to exceed 10,000 psi?

(b) If a hollow shaft, having the same sectional area, has an external diameter of 6 in. what twisting moment will it carry at the same maximum shear stress and what will be the stress at the inner surface?

Solution: (a) For the solid shaft

$$J = \frac{\pi}{32}4^4 = 8\pi \text{ in.}^4$$

The stress of 10,000 psi occurs at the outer surface where r = 2 in

Then,

$$\tau = \frac{Tr}{J}$$

$$10{,}000 = \frac{T \times 2}{8\pi}$$

and $$T = 125{,}700 \text{ lb-in}$$

(b) If the area of the second shaft is the same as that of the first,

$$\frac{\pi}{4}(6^2 - D_1^2) = \frac{\pi}{4} \cdot 4^2$$

or

$$D_1 = \sqrt{20} \text{ in}$$

Then

$$J = \frac{\pi}{32}(6^4 - \sqrt{20}^4) = 28\pi \text{ in}^4$$

Now

$$\tau = 10{,}000 \text{ when } r = 3$$

$$10{,}000 = \frac{T \times 3}{28\pi}$$

and

$$T = 293{,}000 \text{ lb-in}$$

If the stress at the inner surface is τ_1 ,

$$\frac{\tau}{10{,}000} = \frac{T\sqrt{5}/28\pi}{T \times 3/28\pi}$$

or $$\frac{\tau_1}{10,000} = \frac{\sqrt{5}}{3}$$

Hence $\tau_1 = 7450$ psi

• PROBLEM 11-10

> Compare the torsional strength and stiffness of two shafts, one of which is hollow and the other is solid. Both have the same applied load and the same cross-section area, and they are fixed at one end.

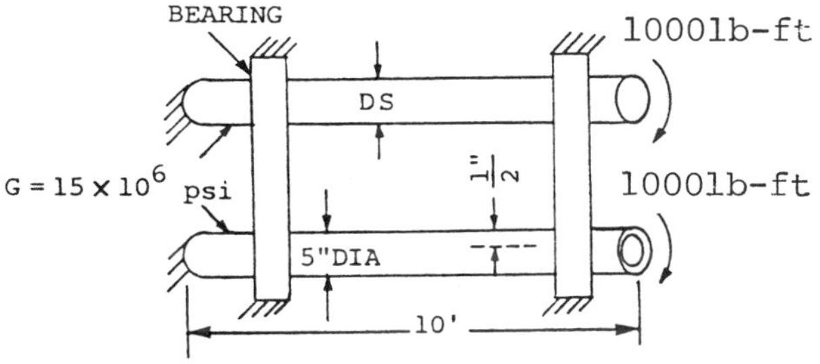

Solution: Since the area of the solid shaft is the same as the hollow shaft, we have

$$\frac{\pi}{4} D_s^2 = \frac{\pi}{4} (D_o^2 - D_i^2)$$

or $$D_s^2 = (5^2 - 4^2)$$

Hence, $D_s = 3$ in.

Next compute the torsional strength for each shaft.

Now, Torsional strength $= \dfrac{T}{\tau}$

Using equation $\tau = \dfrac{Tr}{J}$, we have

$$\frac{T}{\tau_{solid}} = \frac{J}{r} = \frac{\pi d_s^4/32}{d_s/2} = \frac{\pi d_s^3}{16} \tag{1}$$

$$= \frac{\pi(3)^3}{16} = 5.3 \text{ in}^3$$

and

$$\frac{T}{\tau_{hollow}} = \frac{J}{r} = \frac{(\pi/32)(d_o^4 - d_i^4)}{d_o/2}$$

$$= \frac{\pi(d_o^4 - d_i^2)}{16d_o}$$

$$= \frac{\pi(5^4 - 4^4)}{(16 \times 5)} = 14.49 \text{ in}^3 .$$

Hence, the ratio of the torsional strengths between the two cross sections is $\frac{14 \cdot 49}{5 \cdot 3} = 2.73$ in favor of the hollow shaft, showing that the material has been used more efficiently here.

Next we examine the torsional stiffness of the two shafts:

$$\left(\frac{T}{\phi}\right)_{solid} = \frac{GJ_{solid}}{L} = \frac{G}{L}\left(\frac{\pi}{32}(3)^4\right)$$

and

$$\left(\frac{T}{\phi}\right)_{hollow} = \frac{GJ_{hollow}}{L} = \frac{G}{L}\left[\frac{\pi}{32}(5^4 - 4^4)\right]$$

The ratio of the two values for any length of material is then

$$\frac{\left(\frac{T}{\phi}\right)_{hollow}}{\left(\frac{T}{\phi}\right)_{solid}} = \frac{(5^4 - 4^4)}{(3)^4} = 4.56$$

showing an even greater gain in the stiffness for the hollow shaft over the solid shaft than the already significant gain in torsional strength.

TAPERED SHAFT

• PROBLEM 11-11

A tapered bar AB of length L and having a solid, circular cross section (Fig. 1) is twisted by a torque T. Find the angle of twist ϕ of the bar.

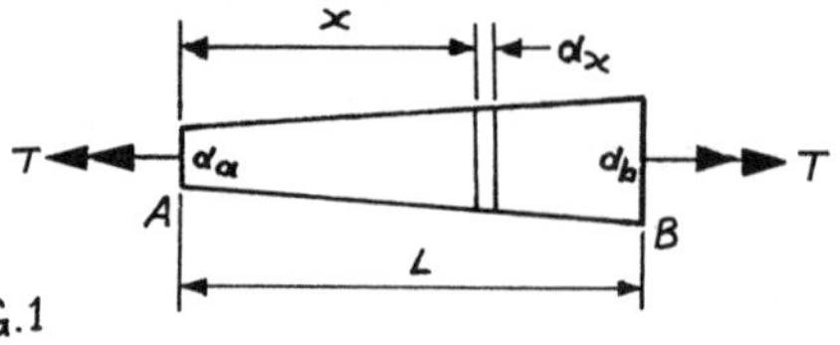

FIG.1

Solution: If the angle of taper of the bar is small, we can find the angle ϕ with good accuracy by applying Eq. $\phi = \frac{TL}{GJ}$ to an element of length dx (Fig. 1). For this element the angle of twist is

$$d\phi = \frac{Tdx}{GJ_x}$$

where J_x represents the polar moment of inertia of the cross section at distance x from the left-hand end. Denoting the diameters at ends A and B by d_a and d_b, respectively, we see that the expression for J_x is

$$J_x = \frac{\pi}{32}\left(d_a + \frac{d_b - d_a}{L}x\right)^4 \qquad (1)$$

The total angle of twist ϕ is

$$\phi = \int_0^L d\phi = \int_0^L \frac{Tdx}{GJ_x} \qquad (2)$$

Substituting Eq. (1) into Eq. (2) and integrating, we find

$$\phi = \frac{32TL}{3\pi G}\left(\frac{1}{d_b - d_a}\right)\left(\frac{1}{d_a^3} - \frac{1}{d_b^3}\right)$$

This example illustrates how the Eq. $\phi = \frac{TL}{GJ}$ can be adapted for use in finding the angle of rotation ϕ when J is a function of x. The same procedure can also be used when T varies along the axis of the bar.

• PROBLEM 11-12

A shaft tapers from 1 in diameter at end B to $\frac{3}{4}$ in diameter at end A. It is 6 in long and is made of steel ($G = 12 \times 10^6$ psi). Find (a) the maximum torque the shaft will transmit if the stress is not to exceed 6000 psi, (b) the angle of twist in the shaft at this torque and (c) the torsional stiffness of the shaft.

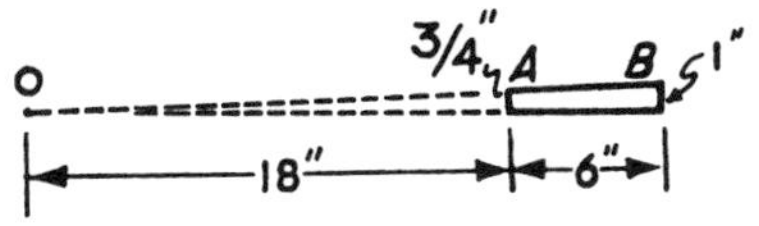

FIG. 1

Solution: (a) The maximum torque is governed by the size of the shaft at the smaller end, A. At A

$$I_p = \frac{\pi \times (\frac{3}{4})^4}{32}$$

$$T = \frac{I_p \times \tau}{r} = \frac{\pi \times (\frac{3}{4})^4}{32}\,\frac{6000}{\frac{3}{8}} = 496 \text{ lb-in}$$

(b) If x is measured from the origin of the taper (Fig. 1), then at any section,

$$d = x/24 \text{ inches}$$

$$I_p = \frac{\pi d^4}{32} = \frac{\pi x^4}{32 \times 24^4}$$

$$\phi = \int_{18}^{24} \frac{T dx}{G I_p} = \frac{T}{G} \frac{32 \times 24^4}{\pi} \int_{18}^{24} \frac{dx}{x^4}$$

$$= \frac{496}{12 \times 10^6} \frac{32 \times 24^4}{\pi} \frac{1}{3} \left(\frac{1}{18^3} - \frac{1}{24^3} \right)$$

$$= 4.625 \times 10^{-3} \text{ radian}$$

$$= 0.265°$$

(c) The stiffness is the torque per unit angular deformation.

$$k = \frac{T}{\phi}$$

$$= \frac{496}{0.265}$$

$$= 1870 \text{ lb-in/degree}$$

DESIGN OF CIRCULAR SHAFTS

• PROBLEM 11-13

Select a solid shaft for a 10-hp motor operating at 1,800 rpm. The maximum shearing stress is limited to 8,000 psi.

Solution: If torque T is in in.-lb, the horsepower transmitted is

$$hp = \frac{2\pi T \eta}{12(33{,}000)} = \frac{T\eta}{63{,}000} \qquad (1)$$

where η = rpm.

From equation (1):

$$T = \frac{63{,}000 \text{ (hp)}}{\eta} = \frac{63{,}000 \text{ (10)}}{1{,}800} = 350 \text{ in-lb.}$$

Now

$$\tau_{max} = \frac{Tr}{J} = \frac{T(d/2)}{J} \quad (2)$$

For solid shaft $J = \frac{\pi d^4}{32}$.

Then equation (2) becomes,

$$\tau_{max} = \frac{T(d/2)}{\pi d^4/32}$$

or

$$d^3 = \frac{16\ T}{\pi\ \tau_{max}}$$

$$= \frac{16 \times 350}{\pi \times 8{,}000} = .2228\ in^3$$

Hence,

$$d = 0.606\ in.$$

For practical purposes a 5/8-in. shaft would probably be selected.

• PROBLEM 11-14

Select solid shafts to transmit 200 hp each without exceeding a shearing stress of 10,000 psi. One of these shafts operates at 20 rpm and the other at 20,000 rpm.

Solution: Subscript 1 applies to the low-speed shaft; 2 to the high-speed shaft.

The expression for hp is

$$hp = \frac{TN}{63{,}000}$$

Hence,

$$T_1 = \frac{(hp)(63{,}000)}{N_1}$$

$$= \frac{200(63{,}000)}{20} = 630{,}000\ in\text{-}lb.$$

Similarly

$$T_2 = \frac{200(63{,}000)}{20{,}000} = 630\ in\text{-}lb.$$

Now,

$$\tau_{max} = \frac{T_1(d_{1/2})}{\pi d_1^4/32}$$

$$= \frac{16T_1}{\pi d_1^3}$$

or $$d_1^3 = \frac{16\ T_1}{\pi\ \tau_{max}} = \frac{16(630,000)}{\pi(10,000)} = 322\ in^3$$

or $$d_1 = 6.85\ in$$

Similarly

$$d_2^3 = \frac{16\ T_2}{\pi\ \tau_{max}} = \frac{16(630)}{\pi(10,000)} \approx .32\ in^3$$

or $$d_2 = 0.685\ in.$$

This example illustrates the reason for the modern tendency to use high-speed machines in mechanical equipment. The difference in size of the two shafts is striking. Further saving in the weight of the material may be effected by making use of hollow tubes.

• PROBLEM 11-15

A Diesel engine for a small commercial boat is to operate at 200 rpm and deliver 800 hp through a gear box with a ratio of 1 to 4 (increase) to the propeller shaft. Both the shaft from engine to gear box, and the propeller shaft are to be solid and made of heat treated alloy steel. Determine the minimum permissible diameters for the two shafts if the allowable stress is 20 ksi and the angle of twist in a 10-ft length of the propeller shaft is not to exceed 4°. Neglect power loss in the gear box and assume (incorrectly because of thrust stresses) that the propeller shaft is subjected to pure torsion.

Solution: The first step is the determination of the torques to which the shafts are to be subjected. By means of the expression, Power = $T\omega$, the torques are obtained as follows:

$$800(33,000) = T_1(200)(2\pi),$$

from which $$T_1 = 66,000/\pi\ \text{ft-lb},$$

which is the torque at the crank shaft of the engine. As the propeller shaft speed is four times that of the crank shaft and power loss in the gear box is to be neglected, the torque on the propeller shaft is one-fourth that on the crank shaft and is equal to $66,000/(4\pi)$ ft-lb. Using the torsion formula, the shaft sizes necessary to satisfy the stress specification are determined. For the main shaft,

$$\frac{J}{r} = \frac{T}{\tau} \tag{1}$$

For solid shaft, $J = \frac{\pi}{2} r^4$

Then equation (1) becomes,

$$\frac{\frac{\pi}{2} r_1^{\,4}}{r_1} = \frac{T_1}{\tau}$$

$$= \frac{66,000(12)/\pi}{(20)(10^3)}$$

or

$$r_1^{\,3} = \frac{66,000(12)(2)}{\pi^2(20)(10^3)}$$

$$= 8.024 \text{ in}^3$$

or

$$r_1 = 2.002 \text{ in}$$

Hence the shaft from engine to gear box should be 4.0 in. in diameter.

The torque on the propeller shaft is one-fourth that on the main shaft, and this is the only change in the expression for $r_1^{\,3}$; therefore,

$$r_2^{\,3} = 8.02/4, \text{ and } r_2 = 1.261 \text{ in.}$$

The size of propeller shaft necessary to satisfy the distortion specification will be determined as follows:

$$\phi = \frac{TL}{GJ} \text{ rad}$$

or

$$4(\pi/180) = \frac{(66,000(12)/4\pi)\ 10(12)}{12(10^6)\ (\pi r_3^{\,4}/2)}$$

from which

$$r_3^{\,4} = \frac{66,000(12)\ 10(12)}{(4\pi)\ 4(\pi/180)\ 12(10^6)(\pi/2)}$$

$$= 5.7422$$

or

$$r_3 = 1.548 > 1.261$$

Therefore, the propeller shaft must be 3.1 inches in diameter.

• PROBLEM 11-16

A first shaft transmits 11,000 hp at a speed of 1800 rpm to a speed reducer having a second output shaft rotating at 107 rpm, and a 90% efficiency in converting the power. Design the two shafts as both solid shafts and hollow shafts. For the hollow shafts assume that I.D.= ½ O.D. The safe yield stress in shear is not to exceed 50,000 psi.

Solution: The power transmitted by a torque T is given as

$$\text{Power} = T\omega \qquad \text{(a)}$$

where ω is the angular velocity in radians per unit time. Hence, the torque T_1 in the first shaft is given by

$$[11{,}000 \text{ hp}]\left(33{,}000\frac{\text{ft-lb/min}}{\text{hp}}\right) = T_1\left(1800\frac{\text{rev}}{\text{min}}\right)\left(\frac{2\pi \text{ rad}}{\text{rev.}}\right) \qquad \text{(b)}$$

$$\therefore\ T_1 = 32{,}100 \text{ ft-lb} \qquad \text{(c)}$$

For the second shaft, the power transmission is decreased to 90% of the original power. Torque T_2 in this shaft is then given by

$$[.90][11{,}000][33{,}000] = T_2(107)(2\pi)$$

$$\therefore\ T_2 = 486{,}000 \text{ ft-lb} \qquad \text{(d)}$$

Applying the relationship for torsional stress and the yield stress of 50,00 psi, for shaft 1,

$$50{,}000 = \left\{\frac{T_1\left(\frac{D_1}{2}\right)}{\frac{\pi(D_1/2)^4}{2}}\right\}$$

or

$$50{,}000 = \frac{T_1 \times 16}{\pi D_1^3}$$

Hence,

$$D_1^3 = \frac{32{,}100(12)16}{\pi(50{,}000)}$$

$$= 39.23615$$

or

$$D_1 = 3.4 \text{ in.}$$

For shaft 2,

$$50{,}000 = \left\{\frac{T_2 \frac{D_2}{2}}{\frac{\pi(D_2/2)^4}{2}}\right\}$$

$$50{,}000 = \frac{T_2 \times 16}{\pi D_2^3}$$

or

$$D_2^3 = \frac{486{,}000(12)(16)}{\pi(50{,}000)}$$

$$= 594.04264$$

Hence

$$D_2 = 8.41 \text{ in.}$$

For the hollow shafts,

$$50{,}000 = \frac{T_1 \frac{D_1}{2}}{\frac{\pi}{2}\left[\left(\frac{D_1}{2}\right)^4 - \left(\frac{1}{2}\frac{D_1}{2}\right)^4\right]}$$

from which

$$D_1 = 3.47 \text{ in.}$$

and

$$50{,}000 = \frac{T_2\left(\frac{D_2}{2}\right)}{\frac{\pi}{2}\left[\left(\frac{D_2}{2}\right)^4 - \left(\frac{1}{2}\frac{D_2}{2}\right)^4\right]}$$

from which

$$D_2 = 8.59 \text{ in.}$$

STATICALLY INDETERMINATE ARRANGEMENTS

• PROBLEM 11-17

A circular bar is constructed of a hollow tube B and solid core A firmly bonded together to act as a solid bar (Fig. 1). The inner material has shear modulus of elasticity G_a, and the outer material has shear modulus G_b. Derive formulas for the maximum shear stresses τ_a and τ_b in the inner and outer materials, respectively, when the composite bar is subjected to a torque T.

FIG. 1

Solution: The angle of twist per unit length θ must be the same for both the tube and the core. Thus,

$$\theta = \frac{\tau_a}{G_a r_a} = \frac{\tau_b}{G_b r_b} \qquad (1)$$

in which τ_a is the shear stress in the inner material at radius r_a, and τ_b is the shear stress in the outer material at radius r_b. Also, the total torque T consists of the torque T_a in the core plus the torque T_b in the tube:

$$T = T_a + T_b = G_a \theta J_a + G_b \theta J_b \qquad (2)$$

The polar moments of inertia J_a and J_b are

$$J_a = \frac{\pi r_a^4}{2} \qquad J_b = \frac{\pi}{2}(r_b^4 - r_a^4)$$

Solving for θ from Eq. (2) yields

$$\theta = \frac{T}{G_a J_a + G_b J_b}$$

which, when combined with Eq. (1) gives

$$\tau_a = T\frac{G_a r_a}{G_a J_a + G_b J_b}, \quad \tau_b = T\frac{G_b r_b}{G_a J_a + G_b J_b}$$

The torques carried by the two parts of the bar are

$$T_a = T \frac{G_aJ_a}{G_aJ_a + G_bJ_b} \quad T_b = T \frac{G_bJ_b}{G_aJ_a + G_bJ_b}$$

Note that this example involves the analysis of a statistically indeterminate system.

• PROBLEM 11-18

A solid, circular shaft AB of two different diameters is fixed at the ends and subjected to a torque T_o as shown in Fig. 1a. Determine the reactive torques T_a and T_b at the ends, and the angle of rotation ϕ_o at the section where T_o is applied.

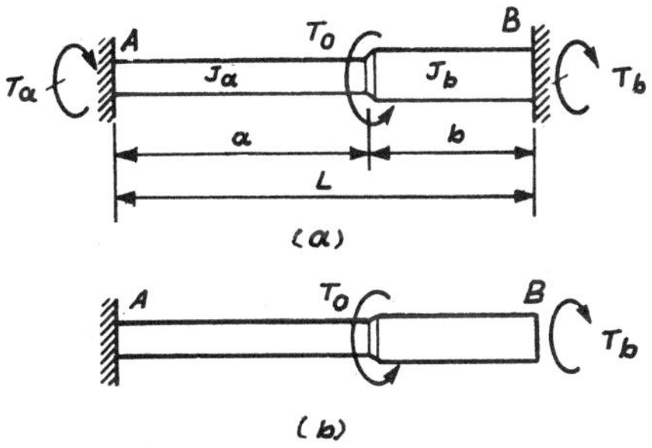

FIG. 1

Solution: The bar is statically indeterminate because there are two unknown torques, T_a and T_b, and only one equation of static equilibrium:

$$T_a + T_b = T_o \qquad \text{(b)}$$

If we select the reactive torque R_b as the redundant and then imagine that end B of the bar is cut free from the support (Fig. 1b), we observe that the total angle of rotation ϕ_b of end B is the sum of the angles of rotation due to T_o and T_b. Thus, we have

$$\phi_b = \frac{T_o a}{GJ_a} - \frac{T_b a}{GJ_a} - \frac{T_b b}{GJ_b}$$

or

$$\phi_b = \frac{a}{GJ_a}\left[T_o - T_b(1 + \frac{bJ_a}{aJ_b})\right]$$

Because the angle of rotation at end B must be equal to zero, the equation of compatibility becomes $\phi_b = 0$. Hence, we obtain the following result for the torque T_b:

$$T_b = \frac{T_o}{1 + \frac{bJ_a}{aJ_b}} \qquad (c)$$

Substituting this result into Eq. (b) gives an analogous expression for the torque T_a:

$$T_a = T_o - \frac{T_o}{1 + \frac{bJ_a}{aJ_b}}$$

$$= T_o \left(1 - \frac{1}{1 + \frac{bJ_a}{aJ_b}} \right)$$

$$= \frac{T_o \frac{bJ_a}{aJ_b}}{1 + \frac{bJ_a}{aJ_b}} = \frac{bJ_a}{aJ_b} T_b \qquad (d)$$

The angle of rotation ϕ_o at the cross section where T_o is applied can be found from either the left- or right-hand portions of the bar, as follows:

$$\phi_o = \frac{T_a a}{GJ_a} = \frac{T_b b}{GJ_b} = \frac{T_o ab}{G(bJ_a + aJ_b)} \qquad (e)$$

• PROBLEM 11-19

A couple of 600 in.-lb is applied to a 1-in.-diameter 2024-0 aluminum-alloy shaft, as shown in Fig. 1a. The ends A and C of the shaft are built in and prevented from rotating. Determine the angle through which the center cross section 0 of the shaft rotates.

Solution: We idealize the situation in Fig. 1b. The shaft is statically indeterminate since we cannot determine M_A and M_C from equilibrium considerations alone. In Fig. 1c we show isolated free bodies of three sections of the shaft.

Satisfying moment equilibrium for the complete shaft shown in Fig. 1b (or for the middle segment in Fig. 1c) yields

$$M_A + M_C - 600 = 0 \qquad (a)$$

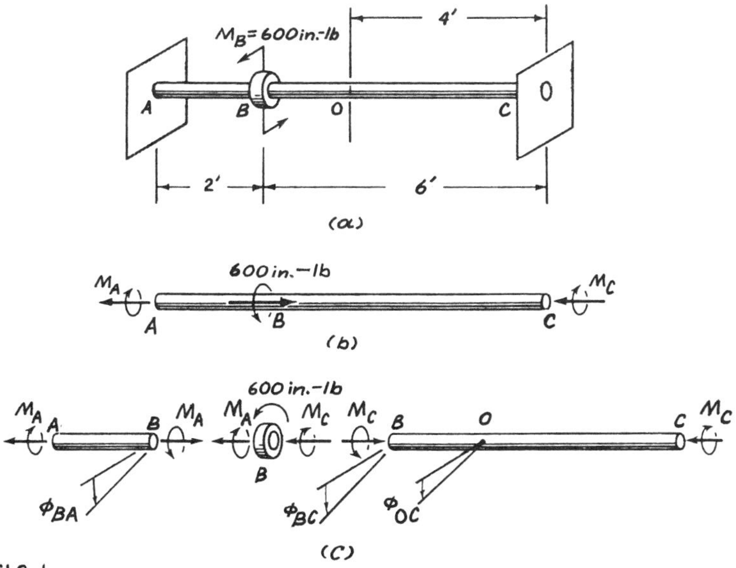

FIG. 1

Continuity of the shaft at the point B requires that

$$\phi_{BC} = \phi_{BA} \tag{b}$$

From the equation $\phi = \frac{ML}{GI_2}$, we have

$$\phi_{BA} = \frac{M_A L_{AB}}{GI_z} \qquad \phi_{BC} = \frac{M_C L_{BC}}{GI_z}$$

$$\phi_{OC} = \frac{M_C L_{OC}}{GI_z} \tag{c}$$

Combining Eqs. (a), (b), and (c), we find

$$M_A = \frac{L_{BC}}{L_{AB}} (600 - M_A)$$

$$= \frac{6 \times 12}{2 \times 12} (600 - M_A)$$

$$= 450 \text{ in.-lb.}$$

and

$$M_C = \frac{L_{AB}}{L_{BC}} M_A$$

$$= \frac{2 \times 12}{6 \times 12} (450)$$

$$= 150 \text{ in.-lb.}$$

Then

$$\phi_{OC} = \frac{M_C L_{OC}}{GI_z}$$

where from table of elastic constants, $G = 37 \times 10^5$ psi.

$$\phi_{OC} = \frac{150 \times 4(12)}{37 \times 10^5 \; [\frac{\pi}{2}(.5)^4]}$$

$$= .02 \text{ rad} = 1.1°$$

• PROBLEM 11-20

A torque is applied to a circular rod fixed at both ends as shown. Calculate the resisting torques generated at the ends.

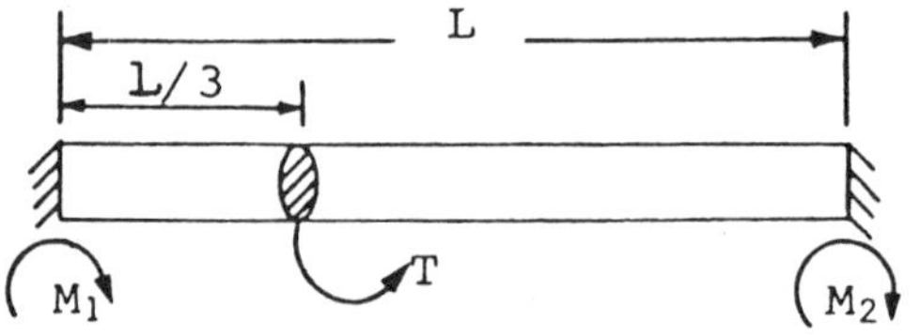

Fig. 1.

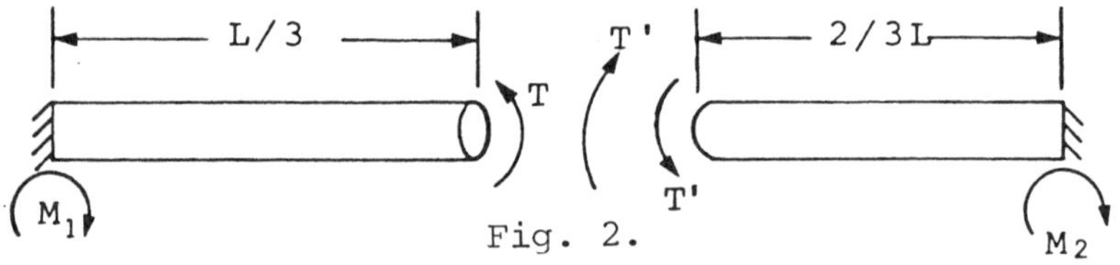

Fig. 2.

Solution: Since only one independent equation is available, and there are 2 unknowns M_1 and M_2, the problem is statically indeterminate.

Since the resisting torques must equal the applied torque,

$$T = M_1 + M_2$$

To study the member, divide the rod into two parts for the free body in Fig. 2. T^1 is transmitted through the severed section. The angle of twist for each severed section is

$$\phi = \frac{TL}{GJ}$$

from which

$$\phi = \frac{(T - T^1)}{GJ}\left(\frac{L}{3}\right)$$

for the left section and

$$\phi_2 = \frac{T^1}{GJ}\left(\frac{2L}{3}\right)$$

for the right section. Since $\phi_1 = \phi_2$,

$$\frac{T - T^1}{GJ}\left(\frac{L}{3}\right) = \frac{T^1}{GJ}\left(\frac{2L}{3}\right)$$

solving for T^1

$$T^1 = \frac{T}{3} .$$

Returning to the left section

$$M_1 = T - T^1,$$

and since $T^1 = \dfrac{T}{3}$,

$$M_1 = \frac{2}{3} T$$

For the right section

$$M_2 = T^1 = \frac{T}{3}$$

• PROBLEM 11-21

The circular shaft AC in Fig. 1a is fixed to rigid walls at A and C. The section AB is solid annealed bronze and the hollow section BC is made of aluminum alloy 2024-T4. There is no stress in the shaft before the 20,000-ft-lb torque, T, is applied. Determine the maximum shearing stress in each shaft after T is applied.

Solution: Figure 1b is a free-body diagram of the shaft. The torques T_A and T_C produced by the supports, are unknown, and the summation of moments about the axis of the shaft gives

$$T_A + T_C = 20,000(12). \qquad \text{(a)}$$

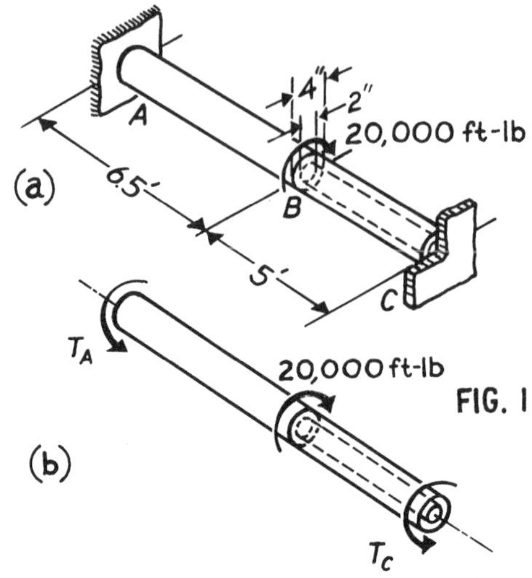

FIG. 1

This is the only independent equation of equilibrium; thus, the problem is statically indeterminate. A second equation can be obtained from the deformation of the shaft, since each section must undergo the same angle of twist; thus,

$$\theta_{AB} = \theta_{BC} . \tag{b}$$

Equations (a) and (b) can both be expressed in terms of the shearing stresses in the two sections. When the torsion formula is applied to Eq. (a) it becomes

$$\frac{\tau_{AB}\pi(2^4)/2}{2} + \frac{\tau_{BC}\pi(2^4 - 1^4)/2}{2} = 240{,}000.$$

or

$$4\pi\tau_{AB} + 3.75\pi\ \tau_{BC} = 240{,}000. \tag{c}$$

Since the angle of twist is

$$\theta = \frac{\gamma L}{r} = \frac{\tau L}{Gr} ;$$

Eq. (b) becomes

$$\frac{\tau_{AB}(6.5)12}{6.5(10^6)2} = \frac{\tau_{BC}(5)12}{4(10^6)2}$$

from which

$$\tau_{AB} = 5\tau_{BC}/4 . \tag{d}$$

Equations (c) and (d) can be solved simultaneously to give

$$\tau_{AB} = 10{,}900 \text{ psi} ,$$

$$\tau_{BC} = 8{,}730 \text{ psi} .$$

Segment CD of Fig. 1a is a solid shaft of cold-rolled bronze, and segment EF is a hollow shaft of aluminum alloy 2024-T4 with a core of low-carbon steel. The ends C and F are to be considered fixed to rigid walls and the steel core of EF is connected to the flange at E so that the aluminum and steel act together as a unit. The two flanges D and E are bolted together and the bolt clearance permits flange D to rotate through 0.03 rad before EF will carry any of the load. Determine the maximum shearing stress in any shaft material when the torque of 20 ft-kips is applied.

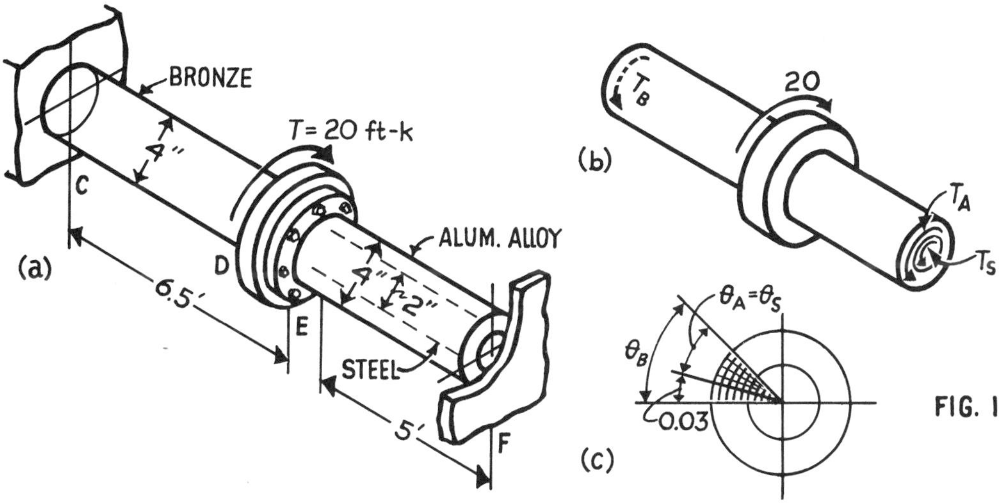

FIG. 1

Solution: Figure 1b is a free-body diagram of the assembly. It is necessary to place two unknown torques T_A and T_S on on the right end because the torques and stresses will need to be related by the torsion formula which is limited to cross sections of homogeneous material. Summing moments with respect to the axis of the shaft gives the following equation:

$$20(12) = T_B + T_A + T_S \,. \qquad \text{(e)}$$

This is the only independent equilibrium equation for this problem and there are three unknown torques; hence, two distortion equations need to be written. A three-dimensional distortion diagram is not easy to draw and the cross-sectional drawing of Fig. 1c is adequate. The angles indicated represent the twist in segment CD at D and in segment EF at E (the coupling is considered rigid). The fact that segment EF is non-homogeneous does not invalidate the assumption of the plane section remaining plane and the diameter remaining straight; the strains are still proportional to the distance from the shaft axis. However, the stresses are not proportional to the radii throughout the entire cross section because G is not single valued.

From Fig. 1c, the distortion equations are

$$\theta_B = \theta_A + 0.03 \qquad \text{(f)}$$

and $$\theta_A = \theta_S \ . \qquad \text{(g)}$$

The three equations (e), (f), and (g) can be written in terms of the same three unknowns (torque, angle, or stress) and solved simultaneously. Since the maximum stress is required, Eq. (f) and (g) will be written in terms of the maximum stress in each material; thus,

$$\theta = \frac{\gamma L}{c} = \frac{\tau L}{Gc} \ ;$$

(f) $$\frac{\tau_B(6.5)(12)}{6.5(10^3)(2)} = \frac{\tau_A(5)(12)}{4(10^3)(2)} + 0.03 \ ,$$

from which $$\tau_B = (5/4)\tau_A + 5 \ ,$$

(therefore $\tau_B > \tau_A$) (h)

and (g) $$\frac{\tau_A(5)(12)}{4(10^3)(2)} = \frac{\tau_S(5)(12)}{11.6(10^3)(1)}$$

from which $$\tau_S = 1.45\tau_A = 1.45(4\tau_B/5 - 4) \ . \qquad \text{(i)}$$

Writing Eq. (e) in terms of maximum stress in each material and using the torsion formula, gives

$$20(12) = \frac{\tau_B(\pi/2)(2^4)}{2} + \frac{\tau_A(\pi/2)(2^4 - 1^4)}{2} + \frac{\tau_S(\pi/2)(1^4)}{1}$$

or

$$960/\pi = 16\tau_B + 15\tau_A + 2\tau_S \qquad \text{(j)}$$

Solving Eq. (h), (i), and (j) simultaneously gives the results

$$\tau_B = 12.44 \text{ ksi} \ ,$$

$$\tau_A = 5.95 \text{ ksi} \ ,$$

and $$\tau_S = 8.63 \text{ ksi} \ .$$

The maximum shearing stress is at the surface of the bronze and is

$$12.44 \text{ ksi} \ .$$

• PROBLEM 11-23

Compare the stresses in a uniform thin-walled circular shaft as predicted by the approximate theory for thin-walled hollow sections and as predicted by the exact theory for the torsion of circular shafts.

Solution: Figure 1 shows the cross section of the shaft. According to the exact theory, the shear stress τ varies linearly with the radius and has its maximum value at the outer radius. Using equations

$$\tau = \frac{Mr_o}{J}$$

and

$$J = \frac{\pi}{2}(r_o^2 - \gamma_i^4)$$

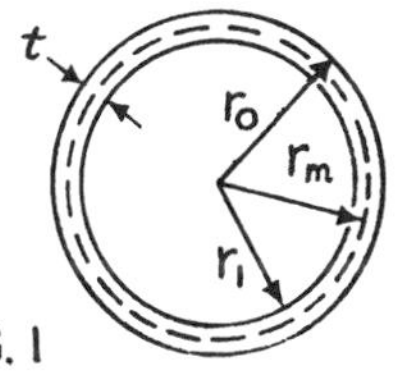

FIG. 1

we have,

$$(\tau)_{max} = \frac{Mr_o}{\frac{\pi}{2}(r_o^4 - r_i^4)}$$

$$= \frac{Mr_o}{\frac{\pi}{2}(r_o^2 + r_i^2)(r_o + r_i)(r_o - r_i)} \qquad (a)$$

$$t = r_o - r_1$$

$$t_m = \frac{r + r}{2}$$

$$A = \pi r_m^2 = \frac{\pi}{4}(r_o + r_i)^2$$

According to the approximate theory of thin-walled hollow sections, the shear stress τ_{sz} is uniformly distributed across the wall thickness. Then,

$$\tau_{sz} = \frac{M_t}{2At}$$

$$= \frac{M_t}{\frac{\pi}{2}(r_o + r_i)^2(r_o - r_i)} \qquad (b)$$

The percentage difference between (a) and (b) would be

computed from the ratio

$$\frac{\tau_{sz} - (\tau_{\theta z})_{max}}{(\tau_{\theta z})_{max}} = \frac{-r_i}{r_o}\frac{r_o - r_i}{r_o + r_i} \qquad (c)$$

If $r_i/r_o = 0.9$, there is only 4.7 percent difference between (a) and (b). As the thickness increases the percent difference increases. For example, the percent difference increases to 11 for $r_i/r_o = 0.75$.

• PROBLEM 11-24

A hollow tube has the cross-section shown in Fig. 1. Find the maximum torque which this tube will withstand if the shear stress is not to exceed 12,000 psi.

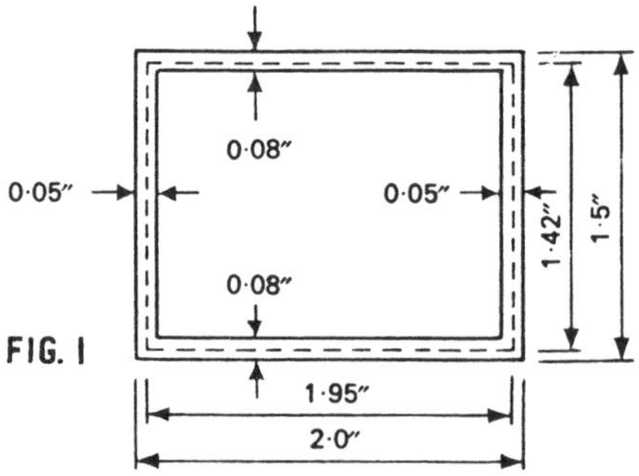

FIG. 1

Solution: The maximum shear stress will occur in the thinner wall. Hence the maximum permissible shear flow is

$$q = \tau t = 12{,}000 \times 0.05 = 600 \text{ lb/in}$$

The area enclosed by the median line of the wall is

$$A_o = 1.42 \times 1.95 = 2.77 \text{ in}^2$$

Then

$$T = 2A_oq$$

$$= 2 \times 2.77 \times 600$$

$$= 3324 \text{ lb-in}$$

• PROBLEM 11-25

A circular and a square tube (Fig. 1) are constructed of the same material. Both tubes have the same length, thickness, and cross-sectional area and both are subjected to the same torque. What are the ratios of the shear stresses and angles of twist for the tubes? (Neglect the effect of stress concentrations at the corners of the square tube.)

Solution: For the circular tube, the Area A_{m1} enclosed by

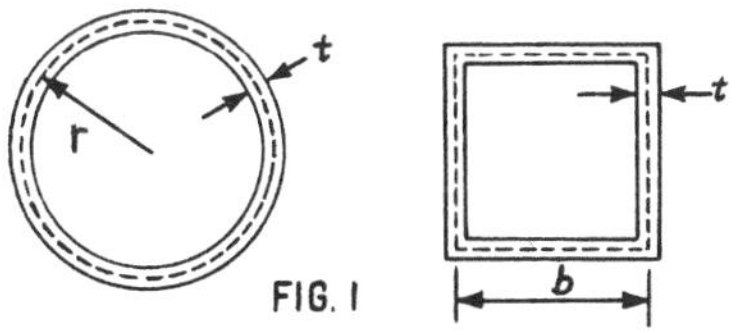

FIG. I

the middle line of the cross section is $A_{m1} = \pi r^2$, where r is the radius to the middle line. Also, the cross-sectional area of the circular tube is $A_1 = 2\pi rt$.

For the square tube the cross-sectional area is $A_2 = 4bt$, where b is the length of one side, measured along the middle line. Inasmuch as the areas of both tubes are the same, we obtain $b = \pi r/2$. Also, the area enclosed by the middle line of the cross-section is $A_{m2} = b^2$.

The ratio τ_1/τ_2 of the shear stress in the circular tube to the shear stress in the square tube is

$$\frac{\tau_1}{\tau_2} = \frac{T/2A_{m1}t}{T/2A_{m2}t} = \frac{A_{m2}}{A_{m1}} = \frac{b^2}{\pi r^2} = \frac{(\pi r/2)^2}{\pi r^2}$$

$$= \frac{\pi}{4} = 0.785$$

The ratio of the angles of twist is

$$\frac{\phi_1}{\phi_2} = \frac{\tau_1 A_{m2}}{\tau_2 A_{m1}} = \left(\frac{\pi}{4}\right)^2 = 0.617$$

These results show that the circular tube not only has a lower shear stress than does the square tube, but it also has greater stiffness against rotation.

INELASTIC BEHAVIOR

• PROBLEM 11-26

A shaft of structural steel 4 in. in diameter is subjected to a pure torque of 7π ft-kips. Assume the steel is elastoplastic and that the yield point in shear is one-half the yield point in tension. Determine the maximum shearing stress in the shaft and the magnitude of the angle of twist in a 10-ft length.

Solution: Assume elastic action first; then

$$\tau = \frac{Tc}{J} = \frac{7\pi(12)(2)}{(\pi/2)(2^4)} = 21 \text{ ksi} > \frac{36}{2} .$$

Therefore, plastic action takes place, and the maximum

stress is 18 ksi, unless strain hardening occurs. To check this, first determine how much of the cross section is behaving elastically by going back to the fundamental concept of resisting torque being the integral of the resisting torques of differential annular areas; thus

$$T = \int^{\text{Area}} \tau (2\pi\rho \, d\rho)(\rho) \; .$$

For the part undergoing elastic action (of radius r),

$$\tau = \frac{T_r}{r} (\rho) = \frac{18}{r} (\rho) \; ,$$

and, for the rest, τ is constant at 18 ksi. Then, the resisting torque is given by

$$T = \int_0^r \frac{18}{r} (\rho)(2\pi\rho d\rho)(\rho) + \int_r^2 (18)(2\pi\rho d\rho)(\rho)$$

or

$$T = \frac{18}{r} (2\pi) \int_0^r \rho^3 d\rho + 18(2\pi) \int_r^2 \rho^2 d\rho \; ,$$

Upon integration one obtains,

$$T = 7\pi(12) = 2\pi \frac{18}{r} \frac{r^4}{4} + 2\pi(18) \frac{1}{3} (2^3 - r^3) \; ,$$

or

$$84 = 9r^3 + 96 - 12r^3$$

from which $r^3 = 4$, and $r = 1.587$ which is the radius of the area undergoing elastic action.

From Hooke's law,

$$\gamma_r = \frac{\tau}{G} = \frac{18}{12,000} = 0.0015 \; ,$$

and, with Eq. (4-2),

$$\gamma_c = \frac{c\theta}{L} \text{ or } \gamma_r = \frac{r\theta}{L}$$

from which

$$\gamma_c = \gamma_r \frac{c}{r} = 0.0015 \frac{2}{1.587} = 0.001,890 \; .$$

This small value of strain indicates that strain hardening does not occur, for the plastic strain at the yield point for structural steel may be on the order of fifteen times the elastic strain before strain hardening occurs; therefore,

$$\tau_{max} = 18 \text{ ksi} .$$

The angle of twist may be obtained as follows:

$$\gamma = \frac{\tau}{G} = \frac{r\theta}{L} = \frac{18}{12(10^3)} = \frac{1.587(\phi)}{10(12)} ,$$

from which $\theta = 0.1134$ rad.

• PROBLEM 11-27

A solid steel shaft of 1-in. diameter is so severely twisted that only a 1/3-in.-diameter elastic core remains on the inside, Fig.1(a). If the material properties can be idealized as shown in Fig. 1(b), what residual stresses and residual rotation will remain upon release of the applied torque?

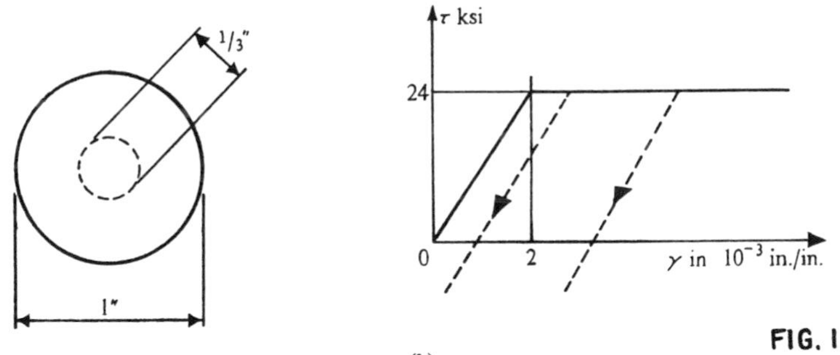

(a) (b)

FIG. 1

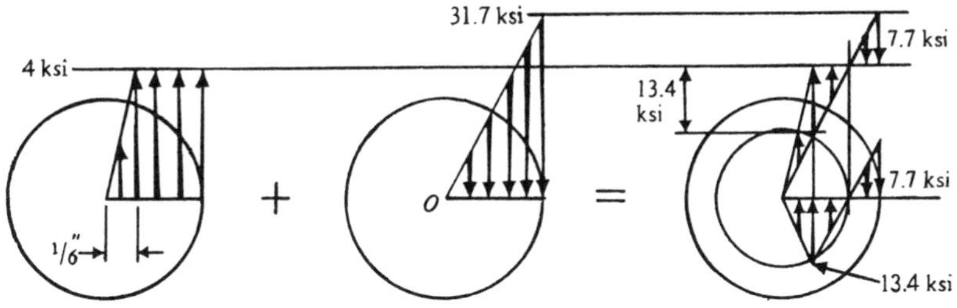

(c) Plastic-plastic stress distribution (d) Elastic rebound stresses (e) Residual stresses

Solution: To begin, the magnitude of the initially applied torque and the corresponding angle of twist must be determined. The stress distribution corresponding to the given condition is shown in Fig. 1(c). The stresses vary linearly from 0 to 24 ksi when $0 \le \rho \le 1/6$ in.; the stress is a constant 24 ksi for $\rho > 1/6$ in. The release of the torque T causes elastic stresses, and the difference between the two stress distributions, corresponding to no external torque, gives the residual stresses.

The applied torque T can be determined by using equation

$$T = \int_{area} \tau(2\pi\rho d\rho)\rho$$

Then,

$$T = \int_{o}^{1/6} \tau(2\pi\rho d\rho)\rho + \int_{1/6}^{1/2} \tau(2\pi\rho d\rho)\rho$$

$$= \int_{o}^{1/6} \left(\frac{\tau}{r}\rho\right) 2\pi\rho^2 d\rho + \int_{1/6}^{1/2} (24)\ 2\pi\rho^2 d\rho$$

$$= \frac{24}{1/6}(2\pi) \int_{o}^{1/6} \rho^3 d\rho + 24(2\pi) \int_{1/6}^{1/2} \rho^2\ d\rho$$

$$= \frac{48\pi}{1/6} \left(\frac{\rho^4}{4}\right)_{o}^{1/6} + 48\pi \left(\frac{\rho^3}{3}\right)_{1/6}^{1/2}$$

$$= 0.17 + 6.05$$

$$= 6.22 \text{ kip-in.}$$

Now,

$$\tau_{max} = \frac{Tc}{J} = \frac{6.22 \times 0.5}{\pi/32} = 31.7 \text{ ksi}$$

At $\rho = 0.5$ in., $\tau_{residual} = 31.7 - 24.0 = 7.7$ ksi. Two diagrams of the residual stresses are shown in Fig. 1(e). For clarity the initial results are replotted from the horizontal line. In the entire shaded portion of the diagram, the residual torque is clockwise; an exactly equal residual torque acts in the opposite direction in the inner portion of the shaft.

The initial rotation is best determined by calculating the twist of the elastic core. At $\rho = 1/6$ in., $\gamma = 2 \times 10^3$. The elastic rebound of the shaft is given by

$$\frac{d\phi}{dx} = \frac{T}{JG}$$

The difference between the inelastic and the elastic twists gives the residual rotation per inch of shaft. If the initial torque is re-applied in the same direction, the shaft responds elastically.

Inelastic: $\frac{d\phi}{dx} = \frac{\gamma_a}{\rho a} = \frac{2 \times 10^{-3}}{1/6} = 12 \times 10^{-3}$ per inch

Elastic: $\frac{d\phi}{dx} = \frac{T}{JG} = \frac{6.22}{(\pi/32)12 \times 10^3} = 5.28 \times 10^{-3}$ per inch

Residual: $\frac{d\phi}{dx}$ $(12 - 5.28)10^{-3} = 6.72 \times 10^{-3}$ radian per inch

• **PROBLEM 11-28**

A shaft of radius 1 in. transmits a torque of 180,000 in.-lb. What is the rate of twist? What is the maximum residual stress on unloading? Finally, what is the residual rate of twist on unloading? Take $G = 15 \times 10^6$ psi and Y_s as 100,000 psi.

Solution: First find out whether we have completely elastic or elastic, plastic behavior or whether a torque has been applied to this shaft in excess of what it can withstand. For this reason we first compute $T_{max\ El}$ and T_{hinge}.

$$T_{max\ El} = \frac{1}{2}\pi R^3 Y_s = 157{,}000 \text{ in.-lb} \qquad (a)$$

$$T_{hinge} = 2\pi Y_s \left(\frac{R^3}{3}\right) = 210{,}000 \text{ in.-lb} \qquad (b)$$

Clearly, both an elastic core and a plastic ring are present. The radius of the core a is,

$$a = \left[(4)(1)^3 - \frac{6}{\pi}\ \frac{180{,}000}{100{,}000}\right]^{1/3} = .825 \text{ in.} \qquad (c)$$

The rate of twist is then

$$\frac{d\phi}{dx} = \frac{Y_s}{Ga} = \frac{100{,}000}{(15 \times 10^6)(.825)} = .00808 \text{ rad/in.} \qquad (d)$$

To get the residual stress distribution we note first that the following is the stress distribution with the given torque applied:

$0 \le r \le .825$:

$$\tau = \left(\frac{r}{.825}\right)(100{,}000) = 121{,}200r \text{ psi} \qquad (e)$$

$.825 \le r \le 1$:

$$\tau = 100{,}000 \text{ psi} \qquad (f)$$

From this we subtract the stress:

$$\tau = \frac{Tr}{J} = \frac{180{,}000}{\frac{1}{2}(\pi)(1^4)}\, r = 115{,}000r \text{ psi} \qquad (g)$$

Hence, the residual stress is given as follows:

$0 \le r \le .825$:

$$\tau_{res} = 121{,}200r - 115{,}000r = 6{,}200r \text{ psi} \quad \text{(h)}$$

$.825 \leq r \leq 1$:

$$\tau_{res} = 100{,}000 - 115{,}000r \text{ psi} \quad \text{(i)}$$

The peak stresses occur at r = .825, and at r = 1. Thus, using Eqs. (h) and (i),

$$(\tau_{res})_A = (6200)(.825) = 5115 \text{ psi} \quad \text{(j)}$$

$$(\tau_{res})_B = 100{,}000 - 115{,}000 = -15{,}000 \text{ psi} \quad \text{(k)}$$

Clearly, we have 15,000 psi as the maximum residual shear stress.

Finally, we compute the final rate of twist on unloading as follows:

$$\left(\frac{d\phi}{dx}\right)_{res} = .00808 - \frac{T}{JG}$$

$$= .00808 - \frac{180{,}000}{\frac{1}{2}\pi(1)^4(15 \times 10^6)}$$

$$= .00808 - .00764 = .000440 \text{ rad/in.} \quad \text{(l)}$$

• PROBLEM 11-29

Determine the torque carried by a solid circular shaft of mild steel when shearing stresses above the proportional limit are reached essentially everywhere. For mild steel, the shearing stress-strain diagram can be idealized to that shown in Fig. 1(a). The shearing yield-point stress τ_{yp} is to be taken as being the same as the proportional limit in shear τ_{pl}.

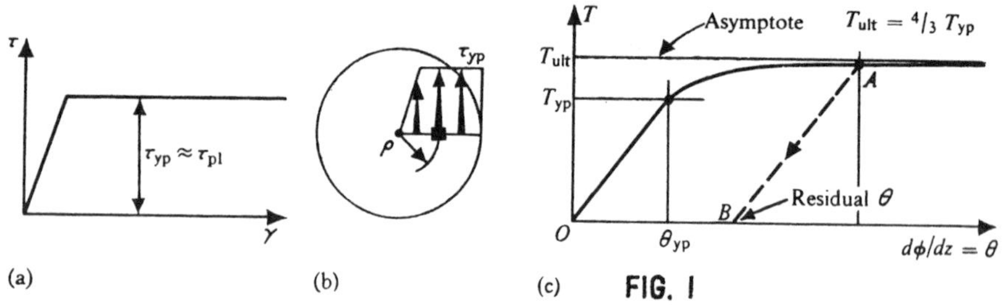

FIG. 1

Solution: If a large torque is imposed on a member, large strains take place everywhere except near the center. Corresponding to the large strains for the idealized material considered, the yield-point shearing stress will be reached everywhere except near the center. However, the resistance to the applied torque offered by the material located near the center of the shaft is negligible as the corresponding ρ's are small, Fig. 1(b). Hence, with a sufficient degree of accuracy it can be assumed that a constant shearing stress τ_{yp} is acting everywhere on the section considered. The torque corresponding to this condition may be considered the ultimate or limit torque. (Figure 1(c) gives a firmer basis for this statement.) Thus

$$T_{ult} = \int_A \tau_{yp} dA \rho = \int_0^c 2\pi\rho^2 \tau_{yp} d\rho$$

$$= \frac{2\pi c^3}{3} \tau_{yp} = \frac{4}{3} \frac{\tau_{yp}}{c} \frac{\pi c^4}{2} = \frac{4}{3} \frac{\tau_{yp} J}{c}$$

Note that the maximum elastic torque capacity of a solid shaft is $T_{yp} = \tau_{yp} J/c$. Therefore since T_{ult} is 4/3 times this value, only 33 1/3 per cent of the torque capacity remains after τ_{yp} is reached at the extreme fibers of a shaft. A plot of torque T vs. θ, the angle of twist per unit distance, as full plasticity develops is in Fig. 1(c). Point A corresponds to the results found in the preceding example; line AB is the elastic rebound; and point B is the residual θ for the same problem.

It should be noted that in machine members, because of the fatigue properties of materials, the ultimate static capacity of the shafts as evaluated above is often of minor importance.

CHAPTER 12

DYNAMIC LOADING & REPEATED LOADING

FREE VIBRATION

• PROBLEM 12-1

A cantilever is 6 ft long. It has a rectangular section 6 in wide and 1 in deep, and its elastic modulus, E, is 4×10^6 psi. A body weighing 10 lb is dropped from a height of 2 in onto the beam at a point 5 ft from the support (Fig. 1). It is assumed that it remains attached to the beam as the latter vibrates.

Find the maximum stress induced in the beam, and the amplitude and frequency of the vibration which is set up. Neglect the weight of the beam.

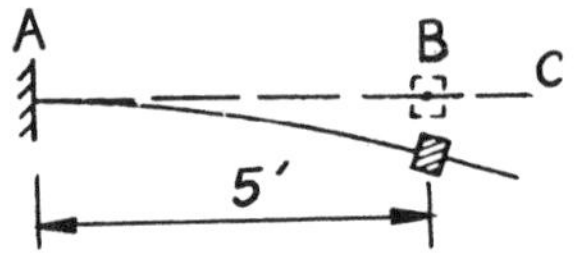

FIG. 1

Solution: To find the flexural stiffness of the beam we need to know the moment of inertia of the cross-section. The moment of inertia of a rectangular section about its own centroid is given by

$$I = \frac{1}{12} \times b \times d^3$$

where

b = width of section

d = depth of section

I = moment of inertia.

i.e. $$I = \frac{6 \times 1^3}{12} = 1/2 \text{ in}^4$$

The cantilever is effectively 5 ft long since the

portion beyond the load does not enter the problem. The bending stiffness of a cantilever in regard to a vertical end force is

$$k = \frac{3EI}{L^3}$$

This is the force required at B (Fig. 1) to produce a deflection of 1 in at B.

$$\therefore \quad k = \frac{3 \times 4 \times 10^6 \times 0.5}{60^3} = 27.8 \text{ lb/in}$$

Let v_{max} = the maximum deflection of the beam at B during the oscillations. Then, equating the energy lost by the falling weight to the strain energy stored in the beam, we obtain

$$10(2 + v_{max}) = \frac{1}{2} kv_{max}^2$$

$$= \frac{1}{2} \times 27.8v_{max}^2$$

whence

$$v_{max} = 0.36 \pm 1.25$$

$$\therefore \quad v_{max} = 1.61 \text{ in}$$

The maximum beam stress clearly occurs at the support, and one way to find this stress is to find the equivalent static load which would produce a deflection of 1.61 in. This is

$$W_{st} = kv = 27.8 \times 1.61 = 44.8 \text{ lb}$$

With a load of 44.8 lb at B, the bending moment at A will be

$$M = 44.8 \times 60 \text{ lb-in}$$

and

$$\sigma = \frac{My}{I} = \frac{44.8 \times 60 \times 0.5}{0.5} = 2690 \text{ psi}$$

It is noted that the stress is 4.48 times the stress which would be produced by a static load of 10 lb.

The amplitude is $v_{max} - v_{st}$. The calculation of the static deflection is simple but unnecessary, since in the solution of the quadratic equation for v_{max} (i.e., $v_{max} = 0.36 \pm 1.25$) the first term represents the static deflection, and the second is the amplitude of vibration. From this we see that the amplitude is 1.25 in.

To find the frequency we first calculate the period, P.

$$P = \frac{kg}{W} = \frac{27.8 \times 386}{10} = 32.7 \text{ radians/sec}$$

Then the frequency, n, is given by

$$n = \frac{P}{2\pi} = 5.2 \text{ cycles/sec}$$

In problems of this kind it is often easier to find the flexibility than the stiffness. For instance, we might apply a unit force at 5 ft from the support of the cantilever, and calculate the deflection at this point as $L^3/3EI$. This is the value of the relevant flexibility coefficient, j, and by inversion we then have $k = 3EI/L^3$.

• PROBLEM 12-2

A steel bar ($E = 30 \times 10^6$ psi) is 100 in long and has a cross-sectional area, A, of 2 in^2. A body weighing 5000 lb is fixed to the lower end (Fig. 1). At the upper end of the bar is a stop which is designed to support the assembly on a platform. When the stop is 0.02 in above the platform the assembly is allowed to fall. It is assumed that when the stop reaches the platform it is restrained from lifting, so that the bar is thereafter capable of being put into compression.

(a) Find the maximum stress induced in the bar.

(b) Find also the amplitude, frequency and period of the oscillations which are set up. Assume that there is no damping, and neglect the mass of the bar.

Solution: (a) The maximum stress in the bar occurs when the deformation is a maximum, i.e., at the lowest point of the travel. The stiffness of the spring k, is given by

$$k = \frac{EA}{L} = \frac{30 \times 10^6 \times 2}{100} = 6 \times 10^5 \text{ lb/in}$$

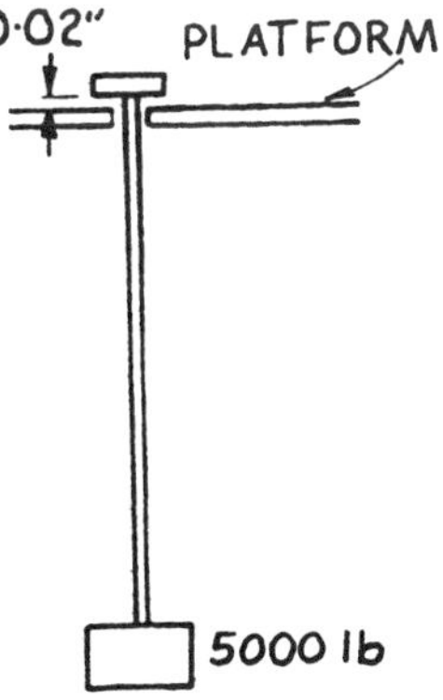

FIG. 1

FIG. 2

The maximum extension is given by

$$u_{max} = \frac{W}{k} + \sqrt{\left(\frac{W}{k}\right)^2 + 2h\frac{W}{k}}$$

$$u_{st} = \frac{W}{k} = \frac{5000}{6 \times 10^5} = \frac{1}{120} \text{ in}$$

$$\therefore u_{max} = \frac{1}{120} + \sqrt{\left(\frac{1}{120}\right)^2 + \left(2 \times 0.02 \times \frac{1}{120}\right)}$$

$$= 0.0083 + 0.0201$$

$$= 0.0284 \text{ in}$$

Note that the static deflection is 0.0083 in and the amplitude of vibration is 0.0201 in. Also, since the amplitude exceeds the static deflection, the bar will at times be in compression. Thus, the maximum force N_{max}, corresponding to the maximum extension is

$$N_{max} = ku_{max} = 6 \times 10^5 \times 0.0284$$

The maximum stress induced in the bar is equivalent to

$$\sigma_{max} = \frac{N}{A} = \frac{6 \times 10^5 \times 0.0284}{2} = 8520 \text{ psi}$$

(b) As noted above, the amplitude of vibration

$$a = 0.0201 \text{ in}$$

To find the period, T, and the frequency, n, we first calculate the circular frequency, p.

$$p = \sqrt{\frac{kg}{W}} = \sqrt{\frac{6 \times 10^5 \times 386}{5000}} = 215 \text{ radians/sec}$$

(note that g is expressed in inch and second units.)

Then the frequency,

$$n = \frac{p}{2\pi} = 34.3 \text{ cycles/sec}$$

and the period

$$T = \frac{1}{n} = 0.029 \text{ sec/cycle}$$

The system which has been examined so far is said to have one degree of freedom since the specification of only one quantity (the extension of the bar in this case) is required to define the configuration of the system at any one instant. The analysis can be applied directly to any elastic system with one degree of freedom provided the relevant stiffness coefficient is known. For instance, we can apply the results to the oscillation of a (weightless) beam supporting a body at any point (Fig. 2). The body can be situated at any point on the beam, and k is computed as the force required, at the point where the body is situated, to produce unit deflection at this same point.

• PROBLEM 12-3

A body of weight W = 100 lb is dropped from a height h = 1 in onto the end of a spring. Find the spring stiffness such that the maximum support reaction R_{max} = 500 lb.

Solution: Let:

K = spring stiffness and

u_{max} = the extension of the bar when the weight finally comes to rest at the lowest point of travel.

Then, from conservation of energy, loss of gravitational energy = gain of strain energy

$$\therefore \quad W(h + u_{max}) = 1/2\ k\ u_{max}^2 \tag{1}$$

Solving for u_{max} in the quadratic equation (1) we get

$$u_{max} = \frac{W}{k} + \sqrt{\left(\frac{W}{k}\right)^2 + 2h\left(\frac{W}{k}\right)} \tag{2}$$

putting

$$u_{st} = \text{static deflection} = \frac{W}{k}, \text{ and}$$

$$R_{max} = k \cdot u_{max} \text{ in equation (2)}$$

we get

$$R_{max} = W\left[1 + \sqrt{1 + \frac{2h}{u_{st}}}\right] \qquad (3)$$

$$500 = 100\left[1 + \sqrt{1 + \frac{2}{u_{st}}}\right]$$

$$\therefore \quad u_{st} = \frac{2}{15} \text{ in}$$

i.e.,

$$\frac{W}{k} = \frac{2}{15}$$

and

$$k = \frac{15W}{2} = 750 \text{ lb/in}$$

For any value of R_{max} greater than 2W it will always be possible to determine a finite value of k. Since from equation (3) the smallest possible value of R_{max} occurs when h = 0

i.e.,

$$R_{max} = W\left[1 + \sqrt{(1 + 0)}\right]$$
$$= 2W$$

FORCED VIBRATION

• PROBLEM 12-4

A cantilever 12 ft long supports two bodies (Fig. 1 (a)), one of weight 10 lb at the free end A, and one of weight 6 lb at the point B, 9 ft from the support. If the value of El for the bar is 120,000 lb-in^2, find the frequencies and amplitudes of each of the two natural modes of vibration.

Solution: The first step in problems of this sort is the calculation of the quantities K_{11}, K_{12}, K_{21} and K_{22}.

The equations of motion for the equivalent mass-spring system (fig. 5) are

$$\left.\begin{aligned} m_1 \ddot{u}_1 + (K_1 + K_2)u_1 - K_2 u_2 &= 0 \\ m_2 \ddot{u}_2 + (K_2 + K_3)u_2 - K_2 u_1 &= 0 \end{aligned}\right\} \qquad (4)$$

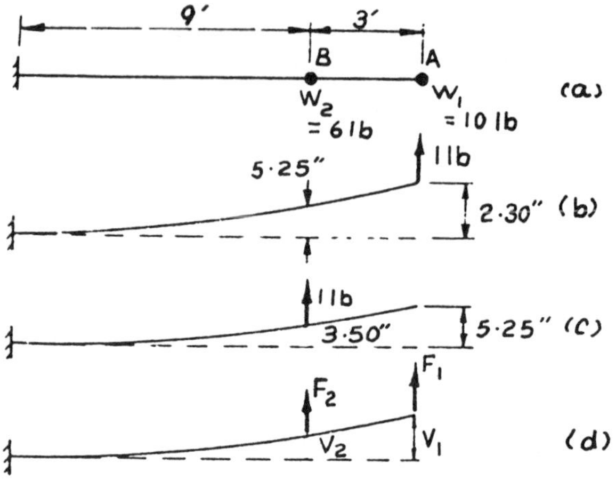

FIG. 1

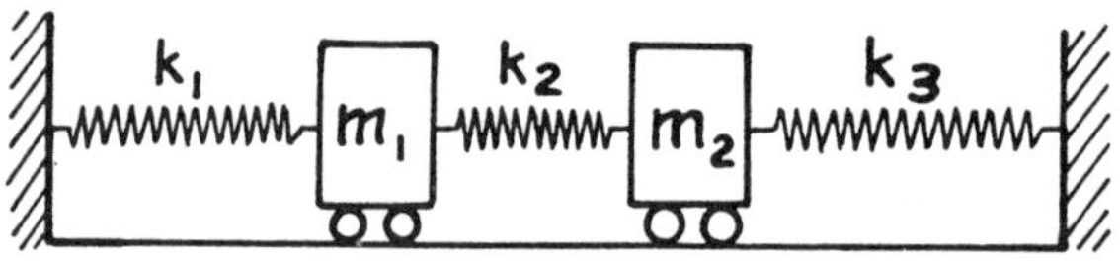

FIG. 5

or,

$$\left.\begin{aligned} m_1 \ddot{u}_1 + K_{11} u_1 + K_{12} u_2 &= 0 \\ m_2 \ddot{u}_2 + K_{22} u_2 + K_{21} u_1 &= 0 \end{aligned}\right\} \qquad (5)$$

In this problem $K_3 = 0$

Thus, comparing equations (4) and (5) the coefficients K_{11}, K_{21}, K_{12} and K_{22} become

$$K_{11} = K_1 + K_2 \quad , \quad K_{12} = - K_2$$

$$K_{22} = K_2 + K_3 = K_2 \quad , \quad K_{21} = - K_2$$

The coefficient K_{11} and K_{12} may be interpreted as the forces which must be exerted on bodies 1 and 2 respectively in order to maintain a configuration where the displacement of the bodies are unity and zero respectively. Similarly, K_{21} and K_{22} are the forces required to maintain displacements of zero and unity. Apply a unit force at each of the points A and B, and calculate the deflections at A and B for each force.

A force of 1 lb is applied at A (Fig. 1(b)). The deflections at A and B are calculated by the moment-area method from the (M/EI) diagram shown in fig. 3.

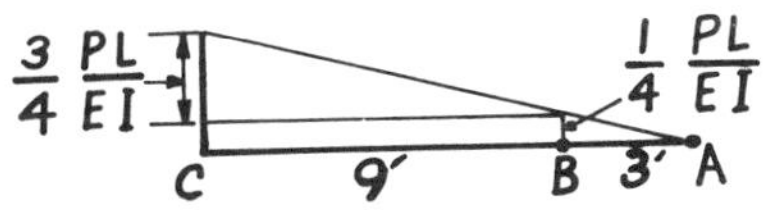

FIG.3

The deflection at A due to a unit force P = lb is given by the moment of the area of the M/EI diagram about A.

i.e.,

$$v_A = 1/2 \times \frac{PL}{EI} \times L \times \frac{2L}{3} = \frac{PL^3}{3EI} = \frac{1 \times (12 \times 12)^3}{3 \times 120{,}000}$$

$$= 8.30 \text{ in}$$

v_B = moment about B

$$= \frac{1}{4} \times \frac{PL}{EI} \times \frac{9}{12} L \left(1/2 \times \frac{9}{12} L\right) + \frac{3}{4} \times \frac{PL}{EI} \times \frac{1}{2} \times \frac{9}{12} L \times \frac{2}{3} \times \frac{9}{12} L$$

$$= \frac{3}{2} \times 1/4 \times \frac{3}{4} \times \frac{3}{4} \frac{PL^3}{EI} = 5.25 \text{ in}$$

Now a force of 1 lb is applied at B (Fig. 1(c)) and the deflections computed.

The $\frac{M}{EI}$ diagram for a unit load at B is shown in fig. 4.

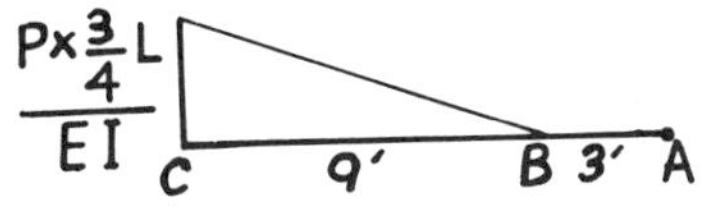

FIG.4

$$v_B = \text{moment of } \frac{M}{EI} \text{ diagram about B}$$

$$= \frac{3}{4} \frac{PL}{EI} \times \frac{1}{2} \times \frac{3}{4} L \times \left(\frac{1}{2} L\right) = \frac{9}{64} \frac{PL^3}{EI}$$

$$= 3.50 \text{ in}$$

$$v_A = \text{moment of } \frac{M}{EI} \text{ diagram about A}$$

$$= \frac{3}{4} \frac{PL}{EI} \times \frac{1}{2} \times \frac{3}{4} L \times \left(\frac{3}{4} L\right) = \left(\frac{3L}{4}\right)^3 \times \frac{P}{2EI} = 5.25 \text{ in}$$

The deflections at A and B due to a combined system of forces F_1 and F_2 (Fig. 1 (d)) are then

$$V_1 = 8.30\ F_1 + 5.25\ F_2$$
$$V_2 = 5.25\ F_1 + 3.50\ F_2 \qquad (1)$$

These equations are solved in order to express F_1 and F_2 in terms of V_1 and V_2.

$$F_1 = 2.35\ V_1 - 3.52\ V_2$$
$$F_2 = -3.52\ V_1 + 5.57\ V_2 \qquad (2)$$

The required K values are obtained directly from these equations

With $V_1 = 1$ and $V_2 = 0$

$$K_{11} = 2.35 \text{ and } K_{21} = -3.52$$

With $V_1 = 0$ and $V_2 = 1$

$$K_{12} = -3.52 \text{ and } K_{22} = 5.57$$

The equations for the amplitudes are

$$\left(K_{11} - m_1 p^2\right) a_1 + K_{12}\, a_2 = 0$$

$$K_{21}\, a_1 + \left(K_{22} - m_2 p^2\right) a_2 = 0$$

i.e.,

$$\left(2.35 - \frac{W_1}{g} p^2\right)a_1 - 3.52a_2 = 0$$
$$-3.52a_1 + \left(5.57 - \frac{W_2}{g} p^2\right)a_2 = 0 \qquad (3)$$

These have solutions only when

$$\begin{vmatrix} \left(2.35 - \frac{10}{386} p^2\right) & -3.52 \\ -3.52 & \left(5.57 - \frac{6}{386} p^2\right) \end{vmatrix} = 0$$

i.e.,

$$p^4 - 386\left(\frac{2.35}{10} + \frac{5.57}{6}\right) + 386^2\left(\frac{2.35 \times 5.57 - 3.52^2}{10 \times 6}\right) = 0$$

Hence

$$p^2 = 3.86 \text{ or } 445$$

and

$$p = 1.96 \text{ or } 21.1 \text{ radians/sec}$$

(a) First natural mode

By substituting $p^2 = 3.86$ into equation (3) we find that $a_2/a_1 = +0.64$. The configuration corresponding to this mode of vibration is therefore as shown in Fig. 2(a).

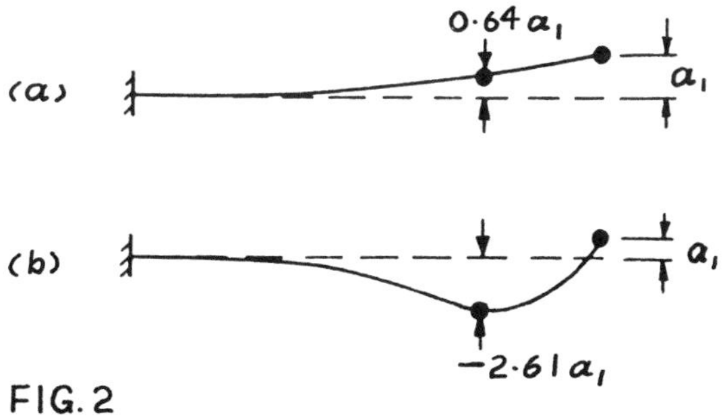

FIG. 2

$$p = 1.96 \text{ radians/sec}$$

$$n_1 = \frac{1.96}{2\pi} = 0.31 \text{ cycles/sec}$$

$$T_1 = \frac{2\pi}{1.96} = 3.2 \text{ sec}$$

(b) Second natural mode

By substituting $p^2 = 455$ into equation (3) we find that $a_2/a_1 = -2.61$. The configuration for this mode is shown in Fig. 2(b).

$$p = 21.1 \text{ radians/sec}$$

$$n_2 = \frac{21.1}{2\pi} = 3.36 \text{ cycles/sec}$$

$$T_2 = \frac{2\pi}{21.1} = 0.30 \text{ sec}$$

It might be noted that the bodies are moving in the same direction at every instant in the first mode of vibration, while in the second mode they are always moving in opposite directions.

Each natural mode of vibration is associated with a particular configuration of deformation, which is a characteristic shape corresponding to the characteristic value of p.

• PROBLEM 12-5

Two blocks are supported by springs as shown. For each natural mode of vibration, find the frequency, the period and the ratio of the amplitudes of the two blocks.

Solution: Apply a time-dependent force, $F_1 = f_1(t)$ to the weight W_1. The equations of motion for the mass-spring

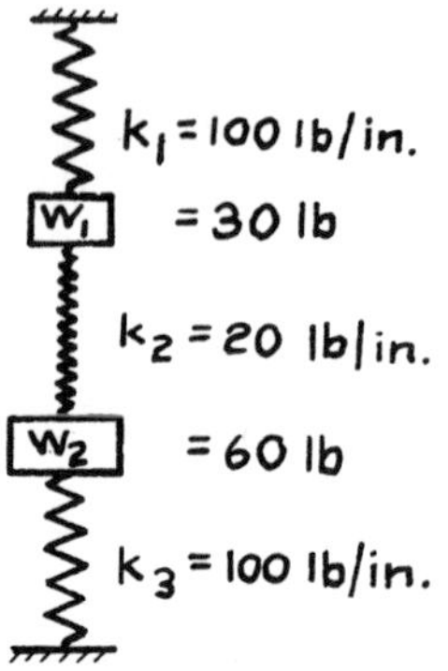

FIG. 1

system shown in fig. 1 may be written as

$$m_1\ddot{x}_1 + (K_1 + K_2)x_1 - K_2\ x_1 = F_1 \tag{1}$$

$$m_2\ddot{x}_2 + (K_2 + K_3)x_2 - K_2\ x_1 = 0 \tag{2}$$

If a harmonic forcing function $F_1 = F_0$ sin wt is applied, then the trial solutions to equations (1) and (2)

i.e., $x_1 = X_1 \sin \omega t$ and $x_2 = X_2 \sin \omega t$ (3)

must satisfy the equations if applicable.
Substituting equations (3) into (1) and (2), we obtain

$$\begin{aligned} X_1(K_1 + K_2 - m_1\ \omega^2) - K_2X_2 &= F_o \\ X_2(K_2 + K_3 - m_2\ \omega^2) - K_2X_1 &= 0 \end{aligned} \tag{4}$$

from which

$$X_1 = \frac{(K_2 + K_3 - m_2\ \omega^2)F_o}{(K_1 + K_2 - m_1\ \omega^2)(K_2 + K_3 - m_2\ \omega^2) - K_2^2} \tag{5}$$

and

$$X_2 = \frac{K_2\ F_o}{(K_1 + K_2 - m_1\ \omega^2)(K_2 + K_3 - m_2\ \omega^2) - K_2^2} \tag{6}$$

The critical frequencies occur when X_1 and X_2 are infinite. i.e., when the denominators in equations (5) and (6) are equal to zero.

$$\therefore \quad (K_1 + K_2 - m_1\ \omega^2)(K_2 + K_3 - m_2\ \omega^2) - K_2^2 = 0 \tag{7}$$

simplifying equation (7),

$$\omega^4 - \left(\frac{K_1 + K_2}{m_1} + \frac{K_2 + K_3}{m_2}\right)\omega^2 + \frac{K_1K_2 + K_1K_3 + K_2K_3}{m_1m_2} = 0 \tag{8}$$

where, ω = cyclic frequency

$$m_1 = \text{mass of } W_1 = \frac{W_1}{g} = \frac{30}{386} \text{ slugs}$$

$$m_2 = \text{mass of } W_2 = \frac{W_2}{g} = \frac{60}{386} \text{ slugs}$$

Equation (8) is a quadratic equation which has the solutions

$$\omega^2 = \frac{K_1 + K_2}{2m_1} + \frac{K_2 + K_3}{2m_2} \pm$$

$$\sqrt{\left(\frac{K_1 + K_2}{2m_1} + \frac{K_2 + K_3}{2m_2}\right)^2 - \frac{K_1K_2 + K_1K_3 + K_2K_3}{m_1m_2}}$$

substituting,

$$\omega^2 = \frac{100 + 20}{2 \times \frac{30}{386}} + \frac{20 + 100}{2 \times \frac{60}{386}} \pm$$

$$\sqrt{\left(\frac{100 + 20}{2 \times \frac{30}{386}} + \frac{20 + 100}{2 \times \frac{60}{386}}\right)^2 - \frac{100 \times 20 + 100 \times 100 + 20 \times 100}{\frac{30}{386} \times \frac{60}{386}}}$$

$$= 386 \times 3 \pm \sqrt{(386 \times 3)^2 - \frac{(386)^2 \times 14{,}000}{30 \times 60}}$$

$$= 1158 \pm 427$$

$\omega^2 = 1585$ gives $\omega_1 = 39.81$ radians/sec

$\omega^2 = 731$ gives $\omega_2 = 27.0$ radians/sec

The natural frequencies of a system are given by,

$$n_i = \frac{\omega_i}{2\pi}, \quad \text{where } i = 1, 2$$

Thus the natural frequencies become

$$n_1 = \frac{\omega_1}{2\pi} = \frac{39.81}{2\pi} = 6.33 \text{ cycles/sec}$$

and $n_2 = \frac{\omega_2}{2\pi} = \frac{27}{2\pi} = 4.30$ cycles/sec

The period, T is given by $T_i = \frac{1}{n_i} \quad i = 1, 2$

$$\therefore \quad T_1 = \frac{1}{n_1} = \frac{1}{6.33} = 0.158 \text{ sec.}$$

$$\text{and } T_2 = \frac{1}{n_2} = \frac{1}{4.30} = 0.232 \text{ sec.}$$

The amplitude ratio for the two motions is given by

$$r = \frac{X_2}{X_1} \quad .$$

Dividing equation (6) by equation (5), we get

$$r_i = \frac{X_2}{X_1} = \frac{\dfrac{K_2}{m_2}}{\dfrac{K_2 + K_3}{m_2} - \omega_i^2} \qquad i = 1, 2$$

$$r_1 = \frac{\dfrac{20}{60/386}}{\dfrac{20 + 100}{30/386} - 1585} = -3.14 \qquad \text{and}$$

$$r_2 = \frac{\dfrac{20}{60/386}}{\dfrac{20 + 100}{30/386} - 729} = 0.158$$

• PROBLEM 12-6

A two-mass system is illustrated in Fig. 1(a). The weights and spring stiffnesses are as shown. Find the two natural frequencies of vibration of the system and the relative amplitudes in each mode of vibration.

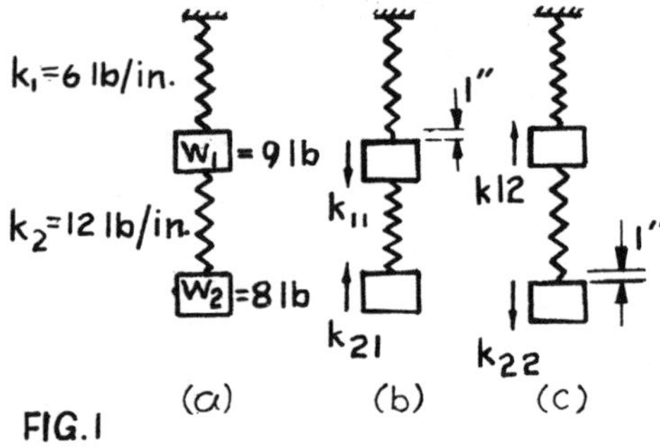

FIG.1

Solution: Suppose that body 1 is displaced 1 in from its equilibrium position (Fig. 1(b)), while body 2 is restrained against displacement. Spring 1 is then stretched by 1 in, while spring 2 is compressed by 1 in. The forces required to maintain the system in this deformed state are (see

Fig. 1(b)).

$$K_{11} = 6 + 12 = + 18 \text{ lb and } K_{21} = - 12 \text{ lb}$$

for every inch of displacement.

A similar operation is now performed with body 2 displaced 1 in (Fig. 1(c)). Now spring 2 is stretched while spring 1 is undeformed. The forces required to maintain this state of deformation are

$$K_{12} = - 12 \text{ lb and } K_{22} = + 12 \text{ lb}$$

We are given that

$$m_1 = \frac{W_1}{g} = \frac{9}{386} \text{ slugs}$$

and

$$m_2 = \frac{W_2}{g} = \frac{8}{386} \text{ slugs}$$

Hence the equations of motion give

$$\left.\begin{aligned} m_1\ddot{u}_1 + (K_1 + K_2)u_1 - K_2u_2 &= 0 \\ m_2\ddot{u}_2 + (K_2 + K_3)u_2 - K_2u_1 &= 0 \end{aligned}\right\} \quad \text{here, } K_3 = 0$$

or

$$m_1\ddot{u}_1 + K_{11}u_1 + K_{12}u_2 = 0 \qquad (1)$$

$$m_2\ddot{u}_2 + K_{22}u_2 + K_{21}u_1 = 0 \qquad (2)$$

For natural modes of vibration, the circular frequency, p, of the motion of each mass is the same.

The solutions to equations (1) and (2) are

$$u_1 = a_1\cos\ (pt + \alpha),$$

and

$$u_2 = a_2\cos\ (pt + \alpha),$$

Now, differentiate u_1 tiwce and substitute into equation (1)

$$\ddot{u}_1 = - p^2a_1\cos(pt + \alpha)$$

$$\therefore \quad m_1(- p^2a_1(\cos pt + \alpha)) + K_{11}(a_1\cos\ (pt + \alpha)) -$$

$$k_{12}a_2 \cos\ (pt + \alpha) = 0$$

which on simplification gives

$$- m_1 p^2 a_1 + K_{11} a_1 - K_{12} a_2 = 0 \qquad (3)$$

similarly, differentiate $u_2 = a_2 \cos(pt + \alpha)$
twice with respect to t and substitute into equation (2)

$$\ddot{u}_2 = - p^2 a_2 \cos(pt + \alpha)$$

$$\therefore m_2(- p^2 a_2 \cos(pt + \alpha)) + K_{21}(a_1 \cos(pt + \alpha)) +$$

$$K_{22} a_2 \cos(pt + \alpha) = 0$$

on cancelling out $\cos(pt + \alpha)$ we get

$$- m_2 p^2 a_2 + K_{22} a_2 + K_{21} a_1 = 0 \qquad (4)$$

Substituting the values of m_1, m_2 and
K_{11}, K_{12}, K_{21}, K_{22} into equation (3) and (4) we get

$$\left(18 - \frac{9}{386} p^2\right) a_1 - 12 a_2 = 0 \qquad (5)$$

$$- 12 a_1 + \left(12 - \frac{8}{386} p^2\right) a_2 = 0 \qquad (6)$$

Equating the determinant of coefficients to zero we have

$$\begin{vmatrix} \left(18 - \frac{9}{386} p^2\right) & -12 \\ - 12 & \left(12 - \frac{8}{386} p^2\right) \end{vmatrix} = 0$$

or $p^4 - (3.5 \times 386) p^2 + 386^2 = 0$. Hence $p^2 = 121$ or 1230

If the two values of $|p|$ are denoted by p_1 and p_2 then

$$p_1 = 11.0 \text{ radians/sec}$$

$$p_2 = 35.1 \text{ radians/sec}$$

These are the circular frequencies associated with the two natural modes of vibration. The natural frequencies are therefore

$$n_1 = \frac{11.0}{2\pi} = 1.75 \text{ cycles/sec}$$

$$n_2 = \frac{35.1}{2\pi} = 5.59 \text{ cycles/sec}$$

The natural periods are $T_1 = 0.572$ sec and $T_2 = 0.179$ sec.

(a) First natural modes

The natural mode of vibration with the lowest frequency is called the fundamental mode. In this case, for the fundamental mode, n = 1.75 and $p^2 = 121$. If this value of p^2 is substituted into equations (5) and (6) the ratio of amplitudes can be found.

$$15.18a_1 - 12a_2 = 0$$

$$-12a_1 + 9.45a_2 = 0$$

Each of these equations is satisfied by the ratio $a_2/a_1 = 1.26$. Thus, when the system is vibrating in the fundamental mode, the frequency of vibration is 1.75 cycles/sec and at every instant the displacement of mass 2 is +1.26 times the displacement of mass 1, that is to say is 1.26 times as great and in the same direction.

(b) Second natural mode

With this system with only two degrees of freedom, there is only one natural mode of vibration higher than the fundamental mode. For the higher mode, $n_2 = 5.59$ cycles/sec and $p^2 = 1230$. When this value of p^2 is substituted into equations (5) and (6) we obtain

$$-10.67a_1 - 12a_2 = 0$$

$$-12a_1 - 13.49a_2 = 0$$

Each of these equations is satisfied by the ratio $a_2/a_1 = -0.89$. Thus for this mode of vibration the frequency is 5.59 cycles/sec and at every instant the displacement of mass 2 is -0.89 times the displacement of mass 1, that is to say 0.89 times as great and in the opposite direction.

IMPACT LOADING

• PROBLEM 12-7

A 1-in. square beam (Fig. 1) is 60 in. long and rests on supports at the ends. A 25-lb weight falls 2 in., striking the beam at its midpoint. What stress is caused (a) if the beam is steel? (b) if the beam is made of an aluminum alloy?

Solution: (a) For the steel beam

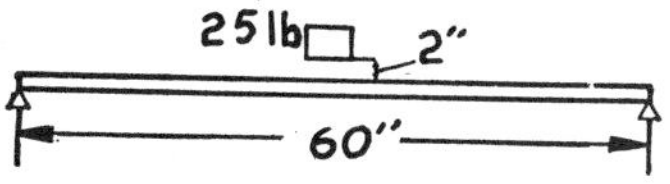

FIG.1

$$\Delta_{st} = \frac{PL^3}{48EI} = \frac{25 \times 60^3}{48 \times 30{,}000{,}000 \times \frac{1}{12}} = 0.045 \text{ in.}$$

The static stress due to a gradually applied weight is given by,

$$S_{st} = \frac{Mc}{I} = \frac{375}{\frac{1}{6}} = 2{,}250 \text{ psi}$$

Since stresses are proportional to deformations or deflections, the stress due to the weight falling a height h and striking the beam is given by,

$$S = S_{st} + S_{st}\sqrt{\frac{2h}{\Delta_{st}} + 1}$$

Substitution of numerical data into above equation yields,

$$S = 2{,}250 + 2{,}250\sqrt{\frac{4}{0.045} + 1} = 2{,}250 + 2{,}250\sqrt{89 + 1}$$

$$= 2{,}250 + 2{,}250 \times 9.5$$

$$= 2{,}250 + 21{,}400 = 23{,}650 \text{ psi}$$

If the weight W is dropped a distance h before striking the beam, the beam will deflect a distance Δ which is given by

$$\Delta = \Delta_{st}\left[1 + \sqrt{\frac{2h}{\Delta_{st}} + 1}\right]$$

If Δ_{st} is small in comparison with h, the above equation can be written as with negligible error.

$$\Delta = \Delta_{st}\left[1 + \sqrt{\frac{2h}{\Delta_{st}}}\right]$$

Substitution of numerical data yields,

$$\Delta = 0.045\left[1 + \sqrt{\frac{2 \times 2}{0.045}}\right]$$

$$= 0.469 \text{ in.}$$

(b) For the aluminum-alloy beam, E = 10,000,000 psi

$$\Delta_{st} = \frac{PL^3}{48EI}$$

$$= \frac{25 \times 60^3}{48 \times 10{,}000{,}000 \times \frac{1}{12}} \doteq 0.135 \text{ in}$$

$$S_{st} = 2{,}250 \text{ psi (for static load)}$$

Then

$$S = 2,250 + 2,250\sqrt{\frac{4}{0.135} + 1} = 2,250 + 2,250\ \sqrt{30.6}$$

$$= 2,250 + 12,500 = 14,750 \text{ psi}$$

If grades of steel and aluminum alloy having the same strength are used, the aluminum-alloy beam has a considerably higher factor of safety. It may be noted, however, that if the load were suddenly applied (without falling, or h = 0), the stress in either beam would be simply twice 2,250 psi, the stress due to static load, or 4,500 psi.

• PROBLEM 12-8

The simply supported 6061-T6 aluminum alloy beam A of Fig. 1a is 3 in. wide by 1 in. deep. The center support is a helical spring with a modulus of 100 lb per in. The spring is initially unstressed and in contact with the beam. When the 50-lb block drops 2 in. onto the top of the beam, 90 percent of the energy is absorbed elastically by the system consisting of beam A and spring B. Determine:

(a) The maximum flexural stress in the beam for this loading.

(b) The load factor.

(c) The proportion of the effective energy absorbed by each of the components A and B.

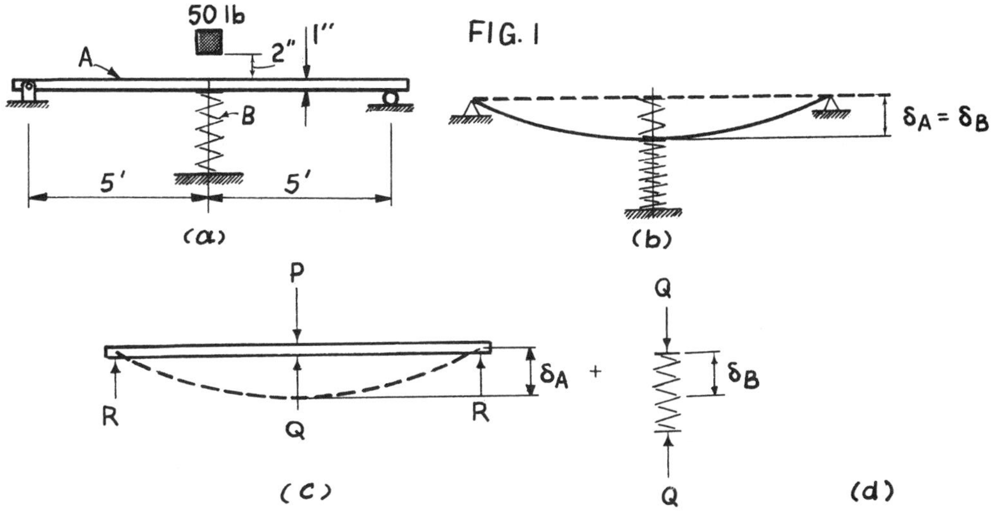

FIG. 1

Solution: In Fig. 1b, c, and d are shown a deflection diagram for the system and free-body diagrams for the component parts. Since the action is assumed to be elastic and the materials obey Hooke's law, the load-deflection relation will be linear, and using the Static

Load concept,

η x Work done by falling weight

= strain energy absorbed elastically by system

i.e.,

$$\eta \cdot W \cdot h = (P - Q) \times \frac{\delta_A}{2} + Q \times \frac{\delta_B}{2} \quad (1)$$

where

η = proportion of potential energy (due to falling weight) that is absorbed by the system

h = total distance travelled by falling weight

P = equivalent static load on beam required to produce a deflection δ_A . Note that the resultant static load is (P - Q).

Q = static load required in spring to produce a deflection δ_B. Since the spring is in contact with the beam, $\delta_A = \delta_B = \Delta$

Thus, equation (1) becomes

$$\eta \cdot W \cdot h = (P - Q)\ \Delta/2 + Q \cdot \Delta/2$$

i.e., $\eta \cdot W \cdot h = P \cdot \Delta/2$

$$\therefore \quad 50(2 + \Delta)(0.9) = P\Delta/2.$$

The fiber stress is wanted; therefore the forces P and Q will be evaluated, and from these forces and Fig. 1c the fiber stress can be determined.

For the simply-supported beam shown in fig. 1c, the central deflection, δ_A is given by

$$\delta_A = \frac{(P - Q)L^3}{48EI} = \frac{(P - Q)(10^3)(12^3)}{48(10^7)(3)(1^3)/12} = \frac{(P - Q)(144)}{(10^4)},$$

and the deflection in the spring is given by

$$\delta_B = \frac{Q}{k} = \frac{Q}{100}$$

where k = spring modulus (or stiffness)

From Fig. 1b,

$$\delta_A = \delta_B = \Delta, \quad \text{or} \quad \frac{(P - Q)(144)}{10{,}000} = \frac{Q}{100},$$

from which $$Q = \frac{36P}{61};$$

then $$\Delta = \frac{Q}{100} = \frac{36P}{6100},$$

and Eq. (c) becomes $$50\left(2 + \frac{36P}{6100}\right) 0.9 = \left(\frac{1}{2}\right) \frac{36P^2}{6100}$$

or $P^2 - 90P = 30{,}500$

from which $P = 225.3$ and -135.3.

The positive root is the magnitude of P necessary to produce the maximum downward deflection of the beam, whereas the negative root is the force necessary to produce the maximum upward deflection.

When the value of 225.3 lb for P is used,

$$Q = \frac{36(225.3)}{61} = 133.0 \text{ lb},$$

and $$P - Q = 92.3 \text{ lb}.$$

(a) From Fig. 1, R is 46.15 lb, and the maximum bending moment occurs at the center of the beam and is 46.15(5)(12) in-lb; therefore, the maximum flexural stress is

$$\sigma = \frac{Mc}{I} = \frac{46.15(60)/2}{3(1^3)/12}$$

$$= 5540 \text{ psi T and C},$$

which is well below the proportional limit, and, therefore, the action is elastic.

(b) The load factor is

$$\frac{P}{W} = \frac{225.3}{50} = 4.51$$

(c) The resultant equivalent static load at the center of beam A is (P - Q) and is 92.3 lb, and the energy absorbed elastically by the beam is

$$U_A = \frac{(92.3)(\Delta)}{2}$$

The elastic energy absorbed by the helical spring is

$$U_B = \frac{(133.0)(\Delta)}{2}$$

The total energy absorbed elastically by the system is

$$U = \frac{(225.3)(\Delta)}{2};$$

therefore the proportions absorbed by each component are

$$\frac{92.3}{225.3} = 41 \text{ per cent for A}$$

and

$$\frac{133.0}{225.3} = 59 \text{ per cent for B.}$$

• PROBLEM 12-9

A 1-in.-diameter steel shaft (Fig. 1) 60 in. long and adequately supported to prevent bending is fixed at one end and carries a 12-in. rigid arm fixed to the other end. A weight of 25 lb falls 2 in., hitting the arm. What stress results in the shaft?

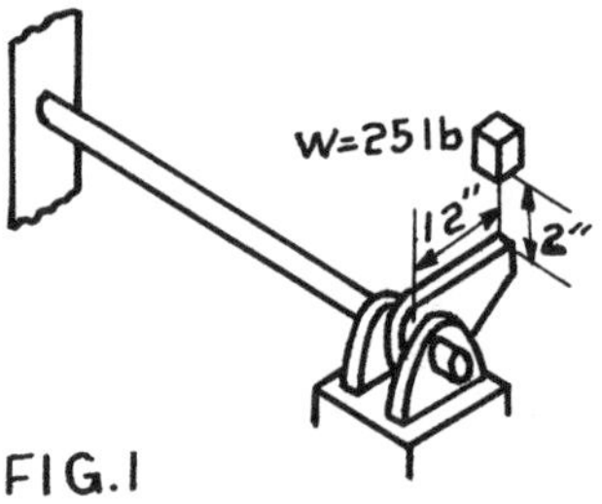

FIG. 1

Solution: The static stress due to the 25-lb weight acting with a moment arm of 12 in. is

$$S_{st} = \frac{Tc}{J} = \frac{300 \times \frac{1}{2} \times 2}{\pi \times \left(\frac{1}{2}\right)^4} = 1{,}530 \text{ psi}$$

$$\theta_{st} = \frac{TL}{E_s J} = \frac{300 \times 60 \times 2}{12{,}000{,}000 \times \pi \times \left(\frac{1}{2}\right)^4} = 0.0153 \text{ radian}$$

$$\Delta_{st} = 12\theta_{st} = 0.184 \text{ in.}$$

Therefore, the resulting stress S is,

$$= S_{st}\left[1 + \sqrt{\frac{2h}{\Delta_{st}} + 1}\right]$$

$$= 1{,}530\left[1 + \sqrt{\frac{2 \times 2}{0.184} + 1}\right]$$

$$= 8{,}880 \text{ psi.}$$

The upper 3 ft of the steel bar AB in Fig. 1a is 2 in. wide by 1/2 in. thick and the lower 2 ft is 1 in. wide by 1/2 in. thick. When the weight, W, is released from rest from a height of 20 in. onto the end A of the bar, the axial stress in the bar (neglecting stress concentration) is not to exceed 16 ksi. Assume that 80 per cent of the energy of the falling block is absorbed elastically by member AB. Determine:

(a) The maximum permissible weight for block W.

(b) The maximum permissible weight for W if the bar AB is 1 in. wide through its entire length. Use the equivalent static load concept and assume a value of E = 30,000 ksi for the Young's modulus of the steel bar.

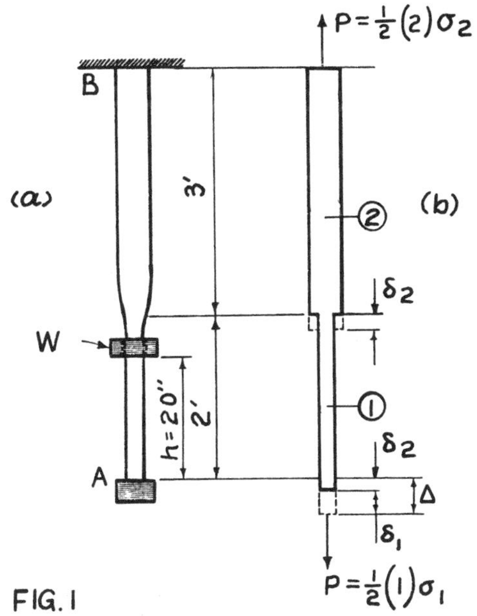

FIG. 1

Solution: (a) Figure 1b indicates the static load applied to the bar and the resulting maximum deflections, δ_1, in bar (1) and δ_2 in bar (2).

Total work done by block = potential energy lost by block in falling through a distance of 20 in + work done by block in stretching bar through a distance Δ in. However, only 80% (η = 0.8) of the total work done is absorbed as strain energy by bar. Thus total work done = ηWh. Equating the total work done to the strain energy ($P\Delta/2$) absorbed, we get

$$\eta Wh = (0.8)W(20 + \Delta) = P\Delta/2. \qquad \text{(b)}$$

where P = equivalent static load required to produce a deflection Δ in bar and h = 20 + Δ

The quantities P and Δ can be calculated directly from the given data. From Fig. lb

$$1(\sigma_2) = 0.5(\sigma_1) \text{ or } \sigma_1 = 2\sigma_2.$$

The expression indicates that σ_1 (equal to 16 ksi) is the limiting stress and that σ_2 must be 8 ksi.

The load P is

$$P = \sigma_1 A_1 = 16(1)(0.5) = 8 \text{ kips},$$

and the deflection Δ is

$$\Delta = \delta_2 + \delta_1 = 36\varepsilon_2 + 24\varepsilon_1 = (36\sigma_2 + 24\sigma_1)/30{,}000$$

$$= \frac{36(8) + 24(16)}{30{,}000} = 0.0224 \text{ in.}$$

Substituting these values of P and Δ into Eq. (b) gives the expression

$$0.8(W)(20.0224) = (8)(0.0224)/2,$$

from which $W = 5.59$ lb.

(b) If the bar is 1 in. wide for its entire length, the deflection Δ is given by total strain in section (1) x its length + total strain in section (2) x its length.

where strain, $\varepsilon = \dfrac{\text{stress}}{\text{Young's modulus}}$

i.e., $$\Delta = \frac{(36 + 24)(16)}{3(10^4)} = 0.032 \text{ in.},$$

and $$0.8(w)(20.032) = (1/2)(8)(0.032),$$

from which $W = 7.99$ lb.

• PROBLEM 12-11

In Fig. la, the bar AB has cross-sectional area = 0.75 sq in. If l = 10 ft; W = 300 lb; h = 2 in.; and E = $15(10)^6$ psi, determine the maximum unit stress and maximum elongation.

Solution: First method (Equivalent static load)

It is often more convenient to solve for the stress or deformation caused by impact by means of an equivalent static load P. The equivalent static load P is defined as the load which, applied gradually, will produce the same maximum stress and deformation as the given impact load W. For vertical impact due to a falling body,

$$W(h + \delta) = P\delta/2$$

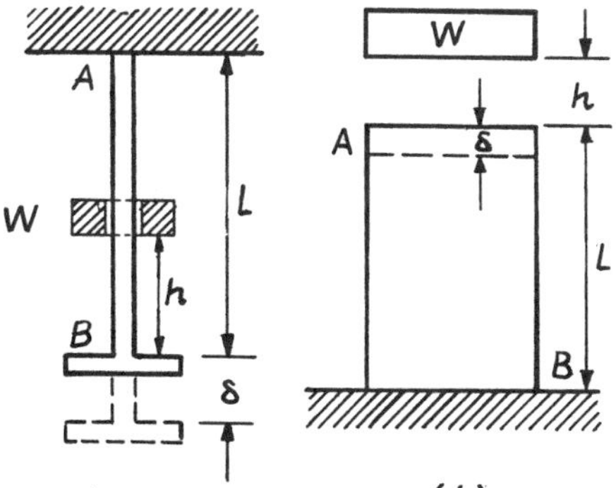

FIG. 1 (a) (b)

For axial loading, $\delta = Pl/AE$. With this substitution, the preceding equation becomes

$$W[h + (Pl/AE)] = P^2 l/2AE \quad \text{or} \quad P^2 - 2WP = 2WhAE/l$$

Thus,

$$P^2 - 2(300)P = 2 \times 300 \times 2 \times 0.75 \times 15(10)^6/120 = 112{,}500{,}000$$

whence $P = 10{,}900$ lb

$$S = P/A = 10{,}900/0.75 = 14{,}500 \text{ psi}$$

$$\delta = Pl/AE = 10{,}900 \times 120/0.75 \times 15(10)^6 = 0.116 \text{ in}$$

If $P = AE\delta/l$ is substituted into the original equation, then

$$W(h + \delta) = AE\delta^2/2l \quad \text{or} \quad \delta^2 - (2Wl/AE)\delta = 2Wlh/AE$$

Thus, $\delta^2 - (2 \times 300 \times 120/0.75 \times 15(10)^6)$

$$= 2 \times 300 \times 120 \times 2/0.75 \times 15(10)^6$$

$$\delta^2 - 0.0064\delta = 0.0128$$

whence $\delta = 0.116$ in.

$$S = E\delta/l = 15(10)^6 \times 0.116/120 = 14{,}500 \text{ psi}$$

Second method (Internal energy)

$$W(h + \delta) = (S^2/2E) \times \text{Volume}$$

But $\delta = Sl/E$. With this substitution, the above equation becomes

$$W[h + Sl/E] = (S^2/2E) \times \text{Volume}$$

Thus,

$$300[2 + 120S/15(10)^6] = \frac{S^2}{2 \times 15(10)^6} \times 0.75 \times 120$$

or $S^2 = 800S = 200{,}000{,}000$

whence $\quad S = 14,500$ psi

and $\quad \delta = Sl/E = 14,500 \times 120/15(10)^6 = 0.116$ in.

The original equation can also be solved by substituting $S = E\delta/l = 15(10)^6\delta/120$, thus obtaining $\delta^2 - 0.0064\delta = 0.0128$, as in the first method.

Third method:

$$S = S_{st}\left[1 + \sqrt{(2h/\delta_{st} + 1}\right]$$

But $S_{st} = W/A = 300/0.75 = 400$ psi

$$\delta_{st} = Wl/AE = 300 \times 120/0.75 \times 15(10)^6 = 0.0032 \text{ in.}$$

Thus, $S = 400\left[1 + \sqrt{(2 \times 2/0.0032) + 1}\right] = 14,500$ psi

$$\delta = \delta_{st}\left[1 + \sqrt{(2h/\delta_{st}) + 1}\right]$$

$$= 0.0032\left[1 + \sqrt{(2 \times 2/0.0032) + 1}\right] = 0.116 \text{ in.}$$

In general, the first method is preferable in that it makes use only of basic stress-strain relations and does not require particular energy expressions as in the second method, or special equations as in the third method. However, situations may arise where a particular method may have certain advantages.

• PROBLEM 12-12

Compute the maximum shearing stress and angle of twist in the shaft AB of Fig. 1 if the diameter of the shaft is 2 in.; l = 3 ft, W = 100 lb; h = 6 in.; q = 12 in; and $G = 12(10)^6$ psi. Assume that all the energy delivered by the impact load W is transmitted to the shaft.

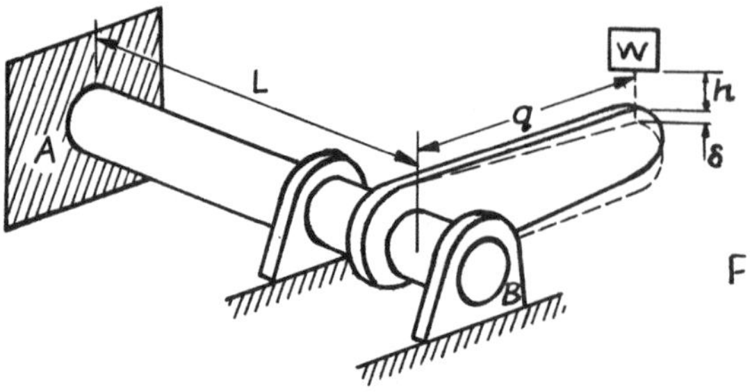

FIG.1

Solution: First method (Equivalent static load). The distance δ through which the end of the arm deflects is $q\theta$, where θ is the angle of twist in radians for the length $l = 36$ in. Also, $\theta = Tl/GJ = Pql/GJ$. Thus, $\delta = Pq^2l/GJ$.

Equating the energy supplied by the impact load W to that supplied by an equivalent static load P, $W(h + \delta) = P\delta/2$. Substituting the expression for δ into the above equation,

$$W[h + (Pq^2 l/GJ)] = P^2 q^2 l/2GJ$$

or $$P^2 - 2WP = 2WhGJ/q^2 l$$

whence

$$P^2 - 2(100)P = \frac{2 \times 100 \times 6 \times 12(10)^6 \times \pi/2}{12^2 \times 36}$$

$$= 4,370,000$$

$$P = 2190 \text{ lb}$$

This is the equivalent static load, and the equivalent static torque T = 2190 x 12 = 26,280 in-lb. The maximum shearing stress developed is:

$$S_s = \frac{Tr}{J} = \frac{26,280 \times 1}{\pi/2} = 16,700 \text{ psi}$$

and the maximum angle of twist is:

$$\Theta = \frac{Tl}{GJ} = \frac{26,280 \times 36}{12(10)^6 \times \pi/2} \times \frac{180}{\pi} = 2.88°$$

Second method (Internal energy). The internal energy for a shaft in torsion is $U = (S_s^2/4G) \times \text{Volume}$. Also, as shown above under the first method, $\delta = q\theta = qS_s l/Gr$. Equating the energy supplied by the impact load to the internal energy of the shaft,

$$W(h + \delta) = U = (S_s^2/4G) \times \text{Volume}$$

or $$W[h + (qS_s l/Gr)] = (S_s^2/4G) \times \pi r^2 l$$

Whence $$S^2 - (4Wq/\pi r^3)S_s = 4WhG/\pi r^2 l$$

$$S_s^2 - [4(100)(12)S_s/\pi] = [4(100)(6)(12 \times 10^6)/\pi(1)^2 \times 36]$$

$$S_s^2 - 1530S_s = 254,000,000 \qquad S_s = 16,700 \text{ psi}$$

$$\theta = S_s l/Gr = (16,700 \times 36/12(10)^6 \times 1) \times (180/\pi) = 2.88°$$

Third method

$$S_s = S_{st}\left[1 + \sqrt{(2h/\delta_{st}) + 1}\right]$$

In this case, $S_{st} = \frac{T_{st} r}{J} = \frac{Wqr}{J} = \frac{100 \times 12 \times 1}{\pi/2} = 765 \text{ psi}$

and $\delta_{st} = q\theta_{st} = \frac{qT_{st}l}{GJ} = \frac{12 \times 100 \times 12 \times 36}{12(10)^6 \times \pi/2}$

$= 0.0275$ in.

Thus, $S_s = 765\left[1 + \sqrt{(2 \times 6/0.0275) + 1}\right]$

$= 16{,}700$ psi

• PROBLEM 12-13

> A cantilever leaf spring 25 in. long consists of 8 leaves, each 4 in. wide and 3/8 in. thick. A 300-lb weight falls from a height of 6 in. upon the free end of the spring. $E = 30(10)^6$ psi. Determine the maximum stress and maximum deflection.

Solution: First method (Equivalent static load). The spring is considered to be equivalent to a cantilever beam of constant strength with depth constant and width varying directly as the distance from the free end. Thus

$b_m = 8 \times 4 = 32$ in.; $d = 3/8$ in.; $I_m = [32\left(\frac{3}{8}\right)^3/12] = 9/64$ in.^{4}

$$W(h + \delta) = P\delta/2$$

Since $\delta = Pl^3/2EI_m$, the above equation becomes

$$W[h + (Pl^3/2EI_m)] = P^2l^3/4\ EI_m$$

or, $P^2 - 2WP = 4WhEI_m/l^3$

Then,

$$P^2 - 2(300)P = \frac{4(300)(6)(30 \times 10^6)(\frac{9}{64})}{(25)^3} = 1{,}944{,}000$$

$$P = 1726 \text{ lb (Equivalent static load)}$$

$$S = \frac{Mc}{I} = \frac{1726 \times 25 \times \frac{3}{16}}{\frac{9}{64}} = 57{,}500 \text{ psi}$$

$$\delta = \frac{Pl^3}{2EI_m} = \frac{1726(25)^3}{2 \times 30(10)^6 \times \frac{9}{64}} = 3.20 \text{ in.}$$

Second method (Internal energy). The energy stored in a leaf spring is $U = (S^2/6E) \times$ Volume. Also, $\delta = Pl^3/2EI_m = Sl^2/2Ec$. Thus,

$$W(h + \delta) = U = (S^2/6E) \times \text{Volume}$$

$$W[h + (Sl^2/2Ec)] = (S^2/6E) \times (b_m dl/2)$$

or, $$S^2 - (12WlS/b_m d^2) = 12WhE/b_m dl$$

whence

$$S^2 - \frac{12(300)(25)S}{32\left(\frac{3}{8}\right)^2} = \frac{12(300(6)(30 \times 10^6)}{32 \times \frac{3}{8} \times 25}$$

$$S^2 - 20{,}000S = 21.6(10)^8$$

$$S = 57{,}500 \text{ psi}$$

$$\delta = \frac{Sl^2}{2Ec} = \frac{57{,}500(25)^2}{2(30 \times 10^5)\left(\frac{3}{16}\right)} = 3.20 \text{ in.}$$

Third method

$$S = S_{st}\left[1 + \sqrt{(2h/\delta_{st}) + 1}\right]$$

In this case,

$$S_{st} = \frac{Wlc}{I_m} = \frac{300 \times 25 \times \frac{3}{16}}{\frac{9}{64}} = 10{,}000 \text{ psi}$$

and $$\delta_{st} = \frac{Wl^3}{2EI_m} = \frac{300(25)^3}{2(30 \times 10^6)\left(\frac{9}{64}\right)} = 0.555 \text{ in.}$$

hence $$S = 10{,}000\left[1 + \sqrt{(2 \times 6/0.555) + 1}\right] = 57{,}500 \text{ psi}$$

• PROBLEM 12-14

Fig. 1 shows two bolts with square threads; they have the same dimensions except that one has the shank turned down to a diameter equal to that at the root of the threads for a length of 10 in. If both bolts are made of steel with a tensile proportional limit of 32,000 lb. per sq. in., find the axial static load and the axial energy load that each bolt will resist when stressed to the proportional limit. Neglect the effect of localized stresses at the root of the threads.

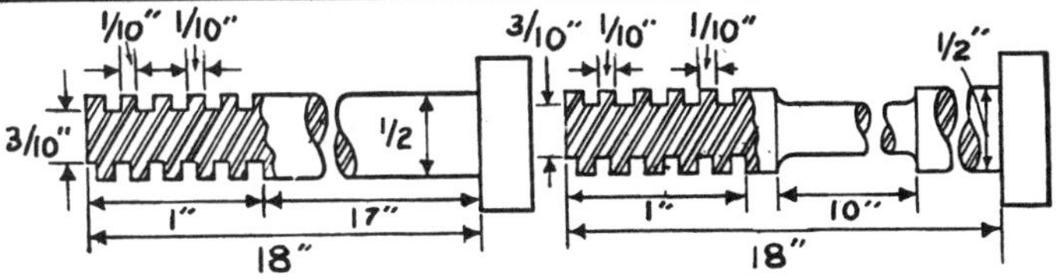

FIG. 1 (a) (b)

Solution: Static Loads. The static loads P that the two bolts can resist are equal since the least cross-sectional areas are equal. Thus,

$$P = as = \frac{\pi(0.3)^2}{4} 32{,}000 = 2265 \text{ lb.}$$

Energy Loads. The cross-sectional area a_1 of each bolt at the root of the threads is 0.0706 sq. in., and area a_2 of the shank is 0.1963 sq. in. Hence when the unit stress s_1 in the first inch of the bolt (the threads are neglected) is 32,000 lb. per sq. in., the unit stress s_2 in the shank of the bolt is only

$$\frac{0.0706}{0.1963} \times 32{,}000 = 11{,}520 \text{ lb. per sq. in.}$$

Therefore, the energy load U that can be absorbed by the bolt in Fig. 1a when it is stressed to 32,000 lb. per sq. in. is

$$U = \frac{1}{2}\frac{s_1^2}{E} a_1 l_1 + \frac{1}{2}\frac{s_2^2}{E} a_2 l_2$$

$$= \frac{1}{2}\frac{(32{,}000)^2}{30{,}000{,}000} 0.0706 \times 1 + \frac{1}{2}\frac{(11{,}520)^2}{30{,}000{,}000}$$

$$\times 0.1963 \times 17$$

$$= 1.21 + 7.38 = 8.59 \text{ in.-lb. or } 0.715 \text{ ft.-lb.}$$

Likewise, the maximum energy load that can be applied to the bolt in Fig. 1b without causing a stress greater than the proportional limit is

$$U = \frac{1}{2}\frac{s_1^2}{E} a_1 l_1 + \frac{1}{2}\frac{s_2^2}{E} a_2 l_2$$

$$= \frac{1}{2}\frac{(32{,}000)^2}{30{,}000{,}000} 0.0706 \times 11 + \frac{1}{2}\frac{(11{,}520)^2}{30{,}000{,}000} 0.1963 \times 7$$

$$= 13.3 + 3.05 = 16.4 \text{ in.-lb. or } 1.36 \text{ ft.-lb.}$$

Therefore, a body weighing only 0.715 lb. falling a distance of only 1 ft. would supply enough energy to the bolt in Fig. 1a to stress it to the proportional limit provided that all the energy were absorbed by the bolt, whereas a body weighing 2265 lb. would be required to cause the same stress if its weight were gradually applied to the bolt. Further, turning down the shank of the bolt as shown in Fig. 1b nearly doubles the energy resistance of the bolt without affecting its static resistance.

The results found in this problem further emphasize the importance of a uniform distribution of stress throughout a body that is required to resist energy loads. The results also indicate the energy loads would be extremely serious if the energy did not distribute itself throughout the whole structure or machine.

ANALYSIS WITH MOVING LOADING

• **PROBLEM 12-15**

Determine the maximum bending moment and the maximum shearing force set up by a truck with axle loads A, B, C, as shown in Fig. 1a when passing over a freely supported span, 22 ft long.

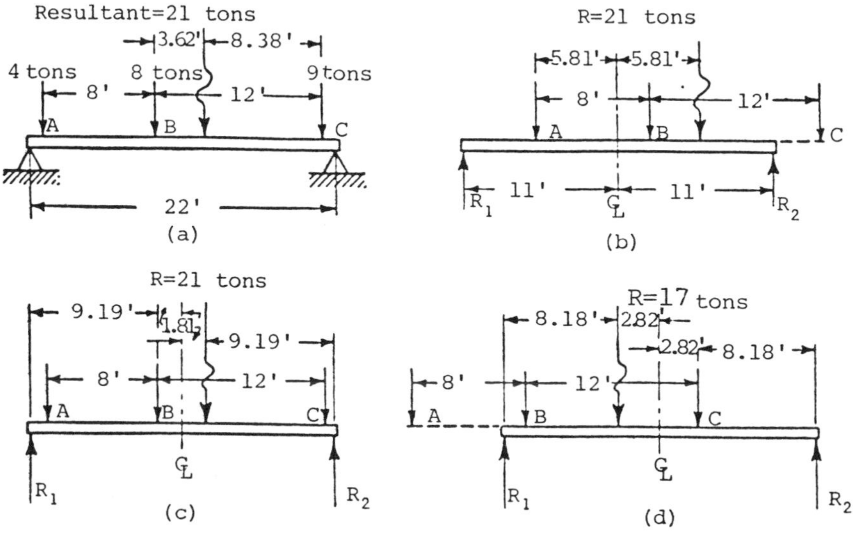

Fig. 1.

Solution: Determination of the Maximum Bending Moment.--All three axle loads on span. The resultant of loads A, B, and C is 21 tons located to the right of B a distance

$$\bar{x} = \frac{9 \times 12 - 4 \times 8}{21} = 3.62 \text{ ft.}$$

Bending Moment may be a Maximum under A when bisector of distance (11.62 ft) between A and the resultant of A, B, and C coincides with center of span. This requirement, however, moves wheel C off the span (Fig. 1b) which is contrary to our assumption.

Bending Moment may be a Maximum under B when the loads are placed as shown in Fig. 1c in accordance with the Rule for location of maximum bending moment. All three wheels are on the span which agrees with assumption made. The reaction R_1 may most easily be determined by equating the moments of R_1 and of the resultant R about the right end of the beam; $22R_1 = 9.19(21)$ and hence $R_1 = 8.78$ tons. The bending moment at B is obtained by summing the moments with respect to B of all forces to the left of B; $M_B = 8.78(9.19) - 4(8) = 48.7$ ft tons.

The condition for the Bending Moment to be a Maximum

under C puts wheel A off the span, which is contrary to our assumption that all three loads are on the span; but this circumstance indicates the likelihood of a maximum bending moment under C when calculated for loads B and C only on the span.

Axle loads B and C only on span. The resultant of B and C = 17 tons, located at (9/17)12 = 6.35 ft to the right of B or 5.65 ft to the left of C.

Bending Moment may be a Maximum under C when the loads are placed as shown in Fig. 1d. A is off the span which is compatible with the assumption made. Here R_2 = (8.18/22)17 = 6.32 tons and M_C = (6.32)(8.18) = 51.7 ft tons.

Bending Moment may be a Maximum under B. Investigation shows that this may occur with loads B and C only on the span and M_B = 47.2 ft tons.

Axle loads A and B only on span. The procedure is the same as above. One finds M_A = 37.9 ft tons and M_B = 51.0 ft tons.

Axle load C at center of span, both A and B coming off, gives M_C = Pl/4 = 49 1/2 ft tons.

The greatest bending moment is therefore M_C = 51.7 ft tons for the case where B and C only are on span.

Determination of the Maximum Shearing Force.--The maximum reaction for any group of loads on a span, and thus the maximum shearing force, occurs either when the left-hand load is over the left-hand support or when the right-hand load is over the right-hand support. Of these two choices, that where the resultant of the group of loads is nearer to the near support will give the greater reaction.

Consider first the group A, B, C. Referring to Fig. 1a, the end load C is nearer the resultant than the end load A so the maximum reaction for this group occurs when C is at R_2; then $22R_2$ = (22 - 8.38)(21) and R_2 = 13 tons.

Other groups must also be considered. The resultant of loads B and C has been found to be 17 tons, 6.35 ft from B and 5.65 ft from C. Although load C is nearer the resultant, it is found that with C over R_2, load A is on the span contrary to our assumption. With load B just to the right of R_1, $22R_1$ = (22 - 6.35)(17) and R_1 = 12.1 tons.

The group A, B need not be considered because the total resultant load of 12 tons is less than the reaction R_2 = 13 tons found above. Load C alone, acting just to the right of R_1, produces a reaction R_1 = 9 tons.

Hence the greatest reaction, and thus the maximum shearing force, is that of 13 tons found in the first case.

The beam of Fig. 1 is subject to a movable uniform load of one kip per ft and a moving concentrated load of 4 kips. Use influence lines to determine (a) maximum downward reaction at point D; (b) maximum bending moment at point C; and (c) maximum shear at point C.

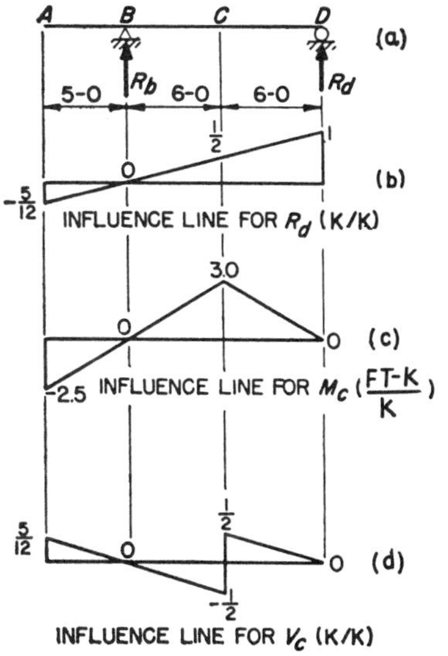

FIG. 1

Solution: To obtain the influence line for R_d, values of R_d must be computed for various positions of a one-kip downward load. For example, if one kip is placed at D, the reaction R_d will be one kip upward, or + 1. If the one-kip load is at point C, the reaction at D is one-half kip upward, or $+\frac{1}{2}$ If the one-kip load is at A, the reaction at D will be $\frac{5}{12}$ kip downward, or $-\frac{5}{12}$. A load at B will cause zero reaction at D. These values of the reaction at D are plotted beneath the position of the unit load which would cause them. The resulting influence line for the reaction at D is shown in Fig. 1(b).

The influence line for R_d shows that downward (negative) values of R_d are caused by loads placed anywhere between points A and B. (Loads between B and D would cause upward reactions at D.) Therefore, to obtain the maximum downard reaction, the 4-kip concentrated load will be placed at A, and uniform load will be placed from A to B only.

The following two rules can be used to obtain the maximum downward reaction.

(1) The amount of a function due to a concentrated load equals the product of the load and the influence ordinate beneath the load.

(2) The amount of a function due to a uniform load equals the load per unit length times the area under the influence line. (If the uniform load does not extend over the full length of the member, use the area under the loaded portions only.)

Applying these two rules,

$$R_d = \left(4 \times \frac{-5}{12}\right) + \left(1 \times \frac{1}{2} \times \frac{-5}{12} \times 5\right)$$

$$= -2.71 \text{ kips, or } 2.71 \text{ kips downward}$$

The influence line for bending moment at point C is computed next. If a unit load is at C, the reaction R_d is $\frac{1}{2}$ kip upward, and M_c is $\frac{1}{2} \times 6$, or 3 ft-kips. If a unit load is at A, R_d is $\frac{5}{12}$ kip downward, and M_c is $-\frac{5}{12} \times 6$, or -2.5 ft-kips. Loads at B or D will cause zero bending moment at C. Plotting these points gives the influence line of Fig. 1(c).

CHAPTER 13

STRUCTURAL ANALYSIS

STATICALLY DETERMINANT TRUSSES

• PROBLEM 13-1

a) In the pin-jointed truss of Fig. 1 calculate the bar forces and the joint displacements.
b) If the truss is made of material for which the stress-strain equation is

$$\varepsilon = 6 \times 10^{-5}(\pm\ 0.04\sigma^2 + \sigma)$$

(the + and - referring to tension and compression respectively, and σ being measured in ksi), find the joint displacements.

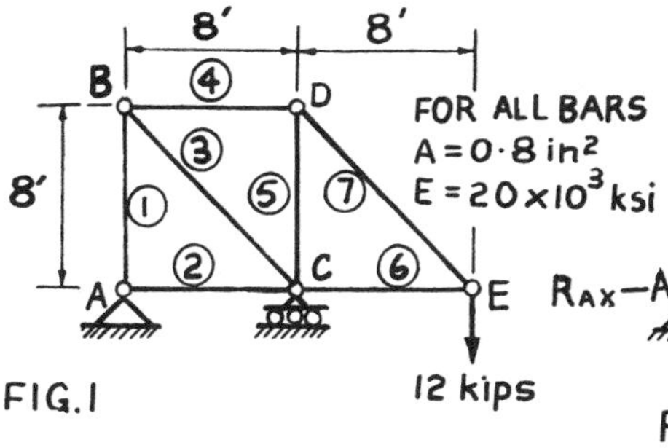

FIG. 1

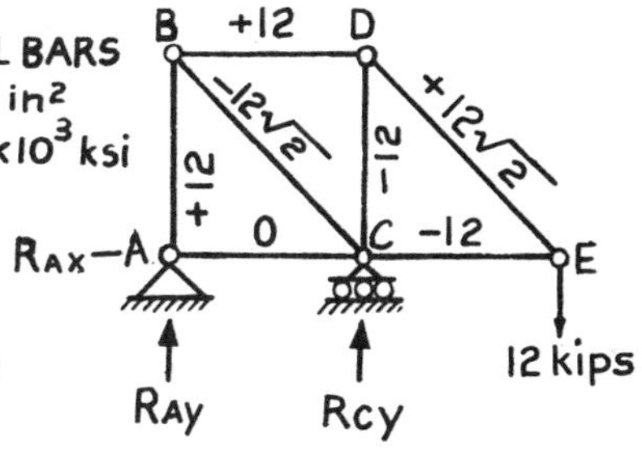

FIG. 2

Solution: a) For convenience the bars are numbered and the joints are lettered. (Fig. 1).

By the method of joint equilibrium the bar forces can be determined. The equilibrium relations for the whole structure are

$$\Sigma F_y = 0\ ,\ -R_{Ay} - R_{Cy} + 12 = 0$$

or,

$$R_{Ay} + R_{Cy} = 12$$

$$\Sigma M_A = 0\ ,\ 8R_{Cy} - 16 \times 12 = 0$$

or,

$$R_{Cy} = 24$$

Hence $$R_{Ay} = -12$$

Now consider joint A. The equilibrium equations are

$$\Sigma F_x = 0 , \quad F_{AC} = 0$$

$$\Sigma F_y = 0 , \quad -R_{Ay} + F_{AB} = 0$$

Hence,

$$F_{AB} = 12$$

Similarly, the forces in other bars can be determined. These are shown in Fig. 2.

Since the bars are uniform and the material is linearly elastic, the extension of any bar is given by $e = NL/EA$. The values are computed in Table 1.

Table 1

Bar	L(in)	N(kips)	$e = \frac{NL}{EA}$
1	96	12	0.072
2	96	0	0.0
3	$96\sqrt{2}$	$-12\sqrt{2}$	-0.144
4	96	12	0.072
5	96	-12	-0.072
6	96	-12	-0.072
7	$96\sqrt{2}$	$12\sqrt{2}$	0.144

The joint displacements are now found.

Joint A $\quad u_A = 0$ (given)

$v_A = 0$ (given)

Joint C $\quad u_C = u_A + e_2 = 0$

$v_C = 0$ (given)

Knowing the locations of A and C we can find the position of B.

Joint B $\quad v_B = e_1 = +0.072$ in

$$e_3 = \frac{-u_B}{\sqrt{2}} + \frac{v_B}{\sqrt{2}} + \frac{u_C}{\sqrt{2}}$$

$$\therefore \; u_B = -\sqrt{2}e_3 + v_B + u_C = 0.204 + 0.072 + 0 = 0.276 \text{ in}$$

From B and C, D can be found.

Joint D $\quad e_4 = u_D - u_B$

$$\therefore \; u_D = e_4 + u_B = 0.072 + 0.276 = 0.348 \text{ in}$$

$$e_5 = v_D - v_C$$

whence

$$v_D = -0.072 \text{ in}$$

Joint E $\quad e_6 = u_E - u_C$

whence

$$u_E = -0.072 \text{ in}$$

Using equation

$$e = (u_B \cos\theta + v_B \sin\theta) - (u_A \cos\theta - v_A \sin\theta)$$

the extension of bar DE is given by

$$e_7 = \left(\frac{u_E}{\sqrt{2}} - \frac{v_E}{\sqrt{2}}\right) - \left(\frac{u_D}{\sqrt{2}} - \frac{v_D}{\sqrt{2}}\right)$$

whence

$$v_E = -\sqrt{2}e_7 + u_E - u_D + v_D = -0.696 \text{ in}$$

b) The bar extensions are determined from equation

$$\varepsilon = 6 \times 10^{-5}(\pm\, 0.04\sigma^2 + \sigma)$$

Table 2

Bar	N	$\sigma = N/A$ (ksi)	ε	L (in)	$e (= \varepsilon L)$
1	12	15	144×10^{-5}	96	0.138
2	0	0.0	0	96	0.0
3	$-12\sqrt{2}$	$-15\sqrt{2}$	-235.3×10^{-5}	$96\sqrt{2}$	-0.320
4	12	15	144×10^{-5}	96	0.138
5	-12	-15	-144×10^{-5}	96	-0.138
6	-12	-15	-144×10^{-5}	96	-0.138
7	$12\sqrt{2}$	$15\sqrt{2}$	235.3×10^{-5}	$96\sqrt{2}$	0.320

The joint displacements are obtained from the bar extensions by the principles of geometry. The expressions obtained in part a) are therefore still valid.

Joint A $\begin{cases} u_A = 0 \text{ (given)} \\ v_A = 0 \text{ (given)} \end{cases}$

Joint C $\begin{cases} u_C = u_A + e_2 = 0 \\ v_C = 0 \text{ (given)} \end{cases}$

Joint B $\begin{cases} v_B = e_1 = 0.138 \text{ in} \\ u_B = -\sqrt{2}e_3 + v_B + u_C = 0.590 \text{ in} \end{cases}$

Joint D $\begin{cases} u_D = e_4 + u_B = 0.728 \text{ in} \\ v_D = e_5 + v_C = -0.138 \text{ in} \end{cases}$

Joint E $\begin{cases} u_E = e_6 + u_C = -0.138 \text{ in} \\ v_E = -\sqrt{2}e_7 + u_E - u_D + v_D = -1.456 \text{ in} \end{cases}$

• PROBLEM 13-2

Consider a pin jointed truss of Fig. 1. Find the vertical and horizontal displacements of joint E by method of virtual forces.

Solution: To find v_E we apply a unit force in the positive v_E direction (Fig. 2 (a)) and compute the corresponding member forces by using the method of joint equilibrium. Fig. 2(a) indicates what

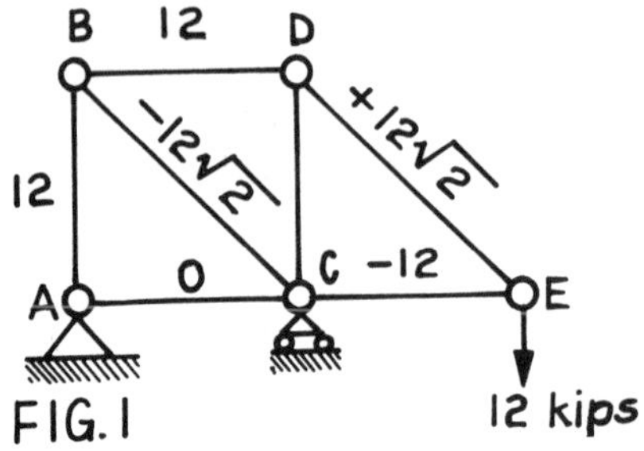

FIG.1

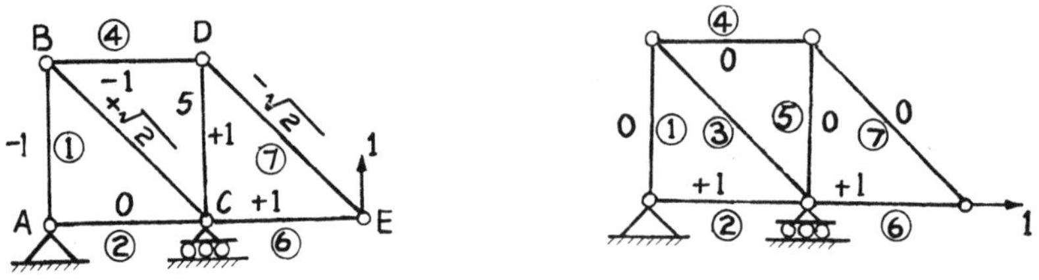

(a) FIG. 2 (b)

we have called the stage 1 forces. In this problem they are virtual forces. The bar forces can be denoted by $n_1 \ldots n_7$.

Suppose that during stage 2 (the real stage in this case) bar 3 undergoes an extension of e_3. The consequent displacement v_E will be $\sqrt{2}e_3$ since n_3 is $\sqrt{2}$.

In the present problem, stage 2 consists of loading the frame with the 12 kip load at E. The bar forces due to the real force can be calculated by using the method of joint equilibrium. Then using equation $e = NL/EA$, the extension can be computed. The values are computed in Table 1.

Table 1

Bar	L (in)	N (kips)	e = NL/EA
1	96	12	0.072
2	96	0	0.0
3	$96\sqrt{2}$	$-12\sqrt{2}$	-0.144
4	96	12	0.072
5	96	-12	-0.072
6	96	-12	-0.072
7	$96\sqrt{2}$	$12\sqrt{2}$	0.144

The internal work done by the virtual n forces during the real deformation e is

$$U_i = n_1e_1 + n_2e_2 + n_3e_3 + n_4e_4 + n_5e_5 + n_6e_6 + n_7e_7$$

$$= -1(0.072) + 0 + \sqrt{2}(-0.144) - 1(0.072) + 1(-0.072) + 1(-0.072)$$

$$- \sqrt{2}(0.144)$$

$$= -0.696$$

The units of U_i are inches and whatever force units we imagine the virtual forces to be measured in.

Since the supports do not move, the total external work done is

$$U_e = 1 \times v_e$$

Hence from the work equation $U_e = U_i$

$$1 \cdot v_e = -0.696 \qquad (1)$$

$$\therefore\ v_E = -0.696 \text{ in}$$

A non-unit virtual force δW at E would simply have caused both sides of equation (1) to be multiplied by δW. Such a procedure is sometimes convenient to simplify the arithmetic in computing the internal virtual force system.

To find the horizontal displacement of E, a unit force is applied in the positive u_E direction, and the corresponding internal forces can be calculated by using the method of joint equilibrium (or any other statical method). These internal forces are shown in Fig. 2(b).

Now,

$$U_e = U_i$$

$$1 \times u_E = 1(e_2) + 1(e_5)$$
$$= 0 - 0.072$$
$$u_E = -0.072 \text{ in}$$

• PROBLEM 13-3

In the frame of Fig. 1 (a) find the force in bar DF and the reaction at G due to the external loads. Use the method of virtual displacements.

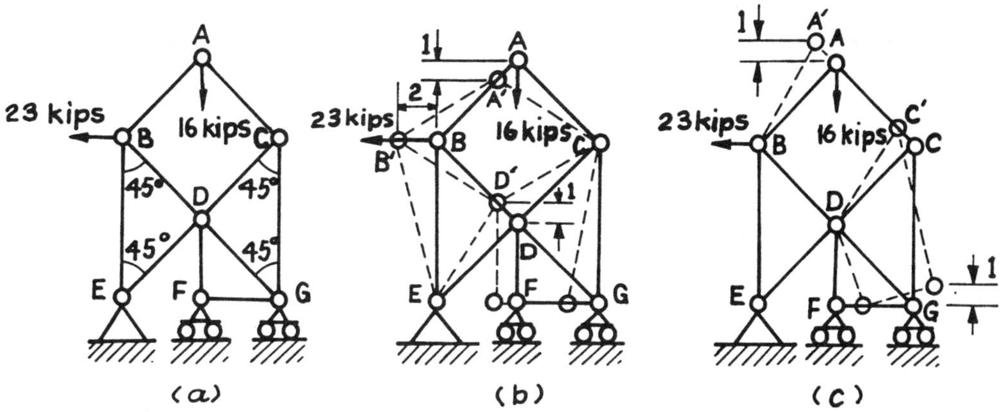

FIG. 1

Solution: Apply the real force system.

To find N_{DF} give member DF a unit extension (1 mm for instance), and calculate by geometry u_B and v_A (Fig. 1(b)). Now D moves vertically upwards by 1 mm and since it must move normally to ED, then D must also move horizontally by 1 mm. Triangle BED rotates about E, and B therefore moves by 2 mm. Since neither B nor C moves vertically, the upward displacement of D must be accompanied by a corresponding downward displacement of A.

Thus

$$U_i = N_{DF} \times 1 \qquad U_e = 23 \times 2 + 16 \times 1 = 62$$

since

$$U_i = U_e,$$

$$N_{DF} \times 1 = 62$$

Hence

$$N_{DF} = +62 \text{ kips}$$

To find the reaction at G we displace G vertically by unit distance (Fig. 1 (c)). To preserve compatibility this must cause a rigid body rotation of section CDFG about D, so that CA moves in the direction of its length. Since GC and CA do not vary in length, joints G, C and A all move vertically by the same amount.

Hence,

$$U_e = R_G \times 1 - 16 \times 1 + 23 \times 0 \quad \text{and} \quad U_i = 0$$

since

$$U_e = U_i$$

$$R_G \times 1 - 16 \times 1 = 0$$

or

$$R_G = 16 \text{ kips}$$

STATICALLY INDETERMINATE STRUCTURES-FORCE METHOD

• PROBLEM 13-4

Find the bar forces in the structure of Fig. 1(a) and the vertical displacement of joint A. The cross-sectional area of each bar is 0.5 in^2 and the material is linearly elastic with $E = 20 \times 10^3$ ksi.

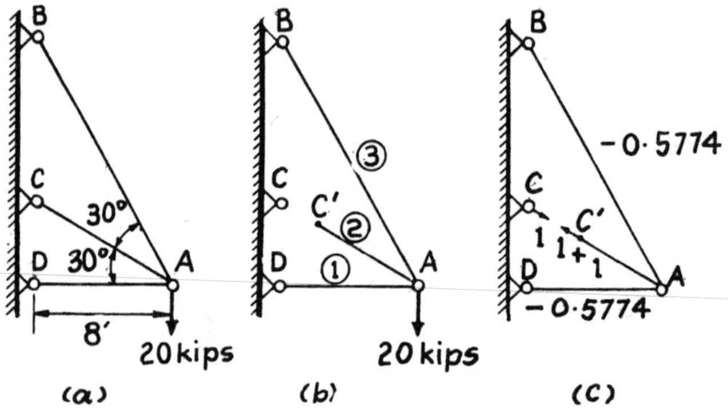

FIG. I

Solution: a) Bar forces. There are two equilibrium equations (for joint A) and three bar forces. Hence we must choose one unknown. Take the force in AC as the unknown, and call it R (for redundant force).

A convenient device is to imagine the bar AC to be detached from joint C while the 20 kip load is applied (Fig. 1(b)). Using equilibrium conditions, we obtain the following equations.

$$20 - AB \sin 60 = 0$$

$$-AD - AB \cos 60 = 0$$

or

$$.866\ AB = 20$$

$$AD + .5\ AB = 0$$

Solving these equations yields,

$$AB = 23.095 \approx 23.1 \text{ kips}$$

$$AD = -11.55 \text{ kips} .$$

A unit value of the redundant force R is now applied in the form of a pair of forces between C and the detached member end C' (Fig. 1 (c)). Then,

$$- R \sin 30 - AB \sin 60 = 0$$

$$-R \cos 30 - AD - AB \cos 60 = 0$$

or

$$-0.5 - .866\ AB = 0$$

$$- .8666 - AD - .5\ AB = 0$$

Solving these equations, one obtains,

$$AB = - .5774$$
$$AD = - .5774$$

With the 20 kip load and the unknown force R, the total bar forces are then

$$AD = N_1 = -11.55 - 0.5774\ R$$

$$AC = N_2 = 0 + R \qquad (1)$$

$$AB = N_3 = 23.1 - 0.5774\ R$$

All we have done up to now is to use the two equations of equilibrium to express the three bar forces in terms of a single unknown which we have called R. This force will be determined from the fact that in the real structure the gap CC' must be zero. Hence we must now find the value of this gap and equate it to zero.

(b) Bar deformations

With a Hookean material it is convenient to evaluate first the bar flexibility coefficients, the extension caused by unit load.

$$f_1 = \frac{L_1 P}{E_1 A_1} = \frac{96}{20 \times 10^3 \times 0.5} = 0.0096 \text{ in/kip}$$

$$f_2 = \frac{L_2 P}{E_2 A_2} = \frac{96/\cos 30^\circ}{20 \times 10^3 \times 0.5} = 0.0111 \text{ in/kip}$$

$$f_3 = \frac{L_3 P}{E_3 A_3} = \frac{96/\cos 60^\circ}{20 \times 10^3 \times 0.5} = 0.0192 \text{ in/kip}$$

Then

$$e_1 = f_1 N_1 = 0.0096(-11.55 - 0.5774R) = -0.111-0.0055R$$

$$e_2 = f_2 N_2 = 0.0111(R) = 0.0111R \qquad (2)$$

$$e_3 = f_3 N_3 = 0.0192(23.10 - 0.5774R) = 0.444 - 0.0111R$$

(c) Compatibility

To find the displacement of C' relative to C we may use the force system of Fig. 1(c) as a convenient virtual force system. This shows that

$$CC' = -0.5774e_1 + 1.0e_2 - 0.5774e_3$$

Hence the bar deformations will be compatible provided

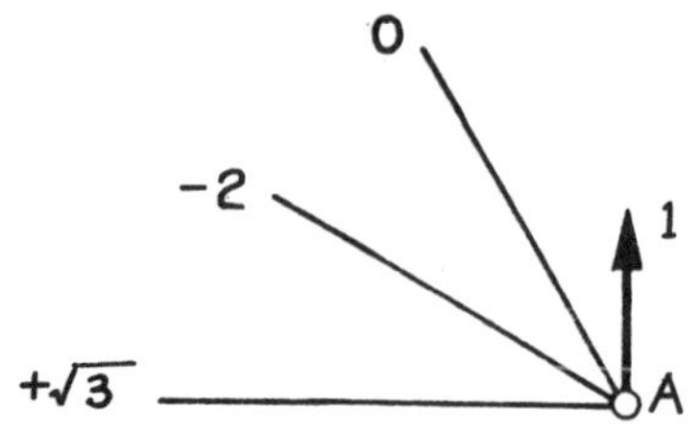

FIG. 2

$$-0.5774(-0.111-0.0055R) + 1.0(0.0111R)-0.5774(0.444 - 0.0111R) = 0$$

$$-0.1929 + 0.0207R = 0$$

$$R = +9.30 \text{ kips}$$

(d) Bar forces

From equations (1) we now have the bar forces

$$AD = -11.55 - 0.5774(9.3) = -16.91 \text{ kips}$$

$$AC = 9.3 \text{ kips}$$

$$AB = 23.1 - 0.5774(9.3) = +17.74 \text{ kips.}$$

(e) Bar deformations

From equations (2) the bar deformations are

$$e_1 = -0.163 \text{ in}; \; e_2 = +0.103 \text{ in}; \; e_3 = +0.341 \text{ in}$$

(f) Joint displacements

The two displacements of joint A can now be found by geometry. Obviously

$$u_A = e_1 = -0.163 \text{ in.}$$

To find v_A a virtual force system is useful. We apply a unit vertical force at A, and any set of bar forces which make equilibrium with the vertical force. The forces shown in Fig. 2 will serve. Then

$$v_A = +\sqrt{3}e_1 - 2e_2 + 0e_3$$

$$= +\sqrt{3}(-.163) - 2(.103) + 0$$

$$= -0.488 \text{ in.}$$

A different choice of virtual forces would produce the same result because the e values are compatible. The only requirement of the virtual force system is that it shall be in equilibrium.

• PROBLEM 13-5

Fig. 1 shows a rigid beam GJH supported by three bars, whose cross sections and spacing are as indicated. A load of 150 kips is attached to the mid-point of the beam.

For the stress range of this problem, bars 1 and 2 are Hookean with $E_1 = 20 \times 10^3$ ksi and $E_2 = 12 \times 10^3$ ksi. For bar 3, the stress-strain law is a straight line with a slope of 10×10^3 ksi up to a stress of 7 ksi and above this stress it is another straight line with half this slope. The equation of the second line is therefore $\sigma = 5 \times 10^3 e + 3.5$ provided that σ is in ksi.

Find the force in each bar.

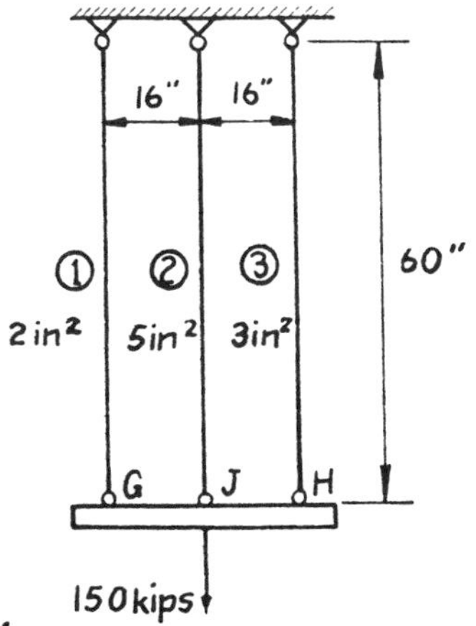

FIG. 1

Solution: The rigidity of beam GJH implies a relationship among the bar deformations. Hence the assembly is statically indeterminate. Since there are three bar forces and two equilibrium equations for beam GJH ($\Sigma Y = 0$ and $\Sigma M = 0$) we must choose one force as an unknown. Any bar force will do.

(a) Bar forces

Let

$$N_2 = R$$

Then $\Sigma Y = 0$ gives

$$N_1 + R + N_3 = 150$$

$\Sigma M = 0$ gives

$$N_1 = N_3$$

$$\therefore N_1 = N_3 = \frac{150 - R}{2}$$

(b) Bar deformations

$$e_1 = \frac{N_1 L_1}{E_1 A_1}$$

$$e_1 = \left(\frac{150 - R}{2}\right)\frac{60}{20 \times 10^3 \times 2} = 7.5 \times 10^{-4}(150 - R)$$

$$e_2 = \frac{N_2 L_2}{E_2 A_2}$$

$$e_2 = (R)\frac{60}{12 \times 10^3 \times 5} = 10 \times 10^{-4}(R)$$

For bar 3, assume that the stress exceeds 7 ksi. Then

$$\sigma_3 = N_3/A_3$$

$$\sigma_3 = \frac{150 - R}{2} \times \frac{1}{3}$$

The equation of the second line is

$$\sigma = 5 \times 10^3 \epsilon + 3.5.$$

Hence,

$$\epsilon_3 = (\sigma_3 - 3.5)/5 \times 10^3$$

$$= \left(\frac{150 - R}{6} - 3.5\right) / 5 \times 10^3$$

$$= \frac{129 - R}{30 \times 10^3}$$

Now,

$$e_3 = L_3 \epsilon_3$$

$$e_3 = 60\epsilon_3 = 20 \times 10^{-4}(129 - R)$$

(c) Compatibility

Since GJH remains straight

$$e_2 = \frac{e_1 + e_3}{2}$$

$$2 \times 10 \times 10^{-4} R = 7.5 \times 10^{-4}(150 - R) + 20 \times 10^{-4}(129 - R)$$

and solving for R gives

$$R = 78 \text{ kips} .$$

Hence

$$N_1 = 36 \text{ kips; } N_2 = 78 \text{ kips; } N_3 = 36 \text{ kips}$$

Since the area of bar 3 is 3 sq. in., the stress in this bar is 12 ksi and therefore the assumption that $\sigma_3 > 7$ was correct.

• PROBLEM 13-6

A bar of aluminium, 2 in² in cross-section, and a bar of copper, 1.5 in² in cross-section, are rigidly connected at their ends (Fig. 1(a)). The compound bar is subjected to a compressive force of 30,000 lb. applied in such a way that the bars remain straight. The elastic moduli for aluminium and copper are $E_A = 10 \times 10^6$ psi and $E_C = 16 \times 10^6$ psi.

Find the force in each bar.

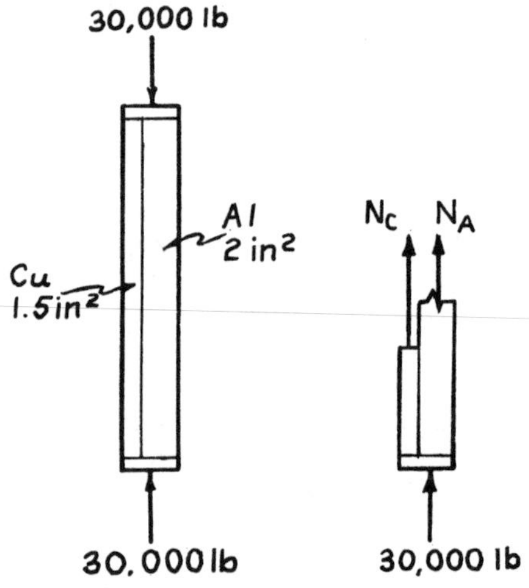

FIG. 1 (a) (b)

Solution: Expressing the bar forces in terms of the force in the aluminium (= R) we have

$$N_A = R$$

The bar forces are assumed to be tensile, and equilibrium (Fig. 1 (b)) then gives $30{,}000 + N_A + N_C = 0$. Hence

$$N_C = -30{,}000 - R$$

The bar flexibilities are

$$f_A = \frac{L}{E_A A_A} = \frac{L}{10 \times 10^6 \times 2} = \frac{L}{20 \times 10^6} \text{ in/lb.,}$$

$$f_C = \frac{L}{E_C A_C} = \frac{L}{16 \times 10^6 \times 1.5} = \frac{L}{24 \times 10^6} \text{ in/lb.}$$

Since

$$e_A = e_C \text{ (for compatibility)}$$

then

$$f_A N_A = f_C N_C$$

$$\frac{L}{20 \times 10^6}(R) = \frac{L}{24 \times 10^6}(-30{,}000 - R)$$

$$R = -13{,}667 \text{ lb.}$$

Thus

$$N_A = -13{,}667 \text{ lb. and } N_C = -16{,}333 \text{ lb.}$$

• PROBLEM 13-7

In the structure of Fig. 1 the properties of the two bars are:

$$L_1 = 60 \text{ in.} \qquad L_2 = 72 \text{ in.}$$

$$A_1 = 1.0 \text{ in}^2 \qquad A_2 = 1.2 \text{ in}^2$$

$$E_1 = 30 \times 10^3 \text{ ksi} \qquad E_2 = 15 \times 10^3 \text{ ksi}$$

Find the location of the 50 kip load so that the beam GH remains horizontal, and find the force in each bar.

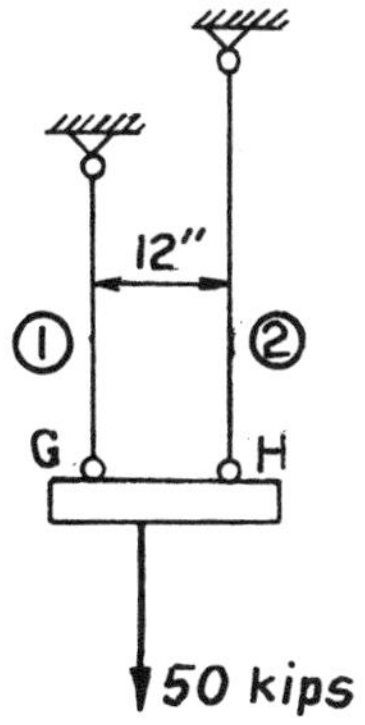

FIG. 1

Solution: Regard the force in bar 1 as the unknown force R. Then,

$$N_1 = R \text{ and } N_2 = 50 - R .$$

The flexibility coefficients are

$$f_1 = \frac{L_1}{E_1 A_1} = 2 \times 10^{-3} \text{ in/kip and } f_2 = \frac{L_2}{E_2 A_2} = 4 \times 10^{-3} \text{ in/kip}$$

The extensions of the bars must be equal, i.e.,

$$f_1 N_1 = f_2 N_2$$

$$2 \times 10^{-3} R = 4 \times 10^{-3}(50 - R)$$

hence

$$R = 33.33 \text{ kips}$$

Thus

$$N_1 = 33.33 \text{ kips} \quad \text{and} \quad N_2 = 16.67 \text{ kips}$$

It would have been sufficient to notice that bar 2 is twice as flexible as bar 1 and hence carries only half as much load.

From the rotational equilibrium of bar GH we see that the 50 kip load must be 4 in. from G.

• PROBLEM 13-8

Three bars are placed end to end (Fig. 1) and overall longitudinal deformation is prevented by rigid end supports. The lengths and areas of the bars are given in Fig. 1. The coefficients of linear thermal expansion are

$$\alpha_1 = 6 \times 10^{-6}, \quad \alpha_2 = 12 \times 10^{-6} \quad \text{and} \quad \alpha_3 = 16 \times 10^{-6} \text{ per } ^\circ\text{F}.$$

For the stress range of this problem $E_1 = 15 \times 10^6$, $E_2 = 30 \times 10^6$ and $E_3 = 10 \times 10^6$ psi.

Find the stress induced in each bar by a fall in temperature of 50°F. Find also the movement of points B and C.

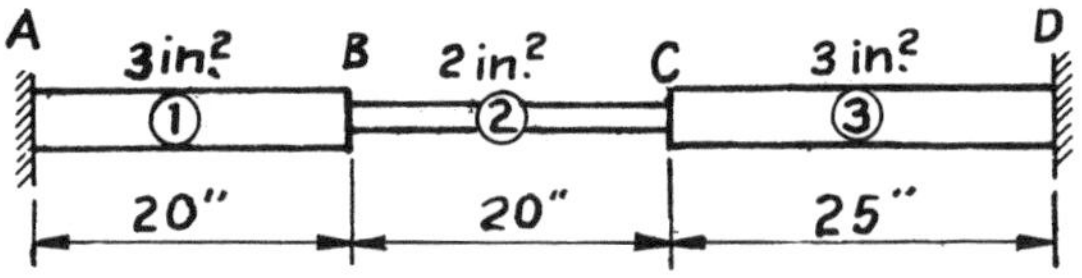

FIG.1

Solution: In this problem, equilibrium of the junctions B and C requires that

$$N_1 = N_2 = N_3 = N(\text{say})$$

The bar flexibility coefficients are

$$f_1 = \frac{L_1}{E_1 A_1} = \frac{20}{15 \times 10^6 \times 3} = 0.444 \times 10^{-6} \text{ in/lb.}$$

$$f_2 = \frac{L_2}{E_2 A_2} = \frac{20}{30 \times 10^6 \times 2} = 0.333 \times 10^{-6} \text{ in/lb.}$$

$$f_3 = \frac{L_3}{E_3 A_3} = \frac{25}{10 \times 10^6 \times 3} = 0.833 \times 10^{-6} \text{ in/lb.}$$

The total deformations are

$$\left.\begin{aligned} e_1 &= f_1 N_1 + \alpha_1 T L_1 = 0.444 \times 10^{-6} N + 6 \times 10^{-6}(-50)20 \\ e_2 &= f_2 N_2 + \alpha_2 T L_2 = 0.333 \times 10^{-6} N + 12 \times 10^{-6}(-50)20 \\ e_3 &= f_3 N_3 + \alpha_3 T L_3 = 0.833 \times 10^{-6} N + 16 \times 10^{-6}(-50)25 \end{aligned}\right\} \quad (1)$$

For compatibility the sum of the three extensions must be zero.

$$e_1 + e_2 + e_3 = 0$$

Substitution from equations (1) gives

$$[.444N + .333N + .833N] \times 10^{-6} + [6 \times 20 + 12 \times 20 + 16 \times 25]10^{-6}(-50)$$
$$= 0$$

or

$$1.611N - 38,000 = 0$$

Hence

$$N = 23,586 \text{ lb.}$$

i.e.,

$$N_1 = N_2 = N_3 = 23,586 \text{ lb.}$$

The stresses are

$$\sigma_1 = \frac{N_1}{A_1} = \frac{23,586}{3} = 7862 \text{ psi}$$

$$\sigma_2 = \frac{N_2}{A_2} = \frac{23,586}{2} = 11,793 \text{ psi}$$

$$\sigma_3 = \frac{N_3}{A_3} = \frac{23,586}{3} = 7862 \text{ psi}$$

To find the movements of B and C we require the deformations of bars 1 and 3. From equation (1),

$$e_1 = -e_2 - e_3$$
$$= [-.333 - .833]10^{-6}(23,586) - [12 \times 20 + 16 \times 25]10^{-6}(-50)$$
$$= [-27501.28 + 32,000] \times 10^{-6}$$
$$= 0.004498 \text{ in.}$$

so that point B moves +0.0045 in.

Again

$$e_3 = -e_1 - e_2$$
$$= [-0.444 - 0.333]10^{6}(23,586) - [120 + 240]10^{-6}(-50)$$
$$= [-18326.32 + 18,000] \times 10^{-6}$$
$$= -0.00033 \text{ in.}$$

so that point C moves +0.00034 in.

• PROBLEM 13-9

The material from which the truss of Fig. 1 is constructed has a stress-strain equation

$$\epsilon = 6 \times 10^{-5}(\pm 0.04\sigma^2 + \sigma)$$

while the stresses are increasing, the + and - signs referring to tension and compression respectively. The cross-sectional area of each bar is 0.5 in². Find the residual bar forces and joint displacements when the 20 kip load is applied.

Solution: Let N_1, N_2 and N_3 be forces in bar AD, AC and AB respectively. Using equilibrium conditions (at joint A), one obtains

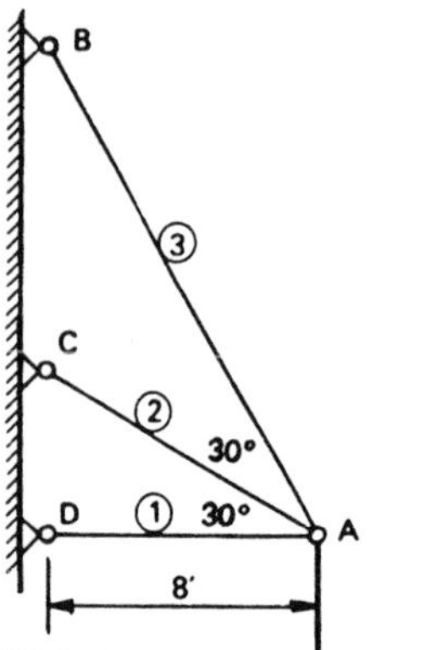

FIG. 1

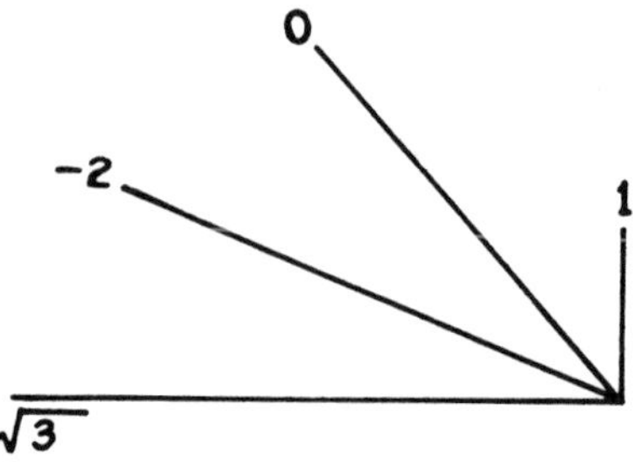

FIG. 2

the following equations.

$$\Sigma F_y = 0 \ , \ 20 - N_2 \sin 30 - N_3 \sin 60 = 0$$

$$\Sigma F_x = 0 \ , \ -N_1 - N_2 \cos 30 - N_3 \cos 60 = 0 \ .$$

There are two equilibrium equations and three bar forces. Hence we must choose one unknown. Take the force in AC as the unknown, and call it R (for redundant force). Using the two equations of equilibrium, express the three bar forces in terms of unknown R. Knowing that $N_2 = R$, we have,

$$N_3 \sin 60 = 20 - R \sin 30$$

$$N_1 = -N_3 \cos 60 - R \cos 30$$

or

$$.866\, N_3 = 20 - 0.5\, R$$

$$N_1 = -0.5\, N_3 - .866\, R$$

Thus,

$$N_3 = -23.1 - 0.5774\, R$$

$$N_1 = 11.55 - 0.5774\, R \qquad (1)$$

$$N_2 = R$$

Next using equation $\sigma = N/A$, obtain the σ for each bar. Thus,

$$\sigma_{AD} = \frac{N_1}{A_1} = \frac{N_1}{0.5} = 2N_1$$

$$\sigma_{AC} = \frac{N_2}{A_2} = \frac{R}{.5} = 2R$$

$$\sigma_{AB} = \frac{N_3}{A_3} = \frac{N_3}{.5} = 2N_3$$

Now the extension of each bar can be computed using equation $e = L\epsilon$. For bar AD,

$$e_{AD} = 96\epsilon_{AD}$$

Then from the stress-strain function, and assuming σ_1 to be compressive,

$$e_{AD} = 96\left[6 \times 10^{-5}(-0.04\sigma_{AD}^2 + \sigma_{AD})\right]$$

$$= 96\left[6 \times 10^{-5}(-0.16N_1^2 + N_1)\right]$$

Substituting the value of N_1 from equations (1) one obtains,

$$e_{AD} = 96\left[6 \times 10^{-5}\{-0.16(-11.55 - 0.5774R)^2 + (-11.55 - 0.5774R)\}\right]$$

or

$$e_{AD} = 10^{-3}(-0.307R^2 - 18.95R - 256) \qquad (2)$$

In the same way (and assuming that σ_2 and σ_3 are tensile), one can obtain the following equations for extension of bars AC and AB.

$$e_{AC} = 10^{-3}(1.066R^2 + 13.33R) \qquad (3)$$

$$e_{AB} = 10^{-3}(0.614R^2 - 62.5R + 1515) \qquad (4)$$

Now for compatibility we require that

$$e_{AD} + e_{AC} + e_{AB} = 0 .$$

Hence,

$$10^{-3}(-0.307R^2 - 18.95R - 256) + 10^{-3}(1.066R^2 + 13.33R) + 10^{-3}(0.614R^2 - 62.5R + 1515) = 0$$

or

$$0.889R^2 + 60.33R - 727 = 0$$

from which,

$$R = 10.4 \text{ kips.}$$

Then from equations (1),

$$N_1 = 11.55 - 0.5774(10.4) = 17.6 \text{ kips}$$

$$N_2 = R = 10.4 \text{ kips.}$$

$$N_3 = 23.1 - 0.5774(10.4) = 17.05 \text{ kips.}$$

Note that our assumptions are correct concerning the signs of these forces.

From equations (2), (3), and (4),

$$e_{AD} = 10^{-3}[-0.307(10.4)^2 - 18.95(10.4) - 256]$$
$$= -0.488 \text{ in.}$$

$$e_{AC} = 10^{-3}[1.066(10.4)^2 + 13.33(10.4)]$$
$$= +0.256 \text{ in.}$$

$$e_{AB} = 10^{-3}[0.614(10.4)^2 - 62.5(10.4) + 1515]$$
$$= +0.927 \text{ in.}$$

The two displacements of joint A can now be found by geometry. Obviously,

$$u_A = e_{AC} = -0.488 \text{ in.}$$

To find v_A a virtual force system is useful. We apply a unit vertical force at A, and any set of bar forces which make equilibrium with the vertical force. The forces shown in Fig. 2 will serve. Then,

$$v_A = +\sqrt{3}\, e_{AD} - 2e_{AC} + 0e_{AB}$$

$= \sqrt{3}\,(-0.488) - 2(0.256) + 0$

$= -1.37$ in.

• PROBLEM 13-10

Three rods are linked together to suspend a load F, as shown in Fig. 1. The rods have the same uniform cross-section and modulus elasticity.

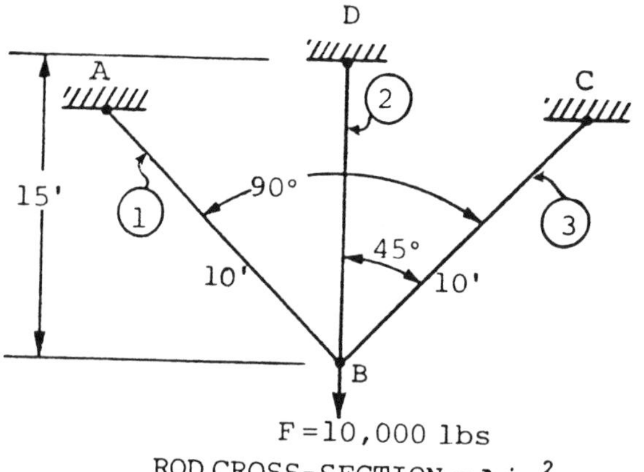

Fig. 1.

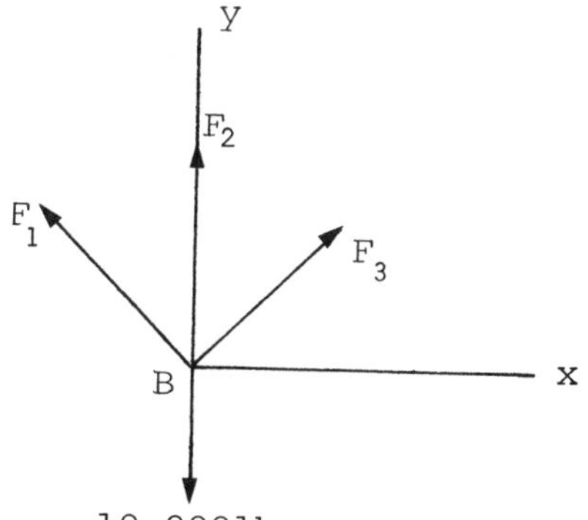

Fig. 2.

Solution: For equilibrium requirements we consider pin B as a free body in Fig. 2. It is clear that $F_1 = F_3$ and that

$$\Sigma F_y = 0\ ,\ F_2 + 2F_1 \cos 45^\circ - 10{,}000 = 0$$

$$\therefore\ F_2 + 1.414F_1 = 10{,}000 \qquad \text{(a)}$$

Calculating the extensions of the rods due to these forces,

$$\delta_1 = \delta_3 = \int_0^{L_1} \epsilon_{zz} dz = \frac{\tau_1}{E} L_1 = \frac{10F_1}{AE} \qquad \text{(b)}$$

$$\delta_2 = \int_0^{L_1} \epsilon_{zz} dz = \frac{\tau_2}{E} L_2 = \frac{15F_2}{AE} \qquad \text{(c)}$$

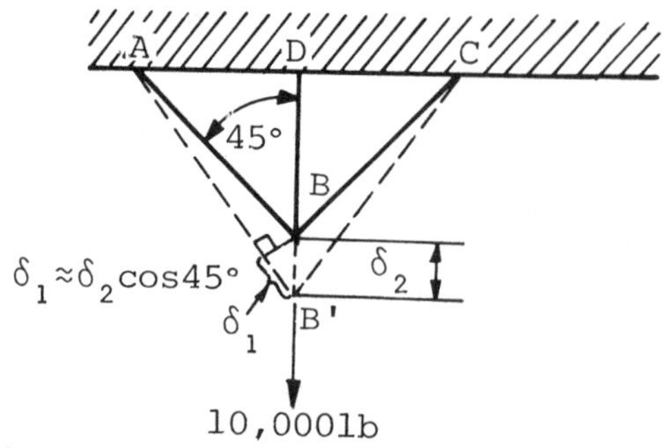

Fig. 3.

The solutions for δ_1 and δ_2 are not all commensurate. A single-value for B is needed, and for this purpose δ_1 and δ_2 must give the same deflection at B. Accordingly,

$$\delta_1 = \delta_2 \cos 45° = .707\delta_2 \quad ,$$

assuming angles AB'D and ABD equal. Solving for forces F_1 and F_2,

$$F_1 = \frac{AE}{10}\delta_1$$

and

$$F_2 = \frac{AE}{15}\delta_2$$

Substitute these values of F_1 and F_2 into equation (a) to obtain

$$\frac{AE}{15}\delta_2 + 1.414\frac{AE}{10}\delta_1 = 10,000$$

from which

$$\delta_2 + 2.12\delta_1 = \frac{150,000}{AE} \tag{e}$$

and

$$\delta_2 = \frac{60,000}{AE}$$

This, then, is the desired deflection of pin B. And we can now determine from Eqs. (b), (c), and (d) the forces F_1, F_2, and F_3.

$$\delta_1 = .707\delta_2$$

then,

$$\frac{10F_1}{AE} = \frac{.707(60,000)}{AE}$$

$$\text{or} \quad F_1 = \frac{.707(60,000)}{10} = 4242.00 \text{ lb.}$$

Since $F_1 = F_3$, $F_3 = 4242.00$ lb. Now,

$$\delta_2 = \frac{15F_2}{AE} = \frac{60,000}{AE}$$

Hence,

$$F_2 = 4,000 \text{ lb.}$$

Thus, the forces in the members are

$$F_1 = 4242 \text{ lb.}$$
$$F_2 = 4000 \text{ lb.}$$
$$F_3 = 4242 \text{ lb.}$$

DISPLACEMENT METHOD

• PROBLEM 13-11

In the structure of Fig. 1 the properties of the bars are:

$$L_1 = 60 \text{ in.} \qquad L_2 = 72 \text{ in.}$$

$A_1 = 1.0 \text{ in}^2 \qquad A_2 = 1.2 \text{ in}^2$

$E_1 = 30 \times 10^3 \text{ksi} \quad E_2 = 15 \times 10^3 \text{ ksi}$

Find the location of the 50 kip load so that the beam GH remains horizontal, and find the force in each bar.

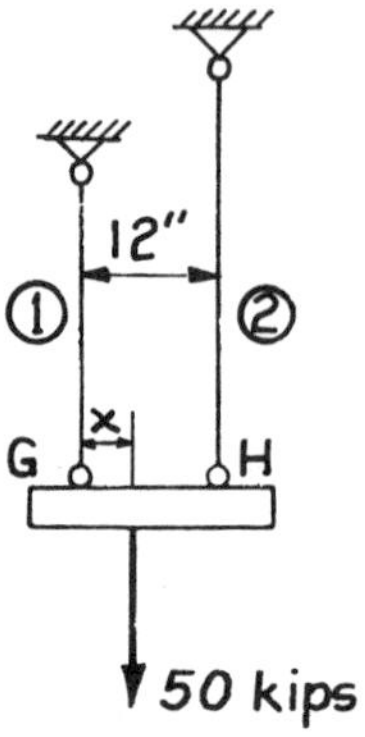

FIG. 1

Solution: Since GH remains horizontal there is only one degree of freedom, expressed by the displacement v. Then,

$$e_1 = e_2 = -v$$

The bar stiffness coefficients are,

$$k_1 = \frac{E_1 A_1}{L_1} = 0.5 \times 10^3 \text{ kips/in}; \; k_2 = \frac{E_2 A_2}{L_2} = 0.25 \times 10^3 \text{kips/in.}$$

Then, the bar forces are,

$$N_1 = k_1 e_1 = -0.5 \times 10^3 v$$
$$N_2 = k_2 e_2 = -0.25 \times 10^3 v \qquad (1)$$

Consider the equilibrium of beam GH

$\Sigma Y = 0$

$$N_1 + N_2 - 50 = 0$$

Substitute the values of N_1 and N_2 from equations (1), to obtain,

$$-0.5 \times 10^3 v - 0.25 \times 10^3 v - 50 = 0$$

or

$$-0.75 \times 10^3 v = 50$$

Hence,

$$v = -66.67 \times 10^{-3} \text{ in.}$$

From equations (1),

$$N_1 = -0.5 \times 10^3 (-66.67 \times 10^{-3}) = 33.33 \text{ kips}$$

$$N_2 = -0.25 \times 10^3 (-66.67 \times 10^{-3}) = 16.67 \text{ kips}$$

We might notice that the bar loads are proportioned to the bar stiffness. The location of the 50 kip load is obtained from the rotational equilibrium of beam GH. Then,

$$\Sigma M_G = 0, \quad -50x - 16.67 \times 12 = 0$$

or

$$x = \frac{16.67 \times 12}{50} = 4.0 \text{ inch.}$$

• PROBLEM 13-12

Find the bar forces in the structure of Fig. 1. For each bar $A = 0.5$ in^2 and $E = 20 \times 10^3$ ksi.

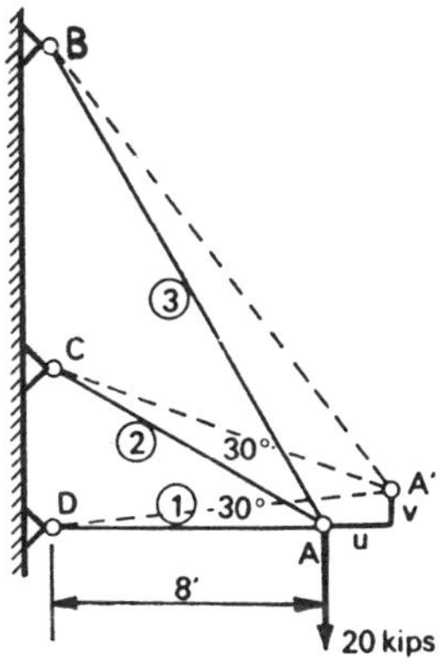

FIG.1

Solution: The primary unknown quantities are the displacements of A (u and v) which are both shown as positive in Fig. 1. It should be kept in mind that, in reality, these displacements are very small so that the changes in bar inclinations are negligible.

To obtain bar deformations, resolve the displacement AA' in the direction of each bar in turn.

$$\begin{aligned} e_1 &= u \cos 0° - v \sin 0° = u \\ e_2 &= u \cos 30° - v \sin 30° = 0.866u - 0.5v \qquad (1) \\ e_3 &= u \cos 60° - v \sin 60° = 0.5u - 0.866v \end{aligned}$$

These equations are based on the laws of geometry.

Then bar forces can be obtained as follows:

With a Hookean material it is convenient to evaluate first the bar stiffness coefficients, the load required to cause unit extension.

$$k_1 = \frac{EA_1}{L_1} = \frac{20 \times 10^3 \times 0.5}{96} = 104.2 \text{ kips/in}$$

$$k_2 = \frac{EA_2}{L_2} = \frac{20 \times 10^3 \times 0.5}{96/\cos 30°} = 90.2 \text{ kips/in}$$

$$k_3 = \frac{EA_3}{L_3} = \frac{20 \times 10^3 \times 0.5}{96/\cos 60°} = 52.1 \text{ kips/in.}$$

Then

$$\begin{aligned} N_1 &= k_1 e_1 = 104.2 \times u = 104.2u \qquad (2) \\ N_2 &= k_2 e_2 = 90.2(0.866u - 0.5v) = 78.0u - 45.1v \\ N_3 &= k_3 e_3 = 52.1(0.5u - 0.866v) = 26.0u - 45.1v \end{aligned}$$

We have now made use of the force-deformation relations for the bars.

Finally, we use the equations of equilibrium which correspond to the displacements u and v.

$\Sigma X = 0$

$$N_1 + N_2 \cos 30^\circ + N_3 \cos 60^\circ = 0$$

or

$$104.2u + (78.0u - 45.1v)0.866 + (26.0u - 45.1v)0.5 = 0$$

$$184.8u - 61.6v = 0 \qquad (3)$$

$\Sigma Y = 0$

$$N_2 \sin 30^\circ + N_3 \sin 60^\circ - 20 = 0$$

or

$$(78.0u - 45.1v)0.5 + (26.0u - 45.1v)0.866 - 20 = 0$$

or

$$61.6u - 61.6v = 20 \qquad (4)$$

solving equations (3) and (4), yields

$$u = -0.162 \text{ in}; \; v = -0.487 \text{ in}.$$

Substituting the values of u and v into equations one obtains the bar forces. Thus,

$$N_1 = 104.2(-0.162) = -16.88 \text{ kips}$$

$$N_2 = 78(-0.162) - 45.1(-0.487) = +9.32 \text{ kips}$$

$$N_3 = 26(-0.162) - 45.1(-0.487) = +17.75 \text{ kips}.$$

• PROBLEM 13-13

Consider the truss of Fig. 1. If the coefficient of linear thermal expansion, α, is 15×10^{-6} per $^\circ$F for each bar, find the bar forces induced by a temperature rise of 60°F. For each bar $A = 0.5$ in^2 and $E = 20 \times 10^3$ ksi.

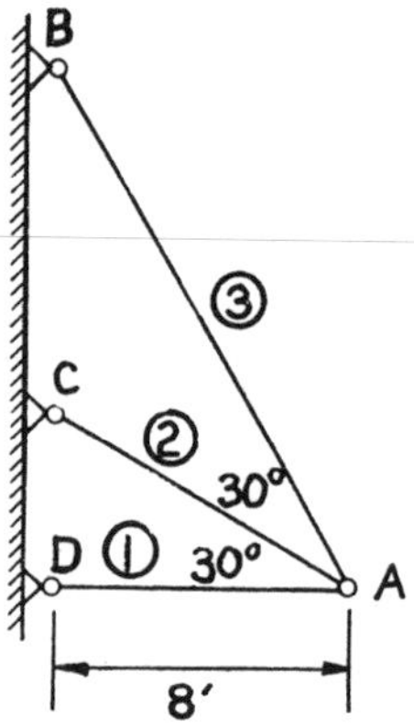

FIG. 1

Solution: From previous example, the bar deformations in terms of the displacements u, v at A are,

$$e_1 = u$$

$$e_2 = 0.866u - 0.5v$$

$$e_3 = 0.5u - 0.866v$$

The bar stiffness coefficients are,

$$k_1 = \frac{EA_1}{L_1} = \frac{20 \times 10^3 \times 0.5}{96} = 104.2 \text{ kips/in.}$$

$$k_2 = \frac{EA_2}{L_2} = \frac{20 \times 10^3 \times 0.5}{96/\cos 30^\circ} = 90.2 \text{ kips/in.}$$

$$k_3 = \frac{EA_3}{L_3} = \frac{20 \times 10^3 \times 0.5}{96/\cos 60^\circ} = 52.1 \text{ kips/in.}$$

The total deformation, e, of each bar is the sum of e_S due to stress and e_T due to temperature.

$$e = e_S + e_T$$

Thus

$$e_S = e - e_T = e - \epsilon_T L$$

where $\epsilon_T = \alpha T = 15 \times 10^{-6} \times 60 = 9 \times 10^{-4}$.

The bar force is obtained by multiplying e_S alone by the bar stiffness coefficient k. Then,

$$N_1 = k_1 e_{1s} = k_1(e_1 - \epsilon_T L_1)$$

$$= 104.2(u - 9 \times 10^{-4} \times 96) = 104.2(u - 0.0864) \quad (1)$$

$$N_2 = k_2 e_{2s} = k_2(e_2 - \epsilon_T L_2)$$

$$= 90.2(0.866u - 0.5v - 9 \times 10^{-4} \times 111)$$

$$= 90.2(0.866u - 0.5v - 0.0998) \quad (2)$$

$$N_3 = k_3 e_{3s} = k_3(e_3 - \epsilon_T L_3)$$

$$= 52.1(0.5u - 0.866v - 9 \times 10^{-4} \times 192)$$

$$= 52.1(0.5u - 0.866v - 0.1728) \quad (3)$$

We have two equations of equilibrium of joint A.

$\Sigma X = 0$

$$N_1 + N_2 \cos 30^\circ + N_3 \cos 60^\circ = 0$$

$\Sigma Y = 0$

$$N_2 \sin 30^\circ + N_3 \cos 60^\circ = 0$$

or

$$N_1 + 0.866 N_2 + 0.5 N_3 = 0$$

$$0.5 N_2 + 0.866 N_3 = 0$$

When the values of N are substituted from equations (1), (2) and (3), these give

$$104.2(u - 0.084) + 0.866[90.2(0.866u - 0.5v - 0.0998)]$$
$$+ 0.5[52.1(0.5u - 0.866v - 0.1728)] = 0$$

$$0.5[90.2(0.866u - 0.5v - 0.0998)]$$
$$+ 0.866N_3[52.1(0.5u - 0.866v - 0.1728)] = 0$$

or

$$184.8u - 61.6v - 21.3 = 0$$

$$61.6u - 61.6v - 12.3 = 0$$

Solving these two equations, one obtains

$$u = +\ 0.073 \text{ in.}$$

$$v = -0.127 \text{ in.}$$

To obtain the bar forces, substitute the values of u, v into equations (1), (2) and (3). Thus,

$$N_1 = -1.39 \text{ kips}$$

$$N_2 = 2.4 \text{ kips}$$

$$N_3 = -1.37 \text{ kips.}$$

• PROBLEM 13-14

A bar of aluminium, 2 in² in cross-section, and a bar of copper, 1.5 in² in cross-section, are rigidly connected at their ends (Fig. 1(a)). The compound bar is subjected to a compressive force of 30,000 lb. applied in such a way that the bars remain straight. The elastic moduli for aluminium and copper are $E_A = 10 \times 10^6$ psi and $E_C = 16 \times 10^6$ psi. Obtain the force in each bar by displacement method.

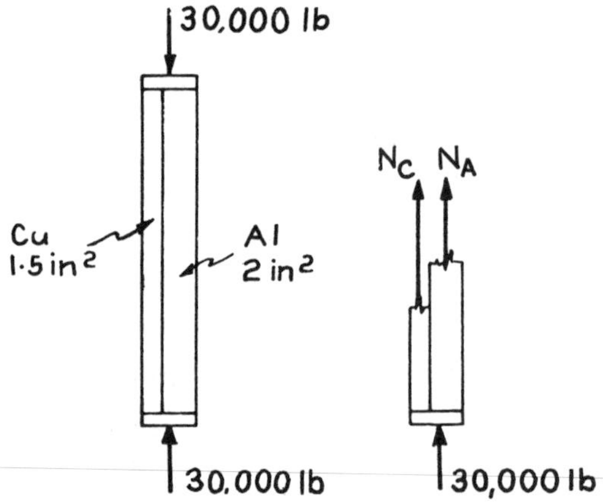

FIG. 1 (a) (b)

Solution: Here the extension, common to both bars, is taken as the main variable.

$$e_A = e_C = e \text{ (say)}$$

Then,

$$k_A = \frac{E_A A_A}{L} = \frac{20 \times 10^6}{L} \text{ lb/in}; \quad k_C = \frac{E_C A_C}{L} = \frac{24 \times 10^6}{L} \text{ lb/in}$$

and

$$N_A = k_A e_A = 20 \times 10^6 \ e/L; \quad N_C = k_C e_C = 24 \times 10^6 \ e/L$$

For equilibrium (of the end connecting plate, Fig. 1 (b)),

$$N_A + N_C + 30{,}000 = 0$$

or

$$20 \times 10^6 \ e/L + 24 \times 10^6 \ e/L + 30{,}000 = 0$$

$$e/L = -0.683 \times 10^{-3}$$

Hence

$$N_A = 20 \times 10^6(-0.683 \times 10^{-3}) = -13,667 \text{ lb.}$$

$$N_C = 24 \times 10^6(-0.683 \times 10^{-3}) = -16,333 \text{ lb.}$$

• PROBLEM 13-15

Fig. 1 shows a rigid beam GJH supported by three bars, whose cross-sections and spacing are as indicated. A load of 150 kips is attached to the mid-point of the beam. For the stress range of this problem, bars 1 and 2 are Hookean with $E_1 = 20 \times 10^3$ ksi and $E_2 = 12 \times 10^3$ ksi. For bar 3, the stress-strain law is a straight line with a slope of 10×10^3 ksi up to a stress of 7 ksi, and above this stress it is another straight line with half this slope. The equation of the second line is therefore $\sigma = 5 \times 10^3\epsilon + 3.5$ provided that σ is in ksi.
Find the force in each bar.

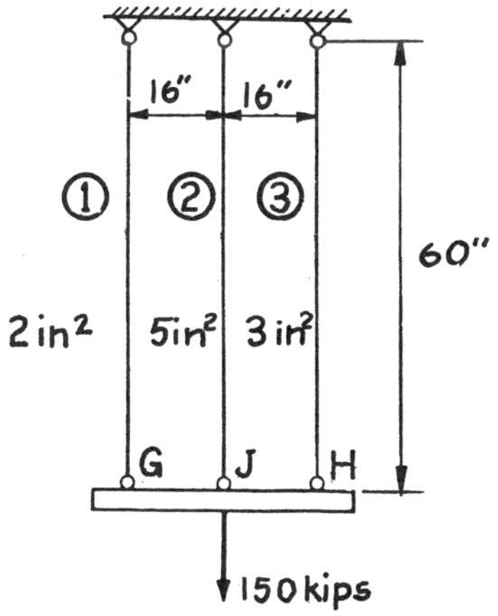

FIG. 1

Solution: In this example the beam GJH has two degrees of freedom. Its displacement can be defined either by the vertical movement of two points, or by the vertical movement of one point and the angular displacement. Suppose we use v_G and v_H as the variables.

Then

$$e_1 = -v_G$$

$$e_2 = -\frac{v_G + v_H}{2}$$

$$e_3 = -v_H$$

Now,

$$N_1 = \frac{E_1A_1}{L_1}e_1 = \frac{20 \times 10^3 \times 2}{60}(-v_G) = -667v_G$$

$$N_2 = \frac{E_2A_2}{L_2}e_2 = \frac{12 \times 10^3 \times 5}{60}\left(-\frac{v_G + v_H}{2}\right) = -500v_G - 500v_H$$

For bar 3,

$$\epsilon = \frac{-v_H}{60}$$

Assuming that the stress exceeds 7 ksi. Then, the stress can be obtained from the equation

$$\sigma = 5 \times 10^3 \epsilon + 3.5 \ .$$

Hence,

$$\sigma = 5 \times 10^3\left(\frac{-v_H}{60}\right) + 3.5$$

and

$$N_3 = \sigma_3 A_3 = \left[5 \times 10^3\left(\frac{-v_H}{60}\right) + 3.5\right] \times 3 \ .$$

$$= -250v_H + 10.5$$

For the equilibrium of bar GH, we have

$$\sum Y = 0, \qquad N_1 + N_2 + N_3 = 150$$

Substituting the values of N_1, N_2, and N_3, gives

$$-667v_G - 500v_G - 500v_H - 250v_M + 10.5 = 150$$

or

$$-1167v_G - 750v_H = 139.5 \qquad (1)$$

Σ M = 0 (about J)

$$N_1 = N_3$$

$$-667v_G = -250v_H + 10.5 \qquad (2)$$

Solving equations (1) and (2), yields,

$$v_G = -0.054 \text{ in. and } v_H = -0.10 \text{ in.}$$

Hence

$$N_1 = -667(-0.054) = 36 \text{ kips.}$$

$$N_2 = -500(-0.054) - 500(-.1) = 78 \text{ kips.}$$

$$N_3 = -250(-0.1) + 10.5 = 36 \text{ kips.}$$

Since the area of bar 3 is 3 sq. in., the stress in this bar is 12 ksi and therefore the assumption that $\sigma_3 > 7$ was correct.

WORK AND ENERGY METHOD

• PROBLEM 13-16

Find the forces in the pin-jointed bars of the steel structure shown in Fig. 1(a) if a force of 3,000 lb. is applied at B.

Solution: The structure may be rendered statically determinate by cutting the bar DB at D. Then the forces in the members can be determined from equilibrium conditions.

$$\Sigma F_y = 0, \ -3000 + N_{AB} \sin\theta - N_{BC} \sin\theta = 0$$

since $\sin\theta = 3/5$, we have

$$N_{AB}(3/5) - N_{BC}(3/5) = 3000 \qquad (1)$$

$$\Sigma F_x = 0, \ N_{AB} \cos\theta + N_{BC} \cos\theta = 0 \ .$$

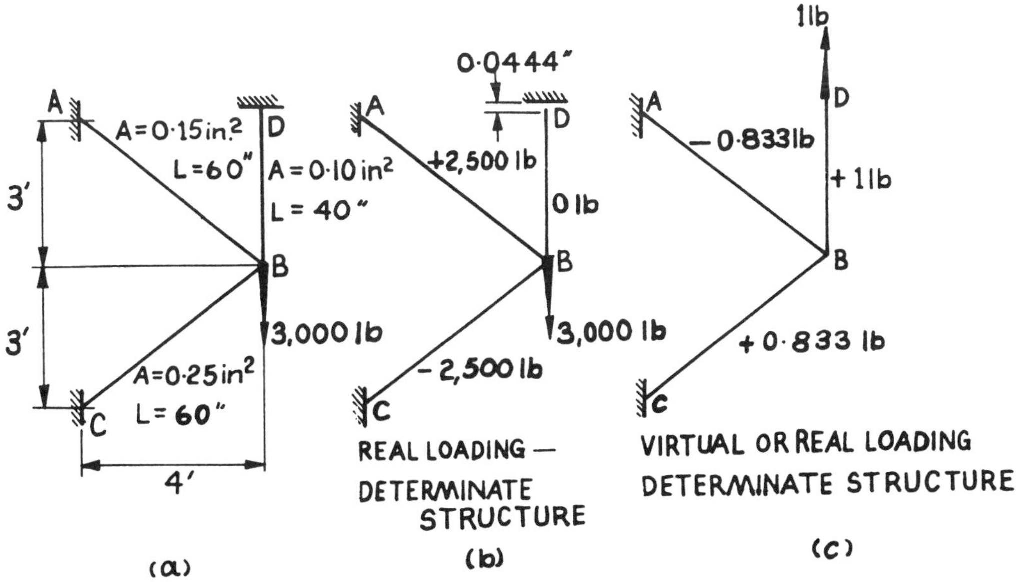

FIG.1.

Since $\cos\theta = 4/5$, we have

$$N_{AB} = -N_{BC}$$

Then, equation (1) becomes,

$$-2N_{BC}(3/5) = 3000$$

or

$$N_{BC} = -\frac{3000 \times 5}{3 \times 2} = -2500 \text{ lb.}$$

Hence $\quad N_{AB} = 2500$ lb.

In this determinate structure, the movement of point D must be found. This can be done by applying a vertical virtual force at D, Fig. 1(c), and using the virtual-work method. However, since the pPL/(AE) term for the member BD is zero, the vertical movement of point D is the same as that of B. The latter quantity was found to be 0.0444 in. down and is so shown in Fig. 1(b).

The movement of point D, shown in Fig. 1(b), violates the conditions of the problem, and a force must be applied to bring it back where it belongs. This can be stated as

$$\Delta_D = f_{DD}X_D + \Delta_{DP} = 0$$

where the gap $\Delta_{DP} \doteq -0.0444$ in.

To determine f_{DD} a 1-lb. real force is applied at D and the virtual-work method is used to find the deflection due to this force. The forces set up in the determinate structure by the virtual and the real forces are numerically the same, Fig. 1(c). To differentiate between the two, forces in members caused by a real force are designated by p', by the virtual force by p. The solution is carried out in tabular form.

Member	p,lb	p',lb	L,in.	A,in.^{2}	pp'L/A
AB	-0.833	-0.833	60	0.15	+278
BC	+0.833	+0.833	60	0.25	+167
BD	+1,000	+1.000	40	0.10	+400

From the table, Σ pp'L/A = +845. Therefore, since

$$1 \times \Delta = \Sigma \frac{pp'L}{AE} = \frac{+845}{30(10)^6} = 0.0000281 \text{ lb.-in.}$$

$$f_{DD} = 0.0000281 \text{ in.,} \quad \text{and} \quad 0.0000281X_D = 0.0444 = 0 .$$

To close the gap of 0.0444 in., the 1-lb. real force at D must be inceased X_D = 0.0444/0.0000281 = 1,580 times. Therefore the actual force in the member DB is 1,580 lb. The forces in the other two members may now be determined from statics,

$$\Sigma F_y = 0, \ -3000 + N_{AB}(3/5) - N_{BC}(3/5) + 1580 = 0$$

since $N_{AB} = -N_{BC}$, we have,

$$-2N_{BC}(3/5) = 3000 - 1580$$

or

$$N_{BC} = -1180 \text{ lb. (compression)}$$

and

$$N_{AB} = 1180 \text{ lb. (tension).}$$

• PROBLEM 13-17

Find the vertical deflection of point B in the pin-jointed steel truss shown in Fig. 1(a) due to the following causes: (a) the elastic deformation of the members, (b) a shortening by 0.125 in. of the member AB by means of a turnbuckle, and (c) a drop in temperature of 120°F occurring in the member BC. The coefficient of thermal expansion of steel is 0.0000065 in. per inch per degree Fahrenheit. Neglect the possibility of lateral buckling of the compression member.

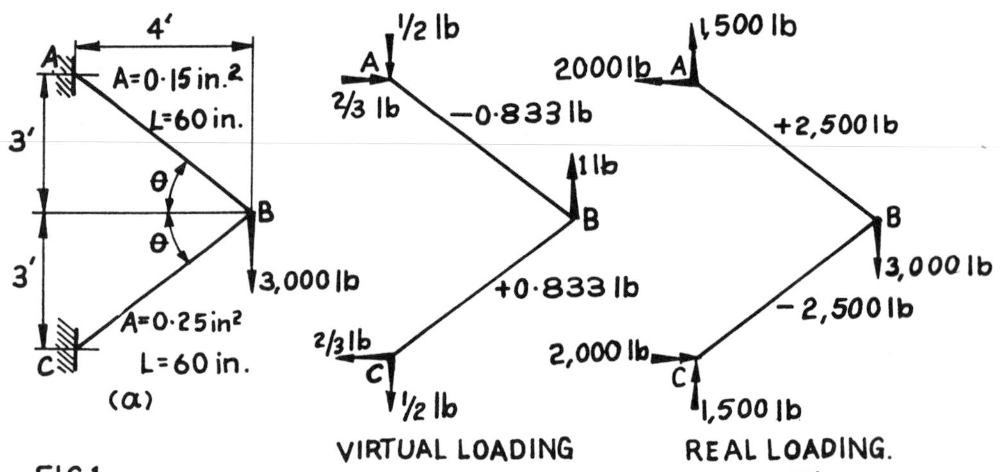

FIG.1.

Solution: Case (a): A virtual unit force is applied in the vertical direction as shown in Fig. 1(b), and the resulting forces p can be determined as follows. From equilibrium equations,

$$\Sigma F_y = 0, \quad 1 + N_{AB} \sin\theta - N_{BC} \sin\theta = 0$$

since $\sin\theta = 3/5$, we have,

$$1 + 3/5\, N_{AB} - 3/5\, N_{BC} = 0 \qquad (1)$$

Now,

$$\Sigma F_x = 0, \quad N_{AB} \cos\theta + N_{BC} \cos\theta = 0$$

Since, $\cos\theta = 4/5$, we have,

$$N_{AB} = -N_{BC} .$$

Substituting this value for N_{AB} into equation (1) yields,

$$1 - 3/5\, N_{BC} - 3/5\, N_{BC} = 0$$

or

$$N_{BC} = 5/6 = 0.833 \text{ lb.}$$

Hence $N_{AB} = -0.833$ lb.

Resolving the force in member AB at joint A, gives,

$$N_{AB_x} = 0.8333(4/5) = 0.666 \text{ lb.}$$

$$N_{AB_y} = 0.8333(3/5) = 0.5 \text{ lb.}$$

Similarly at joint C, we have

$$N_{BC_x} = .8333(4/5) = .666 \text{ lb.}$$

$$N_{BC_y} = .8333(3.5) = 0.5 \text{ lb.}$$

Then, the forces in each member due to the real force can be also determined and they are shown in Fig. 1(c). The equation

$$p\Delta = \Sigma \frac{pPL}{AE}$$

can be used to find the deflection. The work is carried out in tabular form.

Member	p, lb.	P, lb.	L, in.	A, in.^{2}	pPL/A
AB	-0.833	+2,500	60	0.15	-833,000
BC	+0.833	-2,500	60	0.25	-500,000

From this table $\Sigma\, pPL/A = -1,333,000$. Hence

$$1 \times \Delta = \Sigma \frac{pPL}{AE} = \frac{-1,333,000}{(30)10^6} = -0.0444 \text{ lb-in.}$$

and

$$\Delta = -0.0444 \text{ in.}$$

The negative sign means that point B deflects down. In this case, "negative work" is done by the virtual force acting upward when it is displaced in a downward direction. Note particularly the units and the signs of all quantities. Tensile forces in members are taken positive, and vice versa.

Case (b): The forces set up in the bars by the virtual force acting in the direction of the deflection sought are shown in Fig. 1(b). Then, since ΔL is -0.125 in. (shortening) for the member AB and is zero for the member BC,

$$1 \times \Delta = (-0.833)(-0.125) + (+0.833)(0) = +0.1042 \text{ lb-in.}$$

and

$$\Delta = +0.1042 \text{ in. up.}$$

Case (c): Noting that due to the drop in temperature, $\Delta L = -0.0000065(120)60 = -0.0468$ in. in the member BC,

$$1 \times \Delta = (+0.833)(-0.0468)$$

$$= -0.0390 \text{ lb-in.}$$

and

$$\Delta = -0.0390 \text{ in. down}$$

By superposition, the net deflection of point B due to all three causes is $-0.0444 + 0.1042 - 0.0390 = +0.0208$ in.up. To find this quantity, all three effects could have been considered simultaneously in the virtual-work equation.

• PROBLEM 13-18

The truss shown in Fig. 1a is constructed of a material having a stress-strain relationship given by the equation $\sigma = B\sqrt{\varepsilon}$, where B is a constant. Find the axial forces in all three bars by using complementary energy and the force method.

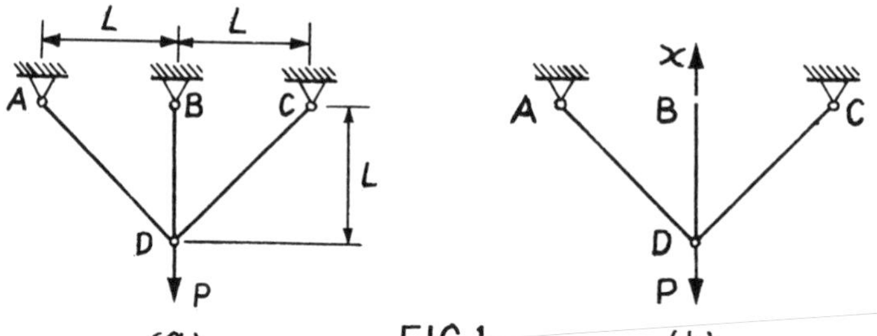

FIG.1.

Solution: Assuming that the reactive force at joint B is the statical redundant X, we obtain the released structure shown in Fig. 1b. The forces in the bars of the released structure can be found from statics.

$$\Sigma F_x = 0, \quad -N_{AD} \cos 45 + N_{CD} \cos 45 = 0$$

from which $N_{AD} = N_{CD}$

$$\Sigma F_y = 0, \quad N_{AD} \sin 45 + N_{BD} - P + N_{cd} \sin 45 = 0$$

since $N_{AD} = N_{CD}$ and $N_{BD} = X$, the above equation can be written as

$$2N_{AD} \sin 45 = P - X$$

or

$$N_{AD} = \frac{P - X}{2 \sin 45} = \frac{P - X}{\sqrt{2}} \tag{1}$$

Then, the corresponding stresses are

$$\sigma_{AD} = \frac{N_{AD}}{A} = \frac{P - X}{\sqrt{2}A} \tag{2}$$

$$\sigma_{CD} = \frac{N_{CD}}{A} = \frac{P - X}{\sqrt{2}A} \tag{3}$$

and

$$\sigma_{BD} = \frac{N_{BD}}{A} = \frac{X}{A} \tag{4}$$

where A is the cross-sectional area of each bar.

The complementary energy per unit volume of bar BD is obtained as follows.

$$u^*_{BD} = \int_0^{\sigma_{BD}} \epsilon \, d\sigma$$

since $\sigma = B\sqrt{\epsilon}$, the above equation can be written as

$$u^*_{BD} = \int_0^{\sigma_{BD}} \frac{\sigma^2}{B^2} \, d\sigma$$

Integration yields,

$$u^*_{BD} = \frac{\sigma_{BD}^3}{3B^2} .$$

Substituting the value of σ_{BD} from equation (4) gives

$$u^*_{BD} = \frac{1}{3B^2} \left(\frac{X}{A}\right)^3$$

Then, the complementary energy per unit volume of bars AD and CD are,

$$u^*_{AD} = \int_0^{\sigma_{AD}} \epsilon \, d\sigma$$

$$= \int_0^{\sigma_{AD}} \frac{\sigma^2}{B^2} \, d\sigma = \frac{\sigma_{BD}^3}{3B^2} = \frac{1}{3B^2} \left(\frac{P - X}{\sqrt{2}A}\right)^3$$

and

$$u^*_{CD} = \frac{1}{3B^2} \left(\frac{P - X}{\sqrt{2}A}\right)^3$$

Finally, we can multiply the complementary energy per unit volume of each bar by the volume of the bar, and then we can sum the results to obtain the total complementary energy of the released structure

$$U^* = u^*_{AD}\, AL_{AD} + u^*_{CD}\, AL_{CD} + u^*_{BD}\, AL_{BD}$$

since, $L_{AD} = L_{CD} = \frac{L}{\cos 45} = \frac{2L}{\sqrt{2}}$, and substituting the values for u^*_{AD}, u^*_{CD} and u^*_{BD}, we have,

$$U^* = \frac{1}{3B^2}\left(\frac{P - X}{\sqrt{2}A}\right)^3 \frac{2L}{\sqrt{2}} + \frac{1}{3B^2}\left(\frac{P - X}{\sqrt{2}A}\right)^3 \frac{2L}{\sqrt{2}} + \frac{1}{3B^2}\left(\frac{X}{A}\right)^3 L$$

or,

$$U^* = \frac{AL}{3B^2A^3}\left[\frac{2 \times 2}{\sqrt{2}(\sqrt{2})^3}(P - X)^3 + X^3\right]$$

$$= \frac{L}{3A^2B^2}\left[(P - X)^3 + X^3\right]$$

This expression for U^* is a nonlinear function of both the load P and the redundant X. The displacement in the original structure corresponding to the redundant X is zero because there is no displacement of support B. Therefore, the Crotti-Engesser theorem, when applied to the redundant X, gives the following equation

$$\frac{dU^*}{dX} = \frac{L}{3A^2B^2}\left[3(P - X)^2(-1) + 3X^2\right] = 0$$

from which

$$X^2 - (P - X)^2 = 0$$

or

$$X^2 - P^2 + 2PX - X^2 = 0$$

or

$$-P(P - 2X) = 0$$

Hence,

$$X = P/2 .$$

Substituting this value for X into equation (1), yields,

$$N_{AD} = \frac{P - P/2}{\sqrt{2}} = \frac{P}{2\sqrt{2}}$$

since, $N_{AD} = N_{CD}$, and $N_{BD} = X$, we have

$$N_{CD} = \frac{P}{2\sqrt{2}} ,$$

and $N_{BD} = P/2$. Thus, the axial forces in the bars of this statically indeterminate, nonlinear truss have been found by the force method.

CHAPTER 14

FAILURE CRITERIA AND DESIGN

• **PROBLEM 14-1**

Using the (a) limit-design criterion and (b) elastic-limit criterion find the difference in the maximum loading intensity.

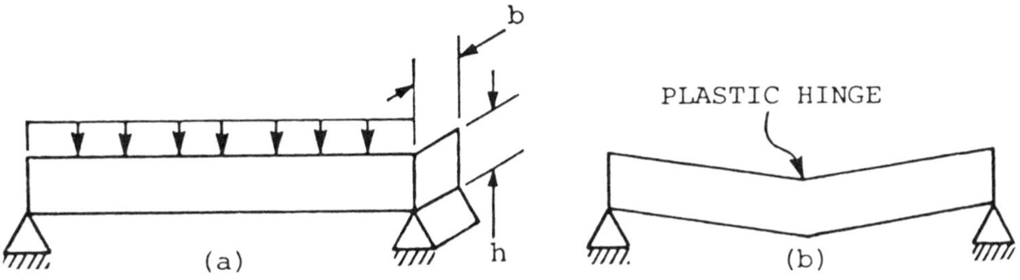

Fig. 1.

Solution: The maximum moment, and therefore, the maximum normal stress occur at the midpoint of the beam. From Fig. 2, the moment at $x = \ell/2$ is

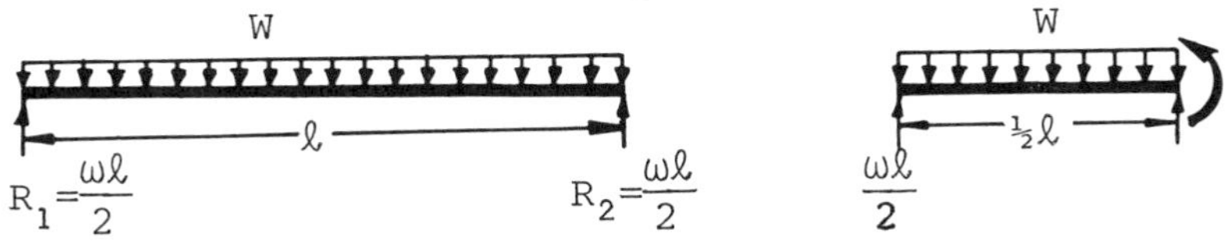

Fig. 2.

$$\Sigma M = 0 \quad \text{about} \quad x = \ell/2$$

$$M + w \tfrac{1}{2}\ell \tfrac{1}{4}\ell - \frac{w\ell}{2}\tfrac{1}{2}\ell = 0$$

$$M = \frac{w\ell^2}{4} - \frac{w\ell^2}{8}$$

Thus, the bending moment M at the center of the beam is

$$M = \frac{w\ell^2}{8} \qquad \text{(a)}$$

Hence, for elastic action, we have for the maximum stress at the center section of the beam

$$\tau_{xx} = \frac{\frac{w\ell^2}{8}\frac{h}{2}}{I} = \frac{w\ell^2 h}{16I} \tag{b}$$

The maximum load possible with the presence of only elastic deformation is then

$$(w_{max})_1 = \frac{16(\tau_{xx})_Y I}{h\ell^2} = \frac{4}{3}\frac{b(\tau_{xx})_Y h^2}{\ell^2} \tag{c}$$

Now let us compute the maximum loading for the limit-design criterion.

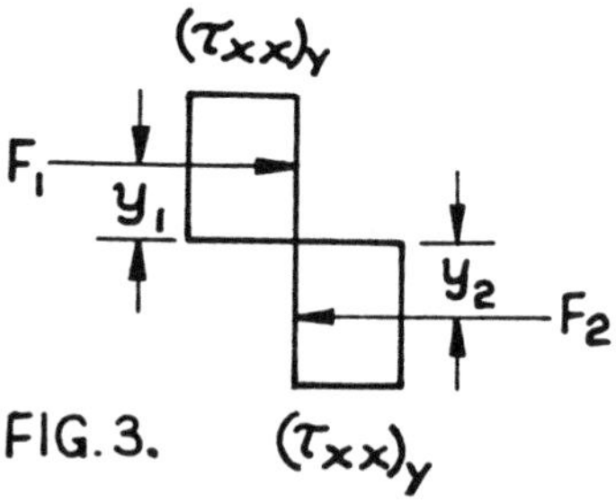

FIG. 3.

In the limit condition, the yield stress has been reached at every fiber, as in Fig. 3. The moment is the sum of the forces times the moment arms. This is the highest moment M_H the beam can withstand without collapsing.

$$F_1 = F_2 = (\tau_{xx})_Y \; bh/z$$

$$y_1 = y_2 = h/4$$

$$M_H = F_1 y_1 + F_2 y_2$$

$$M_H = 2(\tau_{xx})_Y \frac{bh}{2}\left(\frac{h}{4}\right)$$

which reduces to:

$$M_H = \frac{b(\tau_{xx})_Y h^2}{4} \tag{d}$$

Substituting the preceding result for M_H into Eq. (a) and solving for $(w_{max})_2$ we have

$$\frac{b(\tau_{xx})_Y h^2}{4} = \frac{w\ell^2}{8}$$

$$(w_{max})_2 = \frac{2b(\tau_{xx})_Y h^2}{\ell^2} \tag{e}$$

The ratio of the maximum loads according to the two criteria is then

$$\frac{(w_{max})_2}{(w_{max})_1} = \frac{[2b(\tau_{xx})_Y h^2]\ell^2}{\frac{4}{3}[b(\tau_{xx})_Y h^2]\ell^2} = \frac{3}{2}$$

Thus, the limit-design criterion allows for considerably more load.

It is up to the designer to decide on what design criterion he must base his work.

A circular rod of radius r is bent into the shape of a U to form the structure of Fig. 1(a). The material in the rod has a yield stress Y in simple tension. Determine the load P that will cause yielding to begin at some point in the structure.

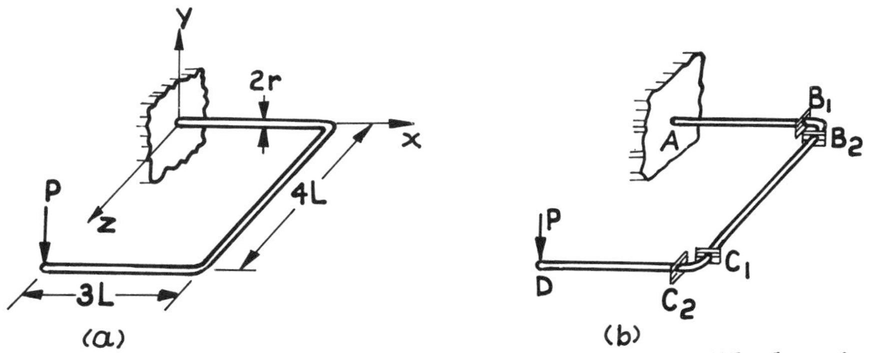

Solution: As indicated in Fig. 1(b), there are five possible locations for the most critically stressed point. The bending and twisting moments acting at these locations are shown in Fig. 1(c) through g.

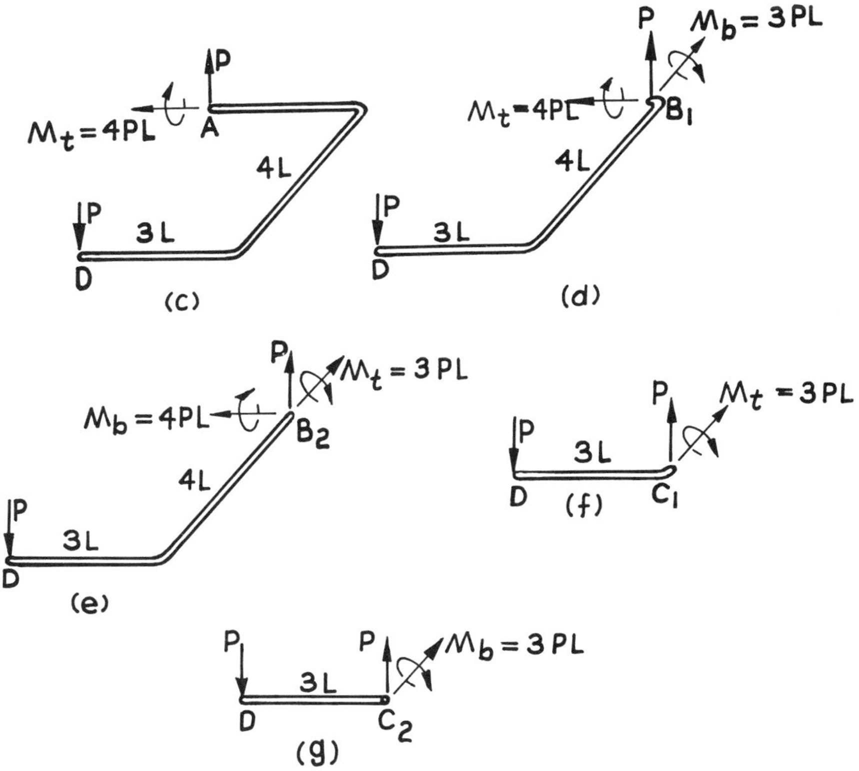

FIG. 1. BENDING AND TWISTING MOMENTS AT FIVE CRITICAL LOCATIONS IN A STRUCTURE.

By comparing the numerical values of the forces and moments at each location the choice narrows down to either location B_1 or B_2, it is not obvious which of these is the more critical.

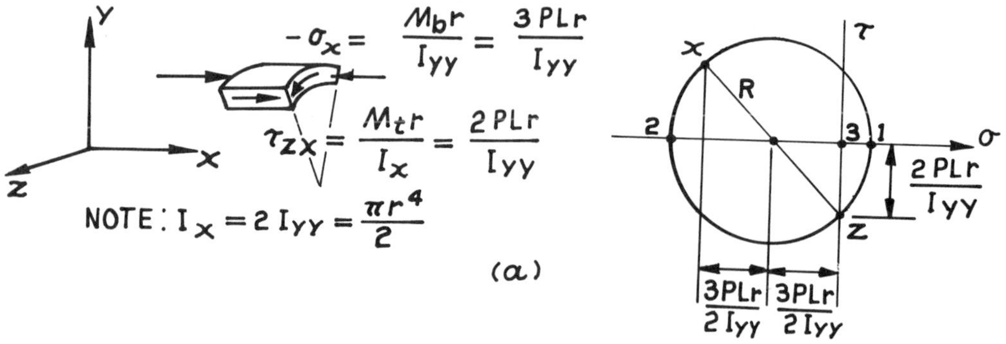

FIG. 2. (a) MAXIMUM STRESS CONDITION AT LOCATION B_1.

The bending and torsional shear stresses acting on an element on the top of the beam at location B_1 are indicated in Fig. 2(a). Although there is a shear force P at this location, the corresponding shear stress τ_{xy} is zero at the top and bottom of the beam where the bending and torsional shear stresses are maximum. The radius of the Mohr's circle for the element at B_1, shown in Fig. 2(a) is

$$R = \sqrt{\left(\frac{3}{2}\frac{PLr}{I_{yy}}\right)^2 + \left(\frac{2PLr}{I_{yy}}\right)^2} = \frac{5}{2}\frac{PLr}{I_{yy}} \qquad \text{(a)}$$

Using (a), we find the principal stresses at the point to be

$$\sigma_1 = +\frac{PLr}{I_{yy}} \qquad \sigma_2 = -4\frac{PLr}{I_{yy}} \qquad \sigma_3 = 0 \qquad \text{(b)}$$

where σ_1 is the distance between point 3 and point 1. σ_2 is the distance between point 3 and point 2. σ_3 is the distance between point 3 and point 3. Substituting (b) into the Mises yield criterion, in terms of principal stresses

$$Y = \sqrt{\tfrac{1}{2}\left[(\sigma_1 - \sigma_2)^2 + (\sigma_2 - \sigma_3)^2 + (\sigma_3 - \sigma_1)^2\right]}$$

$$\sqrt{\tfrac{1}{2}\left[\left(\frac{PLr}{I_{yy}} + 4\frac{PLr}{I_{yy}}\right)^2 + \left(-4\frac{PLr}{I_{yy}} - 0\right)^2 + \left(0 - \frac{PLr}{I_{yy}}\right)^2\right]} = Y \qquad \text{(c)}$$

we obtain the result that yielding begins when

$$P = 0.218\,\frac{I_{yy}Y}{Lr} \qquad \text{(d)}$$

Substituting (b) into the maximum shear-stress criterion,

$$\tau_{max} = \tfrac{1}{2}\left(\frac{PLr}{I_{yy}} + 4\frac{PLr}{I_{yy}}\right) = \frac{Y}{2} \qquad \text{(e)}$$

we find that yielding is predicted when

$$P = 0.200\,\frac{I_{yy}Y}{Lr} \qquad \text{(f)}$$

Note the discrepancy of 9 percent between the loads predicted by the two criteria.

Repeat the foregoing calculations for the element on top of the beam at location B_2.

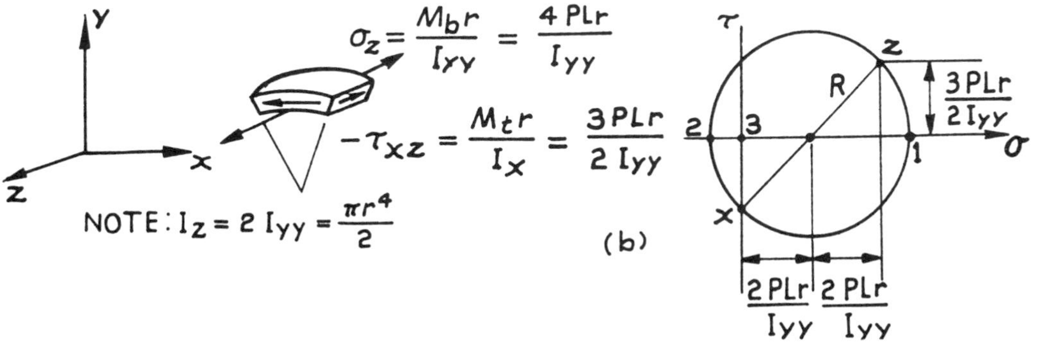

FIG. 2 (b) MAXIMUM STRESS CONDITION AT LOCATION B_2.

The radius of the Mohr's circle for the element at B_2, shown in Fig. 2(b), is

$$R = \sqrt{\left(\frac{2PLr}{I_{yy}}\right)^2 + \left(\frac{3PLr}{2I_{yy}}\right)^2}$$

$$= \frac{5}{2}\frac{PLr}{I_{yy}} .$$

Using Fig. 2(b) we find the principal stresses to be

$$\sigma_1 = +\frac{9}{2}\frac{PLr}{I_{yy}} \qquad \sigma_2 = -\frac{1}{2}\frac{PLr}{I_{yy}} \qquad \sigma_3 = 0 \tag{g}$$

and that according to the Mises criterion, yielding occurs when P satisfies

$$Y = \sqrt{\tfrac{1}{2}\left[\left(\frac{9}{2}\frac{PLr}{I_{yy}} + \frac{1}{2}\frac{PLr}{I_{yy}}\right)^2 + \left(-\frac{1}{2}\frac{PLr}{I_{yy}} - 0\right)^2 + \left(0 - \frac{9}{2}\frac{PLr}{I_{yy}}\right)^2\right]}$$

$$= 4.757\frac{PLr}{I_{yy}}$$

$$\therefore P = 0.210\frac{I_{yy}Y}{Lr} \tag{h}$$

while according to the maximum shear-stress criterion, yielding occurs when

$$\tau_{max} = \tfrac{1}{2}\left(\frac{9}{2}\frac{PLr}{I_{yy}} + \frac{1}{2}\frac{PLr}{I_{yy}}\right) = \frac{Y}{2}$$

$$\therefore P = 0.200\frac{I_{yy}Y}{Lr} \tag{i}$$

The maximum shear-stress criterion predicts yielding at locations B_1 and B_2 at the same load, indicating that the Mohr's circles in Fig. 2(a) and b are of equal size. The Mises criterion identifies B_2 as the critical location and predicts yielding there at a load 5 percent greater than the load for yielding according to the maximum shear-stress criterion.

In a one-dimensional tension test of a specimen, the yield stress was found to be 30,000 psi. Determine whether there will be yielding according to the Tresca criterion and also the maximum distortion strain—energy criterion for the following state of plane stress: $\tau_{xx} = 10,000$ psi; $\tau_{yy} = -20,000$ psi; $\tau_{xy} = 5,000$ psi.

Solution: To find the principal stresses in the xy plane we employ the Mohr's circle diagram for stresses, from which,

$$\tau_{a,b} = \frac{\tau_{xx} + \tau_{yy}}{2} + \frac{\tau_{xx} - \tau_{yy}}{2} \cos 2\theta_{a,b} + \tau_{xy} \sin 2\theta_{a,b}$$

$$\tan 2\theta = \frac{2\tau_{xy}}{\tau_{xx} - \tau_{yy}} = \frac{10,000}{30,000} = \frac{1}{3}$$

$$\therefore \theta_{a,b} = 9.22^\circ, 99.22^\circ \tag{b}$$

The principal stresses are then

$$\tau_{a,b} = \frac{\tau_{xx} + \tau_{yy}}{2} + \frac{\tau_{xx} - \tau_{yy}}{2} \cos\begin{Bmatrix}18.43^\circ\\198.43^\circ\end{Bmatrix} + \tau_{xy} \sin\begin{Bmatrix}18.43^\circ\\198.43^\circ\end{Bmatrix}$$

$$= \frac{10,000 - 20,000}{2} + \frac{10,000 + 20,000}{2}\begin{Bmatrix}.948\\-.948\end{Bmatrix} + (5000)\begin{Bmatrix}.316\\-.316\end{Bmatrix}$$

$$= 10,790, \ -20,790 \text{ psi} \tag{c}$$

Alternatively, the principal stresses may be obtained from the formula

$$\tau_{a,b} = \frac{\tau_{xx} + \tau_{yy}}{2} \pm \sqrt{\left(\frac{\tau_{xx} - \tau_{yy}}{2}\right)^2 + \tau_{xy}^2}$$

$$= \frac{10,000 - 20,000}{2} \pm \sqrt{\left(\frac{10,000 + 20,000}{2}\right)^2 + 5,000^2}$$

$$= 10,810, \ -20,810 \text{ psi}$$

The third principal stress is clearly 0. Hence, for this case we have

$$\tau_1 = 10,790 \text{ psi}$$

$$\tau_2 = 0 \tag{d}$$

$$\tau_3 = -20,790$$

For the Tresca test we now compare

$$\frac{1}{2}(\tau_{max} - \tau_{min}) = \frac{1}{2}[10,790 - (-20,790)] = 15,790 \text{ psi} \tag{e}$$

with τ_{Tr} which is $Y/2 = 15,000$ psi. Clearly, the Tresca condition predicts yielding, since 15,790 psi > Y/2 (= 15,000 psi).

As for the distortional strain-energy test we compare

$$U_{distort} = \frac{1}{6E}(1+\nu)\left[(\tau_1 - \tau_2)^2 + (\tau_1 - \tau_3)^2 + (\tau_2 - \tau_3)^2\right]$$

$$= \frac{1}{6E}(1+\nu)\left[10,790 - 0)^2 + (10,790 + 20,790)^2 + (0 + 20,790)^2\right]$$

$$= \frac{1}{6E}(1+\nu)(116 \times 10^6 + 998 \times 10^6 + 430 \times 10^6)$$

$$= \frac{1}{6E}(1+\nu)(1546) \times 10^6 \qquad \text{(f)}$$

with $(U_{distort})_{tens}$, which from the tensile test is

$$[U_{distort}]_{tens} = \frac{1}{3E}(1+\nu)Y^2 = \frac{1}{6E}(1+\nu)1800 \times 10^6 \qquad \text{(g)}$$

Comparing (f) and (g) it is seen that yielding is not predicted according to the maximum strain-energy of distortion criterion.

• PROBLEM 14-4

A compressed air tank with thin cylindrical walls of thickness t and radius r holds air at gauge pressure p. Calculate the level of p for which yielding will occur according to the Tresca and also the Mises-Hencky criteria.

Solution: The principal stresses τ_1 and τ_2 for an element of the cylinder away from the ends are given approximately as

$$\tau_1 = \frac{pr}{t} \qquad \text{(a)}$$

$$\tau_2 = \frac{1}{2}\frac{pr}{t} \qquad \text{(b)}$$

$$\tau_3 = 0 .$$

According to the Mises-Hencky criterion for the onset of yielding we have

$$\tau_1^2 - \tau_1\tau_2 + \tau_2^2 = Y^2 \qquad \text{(c)}$$

Eliminating p from Eqs. (a) and (b) we get

$$\tau_1 = 2\tau_2 \qquad \text{(d)}$$

Solving Eqs. (c) and (d) simultaneously we have

$$\tau_2 = \frac{Y}{\sqrt{3}}$$

$$\tau_1 = \frac{2Y}{\sqrt{3}} \qquad \text{(e)}$$

From equations (a) and (b) we can conclude that the pressure at which yielding begins to occur according to the Mises-Hencky criterion is

$$p_{M-H} = \frac{2Yt}{\sqrt{3r}} \quad \text{(f)}$$

As for the Tresca condition, for the onset of yielding we have

$$\frac{1}{2}(\tau_{max} - \tau_{min}) = \frac{Y}{2}$$

$$\therefore \; (\tau_1 - 0) = Y \quad \text{(g)}$$

where $\tau_1 (= 2\tau_2)$ clearly is the largest normal stress and 0 is the smallest normal stress. From Eq. (a) and using Eq. (g) we may then solve for the pressure corresponding to the onset of yielding. Thus,

$$p_{Tr} = \frac{Yt}{r} \quad \text{(h)}$$

The Tresca criterion predicts a smaller pressure for the onset of yielding. That is,

$$\frac{p_{Tr}}{p_{M-H}} = \frac{\sqrt{3}}{2} = .866 \quad \text{(i)}$$

• PROBLEM 14-5

A machine member consisting of a suspended shaft and a thin web is subjected to a force F as shown in Fig. 1. Assume the weght of the web is negligible compared to the shaft. Compute the maximum normal stress in a section.

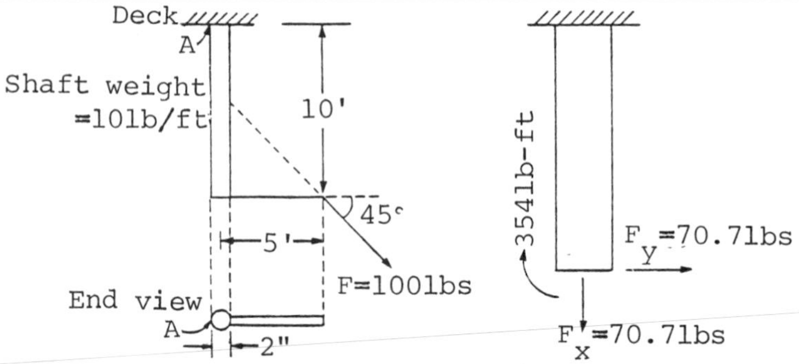

Solution: In the diagram of Fig. 2, the force F has been resolved into its components and the effective moment of 354 lb-ft.

The length of the shaft acts as a lever arm, and as a result the section at maximum stress is at the upper end of the shaft, where the maximum stress is at point A. Condsidering the three normal stress distributions superposed at that section,

$$(\tau_{xx})_1 = \frac{P}{A} = \frac{70.7}{(\pi)(1^2)} = 22.5 \text{ psi}$$

$$(\tau_{xx})_2 = \frac{wL}{A} = \frac{(10)(10)}{(\pi)(1^2)} = 31.8 \text{ psi} \quad \text{(a)}$$

$$(\tau_{xx})_3 = \frac{My}{I} = -\frac{[-(707) + (354)](12)y}{\frac{1}{4}\pi(1^4)} = 5400y$$

from which

$$(\tau_{xx})_{max} = 22.5 + 31.8 + 5400 = 5454 \text{ psi} \qquad \text{(b)}$$

As for the shear stress, we can expect the largest average value $\bar{\tau}_{xy}$ to occur over B-B of the shaft (see Fig. 2 (b)). Furthermore, because the boundaries at the ends of B-B are parallel to the y direction - i.e., the direction of τ_{xy} - we can expect that the average computed by our formula will be close to the value of what may be expected as a uniform distribution of shear stress over B-B. Thus we have,

$$\tau_{xy} = \frac{VQ}{It} = \frac{(70.7)[((\pi 1^2)/2)(.424)(1)]}{\left[\frac{1}{4}\pi(1^4)\right](2)} = 30.0 \text{ psi} \qquad \text{(c)}$$

We get the inconsequential stress of 30 psi.

Clearly, if the end load is increased, we can expect yielding to first occur at point A. Since we have only one nonzero stress there for reference xyz, we can expect yielding to occur when the stress τ_{xx} equals Y, the yield stress from the simple tensile stress. Accordingly, for Y = 100,000 psi, the maximum load that we can have with no yielding is given as follows:

$$Y = \frac{(P_{max})(.707)}{A} + \frac{wL}{A} - \frac{My}{I}$$

Inserting known values,

$$100{,}000 = \frac{(P_{max})(.707)}{\pi(1^2)} + 31.6$$

$$- \frac{[-(.707)P_{max}(10) + (.707)(P_{max})(5)](12)(1)}{\frac{1}{4}(\pi)(1^4)}$$

$$P_{max} = 1843 \text{ lb.}$$

• PROBLEM 14-6

A thin-walled cylinder is subjected to an axial tension of 60,000 lb. and a torque of 800,000 in.-lb. The cylinder has a diameter of 24 in. and a wall thickness of 0.15 in. Will the shell yield according to the maximum shear theory if the material has a tensile yield point of 10,000 psi?

Solution: The principal stresses are obtained by using the following equations:

$$\sigma_1 = \frac{\sigma_x + \sigma_y}{2} + \sqrt{\left(\frac{\sigma_x - \sigma_y}{2}\right)^2 + \tau_{xy}^2} \qquad (1)$$

$$\sigma_2 = \frac{\sigma_x + \sigma_y}{2} - \sqrt{\left(\frac{\sigma_x - \sigma_y}{2}\right)^2 + \tau_{xy}^2} \qquad (2)$$

Here,

$$\sigma = \sigma_x = \frac{P}{A} = \frac{60{,}000}{\pi(24)(0.15)} = 5305 \text{ psi}$$

$$\sigma_y = 0$$

and

$$\tau_{max} = \tau_{xy} = \frac{T}{2\pi r^2 t} = \frac{800,000}{2\pi(12)^2(0.15)} = 5895 \text{ psi}$$

Now using equations (1) and (2), the values of σ_1 and σ_2 can be determined.

$$\sigma_1 = \frac{5305 + 0}{2} + \sqrt{\left(\frac{5305 - 0}{2}\right)^2 + (5895)^2} = 9116 \text{ psi}$$

$$\sigma_2 = \frac{5305 + 0}{2} - \sqrt{\left(\frac{5305 - 0}{2}\right)^2 + (5895)^2} = -3812 \text{ psi}$$

Now, according to the maximum shear criterion, yielding will occur if $\sigma_{max} - \sigma_{min} = \sigma_{yp}$, where σ_{yp} is the yield stress in tension. For this cylinder, $\sigma_1 = \sigma_{max}$ and σ_{min} is given by σ_2 or σ_3, whichever is smaller. The principal stress σ_3, being normal to the shell wall in the radial direction, is zero. Hence, σ_3 is algebraically greater than σ_2(= -3812 psi) and $\sigma_{min} = \sigma_2 = -3812$. Thus,

$$\sigma_{max} - \sigma_{min} = 9116 - (-3812) = 12,928 \text{ psi.}$$

Since this is greater than the prescribed $\sigma_{yp} = 10,000$ psi, yielding will occur according to this failure theory.

• PROBLEM 14-7

A thin-walled cylindrical pressure vessel of radius 1m is subject to an internal pressure of 700 kN/m^2. If the material has a yield point of 250 MN/m^2, determine the required wall thickness according to (a) maximum stress theory and (b) von Mises' theory. Use a factor of safety of 2.

Solution: The principal stresses will be the circumferential stress σ_θ, the longitudinal stress σ_x, and the radial stress σ_r. Set $\sigma_1 = \sigma_\theta$; $\sigma_2 = \sigma_x$, $\sigma_3 = \sigma_r$. From thin-walled shell theory, we have

$$\sigma_1 = \frac{pr}{t} = \frac{700 \times 1}{t} = \frac{700 \text{ kN/m}}{t} \qquad (1)$$

$$\sigma_2 = \frac{pr}{2t} = \frac{700 \times 1}{2t} = \frac{350 \text{ kN/m}}{t} \qquad (2)$$

and

$$\sigma_3 = 0 .$$

According to maximum stress theory, yielding is not influenced by the level of the other principal stresses. Then yielding occurs if

$$\sigma_1 = \sigma_{yp} .$$

Hence, from equation (1),

$$\frac{700 \text{ kN/m}}{t} = \frac{250}{2} \text{ MN/m}^2$$

or

$$t = \frac{700 \times 2}{250} = 5.6 \text{ mm.}$$

(b) von Mises' theory states that yielding takes place when the principal stresses are such that

$$(\sigma_1 - \sigma_2)^2 + (\sigma_2 - \sigma_3)^2 + (\sigma_1 - \sigma_3)^2 = 2\sigma^2_{yp}$$

Substitution of the values for σ_1, σ_2, and σ_3 into the above equation yields,

$$\left[\left(\frac{700}{t} - \frac{350}{t}\right)^2 + \left(\frac{350}{t} - 0\right)^2 + \left(\frac{700}{t} - 0\right)^2\right]\left(\frac{kN}{m}\right)^2 = 2\left(\frac{250}{2}\frac{MN}{m^2}\right)^2$$

or

$$\left[\left(\frac{350}{t}\right)^2 + \left(\frac{350}{t}\right)^2 + \left(\frac{700}{t}\right)^2\right]\left(\frac{kN}{m}\right)^2 = 31250\left(\frac{MN}{m^2}\right)^2$$

or

$$\frac{735000}{t^2}\left(\frac{kN}{m}\right)^2 = 31250\left(\frac{MN}{m^2}\right)^2$$

from which

$$t^2 = 23.52 \text{ mm.}$$

or

$$t = 4.85 \text{ mm.}$$

• PROBLEM 14-8

A spherical tank with an outside diameter of 4 ft. is to contain air at a maximum pressure of 500 psi above the atmosphere. If the yield stress for the material to be used for the tank is 100,000 psi, design the thickness t for a safety factor of 3. Use both the Tresca and Mises-Hencky criteria.

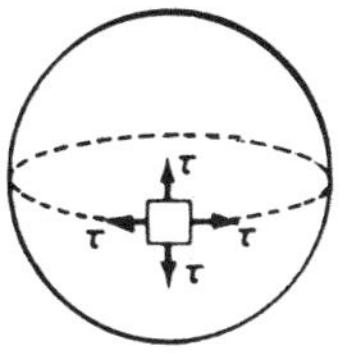

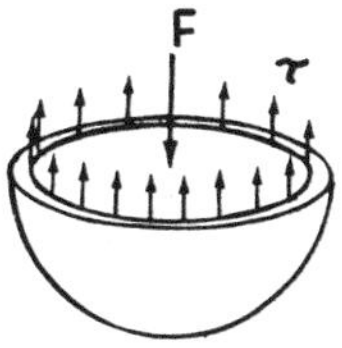

FIG.1. (a) (b)

Solution: We consider an element of the tank as shown in Fig. 1(a). Clearly, there are no shear stresses on the faces of the element, and the normal stresses shown are equal. To compute stress τ we take as a free body half the sphere as shown in Fig. 1(b). Owing to symmetry, the stress τ is uniform over the cut section. The force F is the resultant force from the inside pressure of 500 psi, computed by multiplying the pressure by the projected area in the direction of the desired force. Accordingly, from equilibrium we have

$$\tau(2\pi)\left(r - \frac{t}{2}\right) t = p\pi(r - t)^2$$

$$\therefore \tau = \frac{p(r - t)^2}{2\left(r - \frac{t}{2}\right)t} = \frac{(500)(24 - t)^2}{(48 - t)t} \qquad \text{(a)}$$

We thus have two principal stresses for the element shown in Fig. 1(a). The third principal stress would be some value between 500 psi on the inside surface and 14.7 psi on the outside surface, and accordingly, being so small, we shall consider it to be zero.

One guide that we may follow is to find the smallest thickness t that will just do the job. This will be the lightest design and most likely the most economical design. We could, in this regard, have the tank be just below yielding conditions when we have our maximum pressure of 500 psi. But this would assume complete accuracy of calculations and fabrication-something that is never reached. So instead of using the yield stress Y of 100,000 we employ, for the given safety factor of 3, a stress of 33,330 as a hypothetical "yield stress" while using the Tresca and Mises-Hencky yield criteria.

Considering the Tresca criterion first,

$$\tfrac{1}{2}(\tau_{max} - \tau_{min}) = \frac{Y}{2}$$

where

τ_{max}, τ_{min} = maximum and minimum stresses that could act on the material.

$$\tfrac{1}{2}[\tau_{max} - 0] = \frac{33,330}{2}$$

$$\therefore \quad \frac{500(24 - t)^2}{(48 - t)(t)} = 33,330 \qquad \text{(b)}$$

Solving for t using the quadratic formula we get

$$t = .178 \text{ in.}$$

This is the thinnest design for a safety factor of 3 according to the Tresca condition.

We next consider the Mises-Hencky condition for this design. The Mises-Hencky condition states

$$\tau_1^2 - \tau_1\tau_2 + \tau_2^2 = Y^2$$

where τ_1, τ_2 are the principal stresses. Thus,

$$\frac{\sqrt{2}}{2}\sqrt{2\tau^2} = \tau = \frac{(500)(24 - t)^2}{(48 - t)(t)} = 33,330$$

$$\therefore \quad t = .178 \text{ in.} \qquad \text{(c)}$$

Hence, in this comparatively simple situation both design criteria give the same result.

We point out that finding the appropriate thickness as we have done is but one part of the design. Further design considerations must be made which depend on the method of construction of this sphere. Conceivably, such considerations may require a thickness other than calculated here.

• PROBLEM 14-9

A circular shaft, 4 in. diameter, is tested in combined bending and torsion. At a certain cross-section the bending moment is twice the twisting moment. Determine the value of M and T at which yielding will first occur (a) according to Tresca's criterion and (b) according to the Von Mises criterion. In a simple tension test yielding occurs when the longitudinal tension is 50 ksi.

Solution: The critical point on the section is that which has the greatest bending stress, since this also has the greatest torsion stress.

For the circle, J = 2I

Due to torsion,

$$\tau = \frac{Tr}{J} = \frac{Tr}{2I}$$

At the same point, due to bending,

$$\sigma_x = \frac{Mr}{I} = \frac{2Tr}{I} \text{ (since } M = 2T)$$

For simplicity let $A = Tr/2I$
Then $\tau = A$ and $\sigma = 4A$
The principal stresses are,

$$\sigma_1 = \frac{\sigma_x}{2} + \sqrt{\left(\frac{\sigma_x}{2}\right)^2 + \tau^2} = 2A + \sqrt{4A^2 + A^2} = A(2 + \sqrt{5}) = 4.236A$$

$$\sigma_2 = \frac{\sigma_x}{2} - \sqrt{\left(\frac{\sigma_x}{2}\right)^2 + \tau^2} = A(2 - \sqrt{5}) = -0.236A$$

$$\sigma_3 = 0$$

The principal shear stresses are

$$\tau_1 = \frac{\sigma_2 - \sigma_3}{2} = -0.118A$$

$$\tau_2 = \frac{\sigma_3 - \sigma_1}{2} = -2.118A$$

$$\tau_3 = \frac{\sigma_1 - \sigma_2}{2} = 2.236A$$

(a) According to Tresca
For a given value of A, τ_{max} is 2.236A
In the tension test, $\sigma_1 = 50$, $\sigma_2 = \sigma_3 = 0$

$$\therefore \tau_{max} = \frac{50}{2} = 25 \text{ ksi}$$

Thus the critical value of $\tau_{max} = 25$
Hence yield occurs when $2.236A = 25$

$$A = 11.18$$

Since $I = 12.56 \text{ in}^4$ and $r = 2$ in.

$$\frac{T \times 2}{2 \times 12.56} = A = 11.18$$

Hence $T = 140.3$ kip-in. and $M = 280.6$ kip-in.

(b) According to Von Mises
The octahedral shear stress is

$$\tau_{oct} = \tfrac{2}{3}\sqrt{\tau_1^2 + \tau_2^2 + \tau_3^2} = \tfrac{2}{3} A\sqrt{0.118^2 + 2.118^2 + 2.236^2} = 2.056A$$

In the tension test, $\sigma_1 = 50$, $\sigma_2 = \sigma_3 = 0$

$$\tau_1 = 0,\ \tau_2 = -25,\ \tau_3 = 25$$

$$\therefore \tau_{oct} = \tfrac{2}{3}\sqrt{25^2 + 25^2 + 0} = \sqrt{\tfrac{2}{3}}\ 50 = 23.6 \text{ ksi}$$

$$2.056A = \tau_{oct} = 23.6 \text{ ksi}$$

$$A = 11.48 \text{ ksi}$$

$$\frac{T \times 2}{2 \times 12.56} = 11.48$$

Thus $T = 144.2$ kip-in. and $M = 288.3$ kip-in.

• PROBLEM 14-10

A crankshaft is made of steel having a tensile and compressive proportional limit of 40,000 lb. per sq. in. Determine, by each of the three theories of failure, the diameter d the shaft should have to resist the load P without developing more than one-half of the maximum elastic strength of the material.

Solution: The twisting moment T and the bending moment M have the following values:

$$T = 6P = 60{,}000 \text{ lb.-in. and } M = 8P = 80{,}000 \text{ lb.-in.};$$

and the shearing and normal unit stresses due, respectively, to T and M are

$$S_s = \frac{Tc}{J} = \frac{16T}{\pi d^3} \quad \text{and} \quad S = \frac{Mc}{I} = \frac{32M}{\pi d^3}$$

(a) Maximum Principal Stress Theory. The maximum principal unit stress resulting from the unit stresses S_s and S_1, is

$$S' = \tfrac{1}{2}S + \tfrac{1}{2}\sqrt{S^2 + 4S_s^2}$$

and, according to the maximum stress theory, inelastic action in the material begins when S' exceeds 40,000 lb. per sq. in. Hence the working unit stress is 20,000 lb. per sq. in. Therefore,

$$20{,}000 = \tfrac{1}{2}\,\frac{32M}{\pi d^3} + \tfrac{1}{2}\sqrt{\left(\frac{32M}{\pi d^3}\right)^2 + \left(\frac{2 \times 16T}{\pi d^3}\right)^2}$$

$$= \frac{16}{\pi d^3}\left(M + \sqrt{M^2 + T^2}\right)$$

Hence

$$d^3 = \frac{16}{\pi 20{,}000}\left[80{,}000 + \sqrt{(80{,}000)^2 + (60{,}000)^2}\right]$$

and

$$d^3 = \frac{8}{\pi}\left[8 + \sqrt{(8)^2 + (6)^2}\right] = 45.8 \text{ in.}^3$$

Therefore

$$d = 3.58 \text{ in.}$$

(b) Maximum Strain Theory. According to the maximum strain theory, inelastic action in the material begins when the value of ϵ becomes equal to

$$\frac{S_e}{E} = \frac{40{,}000}{30{,}000{,}000} = 0.00133 \text{ in. per in.}$$

And, the maximum value of ϵ, if μ is assumed to be equal to 0.30, is given by the equation,

$$\epsilon = \frac{1}{E}\left(0.35S + 0.65\sqrt{S^2 + 4S_s^2}\right)$$

The working value of ϵ is $\tfrac{1}{2} \times \dfrac{40{,}000}{E} = \dfrac{20{,}000}{E}$

$$0.000667 = \frac{20,000}{E} = \frac{1}{E}\left[\frac{32}{\pi d^3}(0.35M + 0.65\sqrt{M^2 + T^2})\right]$$

Hence

$$d^3 = \frac{16}{\pi}(0.35 \times 8 + 0.65 \times 10) = 47.4 \text{ in.}^3$$

Therefore

$$d = 3.62 \text{ in.}$$

(c) Maximum Shearing Stress Theory. According to this theory inelastic action in the shaft begins when the maximum shearing unit stress S'_s as given by the equation,

$$S'_s = \tfrac{1}{2}\sqrt{S^2 + 4S_s^2}$$

reaches the shearing elastic limit, which is ½ x 40,000, or 20,000 lb. per sq. in. The working unit stress then is 10,000 lb. per sq. in. Hence,

$$10,000 = \tfrac{1}{2}\sqrt{S^2 + 4S_s^2} = \frac{16}{\pi d^3}\sqrt{M^2 + T^2}$$

Hence,

$$d^3 = \frac{160}{10\pi}\sqrt{8^2 + 6^2} = \frac{1600}{10\pi} = 51.0 \text{ in.}^3$$

Therefore,

$$d = 3.71 \text{ in.}$$

Thus, in this problem the maximum shearing stress theory requires the largest shaft.

• PROBLEM 14-11

The solid circular shaft of Fig. 1 has a proportional limit of 64 ksi and a Poisson's ratio of 0.30. Determine the value of the load R for failure by slip as predicted by each of the four given theories of failure. Assume that point A is the most severely stressed point.

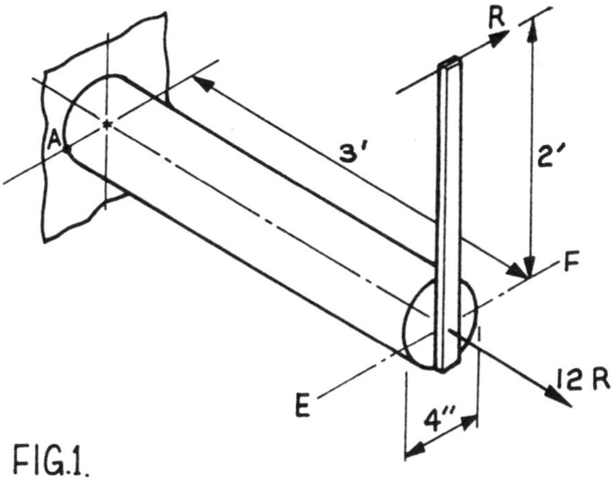

FIG.1.

Solution: When two equal opposite forces R are introduced along line EF of Fig. 1, it is evident that the bending moment at point A is 36R in-kips, the torsional moment is 24R in-kips, and the axial load is 12R kips. The flexural stress at A is

$$\sigma_1 = \frac{Mc}{I} = \frac{36R(2)}{\pi(2^4)/4} = \frac{18R}{\pi}\ T .$$

The direct stress at A is

$$\sigma_2 = \frac{P}{A} = \frac{12R}{\pi(2^2)} = \frac{3R}{\pi}\ T ,$$

and the sum of the two tensile stresses at A becomes

$$\sigma = \sigma_1 + \sigma_2 = \frac{21R}{\pi} .$$

The torsional shearing stress at A is

$$\tau = \frac{Tc}{J} = \frac{24R(2)}{\pi(2^4)/2} = \frac{6R}{\pi} .$$

The maximum stresses at A are

$$\tau_{max} = \sqrt{\left(\frac{10.5R}{\pi}\right)^2 + \left(\frac{6R}{\pi}\right)^2} = \frac{12.1R}{\pi} ,$$

$$\sigma_{p1} = \frac{10.5R}{\pi} + \frac{12.1R}{\pi} = \frac{22.6R}{\pi}\ T ,$$

and

$$\sigma_{p2} = \frac{10.5R}{\pi} - \frac{12.1R}{\pi} = -\frac{1.6R}{\pi} = \frac{1.6R}{\pi}\ C .$$

According to the maximum-normal-stress theory

$$64 = \sigma_f = \sigma_{p1} = 22.6R/\pi ,$$

from which

$$R = 64\pi/22.6 = 8.90 \text{ kips.}$$

According to the maximum-shearing-stress theory

$$64/2 = \tau_f = \tau_{max} = 12.1R/\pi ,$$

from which

$$R = 32\pi/12.1 = 8.31 \text{ kips.}$$

The maximum-normal-strain theory gives

$$\frac{\sigma_f}{E} = \frac{\sigma_{p1} - \mu\sigma_{p2}}{E}$$

or

$$64 = \frac{22.6R}{\pi} - 0.3\left(-\frac{1.6R}{\pi}\right) ,$$

which gives $R = 64\pi/23.1 = 8.71$ kips.

According to the maximum-distortion-energy theory

$$\sigma_f^2 = \sigma_{p1}^2 + \sigma_{p2}^2 - \sigma_{p1}\sigma_{p2}$$

or

$$64^2 = \left(\frac{22.6R}{\pi}\right)^2 + \left(-\frac{1.6R}{\pi}\right)^2 - \frac{22.6R}{\pi}\left(-\frac{1.6R}{\pi}\right) ,$$

which gives $R = 64\pi/23.4 = 8.59$ kips.

In this example the maximum-shearing-stress theory is seen to be the most conservative, and the maximum-normal-stress theory gives the least conservative result.

A torque a vertical force, and an axial load are applied to the free end of a solid steel rod fixed at the other end. (a) compute the maximum principal stress in the rod, and (b) determine the minimum radius of the rod for a yield stress of 100,000 psi and a safety factor of 2. Assume a Poisson's ratio of 3.

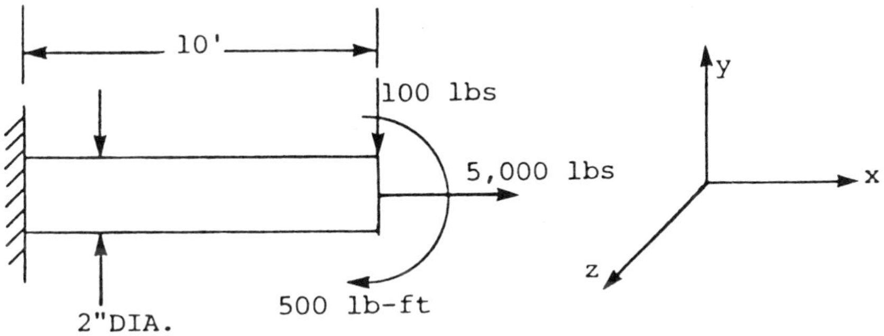

Fig. 1.

Solution: From an inspection of the configuration, it may be seen that the maximum stress τxx is present at point A in Fig. 2 which represents the section of the rod at the fixed end. Maximum torsional shear stress will also be present at this point. As a result, the maximum principal stress will be present at that point A, as follows:

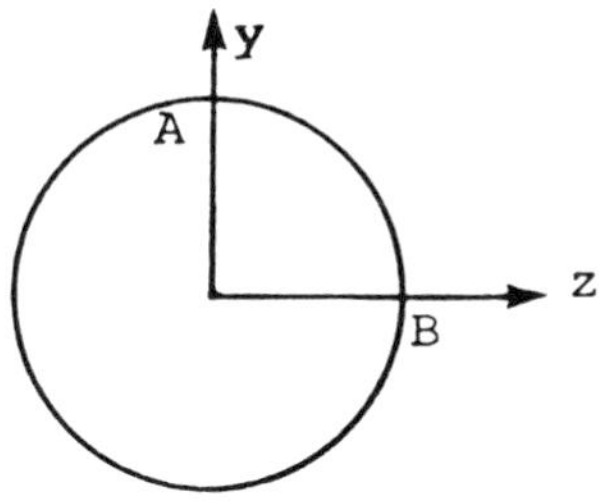

Fig. 2.

From the axial load--tensile distribution:

$$(\tau_{xx})_{tens} = \frac{P}{A} = \frac{5000}{\pi(1^2)} = 1592 \text{ psi}$$

From the vertical force--bending stress:

$$(\tau_{xx})_{bending} = -\frac{M_{max}(-Y_{max})}{I} = \frac{[(100)(10)(12)]\,(I)}{\frac{1}{4}\pi(1^4)} = 15{,}280 \text{ psi}$$

From the vertical force--shear stress:

$$(\tau_{xy})_{shear} = 0$$

From the torque--torsional shear

$$(\tau_{x\theta})_{torsion} = \frac{Tr_{max}}{J} = \frac{[(500)(12)](1)}{\frac{1}{2}\pi(1^4)} = 3820 \text{ psi}$$

at point B there is the maximum shear stress from $(\tau_{xy})_{shear}$ and $\tau_{x\theta}$. The uniform stress $(\tau_{xx})_{tensile}$ is also there.

Thus from the axial load:

$$(\tau_{xx})_{tens} = \frac{P}{A} = 1592$$

From the vertical force (bending)

$$(\tau_{xx})_{bending} = 0$$

From the vertical force (shear)

$$(\tau_{xy})_{shear} = \frac{VQ_{max}}{Ib} = \frac{(100)\left[(\frac{1}{2})(\pi)(1^2)\right](.424)(1)}{\left[\frac{1}{4}\pi\ 1^4\right]\left[2\right]} = 42.4 \text{ psi}$$

From the torque (torsional shear)

$$(\tau_{x\theta})_{torsion} = \frac{Tr_{max}}{J} = 3820 \text{ psi}$$

Considering the four stress distributions evaluated for points A and B, it may be seen that the maximum stress occurs at point A.

From the relationship,

$$\tan 2\theta \equiv \frac{2(\tau_{x\theta})_{torsion}}{(\tau_{xx})_{tens} + (\tau_{xx})_{bending}}$$

and substituting

$$\tan 2\theta = \frac{(2)(-3820)}{16{,}870} = -.453$$

$$2\theta = 155.6^\circ,\ 335.6^\circ$$

The maximum stress is, therefore,

$$\frac{16,870}{2} + \frac{16,870}{2} \cos\begin{Bmatrix}155.6^\circ \\ 335.6^\circ\end{Bmatrix} - 3820 \sin\begin{Bmatrix}155.6^\circ \\ 335.6^\circ\end{Bmatrix}$$

$$= -825 \text{ psi, } 17,690 \text{ psi}$$

(b) Concentrating further on point A,

$$(\tau_{xx})_{tens} = \frac{P}{A} = \frac{5000}{(\pi)(r^2)} = \frac{1590}{r^2}$$

$$(\tau_{xx})_{bending} = -\frac{M_{max}(-Y_{max})}{I} = \frac{[(100)(10)(12)](r)}{(\frac{1}{4})(\pi)r^4} = \frac{15,300}{r^3}$$

$$(\tau_{xy})_{shear} = 0$$

$$(\tau_{x\theta})_{torsion} = \frac{Tr_{max}}{J} = \frac{[(500)(12)](r)}{\frac{1}{2}\pi(r^4)} = \frac{3820}{r^3}$$

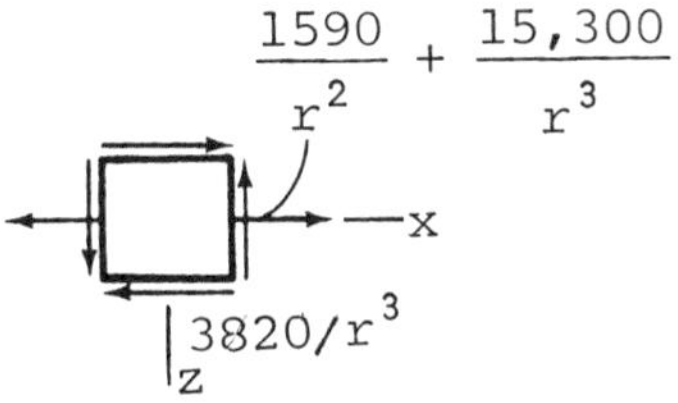

The stresses on an infinitesimal element are then as shown in the figure above, from which the principal stresses are

$$\tau_{a,b} = \frac{\left(\frac{1590}{r^2} + \frac{15,300}{r^3}\right)}{2} \pm \sqrt{\frac{\left(\frac{1590}{r^2} + \frac{15,300}{r^3}\right)^2}{4} + \left(\frac{3820}{r^3}\right)^2} \qquad (1)$$

Using the Tresca condition,

$$(\tau_{max} - \tau_{min}) = 50,000 \qquad (2)$$

Use 50,000 psi for Y (yield strength) in place of its true value of 100,000 psi, for the safety factor of 2. The two principal stresses can be obtained form equation (1) for each value of r. Using a computer it is possible to find that value of r = .715 for which equation (2) is satisfied.

• PROBLEM 14-13

A steel pipe is bent along three equal lengths for the configuration shown in Fig. 1. and is subjected to a force at its free end. If the force is to be resisted safely with a safety factor of 3, find the diameter of the smallest permissible pipe. Neglect the effects at the bends.

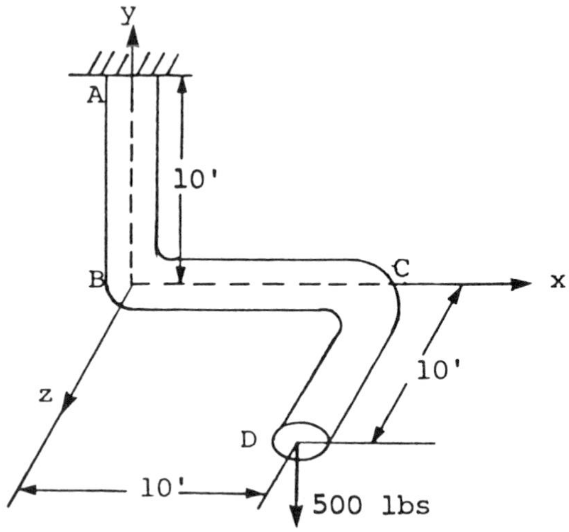

Fig. 1.

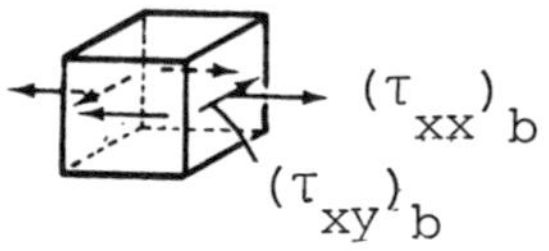

ELEMENT AT POINT (b)
Fig. 2.

Solution: The question now arises as to where the worst state of stress exists. A quick inspection reveals immediately that it might occur toward the left end of pipe section B where we get on the top surface a tensile stress from bending and a shear stress from torsion on the same interface. On the other hand, in member A there will be a combination of bending plus axial load that we shall superpose to compute a possible maximum tensile stress.

Considering length BC, the normal stress at point B is obtained from the relation:

$$(\tau_{xx})_B = -\frac{My}{I} = \frac{[(5000)(12)][D_0/2]}{\frac{\pi}{64}(D_0^4 - D_i^4)} = \left(611{,}000 \frac{D_0}{D_0^4 - D_i^4}\right) \tag{1}$$

Where D_o and D_i are the outside and inside diameters of the pipe, respectively. The torsional stress at B is

$$(\tau_{xy})_B = \frac{[(500)(10)(12)][D_0/2]}{\frac{\pi}{32}(D_0^4 - D_i^4)} = 305{,}500 \frac{D_0}{D_0^4 - D_i^4} \tag{2}$$

Considering length AB, there is a bending moment of 5,000 lb-ft about the x axis and -5,000 lb-ft about the z axis. The total bending moment is between these axes and is obtained from

$$M_T = \sqrt{5000^2 + 5000^2} = 7071 \text{ ft-lb} \tag{3}$$

Using relation (3) to calculate bending stress $(\tau_{yy})_1$ for an element most distant from the neutral axis,

$$(\tau_{yy})_1 = \frac{[(7071)(12)](D_0/2)}{\frac{\pi}{64}\left(D_0^4 - D_i^4\right)} \tag{4}$$

The axial loading on length AB produces a stress

$$(\tau_{yy})_2 = \frac{500}{\frac{\pi}{4}\left(D_0^2 - D_i^2\right)} \tag{5}$$

The principal that need to be considered only are $(\tau_{yy})_1 + (\tau_{yy})_2$; 0; and 0. Using the Mises-Hencky criterion, the octahedral shear stress can be calculated and compared to $\frac{1}{3}\sqrt{2/3}\ Y$.

The octahedral shear stress can be plotted for the mo distant element considered above, as a function of D_o. For the relationships in this problem, the value for D_o is found as 4 in.

CHAPTER 15

ENERGY METHOD

STRAIN-ENERGY CALCULATIONS

• PROBLEM 15-1

A simple beam of length L supports two concentrated loads as shown in Fig. 1. Assuming a = L/4, find the strain energy U stored in the beam. Using this result, determine the deflection δ under one of the loads.

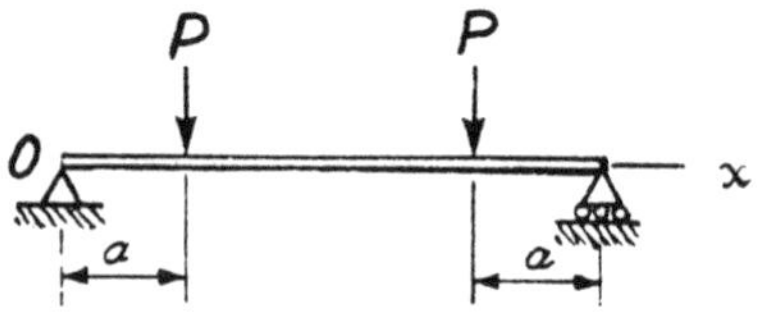

FIG.1

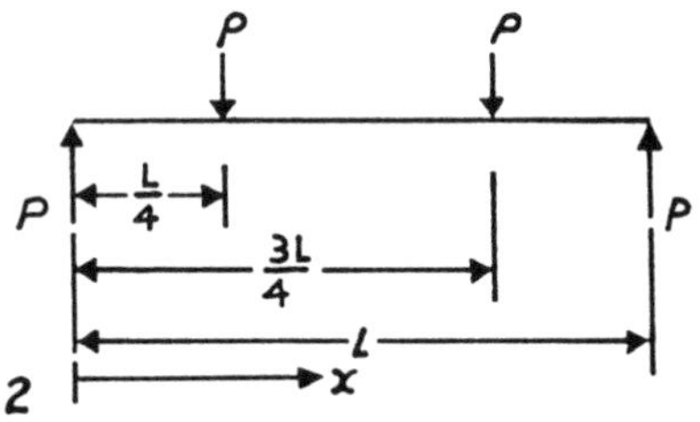

FIG. 2

Solution: The equation for the strain energy stored in a beam is

$$U = \frac{1}{2EI}\int_0^L M^2 dx \tag{1}$$

The moment equations are from Fig. 2:

$0 \le x \le L/4$ $\quad$ $M = Px$

$L/4 \le x \le 3L/4$ $\quad$ $M = PL/4$

$3L/4 \le x \le L$ $\quad$ $M = PL - Px$

Substituting into Eq.(1) gives

$$U = \frac{1}{2EI}\left[\int_0^{L/4} P^2x^2 dx + \int_{L/4}^{3L/4} (P^2L^2/16)dx + \int_{3L/4}^{L} (P^2L^2 - 2P^2Lx + P^2x^2)dx\right]$$

Integrating yields

$$U = \frac{1}{2EI}\left[(P^2 x^3/3)\Big|_o^{L/4} + (P^2L^2 x/16)\Big|_{L/4}^{3L/4}\right.$$

$$\left. + (P^2L^2x - P^2Lx^2 + P^2x^3/3)\Big|_{3L/4}^{L}\right]$$

Substituting in the limits of integration, the equation becomes

$$U = \frac{1}{2EI}\left(\frac{P^2L^3}{192} + \frac{P^2L^3}{32} + P^2L^3 - \frac{3P^2L^3}{4} - P^2L^3 + \frac{9P^2L^3}{16}\right.$$

$$\left. + \frac{P^2L^3}{3} - \frac{9P^2L^3}{64}\right)$$

Simplifying,

$$U = \frac{1}{2EI}\left(\frac{P^2L^3}{192}\right)(1 + 6 + 64 - 27 - 192 + 108 + 192 - 144)$$

$$U = \frac{P^2L^3\ (8)}{2EI(192)}$$

Thus the total strain energy of the beam is

$$U = \frac{P^2L^3}{48EI}$$

The equation for the deflection under the load, P, is

$$\frac{\partial U}{\partial P} = y$$

The deflection is therefore

$$y = \frac{PL^3}{24EI}$$

• PROBLEM 15-2

Derive an expression for the strain energy U stored in a beam in pure bending (Fig. 1) in terms of the maximum normal stress σ_{max} in the beam. Assume that the beam is of rectangular cross section (width b, height h). (Express U as a function of the maximum stress σ_{max}, the modulus of elasticity E, and the dimensions of the beam.)

Solution: Above the neutral axis there is compressive stress in the x direction and below the neutral axis there is tensile stress in the x direction. Stress exists only parallel to the x axis. The strain energy per unit 2

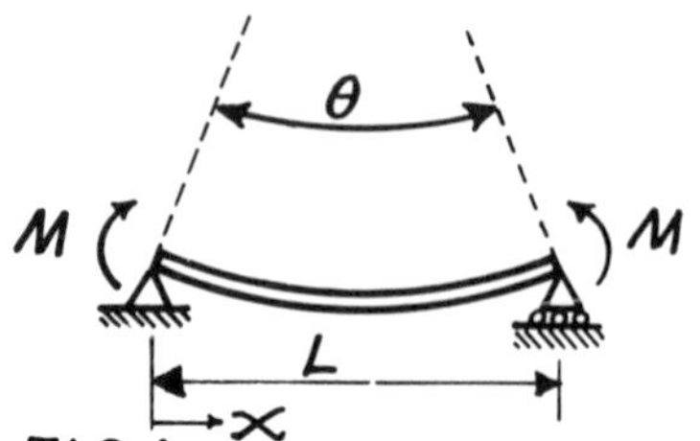

FIG.1

volume due to stress in one direction only is $\sigma^2/(2E)$.
The total strain energy is

$$U = \int_{vol.} \frac{\sigma^2}{2E}\, dV \qquad (1)$$

The relation between the stress and the maximum stress is obtained from the flexure formula

$$\sigma = \frac{My}{I}, \quad \sigma_{max} = \frac{Mh/2}{I}$$

$$\sigma = 2y\sigma_{max}/h$$

Substituting for σ in Eq.(1) gives

$$U = \int_{vol.} \frac{(2y\sigma_{max}/h)^2}{2E}\, dV$$

Squaring the term in parenthesis and simplifying yields

$$U = \int_{vol.} \frac{2y^2\sigma_{max}^2}{Eh^2}\, dV$$

Separating the differential volume into length, width and height terms and taking the constant terms outside the integral gives

$$U = \frac{2\sigma_{max}^2}{Eh^2} \int_o^L \int_{-b/2}^{b/2} \int_{-h/2}^{h/2} y^2 dydzdx$$

Performing the integration gives

$$U = \frac{2bL\sigma_{max}^2}{Eh^2} [(h/2)^3 - (-h/2)^3]$$

Thus

$$U = \frac{bhL\sigma_{max}^2}{6E}.$$

Find the maximum deflection due to a force P applied at the end of an elastic cantilever having a rectangular cross section, Fig. 1(a). Consider the effect of the flexural and shearing deformations.

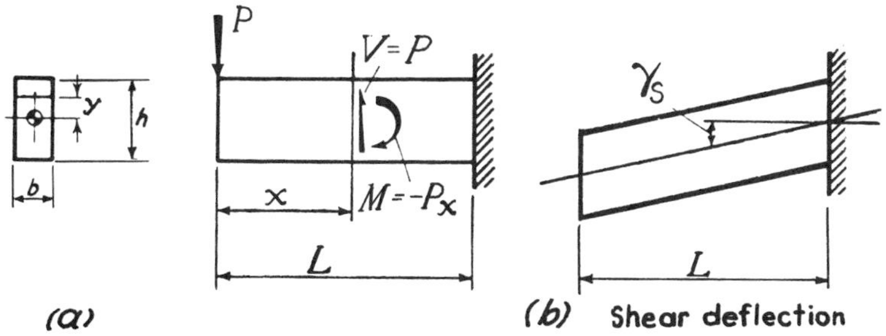

FIG. 1

Solution: As the force P is applied to the beam, the external work $W_e = P\Delta/2$, where Δ is the total deflection of the end of the beam. The internal strain energy consists of two parts. One part is due to the bending stresses, the other is caused by the shearing stresses.

The strain energy in bending is obtained from equation $U = \int M^2 dx/(2EI)$, by noting that $M = -Px$. The strain energy in shear is found by using equation $dU_{shear} = [\tau^2/(2G)]dV$. In this particular problem, the shear at every section is equal to the applied force P while the shearing stress τ, is distributed parabolically as $\tau = [P/(2I)][h/2)^2 - y^2]$. At any one level y, this shearing stress does not vary across either the breadth b or the length L of the beam. Therefore the infinitesimal volume dV in the shear energy expression is taken as Lb dy. By equating the sum of these two internal strain energies to the external work, the total deflection is obtained:

$$U_{bending} = \int_0^L \frac{M^2 dx}{2EI} = \int_0^L \frac{(-Px)^2 dx}{2EI} = \frac{P^2L^3}{6EI}$$

and

$$U_{shear} = \int_{vol} \frac{\tau^2}{2G} dV$$

Substituting the value of τ we obtain,

$$U_{shear} = \frac{1}{2G} \int_{vol} \{\frac{P}{2I}[(\frac{h}{2})^2 - y^2]\}^2 dV$$

Since $dV = Lbdy$, the above equation becomes

$$U_{shear} = \frac{1}{2G}\int_{-h/2}^{h/2}\{\frac{P}{2I}[(\frac{h}{2})^2 - y^2]\}^2 Lbdy$$

$$= \frac{P^2Lb}{2G4I^2}\int_{-h/2}^{h/2}[\frac{h^2}{4} - y^2]^2 dy$$

$$= \frac{P^2Lb}{8GI^2}\int_{-h/2}^{h/2}[\frac{h^4}{16} - \frac{h^2}{2}y^2 + y^4]dy$$

Carrying out the integration yields

$$U_{shear} = \frac{P^2Lb}{8GI^2}\left\{\frac{h^4}{16}y\Big|_{-h/2}^{h/2} - \frac{h^2}{2}\frac{y^3}{3}\Big|_{-h/2}^{h/2} + \frac{y^5}{5}\Big|_{-h/2}^{h/2}\right\}$$

$$= \frac{P^2Lb}{8GI^2}\left\{\frac{h^4}{16}(\frac{h}{2}+\frac{h}{2}) - \frac{h^2}{6}\left[(\frac{h}{2})^3 - (-\frac{h}{2})^3\right] + \frac{1}{5}\left[(\frac{h}{2})^5 - (-\frac{h}{2})^5\right]\right\}$$

$$= \frac{P^2Lb}{8GI^2}\left\{\frac{h^5}{16} - \frac{h^5}{24} + \frac{1}{80}h^5\right\}$$

$$= \frac{P^2Lb}{8GI^2}\left\{\frac{8}{240}h^5\right\}$$

Since $I = \frac{bh^3}{12}$, we have

$$U_{shear} = \frac{P^2Lb}{8G}\frac{h^5}{30}(\frac{12}{bh^3})^2 = \frac{3P^2L}{5Gbh}$$

or

$$U_{shear} = \frac{3P^2L}{5GA}$$

where $A = bh$ is the cross section of the beam. Then

$$W_e = U = U_{bending} + U_{shear}$$

$$\frac{P\Delta}{2} = \frac{P^2L^3}{6EI} + \frac{3P^2L}{5AG} \quad \text{or} \quad \Delta = \frac{PL^3}{3EI} + \frac{6PL}{5AG}$$

The first term in the result, $PL^3/(3EI)$, is the ordinary deflection of the beam due to flexure. The second term is the deflection due to shear and can be interpreted as follows: The ratio P/A = V/A is the average shearing stress τ_{av} across the section. This quantity divided by the shearing modulus G gives the shearing strain for a uniform stress. Since, however, the shearing stress varies across the section, a numerical correction factor, called here α, is necessary. In this problem $\alpha = 6/5$. On this basis (see Fig. 1(b)), for the constant shear occurring along the beam, the end deflection due to shear may be expressed in the following alternative forms:

$$\Delta_{shear} = \gamma_s L = \alpha \frac{\tau_{av}}{G} L = \alpha \frac{VL}{AG} = \frac{6PL}{5AG}$$

The factor α depends on the cross-sectional area of a member. In general, the shear V can vary across the span.

It is instructive to recast the expression for the total deflection Δ as

$$\Delta = \frac{PL^3}{3EI}\left[1 + \frac{18}{5}\frac{EI}{L^2 AG}\right]$$

$$= \frac{PL^3}{3EI}\left[1 + \frac{18E}{5GL^2}\left(\frac{bh^3}{12}\right)\left(\frac{1}{bh}\right)\right]$$

$$= \frac{PL^3}{3EI}\left[1 + \frac{3Eh^2}{10GL^2}\right]$$

where as before, the last term gives the deflection due to shear.

To gain further insight into this problem, replace in the last expression the ratio E/G by 2.5, a typical value for steels. Then

$$\Delta = (1 + 0.75h^2/L^2)\Delta_{bending}$$

From this equation it can be seen that for a short beam--for example, one with L = h--the total deflection is 1.75 times that due to bending. Hence shear deflection is very important in comparable cases. On the other hand, if L = 10h, the deflection due to shear is less than 1 percent. Small deflections due to shear are typical for ordinary, slender beams. This fact may be noted further from the original equation for Δ. There, whereas the deflection due to shear increases directly with the span length, the deflection due to bending increases as the cube of this distance. Therefore, as the length of a beam increases, the deflection due to bending quickly becomes dominant. For this reason it is usually possible to neglect the deflection due to shear. Of course, such a generalization is not always possible.

A structure consisting of two horizontal bars AC and CB, each of length L, is shown in Fig. 1(a). The bars have pinned supports and are linked together at C. The material of the bars is linearly elastic, and each bar has constant axial rigidity EA. If a vertical load P is applied at C, the bars will be incapable of supporting the load as long as they remain in their initial horizontal position. However, as the load is applied gradually, joint C will deflect downward and tensile forces will develop in the bars. Thus, an equilibrium position of the structure can be reached with a small deflection δ under the load (see Fig. 1(b)). Obtain the strain energy and complementary energy for this structure.

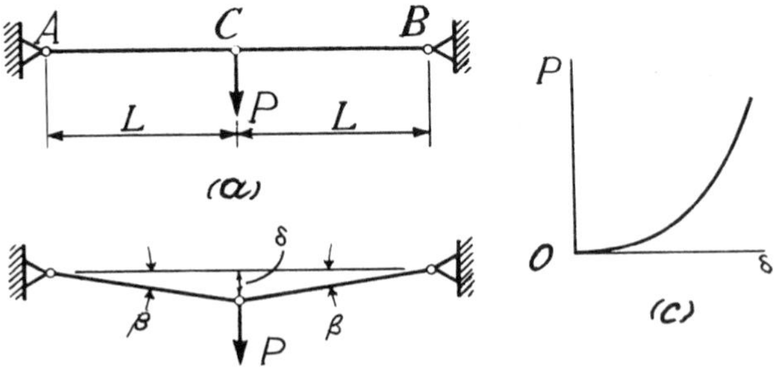

FIG. 1

Solution: In order to evaluate the strain energy and complementary energy for the given structure, we must first obtain the relationship between the load P and the deflection δ. This relation can be found from the expressions for the forces and elongations of the bars. Thus, the tensile force N in each bar, from statics, is

$$N = \frac{P}{2 \sin \beta}$$

where β is the angle of rotation of the bars. However, both the deflection δ and the angle β are assumed to be small quantities, hence we can replace β by δ/L and $\sin \beta$ by β. Therefore, the preceding equation becomes

$$N = \frac{PL}{2\delta} \qquad \text{(a)}$$

The elongation Δ of each individual bar can now be found from Hooke's law:

$$\Delta = \frac{NL}{EA} = \frac{PL^2}{2EA\delta} \qquad \text{(b)}$$

A second equation relating the deflection δ of the structure and the elongation Δ of the bars can be found from the geometry of the deflected structure. The increase in length of each bar (from Fig. 1(b)) is

$$\Delta = \sqrt{L^2 + \delta^2} - L = L\sqrt{1 + (\frac{\delta}{L})^2} - L$$

Expansion of the expression under the radical sign according to the binomial theorem gives

$$\Delta = L[1 + \frac{1}{2}(\frac{\delta}{L})^2 - \frac{1}{8}(\frac{\delta}{L})^4 + \ldots] - L$$

For small deflections we can drop the terms containing powers of δ/L higher than two. Thus keeping only the first two terms in the brackets, the expression for Δ simplifies to

$$\Delta = \frac{\delta^2}{2L} \qquad \text{(c)}$$

Now we can eliminate Δ between Eqs. (b) and (c), thereby producing the desired load-deflection relationship for the structure. This relation may be expressed in either of the following two forms:

$$P = \frac{EA\delta^3}{L^3} \qquad \delta = \sqrt[3]{\frac{PL^3}{EA}}$$

The graph of these equations is shown in Fig. 1(c). It is important to note that the structure analyzed in this example is geometrically nonlinear, even though the material itself follows Hooke's law.

Now we can easily find the strain energy of the structure as follows:

$$U = \int_0^\delta P d\delta = \int_0^\delta \frac{EA\delta^3}{L^3} d\delta = \frac{EA\delta^4}{4L^3}$$

The complementary energy is given by

$$U^* = \int_0^P \delta dP = \int_0^P \sqrt[3]{\frac{PL^3}{EA}} dP = \frac{3P^{4/3}L}{4\sqrt[3]{EA}}$$

Note again that the strain energy is expressed in terms of the displacement and the complementary energy is expressed in terms of the load.

• PROBLEM 15-5

A cantilever beam of length L and rectangular cross section (width b, height h) carries a concentrated load P at the free end (see Fig. 1). The stress-strain diagram is represented by the equation $\sigma = B\sqrt{\varepsilon}$, where B is a constant, and it is the same for both tension and compression. Evaluate the complementary energy for this beam.

Solution: In this example the stresses and strains vary from one end of the beam to the other, since it is necessary to begin by determining the complementary energy u*

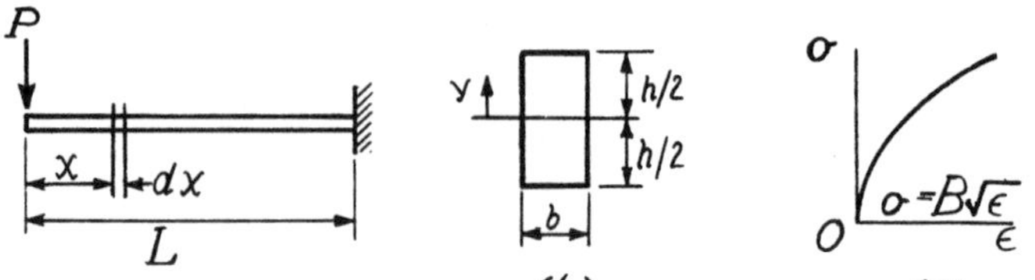

FIG. 1 (a) (b) (c)

per unit volume. Then integrate u* throughout the volume of the beam in order to obtain the total complementary energy U*. The quantity u* will be a function of x (the distance from the free end of the beam) and y (the distance from the neutral axis). In order to find u* we need to know the stress σ_1 existing at any point in the beam having coordinates x and y. This stress can be found if we know the strain ε_1 at the same point, and the strain can be found if the curvature is known. Thus, we must begin our analysis by establishing the curvature of the beam.

The curvature for inelastic bending of beams,

$$\kappa = \frac{\varepsilon_t}{h} \tag{1}$$

where ε_1 is twice the strain at the top fiber of the beam. The expression for the bending moment M at any cross section is

$$M = \frac{2bh^2}{\varepsilon_t^2} \int_0^{\varepsilon_t/2} \sigma \varepsilon d\varepsilon$$

Substituting $\sigma = B\sqrt{\varepsilon}$ and then integrating, we find

$$M = \frac{Bbh^2\sqrt{\varepsilon_t}}{5\sqrt{2}}$$

from which

$$\varepsilon_t = \frac{50M^2}{B^2b^2h^4} \tag{2}$$

The curvature can now be found by eliminating ε_t between Eqs.(1) and (2) and also substituting Px for the bending moment M:

$$\kappa = \frac{50P^2x^2}{B^2b^2h^5} \tag{3}$$

This equation gives the curvature as a function of the distance x measured along the axis of the beam.

The strain ε_1 at any cross section of the beam is $\varepsilon_1 = \kappa y$

The stress can be found from the strain by using the stress-strain relationship:

$$\sigma_1 = B\sqrt{\varepsilon_1} = B\sqrt{\kappa y}$$

Substituting the curvature κ from Eq.(3) gives

$$\sigma_1 = \frac{5\sqrt{2}Py^{1/2}x}{bh^{5/2}} \tag{4}$$

which is the expression for the stress at any point in the beam.

Now we are ready to evaluate the complementary energy per unit volume

$$u^* = \int_0^{\sigma_1} \varepsilon d\sigma = \int_0^{\sigma_1} \frac{\sigma^2}{B^2} d\sigma$$

in which σ_1 is given by Eq.(4). Carrying out the integration yields

$$u^* = \frac{\sigma_1^3}{3B^2}$$

Substituting the value of σ_1 from Eq.(4), we have

$$u^* = \frac{250\sqrt{2}P^3y^{3/2}x^3}{3B^2b^3h^{15/2}} \tag{5}$$

which gives the complementary energy per unit volume as a function of x and y. The complementary energy U* for the entire beam is found by integrating u* throughout the volume of the beam. In setting up the integral, we will let x vary from 0 to L and y from 0 to h/2; the result will then be doubled to account for the two halves of the beam. Thus, the equation for the complementary energy is

$$U^* = \int u^*dV = 2\int_0^L \left[\int_0^{h/2} u^*bdy\right]dx$$

Substitution of expression (5) for u* gives

$$U^* = \frac{500\sqrt{2}P^3}{3B^2b^2h^{15/2}} \int_0^L \left[\int_0^{h/2} y^{3/2}dy\right]x^3dx$$

First integration yields

$$U^* = \frac{500\sqrt{2}P^3}{3B^2b^2h^{15/2}} \int_0^L \left[\frac{y^{5/2}}{5/2}\right]_0^{h/2} x^3dx$$

$$= \frac{500\sqrt{2}P^3}{3B^2b^2h^{15/2}} \frac{(h/2)^{5/2}}{5/2} \int_0^L x^3 dx$$

$$= \frac{100P^3}{6B^2b^2h^5} \int_0^L x^3 dx$$

Now carrying out the second integration yields,

$$U^* = \frac{100P^3}{6B^2b^2h^5} \left[\frac{x^4}{4}\right]_0^L = \frac{25\ P^3L^4}{6B^2b^2h^5}$$

This equation gives the complementary energy in terms of the force P, as expected.

• PROBLEM 15-6

A steel bar AB, of 1 in. diameter, is bent into a quadrant of a circle of radius 24 in. The bar lies in a horizontal plane. It is cantilevered from A and carries a vertical load of 40 lb. at the end B. Find the strain energy stored in the bar due to torsion. Take $G = 12 \times 10^6$ psi.

Solution: It is convenient to determine the position of a cross-section by its angular distance θ from the free end.

Then at θ, $T = WR(1 - \cos\theta)$

$dx = Rd\theta$

Then, $$U = \int \frac{T^2 dx}{2GI_p}$$

Substituting the values of T and dx gives

$$U = \int_0^{\pi/2} \frac{[WR(1-\cos\theta)]^2 Rd\theta}{2GI_p} = \frac{W^2R^3}{2GI_p} \int_0^{\pi/2} (1-2\cos\theta + \cos^2\theta)d\theta$$

Integration yields

$$U = \frac{W^2R^3}{2GI_p} \left[\theta - 2\sin\theta + \frac{\theta}{2} + \frac{\sin 2\theta}{4}\right]_0^{\pi/2}$$

$$= \frac{W^2R^3}{2GI_p} \left[\frac{\pi}{2} - 2(1) + \frac{\pi}{4} + 0\right]$$

$$= \frac{W^2R^3}{2GI_p} (0.36) \qquad (1)$$

Since $I_p = \frac{\pi}{32}$ in^4; R = 24 in; W = 40 lb; G = 12 x 10^6 psi, Eq.(1) becomes

$$U = \frac{40^2 \times 24^3 \times 0.36 \times 32}{2 \times 12 \times 10^6 \times \pi} = 3.38 \text{ lb-in}$$

It might be noted that this is not the total strain energy stored in the bar. The bar is deformed also in bending and in shear, and there will be strain energy corresponding to these types of deformation.

• PROBLEM 15-7

Consider a closely wound coil spring of radius R loaded by a force P (Fig. 1(a)). The spring consists of n turns of wire with wire radius r. Find the deflection of the spring and hence the spring constant.

FIG. 1

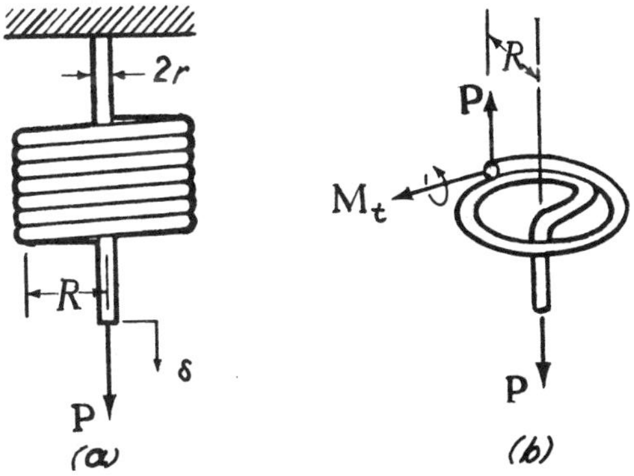

Solution: First we find the internal forces and moments acting on a section of the spring. From the free-body diagram in Fig. 1(b), we see that the twisting moment M_t is independent of position on the spring and is equal to PR. The strain energy associated with the twisting moment is

$$U = \int_L \frac{P^2R^2}{2GI_z}\,dz = \int_0^{2\pi n} \frac{P^2R^2}{2GI_z}\,r\,d\theta$$

Integration yields

$$U = \frac{P^2R^3}{2GI_z}\left[\theta\right]_0^{2\pi n} = \frac{P^2R^3}{2GI_z}\,2\pi n \qquad (1)$$

There is additional strain energy in the spring due to the transverse shear force P. It can be shown, however, that the ratio of strain energy due to transverse shear to strain energy due to torsion is proportional to $(r/R)^2$ and hence is small for springs of usual design. For simplicity we shall neglect the contribution of the transverse force and consider (1) to represent the total strain energy in the spring.

Therefore the deflection in the direction of P is

$$\delta = \frac{\partial U}{\partial P} = \frac{PR^3}{GI_z} 2\pi n \qquad (2)$$

and the spring constant becomes

$$k = \frac{P}{\delta} = \frac{P}{PR^3(2\pi n)/GI_z} = \frac{GI_z}{2\pi n R^3} \qquad (3)$$

Upon substituting for the moment of inertia I_z in (3), we find that

$$k = \frac{G(\pi r^4/2)}{2\pi n R^3} = \frac{Gr^4}{4nR^3}$$

where r is the radius of the wire. We see that the spring constant is inversely proportional to the number of coils n and directly proportional to the fourth power of the wire radius. For example, if we increase the wire radius by 19 percent, the spring constant is doubled.

In this example, Castigliano's theorem has provided a simple means of evaluating an elastic deflection in a system of some geometric complexity.

• PROBLEM 15-8

Calculate the deflection δ of the tightly coiled spring in Fig. 1(a). The wire has radius r and is formed into n complete turns of radius R. The ends of the spring are extended directly from the rim of the coil.

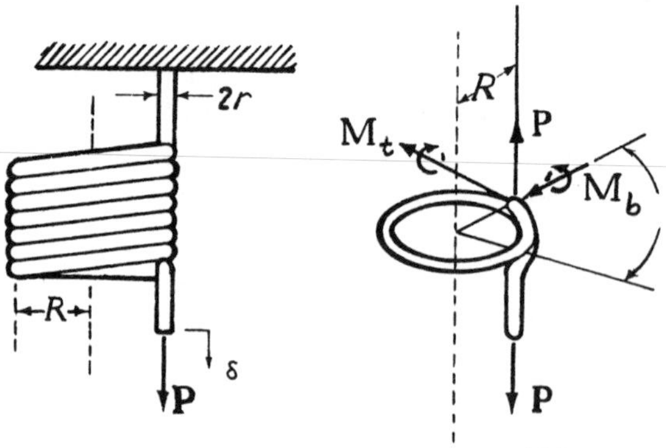

(a) (b)

Solution: This problem will be solved using Castigliano's theorem. At each section of the spring, the wire carries a transverse shear force P, a twisting moment M_t, and a bending moment M_b, as indicated in Fig. 1(b). By applying the equilibrium requirements to this free body, we find

$$M_t = PR(1 - \cos\theta) \qquad M_b = PR\sin\theta \qquad (a)$$

The total strain energy

$$U = \int \frac{M^2}{2EI}\,dx + \int \frac{\tau^2}{2GJ}\,dx$$

in the wire (of uncoiled length $2n\pi R$) due to the twisting and bending contributions is

$$U = \int_0^{2\pi n} \frac{P^2R^2(1-\cos\theta)^2}{2GJ_x} R\,d\theta + \int_0^{2\pi n} \frac{P^2R^2\sin^2\theta}{2EI} R\,d\theta$$

$$= \frac{P^2R^3}{2GJ_x} 3\pi n + \frac{P^2R^3}{2EI} \pi n \qquad \text{(b)}$$

where $J_x = \pi r^4/2$ and $I = \pi r^4/4$. The deflection δ in Fig. 1(a) is, according to $\delta = \frac{\partial U}{\partial P}$:

$$\delta = \frac{\partial U}{\partial P} = PR^3\pi n\left(\frac{3}{GJ_x} + \frac{1}{EI}\right)$$

$$= \frac{4PR^3n}{Gr^4}\left(\frac{3}{2} + \frac{G}{E}\right)$$

$$= \frac{4PR^3n}{Gr^4}\left(\frac{4+3\nu}{2+2\nu}\right) \qquad \text{(c)}$$

where we have used $\frac{G}{E} = \frac{1}{2(1+\nu)}$ to introduce Poisson's ratio.

• PROBLEM 15-9

Consider the plane frame ABC shown in Fig. 1(a). Members AB and BC each have length L and flexural rigidity EI, and the loading on the structure consists of the couple M_o acting at joint B. Calculate the joint displacements D_1 and D_2, which are the angles of rotation at joints B and C.

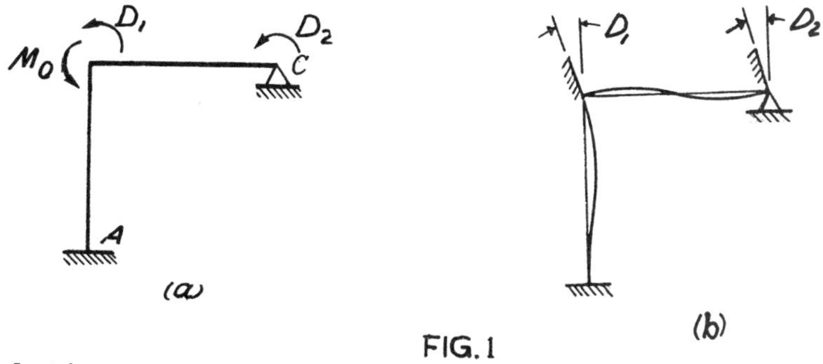

FIG. 1

Solution: An important step in the analysis is finding the strain energy of the structure in terms of the unknown

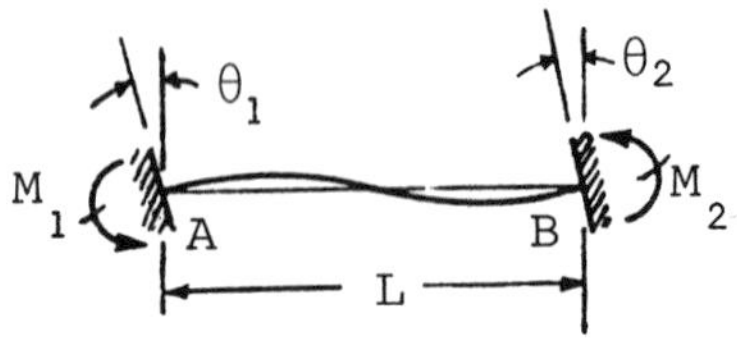

Fig. 2

displacements D_1 and D_2. To accomplish this step for a plane frame, it is sometimes helpful to imagine that the unknown joint displacements are imposed on the structure by the addition of restraints corresponding to those displacements (see Fig. 1(b)). Then each member of the frame is in the condition of a fixed-end beam with rotations at the ends. Thus, if we can obtain a formula for the strain energy stored in such a beam (see Fig. 2), then we can use this formula to obtain the strain energy of the plane frame. In the example of the fixed-end beam shown in Fig. 2, we can make use of the formulas for member stiffnesses, and thus we can immediately write down the expressions for the moments M_1 and M_2 at the ends of the beam in terms of the end rotations θ_1 and θ_2:

$$M_1 = \frac{4EI}{L}\theta_1 + \frac{2EI}{L}\theta_2 \qquad M_2 = \frac{2EI}{L}\theta_1 + \frac{4EI}{L}\theta_2$$

The strain energy stored in this beam is

$$U = \frac{1}{2}M_1\theta_1 + \frac{1}{2}M_2\theta_2$$

or, after substituting the preceding expressions for M_1 and M_2 ,

$$U = \frac{2EI}{L}(\theta_1^2 + \theta_1\theta_2 + \theta_2^2) \tag{1}$$

This equation gives the strain energy in a beam with known rotations at the ends (Fig. 2), provided that the beam behaves linearly.

Now we are ready to return to the plane frame of Fig. 1 and determine the strain energy in terms of the displacements D_1 and D_2. The procedure is to apply Eq. (1) to each member and then sum the results. For member AB we have $\theta_1 = 0$ and $\theta_2 = D_1$, and for member BC we have $\theta_1 = D_1$ and $\theta_2 = D_2$. Thus, the strain energy is

$$U = \frac{2EI}{L}(D_1^2) + \frac{2EI}{L}(D_1^2 + D_1D_2 + D_2^2)$$

$$= \frac{2EI}{L}(2D_1^2 + D_1D_2 + D_2^2)$$

From Castigliano's first theorem we now get the following two equations:

$$M_o = \frac{\partial U}{\partial D_1} = \frac{2EI}{L}(4D_1 + D_2) \tag{2}$$

$$0 = \frac{\partial U}{\partial D_2} = \frac{2EI}{L}(D_1 + 2D_2) \tag{3}$$

These equilibrium equations of the stiffness method can be solved for the joint displacements D_1 and D_2.

From Eqs.(2) and (3),

$$4D_1 + D_2 = \frac{M_oL}{2EI} \qquad D_1 + 2D_2 = 0$$

Solving these equations yields

$$D_1 = \frac{M_oL}{7EI}, \qquad D_2 = -\frac{M_oL}{14EI} .$$

Thus, the joint rotations have been found for the frame.

This example is well suited to the use of strain energy and Castigliano's first theorem because the load M_o corresponds to one of the unknown joint displacements. The only other possible load on the structure would have been a couple corresponding to D_2 , inasmuch as one of the requirements of this method of analysis is that every load must correspond to an unknown joint displacement. This fact raises the question of how to analyze a structure when there are loads at other locations, such as a concentrated load acting at the midpoint of a member. One possibility is to consider every point of loading to be a joint of the structure, thus introducing additional unknown joint displacements that correspond to the loads. The disadvantage of such an approach is that it greatly increases the number of equations of equilibrium to be solved.

CASTIGLIANO'S THEOREM

• **PROBLEM 15-10**

An elastic, prismatic beam is loaded as shown in Fig. 1. Using Castigliano's theorem, find the deflection due to bending caused by the applied force P at the center.

Solution: The expression for the internal strain energy in bending is

$$U = \int M^2/(2EI)dx$$

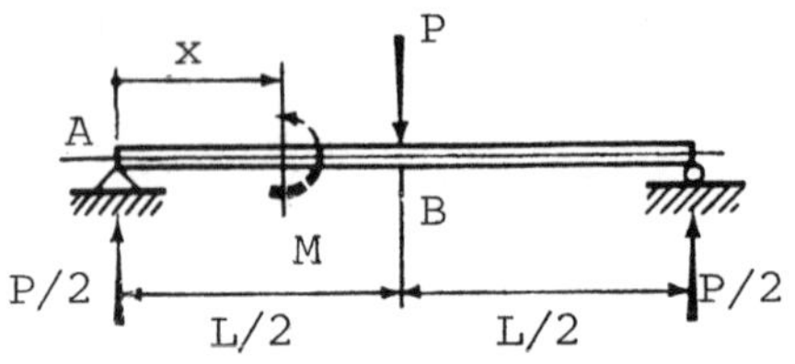

Fig. 1.

Since according to Castigliano's theorem the required deflection is a derivative of this function it is advantageous to differentiate the expression for U before integrating. In problems where M is a complex function, this scheme is particularly useful. In this case the following relation becomes applicable:

$$\Delta = \frac{\partial U}{\partial P} = \int_0^L \frac{M}{EI}\frac{\partial M}{\partial P}\,dx \tag{1}$$

Proceeding on this basis, one has from A to B:

$$M = +\frac{P}{2}x \quad \text{and} \quad \frac{\partial M}{\partial P} = \frac{x}{2}$$

On substituting these relations into Eq.(1) and observing the symmetry of the problem,

$$\Delta = 2\int_0^{L/2} \frac{Px^2}{4EI}\,dx$$

Integration yields

$$\Delta = \frac{2P}{4EI}\frac{x^3}{3}\Bigg|_0^{L/2} = \frac{2P}{4EI}\frac{(L/2)^3}{3} = +\frac{PL^3}{48EI}$$

The positive sign indicates that the deflection takes place in the direction of the applied force P.

• PROBLEM 15-11

For the beam carrying the load shown, calculate the deflection at locations A and B, using energy methods for the solution.

Solution: We shall denote the 100-lb force as P, and we shall introduce a hypothetical or so-called dummy force Q at A. The supporting forces can be found from static equilibrium.

$$\Sigma F_y = 0, \quad R_C - Q - P + R_D = 0$$

$$\text{or} \quad R_C + R_D = Q + P \tag{1}$$

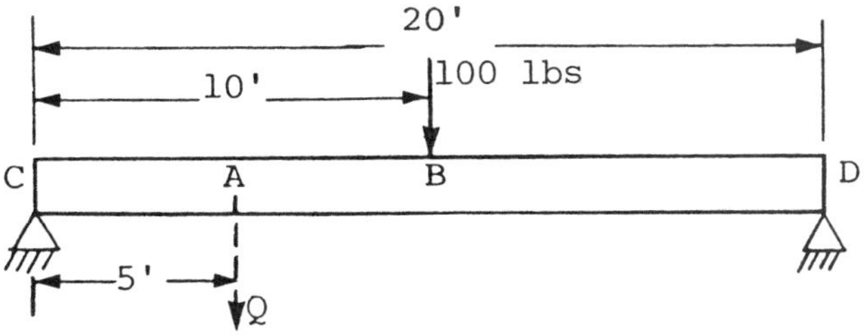

and

$$\Sigma M_C = 0, \quad 5 \times Q + 10 \times P - 20R_D = 0$$

from which $\quad R_D = \frac{5Q+10P}{20} = \frac{Q}{4} + \frac{P}{2}.$

Substituting the value of R_D into Eq.(1) gives

$$R_C = \frac{3}{4}Q + \frac{P}{2}$$

The strain energy in terms of the statically independent external loads can then be given as

$$U = \int_0^L \frac{M_z^2}{2EI_{zz}}\,dx = \int_0^5 \frac{\left[(\frac{P}{2} + \frac{3Q}{4})x\right]^2}{2EI_{zz}}\,dx$$

$$+ \int_5^{10} \frac{\left[(\frac{P}{2} + \frac{3Q}{4})x - Q(x-5)\right]^2}{2EI_{zz}}\,dx \qquad (2)$$

$$+ \int_{10}^{20} \frac{\left[(\frac{P}{2} + \frac{3Q}{3})x - Q(x-5) - P(x-10)\right]^2}{2EI_{zz}}\,dx$$

If U is differentiated with respect to P under the integral sign,

$$\frac{\partial U}{\partial P} = \int_0^5 \frac{\frac{\left((P/2)+3Q/4\right)x^2}{2}}{EI_{zz}}\,dx$$

$$+ \int_5^{10} \frac{\frac{\left\{\left[(P/2)+3Q/4\right]x - Q(x-5)\right\}x}{2}}{EI_{zz}}\,dx \qquad (3)$$

$$+ \int_{10}^{20} \frac{\left[(\frac{P}{2} + \frac{3Q}{4})x - Q(x-5) - P(x-10)\right](-\frac{x}{2}+10)}{EI_{zz}}\,dx$$

Denoting that P = 100 and Q = 0,

$$\Delta_B = \frac{1}{EI_{zz}}\left\{\int_0^5 25x^2dx + \int_5^{10} 25x^2dx\right.$$

$$\left. + \int_{10}^{20} 100(\frac{x^2}{4} - 10x + 100)dx\right\} = \frac{16,670}{EI_{zz}} \qquad (4)$$

$$\Delta_B = \frac{(144)(16,670)}{EI_{zz}} = \frac{2.40 \times 10^6}{EI_{zz}} \text{ ft.} \qquad (5)$$

To obtain Δ_A ,

$$\frac{\partial U}{\partial Q} = \int_0^5 \frac{\left(\frac{P}{2} + \frac{3}{4}Q\right)\frac{3x^2}{4}}{EI_{zz}} dx$$

$$+ \int_5^{10} \frac{\left[(\frac{P}{2} + \frac{3}{4}Q)x - Q(x-5)\right](5 - \frac{x}{4})}{EI_{zz}} dx$$

$$+ \int_{10}^{20} \frac{\left[(\frac{P}{2} + \frac{3}{4}Q)x - Q(x-5) - P(x-10)\right](5-\frac{x}{4})}{EI_{zz}} dx \qquad (6)$$

Substituting Q = 0 and P = 100 and integrating,

$$\Delta_Q = \frac{1}{EI_{zz}}\left\{\int_0^5 \frac{150}{8} x^2dx + \int_5^{10}\left(250x - \frac{50}{4}x^2\right)dx\right.$$

$$\left. + \int_{10}^{20} 100\left(\frac{x^2}{8} - 5x + 50\right)dx\right\} = \frac{10,680}{EI_{zz}}$$

From which

$$\Delta_Q = \frac{(144)(10,680)}{EI_{zz}} = \frac{1.538 \times 10^6}{EI_{zz}} \text{ ft.}$$

A 10 I 25.4 steel beam is loaded as shown. When the deflection at the free end is 0.48 in. downward, determine the force P.

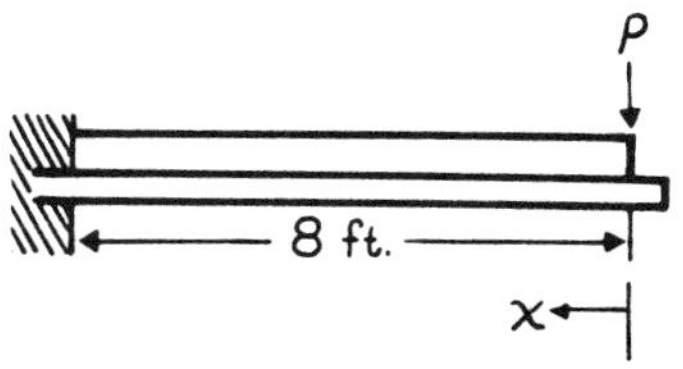

Solution: This problem will be solved using Castigliano's theorem. For the case of strain due to bending this is

$$EIy = \int_0^L M\left(\frac{\partial M}{\partial P}\right) dx \tag{1}$$

The moment equation is, from the figure

$$M = -Px - 3000x^2/2.$$

The partial derivative of M with respect to P is -x. Substituting into Eq.(1) yields

$$EIy = \int_0^L (Px^2 + 3000x^3/2)dx.$$

Performing the integration results in

$$EIy = PL^3/3 + 3000L^4/8. \tag{2}$$

From a steel table, the moment of inertia, I, of a 10 I 25.4 steel beam is 122.1 in.^{4}. Young's modulus, E, for steel is 30 x 10^6 psi, L is given in the figure as 8 ft., and the deflection, y, is given in the statement of the problem as 0.48 inches downward.

Substituting into Eq.(2) and solving for P gives

$$P = \frac{3(30\text{x}10^6)(122.1).48}{8^3(12)^3} - \frac{3(3000)8^4}{8^3(8)}$$

$$P = -3040 \text{ lb.}$$

The minus sign indicates that P is applied in the opposite direction as the deflection.

Thus the force P is 3040 lb. upward.

Using Castigliano's theorem determine the deflection and the angular rotation of the end of a uniformly loaded cantilever, Fig. 1(a). The EI is constant.

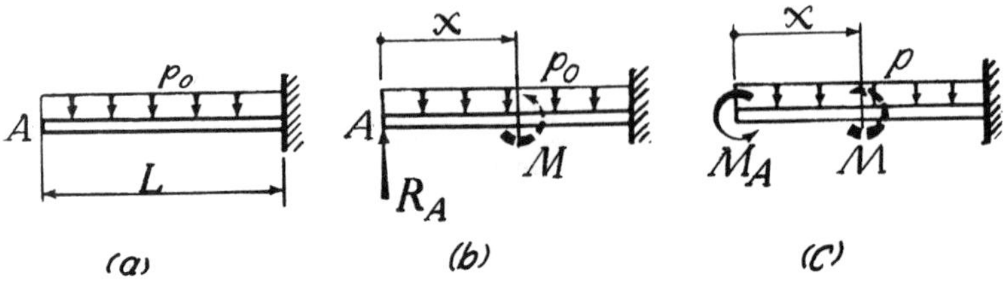

FIG.1

Solution: No forces are applied at the end of the cantilever where the displacements are to be found. Therefore, in order to be able to apply Castigliano's theorem, a fictitious force must be added corresponding to the displacement sought. Thus, as shown in Fig. 1(b), in addition to the specified loading, a force R_A has been introduced. This permits determining $\partial U/\partial R_A$, which with $R_A = 0$ gives the vertical deflection of point A.

The expression for the internal strain energy in bending is

$$U = \int \frac{M^2}{2EI} dx$$

Then the vertical deflection of point A is

$$\Delta_A = \frac{\partial U}{\partial R_A} = \int_0^L \frac{M}{EI} \frac{\partial M}{\partial R_A} dx \qquad (1)$$

Now,

$$M = \frac{-p_o x^2}{2} + R_A x$$

Hence, $\dfrac{\partial M}{\partial R_A} = x$

Substitution of these relations into Eq.(1) yields

$$\Delta_A = \frac{1}{EI} \int_0^L \left(\frac{-p_o x^2}{2} + R_A x \right) x \, dx$$

Since $R_A = 0$, the above equation becomes

$$\Delta_A = \frac{1}{2EI} \int_0^L (-p_o x^3) dx$$

Integration gives

$$\Delta_A = \frac{-p_o L^4}{8EI}$$

where the negative sign shows that the deflection is in the opposite direction to that assumed for force R_A. If R_A in the above integration were not set equal to zero, the end deflection due to p_o and R_A would be found.

The angular rotation of the beam at A can be found in a manner analogous to the above. A fictitious moment M_A is applied at the end, Fig. 1(c), and the calculations are made in much the same manner as before:

$$M = -\frac{p_o x^2}{2} - M_A \qquad \text{and} \qquad \frac{\partial M}{\partial M_A} = -1$$

$$\Delta_A = \frac{\partial U}{\partial M_A} = \frac{1}{EI}\int_0^L \left(-\frac{p_o x^2}{2} - \cancel{M_A}^{\,0}\right)(-1)\,dx = +\frac{p_o L^3}{6EI}$$

where the sign indicates that the sense of the rotation of the end coincides with the assumed sense of the fictitious moment M_A.

• PROBLEM 15-14

Determine the horizontal deflection for the simple elastic frame shown in Fig. 1(a). Consider only the deflection caused by bending. The flexural rigidity EI of both members is equal and constant.

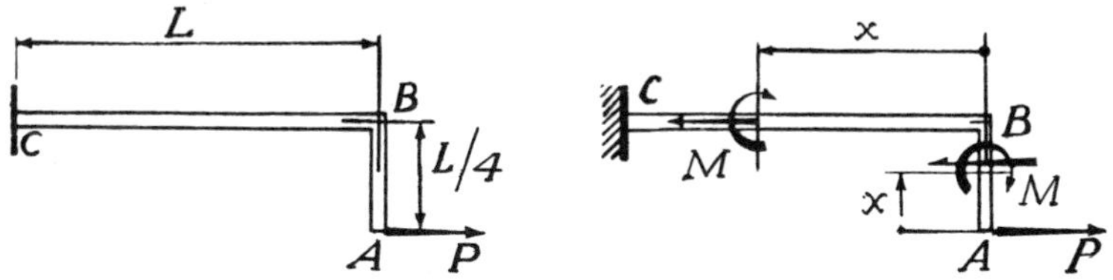

FIG.1 (a) (b)

Solution: The strain energy function is a scalar. Therefore, the separate strain energies for the different elements of an elastic system can be added algebraically. After the total strain energy is determined, its partial derivative with respect to a force gives the displacement of that force. The equation for the strain energy stored in a beam is

$$U = \frac{1}{2EI}\int_0^L M^2 dx$$

From A to B: $M = +Px$

From B to C: $M = +\frac{PL}{4}$

Then

$$U = \frac{1}{2EI}\int_0^{L/4}(Px)^2 dx + \frac{1}{2EI}\int_0^{L}\left(\frac{PL}{4}\right)^2 dx$$

Integration yields

$$U = \frac{1}{2EI}\left[\left(\frac{P^2x^3}{3}\right)\Bigg|_0^{L/4} + \frac{P^2L^2}{16}(x)\Bigg|_0^{L}\right]$$

$$= \frac{1}{2EI}\left[\frac{P^2(L/4)^3}{3} + \frac{P^2L^2}{16}L\right]$$

$$= \frac{1}{2EI}\left[\frac{13P^2L^3}{192}\right]$$

Now,

$$\Delta_A = \frac{\partial U}{\partial P}$$

Hence,

$$\Delta_A = \frac{1}{2EI}\,\frac{13L^3 2P}{192} = \frac{13PL^3}{192EI}$$

Often it is possible to determine the displacements of the individual points in complex frames very simply by using an energy method. The complete freedom of choice in the sign convention of moments and in the location of the origin for each part or piece of a structure is an added attraction of the method.

• PROBLEM 15-15

Determine the deflection at the free end of a cantilever beam of constant cross section and length L, loaded with a force P at the free end and a distributed load which varies linearly from zero at the free end to w at the support.

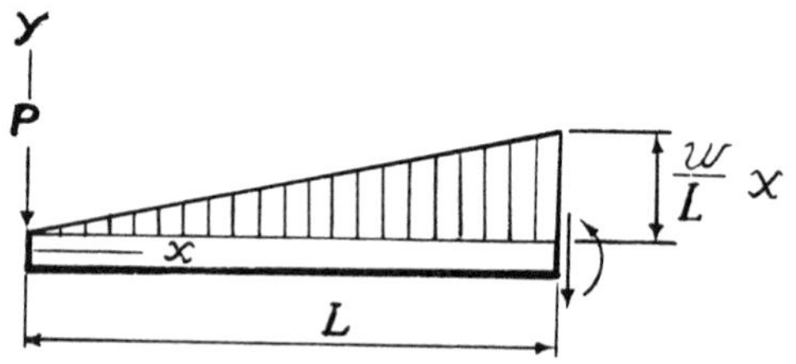

Solution: This problem will be solved using Castigliano's theorem. Castigliano's theorem can be stated mathematically for the case of strain energy due to bending moment as follows:

$$EIy = \int_0^L M(\frac{\partial M}{\partial P})dx \qquad (1)$$

From the free-body diagram, the moment equation is

$$M = -Px - \frac{wx^3}{6L} .$$

The partial derivative of M with respect to P is -x, and Eq.(1) becomes

$$EIy = \int_0^L (Px^2 + \frac{wx^4}{6L})dx = + \frac{PL^3}{3} + \frac{wL^4}{30} .$$

The positive signs indicate deflection in the direction of the force P; hence

$$y = \frac{PL^3}{3EI} + \frac{wL^4}{30EI} \quad \text{downward.}$$

The result may be verified by reference to a table of beam deflections.

• PROBLEM 15-16

Determine the deflection at the center of a simply supported beam of constant cross section and span L carrying a uniformly distributed load w lb. per ft. over its entire length.

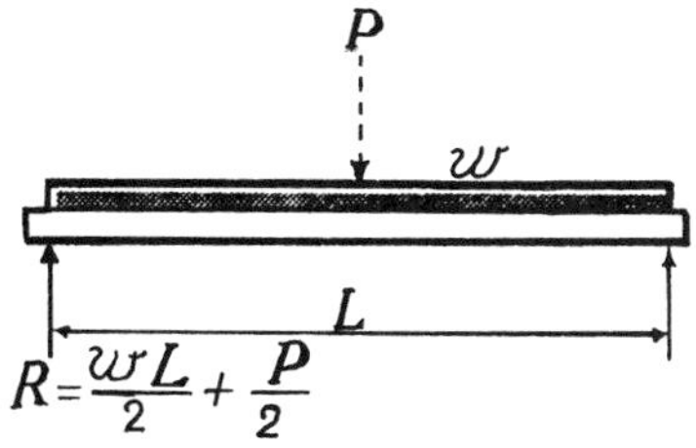

Solution: This problem will be solved by the Castigliano strain energy method. The mathematical statement of Castigliano's theorem is:

$$\frac{\partial U}{\partial P_x} = yx,$$

where U is the strain energy, P_x is a concentrated load at point x, and y is the deflection of the beam at point x. When y is positive, a deflection in the direction of the load is indicated.

When there is no concentrated load at the point at which it is desired to find the deflection, a dummy force is used. This is an imaginary force that gives the equations the proper form. It is set equal to zero when the deflection is evaluated.

The equation for the strain energy, U, in terms of the bending moment is

$$U = \int_0^L \frac{M^2}{2EI}\,dx$$

The deflection is then:

$$yx = \frac{\partial U}{\partial P_x} = \int_0^L \frac{1}{2EI}\frac{\partial(M^2)}{\partial P_x}\,dx = \int_0^L \frac{2M}{2EI}\frac{\partial M}{\partial P_x}\,dx$$

$$yx = \int_0^L \frac{M}{EI}\frac{\partial M}{\partial P_x}\,dx \tag{1}$$

The figure shows the free-body diagram in which the dashed force P represents a fictitious load applied at the location and in the direction of the desired deflection. The moment equation is

$$M = \frac{wLx}{2} + \frac{Px}{2} - \frac{wx^2}{2} - P\left(x - \frac{L}{2}\right)^1, \tag{2}$$

where the quantity $(x - L/2)^1$ is zero for all $x \leq L/2$. The partial derivative of M with respect to P is

$$\frac{\partial M}{\partial P} = \frac{x}{2} - \left(x - \frac{L}{2}\right)^1. \tag{3}$$

Substituting (2) and (3) into (1) yields:

$$y = \int_0^L \frac{\left[\frac{wLx}{2} + \frac{Px}{2} - \frac{wx^2}{2} - P\left(x - \frac{L}{2}\right)^1\right]\left[\frac{x}{2} - \left(x - \frac{L}{2}\right)^1\right]}{EI}\,dx$$

The dummy force P is equated to zero and the deflection is given by

$$EIy = \int_0^L \left[\frac{wLx}{2} - \frac{wx^2}{2}\right]\left[\frac{x}{2} - \left(x-\frac{L}{2}\right)^1\right]dx$$

which can be written as

$$EIy = \frac{w}{4}\int_0^{L/2} (Lx^2-x^3)\,dx + \frac{w}{4}\int_{L/2}^{L} (L^2x-2Lx^2+x^3)\,dx$$

$$= \frac{5wL^4}{384EI}$$

Since the deflection is positive in the direction of the force, the deflection is downward and

$$y = \frac{5wL^4}{384EI} \text{ downward.}$$

• PROBLEM 15-17

A uniform cantilever beam has bending modulus EI and length L. It is built in at A and subjected to a concentrated force P and moment M applied at B, as shown in the figure. Using Castigliano's theorem, find the deflection δ and the slope angle ϕ at B due to these loads.

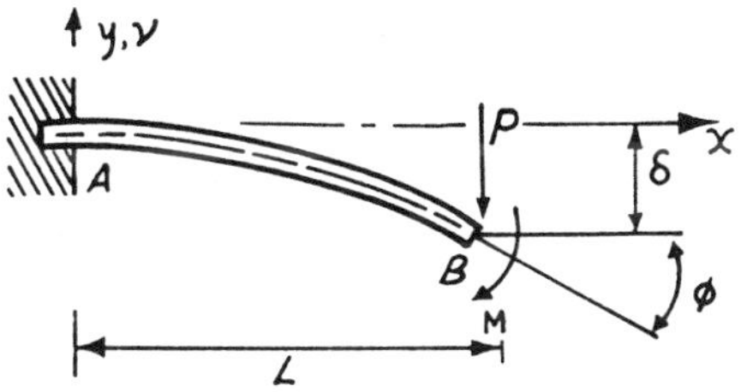

Solution: Castigliano's theorem states that the rate of change of the strain energy for a body with respect to any statically independent force P gives the deflection component of the point of application of this force in the direction of the force, i.e. $\delta = \frac{\partial U}{\partial P}$. A similar statement is made for moments and rotations: The rate of change of strain energy with respect to a statically independent point couple M gives the amount of rotation at the point of application of the point couple about an axis collinear with the couple moment,

$$\text{i.e.} \quad \frac{\partial U}{\partial M} = \theta$$

In most beams, the bending stress, $\sigma = M_b y/I$, is the only stress that causes significant deflection. The bending stress acts only in the direction of the axis of the beam, therefore the equation for the strain energy due to stress that acts in only one direction can be used:

$$U = \int \frac{\sigma^2}{2E}\, dV$$

The integral is taken over the whole volume, V, of the beam. Substituting $M_b y/I$ for σ and $(\int dA)dx$ for dV results in

$$U = \int_0^L \frac{M_b^2}{2EI^2} (\int y^2 dA) dx$$

Since I is defined as $\int y^2 dA$, the integral cancels with one of the I's.

i.e. $$U = \int_0^L \frac{M_b^2}{2EI} dx$$

The bending moment at any point along the x-section is

$$M_b = -P(L-x) - M = (-1)[P(L-x)+M]$$

Since $(-1)^2 = 1$, the strain energy is:

$$U = \int_0^L \frac{M_b^2}{2EI} dx = \int_0^L \frac{[P(L-x)+M]^2}{2EI} dx$$

The terminal deflection δ is in line with the load P, and so according to Castigliano's theorem, $\delta = \frac{\partial U}{\partial P}$, where δ is positive downward, the direction of the applied load P. By Leibnitz' rule for differentiation under the integral sign:

$$\frac{\partial U}{\partial P} = \frac{\partial \int_0^L \frac{M_b^2}{2EI} dx}{\partial P} = \int_0^L \frac{1}{2EI} \frac{\partial (M_b^2)}{\partial P} dx$$

$$= \int_0^L \frac{1}{2EI} 2M_b \frac{\partial M_b}{\partial P} dx = \int_0^L \frac{M_b}{EI} \frac{\partial M_b}{\partial P} dx$$

The partial derivative of the bending moment, M_b, with respect to the load, P, is:

$$\frac{\partial M_b}{\partial P} = \frac{\partial[-P(L-x)-M]}{\partial P} = -(L-x).$$

Multiplying this by the bending moment:

$$M_b \frac{\partial M_b}{\partial P} = [-P(L-x)-M][-(L-x)] = P(L-x)^2 + M(L-x).$$

Substituting this result into the equation for deflection yields:

$$\delta = \frac{\partial U}{\partial P} = \int_0^L \frac{M_b}{EI}\frac{\partial M_b}{\partial P}\,dx = \int_0^L \frac{P(L-x)^2 + M(L-x)}{EI}\,dx$$

$$\delta = \left[\frac{P(L-x)^3}{3EI} + \frac{M(L-x)^2}{2EI}\right]\Bigg|_0^L$$

The deflection is thus:

$$\delta = \frac{PL^3}{3EI} + \frac{ML^2}{2EI} \quad \text{downwards because P is downwards.}$$

The terminal slope $\emptyset$ may be considered to be the in-line displacement corresponding to the moment load M. Thus a second application of Castigliano's theorem yields

$$\emptyset = \frac{\partial U}{\partial M_b}$$

By Leibnitz' rule for differentiation under the integral sign:

$$\frac{\partial U}{\partial M_b} = \frac{\partial \int_0^L \frac{M_b^2}{2EI}\,dx}{\partial M_b} = \int_0^L \frac{1}{2EI}\frac{\partial M_b^2}{\partial M_b}\,dx = \int_0^L \frac{2M_b}{2EI}\,dx$$

$$= \int_0^L \frac{M_b}{EI}\,dx$$

Substituting for M_b:

$$\emptyset = \frac{\partial U}{\partial M_b} = \int_0^L \frac{-P(L-x)-M}{EI}\,dx$$

$$\emptyset = \left[\frac{-P(-1)(L-x)^2}{2EI} - \frac{Mx}{EI}\right]\Bigg|_0^L = \left(0 - \frac{ML}{EI}\right) - \left(\frac{+PL^2}{2EI} - 0\right)$$

The slope is thus:

$$\emptyset = -\frac{ML}{EI} - \frac{PL^2}{2EI}\,.$$

In the five-storied structure shown, the vertical columns, into which the flexible horizontal beams are built, can be considered rigid. Estimate the maximum bending moment that would be induced in the horizontal beams if the foundation B were to settle a distance δ.

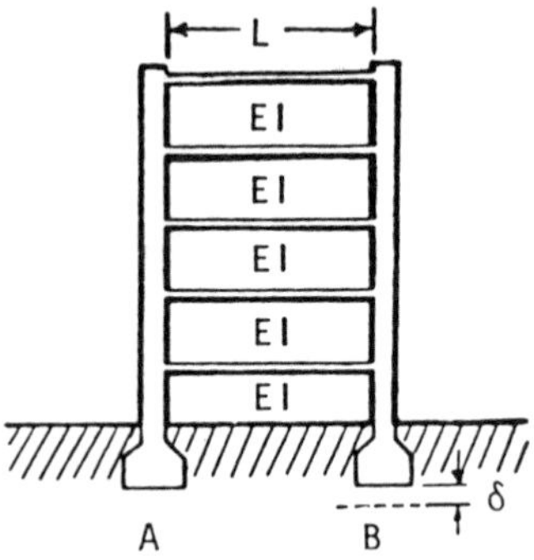

Fig. 1

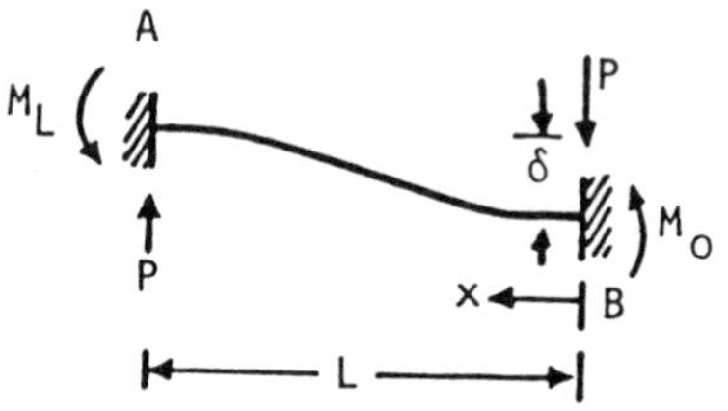

Fig. 2

Solution: This problem will be solved using Castigliano's theorem. In this problem the strain energy is due to the bending moment, so Castigliano's theorem can be written

$$EIy = \int_0^L M\left(\frac{\partial M}{\partial P}\right) dx \tag{1}$$

The vertical columns are assumed to remain rigid and parallel. The horizontal beams all have the same length and stiffness. Thus the moment distributions in all the horizontal beams are identical. Only one has to be examined. The maximum bending moment in one horizontal beam will be the same as the maximum in each of the others.

Figure 2 shows one of the horizontal beams. In order to use Eq. (1), the moment and the partial derivative of the moment with respect to P are needed. From Fig. 2,

$$M = -Px + M_o \tag{2}$$

$$\frac{\partial M}{\partial P} = -x$$

Substituting into Eq. (1) yields

$$EIy = \int_0^L (Px^2 - M_o x)\,dx$$

Upon integration this becomes

$$EIy = PL^3/3 - M_o L^2/2.$$

In Fig. 2, from symmetry $M_o = M_L$. By moment equilibrium about the point x = L,

$$\Sigma M = 0 = M_L - PL + M_o$$

Substituting M_o for M_L and solving for P yields

$$P = 2M_o/L$$

The deflection under the load P is $y = \delta$.

Making the substitutions and solving for M_o results in

$$M_o = -\frac{6EI\delta}{L^2}$$

Substituting for P and M_o in Eq.(2) gives a general equation for the moment:

$$M = \frac{2(6EI\delta/L^2)}{L}x - 6EI\delta/L^2$$

The minimum value of M occurs when x is zero and the maximum moment occurs when x equals L. Substituting L for x yields

$$M = 6EI\delta/L^2$$

Thus the maximum bending moment induced in the horizontal beams is $6EI\delta/L^2$.

• PROBLEM 15-19

Calculate the deflection at joint C due to loads at joints B and D of the statically-determinate truss.

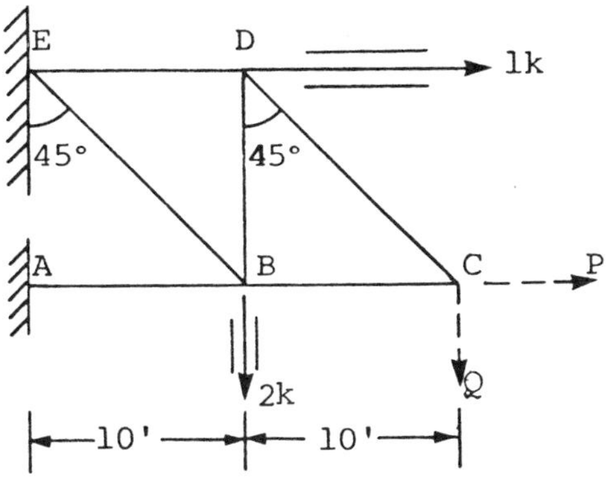

Fig. 1.

Solution: To use Castiglino's theorem, assume force components P and Q at joint C to enable calculation of the total deflection. To find the strain energy from the loads including P and Q,

AB = P - 2(1 + Q) tension   DE = 1 + Q tension

BC = P - Q tension   DB = Q compression

$CD = \frac{Q}{.707}$ tension $EB = \frac{2 + Q}{.707}$ tension

is obtained from

$$U = \sum_i \frac{F_i^2 L_i}{2A_i E_i}$$

Assuming uniform links in the truss,

$$U = \frac{1}{2AE}\Big\{[P - 2(1 + Q)]^2(10) + (P - Q)^2(10)$$

$$+ \left(\frac{Q}{.707}\right)^2\left(\frac{10}{.707}\right) + (1 + Q)^2(10) + Q^2(10)$$

$$+ \left(\frac{2 + Q}{.707}\right)^2\left(\frac{10}{.707}\right)\Big\}$$

To calculate the horizontal and vertical components at joint C,

$$\Delta_H = \left(\frac{\partial U}{\partial P}\right)_{P=Q=0} = \frac{1}{2AE}[2(P-2-2Q)(10) + 2(P-Q)10]_{P=Q=0}$$

$$= \frac{1}{2AE}[(2)(-2)(10)] = -\frac{20}{AE} \text{ ft}$$

The horizontal deflection component of joint C is opposite in sense to the direction of the force P accordingly,

$$\Delta_V = \left(\frac{\partial U}{\partial Q}\right)_{P=Q=0} = \frac{1}{2AE}\Big[2(P-2-2Q)(10)(-2) + 2(P-Q)(10)(-1)$$

$$+ \frac{2Q}{(.707)^2}\left(\frac{10}{.707}\right) + 2(1+Q)(10) + 20Q$$

$$+ \frac{2(2+Q)}{(.707)^2} \frac{10}{.707} \Bigg]_{P=Q=0}$$

$$\therefore \ \Delta_V = \frac{1}{2AE}(80 + 20 + 1132) = \frac{106.6}{AE} \text{ ft.}$$

total deflection at joint C, therefore, is

$$\Delta_c = \frac{1}{AE}(-20i+106.6j) \text{ ft.}$$

STATICALLY INDETERMINATE PROBLEMS

• PROBLEM 15-20

For the beam shown, find the supporting force system.

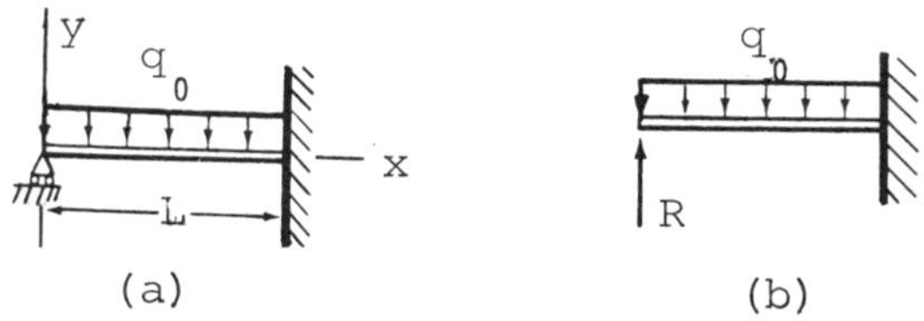

Fig. 1.

Solution: In this statically indeterminate system, there is one redundant constraint, R. Using Castigliano's theorem to find R,

$$\frac{\partial U}{\partial R} = 0$$

The bending moment for $0 \leq x < L$ is

$$M_z = Rx - \frac{q_o x^2}{2}$$

and therefore

$$U = \int_0^L \frac{(Rx - \frac{q_o x^2}{2})^2}{2EI_{zz}} dx$$

from which

$$\frac{\partial U}{\partial R} = \int_0^L \frac{\left(Rx - \frac{q_o x^2}{2}\right)x}{EI_{zz}}\,dx$$

Integrating and equating the resulting expression to zero,

$$\frac{1}{EI_{zz}}\left[R\frac{x^3}{3} - \frac{q_o}{8}x^4\right]\Big|_0^L = \frac{1}{EI_{zz}}\left(\frac{RL^3}{3} - \frac{q_o L^4}{8}\right) = 0$$

Solving for R,

$$R = \frac{3}{8}q_o L$$

• PROBLEM 15-21

> Determine the supporting force system for beam carrying a uniform load and supported by a roller as shown in Fig. 1.

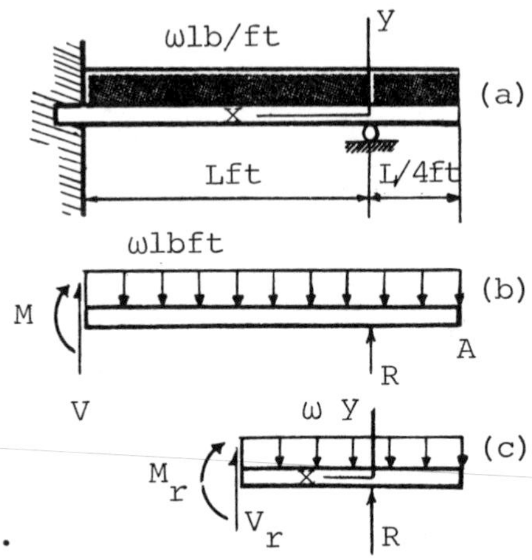

Fig. 1.

Solution: The free-body diagram of Fig. 1(b) indicates that the problem is statically indeterminate, since there are three unknown reaction components and only two independent equations of equilibrium available.

If the portion of the beam to the right of the reaction R were removed and replaced by an equivalent shearing force and bending moment at the transverse section above R, neither R nor the elastic curve in the interval $0 \leq x \leq L$ would be changed. Hence, it is necessary to deal with only the strain energy of the beam in the interval $0 \leq x \leq L$. With the coordinate system placed as shown, the resulting moment equation obtained from the free-body diagram in Fig. 1(c) is

$$M = Rx - \frac{w}{2}(x + \frac{L}{4})^2 = Rx - \frac{wx^2}{2} - \frac{wLx}{4} - \frac{wL^2}{32}.$$

The deflection at the right support is given by

$$y_o = \frac{\partial U}{\partial R} = \frac{1}{EI}\int_0^L M \frac{\partial M}{\partial R}\,dx.$$

Since the partial derivative of M with respect to R is x, the expression for the deflection is

$$y_o = \frac{1}{EI}\int_0^L (Rx^2 - \frac{wx^3}{2} - \frac{wLx^2}{4} - \frac{wL^2x}{32})\,dx,$$

which upon integration and substitution of limits becomes

$$y_o = \frac{1}{EI}(\frac{RL^3}{3} - \frac{wL^4}{8} - \frac{wL^4}{12} - \frac{wL^4}{64}).$$

Since the support is unyielding (y = 0 when x = 0), the above expression can be equated to zero and solved for R, yielding

$$R = \frac{43wL}{64} \text{ lb upward.}$$

The other reaction components (M and V) are obtained from the equilibrium equations, $\Sigma M_A = 0$ and $\Sigma F_y = 0$,

$$\Sigma Fy = 0$$

$$V + R - w(\frac{5}{4}L) = 0$$

or $$V = \frac{5}{4}wL - \frac{43wL}{64} = \frac{37wL}{64} \text{ lb. upward.}$$

Then

$$\Sigma M_A = 0$$

$$M + V(\frac{5}{4}L) - \frac{5}{4}wL\ (\frac{5}{8}L) + R(\frac{L}{4}) = 0$$

or $$M = \frac{25}{32}\,wL^2 - \frac{37(5)}{64(4)}\,wL^2 - \frac{43}{64x4}\,wL^2 = -\frac{28wL^2}{64(4)}$$

or $$M = \frac{7wL^2}{64} \text{ ft lb counterclockwise.}$$

Determine the vertical deflection of the midpoint of the beam (see Fig. 1(a)) and the slope of the deflection curve at this point.

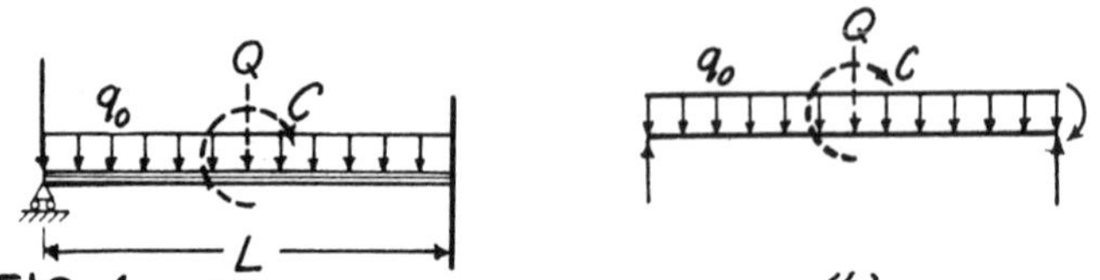

FIG. 1 (a) (b)

Solution: To find the vertical deflection of the midpoint, assume a point force Q at this point and a point couple C also at this point (see Fig. 1(b)). First step will be to get the strain energy in terms of R (the redundant constraint), Q, C, and the uniform loading q_o. Thus,

$$U = \int_0^L \frac{1}{2}\frac{M_z^2}{EI_{zz}}\,dx = \frac{1}{2EI_{zz}}\left\{\int_0^{L/2}\left(Rx - \frac{q_o x^2}{2}\right)^2 dx\right.$$

$$\left. + \int_{L/2}^{L}\left[Rx - \frac{q_o x^2}{2} + C - Q\left(x - \frac{L}{2}\right)\right]^2 dx\right\} \qquad \text{(a)}$$

To determine Δ_A at the midpoint, we proceed as follows:

$$\Delta_A = \left(\frac{\partial U}{\partial Q}\right)_{\substack{Q=0\\C=0}} = \frac{1}{2EI_{zz}}\left[\int_{L/2}^{L} -2\left(Rx - \frac{q_o x^2}{2} + C - Q\left(x - \frac{L}{2}\right)\right)\right.$$

$$\left. \times \left(x - \frac{L}{2}\right)dx\right]_{\substack{Q=0\\C=0}}$$

$$= \frac{1}{EI_{zz}}\int_{L/2}^{L}\left(Rx - \frac{q_o x^2}{2}\right)\left(\frac{L}{2} - x\right)dx$$

Upon integration one obtains

$$\Delta_A = \frac{1}{EI_{zz}}\left[\frac{RL}{2}\frac{x^2}{2} - \frac{Rx^3}{3} - \frac{q_o L}{4}\frac{x^3}{3} + \frac{q_o}{2}\frac{x^4}{4}\right]_{L/2}^{L}$$

$$\therefore\ \Delta_A = \frac{L^3}{8EI_{zz}}\left[q_o L(.354) - .83R\right] \qquad \text{(b)}$$

Our solution, however, is in terms of R. To obtain the value of R, set $\left(\frac{\partial U}{\partial R}\right)_{\substack{C=0\\Q=0}} = 0.$

From Eq.(a), we have

$$\left(\frac{\partial U}{\partial R}\right)_{\substack{C=0\\Q=0}} = \frac{1}{2EI_z}\left\{\int_0^{L/2} 2\left(Rx - \frac{q_o x^2}{2}\right) xdx + \int_{L/2}^{L} 2\left(Rx - \frac{q_o x^2}{2}\right)xdx\right\} = 0$$

Integration yields

$$\frac{1}{EI_z}\left\{\left[\frac{Rx^3}{3} - \frac{q_o x^4}{8}\right]\Bigg|_0^{L/2} + \left[\frac{Rx^3}{3} - \frac{q_o x^4}{8}\right]\Bigg|_{L/2}^{L}\right\} = 0$$

or

$$\left[\frac{RL^3}{24} - \frac{q_o L^4}{128} + \frac{RL^3}{3} - \frac{q_o L^4}{8} - \frac{RL^3}{24} + \frac{q_o L^4}{128}\right] = 0$$

$$\frac{RL^3}{3} - \frac{q_o L^4}{8} = 0$$

from which

$$R = \frac{3}{8} q_o L$$

Substituting this value of R into Eq.(b), we have

$$\Delta_A = \frac{L^3}{8EI_{zz}} (.354q_o L - .311q_o L) = .0043 \frac{q_o L^4}{EI_{zz}} \tag{c}$$

Because Δ_A is positive the deflection is in the same direction as the dummy load P that was used and hence the movement is downward.

To get the slope at A, we have

$$\left(\frac{\partial U}{\partial C}\right)_{\substack{C=0\\Q=0}} = \theta_A \tag{d}$$

We get

$$\theta_A = \frac{1}{2EI_{zz}} \left(\int_{L/2}^{L} 2\ Rx - \frac{q_o x^2}{2} + C - Q(x - \frac{L}{2})\ dx\right)_{\substack{C=0\\Q=0}}$$

$$= \frac{1}{EI_{zz}}\left[\frac{Rx^2}{2} - \frac{q_o x^3}{6}\right]\Bigg|_{L/2}^{L} = \frac{1}{EI_{zz}}\left[\frac{R}{2}(L^2 - \frac{L^2}{4}) - \frac{q_o}{6}(L^3 - \frac{L^3}{8})\right]$$

$$= \frac{1}{EI_{zz}}(\frac{3}{8}RL^2 - \frac{7}{48}q_o L^3) = \frac{L^2}{8EI_{zz}}(3R - \frac{7}{6}q_o L) \qquad \text{(e)}$$

Now substitute the value $R = \frac{3}{8}q_o L$. We get

$$\theta_A = \frac{q_o L^3}{8EI_{zz}}(\frac{9}{8} - \frac{7}{6}) = -\frac{q_o L^3}{192EI_{zz}} \qquad \text{(f)}$$

because θ_A is negative, the rotation must be opposite in sense to the dummy couple C and is hence counterclockwise. Since the beam was originally horizontal and since we are considering only small deformations, $q_o L^3/192EI_{zz}$ is clearly the slope of the deflection curve.

• PROBLEM 15-23

Beam BC of Fig. 1(a) is a rolled steel 8-in., 15-lb light beam having a cross-sectional moment of inertia of 48 $in.^4$ The beam is fixed at B and supported at C by an aluminum alloy tie rod having a cross-sectional area of 0.15 sq.in. Determine the force in the tie rod due to the distributed load of 800 lb per ft. Use 30,000 ksi and 10,000 ksi for the moduli of elasticity of the steel and aluminum, respectively.

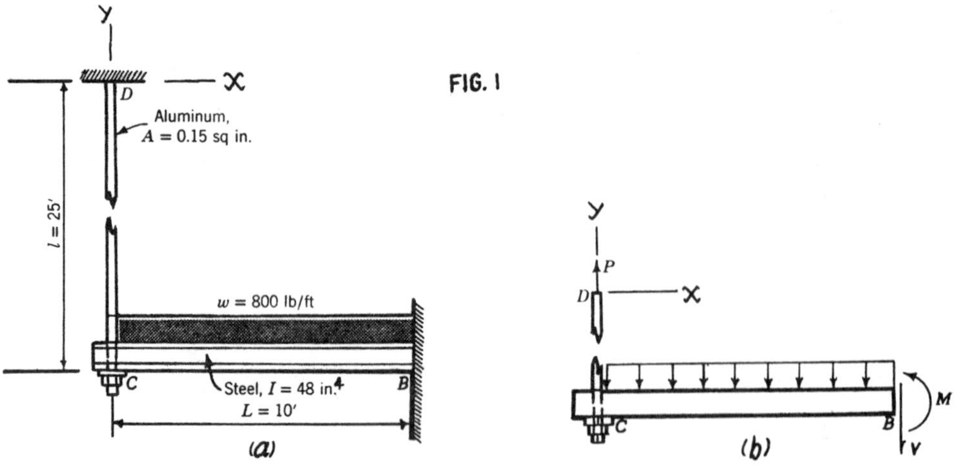

FIG. 1

Solution: The free-body diagram of the beam and tie rod is shown in Fig. 1(b) with the origin of coordinates at the top of the tie rod where the boundary condition is $x = 0$, $y = 0$. The total strain energy in the system is the sum of the energies in the tie rod and the beam, that is

$$U = \frac{\sigma^2}{2E_a} Al + \int_0^L \frac{M^2}{2E_sI} dx = \frac{P^2 l}{2AE_a} + \int_0^L \frac{M^2}{2E_sI} dx.$$

The deflection at D is

$$y_o = \frac{\partial U}{\partial P} = \frac{Pl}{AE_a} + \frac{1}{E_sI} \int_0^L M\frac{\partial M}{\partial P} dx = 0.$$

The moment in the beam is

$$M = Px - \frac{wx^2}{2},$$

and

$$\frac{\partial M}{\partial P} = x.$$

Therefore

$$y_o = \frac{Pl}{AE_a} + \frac{1}{E_sI} \int_0^L (Px - \frac{wx^2}{2}) x \, dx = 0$$

or

$$y_o = \frac{Pl}{AE_a} + \frac{1}{E_sI} \int_0^L (Px^2 - \frac{wx^3}{2}) dx$$

Integration gives

$$y_o = \frac{Pl}{AE_a} + \frac{1}{E_sI} [P \frac{x^3}{3} - \frac{wx^4}{8}] \Big|_0^L$$

$$= \frac{Pl}{AE_a} + \frac{PL^3}{3E_sI} - \frac{wL^4}{8E_sI}$$

Since the structure is fixed at D, y_o is zero and substitution of the given data yields

$$0 = \frac{P(25)12}{.15(10^7)} + \frac{P(10^3)(12^3)}{3x(3x10^7)48} + \frac{800(10)(10^3)(12^3)}{8(3x10^7)48}$$

or $2000P + 4000P = 1200 \times 10^3$

from which $P = 2000$ lb. T.

Find the horizontal reaction X at point C in Fig. 1(a) using Castigliano's theorem.

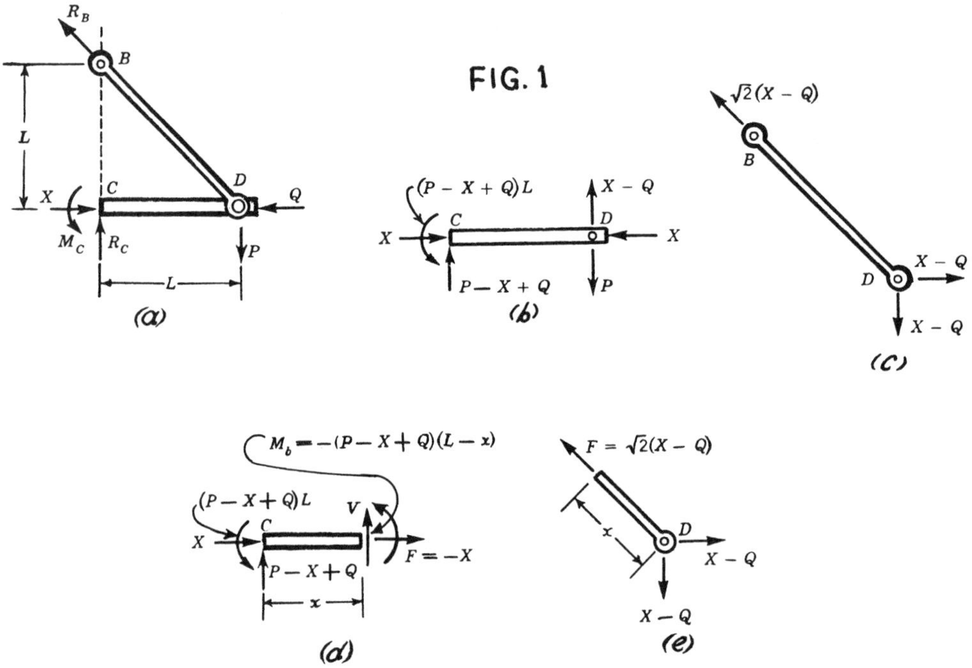

Solution: This problem illustrates the application of energy methods to statically indeterminate systems in which slender members carry both longitudinal and bending loads. In order to obtain the horizontal deflection of point D by Castigliano's theorem, insert the fictitious force Q in Fig. 1(a). If the horizontal reaction X at point C is temporarily considered as an external load, the system becomes statically determinate. Using the equilibrium requirements it is possible to express all external forces and moments on the members CD and BD in terms of P, Q, and X, as indicated in the free-body diagrams of Fig. 1(b) and (c). The internal forces and moments acting on the section at the location x in CD are displayed in Fig. 1(d), and the internal force acting in BD is indicated in Fig. 1(e). The total strain energy in this case is due to longitudinal and bending loading in CD and to longitudinal loading in BD.

$$U = \int_0^L \frac{X^2}{2A_{CD}E}\, dx + \int_0^L \frac{(P-X+Q)^2(L-x)^2}{2EI}\, dx$$

$$+ \int_0^{\sqrt{2}L} \frac{[\sqrt{2}(X-Q)]^2}{2A_{BD}E}\, dx \qquad \text{(a)}$$

The vertical and horizontal deflections at point D are

$$\delta_V = \left(\frac{\partial U}{\partial P}\right)_{Q=0} = \int_0^L \frac{(P-X)(L-x)^2}{EI}\,dx$$

$$= \frac{(P-X)L^3}{3EI} \qquad \text{(b)}$$

$$\delta_H = \left(\frac{\partial U}{\partial Q}\right)_{Q=0} = \int_0^L \frac{(P-X)(L-x)^2}{EI}\,dx - \int_0^{\sqrt{2}L} \frac{2X}{A_{BD}E}\,dx$$

$$= \frac{(P-X)L^3}{3EI} - \frac{2\sqrt{2}XL}{A_{BD}E} \qquad \text{(c)}$$

in terms of the statically indeterminate reaction X. To determine X use the fact that the deflection at point C in Fig. 1(a) is zero; i.e.,

$$0 = \left(\frac{\partial U}{\partial X}\right)_{Q=0} = \int_0^L \frac{X}{A_{CD}E}\,dx - \int_0^L \frac{(P-X)(L-x)^2}{EI}\,dx$$

$$+ \int_0^{\sqrt{2}L} \frac{2X}{A_{BD}E}\,dx$$

$$= \frac{XL}{A_{CD}E} - \frac{(P-X)L^3}{3EI} + \frac{2\sqrt{2}XL}{A_{BD}E} \qquad \text{(d)}$$

Solve for X

$$X = \frac{P}{1 + 3I/A_{CD}L^2 + 6\sqrt{2}I/A_{BD}L^2} \qquad \text{(e)}$$

• PROBLEM 15-25

In the truss supporting three loads, (Fig. 1) find the forces in the links and the displacement of joint A.

Solution: The truss is supported in a statically determinate manner. There are six bars and four joints so that we have clearly one redundant member, making the truss statically indeterminate in the first degree.

Replace link AB with force F_{AB} at joints A and B (Fig. 2). From statics it is possible to find the reaction forces at the supports. Using the method of joints, the forces in the links can be expressed as a function of F_{AB}, as

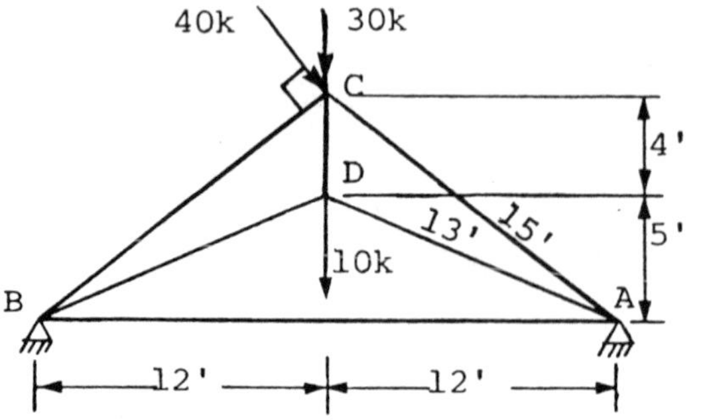

Fig. 1.

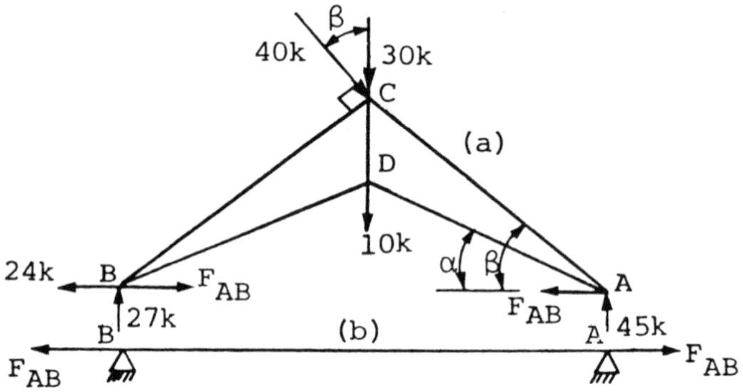

Fig. 2.

$$AD = -146.2 + 2.437F_{AB}$$

$$AC = -168.8 - 1.562F_{AB}$$

$$BC = 138.8 - 1.562F_{AB}$$

$$DC = -122.5 + 1.874F_{AB}$$

$$BD = -146.2 + 2.437F_{AB}$$

Calculating the strain energy in the system without link AB, assuming that the links are of identical materials and cross-sections,

$$U = \frac{1}{2AE}[(AD)^2(13) + (AC)^2(15) + (DC)^2(4)$$

$$+ (BD)^2(13) + (BC)^2(15)]$$

Substituting,

$$U = \frac{1}{2AE}\Big[(-146.2 + 2.437F_{AB})^2(13) + (-168.8 - 1.562F_{AB})^2(15)$$
$$+ (-122.5 + 1.874F_{AB})^2(4) + (138.8 - 1.562F_{AB})^2(15)$$
$$+ (-146.2 + 2.437F_{AB})^2(13)\Big]$$

Since

$$\frac{\partial U}{\partial F_{AB}} = -\frac{F_{AB}L_{AB}}{AE}$$

From which F_{AB} can be calculated

$$(-146.2 + 2.437F_{AB})(2.437)(13)$$
$$+ (-168.8 - 1.562F_{AB})(1.562)(15)$$
$$+ (-122.5 + 1.874F_{AB})(1.874)(4)$$
$$+ (138.8 - 1.562F_{AB})(-1.562)(15)$$
$$+ (-146.2 + 2.437F_{AB})(2.437)(13) = -(F_{AB})(24)$$

and $\quad F_{AB} = 35.7$ kips

Calculating the displacement of joint A

$$\Delta_A = \frac{F_{AB}L}{AE} = \frac{(35.7)(1000)(24)}{AE} = \frac{.857 \times 10^6}{AE}$$

CHAPTER 16

COLUMNS

BUCKLING LOAD

• PROBLEM 16-1

A beam-column is subjected to an axial force P and an upward transverse force F at its midspan, Fig. 1(a). Determine the equation of the elastic curve, and the critical axial force P_{cr} . Let EI = constant.

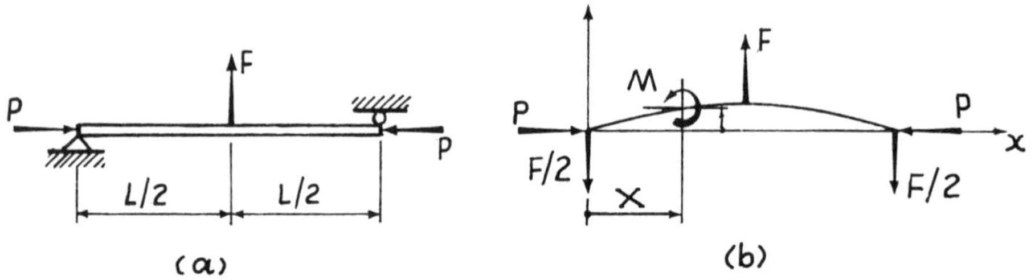

FIG.1

Solution: The free-body diagram for the deflected beam-column is shown in Fig. 1(b). This diagram permits the formulation of the total bending moment M which includes the effect of the axial force P multiplied by the deflection v. The total moment divided by EI could be set equal to the expression for the exact curvature, i.e.,

$$\rho = \frac{1}{R} = \frac{d^2v/dx^2}{\left[1 + \left(\frac{dv}{dx}\right)^2\right]^{3/2}} \tag{1}$$

where ρ = curvature
R = radius .

However, as is customary, since for small deflections $\left(\frac{dv}{dx}\right)^2 \simeq 0$, this curvature will be taken as d^2v/dx^2 ; i.e., the expression $M = EIv''$ will be accepted. This yields accurate results only for small deflections and rotations.
Thus, using the relation $M = EIv''$ and noting that for the left side of the span $M = -(F/2)x - Pv$, one has

$$EIv'' = M = -Pv - (F/2)x \qquad (0 \le x \le L/2)$$

or

$$EIv'' + Pv = -(F/2)x .$$

By dividing through by EI and letting

$$\lambda^2 = P/(EI) \tag{2}$$

after some simplification, the governing differential equation becomes

$$\frac{d^2v}{dx^2} + \lambda^2 v = - \frac{\lambda^2 F}{2P} x \qquad (0 \le x \le L/2) \tag{3}$$

The homogeneous solution for this differential equation has the well-known form of the one for simple harmonic motion; the particular solution equals the right-hand term divided by λ^2. Therefore, the complete solution is

$$v = C_1 \sin \lambda x + C_2 \cos \lambda x - (F/2P)x \tag{4}$$

The constants C_1 and C_2 follow from the boundary condition $v(0) = 0$ and from a condition of symmetry $v'(L/2) = 0$. The first condition gives

$$v(0) = C_2 = 0 .$$

Since

$$v' = C_1 \lambda \cos \lambda x - C_2 \lambda \sin \lambda x - F/(2P)$$

with C_2 already known to be zero, the second condition gives

$$v'(L/2) = C_1 \lambda \cos \lambda L/2 - F/(2P) = 0$$

or

$$C_1 = F/[2P\lambda \cos(\lambda L/2)] .$$

On substituting this constant into Eq. (4),

$$v = \frac{F}{2P\lambda} \frac{1}{\cos \lambda L/2} \sin \lambda x - \frac{F}{2P} x \tag{5}$$

The maximum deflection occurs at $x = L/2$. Thus, after some simplifications,

$$v_{max} = [F/(2P\lambda)](\tan \lambda L/2 - \lambda L/2) \tag{6}$$

From this it may be concluded that the absolute maximum moment, occurring at the midspan, is

$$M_{max} = \left| - \frac{FL}{4} - Pv_{max} \right| = \frac{F}{2\lambda} \tan \frac{\lambda L}{2} \tag{7}$$

Note that the expressions given by Eqs. (5), (6) and (7) become infinite if $\lambda L/2$ is a multiple of $\pi/2$ since this makes $\cos \lambda L/2$ equal to zero and $\tan \lambda L/2$ infinite. Stated algebraically this occurs when

$$\frac{\lambda L}{2} = \sqrt{\frac{P}{EI}} \frac{L}{2} = \frac{n\pi}{2} \tag{8}$$

where n is an integer. Solving this equation for P, one obtains the magnitude of P causing either infinite deflections or bending moment. This corresponds to the condition of the critical axial force P_{cr} for this bar:

$$P_{cr} = \frac{n^2 \pi^2 EI}{L^2} \tag{9}$$

For the smallest critical force the integer $n = 1$. This result was first established by the great mathematician Leonhard Euler in 1757 and is often referred to as the Euler buckling load.

A slender column of length L is fixed at the lower end and simply supported at the upper end. Derive an expression for the lowest critical load for this column and determine the corresponding buckled mode shape.

Solution: When this column buckles, a horizontal reactive force R is developed at the upper end of the column. At the fixed end, both a horizontal force and a couple are induced. From static equilibrium, we see that the two forces are equal in magnitude but opposite in direction and that the couple M is equal to RL. The bending moment at distance x from the base is

$$M = Pv - R(L - x)$$

and the differential equation of the deflection curve is

$$EIv'' = -Pv + R(L - x)$$

The general solution of this equation is

$$v = C_1 \sin kx + C_2 \cos kx + R(L - x)/P \qquad (1)$$

where $k^2 = P/EI$.

For determining the constants C_1 and C_2 and the unknown reaction R, we have the following three conditions at the ends:

$$v = v' = 0 \quad \text{at} \quad x = 0$$
$$v = 0 \quad \text{at} \quad x = L$$

Applying these conditions to Eq. (1) yields

$$C_2 + RL/P = 0 \qquad C_1k - R/P = 0 \qquad C_1 \tan kL + C_2 = 0 \qquad (2)$$

All these equations will be satisfied by taking $C_1 = C_2 = R = 0$, in which event the deflection vanishes, and we have the straight, unbuckled form of equilibrium. In order to have the possibility of a buckled shape of equilibrium, we need a solution of Eqs. (2) other than the trivial one. We may observe that Eqs. (2) are homogeneous equations with C_1, C_2, and R as the unknowns; such a set of equations has a non-trivial solution only if the determinant of the coefficients is equal to zero. Thus, we get for the buckling equation the following:

$$\begin{vmatrix} 0 & 1 & L/P \\ k & 0 & -1/P \\ \tan kL & 1 & 0 \end{vmatrix} = 0$$

or, upon expanding the determinant,

$$-1 \begin{vmatrix} k & -1/P \\ \tan kL & 0 \end{vmatrix} + L/P \begin{vmatrix} k & 0 \\ \tan kL & 1 \end{vmatrix} = 0 \qquad (3)$$

or

$$-(1/p) \tan kL + (L/P)k = 0$$

or

$$KL = \tan kL$$

This transcendental equation defines the critical load. The smallest nonzero value of kL which satisfies the equation is kL = 4.493, which may be found by trial and error. The corresponding critical load is

$$P_{cr} = (kL)^2 \frac{EI}{L^2} = \frac{20.19\ EI}{L^2} \tag{4}$$

which is intermediate between the values of the critical loads for columns with pinned ends and with fixed ends.

We may now return to Eqs. (2) and evaluate C_1 and C_2 in terms of R:

$$C_1 = \frac{R}{kP} \qquad C_2 = -\frac{RL}{P}$$

Substituting into Eq. (1) gives the equation of the deflection curve:

$$v = \frac{R}{Pk}\left[\sin kx - kL \cos kx + kL\left(1 - \frac{x}{L}\right)\right] \tag{5}$$

The term in square brackets represents the mode shape for the deflection of the buckled column, but the amplitute of the deflection remains undefined because R is arbitrary.

• PROBLEM 16-3

A slender bar of constant EI is simultaneously subjected to the end moments M_0 and an axial force P as shown in Fig. 1(a). Determine the maximum deflection and the largest bending moment.

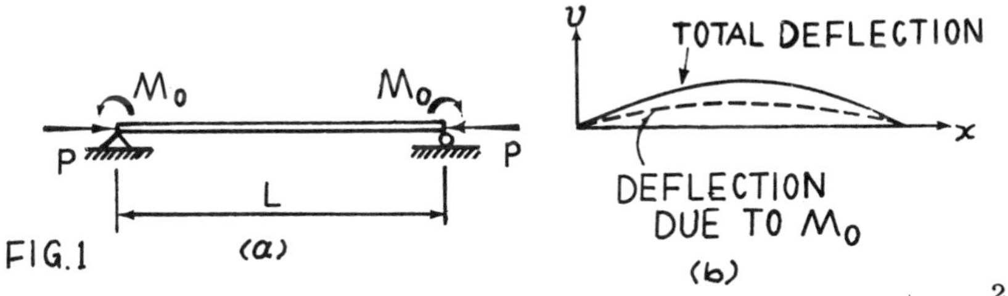

FIG.1

Solution: If we make the small deflection approximation $\left(\frac{1}{R} = \frac{d^2v}{dx^2}\right)$, the internal bending stresses form a couple equal to $EI(d^2v/dx^2)$, therefore we have the external moment $M_{ext} = -P(M_0/P + v)$ and the internal moment $M_{int} = +EI\, d^2v/dx^2$. For equilibrium

$$EI \frac{d^2v}{dx^2} = -P\left(\frac{M_0}{P} + v\right)$$

or

$$\frac{d^2v}{dx^2} + \frac{P}{EI} \cdot v = -\frac{M_0}{EI} \tag{1}$$

If we let

$$\lambda = \sqrt{P/EI}$$

equation (1) becomes

$$\frac{d^2v}{dx^2} + \lambda^2 v = -\lambda^2 \cdot \frac{M_0}{P} \tag{2}$$

The solution to equation (2) is

$$v(x) = C_1 \sin \lambda x + C_2 \cos \lambda x + C_3 x + C_4 \ldots \tag{3}$$

Differentiating equation (3) twice yields,

$$v'' = -C_1 \lambda^2 \sin \lambda x - C_2 \lambda^2 \cos \lambda x$$

Since $M = EIv''$, the above equation can be written as,

$$M = -C_1 EI\,\lambda^2 \sin \lambda x - C_2 EI\,\lambda^2 \cos \lambda x \tag{4}$$

The boundary conditions are

$$v(0) = 0, \quad v(L) = 0, \quad M(0) = -M_0, \text{ and } M(L) = -M_0$$

Substitution of these boundary conditions into equations (3) and (4) yields,

$$v(0) = \quad + C_2 \quad + C_4 = 0 \tag{5}$$

$$v(L) = + C_1 \sin \lambda L + C_2 \cos \lambda L + C_3 L + C_4 = 0 \tag{6}$$

$$M(0) = \quad - C_2\, EI\lambda^2 = - M_0 \tag{7}$$

$$M(L) = -C_1 EI\lambda^2 \sin \lambda L - C_2 EI\lambda^2 \cos \lambda L = - M_0 \tag{8}$$

From equation (7),

$$C_2 = \frac{M_0}{EI\lambda^2}$$

since $\lambda = \sqrt{P/EI}$,

$$C_2 = \frac{M_0}{P}$$

and from equation (5) $C_2 = -C_4$

Hence, $C_4 = -\frac{M_0}{P}$

To obtain the value of C_1, substitute the value for C_2 into equation (8). Thus,

$$-C_1\, EI\lambda^2 \sin \lambda L - \left(M_0/P\right) EI\lambda^2 \cos \lambda L = - M_0$$

or

$$C_1 = \left(M_0 - \left(M_0/P\right) EI\lambda^2 \cos \lambda L\right) \Big/ EI\lambda^2 \sin \lambda L$$

Since $\lambda = \sqrt{P/EI}$, the above equation becomes,

$$C_1 = \frac{M_0 - M_0 \cos \lambda L}{P \sin \lambda L}$$

or

$$C_1 = \frac{M_0}{P}\left[\frac{1 - \cos \lambda L}{\sin \lambda L}\right]$$

Substitute the values of C_1, C_2 and C_4 into equation (6), to obtain

$$\frac{M_0}{P}\left[\frac{1 - \cos \lambda L}{\sin \lambda L}\right] \sin \lambda L + \frac{M_0}{P} \cos \lambda L + C_3 L - \frac{M_0}{P} = 0$$

from which

$$C_3 = 0 .$$

Therefore, the equation of the elastic curve is

$$v = \frac{M_0}{P}\left(\frac{1 - \cos \lambda L}{\sin \lambda L} \sin \lambda x + \cos \lambda x - 1\right) \tag{9}$$

The maximum deflection occurs at $x = L/2$. After some simplifications, it is found to be

$$v_{max} = \frac{M_0}{P}\left(\frac{\sin^2 \lambda L/2}{\cos \lambda L/2} + \cos \frac{\lambda L}{2} - 1\right) = \frac{M_0}{P}\left(\sec \frac{\lambda L}{2} - 1\right) \tag{10}$$

The largest bending moment also occurs at $x = L/2$. Its absolute maximum is

$$M_{max} = \left| - M_0 - Pv_{max} \right| = M_0 \sec \lambda L/2 \tag{11}$$

It is important to note that in slender members bending moments may be substantially increased by the presence of axial compressive forces. When such forces exist, the deflection caused by the transverse loading is magnified, Fig. 1(b). For tensile forces the deflections are reduced.

• PROBLEM 16-4

A strut with hinged ends AB, Fig. 1, is compressed by forces P_1 and P_2. Find the critical value of the force $P_1 + P_2$ if $(P_1 + P_2)$:

$$P_1 = m, \; I_2 : I_1 = n, \; \ell_2/\ell_1 = r .$$

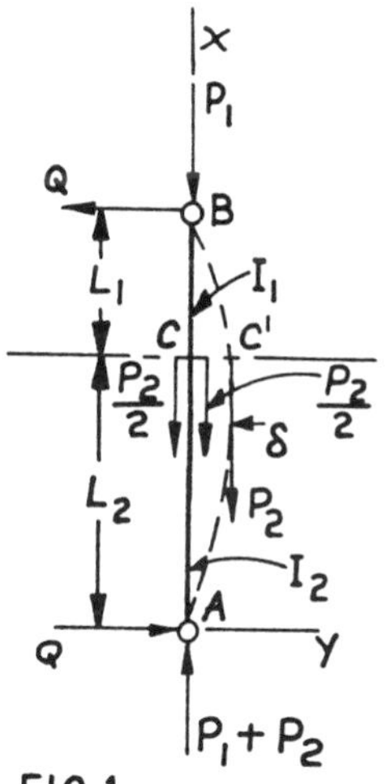

FIG.1.

Solution: Assuming that the buckled shape of the strut is as shown in Fig. 1 by the dotted line, there will be horizontal reactions $Q = \delta P_2/\ell$ produced during buckling. The differential equations of the upper and the lower portions of the deflection curve are

$$\left.\begin{aligned} EI_1 \frac{d^2y_1}{dx^2} &= - P_1 y_1 - \frac{\delta P_2}{\ell}(\ell - x), \\ EI_2 \frac{d^2y_2}{dx^2} &= - P_1 y_2 - \frac{\delta P_2}{\ell}(\ell - x) + P_2(\delta - y_2) \end{aligned}\right\} \tag{1}$$

Using notations

$$\frac{P_1}{EI_1} = p_1^2, \quad \frac{P_2}{EI_2} = p_2^2, \quad \frac{P_1 + P_2}{EI_2} = p_3^2, \quad \frac{P_2}{EI_1} = p_4^2, \tag{2}$$

we obtain the solutions of equations (1):

$$y_1 = C_1 \sin p_1 x + C_2 \cos p_1 x - \frac{\delta}{\ell}\frac{p_4^2}{p_1^2}(\ell - x)$$

$$y_2 = C_3 \sin p_3 x + C_4 \cos p_3 x + \frac{\delta}{\ell}\frac{p_2^2}{p_3^2}x .$$

The constants of integration are obtained from the end conditions of the two portions of the buckled bar:

$$(y_1)_{x=1} = 0, \quad (y_1)_{x=\ell_2} = \delta , \quad (y_2)_{x=\ell_2} = \delta , \quad (y_2)_{x=0} = 0 .$$

From these,

$$C_1 = \frac{\delta\left(p_1^2\ell + p_4^2\ \ell_1\right)}{p_1^2\ell(\sin p_1\ell_2 - \tan p_1\ell \cos p_1\ell_2)} , \qquad C_2 = - C_1 \tan p_1\ell$$

$$C_3 = \frac{\delta(p_3^2\ell - p_2^2\ell_2)}{p_3^2\ell \sin p_3\ell_2} , \qquad C_4 = 0 .$$

Substituting these in the continuity condition

$$\left(\frac{dy_1}{dx}\right)_{x=\ell_2} = \left(\frac{dy_2}{dx}\right)_{x=\ell_2}$$

we obtain the following transcendental equation for calculating critical loads:

$$\frac{p_4^2}{p_1^2} - \frac{p_1^2\ell + p_4^2\ell_1}{p_1 \tan p_1\ell_1} = \frac{p_2^2}{p_3^2} + \frac{p_3^2\ell - p_2^2\ell_2}{p_3 \tan p_3\ell_2} \tag{t}$$

which can be solved in each particular case by trial and error or by plotting both sides of the equation and determining the intersection point of the two curves. Taking, as an example, $\ell_1 = \ell_2$, $I_1 = I_2 = I$ and $P_1 = P_2$, we obtain

$$(P_1 + P_2)_{cr} = \frac{\pi^2 EI}{(0.87\,\ell)^2} .$$

• PROBLEM 16-5

Find the critical load for the column built-in at the bottom and free at the top and consisting of the two prismatical portions with moments of inertia I_1 and I_2 , Fig. 1.

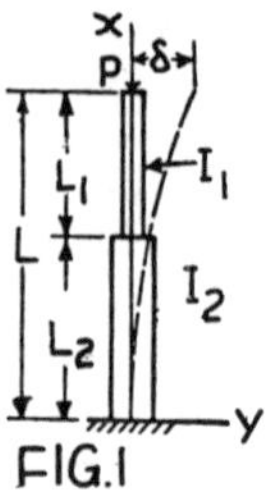

FIG.1

Solution: If δ is the deflection at the top during buckling the differential equations for the two portions of the deflection curve are

$$EI_1 \frac{d^2y_1}{dx^2} = P(\delta - y_1) ,$$

$$EI_2 \frac{d^2y_2}{dx^2} = P(\delta - y_2) .$$

Letting, $\frac{P}{EI_1} = p_1^2$, $\frac{P}{EI_2} = p_2^2$, the solutions of these equations are reached:

$$y_1 = \delta + C \cos p_1x + D \sin p_1x ,$$

$$y_2 = \delta(I - \cos p_2x) .$$

The constants of integration are obtained from the conditions:

$$(y_1)_{x=\ell} = \delta , \quad (y_1)_{x=\ell_2} = (y_2)_{x=\ell_2}$$

which gives

$$\delta + C \cos p_1\ell + D \sin p_1\ell = \delta ,$$

$$\delta + C \cos p_1\ell_2 + D \sin p_1\ell_2 = \delta(1 - \cos p_2\ell_2) ,$$

from which

$$C = - D \tan p_1\ell , \; D = \frac{\delta \cos p_2\ell_2 \cos p_1\ell}{\sin p_1\ell_1} .$$

Since the two portions of the deflection curve have the same tangent at $x = \ell_2$ we have the equation:

$$\delta p_2 \sin p_2\ell_2 = - Cp_1 \sin p_1\ell_2 + Dp_1 \cos p_1\ell_2 .$$

Substituting for C and D the above values, we finally obtain the following equation for calculating P_{cr}:

$$\tan p_1\ell_1 \tan p_2\ell_2 = \frac{p_1}{p_2} .$$

In the particular case when

$$p_1\ell_1 = p_2\ell_2 = \frac{\ell}{2}\sqrt{\frac{P}{EI}} ,$$

we obtain

$$\tan^2\left(\frac{\ell}{2}\sqrt{\frac{P}{EI}}\right) = I ,$$

$$\frac{\ell}{2}\sqrt{\frac{P}{EI}} = \frac{\pi}{4}$$

and

$$P_{cr} = \frac{\pi^2 EI}{4\ell^2} .$$

This is the critical load for a column of constant cross section.

• PROBLEM 16-6

Design the support for a load shown, using two identical angle irons AB made of steel. For safety purposes, three times the load is to be used.

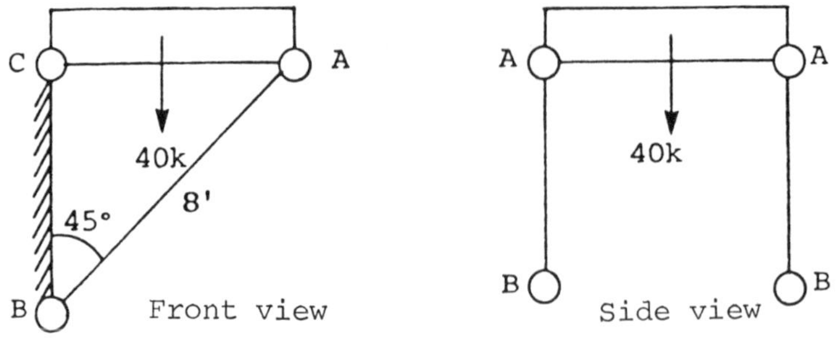

Solution: The total load to be designed for, using the safety factor of 3

$$W = 3 \times 40{,}000 \text{ lb.} = 120{,}000 \text{ lb.}$$

The load is supported at four points (2 points on the links and 2 points against the wall). Each point suports therefore 120K ÷ 4 = 30 K. Considering the buckling aspects of the angle iron links, the axial force in the links are

$$F_{AB}(.707) = 30{,}000$$

$$F_{AB} = 42{,}433$$

Assuming incipient buckling at, F_{AB}, and using Euler's equation,

$$P_{cr} = \frac{\pi^2 EI}{L^2}$$

$$42{,}434 = \frac{\pi^2(30 \times 10^6)(I)}{(8^2)(144)}$$

$$\therefore I = 1.320 \text{ in.}$$

In searching through a standard table of angles, it may be seen that corresponding to such value of I, there is an angle of $3 \times 3 \times \frac{3}{8}$. The angle has an area of 2.11 in^2 which results in an acceptable stress of

$$\tau = \frac{42{,}433}{2.11} = 20{,}110 \text{ psi}$$

• PROBLEM 16-7

Find the shortest length L for a pinned-ended steel column having a cross-sectional area of 2 in. by 3 in. for which the elastic Euler formula applies. Let $E = 30 \times 10^6$ psi and assume the proportional limit to be at 36 ksi.

Solution: The minimum moment of inertia of the cross-sectional area $I_{min} = 3(2)^3/12 = 2 \text{ in.}^4$. Hence

$$r = r_{min} = \sqrt{\frac{I_{min}}{A}} = \sqrt{\frac{2}{2(3)}} = \frac{1}{\sqrt{3}} \text{ in.}$$

Then using $\sigma_{cr} = \pi^2\left(E/(L/r)^2\right)$ and solving it for the L/r ratio at the proportional limit

$$\left(\frac{L}{r}\right)^2 = \frac{\pi^2 E}{\sigma_{cr}} = \frac{\pi^2(30)10^6}{(36)10^3} = 8,220$$

or

$$\frac{L}{r} = 90.7 \quad \text{and} \quad L = \frac{90.7}{\sqrt{3}} = 52.3 \text{ in.}$$

Therefore, if this column is 52.3 in. or more in length, it will buckle elastically as for such dimensions of the column the critical stress at buckling will not exceed the proportional limit for the material.

• PROBLEM 16-8

A spirally reinforced column is shown in Fig. 1. The laterally unsupported length of the column is 17 ft. 6 in. The steel is intermediate grade and the concrete has a 28-day strength f'_c of 3,000 psi. What is the allowable axial load for the column?

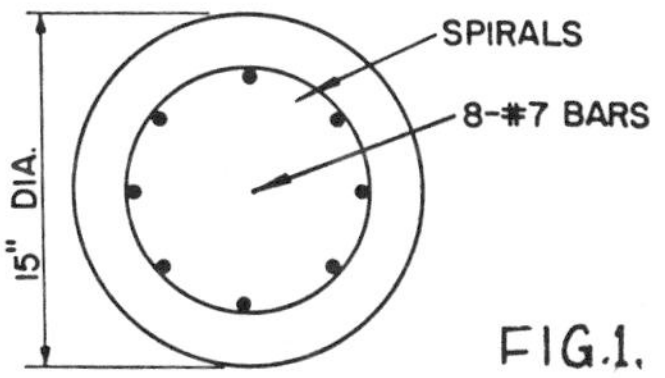

FIG.1.

Solution: Buckling is a factor to consider in concrete column design only when the laterally unsupported length h exceeds ten times the least lateral dimension d. The column is then classed as a long column. The load allowed on a long column is reduced from that for a short column of the same cross section. The reduction (for ACI Code) is given by

$$P' = P(1.3 - 0.03 \frac{h}{d}) \tag{1}$$

In this, P' is the allowable load for the long column, and P is the load for a short column of the same cross section. The factor in parentheses gives no reduction in load allowed for h/d ratios up to 10. For ratios over 10, the allowable load P' reduces in a straight-line variation.

For given problem, the ratio of unsupported length to least lateral dimension is $210/15 = 14$. The ratio exceeds 10, so the column is treated as a long column. The allowable load will be computed first as if the column were short. Then use equation (1) to determine the allowable load for the actual column.

The load allowed for a short column of the same cross section is

$$P = A_g(0.225f'_c + f_s p_g)$$

$$A_g = \frac{\pi(15)^2}{4} = 177 \text{ sq. in.}$$

Allowed $f_s = 0.40f_y = 16,000$ psi

$$p_g = \frac{A_s}{A_g} = \frac{4.80}{177} = 0.0272$$

$$P = 177[(0.225 \times 3,000) + (16,000 \times 0.0272)]$$
$$= 196,000 \text{ lb, or } 196 \text{ kips.}$$

The allowable axial load for the long column is

$$P' = 196(1.3 - 0.03 \frac{h}{d})$$
$$= 196(1.3 - 0.03 \times 14)$$
$$= 173 \text{ kips.}$$

• PROBLEM 16-9

Determine the dimensions necessary for a 20-in. rectangular strut to carry an axial load of 1500 lb. with a factor of safety of 2. The material is aluminum alloy 2024-T4, and the width of the strut is to be twice the thickness.

(a) Use Code No. 4.

(b) Use the parabolic equation $R = 1 - C_3 S^2$ (1)

where the general equation for the Euler part of the curve is

$$R = \frac{1}{S^2} \quad (2)$$

and the straight-line equation

$$R = 1 - C_2 S \quad (3)$$

$C_2 = 0.385$ for $0 \le S \le 1.732$

$C_3 = 0.250$ for $0 \le S \le 1.414$

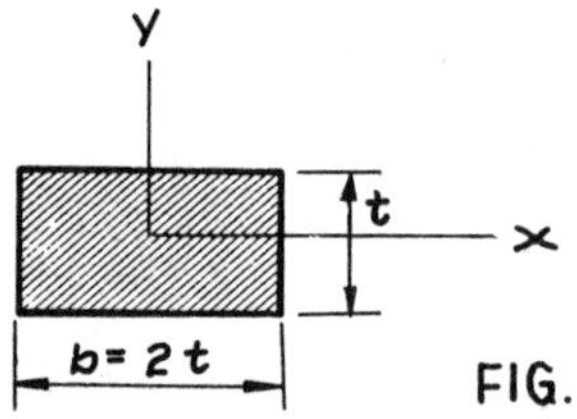

FIG.1.

Solution: (a) The code is represented by two different equations which depend upon the value of L/r, which in turn will depend on the equation used. Thus it will be necessary to assume that one of the equations applies and use it to obtain the dimensions of the column, after which the value of L/r must be calculated and used to check the validity of the equation used. Assume L/r is less than 64, in which case the straight-line equation is valid. The cross section is shown in Fig. 1, and the least moment of inertia, I_x, is equal to $bt^3/12$; the area, A, is equal to bt or $2t^2$; and the least radius of gyration is

$$r = \left(\frac{bt^3/12}{bt}\right)^{1/2} = \frac{t}{\sqrt{12}}$$

The slenderness ratio is

$$\frac{L}{r} = \frac{20\sqrt{12}}{t},$$

and, when this value and the expression for the area are substituted in the straight-line formula of Code 4, it becomes

$$k\left(\frac{P}{A}\right) = \frac{2(1500)}{2t^2} = 44,800 - 313\left(\frac{20\sqrt{12}}{t}\right),$$

from which

$$t = 0.546 \text{ in.}$$

The value of L/r for this thickness is

$$\frac{L}{r} = \frac{20\sqrt{12}}{0.546} = 127$$

which is greater than 64 and indicates that the straight-line formula is not valid. The problem must be solved again using the Euler equation. Thus

$$\frac{P}{A} = \frac{1500}{2t^2} = \frac{\pi^2 E}{2(L/r)^2} = \frac{9.87(10.6)(10^6)}{2\left[(20)\sqrt{12}/t\right]^2},$$

from which

$$t^4 = 0.06882 \quad \text{and} \quad t = 0.512 \text{ in.}$$

The value of L/r is 135.3 for this thickness which confirms the use of the Euler formula. The dimensions of the cross section are

$$t = 0.512 \text{ in. and } b = 1.024 \text{ in.}$$

(b) Assume S is less than 1.732 in which case the straight-line formula applies. The parameter $\pi\sqrt{E/\sigma_0}$ becomes

$$\pi\sqrt{10.6(10^3)/44.8} = 48.3;$$

consequently,

$$S = \frac{L/r}{\pi\sqrt{E/\sigma_0}} = \frac{20\sqrt{12}}{48.3t} = \frac{1.433}{t}$$

when this value is substituted into Eq. (3), R is found to be

$$R = 1 - 0.385\left(\frac{1.433}{t}\right) = \frac{k(P/A)}{\sigma_0} = \frac{2(1500)}{2t^2(44.800)} = \frac{0.0335}{t^2},$$

from which

$$t = 0.607 \text{ in.}$$

Upon substituting this value for t in the equation for S,

$$S = \frac{1.433}{0.607} = 2.36,$$

which is greater than the 1.732 assumed and, therefore, the slender-range formula must apply. Equation (1) yields

$$R = \frac{k(P/A)}{\sigma_0} = \frac{0.0335}{t^2} = \frac{1}{S^2} = \left(\frac{t}{1.433}\right)^2$$

from which

$$t^4 = 0.0688 \quad \text{and} \quad t = 0.512 \text{ in.}$$

Therefore, the dimensions of the cross section are

$$t = 0.512 \text{ in. and } b = 1.024 \text{ in.}$$

DESIGN FORMULAS

• PROBLEM 16-10

Using AISC column formulas select a 15-ft-long, pin-ended column to carry a concentric load of 200 kips. The structural steel is to be A441, having $\sigma_{yp} = 50$ ksi.

Solution: The required size of the column may be found directly from the tables in the AISC Steel Construction Manual. However, this example provides an opportunity to demonstrate the trial-and-error procedure which is so often necessary in design, and the solution presented follows from using this method.

First try: Let $L/r = 0$ (a poor assumption for a column 15 ft long). Then, since F.S. = 5/3, $\sigma_{allow} = 50/(F.S.) = 30$ ksi and $A = P/\sigma_{allow} = 200/30 = 6.67$ in.^{2}. From Table, this requires an 8 WF 24 section, whose $r_{min} = 1.61$ in. Hence $L/r = 15(12)/(1.61) = 112$. To find the allowable stress, first obtain the value of C_c. Thus,

$$C_c = \sqrt{2\pi^2 E/\sigma_{yp}}$$

$$= \sqrt{2\pi^2 \times 29 \times 10^3/50} = 107.$$

Since $C_c \leq L/r$, the equation $\sigma_{allow} = \frac{149{,}000}{(L/r)^2}$ is applicable to determine allowable stress. Hence,

$$\sigma_{allow} = \frac{149{,}000}{(112)^2} = 11.9 \text{ ksi.}$$

This is much smaller than the initially assumed stress of 30 ksi, and another section must be selected.

Second try: Let $\sigma_{allow} = 11.9$ ksi as found before. Then $A = 200/11.9 = 16.8$ in.^{2} requiring an 8 WF 58 section having $r_{min} = 2.10$ in. Now $L/r = 15(12)/(2.10) = 85.7$, which is less than C_c found before. Therefore equation

$$\sigma_{allow} = \frac{\sigma_{yp}}{F.S.}\left[1 - \frac{(L/r)^2}{2C_c^2}\right]$$

is applicable. Then

$$F.S. = \frac{5}{3} + \frac{3(L/r)}{8C_c} - \frac{(L/r)^3}{8C_c^3}$$

$$F.S. = \frac{5}{3} + \frac{3(85.7)}{8 \times 107} - \frac{(85.7)^3}{8(107)^3}$$

$$= 1.9$$

Hence,

$$\sigma_{allow} = \frac{50}{1.9}\left[1 - \frac{(85.7)^2}{2(107)^2}\right]$$

$$= 17.9 \text{ ksi}$$

The stress requires $A = 200/17.9 = 11.2$ in.^{2}, which is met by an 8 WF 40 section with $r_{min} = 2.04$ in. The allowable axial load is $\sigma_A = 17.9 \times 11.2 = 200$ kips, which meets the requirements of the problem.

• PROBLEM 16-11

Select a steel I section for a column 9 ft. long to carry an axial compressive load of 90,000 lb., assuming the column to have round ends.

Solution: An approximate value of the area of section needed may be found by considering the member to be a compression block, for which

$P/a = 15{,}000$, and hence $a = \frac{90{,}000}{15{,}000} = 6.0 \text{ in.}^2$.

From Table of properties of steel section, it is found that the minimum radius of gyration for I sections having areas of 6 to 7 in.^{2} is about 1.0, and hence ℓ/r is approximately 108, which means that the a in $P/a = 18{,}000 - 60\ \ell/r$ must be considerably larger than 6.0 if P is equal to 90,000 lb. when $\ell/r = 108$.

As a second trial, select a 10-in. 25.4-lb. I section for which $a = 7.38 \text{ in.}^2$, and $r_{min} = 0.97$ in. Then

$$\ell/r = \frac{108}{0.97} = 111.$$

Hence

$$\frac{90.000}{a} = 18{,}000 - 60 \times 111$$

or $a = 8.0 \text{ in.}^2$ approximately. Therefore, a section having an area larger than 7.38 in.^{2} is needed. As a further trial, select a 10-in. 30-lb. I section, for which $a = 8.76 \text{ in.}^2$, $r_{min} = 0.93$ in., and hence $\ell/r = 116$. Then

$$a = \frac{90{,}000}{18{,}000 - 60 \times 116} = 8.15 \text{ in.}^2$$

Therefore, a 12-in. 27.9-lb. I section having an area of 8.15 in.^{2} would be adequate.

• PROBLEM 16-12

A column made of a 10-in. 35-lb. I beam and two plates 5/8 in. by 11 in., as shown in Fig. 1, is 20 ft. long and is subjected, in a testing machine, to an axial load applied through spherical-seated bearings. Calculate the least radius of gyration r and the corresponding slenderness ratio ℓ/r . Find the allowable or working load for the column.

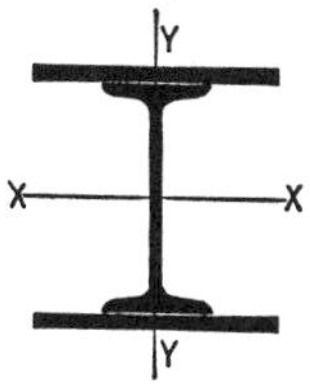

FIG.1.

Solution: The moment of inertia of the cross-sectional area about the x axis may be found as follows: Area of each plate, $a_1 = 6.87$ sq. in. A steelmaker's handbook gives:

$$\text{Area of the I section} = 10.29 \text{ sq. in.}$$

$$I_x \text{ of the I section} = 146.4 \text{ in.}^4$$

$$I_y \text{ of the I section} = 8.5 \text{ in.}^4$$

Hence,

$$\text{Total area of cross section } a = 24.03 \text{ sq. in.}$$

$$I_x \text{ of the two plates} = 2(I + a_1 d^2),$$

$$= 2a_1 d^2, \text{ approximately}$$

$$= 2 \times 6.87 \times (5.3)^2$$
$$= 386 \text{ in.}^4$$

I_x for whole area $= 146.4 + 386 = 532.4 \text{ in.}^4$

I_y for whole area $= 8.5 + 2\left(\frac{1}{12} \times \frac{5}{8}\right)(11)^3$
$$= 8.5 + 138.6 = 147.1 \text{ in.}^4$$

Since I_y is smaller than I_x, the column will bend so that the y axis is the neutral axis, that is, in a plane perpendicular to the y axis.

The least radius of gyration, $r = \sqrt{\frac{I_y}{a}} = \sqrt{\frac{147.1}{24.03}} = 2.47$ in. Therefore,

$$\frac{\ell}{r} = \frac{20 \times 12}{2.47} = 97.0$$

For this intermediate value of ℓ/r,

$$\frac{P_w}{a} = 18{,}000 - 60 \times 97 = 12{,}180 \text{ lb./in}^2$$

$$P_w = 12{,}180 \times 24.03 = 292{,}000 \text{ lb., allowable load.}$$

• PROBLEM 16-13

Select the lightest WF steel section to support a centric load of 150 kips as a 15-ft. column. Use Code No. 2.

Solution: If L/r were small, P/A would be 15,000 psi, and the area would be

$$A = 150{,}000/15{,}000 = 10 \text{ sq. in.}$$

A column should be selected from Table of Steel Properties with an area greater than 10.00 sq. in. for the first trial. In this case try an 8 WF 40 section for which A is 11.76 sq. in. and r_{min} is 2.04 in. The value of L/r for this column is

$$\frac{L}{r} = \frac{180}{2.04} = 88.2,$$

and the load that it can support is

$$P = A\left[15{,}000 - \frac{(L/r)^2}{3}\right] = 11.76\left[15{,}000 - \frac{88.2^2}{3}\right] = 146{,}000 \text{ lb.}$$

This load is less than the design load; therefore a column with either a larger area, a larger radius of gyration, or both must be investigated. As a second trial value use a 10 WF 45 section for which A is 13.24 sq. in. and r is 2.00 in. For this section L/r is equal to 90, and the load is

$$P = 13.24[15{,}000 - 90^2/3] = 163{,}000 \text{ lb.}$$

Since the 45-lb. column is stronger than necessary and the 40-lb. column is not strong enough, any other sections investigated should weigh between 40 and 45 lb. per ft. The only WF section in a table of properties of steel section which might satisfy the requirements is a 14 WF 43 section for which A is 12.65 sq. in. and r is 1.89 in. The slenderness ratio and allowable load for this column are

$$(L/r) = 95.2 \quad \text{and} \quad P = 151{,}500 \text{ lb.}$$

Thus the lightest column is a 14 WF 43 section.

• PROBLEM 16-14

What is the axial load capacity of a 10 WF 33 section, used as a column? The length is 14 ft. The column is laterally supported at its ends only. Use the AISC Specification.

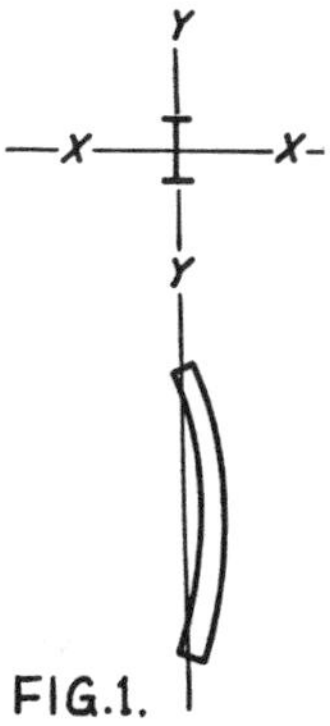

FIG.1.

Solution: The column will buckle in the direction of least stiffness. The radii of gyration for the section are given by the tables as 4.20 in. about axis X-X, and 1.94 in. about axis Y-Y. The ratio L/r is

$$\frac{14 \times 12}{4.20} = 40.0 \text{ for axis X-X}$$

or

$$\frac{14 \times 12}{1.94} = 86.5 \text{ for axis Y-Y}$$

The larger L/r ratio determines the allowable capacity and the direction of buckling that would occur at ultimate load. This column would buckle as shown in Fig. 1, so that it bends about axis Y-Y as a neutral axis.

$$\text{Allowable } \frac{P}{A} = 17{,}000 - 0.485(86.5)^2 = 13{,}370 \text{ psi}$$

From the tables of WF sections, the area of the section is 9.71 sq. in. The allowable axial load is

$$P = 9.71 \times 13.37 = 130 \text{ kips.}$$

• PROBLEM 16-15

Select a WF section to use for a column 13 ft. long having 120 kips of axial load.

Solution: The design of a column is a trial-and-error procedure. This is sometimes more elegantly referred to as successive approximation. Such a process should not be frowned upon as unscientific or inaccurate. On the contrary, it is a process used in much engineering and scientific work. For example, long division and the extraction of square roots are trial-and-error methods.

The allowable P/A is not known until L/r is known, and L/r is not known until the selection of a section is made. Something must be assumed in order to get started. A 13-ft. column is not very long so why not assume some middle-of-the-road value of L/r, say about 50? For L/r of 50, the allowable P/A would be $17{,}000 - 0.485(50)^2 =$

15,790 psi, or about 16 kips per sq. in. If L/r were 50, the required area would then be 120/16 = 7.50 sq. in. A section with an area somewhere near 7.5 sq. in. will be tried.

Trial No. 1: Try 12 WF 27 (A = 7.97 sq. in.).

$$\text{Maximum } \frac{L}{r} = \frac{13 \times 12}{1.44} = 108$$

$$\text{Allowable } \frac{P}{A} = 17{,}000 - 0.485(108)^2 = 11{,}340 \text{ psi}$$

$$\text{Actual } \frac{P}{A} = \frac{120{,}000}{7.97} = 15{,}050 \text{ psi} \quad \text{Not Satisfactory}$$

Since the actual stress would exceed the allowable, the 12 WF 27 is unsatisfactory. For the next trial, use a section with either larger r, or larger A, or both.

Trial No. 2: Try 10WF 33 (A = 9.71 sq. in.).

$$\text{Maximum } \frac{L}{r} = \frac{13 \times 12}{1.94} = 80.5$$

$$\text{Allowable } \frac{P}{A} = 17{,}000 - 0.485(80.5)^2 = 13{,}860 \text{ psi}$$

$$\text{Actual } \frac{P}{A} = \frac{120{,}000}{9.71} = 12{,}350 \text{ psi} \quad \text{Satisfactory}$$

The actual stress would not exceed the allowable, so the 10 WF 33 would be satisfactory. There are many other sections that will work, however. The object is usually to find the lightest satisfactory section. Further trials should be made on lighter sections.

Trial No. 3: Try 8 WF 31 (A = 9.12 sq.in.).

$$\text{Maximum } \frac{L}{r} = \frac{13 \times 12}{2.01} = 77.6$$

$$\text{Allowable } \frac{P}{A} = 17{,}000 - 0.485(77.6)^2 = 14{,}080 \text{ psi}$$

$$\text{Actual } \frac{P}{A} = \frac{120{,}000}{9.12} = 13{,}150 \text{ psi} \quad \text{Satisfactory}$$

The next lighter sections are the 10 WF 29 and 8 WF 28, both of which have much lower r values than the 8 WF 31. They will prove to be unsatisfactory. Use the 8 WF 31.

Even when the first guess is extremely poor, the designer can arrive at the most economical section after two, three, or four trials at the most. He can use the amount of error on the first trial as a guide to how much heavier, or lighter, the second trial section should be.

• PROBLEM 16-16

Select a WF Beam Section to serve as a column, 25 ft. long, with fixed ends, carrying a concentric load of 200,000 lb. Use the A.I.S.C. formula.

Solution: For fixed ends, the modified length is $\frac{1}{2}\ell = \frac{25 \times 12}{2} = 150$ in.

A.I.S.C. formula is

$$\frac{P}{A} = 17{,}000 - 0.485\frac{\ell^2}{r^2} \quad (\ell/r \leq 120) \qquad (1)$$

Substituting P and ℓ in the above formula,

$$\frac{200,000}{A} = 17,000 - 0.485 \frac{150^2}{r^2} . \qquad (2)$$

This solution is obtained by trial methods, selecting a section such that A and r for that section satisfies the above relation. A trial solution giving a minimum area may be found by assuming $P/A = 17,000$ as for a very short column (that is, with $\ell/r = 0$); hence $A = 11\frac{3}{4}$ sq.in. We, therefore, need not try any section which has an area less than $11\frac{3}{4}$ sq. in.

For a first trial, select a 12 WF 45 Beam Section, A = 13.24 sq.in., least r = 1.94, and $\ell/r = 77.2$ which lies between the limits where Eq. (1) applies. The actual stress, given by the left side of (1), is 15,100 psi. The safe stress, given by the right side, is 14,100 psi. A somewhat larger section is therefore needed; try a 12 WF 50 Section, A = 14.71 sq.in., least r = 1.96, $\ell/r = 76.5$. The actual stress now is 200,000/14.71 = 13,600 psi and the safe stress, from Eq. (1) is 14,160 psi. This latter section is amply safe.

The result may be obtained more readily by using tables of allowable concentric loads, as found in the A.I.S.C. handbook, and a modified length of $12\frac{1}{2}$ ft.

As a rough check, calculate the safe load the above section will carry using the A.R.E.A. formula.

$$s_w = 17,000 - 0.35(\ell/r)^2 = 14,950 \text{ psi.}$$

$$P = s_w A = 14,950 \times 14.71 = 220,000 \text{ lb.}$$

This is higher than the design load of 200,000 lb. partly because the available section is larger than that theoretically needed.

• PROBLEM 16-17

Select a section for a building column 18 ft. long, subject to an axial compressive load of 25 kips. Lateral support is provided at the ends only. Use the 1946 AISC Specification.

Solution: The use of AISC Specifications previous to the 1946 issue would result in the selection of an 8 WF 31 for this member. The selection would be controlled not by stress considerations but by the requirement that the slenderness ratio L/r not exceed 120 for main members. The 8 WF 31 is the lightest section for which L/r is not over 120, but its axial load capacity is 104 kips, or over four times the load to be applied.

It will now be shown that, by application of the 1946 AISC Specification provision for main compression members with L/r of over 120, much saving is possible. The following analysis is for a 5 WF 18.5 section:

$$A = 5.45 \text{ in.}^2$$

$$r_{min} = 1.28 \text{ in.}$$

$$\frac{L}{r} = \frac{12 \times 18}{1.28} = 169$$

The allowable P/A for secondary members with L/r = 169 is

$$\frac{18,000}{1 + (1/18,000)(\ell/r)^2}$$

or

$$\frac{18{,}000}{1 + \frac{1}{18{,}000}\,(169)^2} = 6{,}960 \text{ psi}$$

For a main member having L/r of 169, the stress P/A allowed is given by

$$\left(\frac{P}{A}\right)_{\text{allowable}} = \frac{18{,}000}{1 + (1/18{,}000)(\ell/r)^2}\left[1.6 - \frac{(\ell/r)}{200}\right]$$

$$= \frac{18{,}000}{1 + (1/18{,}000)(169)^2}\left[1.6 - \frac{169}{200}\right]$$

$$= 0.755$$

The allowable P/A for the column is 0.755 x 6,960, or 5,250 psi.

The actual P/A for the section is 25,000/5.45, or 4,590 psi. The allowable exceeds the actual; therefore, the section is satisfactory. A saving of 225 lb. of steel per column is made possible by use of the provision quoted.

ECCENTRICALLY LOADED COLUMNS

• PROBLEM 16-18

A load is applied offset from the longitudinal axis of the steel beam, as shown. Find the magnitude of the load so as not to develop a working stress exceeding 40,000 psi in compression.

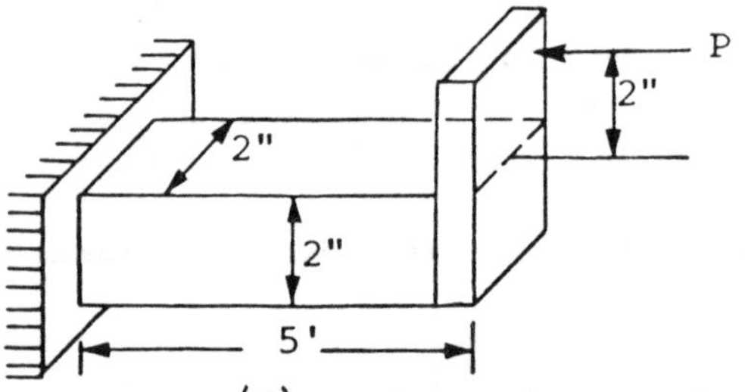

(a)

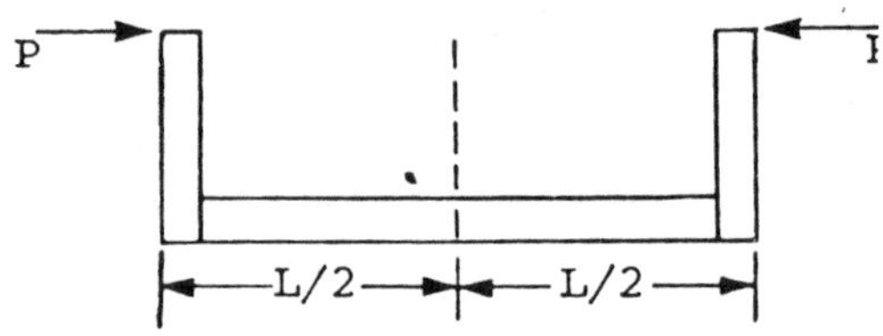

(b)

Solution: Applying the secant formula and considering that the beam is half of the column shown in Fig. (b) to which the formula is applicable,

$$\sigma_{max} = \frac{P}{A}\left\{1 + \frac{ec}{r^2}\sec\left(\frac{L}{2r}\sqrt{\frac{P}{EA}}\right)\right\} \qquad (1)$$

where,

$$\sigma_{max} = 40{,}000 \text{ psi}$$

$$e = 3 \text{ in.}$$

$$c = 2 \text{ in.}$$

$$r^2 = I/A = \frac{1/12 \times 2 \times 2^3}{2 \times 2} = 1/3 \text{ in.}^2$$

$$L = 10 \times 12 \text{ in.}$$

Substituting into equation (1),

$$40{,}000 = -\frac{P}{4}\left\{1 + \frac{(3)(2)}{1/3}\sec\left[\frac{(10)(12)}{2(1/\sqrt{3})}\sqrt{\frac{P}{(30 \times 10^6)(4)}}\right]\right\}$$

simplifying

$$160{,}000 = P[1 + 18 \sec .00949\sqrt{P}] .$$

from which (using trial and error)

$$P = 6250 \text{ lb.}$$

• PROBLEM 16-19

A 25-ft. 18 WF 96 steel column supports an eccentric load which is applied 5 in. from the center of the section measured along the web. Determine the maximum safe load the column can support (using Code No. 2):

(a) According to the modified column formula.
(b) According to the interaction formula with σ_b equal to 18 ksi.

The properties of the steel section are as follows:

$$A = 28.22 \text{ sq. in.}, \quad r_{min} = 2.71 \text{ in.}$$

$$r_{max} = 7.70 \text{ in., and} \quad c = 18.16/2 = 9.08 \text{ in.}$$

Solution: (a) Assume first that the column tends to buckle about the axis parallel to the web. Note that there is no eccentricity about this axis. The value of L/r is

$$\frac{L}{r} = \frac{25(12)}{2.71} = 110.7,$$

which is in the intermediate range. The average unit load is

$$P/A = 15{,}000 - 0.333(110.7^2) = 10{,}920 \text{ psi.}$$

For bending about the axis perpendicular to the web, the radius of gyration is 7.70 in. (L/r will be much less than 110.7), and the modified column formula becomes

$$\frac{P}{A} + \frac{Mc}{I} = 15{,}000 - 0.333(L/r)^2 .$$

The bending moment is Pe, and, when numerical values are substituted in the equation, it becomes

$$\frac{P}{A} + \frac{P(5)9.08}{A(7.70^2)} = 15{,}000 - 0.333\left(\frac{300}{7.70}\right)^2 ,$$

from which

$$P/A = 8210 \text{ psi.}$$

Since this last unit load is less than that for buckling about the web, the maximum allowable load is

$$P = 8210(28.22) = 232{,}000 \text{ lb.}$$

(b) The interaction formula for eccentrically loaded columns is

$$\frac{P/A}{\sigma_a} + \frac{Mc/I}{\sigma_b} = \frac{P/A}{\sigma_a} + \frac{Pec/(Ar^2)}{\sigma_b} = 1 .$$

The value of σ_a was found to be 10,920 psi in part a, and, when numerical data are substituted in the expression, it becomes

$$\frac{P}{A}\left[\frac{1}{10{,}920} + \frac{5.00(9.08)/(7.70^2)}{18{,}000}\right] = 1 ,$$

which gives

$$P/A = 7456 \text{ psi}.$$

The allowable load using this specification is

$$P = 7456(28.22) = 210{,}000 \text{ lb}.$$

The two results are about 10 percent apart in this case.

• PROBLEM 16-20

A 10 WF 33 column is laterally braced at its ends only. The length is 15 ft. A load of 55 kips is applied to a seat connection 2 ft. from the top of the column as shown in Fig. 1(a). Is the section satisfactory under the AISC Specification?

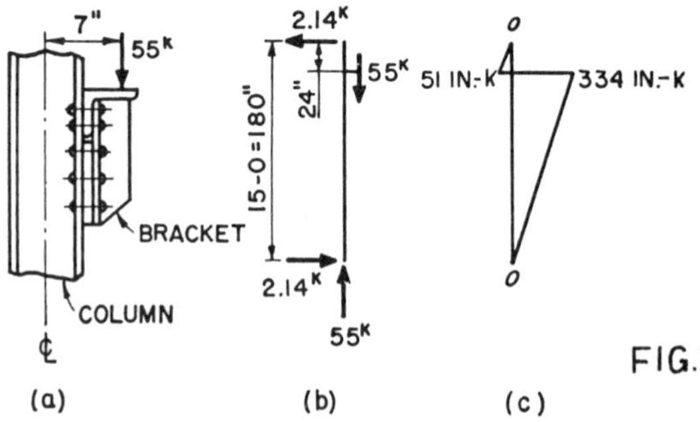

FIG.1.

Solution: Fig. 1(b) shows the free-body diagram, and part (c) the moment diagram. Normally, unless the load is applied at a considerable distance from the end, the bending moment is assumed to be the product of P and e. In this case, the moment would be taken as

$$7 \times 55 = 385 \text{ in.-kips}.$$

The custom is obviously a conservative one. The usual excuse for using it though, is merely the failure to recognize the support condition and the shape of the moment diagram. In this example, it will be assumed that the support conditions are known and recognized. The 334 in.-kip moment will be used.

$$L/r = 180/1.94 = 92.8$$

Now, allowable P/A for AISC Specification is

$$P/A = 17{,}000 - 0.485(L/r)^2 \quad (L/r \leq 120)$$

Hence,

$$(P/A)_{\text{allowable}} = 17{,}000 - 0.485(92.8)^2$$

$$= 12{,}830 \text{ psi}$$

$$\text{Actual } P/A = 55{,}000/9.71 = 5{,}660 \text{ psi}$$

$$\text{Allowable } F_b = \frac{12{,}000{,}000}{180 \times 9.75/7.96 \times 0.433} = 23{,}600 \text{ psi}$$

(Use 20,000 psi.)

$$\text{Actual } f_b = 334{,}000/35 = 9{,}550 \text{ psi}$$

$$\frac{f_a}{F_a} + \frac{f_b}{F_b} = \frac{5.66}{12.83} + \frac{9.55}{20} = 0.441 + 0.477 = 0.918 < 1.0$$

Therefore, the column is satisfactory.

Select a WF Beam Section to serve as a column 25 ft. long, hinged ends, if it carries a concentric load of 100,000 lb. and an eccentric load of 50,000 lb. lying on the axis 2-2, 10 in. from the center of the section

(a) by use of the A.I.S.C. formula and the method of eq.

$$s = \frac{\Sigma P}{A} + \frac{Mc}{I} = \frac{P + P_0}{A} + \frac{Pec}{I}, \tag{1}$$

where P_0 represents a centrally placed load.

(b) by the method of eq.

$$1 = \frac{\Sigma P/A}{s_c} + \frac{Mc/I}{s_b} \tag{2}$$

Assume s_c to be given by the A.I.S.C. formula; and s_b = 20,000 psi.

(c) by the secant formula assuming a factor of safety n = 2.5 and $s_{y,p}$ = 40,000 psi.

Solution: Method (a). The A.I.S.C. formula is

$$P/A = 17,000 - 0.485(\ell/r)^2$$

The minimum area may be found by assuming P/A = 17,000 as for a very short column (that is, with $\ell/r = 0$). Hence, A = 150,000/17,000 = 8.82 sq.in. No areas less than 8.82 sq.in. need be tried for then the actual stress would exceed the safe allowable stress of 17,000 psi for very short columns. From eq.(1),upon substitution

$$17,000 - 0.485\frac{300^2}{r^2} = \frac{150,000}{A} + \frac{50,000(10)}{Z}$$

This equation is to be solved by trial as follows:

Try 12 WF 40 section, for which least r = 1.94 in. But this makes ℓ/r = 300/1.94 = 155 which is higher than usual for a main compression member.

Try 12 WF 58 section; least r = 2.51 in., ℓ/r = 119 1/2, A = 17.06, Z = 78.1.

$$17,000 - \frac{43,650}{(2.51)^2} = \frac{150,000}{17.06} + \frac{500,000}{78.1}$$

$$10,070 \neq 15,200.$$

Safe stress 10,070 < actual stress 15,200, therefore the section is too small.

Try 14 WF 78 section; least r = 3.00 in., ℓ/r = 100, A = 22.94, Z = 121.1.

Safe stress 12,150 > actual stress 10,650. This section would be satisfactory, but the following further investigation shows that there is a 12-in. section of less weight which is also satisfactory.

Try 12 WF 72 section; least r = 3.04, ℓ/r = 98.7, A = 21.16, Z = 97.5. The safe stress 12,280 > actual stress 12,220. Therefore this section is also satisfactory.

Method (b). Using eq. (2)

$$1 \geqq \frac{\Sigma P/A}{s_c} + \frac{Mc/I}{s_b},$$

one obtains

$$1 \geqq \frac{100,000 + 50,000}{As_c} + \frac{50,000(10)}{Zs_b} \tag{3}$$

where s_c is the working stress in compression given by eq.

$$P/A = 17{,}000 - 0.485(\ell/r)^2$$

when $\ell/r < 120$. Z is taken with respect to the axis of bending; r is always the least radius of gyration.

Try 12 WF 65 section; A = 19.11, least r = 3.02, $\ell/r = 99.3$

$$s_c = P/A = 17{,}000 - 0.485(99.3)^2$$

$$= 12{,}220 \text{ psi.}$$

Z = 88.0, b = 12.00. Then $\ell/b = 300/12 = 25$ and from the equation for the reduced compressive stress in bending

$$s_b = \frac{22{,}500}{1 + \dfrac{300^2}{1{,}800(12)^2}} \doteq 16{,}700 \text{ psi.}$$

Substituting these values in eq. (3),

$$1 \geqq \frac{150{,}000}{(19.11)(12{,}220)} + \frac{500{,}000}{(88.0)(16{,}700)}$$

$$1 \geqq 0.642 + 0.340 \quad \text{or} \quad 1 \geqq 0.982.$$

This would be a satisfactory selection because the fraction 0.982 indicates that the actual maximum stress set up in the column is 0.982 of the allowable maximum stress, and the section is therefore safe. It is also near enough to unity to indicate good utilization of the strength of the material. (The most economical section as regards weight gives a fraction or factor or utilization which is less than and not far from unity. This fraction, however, is not necessarily the one closest to unity.)

Method (c). To use secant formula, it is necessary that the two given loads, 50,000 lb. and 100,000 lb., be expressed as a single resultant force of 150,000 lb. magnitude applied with an eccentricity of 3.33 in. The secant formula is

$$\frac{s_{y.p.}}{n} = \frac{P}{A} + \frac{Pe}{Z} \sec \frac{1}{2}\sqrt{\frac{nP}{EI}}$$

where Z = section modulus and I = moment of inertia of area with respect to axis about which bending occurs. The right-hand side of the above equation must not exceed $s_{y.p.}/n = 40{,}000/(2.5) = 16{,}000$.

Try 14 WF 78 section. Right-side = 11,450 psi.
Try 14 WF 68 section. Right-side = 13,500 psi.
Try 14 WF 61 section. Right-side = 15,270 psi.
Therefore this last section is suitable.

If the section selected be investigated for buckling about axis 2-2, treating the load as a centrally applied load of 150,000 lb., the actual compressive stress is 150,000/17.94 or 8,350 psi. The allowable stress is only 7,900 psi. The difference is relatively small and probably the column section selected might be satisfactory; it will be better practice, however, to select a slightly heavier section.

CHAPTER 17

TIMBER DESIGN

• PROBLEM 17-1

Determine the thickness required for a wood flooring and the size of wood joists for a living quarters location. The allowable live load is 70 lb/ft^2. It is estimated that an additional load of 10 lb/ft^2 would be sufficient to account for the dead load due to building materials. The joists are spaced at 16" center to center and are 10 feet long. Assume end conditions to be simply supported. The allowable stresses for wood are f_w (flexure) = 1200 psi and τ(shear) = 110 psi.

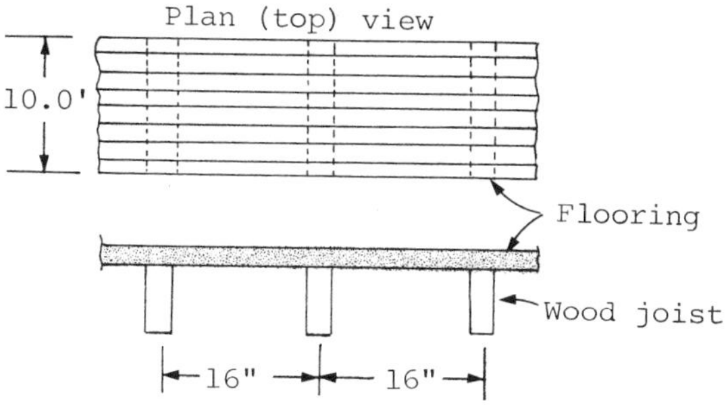

Solution:

(1) FLOOR THICKNESS:

$$\text{Total load} = \text{live load} + \text{dead load}$$

$$= 70 + 10 = 80 \ lb/ft^2.$$

Flexural Analysis:

$$\text{Maximum Bending Moment } M = \frac{Wl^2}{12}$$

$$= \frac{1}{12}\ (80 \times 1\ ft^*) \times \left(\frac{16}{12}\right)^2$$

$$= 11.85\ lb - ft$$

$$M = 142.22\ lb\text{-}in$$

$$f_w = \frac{M}{Z} \text{ or } Z = \frac{M}{f_w} \qquad (1)$$

$$f_w = 1200\ psi\ (\text{given})$$

$$M = 142.22\ lb\text{-}in$$

Substituting these values of f_w and M in equation (1),

$$Z = \frac{142.22}{1200} = 0.1185\ in^3.$$

Z (section modulus) would be the required section modulus for the floor to bear the given loading conditions.

$$Z(\text{section modulus}) = \frac{1}{6}\ bt^2 \qquad (2)$$

where b = 12" (because of 1 ft x 1 ft basis)

and t = thickness of the floor.

But $Z = 0.1185\ in^3$. (obtained previously)

Using these values of Z and b in equation (2),

$$0.1185 = \frac{1}{6} \times 12 \times t^2$$

or $t = 0.24$ in.

The floor's thickness, based on flexural analysis, is obtained as 0.24 in. (a)

<u>Shear Analysis</u>:

$$V = \frac{Wl}{2} \qquad (V = \text{vertical load})$$

$$= \frac{1}{2}\ (80 \times 1\ ft)\ \frac{16}{12}$$

$$V = 53.33\ lbs.$$

$$\tau = \frac{3}{2}\ \frac{V}{b \cdot h} \qquad (\text{shear stress}) \qquad (3)$$

But $\tau = 110$ psi (given)

* Designs for floors are generally done considering 1' x 1' section (1 foot basis)

and $b = 1$ ft $= 12$ in. (since design is based on 1 ft x 1 ft basis)

h = thickness of the floor

$V = 53.33$ lbs (obtained previously)

Using these values of τ, b in equation (3),

$$110 = \frac{3}{2} \times \frac{53.3}{12(t)}$$

or $t = 0.0606$ in.

This is less than 0.24 in. on the basis of flexural analysis. Therefore, the controlling floor thickness is 0.24 in. Hence, select $\frac{1}{4}$ in plywood.

(ii) DESIGN OF JOIST'S SIZE:

Flexural Analysis:

Maximum bending moment $M = \frac{Wl^2}{8}$ (simply supported condition)

The joists are spaced 16 in. center to center and therefore, each joist carries 16 in. of load (total).

$\therefore$ The total load/unit length $W = 80 \times \frac{16}{12}$

$= 106.66$ lb/ft

$$M = \frac{Wl^2}{8}$$

$$l = 10 \text{ ft}$$

$$\therefore \quad M = \frac{1}{8}(106.66)(10)^2 \times 12 \text{ in}$$

$$= 15999 \text{ lb-in.}$$

But, according to flexure equation

$$f_w = \frac{M}{Z}$$

$$\therefore \quad Z \text{ (required)} = \frac{M}{f_w}$$

$$M = 15999$$

$$f_w = 1200 \text{ lb/in}^2$$

Therefore, Z (section modulus) $= \frac{15999}{1200}$

$$= 13.33 \text{ in}^3.$$

The required section modulus for the joists to resist flexure is $Z = 13.33 \text{ in}^3$.

Shear Analysis:

$$V = \frac{Wl}{2} \qquad (V = \text{vertical load})$$

$W = 106.66$ lb/ft (obtained previously)

$l = 10$ ft

$$\therefore \quad V = \frac{106.66 \times 10}{2} = 533.3 \text{ lbs.}$$

But according to shear equation,

$$\tau = \frac{3}{2}\frac{V}{A}$$

$\tau = 110 \text{ lb/in}^2$ (given)

$V = 533.3$

$$\therefore \quad 110 = \frac{3}{2} \times \frac{533.3}{A}$$

or $\quad A = 7.27 \text{ in}^2$.

Therefore, the required $Z = 13.33 \text{ in}^3$

and the required area $\quad A = 7.27 \text{ in}^2$.

Referring to the table for lumber sizes, select a nominal size of 2 in x 8 in. joist having a section modulus $Z = 13.141 \text{ in}^3$ and A (S_4S) = 10.875 in^2.

Note that in this design, the required Z was 13.33 in^3 whereas the one obtained through the table has $Z = 13.141 \text{ in}^3$ slightly less than the required value. To be conservative, the next higher selection of 2 in. x 10 in. joist could be made which gives us $Z = 21.391^3$ in. and A = 13.875, both considerably higher than the required values. Selection of such a section would result in wasteful expense. Selection should therefore be prudently made, drawing a balance between safety and economy and guided by experience.

• PROBLEM 17-2

A concrete wall is poured at the rate of 2 feet per hour. The setting time for concrete is $1\frac{1}{2}$ hours. If 1 x 6 sheathing, studs and double walls, spaced at 2'6", are used for a wall form, design the wall form. Compute at what distance $\frac{1}{2}$" ϕ unthreaded ties are to be used along the wales. The permissible stresses for wood in flexure and shear are f_w = 1800 psi and τ = 150 psi and in steel the maximum tensile stress f_t = 25000 psi.

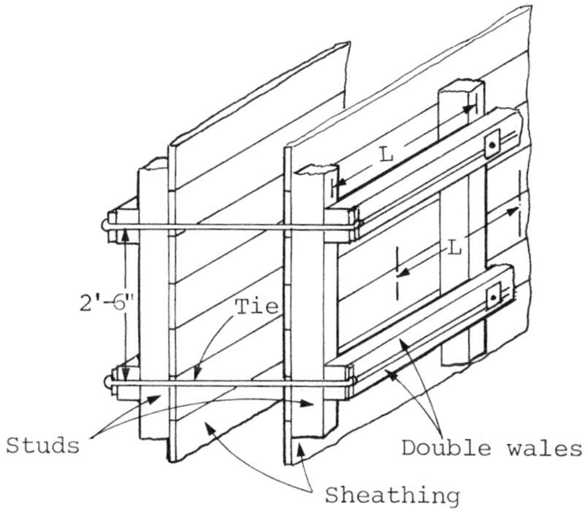

Solution: The weight per unit length of concrete,

$$= 2 \text{ ft/hr} \times 1\tfrac{1}{2} \text{ hrs.} \times 140 \text{ lbf/ft}^3.$$

or $$W = 420 \text{ lbf/ft}^2 \quad \text{(since the sheathing is continuous)}$$

Flexure:

The moment is,

$$M = \frac{1}{12} Wl^2 = fZ$$

or $$\frac{1}{12}(420)(1) \times L^2 \times 12 \text{ in/ft} = 1800 \times \frac{1}{6} \times 12'' \times \frac{3}{4} \times \frac{3}{4}$$

where L is the spacing of stud.

Solving for L = 2.20 ft.

Shear:

$$\tau = \frac{3}{2}\frac{V}{bd} = 150 = \frac{3}{2}\,\frac{420 \times \frac{L}{2}}{12 \times \frac{3}{4}}$$

Solving,

$$L \simeq 4.28 \text{ ft.}$$

Choosing minimum value of L, we have

$$L = 2.2 \text{ ft}$$

$$= 2'2''$$

For flexure, Load per unit length is,

$$W = 420 \times 2.17 = 911 \text{ lbf/ft.}$$

$$M = \frac{1}{10} Wl^2 = fZ$$

$$= \frac{1}{10} \times 911 \times 2.5^2 \times 12 \text{ in/ft} = 180 \times Z$$

Solving,

$$Z \simeq 3.80 \text{ in}^3$$

For shear, $\tau = \frac{3}{2}\frac{V}{A} = 150 \text{ lbs/in}^2$

$$\tau = 150 = \frac{3}{2} \times \frac{911 \times \frac{2.5}{2}}{A}$$

Solving,

$$A \simeq 11.4 \text{ in}^2$$

From Table I (see end of this chapter), select a standard 4 x 4 lumber ($A = 12.25 \text{ in}^2$)

For the ties,

$$f = \frac{P}{A}$$

where for $\phi = \frac{1}{2}''$ $\qquad A = \frac{\pi}{4}\left(\frac{1}{2}\right)^2$

Substituting,

$$25{,}000 = \frac{P}{\frac{\pi}{4}\left(\frac{1}{2}\right)^2}$$

Solving,

$$P \simeq 4910 \text{ lb/tie}$$

But as wales are 2.5 feet apart, wales carry (420 lb/ft^2)(2.5 ft)

$$= 1050 \text{ lbf/ft.}$$

Tie spacing,

$$= \frac{4910}{1050}$$

$$\simeq 4.67 \text{ ft/tie}$$

For continuous wales between ties (as supports),

$$M = \frac{1}{12} Wl^2 = (fZ)$$

where W = 1050 lbf/ft.

$$M = \frac{1}{12} \times 1050 \times (4.67)^2 \times 12''/\text{ft} = (1800)Z$$

Solving, $Z \simeq 12.7 \text{ in}^3$

$$(\tau = \frac{3}{2}\frac{V}{bh} = \frac{Wl}{2})$$

For shear,

$$\tau = 150 = \frac{3}{2}\frac{1050 \times \frac{4.66}{2}}{A}$$

Solving,

$$A_{required} = 24.50 \text{ in}^2 \text{ for 2 wales.}$$

For each wale, A = 12.25 in^2/wale.

From table I (see end of this chapter), use two 4 x 4 size wales. (A = 12.25 in^2)

• PROBLEM 17-3

A floor system consists of an 8" thick slab having a clear span of 8 feet between beams. The beams are 12" wide and 18" deep (including the 8" slab). Design wood forms to support this floor system. If 1" x 6" (S4S) sheathing, 4 x 4 (S4S) posts are used, design the stud size and the soffit beam thickness if it is $13\frac{1}{2}$" wide. Assume posts to be 12 feet high. The construction load is 60 lb/ft^2. The allowable stresses are $(f_w) = 1800$ lb/in^2, $\tau = 160 \text{ lb/in}^2$. For posts, use f = 1200(1 - L/80D). Use $M = \frac{Wl^2}{12}$ for full continuity and $M = \frac{Wl^2}{8}$ for simply supported spans in your computations.

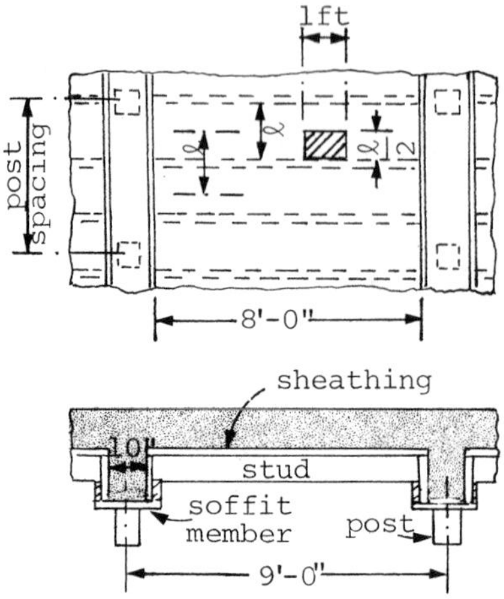

Solution:

Load due to weight of the slab $= 150 \times \frac{8}{12} = 100$ lb/ft^2

Construction load $= 60$ lb/ft^2

Total load $= 160$ lb/ft^2

For a fully continuous sheathing, $M = \frac{Wl^2}{12}$

But $f_w = \frac{M}{Z}$ (flexure)

Therefore $M = \frac{Wl^2}{12} = f_w \cdot Z$

Substituting the value, $\frac{1}{12}(160 \times 1) \times l^2 = 1800 \times \frac{1}{6}(1)\left(\frac{3}{4}\right)^2$

Solving, $l \simeq 3.56$ ft use $\ell = 3'7''$

From shear considerations,

$$\tau = \frac{3}{2} \cdot \frac{V}{bh} \qquad (V = \text{vertical load})$$

But $V = \frac{Wl}{2}$

$$V = 160 \times 1 \text{ ft basis} \times \frac{1}{2} \quad \text{(considering a 1 foot strip)}$$

$$= 80(l) \text{ lbf/ft.}$$

Substituting,

$$\tau = 160 = \frac{3}{2}\,\frac{80\ell}{12'' \times \frac{3''}{4}}$$

Solving for l,

$$l = 12.0 \text{ ft. (by shear)}$$

Comparing the two l's obtained by flexure and shear, $l_{flexure} < l_{shear}$. Therefore, adopt l = 3'7"

Studs Design

For simply supported spans,

$$M = \frac{1}{8} Wl^2$$

But $\frac{M}{Z} = f_w$ (flexure), thus, $M = \frac{Wl^2}{8} = f_w \cdot Z$

where W = uniformly distributed load

$$= (160) \times (3' \tfrac{3}{4}) = 600 \text{ lbf/ft.}$$

and l = span length = 8 ft.

$$M = \frac{1}{8} \times (600) \times 8^2 = \frac{1800}{12} \times Z$$

or $Z = 32.0 \text{ in}^3$

From shear considerations,

$$\tau = \frac{3}{2}\frac{V}{bh} \qquad (V = \frac{Wl}{2})$$

$$\tau = 160 = \frac{3}{2}\frac{V}{bh} = \frac{\frac{3}{2}(\frac{8}{2} \times 600)}{A}$$

Solving,

$$A_{req.} = 22.5 \text{ in}^2$$

Referring to table I for standard lumber sizes,(at the end of this section) choose a 3 x 10 lumber giving $Z = 35.65 \text{ in}^3$ ($> 32 \text{ in}^3$) and $A = 23.125 \text{ in}^2$ ($> 22.5 \text{ in}^2$).

• PROBLEM 17-4

Compute the uniform load carrying capacity of an attic floor made up of smooth-four-sides (S4S) 2" x 6" southern pine joists. The joists are spaced 14" apart and are 20 feet long. Assume simply supported end conditions. The allowable stresses in bending and shear are $f_w = 1200 \text{ lb/in}^2$ and $\tau = 100 \text{ lb/in}^2$, respectively.

Solution: Flexure strength:

$$f_w = \frac{Mc}{I} = \frac{M}{Z} \text{ (for flexure)}$$

or $$M = f_w \cdot Z \qquad (1)$$

where M = maximum bending moment

f_w = bending stress

Z = section modulus

f_w = bending stress = 1200 lb/in^2 (given)

The value of Z for the given joist section 2" x 6" S4S, is obtained from Table I (see end of this chapter) to be 7.563 in^3.

Therefore, Z = 7.563 in^3.

The maximum bending moment for a uniformly loaded simply-supported beam is $\frac{Wl^2}{8}$

$$\therefore \quad M = \frac{Wl^2}{8}$$

Using these values of f_w, Z and M in equation (1), we have,

$$\frac{Wl^2}{8} = 1200 \times 7.563$$

or $$W = \frac{1200 \times 7.563 \times 8}{(20)^2 (12)}$$

$$\simeq 15 \text{ lb/ft}$$

So, the load per unit area of the attic floor is

$$W = 15 \times \frac{12}{14} \simeq 12.86 \text{ lb/ft}^2.$$

Shear Strength:

$$\tau = \frac{3}{2}\frac{V}{A} \qquad (2)$$

where τ = shear stress

V = vertical load

A^* = area of the section

*NOTE: A = area of the given joist section obtained from Table I (see end of this chapter) and not 2" x 6" = 12 in^2.

τ = 100 lb/in^2 (given)

A = 8.25 in^2 obtained from Table I (see end of this chapter) for 2" x 6" section S4S area.

Using these values of τ and A in equation (2),

$$100 = \frac{3}{2} \times \frac{V}{8.25}$$

$$\therefore \qquad V = 550 \text{ lb}$$

But shear force induced in the joist is

$$V = \frac{Wl}{2}$$

$$\therefore \qquad 550 = W \times \frac{20}{2}$$

$$\text{or} \qquad W = 55 \text{ lb/ft}$$

Therefore, Load per unit area of the attic floor is

$$W = 55 \times \frac{12}{14} \quad 47 \text{ lb/ft}^2$$

Comparing these two values of w obtained on the basis of flexure strength and shear strength, it is obvious that the uniform load carrying capacity of the floor is 12.86 lb/ft^2. In other words, the floor is safe under bending and not under shear.

• PROBLEM 17-5

A house flooring consists of 1" x 8" boards (S4S lumber) placed across joists which are spaced 20" centre to centre. 1) What load would the floor take if it is to be used as a store room? 2) How much more load can be added to the floor if the planks were replaced by a 1" thick plywood? The permissible stresses in bending and shear are f_w = 1300 psi and τ = 130 psi respectively. For continuity purposes take the moment equation $M = \frac{Wl^2}{10}$. Assume the boards remain horizontal.

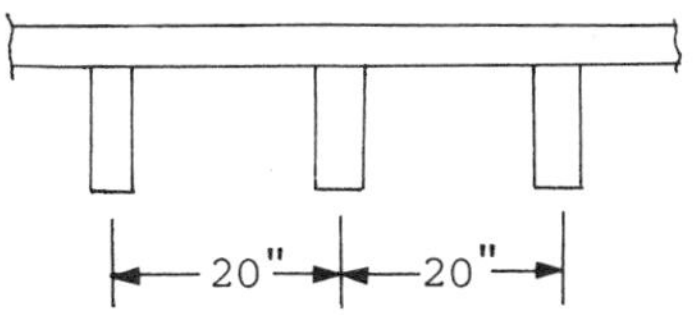

Solution:

(1) Flexural Analysis:

$$\text{Maximum bending moment } M = \frac{Wl^2}{10}$$

$$\text{But } M = f_w Z \qquad \text{since } f_w = \frac{M}{Z}$$

Considering a 1' x 1' section,

$$M = \frac{1}{10} \times \left[(w \text{ lbs/ft}^2 \times 1 \text{ ft}) \times \left(\frac{20}{12}\right)^2 \times 12''\right]$$

Using $M = f_w \cdot Z$

where f = 1300 psi (given)

$$Z = \frac{1}{6} bt^2$$

Solving for W

$$\frac{1}{10} (W \text{ lbs/ft}^2 \times 1 \text{ ft}) \times \left(\frac{20}{12}\right)^2 \times 12'' = 1300 \times \frac{1}{6}(12'')\times\frac{3}{4}\times\frac{3}{4}$$

$$\therefore \quad W = 438.75 \text{ lbs/ft}^2$$

Shear Analysis:

$$\tau = \frac{3}{2}\frac{V}{bh}$$

$$\text{i.e. } V = \frac{2}{3}\tau \cdot bh$$

where V = shear force = $\frac{Wl}{2}$

τ = shear stress

$$\text{Therefore, } V = \frac{2}{3}\tau \cdot bh = \frac{Wl}{2}$$

$$\text{or, } \frac{2}{3}(130)\left(\frac{3}{4}\right)(12) = \frac{1}{2}(W \text{ lb/ft}^2 \times 1 \text{ ft})\left(\frac{20}{12}\right)$$

i.e. $W \simeq 936 \text{ lb/ft}^2$

Thus, $W = 438.75 \text{ lb/ft}^2$ by flexure

and $W = 936 \text{ lb/ft}^2$ by shear

The least W i.e. $\simeq 438 \text{ lb/ft}^2$ governs.

Therefore, the maximum permissible loading on the floor if it were to be used as storeroom is 438 lb/ft^2.

2) If we replace the planks by a 1" thick plywood,

the section modulus $Z = \frac{1}{6} bt^2$

where b = width = 1' or 12"

and t = thickness

Therefore, $Z = \frac{1}{6} \times 12 \times 1 \times 1$

$= 2 \text{ in}^3.$

Using this value of Z in the previous computations, w is obtained:

For flexure: $W = 780 \text{ lb/ft}^2$

For shear: $W = 1248 \text{ lb/ft}^2$

The minimum W controls.

Therefore the load that can be carried by the floor if the planks were replaced by a 1" thick plywood is 780 lb/ft^2.

The extra load that the floor can carry by replacing the wooden planks with the 1" thick plywood is the difference of w for planks and w for plywood.

i.e. $= 780 - 438$

$= 342 \text{ lbs/ft}^2.$

• PROBLEM 17-6

A 6" thick slab spans 9' between beams and uses 1 x 6 wood sheathing (S4S) and studs. If the estimated construction load is 5 lbs/ft^2, design wood forms to support this slab. The slab forms part of a floor system having beams 12" wide and 15" deep (including the 6" slab). Compute the spacing of 4 x 4 posts used to shore the forms and placed under the beam forms. The posts are 12 feet high. Also design the soffit (bottom) beam form member which is $15\frac{1}{2}$" wide. Neglect the weight of wood. The permissible stresses in flexure and shear are(f_w = 1800 lb/in^2) and τ = 150 lb/in^2 respectively.
Use f = 1200(1 - L/80D) for columns.

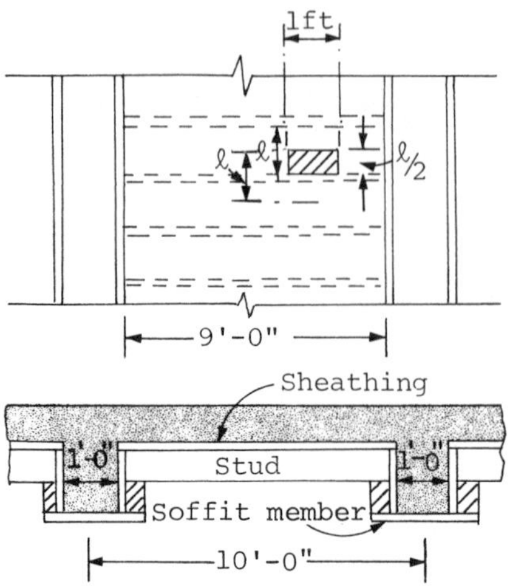

Solution: Sheathing:

Flexure:

$$\text{weight of slab} = 150 \text{ lb/ft}^3 \times \frac{6}{12}$$

$$= 75 \text{ lb/ft}^2$$

$$\text{construction load} = 50 \text{ lb/ft}^2$$

$$\text{Total load} = 125 \text{ lb/ft}^2$$

For fully continuous sheathing, we have

$$M = \frac{Wl^2}{12} = fZ \qquad \left(f_w = \frac{M}{Z}\right)$$

where $W = 125 \text{ lb/ft}^2$

$$f_w = 1800 \text{ lb/in}^2 \text{ and } Z = \frac{1}{6} bt^2$$

Considering 1 ft strip, we have,

$$M = \frac{1}{12} (125 \times 1 \text{ ft wide}) \times l^2 \times 12 \text{ in/ft}$$

$$M = 1800 \times \frac{1}{6} (12)(3/4)^2$$

Solving for l,

$$l \simeq 4 \text{ ft.}$$

Shear:

$$\tau = \frac{3}{2} \frac{V}{bh}$$

where $V = \frac{Wl}{2}$

$= 125 \times (1 \text{ ft basis} \times \frac{1}{2})$

Therefore,

$$\tau = 150 = \frac{125 \times \frac{1}{2}}{12 \times \frac{3}{4}} \times \frac{3}{2}$$

Solving for l,

$$l = 14.4 \text{ ft} \quad > \quad l = 4'$$

Thus, choosing the minimum value for l, we have 'l', stud spacing = 4 ft.

Flexure:

For simply supported studs,

$$M = \frac{1}{8} Wl^2 = fZ$$

The load on the stud,

$W = 125 \times$ width for which load acts upon

$= 125 \times 4 = 500$ lb/ft

Thus,

$$\frac{1}{8} (500)(9)^2(12 \text{ in/ft}) = fZ = 1800 \times Z(\text{in})^3$$

Solving for Z,

$$Z = 33.8 \text{ in}^3$$

Shear:

$$\tau = \frac{3}{2} \frac{V}{bh}$$

and $V = \frac{Wl}{2}$

Therefore, $150 = \frac{3}{2} \frac{(\frac{1}{2} \times \text{length of span} \times 500)}{A}$

or $150 = \frac{3}{2} \frac{(\frac{1}{2} \times 9 \times 500)}{A}$

Solving, $A = 22.5 \text{ in}^2$

required area $A = 22.5 \text{ in}^2$

and required section modulus $Z = 33.8 \text{ in}^3$

Select 3 x 10 size using Table I (see end of this chapter) which gives $A = 23.125\ in^2$ and $Z = 35.651\ in^3$.

For posts,

$$f = 1200\left(1 - \frac{L}{80D}\right) \qquad (1)$$

where $L = 12' = 144''$

and $D = 80 \times 3\frac{1}{2}'' = 280$

Substituting these values of L and D in equation (1)

$$f = 1200\left(1 - \frac{144}{280}\right)$$

$$\simeq 583 \text{ psi (allowable)}$$

Area, $A = 3\frac{1}{2}'' \times 3\frac{1}{2}''$

$$= 12.25\ in^2$$

Load carrying capacity per post is,

$$= 12.25 \times 583$$

$$= 7140 \text{ lbs.}$$

Load per unit lengtn is,

$$= (9' \text{ of slab} + 1' \text{ of beam}) \times 125$$

$$= 1250 \text{ lbs/ft}$$

Also, contribution by "stem" (below slab)

$$= \frac{9 \times 12}{144} \times 150 \simeq 113$$

Total load = 1250 + 113

$$= 1363 \text{ lb/ft (load/unit length)}$$

Spacing,

$$= \frac{\text{total weight}}{\text{wt. per unit length}}$$

$$= \frac{7140}{1363}$$

$$= 5.23 \text{ ft/post}$$

Spacing of the posts is 5'3"

Considering 1 ft strip,

For a fully continuous soffit beam,

$$M = \frac{1}{12} Wl^2 = f_w Z \qquad (Z = \frac{1}{6} bt^2)$$

or $$M = \frac{1}{12} \times 1363 \times (5.25)^2 \times 12 \text{ in/ft}$$

$$= 1800 \times \frac{1}{6} (15\tfrac{1}{2})(t \text{ in})^2$$

Solving for

$$t \simeq 2.84''$$

Use standard size (refer to table I at the end of this chapter) t = 3.5" (std. 4" x 16")(S4S).

For shear,

$$150 = \frac{3}{2} \frac{1363 \times \frac{5.25}{2}}{15\frac{1}{2} \times (t \text{ in})}$$

Solving,

$$t \simeq 2.31 \text{ in}$$

Use standard (refer to table I at the end of this chapter) 3" x 16" with t = 2.5in.

Choosing the bigger size we have the soffit beam size 4" x 16" (standard size obtained from table I at the end of this chapter).

CHAPTER 18

DESIGN OF REINFORCED CONCRETE STRUCTURES

DESIGN OF SINGLY REINFORCED RECTANGULAR BEAMS BY WORKING STRESS METHOD

• PROBLEM 18-1

Compute the maximum moment for the given rectangular reinforced concrete beam as per ACI code requirements. f'_c = 3 kips and f_s = 20 kips.

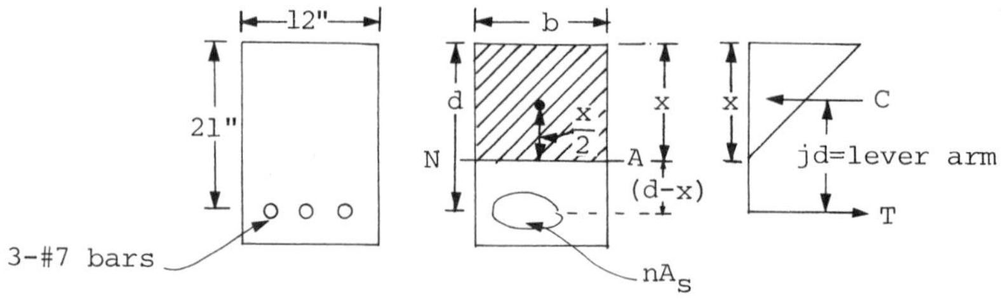

Note: d-effective depth

Solution: We have n = 9 (for f'_c = 3 kips)(See table V at end of chapter ACI code).

Taking moments about the neutral axis (NA), we have

$$(12)(x)(x/2) = 9(1.8)(21 - x) \qquad (1.8 \text{ is } A_s)$$

or $\quad 6x^2 = 340.2 - 16.2\,x$

or $\quad 6x^2 + 16.2\,x - 340.2 = 0$

This is a quadratic equation in x. Solving for x, we get x = + 6.30 and x = - 9.0

Therefore, taking the positive value of $x = 6.30''$

Now, lever arm $jd = d - \frac{x}{3} = 21 - \frac{6.3}{3} = 18.9''$

Moment:

M_c (Moment on the concrete side)

$= f_c(bx/2)(jd)$

$\therefore \quad M_c = 1350\ (12 \times 6.30/2)(18.9)$

$= 964467$ lb-in.

M_s (Moment on the steel side)

$= f_s \cdot jd \cdot A_s$

$= 20{,}000 \times 18.9 \times 1.8$

$= 680{,}400$ lb-in $< M_c$

$\therefore \quad M_s$ controls or steel governs.

$$\therefore \quad M = M_s = \frac{680400}{12 \times 1000} = 56.7 \text{ kip-ft}$$

• PROBLEM 18-2

For the beam shown in figure, compute the moment carrying capacity of the beam. Assume $f'_c = 4000$ lbs/in^2 and $f_s = 20{,}000$ lbs/in^2.

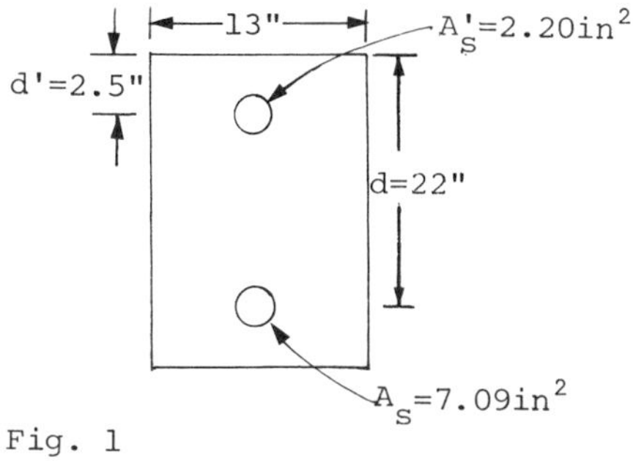

Fig. 1

Solution: For $f'_c = 4000$ lb/in^2, from ACI code table V (see end of this chapter), we have $n = 8$, $f_c = 1800$ lb/in^2.

Taking moments about neutral axis where $A_s = 7.09$ in^2

$$13x(x/2) + [(2)(8) - 1]\ 2.20(x - 2.5) = 8(7.09)(22 - x)$$

or $6.5x^2 + 33x - 82.5 = 1248 - 56.7x$

or $6.5x^2 + 89.7x = 1330.5$

This is a quadratic equation in x.

Solving for the positive x, we get

$$x = 8.98''.$$

We have, $jd = \dfrac{(M_1 + M_2)}{(C_1 + C_2)}$

where $M_1 = c_1 a_1$ and $M_2 = c_2 \cdot a_2$.

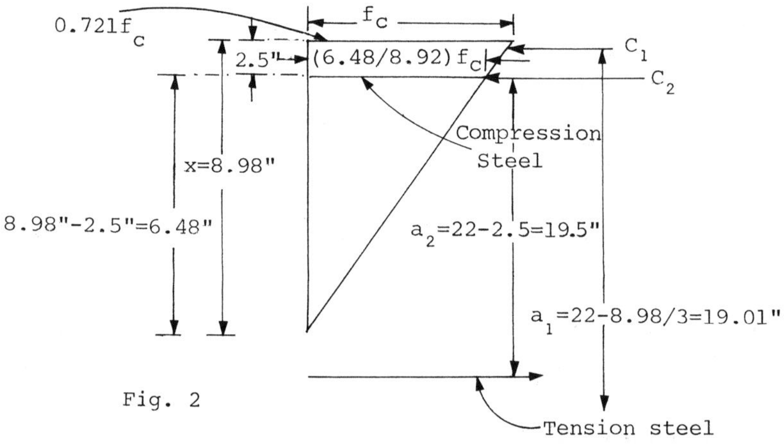

Fig. 2

$$c_1 = \frac{1}{2} f_c (b)(x)$$

$$= \frac{1}{2} f_c (13)(8.98) = 58.3\ f_c$$

$$a_1 = 19.01$$

Thus, $M_1 = 58.3\ f_c \times 19.01 \simeq 1110\ f_c$.

$$c_2 = \left[(2)(8) - 1\right] 2.20(0.721\ f_c)$$

$$= 23.8\ f_c$$

$$a_2 = 19.5''$$

Thus, $M_2 = 23.8\ f_c \times 19.5'' \simeq 465\ f_c$.

$$c_1 + c_2 = 58.3 + 23.8 = 82.1\ f_c$$

and $M_1 + M_2 = 1110\ f_c + 465\ f_c = 1575\ f_c$.

Therefore, $jd = \frac{M_1 + M_2}{c_1 + c_2} = \frac{1575 f_c}{82.1 f_c} = 19.2''$

and the maximum moment in concrete

$$M_c = 1575 f_c = 1575 \times 1800 = 2{,}835{,}000 \text{ lb-in}$$
$$= 236.25 \text{ kip-ft.}$$

and the maximum moment in steel

$$M_s = A_s f_s jd = 7.09(20{,}000)(19.2) = 2{,}722{,}560 \text{ lb-in}$$
$$= 226.88 \text{ kip-ft}$$

Note that $M_s < M_c$

Thus the steel governs.

And the maximum moment the section can withstand = 226.88 kip-ft.

Check, however, to see if $f_{sc} > 20{,}000$ lb/in².

If M = 2,722,560 lb-in, $f_c = \frac{M}{1575}$

$$= 1729 \text{ lb/in}^2.$$

Then, concrete stress next to compression steel

$$= 0.721 f_c = 1247 \text{ lb/in}^2.$$

or $f_{sc} = 0.721 f_c \times 2 \times 8$

$$= 1247 \times 16 = 19952 < 20{,}000$$

Therefore, OK.

• PROBLEM 18-3

Compute the maximum resisting moment for the given section. The ultimate stress in concrete is 2500 psi. Steel is of structural grade with a working stress of 18000 psi.

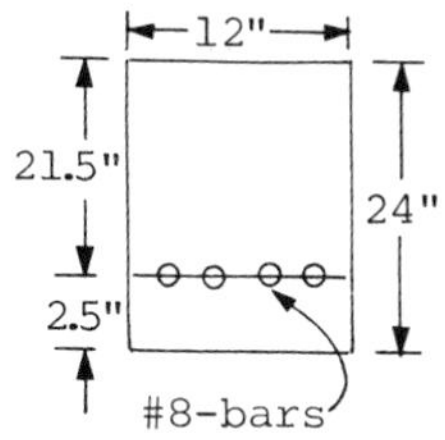

Solution: From table I (see end of this chapter) for Bar # 8 Area = 0.79 in^2

$$\therefore \qquad A_s = 4 \times 0.79 = 3.16 \text{ in}^2$$

The effective depth, d = 24 - 2.5 = 21.5"

From ACI code (table V - see end of this chapter)

for $f_s = 18000$ psi

and $f'_c = 2500$ psi $\quad n = 10$

Applying the transformed area principle,

$$bx\left(\frac{x}{2}\right) = nA_s(d - x)$$ where x is the distance between the top fibre and the neutral axis.

or $$\frac{12x^2}{2} = 10(3.14)(21.5 - x)$$

Solving, x = 8.34"

Moment arm,

$$jd = d - x/3$$

$$= 21.5 - 8.34/3$$

or $$jd = 18.72''$$

Moment on the concrete side

$$M_c = \frac{1}{2} f_c \, bx \, jd$$

$$= \frac{1}{2}(1125)(12)(8.34)(18.72)$$

$$= 1053842 \text{ lb-in}$$

$$= 87{,}820 \text{ lb-ft}$$

Moment on the steel side,

$$M_s = A_s f_s jd$$

$$= 3.14 \times 18000 \times 18.72$$

$$= 1058054 \text{ lb-in}$$

$$= 88{,}171 \text{ lb-ft}$$

$$M_s > M_c$$

Therefore, the maximum resisting moment is $M_c = 87{,}820$ lb-ft.

Compute the stresses for a reinforced concrete slab given that M = 2000 kip-in. $E_c = 3 \times 10^6$ psi and $E_s = 30 \times 10^6$ psi.

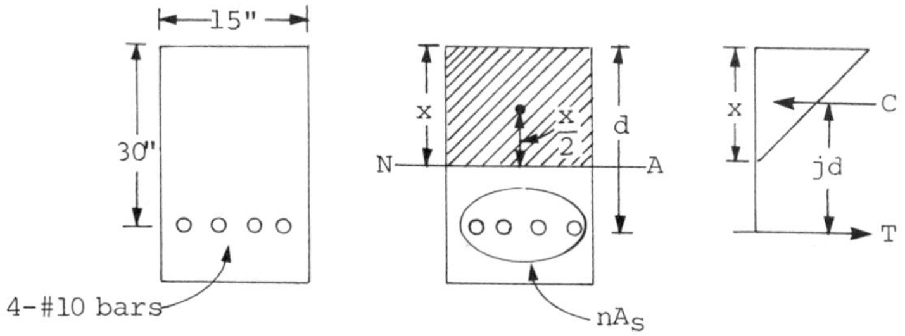

Solution:

$$n = \frac{E_s}{E_c} = \frac{30 \times 10^6}{3 \times 10^6} = 10$$

$\therefore \quad (n \cdot As) = 10 \times 5.08 = 50.80$

Taking moments about the neutral axis (NA), we have,

$$(15)(x)(x/2) = (10)(5.08)(30 - x)$$

i.e. $\quad 7.5x^2 = 1524 - 50.8x$

or $\quad 7.5x^2 + 50.8x - 1524 = 0$

This is a quadratic equation in x.

Solving for x, we get

$$x = +11.26" \quad \text{and} \quad x = -18.0"$$

Therefore, x = 11.26"

Now, lever arm $jd = d - \frac{x}{3}$

$$= 30 - \frac{11.26}{3} = 26.24"$$

Moment on concrete side $M_c = f_c \cdot \frac{bx}{2} \cdot jd$

But $M = M_s = M_c = 2000 \times 10^3$ lb-in (given)

Therefore, $2000 \times 10^3 = f_c \cdot \frac{15 \times 11.26}{2} \times 26.24"$

or $\quad f_c = \frac{2000 \times 10^3 \times 2}{15 \times 11.26 \times 26.24}$

$$= 902.5 \text{ psi}$$

Now, $M_s = A_s \cdot f_s \cdot jd$

But $M = M_s = 2000 \times 10^3$ lb-in

$\therefore \quad 2000 \times 10^3 = 5.08 \cdot f_s \cdot 26.24$

$$\therefore \quad f_s = \frac{2000 \times 10^3}{5.08 \times 26.24}$$

$$= 15004 \text{ psi}$$

• **PROBLEM 18-5**

A rectangular concrete beam is to resist a moment of 30,000 lb-ft. Using 2500 psi concrete and intermediate grade steel (f_s = 20,000 psi), design the beam. Provide a clear cover of 4/3" for the steel. Assume that b is approximately equal to 2d/3.

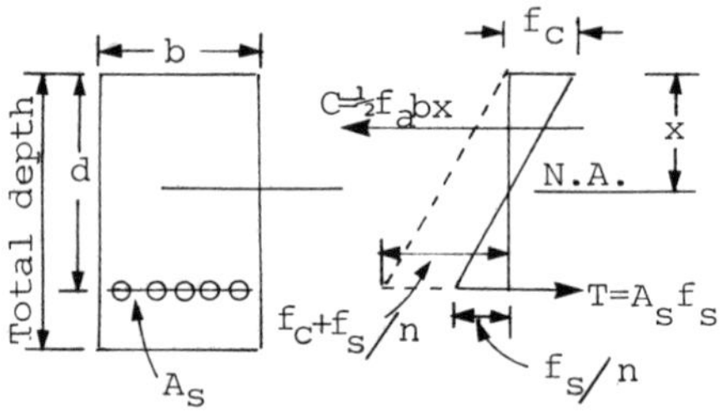

Solution: Referring to the stress diagram, by similar triangles, we have,

$$\frac{x}{d} = \frac{f_c}{f_c + f_s/n} \qquad \text{or} \qquad x = \frac{f_c d}{f_c + f_s/n}$$

where n = 10 (from ACI code)

From table V of ACI code (see end of this chapter)

For f_s = 20,000 psi and 2500 psi

f_c = 1125 psi

$$\text{Thus,} \quad x = \frac{1125 \cdot d}{1125 + \frac{20,000}{10}}$$

or $\quad x = 0.360$ d

Then, moment arm, $jd = d - x/3$

$$= d - 0.120 \text{ d}$$

$$\text{or} \quad jd = 0.88\ d$$

We have, moment $M = \frac{1}{2} f_c\ bx \cdot jd$

Thus, $M = \frac{1}{2}(1125)(b)(0.360\ d \times 0.88\ d)$

or $\quad 30{,}000 \times 12 = 178bd^2$

or $\quad bd^2 = 2020$

But we know that $b \simeq \frac{2}{3} d$

Therefore, $\frac{2}{3} d \cdot d^2 = 2020$

or $\quad d = 14.5$ in

Let us use d = 15"

Then, $\quad b = \dfrac{2020}{(15 \times 15)} = 8.98'' \simeq 9''$

After providing a cover of 4/3" for steel, total depth ≃ 17"

Therefore, let us use a 9" x 17" beam.

Moment on the steel side

$$M_s = A_s f_s jd$$

$$\text{or} \quad A_s = \frac{30{,}000 \times 12}{20{,}000 \times 0.880 \times 15} \simeq 1.36\ \text{in}^2$$

Use #8 bars ($A_s = 1.57\ \text{in}^2$)

• PROBLEM 18-6

Determine the cross-section b, d and area of steel A_s for the given rectangular reinforced concrete beam. M = 100 kip-ft; $f_c' = 3$ kips and $f_s = 20$ kips. Assume that b is approximately equal to 2d/3. Analyse using ACI code.

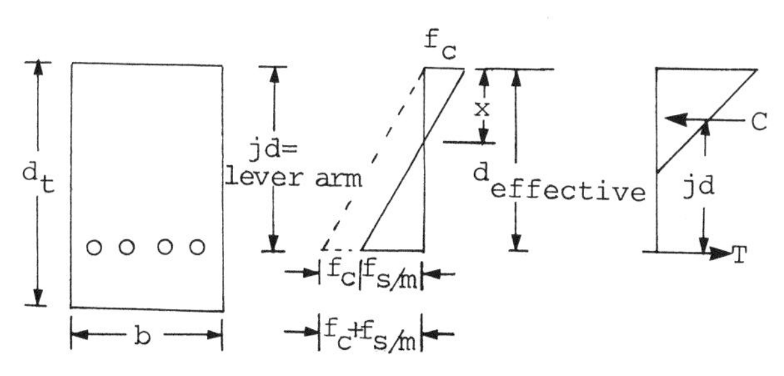

Fig. 1

Solution: As per ACI code (see table V at end of this chapter) the modular ratio n = 9

and $f_s = 1350$ for $f'_c = 3$ kips & $f_s = 20$ kips

Referring to the stress diagram, (fig. 1), we have, from similar triangles,

$$\frac{x}{d} = \frac{f_c}{f_c + f_s/m}$$

or $$x = \frac{f_c \cdot d}{f_c + f_s/m}$$

Thus, $$x = \frac{1350 \cdot d}{1350 + \frac{20,000}{9}}$$

$$= 0.378\ d$$

We have, $jd = d - \frac{1}{3}x$

or $$jd = d - \frac{1}{3}(0.378\ d) = d - 0.126\ d$$

or $$jd = 0.874\ d.$$

We further have,

Moment M = Force x distance (perpendicular)

= stress x area x distance

$\therefore \quad M = 100 \times 1000 \times 12 = f_c \times (\frac{1}{2}\ bx)(jd)$

(d here refers to the effective depth and not to the total depth)

where jd is the lever arm or the perpendicular distance between the two forces C (compressive) and T (tensile). Refer to figure.

Therefore,

$$M = 100 \times 1000 \times 12 = f_c \times (\tfrac{1}{2}\ b \cdot x) \times jd$$

$$= 1350\ (\tfrac{1}{2} \times b \times 0.378\ d) \times (0.87\ d)$$

Since x = 0.378 d (found previously)

and j = 0.87 (as per ACI code, see table V at end of this chapter)

$\therefore\ bd^2 = 5406\ in^3.$

but $b \simeq \frac{2}{3}\ d$

$\therefore\ \frac{2}{3} d \times d^2 = 5406 \text{ in}^3.$

or $\quad d = \left(\frac{5406 \times 3}{2}\right)^{1/3} \simeq 20$ in.

and $\quad b = \frac{2}{3} d = \frac{2}{3} \times 20 = 13.33$

Thus, taking b = 14" and d* = 20"

i.e. the section is 14" x 20".

We have,

$$M = f_s \times A_s \times jd$$

where d = effective depth

and A_s = area of steel

$$\therefore \quad A_s = \frac{M}{f_s \times jd}$$

$$= \frac{100 \times 12 \times 1000}{20{,}000 \times 0.874(20)}$$

$$= 3.43 \text{ in}^2.$$

As per code requirements (Article 7.7.1 for slabs walls, etc.) minimum cover for concrete is 1½" plus ½ of 1" dia bar.

$\therefore$ Total depth = effective depth + cover + bar dia.

= 20" + 1½" + ½" = 22"

(See table I at end of this chapter) Select 4 #9 bars giving a total area of $A_s = 4 \text{ in}^2$ (each 1 in^2).

Thus, the beam's cross-section and area of steel A_s, required to resist the external forces due to moment are as follows:

b = 14"

d_t = 22" (total depth) Allow a cover of 1½".

or effective depth d_e = 20"

$A_s = 4 \text{ in}^2$ i.e. providing 4 #9 bars.

Refer to fig. 2.

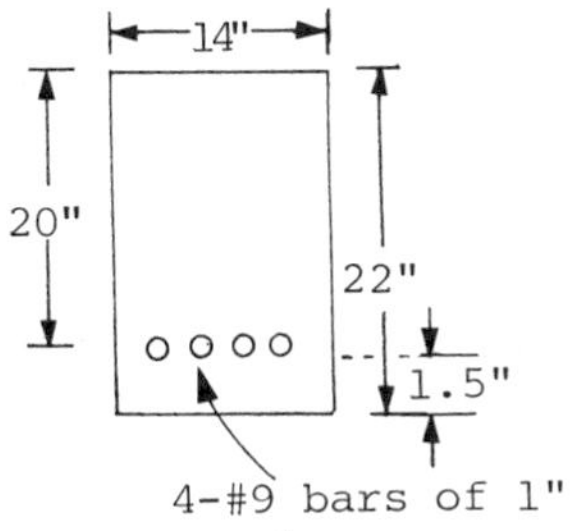

Fig. 2

A beam 20 feet long with b = 10" and d = 24" carries a load of 3200 lbs/ft. Using f'_c = 2500 psi and f_s = 20,000psi, design #3 vertical stirrups required for the beam. Base your computations on the 'Alternate Design' method of approach.

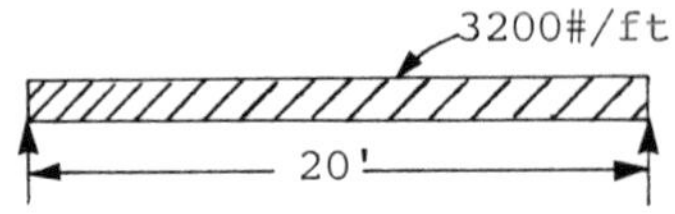

Fig. 1

Solution:

Maximum end shear = $\frac{wl}{2}$ = 3200 #/ft x 10' = 32000 lbs.

Shear @ a distance 'd' from support (ACI B.7.2)

= 3200 #/ft x 8 ft = 25600 lbs. (ACI 11.2.1 is similar)

Therefore shear stress 'ν' @ a distance 'd' from support is

$$\nu = \frac{V}{bd} = \frac{25600}{10'' \times 24''} = 107 \text{ psi.}$$

Shear stress taken by concrete $\nu_c = 1.1\sqrt{f'_c} = 1.1\sqrt{2500}$

$= 55$ psi (ACI 8.3.1.b)

Remaining shear to be carried by stirrups,

$$\nu' = \nu - \nu_c = 107 - 55 = 52 \text{ psi.}$$

We have $A_\nu \cdot f_\nu = \nu' bs$

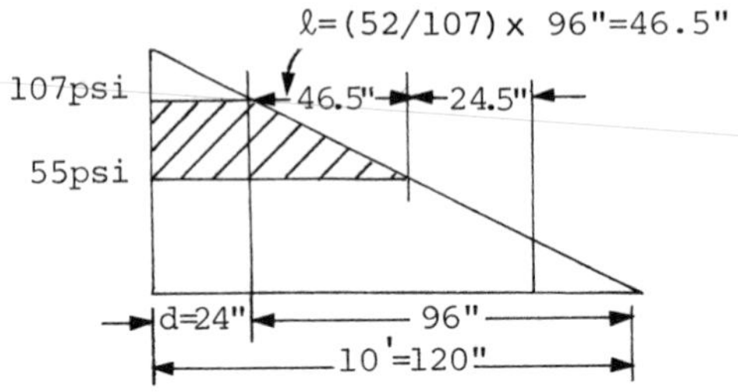

Fig. 2

$$S_{end} = \frac{A_\nu \cdot f_\nu}{\nu' b} = \frac{2 \times 0.11 \text{ in}^2 \times 20{,}000 \text{ psi}}{52 \text{ psi} \times 10''} = 8.46''.$$

Maximum spacing (ACI B.7.5.4.1) = 0.5 d = 0.5(24") = 12".

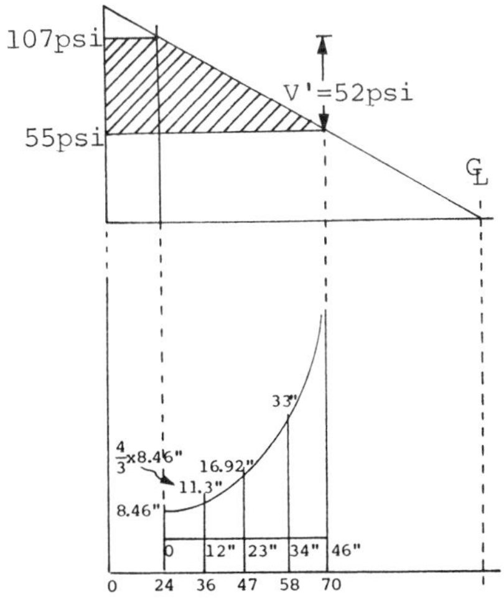

Fig. 3

Length where stirrups are required (Refer to fig. 3)

46.5" + 24" + half the difference to ℄ (ACI B.7.5.5.1)

$$= 46.5'' + 24'' + \frac{120 - 70.5}{2} = 95.3''$$

Maximum spacing as per ACI B.7.5.5.3

$$S = \frac{A_\nu \cdot f_y}{50\ bw} \qquad (A_\nu = 50\ \frac{bwS}{f_y})$$

Thus $S = \dfrac{2 \times 0.11 \times 40{,}000}{50'' \times 10''} = 17.6''$

$$S = \frac{A_\nu \cdot f_\nu}{\nu' b} \text{ and } \frac{A_\nu \cdot f_\nu}{b} \text{ would be a constant.}$$

Thus, S can be rewritten as $S = \dfrac{k}{\nu'}$

Then, $\frac{1}{2}\nu'$ gives $2S_1$, 3/4 ν' yields 4/3of S_1 and so on, where S_1 is the first or end value of S. The spacing is then obtained from the rough curve as shown in fig. 3.

Thus, let us provide #3 stirrups

1 @ 4, 3 @ 8, 1 @ 11, 5 @ 12 at each end.

Note for curve: Additional points may be obtained at eighths also, if desired but savings are not often warranted. Note also that full inches are always used and the first stirrup must be half the first 'S' value.

• PROBLEM 18-8

Using ACI prescribed moment coefficients, determine the positive moments required for the design of the beam shown in figure below. The factored live and dead loads are 2 $^{k/ft}$ and 1 $^{k/ft}$ respectively.

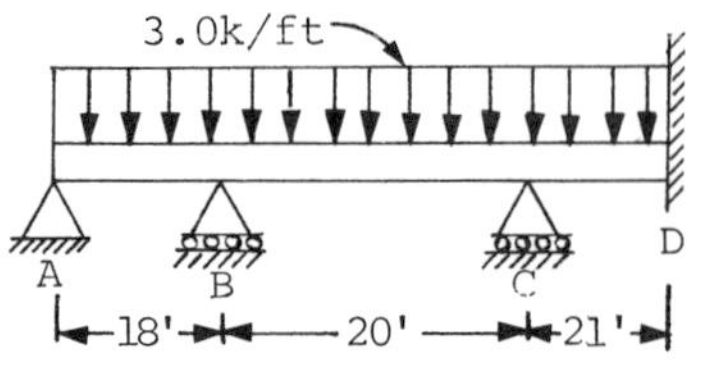

Solution: Approximate moments for the analysis of (ACI code prescribed coefficients) continuous beams can be utilised, provided that the following criteria are satisfied:

a) Two or more spans.

b) Adjacent spans not larger than 20% of neighboring spans.

c) Uniform loads.

d) Live load is less than or equal to three times dead load.

Criterion (a) is satisfied since the beam has more than two spans.

Criterion (b) is also satisfied since

$$20' < 1.2(18') \quad \text{or} \quad 1.2(21') \quad (\text{where } 1.2 \text{ is } 20\%)$$

Loads on the beam are uniform and therefore criterion (c) is also satisfied.

Live load = 2 $^{k/ft}$

Dead load = 1 $^{k/ft}$

and 3 (dead load) = 3 $^{k/ft}$

Thus, live load < 3 times dead load and therefore criterion (d) is also satisfied.

We can therefore utilise code prescribed moment coefficients to determine the positive moments.

For interior span BC, $M = \dfrac{Wl^2}{16}$

or $(M_{BC})_{positive} = \frac{3.0^{\ k/ft}(20')^2}{16} = 75^{\ k\text{-}ft}$

For end span AB, (discontinuous end unrestrained)

$$M = \frac{Wl^2}{11}$$

or $(M_{AB})_{positive} = \frac{3.0^{\ k/ft}(18')^2}{11} \simeq 88.4^{\ k\text{-}ft}$

For end span CD (discontinuous and integral with support)

$$M = \frac{Wl^2}{14}$$

or $(M_{CD})_{positive} = \frac{3.0^{\ k/l} \times (21')^2}{14} = 94.5^{\ k\text{-}ft}$

Therefore, the positive moments $M_{AB} = 88.4^{\ k\text{-}ft}$, $M_{BC} = 75^{k\text{-}ft}$ and $M_{CD} = 94.5^{\ k\text{-}ft}$.

• PROBLEM 18-9

Using ACI 318-77 provisions, compute the minimum thickness 'h' required for the beam shown in figure below. Neglect the considerations of computing deflections.

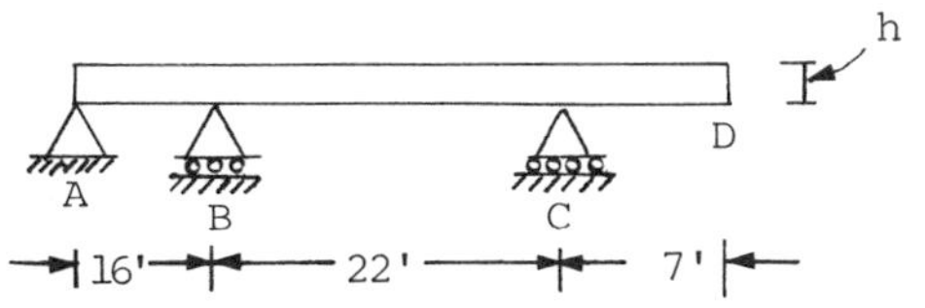

Solution: ACI 318-77, Table 9.5(a) lists the minimum thickness of beams in terms of span length.

The minimum thickness 'h' for different end conditions, from the same table, are as follows:

Simple support	$h \geq \frac{1}{16}$
One end continuous	$h \geq \frac{1}{18.5}$
Both ends continuous	$h \geq \frac{1}{21}$
Cantilever	$h \geq \frac{1}{8}$

where 'l' is the span in inches.

Thus, in our problem,

for span AB $\quad h \geq \dfrac{16' \times 12''}{18.5} = 10.4$ inches

for span BC $\quad h \geq \dfrac{22' \times 12''}{21} = 12.6$ inches

for span CD $\quad h \geq \dfrac{7' \times 12''}{8} = 10.5$ inches

Span BC governs.

And therefore, minimum thickness of the given beam is 12.6 inches.

• PROBLEM 18-10

Determine the minimum width required for a cast-in-place beam reinforced with 4-#6 bars and #2 stirrup.

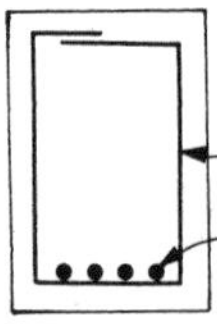

Solution:

As per ACI 318-77 sec. 7.7.1, the minimum cover for an interior cast-in-place beam shall be $1\frac{1}{2}''$.

Also, from sec. 7.6.1 of ACI 318-77, the minimum clear distance between parallel bars in a layer shall not be less than 1" or d_b, the bar diameter.

We have d_b, the bar diameter for a #6 bar equal to 6/8".

Thus, let us provide 1" clear distance.

Hence, the minimum beam width is the sum of the following:

Two covers $= 2 \times 1\frac{1}{2}'' = 3.00''$

Two stirrup diameters (#2) $= 2 \times 2/8 = 0.50''$

Four #6 bar diameters $= 4 \times 6/8 = 3.00''$

Three clear distances $= 3 \times 1'' = 3.00''$

Thus, minimum beam width $= 3.00'' + 0.50'' + 3.00'' + 3.00''$

$= 9.50''$.

Determine the distance "L" where the top #6 bars may be terminated. Use concrete with f'_c = 4 ksi, steel reinforcements with f_y = 60 ksi, and relevant ACI provisions.

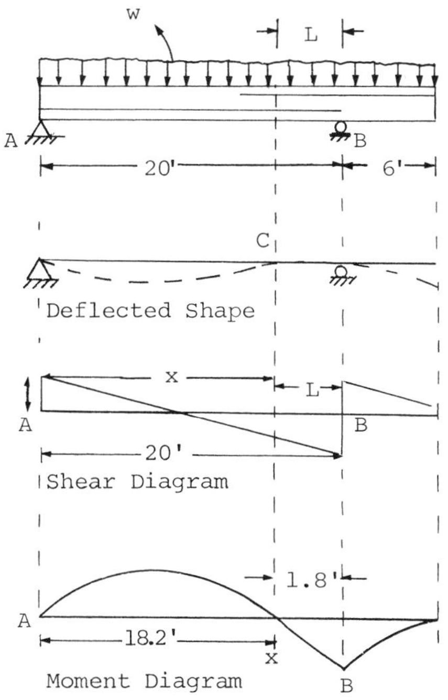

Fig. 1

Solution: Computing reactions by taking moment about A & B

$$R_B = \frac{(26W)(26/2)}{20} = 16.9W$$

$$R_A = 26W - R_B = 9.1W$$

As shown in fig. 1, bending moment at the inflection point c is zero.

Taking moments about a section x-x at a distance 'x' from the left support 'A' and passing through point c.

$$M_{xx} = (R_A \cdot x) - W \cdot x \cdot \frac{x}{2}$$

But the moment at the section xx (at the inflection point c) is zero.

Therefore, $R_A x - W\frac{x^2}{2} = 0$

But $R_A = 9.1\ W$

$$9.1W \cdot x = \frac{Wx^2}{2}$$

Therefore, $x = 9.1 \times 2 = 18.2$ from 'A'.

According to ACI sec. 12.13.3, negative moment reinforcement must extend beyond the inflection point by the largest of the three below:

effective depth = 20" ← controls

12 bar diameters = 12(6/8) = 9"

1/16 of clear span = 15"

Consequently L = 1.8' + 20" = 41.6" (Refer fig. 1)

Next, check to ensure that L exceeds the development length of #6 bars.

According to ACI sec. 12.2, #6 bar development length is 25" < L of 41.6". Therefore OK. Hence L = 41.6 say 42".

• PROBLEM 18-12

Two #8 flexural bars are being terminated in a zone of tension at point A. The continuing flexural reinforcement consists of 2-#8 bars. The factored shear and moment at point A are 43^k and $67^{k\text{-}ft}$ respectively. The shear reinforcement consists of #3 stirrup spaced at 6 inches, $f'_c = 4$ ksi and $f_y = 60$ ksi. Determine if extra "binder" stirrups are needed at point A as per ACI 318-77.

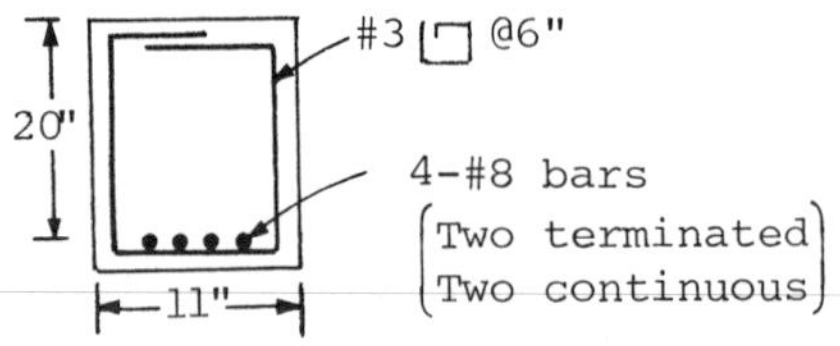

Fig. 1

Solution: Extra binder-stirrups are required, unless

I) $\nu_{reqd} \leq 2/3\ \nu_{prov}$

or

II) $\nu_{reqd} \leq 3/4\ \nu_{prov}$

and

$$A_{reqd} \leq 1/2\ A_{prov}$$

where

ν_{reqd} = shear resistance required at cut off

ν_{prov} = shear resistance provided at cut off

A_{reqd} = flexural steel area required at cut off

A_{prov} = flexural steel area provided at cut off.

The shear resistance provided at cut off is (ACI sections 11.1.1, 11.3.1.1, 11.5.6.2)

$$\nu_{prov} = \phi\cdot(\nu_c + \nu_s) \qquad (1)$$

where

$$\nu_c = 2\sqrt{f'_c}\ b\cdot d$$

and $\nu_s = \dfrac{A_\nu f_y d}{s}$ and $\phi = 0.85$

Substituting the values in equation (1),

$$\nu_{prov} = 0.85\left[2\sqrt{4000}\ (11)(20) + \frac{0.22(60000)20}{6}\right]$$

$$= 61{,}050^{\#} = 61.1^k$$

The given required shear resistance $\nu_{reqd} = 43^k$ (given)

Since $2/3(61.1^k) = 40.7^k$ is less than 43^k, criterion I is not met, however, $3/4(61.1^k) = 45.8^k$ is larger than 43^k and thus, the shear part of criterion II is met. The flexure part of criterion II must now be checked.

The area provided is the continuing steel (2 -#8's)

or $A_{prov} = 2(0.79) = 1.58\ in^2$

The required area can be calculated from the normalized moment

$$K = \frac{M_u}{\phi bd^2} = \frac{67^{k-ft}(12'')}{0.9(11'')(20'')^2} = 0.203\ ksi$$

From K vsρ graphs (Refer Fig. I at end of this chapter), ρ corresponding to K = 0.2038 (for n = 7)

$$\rho = 0.0035$$

Hence, the required area

$$A_{reqd} = \rho bd$$
$$= 0.0035(11)(20) = 0.77\ in^2 (A = \rho bd)$$

Since $0.77\ in^2 < \frac{1}{2}(1.58) in^2$, the second part of criterion II is also met.

Therefore, no extra "binder" stirrups are required.

• PROBLEM 18-13

Determine the location for half positive flexural reinforcement to be theoretically terminated, if the factored dead and live loads are as shown in figure 1.

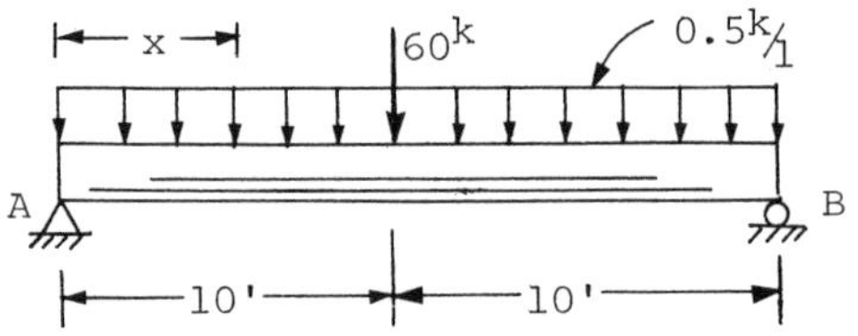

Fig. 1

Solution: One half of the positive steel may theoretically be terminated where the bending moment is less than one half of the maximum value.

The maximum moment occurs at midspan,

$$M_{max} = \frac{Wl^2}{8} + \frac{Pl}{4} = \frac{0.5(20')^2}{8} + \frac{60(20)}{4} = 325^{k\text{-}ft}$$

The reaction at support A (or B) is

$$R_A = \frac{Wl}{2} + P/2 = \frac{0.5(20)}{2} + \frac{60}{2} = 35^k$$

Thus, half positive steel can be theoretically terminated where

$$M = \tfrac{1}{2}(325^{k\text{-}ft}) = 162.5^{k\text{-}ft}$$

Considering the F.B.D. of left half span $0.5^{k/1}$

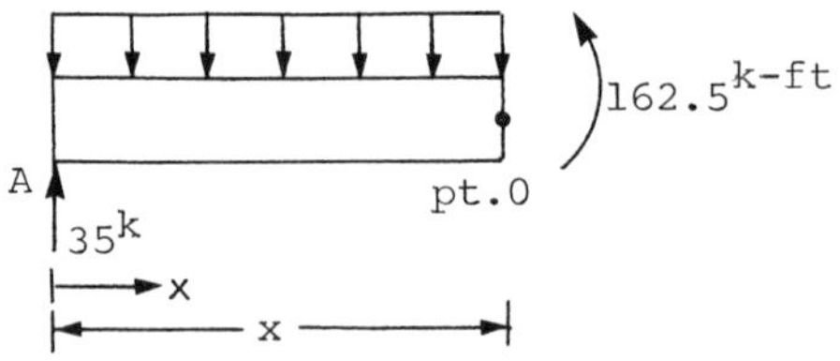

Fig. 2

Moment about point 0 is

$$162.5 = 35(x) - \frac{0.5(x^2)}{2}$$

or

$$x^2 - 140x + 650 = 0$$

$$x = \frac{-(-140) \pm \sqrt{(140)^2 - 4(1)(650)}}{2(1)} = \frac{140 \pm 130.4}{2}$$

$$x = 4.81'$$

Therefore terminate half positive steel at x = 4.81 ft from supports.

• PROBLEM 18-14

A R/C beam, shown in figure, is subjected to pure moment. Determine the bending moment to cause an initial crack in the beam.

Assume modular ratio $n = E_s/E_c = 8$

maximum tensile strength of concrete = 400 psi

and reinforcement area = 1.8 in^2.

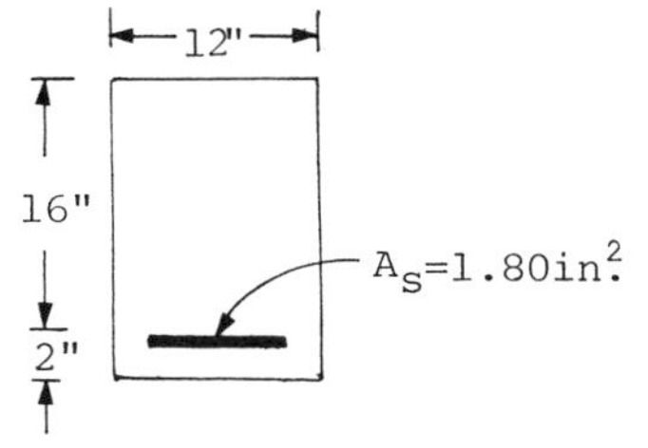

Fig. 1

Solution: Transforming steel into equivalent concrete, we have,

$$A_s(n - 1) = 1.80(8 - 1) = 12.6$$

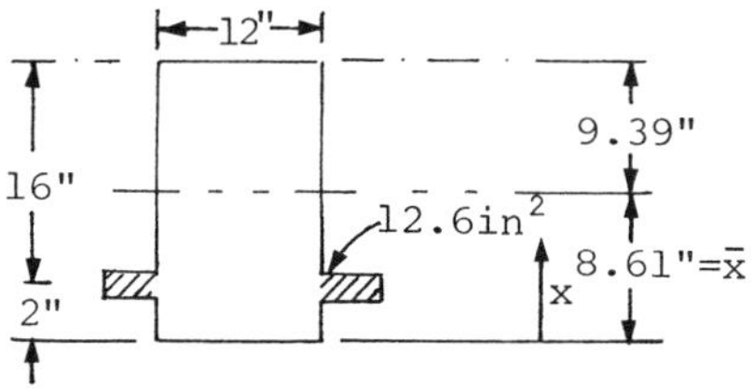

Fig. 2

The neutral axis of the transformed section is

$$\bar{x} = \frac{\bar{Z} x_i A_i}{\bar{Z} A_i} = \frac{9(18 \times 12) + 2(12.6)}{18 \times 12 + 12.6} = 8.61 \text{ in}$$

The moment of inertia of transformed section about neutral axis:

concrete above N.A. $I_1 = 1/3\ bh^3 = 1/3(12)(9.39)^3 = 3311 \text{ in}^4$

concrete below N.A. $I_2 = 1/3\ (12)(8.61)^3 = 2553 \text{ in}^4$

transformed steel $I_3 = Ad^2 = 12.6(8.61 - 2)^2 = 550 \text{ in}^4$

Note, moment of inertia of transformed steel about its own centriodal axis is neglected as it is negligibly small compared to its moment of inertia about the neutral axis.

$$I_{TR} = I_1 + I_2 + I_3 = 3311 + 2553 + 550 = 6414 \text{ in}^4$$

initial cracking occurs when flexural stress at bottom equals 400 psi

$$f = \frac{M_{cr}\bar{x}}{I_{TR}} \quad \text{or} \quad 400 \text{ psi} = \frac{M_{cr} \cdot 8.61''}{6414 \text{ in}^4}$$

$$M_{cr} = \frac{400 \text{ psi}(6414 \text{ in}^4)}{8.61''} \simeq 299000 \text{ lb-in}$$

or $M_{cr} = 299^{\text{k-in}}$

• PROBLEM 18-15

Determine the overall depth (h) and width (b) required for an interior cast-in-place (c.i.p.) flexural beam shown in figure.

Assume flexural reinforcement to contain 8 #9 bars. (Use relevant ACI code provisions).

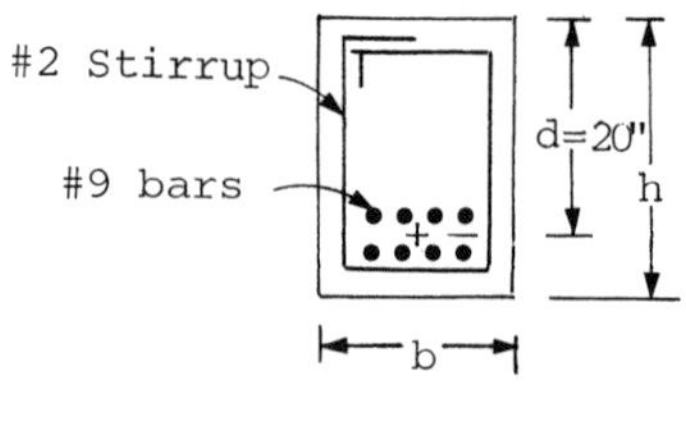

Solution: As per ACI 318-77 sec. 7.6.1 a) the clear distance between bars in a layer shall not be less than the bar diameter (1") b) the clear distance between layers shall not be less than 1" and c) for cast-in-place (c.i.p.) beams the concrete cover shall not be less than $1\frac{1}{2}$" (ACI sec. 7.7.1).

The diameter of #9 bar is 9/8in, therefore the bar spacing is taken as equal to bar diameter.

Therefore the beam width b:

two covers	$2(1\frac{1}{2}")$	→ 3.00"
two stirrups	$2(2/8")$	→ 0.50"
four bars	$4(9/8)$	→ 4.50"
three spaces	$3(9/8)$	→ 3.375"
Total		→ 11.375" ≃ $11\frac{1}{2}$"

and beam depth h:

depth at centroid		→ 20.0"
half of layer spacing	$\frac{1}{2}(1")$	→ 0.50"
1 bar	$1(9/8")$	→ 1.125"
1 stirrup	$1(2/8)$	→ 0.25"
	Total	→ 23.375 or ≃ $23\frac{1}{2}$ in.

Therefore use b = $11\frac{1}{2}$ in and h = $23\frac{1}{2}$ in.

• PROBLEM 18-16

Determine the point at which #8 top bars may be terminated for the beam shown in figure 1. $f'_c = 4$ ksi. $f_y = 60$ ksi. Use relevant ACI 318-77 provisions.

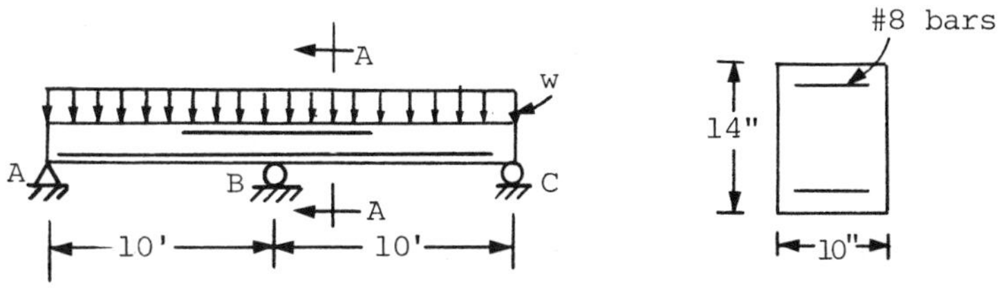

Fig. 1

Solution: From standard beam tables,

$R_A = R_C = 3\ wl/8$ (or AISC Manual of steel construction)

$R_B = 5\ wl/4$

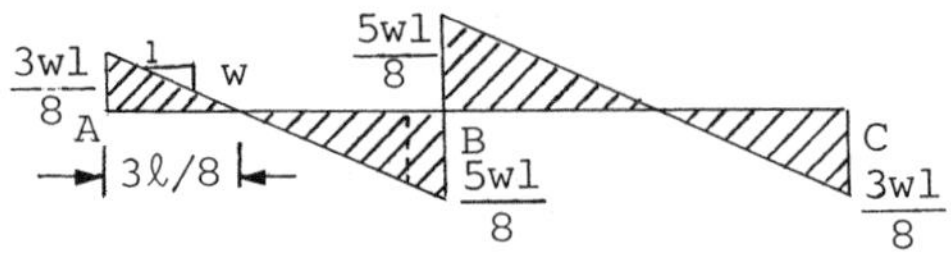

Fig. 2 SHEAR FORCE DIAGRAM

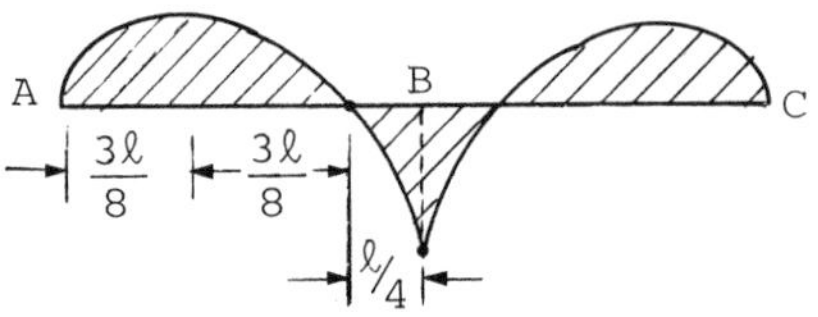

Fig. 3 BENDING MOMENT DIAGRAM

The moment is zero where the shear areas cancel, hence the inflection point is at 1/4 = 10'/4 = 2.5 ft to left of B (another inflection point is 2.5' to right of B by symmetry).

In negative moment area, the steel must extend beyond the inflection points by a length, whichever is maximum of the following: (i) effective depth 14 in

(ii) 12 bar diameter 12(8/8) = 12 in

(iii) 1/16 clear span 1/16(10') = 7.5 in

Therefore, use 14 in. The length of the rear for the distance from the point of (ACI 12.13.2) maximum moment to the termination point must be larger than the development length of the bars. From tables, the development length for #8 top bars is 42" (ACI sec. 12.2).
We have, 2.5' + 14" = 44" > 42" which is valid.

Therefore, terminate negative steel 44" from support B.

• PROBLEM 18-17

An interior reinforced concrete beam has 4-#7 bars in one layer as its flexural reinforcement. Determine the maximum beam width considering crack control. f'_c = 4 ksi f_y = 60 ksi. Use ACI 318-77. Assume that the stirups are #3.

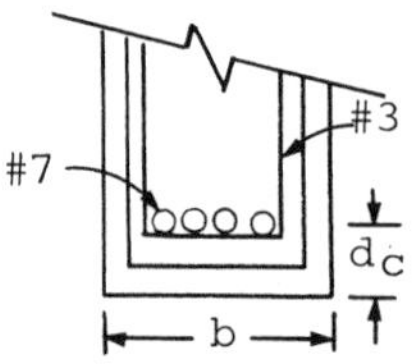

Solution: For interior exposure $f_s \sqrt[3]{d_c \cdot A} \leq 175$ k/in

where $f_s = 0.6\ f_y = 0.6 \times 60 = 36$ ksi (ACI sec. 10.6.4)

The parameter d_c is equal to

cover	$1\frac{1}{2}''$
stirrup	3/8
half bar diam	$\frac{1}{2}(7/8)$
	2.31 in.

The area surrounding one bar is

$$A = \frac{2 \cdot d_c \cdot b}{\#\text{ of bars}} = \frac{2(2.31)(b)}{4} = 1.155(b)$$

or

or $$175 \geq 36\ \sqrt[3]{2.31(1.155\ b)}$$

$$b \leq 43.05 \text{ in.}$$

Thus, for crack control considerations, the beam width b should be less than or equal to 43 in.

DESIGN OF DOUBLY REINFORCED RECTANGULAR BEAMS BY WORKING STRESS METHOD

• PROBLEM 18-18

A doubly reinforced concrete beam has a resisting moment of 60,000 ft-lbs. The stresses in the beam are: $f' = 1400$ lb/in^2; $f_c = 650$ lb/in^2; $f_s = 16000$ lb/in^2; and $n = 15$. The beam dimensions are $b = 10''$, $d = 20''$ and $d = 3''$. Determine the amount of tension (A_s) and compression (A_s') steel required.

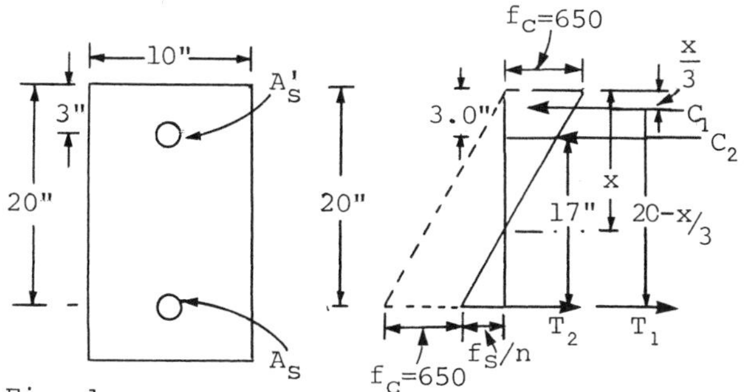

Fig. 1

Solution: Referring to the stress diagram and by similar triangles,

$$\frac{x}{d} = \frac{f_c}{f_c + f_s/n}$$

or

$$x = \frac{f_c \cdot d}{f_c + f_s/n} = \frac{650 \times 20}{650 + \frac{16000}{15}} = 7.57''$$

Consider the reinforcements of the tension side and compression side separately.

a) Rectangular beam reinforced on the tension side:

$$\text{moment } M = \tfrac{1}{2} f_c bxjd$$

$$= \tfrac{1}{2}(650)(10)(7.57)(17.48)$$

where $jd = d - \frac{x}{3} = 20 - \frac{7.57}{3} = 17.48''.$

i.e. $M = 430{,}000$ lb-in.

But total moment = 60,000 lb-ft = 720,000 lb-in.

Therefore balance M = 720,000 - 430,000 = 290,000 lb-in. This is to be taken up by the reinforced compression side of the beam.

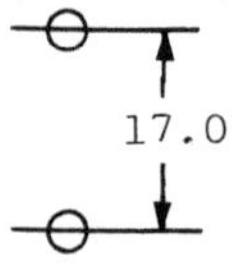

Fig. 2

b) Computing the force,

$$\frac{290{,}000 \text{ lb-in}}{17.00''} \simeq 17{,}060 \text{ lbs. approximating to } 17{,}100 \text{ lbs.}$$

Tension steel:

Beam (a) $A_s = \frac{M}{f_s jd} = \frac{430{,}000}{16000 \text{ lb/in}^2 \times 17.48''} \simeq 1.54 \text{ in}^2 = A_{s1}$

Beam (b) $A_s = \frac{T_2}{f_s} = \frac{17100 \text{ lb}}{16{,}000 \text{ lb/in}^2} \simeq 1.06 \text{ in}^2 = A_{s2}$

Total $A_s = A_{s1} + A_{s2} = 1.54 + 1.06 = 2.60 \text{ in}^2$ (Total tension steel)

Compression steel:

By the theory of elasticity, the allowable stress of the compression steel is 'n' times that of the concrete. However, article 8.10.1 of the ACI code suggests the use of 2n.

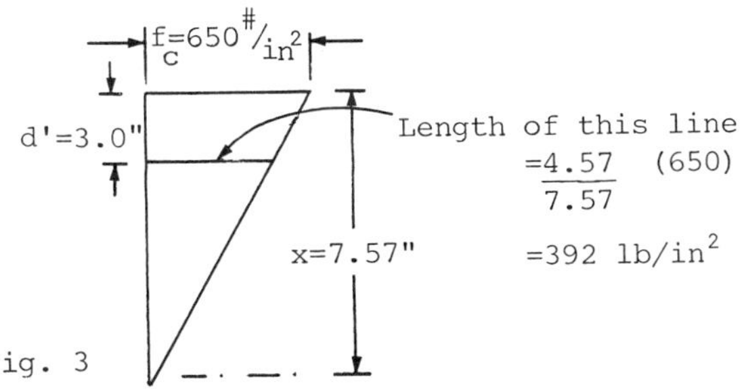

Fig. 3

Therefore, the stress at this level of compression steel is $392(2)(15) = 11{,}760\ lb/in^2$ (ACI code "2n").

This stress is less than $f_s = 16{,}000\ lb/in^2$, and hence no adjustment is necessary.

To obtain the actual area of the steel, allowance is made for the area of concrete "replaced" by the steel (but included in the (a) beam above). Using (2n - 1)... or the 1/2n-1 part of the area of concrete that would be required.

Then A'_s (area of compression steel)

$$= \frac{17{,}100}{392\ lb/in^2} \times \frac{1}{2 \times (15 - 1)} \approx 1.56\ in^2$$

• PROBLEM 18-19

Compute the maximum moment that the beam shown can carry if $f_c = 1000\ lbs/in^2$, $n = 10$ and $f_s = 18000\ lbs/in^2$.

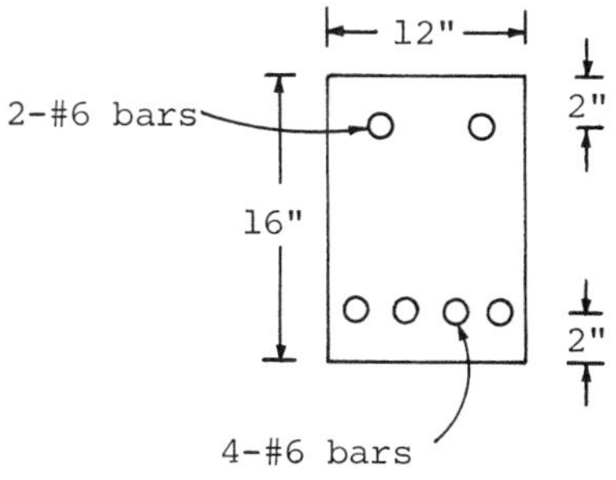

Fig. 1

Solution:

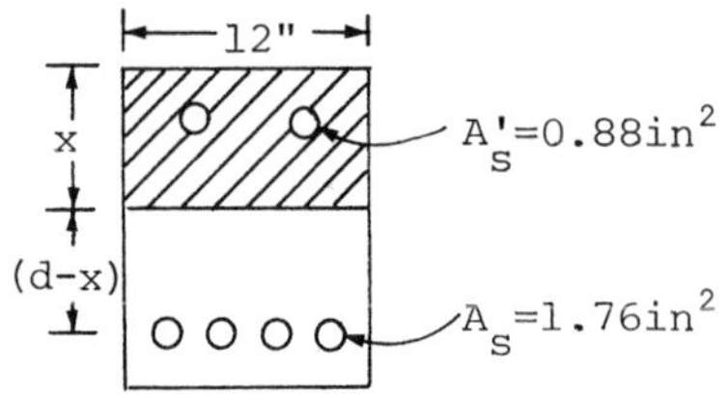

Fig. 2

Referring to figure 2:

$$12 \cdot x(x/2) + (2n - 1)(0.88)(x - 2) = 10(1.76)(14 - x) \text{ (Moment about neutral axis)}$$

where $n = 10$

Thus $12 \cdot x(x/2) + (19)(0.88)(x - 2) = 10(1.76)(14 - x)$

or $6x^2 + 16.7x - 33.4 = 246.4 - 17.6x$

or $6x^2 + 34.3x - 279.8 = 0$

Solving for $x = + 4.54$ in. (positive root)

To find jd:

$$jd \neq d - \frac{x}{3}$$

Instead, jd is found out by using the relation

$$jd = \frac{M}{C} = \frac{M_1 + M_2}{C_1 + C_2}$$

Refering to the following stress diagram,

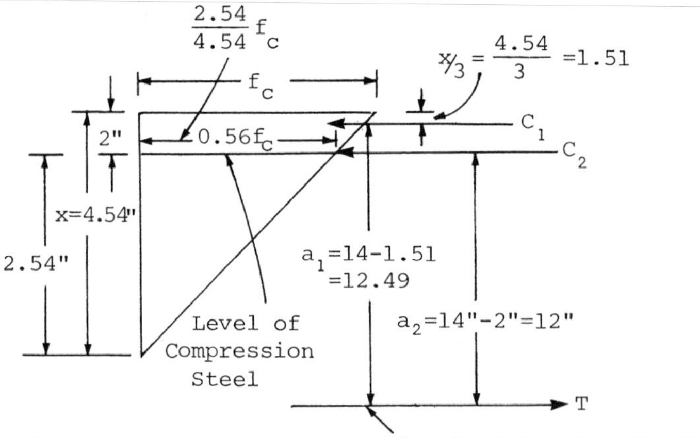

Fig. 3

$$M_1 = C_1 \times a_1$$

where $C_1 = \frac{1}{2} f_c bx = \frac{1}{2} f_c \times 12 \times 4.54 = 27.24 f_c$

and $a_1 = 14 - 1.51 = 12.49''$

Thus $M_1 = 27.24 \times 12.49(f_c) = 340 f_c$.

Similarly $M_2 = C_2 \times a_2$

where $C_2 = (2n - 1)(0.56 f_c)(0.88) = 9.36 f_c$

and $a_2 = 12''$

Therefore, $M_2 = 9.36 f_c \times 12 \simeq 112 f_c$.

$$C_1 + C_2 = 27.24 f_c + 9.36 f_c = 36.6 f_c$$

and $M_1 + M_2 = 340 f_c + 112 f_c = 452 f_c$.

Therefore, $jd = \dfrac{M_1 + M_2}{C_1 + C_2} = \dfrac{452 f_c}{36.6 f_c} = 12.35''$.

Maximum moment on the concrete side = $452 f_c$.

$$M_c = 452 \times 1000 = 452{,}000 \text{ lb-in.}$$

Maximum moment on the steel side $M_s = A_s \cdot f_s \cdot jd$

$= 1.76 \times 18{,}000 \times 12.35 = 391{,}248$ lb-in.

Check for stresses:

f_{sc} (stress in compression steel) as per ACI 1102(c) is

$$f_{sc} = (2n)(0.56)f_c$$

$$= 20(0.56)f_c.$$

But $f_c = \dfrac{391{,}248}{452}$ (because $M = 452 f_c$)

$= 865.6 \simeq 866 \text{ lb/in}^2$.

and $f_{sc} = 20(0.56)(866) \simeq 9700 \text{ lb/in}^2 < 18{,}000 \text{ lb/in}^2$.

The calculated value of f_{sc} is less than f_s and hence the selected beam is safe.

A doubly reinforced concrete beam has M = 105 ft-kips, b = 13", d = 16" and d' = 2.5". If f'_c = 3000 lbs/in^2 and f_s = 20,000 lbs/in^2, determine the tension and compression steel required.

Solution:

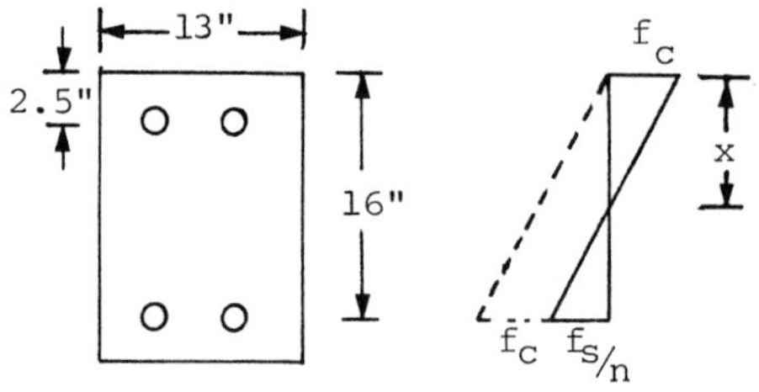

Fig. 1

Referring to the stress diagram, by similar triangles, we have

$$\frac{x}{d} = \frac{f_c}{f_c + f_s/n}$$

or $$x = \frac{f_c \cdot d}{f_c + f_s/n}$$

$$= \frac{1350 \times 16"}{1350 + (20{,}000/9)} \simeq 6.05" \quad (f_c = 1350 \text{ for a } 3000\# \text{ concrete})$$

$$jd = d - \frac{x}{3} = 16 - \frac{6.05}{3} \simeq 14"$$

Let us consider the tension and compression steel separately.

First, the beam reinforced on the tension side only:

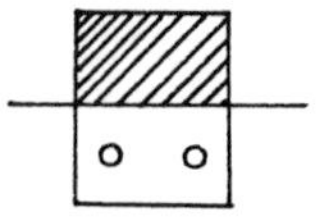

Fig. 2

We have,

$$M_1 = \tfrac{1}{2} f_c b \cdot x \cdot jd$$

$$= \tfrac{1}{2}(1350)(13)(6.05)(14)$$

$$\simeq 743242 \text{ lb-in.}$$

$$A_{s1} = \frac{M}{f_s \cdot jd} = \frac{743242}{20{,}000 \times 14} \simeq 2.66 \text{ in}^2.$$

We have total moment = 105 ft-kip

= 105 x 1000 x 12 lb-in

= 1260000 lb-in.

Moment resisted by tension steel = 743242 lb-in.

Therefore, remaining moment to be resisted by the other reinforcement = 1260000 - 743242 = 516758 lb-in

Considering now the beam with compression steel, we have,

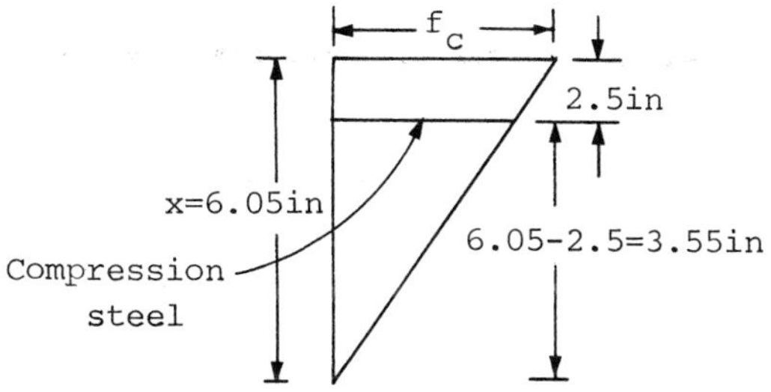

Fig. 3

Referring to the figure,

stress at the level of compression steel

$$= \frac{3.55}{6.05}(1350) \simeq 792 \text{ lb/in}^2.$$

Checking this with 792 x (2)(9) = 14,260 $\text{lb/in}^2 < 20{,}000$

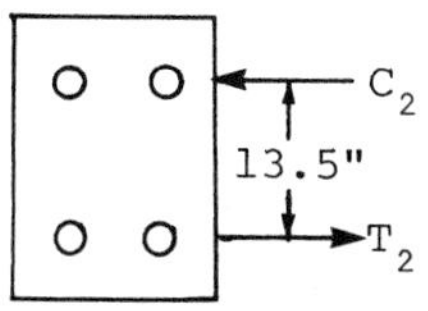

Fig. 4

The stress is within safe limit.

$$C_2 = T_2 = \frac{516758}{13.5''} = 38278.37 \simeq 38279 \text{ lb}.$$

$n = 9$

and $A'_s = \dfrac{38279}{792 \text{ lb/in}^2} \times \dfrac{1}{(2n-1)} \simeq 2.84 \text{ in}^2.$

$$\text{Required } As_2 = \frac{38279 \text{ lb}}{20000 \text{ lb/in}^2} = 1.91 \text{ in}^2.$$

Therefore, total area of steel required

$$= 2.66 + 1.91 = 4.57 \text{ in}^2.$$

i.e. taking standards $\simeq 4\ 5/8 \text{ in}^2$.

• PROBLEM 18-21

Determine the spacing of #3 stirrups (f_y = 40 ksi) at the fixed support for cantilever beam shown below. Factored dead and live loads are as indicated in the figure. f'_c = 4 ksi. Use relevant ACI code provisions.

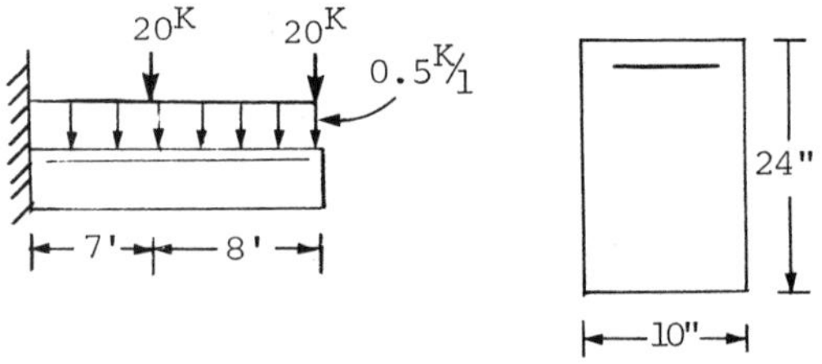

Solution: The shear force at support end is

$$V = 20^k + 20^k + 15'(0.5^{k/in}) = 47.5^k$$

The shear force at a distance "d" (effective depth) away from support end is (ACI sec. 11.1.3.1)

$$V_u = 47.5^k - 0.5^{k/1}\ (2') = 46.5^k$$

Shear carried by concrete

$$V_c = 2\sqrt{f'_c}\ bwd = 2\sqrt{4000}\ (10")(24") = 30{,}358^k \quad \text{(ACI sec. 11.3.1.1)}$$

Since $\frac{V_u}{\phi} > \frac{V_c}{Z}$ need stirrups. The shear force carried by stirrups

$$V_s = \frac{V_u}{\phi} - V_c$$

$$= \frac{46.5}{0.85} - 30.4^k = 24.3^k$$

Shear area of a #3 stirrup $A_u = 2(0.11") = 0.22 \text{ in}^2$

hence,

$$.S \le \frac{A_u f_y d}{V_s} = \frac{0.22(40 \text{ ksi})(24")}{24.3^k} = 8.69 \text{ in. (ACI sec. 11.5.6.7)}$$

Also,

$$.S \le \frac{A_u f_y}{50bw} = \frac{0.22(40000 \text{ psi})}{50(10")} = 17.5 \text{ in. (ACI sec. 11.5.5.3)}$$

$$.S \le 24"$$

$$.S \le d/2 = 24"/2 = 12 \text{ in.} \quad \text{(ACI sec. 11.5.4.1)}$$

Thus, stirrup spacing at support is the least of all S calculated above, that is, 8.68" say $S = 8\frac{1}{2}"$.

• PROBLEM 18-22

Determine at what moment the maximum concrete compressive stress is equal to $0.45\ f'_c$ for the beam shown in fig. 1 Assume $A_s = 3.93\ \text{in}^2$, $f'_c \cong 4$ ksi, & $f_y = 60$ ksi.

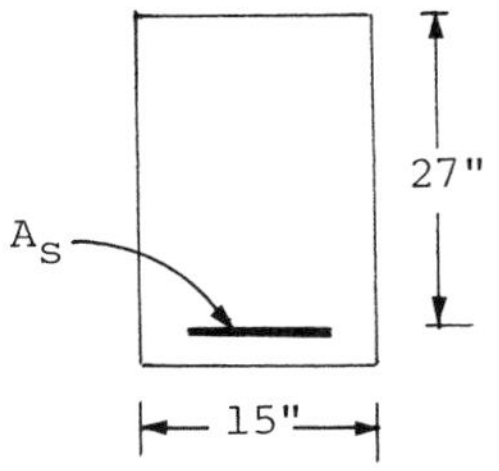

Fig. 1

Solution: At maximum stress of $0.45\ f'_c$, cracks will develop under tensile stresses. However, concrete remains elastic under compressive stresses. The distribution of force is as shown in figure 2.

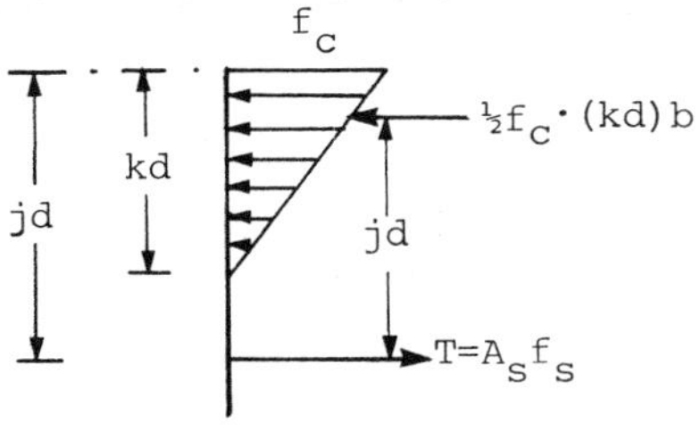

Fig. 2

The depth of neutral axis kd from the top is

$$kd = \left[\sqrt{2\rho n + (\rho n)^2} - \rho n\right]d \qquad (1)$$

where

$$\rho = A_s/bd = \frac{3.93 \text{ in}^2}{15''(27)''} = 0.0097$$

The modulus of elasticity for concrete is $E_c = 57,000 \sqrt{f'_c}$ $= 57000 \sqrt{4000} = 3.6 \times 10^6$psi (ACI section 8.5.1)

Hence, the modular ratio $n = E_s/E_c$ ($E_s = 29 \times 10^6$ psi)

$$n = \frac{29 \times 10^6 \text{ psi}}{3.6 \times 10^6 \text{ psi}} = 8.05 \text{ say } 8.0$$

$$\therefore \quad \rho n = 0.0097(8) = 0.0776$$

and

$$k = \left[\sqrt{2(0.0776) + (0.0776)^2}\right] - 0.0776 = 0.324$$

Substituting in equation (1)

and $j = 1 - k/3 = 1 - 0.324/3 = 0.892$

From figure 2, we have

$$M = \tfrac{1}{2} f_c(kd)(b) \times (jd)$$

or $M = \tfrac{1}{2} f_c kjbd^2$

or $M = \tfrac{1}{2}(0.45 \times 4.0 \text{ ksi})(0.324)(0.892)(15)(27)^2$

$= 2844$k-in

Thus @ compressive stress $= 0.45 f'_c$, moment M is 2844k-in ($k = 0.324$ and $j = 0.892$ for a $4000^{\#}$ concrete)

• PROBLEM 18-23

Determine over what portion of the beam stirrups are not required as per ACI 318-77. Use $f'_c = 3$ ksi. Load shown in the figure below is factored dead and live load acting together.

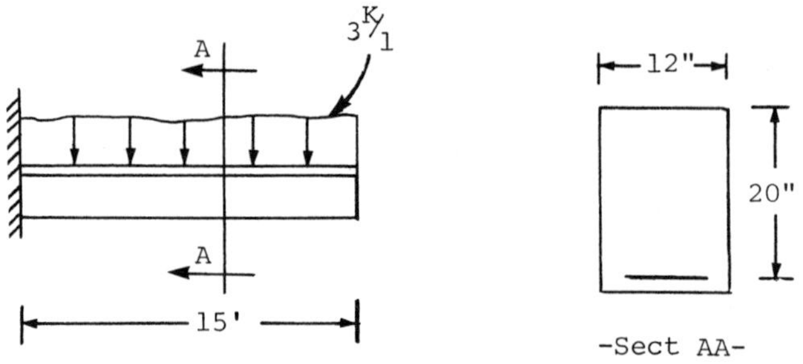

Solution: Stirrups are not needed where

$$V_u < \frac{1}{2}\,\phi V_c \quad \text{(ACI sec. 11.5.5)}$$

The shear force carried by the concrete V_c is given by

$$V_c = 2\sqrt{f'_c}\,b\cdot d \quad \text{(ACI sec. 11.3.1.1)}$$

$$= 2\sqrt{3000}\,(12)(20) = 26{,}290 = 26.3^k$$

hence, stirrups are not needed where

$$V_u < \tfrac{1}{2}(0.85)(26.3^k)$$

$$V_u < 11.2^k$$

Since the shear force is zero at free end and increases linearly at the rate of 3^kft, $V_u = 11.2^k$ at

$$x = \frac{11.2^k}{3^{k/1}} = 3.72 \text{ ft from free end.}$$

Thus, stirrups are not needed beyond 15' - 3.72 = 11.28 ft from fixed end support.

• PROBLEM 18-24

Determine over what length of the beam stirrups are not required as per ACI 318-77. Use f'_c = 4 ksi. The loads shown in Fig. 1 are factored dead plus live loads.

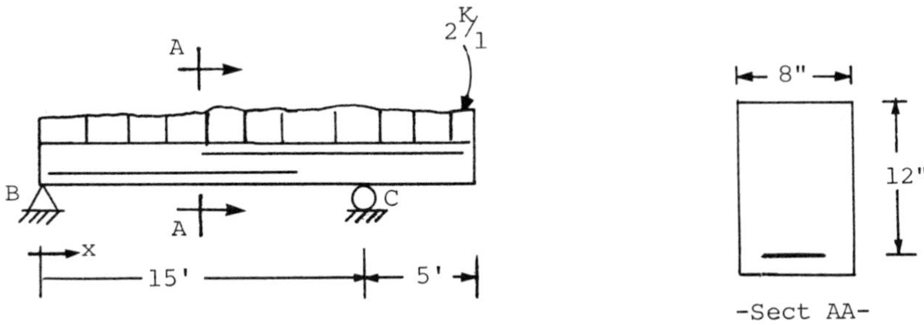

Fig. 1

Solution: Stirrups are not required where

$$V_u \leq \frac{1}{2}\,\phi V_c \quad \text{(ACI section 11.5.5)}$$

The shear force carried by the concrete V_c is given by

$$V_c = 2\sqrt{f'_c}\cdot b\cdot d \quad \text{(ACI section 11.3.1.1)}$$

$$= 2\sqrt{4000}\times 8 \times 12 = 12{,}143 = 12.1^k$$

or stirrups are not required where

$$V_u < \tfrac{1}{2}(0.85)(12.1^k) = 5.16^k$$

The reaction at point C is given by the sum of moments about A.

$$\text{Reaction force } R_c = \frac{2.0(20)^2/2}{15} = 26.7^k$$

The reaction at A is the algebraic sum of vertical forces.

Therefore, $R_A = 2.0(20) - 26.7 = 13.3^k$

The shear force diagram is as given in fig. 2.

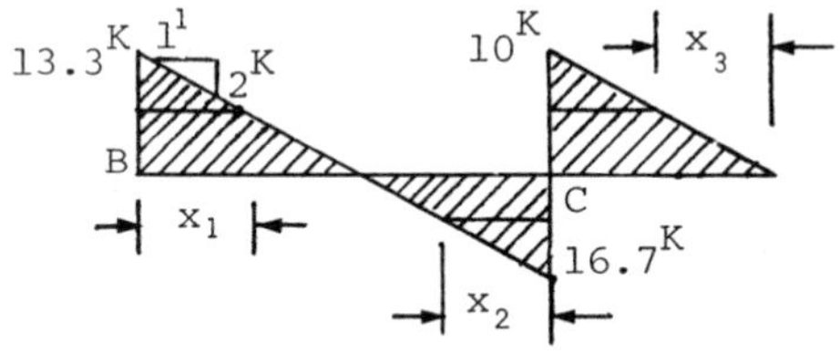

Fig. 2

Let the distances x_1, x_2 and x_3, as shown in fig. 2, denote the locations where $V_u = 5.16^k$. The slope of the shear diagram is 2^k/ft (intensity at uniform load).

$$\therefore \quad 5.16^k = 13.3^k - x_1(2^{k/1}) \quad \text{or} \quad x_1 = 4.07 \text{ ft.}$$

$$\text{Again, } 5.16^k = 16.7^k - x_2(2^{k/1}) \text{ or } x_2 = 5.77 \text{ ft.}$$

$$\text{and, } \quad 5.16^k = x_3 \cdot 2^{k/1} \quad \text{or} \quad x_3 = 2.58 \text{ ft.}$$

Since, stirrups are not required where $V_u \leq 5.16^k$, stirrups are not required in the shaded area of figure 3.

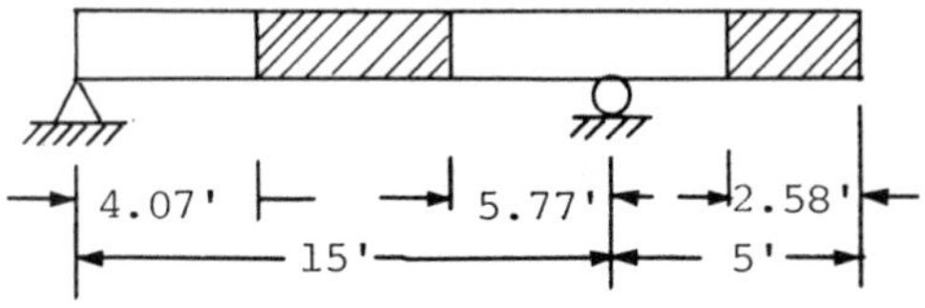

Fig. 3

• PROBLEM 18-25

Design stirrup spacing using #4 vertical U stirrups and 2500# concrete for a concrete beam loaded as shown. f_v = 18,000 lb/in^2. Neglect dead load.

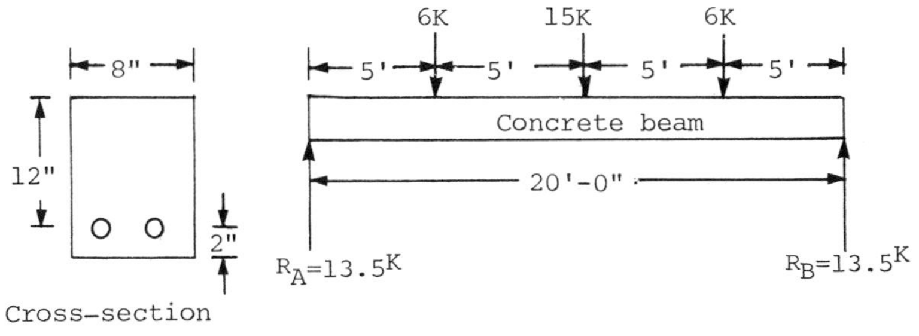

Fig. 1

Solution: We have, reactions at both ends $R_A = R_B = \frac{27}{2} = 13.5$ k (symmetrical loading)

The shear stress $v = \frac{V}{bd}$

where $V = R_A = R_B = 13.5$ k = 13500 lbs

Thus, $v_1 = \frac{13500}{8 \times 12} = 141$ lbs/in^2. (@ edge)

We have v_c (shear taken by concrete) = $1.1\sqrt{f'_c} = 55$ #/in^2

Thus $v'_o = v - v_c = 141 - 55 = 86$ lbs/in^2. (ACI 8.3.1(b)

$$A_V \cdot f_V = V' \cdot b \cdot S$$

$$\text{or} \quad S_1 = \frac{A_V \cdot f_V}{v'b}$$

$$\text{Thus} \quad S_1 = \frac{2 \times (0.20) \times 18000}{86 \times 8''} = 10.5''$$

$$v_2 = \frac{7500}{8 \times 12} = 78\#/\text{in}^2$$

and $v_c = 55\#/\text{in}^2$ (as before)

Therefore, $v'_1 = 78 - 55 = 23$.

$$\text{and} \quad S_2 = \frac{2 \times (0.20) \times 18000}{23 \times 8} = 39.1''$$

But max. spacing $S = \frac{d}{2} = \frac{12}{2} = 6''$ (ACI code sec. 13.7.5.4.1)

Therefore use #4 stirrups, 1 @ 3, 19@ 6@ each end.

Note, however, that ACI code provisions of sec. B7.5.4.3 should be checked. If the value of v' be more than $2\sqrt{f'_c}$, then S_1 should be $= \frac{d}{4} = \frac{12}{4} = 3''$ (@ end bays) and the answer would have been #4 U stirrups 1 @ 1, 20 @ 3 and 9 @ 6 at each end. Check also to see if v' is under $4.4\sqrt{f'_c}$. (ACI B.7.5.6.8)

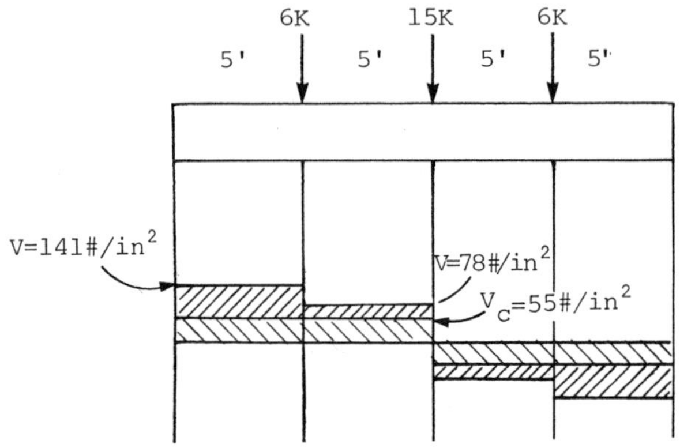

Fig. 2

• PROBLEM 18-26

> Compute the ultimate moment for the given section if $f_y = 60{,}000$ psi and $f'_c = 5000$ psi.

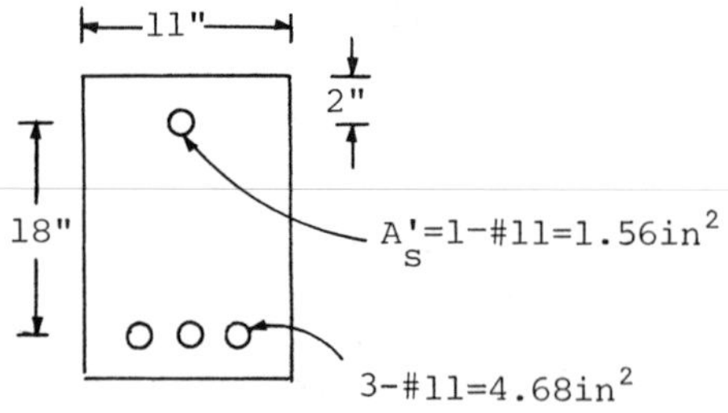

Fig. 1

Solution: Applying ultimate design method of ACI:

$$\rho = \frac{A_s}{bd} = \frac{4.68}{11 \times 20} = 0.0212$$

$$\rho' = \frac{A'_s}{bd} = \frac{1.56}{11 \times 20} = 0.0071$$

and $(\rho - \rho') = 0.0141$

$$\rho_b = \frac{0.85\ f'_c}{f_y} \cdot \frac{\beta_1 d'}{d} \cdot \frac{87000}{87000 - f_y}$$

$$= \frac{0.85 \times 0.80 \times 5000 \times 2}{60{,}000 \times 20} \cdot \frac{87000}{87000 - 60000}$$

$$= 0.0183 > (\rho - \rho')$$

First method of analysis:

Let us ignore compression steel, so that

$$M_u = \phi f'_c bd^2 q\ (1 - 0.59q)$$

$$\text{where}\quad q = \rho \cdot \frac{f_y}{f'_c} = 0.0212\ \frac{60{,}000}{5000} = 0.2544$$

$$\phi = 0.9$$

$$\text{Therefore,}\ M_u = 0.9 \times 5000 \times 11 \times 20^2 \times 0.2544 \left[1 - 0.59(0.254)\right]$$

$$= 4282257 \text{ in-lbs}$$

$$= 357 \text{ ft-kips.}$$

Second method of analysis:

We have tension = compression

so that $A_s \cdot f_y = 0.85\ f'_c ba$

$$\text{Therefore}\quad a = \frac{A_s \cdot f_y}{0.85\ f'_c b}$$

Assuming that area of steel $= A_s - A'_s = 4.68 - 1.56 = 3.12\ in^2$,

we have $A_s = 3.12\ in^2$

Substituting these values in the expression for a, we have

$$a = \frac{3.12 \times 60000}{0.85 \times 5000 \times 11} = 4.00''$$

Also, $a = \beta_1 C$ where $\beta_1 = 0.80$ for a $5000^{\#}$ concrete

$$\text{Therefore}\quad C = \frac{a}{\beta_1} = \frac{4}{0.8} = 5.00''.$$

Referring to the resulting strain diagram below:

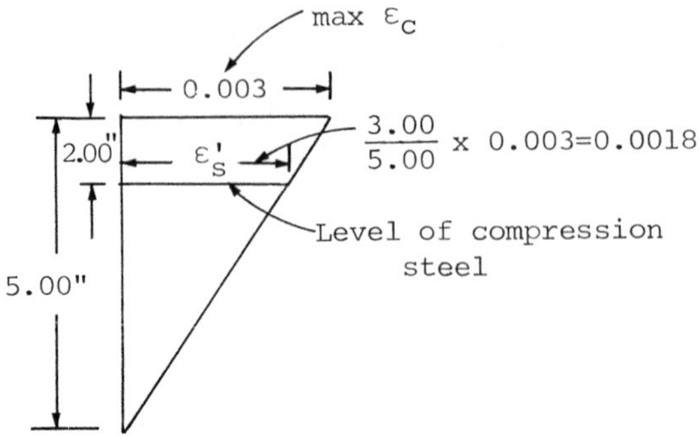

Fig. 2

From similar triangles,

$$\frac{\varepsilon_s'}{0.003} = \frac{3}{5}$$

or $$\varepsilon_s' = \frac{3 \times 0.003}{5} = 0.0018$$

From which $f_{sc} = \varepsilon_s' \times E_s = 0.0018 \times 29 \times 10^6 \#/in^2$

$= 52{,}200 \#/in^2$ (compare with $f_y = 60{,}000 \#/in^2$)

Therefore, $A_s' = 1.56\ in^2$ will now become $= \frac{52{,}200}{60{,}000} \times 1.56$

$= 1.36\ in^2$.

Whence $4.68\ in^2 - 1.36\ in^2 = 3.32\ in^2$.

Having 2 beams,

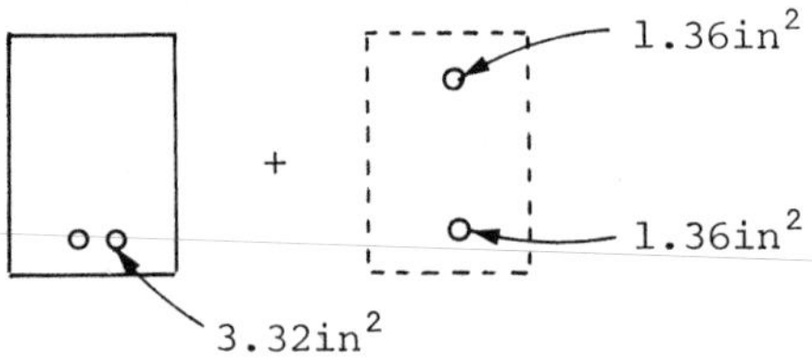

Fig. 3

$$M_u = \phi\left[(A_s - A_s')(d - a/2) + A_s \cdot f_y(d - d')\right]$$
$$= \phi\left[f_c' bd^2 q_1(1 - 0.59\ q_1) + A_s' f_y(d - d')\right]$$

where $q_1 = \rho_1 \quad \frac{f_y}{f_c'} = \frac{3.32}{11 \times 20} \times \frac{60000}{5000} \quad (\rho = \frac{A_s}{bd})$

$= 0.180$ and $\phi = 0.90$ as usual.

Therefore, $M_u = 0.90 \Big[5000 \times 11 \times 20^2 \times 0.180(1 - 0.59 \times 0.180)$

$+ 1.36(60{,}000)(18'')\Big]$

$= 4507423$ in-lbs

$= 376$ ft-kips.

NOTE: In the above illustration, a very slight error is introduced by using 3.12 in^2 to find 'a' when the actual value of $(A_s - A_s')$ was 3.32 in^2(found later). However, since the difference is small, it can be neglected. Where the difference is significantly large, the new value of $A_s - A_s'$ must be substituted and the process repeated.

DESIGN OF RECTANGULAR BEAMS BY ULTIMATE DESIGN METHOD

• PROBLEM 18-27

Determine the ultimate moment capacity of the given rectangular beam. $f_c' = 5000$ lbs/in^2 and $f_y = 40{,}000$ lbs/in^2.

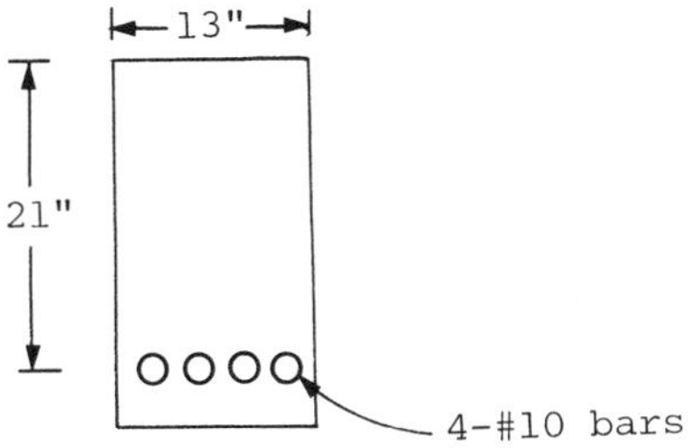

Solution: Referring to table III (see end of this chapter)

Area of 4-#10 bars = 5.06 in^2.

$$\rho = \frac{A_s}{bd} = \frac{5.06}{13'' \times 21''}$$

$$= 0.0185$$

and $$\rho_b = \frac{0.85\ \beta_1 f_c'}{f_y} \times \frac{87000}{87000 + f_y}$$

$$= \frac{0.85 \times 0.80 \times 5000}{40{,}000} \times \frac{87000}{87000 + 40{,}000} = 0.0582$$

Maximum allowable $\rho = 0.75\ \rho_b$

$$= 0.75 \times 0.0582 = 0.0437$$

Using $\rho = 0.0185$.

$$q = \rho \cdot \frac{f_y}{f'_c}$$

$$= 0.0185 \times \frac{40,000}{5000}$$

$$= 0.148$$

$$M_u = \phi b d^2 f'_c q(1 - 0.59q)$$

$$= 0.90 \times 13 \times 21^2 \times 5000 \times 0.148 \left[1 - 0.59(0.148)\right]$$

$$= 3484775 \text{ lb-in}$$

$$= 290.4 \text{ kip-ft.}$$

Working stress method:

We have $\rho = 0.0185$ and $n = 7$.

From curves, (see Fig. I at end of this chapter) $j = 0.864$ and $k = 0.400$.

Moment on the steel side $M_s = A_s \cdot f_s jd$

$$= 5.06 \times 20,000 \times 0.864 \times 21$$

$$= 1836173 \text{ lb-in} = 153 \text{ kip-ft.}$$

Moment on the concrete side $M_c = \frac{1}{2} f_c bkdjd$

$$= \frac{1}{2} \times 2250 \times 13 \times 0.400 \times 21 \times 0.864 \times 21$$

$$= 2228990 \text{ lb-in} = 186 \text{ kip-ft.}$$

Therefore allowable moment = 153 kip-ft.

Comparison of the two methods:

To compare both the methods, an assumption usually made is that Live Load = Dead Load so that equation 9 - 1 of ACI 9.3.1 becomes $U = 1.4D + 1.7L = 1.55\ (D + L)$

The ultimate moment obtained previously now becomes $M_u = \frac{290.4}{1.55}$

$$= 187 \text{ kip-ft.}$$

Thus, extra moment carried by the section in the ultimate design method is 187 - 153 = 34 kip-ft

Percentage benefit of ultimate design over working stress method

$$= 100 \times \frac{34}{153} = 22.2\%.$$

• PROBLEM 18-28

Determine the ultimate moment carrying capacity of a rectangular beam for the following specifications:

$b = 11''$, $d = 20''$, $A_s = 3 - \#8$, $f'_c = 3000$ psi,

$f_y = 40{,}000$ psi.

Solution: We have M_u = ultimate moment $= \phi f'_c bd^2 q(1 - 0.59q)$

where $q = \rho \cdot \frac{f_y}{f'_c}$ and $\rho = \frac{A_s}{bd}$, $\phi = 0.9$

From table I (see end of this chapter) Area of #8 bar = $0.79 in^2$.

Area of steel $A_s = 3 \times 0.79\ in^2 = 2.37\ in^2$

Therefore, $\rho = \frac{2.37}{11'' \times 20''} \simeq 0.0107$

and $q = \rho \cdot \frac{f_y}{f'_c} = 0.0107 \times \frac{40{,}000}{3000} = 0.143$

Substituting these values in the expression for M_u, we have,

$$M_u = (0.9)(3000)(11)(20^2)0.143 \left[1 - 0.59(0.143)\right]$$

$$\simeq 1555510 \text{ lb-in} = 130 \text{ kip-ft}.$$

Check to see if ρ_b is exceeded.

We have, $\rho_b = \frac{\beta_1 \cdot 0.85\ f'_c}{f_y} \cdot \frac{87000}{87000 + f_y}$

$$= \frac{(0.85)(0.85)(3000)}{40000} \cdot \frac{87000}{87000 + 40{,}000}$$

$$= 0.0371$$

and $0.75\rho_b = 0.0278$ OK since > 0.0107

NOTE: Generally in designs ρ is taken to be about $0.5(\rho_b \times 0.75)$.

• PROBLEM 18-29

> Design a rectangular beam reinforced on the tension side to carry an ultimate moment of 400 ft-kips. $f'_c = 4000$ psi and $f_y = 40,000$ psi. Assume that 'b' is approximately '2/3 d'.

Solution: We have

$$\rho_b = \frac{0.85\ \beta_1 f'_c}{f_y} \times \frac{87000}{87000 + f_y}$$

$$= \frac{0.85 \times 0.85 \times 4000}{40,000} \times \frac{87000}{87000 + 40000}$$

$$= 0.0495.$$

Maximum allowable $\rho = 0.75\ \rho_b = 0.0371.$

However, such a large value of ρ may lead to deflections. To avoid this, let us choose $\rho = \frac{1}{2}(0.75\ \rho_b)$

$$= \tfrac{1}{2}(0.0371) = 0.0186;$$

$$q = 0.0186 \left(\frac{f_y}{f'_c}\right) = 0.186$$

Ultimate moment $M_u = \phi b d^2 f'_c q(1 - 0.59\ q)$

Substituting the various values in the above equation, we have

$$400 \times 12 \times 1000 = 0.90 \times b \times d^2 \times 4000 \times 0.186\ \{1-0.59(0.186)\}$$

$$= 596.12\ bd^2$$

or $\quad bd^2 = 8052$

But $\quad b = \frac{2}{3}\ d$

Therefore $\frac{2}{3}\ d^3 = 8052$

or $\quad d = 22.95''$ say $23''$.

Therefore $\quad b = 15.22''$ say $16''$.

Area of steel $A_s = \rho \cdot bd = 0.0186 \times 23'' \times 15.3'' = 6.55\ in^2$.

Referring to table III (see end of this chapter)

Let us use 5 - #11 bars giving an area of 7.81 in^2.

Assuming that 'b' is approximately '$\frac{1}{2}$d' and using f'_c = 3000 psi and f_y = 60,000 psi, design a rectangular beam to carry 'service moments' of 40 ft-kips for dead load and 100 ft-kips for live load.

Solution: As per ACI sec. 318 of 1977 and article 9.2.1

$$U = 1.4 \text{ (Dead Load + 1.7 Live Load)}$$

Using these factors of 1.4 and 1.7 for our problem,

$$\text{Ultimate moment} = M_u = 1.4(40) + 1.7(100) = 226 \text{ ft-kips}$$
$$= 2712000 \text{ in-lbs.}$$

At this point some determination of ρ must be made. Sec. 318 of ACI, 1963 provided for

$$\rho = 0.18 \frac{f'_c}{f_y} \quad \text{exceeding which deflection computations}$$

must be made unless $f_y > 40{,}000$ psi as is the case in this problem. ACI code of 1977 makes no such provision for the determination of ρ. However, a guideline leading to a good design generally is that ρ can be taken to be about $\frac{1}{2}$ of 0.75 ρ_b

$$\text{where} \quad \rho_b = \frac{\beta_1(0.85)(f'_c)}{f_y} \cdot \frac{87000}{87000 + f_y}$$

$$\text{Thus,} \quad \rho_b = \frac{0.85(0.85)(3000)}{60{,}000} \cdot \frac{87000}{87000 + 60{,}000}$$

$$= 0.0214$$

$$\text{whence} \quad 0.75\,\rho_b = 0.75 \times 0.0214 = 0.0160$$

$$\text{and} \quad \tfrac{1}{2}(0.75\,\rho_b) = \frac{0.0160}{2} = 0.008$$

$$q = \rho \cdot \frac{f_y}{f'_c} = 0.008 \cdot \frac{60{,}000}{3000} = 0.16$$

$$\text{But} \quad M_u = 2712000 = \phi \cdot f'_c bd^2 q \left[1 - 0.59(q)\right]$$

$$\text{Therefore, } 2712000''^{\#} = 0.9(3000)(bd^2)(0.16)\left[1 - 0.59(0.16)\right]$$

$$\text{or} \quad bd^2 = 6932$$

$$\text{But} \quad b = \tfrac{1}{2}\,d$$

Thus $\frac{d^3}{2} = 6932$

or $d = 24''$.

Hence $b = \frac{1}{2} d = \frac{24}{2} = 12''$.

$$\rho = \frac{A_s}{bd} \quad \text{or} \quad A_s = \rho \cdot bd$$

Therefore $A_s = 0.008 \times 12 \times 24 = 2.30 \text{ in}^2$.

Referring to table III (see end of this chapter)

Selecting 4 - #7 bars giving a total area of 2.41 in^2.

The designed section is as illustrated below in the fig. 1.

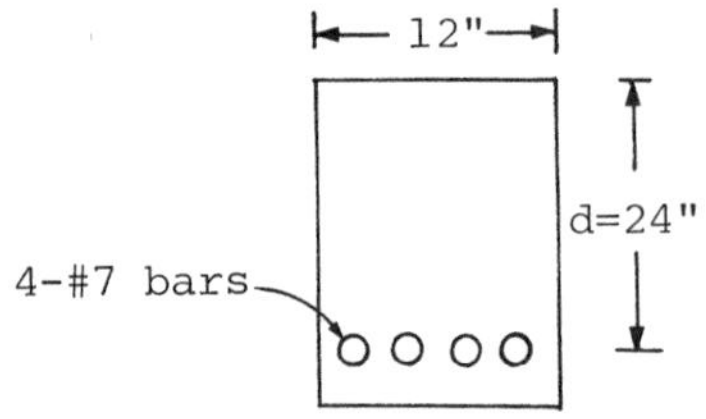

Fig. 1

• PROBLEM 18-31

Determine the amount of tension steel (A_s) and compression steel (A_s') required for a beam with the following specifications: $b = 13''$, $d = 16''$, $d' = 2.5''$, $f_c' = 3000$psi, $f_s = 20{,}000$ psi (grade 40 steel, $f_t = 40{,}000$ psi). The beam is to carry a moment of 105 ft-kips (Dead load contributes 40 ft-kips and the live load 65 ft-kips).

Solution:

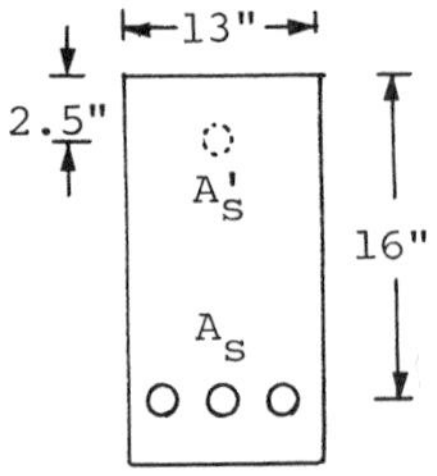

Fig. 1

First, consider the section without compression reinforcement.

$$0.75\ \rho_b = 0.75 \times \beta_1 \times 0.85 \times \frac{f'_c}{f_y} \cdot \frac{87000}{87000 + f_y}$$

$$= 0.75 \times 0.85 \times 0.85 \times \frac{3000}{40000} \cdot \frac{87000}{87000 + 40000}$$

$$= 0.0278$$

Using $\rho = \frac{0.75\rho_b}{2}$,

$$\rho = \frac{0.0278}{2} = 0.0139$$

$$U = 1.4D + 1.7L$$

Therefore, ultimate moment $M_u = 1.4 \times 40 + 1.7 \times 65$
$= 166.5$ ft-kips
$= 1998000$ in-lbs

But $M_u = \phi f'_c bd^2 q \left[1 - 0.59(q)\right]$

where $q = \rho \cdot \frac{f_y}{f'_c} = 0.0139 \times \frac{40,000}{3000} = 0.185$

Therefore, $M_u = 0.9 \times 3000 \times 13 \times 16^2 \times 0.185 \left[1 - 0.59(0.185)\right]$
$= 1480892$ lb-in

But Total Ultimate Moment = 1998000 lb-in.

Thus, remaining moment to be taken by compression steel = 1998000 - 1480892 = 517108 in-lbs.

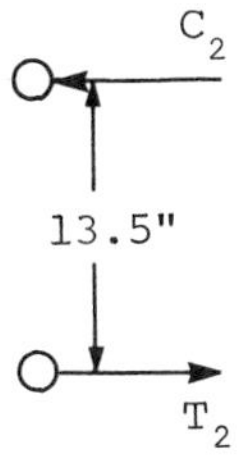

Fig. 2

$$C_2 = T_2 = \frac{517108}{13.5} = 38304 \text{ lbs}$$

But $38304 = \phi \cdot A'_s \cdot f_y$

where A'_s is compression steel.

Therefore, $A'_s = \frac{38304}{0.9 \times 40{,}000} = 1.06 \text{ in}^2.$

Note that this is true only if the stress in compression steel is in the region where strain exceeds $\frac{f_y}{E_s}$.

Check:

$$\text{We have,} \quad a = \frac{A_s \cdot f_y}{0.85 f'_c b} = \frac{\rho \cdot \not{b} d \cdot f_y}{0.85 f'_c \not{b}} = \frac{\rho \cdot d \cdot f_y}{0.85 f'_c}$$

$$= \frac{0.0139 \times 16 \times 40{,}000}{0.85 \times 3000} = 3.49''$$

But $\quad a = \beta_1 C = 0.85C$

Therefore, $C = \frac{3.49}{0.85} = 4.1''$

and the resulting strain diagram is:

Strain at the level of compression steel $\varepsilon'_s = \frac{f_{sc}}{E_s}$

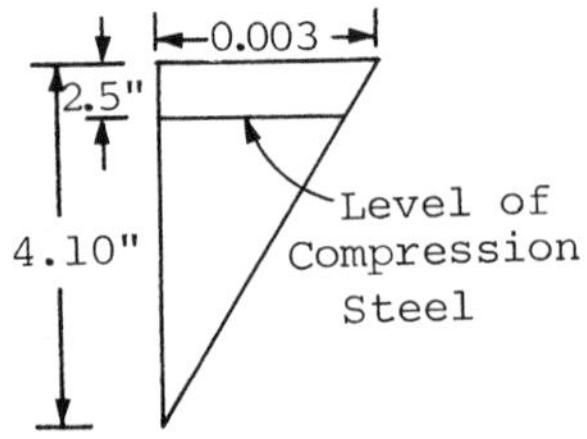

Fig. 3

Referring to the above figure, we have

$$\varepsilon'_s = \frac{f_{sc}}{E_s} = \frac{4.10 - 2.50}{4.10}(0.003) = 0.00118 = \frac{f_{sc}}{29 \times 10^6}$$

From which, $f_{sc} = 34220 \text{ lbs/in}^2 < 40{,}000 \text{ lbs/in}^2.$

Therefore, $A'_s = \frac{40{,}000}{34220} \times 1.06 = 1.24 \text{ in}^2.$

For tension steel,

$As_1 = \rho bd = 0.0139 \times 13 \times 16 = 2.89 \text{ in}^2.$

and

$AS_2 = 1.06 \text{ in}^2$ (obtained above)

Therefore $A_s = 2.89 + 1.06 = 3.95 \text{ in}^2.$

Check for ρ:

$$\text{Actual } \rho \text{ (tension steel)} = \frac{3.95}{13 \times 16} \quad (\rho = A_s/bd)$$

$$= 0.0189$$

$$\text{and } \rho' \text{ (compresion steel)} = \frac{1.06}{13 \times 16} \quad (\rho' = A_s'/bd)$$

$$= 0.0046$$

Therefore, $(\rho - \rho') = 0.0139$

$$\text{Maximum allowable } \rho = \frac{0.85\ \beta_1 f_c' d'}{f_y \cdot d} \cdot \frac{87000}{87000 - f_y}$$

$$= \frac{0.85 \times 0.85 \times 3000 \times 2.5}{40000 \times 16} \cdot \frac{87000}{87000 - 40000}$$

$$= 0.0156 > 0.0139. \quad \text{Therefore OK.}$$

This checks that f_y = 40000 psi is not exceeded.

• PROBLEM 18-32

A simply supported beam spanning 22' is 8" wide and 20" deep (d = 18"). If it is to carry a load of 2000#/ft, design #3 U stirrups. Assume f_c' = 2500 psi, f_s = 20,000 psi and f_y = 40,000 psi. Design using (i) Ultimate Design Method) (ii) Working Stress Method.

Assume that half of the load is live load.

Solution:

(1) Ultimate Design Method:

$$U = 1.4(1000^{\#/ft}) + 1.7\ (1000^{\#/ft}) \text{ (Dead load = live load)}$$

$$= 3100\ \#\cdot ft.$$

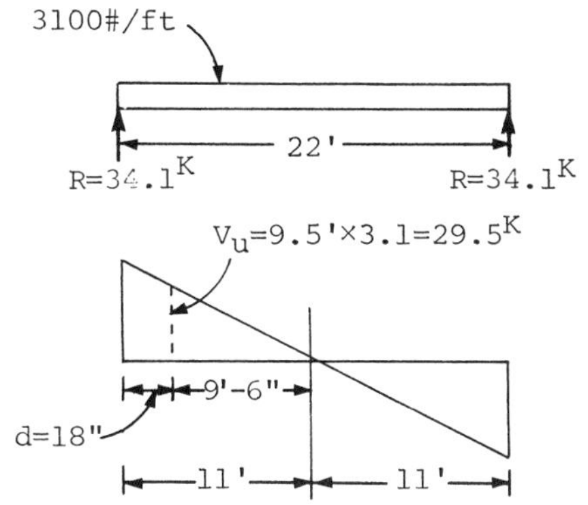

Fig. 1

Going out a distance d = 18" from support,

$$V_u = 9.5 \text{ ft} \times 3.1^{k/ft} = 29.5^k$$

Therefore shear stress $v_u = \dfrac{V_u}{\phi bd} = \dfrac{29500^{\#}}{0.85 \times 8'' \times 18''} = 241 \text{ lbs/in}^2$

But maximum allowable shear $v_c = 2\sqrt{f'_c} = 2\sqrt{2500} = 100 \text{ lbs/in}^2$ (ACI 11.3.1.1)

Therefore, extra shear = 241 - 100 = $141^{\#/in^2}$

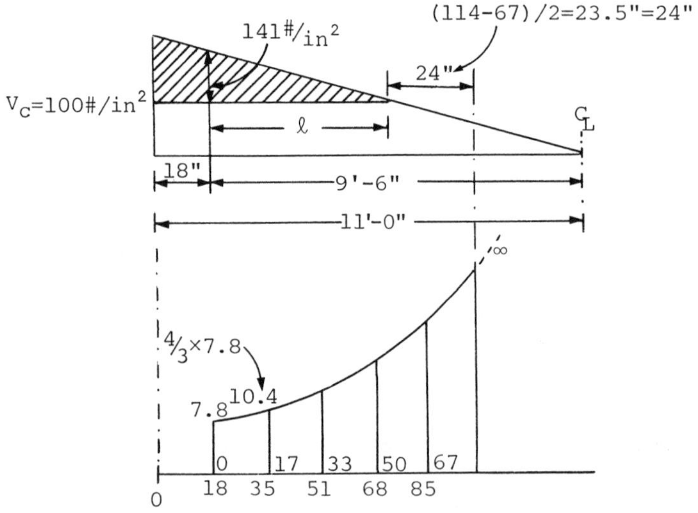

Fig. 2

Theoretical length $l = \dfrac{141}{241} \times 114'' = 67''$

Total length = 67" + 18"(left end) + 24" (right end)

= 109".

As per ACI 11.5.6.2, $A_v \cdot f_y = (v_u - v_c)bs$

or $S_1 = \dfrac{A_v \cdot f_y}{(v_u - v_c)b} = \dfrac{2 \times 0.11 \times 40{,}000}{141 \times 8} = 7.8''$ (two bars area)

And maximum spacing S = d/2 = 18/2 = 9".

Based on the curve obtained, spacing of stirrups #3U are 1 @ 3, 4 @ 7, 10 @ 9 on each side.

(ii) Working Stress Method:

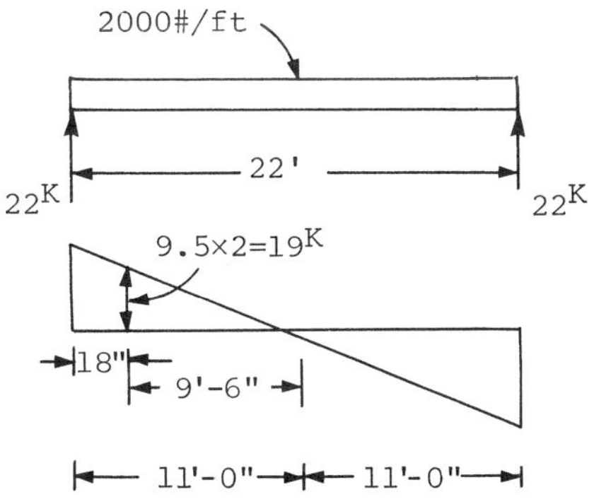

Fig. 3

We have, shear stress $v = \frac{V}{bd}$

$$V = 2^{k/ft} \times 9'\text{-}6'' = 2 \times 9.5 = 19 \text{ kips} = 19000 \text{ lbs.}$$

Therefore, $v = \frac{19000}{8'' \times 18''} = 132 \text{ lbs/in}^2$.

Using 55% of $2\sqrt{f'_c}$ (ACI 8.10.3), we have

$$= 2\sqrt{2500} \times 0.55 = 55 \text{ lbs/in}^2.$$

Therefore remaining shear $v' = 132 - 55 = 77 \text{ lbs/in}^2$.

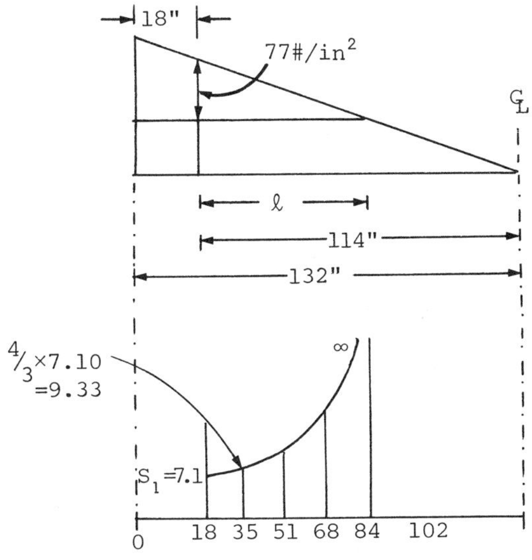

Fig. 4

The theoretical length $l = \frac{77}{132} \times 114'' = 66''$

Therefore, total length = 66" + 18" (left edge) + 24" (right edge)

= 108".

We have $A_v \cdot f_v = v'bS$

Therefore, $S = \frac{A_v \cdot f_v}{v'b} = \frac{2 \times 0.11 \times 20{,}000}{77 \times 8}$

$= 7.1''.$

Maximum spacing $S = d/2 = 18/2 = 9''$.

Based on the curve obtained above, the stirrup's spacings are: #3 U stirrups, 1 @ 3, 4 @ 7, 9 @ 9 and 1 @ 3 on each side.

NOTE: As per ACI 11.5.5.3 (1977), Min $A_v = \frac{50 b_w \cdot S}{f_y}$

$= \frac{50 \times 8'' \times 9''}{40{,}000} = 0.09 \text{ in}^2.$

from which $S = \frac{A_v \cdot f_y}{50\ bw} = 22''$ (having $A_V = 0.22 \text{ in}^2$.)

This means that additional stirrups be used toward the center @ a usual spacing of say 18''.

• PROBLEM 18-33

Determine the positive flexural steel needed in span AB and the negative steel needed at support B for the beam shown in fig. 1. The total factored live and dead load is $1.5^{k/ft}$. $f'_c = 4$ ksi, $f_y = 60$ ksi. Use ACI 318.

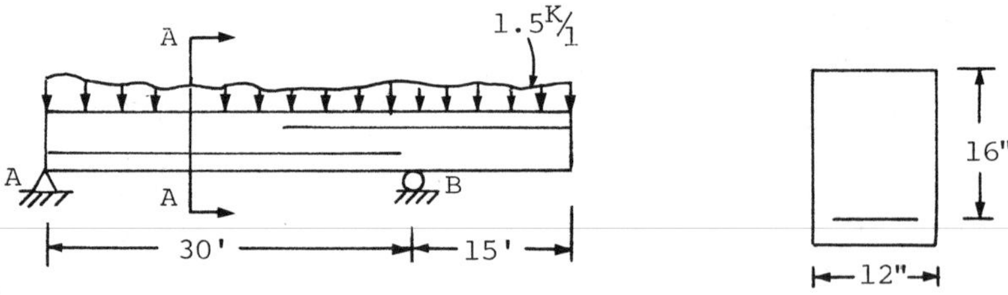

Fig. 1

Solution: The reaction at B is obtained by taking moment about A.

$$R_B = \frac{(1.5)(45)(45/2)}{30} = 50.6^k$$

the reaction at A, then is, $R_A = 1.5(45) - R_B = 16.9^k$

The shear and moment diagrams for beam is as follows: (Refer Fig. 2)

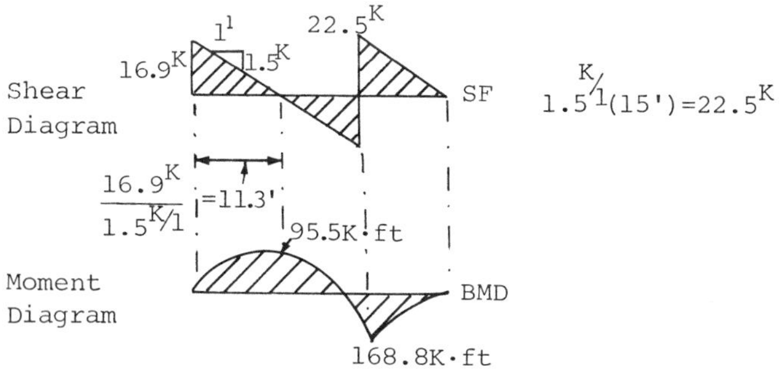

Fig. 2

The maximum positive midspan moment occurs where shear force is zero. From area under shear diagram

$$M_{AB} = \tfrac{1}{2}(16.9^k)(11.3) = 95.5 \text{ k-ft.}$$

The maximum negative moment occurs at support B, and equal to area under shear diagram to right of B

$$M_B = \tfrac{1}{2}(22.5^k)(15) = 168.8 \text{ k-ft}$$

Positive Moment:

the normalized positive moment

$$k = \frac{M_u}{\phi bd^2} = \frac{95.5(12)}{0.9(12)(16)^2} = 0.414 \text{ ksi}$$

From the graph such as on pg. 614 in "Design of Concrete Structure" by Winter and Nilson.

The required steel ratio is

$$\rho_{req'd} = 0.0074$$

Therefore, $A_s = \rho \cdot b \cdot d = 0.0074(12)(16) = 1.42 \text{ in}^2$

Negative Moment:

the normalized negative moment

$$k = \frac{M_u}{\phi bd^2} = \frac{168.8(12)}{(0.9)(12)(16)^2} = 0.732 \text{ ksi}$$

From the same graph

$$\rho = 0.0140$$

$\therefore \quad A_s = \rho \cdot b \cdot d = 0.014(12)(16) = 2.69 \text{ in}^2$

The cross-sectional area of steel required is

A_s for positive moment $= 1.42 \text{ in}^2$

and A_s for negative moment $= 2.69 \text{ in}^2$.

DESIGN OF SLABS BY WORKING STRESS METHOD

• PROBLEM 18-34

Compute the moment carrying capacity of a $4\frac{1}{2}$" slab reinforced with #6 bars @ 8" center to center. Use f'_c = 5000 lbs/in^2 and Grade 40 steel.

Solution: Effective depth d = $4\frac{1}{2}$ - 1" (cover) = $3\frac{1}{2}$"

For f'_c = 5000 lbs/in^2, n = 7, $\rho = \frac{A_s}{bd} = \frac{0.66}{12 \times 3.5} = 0.0157$.

From the design tables and curves for n = 7,

k = 0.376 and j = 0.873 (Refer Fig. 1 at end of this chapter)

Thus, x = kd = 0.376 x 3.5 = 1.32

jd = 0.873 x 3.5 = 3.06

Moment on the concrete side $M_c = \frac{1}{2} f_c b \cdot x \cdot jd$

f_c = 2250 #/in^2

Therefore, $M_c = \frac{1}{2}$ x 2250 x 12" x 1.32 x 3.06 (for a 1' strip, b = 12").

= 54530 #-in

Moment on the steel side $M_s = A_s \cdot f_s \cdot jd$

f_s = 20,000 lbs/in^2

A_s for #6 bar = 0.66 in^2

Therefore, M_s = 0.66 x 20,000 x 3.06

= 40392 lb-in

Thus controlling moment = M_s = 40392 lb-in.

• PROBLEM 18-35

A 6" slab simply supported with effective depth of 5" spans between walls for 11 feet. #4 bars spaced at 5.5" center to center are used for reinforcing the slab. If the stresses in concrete and steel are f'_c = 3 kips and f_s = 24 kips respectively, compute the uniform live load that the slab can carry.

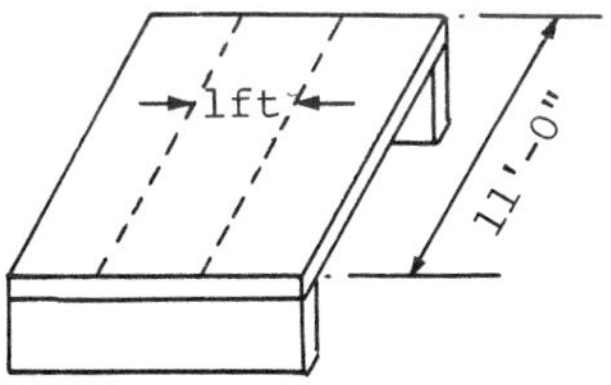

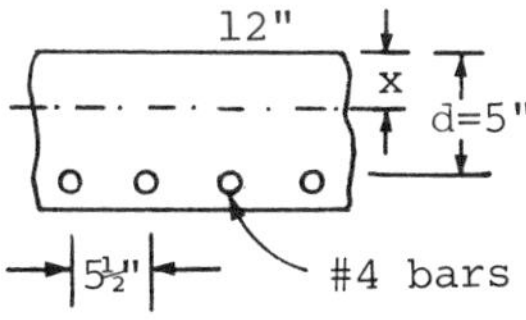

Solution: We have n = 9 (ACI code provisions)(Refer Table V- at end of this chapter)

Considering a 1 foot strip of the slab, we have, no. of bars in each foot,

$$= \frac{12 \text{ in}}{5.5} = 2.182 \text{ bars/foot.}$$

and $A_s = (2.182)(0.20) = 0.436 \text{ in}^2$

$n = 9$

$A = 0.437$

Therefore,

$$12(x)\left(\frac{x}{2}\right) = 9(0.436)(5 - x)$$

Solving, x = 1.51 or - 2.16

Let us use x = 1.51"

lever arm $jd = d - \frac{x}{3} = 5 - \frac{1.51}{3}$

or $jd = 4.497''$

Moment on the steel side,

$M_s = A_s f_s jd$

$= 0.436 \times 24{,}000 \times 4.497$

or $M_s = 47057$ lb-in governs.

Moment on the concrete side,

$M_c = \frac{1}{2} bx\ f_c\ jd$

$= \frac{1}{2}(12)(1.51)(1350)(4.497)$

or $M_c = 55{,}003$ lb-in > f_{all}

$M_c > M_s$ Therefore M_s controls and maximum allowable moment is $= 47057$ lb-in

$= 47057 \times \frac{1}{12}$

or $M = 3921$ lb-ft.

For a simply supported span, we have

$$M = \frac{1}{8} wl^2$$

or $$3921 = \frac{1}{8} w(11)^2$$

or $$w = 259 \text{ lbs/ft.}$$

Therefore, total loading (for one foot strip),

$$w = 259 \text{ lbs/ft}^2$$

The dead load is,

$$= \frac{6}{12} \times \left(150 \text{ lbs/ft}^3\right)$$

$$= 75 \text{ lbs/ft}^2 \text{ (slab weight)}$$

Thus, the live load $= 259 - 75$

$$= 184 \text{ lb/ft}^2$$

• PROBLEM 18-36

Design a simply supported reinforced concrete slab to carry a live load of 200 lbs/ft^2 on a 12 foot span. Allowable stresses in concrete and steel are 5000 psi and 20,000 psi respectively.

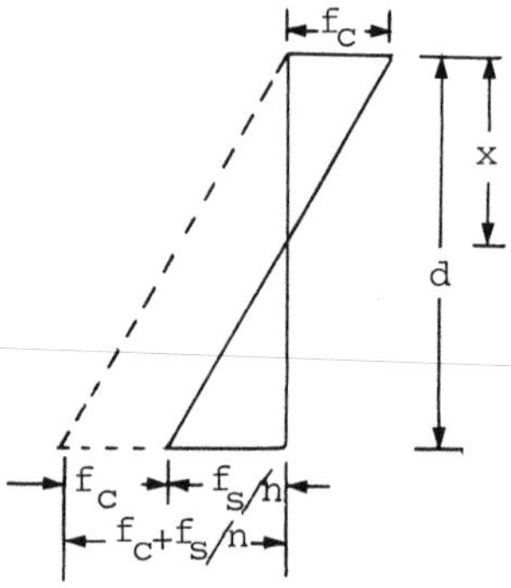

Fig. 1 Stress Diagram

Solution: For a 5000 psi concrete, $f_c = 2250$ psi and $n = 7$ (ACI code. Refer Table V at end of this chapter)

Let us initially, assume a slab thickness of, say, 6".

Dead load due to self weight of slab $= \frac{6}{12} \times \left(150 \text{ unit wt of concrete}\right)$

$= 75 \text{ lb/ft}^2$

NOTE: It is usual to consider 1 ft strip of slabs for design purposes.

Live load on the slab = 200 lb/ft^2 (given)

$\therefore$ Total load = Dead load + Live load = 200 + 75 = 275 lb/ft^2.

The maximum moment for a simply supported end condition is

$$M = \frac{Wl^2}{8}$$

Therefore, $M = \frac{(275 \times 1 \text{ ft}) \times 12^2}{8}$

$= 4950 \text{ lb ft}$

$= 59400 \text{ lb-in.}$

Consider the stress diagram:

By similar triangles,

$$\frac{x}{d} = \frac{f_c}{f_c + f_s/n}$$

Therefore, $x = \frac{f_c \cdot d}{f_c + f_s/n}$

We have $f_c = 2250$ psi, $f_s = 20{,}000$ psi and $n = 7$

Therefore $x = \frac{2250 \cdot d}{2250 + 20000/7}$

Thus, $x = 0.44\ d$

And, the lever arm $jd = d - \frac{x}{3}$

$= d - \frac{0.44\ d}{3}$

Thus, $jd = 0.853\ d$

The moment $M = \frac{1}{2} f_c \cdot bx \cdot jd$

But $M = 59400$ lb-in (found previously)

Therefore, $59400 = \frac{1}{2} \cdot (2250) \cdot (12)(0.44\ d)(0.853\ d)$

$= 5067 \cdot d^2$

$\therefore \quad d = 3.42''$ NOTE: d = effective depth.

Therefore, total depth $= 3.42 + \frac{3''}{4}$ (concrete cover)

$+ \frac{1}{2}$ of a $\frac{1}{2}'' \phi$ bar (ACI code provisions)

$= 3.42 + \frac{3''}{4} + \frac{1''}{4}$

$= 4.42''$ say $4\frac{1}{2}''$

Therefore, actual dead load $= \frac{4\frac{1}{2}''}{12''} \times 150 \simeq 56 \text{ lb/ft}^2$

$\therefore$ Total load $= 200 + 56 = 256 \text{ lb/ft}^2$

$$M = \frac{Wl^2}{8} = \frac{256 \times 1' \times 12^2 \times 12}{8}$$

$$= 55296 \text{ lb-in}$$

Also, $M = \frac{1}{2} f_c \cdot bx \cdot jd$

i.e. $55296 = \frac{1}{2} \times 2250 \times 12\ (0.44\ d)(0.853\ d)$

$= 5067\ d^2$

Therefore, $d = 3.3''$ say $3\frac{1}{2}''$

Thus, total depth $= 3/3 + \frac{3''}{4} + \frac{1''}{4}$

$= 4.3''$

We have, $M = A_s \cdot f_s \cdot jd$

Therefore $A_s = \frac{M}{f_s(jd)} = \frac{55296}{20{,}000 \times 0.853 \times 3\frac{1}{2}''}$

$= 0.92 \text{ in}^2.$

Let us assume a 6'' spacing*

Thus, $A_s = \frac{0.92}{2/\text{ft}} = 0.46 \text{ in}^2.$

Let us select a #6 bar giving an area of $0.44 \text{ in}^2/\text{bar}$.

Spacing $S = \frac{12'' \times 0.44}{0.92} = 5.74''$

*NOTE: Spacings for slab reinforcement generally (normal) vary between 4'' to 8'' and therefore an assumption of 6'' spacing is reasonable.

Therefore, let us select a spacing of $5\frac{1}{2}$" (<5.74")

Thus, let us select a $4\frac{1}{2}$" thick slab, reinforced with #6 bars at a spacing of $5\frac{1}{2}$" center to center.

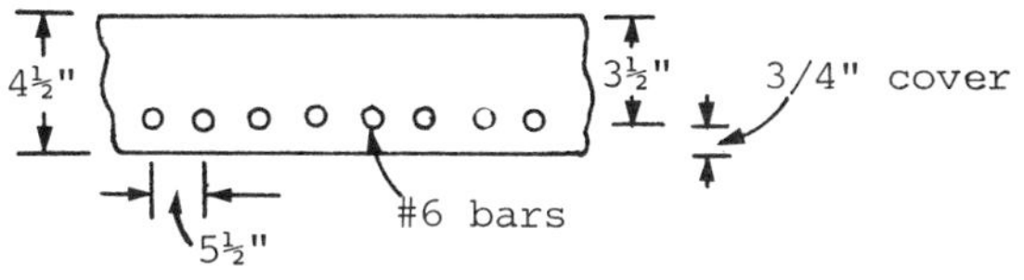

CROSS-SECTION OF THE DESIGNED SLAB SHOWING REINFORCEMENT DETAILS.

Fig. 2

• PROBLEM 18-37

Design a flat slab conforming to ACI code prescribed provisions for the following specifications:

Assume bays to be 20'-0" x 22'-0" and supports provided by 20" square columns with dropped heads (without column capitals). The floor is estimated to carry a live load of 180 #/ft². f'_c = 3000 psi and f_y = 40,000 psi.

Also assume that there are no edge beams and that the column height (floor height) is 12 feet.

Solution:

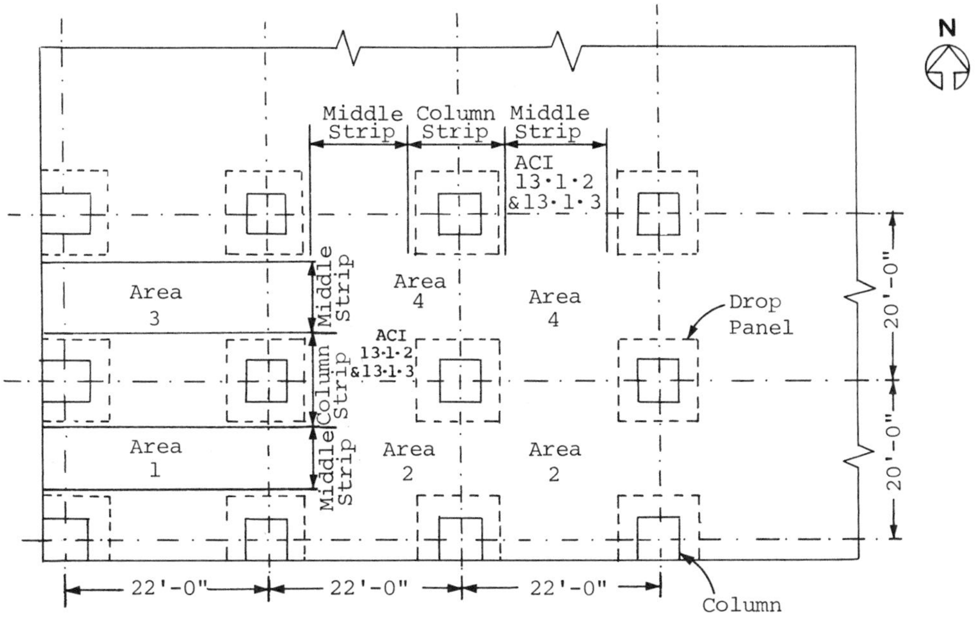

Fig. 1. PLAN OF FLOOR

I SLAB DESIGN

a) Panel ratio: β(clear span ratio): $\frac{\text{Longer span}}{\text{Shorter span}} = \frac{22}{20} = 1.10$

OK since < 2.0 (ACI section 13.6.1.2)

b) Length $l_n = \left(22'\text{-}0'' - \frac{20}{12}\right) = 20.33 \text{ ft} = 244''$.

$$= \frac{244''(800 + 0.005 \times 40{,}000)}{36000 + 5000\left(\frac{20.33}{18.33}\right)(1 + 1.0)}$$

$= 5.2''$.

Article (9.5.3.2) [drop panels] specifies reducing this by 10%, but article (9.5.3.3) [absence of edge beams] specifies addition of extra 10%.

Provide 7" minimum for interior slab.

b) For exterior slab, panel 2, β is $\frac{20.33}{18.33} = 1.11$, but $\beta_s = 0.74$

From equation (9-12),

$$h = \frac{244''(800 + 0.005 \times 40{,}000)}{36000 + 5000(1.11)\left[0 - 0.5(1 - 0.74)\left(1 + \frac{1}{1.11}\right)\right]}$$

$= 7.05''$ ← largest

Using equation (9-11), $h = \frac{244''(800 + 0.005 \times 40{,}000)}{36000 + 5000(1.11)(1 + 0.74)}$

$= 5.34''$.

c) For the corner slab, panel 1, equation (9-10) is again the same and equation (9-11) will change little.

However, using equation (9-10), we have,

β_s is the ratio of continuous edge to total slab perimeter

For interior panel (area 4 on fig. 1), $\beta_s = 1.0$

For panel 2, $\beta_s = \frac{62.0}{84.0} = 0.74$

For panel 3, $\beta_s = \frac{64.0}{84.0} = 0.76$

For panel 1, $\beta_s = \frac{42.0}{84.0} = 0.50$

(i) For drop panel (13.4.7.1), use 1/3 of larger span (each way)

1/3 x 22'-0" = 7'-4" (use square drop panel)

(ii) Minimum slab thickness (9.5.3.1)

a) For interior slabs (type 4), since $1 - \beta_s = 1 - 1.0 = 0$,

and $L_m = 0$ (no beams), equations (9-10) and (9-12) (page 31 ACI code)

are identical.

$$h = \frac{l_n(800 + 0.005\ f_y)}{36000} = \frac{244''(800 + 0.005 \times 40,000)}{36000}$$

$$= 6.77''$$

Using equation (9-11), $h = \dfrac{l_n(800 + 0.005\ f_y)}{36000 + 5000\beta(1 + \beta_s)}$

$$h = \frac{l_n(800 + 0.005\ f_y)}{36000 + 5000\ (L_m - \beta_s)(1 - \beta_s)(1 + 1/\beta)}$$

$$= \frac{244''(800 + 0.005 \times 40,000)}{36000+5000(1.11)(0 - 0.5)(1-0.5)(1 + 1/1.11)}$$

$$= 7.31''.$$

Try $7\frac{1}{2}''$ slab (d = 6" without preference for bars)

II SLAB DESIGN BY MOMENT

a) Check for limitations of (13.6.1) of direct design method. Referring to fig. 1 (13.6.1.1), (13.6.1.2), (13.6.1.3) and (13.6.1.4) are all satisfied. Item (13.6.1.6) does not apply. Check for Item (13.6.1.5): Live load should not exceed 3 times dead load.

We have slab thickness = $7\frac{1}{2}''$

Dead load due to slab = $\dfrac{7\frac{1}{2}''}{12''} \times 150^{\#/ft^3} = 94^{\#/ft^2}$

3 times dead load = $3 \times 94^{\#/ft^2} = 282^{\#/ft^2}$

Live load = $180^{\#/ft^2} < 282^{\#/ft^2}$

Therefore OK

b) Clear span l_n (ACI 13.6.2.5) = $22'\text{-}0'' - \dfrac{20}{12} = 20.33$ ft.

(Lower) limitation is $0.65\ (l_1) = 0.65(22'\text{-}0'') = 14.3$ ft. OK.

(Note: This limitation is critical where capitals are large)

c) Total static design moment (13.6.2.2)

(Note that l_1 is the span considered and l_2 is the span other way)

$$M_o = \frac{w l_2 l_n^2}{8}$$

Neglecting extra weight at the drop panel, we have,

$$U = 1.4 \text{ (Dead load)} + 1.7 \text{ (Live load)}$$

$$= 1.4(94^{\#/ft^2}) + 1.7(180^{\#/ft^2})$$

$$= 132^{\#/ft^2} + 306^{\#/ft^2} = 438^{\#/ft^2} = W$$

Therefore, $M_o = \dfrac{0.438^{k/ft^2}(20)(20.33)^2}{8} = 453$ ft-kips.

d) Distribution of the moment M_O is 65% negative and 35% positive in the interior spans (13.6.3.2).

The constant α_{EC} of equations in (13.6.3.3) is obtained from the notation (13.0) and article (13.7.4.2), equations (13-6), (13-7) and (13-8). For a preliminary design, equations (13-7) and (13-8) can be ignored, making equation (13-6) $\dfrac{1}{K_{EC}} = \dfrac{1}{\Sigma Kc}$

or $K_{EC} = \Sigma K_c$.

For equation (13-8) x is the smaller dimension, y the larger, of a column wide strip of slab

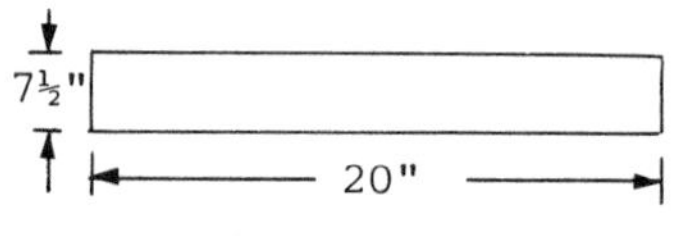

Fig. 2

$$C = \left(1 - 0.63\frac{x}{y}\right)\left(\frac{x^3 y}{3}\right)$$

$$= \left(1 - 0.63\frac{7.5}{20}\right)\left(\frac{7.5^3 \times 20}{3}\right)$$

$$= (1 - 0.236)(2810) = 2147.$$

From equation (13-7), we have

$$K_t = \Sigma \frac{9E_{CS}\cdot C}{l_2\left(1 - \frac{C_2}{l_2}\right)^3} = 2 \text{ sides} \left[\frac{9E_{CS}(2140)}{240''\left(1 - \frac{20''}{240''}\right)^3}\right]$$

$$= 2 \left(\frac{19260\ E_{CS}}{240 \times 0.916^3} \right)$$

$$= 209\ E_{CS}$$

Equation (13-6) uses $K_c = \frac{4\ E_{CC} \cdot I}{L} = \frac{4\ E_{CC}\left(\frac{1}{12}\right)(20'')(20'')^3}{12' \times 12''}$

$$= 370\ E_{CC}.$$

Assuming that concrete is of same grade throughout,

$$\frac{1}{K_{EC}} = \frac{1}{\Sigma K_c} + \frac{1}{K_t} = \frac{1}{2(370)E_C} + \frac{1}{209\ E_C}$$

$$= \frac{1}{163.0\ E_C}$$

Using the consideration of item a of (13.7.3) of the ACI commentary, let us take only the slab for 20'-0" wide and 7½" thick.

Then $K_s = \frac{4\ E_C I_C}{l_1} = \frac{4\ E_C\left(\frac{1}{12}(240)(7\frac{1}{2})^3\right)}{264''} = 128\ E_C.$

and $\alpha_{EC} = \frac{K_{EC}}{\Sigma K_s} = \frac{163.6\ E_C}{128\ E_C} = 1.28$

For interior negative design moment, $0.75 - \frac{0.10}{1 + \frac{1}{\alpha_{EC}}}$

$$= 0.75 - \frac{0.10}{1 + \frac{1}{1.28}} = 0.694$$

For positive design moment, $0.63 - \frac{0.28}{1 + \frac{1}{\alpha_{EC}}}$

$$= 0.63 - \frac{0.28}{1 + \frac{1}{1.28}} = 0.473$$

For exterior negative design moment, $\frac{0.65}{1 + \frac{1}{\alpha_{EC}}}$

$$= \frac{0.65}{1 + \frac{1}{1.28}} = 0.365$$

e) Since the slab design is governed by the positive moment in the end span and the column strip takes 60% of this (Table of Article 13.6.4) and also noting that since there are no beams, $\alpha_1 \frac{l_2}{l_1} = 0$,

we have, the moment across a column strip ($\frac{1}{2}$ of 20' = 10' wide) to be

$$M = 0.473(M_o)(60\%) = 0.473(448^{1k})(0.60)$$

$$= 1.27^{1k} \text{ per foot width (10' strip)}$$

Using the design tables for beams, for f'_c = 3000 psi, f_y = 40,000 psi, for ρ = 0.0139, (12" beam), we obtain d = 6" for a moment of 16.05^{1k}. Thus, the slab depth checks by moment. (Refer Table VI at end of this chapter).

III NEGATIVE MOMENTS (and drop panel)

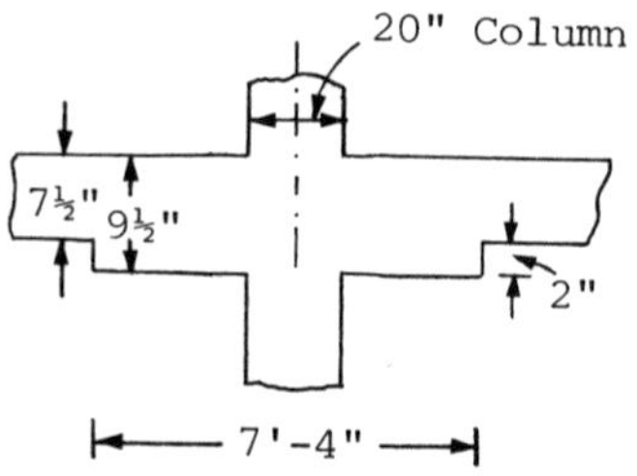

Fig. 3

a) ACI (9.5.3.2) suggests that the projection below the slab be at least $\frac{h}{4}$. We have $\frac{7.5}{4}$ = 1.88" say 2" so that total depth = 7½" + 2" = 9½" (Refer fig. 3)

For maximum negative moment, M = 0.694 M_o (Refer sec. IId above).

Since there are no beams $\alpha_1 \; l_2/l_1 = 0$ and so 75% of the moment is taken by the column strip (Table in 13.6.4.1 of ACI)

Therefore, M = 75% x 0.694 M_o

= 0.75 x 0.694 x 448

= 233 kips-ft. or 23.3 kips-ft per foot

But this is for a 10' strip of which only 7'-4" has d = 8" (exercising no preference for bars).

Thus average depth = $\frac{(8'' \times 7.33) + (6'' \times 2.67)}{10'}$ = 7.46" for 23.3 kips-ft per foot.

Referring to the ultimate design tables (Tables VI at end of this chapter) for a 3000 psi concrete and grade 40 steel, for $\rho = 0.0139$, for d = 7.5", M is obtained to be 25.07^{1k} and by interpolation for d = 7.46", M = 24.81^{1k} > our obtained value of 23.3^{1k}

Our design is therefore satisfactory.

b) We have exterior negative moment = $0.365\ M_o$

Since there are no edge beams $\alpha_1 \frac{l_2}{l_1} = 0$, $\beta_t = 0$

Therefore 100% of the exterior moment goes to the column strip.

(Note that the middle strip still has minimum reinforcing steel - 105.3 and 7.12)

Thus, M = 100% x 0.365 x $448^{1k} = 164^{1k}$.

c) Moment for span "the other way":

Note that l_1 is the direction being considered with l_2 the other span distance.

Thus for moments in the North-South direction (Refer fig. 1)

$$\text{we have } M_o = \frac{w l_2 l_n^2}{8}$$

$$= \frac{438^{\#/ft^2}(22')(20 - 20/12)^2}{8} = 405 \text{ ft-kips.}$$

Again, let us use 65% and 35% for interior slab distributions to middle and column strips. The coefficients obtained previously are close enough for exterior panels.

Average depth through panel is

$$d = \frac{(8" \times 7.33') + (6" \times 3.67')}{11'\text{-}0"} = 7.3".$$

IV. SHEAR:

a) Just beyond the column:

Refer sections (15.5.1),(15.4.2(a),(11.11.1.2),(11.11.2)

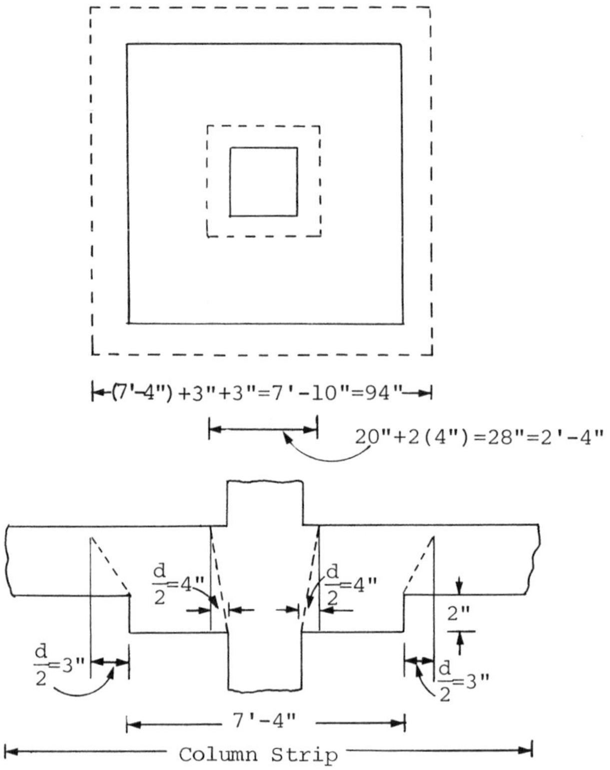

Fig. 4

We have shear stress $v_u = \dfrac{V_u}{\phi b_o d}$

where V_u = shear force $= \left[22' \times 20' - (2.33)^2\right] \times 438^{\#/ft^2}$

$= 190.3^k$.

Add 2" for drop panel

Load due to drop panel $= \dfrac{2''}{12''} \times 150^{\#/ft^3}$

$= 25^{\#/ft^2}$

Thus V_u due to drop panel $= 25^{\#/ft^2}\left[(7.33)^2 - (2.33)^2\right] \times 1.4$

$= 1.7^k$.

Thus total $V_u = 190.3^k + 1.7^k = 192^k$.

Thus shear stress $v_u = \dfrac{192000^{\#}}{0.85 \times (4 \times 28'') \times 8''}$

$(\phi = 0.85,\ b_o = \text{perimeter} = 4 \times 28)$

$v_u = 252^{\#/in^2}$.

Allowable v_c (ACI sec. 11.11.2) $= 4\sqrt{f'_c} = 4\sqrt{3000} = 220^{\#/in^2}$.

But if stirrups are provided, allowable $v_c = 6\sqrt{f'_c}$

$$= 6\sqrt{3000} = 330^{\#/in^2}.$$

Two alternates are possible:

(i) Increase the depth of the drop panel.

$$d \simeq \frac{V_u}{\phi v_u b_o}$$

Limiting v_u to the allowable $220^{\#/in^2}$, we have,

$$d \simeq \frac{192,000 \times 107.5\%}{0.85 \times 220 \times 28 \times 4} = 9.9'' \text{ say } 9''.$$

But using d = 9" gives $v_u = 230^{\#/in^2} >$ allowable $220^{\#/in^2}$.

Let us try d = 9½".

$$v_u = \frac{206,400}{0.85\left[4(20 + 2(4\ 3/4))\right](9\tfrac{1}{2})} = 215^{\#/in^2} < 220^{\#/in^2}$$

Therefore OK.

(NOTE: Most designers prefer to consider the shear of $\frac{1.15wl_n}{2}$ of section (8.3.3) for the end bay. The average two spans = $\frac{100\% + 115\%}{2} = 107.5\%$).

Thus, one possibility is to deepen the drop panel to a total depth of 9½" + 1½" = 11".

(ii) The second alternative is to provide stirrups. (ACI 11.11.4). ACI Article (11.11.3) indicates that where stirrups are used v_c (carried by the concrete) be considered only by $2\sqrt{f'_c}$ in computation of stirrups as per ACI 11.11.3.4.

From equation (11-17) we have $A_v = \left(\frac{v_u - v_c}{f_y}\right) b_w \cdot S$ or

$$S = \frac{A_v \cdot f_v}{(v_u - v_c)b}$$

Stirrups are generally of 6 to 12 legs. Choosing 10 legged stirrups, we have $A_v = 1.96\ in^2$, so that

$$S = \frac{(1.96)(40,000)}{(252 - 110)(112)} = 4.9''$$

But maximum spacing as per (ACI 11.5.4.1) is S = 0.5d

$$= 0.5(8) = 4.0''$$

So, provide a spacing of 10 leg #4 stirrups 1 @ 2 @ 4 at each side from the column.

Going out a distance of 2" + 4" + 4" + 4" (4" = $\frac{d}{2}$).
from the column on each side, b_o (periphery) =

(14" + 20" + 14") x 4 sides

= 192".

$$\text{Thus } v_u = \frac{V_u}{\phi b_o d} = \frac{206,400}{0.85 \times 192 \times 8''} = 158^{\#/in^2} < 220^{\#/in^2}.$$

Therefore OK.

b) Just beyond the drop panel: (Refer fig. 4)

$$V_u = \left[(22' \times 20') - (7' - 10'')^2\right] 438^{\#/ft^2}$$

$$= 166,000 \text{ lbs}$$

Perimeter b_o = 4(7' - 10") = 376".

d = 7½" - 1½" = 6".

$$v_u = \frac{V_u}{\phi b_o d} = \frac{166,000}{0.85 \times 376 \times 6} = 87^{\#/in^2} < 220^{\#/in^2}.$$

Therefore OK.

V REINFORCING:

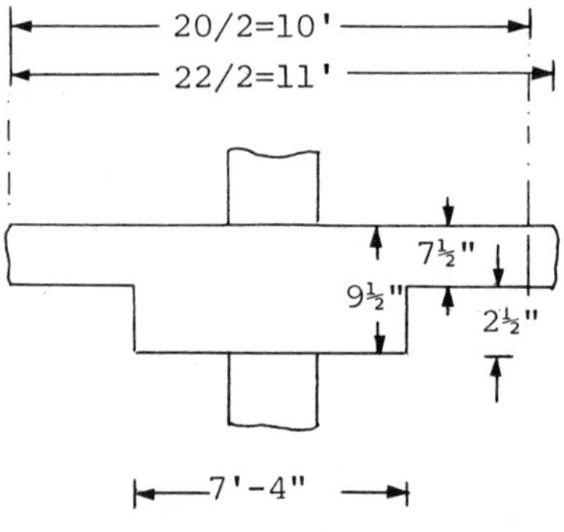

Fig. 5

a) Reinforcing details are shown in the following table.
Steel must be placed roughly 6" apart (Maximum spacing as per (13.4.2) is 2 times slab thickness = 2 x 7½" = 15").

b) For minimum steel, we have from design tables (10.5.3) and (7.12).

A_s = 0.17/in²/ft wide for 3000# concrete & grade 40 steel.

Along 10' width, 0.0020 x 10' x 12" x 7½" = 1.80 in² (ACI 13.4.2) 2 x 7½" = 15" ←

Along 11'-0" width, 0.0020 x 11'-0" x 12" x $7\frac{1}{2}$" = 1.98 in^2

or (7.6.5 says) 3 x depth = 18".

Then $\frac{132''}{15''/bar}$ = 8.8 bars, or 9 - #4 bars = 1.77 in^2.

But minimum A_s = 1.96^2 = 10 - #4 bars.

c) Using design tables (Table VI at end of this chapter), Interpolating for 'd' between 7" and 7.5", M = 24.81^{1k} and A_s = 1.24 in^2 for 7.46" d.

Similarly, M = 25.07 - $\frac{0.22}{0.50}$ (25.07 - 21.84) = 23.65^{1k} and

A_s = 1.21 in^2 for d = 7.28". These are for values which are not exceeded here as taken from ρ = 0.0139 column.

From the same table for 6", M = 16.05^{1k}, for A_s = 1.00 in^2.

where ρ = 0.0139.

(NOTE: Where moments are considerably less, ρ = 0.0094 and ρ = 0.0050 tables may be used. The errors if any are small and on the conservative side).

Thus, for:

Long way through slab, $A_s = M_u^{1k} \times \frac{1.00 \text{ in}^2}{16.05^{1k}} = 0.0623\ M_u$

$$\left(\frac{0.68 \text{ in}^2}{11.29} = 0.0602 \text{ if } M_u < 112.9^{1k}\right).$$

Short way through slab, $A_s = 0.0623\ M_u$ also

or 0.0602 if $M_u < 11' \times 11.29^{1k} = 124.2^{1k}$

Long way through drop panel, $A_s = M_u^{1k} \times \frac{1.24 \text{ in}^2}{24.06^{1k}} = 0.0515\ M_u$

Short way through drop panel, $A_s = M_u^{1k} \times \frac{1.21 \text{ in}^2}{23.65} = 0.0512\ M_u$

Preferred number of bars:

Long way, $\frac{10'\text{-}0'' \text{ width}}{6''/bar}$ = 20 bars.

Minimum number = $\frac{120''}{15''/bar}$ = 8 bars.

Short way, $\frac{11'\text{-}0'' \text{ width}}{6''/bar}$ = 22 bars.

Minimum number $= \frac{132''}{15''/\text{bar}} = 8.8$ or 9 bars.

d) To determine whether the positive bending moments are to be modified according to (13.6.10), then,

$$\beta_a = \frac{\text{dead load}}{\text{live load}} = \frac{94}{180} = 0.522 < 2$$

$$\frac{l_2}{l_1} = \frac{20'}{22'} = 0.91 \qquad \alpha = 0 \text{ (no beams)}$$

From table 13.3.6.1 of ACI, $\alpha_{min} = 1.55$

Checking, $\alpha_C \left[\text{sec } 13.3.6.1(a)\right]$ then,

$$\frac{\Sigma K_c}{\Sigma(K_s + K_t)} = \frac{2(370)E_C}{2(4)\left[\frac{1/12(246)(7.5)}{22' \times 12''}\right] E_C} = 2.90$$

Since $\alpha_C > 1.55$ no correction need be made as per 13.6.10.

V(f) Length of bars:

Bar details are illustrated in ACI fig. 13.5.8 for both straight or bent bars.

V(g) "Half-column" strips at wall:

The column strips at the edges of the floor may have reinforcement proportional to interior column strips, but this would be increased to provide for wall or window loads if applicable.

DESIGN OF T-BEAMS BY WORKING STRESS METHOD

• PROBLEM 18-38

Determine the maximum moment that the following T beam can carry. 3000 lb/in^2 concrete (n = 9) and intermediate grade steel f_s = 20000 lb/in^2 are used.

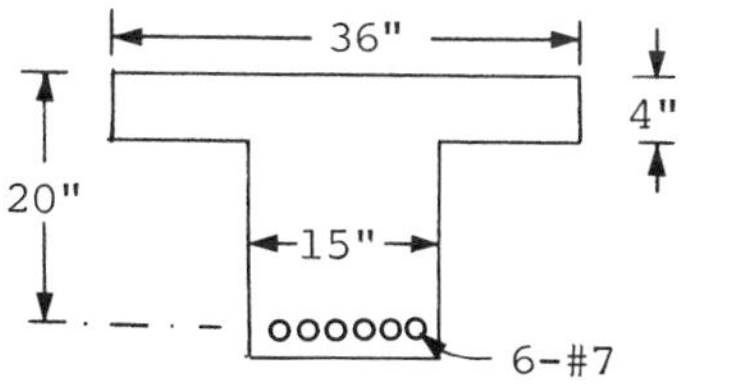

Fig. 1

Solution: Referring to figure, we have

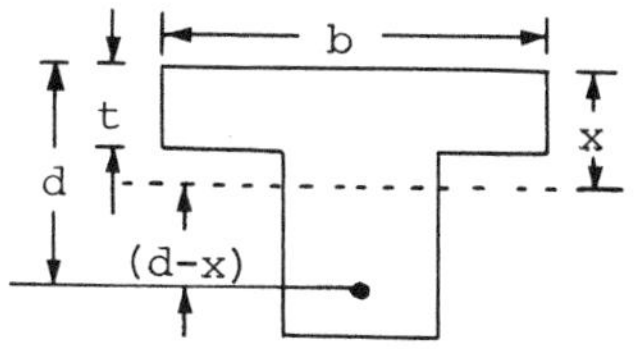

Fig. 2

$$bt(x - t/2) = nA_s(d - x) \qquad (1)$$

where $b = 36''$, $t = 4''$, $n = 9$, $A_s = 3.60$, $d = 20''$

Substituting these values in equation (1), we have

$$36 \times 4(x - 4/2) = 9 \times 3.60(20 - x)$$

or $\quad 144(x - 2) = 32.40(20 - x)$

From which,

$$x = 5.30''$$

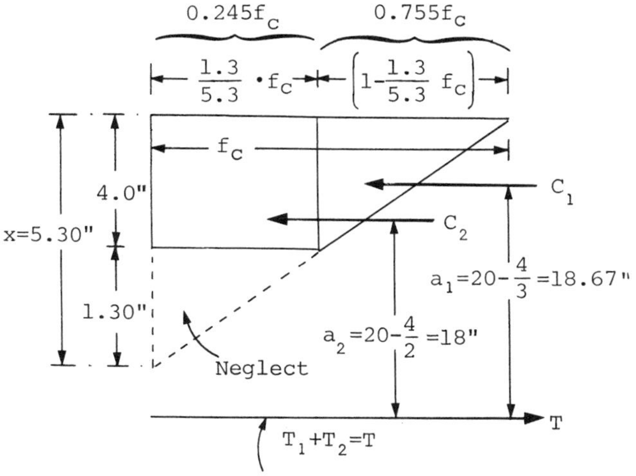

Fig. 3

By taking moments about the steel of the two compressive forces C_1 and C_2, we have

$$(M_1 + M_2) = jd(C_1 + C_2)$$

Note however, that $jd \neq d - \frac{x}{3}$

Thus $$jd = \frac{(M_1 + M_2)}{(C_1 + C_2)}$$

Referring to the figure, we have,

$$M_1 = C_1 \times a_1$$

$$= \frac{1}{2}\left\{(0.755\ f_c)(36)(4)\right\} \times (18.67)$$

$$C_1 = \tfrac{1}{2}(0.755 f_c)(36)(4)$$

$$M_1 = 54.36\ f_c \times 18.67$$

$$= 1015\ f_c$$

$$M_2 = C_2 \times a_2$$

$$= \left\{(0.245\ f_c)(36)(4)\right\} \times (18.0)$$

where $C_2 = (0.245\ f_c)(36)(4)$

$$M_2 = 35.28\ f_c \times 18.0$$

$$= 635\ f_c$$

$$C_1 + C_2 = 54.36\ f_c + 35.28\ f_c = 89.64\ f_c.$$

$$M_1 + M_2 = 1015\ f_c + 635\ f_c = 1650\ f_c.$$

$\therefore$ Lever arm $$jd = \frac{(M_1 + M_2)}{(C_1 + C_2)}$$

$$= \frac{1650\ f_c}{89.64\ f_c} = 18.40''$$

We have,

Maximum moment on the steel side

$$M_s = A_s \cdot f_s \cdot jd$$

where, $A_s = 3.60\ \text{in}^2$, $f_s = 20{,}000\ \text{lbs/in}^2$, $jd = 18.40''$

Therefore $M_s = 3.60 \times 20{,}000 \times 18.40$

$= 1{,}324{,}800$ lb-in.

$= 110{,}400$ lb-ft

Maximum moment on the concrete side

$$M_c = M_1 + M_2 = 1650\ f_c$$

But f_c for a $3000^{\#}$ concrete is 1350 lb/in^2 (ACI code provision, Table V at end of this chapter)

Thus, $M_c = 1650\ f_c = 1650 \times 1350 = 2{,}227{,}500$ lb-in.

$= 185{,}625$ lb-ft

But $M_s < M_c$

Therefore steel governs and maximum moment the section can carry $= M = M_s = 110{,}400$ lb-ft.

• PROBLEM 18-39

Determine the maximum moment that the T beam (shown) can carry if the allowable stresses in concrete and steel are $f'_c = 3000$ lbs/in^2 ($f_c = 1350$ lbs/in^2) and $f_s = 20{,}000$ lbs/in^2.

NOTE: The width of the T-beam is obtained as per the provisions set out by ACI code sec. 8.7.2.

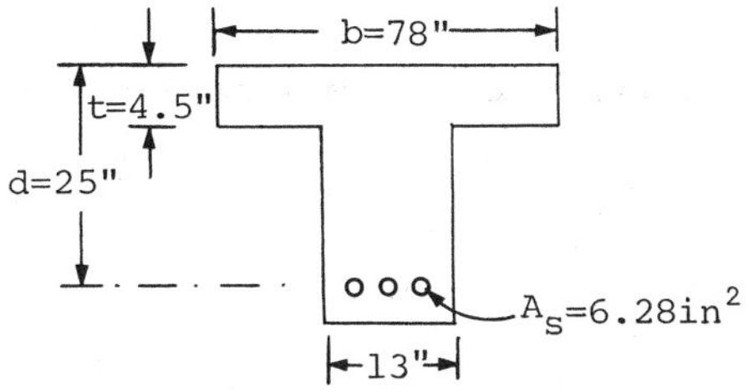

Solution:

We have $\rho = \dfrac{A_s}{bd} = \dfrac{6.28}{78 \times 25} = 0.00322$

$n = 9$

Thus $\rho n = 0.00322 \times 9 = 0.029$

Ratio of thickness to depth $\dfrac{t}{d} = \dfrac{4.5}{25} = 0.18$

Let us find out the values of k and j corresponding to $\rho n = 0.029$ and $\dfrac{t}{d} = 0.18$.

Referring to the curves with t/d on x - axis and ρn on the y-axis with curves plotted giving the corresponding values for k and j, we have, for $t/d = 0.18$ and $\rho n = 0.029$, the value of $k = 0.215$ and $j = 0.930$.

Therefore, $kd = 0.215 \times 25 = 5.4''$

and $jd = 0.930 \times 25 = 23.3''$

Moment M is given by

$$M = A_s \cdot f_s \cdot jd$$

$$= 6.28 \times 20,000 \times 23.3 = 2926480 \text{ lb-in}$$

$$= 243.8 \text{ kip-ft.}$$

However, we will have to check for stress in concrete and if it is greater than $f_c = 1350 \text{ lbs/in}^2$.

Referring to the equation on the sheet of curves, we have

$$f_c = \frac{f_s \cdot k}{n(1 - k)}$$

$$= \frac{20,000 \times (0.215)}{9(1 - 0.215)}$$

$$= 609 \text{ lbs/in}^2 < 1350 \text{ lbs/in}^2$$

Therefore, the section is safe.

• PROBLEM 18-40

A T-beam consists of a $4\frac{1}{2}''$ thick slab with a floor beam projection of $13'' \times 24''$ (effective depth $d = 25''$) and is reinforced with 8 - #8 bars of steel. The beam spans for a length of 26 feet. The beams are spaced 13 feet apart center to center. Using $f'_c = 3000$ psi (concrete) and $f_s = 20,000$ psi (steel), compute the allowable moment the section can carry.

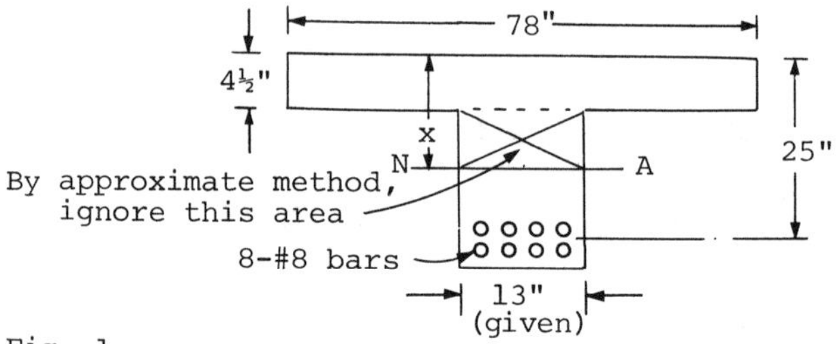

Fig. 1

Solution: The width of 'b' is the minimum of the following: (Refer ACI code sec. 8.10.2)

1) 1/4 span = $\frac{26'}{4}$ = 6'6" = 78"

2) Twice of $8t + w_b = (8 \times 4.5) + 13'' = 85''$
(where W_b = web width)

3) Center to center distance of webs = 13' = 156"

Therefore select b = 78" which is the minimum of the three criteria.

By taking moments about neutral axis, we have,

$$78(4.5)(x - 2.25) = 9 \times (6.32)(25 - x)$$

where $A_s = 8 \times 0.79 = 6.32 \text{ in}^2$.

Thus $351x - 789 = 1420 - 56.8x$

or $351x + 56.8x = 1420 + 789$

or $407.8x = 2209$

Thus $x = 5.41''$.

Taking moments about the steel, we have

$$M = M_1 + M_2 = C_1 a_1 + C_2 a_2$$

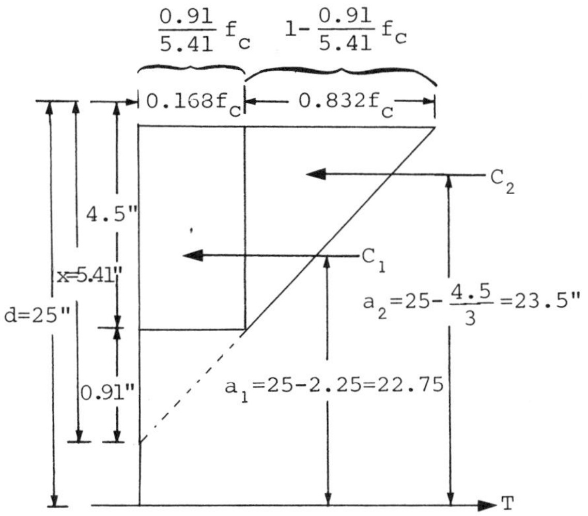

Fig. 2

If the stress distribution is as shown, then the proportions of f_c for the rectangular and triangular parts are $\frac{0.91}{5.41} f_c$ and $\left(1 - \frac{0.91}{5.41} f_c\right)$ respectively.

Therefore, $M_1 = C_1 \times a_1$, where

$$C_1 = 0.168 f_c(78'')(4\tfrac{1}{2}'') = 59 f_c$$

and $a_1 = 22.75$

Thus $M_1 = 59\ f_c \times 22.75 = 1341\ f_c$.

$M_2 = C_2 \times a_2$

where $C_2 = \frac{1}{2}(0.832\ f_c)(78'')(4\frac{1}{2}'')$

$= 146\ f_c$

and $a_2 = 23.5''$

Thus $M_2 = 146\ f_c \times 23.5 = 3434\ f_c$.

$$jd = \frac{M}{C} = \frac{M_1 + M_2}{C_1 + C_2}$$

$$M_1 + M_2 = 1341\ f_c + 3434\ f_c = 4775\ f_c$$

$$C_1 + C_2 = 59.0\ f_c + 146\ f_c = 205\ f_c$$

Therefore, $jd = \dfrac{4775\ f_c}{205\ f_c} = 23.3''$.

Moment on the concrete side $= 4775\ f_c$

$$M_c = 4775 \times 1350\ \text{lb/in}^2 = 6480000\ \text{lb-in}.$$

Moment on the steel side $= M_s = A_s f_s jd$

$= 6.32(20,000\ )(23.3) = 2,950,000$ lb-in

$M_s < M_c$

Thus, steel governs

and the moment $= 2,950,000$ lb-in $= \dfrac{2950}{12} =$ k-ft

$= 246$ k-ft.

• PROBLEM 18-41

Determine the flexural reinforcement required for the T-beam shown in fig. 1, if the ultimate factored moment on the section is 900 k-ft. Assume $f'_c = 4000$ psi and f_y (steel) $= 60,000$ psi.

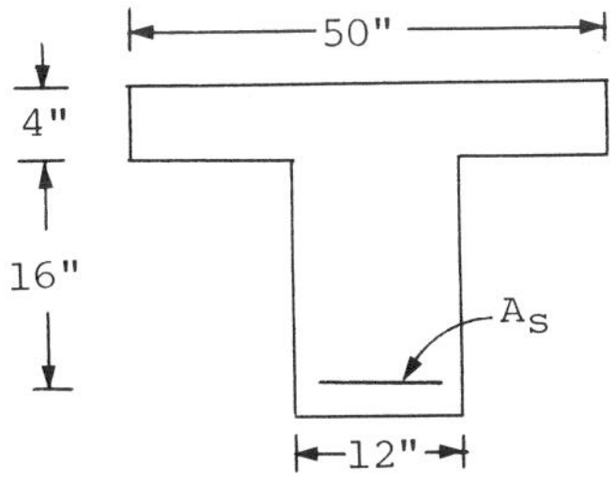

Fig. 1

Solution: Let us assume that the Whitney's Stress Block (WSB) lies within the flange of the T-beam ($a < 4''$). The given T-beam can then be analysed as a rectangular beam with depth $d = 20''$ and width $b = 50''$.

Thus, the normalized moment is

$$K = \frac{M_u}{\phi bd^2} = \frac{900 \times 12}{0.9(50'')(20'')^2} = 0.6 \text{ ksi}.$$

From fig. 2 (graph), the value of ρ corresponding to $K = 0.600$ is $\rho = 0.0111$.

Thus, $A_s = \rho \cdot bd$

$$= 0.0111 \times 50'' \times 20'' = 11.1 \text{ in}^2.$$

Check to see if $a < 4''$ as assumed:

We have $A_s \cdot f_y = 0.85 \, f'_c \cdot b \cdot a$.

$$\text{or} \qquad a = \frac{A_s \cdot f_y}{0.85 \, f'_c \cdot b} = \frac{11.1 \times 60^{\text{ksi}}}{0.85 \times 4^{\text{ksi}} \times 50''}$$

$$= 3.91'' < 4'' \text{ as assumed}$$

Therefore OK.

Thus, the required steel reinforcement for the given section is $A_s = 11.1 \text{ in}^2$.

• PROBLEM 18-42

Compute the moment capacity of the shown reinforced T beam according to ACI. Yield strength of the steel reinforcement $f_y = 60$ ksi and its area $A_s = 5 \text{ in}^2$. Use concrete with $f'_c = 4$ ksi.

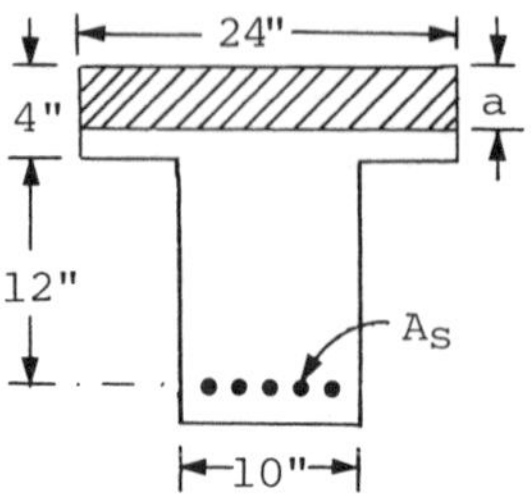

Solution: The given T beam can be analysed as a rectangular beam with b = 24" and d = 16".

If the Whitney's Stress Block falls within its flange, that is, "a", depth of Whitney's, then block should be less than '4' - the thickness of the given flange.

Let us assume a < 4:

Then, $A_s f_y = 0.85\ f'_c \cdot a \cdot b$

or $$a = \frac{A_s f_y}{0.85\ f'_c b} = \frac{5.0 \times 60}{0.85 \times 4 \times 24} = 3.67\text{in} < 4\text{in}$$

as assumed.

Hence the T-beam can be analysed as a 24" x 16" rectangular beam.

Bending moment capacity, $M_o = \phi A_s f_y (d - a/2)$

where ϕ is the bending moment capacity reduction factor and is equal to 0.9 (ACI).

Thus, $M_o = 0.9 \times 5.0 \times 60(16 - \frac{3.67}{2})$

$= 3825$ in-kips.

• PROBLEM 18-43

Determine the moment carrying capacity of the T-beam shown in fig. 1. $f'_c = 4$ ksi, $f_y = 60$ ksi and $A_s = 5.8$ sq. in. Use relevant ACI provisions.

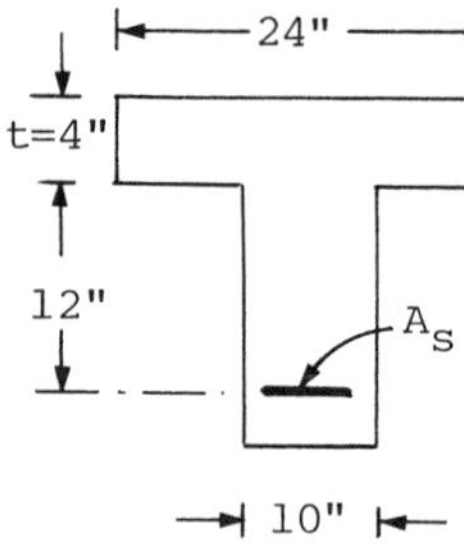

Fig. 1

Solution: Assume that the depth of Whitney Stress Block (a) is less than 4" (flange thickness)

We have $A_s f_y = 0.85\, f'_c \cdot a \cdot b$

or $$a = \frac{A_s f_y}{0.85\, f'_c b} = \frac{5.8(60)}{0.85(4)(24)} = 4.26''$$

Since a > 4", a "T-beam" analysis is required.

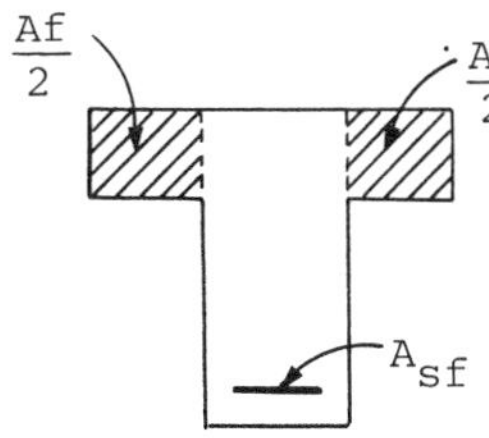

Fig. 2

Determine moment M_1 due to concrete in overhanging portion of flange.

A_f is overhanging flange area
(Refer fig. 2)

$A_f = 4''(24'' - 10'') = 56$ sq. in.

If the flexural steel needed to balance A_f is A_{sf}, then,

$$A_{sf} \cdot f_y = 0.85\, f'_c \cdot A_f$$

or $$A_{sf} = \frac{0.85\, f'_c A_f}{f_y} = \frac{0.85(4\text{ ksi})(56\text{ sq. in.})}{60\text{ ksi}}$$

$$= 3.17\text{ sq. in.}$$

The moment M_1 due to A_{sf} is now

$$M_1 = \phi A_{sf} \cdot f_y (d - t/2) \qquad (\therefore\ \phi = 0.9)$$

$$= 0.9(3.17\text{ sq. in.})(60\text{ ksi})(16 - 4/2) = 2397\text{ k-in.}$$

The remaining steel $(A_s - A_{sf})$ balances the concrete stress in the web. The depth of the Whitney Stress Block for the web is given by

$$a = \frac{(A_s - A_{sf})\, f_y}{0.85\, f'_c \cdot b_w}$$

where b_w is the web width = 10 in.

or

$$a = \frac{(5.8 - 3.17)(60\text{ ksi})}{0.85(4\text{ ksi})(10)} = 4.64\text{ in.}$$

The moment M_2 due to $(A_s - A_{sf})$ is then

$$M_2 = \phi(A_s - A_{sf})f_y(d - a/2)$$

$$= 0.9(5.8 - 3.17)(60)(16 - 4.64/2)$$

$$= 1942 \text{ k-in.}$$

Thus, the total moment carrying capacity of the beam is

$$M = M_1 + M_2 = 2397 + 1942 = 4339 \text{ k-in.}$$

• **PROBLEM 18-44**

Determine the allowable spacing of #3 (f_y = 40,000 psi) stirrups required for the supports of the reinforced concrete beam loaded as shown in fig. Assume f'_c = 4000 psi. Use relevant ACI provisions.

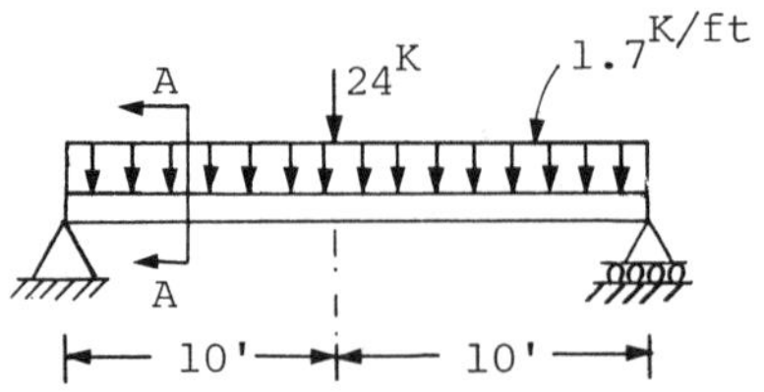

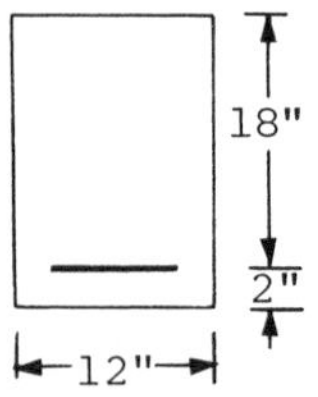

Solution: We have U = 1.7 (live load) + 1.4 (dead load)

$$= 1.7(24^k + 1.7^{k/ft} \times 20') +$$

$$1.4\left(\frac{12''}{12} \times \frac{20''}{12} \times 0.15^{k/ft} \times 20'\right)$$

$$= 98.6^k + 5.0^k = 103.6^k$$

Thus maximum shear at support $= \dfrac{103.6^k}{2} = 51.8^k$.

But, as per ACI, maximum shear occurs at a distance'd' from support (sec. 11.1.3.1).

$$\text{Thus, } V_u = 51.8^k - \left\{\left(\frac{12''}{12''} \times \frac{20''}{12''} \times 0.150^{k/ft^3}\right)(1.4) + (1.7^{k/ft})(1.7)\right\}\left(\frac{18''}{12''}\right)$$

$$= 46.9^k.$$

Amount of shear carried by concrete $V_c = 2\sqrt{f'_c}\, b_w \cdot d$.

(Refer ACI sec. 11.3.1.1).

Thus, $V_c = 2\sqrt{4000} \cdot 12 \times 18 = 27322$ lbs

$$= 27.3^k$$

Thus, remaining shear to be carried by stirrups

$$V_s = \frac{V_u}{\phi} - V_c \qquad \text{(ACI sec. 11.1.1)}$$

$$= \frac{46.9^k}{0.9} - 27.3^k = 28^k$$

(ϕ = capacity reduction factor = 0.85, generally)

$$\text{Spacing } S = \frac{A_v \cdot f_y \cdot d}{V_s} \qquad \text{(ACI sec. 11.5.5·2)}$$

where A_v = area of #3 stirrups = $2(0.11 \text{ in}^2) = 0.22 \text{ in}^2$.

f_y = 40,000 psi = 40 ksi

$$\text{Therefore} \quad S = \frac{0.22 \times 40^{\text{ksi}} \times 18''}{28^k} = 5.65 \text{ in.}$$

$$\text{Also,} \quad S = \frac{A_v \cdot f_y}{50\ b_w} \qquad \text{(ACI sec. 11.5.5.3)}$$

$$= \frac{0.22 \times 40{,}000 \text{ psi}}{50 \times 12''} = 14.66 \text{ in}^2.$$

However, as per ACI 11.5.4.1, S is not to exceed $d/2 = 18/2 = 9''$.

Thus, choosing the smaller of all the 'S' obtained above, we have S = 5.65 in (smallest), say 5 in.

• PROBLEM 18-45

Design a T-beam for the following specifications: slab thickness = $4\frac{1}{2}''$; effective depth = 25" The designed section is to carry a moment of 240 ft-kips. Stresses in concrete and steel (f'_c and f_s) are not to exceed 3000 lb/in² and 20,000 lb/in² respectively.

Solution: For a 3000 lb/in² concrete, f_c = 1350 lb/in² (ACI code provision)

and n = 9. (Table V at end of this chapter)

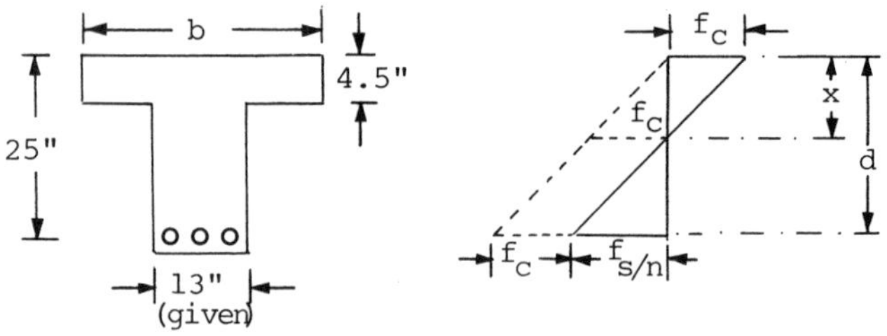

Fig. 1

Referring to the stress diagram and by similar triangles, we have,

$$\frac{x}{d} = \frac{f_c}{f_c + f_s/n}$$

or $$x = \frac{f_c \cdot d}{f_c + f_s/n}$$

where $f_c = 1350^{\#}/\text{in}^2$ (ACI code) (Table V at end of this chapter)

$f_s = 20{,}000^{\#}/\text{in}^2$ (given)

and $n = 9$ (ACI code)

Thus, $$x = \frac{1350 \cdot d}{1350 + 20{,}000/9} = 0.378\ d$$

But $d = 25''$ (given)

Therefore, $x = 0.378 \times 25 = 9.45''$.

Note again that $jd \neq d - \frac{x}{3}$.

$$jd = \frac{(M_1 + M_2)}{(C_1 + C_2)}$$

where C_1 and C_2 are the compressive forces (Refer fig.)

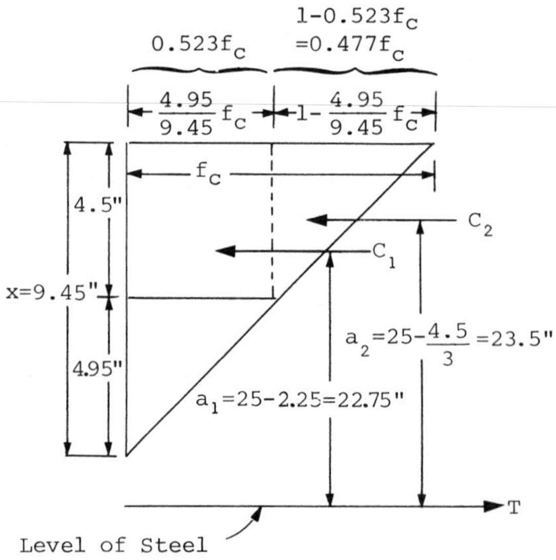

Fig. 2

We have,

$$M_1 = C_1 \times a_1$$

where $C_1 = (0.523\ f_c)(4.5)(b) = 2.35\ f_cb.$

and $a_1 = 22.75''$

Thus, $M_1 = (0.523\ f_c)(4.5)(b)(22.75)$

$= 53.5\ f_cb$

$$M_2 = C_2 \times a_2$$

where $C_2 = \frac{1}{2}(0.477\ f_c)(4.5)(b) = 1.07\ f_cb.$

and $a_2 = 23.5''$

Thus $M_2 = \frac{1}{2}(0.477\ f_c)(4.5)(b) \times 23.5 = 25.2\ f_cb.$

Therefore, $(C_1 + C_2) = 2.35\ f_cb + 1.07\ f_cb$

$= 3.42\ f_cb$

and $(M_1 + M_2) = 53.5\ f_cb + 25.2\ f_cb$

$= 78.7\ f_cb.$

Therefore $jd = \dfrac{(M_1 + M_2)}{(C_1 + C_2)} = \dfrac{78.7\ f_cb}{3.42\ f_cb} = 23.0''$

And, moment on the concrete side,

$$M_c = M_1 + M_2 = 78.7\ f_cb$$

But $f_c = 1350\ lb/in^2$ (for a $3000^{\#}$ concrete, ACI code)

Thus $M_c = 78.7 \times 1350\ b$

But the maximum moment the section can carry = 240 k-ft = $240 \times 10^3 \times 12$ lb-in (given)

Therefore, $240 \times 1000 \times 12 = 78.7 \times 1350\ b$

or $b = 27.10''$.

Also, moment on the steel side,

$M_s = A_sf_sjd$, where $f_s = 20{,}000\ lb/in^2$, $jd = 23''$

But the maximum moment the section can carry = 240 k-ft = $240 \times 10^3 \times 12$ in-lb

Thus $240 \times 10^3 \times 12 = A_s \times 20{,}000 \times 23$

or $A_s = 6.26\ in^2.$

Let us select 8 - #8 bars giving a total area of 6.28 in^2. However, the steel will have to be arranged in 2 rows of 4 bars each. Alternately, we can select 4 - #11 bars giving an area of 6.29 in^2. which can then be arranged in one row.

Thus, the designed T beam has a width b ≃ 27" and the area of steel required as 6.28 in^2.

• PROBLEM 18-46

Determine the effective width of the concrete flange for T-beam construction if the beam spans for 21 ft. Use relevant ACI code provisions.

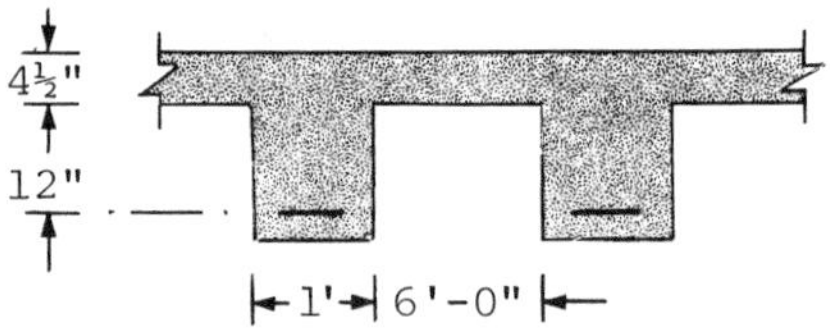

Solution: As per ACI 318-77 sec. 8.10.2, the width of slab effective as a T-beam flange shall not exceed 1/4 of the beam span.

i.e., $b \le (1/4)(21') = 63$ in.

Also, the effective overhang shall neither exceed 8 times the slab thickness nor 1/2 the clear distance on each side of web.

Thus, $b \le 12 + 2 \times 8 \times 4\frac{1}{2} = 84$ in.

or $b \le 12 + 2(\frac{1}{2} \times 6 \times 12) = 84$ in.

Using the least value of b, effective width = 63 in.

• PROBLEM 18-47

Determine the effective width of the concrete flange for T-beam constrcution shown in fig. The beam spans for 25 ft. Use relevant ACI code provisions. (ACI 318-77)

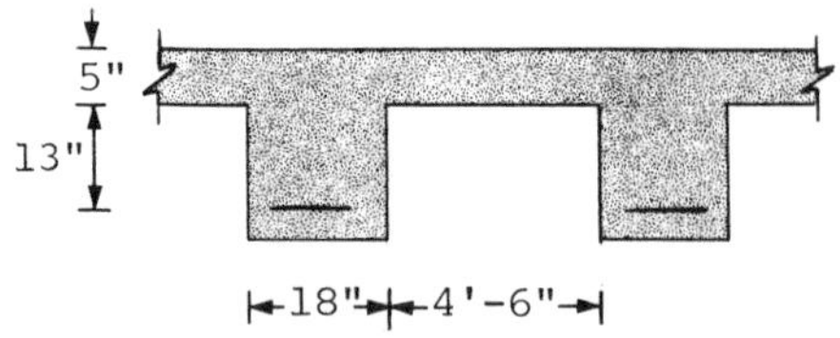

Solution: As per ACI 318 sec. 8.10.2, the effective width of the slab shall not exceed 1/4 of beam span.

That is, $b \leq 1/4(25') = 75$ in.

The effective overhang shall not exceed 8 times slab thickness nor ½ clear span between webs.

$$b \leq 18'' + 2\ (8 \times 5'') = 98''$$

$$b \leq 18'' + 2(4' - 6''/2) = 72'' \leftarrow$$

Choosing the minimum b,

The clear span between web governs and effective width = 72''.

• PROBLEM 18-48

A T-beam has an effective depth d = 18'' and thickness of slab t = 4''. Determine the amount of steel required (A_s) and the width (b) if the section is to carry a moment (M) of 100,000 lb-ft. The allowable stresses in concrete and steel are f'_c = 3000 lb/in² and f_s = 20,000 lb/in² respectively.

Solution:

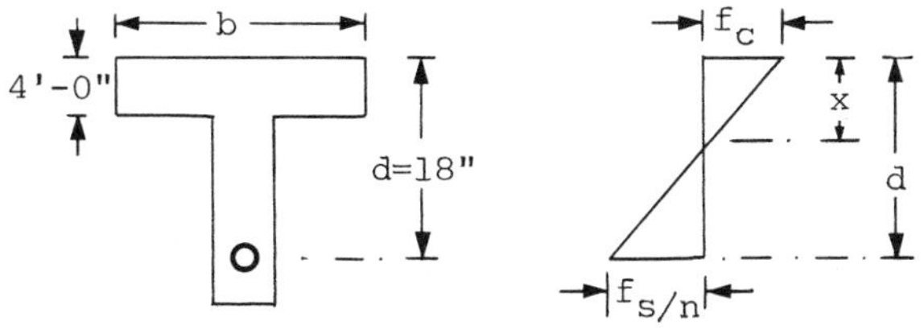

Fig. 1

Referring to the stress diagram, by similar triangles, we have,

$$\frac{x}{d} = \frac{f_c}{f_c + f_s/n} \quad \text{or} \quad x = \frac{f_c \cdot d}{f_c + f_s/n}$$

But $f_c = 1350$ lb/in², n = 9 (ACI code. Refer Table V at end of this chapter)

and $f_s = 20{,}000$ lb/in².

$$\text{Thus} \quad x = \frac{1350 \cdot d}{1350 + \dfrac{20{,}000}{9}}$$

and $\quad d = 18''$

$$\text{Therefore,} \quad x = \frac{1350 \times 18}{1350 + \frac{20,000}{9}} = 6.81''$$

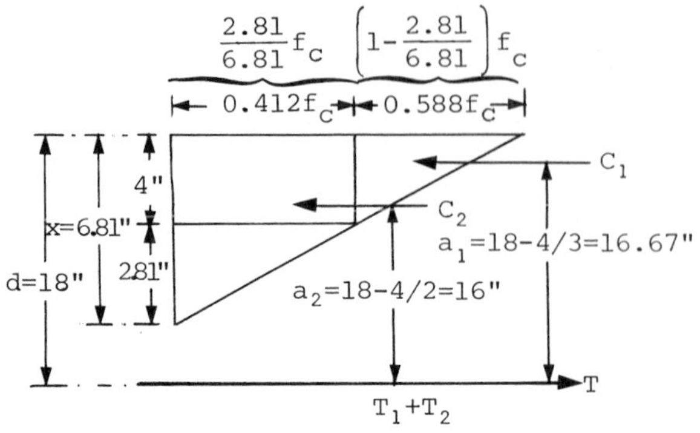

Fig. 2

We have,

$$M_1 = C_1 \times a_1$$

where $C_1 = \frac{1}{2}(0.588\ f_c)(b)(4) = 1.176\ f_c b$

and $a_1 = 16.67''$

Thus, $M_1 = 1.176\ f_c b \times 16.67 = 19.60\ f_c b$

$M_2 = C_2 \times a_2$

where $C_2 = (0.412\ f_c)(b)(4) = 1.648\ f_c b$

and $a_2 = 16''$

Thus, $M_2 = 1.648\ f_c b \times 16 = 26.35\ f_c b$

$C_1 + C_2 = 1.176\ f_c b + 1.648\ f_c b = 2.824\ f_c b$

$M_1 + M_2 = 19.60\ f_c b + 26.35\ f_c b = 45.95\ f_c b.$

$$\text{Thus,}\ jd = \frac{M_1 + M_2}{C_1 + C_2} = \frac{45.95\ f_c b}{2.824\ f_c b} = 16.26''$$

Moment on the concrete side

$$M_c = 45.95\ f_c b$$
$$= 45.95 \times 1350\ (b)$$

But the maximum moment, the section can carry $= 100,000 \times 12$
$= 1,200,000$ lb-in.

Therefore, $1,200,000 = 45.95 \times 1350\ (b)$

or $b = 19.3''$

Moment on the steel side

$$M_s = A_s \cdot f_s \cdot jd$$

But again, the moment carrying capacity of the section is restricted to $M = 100{,}000 \times 12 = 12 \times 10^5$ lb-in.

Thus $1{,}200{,}000 = A_s \times 20{,}000 \times 16.26$

Therefore, $A_s = 3.69 \text{ in}^2$. Let us use 4 - #9 bars giving an area of 4.00 in^2.

The required section is $b \cong 19.3''$ and $A_s = 3.69 \text{ in}^2$

DESIGN OF T-BEAMS BY ULTIMATE DESIGN METHOD

• PROBLEM 18-49

A beam is cast monolithically with a 4" slab and has $d = 18''$ and $b = 15''$. If the beam is to support a moment of 240,000 ft-lbs (1/3 of which is due to dead load). Determine

a) The amount of steel (A_s) required

b) The effective flange width.

Assume that $\rho - \rho_f$ is 1/2 of $0.75\ \rho_b$; $f'_c = 4000$ psi, $f_y = 40000$ psi.

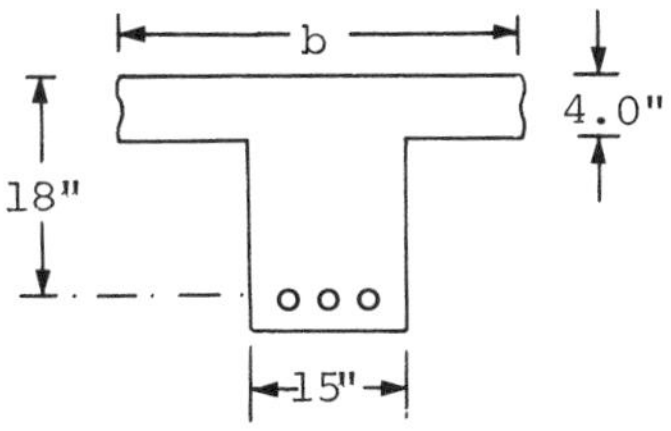

Solution:

$$M_u = \phi(A_s - A_{sf})f_y(d - a/2) \quad \text{(for web portion)}$$

and $$M_u = A_{sf}\ f_y(d - 0.5\ t) \quad \text{(for flange portion)}$$

But M_u for web is also equal to $\phi f'_c b d^2 q\ (1 - 0.59\ q)$

where $q = \rho \cdot \frac{f_y}{f'_c}$ (In this case ρ is equivalent to $\rho - \rho_f$)

$$\rho_b = \frac{\beta_1 \cdot 0.85\ f'_c}{f_y} \cdot \frac{87000}{87000 + f_y}$$

$$= \frac{0.85 \times 0.85 \times 4000}{40000} \cdot \frac{87000}{87000 + 40000}$$

$$= 0.0495$$

and 1/2 of $0.75\rho_b = \frac{1}{2}(0.75 \times 0.0495) = 0.0185 = \rho$

Thus, $q = 0.0185 \times \frac{40,000}{4000} = 0.185$

Therefore, for web, $M_u = \phi f'_c b d^2 q(1 - 0.59\ q)$

$$= 0.90 \times 4000 \times 15 \times 18^2 \times 0.185\ \left(1 - 0.59(0.185)\right)$$

$$= 2883468 \text{ in-lbs}$$

Total M_u provided $= 1.4 \left[\frac{1}{3} \times 240000 \times 12\right] + 1.7 \left[\frac{2}{3} \times 240,000 \times 12\right]$

$$= 4608000 \text{ in-lbs.}$$

The remaining moment accounted for by the flange

$$= 4,608,000 - 2,883,468 = 1,724,532 \text{ lb-in}$$

But M_u for flange $= \phi A_{sf}\ f_y(d - 0.5t)$

Therefore, $\phi A_{sf}\ f_y(d - 0.5t) = 1,724,532$

or $A_{sf} = \frac{1,724,532}{\phi \cdot f_y(d - 0.5t)} = \frac{1,724,532}{0.9 \times 40,000(18 - 0.5 \times 4)}$

$$= 2.99 \text{ in}^2$$

But $A_{sf} = 0.85(b - b')t\ f'_c/f_y$

or $2.99 = 0.85(b - b')4 \cdot (4000/40000)$

Thus $b - b' = \frac{2.99 \times 40000}{0.85 \times 4 \times 4000} = 8.8''$

Total b required $= 15 + 8.8 = 23.8''$

$(A_s - A_{sf}) = (\rho - \rho_f)b'd = 0.0185 \times 15 \times 18 = 4.99\ in^2$

and $A_{sf} = 2.99$ (obtained previously)

Therefore total area of steel $A_s = 7.98\ in^2$

Use 8 - #9 bars giving an area of 8.00 in^2.

NOTE: This design procedure would work only if C exceeds flange thickness. In our case, we have,

$$a = \frac{A_s f_y}{0.85\ f'_c b} = \frac{4.99 \times 40{,}000}{0.85 \times 4000 \times 15} = 3.91''$$

$$\text{and } C = \frac{a}{\beta_1} = \frac{3.91}{0.85} = 4.6'' > 4.0''\ \text{(thickness of flange)}$$

However, if C falls within the flange, the design can be worked out using the rectangular beam theory only.

• PROBLEM 18-50

Determine the flexural reinforcement necessary if the ultimate factored moment on the section shown below is 950 $^{k\text{-}ft}$. Given $f'_c = 4$ ksi, $f_y = 60$ ksi. Apply relevant ACI code provisions.

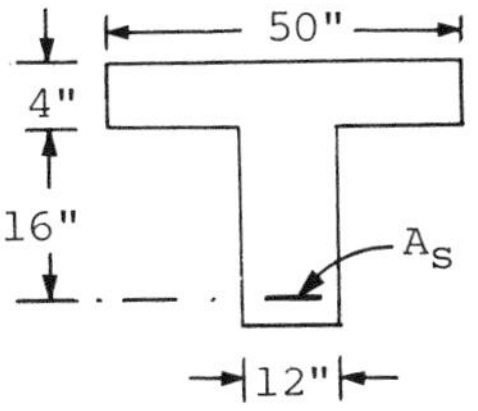

Fig. 1 CROSS-SECTION OF T-BEAM

Solution: Assume Whitney Stress Block lies partly within web, that is, a "T-beam" approach is necessary.

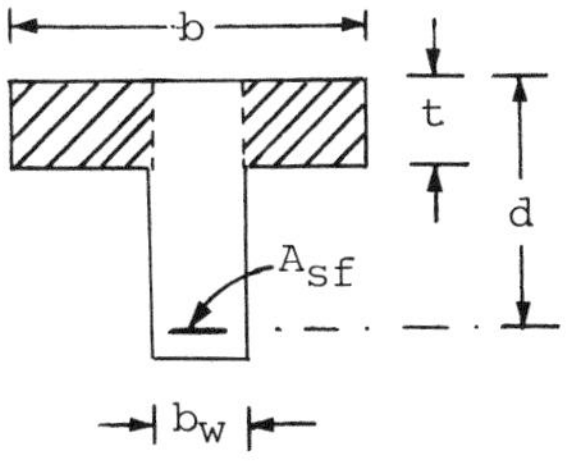

Fig. 2 UNSUPPORTED PORTION OF FLANGE

Moment due to stress in concrete in overhanging portion of flange:

$$A_{sf} \cdot f_y = 0.85\, f'_c \cdot (b - b_w)t$$

$$A_{sf} = \frac{0.85\, f'_c}{f_y}(b - b_w)t$$

$$= \frac{0.85(4)}{60}(50 - 12)(4) = 8.61 \text{ in}^2.$$

Moment M_1

$$M_1 = \phi A_{sf} \cdot f_y (d - t/2)$$

$$= 0.9(8.61)(60)(20 - 4/2) = 8369 \text{ k-in} = 697 \text{ k-ft}.$$

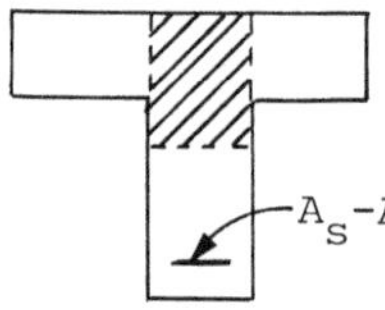

Fig. 3

The remaining moment $950^{k\text{-}ft} - 697^{k\text{-}ft} = 253^{k\text{-}ft}$ is provided by steel area $(A_s - A_{sf})$ acting in conjunction with rectangular beam of width $b_w = 12$ in.

The normalized moment is

$$K = \frac{M_u}{\phi b_w d^2} = \frac{253^{k\text{-}ft}(12''/1)}{0.9(12'')(20'')^2} = 0.702 \text{ ksi}$$

From figure 4 (graph)

the required steel ratio $\rho = \dfrac{A_s - A_{sf}}{b_w d} = 0.0133$

Thus, $A_s - A_{sf} = 0.0133(12)(20) = 3.19 \text{ in}^2$

or $A_s = 3.19 + 8.61 = 11.8 \text{ in}^2$

T-beam analysis approach is checked by calculating the depth of Whitney Stress Block corresponding to $(A_s - A_{sf})$

$$(A_s - A_{sf})f_y = 0.85\, f'_c \cdot b_w \cdot a$$

or $$a = \frac{(A_s - A_{sf})f_y}{0.85\, f'_c \cdot b_w} = \frac{3.19(60)}{0.85(4)(12)} = 4.69'' > 4''$$

Thus, a > 4", therefore, T-beam analysis is appropriate.

A final check is performed to ensure that the balanced steel ratio is not exceeded by the limit of 0.75 (ACI sec. 10.3.3).

$$\rho_{bal} = 0.72 \cdot \frac{f'_c}{f_y} (0.003) \left[\frac{1}{0.003 + f_y/E_s} \right]$$

for $f_y = 60$ ksi, $f'_c = 4$ ksi, $E_s = 29 \times 10^6$ psi, $\rho_{bal} = 0.028$

Thus, $0.75\ \rho_{bal} = 0.021 > 0.0133$ Therefore OK.

Use $A_s = 11.8\ in^2$

DESIGN OF BEAMS AND SLABS USING DESIGN TABLES

• **PROBLEM** 18-51

Determine the amount of steel required for a rectangular reinforced concrete beam carrying a moment of 105 ft-kips with the following specifications:

$b = 13''$, $d = 16''$, $d' = 2.5''$, $f'_c = 3000\ \#/in^2$ and $f_s = 20{,}000\ \#/in^2$.

Solution:

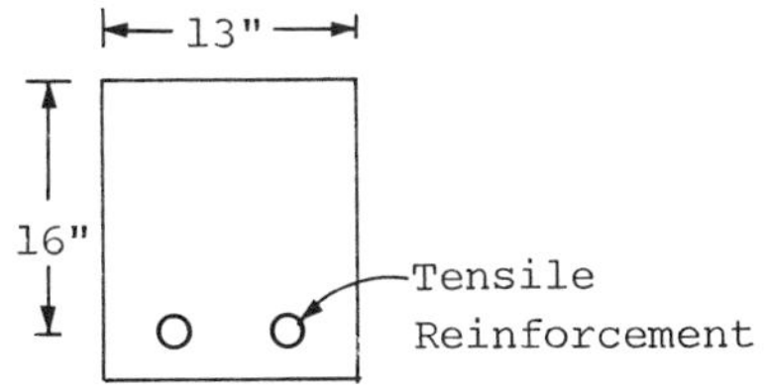

Fig. 1

From the tables, K = 224, k = 0.378, n = 9 and j = 0.874 (Refer Table V at end of this chapter)

Let us first consider the rectangular beam with tensile reinforcement.

$$M_1 = Kbd^2 = 223 \times 13 \times 16 \times 16 = 742144 \text{ lb-in}$$

$$= 61846 \text{ lb-ft.}$$

Therefore $$A_{s_1} = \frac{M_1}{f_s jd} = \frac{742144}{20{,}000 \times (0.874)(16)} = 2.65\ in^2.$$

Moment carried by A_{s_1} = 61846 lb-ft

Total moment carried by beam = 105000 lb-ft

Therefore, remaining moment = 105,000 - 61846

= 43154 lb-ft.

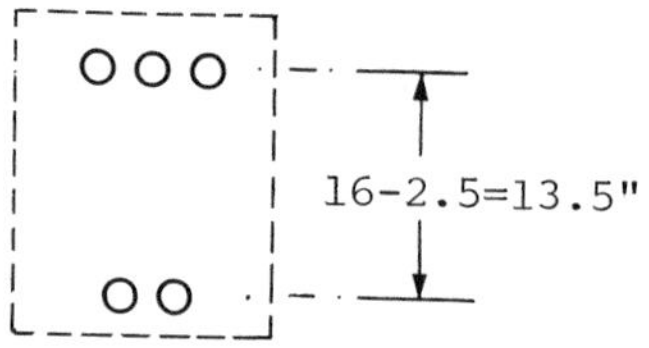

Fig. 2

We have, $C_2 = T_2 = \frac{43154 \times 12}{13.5} = 38360$ lb

Therefore $A_{s_2} = \frac{38360 \text{ lbs}}{20000 \text{ lb/in}^2} = 1.92 \text{ in}^2$.

Therefore total tensile steel required

$= A_{s_1} + A_{s_2} = 2.65 + 1.92 = 4.57 \text{ in}^2$

Compression steel:

$x = kd = 0.378 \times 16 = 6.05''$

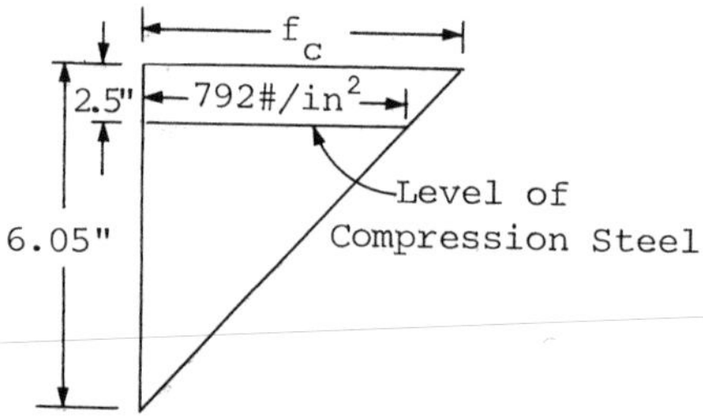

Fig. 3

Stress at level of compression steel $= \frac{3.55}{6.05}(1350) = 792 \text{ \#/in}^2$

Thus $A'_s = \frac{38360\#}{792 \text{ \#/in}^2} \times \frac{1}{\underbrace{(2 \times 9 - 1)}_{(2n - 1)}}$

$= 2.85 \text{ in}^2$.

Check for stress f_s:

We have stress = $2n\ f_{cs} = 2 \times 9 \times 792\ lb/in^2$

$= 14256\ lbs/in^2 < 20{,}000\ lb/in^2$

NOTE: The sizes of steel should be determined.

Therefore, OK.

• PROBLEM 18-52

Design a slab system with multiple rectangular panels of 22'-0" to 20'-0" bays (these distances being measured to the centers of 20" square columns, 12'-0" story heights) and peripheral beams. It is estimated that the floor would eventually carry a live load of 180 $\#/ft^2$. The concrete to be used shall be of 3000# quality and the reinforcing steel that of grade 40 (f_y = 40,000 psi) quality.

Solution:

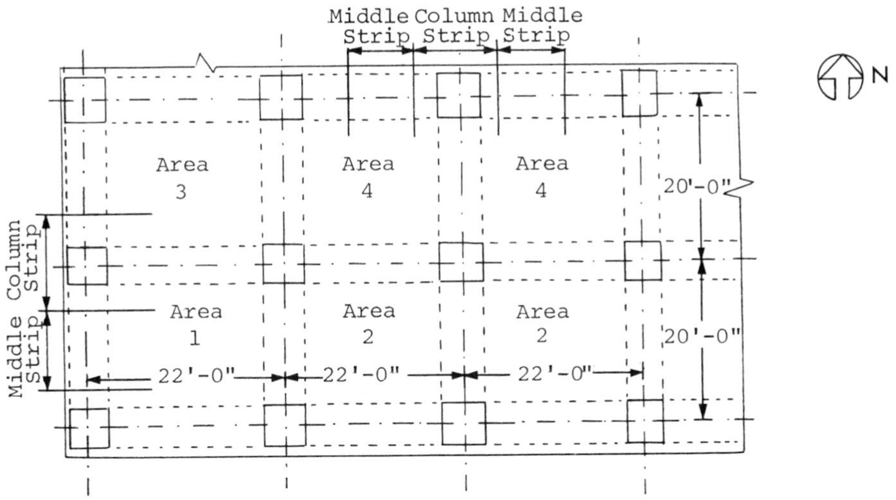

Fig. 1

1 PRELIMINARY DESIGN:

To get at a reasonable beam size, let us assume the slab thickness to be, say 6".

Thus, self weight of slab = $\frac{6''}{12''} \times 150^{\#/ft^3} = 75\ ^{\#/ft^2}$.

Live load = $180^{\#/ft^2}$

But as per ACI section 9.2.1, we have

U = 1.4 (Dead load) + 1.7 (Live load)

$= 1.4\ (75) + 1.7(180)$

$= 411^{\#/ft^2}.$

Width $= 20'$

Therefore, distributed load $= 20' \times 411^{\#/ft^2}$

$= 8220^{\#/ft}.$

Load due to, say, 2 ft^2 of beam $= 2 \times 150^{\#/ft^3}$

$= 300^{\#/ft}.$

Thus, total load w $= 8220^{\#/ft} + 300^{\#/ft}$

$= 8520^{\#/ft}.$

For the 'first interior support', we have,

$$M = \frac{1}{10}\, wl_n^2 = \frac{1}{10}\,(8520)(22' - 1.67')^2$$

$$= 352 \text{ ft-kips}$$

Using the highest permissible percentage of reinforcement, we have $\rho = 0.75\ \rho_b = 0.0278$.

A 12" x 22" beam would be a distinct possibility. Let us, however, try a 16" wide beam so that $M = \frac{12}{16} \times 352 = 264$ ft-kips per ft wide.

From design tables, d corresponding to this (Refer to Table VI at end of this chapter) M is 19" ($M = 282.3^{1k}$)[for $\rho = 0.0139$, $M = 257^{1k}$ and d = 24"]

Let us try using a 16" x (21" + 3") beam (including the slab as shown in fig. 2). Note that normally, design at 0.75 ρ_b is a poor choice and at best is only an approximation which must be checked fully.

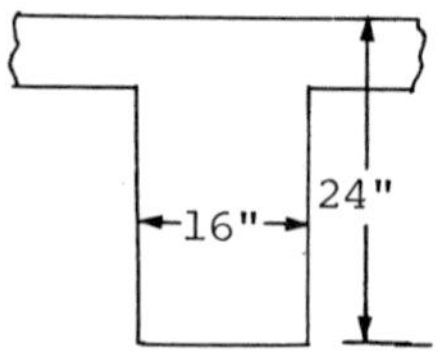

Fig. 2

2. MINIMUM SLAB THICKNESS:

β(ratio of clear long span to short span) $= \frac{20.33}{18.33} = 1.11.$

β_s(edge to perimeter ratio) $= \frac{84}{84} = 1$ at interior bays.

$$\beta_s = \frac{62.0}{84.0} = 0.74 \text{ in panel 2 (area 2)}$$

$$\beta_s = \frac{64}{84} = 0.76 \text{ in area 3}$$

$$\beta_s = \frac{42}{84} = 0.5 \text{ in area 1.}$$

Using equation 9-11 of ACI sec. 9.5.3.1 for minimum slab, $\beta = \frac{20.33' \text{ (clear)}}{18.33' \text{ (clear)}} = 1.11$. For the lowest β_s (corner panel, area 1, $\beta_s = 0.50$)

$$h = \frac{l_n(800 + 0.005\ f_y)}{36{,}000 + 5000\ \beta(1 + \beta_s)} = \frac{244''\ (800 + 0.005(40{,}000))}{36000 + 5000(1.11)(1.5)}$$

$$= 5.52'' \text{ say } 5\tfrac{1}{2}''.$$

However, the thickness need not exceed

$$h = \frac{l_n(800 + 0.005 \times 40{,}000)}{36{,}000} = 6.78''$$

(Refer to equation 9-12)

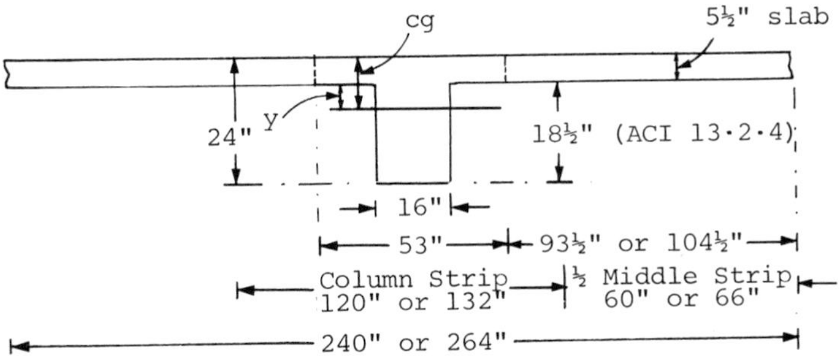

To use equation (9-10) we need α_m (average α).

$$A_s d = \frac{E_{cb} I_b}{E_{cs} I_s} \text{ and using (ACI 13.2.4) and a } 5\tfrac{1}{2} \text{ thick slab,}$$

$$\text{Centroid of the beam} = \frac{(53'' \times 5\tfrac{1}{2}'')(2.75'') + (16'' \times 18.5'')(5\tfrac{1}{2} + 9\tfrac{1}{4}'')}{292 \text{ in}^2 + 296 \text{ in}^2}$$

$$= \frac{5202}{588} = 8.90''$$

Then y in fig. 3 = 8.90" - 5.50" = 3.40"

$$I_b = \frac{1}{3}(16)(15.1)^3 + \frac{1}{3}(16)(3.4)^3 + \frac{1}{12}(53)(5.5)^3$$

$$+ 53 \times 5.5(2.75 + 3.4)^2 = 30332 \text{ in}^4.$$

I_s (both sides) $(5.5)^3/12 \times (240'' - 53'') = 2590 \text{ in}^4$

Two ways $(5.5)^3/12 \times (264'' - 53'') = 2925 \text{ in}^4$

Thus, average $I_s = \dfrac{2590 + 2925}{2} = 2758 \text{ in}^4$.

$$\alpha_m = \frac{E_c I_b}{E_c I_s} = \frac{30332}{2758} = 11 \text{ (Interior)}$$

$$\alpha_m = \frac{30332}{\dfrac{2(2740) + 2(1379)}{4}} = 14.7$$

(at edge, beams have one side of slab so I_s = 1295 or 1463 in^4 for an average of 1379 in^4).

$$M_o = \frac{w l_2 l_n^2}{8}$$

where $l_n = 264'' - 20'' = 244'' = 20.33'$

$l_2 = 240''$ (other way) $= 20'$.

Dead load $= \dfrac{5.5'}{12} \times 150^{\#/ft^3} = 69^{\#/ft^2} \times 20'$ (slab)

$= 1380^{\#/ft}$.

beam, $\dfrac{18\frac{1}{2}'' \times 16''}{12'' \times 12''} \times 150^{\#/ft^3} = 310^{\#/ft}$

Total dead load $= 1380 + 310 = 1690^{\#/ft}$

Live load $= 180^{\#/ft^2} \times 20' = 3600^{\#/ft}$

Thus $U = 1.4(D) + 1.7(L)$

$= 1.4(1690) + 1.7(3600)$

Total $= 8486^{\#/ft}$.

Check with ACI sec. 13.6.1.5.

$3 \times 1690 = 5070^{\#/ft} > 3600^{\#/ft}$

[3(dead load) > live load]

For interior panels, using equation 9-10 (ACI code)

$$h = \frac{l_n(800 + 0.005 f_y)}{36000 + 5000\beta \left[\alpha_m - 0.5(1 - \beta_s)(1 + \frac{1}{\beta})\right]}$$

$$= \frac{244(800 + 200)}{36000 + 5000(1.11) \left[11 - 0.5(1 - 1.0)(1 + \frac{1}{1.11})\right]}$$

$= 2.51'' < 5\frac{1}{2}''$

For corner panels,

$$h = \frac{l_n(800 + 0.005\ f_y)}{36000 + 5000(1.11)\left(14.7 - 0.5(1.0 - 0.5)(1 + \frac{1}{1.11})\right)}$$

$$= \frac{244(800 + 200)}{36000 + 5000(1.11)(14.2)} = 2.12'' < 5\tfrac{1}{2}''$$

Thus $5\frac{1}{2}''$ thick slab seems OK.

III TOTAL STATIC DESIGN MOMENT:

We have U = 1.4 (Dead load) + 1.7(Live load) (ACI 13.6.2.2)

Thus Maximum Moment $M_o = \dfrac{(wl_2)l_n^2}{8}$ (East-West)

$$= \frac{8486 \times (20.33)^2}{8}$$

= 438 ft-kips.

IV DISTRIBUTION:

At interior spans, negative moment = 65% x $438^{1k} = 285^{1k}$

And positive moment = 35% x $438^{1k} = 153^{1k}$.

For exterior spans, we will have to obtain α_{BC}(from K_{EC}, k_t and C).

Starting with equation 13-14 of ACI sec. 13.7.5.2

$$C = \Sigma(1 - 0.63\cdot\frac{x}{y})\ \frac{x^3y}{3}$$

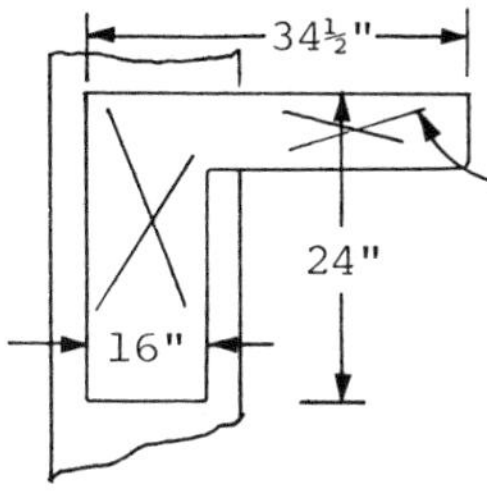

Fig. 4

$$C = \left(1 - 0.63\ \frac{5.5}{18\frac{1}{2}}\right)\left(\frac{\overline{5.5}^3 \times 18.5}{3}\right) + \left(1 - 0.63 \times \frac{16}{24}\right)\left(\frac{16^3(24)}{3}\right)$$

= 19840

$$K_t = \Sigma\frac{9\ E_{CS}C}{l_2\left(1 - \frac{C_2}{l_2}\right)^3}$$

$$= 2\ (\text{sides}) \left[\frac{9\ E_{CS}(19840)}{240''\left(1 - \frac{20''}{240''}\right)^3} \right]$$

$$= \frac{2(178{,}560)E_{CS}}{240(0.770)} = 1930\ E_{CS}$$

For columns, $K_C = \frac{4\ E_{CC} I_s}{l_c} = \frac{4\ E_{CC}(1/12)(20'')(20)^3}{12\ \text{ft col x } 12''/\text{ft}}$

$$= 370\ E_{CC}$$

Then $\frac{1}{K_{EC}} = \frac{1}{\Sigma K_C} + \frac{1}{K_t} = \frac{1}{2(370)E_{CC}} + \frac{1}{1930\ E_{CS}}$

$$= \frac{0.00135 + 0.00052}{\text{Assume same } E_C} = \frac{0.0187}{E_C}$$

$$= \frac{1}{535\ E_C}$$

$$K_{EC} = 535\ E_C.$$

$$\Sigma(K_s + K_b) = 4\ \frac{(I_b + I_s)}{l_1}\ E_C = 4\ \frac{(30332 + 2740)}{264''}\ E_C$$

$$= 4(125.2)E_C = 500\ E_C$$

Then $\alpha_{EC} = \frac{K_{EC}}{\Sigma(K_s + K_b)} = \frac{535\ E_C}{500\ E_C} = 1.07$

Coefficients:
(ACI sec. 13.6.3.3)

For Interior Negative Moment

$$= 0.75 - \frac{0.10}{1 + \frac{1}{1.07}} = 0.698$$

For positive (Exterior Bay Moment) $= 0.63 - \frac{0.28}{1 + \frac{1}{1.07}}$

$$= 0.485$$

For Exterior Negative Moment $= \frac{0.65}{1 + \frac{1}{1.07}}$

$$= 0.335$$

For long way, $\alpha_1 = \frac{E_{cb} I_b}{E_{cs} I_s} = \frac{30332\ E_C}{2590\ E_C}$

$= 11.7$

Other way, $\alpha_1 = \frac{30332}{2925} = 10.3$

(long way) And $\alpha_1 l_2/l_1 = 11.7(20'/22'') = 10.6 > 1.0$

And $\alpha_1 l_2/l_1$ (other way)

$= 10.3(22'/20') = 11.33 > 1.0$

V SLAB CHECK:

Maximum Positive Moment $= 0.485(438^{1k}) = 212^{1k}$

$$\frac{l_2}{l_1} = \frac{20'}{22'} = 0.91$$

Distribution @ column strip $= 75 + \frac{1.0 - 0.91}{1.0 - 0.50}(90 - 75)$

$= 77.7\%$ $(100 - 77.7 = 22.3\%)$

(ACI sec. 13.6.4.1)

Middle Strip Moment $= 0.223 \times 212^{1k} = 47.2^{1k}$

Maximum Negative Moment $= 0.698 \times 438^{1k} = 305^{1k}$.

Distribution @ column strip $= 75 + \frac{1.0 - 0.91}{1.0 - 0.50}(90 - 75)$

$= 77.7\%$ $(100 - 77.7 = 22.3\%)$

Middle strip moment $= 22.3\% \times 305^{1k}$ 68^{1k} – governs.

Since this moment is for a 10 ft strip, M per foot

$= \frac{67.1}{10} = 6.71^{1k/ft}$

Provide effective depth d = 4" (exercising no preference of bars)

From design tables, for $\rho = 0.0139$, $M_u = 7.14^{1k}$

Therefore, design is OK.

VI BEAM CHECK:

Maximum Negative Moment $= 0.698\ M_o$

$= 0.698 \times 438 = 305^{1k}$.

M for column strip = $0.777 \times 305 = 237^{1k}$

Since $\alpha_1 l_2/l_1 > 1.0$ take 85% for beam

$= 0.85 \times 237 = 201^{1k}$ (ACI sec. 13.6.5.1)

On a 12" basis, $M = \frac{12}{16} \times 201'K = 150^{1k}$

From $\rho = 0.0139$ (design tables)

$M_u = 196.6^{1k}$ for d = 21" and $M_u = 160.9^{1k}$ for d = 19"

Since shear may be critical, let us try a total depth of 24" (21" + 3" for 2 rows of bars).

VII REINFORCEMENT:

Coefficients for Exterior Negative Moments depend on

$$\beta_t = \frac{E_{cb}C}{2\ E_{cs}I_s}$$

where $I_s = \frac{1}{12}(264'')(5.5)^3 = 3660\ in^4.$

$$\beta_t = \frac{E_{cb}(20{,}850)}{2\ E_{cs}(3660)} = 2.85 \geq 1.0$$

Thus, the distribution here too is $75\% + \frac{1.0 - 0.91}{1.0 - 0.50}(90 - 75)$

$= 77.7\%$ in column strips.

Note that at column strips, the beams take 85% of the moments.

VIII Check against table 13.6.10

$$\beta_a = \frac{\text{Dead Load}}{\text{Live Load}} = \frac{1690^{\#/ft}}{3600^{\#/ft}} = 0.47$$

α is over 4.0

$$\frac{l_2}{l_1} = \frac{20}{22} = 0.91$$

Minimum α permitted from above data is 0.0 from the table.

(Note: Compare with $\alpha_c = \frac{\Sigma K_c}{\Sigma(K_s + K_b)} = \frac{2(370)E_{\mathcal{C}}}{2(333)E_{\mathcal{C}}} = 1.11$)

IX <u>Shear Check</u>:

a) Slab: (ACI section 13.6.8.4 and 13.6.8.1)

Refer to fig. 5.

For distance 'L', $(10'\text{-}0'') - \left(\frac{16''}{2} + 2''\right) = 9'\text{-}2''$

Area $= (9'\text{-}2'')\left[\frac{(20'\text{-}4'') + (2'\text{-}0'')}{2}\right] = 102.2\ ft^2$.

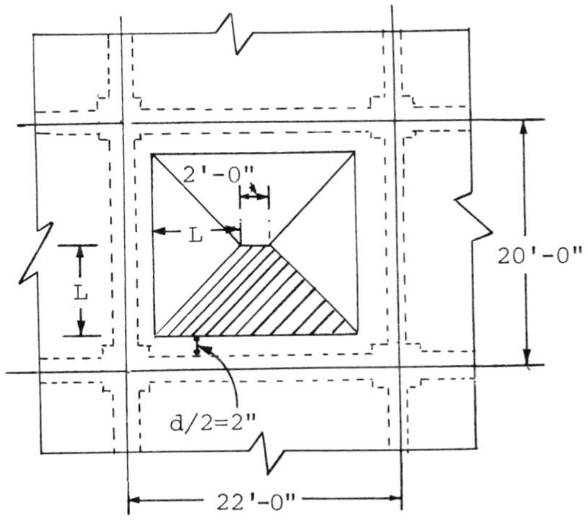

Fig. 5

Live load = 180 x 1.7 = $306^{\#}/ft^2$

Slab = 69 x 1.4 = $96^{\#}/ft^2$

Total load = 306 + 96 = $402^{\#}/ft^2$

$$V_u = 402 \times 102.2 = 41000^{\#}$$

V_u for first interior support = 41000 x 1.15 ≃ $47{,}200^{\#}$
(ACI 8.3.3)

Thus, shear stress $v_u = \frac{V_u}{\phi bd} = \frac{47{,}200}{0.85(20.33)(12'')(4'')}$

$$= 57^{\#}/in^2$$

Allowable is $4\sqrt{f'_c} = 4\sqrt{3000} = 220^{\#}/in^2$

(ACI sec. 11.11.2 - 2 way shear)

Therefore OK.

b) Beam:

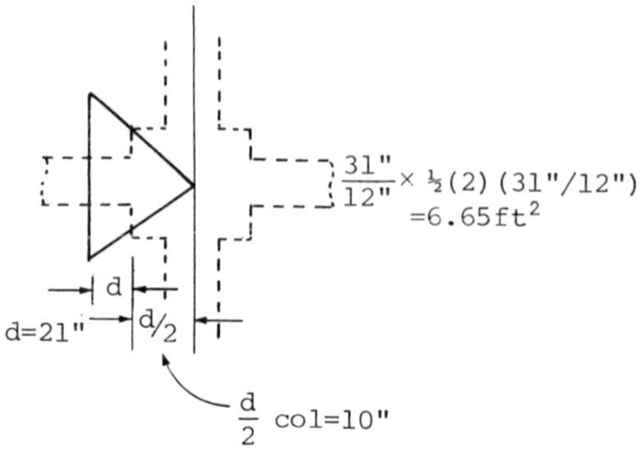

Fig. 6

Half area to beam $= \frac{1}{2}\,(2)\left(\frac{22' + 2'}{2}\right)(10') = 120\ \text{ft}^2$

less $\frac{31''}{12} \times \frac{1}{2}\,(2)\left(\frac{3'}{12}\right) = 6.65\ \text{ft}^2$

Thus net area $= 120 - 6.65 = 113.35\ \text{ft}^2$

Net $V_u = (113.35)\text{ft}^2 \times 402^{\#/\text{ft}^2} = 45600^{\#}$.

Beam contributes $(11'\text{-}0') - \left(\frac{31'}{12}\right) \times \frac{18.5 \times 16''}{12'' \times 12''} \times 150^{\#/\text{ft}^3}$

$= 2600^{\#}$

Thus, total $V_u = 45600 + 2600 = 48{,}200^{\#}$

And shear stress $v_u = \frac{V_u}{\phi bd} = \frac{48200}{0.85 \times 16'' \times 21''}$

$= 169^{\#/\text{in}^2}$

At first interior support $v_c = \frac{\frac{1.15\ wl_n}{2}}{\phi b_o d} = 1.15(169)$

$= 195^{\#/\text{in}^2}$

(ACI sec. 8.3.3)

Allowable $v_c = 2\sqrt{f'_c}$ (ACI sec. 11.3.1.1)

$= 2\sqrt{3000} = 1100^{\#/\text{in}^2}$

or from ACI sec. 11.3.2.1 we have,

$$v_c = 1.9\sqrt{f'_c} + 2500\rho\,\frac{V_u d}{M_u} = 1.9\sqrt{3000} + 2500(0.0135) \times \left(\frac{1.15 \times 48300 \times 21''}{202{,}000 \times 12''}\right)$$

$= 120^{\#/\text{in}^2}$.

Then $(v_u - v_c) = 195 - 120 = 75^{\#/\text{in}^2}$

We will therefore have to provide shear reinforcement for this shear.

Proving a #3 stirrup,

$$\text{Spacing } S_1 = \frac{A_v \cdot f_y}{(v_u - v_c)(b_w)} = \frac{(2 \times 0.11 \text{ in}^2)(40{,}000)}{75 \times 16}$$

$$= 7.3''$$

For first stirrup, $\frac{7.3}{2} = 3.6$ say 3".

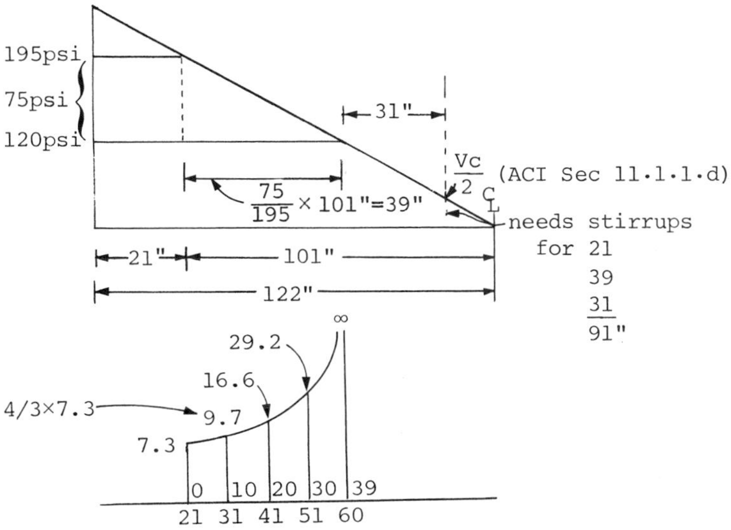

Fig. 7 FIRST INTERIOR BEAMS

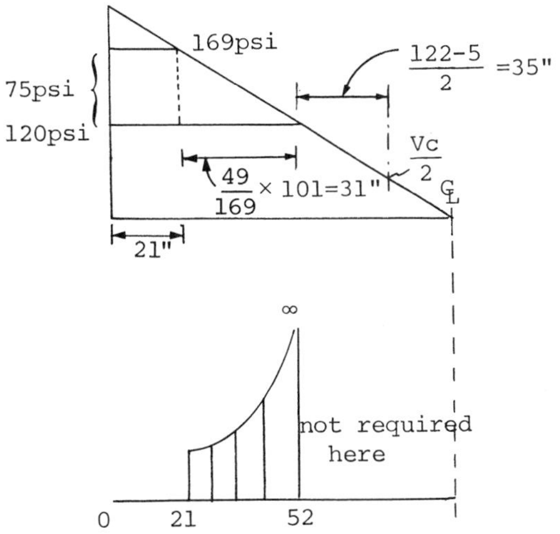

Fig. 8 ALL OTHER BEAMS

For the first interior beams, using #4 stirrups,

use 1 @ 3, 3 @ 7, 1 @ 9, 6 @ 10 at each end. (Refer to Fig. 7)

Note: Could add 1 @ 14" as beam tie.

For all other beams, $(v_u - v_c) = 169 - 120 = 49$ psi,

$$S_1 = \frac{(0.11 \times 2)(40,000)}{49 \times 16''} = 11.2''$$

$$\text{Maximum spacing} = \frac{d}{2} = 10''$$

Using a similar distribution, (refer to fig. 8) and #3 stirrups, we have spacing of 1 @ 5, 8 @ 10 at each end.

Note: We could add 2 @ 14" as ties.

X SLAB REINFORCEMENT:

a) Minimum Steel: From ACI section 7.6.5, $3 \times 5\frac{1}{2} = 16''$(or 18").

From ACI section 13.4.2, $2 \times 5\frac{1}{2} = 11''$.

Middle strips: 10'-0" width $\times 0.0020 \times 12'' \times 5\frac{1}{2}'' = 1.32$ in^2

Use 7 - #4 bars @ 120"/11"/bar = 10.9 bars

11'-0" width $\times 0.002 \times 12'' \times 5\frac{1}{2}'' = 1.45$ in^2

Use 8 - #4 bars @ 132"/11"/bar = 12 bars

Column strips: (Sides of 16" beam)

$$\left(\frac{120'' - 16''}{12}\right) \times 0.002 \times 12'' \times 5\tfrac{1}{2}'' = 1.14 \text{ in}^2, \quad \text{use 6 \#4 bars.}$$

$$\text{No. of bars} = \frac{104''}{11''/\text{bar}} = 9.5 \text{ bars}$$

$$\left(\frac{132'' - 16''}{12''}\right) \times 0.002 \times 12'' \times 5\tfrac{1}{2}'' = 1.28 \text{ in}^2.$$

Use 7 - #4 bars.

$$\text{No. of bars} = \frac{116''}{11''/\text{bar}} = 10.5 \text{ bars}$$

b) Using beam tables, for $\rho = 0.0139$ @ $d = 4''$,

$$M = 7.14^{k-ft} \text{ for } A_s = 0.67 \text{ in}^2,$$

or $$A_s = \frac{M_u \times 0.67}{7.14} = 0.00939\, M_u$$

(Note: for less than 5.02^{1k} for 12" (or $50.2'^{k-ft}$ for 10'-0"),

$$A_s = \frac{0.45}{5.02} M_u = 0.00897\, M_u.$$

Note also that in a column strip, only 15% of M_u is in slab and the rest 85% in the beam.

c)

TABLE OF SLAB REINFORCEMENT

22'-0"x20'-0" Bays		f'_c = 3000psi	f_y = 40,000psi	SLAB SYSTEM WITH PERIPHERAL BEAMS				
DIRECTION PANEL TYPE AND M_o	TYPE of STRIP	TYPE OF MOMENT	COEFICIENTS ACI SECTIONS 13.3.3.2 & 3; 13.3.4.1,2 & 3	MOMENT M_U kip-ft	FORMULA FOR A_S (REFER $\bar{X}$ b ABOVE)	A_S in^2	BAR SELECTION (Try for about 6" maximum spacing	REMARKS
LONG SPAN (E-W) 22'-0" Interior Bay M_o=438 k-ft	COLUMN STRIP	NEGATIVE	0.65x0.777x0.15xM_o	33.2	0.0897M_U	2.98	15-#4=3.0in^2	10% Rule (13.6.7) 104"/16=6.5"apart
		POSITIVE	0.35x0.777x0.15xM_o	17.9	0.0897M_U	1.61	8-#4=1.6in^2	
	MIDDLE STRIP	NEGATIVE	0.65x0.223xM_o	63.5	0.0939M_U	5.96	20-#5=6.2in^2	120"/20=6"apart
		POSITIVE	0.35x0.223xM_o	34.2	0.0897M_U	3.06	16-#4=3.2in^2	
SHORT SPAN (N-S) 20'-0" Interior Bay $M_o=445\text{x}\left(\frac{18.3}{20.3}\right)^2\text{x}\ \frac{22}{20}=391^k$	COLUMN STRIP	NEGATIVE	0.65x0.720x015xM_o	27.4	0.0897M_U	2.46	13-#4=2.6in^2	
		POSITIVE	0.35x0.720x0.15xM_o	14.8	0.0897M_U	1.33	12-#4=2.8in^2	Min Steel=1.28in^2
	MIDDLE STRIP	NEGATIVE	0.65x0.280xM_o	71.1	0.0939M_U	6.68	22-#5=6.82in^2	
		POSITIVE	0.35x0.280xM_o	38.3	0.0897M_U	3.44	18-#4=3.6in^2	
LONG SPAN (E-W) 22'-0" Exterior Bays Spandrel beams M_o=438 k-ft	COLUMN STRIP	Ext. Neg. Spandrel	0.335x0.777x0.15xM_o	17.1	0.0897M_U	1.53	8-#4=1.6in^2	
		POSITIVE	0.485x0.777x0.15xM_o	24.8	0.0897M_U	2.22	11-#4=2.2in^2	
		Int. Neg.	0.698x0.777x0.15xM_o	35.6	0.0897M_U	3.19	16-#4=3.2in^2	10% Rule (13.6.7)
	MIDDLE STRIP	Ext.Neg. Spandrel	0.335x0.223xM_o	32.7	0.0897M_U	2.93	15-#4=3.0in^2	
		POSITIVE	0.485x0.223xM_o	47.3	0.0897M_U	4.24	21-#4=4.20in^2	10% Rule (13.6.7)
		Int. Neg.	0.698x0.223xM_o	68.1	0.0939M_U	6.39	21-#5=6.51in^2	120"/21 =5.71"/bar
SHORT SPAN (N-S) 20'-0" Exterior Bays Spandrel Beams M_o=391 k-ft	COLUMN STRIP	Ext. Neg. Spandrel	0.335x0.723x0.15xM_o	14.2	0.0897M_U	1.27	12-#4=2.4in^2	Minimum Steel
		POSITIVE	0.485x0.723x0.15xM_o	20.6	0.0897M_U	1.85	12-#4=2.4in^2	Minimum Steel
		Int. Neg.	0.698x0.723x0.15xM_o	29.6	0.0897M_U	2.66	14-#4=2.8in^2	
	MIDDLE STRIP	Ext. Neg. Spandrel	0.335x0.277xM_o	36.2	0.0897M_U	3.25	17-#4=3.4in^2	
		POSITIVE	0.485x0.277xM_o	52.5	0.0897M_U	4.71	24-#4=4.8in^2	10% Rule (13.6.7)
		Int. Neg.	0.698x0.277xM_o	75.6	0.0939M_U	7.10	23-#5=7.13in^2	132"/23 Bars= 5.7"/bar

NOTE: From ACI Sec. 13.6.6.1, as column strip moment is divided into two pools by the beam, an extra bar is added where an odd number of bars result.

XI BEAM REINFORCEMENT:

Minimum steel:

$$\rho_{min} = \frac{200}{f_y} = \frac{200}{40,000} = 0.005$$

Thus $A_s = \rho_{min} \times b \times d$

$= 0.005 \times 16'' \times 21''$

$= 1.68 \text{ in}^2.$

Use 4 - #6 bars giving a total area of 1.76 in^2.

Coefficients: Using a 16" width and design tables, for d = 21", we have,

Below $\rho = 0.0139$, use $A_s = \frac{3.50}{196.6} M_u = 0.0178 M_u$

below $M_u = \frac{16}{12} \times 196.6 = 262$ kips-ft.

Below $\rho = 0.0094$, use $A_s = \frac{2.37}{138.25} M_u = 0.0171 M_u$

below $M_u = \frac{16}{12} \times 138.25 = 184$ kips-ft

Below $\rho = 0.0050$, use minimum steel

Minimum moment $= 76.3 \times \frac{16}{12} = 102$ kips-ft.

TABLE OF BEAM REINFORCEMENT FOLLOWS NEXT PAGE

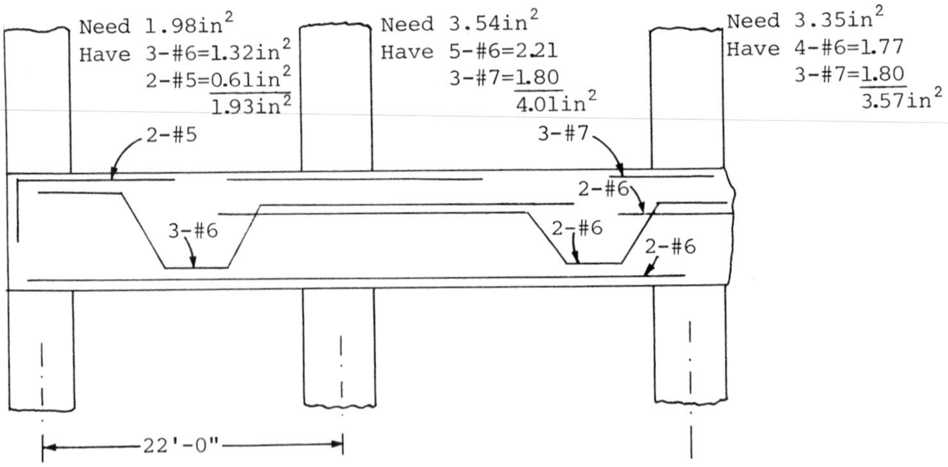

Fig. 9 FOR LENGTH OF BARS, EMBEDMENT, FOLLOW PROVISIONS OF ACI CODE, CHAPTER 12.

TABLE OF BEAM REINFORCEMENT NOTE: ALL ARE 85% OF COLUMN STRIPS

DIRECTION PANEL TYPE M_O	TYPE OF MOMENT	COEFFICIENTS MULTIPLIED BY M_O	MOMENT M_U kip-ft	FORMULA FOR A_S	A_S IN^2	BAR SELECTION	REMARKS
LONG SPAN 22'-0" Interior Bay M_O=438 kip-ft	NEGATIVE	$0.65 x 0.777 x 0.85 x M_O$	188	$0.0178 M_U$	3.35	8-#6, $A_S=3.52 in^2$	6-#7=$3.61 in^2$
	POSITIVE	$0.35 x 0.777 x 0.85 x M_O$	101	$0.0171 M_U$	1.73	4-#6, $A_S=1.76 in^2$	
SHORT SPAN 20'-0" Interior Bay M_O=391 kip-ft	NEGATIVE	$0.65 x 0.723 x 0.85 x M_O$	156	$0.0171 M_U$	2.67	6-#6, $A_S=2.64 in^2$	5-#7=$3.01 in^2$
	POSITIVE	$0.35 x 0.723 x 0.85 x M_O$	84	$0.0171 M_U$	1.44	4-#6, $A_S=1.76 in^2$	$1.68 in^2$ Minimum Steel
LONG SPAN (E-W) 22'-0" Exterior Bays M_O=438ft-kips	Ext Neg @ Spandrel	$0.335 x 0.777 x 0.85 x M_O$	97	$0.0171 M_U$	1.66	4-#6, $A_S=1.76 in^2$	$1.68 in^2$ Minimum Steel
	POSITIVE	$0.485 x 0.777 x 0.85 x M_O$	140	$0.0171 M_U$	2.39	6-#6, $A_S=2.64 in^2$	10% Rule(13.6.7)
	Int. Neg	$0.698 x 0.777 x 0.85 x M_O$	202	$0.0178 M_U$	3.59	8-#6, $A_S=3.52 in^2$	10% Rule(13.6.7)
SHORT SPAN (N-S) 20'-0" Exterior Bays M_O=391 kip-ft	Ext. Neg @ Spandrel	$0.335 x 0.723 x 0.85 x M_O$	81	$0.0171 M_U$	1.39	4-#6, $A_S=1.76 in^2$	$1.68 in^2$ Minimum Steel
	POSITIVE	$0.485 x 0.723 x 0.85 x M_O$	116	$0.0171 M_U$	1.98	5-#6, $A_S=2.2 in^2$	
	Interior Neg.	$0.698 x 0.723 x 0.85 x M_O$	168	$0.0178 M_U$	2.99	7-#6, $A_S=3.08 in^2$	

NOTE: THE ABOVE TABLE IS SUFFICIENT FOR STRAIGHT BARS

FOR BENT BARS, REFER TO FIG.9

• **PROBLEM 18-53**

Design a rectangular reinforced concrete beam to carry a moment of 105 ft-kips such that 'b' is approximately '2/3 d'. Assume $f'_c = 3000 \#/in^2$ and $f_s = 20,000 \#/in^2$.

Solution: Referring to the design tables (Table VIII at end of this chapter), for b = 12", for a $3000 \#/in^2$ concrete and $20,000 \#/in^2$ steel, corresponding to a moment of about 108ft-kips (nearest to our 105 ft-kips requirement) we have an effective depth of 22.0". But the requirement is that b should be approximately 2/3 d. Let us therefore try a wider beam, say, 13".

Each 12" carries $\frac{12''}{13''} \times 105^{1k} = 96.9^{1k}$.

Referring to the same table, we have 'd' corresponding to this moment of 96.9 equal to 21" and 2/3 d = 2/3 x 21 = 14" which is close enough.

Further, $M = A_s \cdot f_s \cdot jd$

or $$A_s = \frac{M}{f_s \cdot jd}$$

$$= \frac{105 \times 10^3 \times 12 \text{ lb-in}}{20,000 \times 0.874 \times 21} = 3.44 \text{ in}^2.$$

Let us use 3 - #10 bars giving an area of 3.79 in^2.

Thus the designed section is 13" x 21" (21" = d-effective depth) and reinforced with 3 - #10 bars.

NOTE: We could also choose b = 14" and repeat the computations to get the value of 'd' (effective depth) from tables.

• **PROBLEM 18-54**

Determine the maximum allowable bending moment for the given section if f'_c = 3000 psi and f_s = 20,000 psi.

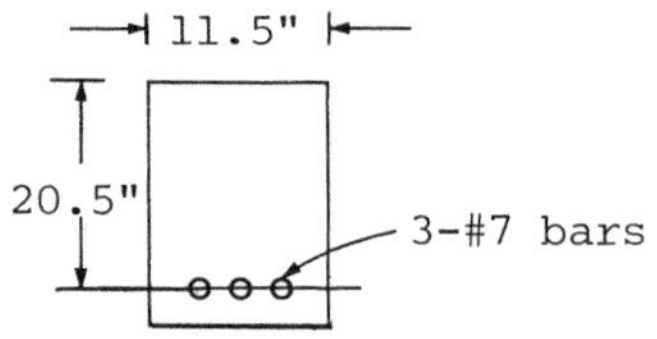

Solution:

$$\rho = \frac{A_s}{bd} \quad ; \quad A_s = 1.80 \text{ in}^2.$$

Thus $$\rho = \frac{1.80}{11.5 \times 20.5} = 0.0076$$

From the curves, we have (Refer to Fig. I at end of chapter).

$$k = 0.308 \quad \text{and} \quad j = 0.898$$

Therefore $kd = 0.308 \times 20.5 = 6.30''$

and $jd = 0.898 \times 20.5 = 18.41''$

Moment on the concrete side $M_c = \frac{1}{2} f_c b \cdot kd \cdot jd$

$$= \frac{1}{2} \times 1350 \times 11.5'' \times 6.30'' \times 18.41''$$

$$= 900318 \text{ lb-in}$$

Moment on the steel side $M_s = A_s \cdot f_s \cdot jd$

$$= 1.80 \times 20,000 \times 18.41$$

$$= 662,760 \text{ lb-in}$$

Thus the allowable moment for the given section = M_s = 662,760 lb-in (choosing the lower of the two values).

• PROBLEM 18-55

Design a rectangular reinforced concrete beam to carry a moment of 105 ft-kips. Use $f'_c = 3000 \text{ lbs/in}^2$ and $f_s = 20,000 \text{ lbs/in}^2$. Assume that 'b' is approximately '2/3 d'.

Solution: From tables, we have $n = 9$, $k = 0.378$, $j = 0.874$ form which $K = 223$ (Refer to Table V at end of this chapter).

Moment $M = K \cdot bd^2$.

Therefore, $105 \times 12 \times 1000 = 223\, bd^2$

$$\text{or} \quad bd^2 = 5650$$

$$\text{But} \quad b \simeq (2/3)d$$

Therefore $\frac{2}{3} d.d^2 = 5650$

or $\quad d = 20.38''$

Let us select $d = 21''$ from which

$$bd^2 = 5650$$

or $b \times 21^2 = 5650$

or $\quad b = 12.7''$ say $13''$

$$\text{Area of steel } A_s = \frac{M}{f_s \cdot jd}$$

$$= \frac{105 \times 12 \times 1000}{20{,}000 \times 0.874 \times 21}$$

$$= 3.43 \text{ in}^2.$$

Let us use 3 - #10 bars giving an area of 3.79 in^2.

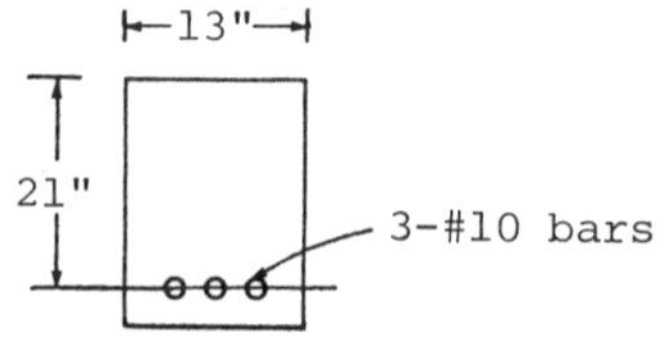

Fig. 1

• PROBLEM 18-56

Compute the maximum allowable bending moment that the given beam can carry if $f'_c = 4000 \text{ lbs/in}^2$, $f_s = 20{,}000 \text{ lbs/in}^2$. Relevant ACI code provisions may be used.

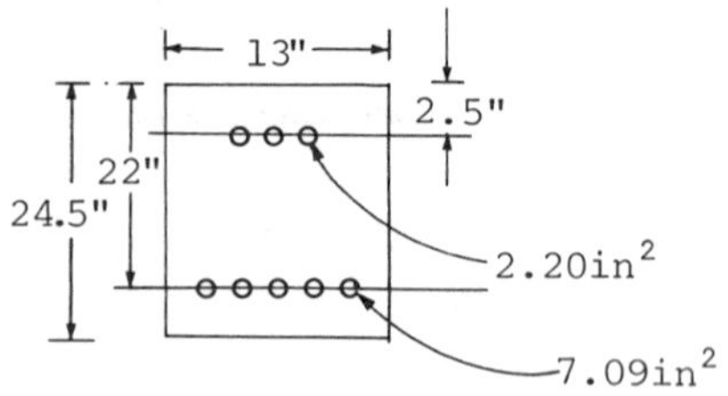

Solution: For concrete with $f'_c = 4000 \text{ lbs/in}^2$, $n = 8$ and

$f_c = 1800 \text{ lbs/in}^2$. (Refer to Table V at end of this chapter).

$$\rho = \frac{7.09 \text{ in}^2}{13 \times 22} = 0.0248$$

and $\rho' = \frac{2.20}{13 \times 22} = 0.00769$

Thus, $\rho \cdot n = 8 \times 0.0248 = 0.198$

and $\rho' n = 8 \times 0.00769 = 0.0615$

The ratio $\frac{d'}{d} = \frac{2.5}{22} = 0.114.$

For $\frac{d'}{d} = 0.10$, K = 0.404 and j = 0.875

and for $\frac{d'}{d} = 0.20$, K = 0.418 and j = 0.848

Establishing a table, we have

	d'/d = 0.10	d'/d = 0.20
K	0.404	0.418
j	0.875	0.848

But $\frac{d'}{d}$ in our problem = 0.114 which lies between 0.10 and 0.20 for which we have the values of K and j.

We will have to determine the value of j for $\frac{d'}{d} = 0.114$ so that we could use the equation $M = A_s \cdot f_s \cdot jd$ as required.

We will have to determine the value of K to check if f_c is exceeded by using the relation $f_c = \frac{f_s k}{n(1 - k)}$

We will therefore have to interpolate to obtain the required j and K values.

Let us first determine the value of K. For a difference of $\frac{d'}{d}$ (increase) of 0.1 (i.e. from 0.1 to 0.2) there is an increase in the value of K from 0.404 to 0.418 = 0.014.

Therefore, for an increase in value of $\frac{d'}{d}$ from 0.1 to 0.114 (= 0.014) there is an increase in K value for $\frac{0.014 \times 0.014}{0.1}$ = 0.002.

Therefore, value of K for $\frac{d'}{d} = 0.114$ is 0.404 + 0.002 = 0.406.

Similiarly, let us determine the value of 'j' for $\frac{d'}{d} = 0.114$.

For an increase from $\frac{d'}{d}$ = 0.1 to 0.2 'j' <u>decreases</u> from 0.875 to 0.848.

That is, for an increase in $\frac{d'}{d}$ for 0.1 there is a decrease in j for (0.875 - 0.848)= 0.027. Thus, for an increase in $\frac{d'}{d}$ for 0.014, there is a decrease in j for $\frac{0.014 \times 0.027}{0.1} = 0.004$.

Therefore, value of 'j' for $\frac{d'}{d}$ = 0.114 is 0.875 - 0.004 = 0.871.

We now have,

$$M = A_s \cdot f_s \cdot jd$$

$$= (7.09)(20{,}000)(0.871)(22) = 2717172 \text{ lb-in}$$

$$= 226431 \text{ lb-ft.}$$

Check for f_c:

$$f_c = \frac{f_s k}{n(1 - k)} = \frac{20{,}000\ (0.406)}{8(1 - 0.406)} = 1709 \text{ lb/in}^2 < 1800 \text{ lb/in}^2.$$

Therefore, OK.

• PROBLEM 18-57

> Determine the steel reinforcement required for a doubly reinforced concrete beam of section 10" x 22" (d = 20") using 3000# concrete and $f_s = 20{,}000\#/\text{in}^2$. Adopt d' = 2". The beam carries a moment of 100,000 ft-lb.

<u>Solution</u>: This problem can be done using tables to obtain the values of K for different concrete grades.

Let us first determine if the section can carry the external moment without compression steel.

We have $M = K \cdot bd^2$

K = 223 (for a 3000# concrete from Table V at end of this chapter).

Therefore $M = 223 \times 10 \times 20^2 = 892{,}000 < 1{,}200{,}000$

Therefore we will have to provide compression steel to account for an extra moment of 1,200,000 - 892,000 = 308,000 lb-in.

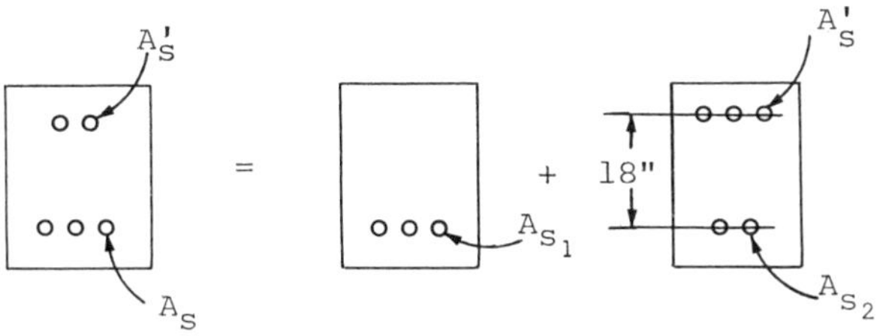

Fig. 1

We have $C_2 = T_2 = \frac{308,000}{18} = 17111$ lbs. (M for compression steel)

Therefore, $A_s = \frac{17111}{20,000} = 0.85 \text{ in}^2$.

$$A_{s_1} = \frac{M}{f_s jd} = \frac{892,000}{20,000 \times 0.874 \times 20} = 2.55 \text{ in}^2$$

Note $M = 892,000$ (tension steel)

and $jd = 0.874$ (from Table V at end of this chapter).

Therefore,

Total $A_s = 3.40 \text{ in}^2$.

Use 3 - #10 bars giving a total area of 3.79 in^2.

To determine A'_s:

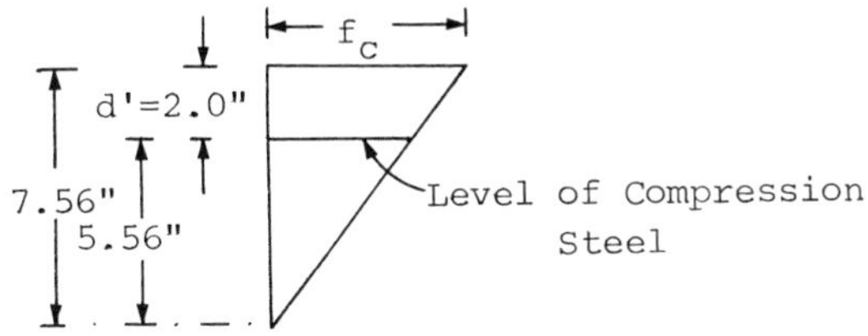

Fig. 2

$kd = 0.378 \times 20'' = 7.56''$ (k value obtained from table)

Stress at the level of compression steel

$= \frac{5.56}{7.56} f_c = \frac{5.56}{7.56} \times 1350$ ($f_c = 1350^{\#}/\text{in}^2$ for a $3000^{\#}$ concrete)

$= 993^{\#}/\text{in}^2$ (Refer to Table V at end of this chapter).

$$A'_s = \frac{17000^{\#}}{995^{\#}/\text{in}^2} \times \frac{1}{(2n - 1)}$$

$$= \frac{17000}{995 \times 17} = 1.00 \text{ in}^2$$

Let us provide 2 - #7 bars giving an area of 1.20 in^2 as compression steel.

• PROBLEM 18-58

> If a T-beam has a slab thickness 't' = $4\frac{1}{2}$", effective depth d = 25", web thickness = 13", determine the required effective width and the area of steel reinforcement. The beam spans for 26' with beams (intermediate) spaced at 13' center to center.
> $f'_c = 3000^{\#}/\text{in}^2$; $f_s = 20{,}000^{\#}/\text{in}^2$, M = 240 kips-ft.

Solution: Referring to tables for values of K for T-beams (Table XV at end of this chapter).

we have for $\frac{t}{d} = \frac{4.5}{25} = 0.18$ and $f_c = 1350$ ($f'_c = 3000$).

We have, $K = 173$.

Further, $M = Kbd^2$

Therefore $b = \frac{M}{Kd^2} = \frac{240 \times 10^3 \times 12}{173 \times 25^2} \simeq 27''$.

Section 8.7.2 of ACI code provides that, the effective width 'b' is the minimum of the following:

i) $\frac{1}{4}$ span length $= \frac{1}{4} \times 26 \times 12 = 78''$

ii) 8t of each side + web thickness $= (8 \times 4.5 \times 2) + 13''$
$= 85''$

iii) center to center distance of beams $= 13' \times 12 = 156''$

However, as per our computations, 'b' works out to be equal to 27". Therefore OK.

To determine area of steel:

The value of k for a $3000^{\#}$ concrete is obtained from design table to be equal to 0.378. (Table V at end of this chapter)

Now, using the T-beam review curves (Fig. 2 at end of this chapter) proceed along t/d = 0.18 and locate 0.378 on the k-line and find the value of j corresponding to this point to be 0.920.

and $A_s = \frac{M}{f_s \cdot jd} = \frac{240 \times 10^3 \times 12}{20{,}000 \times 0.92 \times 25} = 6.26 \text{ in}^2$.

Compute the moment carrying capacity of the given beam if f'_c = 2500 psi and f_y = 40,000 psi.

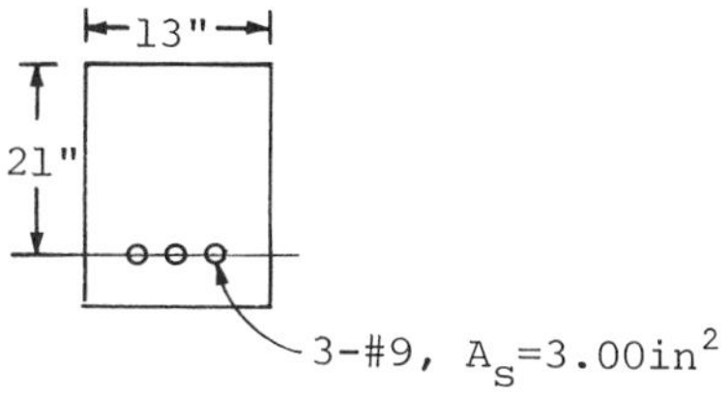

Solution:

$$\rho = \frac{A_s}{bd} = \frac{3.00\ in^2}{13'' \times 21''} = 0.0110$$

Referring to the design tables for a 2500 psi concrete and f_y = 40,000 psi for steel, corresponding to d = 21" and ρ= 0.0116 (next higher value to 0.0110), we have $M_u = 164.05^{1k}$ and A_s = 2.92 in². (Table VI at end of this chapter).

Therefore, actual moment carried by the given sector for

$$A_s = 3.00\ in^2 \text{ is } \frac{3.00\ in^2}{2.92} \times 164.05^{1k}$$

$$= 168.5 \text{ ft-kips.}$$

Working Stress Method:

For a rough and quick estimate of moment using working stress method, let us assume that live load = dead load (since not specified in problem).

$$\text{Therefore load factor} = \frac{1.4 + 1.7}{2} = 1.55$$

$$\text{and working stress moment} = \frac{168.5}{1.55} = 108.7 \text{ ft-kips.}$$

Alternately, using design curves for working stress method, for ρ = 0.0110 and n = 10, we obtain k = 0.388 and j = 0.874.

$$\text{Moment on the steel side } M_s = A_s \cdot f_s \cdot jd$$

$$= 3.00\ in^2 \times 20000^{\#/in^2} \times 0.874 \times 21''$$

$$= 1101240 \text{ in-lbs}$$

$$= 91.8 \text{ ft-kips (dividing by } 12'' \times 1000^{lbs}).$$

Moment on the concrete side $M_c = \frac{1}{2} f_c bkdjd$

$$= \frac{1}{2} \times 1125^{\#/in^2} \times 13'' \times 0.388 \times 21 \times 0.874 \times 21$$

$$= 1093573 \text{ in-lbs}$$

$$= 91.1 \text{ ft-kips} \quad (\text{dividing by } 12'' \times 1000^{\#}).$$

Therefore, concrete controls and $M = M_c = 91.1$ ft-kips.

NOTE: A comparison of values for moment obtained by the two working stress methods using load factors and design curves reveals that there is a difference. It should be noted that analysis using such curves and load factors are only approximate and at best only provide a rough and quick estimate.

• PROBLEM 18-60

> Design a rectangular beam to carry a moment (service) of 95 ft-kips (35% of which is dead load) using $2500^{\#}$ concrete and grade 40 steel. Assume that 'b' is approximately $\frac{'d'}{2}$.

Solution:

$$M_u = 1.4(0.35 \times 95^{1k}) + 1.7(0.65 \times 95^{1k})$$

$$= 46.55^{1k} + 104.98^{1k} = 151.53^{1k}$$

$$\rho = 0.75 \frac{\rho_b}{2} \quad (\text{for a good design})$$

where $$\rho_b = \frac{\beta_1(0.85)f'_c}{f_y} \cdot \frac{87000}{87000 + f_y}$$

$$= \frac{0.85 \times 0.85 \times 2500}{40,000} \cdot \frac{87000}{87000 + 40,000}$$

$$= 0.0309$$

Therefore, $$\rho = 0.75 \frac{\rho_b}{2} = \frac{0.75(0.0309)}{2}$$

$$= 0.0116.$$

Referring to design tables for $\rho = 0.0116$, for $d = 21''$ and $b = 12''$ (b is slightly greater than $d/2$) we have (Table XIX at end of this chapter) $M_u = 164.05^{1k}$ which is slightly higher than the required value of 151.53^{1k}.

Let us try b = 10" so that a 12" beam would have

$\frac{12}{10} \times 151.53 = 182^{1k}$ (slightly over d = 22", i.e., 23" - refer to tables for M_u = 182' k and ρ = 0.0116).

Let us try b = 11" so that a 12" beam would have M_u = $\frac{12}{11} \times 151.53 = 165.30^{1k}$ corresponding to which we have d = 22".

(M_u = 180.04), A_s = 3.06 in^2.

Therefore, $A_s = \frac{151.53}{180.04} \times 3.06 = 2.57$ in^2.

Let us use 3 - #9 bars giving an area of 3.00 in^2.

Therefore, select a 11" x 22" (d) beam reinforced with 3 - #9 bars.

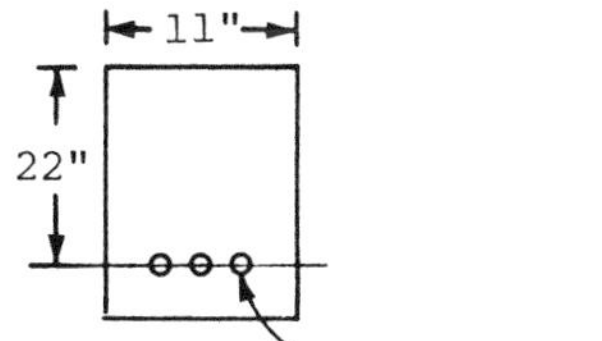

Fig. 1

Working Stress Method:

Referring to the design ('quick') tables for working stress for b = 12" and d = 23" we have M = 94.3^{1k} (Table VII at end of this chapter). While we require 95^{1k}. For d = 24", M = 102.7^{1k}, A_s = 2.92.

Therefore, $A_s = \frac{95}{102.7} \times 2.92 = 2.70$ in^2.

Use 3 - #9 bars giving an area of 3.00 in^2.

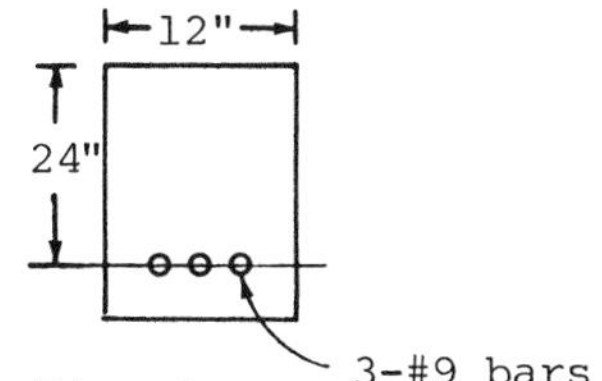

Fig. 2

• PROBLEM 18-61

Design a slab to carry a moment of 10.5 kip-ft per foot width using $3000^{\#}/in^2$ concrete and $20,000^{\#}/in^2$ steel.

Solution: Reading off from the table (Refer to Table VIII at end of this chapter) corresponding to a moment of 10.93 k-ft (nearest to our requirement of 10.5 k-ft) we have effective depth equal to 7" (for a $3000^{\#}$ concrete and $20,000^{\#}$ steel). Adding 1" for cover, let us select total depth of slab = 8".

$$\text{Area of steel} \quad A_s = \frac{M}{f_s jd} = \frac{10.5 \times 10^3 \times 12}{20,000 \times 0.874 \times 7}$$

$$= 1.03 \text{ in}^2.$$

Let us select #6 bars @ 5" center to center.

NOTE: The actual moment carried by the section = 10.93 k-ft where as the required moment carried by the section is

10.5 k-ft. Thus, to arrive at a closer value for area of steel, the moment may be taken as the ratio $\frac{10.5}{10.93}$. There is no significant difference, however, in this instance since both the figures are quite close to each other.

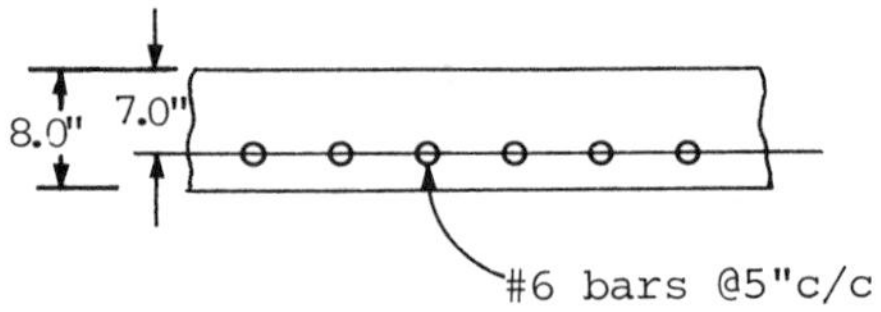

Fig. 1 CROSS-SECTION SHOWING THE REINFORCEMENT DETAILS

• PROBLEM 18-62

Using $f'_c = 2500 \text{ lbs/in}^2$ and grade 40 steel, design a slab to carry a moment of 4 ft-kips.

Solution: From the tables, we have

k = 0.360 and j = 0.880 (Table V at end of the chapter).

$$\text{Further, } M = \frac{1}{2} f_c b \cdot kd \cdot jd$$

$$\text{Also} \quad M = K \cdot bd^2 \qquad (1)$$

$$\text{Therefore } \frac{1}{2} f_c b \cdot kd \cdot jd = K \cdot bd^2$$

or $K = \frac{1}{2} f_c kj$

$= \frac{1}{2} \times 1125 \times 0.360 \times 0.880 = 179$

Using equation (1), we have

$M = 4 \times 12 \times 1000$ lb-in $= 179 \times 12'' \times d^2$ (b = 12'', considering 1 foot strip)

Therefore d = 4.73'' say 5''.

And $A_s = \frac{M}{f_s jd} = \frac{4 \times 12 \times 1000}{20{,}000 \times 0.880 \times 5''} = 0.55 \text{ in}^2$.

Let us use #5 bars at 6'' center to center.

• PROBLEM 18-63

A floor slab is to carry a uniform live load of 350 lbs/ft^2 and is simply supported over a span of 23 ft. If $f'_c = 3000$ lbs/in^2 and $f_y = 40{,}000$ lbs/in^2, design the slab using ultimate design. For the purpose of reducing deflection, assume that $\rho = \frac{1}{2}$ of $0.75\ \rho_b$. Also assume that the only dead load is the weight of the slab.

Solution: Let us assume a slab thickness of say, 14''

Then Dead Load $= \frac{14}{12} \times 150\#/\text{ft}^3 = 175\ \#/\text{ft}^2$

Live Load $= 350\ \#/\text{ft}^2$

Thus, Ultimate load = 1.4 (DL) + 1.7(LL)

$= 1.4(175) + 1.7(350) = 840\ \#/\text{ft}^2$.

Considering a 1 ft strip of the floor slab, we have

Ultimate Moment $M_u = \frac{W_u l^2}{8}$ (simply supported)

where W_u = ultimate load = 840 #/ft^2,

Therefore $M_u = \frac{840 \times 1 \text{ ft} \times 23 \times 23 \times 12}{8} = 666540$ lb-in.

We have $\rho_b = \frac{0.85\ \beta_1 f'_c}{f_y} \times \frac{87000}{87000 + f_y}$

$= \frac{0.85 \times 0.85 \times 3000}{40000} \times \frac{87000}{87000 + 40000}$

$= 0.0371$

Thus $0.75\ \rho_b = 0.0278$

$$\text{Therefore } \rho = \frac{0.75\ \rho_b}{2} = \frac{0.0278}{2} = 0.0139$$

$$q = \rho \cdot \frac{f_y}{f'_c} = 0.0139 \times \frac{40{,}000}{3000} = 0.185$$

Ultimate Moment $M_u = \phi f'_c bd^2 q(1 - 0.59\ q)$

Substituting the various values in the above equation,

$$666540 = 0.90 \times 3000 \times bd^2 \times 0.185\ \{1 - 0.59(0.185)\}$$

or $666540 = 445\ bd^2$

or $bd^2 = 1498$

But $b = 12''$ since we are considering a 1 foot strip.

Therefore $d^2 = \frac{1498}{12}$ or $d = 11.2''$.

Adding $\frac{3''}{4}$ cover + $\frac{1''}{4}$ for bar, total depth of slab

$= 11.2 + 1.0 = 12.2''$ say $12\frac{1}{2}''$.

Area of steel $A_s = \rho \cdot bd = 0.0139 \times 12'' \times 11.2'' = 1.87\ in^2$.

We will have to revise our calculations since $d = 12\frac{1}{2}''$ and not $14''$ as we initially assumed.

$$\text{Weight of slab} = \frac{12\frac{1}{2}''}{12''} \text{ X } 150\ \#/ft^3 = 156\ \#/ft^2$$

and ultimate load $U = 1.4(156) + 1.7(350) = 813\ \#/ft^2$

and Moment $M_u = \frac{813}{840} \times 666540 = 645115$ lb-in

and $d = \sqrt{\frac{645115}{12 \times 445}} = 11''$. $(b = 12'')$

and Area of steel $A_s = \rho \cdot bd = 0.0139 \times 12 \times 11 = 1.84\ in^2$.

Let us use #9 bars each of $1.00\ in^2$ at a spacing of

$$\frac{12 \times 1.00\ in^2/bar}{1.84\ in^2} = 6.5''$$

Therefore, select a $12\frac{1}{2}''$ thick slab reinforced with #9 bars spaced at $6\frac{1}{2}''$ center to center.

Working Stress Method:

Let us assume a 14" thick slab as before.

Dead Load = 175 $\#/ft^2$

Live Load = 350 $\#/ft^2$

Total Load = 175 + 350 = 525 $\#/ft^2$.

$$\text{and Moment } M = \frac{Wl^2}{8} = \frac{525\ \#/ft^2 \times 1\ ft \times 23^2}{8}$$

$$= 34716 \text{ lb-ft} = 416587 \text{ lb-in}$$

From tables, for $f_c' = 3000$ psi and $f_s = 20{,}000$ psi, K = 224

and j = 0.874 (Table V at end of this chapter).

Recall, $M = Kbd^2$ (b = 12", K = 224)

Therefore $416587 = 224 \times 12 \times d^2$

or $d = 12.45"$

Adding 1" cover, total depth = 12.45" + 1.00" = 13.45" say 14"

$$\text{Area of steel } A_s = \frac{M}{f_s \cdot jd} = \frac{416587}{20{,}000 \times 0.874 \times 13"}$$

$$= 1.83 \text{ in}^2.$$

Let us use #9 bars at a spacing of $\frac{12 \times 1.00 \text{ in}^2/\text{bar}}{1.83 \text{ in}^2} = 6.56"$

Thus, use a 14" slab reinforced with #9 bars spaced at $6\frac{1}{2}"$ center to center.

• PROBLEM 18-64

A reinforced concrete slab is to be simply supported on a span of 23 ft. Using $f_c' = 3000$ psi and grade 40 steel, design the slab by the Ultimate (strength) Design Method. Compare this design with the design obtained by the Working Stress Method. You may assume that $\rho = \frac{1}{2}$ of $0.75\ \rho_b$ nd that the only dead load is the weight of the slab. It is estimated that the slab would likely carry a live load of 350 lbs/ft^2. (uniform)

Solution:

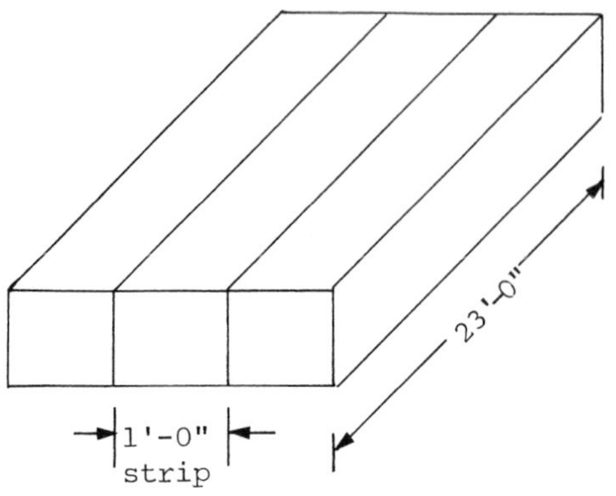

1. ULTIMATE DESIGN:

Let us consider a 1 foot strip of the slab. Assume, thickness of slab = 12" (say)

Therefore dead load = 150 lbs/ft^3 x 1 ft basis

= 150 lbs/ft.

Live load = $350^{\#/ft^2}$ x 1 ft basis = $350^{\#/ft}$.

Ultimate Load = 1.4(Dead Load) + 1.7 (Live Load)
(ACI specification)

Therefore, Ultimate Load U = 1.4(150) + 1.7(350)

= 805 lbs/ft

Moment due to this Ultimate load = $\frac{Wl^2}{8}$ (simply supported)

$= \frac{805 \times 23 \times 23}{8} \times 12''$

= 638768 lb-in.

Further, $\rho_b = \frac{0.85\ \beta_1 f'_c}{f_y} \cdot \frac{87000}{87000 + f_y}$

$= \frac{0.85 \times 0.85 \times 3000}{40{,}000} \times \frac{87000}{87000 + 40000}$

= 0.0371

But $\rho = \frac{1}{2}(0.75\ \rho_b)$ given

Therefore $\rho = \frac{1}{2}(0.75 \times 0.0371)$

= 0.0139

From which, $q = \rho \cdot \frac{f_y}{f'_c}$

$= 0.0139 \times \frac{40,000}{3000}$

$= 0.185$

Thus $0.59\ q = 0.59\ (0.185)$

$= 0.109$

and $(1 - 0.59\ q) = (1 - 0.109) = 0.891$

Ultimate Moment $M_u = \phi f'_c bd^2 q\ (1 - 0.59\ q)$ (1)

But ultimate moment obtained above = 638768 lb-in

Therefore $638768 = \phi f'_c bd^2 q\ (1 - 0.59\ q)$

where ϕ is generally 0.9 (ACI section 9.2.1)

Substituting the various values in the above equation, we have,

$638768 = 0.9 \times 3000 \times 12'' \times d^2 \times 0.185 \times 0.891$

(b = 12" since we are considering a 1 foot strip)

from which,

$d = 10.94''$ (effective depth)

Adding $\frac{3''}{4}$ (cover) and $\frac{1}{2}$ of one bar dia say $\frac{1''}{2}$ we have, total

depth = 10.94" + 1" = 11.94" say 12".

Our assumption of 12" was a fairly good guess!

Area of steel $A_s = \rho \cdot bd = 0.0139 \times 12'' \times 10.94''$

$= 1.82\ in^2$.

provide #8 bars each having an area = 0.79 in^2 @ a spacing

$\frac{12 \times 0.79}{1.82} = 5.21''$ say 5" C/C.

Thus, the slab designed by the Ultimate Design Method is 12" thick and is provided with #8 bars spaced @ 5" C/C.

2. WORKING STRESS METHOD:

Assuming a 12" thick slab,

Dead load = $150\#/ft^2 \times 1$ (for 1 ft thick)

$= 150\#/ft^2$

Live load = $350\ \#/ft^2$

Therefore, total load = $500\ \#/ft^2$

Maximum Moment = $\frac{Wl^2}{8}$ (simply supported)

Therefore $M = \frac{500 \times 23^2 \times 23 \times 12''}{8}$

$= 396750$ lb-in

Using tables we have K = 224 (Table V at end of this chapter).

$M = Kbd^2$

that is, $396750 = 224 \times 12'' \times d^2$ (b = 12" for a 1 ft strip)

or $d = 12.15'' > 12''$

Using d = 12.5" and adding 1" for cover, total thickness of slab = 13.5".

Revising the computations again,

Dead load = $\frac{13.5}{12} \times 150 = 169\ \#/ft^2$

Live load = $350\ \#/ft^2$

And total load = $169 + 350 = 519\ \#/ft^2$.

and Moment $M = \frac{Wl^2}{8} = \frac{519 \times 23 \times 23}{8} \times 12'' = 411827$ lb-in

and $M = Kbd^2$

$411827 = 224 \times 12 \times d^2$

from which d = 12.38

Thus, let us choose a slab with thickness

$$= 12.5'' + 1'' = 13.5'' \text{ (overall)}$$

$$\text{Area of steel } A_s = \frac{M}{f_s jd} = \frac{411827}{20{,}000 \times 0.874 \times 12.5}$$

$$= 1.88 \text{ in}^2.$$

Let us use #8 bars spaced @ 5" C/C as before.

Thus, by the working stress method the thickness of the slab is $13\frac{1}{2}''$ and it is to be reinforced with #8 bars @ 5" C/C (center to center)

COMPARISON: Comparing the designs obtained by both the methods, we find that the thickness of slab is higher by the working stress method than by the Ultimate Design Method, though the reinforcement details remain the same in both the cases.

DESIGN OF COLUMNS BY WORKING STRESS METHOD

• PROBLEM 18-65

Using $3000^{\#}$ concrete and grade 40 steel, for the given column section, draw the interaction diagram. Indicate on it P_u, ϕP_o, M_b, P_b and maximum moment with zero load (M_o). Note that ACI 318-77 sec. 7.7.1 (c) indicates that there is $1\frac{1}{2}''$ (clear) concrete over #3 ties.

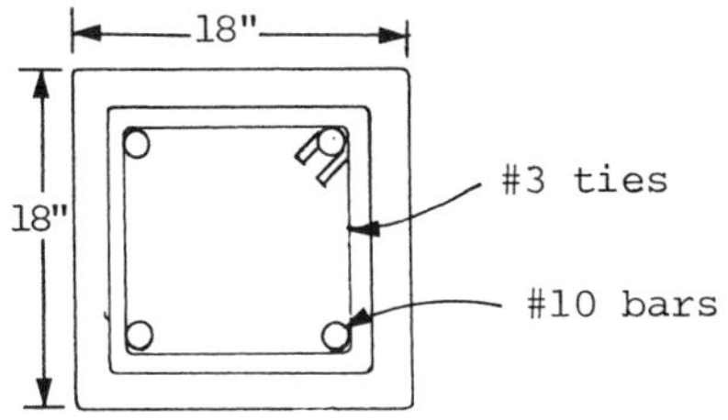

Fig. 1

Solution:

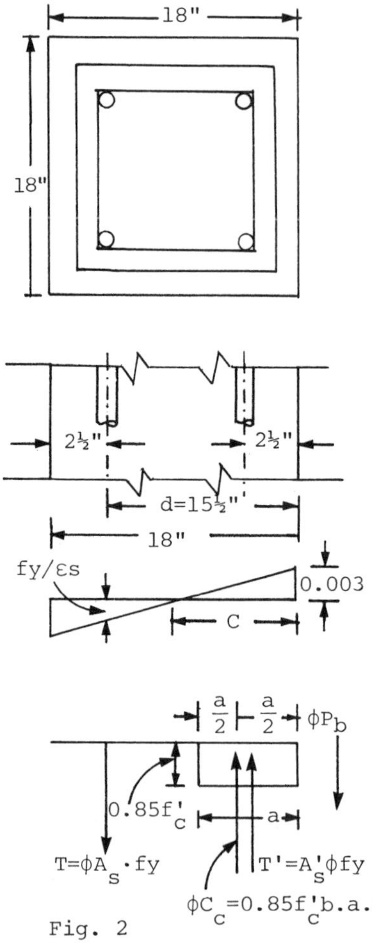

Fig. 2

$$\text{Area of steel } A_{st} = 4 - \#10 \text{ bars} = 4 \times 1.27$$
$$= 5.08 \text{ in}^2.$$

Therefore, $A_s = A_s' = 2.54 \text{ in}^2$.

We have, $0.80\,\phi\left[0.85\, f_c'\,(A_g - A_{st}) + f_y A_{st}\right] = 0.80\, P_o$

$= P_u\ (\max)$

(Refer to ACI 10.3.5.2)

where $\phi P_o = \phi\left[0.85\, f_c'\,(A_g - A_{st}) + f_y A_{st}\right]$

Therefore

$$P_u(\max) = 0.8 \times 0.7\ \left[0.85 \times 3^{k/in^2}(18^2 - 5.08) + 40^{k/in^2}(5.08)\right]$$
$$= 569^k.$$

And $\phi P_o = 0.7\left[0.85 \times 3^{k/in^2}(18^2 - 5.08) + 40^{k/in^2}(5.08)\right]$
$= 711^k$

Distance to center of bar $= 1\frac{1}{2}'' + \frac{3}{8} + \frac{10/8}{2} = 2\frac{1}{2}''$

(ACI 7.7.1 C)

Therefore $d = 18'' - 2\frac{1}{2}'' = 15\frac{1}{2}''$

We have $C = \dfrac{0.003\ d}{0.003 + \dfrac{f_y}{E_s}}$

where $f_y = 40{,}000$ psi and $E_s = 29 \times 10^6$ psi

Therefore $C = \dfrac{0.003 \times 15\frac{1}{2}}{0.003 + \dfrac{40{,}000}{29000000}}$

$= \dfrac{0.003 \times 15\frac{1}{2} \times 29000000}{(0.003 \times 29000000) + 40{,}000}$

$= 10.62''$.

Also, $a = \beta_1 C$ where $\beta_1 = 0.85$ (ACI 10.2.7.C')

Therefore $a = 0.85 \times 10.62 = 9.02''$.

Summing the forces in the vertical direction,

$\Sigma f_y = 0$,

or $\phi P_b = \phi C_c = 0.85(3^{k/in^2})(18'')(9.02)(0.7) = 290^k$

(Using $\phi C_c = 0.85\ f'_c ba\phi$)

Note that in the figure illustrated above, two couples constituted by T, T' and ϕC_c, ϕP_b are equal.

$\phi A_s f_y(15\frac{1}{2} - 2\frac{1}{2}) = \phi P_b(\text{or } C_c) \times \text{lever arm}$

that is, $0.7 \times 2.54 \times 40^{k/in^2} \times 13'' = 290^k \times \text{lever arm}$

Therefore, lever arm $= \dfrac{0.7 \times 2.54 \times 40 \times 13}{290} = 3.18''$.

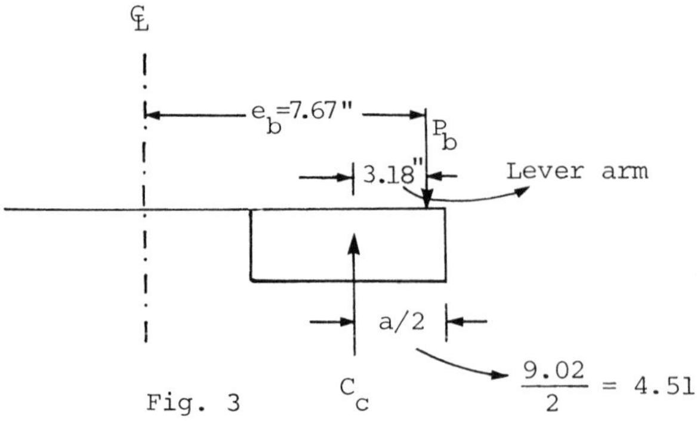

Fig. 3

e_b (distance of P_b from center line; eccentricity)

$= 9'' - (4.51 - 3.18) = 7.67''$

$$\phi M_b = \phi P_b e_b = \frac{290^k \times 7.67''}{12''} = 185.4^{\text{ft-kips}}$$

To find M_o, let us ignore the concrete,

$$M_o = \phi A_s f_y (d - d') \quad \text{(Note that } \phi \text{ is now} = 0.90)$$

$$M_o = \phi A_s f_y (d - d') = 0.9 \times 2.54 \times 40^{k/in^2} \times \frac{13''}{12''}$$

$$= 99 \text{ ft-kips}$$

Ignoring compression steel, $\rho = \dfrac{2.54}{18'' \times 15\frac{1}{2}''} \quad \left(\rho = \dfrac{A_s}{bd}\right)$

$$= 0.0091$$

and $\quad q = \rho \cdot \dfrac{f_y}{f'_c} = 0.0091 \times \dfrac{40{,}000}{3000} = 0.1213.$

$$M_o = \phi f'_c bd^2 q\,(1 - 0.59\,q)$$

$$= 0.9 \times 3^{k/in^2} \times 18'' \times (15.5'')^2(0.1213)\left[1 - 0.59(0.1213)\right] \times \frac{1}{12}$$

$= 109$ ft-kips (slightly higher than 99 ft-kips)

P_u (max) = 569 kips

ϕP_o = 711 kips

ϕM_b = 185 ft-kips

ϕP_b = 290 kips

e_b = 7.67" ; M_o = 109 ft-kips

The resulting interaction diagram for the given column section is as follows:

Figure not to scale

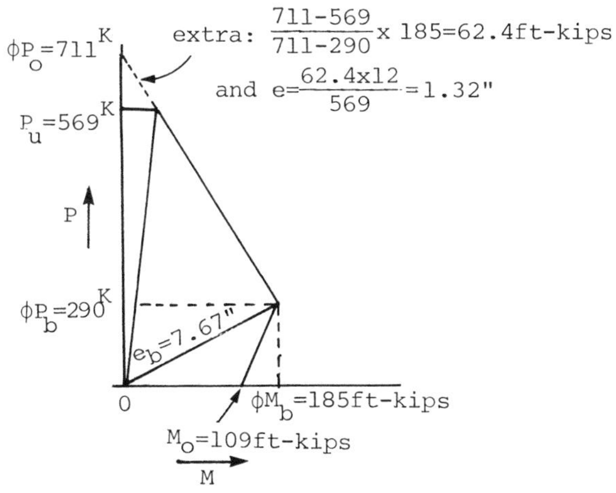

INTERACTION DIAGRAM

Fig. 4

• PROBLEM 18-66

Design a tied column for minimum eccentricity to carry a dead load of 180 kips and a live load of 300 kips. Assume f'_c = 4000 psi and f_y = 60,000 psi.

Solution: Let us assume that the area of steel is 1% of the gross area for greater economy.

$$\phi P_n(max) = 0.80\phi \left[0.85 f'_c(A_g - A_{st}) + f_y A_{st}\right]$$

(ACI sec. 10.3.5.2)

But $P_u = 1.4D + 1.7L = 1.4(180) + 1.7(300) = 762 \text{ kips} = \phi P_{n(max)}$

Therefore $762 = 0.80\phi \left[0.85 f'_c(A_g - A_{st}) + f_y A_{st}\right]$

$$= 0.80 \times 0.70 \left[0.8 \times 4^{k/in^2}(A_g - 0.01 A_g) + 60^{k/in^2}(0.01 A_g)\right]$$

$$762 = 2.22 A_g$$

or $A_g = 343.2$

Assuming a square column,

side of the column = $\sqrt{343.2}$ = 18.5" say 18" side.

Thus $A_g = 18 \times 18 = 324 \text{ in}^2$

Now, $762^k = (0.80)(0.70)\left[0.85 \times 4^{k/in^2}(324 - A_{st}) + 60^{k/in^2}(A_{st})\right]$

from which, $A_{st} = 4.5 \text{ in}^2$.

Select 6 - #8 bars giving an area of 4.71 in².

$A_{st} = 4.71 \text{ in}^2, \quad A_g = 324 \text{ in}^2$

Substituting these values in the expression for

$$P_u = \phi P_n(\text{max}) = 0.80\phi\left[0.85f'_c(A_g - A_{st}) + f_y A_{st}\right]$$

$$P_u = 0.80 \times 0.70\left[0.85 \times 4^{k/in^2}(324 - 4.71) + 60^{k/in^2} \times 4.71\right]$$

$= 766$ kips (actual $P_u = 762$)

Therefore OK.

NOTE: If we would have selected a 19" x 19" column, gross area A_g = 19" x 19" = 361 in².

Providing 1% of A_g as area of steel (A_{st})

$A_{st} = 0.01 \times 361 = 3.61 \text{ in}^2$.

Substituting these values in the expression for P_u,

$$P_u = \phi P_n(\text{max}) = 0.80\phi\left[0.85f'_c(A_g - A_{st}) + f_y A_{st}\right]$$

$$= 0.80 \times 0.70\left[0.85 \times 4^{k/in^2}(361 - 3.61) + 60^{k/in^2} \times 3.61\right]$$

$= 802$ kips >> the required $P_u = 762$ kips.

Thus, if we had selected a 19" x 19" column, its load carrying capacity would have been much greater than the required value.

TIE DESIGN: (Refer ACI 7.10.5.2)

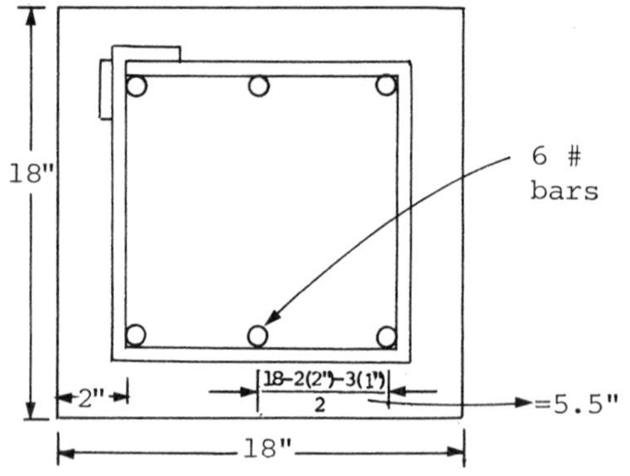

Spacing of ties is the least of:

(i) 16 x 9/8 (#8 bars) = 18"

(ii) 48 x dia (#3) = 48 x 3/8 = 18"

(iii) Least dimension = 18"

Therefore provide #3 @ 18" on center.

• PROBLEM 18-67

> Design a column to carry a live load of 170 kips, dead load of 80 kips at an eccentricity e = 11". Assume f'_c = 3000 psi and f_y = 40,000 psi. Permissible range of ρ_g is 2 to 3%.

Solution: Steel and concrete will be stressed to their maximum capacities when $P_u = P_b$ (large eccentricities)

$$P_u = P_b = 1.40 \times 80^k + 1.70 \times 170^k = 401^k$$

But $P_b = \phi\left(0.85\ f'_c ba + A'_s f_y - A_s f_y\right)$ (assuming $A_s = A'_s$)

where $a = \beta_1 C$ and $C = \dfrac{0.003\ d}{0.003 + \dfrac{f_y}{E_s}}$, $\phi = 0.7$

Substituting these values in the above expression for P_b,

$$P_b = 0.7\left[0.85 \times 3^{k/in^2} \times bd \times \beta_1 \times \frac{0.003}{0.003 + \frac{f_y}{E_s}}\right]$$

Substituting for $\beta_1 = 0.85$, $f_y = 40{,}000$ and $E_s = 29 \times 10^6$ psi,

$$P_b = 0.7\left[0.85 \times 3 \times bd \times 0.85 \times \frac{87000}{87000 + 40{,}000}\right]$$

$$= 1.039\ bd$$

But $P_b = 401^k$

Therefore 1.039 bd = 401

or $bd = \dfrac{401}{1.039} = 386\ in^2$.

Assuming that d = 0.85 t

$$t^2 = \frac{386}{0.85} \quad \text{(Assuming a square column)}$$

$$= 454$$

or $\quad t = 21.3''$

Let us try a 21" x 21" column.

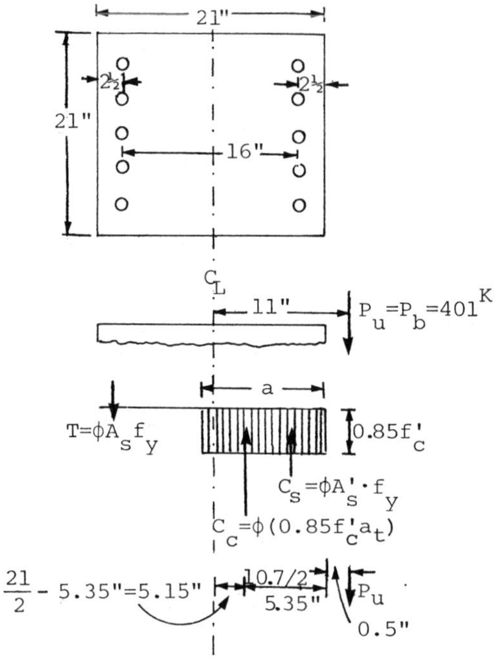

To find a, sum forces about the y-axis so that

$$\Sigma F_y = 0 \qquad \text{(Note that } A_s \cdot f_y = A'_s \cdot f_y\text{)}$$

Therefore, $P_u = P_b = 401^k = \phi \left[0.85\ f'_c at + A'_s \cdot f_y - A_s \cdot f_y \right]$

$$401^k = 0.7 \times 0.85 \times 3^{k/in^2} \times a \times 21'' \quad (t = 21'')$$

or $\quad a = 10.70''$

To get A_s, let us take moment about the center. Considering the force system indicated in the diagram. It consists of two couples, P_u, C_c and T, C_s.

$$M\ C_L = 0$$

Therefore, $401^k(5.35 + 0.5) = A_s(40^{k/in^2})(0.7)(16'')$

or $\quad A_s = 5.22\ in^2$, on each side

Let us try 6 - #9 bars on each side giving 6.00 in^2 each. (Table I at end of this chapter).

Check for ρ_g:

$$\rho_g = \frac{2 \times 5.22}{21 \times 21} \times 100 = 2.36\% < 3\%$$

Therefore OK.

Ties:

Let us try minimum #3 ties @ the least of the following

(i) $16 \times \frac{9}{8} = 18''$

(ii) $48 \times$ dia of #3 $= 48 \times \frac{3}{8} = 18''$

(iii) Least dimension = 21''

Therefore, provide #3 ties at 18'' center.

• PROBLEM 18-68

> Using grade 40 steel and 3000# concrete, design an economical square tied column to carry 200,000 lbs. (minimal eccentricity)

Solution: Let us assume that 1% steel is used as most economical from a material standpoint.

$$A_{st} = 0.01\ A_g$$

$$P_n\ (max) = 200{,}000 \text{ lbs} \quad \text{(given)}$$

For columns with ties, $P_n\ (max) = 0.80\phi\left[0.85f'_c(A_g - A_{st}) + f_yA_{st}\right]$

(ACI code 10.3.5.1 and 10.3.5.2)

Therefore,

$$P_n(max) = 200{,}000 = 0.40 \times 0.80\left[0.85(3000)(A_g - 0.01\ A_g) + 40{,}000\ (0.01\ A_g)\right]$$

or $\qquad 200{,}000 = 935.8\ A_g$

or $\qquad A_g = 213.7 \text{ in}^2$

Size of column $= \sqrt{213.7} = 14.6''$ (14 x 14 square column)

Note here that instead of rounding off the size obtained to the next highest number, we have rounded off to the next lowest number. This is because a 15" square column must have 1% steel and so its capacity will exceed 200,000 lbs.

$$P = 200,000 = 0.40 \times 0.80 \left(0.85(3000)(14^2 - A_{st}) + 40,000(A_{st})\right)$$

So, $A_{st} = 3.346\ in^2$.

Check for % of A_g: $\frac{3.35}{14 \times 14} = 0.171$ OK since > 0.01 but < 0.08.

Let us use 4 - #9 bars giving an area of 4.00 in^2. Note, however, that the design of a tied column also includes Tie Design.

Referring to sec. 7.10.5.1 and 7.10.5.2 of ACI code

16 x 9/8" - #9 bars = 18"

or 48 x 3/8" - #3 (min) bars = 18"

and least dimension = 14"

Therefore, the column will be a 14" square reinforced with 4 - #9 bars and #3 ties @ 14" O.C.

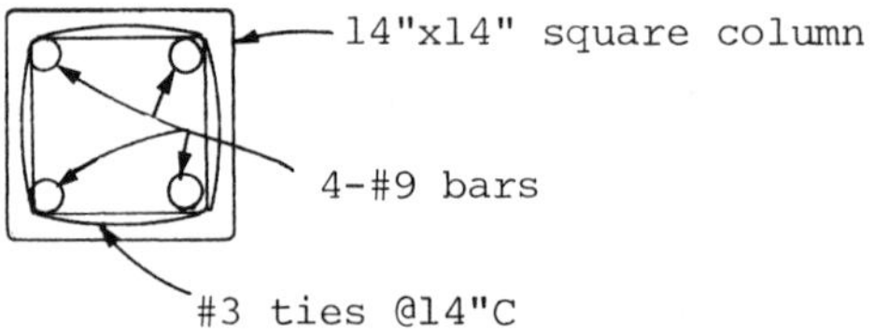

Fig. 1 SECTION SHOWING DETAILS OF DESIGN AND REINFORCEMENT OF THE COLUMN.

DESIGN OF COLUMNS BY ULTIMATE DESIGN METHOD

• PROBLEM 18-69

Determine the concentric load that the given column can carry. Assume that grade 40 steel and 3000# concrete are used.

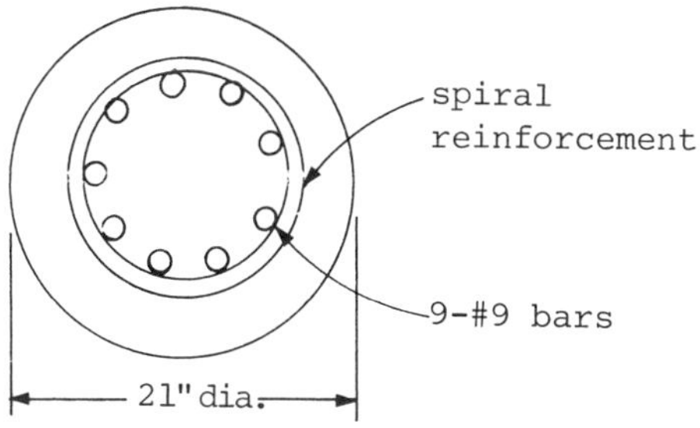

Solution: $A_{st} = 9 \text{ in}^2$

A_g (gross area) = 346 in^2

$\rho_g = \frac{9 \text{ in}^2}{346} = 0.0260$ OK since between 0.01 to 0.08 (ACI 10.9.1)

According to ACI, sec. B.6.1 requires to use 40% of strength design.

According to sec. 10.3.5.1 and 10.3.5.2 for spirally reinforced columns,

$$P_n(\max) = 0.85\phi \left(0.85 f'_c (A_g - A_{st}) + f_y \cdot A_{st}\right) \tag{1}$$

Thus, for our problem, we have $\phi = 40\%$,

$f'_c = 3000 \text{ lb/in}^2$, $A_g = 346 \text{ in}^2$, $A_{st} = 9 \text{ in}^2$,

$f_y = 40{,}000 \text{ lb/in}^2$

Substituting these values in equation (1),

$$P_n(\max) = 40\% \times 0.85 \left[0.85(3000)(346 - 9) + (40{,}000 \times 9)\right]$$

$$= 414{,}600 \text{ lbs.}$$

• PROBLEM 18-70

A 12 in. square R/C column is supported by a sq. footing. The unfactored dead and live loads on the column are 300^k and 140^k respectively. The allowable soil pressure is $5.0^{k/ft^2}$. Determine the required effective depth of the footing using ACI 318-77 if $f'_c = 4$ ksi.

Solution: The load factors for dead and live loads are 1.4 and 1.7. Hence the factored column load is

$$P_f = 1.7 \text{ (Live Load)} + 1.4 \text{ (Dead Load)}$$

i.e. $P_f = 1.4\,(300^k) + 1.7\,(140^k) = 658^k$

The unfactored column load is

$$P = 300^k + 140^k = 440^k$$

Assuming the weight of the footing to be about 6% of the unfactored column loads, and an allowable soil pressure of $5^{k}/ft^2$, the required base area of the footing is,

$$A = \frac{1.06\ P}{\text{allow. soil pr.}} = \frac{1.06(440^k)}{5} = 93.3\ ft^2.$$

The plan dimension based on unfactored column loads is then,

$$B = \sqrt{A_{req'd}} = \sqrt{93.3} = 9.66\ ft \text{ (assuming a square)}$$

Use B = 10 ft

The depth of the footing is based upon factored column loads $= 658^k$ and factored soil pressure is $658^k/10 \times 10 = 6.58\ k/ft^2$.

Footing Depth based on beam shear and punching shear:

By trial and error:

Let us try d = 22 in.

Beam Shear:

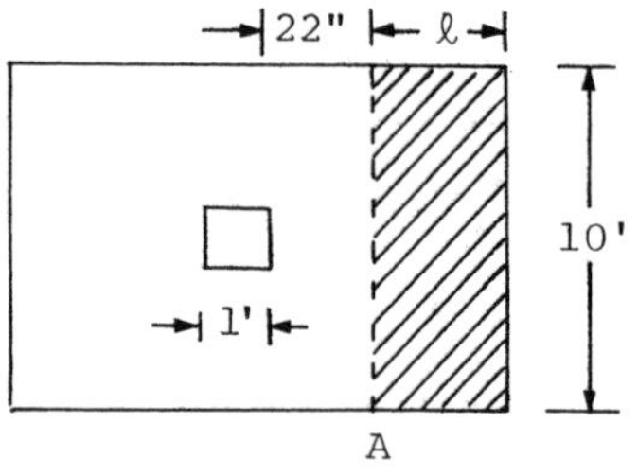

Fig. 1

Evaluating beam shear depth "d" from column face (Refer to fig. 1)

$$2(\ell) = 10' - 1' - 2(22'')$$

$$\text{or } l = 2.66\ ft$$

The shear force carried along face A by concrete is

$$V_c = 2\sqrt{f'_c}\cdot b_w \cdot d = 2\sqrt{4000}\ (10 \times 12'')(22)\ \text{lbs.}$$
$$= 333.9^k$$

The factored shear force acting along face A is

$$V_u = w \cdot l = 6.58 \times 10 \times 2.66 = 175^k$$

Since $V_c > V_u/\phi$ that is $333.9 > 175/0.85$, therefore, d = 22" is OK for beam shear.

Punching Shear:

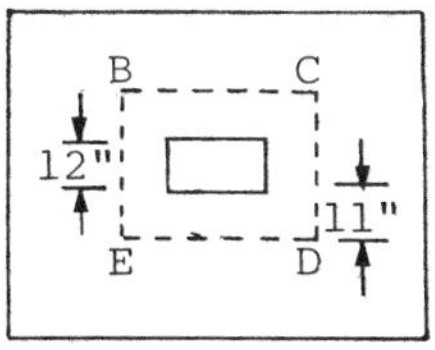

Fig. 2

The critical section for punching shear is "d/2" distance away from column face. (refer to fig. 2)

The net factored shear force along BCDE is column load minus upward soil pressure.

$$V_o = 658^k - 6.58\left(\frac{34}{12}\right)^2 = 605^k$$

The shear force carried by concrete along BCDE is (ACI sec. 11.11.2)

$$V_c = 4\sqrt{f'_c}\, b_o d$$

where b_o is perimeter = 4(34") = 136 in.

$$V_c = 4\sqrt{4000}\,(136)(22) = 757^k$$

Since $V_c > V_u/\phi$ that is $757^k > 605/0.85$, therefore, d = 22" is OK for punching shear.

Therefore, use d = 22" for footing.

DESIGN OF FOOTINGS BY WORKING STRESS METHOD

• PROBLEM 18-71

Design a square concrete (plain) footing for an 18" diameter round column which carries a load of 250,000lbs. 3000 lb concrete and a 2 ton soil (bearing capacity of 4000 lbs/ft^2) are to be used. Assume that the weight of the footing is approximately $12\frac{1}{2}\%$ of the column load.

Solution:

(i) To find the size of the footing:

Load of the footing = $12\frac{1}{2}\%$ x 250,000 lbs = 31,250 lbs

Therefore total bearing on the soil = 250,000 + 31,250 lbs

= 281,250 lbs.

Therefore, bearing area required for footing $= \frac{281,250 \text{ lbs}}{4000 \text{ lbs/ft}^2}$

$\simeq 70.3 \text{ ft}^2$.

side of a square $= \sqrt{70.3} \simeq 8.39$ ft.

Using a square of side 8' - 6".

(ii) To find depth of the footing : (Moment Considerations)

a) An equivalent square column is assumed

Side of the column $= \sqrt{\frac{\pi \times 18^2}{4}} \simeq 15.95 \simeq 1.33$ ft.

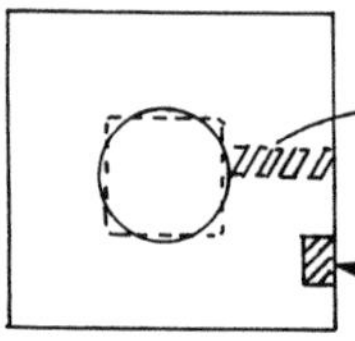

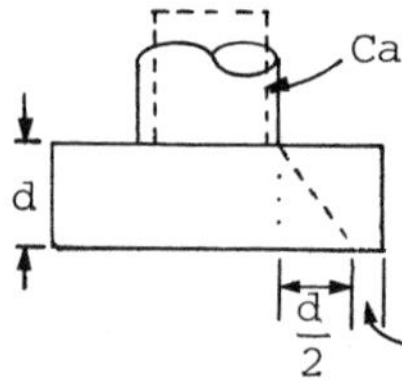

b) Length of cantilever for moment:

$$\frac{8.50 - 1.33}{2} \simeq 3.59 \text{ ft.}$$

c) Maximum Tension $= f_c = 1.6 \sqrt{f'_c} = 88 \text{ lbs/in}^2$

(ACI 15.7.2, 1971 code)

$$f_t = \frac{M_c}{I} = \frac{6M}{bd^2}$$

Therefore, $d = \sqrt{\frac{6M}{b \cdot f_t}}$

and $f_{bearing} = \frac{250,000}{(8.5)^2} \simeq 3460 \text{ lbs/ft}^2$

Note that the load used above is not total load but load on the column only.

Considering a 1 ft width,

$$M = 3460 \times 1 \text{ ft width} \times 3.59 \times \frac{3.59}{2} \simeq 22,300 \text{ lb-ft}$$

$$= 22,300 \times 12 = 267600 \text{ lb-in}$$

$$d = \sqrt{\frac{6 \times 267600}{12 \times 88}} \simeq 39'' = 3'3''$$

d) Shear: (CHECK)

Shear cantilever length = 3.59' - 1.58' = 2.01'

$$v = \frac{V}{bd} = \frac{2.01 \times 3460 \text{ lb/ft}^2 \times 1 \text{ ft width}}{12 \times 38} = 153 \text{ lb/in}^2$$

The value obtained is reasonable since allowable $= 2\sqrt{f'_c}$

$= 110 \text{ lb/in}^2$

(ACI 8.7.7.3)

Therefore an 8' - 6" square concrete footing with a depth of 3' - 2" is selected.

• PROBLEM 18-72

Determine the plan dimensions for a double column footing shown in figure below. The footing base is located 5 ft below ground level. Unfactored dead and live loads are indicated in the figure. Assume that the safe bearing capacity of soil at 5 ft below ground level is 3.8 k/ft^2.

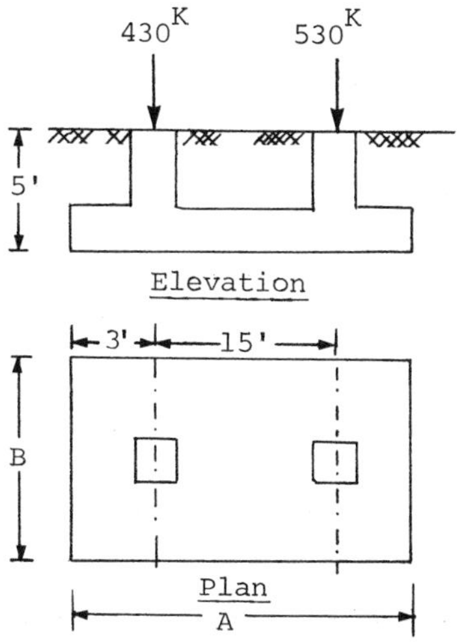

Solution: The dimension 'A' should be such that the resultant of the column loads passes through the centroid of the dual column footing. This would result in a uniform settlement of the footing.

Assuming that the resultant of the column loads is located at a distance 'x' from the left,

$$\text{then} \quad x = \frac{3'(430^k) + 18'(530^k)}{430^k + 530^k}$$

$$= 11.28 \text{ ft.}$$

Thus, A = 2x = 2 x 11.28' = 22.56 ft say 22.5 ft

Based on the safe bearing capacity of the soil, the other plan dimension 'B' can be determined as follows:

If the unit weight of soil and concrete together is taken to average about 125 lbs/ft^3 above the base of the footing, then the net allowable soil pressure P_{net} is

$$P_{net} = 3.8^{k/ft^2} - 5'(0.125^{k/ft^3})$$

$$= 3.18 \ k/ft^2$$

Thus, 'B' must now be large enough to ensure that the pressure due to column loads does not exceed $3.18^{k/ft^2}$.

$$\text{Hence,} \quad \frac{430^k + 530^k}{22.5' \times B} = 3.18^{k/ft^2}$$

$$\text{from which,} \quad B = \frac{430^k + 530^k}{22.5' \times 3.18^{k/ft^2}}$$

$$= 13.4 \text{ ft say, } 13.5 \text{ ft.}$$

Therefore the plan dimensions for the given dual column footing are:

A = 22.5 ft.

B = 13.5 ft.

• PROBLEM 18-73

Design a reinforced concrete footing to rest on a two-ton soil for a total load of 27 k/ft on a 13" brick wall. 3000# concrete and grade 40 steel are to be used. Use "Alternate Design" (working stress) scheme.

Solution:

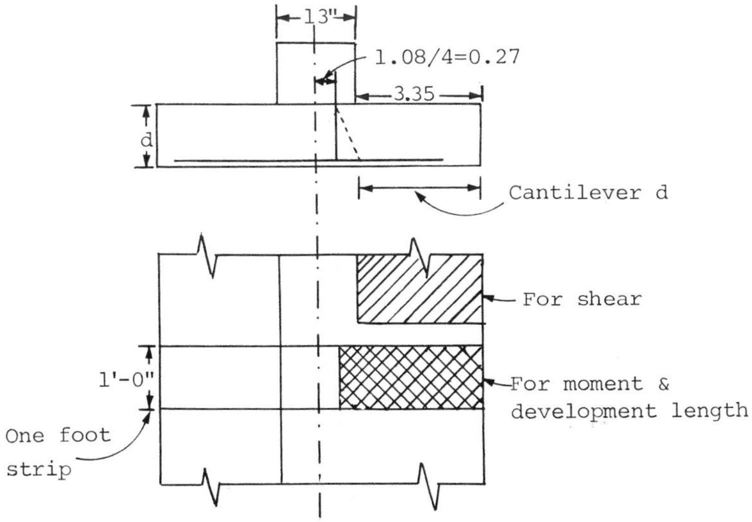

Fig. 1

Let us assume that footing weight is approximately 7% of the wall load.

Therefore, footing weight = 0.07 x 27 = 1.9 k/ft.

Thus, total load = $27^k + 1.9^{k'} = 28.9^{k'}$ = 28,900 lbs/ft

Considering a 1 foot width strip,

$$b = \frac{28{,}900 \text{ x } 1 \text{ ft}}{4000^{\#}/\text{ft}^2} = 7.23 \text{ ft}^2 = 1' \text{ x } 7.23'$$

Let us use a width of 7.3' = 7.25'

$$\text{Net soil pressure} = \frac{27000^{\#}/\text{ft}}{7.25} = 3{,}720 \text{ lb/ft}^2.$$

Note that the footing weight does not contribute to either moment or shear. It only adds to the total soil pressure.

$$\text{Cantilever} = \frac{7.25}{2} - \frac{1.08}{4} = 3.36 \text{ ft} \quad \left(\text{ACI } 15.4.2(\text{b})\right) = 1$$

$$\text{Therefore, } M_u = \frac{Wl^2}{2} = \frac{3720 \text{ x } 1 \text{ ft x } 3.36^2}{2} = 20{,}900 \text{ ft-lbs.}$$

$$= 20{,}900 \text{ x } 12 \text{ in-lb} = 251{,}000 \text{ lb-in} = Kb \cdot d^2.$$

But K = 224 for a $3000^{\#}$ concrete

Thus $M = Kbd^2 = 224 \text{ x } 12'' \text{ x } d^2 = 251{,}000$

Therefore d = 9.35"

Let us try d = 9.5"

Adding 3" clear cover + $\frac{1}{2}$ of a 1" ϕ bar, (ACI 7.71(a))

We have depth d = 9.5" + 3.5" = 13.00"

Check for shear:

$$\text{Now, cantilever} = 3.36 - \frac{9.5}{12} = 2.59 \text{ ft.}$$

$$\text{Then, shear stress } v = \frac{V}{bd} = \frac{3720 \times 1 \text{ ft} \times 2.59}{12'' \times 9.5''} = 84.4 \ \#/\text{in}^2.$$

But maximum allowable $v = 1.1\sqrt{f'_c} = 1.1\sqrt{3000} = 60 \ \#/\text{in}^2$

Therefore, d will have to be revised.

$$v = \frac{V}{bd}$$

or
$$d = \frac{V}{b \cdot v}$$

$$V = 3720 \times 2.59$$

$$b = 1' = 12''$$

and v is not to exceed 60 lbs/in^2.

$$\text{Therefore,} \quad d = \frac{3720 \times 2.59 \times 1'}{12''(60)} = 13.4''.$$

Let us use the average of the two d's so obtained

$$= \frac{9.5 + 13.4}{2} \simeq 11.5''$$

$$\text{from which } v = \frac{3720 \times 2.59}{12 \times 11.5} = 65 \ \#/\text{in}^2 > 60$$

No good.

By trial and error, obtain d = 12.5" to yield

$$v = 58 \ \#/\text{in}^2 < 60 \ \#/\text{in}^2$$

Therefore OK.

Therefore, let us use d = 12.5"

To obtain the area of steel, A_s, we have

$$M = A_s \cdot f_s \cdot jd$$

or
$$A_s = \frac{M}{f_s \cdot jd} = \frac{20{,}900 \times 12}{20000 \times 0.874 \times 12.5} = 1.15 \text{ in}^2.$$

Note that the value of j = 0.874 is obtained from design table.

Using #7 bars, the spacing $S = \frac{12 \times 0.60}{1.15} = 6.27'$

Therefore, use #7 bars @ 6 inches center to center or #8 bars @ 8 inches center to center. (obtained by repeating the above calculation for S)

Development Length:

As per ACI 12.2.2(a), the basic development length is

$$0.4\ A_b(f_y/\sqrt{f_c'}) = 0.4(0.66)\left((40{,}000)/\sqrt{3000}\right) = 17.5'$$

but not less than $0.0004\ d_b f_y = 0.0004(0.875)(40{,}000)$

$= 14.0''$

We have 3.36' - 3" = 3.11' = 37.4" > 14.00

Therefore OK.

Check for weight:

Wt. of footing $= 7.25 \times \frac{16}{12} \times 150\ \#/ft^3 = 1450\ \#/ft <$ assumed weight of 1900 #/ft

Therefore, OK.

Thus, let us provide a 16" thick footing with #7 bars (transverse direction) @ 6" center to center @ bottom.

Note that in general practice, 3 to 4, #4 or #5 bars are often added in the longitudinal direction to tie the main transverse bars but more to give the effect of bridging over 'soft spots' in the soil.

Refer to figure.

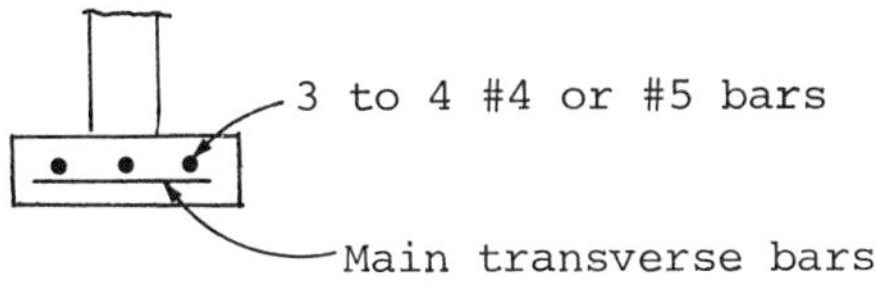

Fig. 2

Design a reinforced concrete footing for a W12 x 99 column (12" x 12" steel section) which carries a load of 813 kips. The footing is to use 2500# concrete and grade 40 steel. It is assumed that the footing will rest on a $2\frac{1}{2}$ ton soil. The column rests on a 28" x 28" base plate.

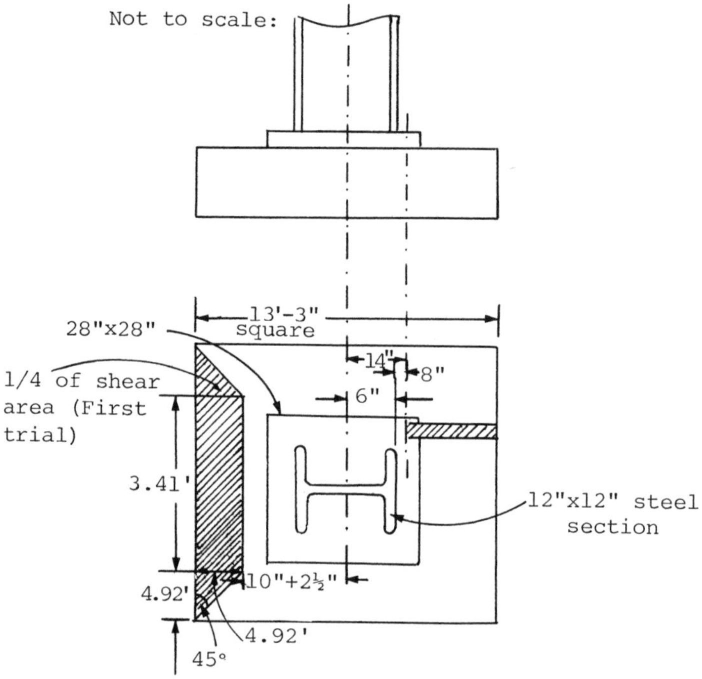

Solution: Let us assume that footing weight is 8% of the load on the column.

(Generally varies between 6 to 10%. In this case, 8% would be a good guess since concrete strength is 2500 $\#/in^2$)

Therefore, footing weight = 8% of 813 k = $65040^{\#}$

Thus total load = 813000 + 65040 = $878040^{\#}$.

Bearing capacity of a $2\frac{1}{2}$ ton soil = 5000 $\#/ft^2$.

$$\text{Therefore bearing area} = \frac{\text{Total load}}{\text{Bearing capacity}} = \frac{878040^{\#}}{5000\ \#/ft^2}$$

$$= 175.6\ ft^2.$$

Assuming a square footing,

Size of the footing = $\sqrt{175.6}$ = 13.25 ft say 13'-3".

Cantilever length = $\frac{13'-3''}{2} - 10'' = 69\frac{1}{2}'' = 5.79'$.

Moment $M = \frac{Wl^2}{2}$

Bearing area = 175.6 ft^2

Load on the column = $813^k = 813000^{\#}$

Therefore, bearing pressure = $\frac{813000}{175.6} = 4630$ lbs/ft^2 = W.

Thus, moment $M = 4630 \times \frac{5.79^2}{2} = 77608$ lb-ft

$= 931296$ lb-in.

But $M = Kbd^2$ where K = 179 (for a $2500^{\#}$ concrete from tables)

Therefore, $931296 = 179 \times 12'' \times d^2$ (considering a 1' strip, b = 1' = 12")

Thus d = 20.8" say 21".

Check for shear:

To check for shear let us go out d/2 distance

$$= 5.79' - \frac{21}{2} \times \frac{1}{12} = 4.92' \quad \text{(ACI code)}$$

Referring to the first trial trapezoid in the figure, we have

$$b = 13.25 - 2(4.92) = 3.41'$$

Shear stress $v = \frac{V}{b \cdot d}$

where $V = 4630 \times 4.92' \times (13.25 + 3.41)/2$ (Trapezoid)

$= 189754$ lbs.

Therefore $v = \frac{189754}{(3.41 \times 12)'' \times 21''}$

$= 221$ #/in^2.

But maximum permissible shear stress $v = 2\sqrt{f'_c}$

$= 2\sqrt{2500} = 100$ #/in^2

Therefore $v > v_{allowable}$

Hence 'd' will have to be revised.

$$v = \frac{V}{bd}$$

or $$d = \frac{V}{b \cdot v}$$

Limiting v to 100 $\#/in^2$, we have

$$d = \frac{189754}{41 \times 100} = 46''$$

Let us try an average 'd' $= \frac{46 + 21}{2} \simeq 33''$.

Considering the new trapezoid:

All dimensions in feet

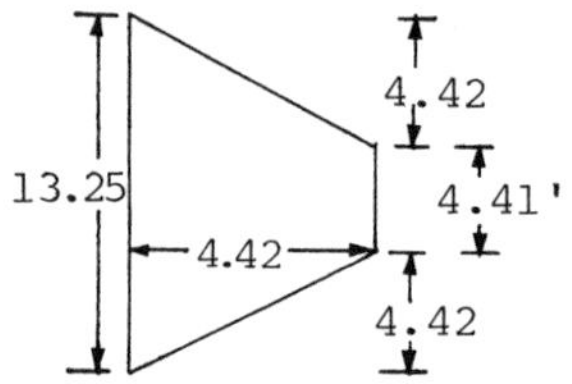

Fig. not to scale

Fig. 2

$$5.79' - \frac{33}{2} \times \frac{1}{12} = 4.42'$$

and $b = 13.25 - 2(4.42) = 4.41'$

$$\text{Thus } v = \frac{4630 \times 4.42 \times (13.25 + 4.41)/2}{(4.41 \times 12) \times 33''}$$

$$= 104 \ \#/in^2 > 100 \ \#/in^2.$$

Let us therefore try d = 34", giving us:

For the new trapezoid,

$$5.79 - \frac{34}{2} \times \frac{1}{12} = 4.37'$$

and $b = 13.25 - 2(4.37) = 4.51'$

All dimensions in feet

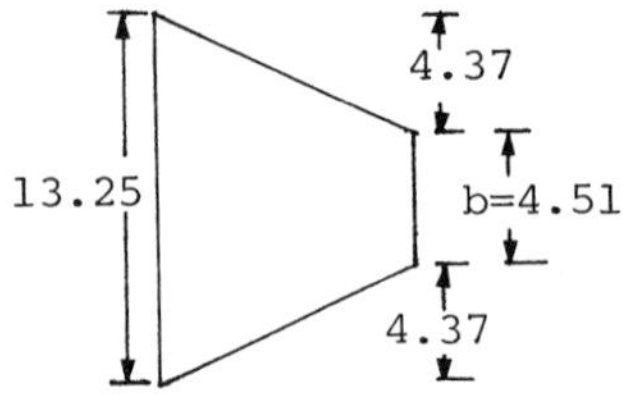

Fig. not to scale

Fig. 3

Thus $v = \dfrac{4630(4.37)(13.25 + 4.51)/2}{(4.51 \times 12) \times 34}$

$= 97.6\ \#/in^2 < 100\ \#/in^2.$

Therefore, let us select d = 34".

To find reinforcement steel:

Moment $M = A_s \cdot f_s \cdot jd$

where j = 0.880 from tables for a $2500^{\#}$ concrete

$M = 13.25 \times 931296 = 12339672$

Thus $A_s = \dfrac{M}{f_s \cdot jd}$

$= \dfrac{12339672}{20{,}000 \times 0.880 \times 34} = 20.6\ in^2.$

Using a 6" minimum spacing,

$\dfrac{20.6}{2 \times 13.25} = 0.78\ in^2.$ (2 bars/ft)

Let us select #8 bars each of 0.79 in^2.

Thus, use 27 - #8 bars @ 6" center to center.

Check for bond:

The development length $L = 0.04\ A_b f_y/\sqrt{f'_c}$

$= 0.04 \times 0.79 \times 40{,}000/\sqrt{2500} = 25.3"$

but not less than $0.0004\ d_b \cdot f_y$

$= 0.0004\ (1.0)(40{,}000) = 16"$

We have cantilever of 5.79' or 69½" minus 3" for cover

= 66.5" > 16"

Therefore, OK.

Total depth d = 34" + 3" + 1" (bar dia) = 38"

Thus, let us provide a square footing of side 13'-3" and 3'-2" deep reinforced with 27 - #8 bars spaced @ a minimum 6" center to center.

Design a reinforced concrete footing to rest on a two-ton soil for a total load of 20 k/ft (service load) on a 13" brick wall. Use 3000# concrete, grade 40 steel. Employ the ultimate strength design and the relevant ACI code provisions.

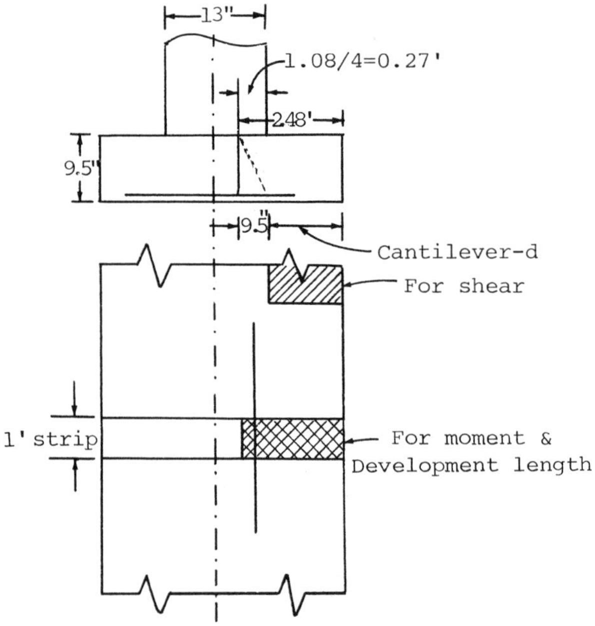

Solution: Let us assume that footing weight is 8% of the total load.

Therefore, footing weight = $0.08 \times 20^{k/1} = 1.6$ k/ft

Hence, total load on the soil = 20 + 1.6 = 21.6 k/ft

= 21600 #/ft

Bearing capacity of a 2-ton soil = 4000 $\#/ft^2$

Considering a 1 ft width strip,

$$\text{Bearing area} = \frac{21{,}600\ \#/\text{ft} \times 1\ \text{ft}}{4000\ \#/\text{ft}^2} = 5.40\ \text{ft}^2$$

$$= 1' \times 5.4'$$

Let us select a width of 5'-6" (5.5 ft)

$$\text{Therefore net soil pressure} = \frac{20 \times 1000\ \#/\text{ft}}{5.5'} = 3636\ \#/\text{ft}^2$$

Assuming that Dead load = Live load (in the absence of any specific data in the problem)

Ultimate load U = 1.4D + 1.7L = 1.55 (D + L)

$$= 1.55(3636\ \#/ft^2) = 5636\ \#/ft^2.$$

Length of cantilever for moment $= \frac{5.5}{2} - \frac{1.08}{4} = 2.48$ ft

(Refer ACI 15.4.2(b))

Thus, ultimate moment $M_u = \frac{Wl^2}{2} = \frac{5636\ \#/ft^2 \times 1\ ft \times (2.48)^2}{2}$

$$= 17332 \text{ ft-lbs} = 17.332 \text{ ft-kips.}$$

The maximum allowable $\rho = \frac{0.75\ \rho_b}{2}$

where $\rho_b = \frac{\beta_1 \times 0.85\ f'_c}{f_y} \cdot \frac{87000}{87000 + f_y}$

In our case, $\beta_1 = 0.85$, $f'_c = 3000$ psi

and f_y for grade 40 steel = 40,000 psi

Substituting these values in the above expression for ρ_b, we have,

$$\rho_b = \frac{0.85 \times 0.85 \times 3000}{40{,}000} \cdot \frac{87000}{87000 + 40{,}000}$$

$$= 0.0371$$

Therefore $\rho = \frac{0.75\ \rho_b}{2} = \frac{0.75 \times 0.0371}{2} = 0.0139$

Referring to the strength design tables for a 3000 psi concrete, 40,000 psi steel for f_y and ρ equal to 0.0139 corresponding to $M_u = 17.3$ ft-kips we have $M_u = 18.84$ ft-kips (Refer to Table XX at end of this chapter).
in the column for $\rho = 0.0139$. Reading off the values of A_s and effective depth for this M_u, we have $A_s = 1.08$ in^2 and effective depth = 6.5 in.

Providing a cover of 3" + ½ of 1" ϕ bar (ACI 7.14.1.1)

$$d = 6.5 + 3.5 = 10''$$

However, for a wall footing of 12", the minimum practical depth would be d = 12" - 3.5" = 8.5".

Note now that length of cantilever $= 2.48' - \frac{8.5''}{12''} + 1.77$ ft.

Check for shear:

$$\text{Shear stress } v_u = \frac{V_u}{\phi bd} = \frac{5636 \text{ \#/ft}^2 \times 1 \text{ ft} \times 1.77}{0.85 \times 12'' \times 8.50''}$$

$$= 115 \text{ \#/in}^2.$$

But permissible shear stress is $2\sqrt{f'_c} = 2\sqrt{3000} = 110 \text{ \#/in}^2$

We will therefore, have to revise our 'd'.

$$v_u = \frac{V_u}{\phi bd}$$

or $$d = \frac{V_u}{\phi b v_u}$$

Since v_u is not to exceed 110 #/in²,

$$d = \frac{5636 \text{ \#/ft}^2 \times 1' \times 1.77'}{0.85 \times 12'' \times 110 \text{ \#/in}^2} = 8.90''$$

As before, providing a cover of 3½", d = 8.9 + 3.5 = 12.4"
say 13" (total depth)

To obtain area of steel A_s, effective depth = 13"-3.5" = 9.5"

Again, referring to the strength design tables, for $\rho = 0.0094$, corresponding to an effective depth of 9.5", we have $A_s = 1.07 \text{ in}^2$ and $M_u = 28.29$ ft-kips (Table XX at end of this chapter).

But actual $M_u = 17.332$ ft-kips

Therefore, required $A_s = \frac{17.332}{28.29} \times 1.07 = 0.656 \text{ in}^2$

Let us use, say #6 bars at a spacing of $\frac{12 \times 0.44}{0.656} = 8''$

Therefore, use #6 bars @ 8" center to center.

Check for development length:

For #6 bars, as per ACI 12.5, the basic development length is $0.04\, A_b f_y/\sqrt{f'_c} = 0.04(0.44 \text{ in}^2)(40{,}000 \text{ \#/in}^2)/\sqrt{3000}$

$$= 12.85 \text{ in.}$$

but not less than $0.0004\, d_b \cdot f_y = 0.0004(0.75'')(40{,}000)$

$$= 12''.$$

We have 2.48' - 3" = 2.23' = 26.8" > 12"

Therefore, OK.

Check for weight:

$$\text{Weight of footing} = 5.5' \times \frac{13}{12} \times 150\ \#/ft^3$$

$$= 894\ \#/ft < \text{our assumed } 1600\ \#/ft$$

Therefore, OK.

Final Design: Provide a 5'-6" wide, 13" thick footing reinforced with #6 bars spaced @ 8" center to center. 3 or 4 #4 or #5 bars may be provided longitudinally to bridge over 'soft spots' in the soil.

• PROBLEM 18-76

A 16" x 16" square column carries a load of 350 kips and rests on a two-ton soil. If there is to be a space restriction of four feet from the centerline of the column to the edge of the footing, design an isolated reinforced concrete footing. $f_s = 20000\ lbs/in^2$ and $f_c' = 4000\ lbs/in^2$.

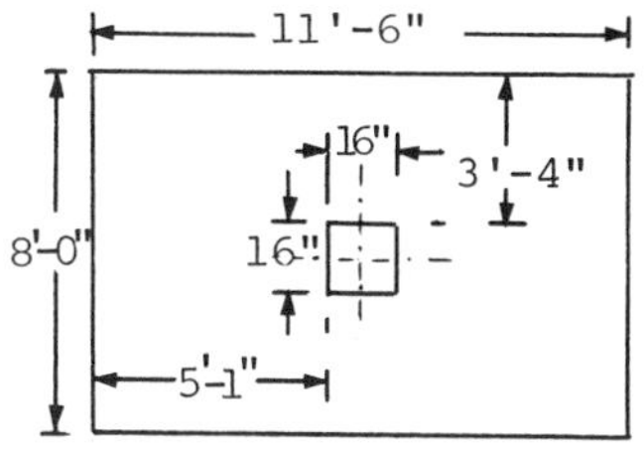

Fig. 1

Solution:

The footing dimension on one side is restricted to 8'-0".

Let us now find out the area of the footing (bearing area) so that we can determine the other dimension of the footing and at the same time restricting the one dimension to 8'-0".

Column load = 350 kips

Assuming dead load to be 6% of column load, we have, dead load = 21 kips.

Total load = 350k + 21k = 371 kips

Therefore, bearing area = $\frac{371^k}{4000 \text{ lb/ft}^2}$ = 92.5 ft^2.

(for a 2 ton soil) [arrow pointing to 4000]

Therefore, dimension of the other side = $\frac{92.5}{8}$ = 11.51'

say 11'-6".

Thus, bearing pressure to be used for moment and shear $\Bigg\}$ = $\frac{350,000}{8' \times 11.5'}$ = 3810 lb/ft^2

Maximum moment (along length) M = 3810 x 1 ft x 5.08' x $\frac{5.08'}{2}$

= 49000 lb-ft. (5'-1" arm)

We have, M= Kbd^2

or $\quad d = \sqrt{\frac{M}{Kb}} = \sqrt{\frac{49,000 \times 12}{324 \times 12}}$ = 12.3" say 13"

Providing a cover of 3" + bars we have

depth d = 13" + 4" = 17".

Check for shear:

(i) Assuming a one-way beam,

Shear force V for a length (5'- 1") - 13" = 4'-0", is

V = 1'-0" x 3810 lb/ft^2 x 4'-0" = 15,240 lbs.

Thus, shear stress v = $\frac{V}{bd} = \frac{15,240}{12 \times 13}$

= 928 lb/in^2.

But allowable v = 70 lbs/in^2

Limiting shear stress v to 70 lbs/in^2, we have

$d = \frac{V}{vb} = \frac{15240}{70 \times 12''}$ = 18.2".

Let us try d = 16".

Shear force V =(1'- 0") x 3810 lb/ft^2 x {(5'-1") - (1'-4")}

= 14,300 lbs.

Thus, shear stress = v = $\frac{14300}{12'' \times 16''}$ = 75 lbs/in^2 > 70 lb/in^2

No good.

Let us try d = 17".

Shear force $V = (1'\text{-}0'') \times 3810\ \text{lb/ft}^2 \times \{(5'\text{-}1'') - (1'\text{-}5'')\}$

$= 14{,}000$ lbs.

Thus, shear stress $= v = \frac{V}{bd} = \frac{14000}{12 \times 17} = 68.6\ \text{lb/in}^2 < 70\ \text{lb/in}^2$

Therefore, OK.

(ii) Assuming a two-way beam,

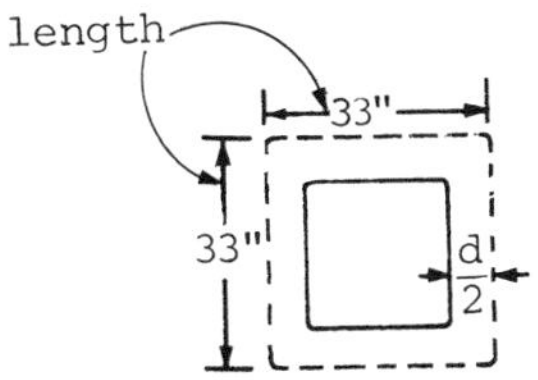

Fig. 2

let us try d = 17" so that $\frac{d}{2} = \frac{17}{2} = 8.5''$

We have, $v = \frac{V}{bd} = \frac{[(11.5 \times 8) - (2.75)^2]\ (3810\ \text{lb/in}^2)}{4 \times 33 \times 17''}$

$= 143\ \text{lb/in}^2$.

But allowable $v = 2\sqrt{f'_c} = 126\ \text{lb/in}^2$.

Let us try d = 18"

Then length = 34" = 2'-10"

Thus, $v = \frac{[(11.5 \times 8.0) - (2.83\ )^2]\ (3810)}{4 \times 34 \times 18} = 131\ \text{lb/in}^2$

$> 126\ \text{lb/in}^2$.

Trying d = 19", we get (using the same procedure as above)

$v = 120\ \text{lb/in}^2 < 126\ \text{lb/in}^2$.

Therefore, OK.

Using d = 19", we get a total depth of 23" (providing 3" cover + 1" for bars).

Steel Reinforcement:

Long bars:

Total $A_s = \frac{M}{f_s \cdot jd} = \frac{49000 \times 8 \times 12}{20{,}000 \times 0.816 \times 19} = 12.38\ \text{in}^2$.

where jd = 0.816 for 4000 lb concrete

Let us provide 16 - #8 bars giving a total area of $12.56\ \text{in}^2$.

Check for development length: $l_d = 0.04\ A_b f_y/\sqrt{f'_c}$

$= 0.04(0.79)(40{,}000)/\sqrt{4000} = 20''$

But this should not be less than, $0.0004\ d_b \cdot f_y$

$= 0.0004(1.0)(40{,}000) = 16''$.

We have 61" - 3" clear = 58"   OK.

Short bars:

$$\text{Total } A_s = \frac{M}{f_s \cdot jd} = \frac{3810 \times 3'\text{-}4'' \times (3'\text{-}4''/2) \times 11'\text{-}6'' \times 12''}{20{,}000 \times 0.861 \times 19''}$$

$$= 8.95 \text{ in}^2.$$

Let us use 12 - #8 bars giving an area of 9.43 in^2.

Check for development length:

We need $l_d = 0.04\ A_b \cdot f_y/\sqrt{f'_c} = 0.04(0.79 \text{ in}^2)(40{,}000)/\sqrt{4000}$

$= 20''$

But we have(3' - 4") - 3" clear = 37". So, OK.

However, as per ACI 15.4.4, center 8'-0" (of the 11'-6")

must have $\dfrac{2}{\beta + 1} = \dfrac{2}{\frac{11.5}{8} + 1} = 82\%$ of the short bars.

For a uniform distribution, 82% of 8.95 = 7.35 in^2.

The same frequency of steel is used throughout such that $A_s = \dfrac{11.5}{8.0} \times 7.35 = 10.60 \text{ in}^2$.

Let us use 14 - #8 bars giving an area of 11.00 in^2.

Check for weight:

$$8'\text{-}0'' \times 11'\text{-}6'' \times \frac{23}{12} \text{ ft} \times 150 \text{ lbs/ft}^3 = 26.4 \text{ k}$$

But we assumed a wt of 21 k which is less than 26.4 k (actual) by 5.4 k and the percentage is $\frac{5.4}{371} = 1.45\%$ only which can be ignored. The above design can therefore be accepted or a 11'-9" instead of 11'-6" can be used. Note however that the steel reinforcement remains the same.

Two reinforced concrete coloumns 12" square, each carry a load of 140,000 lbs. Design for these two columns, a combined footing if it is to rest on a 3 ton soil, using f'_c = 3000 psi and f_s = 20,000 psi. The footing is to be deep enough to eliminate the need for stirrups. Also, the footing is not to extend beyond the edge of the columns which are apart by 12 feet measured center to center. Assume that the footing weight is approximately 8% of the column load.

Solution: Load on each column = 140,000 lbs = 140^k

Therefore, total column load = 2 x 140^k = 280^k.

Thus footing weight = 8% of column load = 0.08 x 280^k = 22.4^k

Hence, total load = 280^k + 22.4^k = 302.4^k

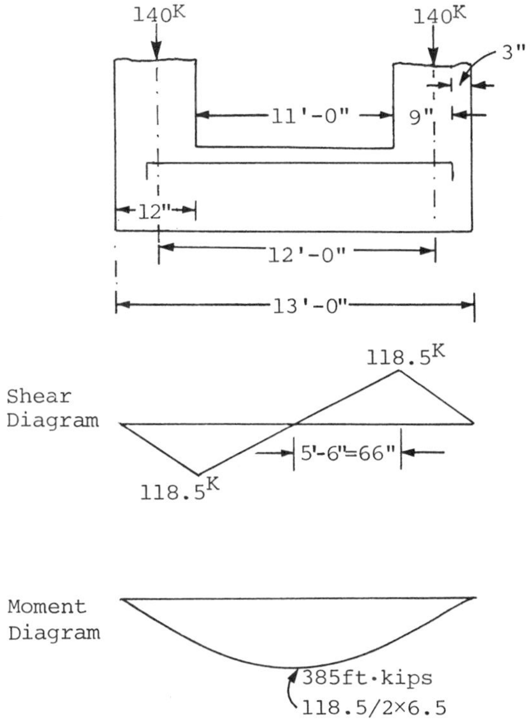

Fig. 1

Bearing capacity of a 3 ton soil = 6000 lbs/ft^2 = $6^{k/ft^2}$.

and total load = 302.4^k.

Therefore bearing area = $\dfrac{302.4^k}{6^{k/ft^2}}$ = 50.4 ft^2.

Thus, width of the footing (l = 13'-0") = $\frac{50.4}{13}$ = 3.88 wide

say 4'-0" wide.

$M = Kbd^2$ for compression in concrete

where K = 224 (obtained from design table for f'_c = 3000 psi concrete, Table V at end of this chapter).

$$\text{Therefore } d = \sqrt{\frac{M}{Kb}} = \sqrt{\frac{385000^{\text{lb-ft}} \times 12''}{224 \times 4' \times 12''}}$$

= 20.8" say 21".

Adding 4" clear cover, overall depth = 21" + 4" = 25".
(can use $3\frac{1}{2}$" cover also)

Check for shear.

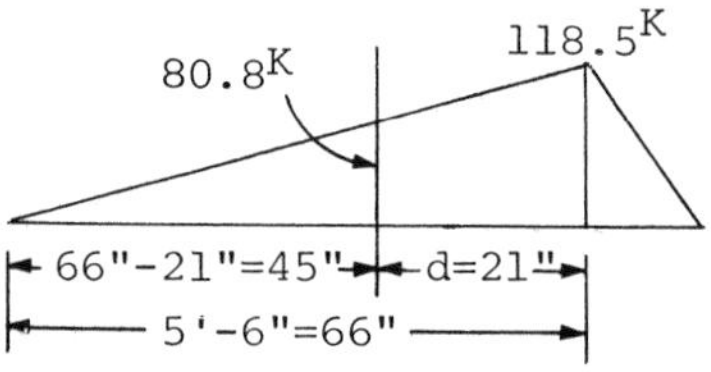

Fig. 2

Going out a distance of d = 21", shear at that point =

$\frac{45}{66} \times 118.5^k$ (refer to the figure and by similar triangles)

$= 80.8^k$

Therefore, shear stress $v = \frac{V}{bd} = \frac{80.8 \times 1000}{48'' \times 21''} = 80.2\ \#/in^2$.

But maximum permissible shear stress $= 1.1\sqrt{f'_c}$

$= 1.1\sqrt{3000} = 60\ \#/in^2$.

Therefore, 'd' will have to be revised.

$$v = \frac{V}{bd} \quad \text{or} \quad d = \frac{V}{b \cdot v}$$

Limiting v to the allowable 60 $\#/in^2$,

$$d = \frac{80.8^k \times 1000}{48'' \times 60} = 28''$$

Let us try 'd' somewhere between 21" and 28".

Let us try d = 26" so that,

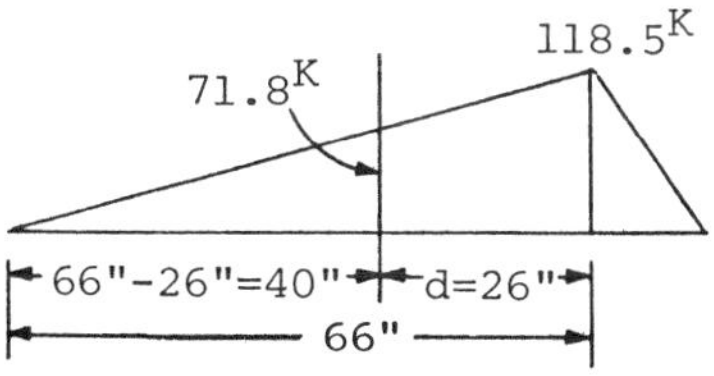

Fig. 3

Shear force at d = 26" = $118.5 \times \frac{40}{66}$ (Refer to fig. 2 and similar triangles)

$= 71.8^k = 71800$ lbs.

Therefore, shear stress $v = \frac{V}{bd} = \frac{71800}{48" \times 26"} = 57.5^{\#}/in^2 < 60^{\#}/in^2$

Therefore, OK.

Using 4" cover (can be $3\frac{1}{2}$" also), overall depth = 26" + 4" = 30".

Area of steel $A_s = \frac{M}{f_s \cdot jd}$ $(M = A_s \cdot f_s \cdot jd)$

$= \frac{385{,}000 \times 12"}{20{,}000 \times 0.874 \times 26"} = 10.16\ in^2$ ($j = 0.874$ from design tables for $f'_c = 3000$ psi concrete, Table V)

Let us select 7 - #11 bars giving an area = $10.92\ in^2$ ($7 \times 1.56\ in^2$)

(Top bars)

Check for bond (Development length):

Development length $l_d = 1.4 \times 0.04\ A_b\ f_y/\sqrt{f'_c}$

$= 1.4 \times 0.04 \times (1.56) \times 40{,}000/\sqrt{3000}$

$= 63.8"$

Maximum length beyond inside of column (refer to fig. 1)

= 9" + 30" - (3" + 3") = 33" (Not sufficient)

Limiting development length $l_d = 33"$,

we have $l_d = 33" = 1.4 \times 0.04\ A_b\ (40{,}000/\sqrt{3000})$

Therefore $A_b = 0.807\ in^2$.

We can select #8 bars or smaller bars (See Sec. 12 of ACI)

Let us use 13 - #8 bars giving an area of 10.27 in^2.

(Table I at end of this chapter)

Thus $l_d = 1.4 \times 0.04(0.79\ in^2)(40{,}000/\sqrt{3000})$

$= 32.3'' - 9'' = 23.2''$ say 24".

Transverse Steel:

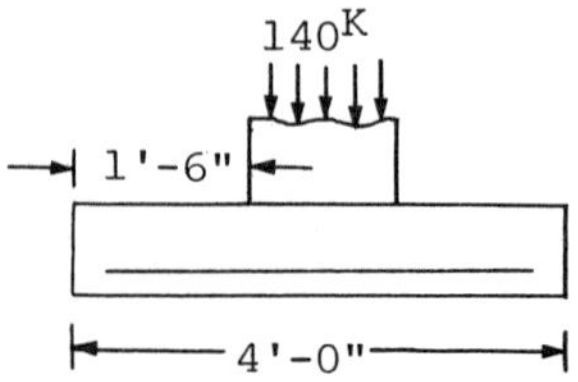

Let us assume that the 140^k load is spread over last two feet = 24" (wide) and 4'-0" width.

Therefore distributed load $= \dfrac{140^k}{4^{ft}} = 35^{k/ft}$

and $M = \dfrac{wl^2}{2} = \dfrac{35 \times (1.5)^2}{2} = 39.4$ ft-kips.

But $M = fz = 39400 \times 12'' = 88^{\#/in^2} \times \frac{1}{6} \times 24'' \times d^2$

(Note $f = 88^{\#/in^2}$, from ACI code)

Therefore $d = 36.6''$.

But we have only 30".

Therefore, steel bars have to be used.

Area of steel $A_s = \dfrac{M}{f_s jd} = \dfrac{39400 \times 12''}{20{,}000 \times 0.874 \times 26''}$

$= 1.04\ in^2$.

Let us provide 3 - #6 bars on the 2' end each side, giving an area = 1.32 in^2.

Check for bond (development length):

$l_d = 0.04 \times A_b\ (f_y/\sqrt{f'_c})$

$= 0.04 \times 0.44\ (40{,}000/\sqrt{3000}) = 12.8''$.

We have, beyond column, 18"-3" = 15"

Therefore, OK.

Check for shear: A 45^0 line drawn from column touches side of footing before coming to the bottom. Therefore, shear is OK.

Longitudinal steel:

Let us assume that there is no support for 12'-0".

$w = 2'\text{-}6" \times 4' \times 150^{\#/ft^3}$ ($150^{\#/ft^3}$ = unit wt. of concrete).

$= 1.5^{k/ft}$

And M for simply supported section

$= \frac{1}{8} wl^2$

$= \frac{1}{8} \times 1.5^{k/ft} \times 12^2$

$= 27^{k/ft}$

whence $A_s = \dfrac{27000 \times 12"}{20{,}000 \times 0.874 \times 26"}$ (j = 0.874 from design table)

$= 0.71\ in^2$.

Let us provide 3 - #5 bars longitudinally.

Final Design Summary:

Let us provide a combined footing, 13'-0" long, 4'-0" wide and 2'-6" deep (d = 26") with 13 - #8 bars as top reinforcement (long bars @ top), 13 - #6 short bars, (bottom bars) and 3 - #5 bars long (longitudinally).

Check for weight:

Footing weight = $2'\text{-}6" \times 13' \times 4' \times 150^{\#/ft^3}$

$= 19.5^k$ - OK since we assumed 22.4^k.

• **PROBLEM 18-78**

An 18" round diameter concrete column carries a load of 250,000 lbs. Design a square reinforced concrete footing for this column, to rest on a 2 ton soil using 3000# concrete. You may assume that $f_s = 20,000$ lbs/in^2 (deformed, intermediate grade). Specifications require that you use steel bars not smaller than #6.

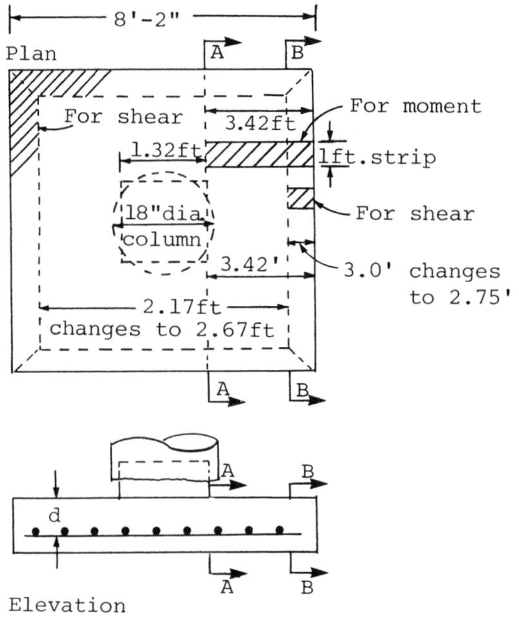

Fig. 1

Solution: Let us assume footing weight to be 6% of the column load.

(Generally such an assumption for weight of footing is in the range of 6 to 10% of the load on the column. Note however, that this assumption will eventually have to be checked to see if the deviation from actual weight is within permissible limits).

Thus, footing weight = 6% of 250,000 lbs = 15000 lbs.

Bearing capacity of a 2 ton soil = 4000 lbs/ft^2.

$$\text{Therefore, required bearing area} = \frac{250,000 \text{ lbs} + 15000 \text{ lbs}}{4000 \text{ lbs/ft}}$$

$$= 66.25 \text{ ft}^2.$$

Since the footing is a square, size of the footing = $\sqrt{66.25}$ = 8.15 ft. = 8'2" side.

Since the column is round, we will utilize an equivalent square column for our computations (Refer to ACI code Sec. 15.3).

Therefore, side of the equivalent square column

$$= \sqrt{\frac{\pi \times 18}{4}} = 15.8'' = 1.32 \text{ ft}$$

Moment - Concrete:

Length of cantilever = (8.15 - 1.32)/2 = 3.42 ft

(Refer to ACI sec. 15.4.1 and 15.4.2 (a))

Considering a 1 foot strip, we have

$$M = \frac{wl^2}{2}$$

Bearing area ≃ 67 ft^2

Thus, bearing pressure $= \frac{250,000}{67} = 3732$ lbs/ft^2

NOTE: w = load on column only.

Therefore w for a 1 ft strip = 3732 x 1 ft

= 3732 lbs/ft.

$$\text{Thus, } M = \frac{wl^2}{2} = \frac{3732 \times 3.42 \times 3.42}{2}$$

= 21826 lb-ft

= 261906 lb-in (Multiplying by 12")

From the tables, we have K for a 3000# concrete to be 224.

We know that $M = Kbd^2$, (M = 261906 lb-in)

For a 1 ft strip, (substituting values in the above equation)

$$261906 = 224 \times 12 \times d^2 \qquad (b = 1' = 12")$$

Thus d = 9.9".

Let us try d = 10".

Check for shear:

Edge width (Bearing surface) $= 3.42 \text{ ft} - \frac{5}{12} \text{ ft}$

= 3.00 ft

(Refer to ACI B.7.7.12 and B.7.7.2)

(where the length is very short, a one foot basis may be used). For any appreciable width, the trapezoid may be used.

Fig. 2

$$\text{Shear stress } v = \frac{V}{b \cdot d} = \frac{3740 \times 3 \times (2.17 + 8.17)/2}{(2.17)(12'')(10'')}$$

$$= 223 \text{ lbs/in}^2.$$

But permissible shear stress as per ACI $= 2\sqrt{f'_c}$

$$= 110 \text{ lbs/in}^2.$$

Therefore, the 'd' will have to be revised.

$$v = \frac{V}{bd}$$

$$\text{or} \quad d = \frac{V}{b \cdot v}$$

Limiting v to 110 lbs/in^2, we have

$$d = \frac{3740 \times 3 \times (2.17 + 8.17)/2}{12 \times 110 \times 2.17} = 20.3''$$

Let us try d = 16'' so that $\frac{d}{2} = 8''$ and edge width

$$= 3.42 - 0.67' = 2.75'$$

$$\text{Now, } v = \frac{V}{b \cdot d} = \frac{3740 \times 2.75 \times (2.67 + 8.17)/2}{2.67 \times 12 \times 16}$$

$$= 109 \text{ lb/in}^2 < 110 \text{ lb/in}^2.$$

Therefore, OK.

Moment - Steel:

Considering on an entire footing basis,

$M = A_s \cdot f_s \cdot jd$ where j = 0.874 (from tables)

$$\text{Therefore } A_s = \frac{M}{f_s \cdot jd} = \frac{261906 \times 8.17}{20{,}000 \times 0.874 \times 16} = 7.65 \text{ in}^2.$$

Using a spacing of 6" (minimum), then,

$$\frac{7.69 \text{ in}^2}{2 \text{ bars/ft} \times 8.17 \text{ ft}} = 0.467 \text{ in}^2/\text{bar}.$$

Let us use #6 bars each of 0.44 in^2.

Check for bond:

Bond calculations are based on development length 'L' (Refer to 1977 ACI sec. 12.2.2 (a))

$$L = 0.04\, A_b\, f_y/\sqrt{f'_c}$$

For #6 bars, $L = 0.04(0.44)(40{,}000)/\sqrt{3000}$

$= 12.9"$

but should not be less than $0.0004\, d_b \cdot f_y$

$= 0.0004(0.75")(40{,}000) = 12"$

In our example, we have, from the theoretical column face, a length of (3.42' x 12) - 3" clear = 38" > 12"

Therefore, OK.

Thus, the 18 - #6 bars will be sufficient for bond.

Check for weight:

Adding 3" + one dia. of 2 bars as cover (Refer to ACI 7.7.1 (a))

we have total cover = 3" + 3/4" = 3 3/4 say 4".

Therefore total depth = 16" + 4" = 20".

And, weight $= \frac{20'}{12} \times 8.17 \times 8.17 \times 150^{\#/\text{ft}^3}$

$= 16{,}700^{\#}$ $(150^{\#/\text{ft}^3}$-unit weight of concrete)

We assumed weight of footing $= 15{,}000^{\#}$

giving a difference of $16700 - 15000 = 1700^{\#}$.

Thus, percentage deviation $= \frac{1700}{265000} \times 100 = 0.64\%$

which is less than 1%. Hence our assumption and, therefore, the design, is acceptable. Thus, let us provide a square footing of 8'-2" square, 20" overall depth and reinforced with 18 - #6 bars each way.

Design a reinforced concrete combined footing (rectangular) for the following specifications:

Bearing capacity of soil = 5000 lbs/ft^2

f'_c (concrete) = 3000 psi @ 28 days

f_s (steel) = 20,000 psi

Exterior column is 12" square

Interior column is 1.6 feet square

Load carried by exterior column = 195 kips

Load carried by interior column = 310 kips

Columns are spaced 19'-6", measured center to center

Restriction: Exterior face of footing must be flush with the edge of the exterior column.

Solution:

Step 1: Length of footing:

First, let us determine the centroid of the loads which should equal the centroid of the footing.

$$\text{Centroid of the loads} = \frac{(19.5' \times 310^k)}{(310^k + 195^k)} = 11.97 \text{ ft.}$$

$$1/2 \text{ of exterior column} = \frac{12''}{2} = 0.50 \text{ ft}$$

Therefore 1/2 of footing length = 11.97 + 0.50 = 12.47' say 12.5'

Therefore, length of footing = 12.5' x 2 = 25.0'.

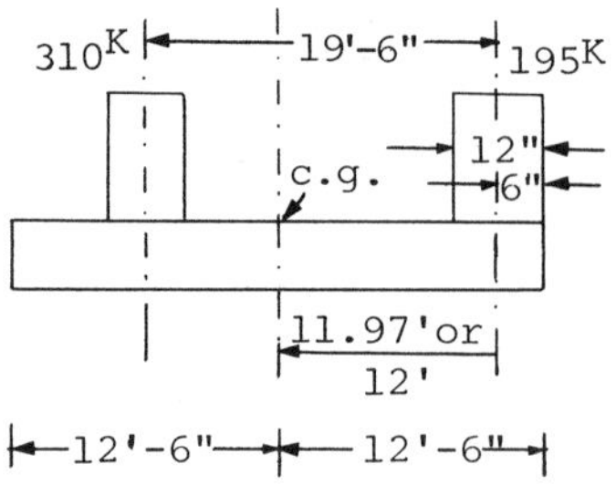

Fig. 1

Step 2: Width of footing:

Assume weight of footing is approximately 10% of column load.

Load on the exterior column = 195,000 lbs

Load on the interior column = 310,000 lbs

Therefore, total column load = 195,000 + 310,000 = 505,000 lbs

Hence, weight of footing = 0.1 x 505000 = 50500 lbs

Thus, total load = 505000 + 50500 = 555500 lbs.

Bearing capacity of the soil = 5000 lbs/ft^2

Therefore, bearing area = $\frac{555500}{5000}$ = 111.1 ft^2

Length of footing = 25 ft.

Thus, width of footing = $\frac{111.1}{25}$ = 4.44 ft say 4.5'

or 4'-6" wide.

Step 3: Compute Shear and Moment: (Diagrams)

Net soil pressure = $\frac{505000}{4.5' \times 25'}$ = 4489 lbs/ft^2

(Note that only the column load is taken into account)

or converting it to a uniform scale,

4489 x 4.5' = 20,200 lbs/linear foot.

Shear: (Refer to fig. No. 2)

$20.2^{k/ft} \times 1.6^{ft} = 32.3^k$, Load on the interior column = 310^k

Shear = $32.3^k - 310^k = -277.7^k$

$4.2^{ft} \times 20.2^{k/ft} = 85.0^k$ (shear @ 4.2 ft from left)

$85.0^k - 277.7^k = -192.7^k$ (shear @ 5.8 ft from left)

$20.2^{k/1} \times 1' = 20.2^k$

Load on the exterior column = 195^k

$-20.2 + 195^k = 174.8^k$ (shear @ 1 ft from right)

Moment: (Refer to fig. no. 2 shear diagram)

Maximum moment occurs @ a distance of $\frac{174.8}{174.8 + 192.7}$

x 18.2' i.e. 8.65' + 1.0'

= 9.65' (from right)

Therefore moment $M_1 = \frac{174.8^k \times 9.65'}{2}$ = 843 k-ft (positive)

Moment M_2 occurs @ a distance of $\frac{85.0}{85.0 + 192.7} \times 1.6$

i.e. 0.49' + 4.2' = 4.69' (from left)

Thus $M_2 = \frac{85 \times 4.69}{2}$ = 199 k-ft (negative)

Therefore depth 'd' $= \sqrt{\frac{M}{Kb}}$ (since $M = Kbd^2$)

where M = maximum moment, K = 223 (from Table V at end of this chapter)

Thus $d = \sqrt{\frac{843 \times 1000 \times 12''}{223 \times 54''}}$ (because b = 4'-6" = 54")

= 28.98" say 29".

Note: Fig. not to scale
All dimensions in feet

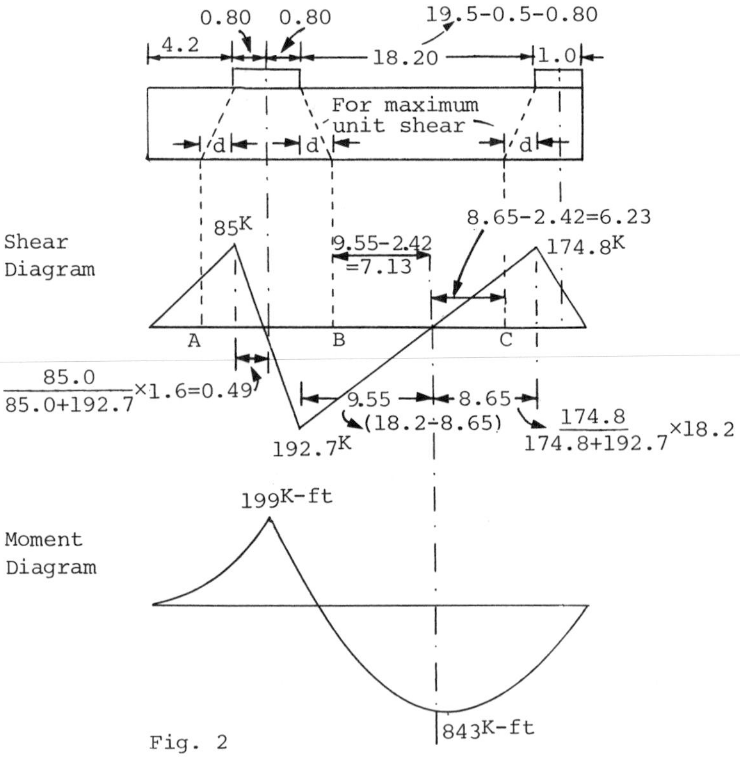

Fig. 2

Check for shear: (Assume that maximum shear occurs @ a distance 'd' from column face)

Shear force V @ point A in fig. 2 = $\frac{4.2 - 29/12}{4.2} \times 85^k = 36^k$

Thus, shear stress $v = \frac{V}{bd} = \frac{36000^{\#}}{54'' \times 29''} = 23^{\#/in^2}$ OK

since $< 60^{\#/in^2}$

(Max. allowable shear stress $= 1.1\underbrace{\sqrt{3000}}_{f'_c} = 60^{\#/in^2}$

Shear force V @ point B in fig. 2 = $\frac{9.55 - 29/12}{9.55} \times 192.7$

$= 144^k$

And shear stress $v = \frac{V}{bd} = \frac{144000}{54'' \times 29''} = 92^{\#/in^2} > 60^{\#/in^2}$

and $v' = 92 - 60 = 32^{\#/in^2}$

Shear force V @ point C in fig. 2 = $\frac{\left(8.65 - \frac{29}{12}\right)}{8.65} \times 174.8^k$

$= 126^k$

Thus, shear stress $v = \frac{V}{bd} = \frac{126000}{54'' \times 29''} = 80.5^{\#/in^2} > 60^{\#/in^2}$

$v' = 80.5 - 60 = 20.5^{\#/in^2}$

Thus points B and C are critical.

Stirrups: A does not need any stirrups.

For B, let us try #4 stirrups, 6 legged so that

$$S = \frac{A_v f_v}{v'b} = \frac{6 \times 0.20^{in^2} \times 20{,}000^{\#/in^2}}{32^{\#/in^2} \times 54''}$$

$= 14.3''$

However, maximum spacing permissible = $d/2 = \frac{29}{2} = 14.5''$

Let us use 14".

Note: As B is more critical than C, only B need be considered.

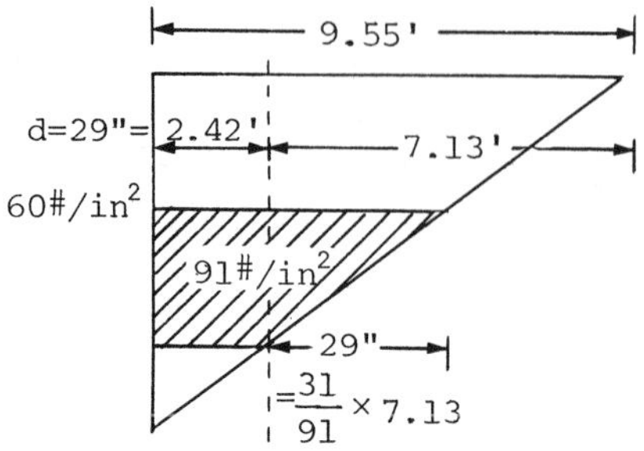

Fig. 3

Refer to sec. 11.1.1.(d) of ACI.

(9.55' = 115" - (29" + 29") = 57"/2 = 28.5")

We need stirrups for 29" + 29" + 29" = 87".

Let us use #4 stirrups 1 @ 7, 5 @ 14 from each column face.

Tension steel:

$$M_1 = A_{s_1} f_s \cdot jd$$

Therefore, $A_{s1} = \frac{M_1}{f_s \cdot jd}$ where M_1 = max. moment and j = 0.874 from tables.

Therefore $A_{s1} = \frac{843000 \text{ x } 12''}{20,000 \text{ x } 0.874 \text{ x } 29''} = 19.95 \text{ in}^2$

Let us use 13 - #11 bars in two rows giving an area of 20.31 in^2.

Moment $M_2 = A_{s_2} f_s jd$

or $A_{s2} = \frac{M_2}{f_s \cdot jd} = \frac{199000 \text{ x } 12''}{20,000 \text{ x } 0.874 \text{ x } 29''} = 4.71 \text{ in}^2$

Let us provide 5 - #9 bars = 5.00 in^2

(or bend 4 - #11 bars = 6.25 in^2)

Bond (Development length):

For #11 bars, $l_d = 1.4 \text{ x } 0.4\ A_b(f_y/\sqrt{f'_c})$

$= 1.4 \text{ x } 0.4 \text{ x } 1.56(40,000/\sqrt{3000})$

$= 64''$

We have 12" - 3" + 2'-9" - 3" - 3" = 37" < 64"

Therefore we will have to consider using smaller bars or hooks or check ACI provisions of 12.12.3.

For #9 bars, $l_d = 0.04(100)(40{,}000/\sqrt{3000})$

$= 29.2''$

We have, 4.2' - 3" = 47.4"

Transverse steel and shear:

For shear, let us extend 29" from each side

= 58" + column width

We have only 54" (4'-6"). Thus shear is within limits.

For moment, let us assume 'extent of equivalent beam' as 3x column width.

a) Interior column:

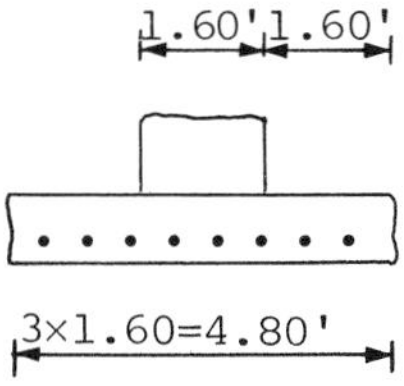

Fig. 4

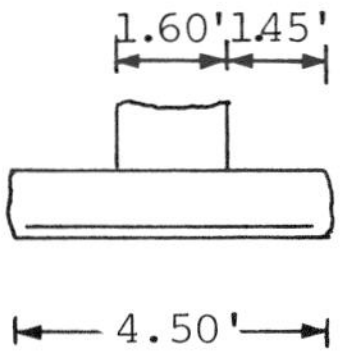

Fig. 5

$$\text{Uniform load} = 4.80\ f_b = \frac{310^k}{4.50\ \text{ft(wide)}} = 68889\ \#\text{ft}$$

(fig. no. 4)

Note: $\frac{68889}{4.80} = f_b = 14352^{\#/ft^2}$ is not soil pressure but pressure in the longitudinal concrete 'beam'.

Referring to fig. no. 5,

$$M = 68889 \times \frac{1.45^2}{2} = 72{\cdot}420 \text{ ft-kips}$$

Using d = 28" (place above transverse steel)

$$A_s = \frac{72.42 \times 1000 \times 12}{20{,}000 \times 0.874 \times 28''} = 1.78 \text{ in}^2$$

$$M = Kbd^2$$

or $d = \sqrt{\frac{M}{Kb}} = \sqrt{\frac{72420 \times 12}{223 \times 54''}}$

$= 8.5''$ required

Compression, OK.

Exterior column:

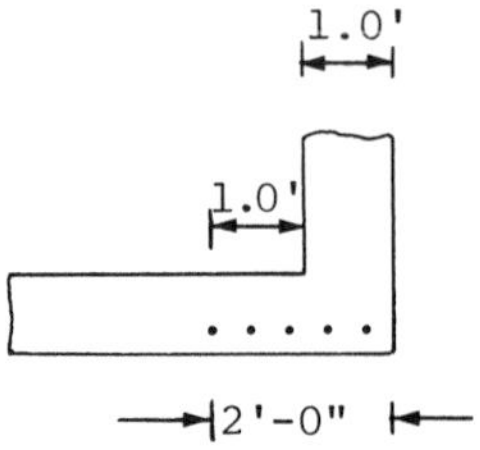

Fig. 6

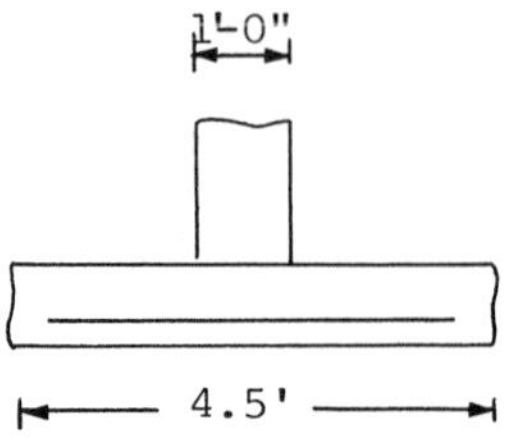

Fig. 7

$$\text{Uniform load} = 2.0\ f_b = \frac{195^k}{4.5'} = 43333\ \#/\text{ft}$$

$$\text{Therefore, } M = 43{\cdot}33 \times \frac{1.75^2}{2} = 66.3 \text{ kip-ft}$$

$$\text{Thus,} \quad A_s = \frac{66300 \times 12''}{20{,}000 \times 0.874 \times 28''} = 1.62 \text{ in}^2.$$

Let us provide 4 - #6 bars giving an area = 1.77 in^2.

Final Design:

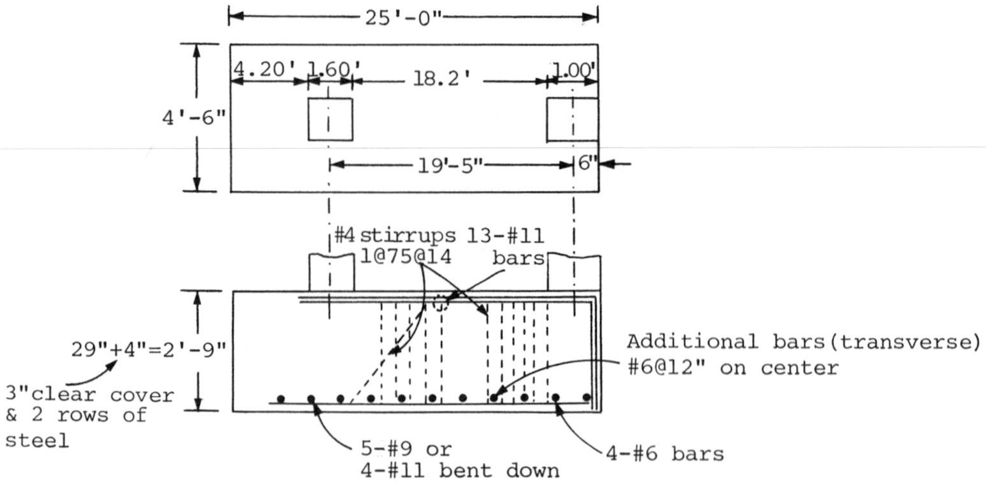

Fig. 8

Alternate Design:

Let us increase the depth of the footing so that we can eliminate the need for stirrups.

Since point B is more critical, where $V = 144^k$.

$$v = \frac{V}{bd}$$

or $$d = \frac{V}{vb} = \frac{144000}{60^{\#/in^2} \times 54''}$$

(limiting 'v' to the maximum allowable)

$$= 44.4''.$$

Let us try d = 40" so that

$$V = \frac{(9.55 - 3.33)}{9.55} \times 192700 = 125508^{\#}$$

Thus, $$v = \frac{125508}{54'' \times 40''} = 58.1^{\#/in^2} < 60^{\#/in^2}$$

Therefore OK.

Let us select d = 40".

$$M_1 = A_{s_1} f_s jd \text{(exterior column)}$$

or $$A_{s1} = \frac{M_1}{f_s jd} = \frac{843000 \times 12''}{20{,}000 \times 0.874 \times 40''}$$

$= 14.5\ in^2$ Use 10 - #11 bars, area = $15.62\ in^2$

Similarly $$M_2 = A_{s_2} f_s jd \text{ (exterior column)}$$

or $$A_{s2} = \frac{M_2}{f_s \cdot jd} = \frac{199000 \times 12}{20{,}000 \times 0.874 \times 40}$$

$$= 3.42\ in^2.$$

Provide 5 - #8 bars of area = $3.93\ in^2$ or can bend 3 - #11 bars, area = $4.68\ in^2$.

Transverse steel:

As before, let us assume that the extent of an 'equivalent beam' is equal to width of column on each side.

Therefore as before, we have

a) Interior column:

$$M = 68889^{\#/ft} \times \frac{1.45^2}{2} = 72{\cdot}420 \text{ ft-kips}$$

Therefore $A_s = \frac{72420 \times 12''}{20{,}000 \times 0.874 \times 39''} = 1.27 \text{ in}^2$

Let us use 3 - #6 bars giving an area of 1.32 in^2.

b) Exterior column:

$M = 66300^{\#/ft}$ as before.

Therefore A_s required $= \frac{66300 \times 12''}{20{,}000 \times 0.874 \times 39''}$

$= 1.06 \text{ in}^2$.

Let us provide 3 - #6 bars, giving an area of 1.32 in^2 in 2'-0" width of the beam.

For transverse reinforcement, let us provide a minimum size of #6 bars at 12" center to center (should be ample).

Final Design:

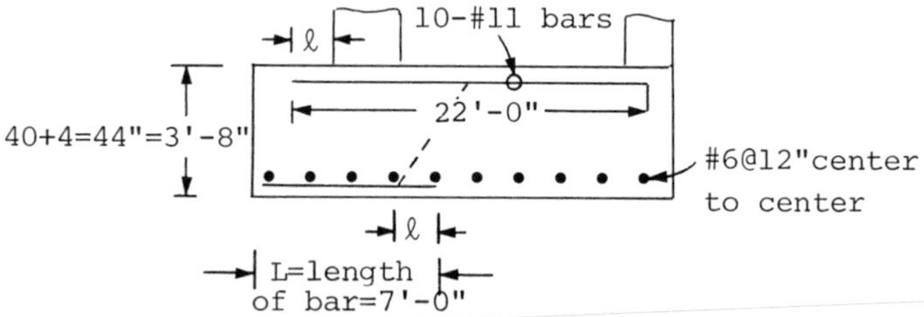

Fig. 9

Note: It is common practice to use 12 diameters beyond column rather than curtailing at point of zero moment.

L = 12" x 1.410 = 16.95" = 1.41'

Top bar length = L + 1.6' + 18.2' + 1.0' - 3" (clear)

= 21.94' = 22'

where (1.6' and 1.0' are the column sizes, interior and exterior, respectively)

Design a combined footing to rest on a $2\frac{1}{2}$ ton soil for two columns of 1 ft square and 1.6 ft square carrying loads of 195^k and 310^k respectively. The columns are spaced 19.5 ft apart measured center to center. Assume f'_c = 3000 psi and f_s = 20,000 psi.

Solution: Since the column loads are unequal, this becomes a trapezoidal combined footing.

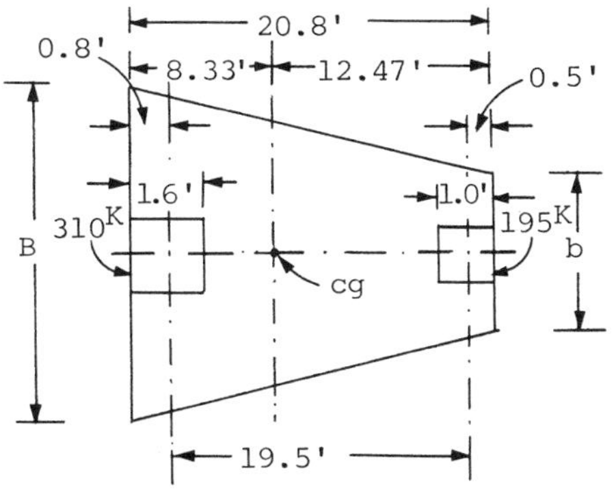

Fig. 1

Total length of footing = 19.5' + 0.5' + 0.8' = 20.8 ft.

Centroid of the loads must be equal to the centroid of the footing.

$$\text{Centroid of the loads} = \frac{19.5 \times 310^k}{(310^k + 195^k)} = 11.97' + \tfrac{1}{2} \text{ of column}$$

$$= 11.97' + 0.5' = 12.47 \text{ ft.}$$

Load on the exterior column = 195^k

Load on the interior column = 310^k

Total column load = 505^k $(195^k + 310^k)$

Assuming that weight of the footing is about 10% of the column load, we have,

weight of the footing = $0.1 \times 505^k = 50.5^k$

Thus, total load = $505^k + 50.5^k = 555.5^k$

Bearing capacity of a $2\frac{1}{2}$ ton soil = 5000 lbs/ft^2

Therefore bearing area required = $\frac{555.5^k}{5^{k/ft}}$ = 111.1 ft^2.

Let us assume that one width of the footing = 'B' and the other 'b'.

To obtain these two values of 'B' and 'b', let us use two equations.

Equation (1)... $\left(\frac{b + B}{2}\right)(20.8) = 111.1 \; ft^2$.

Equation (2)... Centroid of area = $\frac{\text{Moment of area}}{\text{Total area}}$

$$\text{or} \quad \frac{\left[\frac{(B - b)(20.8)}{2} \times \frac{2}{3}(20.8)\right] + \left[b(20.8)\left(\frac{20.8}{2}\right)\right]}{20.8\left(\frac{B + b}{2}\right)} = 12.47$$

(Refer to fig. 2)

Note that, generally $C = \frac{L(2B + b)}{3(B + b)}$ (form)

Also note that a general solution of equations (1) and (2)

becomes $B = \frac{2A}{L^2}(3C - L)$ and $b = \frac{2A}{L^2}(2L - 3C)$

Solving (1) and (2) yields

$b + B = \frac{111.1}{10.4} = 10.68$ and $12.47(3)(10.68) = (B + 10.68)(20.8)$

Thus, B = 19.21 - 10.68 = 8.53' say 8'-7"

and b = 10.68 - B = 2.15 say 2'-2".

Let us check this with the bearing area originally obtained (111.1 ft^2).

We have $\frac{2.18 + 8.58}{2} \times 20.8' = 112 \; ft^2$

Therefore OK.

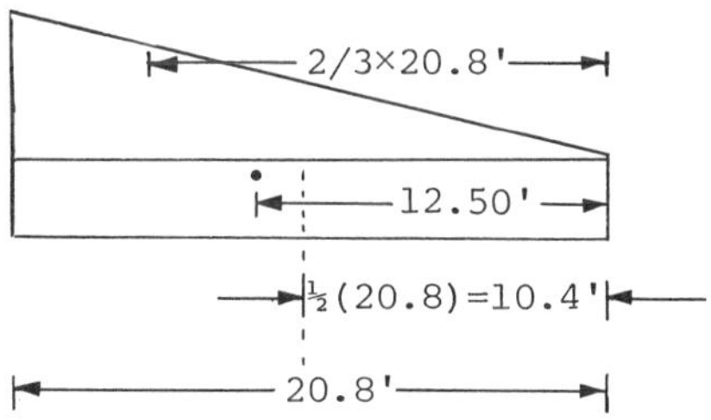

Fig. 2

Bearing pressure = $\frac{505000^{\#}}{112\ ft^2} = 4510^{\#/ft^2}$

(Note the use of $505000^{\#}$, column loads only)

As a uniformly distributed load, bearing pressure is

$4510 \times 2.18'$ (width) $= 9832^{\#/ft}$.

and for a width of 8.58', it is $4510 \times 8.58 = 38700^{\#/ft}$

Difference of these two = $38,700 - 9832 = 28868^{\#/ft}$

$= \frac{28868}{20.8} = 1390^{\#/ft}$

difference in uniform loading

Shear and Moment Diagrams:

Shear: Left End: $38700 - (1.6 \times 1390) = 36476$ lbs

and average $= \frac{38700 + 36476}{2} = 37588$ lbs.

Therefore shear @ the edge of the exterior column

$= 37588 \times 1.6'$ (width) $- 310000$ (load)

$= 249860^{\#} \simeq 249.8^{k}$.

Right End: 9832 + 1390 = 11222lbs

and average $= \frac{11222 + 9832}{2} = 10527$ lbs

Therefore shear @ the inner edge of the interior column

$$= 10527 \times 1.0 - 195000 \text{ (load)} = 184.5^k$$

To find the distance x, where the shear force V = 0:

$$11222x + \frac{1390 \times x \times x}{2} = 184500$$

or $695\ x^2 + 11222x = 184500$

or $695\ x^2 + 11222x - 184500 = 0$

This is a quadratic equation in x, solving which yields x = 9.84'.

Moment:

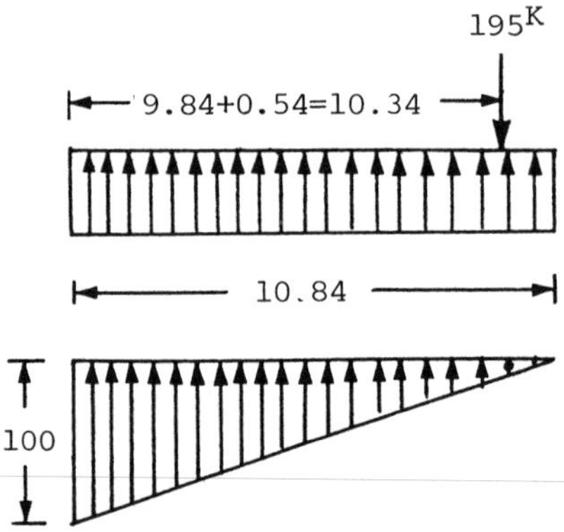

Fig. 3

$$\text{Moment } M(\text{maximum}) = 195^k(10.34) - 9832^{\#/ft} \times 10.84 \times \frac{10.84}{2}$$

$$- 15100^{\#/ft} \times \frac{1}{2} \times 10.84 \times \frac{1}{3} \times 10.34$$

$$= 2016 - 577 - 282 = 1157 \text{ ft-kips.}$$

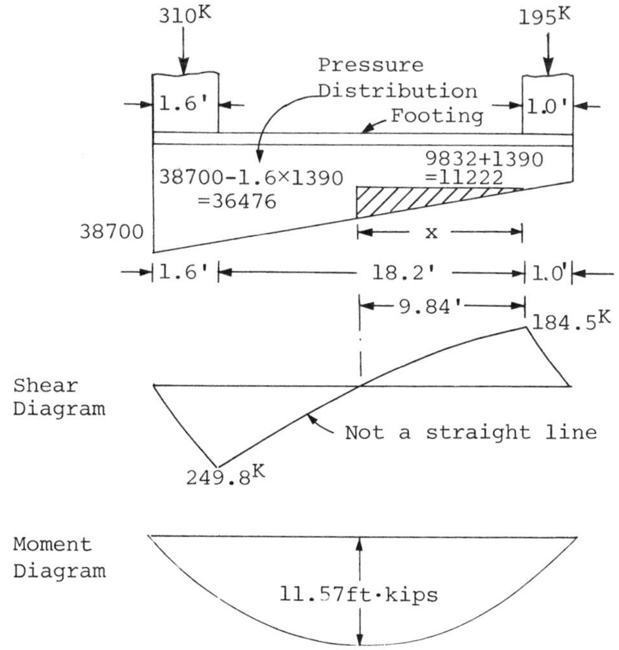

Fig. 4

Depth of footing:

$$M = Kbd^2 \quad \text{or} \quad d = \sqrt{\frac{M}{Kb}}$$

where K = 224 and b is obtained from fig. 5 as follows:

(Table V at end of this chapter)

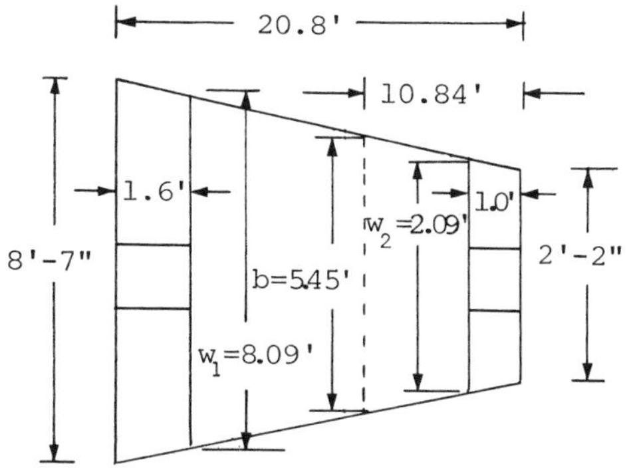

Fig. 5

$$(8'\text{-}7'') - (2'\text{-}2'') = 6'\text{-}5''$$

$$b = (2'\text{-}2'') + \frac{10.64}{20.80}(6'\text{-}5'') = 5.45'$$

Therefore $d = \sqrt{\frac{1157 \times 12'' \times 1000^{\#}}{224 \times 5.45 \times 12''}} = 30.8''$

Shear:

Width at the face of the interior column

$$W_1 = 8'\text{-}7'' - \frac{1.6'}{20.8}(6'\text{-}5'') = 8.09'$$

Width at a distance 'd' ($d \simeq 31''$) = ($d = 2.58'$)

$$W_3 = 8'\text{-}7'' - \frac{1.6' + 2.58'}{20.8'}(6'\text{-}5'') = 7.29'$$

$$= 87\tfrac{1}{2}''$$

Width @ 30'' away $= W_4 = 2'\text{-}2'' + \frac{1.0 + 2.5}{20.80}(6'\text{-}5'') = 3.25' =$ 39''.

Therefore, shear force $V = 184.5 - \frac{2.49 + 3.25}{2}(2.50')$ $(4.51^{k/ft})$

$$= 152.14^{k}$$

Limiting shear stress v to the allowable value

$$= 1.1\sqrt{f'_c} = 1.1\sqrt{3000} = 60^{\#/in^2},$$

we have $v = \frac{V}{bd}$

or $d = \frac{V}{bv} = \frac{152140^{\#}}{(60^{\#/in^2}) \times 39''}$

$$= 65''$$

Average is $(39'' + 65'')/2 = 52''$.

Thus, we could select a depth of 52". However, the total depth would then be 52" + 4" (cover) = 56" which would be quite deep though it obviates the need for stirrups. Stirrups could sometimes be cheaper since excavation is costlier. However, shallower depths may necessitate the need of tension bars making it costlier. Keeping these factors in mind, let us select arbitrarily, say, a depth of 3'-6" (42").

Effective depth d = 42" - 3" (clear) - 1/2 of one bars

$$= 38\tfrac{1}{2}" \text{ or } 3'\text{-}2"$$

Stirrups may then be needed at the exterior column only.

$$\text{Then } W = \left(2'\text{-}2"\right) + \frac{2.49 + 3.2}{20.8}\,(6'\text{-}5") = 4.0' = 48".$$

$$\text{Shear force } V = 184.5 - \left(\frac{2.49 + 4.0}{2}\right)(3.2)(4.51^{k/ft^2})$$

$$= 137.7^{k}$$

$$\text{and shear stress } v = \frac{V}{bd} = \frac{137700^{\#}}{47" \times 38\frac{1}{2}"} = 76^{\#/in^2} > \text{allowable } 60^{\#/in^2}$$

$$\text{Hence } v' \text{ (excess shear)} = 76 - 60 = 16^{\#/in^2}.$$

Let us use #5 stirrups (4-legged)

$$\text{Thus spacing } S = \frac{A_v \cdot f_v}{v'b} = \frac{4(0.31)(20{,}000^{\#/in^2})}{16^{\#/in^2}\ (47")}$$

$$= 33".$$

$$\text{Maximum spacing allowable} = \frac{d}{2} = \frac{44.5}{2} = 22\tfrac{1}{4}".$$

Let us try 1 @ 10" and 4 @ 20" (from exterior column) and check shear @ 10" + 80" + 10" = 100" out.

$$W = \frac{100''/12 + 1.0'}{20.8'} (6'\text{-}5'') + 2'\text{-}2'' = 5.05 \text{ ft.}$$

$$\text{and } V = 184.5 - \frac{2.49 + 5.05}{2} (8.33')(4.51^{k/ft^2}) = 42.9^k$$

$$\text{Therefore, shear stress } v = \frac{42900^{\#}}{60.6'' \times 38.5''} = 18.4^{\#/in^2} < 60^{\#/in^2}$$

Therefore OK.

Since shear is below $30^{\#/in^2}$, then let us go to 1/2 of

$v_c = 1/2 \times 60 = 30^{\#/in^2}$ (ACI 11.1.1)

The stirrups are #5 (4-legged), 1 @ 10'' and 4 @ 20'' from the exterior column.

(Note that each stirrup has a different width)

Main Longitudinal Steel:

$$\text{Area of steel } A_s = \frac{M}{f_s jd} = \frac{1157 \times 12 \times 1000}{20{,}000 \times 0.874 \times 38\tfrac{1}{2}''}$$

$$= 20.6 \text{ in}^2$$

Let us provide 14 - #11 bars (top)

Bond (Development Length):

$$l_d = 0.04\, A_b(f_y/\sqrt{f'_c}) = 0.04(1.56)(40{,}000/\sqrt{3000}) \times 1.4 \rightarrow \text{top bars}$$

$$= 63.8''$$

We have, as per ACI 12.2.3,

$$1.3 \times \frac{M_b}{V_u} + l_a = \frac{1.3 \times 1157^{1k} \times 12''}{249.8^k} + \left[\frac{1.6'}{2} \times 12'' - 3''\right]$$

(1.3 - for compressive reaction)

$$= 70.7'' + 6.6'' = 77.3'' > 63.8''$$

Therefore, OK.

In one row, we would need a width of

2 x 3" (clear) + 14 x(11/8")(bars) + 13 x(11/8")(spacing) +

2 x (5/8)"(stirrups)

= 44"

Using two rows of bars, the depth would increase to 46" or 3'-10".

Transverse steel:

Using one row, we have d = 46" - $3\frac{1}{2}$" = $42\frac{1}{2}$".

Assume that "beam width" = 2 x column width, so that length = width of footing at inside of column.

Interior Column:

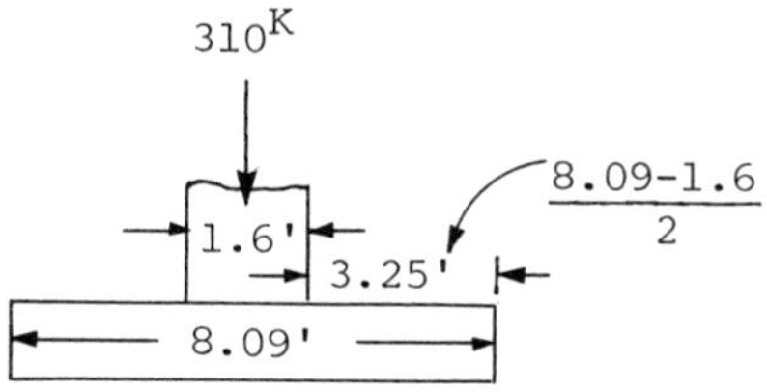

Fig. 6

$$W \text{ (load)} = \frac{310}{8.09} = 38.3^{k/ft}.$$

Therefore, moment $M = 38.3 \times \frac{3.25^2}{2} = 202$ ft-kips.

$$M = A_s f_s \cdot jd$$

or $$A_s = \frac{M}{f_s jd} = \frac{202 \times 1000 \times 12}{20{,}000 \times 0.874 \times 43\frac{1}{2}} = 3.19 \text{ in}^2$$

Let us provide 8 - #6 bars giving a total area of 3.53 in^2.

EXTERIOR COLUMN:

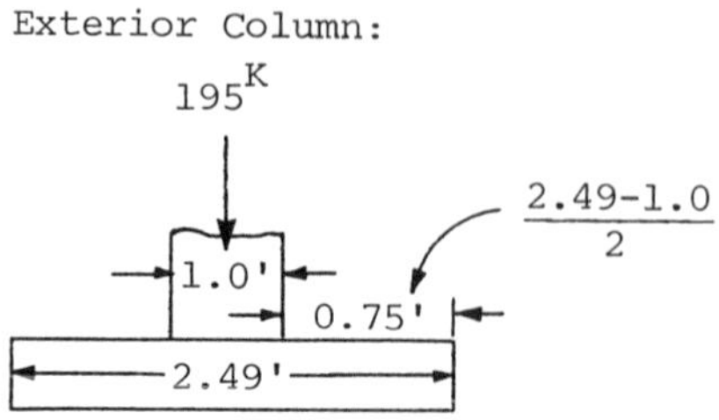

Fig. 7

Uniform load $W = \frac{195^k}{2.49'} = 78.3$ kips/ft

And moment $M = \frac{wl^2}{2} = 78.3 \times \frac{0.75^2}{2} = 22$ ft-kips

Therefore, area of steel $A_s = \frac{22000^{\#} \times 12''}{20{,}000 \times 0.874 \times 43\frac{1}{2}}$

$= 0.35 \text{ in}^2$

Use #6 @ 18" on center for balance of footing.

Final Design:

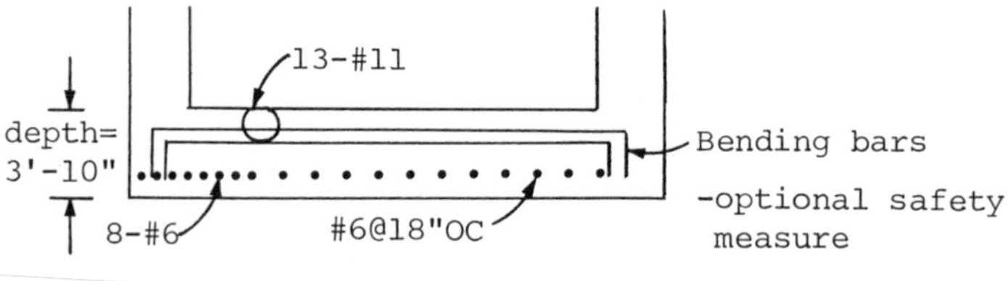

Fig. 8

Check for weight:

$112 \text{ ft}^2 \times 3.67 \text{ ft} \times 150^{\#/\text{ft}^3} = 61.6^k >$ our assumed 50.5^k as footing weight.

This weight gives a total soil pressure of $\frac{567^k}{112^{\text{ft}^2}}$

$= 5070^{\#/ft^2}$ which is not too high. However, let us add 1" to the shorter end and 2" to the longer end, giving us an area of 114 ft^2 and the corresponding soil pressure of $4970^{\#/ft^2}$.

Note: There is no change in reinforcement.

• PROBLEM 18-80

Design a strap type combined footing to rest on a $2\frac{1}{2}$ ton soil for two columns loaded as shown in figure. The columns are spaced at 19'-6" center to center. Assume $f'_c = 3000$ psi, $f_s = 20{,}000$ psi and $f_y = 40{,}000$ psi.

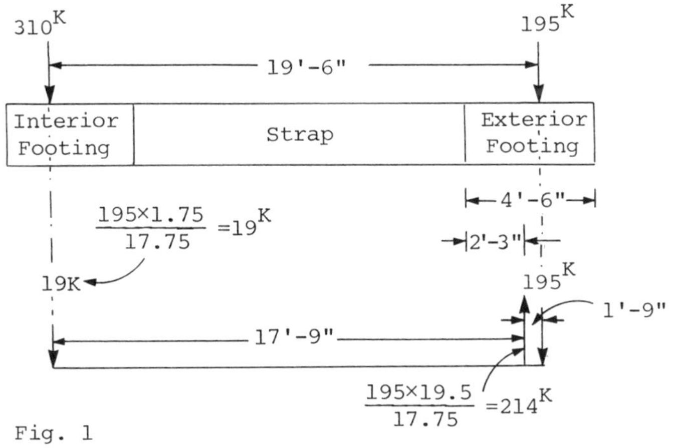

Fig. 1

Solution: Since a narrow width of the exterior footing would result in a shorter moment arm, let us, as an approximation, assume that d = 2b where d = depth and b = width.

Thus, area of the footing = $2b \times b = 2b^2$.

Bearing capacity of a $2\frac{1}{2}$ ton soil = $5000^{\#/ft^2} = 5^{k/ft^2}$

Load on the exterior column = 195^k.

Thus, $5^{k/ft^2} = \dfrac{195}{2b^2}$

form which, b = 4.41' say 4'-6" (indicated in fig. 1)

Reaction R at the interior support = $\frac{195^k \times 1.75}{17.75} = 19^k$

(footing) (Refer to fig. 1)

Reaction at the exterior footing = $\frac{195^k \times 19.5}{17.75} = 214^k$.

(This is the figure to be used for the design of the exterior footing)

Generally, the exterior footing is designed first since the strap footing design follows the exterior footing depth.

Exterior footing design:

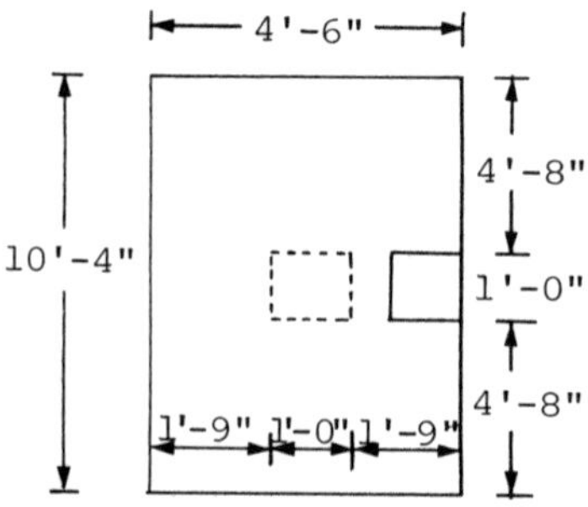

Fig. 2

Exterior column load adjusted for eccentricity = 214^k

Assuming footing weight to be 8% of the column load,

footing weight = $0.08 \times 214^k = 17^k$ (To be rechecked later)

Therefore, total load = $214^k + 17^k = 231^k$.

Bearing capacity of soil = $5^{k/ft^2}$

Thus, bearing area required = $\frac{231^k}{5^{k/ft^2}} = 46.2\ ft^2$.

$b = 4.5'$

Therefore, length $l = 46.2/4.5 = 10.27'$ say 10'-4".

Assuming that the strap removes any eccentric effect induced, we can design as if the column were 12" square located centrally.

Thus the long arm = (10'-4" - 1'-0")/2 = 4'-8" (refer to fig. 2)

Uniform load of soil $= \frac{214^k}{10'\text{-}4''} = 20.5^{k/ft} = W$

Moment $M = \frac{wl^2}{2} = 20.5 \times \frac{4.67^2}{2} = 224$ ft-kips.

And depth $d = \sqrt{\frac{224 \times 12 \times 1000}{223 \times 54''}}$ $(M = Kbd^2)$

$= 15''$.

However, the general practice is to provide a minimum total depth of 24".

Check for shear:

Total depth = 24"

Therefore, effective depth d = 24" - $3\frac{1}{2}$" = $20\frac{1}{2}$"

For maximum shear, let us go out a distance 'd' so that,

4'-8" - $20\frac{1}{2}$" = 2'-$11\frac{1}{2}$"

Thus shear force V = 2'-$11\frac{1}{2}$" x $20.5^{k/ft} = 61^k$.

Thus, if we limit the shear stress 'v' to $60^{\#/in^2}$

(Max. allowable shear stress $= 1.1\sqrt{f'_c}$

$= 1.1\sqrt{3000} = 60^{\#/in^2}$)

we have $v = \frac{V}{bd}$ or $d = \frac{V}{b \cdot v}$

Thus $d = \dfrac{61{,}000^{\#}}{54'' \times 60^{\#}/in^2} = 18.8'' <$ our value of $d = 20\frac{1}{2}''$

Therefore, OK.

Longitudinal steel:

A_s (area of steel) $= \dfrac{M}{f_s jd}$ $\quad (M = A_s \cdot f_s \cdot jd)$

where $j = 0.874$ from tables for a $3000^{\#}$ concrete (Table V at end of this chapter)

Thus, $A_s = \dfrac{224 \times 1000 \times 12''}{20{,}000 \times 0.874 \times 20.5''} = 7.50$ in^2.

Let us provide 10 - #8 bars giving a total area of 7.85 in^2. (nominal spacing of 6" c/c can be used).

Check for Bond:

As per ACI 12.5,

l_d (development length) $= 0.04\ A_b \cdot (f_y/\sqrt{f'_c})$

$= 0.04 \times 0.79\ (40{,}000/\sqrt{3000})$

$= 23''$

or $l_d = 0.0004\ d_b \cdot f_y = 0.0004(1.0)(40{,}000)$

$= 16''$

We have, a cantilever of length 4'-8" less 3"

$= 4'\text{-}5'' = 53'' > 16''$ or $23''$

Therefore, OK.

Short bars:

Length of arm = 1'-9" for moment

and uniform load $W = \frac{214^k}{4.5} = 47.5^{k/ft}$

Thus moment $M = \frac{wl^2}{2} = 47.5 \times \frac{1.75^2}{2} = 72.7$ ft-kips

$$M = Kbd^2$$

from which $d = \sqrt{\frac{M}{Kb}} = \sqrt{\frac{72.7 \times 1000 \times 12}{223 \times 124''}}$

$= 5.6''$ and we have

$d = 20.5''$ Therefore, OK.

(Value of K obtained from Table V at end of this chapter)

Area of steel, $A_s = \frac{M}{f_s \cdot jd} = \frac{72.7 \times 12 \times 1000}{20{,}000 \times 0.874 \times 20.5}$

$= 2.43\ in^2$.

But as per ACI 15.4.4(b), % reinforcement $= \frac{2}{\beta + 1}$

where $\beta = \frac{10'\text{-}4''}{4'\text{-}6''} = \frac{10.33}{4.5} = 2.29$

Thus % reinforcement $= \frac{2}{2.29 + 1} = 0.607$ or 60.7%

Thus 60.7% x 2.43 in^2 = 1.47 in^2.

Using the same distribution across the entire footing,

area of steel $A_s = 1.47 \times \frac{10.33}{4.5} = 3.37\ in^2$.

Let us provide 8 - #6 bars giving an area of 3.53 in^2.

Check for weight:

weight of footing = 4'-6" x 10'-4" x 2'-0" (24" deep)

x $150^{\#/ft^3}$ (unit weight of concrete)

= 14^k < our assumed 17^k

Therefore, OK.

Final Design of Exterior Footing:

Let us provide 4'-6" x 10'-4" and 2'-0" deep footing with 10 - #8 long bars and 8 -#6 short bars as reinforcement.

Design of strap:

Let us first draw the shear force and moment diagrams:

Shear at the inner face of interior footing = 19^k (as before)

Shear at the inner face of exterior footing,

$$\frac{214^k}{4.5} = 47.6^{k/ft} = 47.6 \times 1'\text{-}0'' = 47.6^k$$

Load on column (exterior) = 195^k

Thus shear = $195.0^k - 47.6^k = 147.4^k$.

Moment M = 15.5' x 19^k = 295 ft-kips(@ $15\frac{1}{2}$' from center of interior support)

(Refer to fig. 3)

and max. moment = $295^k + \frac{0.4}{2}(19) \simeq 298.8 \simeq 299$ ft-kips

where $0.4 = \frac{19^k}{166.4^k} \times 3.5 = 0.40'$

(Refer to fig. 3)

However, we can use M = 295 ft-kips as b = 10'-4" width beyond edge of exterior footing.

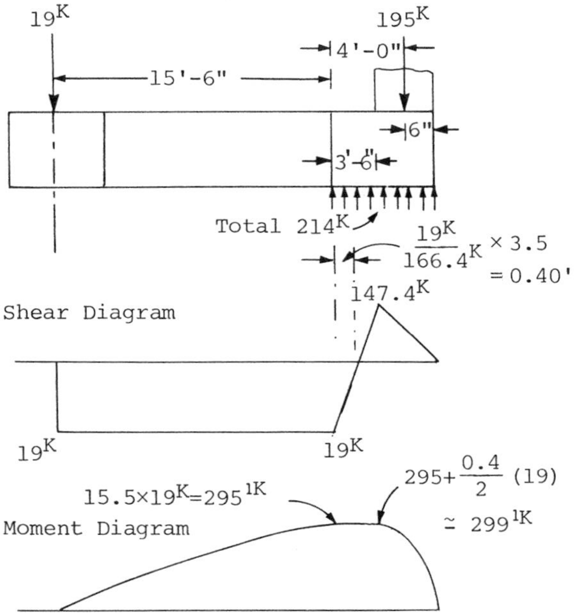

Fig. 3

Therefore, let us use $295^{ft\text{-}k}$ for designing width of strap.

$$M = Kbd^2$$

or $$b = \frac{M}{Kd^2}$$

Thus $$b = \frac{295 \text{ x } 1000^{\#} \text{ x } 12''}{223 \text{ x } 20.5} = 37.8'' \text{ or } 3'\text{-}2''$$

wide strap.

Width from shear requirements:

We have $$v = \frac{V}{bd}$$

or $$b = \frac{V}{v \cdot d} = \frac{19^k \text{ x } 1000^{\#}}{60^{\#}/\text{in}^2 \text{ x } 20.5''} = 15.5'' < 38''$$

$$(v = 1.1\sqrt{f'_c} = 60^{\#}/\text{in}^2)$$

Therefore, OK.

Area of steel: $A_s = \frac{M}{f_s \cdot jd} = \frac{299 \times 1000 \times 12}{20{,}000 \times 0.874 \times 20.5} = 10.01 \text{ in}^2$

Let us provide 7 - #11 bars giving an area of 10.94 in^2.

(Table I at end of this chapter)

Note that we can drop some bars partway but we need some bars beyond the center line of the interior column for a distance of 12 diameters (ACI 12.11.3) or 6" (ACI 12.12.2).

Let us use 12 x 1.41 (ϕ of #11) = 16.9" or 1'-5" minimum.

Check for development length l_d:

$$l_d = 0.04\, A_b \cdot (f_y/\sqrt{f'_c}) = 0.04(1.56)(40{,}000/\sqrt{3000})$$

$$= 45.5''$$

Bend bars down at the right side.

From ACI 12.2.3(a), 1.4 x 45.5 = 63.7" (check with ACI 12.12.3)

Bottom bars in strap to support dead load at erection:

Interior footing - 8'-3" square (refer to the following interior column footing for details)

$$(15'\text{-}6'') - \left(\frac{8'\text{-}3''}{2}\right) = 11'\text{-}4\tfrac{1}{2}''.$$

Assuming a simple span, $M = \frac{1}{8} \times 300^{\#/\text{ft}} \times 3.17 \text{ wide} \times (11.375)^2$

$$= 15382 \text{ ft-pounds}$$

Area of steel required $= \frac{15382 \times 12''}{20{,}000 \times 0.874 \times 20.5} = 0.515 \text{ in}^2$.

Let us provide 4 - #6 bottom bars as a minimum.

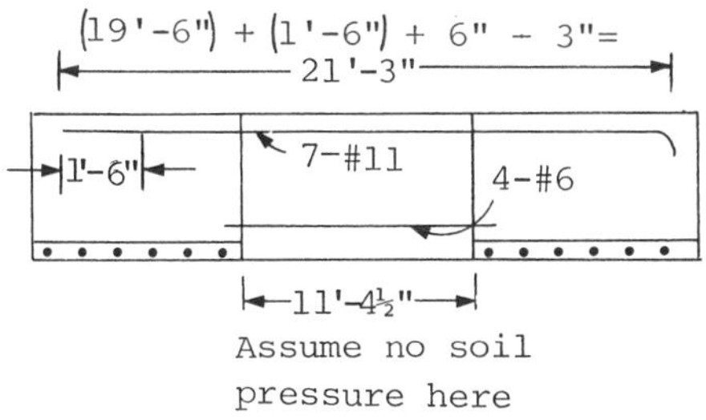

Fig. 4

Interior column footing design:

Let us start with a depth of 20.5" which is the same as the depth for the exterior column footing.

Load on the interior column = 310^k

Assuming footing weight to be 8% of the column load,

footing weight = $0.08 \times 310^k = 25^k$

Therefore, total load = $310^k + 25^k = 335^k$.

Bearing capacity of soil = $5^{k/ft^2}$.

Therefore, bearing area = $\dfrac{335^k}{5^{k/ft^2}} = 67\ ft^2$.

Assuming a square, side of the footing = $\sqrt{67}$ = 8'-3".

Uniform load W = $\dfrac{310^k}{(8.25)^2} = 4550^{\#/ft^2} \times 1\ ft = 4550^{\#/ft}$

(1 foot basis)

Moment M = $\dfrac{wl^2}{2} = 4550 \times 1' \times \dfrac{3.33^2}{2}$

= 25228 ft-pounds

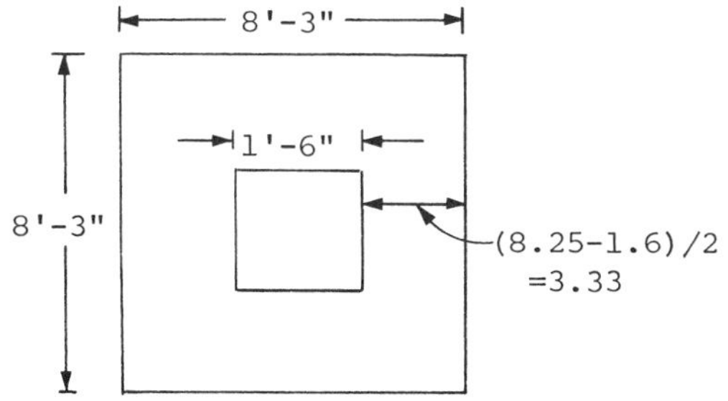

Fig. 5

$$M = Kbd^2$$

or $$d = \sqrt{\frac{M}{Kb}} = \sqrt{\frac{25228 \times 12}{223 \times 12}} = 10.6''.$$

We have 20.5". OK for concrete compression

Minimum depth, however, is 24" = 2'

Thus, effective depth 'd' = 2' - $3\frac{1}{2}$" (clear + 1/2 of ϕ)

= 20.5".

Check for shear:

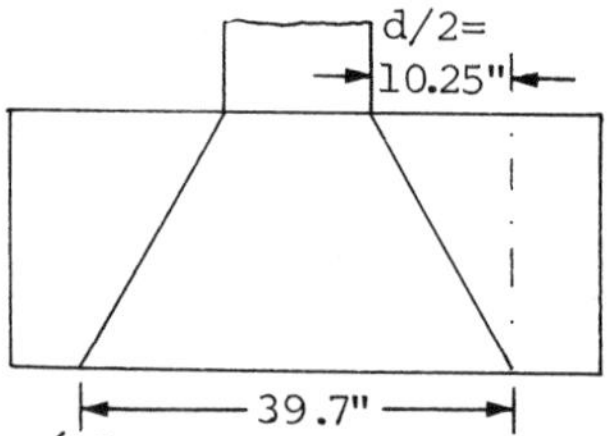

Fig. 6

Going out a distance d/2 = 10.25",

Area within the periphery of d/2 = $(3.31')^2$ = 10.95 ft^2

(Refer to fig. 6)

Thus, shear area outside this periphery = $8.25^2 - 3.31^2$

= 57.2 ft^2.

Shear force V = $4550^{\#/ft^2} \times 57.2\ ft^2 = 260260^{\#}$.

And shear stress $v = \frac{V}{bd} = \frac{260260}{4 \times 39.7'' \times 20.5''} = 80^{\#/in^2}$.

Allowable shear stress = $2\sqrt{f'_c} = 2\sqrt{3000} = 110^{\#/in^2}$.

Therefore, OK.

Steel reinforcement in each direction:

Area of steel $A_s = \frac{25228 \times 12'' \times 8.25'}{20,000 \times 0.874 \times 20.5'} = 6.96 \text{ in}^2$.

Let us use 12 - #7 bars ($A_s = 7.22 \text{ in}^2$) each way @ $\frac{94}{12}$ bars =

8.3" apart.

Check for bond:

Development length $l_d = 0.04\ A_b\ f_y/\sqrt{f'_c}$

$= 0.04(0.60)(40,000/\sqrt{3000})$

$= 17{\cdot}5''$

or $l_d = 0.0004\ d_b\ f_y = 0.0004(0.875)(40,000)$

$= 14''$

We have 3'-4" less 3" edge distance = 37" < 14" or 17·5"

Therefore, OK.

Check for weight:

$(8.25)^2 \times 2'\text{-}0'' \times 150^{\#/ft^3} = 20.4^k$ < our assumed

footing weight of 25^k. Therefore, OK.

Final Interior Column Footing Design:

Provide a 8'-3" square footing with a total depth of 24" and 12-#7 bars both ways in the bottom of the footing.

DESIGN OF FOOTINGS BY ULTIMATE DESIGN METHOD

• PROBLEM 18-82

Determine the effective depth required for the column footing shown below in fig. 1. The unfactored column dead and live loads are 325^k and 280^k respectively. Use relevant ACI code provisions. Assume that f'_c = 3.5 ksi.

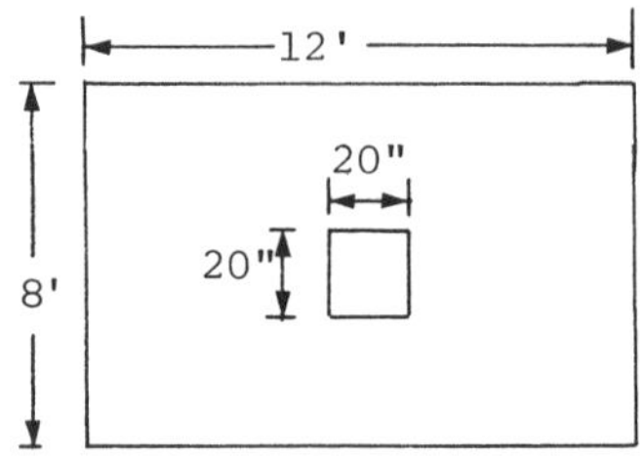

Fig. 1 PLAN

Solution:

$$\text{Total load } U = 1.4 \text{ (Dead load)} + 1.7 \text{ (Live load)}$$

$$= 1.4\ (325^k) + 1.7(280^k) = 931^k$$

Bearing pressure at base of the footing due to this load

$$= \frac{P}{A} = \frac{931^k}{12' \times 8'} = 9.69 \text{ k/ft}^2.$$

To determine the depth 'd' of the footing (without shear reinforcement) by trial and error:

Try by assuming d = 25".

Beam shear:

Beam shear is to be evaluated at a distance 'd' from the face of the column (ACI sec. 11.1.3.1).

The critical section 'AA' for beam shear can be determined as follows: (Refer to fig. 2)

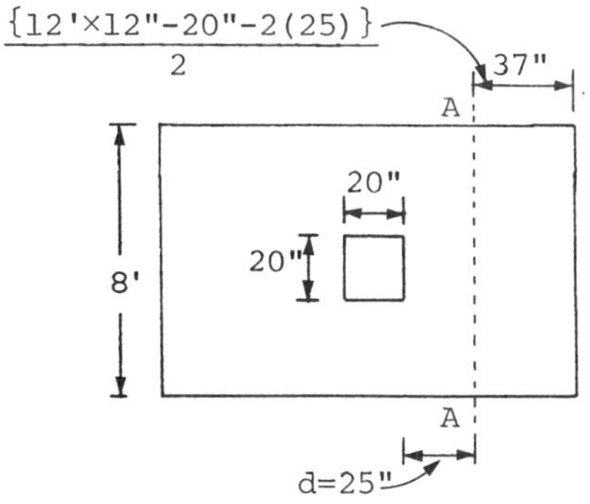

Fig. 2

Shear force at section AA is

$$V_u = 9.69^{k/ft^2} \times 8' \times \frac{37''}{12''} = 239^k$$

Shear force carried by concrete is

$$V_c = 2\sqrt{f'_c} \cdot b_w \cdot d \qquad \text{(ACI 11.3.1.1)}$$

where b_w = width of beam = 8' x 12" = 96 in.

Therefore $V_c = 2\sqrt{3500}\ (96'')(25'') = 283{,}971^{\#} \simeq 284^k$

$$V_u \simeq \phi V_c \qquad \text{(ACI sec. 11.1.1)}$$

where $\phi = 0.85$

$239 < 0.85\ (284)$

i.e. $239 < 241$

Therefore, the assumed depth d = 25" is OK for beam shear.

Punching shear: (Fig. 3)

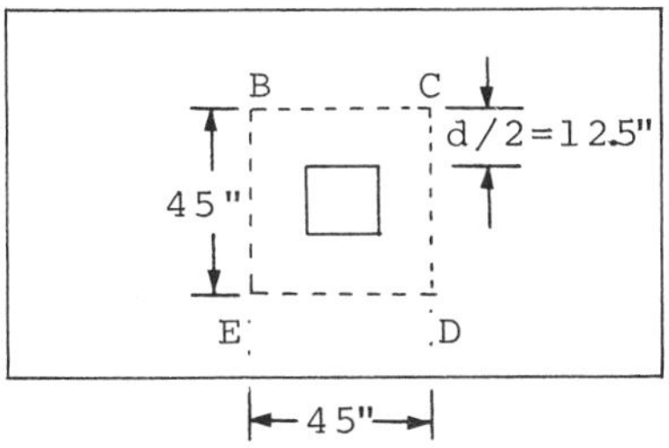

Fig. 3

The critical section for punching shear is at a distance 'd/2' away from the column face (ACI sec. 11.11.1.2).

Critical perimeter $b_o = 4\ (45'') = 180''$

Shear force V_u along BCDE $= 931^k - 9.69^{k/ft} \times \left(\frac{45''}{12''}\right)^2$

$$\simeq 794^k.$$

Punching shear force carried by concrete is

$V_c = 4\sqrt{f'_c} \cdot b_o \cdot d$ (ACI sec. 11.11.2)

$= 4\sqrt{3500}\ (180'')(25'')$

$= 1{,}064{,}890^{\#} \simeq 1065^k$

$V_u < \phi V_c$ (ACI sec. 11.1.1)

or $794^k < 0.85\ (1065)$

or $794^k < 905^k$

Therefore our assumed depth 'd' = 25" is also valid for punching shear.

Hence, provide an effective depth d = 25" for the given column footing.

• PROBLEM 18-83

Using Ultimate Design Method, design a square plain concrete footing for a circular column of 18" diameter carrying a load of 250,000 lbs. The footing is to rest on a soil of bearing capacity 4000 lbs/ft^2. Use a $3000^{\#}$ concrete and relevant ACI code provisions. Assume that the footing weight is approximately $12\frac{1}{2}\%$ of the column load. Also assume that 30% of the load is dead load.

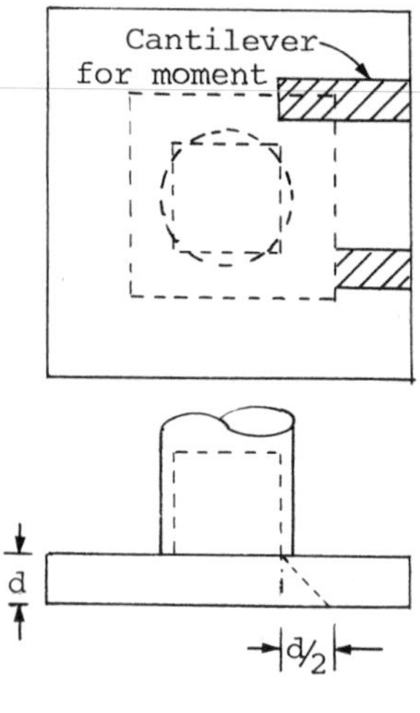

Solution:

Weight of the footing = $12\frac{1}{2}\%$ of 250,000 lbs = 31,250 lbs

Column load = 250,000 lbs

Therefore, total load = 250,000 + 31,250 = 281,250 lbs

Bearing capacity of soil = 4000 lbs/ft^2

$$\text{Thus bearing area of footing} = \frac{\text{Total load}}{\text{Bearing Capacity of Soil}} = \frac{281{,}250^{\#}}{4000^{\#/ft^2}} = 70.3\ ft^2$$

Hence, for a square footing, side = $\sqrt{70.3} \simeq 8.4$ ft, say 8'-6" side

By the Ultimate Strength Method, we have

$$P_u = 1.4\ D + 1.7\ L = 1.4(0.3 \times 250{,}000) + 1.7(0.7 \times 250{,}000)$$

(Since dead load is 30% of the total column load)

Therefore, P_u = 402,500 lbs

bearing pressure = $\frac{402{,}500}{(8.5)^2} \simeq 5571\ lbs/ft^2$

Assuming an equivalent square column as per ACI 15.8,

Side of the square column = $\sqrt{\frac{\pi}{4} \times 18^2} \simeq 15.95'' \simeq 1.33$ ft.

Therefore, length of cantilever = $\frac{8.5 - 1.33}{2} \simeq 3.59$ ft. = l

Moment/ft = $5571^{\#/ft^2} \times 1\ ft \times \frac{1}{2} \times 3.59^2$ $(M = wl^2/2)$

$\simeq$ 35900 ft-lbs

Allowable f_c in tension as per ACI 15.11.1, is

$$5\phi\sqrt{f'_c} = 5(0.65)\sqrt{3000} = 178\ lbs/in^2$$

Further, M= fz or z = $\frac{M}{f}$ and z is also = $\frac{1}{6}$ bd^2

For a 1 foot strip, b = 12".

$$z = \frac{M}{f} = \frac{35900 \times 12''}{178\ \#/in^2} = 2420.2\ in^3$$

But $z = \frac{1}{6}\ bd^2$ where b = 12"

Therefore, $2420.2 = \frac{1}{6} \times 12 \times d^2$

or d = 34.8", take d = 35"

Check for shear:

Going out a distance of d/2 from the column,

$$3.59\ ft - \frac{(35'')/2}{12''} = 2.13\ ft$$

Shear stress $v_u = \frac{V_u}{\phi \cdot bd}$ where $\phi = 0.85$

Therefore, $v_u = \frac{2.13' \times 5571\ \#/ft^2 \times 1\ ft}{0.85 \times 12'' \times 35''} = 33.3\ \#/in^2$

Maximum allowable shear stress according to ACI 11.11.2 is

$4\sqrt{f'_c} = 4\sqrt{3000} = 219\ \#/in^2 >> \text{actual}\ 33.3\ \#/in^2$

Therefore, the value is OK.

Check for weight:

Weight of footing = $(8.5\ ft)^2 \times 2.92\ ft \times 140\ \#/ft^3$

(unit wt. of concrete = $140\ \#/ft^3$)

= 29536 lbs < our assumed 31,250 lbs.

Hence within limits.

Final Design: Provide an 8'-6" side square footing, 35" deep.

A 12 x 12 steel column (12" wide flange) carries a load of 420 kips, half of which is live load. The column rests on a 18" x 18" steel base plate. Design a square reinforced concrete footing for this column, if it is to rest on a $2\frac{1}{2}$ ton soil (based on service load). The allowable stresses are $f_c' = 4000$ psi, $f_s = 24000$ psi and $f_y = 60,000$ psi. The depth of footing shall not be less than 20". Assume footing weight to be 6% of column load and use magnitude of width in 3" intervals and depth in full inches.

Solution:

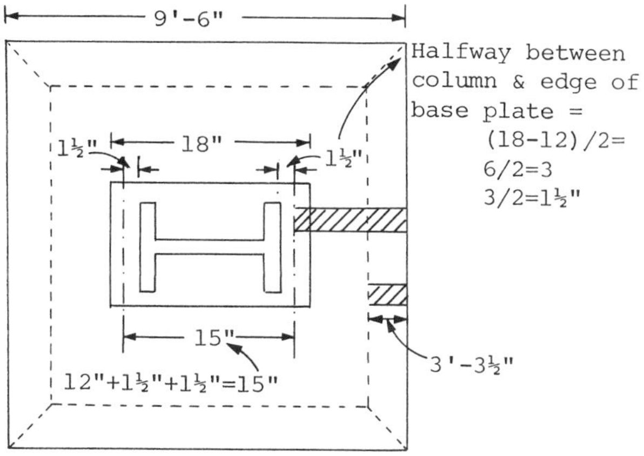

Footing weight = 6% of column load

$= 0.06 \times 420^k = 25.2^k$

Therefore, total load $= 420^k + 25.2^k = 445.2^k$

Bearing capacity of a $2\frac{1}{2}$ ton soil = 5 kips/ft²

$$\text{Therefore, bearing area} = \frac{\text{Total load}}{\text{Bearing capacity of soil}}$$

$$= \frac{445.2^k}{5^k/\text{ft}^2} = 89.04 \text{ ft}^2.$$

Therefore each side of the square footing

$= \sqrt{89.04} \simeq 9.44$ ft $\simeq$ 9'-6"

$$\text{Therefore, bearing pressure to be used} = \frac{420,000^{\#}}{(9.5)^2}$$

$$\simeq 4654 \text{ \#/ft}^2$$

Moment:

Length of cantilever = 9'-6" - 15" = (9'-6") - (1'-3")

= (8'-3")/2

= 4.125 ft each side

Moment $M = \frac{wl^2}{2}$ where $w = 4654$ #/ft^2 and $l = 4.125$ ft

Therefore $M = \frac{4654 \text{ #/ft}^2 \times 1 \text{ ft} \times (4.125)^2}{2} \simeq 39596$ ft-lbs.

(considering a 1 ft strip)

= 475152 in-lbs.

But U = 1.4 D + 1.7 L and dead load = live load

Hence, Ultimate Moment M_u will now be obtained by multiplying

M with a factor $\frac{1.4 + 1.7}{2} = 1.55$.

Therefore, $M_u = 1.55 \times 475152 = 736486$ in-lbs.

For balanced conditions ρ is not to exceed $0.75\ \rho_b$

where $$\rho_b = \frac{\beta(0.85)f'_c}{f_y} \cdot \frac{87000}{87000 + f_y} \qquad \text{(ACI 10.3.2)}$$

So in our case $$\rho_b = \frac{0.85 \times 0.85 \times 4000}{60000} \cdot \frac{87000}{87000 + 60000}$$

$= 0.0285$

and $0.75\ \rho_b = 0.75 \times 0.0285 = 0.0214$

However, for a realistic design ρ is generally taken to be equal to 1/2 of $0.75\ \rho_b$.

Therefore, $$= \frac{0.75\ \rho_b}{2} = \frac{0.0214}{2} = 0.0107$$

and $$q = \rho \cdot \frac{f_y}{f'_c} = 0.0107 \times \frac{60000}{4000} = 0.160$$

Also, Ultimate Moment $M_u = \phi \left[f'_c b d^2 q(1 - 0.59\ q)\right]$

$$M_u = 0.90 \times 4000 \times 12'' \times d^2 \times 0.160(1 - 0.59 \times 0.160)$$
$$= 6260\ d^2$$

But $M_u = 736486$ (obtained before)

Therefore, $6260\ d^2 = 736486$

Hence $d = 10.85''$

However, 'd' shall not be less than 20".

Therefore d = 20" will be binding.

Check for shear:

Bearing pressure = $4654^{\#/ft^2}$ (obtained previously)

To obtain ultimate bearing pressure, we multiply bearing pressure by a factor $\frac{1.4 + 1.7}{2} = 1.55$ (since dead load = live load)

Hence, ultimate bearing pressure = $1.55 \times 4654 = 7214^{\#/ft^2}$

From ACI 11.10.1(b) and 11.10.2, we have

cantilever length (d/2 from other cantilever)

$$= (4'\text{-}1\tfrac{1}{2}'') - (10'') = 3'\text{-}3\tfrac{1}{2}'' = 39\tfrac{1}{2}''$$
$$= 3.29 \text{ ft.}$$
$$9.50 - 2(3.29) = 2.92 \text{ ft.}$$

Again from ACI 11.10.3, shear stress $v_u = \frac{V_u}{\phi bd}$

$$\text{Therefore, } v_u = \frac{7214^{\#/ft^2} \times 3.29' \times (9.5 + 2.92)/2}{0.85 \times 35'' \times 20''}$$
$$= 248^{\#/in^2}$$

Maximum permissible shear stress = $4\sqrt{f'_c} = 4\sqrt{4000} = 253^{\#/in^2}$

Since the value is within limits, it is OK.

Steel:

We have $\rho = \frac{A_s}{bd}$ or $A_s = \rho bd$, b = 9'-6", d = 10.8"

Therefore $A_s = 0.0107 \times 114" \times 10.8" = 13.2\ in^2$.

But d = 20" (minimum)

Therefore $A_s = \frac{10.8}{20} \times 13.2 = 7.13\ in^2$.

NOTE: As can also be found by first determining q and then ρ from the equation $M_u = \phi\ f'_c bd^2 q(1 - 0.59\ q)$

$$\text{and} \qquad q = \rho \cdot \frac{f_y}{f'_c}$$

Assuming, bars are spaced 6" apart, number of bars = 2 x 9.5 (2 bar/ft) = 19 bars.

Let us use 16 - #6 bars giving an area of $7.06\ in^2$.

Check for development length:

As per ACI 12.5, development length $l_d = 0.04\ A_b(f_y/\sqrt{f'_c})$ but not less than $0.0004\ d_b \cdot f_y$

$$0.04\ A_b(f_y/\sqrt{f'_c}) = 0.04 \times 0.44(60{,}000/\sqrt{4000}) = 16.7"$$

and $0.0004\ d_b \cdot f_y = 0.0004 \times 0.75 \times 60{,}000 = 18"$.

We have cantilever length = 4.125 ft = 49.5"

Deducting 3" to edge, development length = 49.5" - 3"

= 46.5" > 18"

Therefore, OK.

Effective depth d = 20". Adding 3" cover + 1" (bar dia), overall depth = 20 + 4 = 24" or 2 feet.

Final Design:

Provide a square footing of side 9'-6" and 24" deep, reinforced with 16 - #6 bars each way.

Assuming that live load = dead load, compute the allowable moment for the beam illustrated in the previous problem. The beam is reinforced with 8 - #9 bars (8.00 in^2) and spans for 20'-0" with the webs spaced at 8'-0" center to center. f_y = 40000 psi, f'_c = 4000 psi.

Solution: As per ACI 8.10.2, 'b' is the least of the following:

(i) 1/4 span length = 1/4 x 20' = 5' = 60"

(ii) 8 flange depths each side = (2 x 8 x 4) + 15" = 79"

(iii) Center to center distance of webs = 8' = 96"

Therefore select b = 60".

$$\rho = \frac{A_s}{bd} = \frac{8.00}{60 \times 18} = 0.0074$$

$$q = \rho \cdot \frac{f_y}{f'_c} = 0.0074 \times \frac{40{,}000}{4000} = 0.074$$

$$\text{Therefore } 1.18\, q \cdot \frac{d}{\beta_1} = \frac{1.18(0.074)(18)}{0.85} = 1.85'' < 4.00''$$

Hence the analysis can be made using rectangular beam, for which

$$M_u = \phi f'_c\, bd^2 q(1 - 0.59\, q)$$

$$= 0.90 \times 4000 \times 60 \times 18^2 \times 0.074 \times \left[1 - 0.59(0.074)\right]$$

$$= 4952709 \text{ lb-in} = 412.7 \text{ ft-kips}$$

$$\text{Service Moment} = \frac{412.7}{(1.4 + 1.7)/2} \quad \text{(Live Load = Dead Load)}$$

$$= 266 \text{ ft-kips}$$

NOTE: In analysis problems by the ultimate design methods, most of the T-beam problems are treated as rectangular beam problems.

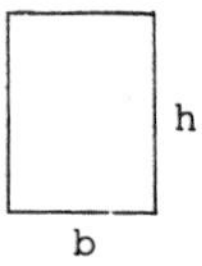

TABLE FOR COMMERCIAL LUMBER SIZES

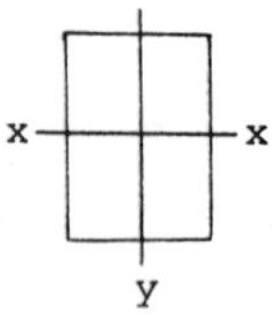

Nominal Size	Actual Size inches bxh	Area sq. in.	Axis X-X		Axis Y-Y		Weight per Foot* lbs.
			I $in.^4$	Z $in.^3$ (Section Modulus)	I $in.^4$	Z $in.^3$ (Section Modulus)	
1x3	3/4x2½	1.88	0.98	0.78	0.09	0.23	0.47
1x4	3/4x3½	2.63	2.68	1.53	0.12	0.33	0.64
1x6	3/4x5½	4.13	10.40	3.78	0.19	0.52	1.00
1x8	3/4x7¼	5.44	23.82	6.57	0.26	0.768	1.32
1x10	3/4x9¼	6.94	49.47	10.70	0.33	0.87	1.69
1x12	3/4x11¼	8.44	88.99	15.82	0.40	1.06	2.05
2x3	1½x2½	3.75	3.75	1.95	1.56	0.70	0.94
2x4	1½x3½	5.25	5.36	3.06	0.98	1.31	1.28
2x6	1½x5½	8.25	20.80	7.56	1.55	2.06	2.00
2x8	1½x7¼	10.88	47.64	13.14	2.04	2.72	2.64
2x10	1½x9¼	13.88	98.93	21.39	2.60	3.47	3.37
2x12	1½x11¼	16.88	177.98	31.64	3.16	4.22	4.10
2x14	1½x13¼	19.88	290.78	43.89	3.73	4.97	4.83
3x3	2½x21	6.25	3.25	2.60	3.25	2.60	1.52
3x4	2½x3½	8.75	8.93	5.10	4.56	3.65	2.13
3x6	2½x5½	13.75	34.66	12.60	7.16	5.73	3.34
3x8	2½x7¼	18.13	79.39	21.90	9.44	7.55	4.41
3x10	2½x9¼	23.13	164.89	35.65	12.04	9.64	5.62
3x12	2½x11¼	28.13	296.63	52.73	14.65	11.72	6.84
3x14	2½x13¼	33.13	484.63	73.15	17.25	13.80	8.05
3x16	2½x15¼	38.13	738.87	96.90	20.18	16.15	9.27
4x4	3½x3½	12.25	12.51	7.15	12.51	7.15	2.98
4x6	3½x5½	19.25	48.53	17.65	19.65	11.23	4.68
4x8	3½x7¼	25.38	111.15	30.66	25.90	14.80	6.17
4x10	3½x9¼	32.38	230.84	49.91	33.05	18.89	7.87
4x12	3½x11¼	39.38	415.28	73.83	40.20	22.97	9.57
4x14	3½x13¼	46.38	678.46	102.41	47.44	27.11	11.28
4x16	3½x15¼	53.38	1034.40	135.66	54.60	31.20	12.98
6x6	5½x5½	30.25	76.26	27.73	76.26	27.73	7.35
6x8	5½x7½	41.25	193.36	51.56	103.98	37.81	10.03
6x10	5½x9½	52.25	392.96	82.73	131.71	47.90	12.70
6x12	5½x11½	63.25	697.07	121.23	159.44	57.98	15.37
6x14	5½x13½	74.25	1127.67	167.06	187.17	68.06	18.05
6x16	5½x15½	85.25	1706.78	220.23	214.90	78.15	20.72
6x18	5½x17½	96.25	2456.38	280.73	242.63	88.23	23.29
8x8	7½x7½	56.25	263.67	70.31	263.67	70.31	13.67
8x10	7½x9½	71.25	535.86	112.81	334.10	89.06	17.32
8x12	7½x11½	86.25	950.55	165.31	404.30	107.81	20.96
8x14	7½x13½	101.25	1537.73	227.81	474.61	126.56	24.61
8x16	7½x15½	116.25	2327.42	300.31	544.92	145.31	28.26
8x18	7½x17½	131.25	3349.61	382.81	615.23	164.06	31.90
10x10	9½x9½	90.25	678.76	142.90	678.76	142.90	21.94
10x12	9½x11½	109.25	1204.03	209.40	821.65	172.98	26.55
10x14	9½x13½	128.25	1947.80	288.56	964.55	203.06	31.17
10x16	9½x15½	147.25	2948.07	380.40	1107.44	233.15	35.79
10x18	9½x17½	166.25	4242.84	484.90	1250.34	263.23	40.41
12x12	11½x11½	132.25	1457.51	253.48	1457.51	253.48	32.14
12x14	11½x13½	155.25	2357.86	349.31	1710.98	297.56	37.73
12x16	11½x15½	178.25	3568.71	466.48	1964.46	341.65	43.33
12x18	11½x17½	201.25	5136.98	2217.94	385.73	48.92	

*Based on 35 lbs./cu. ft. actual volume and weight.

FLEXURE: For rectangular homogeneous beams, $I/c = 1/6\ bd^2$, $f = \frac{Mc}{I} = \frac{M}{Z}$

Stress in normal construction: 1,200 $\#/in^2$, in forms, 1,800 $\#/in^2$

LONGITUDINAL SHEAR: For rct. beams, $\tau = \frac{3V}{2bd}$

Stress in normal construction: 100 $\#/in^2$, in forms 150 $\#/in^2$

COLUMNS: There are several column formulas in use, one of these being:

for normal construction: $f = 800(1 - \frac{L}{80D})$,

for forms, $f = 1{,}200(1 - \frac{L}{80D})$,

Coefficients for conditions of fixity (multiply by wl^2)
Simple span: 1/8 Partial fixity: 1/10 Full continuity: 1/12

TABLE I

Designations, areas, perimeters and weights of standard bars.

Bar No.*	Diameter, in.	Cross-sectional area, in.^{2}	Perimeter, in.	Unit weight per foot, lb
2	1/4 = 0.250	0.05	0.79	0.167
3	3/8 = 0.375	0.11	1.18	0.376
4	1/2 = 0.500	0.20	1.57	0.668
5	5/8 = 0.625	0.31	1.96	1.043
6	3/4 = 0.750	0.44	2.36	1.502
7	7/8 = 0.875	0.60	2.75	2.044
8	1 = 1.000	0.79	3.14	2.670
9	1 1/8 = 1.128	1.00	3.54	3.400
10	1 1/4 = 1.270	1.27	3.99	4.303
11	1 3/8 = 1.410	1.56	4.43	5.313
14	1 3/4 = 1.693	2.25	5.32	7.650
18	2 1/4 = 2.257	4.00	7.09	13.600

*Based on the number of eighths of an inch included in the nominal diameter of the bars. The nominal diameter of a deformed bar is equivalent to the diameter of a plain bar having the same weight per foot as the deformed bar. Bar No. 2 is available in plain rounds only. All others are available in deformed rounds.

TABLE II Areas of groups of standard bars (in square inches)

Bar No.	Number of bars												
	2	3	4	5	6	7	8	9	10	11	12	13	14
4	0.39	0.58	0.78	0.98	1.18	1.37	1.57	1.77	1.96	2.16	2.36	2.55	2.75
5	0.61	0.91	1.23	1.53	1.84	2.15	2.45	2.76	3.07	3.37	3.68	3.99	4.30
6	0.88	1.32	1.77	2.21	2.65	3.09	3.53	3.98	4.42	4.86	5.30	5.74	6.19
7	1.20	1.80	2.41	3.01	3.61	4.21	4.81	5.41	6.01	6.61	7.22	7.82	8.42
8	1.57	2.35	3.14	3.93	4.71	5.50	6.28	7.07	7.85	8.64	9.43	10.21	11.00
9	2.00	3.00	4.00	5.00	6.00	7.00	8.00	9.00	10.00	11.00	12.00	13.00	14.00
10	2.53	3.79	5.06	6.33	7.59	8.86	10.12	11.39	12.66	13.92	15.19	16.45	17.72
11	3.12	4.68	6.25	7.81	9.37	10.94	12.50	14.06	15.62	17.19	18.75	20.31	21.87
14	4.50	6.75	9.00	11.25	13.50	15.75	18.00	20.25	22.50	24.75	27.00	29.25	31.50
18	8.00	12.00	16.00	20.00	24.00	28.00	32.00	36.00	40.00	44.00	48.00	52.00	56.00

TABLE III Perimeters of groups of standard bars (in inches)

Bar No.	Number of bars												
	2	3	4	5	6	7	8	9	10	11	12	13	14
4	3.1	4.7	6.2	7.8	9.4	11.0	12.6	14.1	15.7	17.3	18.8	20.4	22.0
5	3.9	5.9	7.8	9.8	11.8	13.7	15.7	17.7	19.5	21.6	23.6	25.5	27.5
6	4.7	7.1	9.4	11.8	14.1	16.5	18.8	21.2	23.6	25.9	28.3	30.6	33.0
7	5.5	8.2	11.0	13.7	16.5	19.2	22.0	24.7	27.5	30.2	33.0	35.7	38.5
8	6.3	9.4	12.6	15.7	18.9	22.0	25.1	28.3	31.4	34.6	37.7	40.9	44.0
9	7.1	10.6	14.2	17.7	21.3	24.8	28.4	31.9	35.4	39.0	42.5	46.0	49.6
10	8.0	12.0	16.0	20.0	23.9	27.9	31.9	35.9	39.9	43.9	47.9	51.9	55.9
11	8.9	13.3	17.7	22.2	26.6	31.0	35.4	39.9	44.3	48.7	53.2	57.6	62.0
14	10.6	16.0	21.3	26.6	31.9	37.2	42.6	47.9	53.2	58.5	63.8	69.2	74.5
18	14.2	21.3	28.4	35.5	42.5	49.6	56.7	63.8	70.9	78.0	85.1	93.2	100.3

TABLE IV Areas of bars in slabs (in square inches per foot)

Spacing, in.	Bar No.								
	3	4	5	6	7	8	9	10	11
3	0.44	0.78	1.23	1.77	2.40	3.14	4.00	5.06	6.25
3½	0.38	0.67	1.05	1.51	2.06	2.69	3.43	4.34	5.36
4	0.33	0.59	0.92	1.32	1.80	2.36	3.00	3.80	4.68
4½	0.29	0.52	0.82	1.18	1.60	2.09	2.67	3.37	4.17
5	0.26	0.47	0.74	1.06	1.44	1.88	2.40	3.04	3.75
5½	0.24	0.43	0.67	0.96	1.31	1.71	2.18	2.76	3.41
6	0.22	0.39	0.61	0.88	1.20	1.57	2.00	2.53	3.12
6½	0.20	0.36	0.57	0.82	1.11	1.45	1.85	2.34	2.89
7	0.19	0.34	0.53	0.76	1.03	1.35	1.71	2.17	2.68
7½	0.18	0.31	0.49	0.71	0.96	1.26	1.60	2.02	2.50
8	0.17	0.29	0.46	0.66	0.90	1.18	1.50	1.89	2.34
9	0.15	0.26	0.41	0.59	0.80	1.05	1.33	1.69	2.08
10	0.13	0.24	0.37	0.53	0.72	0.94	1.20	1.52	1.87
12	0.11	0.20	0.31	0.44	0.60	0.78	1.00	1.27	1.56

TABLE V <u>DESIGN COEFFICIENTS FOR RECTANGULAR SECTIONS BASED ON 1977 ACI CODE</u>

f_s	f'_c	f_c	n	k	j	ρ	K
18000	2000	900	11	0.355	0.882	0.0089	142
	2500	1125	10	0.385	0.872	0.0121	189
	3000	1350	9	0.403	0.866	0.0152	236
	4000	1800	8	0.445	0.852	0.0223	342
	5000	2250	7	0.467	0.845	0.0292	444
20000	2000	900	11	0.332	0.890	0.0075	133
	2500	1125	10	0.360	0.880	0.0102	179
	3000	1350	9	0.378	0.874	0.0128	224
	4000	1800	8	0.419	0.861	0.0189	325
	5000	2250	7	0.441	0.853	0.0249	424
24000	2000	900	11	0.893	0.903	0.0055	119
	2500	1125	10	0.320	0.894	0.0075	161
	3000	1350	9	0.337	0.888	0.0095	202
	4000	1800	8	0.376	0.875	0.0141	296
	5000	2250	7	0.397	0.868	0.0186	388
30000	2000	900	11	0.249	0.918	0.0038	103
	2500	1125	10	0.273	0.909	0.0052	140
	3000	1350	9	0.289	0.904	0.0065	177
	4000	1800	8	0.325	0.892	0.0098	261
	5000	2250	7	0.345	0.886	0.0130	344

For coefficients not indicated above:

$$n = \frac{E_s}{E_c}$$

$$k = \frac{f_c}{f_c + f_s/n} = \frac{1}{1 + r/n} = \frac{n}{n + r} \quad \text{where } r = f_s/f_c$$

$$j = 1 - k/3$$

$$K = 1/2\ f_c\ kj$$

TABLE VI

STRENGTH DESIGN TABLE

MU IN FT-KIPS FOR 12 INCH WIDTH — AS IN SQUARE IN.

3000 PSI CONCRETE — 40,000 PSI STEEL = FY

E.D.	MIN. SLAB		ρ = 0.0050		ρ = 0.0094		ρ = 0.0139		ρ = 0.0278	
	MU	AS	MU	AS	MU	AS	MU	AS	MU	AS
3.0	0.85	0.10	1.56	0.18	2.83	0.34	4.02	0.50	7.04	1.00
3.5	1.12	0.11	2.12	0.21	3.84	0.39	5.46	0.58	9.58	1.17
4.0	1.42	0.12	2.77	0.24	5.02	0.45	7.14	0.67	12.52	1.33
4.5	1.75	0.13	3.51	0.27	6.35	0.51	9.03	0.75	15.84	1.50
5.0	2.12	0.14	4.33	0.30	7.84	0.56	11.15	0.83	19.55	1.67
5.5	2.53	0.16	5.24	0.33	9.48	0.62	13.49	0.92	23.66	1.83
6.0	2.97	0.17	6.23	0.36	11.29	0.68	16.05	1.00	28.15	2.00
6.5	3.45	0.18	7.31	0.39	13.25	0.73	18.84	1.08	33.04	2.17
7.0	3.96	0.19	8.48	0.42	15.36	0.79	21.84	1.17	38.32	2.34
7.5	4.51	0.20	9.73	0.45	17.63	0.85	25.07	1.25	43.99	2.50
8.0	5.10	0.22	11.07	0.48	20.06	0.90	28.53	1.33	50.05	2.67
8.5	5.72	0.23	12.50	0.51	22.65	0.96	32.21	1.42	56.50	2.84
9.0	6.37	0.24	14.01	0.54	25.39	1.02	36.11	1.50	63.34	3.00
9.5	7.06	0.25	15.61	0.57	28.29	1.07	40.23	1.58	70.57	3.17
10.0	7.79	0.26	17.30	0.60	31.34	1.13	44.57	1.67	78.20	3.34
10.5	8.55	0.28	19.07	0.63	34.55	1.18	49.14	1.75	86.21	3.50
11.0	9.35	0.29	20.93	0.66	37.92	1.24	53.93	1.83	94.62	3.67
12.0			24.95	0.72	45.18	1.35	64.23	2.00	112.65	4.00
13.0			29.27	0.78	53.01	1.47	75.37	2.17	132.20	4.34
14.0			33.94	0.84	61.47	1.58	87.40	2.34	153.31	4.67
15.0			38.96	0.90	70.56	1.69	100.33	2.50	175.98	5.00
16.0			44.32	0.96	80.27	1.80	114.14	2.67	200.22	5.34
17.0			50.02	1.02	90.62	1.92	128.85	2.84	226.03	5.67
18.0			56.08	1.08	101.58	2.03	144.45	3.00	253.40	6.00
19.0			62.47	1.14	113.18	2.14	160.94	3.17	282.33	6.34
20.0			69.22	1.20	125.40	2.26	178.32	3.34	312.82	6.67
21.0			76.31	1.26	138.25	2.37	196.60	3.50	344.88	7.01
22.0			83.74	1.32	151.72	2.48	215.76	3.67	378.50	7.34
23.0			91.52	1.38	165.83	2.59	235.82	3.84	413.69	7.67
24.0			99.65	1.44	180.55	2.71	256.76	4.00	450.44	8.01
26.0			116.94	1.56	211.89	2.93	301.33	4.34	528.63	8.67
28.0			135.62	1.68	245.74	3.16	349.46	4.67	613.08	9.34
30.0			155.68	1.80	282.09	3.38	401.16	5.00	703.79	10.01
32.0			177.12	1.92	320.95	3.61	456.43	5.34	800.75	10.68
34.0			199.95	2.04	362.31	3.84	515.26	5.67	903.96	11.34
36.0			224.15	2.16	406.19	4.06	577.65	6.00	1013.43	12.01

(E.D. = EFFECTIVE DEPTH)

CAUTION: CHECK DEFLECTIONS

NOTES:

(1) FOR MIN. SLAB, AS = .0018BH FOR 60,000FY AND .0020BH FOR LESSER FY. (E.D. PLUS ONE INCH EQUALS H)

(2) MU FOR NEXT ρ IS MINIMUM FOR BEAMS.

(3) MU FOR NEXT TO LAST ρ IS FOR ABOUT HALF OF THE MAXIMUM ρ, WHICH NORMALLY RESULTS IN A DESIGN WHERE THE DEFLECTION IS NOT EXCESSIVE ($= \frac{1}{2} \times .75\,\rho_b$)

(4) MU FOR LAST ρ IS MAXIMUM FOR BEAMS, BUT DEFLECTIONS MUST BE CHECKED.

(5) AS FOR OTHER VALUES OF MU TO BE PROPORTIONAL TO AS FOR NEXT HIGHER VALUE OF MU.

CAUTION: Tables VII through XIV are design tables and should not be used for investigation (analysis) problems. The tables are based on

$$M = \tfrac{1}{2} f_c \; b \; kdjd = Kbd^2 \quad \text{where}$$

$$kd = \frac{f_c}{f_s + f_s/n} \cdot d \quad \text{and} \quad jd = d - \frac{kd}{3},$$

$$M = A_S \cdot f_S \cdot jd \quad \text{and a width 'b' equalling 12"}$$

TABLE VII REINFORCED CONCRETE DESIGN TABLE, USING WORKING STRESS METHODS
BASIS: 12" WIDE BEAMS
STEEL STRESS(FS) = 20,000 LB./IN^2 AND
CONCRETE IS 2,500 LBS./IN^2 (ULTIMATE)
N = 10

E.D. = EFFECTIVE DEPTH

E.D. INCHES	M FT. KIPS	AS SQ.IN.	E.D. INCHES	M FT. KIPS	AS SQ.IN.	E.D. INCHES	M FT. KIPS	AS SQ.IN.
0.5	0.05	0.07	12.0	25.7	1.47	24	102.7	2.92
1.0	0.18	0.13	12.5	27.9	1.53	26	120.5	3.17
1.5	0.41	0.19	13.0	30.2	1.59	28	139.8	3.41
2.0	0.72	0.25	13.5	32.5	1.65	30	160.4	3.65
2.5	1.12	0.31	14.0	35.0	1.71	32	182.5	3.89
3.0	1.61	0.37	14.5	37.5	1.77	34	206.0	4.14
3.5	2.19	0.43	15.0	40.1	1.83	36	231.0	4.38
4.0	2.86	0.49	15.5	42.9	1.89	38	257.4	4.62
4.5	3.61	0.55	16.0	45.7	1.95	40	285.2	4.87
5.0	4.46	0.61	16.5	48.6	2.01	42	314.4	5.11
5.5	5.40	0.67	17.0	51.5	2.07	44	345.0	5.35
6.0	6.42	0.73	17.5	54.6	2.13	46	377.1	5.59
6.5	7.53	0.80	18.0	57.8	2.19	48	410.6	5.84
7.0	8.74	0.86	18.5	61.0	2.25	50	445.5	6.08
7.5	10.03	0.92	19.0	64.4	2.32	52	481.9	6.32
8.0	11.41	0.98	19.5	67.8	2.38	54	519.7	6.57
8.5	12.88	1.04	20.0	71.3	2.44	56	558.9	6.81
9.0	14.44	1.10	20.5	74.9	2.50	58	599.5	7.05
9.5	16.09	1.16	21.0	78.6	2.56	60	641.6	7.30
10.0	17.82	1.22	21.5	82.4	2.62	62	685.0	7.54
10.5	19.65	1.28	22.0	86.3	2.68	64	730.0	7.78
11.0	21.57	1.34	22.5	90.3	2.74	66	776.3	8.02
11.5	23.57	1.40	23.0	94.3	2.80	68	824.0	8.27

TABLE VIII

REINFORCED CONCRETE DESIGN TABLE, USING WORKING STRESS METHODS
BASIS: 12" WIDE BEAMS
STEEL STRESS (FS) = 20,000 LB./IN^2 AND
CONCRETE IS 3,000 LBS./IN^2 (ULTIMATE)
N = 9

E.D. INCHES	M FT. KIPS	AS SQ.IN.	E.D. INCHES	M FT. KIPS	AS SQ.IN.	E.D. INCHES	M FT. KIPS.	AS SQ.IN.
0.5	0.06	0.09	12.0	32.2	1.84	24	128.5	3.68
1.0	0.23	0.16	12.5	34.9	1.92	26	150.8	3.99
1.5	0.51	0.24	13.0	37.7	2.00	28	174.8	4.29
2.0	0.90	0.31	13.5	40.7	2.07	30	200.7	4.60
2.5	1.40	0.39	14.0	43.7	2.15	32	228.4	4.90
3.0	2.01	0.47	14.5	46.9	2.23	34	257.8	5.21
3.5	2.74	0.54	15.0	50.2	2.30	36	289.0	5.52
4.0	3.57	0.62	15.5	53.6	2.38	38	322.0	5.82
4.5	4.52	0.69	16.0	57.1	2.46	40	356.8	6.13
5.0	5.58	0.77	16.5	60.8	2.53	42	393.3	6.43
5.5	6.75	0.85	17.0	64.5	2.61	44	431.7	6.74
6.0	8.03	0.92	17.5	68.3	2.69	46	471.8	7.05
6.5	9.43	1.00	18.0	72.3	2.76	48	513.7	7.35
7.0	10.93	1.08	18.5	76.4	2.84	50	557.4	7.66
7.5	12.55	1.15	19.0	80.5	2.91	52	602.9	7.96
8.0	14.27	1.23	19.5	84.8	2.99	54	650.2	8.27
8.5	16.11	1.31	20.0	89.2	3.07	56	699.2	8.58
9.0	18.06	1.38	20.5	93.7	3.14	58	750.1	8.88
9.5	20.13	1.46	21.0	98.4	3.22	60	802.7	9.19
10.0	22.30	1.54	21.5	103.1	3.30	62	857.1	9.50
10.5	24.59	1.61	22.0	108.0	3.37	64	913.3	9.80
11.0	26.98	1.69	22.5	112.9	3.45	66	971.3	10.11
11.5	29.49	1.77	23.0	118.0	3.53	68	1031.0	10.41

E.D. = EFFECTIVE DEPTH

TABLE IX

REINFORCED CONCRETE DESIGN TABLE, USING WORKING STRESS METHODS
BASIS: 12" WIDE BEAMS
STEEL STRESS(FS) = 20,000 LB./IN^2 AND
CONCRETE IS 4,000 LBS./IN^2 (ULTIMATE)
N = 8

E.D. INCHES	M FT. KIPS	AS SQ.IN.	E.D. INCHES	M FT. KIPS	AS SQ.IN.	E.D. INCHES	M FT. KIPS	AS SQ.IN.
0.5	0.09	0.12	12.0	46.7	2.72	24	186.8	5.43
1.0	0.33	0.23	12.5	50.7	2.83	26	219.2	5.88
1.5	0.73	0.35	13.0	54.8	2.95	28	254.2	6.34
2.0	1.30	0.46	13.5	59.1	3.06	30	291.8	6.79
2.5	2.03	0.57	14.0	63.6	3.17	32	332.0	7.24
3.0	2.92	0.68	14.5	68.2	3.29	34	374.8	7.69
3.5	3.98	0.80	15.0	73.0	3.40	36	20.2	8.14
4.0	5.19	0.91	15.5	77.9	3.51	38	468.2	8.60
4.5	6.57	1.02	16.0	83.0	3.62	40	518.7	9.05
5.0	8.11	1.14	16.5	88.3	3.74	42	571.9	9.50
5.5	9.81	1.25	17.0	93.7	3.85	44	627.7	9.95
6.0	11.68	1.36	17.5	99.3	3.96	46	686.0	10.40
6.5	13.70	1.47	18.0	105.1	4.08	48	746.9	10.86
7.0	15.89	1.59	18.5	111.0	4.19	50	810.5	11.31
7.5	18.24	1.70	19.0	117.1	4.30	52	876.6	11.76
8.0	20.75	1.81	19.5	123.3	4.41	54	945.3	12.21
8.5	23.43	1.93	20.0	129.7	4.53	56	1016.7	12.66
9.0	26.26	2.04	20.5	136.3	4.64	58	1090.6	13.12
9.5	29.26	2.15	21.0	143.0	4.75	60	1167.1	13.57
10.0	32.42	2.27	21.5	149.9	4.87	62	1246.2	14.02
10.5	35.75	2.38	22.0	157.0	4.98	64	1327.9	14.47
11.0	39.23	2.49	22.5	164.2	5.09	66	1412.2	14.92
11.5	42.88	2.60	23.0	171.5	5.21	68	1499.0	15.38

E.D. = EFFECTIVE DEPTH

TABLE X

REINFORCED CONCRETE DESIGN TABLE, USING WORKING STRESS METHODS
BASIS: 12" WIDE BEAMS
STEEL STRESS(FS) = 20,000 LB./IN^2 AND
CONCRETE IS 5,000 LBS./IN^2 (ULTIMATE)
N = 7

E.D. INCHES	M FT. KIPS	AS SQ.IN.	E.D. INCHES	M FT. KIPS	AS SQ.IN.	E.D. INCHES	M FT. KIPS	AS SQ.IN.
0.5	0.11	0.16	12.0	60.9	3.58	24	243.6	7.14
1.0	0.43	0.31	12.5	66.1	3.73	26	285.9	7.74
1.5	0.96	0.45	13.0	71.5	3.87	28	331.6	8.33
2.0	1.70	0.60	13.5	77.1	4.02	30	380.6	8.93
2.5	2.65	0.75	14.0	82.9	4.17	32	433.0	9.52
3.0	3.81	0.90	14.5	89.0	4.32	34	488.9	10.12
3.5	5.18	1.05	15.0	95.2	4.47	36	548.1	10.71
4.0	6.77	1.20	15.5	101.6	4.62	38	610.6	11.31
4.5	8.57	1.34	16.0	108.3	4.77	40	676.6	11.90
5.0	10.58	1.49	16.5	115.2	4.91	42	745.9	12.50
5.5	12.80	1.64	17.0	122.3	5.06	44	818.7	13.09
6.0	15.23	1.79	17.5	129.5	5.21	46	894.8	13.69
6.5	17.87	1.94	18.0	137.1	5.36	48	974.3	14.28
7.0	20.72	2.09	18.5	144.8	5.51	50	1057.2	14.87
7.5	23.79	2.24	19.0	152.7	5.66	52	1143.4	15.47
8.0	27.07	2.38	19.5	160.8	5.81	54	1233.1	16.06
8.5	30.56	2.53	20.0	169.2	5.95	56	1326.1	16.66
9.0	34.26	2.68	20.5	177.8	6.10	58	1422.5	17.25
9.5	38.17	2.83	21.0	186.5	6.25	60	1522.3	17.85
10.0	42.29	2.98	21.5	195.5	6.40	62	1625.5	18.44
10.5	46.62	3.13	22.0	204.7	6.55	64	1732.0	19.04
11.0	51.17	3.28	22.5	214.1	6.70	66	1842.0	19.63
11.5	55.93	3.43	23.0	223.7	6.85	68	1955.3	20.23

E.D. = EFFECTIVE DEPTH

TABLE XI

REINFORCED CONCRETE DESIGN TABLE, USING WORKING STRESS METHODS
BASIS: 12" WIDE BEAMS
STEEL STRESS(FS) = 24,000 LB./IN^2 AND
CONCRETE IS 2,500 LBS./IN^2 (ULTIMATE)
N = 10

E.D. INCHES	M FT. KIPS	AS SQ.IN.	E.D. INCHES	M FT. KIPS	AS SQ.IN.	E.D. INCHES	M FT. KIPS	AS SQ.IN.
0.5	0.05	0.06	12.0	23.2	1.08	24	92.5	2.16
1.0	0.17	0.10	12.5	25.1	1.13	26	108.5	2.34
1.5	0.37	0.14	13.0	27.2	1.17	28	125.8	2.52
2.0	0.65	0.19	13.5	29.3	1.22	30	144.4	2.70
2.5	1.01	0.23	14.0	31.5	1.26	32	164.3	2.88
3.0	1.45	0.28	14.5	33.8	1.31	34	185.5	3.06
3.5	1.97	0.32	15.0	36.1	1.35	36	208.0	3.24
4.0	2.57	0.36	15.5	38.6	1.40	38	231.7	3.42
4.5	3.25	0.41	16.0	41.1	1.44	40	256.7	3.60
5.0	4.02	0.45	16.5	43.7	1.49	42	283.0	3.78
5.5	4.86	0.50	17.0	46.4	1.53	44	310.6	3.96
6.0	5.70	0.54	17.5	49.2	1.58	46	339.5	4.13
6.5	6.78	0.59	18.0	52.0	1.62	48	369.7	4.31
7.0	7.87	0.63	18.5	55.0	1.67	50	401.1	4.49
7.5	9.03	0.68	19.0	58.0	1.71	52	433.8	4.67
8.0	10.27	0.72	19.5	61.1	1.76	54	467.8	4.85
8.5	11.60	0.77	20.0	64.2	1.80	56	503.1	5.03
9.0	13.00	0.81	20.5	67.5	1.85	58	539.7	5.21
9.5	14.48	0.86	21.0	70.8	1.89	60	577.6	5.39
10.0	16.05	0.90	21.5	74.2	1.94	62	616.7	5.57
10.5	17.69	0.95	22.0	77.7	1.98	64	657.1	5.75
11.0	19.42	0.99	22.5	81.3	2.03	66	698.9	5.93
11.5	21.22	1.04	23.0	84.9	2.07	68	741.8	6.11

E.D. = EFFECTIVE DEPTH

TABLE XII

REINFORCED CONCRETE DESIGN TABLE, USING WORKING STRESS METHODS
BASIS: 12" WIDE BEAMS
STEEL STRESS(FS) = 24,000 LB./IN^2 AND
CONCRETE IS 3,000 LBS./IN^2 (ULTIMATE)
N = 9

E.D. INCHES	M FT. KIPS	AS SQ.IN.	E.D. INCHES	M FT. KIPS	AS SQ.IN.	E.D. INCHES	M FT. KIPS	AS SQ.IN.
0.5	0.06	0.07	12.0	29.1	1.37	24	116.1	2.73
1.0	0.21	0.12	12.5	31.5	1.43	26	136.2	2.96
1.5	0.46	0.18	13.0	34.1	1.48	28	158.0	3.18
2.0	0.81	0.23	13.5	36.8	1.54	30	181.4	3.41
2.5	1.26	0.29	14.0	39.5	1.60	32	206.3	3.64
3.0	1.82	0.35	14.5	42.4	1.65	34	232.9	3.86
3.5	2.47	0.40	15.0	45.4	1.71	36	261.1	4.09
4.0	3.23	0.46	15.5	48.4	1.77	38	290.9	4.32
4.5	4.08	0.52	16.0	51.6	1.82	40	322.4	4.54
5.0	5.04	0.57	16.5	54.9	1.88	42	355.4	4.77
5.5	6.10	0.63	17.0	58.3	1.94	44	390.1	5.00
6.0	7.26	0.69	17.5	61.7	1.99	46	426.3	5.22
6.5	8.52	0.74	18.0	65.3	2.05	48	464.2	5.45
7.0	9.88	0.80	18.5	69.0	2.11	50	503.7	5.68
7.5	11.34	0.86	19.0	72.8	2.16	52	544.8	5.90
8.0	12.90	0.91	19.5	76.7	2.22	54	587.5	6.13
8.5	14.56	0.97	20.0	80.6	2.28	56	631.8	6.36
9.0	16.32	1.03	20.5	84.7	2.33	58	677.7	6.58
9.5	18.19	1.08	21.0	88.9	2.39	60	725.3	6.81
10.0	20.15	1.14	21.5	93.2	2.45	62	774.4	7.04
10.5	22.21	1.20	22.0	97.6	2.50	64	825.2	7.27
11.0	24.38	1.25	22.5	102.0	2.56	66	877.6	7.49
11.5	26.65	1.31	23.0	106.6	2.62	68	931.6	7.72

E.D. = EFFECTIVE DEPTH

TABLE XIII

REINFORCED CONCRETE DESIGN TABLE, USING WORKING STRESS METHODS
BASIS: 12" WIDE BEAMS
STEEL STRESS(FS) = 24,000 LB./IN^2 AND
CONCRETE IS 4,000 LBS./IN^2 (ULTIMATE)
N = 8

E.D. INCHES	M FT. KIPS	AS SQ.IN.	E.D. INCHES	M FT. KIPS	AS SQ.IN.	E.D. INCHES	M FT. KIPS	AS SQ.IN.
0.5	0.08	0.10	12.0	42.6	2.03	24	170.2	4.06
1.0	0.30	0.18	12.5	46.2	2.12	26	199.7	4.39
1.5	0.67	0.26	13.0	50.0	2.20	28	231.6	4.73
2.0	1.19	0.34	13.5	53.9	2.29	30	265.8	5.07
2.5	1.85	0.43	14.0	57.9	2.37	32	302.5	5.41
3.0	2.66	0.51	14.5	62.1	2.45	34	341.4	5.74
3.5	3.62	0.60	15.0	66.5	2.54	36	382.8	6.08
4.0	4.73	0.68	15.5	71.0	2.62	38	426.5	6.42
4.5	5.99	0.77	16.0	75.7	2.71	40	472.6	6.76
5.0	7.39	0.85	16.5	80.4	2.79	42	521.0	7.09
5.5	8.94	0.93	17.0	85.4	2.88	44	571.8	7.43
6.0	10.64	1.02	17.5	90.5	2.96	46	624.9	7.77
6.5	12.48	1.10	18.0	95.7	3.04	48	680.5	8.11
7.0	14.48	1.19	18.5	101.1	3.13	50	738.3	8.44
7.5	16.62	1.27	19.0	106.7	3.21	52	798.6	8.78
8.0	18.91	1.36	19.5	112.3	3.30	54	861.2	9.12
8.5	21.34	1.44	20.0	118.2	3.38	56	926.2	9.46
9.0	23.93	1.52	20.5	124.2	3.47	58	993.5	9.79
9.5	26.66	1.61	21.0	130.3	3.55	60	1063.2	10.13
10.0	29.54	1.69	21.5	136.6	3.63	62	1135.2	10.47
10.5	32.56	1.78	22.0	143.0	3.72	64	1209.7	10.81
11.0	35.74	1.86	22.5	149.6	3.80	66	1286.4	11.14
11.5	39.06	1.95	23.0	156.3	3.89	68	1365.6	11.48

E.D. = EFFECTIVE DEPTH

TABLE XIV

REINFORCED CONCRETE DESIGN TABLE, USING WORKING STRESS METHODS
BASIS: 12" WIDE BEAMS
STEEL STRESS(FS) = 24,000 LB./IN^2 AND
CONCRETE IS 5,000 LBS./IN^2 (ULTIMATE)
N = 7

E.D. INCHES	M FT. KIPS	AS SQ.IN.	E.D. INCHES	M FT. KIPS	AS SQ.IN.	E.D. INCHES	M FT. KIPS	AS SQ.IN.
0.5	0.10	0.12	12.0	55.8	2.68	24	222.9	5.36
1.0	0.39	0.23	12.5	60.5	2.79	26	261.6	5.80
1.5	0.88	0.34	13.0	65.4	2.90	28	303.4	6.25
2.0	1.55	0.45	13.5	70.6	3.02	30	348.2	6.69
2.5	2.42	0.56	14.0	75.9	3.13	32	396.2	7.14
3.0	3.49	0.67	14.5	81.4	3.24	34	447.3	7.58
3.5	4.74	0.79	15.0	87.1	3.35	36	501.4	8.03
4.0	6.20	0.90	15.5	93.0	3.46	38	558.7	8.48
4.5	7.84	1.01	16.0	99.1	3.57	40	619.1	8.92
5.0	9.68	1.12	16.5	105.4	3.68	42	682.5	9.37
5.5	11.71	1.23	17.0	111.9	3.80	44	749.1	9.81
6.0	13.93	1.34	17.5	118.5	3.91	46	818.7	10.26
6.5	16.35	1.45	18.0	125.4	4.02	48	891.4	10.70
7.0	18.96	1.57	18.5	132.5	4.13	50	967.3	11.15
7.5	21.77	1.68	19.0	139.7	4.24	52	1046.2	11.60
8.0	24.77	1.79	19.5	147.2	4.35	54	1128.2	12.04
8.5	27.96	1.90	20.0	154.8	4.46	56	1213.3	12.49
9.0	31.34	2.01	20.5	162.6	4.58	58	1301.5	12.93
9.5	34.92	2.12	21.0	170.7	4.69	60	1392.8	13.38
10.0	38.69	2.23	21.5	178.9	4.80	62	1487.2	13.82
10.5	42.66	2.35	22.0	187.3	4.91	64	1584.7	14.27
11.0	46.82	2.46	22.5	195.9	5.02	66	1685.3	14.72
11.5	51.17	2.57	23.0	204.7	5.13	68	1789.0	15.16

E.D. = EFFECTIVE DEPTH

VALUES OF K FOR TEE BEAMS

TABLE XV

F_S = 18,000 PSI

N	F_C	.06	0.08	0.10	0.12	0.14	0.16	0.18	0.20	0.24	0.28	0.32	0.36	0.40
10	1125	60	78	93	108	120	132	143	152	167	178	185	188	188
9	1350	73	94	113	130	146	160	173	185	204	218	228	234	235
8	1800	98	126	152	176	198	219	237	254	282	304	321	332	338
7	2250	123	158	191	222	250	276	300	321	359	388	411	427	437

(Columns .06–0.40: VALUES OF T/D)

TABLE XVI

F_S = 20,000 PSI

N	F_C	.06	0.08	0.10	0.12	0.14	0.16	0.18	0.20	0.24	0.28	0.32	0.36	0.40
10	1125	60	77	92	106	119	130	140	148	162	171	177	178	177
9	1350	72	93	112	129	144	158	170	181	199	211	219	223	222
8	1800	97	125	151	175	196	216	234	249	276	296	311	320	324
7	2250	122	157	190	220	248	273	296	316	352	379	399	413	420

(Columns .06–0.40: VALUES OF T/D)

TABLE XVII

F_S = 24,000 PSI

N	F_C	.06	0.08	0.10	0.12	0.14	0.16	0.18	0.20	0.24	0.28	0.32	0.36	0.40
10	1125	59	76	90	104	115	125	134	141	152	159	160	159	153
9	1350	72	92	110	126	140	153	164	173	188	197	201	201	196
8	1800	96	124	149	171	192	210	226	241	264	280	291	295	294
7	2250	121	156	187	216	242	266	288	307	338	361	376	385	387

(Columns .06–0.40: VALUES OF T/D)

TABLE XVIII

F_S = 30,000 PSI

N	F_C	.06	0.08	0.10	0.12	0.14	0.16	0.18	0.20	0.24	0.28	0.32	0.36	.40
10	1125	58	74	88	100	110	118	125	131	138	139	136	129	118
9	1350	70	89	106	121	134	145	154	162	172	176	174	168	157
8	1800	95	121	145	166	185	201	216	228	246	256	260	258	250
7	2250	120	153	183	211	235	256	275	292	317	333	342	340	337

(Columns .06–.40: VALUES OF T/D)

CAUTION: Tables XIX through XXVI are strength design tables and must be used with great care. At best these tables provide a quicker and approximate design and must be necessarily cross-checked with detailed analysis.

NOTE: The following apply for all the tables:

(1) FOR MIN. SLAB, AS = .0018BH FOR 60,000 FY AND .0020BH FOR LESSER FY. (E.D. PLUS ONE INCH EQUALS H)
(2) MU FOR NEXT ρ IS MINIMUM FOR BEAMS
(3) MU FOR NEXT TO LAST IS FOR ABOUT HALF OF THE MAXIMUM ρ, WHICH NORMALLY RESULTS IN A DESIGN WHERE THE DEFLECTION IS NOT EXCESSIVE.
(4) MU FOR LAST ρ IS MAXIMUM FOR BEAMS, BUT DEFLECTIONS MUST BE CHECKED.
(5) AS FOR OTHER VALUES OF MU TO BE PROPORTIONAL TO AS FOR NEXT HIGHER VALUE OF MU.

TABLE XIX

STRENGTH DESIGN TABLE

MU IN FT-KIPS FOR 12 INCH WIDTH — AS IN SQUARE IN.

2500 PSI CONCRETE — 40,000 PSI STEEL = FY

E.D.	MIN. SLAB MU	MIN. SLAB AS	ρ = 0.0050 MU	ρ = 0.0050 AS	ρ = 0.0083 MU	ρ = 0.0083 AS	ρ = 0.0116 MU	ρ = 0.0116 AS	ρ = 0.0232 MU	ρ = 0.0232 AS
3.0	0.85	0.10	1.55	0.18	2.48	0.30	3.35	0.42	5.88	0.84
3.5	1.11	0.11	2.11	0.21	3.38	0.35	4.56	0.49	8.00	0.97
4.0	1.41	0.12	2.75	0.24	4.41	0.40	5.95	0.56	10.44	1.11
4.5	1.75	0.13	3.48	0.27	5.58	0.45	7.54	0.63	13.21	1.25
5.0	2.12	0.14	4.29	0.30	6.89	0.50	9.30	0.70	16.31	1.39
5.5	2.52	0.16	5.19	0.33	8.34	0.55	11.25	0.77	19.74	1.53
6.0	2.96	0.17	6.18	0.36	9.92	0.60	13.39	0.84	23.49	1.67
6.5	3.44	0.18	7.25	0.39	11.64	0.65	15.72	0.90	27.56	1.81
7.0	3.95	0.19	8.41	0.42	13.50	0.70	18.23	0.97	31.97	1.95
7.5	4.50	0.20	9.65	0.45	15.50	0.75	20.92	1.04	36.70	2.09
8.0	5.08	0.22	10.98	0.48	17.63	0.80	23.80	1.11	41.75	2.23
8.5	5.70	0.23	12.40	0.51	19.90	0.85	26.87	1.18	47.13	2.37
9.0	6.35	0.24	13.90	0.54	22.31	0.90	30.13	1.25	52.84	2.51
9.5	7.04	0.25	15.48	0.57	24.86	0.95	33.57	1.32	58.87	2.64
10.0	7.76	0.26	17.16	0.60	27.54	1.00	37.19	1.39	65.23	2.78
10.5	8.52	0.28	18.91	0.63	30.37	1.05	41.00	1.46	71.92	2.92
11.0	9.31	0.29	20.76	0.66	33.33	1.10	45.00	1.53	78.93	3.06
12.0			24.75	0.72	39.71	1.20	53.60	1.67	93.98	3.34
13.0			29.03	0.78	46.59	1.29	62.90	1.81	110.29	3.62
14.0			33.66	0.84	54.03	1.39	72.94	1.95	127.90	3.90
15.0			38.64	0.90	62.01	1.49	83.72	2.09	146.81	4.18
16.0			43.95	0.96	70.55	1.59	95.25	2.23	167.03	4.45
17.0			49.61	1.02	79.64	1.69	107.52	2.37	188.56	4.73
18.0			55.62	1.08	89.28	1.79	120.54	2.51	211.39	5.01
19.0			61.96	1.14	99.47	1.89	134.30	2.64	235.52	5.29
20.0			68.65	1.20	110.21	1.99	148.80	2.78	260.96	5.57
21.0			75.68	1.26	121.50	2.09	164.05	2.92	287.71	5.85
22.0			83.06	1.32	133.34	2.19	180.04	3.06	315.76	6.12
23.0			90.78	1.38	145.73	2.29	196.77	3.20	345.11	6.40
24.0			98.84	1.44	158.67	2.39	214.25	3.34	375.77	6.68
26.0			115.99	1.56	186.21	2.59	251.43	3.62	440.99	7.24
28.0			134.51	1.68	215.95	2.79	291.60	3.90	511.44	7.80
30.0			154.40	1.80	247.90	2.99	334.73	4.18	587.11	8.35
32.0			175.67	1.92	282.05	3.19	380.85	4.45	667.99	8.91
34.0			198.31	2.04	318.40	3.39	429.93	4.73	754.09	9.47
36.0			222.32	2.16	356.95	3.59	481.99	5.01	845.41	10.02

(E.D. = EFFECTIVE DEPTH)

CAUTION: CHECK DEFLECTIONS

TABLE XX

STRENGTH DESIGN TABLE

MU IN FT-KIPS FOR 12 INCH WIDTH — AS IN SQUARE IN.

3000 PSI CONCRETE — 40,000 PSI STEEL = FY

E.D.	MIN. SLAB		ρ = 0.0050		ρ = 0.0094		ρ = 0.0139		ρ = 0.0278	
	MU	AS	MU	AS	MU	AS	MU	AS	MU	AS
3.0	0.85	0.10	1.56	0.18	2.83	0.34	4.02	0.50	7.04	1.00
3.5	1.12	0.11	2.12	0.21	3.84	0.39	5.46	0.58	9.58	1.17
4.0	1.42	0.12	2.77	0.24	5.02	0.45	7.14	0.67	12.52	1.33
4.5	1.75	0.13	3.51	0.27	6.35	0.51	9.03	0.75	15.84	1.50
5.0	2.12	0.14	4.33	0.30	7.84	0.56	11.15	0.83	19.55	1.67
5.5	2.53	0.16	5.24	0.33	9.48	0.62	13.49	0.92	23.66	1.83
6.0	2.97	0.17	6.23	0.36	11.29	0.68	16.05	1.00	28.15	2.00
6.5	3.45	0.18	7.31	0.39	13.25	0.73	18.84	1.08	33.04	2.17
7.0	3.96	0.19	8.48	0.42	15.36	0.79	21.84	1.17	38.32	2.34
7.5	4.51	0.20	9.73	0.45	17.63	0.85	25.07	1.25	43.99	2.50
8.0	5.10	0.22	11.07	0.48	20.06	0.90	28.53	1.33	50.05	2.67
8.5	5.72	0.23	12.50	0.51	22.65	0.96	32.21	1.42	56.50	2.84
9.0	6.37	0.24	14.01	0.54	25.39	1.02	36.11	1.50	63.34	3.00
9.5	7.06	0.25	15.61	0.57	28.29	1.07	40.23	1.58	70.57	3.17
10.0	7.79	0.26	17.30	0.60	31.34	1.13	44.57	1.67	78.20	3.34
10.5	8.55	0.28	19.07	0.63	34.55	1.18	49.14	1.75	86.21	3.50
11.0	9.35	0.29	20.93	0.66	37.92	1.24	53.93	1.83	94.62	3.67
12.0			24.95	0.72	45.18	1.35	64.23	2.00	112.65	4.00
13.0			29.27	0.78	53.01	1.47	75.37	2.17	132.20	4.34
14.0			33.94	0.84	61.47	1.58	87.40	2.34	153.31	4.67
15.0			38.96	0.90	70.56	1.69	100.33	2.50	175.98	5.00
16.0			44.32	0.96	80.27	1.80	114.14	2.67	200.22	5.34
17.0			50.02	1.02	90.62	1.92	128.85	2.84	226.03	5.67
18.0			56.08	1.08	101.58	2.03	144.45	3.00	253.40	6.00
19.0			62.47	1.14	113.18	2.14	160.94	3.17	282.33	6.34
20.0			69.22	1.20	125.40	2.26	178.32	3.34	312.82	6.67
21.0			76.31	1.26	138.25	2.37	196.60	3.50	344.88	7.01
22.0			83.74	1.32	151.72	2.48	215.76	3.67	378.50	7.34
23.0			91.52	1.38	165.83	2.59	235.82	3.84	413.69	7.67
24.0			99.65	1.44	180.55	2.71	256.76	4.00	450.44	8.01
26.0			116.94	1.56	211.89	2.93	301.33	4.34	528.63	8.67
28.0			135.62	1.68	245.74	3.16	349.46	4.67	613.08	9.34
30.0			155.68	1.80	282.09	3.38	401.16	5.00	703.79	10.01
32.0			177.12	1.92	320.95	3.61	456.43	5.34	800.75	10.68
34.0			199.95	2.04	362.31	3.84	515.26	5.67	903.96	11.34
36.0			224.15	2.16	406.19	4.06	577.65	6.00	1013.43	12.01

(E.D. = EFFECTIVE DEPTH)

CAUTION: CHECK DEFLECTIONS

TABLE XXI

STRENGTH DESIGN TABLE

MU IN FT-KIPS FOR 12 INCH WIDTH							AS IN SQUARE IN.			
4000 PSI CONCRETE						40,000 PSI STEEL = FY				
E.D.	MIN. SLAB		ρ = 0.0050		ρ = 0.0117		ρ = 0.0185		ρ = 0.0370	
	MU	AS	MU	AS	MU	AS	MU	AS	MU	AS
3.0	0.86	0.10	1.58	0.18	3.53	0.42	5.34	0.67	9.38	1.33
3.5	1.12	0.11	2.14	0.21	4.81	0.49	7.27	0.78	12.76	1.55
4.0	1.42	0.12	2.80	0.24	6.28	0.56	9.50	0.89	16.66	1.78
4.5	1.76	0.13	3.54	0.27	7.95	0.63	12.02	1.00	21.09	2.00
5.0	2.13	0.14	4.37	0.30	9.81	0.70	14.84	1.11	26.04	2.22
5.5	2.54	0.16	5.29	0.33	11.87	0.77	17.95	1.22	31.50	2.44
6.0	2.99	0.17	6.29	0.36	14.12	0.84	21.36	1.33	37.49	2.66
6.5	3.47	0.18	7.39	0.39	16.57	0.91	25.07	1.44	44.00	2.89
7.0	3.98	0.19	8.56	0.42	19.22	0.98	29.08	1.55	51.02	3.11
7.5	4.53	0.20	9.83	0.45	22.06	1.05	33.38	1.66	58.57	3.33
8.0	5.12	0.22	11.19	0.48	25.10	1.12	37.98	1.78	66.64	3.55
8.5	5.74	0.23	12.63	0.51	28.34	1.19	42.87	1.89	75.23	3.77
9.0	6.40	0.24	14.15	0.54	31.77	1.26	48.06	2.00	84.34	4.00
9.5	7.09	0.25	15.77	0.57	35.39	1.33	53.55	2.11	93.98	4.22
10.0	7.82	0.26	17.47	0.60	39.22	1.40	59.34	2.22	104.13	4.44
10.5	8.59	0.28	19.26	0.63	43.24	1.47	65.42	2.33	114.80	4.66
11.0	9.39	0.29	21.14	0.66	47.45	1.54	71.80	2.44	125.99	4.88
12.0			25.21	0.72	56.52	1.68	85.49	2.66	149.99	5.33
13.0			29.57	0.78	66.32	1.83	100.32	2.89	176.02	5.77
14.0			34.29	0.84	76.91	1.97	116.34	3.11	204.13	6.22
15.0			39.36	0.90	88.28	2.11	133.54	3.33	234.33	6.66
16.0			44.77	0.96	100.43	2.25	151.94	3.55	266.60	7.10
17.0			50.54	1.02	113.37	2.39	171.52	3.77	300.96	7.55
18.0			56.65	1.08	127.10	2.53	192.28	4.00	337.41	7.99
19.0			63.11	1.14	141.61	2.67	214.23	4.22	375.93	8.44
20.0			69.93	1.20	156.90	2.81	237.37	4.44	416.54	8.88
21.0			77.09	1.26	172.98	2.95	261.70	4.66	459.23	9.32
22.0			84.60	1.32	189.84	3.09	287.21	4.88	504.00	9.77
23.0			92.46	1.38	207.48	3.23	313.91	5.11	550.86	10.21
24.0			100.67	1.44	225.91	3.37	341.79	5.33	599.79	10.66
26.0			118.14	1.56	265.13	3.65	401.12	5.77	703.92	11.54
28.0			137.01	1.68	307.48	3.93	465.20	6.22	816.37	12.43
30.0			157.27	1.80	352.96	4.21	534.03	6.66	937.15	13.32
32.0			178.93	1.92	401.59	4.49	607.60	7.10	1066.26	14.21
34.0			201.99	2.04	453.35	4.77	685.91	7.55	1203.70	15.10
36.0			226.45	2.16	508.24	5.05	768.97	7.99	1349.48	15.98

(E.D. = EFFECTIVE DEPTH)

CAUTION: CHECK DEFLECTIONS

TABLE XXII

STRENGTH DESIGN TABLE

MU IN FT-KIPS FOR 12 INCH WIDTH						AS IN SQUARE IN.				
5000 PSI CONCRETE						40,000 PSI STEEL = FY				
	MIN. SLAB		ρ = 0.0050		ρ = 0.0134		ρ = 0.0219		ρ = 0.0438	
E.D.	MU	AS	MU	AS	MU	AS	MU	AS	MU	AS
3.0	0.86	0.10	1.59	0.18	4.07	0.48	6.37	0.79	11.26	1.58
3.5	1.13	0.11	2.16	0.21	5.54	0.56	8.66	0.92	15.33	1.84
4.0	1.43	0.12	2.82	0.24	7.24	0.64	11.32	1.05	20.02	2.10
4.5	1.77	0.13	3.56	0.27	9.16	0.72	14.32	1.18	25.33	2.37
5.0	2.14	0.14	4.40	0.30	11.30	0.80	17.68	1.31	31.28	2.63
5.5	2.55	0.16	5.32	0.33	13.67	0.88	21.39	1.45	37.84	2.89
6.0	3.00	0.17	6.33	0.36	16.27	0.96	25.45	1.58	45.03	3.15
6.5	3.48	0.18	7.43	0.39	19.10	1.05	29.87	1.71	52.85	3.42
7.0	3.99	0.19	8.62	0.42	22.15	1.13	34.64	1.84	61.30	3.68
7.5	4.55	0.20	9.89	0.45	25.42	1.21	39.77	1.97	70.36	3.94
8.0	5.13	0.22	11.25	0.48	28.93	1.29	45.25	2.10	80.06	4.20
8.5	5.76	0.23	12.70	0.51	32.65	1.37	51.08	2.23	90.38	4.47
9.0	6.42	0.24	14.24	0.54	36.61	1.45	57.26	2.37	101.32	4.73
9.5	7.11	0.25	15.87	0.57	40.79	1.53	63.80	2.50	112.89	4.99
10.0	7.84	0.26	17.58	0.60	45.19	1.61	70.70	2.63	125.09	5.26
10.5	8.61	0.28	19.38	0.63	49.83	1.69	77.94	2.76	137.91	5.52
11.0	9.41	0.29	21.27	0.66	54.68	1.77	85.54	2.89	151.35	5.78
12.0			25.36	0.72	65.12	1.93	101.84	3.15	180.17	6.31
13.0			29.75	0.78	76.42	2.09	119.52	3.42	211.44	6.83
14.0			34.50	0.84	88.62	2.25	138.60	3.68	245.21	7.36
15.0			39.59	0.90	101.73	2.41	159.10	3.94	281.48	7.88
16.0			45.04	0.96	115.73	2.57	181.02	4.20	320.26	8.41
17.0			50.84	1.02	130.65	2.73	204.35	4.47	361.54	8.94
18.0			56.99	1.08	146.46	2.89	229.09	4.73	405.31	9.46
19.0			63.50	1.14	163.18	3.06	255.24	4.99	451.59	9.99
20.0			70.35	1.20	180.81	3.22	282.81	5.26	500.38	10.51
21.0			77.56	1.26	199.33	3.38	311.79	5.52	551.66	11.04
22.0			85.11	1.32	218.76	3.54	342.19	5.78	605.45	11.56
23.0			93.02	1.38	239.10	3.70	374.00	6.04	661.73	12.09
24.0			101.28	1.44	260.34	3.86	407.23	6.31	720.52	12.61
26.0			118.86	1.56	305.53	4.18	477.92	6.83	845.60	13.67
28.0			137.84	1.68	354.33	4.50	554.26	7.36	980.69	14.72
30.0			158.23	1.80	406.75	4.82	636.26	7.88	1125.79	15.77
32.0			180.02	1.92	462.78	5.15	723.92	8.41	1280.89	16.82
34.0			203.22	2.04	522.43	5.47	817.23	8.94	1445.99	17.87
36.0			227.82	2.16	585.70	5.79	916.20	9.46	1621.11	18.92

(E.D. = EFFECTIVE DEPTH)

CAUTION: CHECK DEFLECTIONS

TABLE XXIII

STRENGTH DESIGN TABLE

MU IN FT-KIPS FOR 12 INCH WIDTH						AS IN SQUARE IN.				
2500 PSI CONCRETE					60,000 PSI STEEL = FY					
	MIN. SLAB		ρ = 0.0033		ρ = 0.0050		ρ = 0.0067		ρ = 0.0133	
E.D.	MU	AS	MU	AS	MU	AS	MU	AS	MU	AS
3.0	1.13	0.09	1.53	0.12	2.26	0.18	2.95	0.24	5.25	0.48
3.5	1.49	0.10	2.09	0.14	3.08	0.21	4.02	0.28	7.15	0.56
4.0	1.89	0.11	2.72	0.16	4.02	0.24	5.24	0.32	9.33	0.64
4.5	2.34	0.12	3.44	0.18	5.09	0.27	6.64	0.36	11.81	0.72
5.0	2.83	0.13	4.25	0.20	6.28	0.30	8.19	0.40	14.58	0.80
5.5	3.38	0.14	5.14	0.22	7.59	0.33	9.91	0.44	17.64	0.88
6.0	3.97	0.15	6.12	0.24	9.04	0.36	11.79	0.48	20.99	0.96
6.5	4.60	0.16	7.18	0.26	10.60	0.39	13.84	0.52	24.63	1.04
7.0	5.29	0.17	8.33	0.28	12.30	0.42	16.05	0.56	28.57	1.12
7.5	6.02	0.18	9.56	0.30	14.12	0.45	18.43	0.60	32.80	1.20
8.0	6.80	0.19	10.88	0.32	16.06	0.48	20.96	0.64	37.31	1.28
8.5	7.63	0.21	12.28	0.34	18.13	0.51	23.67	0.68	42.12	1.36
9.0	8.51	0.22	13.76	0.36	20.33	0.54	26.53	0.72	47.22	1.44
9.5	9.43	0.23	15.34	0.38	22.65	0.57	29.56	0.76	52.62	1.52
10.0	10.40	0.24	16.99	0.40	25.09	0.60	32.75	0.80	58.30	1.60
10.5	11.41	0.25	18.73	0.42	27.66	0.63	36.11	0.84	64.27	1.68
11.0	12.48	0.26	20.56	0.44	30.36	0.66	39.63	0.88	70.54	1.76
12.0			24.51	0.48	36.18	0.72	47.21	0.96	83.99	1.92
13.0			28.76	0.51	42.45	0.78	55.39	1.05	98.57	2.07
14.0			33.35	0.55	49.22	0.84	64.24	1.13	114.31	2.23
15.0			38.27	0.59	56.50	0.90	73.73	1.21	131.21	2.39
16.0			43.54	0.63	64.28	0.96	83.88	1.29	149.28	2.55
17.0			49.14	0.67	72.56	1.02	94.69	1.37	168.52	2.71
18.0			55.09	0.71	81.34	1.08	106.15	1.45	188.92	2.87
19.0			61.37	0.75	90.62	1.14	118.27	1.53	210.49	3.03
20.0			68.00	0.79	100.40	1.20	131.04	1.61	233.23	3.19
21.0			74.96	0.83	110.69	1.26	144.47	1.69	257.13	3.35
22.0			82.27	0.87	121.48	1.32	158.55	1.77	282.19	3.51
23.0			89.91	0.91	132.77	1.38	173.28	1.85	308.43	3.67
24.0			97.90	0.95	144.56	1.44	188.68	1.93	335.82	3.83
26.0			114.88	1.03	169.65	1.56	221.42	2.09	394.12	4.15
28.0			133.23	1.11	196.74	1.68	256.79	2.25	457.08	4.47
30.0			152.94	1.19	225.85	1.80	294.78	2.41	524.70	4.79
32.0			174.00	1.27	256.95	1.92	335.38	2.57	596.98	5.11
34.0			196.42	1.35	290.07	2.04	378.61	2.73	673.93	5.43
36.0			220.21	1.43	325.20	2.16	424.46	2.89	755.54	5.75

(E.D. = EFFECTIVE DEPTH)

CAUTION: CHECK DEFLECTIONS

TABLE XXIV

STRENGTH DESIGN TABLE

MU IN FT-KIPS FOR 12 INCH WIDTH						AS IN SQUARE IN.				
3000 PSI CONCRETE						60,000 PSI STEEL = FY				
E.D.	MIN. SLAB		ρ = 0.0033		ρ = 0.0057		ρ = 0.0080		ρ = 0.0160	
	MU	AS	MU	AS	MU	AS	MU	AS	MU	AS
3.0	1.14	0.09	1.55	0.12	2.59	0.21	3.53	0.29	6.31	0.58
3.5	1.49	0.10	2.10	0.14	3.52	0.24	4.80	0.34	8.59	0.67
4.0	1.90	0.11	2.75	0.16	4.60	0.27	6.26	0.38	11.22	0.77
4.5	2.35	0.12	3.47	0.18	5.82	0.31	7.93	0.43	14.20	0.86
5.0	2.85	0.13	4.29	0.20	7.18	0.34	9.79	0.48	17.53	0.96
5.5	3.39	0.14	5.19	0.22	8.69	0.38	11.84	0.53	21.21	1.06
6.0	3.99	0.15	6.17	0.24	10.34	0.41	14.09	0.58	25.24	1.15
6.5	4.63	0.16	7.24	0.26	12.13	0.44	16.53	0.62	29.62	1.25
7.0	5.32	0.17	8.40	0.28	14.07	0.48	19.17	0.67	34.35	1.34
7.5	6.05	0.18	9.64	0.30	16.15	0.51	22.01	0.72	39.43	1.44
8.0	6.84	0.19	10.97	0.32	18.38	0.55	25.04	0.77	44.86	1.54
8.5	7.67	0.21	12.38	0.34	20.75	0.58	28.27	0.82	50.64	1.63
9.0	8.55	0.22	13.88	0.36	23.26	0.62	31.69	0.86	56.78	1.73
9.5	9.47	0.23	15.46	0.38	25.92	0.65	35.31	0.91	63.26	1.82
10.0	10.45	0.24	17.13	0.40	28.71	0.68	39.13	0.96	70.09	1.92
10.5	11.47	0.25	18.89	0.42	31.66	0.72	43.14	1.01	77.28	2.02
11.0	12.54	0.26	20.73	0.44	34.74	0.75	47.34	1.06	84.81	2.11
12.0			24.71	0.48	41.39	0.82	56.39	1.15	100.98	2.30
13.0			28.99	0.51	48.57	0.89	66.17	1.25	118.50	2.50
14.0			33.62	0.55	56.32	0.96	76.73	1.34	137.42	2.69
15.0			38.58	0.59	64.65	1.03	88.07	1.44	157.75	2.88
16.0			43.89	0.63	73.55	1.09	100.20	1.54	179.47	3.07
17.0			49.54	0.67	83.02	1.16	113.11	1.63	202.60	3.26
18.0			55.54	0.71	93.07	1.23	126.81	1.73	227.13	3.46
19.0			61.88	0.75	103.69	1.30	141.28	1.82	253.07	3.65
20.0			68.55	0.79	114.89	1.37	156.54	1.92	280.40	3.84
21.0			75.58	0.83	126.66	1.44	172.58	2.02	309.14	4.03
22.0			82.94	0.87	139.01	1.50	189.40	2.11	339.27	4.22
23.0			90.65	0.91	151.92	1.57	207.00	2.21	370.81	4.42
24.0			98.70	0.95	165.42	1.64	225.39	2.30	403.75	4.61
26.0			115.82	1.03	194.13	1.78	264.51	2.50	473.84	4.99
28.0			134.32	1.11	225.13	1.92	306.77	2.69	549.54	5.38
30.0			154.18	1.19	258.44	2.05	352.15	2.88	630.84	5.76
32.0			175.42	1.27	294.04	2.19	400.66	3.07	717.75	6.14
34.0			198.03	1.35	331.93	2.33	452.30	3.26	810.26	6.53
36.0			222.00	1.43	372.13	2.46	507.07	3.46	908.39	6.91

(E.D. = EFFECTIVE DEPTH)

CAUTION: CHECK DEFLECTIONS

TABLE XXV

STRENGTH DESIGN TABLE

MU IN FT-KIPS FOR 12 INCH WIDTH							AS IN SQUARE IN.			
4000 PSI CONCRETE						60,000 PSI STEEL = FY				
	MIN. SLAB		ρ = 0.0033		ρ = 0.0070		ρ = 0.0107		ρ = 0.0214	
E.D.	MU	AS	MU	AS	MU	AS	MU	AS	MU	AS
3.0	1.15	0.09	1.56	0.12	3.20	0.25	4.71	0.39	8.44	0.77
3.5	1.50	0.10	2.12	0.14	4.35	0.29	6.41	0.45	11.48	0.90
4.0	1.91	0.11	2.77	0.16	5.68	0.34	8.37	0.51	14.99	1.03
4.5	2.36	0.12	3.51	0.18	7.19	0.38	10.60	0.58	18.97	1.16
5.0	2.87	0.13	4.33	0.20	8.87	0.42	13.08	0.64	23.42	1.28
5.5	3.41	0.14	5.24	0.22	10.73	0.46	15.83	0.71	28.34	1.41
6.0	4.01	0.15	6.23	0.24	12.77	0.50	18.84	0.77	33.73	1.54
6.5	4.66	0.16	7.31	0.26	14.99	0.55	22.11	0.83	39.58	1.67
7.0	5.35	0.17	8.48	0.28	17.38	0.59	25.64	0.90	45.91	1.80
7.5	6.09	0.18	9.74	0.30	19.95	0.63	29.43	0.96	52.70	1.93
8.0	6.88	0.19	11.08	0.32	22.70	0.67	33.48	1.03	59.96	2.05
8.5	7.71	0.21	12.50	0.34	25.62	0.71	37.80	1.09	67.68	2.18
9.0	8.60	0.22	14.02	0.36	28.73	0.76	42.37	1.16	75.88	2.31
9.5	9.53	0.23	15.62	0.38	32.01	0.80	47.21	1.22	84.55	2.44
10.0	10.51	0.24	17.30	0.40	35.46	0.84	52.31	1.28	93.68	2.57
10.5	11.54	0.25	19.08	0.42	39.10	0.88	57.68	1.35	103.28	2.70
11.0	12.61	0.26	20.94	0.44	42.91	0.92	63.30	1.41	113.35	2.82
12.0			24.96	0.48	51.11	1.01	75.37	1.54	134.94	3.08
13.0			29.29	0.51	59.97	1.09	88.45	1.67	158.36	3.34
14.0			33.96	0.55	69.55	1.18	102.57	1.80	183.65	3.60
15.0			38.97	0.59	79.83	1.26	117.74	1.93	210.82	3.85
16.0			44.34	0.63	90.82	1.34	133.96	2.05	239.86	4.11
17.0			50.05	0.67	102.52	1.43	151.22	2.18	270.77	4.37
18.0			56.10	0.71	114.93	1.51	169.53	2.31	303.55	4.62
19.0			62.50	0.75	128.05	1.60	188.88	2.44	338.21	4.88
20.0			69.25	0.79	141.88	1.68	209.28	2.57	374.75	5.14
21.0			76.34	0.83	156.42	1.76	230.73	2.70	413.15	5.39
22.0			83.78	0.87	171.67	1.85	253.22	2.82	453.43	5.65
23.0			91.56	0.91	187.62	1.93	276.76	2.95	495.59	5.91
24.0			99.70	0.95	204.29	2.02	301.35	3.08	539.61	6.16
26.0			116.99	1.03	239.75	2.18	353.66	3.34	633.29	6.68
28.0			135.68	1.11	278.04	2.35	410.15	3.60	734.45	7.19
30.0			155.75	1.19	319.17	2.52	470.83	3.85	843.12	7.70
32.0			177.20	1.27	363.14	2.69	535.69	4.11	959.27	8.22
34.0			200.03	1.35	409.95	2.86	604.74	4.37	1082.92	8.73
36.0			224.25	1.43	459.59	3.02	677.97	4.62	1214.07	9.24

(E.D. = EFFECTIVE DEPTH)

CAUTION: CHECK DEFLECTIONS

TABLE XXVI

STRENGTH DESIGN TABLE

MU IN FT-KIPS FOR 12 INCH WIDTH						AS IN SQUARE IN.				
5000 PSI CONCRETE						60,000 PSI STEEL = FY				
E.D.	MIN. SLAB		ρ = 0.0033		ρ = 0.0080		ρ = 0.0126		ρ = 0.0251	
	MU	AS	MU	AS	MU	AS	MU	AS	MU	AS
3.0	1.15	0.09	1.57	0.12	3.67	0.29	5.58	0.45	10.04	0.90
3.5	1.51	0.10	2.14	0.14	5.00	0.34	7.60	0.53	13.66	1.05
4.0	1.92	0.11	2.79	0.16	6.53	0.38	9.92	0.60	17.84	1.20
4.5	2.37	0.12	3.53	0.18	8.26	0.43	12.55	0.68	22.57	1.36
5.0	2.88	0.13	4.36	0.20	10.19	0.48	15.50	0.76	27.87	1.51
5.5	3.43	0.14	5.27	0.22	12.33	0.53	18.75	0.83	33.72	1.66
6.0	4.03	0.15	6.27	0.24	14.68	0.58	22.31	0.91	40.13	1.81
6.5	4.67	0.16	7.36	0.26	17.22	0.62	26.19	0.98	47.09	1.96
7.0	5.37	0.17	8.53	0.28	19.97	0.67	30.37	1.06	54.62	2.11
7.5	6.11	0.18	9.79	0.30	22.93	0.72	34.86	1.13	62.70	2.26
8.0	6.90	0.19	11.14	0.32	26.09	0.77	39.67	1.21	71.34	2.41
8.5	7.74	0.21	12.58	0.34	29.45	0.82	44.78	1.29	80.53	2.56
9.0	8.63	0.22	14.10	0.36	33.02	0.86	50.20	1.36	90.28	2.71
9.5	9.56	0.23	15.71	0.38	36.78	0.91	55.93	1.44	100.59	2.86
10.0	10.55	0.24	17.41	0.40	40.76	0.96	61.98	1.51	111.46	3.01
10.5	11.58	0.25	19.19	0.42	44.94	1.01	68.33	1.59	122.88	3.16
11.0	12.66	0.26	21.06	0.44	49.32	1.06	74.99	1.66	134.86	3.31
12.0			25.11	0.48	58.73	1.15	89.29	1.81	160.54	3.61
13.0			29.46	0.51	68.92	1.25	104.78	1.97	188.41	3.92
14.0			34.16	0.55	79.93	1.34	121.51	2.12	218.50	4.22
15.0			39.21	0.59	91.74	1.44	139.48	2.27	250.82	4.52
16.0			44.60	0.63	104.38	1.54	158.69	2.42	285.37	4.82
17.0			50.35	0.67	117.83	1.63	179.14	2.57	322.15	5.12
18.0			56.44	0.71	132.09	1.73	200.83	2.72	361.16	5.42
19.0			62.88	0.75	147.17	1.82	223.76	2.87	402.40	5.72
20.0			69.66	0.79	163.06	1.92	247.93	3.02	445.86	6.02
21.0			76.80	0.83	179.77	2.02	273.34	3.18	491.56	6.33
22.0			84.28	0.87	197.30	2.11	299.99	3.33	539.48	6.63
23.0			92.12	0.91	215.63	2.21	327.87	3.48	589.64	6.93
24.0			100.29	0.95	234.79	2.30	357.00	3.63	642.02	7.23
26.0			117.70	1.03	275.54	2.50	418.97	3.93	753.47	7.83
28.0			136.49	1.11	319.55	2.69	485.90	4.23	873.84	8.43
30.0			156.68	1.19	366.83	2.88	557.78	4.54	1003.13	9.04
32.0			178.26	1.27	417.36	3.07	634.63	4.84	1141.33	9.64
34.0			201.24	1.35	471.16	3.26	716.43	5.14	1288.45	10.24
36.0			225.60	1.43	528.21	3.46	803.18	5.44	1444.49	10.84

(E.D. = EFFECTIVE DEPTH)

CAUTION: CHECK DEFLECTIONS

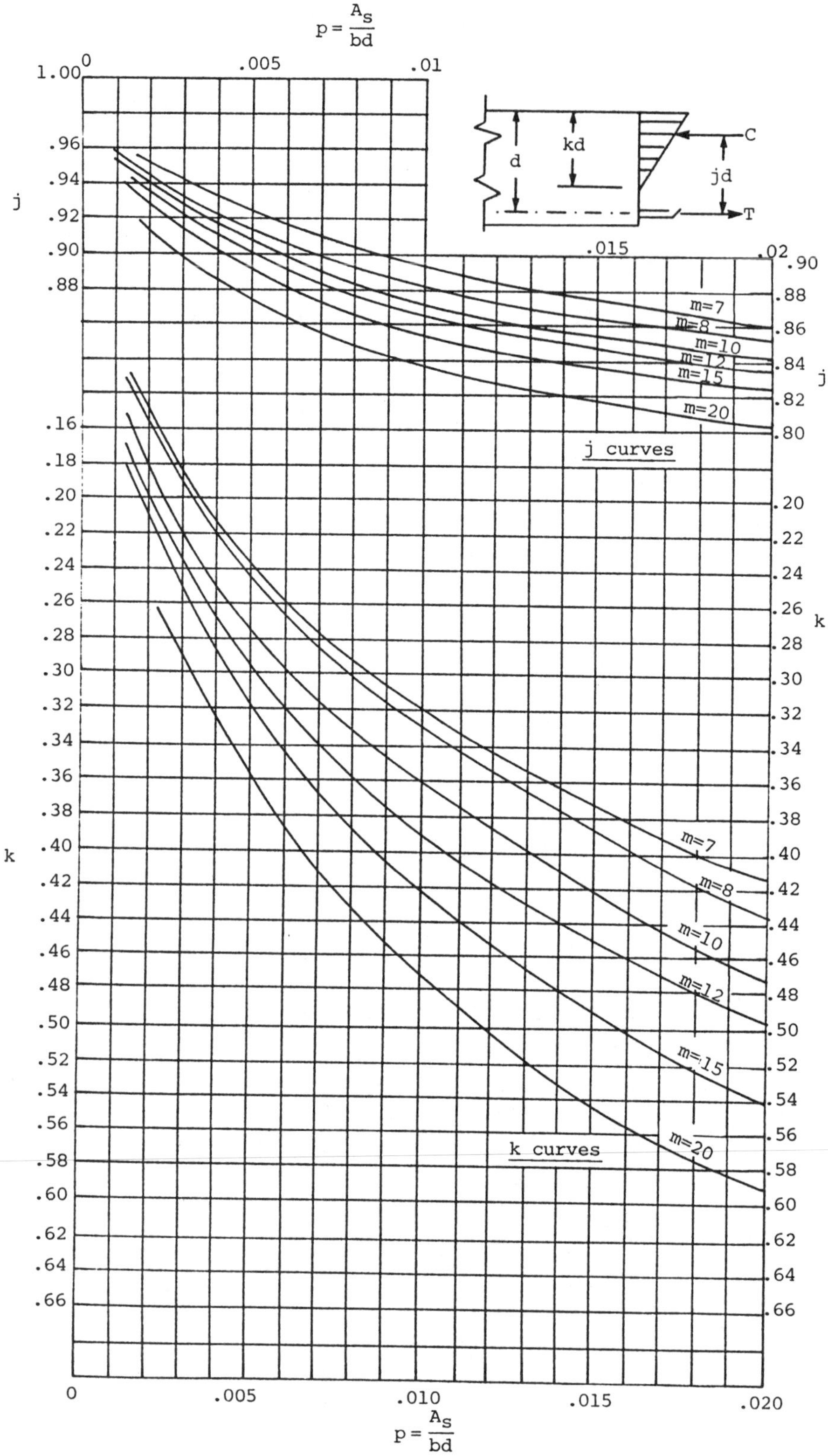

Fig. 1 REVIEW (INVESTIGATION) CURVES FOR BEAMS WITH TENSILE REINFORCEMENT

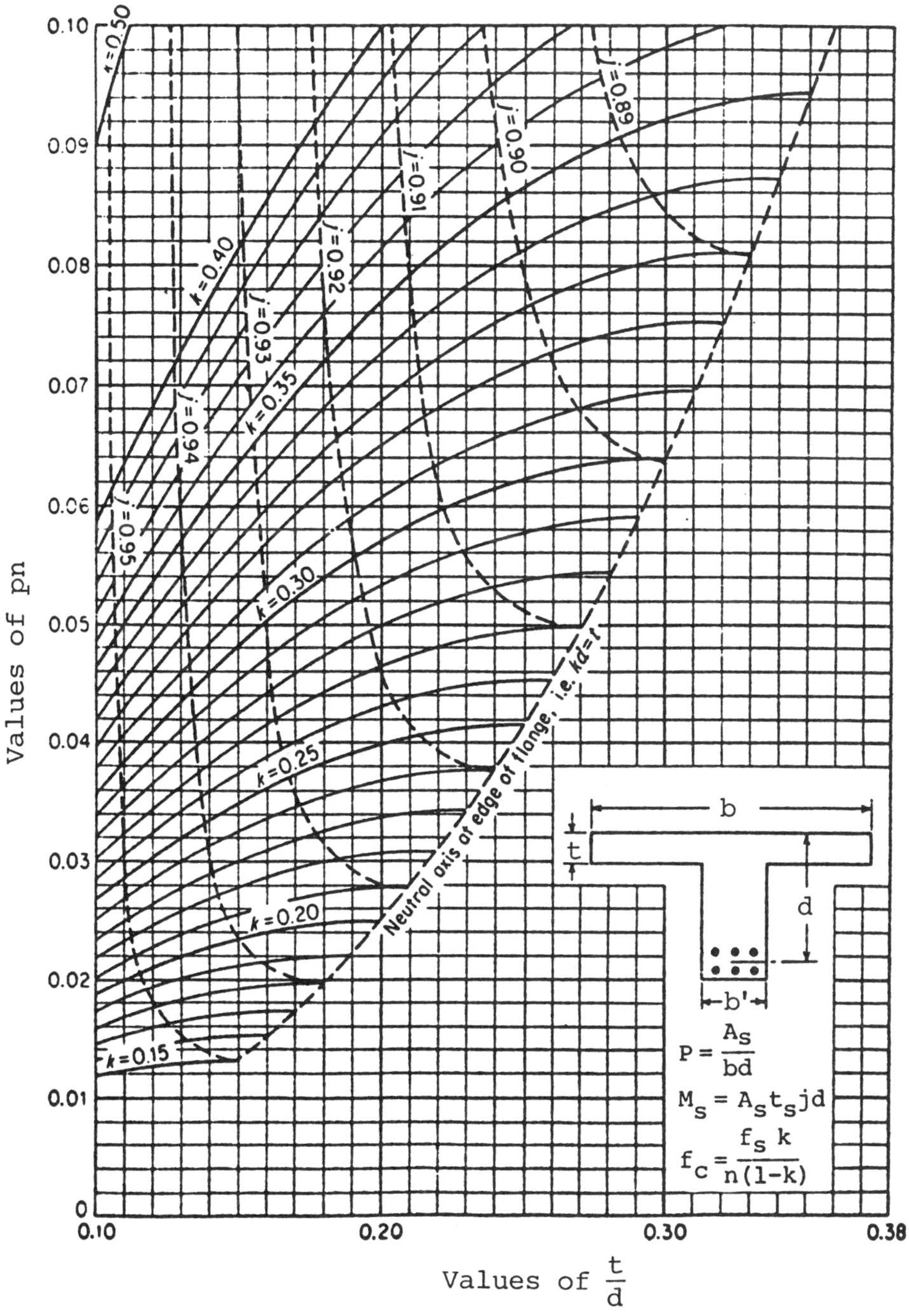

Fig. 2 T-BEAM REVIEW CURVE (INVESTIGATION)

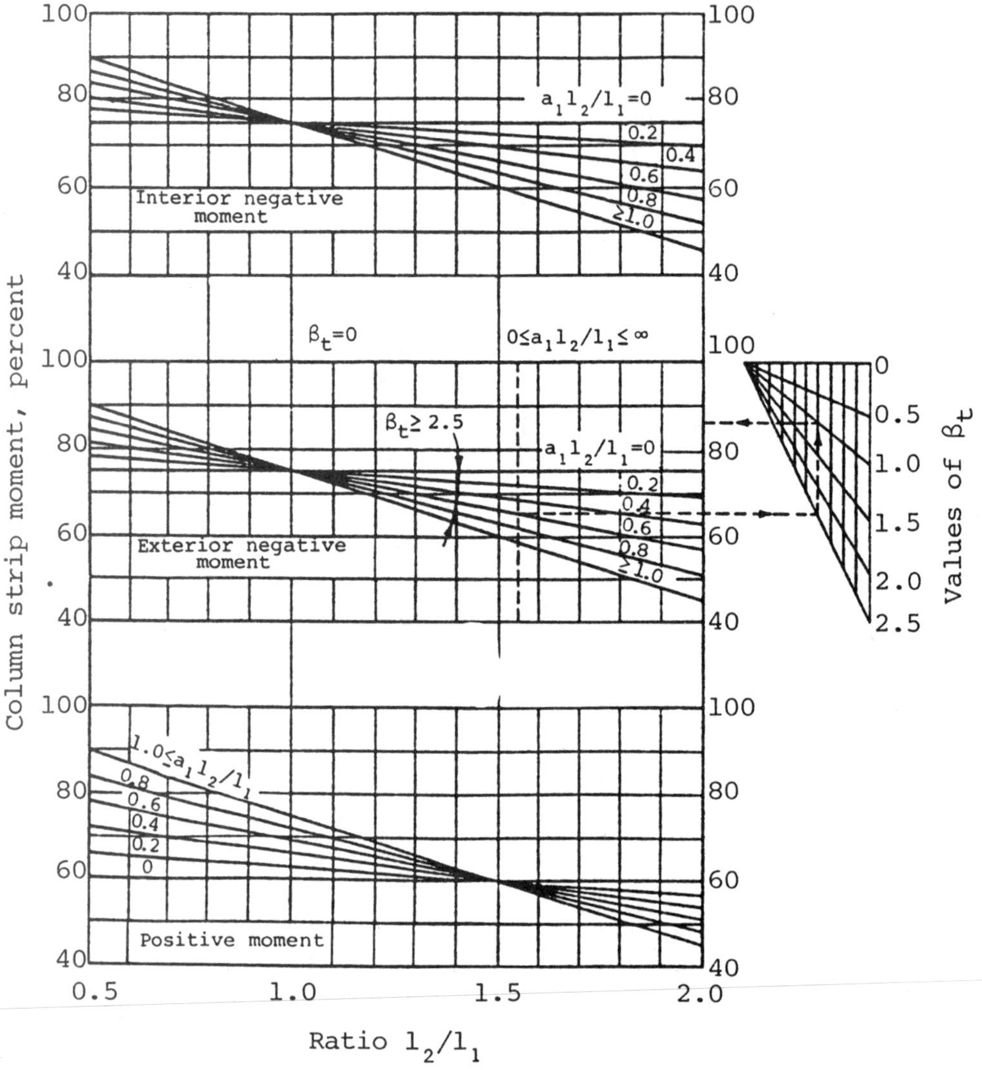

Fig. 3 INTERPOLATION CHARTS FOR LATERAL DISTRIBUTION OF THE SLAB MOMENTS

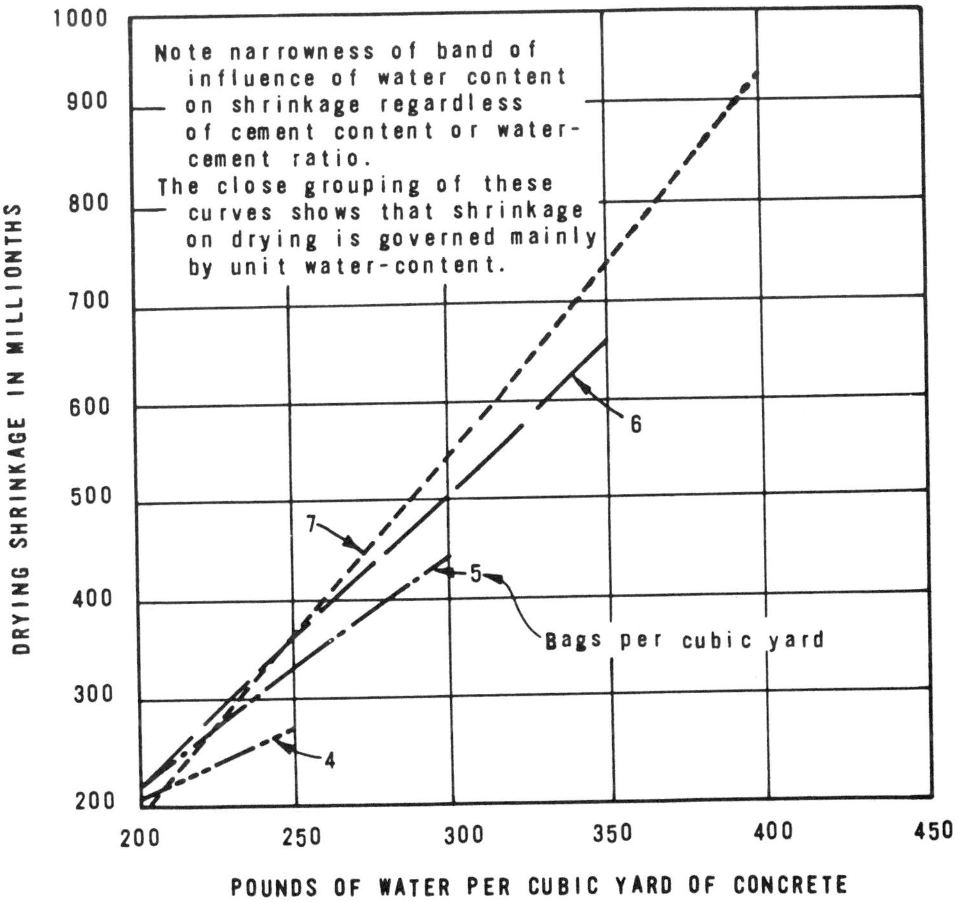

The interrelation of shrinkage, cement content, and water content. The chart indicates that shrinkage is a direct function of the unit water content of fresh concrete.

Observed average weight of fresh concrete

(Pounds per cubic foot)

Maximum size of aggregate, inches	Average values			Unit weight, pounds per cubic foot [1]				
				Specific gravity of aggregate [2]				
	Air content, percent	Water, pounds per cubic yard	Cement, pounds per cubic yard	2.55	2.60	2.65	2.70	2.75
¾	6.0	283	566	137	139	141	143	145
1½	4.5	245	490	141	143	146	148	150
3	3.5	204	408	144	147	149	152	154
6	3.0	164	282	147	149	152	154	157

[1] Weights indicated are for air-entrained concrete with indicated air content.
[2] On saturated surface-dry basis.

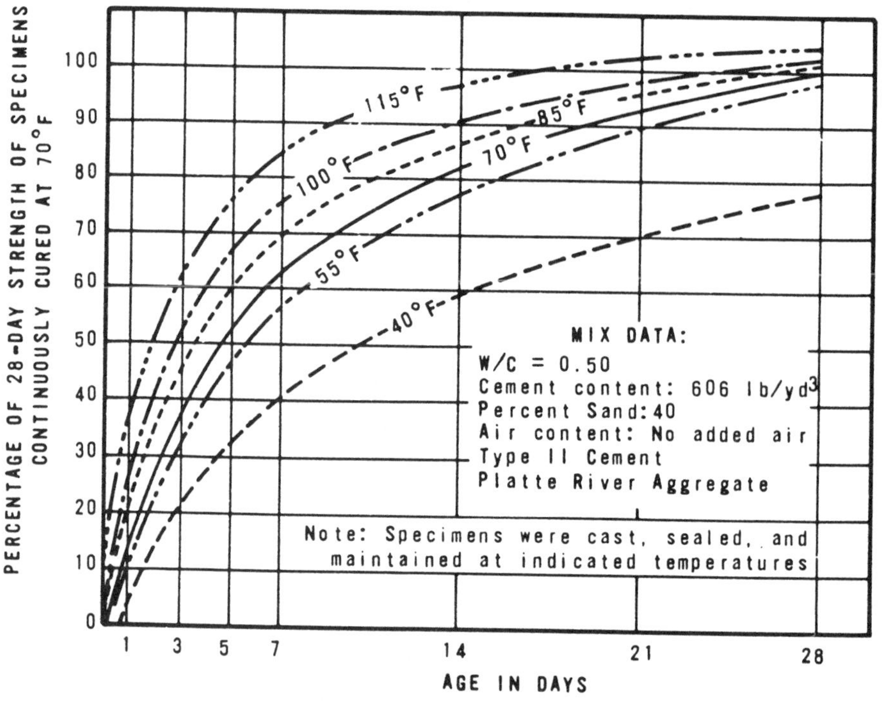

Effect of curing temperature on compressive strength of concrete.

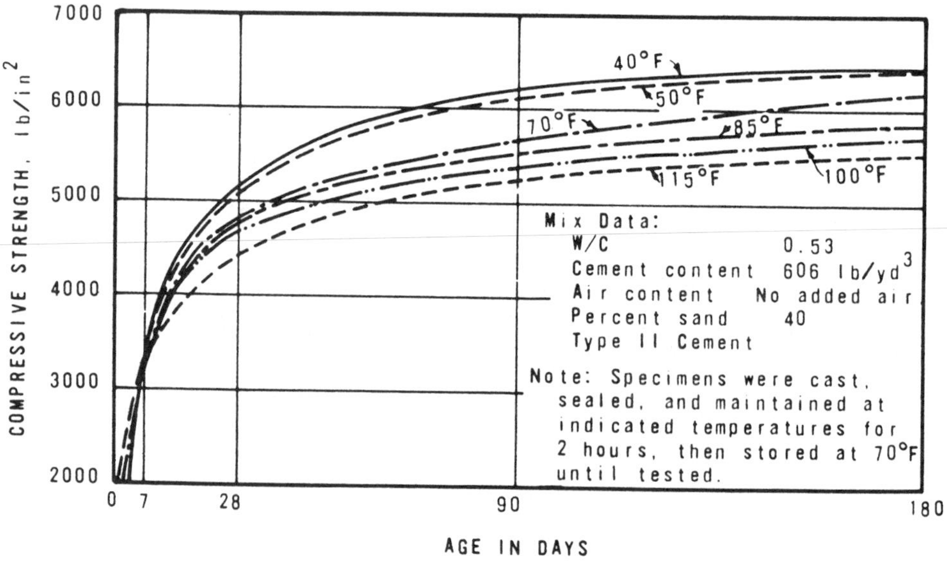

Effect of initial temperature on compressive strength of concrete.

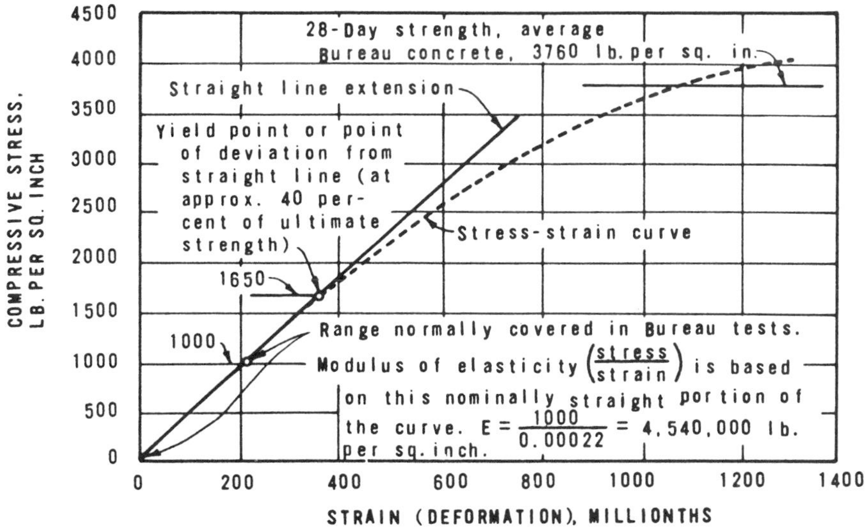

Typical stress-strain diagram for thoroughly hardened concrete that has been moderately preloaded. The stress-strain curve is very nearly a straight line within the range of usual working stresses.

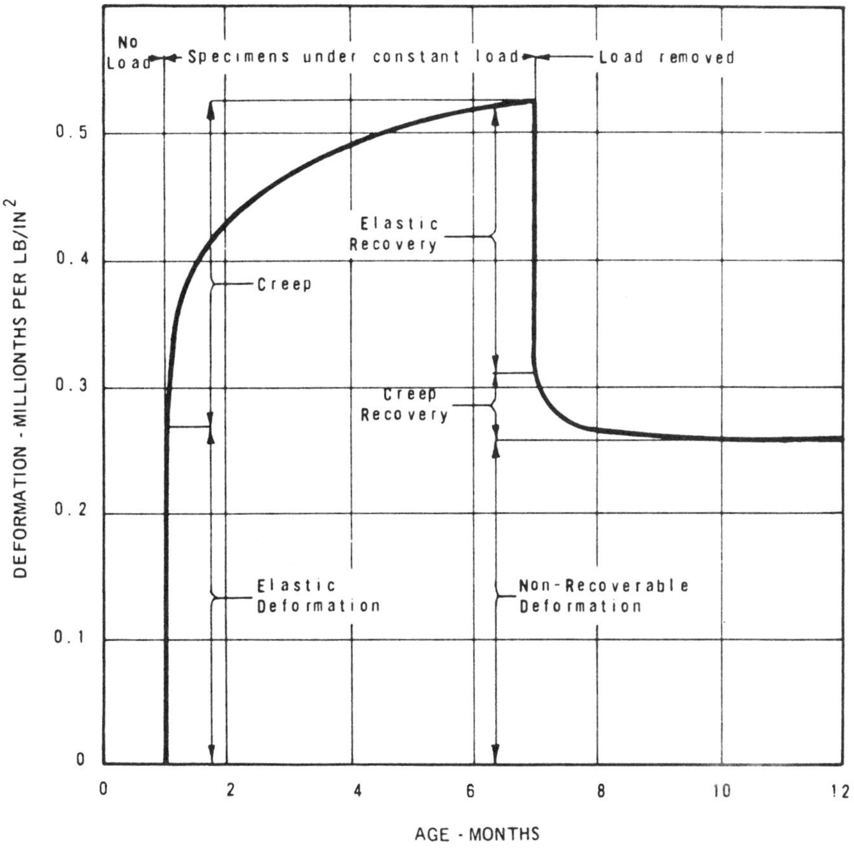

Elastic and creep deformations of mass concrete under constant load followed by load removal.

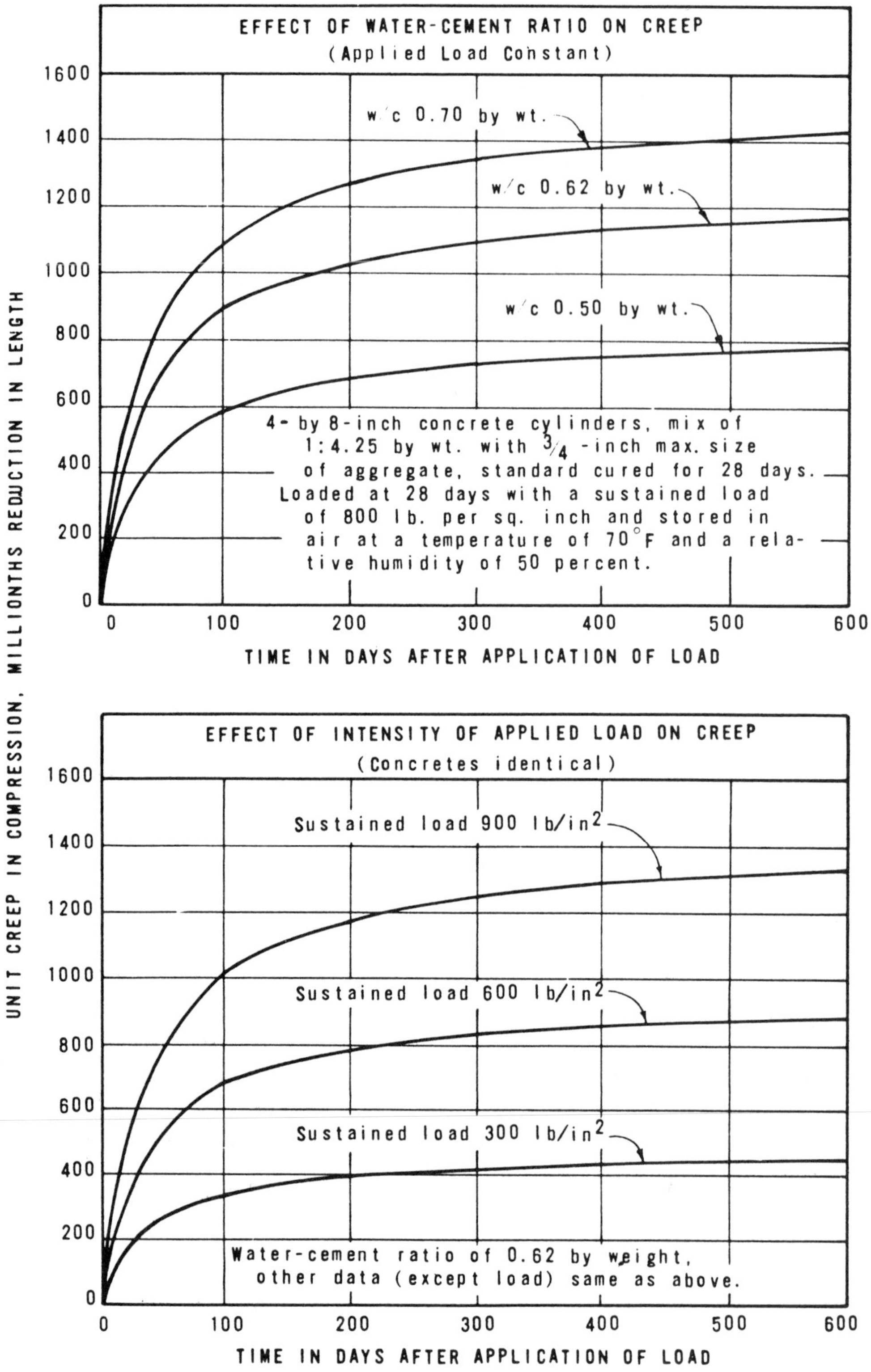

Rate of creep in concrete as affected by variation in water-cement ratio and intensity of applied load.

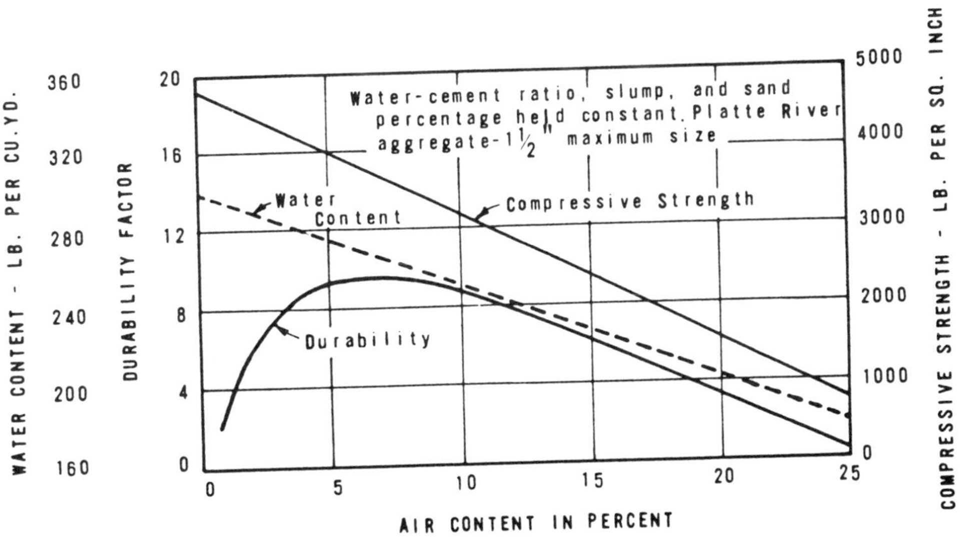

Effects of air content on durability, compressive strength, and required water content of concrete. Durability increases rapidly to a maximum and then decreases as the air content is increased. Compressive strength and water content decrease as the air content is increased.

MINIMUM DESIGN LOADS IN BUILDINGS AND OTHER STRUCTURES

UNIFORMLY DISTRIBUTED FLOOR LOADS

The live loads assumed for purposes of design shall be the greatest loads that probably will be produced by the intended occupancies or uses, provided that the live loads to be considered as uniformly distributed shall be not less than the values given in the following table.

Occupancy or Use	Live Load Lb. per Sq. Ft.	Occupancy or Use	Live Load Lb. per Sq. Ft.
Apartment houses:		Hotels:	
Private apartments	40	Guest rooms	40
Public stairways	100	Corridors serving public rooms	100
Assembly halls:		Public rooms	100
Fixed seats	60	Loft buildings	125
Movable seats	100	Manufacturing, light	125
Corridors, upper floors	100	Office buildings.	
Corridors:		Offices	80
First floor	100	Lobbies	100
Other floors, same as occupancy served except as indicated		Schools:	
Courtrooms	80	Classrooms	40
Dance halls	100	Corridors	100
Dining rooms, public	100	Stores	125
Dwellings	40	Theatres:	
Hospitals and asylums:		Aisles, corridors, and lobbies	100
Operating rooms	60	Orchestra floor	60
Private rooms	40	Balconies	60
Wards	40	Stage floor	150
Public space	80		

Note: These are suggested loads only. The local codes should also be consulted.

Kq is a relative measure of the flow of water thru concrete in cubic feet per year per square foot of area for a unit hydraulic gradient.
COEFFICIENT OF PERMEABILITY, Kq x 10^4
140
130
120
110
100
90
80
70
60
50
40
30
20
10
0
4½-In. Max. Agg.
3 In. Max. Agg.
1½ In. Max. Agg.
Mortar, No. 4 Max. Agg.
0.4
0.5
0.6
0.7
0.8
0.9
WATER - CEMENT RATIO BY WEIGHT

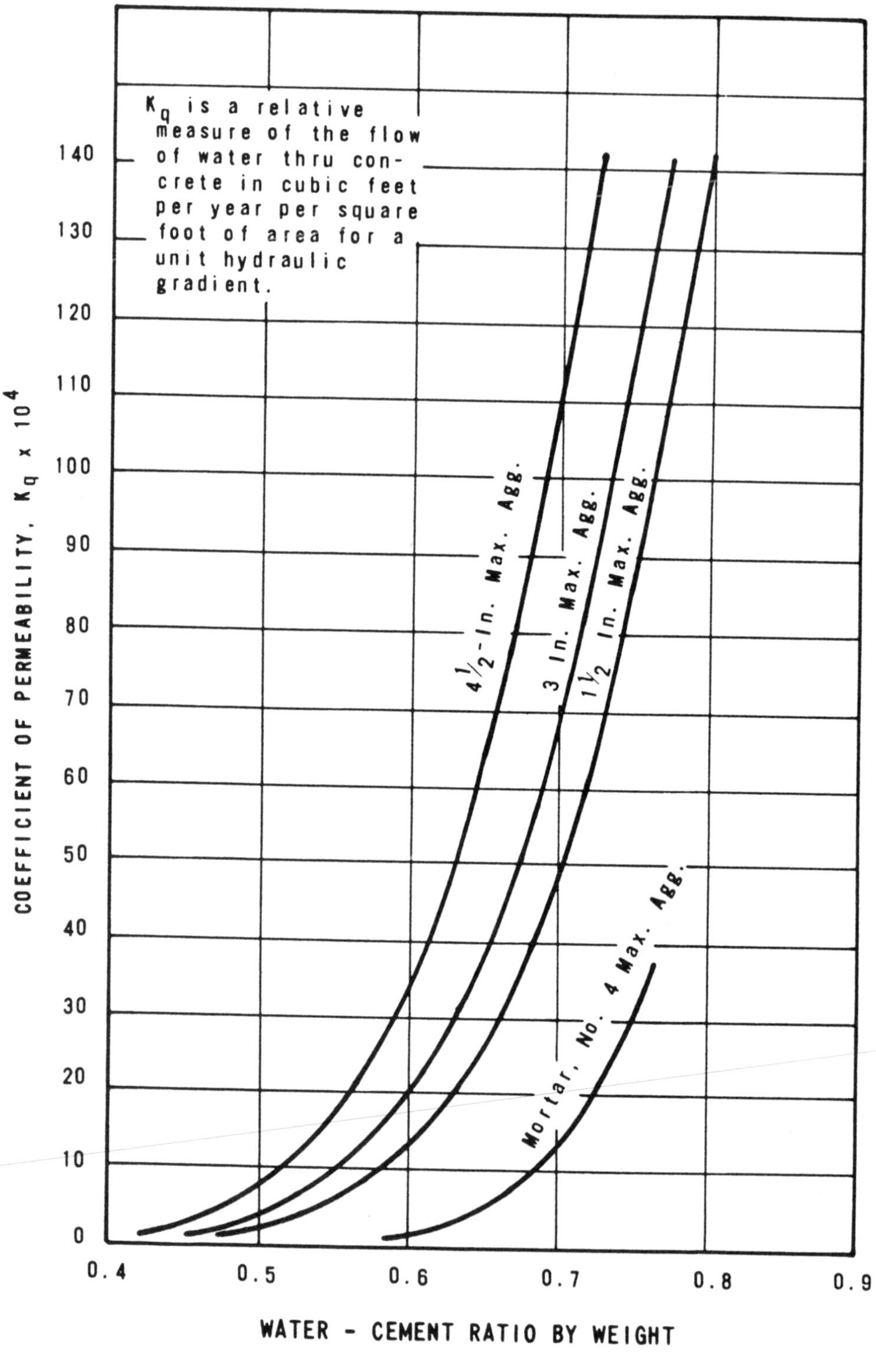

Relationship between coefficient of permeability and water-cement ratio, for mortar and concrete of three maximum sizes. Relatively low water-cement ratios are essential to impermeability of concrete.

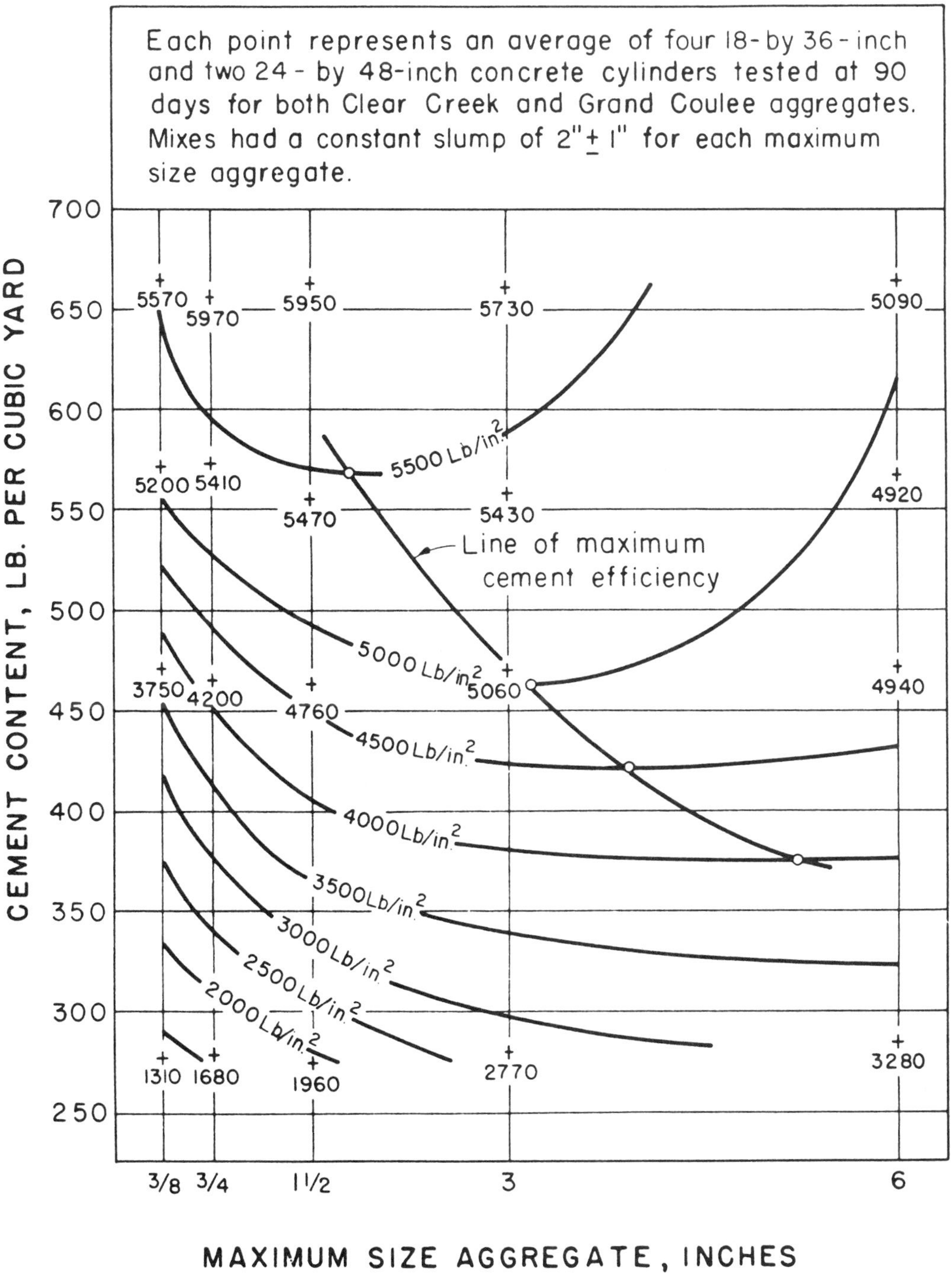

Variation of cement content with maximum size of aggregate for various compressive strengths. Chart shows that compressive strength varies inversely with maximum size of aggregate for minimum cement content.

WEIGHTS OF BUILDING MATERIALS

Materials	Weight Lb. per Sq. Ft.
CEILINGS	
Gypsum ceiling block, 2″ thick, unplastered	10
Plaster board, unplastered	3
Plaster, ¾″, and wood lath	8
Plaster, ¾″, and metal lath	8
Plaster, on tile or concrete	5
Suspended, metal lath and plaster	10
FLOORS	
Hardwood flooring, ⅞″ thick	4
Sheathing, white, red and Oregon pine, spruce or hemlock, ⅞″ thick	2½
Sheathing, yellow pine, 1″ thick	4
Wood block, creosoted, 3″ thick	15
Cement finish, per inch thick	12
Cinder concrete, per inch thick	9
Cinder concrete fill, per inch thick	5
Terrazzo, Tile, Mastic, Linoleum, per inch thick, including base	12
Gypsum slab, per inch thick	5
ROOFS	
Corrugated metal	Page 143
Roofing felt, 3 ply and gravel	5½
Roofing felt, 5 ply and gravel	6½
Roofing felt, 3 ply and slag	4½
Roofing felt, 5 ply and slag	5½
3-ply ready roofing	1
Shingles, wood	2
Tile or slate	5-20

Materials	Weight Lb. per Sq. Ft.
PARTITIONS	
Channel studs, metal lath, cement plaster, solid, 2″ thick	20
Studs, 2″ x 4″, wood or metal lath, ¾″ plaster both sides	18
Studs, 2″ x 4″ plaster board, ½″ plaster both sides	18
Plaster, ½″, on gypsum block or clay tile (one side)	4
Hollow clay tile, 2″	13
Hollow clay tile, 3″	16
Hollow clay tile, 4″	18
Hollow clay tile, 5″	20
Hollow clay tile, 6″	25
Hollow clay tile, 8″	30
Hollow clay tile, 10″	35
Hollow gypsum block, 3″	10
Hollow gypsum block, 4″	13
Hollow gypsum block, 5″	15½
Hollow gypsum block, 6″	16½
Solid gypsum block, 2″	9½
Solid gypsum block, 3″	13
Steel partitions	4
WALLS	
Brick, 9″ thick	84
Brick, 13″ thick	121
Brick, 18″ thick	168
Brick, 22″ thick	205
Brick, 26″ thick	243
Wall tile, 6″ thick	30
Wall tile, 8″ thick	33
Wall tile, 10″ thick	40
Wall tile, 12″ thick	45
Brick 4″, tile backing 4″	60
Brick 4″, tile backing 8″	75
Brick 9″, tile backing 4″	100
Brick 9″, tile backing 8″	115
Limestone 4″, brick 9″	140
Limestone 4″, brick 13″	175
Limestone 4″, tile 8″	90
Limestone 4″, tile 12″	100
Corrugated metal siding	Page 143
Windows, glass, frame and sash	8

RECOMMENDED LIVE LOADS
FOR
STORAGE WAREHOUSES

United States Department of Commerce, National Bureau of Standards

Material	Weight per Cubic Foot of Space Lb.	Height of Pile Feet	Weight per Square Foot of Floor Lb.	Recommended Live Load Lb. per Sq. Foot
BUILDING MATERIALS				
Asbestos	50	6	300	
Bricks, Building	45	6	270	
Bricks, Fire Clay	75	6	450	
Cement, Natural	59	6	354	300
Cement, Portland	72 to 105	6	432 to 630	to
Gypsum	50	6	300	400
Lime and Plaster	53	5	265	
Tiles	50	6	300	
Woods, bulk	45	6	270	
DRUGS, PAINTS, OIL, ETC.				
Alum, Pearl, in barrels	33	6	198	
Bleaching Powder, in hogsheads	31	3½	102	
Blue Vitriol, in barrels	45	5	226	
Glycerine, in cases	52	6	312	
Linseed Oil, in barrels	36	6	216	
Linseed Oil, in iron drums	45	4	180	
Logwood Extract, in boxes	70	5	350	
Rosin, in barrels	48	6	288	
Shellac, Gum	38	6	228	200
Soaps	50	6	300	to
Soda Ash, in hogsheads	62	2¾	167	300
Soda, Caustic, in iron drums	88	3⅜	294	
Soda, Silicate, in barrels	53	6	318	
Sulphuric Acid	60	1⅝	100	
Toilet Articles	35	6	210	
Varnishes	55	6	330	
White Lead Paste, in cans	174	3½	610	
White Lead, dry	86	4¾	408	
Red Lead and Litharge, dry	132	3¾	495	
DRY GOODS, COTTON, WOOL, ETC.				
Burlap, in bales	43	6	258	
Carpets and Rugs	30	6	180	
Coir Yarn, in bales	33	8	264	
Cotton, in bales, American	30	8	240	
Cotton, in bales, Foreign	40	8	320	
Cotton Bleached Goods, in cases	28	8	224	
Cotton Flannel, in cases	12	8	96	
Cotton Sheeting, in cases	23	8	184	
Cotton Yarn, in cases	25	8	200	
Excelsior, compressed	19	8	152	200
Hemp, Italian, compressed	22	8	176	to
Hemp, Manila, compressed	30	8	240	250
Jute, compressed	41	8	328	
Linen Damask, in cases	50	5	250	
Linen Goods, in cases	30	8	240	
Linen Towels, in cases	40	6	240	
Silk and Silk Goods	45	8	360	
Sisal, compressed	21	8	168	
Tow, compressed	29	8	232	
Wool, in bales, compressed	48			
Wool, in bales, not compressed	13	8	104	
Wool, Worsteds, in cases	27	8	216	

RECOMMENDED LIVE LOADS
FOR
STORAGE WAREHOUSES

United States Department of Commerce, National Bureau of Standards

Material	Weight per Cubic Foot of Space Lb.	Height of Pile Feet	Weight per Square Foot of Floor Lb.	Recommended Live Load Lb. per Sq. Ft.
GROCERIES, WINES, LIQUORS, ETC.				
Beans, in bags	40	8	320	
Beverages	40	8	320	
Canned Goods, in cases	58	6	348	
Cereals	45	8	360	
Cocoa	35	8	280	
Coffee, Roasted, in bags	33	8	264	
Coffee, Green, in bags	39	8	312	
Dates, in cases	55	6	330	
Figs, in cases	74	5	370	
Flour, in barrels	40	5	200	250
Fruits, Fresh	35	8	280	to
Meat and Meat Products	45	6	270	300
Milk, Condensed	50	6	300	
Molasses, in barrels	48	5	240	
Rice, in bags	58	6	348	
Sal Soda, in barrels	46	5	230	
Salt, in bags	70	5	350	
Soap Powder, in cases	38	8	304	
Starch, in barreis	25	6	150	
Sugar, in barrels	43	5	215	
Sugar, in cases	51	6	306	
Tea, in chests	25	8	200	
Wines and Liquors, in barrels	38	6	228	
HARDWARE, ETC				
Automobile Parts	40	8	320	
Chain	100	6	600	
Cutlery	45	8	360	
Door Checks	45	6	270	
Electrical Goods and Machinery	40	8	320	
Hinges	64	6	384	
Locks, in cases, packed	31	6	186	
Machinery, Light	20	8	160	
Plumbing, Fixtures	30	8	240	300
Plumbing, Supplies	55	6	330	to
Sash Fasteners	48	6	288	400
Screws	101	6	606	
Shafting Steel	125			
Sheet Tin, in boxes	278	2	556	
Tools, Small, Metal	75	6	450	
Wire Cables, on reels			425	
Wire, Insulated Copper, in coils	63	5	315	
Wire, Galvanized Iron, in coils	74	4½	333	
Wire, Magnet, on spools	75	6	450	
MISCELLANEOUS				
Automobile Tires	30	6	180	
Automobiles, uncrated	8		64	
Books (solidly packed)	65	6	390	
Furniture	20			
Glass and Chinaware, in crates	40	8	320	
Hides and Leather, in bales	20	8	160	
Hides, Buffalo, in bundles	37	8	296	
Leather and Leather Goods	40	8	320	
Paper, Newspaper, and Strawboards	35	6	210	
Paper, Writing and Calendared	60	6	360	
Rope, in coils	32	6	192	
Rubber, Crude	50	8	400	
Tobacco, bales	35	8	280	

AREAS AND PERIMETERS OF CONCRETE REINFORCING BARS IN ONE-FOOT WIDTHS OF SLAB

Top number gives area A_s in square inches per foot width of slab. Bottom number gives perimeter Σo in inches per foot width of slab. Interpolate for $\frac{1}{4}$-in. increments of spacing.

Spacing	Bar Size Number									
	2	3	4	5	6	7	8	9	10	11
2	0.29 4.6	0.66 7.1	1.20 9.4	1.86 11.8	2.64 14.2					
2½	0.24 3.8	0.53 5.7	0.96 7.5	1.49 9.4	2.11 11.3	2.88 13.2	3.79 15.1			
3	0.20 3.1	0.44 4.7	0.80 6.3	1.24 7.8	1.76 9.4	2.40 11.0	3.16 12.6			
3½	0.17 2.7	0.38 4.0	0.69 5.4	1.06 6.7	1.51 8.1	2.06 9.4	2.71 10.8	3.42 12.2		
4	0.15 2.4	0.33 3.5	0.60 4.7	0.93 5.9	1.32 7.1	1.80 8.3	2.37 9.4	3.00 10.6	3.81 12.0	4.68 13.3
4½	0.13 2.1	0.29 3.1	0.53 4.2	0.83 5.2	1.17 6.3	1.60 7.3	2.11 8.4	2.67 9.4	3.39 10.7	4.16 11.8
5	0.12 1.9	0.26 2.8	0.48 3.8	0.74 4.7	1.06 5.7	1.44 6.6	1.90 7.5	2.40 8.5	3.05 9.6	3.74 10.6
5½	0.11 1.7	0.24 2.6	0.44 3.4	0.68 4.3	0.96 5.1	1.31 6.0	1.72 6.9	2.18 7.8	2.77 8.7	3.40 9.7
6	0.10 1.6	0.22 2.4	0.40 3.1	0.62 3.9	0.88 4.7	1.20 5.5	1.58 6.3	2.00 7.1	2.54 8.0	3.12 8.8
6½	0.09 1.5	0.20 2.2	0.37 2.9	0.57 3.6	0.81 4.4	1.11 5.1	1.46 5.8	1.85 6.5	2.35 7.4	2.88 8.2
7	0.09 1.4	0.19 2.0	0.34 2.7	0.53 3.4	0.75 4.0	1.03 4.7	1.35 5.4	1.71 6.1	2.18 6.8	2.67 7.6
7½	0.08 1.3	0.18 1.9	0.32 2.5	0.50 3.1	0.70 3.8	0.96 4.4	1.26 5.0	1.60 5.7	2.03 6.4	2.50 7.1
8	0.08 1.2	0.17 1.8	0.30 2.4	0.47 2.9	0.66 3.5	0.90 4.1	1.19 4.7	1.50 5.3	1.91 6.0	2.34 6.6
8½	0.07 1.1	0.16 1.7	0.28 2.2	0.44 2.8	0.62 3.3	0.85 3.9	1.12 4.4	1.41 5.0	1.79 5.6	2.20 6.3
9	0.07 1.1	0.15 1.6	0.27 2.1	0.41 2.6	0.59 3.1	0.80 3.7	1.05 4.2	1.33 4.7	1.69 5.3	2.08 5.9
9½	0.06 1.0	0.14 1.5	0.25 2.0	0.39 2.5	0.56 3.0	0.76 3.5	1.00 4.00	1.26 4.5	1.60 5.0	1.97 5.6
10	0.06 1.0	0.13 1.4	0.24 1.9	0.37 2.4	0.53 2.8	0.72 3.3	0.95 3.8	1.20 4.2	1.52 4.8	1.87 5.3
10½	0.06 0.9	0.13 1.3	0.23 1.8	0.35 2.2	0.50 2.7	0.69 3.1	0.90 3.6	1.14 4.0	1.45 4.6	1.78 5.0
11	0.05 0.9	0.12 1.3	0.22 1.7	0.34 2.2	0.48 2.6	0.65 3.0	0.86 3.4	1.09 3.9	1.39 4.4	1.70 4.8
11½	0.05 0.8	0.11 1.2	0.21 1.6	0.32 2.0	0.46 2.5	0.63 2.9	0.82 3.3	1.04 3.7	1.33 4.2	1.63 4.6
12	0.05 0.8	0.11 1.2	0.20 1.6	0.31 2.0	0.44 2.4	0.60 2.7	0.79 3.1	1.00 3.5	1.27 4.0	1.56 4.4

ALLOWABLE SOIL BEARING PRESSURES

(Note: This list is acceptable in many areas, but local codes should be consulted.)

Material	Allowable Bearing Value (tons/sq ft)
Laminated rocks such as slate and schist, in sound condition (some cracks allowed)	35
Shale in sound condition (some cracks allowed)	10
Hardpan	10
Gravel, sand-gravel mixtures, compact	5
Gravel, sand-gravel mixtures, loose; sand, coarse, compact	4
Sand, coarse, loose; sand, fine, compact	3
Sand, fine, loose	1
Hard clay	6
Medium clay	4
Soft clay	1

APPENDIX

STRENGTH OF MATERIALS

METALS AND ALLOYS

Material	Stress in Kips per Square Inch: Tension Ultimate	Elastic Limit	Compression Ultimate	Bending Ultimate	Shearing Ultimate	Modulus of Elasticity Pounds per Sq. In.	Elongation Per cent
Aluminum, bars, sheets	24-28	12-14					
" wire, annealed	20-35	14					
Brass, 50% Zn	31	17.9	117	33.5			5.0
" cast, common	18-24	6	30	20	36	9,000,000	
" wire, hard	80						
" " annealed	50	16				14,000,000	
Bronze, aluminum 5 to 7½%	75	40	120				
" Tobin, cast } 38% Zn	66						
" " rolled } 1½% Sn	80	40				14,500,000	
" " c. " } ⅓% Pb	100						
Copper, plates, rods, bolts	32-35	10	32				
Iron, cast, gray	18-24			25-33			
" " malleable	27-35	15-20	46	30	40		
" wrought, shapes	48	26	Tensile	Tensile	⅚ Tens.	28,000,000	
Steel, plates for cold pressing	48-58	½ Tens.	Tensile	Tensile	¾ Tens.	29,000,000	*1,500,000 / Tensile Strength
" cars	50-65	½ Tens.	Tensile	Tensile	¾ Tens.	29,000,000	
" locos., stat. boilers	55-65	½ Tens.	Tensile	Tensile	¾ Tens.	29,000,000	
" bridges and bldgs., ships	60-72	33	Tensile	Tensile	¾ Tens.	29,000,000	
" structural silicon	80-95	45	Tensile	Tensile	¾ Tens.	29,000,000	
" struc. nickel (3.25% Ni)	85-100	50	Tensile	Tensile	¾ Tens.	29,000,000	
Steel, rivet, boiler	45-55	½ Tens.	Tensile	Tensile	¾ Tens.	29,000,000	
" " br.,bldg.,loco., cars	52-62	28	Tensile	Tensile	¾ Tens.	29,000,000	
" " ships	55-65	30	Tensile	Tensile	¾ Tens.	29,000,000	
" " high-tensile	70-85	38	Tensile	Tensile	¾ Tens.	29,000,000	
Steel, cast, soft	60	27	Tensile	Tensile	¾ Tens.	29,000,000	†24
" " medium	70	31.5	Tensile	Tensile	¾ Tens.	29,000,000	†20
" " hard	80	36	Tensile	Tensile	¾ Tens.	29,000,000	†17
Steel wire, unannealed	120	60					
" " annealed	80	40					
" " bridge cable	215	95					

* 8″ gage length
† 2″ gage length

BUILDING MATERIALS

Material	Average Ultimate Stress Pounds per Square Inch: Compression	Tension	Bending	Safe Working Stress Pounds per Square Inch: Compression	Bearing	Shearing	Modulus of Elasticity Pounds per Sq. In.
Masonry, granite				420	600		
" limestone, bluestone				350	500		
" sandstone				280	400		
" rubble				140	250		
" brick, common	10000	200	600				
Ropes, cast steel hoisting		80000					
" standing, derrick		70000					
" manila		8000					
Stone, bluestone	12000	1200	2500	1200	1200	200	7,000,000
" granite, gneiss	12000	1200	1600	1200	1200	200	7,000,000
" limestone, marble	8000	800	1500	800	800	150	7,000,000
" sandstone	5000	150	1200	500	500	150	3,000,000
" slate	10000	3000	5000	1000	1000	175	14,000,000

TRIGONOMETRIC FORMULAS

TRIGONOMETRIC FUNCTIONS

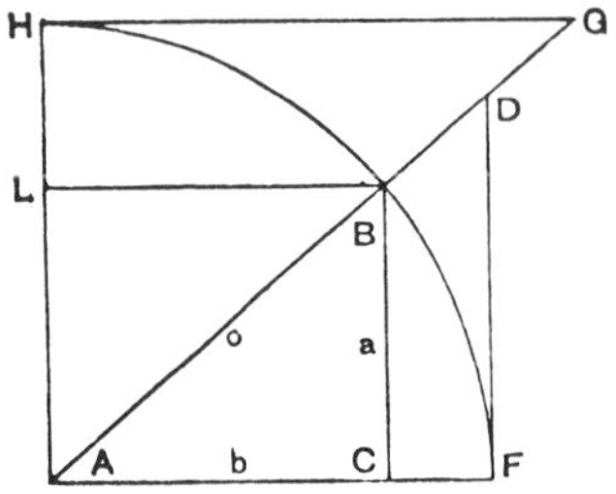

Radius AF $= 1$
$= \sin^2 A + \cos^2 A = \sin A \operatorname{cosec} A$
$= \cos A \sec A = \tan A \cot A$

Sine A $= \dfrac{\cos A}{\cot A} = \dfrac{1}{\operatorname{cosec} A} = \cos A \tan A = \sqrt{1-\cos^2 A} = BC$

Cosine A $= \dfrac{\sin A}{\tan A} = \dfrac{1}{\sec A} = \sin A \cot A = \sqrt{1-\sin^2 A} = AC$

Tangent A $= \dfrac{\sin A}{\cos A} = \dfrac{1}{\cot A} = \sin A \sec A = FD$

Cotangent A $= \dfrac{\cos A}{\sin A} = \dfrac{1}{\tan A} = \cos A \operatorname{cosec} A = HG$

Secant A $= \dfrac{\tan A}{\sin A} = \dfrac{1}{\cos A} = AD$

Cosecant A $= \dfrac{\cot A}{\cos A} = \dfrac{1}{\sin A} = AG$

RIGHT ANGLED TRIANGLES

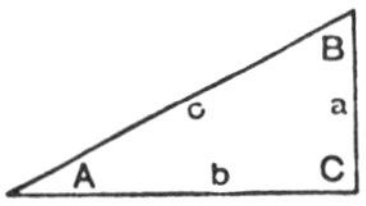

$a^2 = c^2 - b^2$

$b^2 = c^2 - a^2$

$c^2 = a^2 + b^2$

Known	Required					
	A	B	a	b	c	Area
a, b	$\tan A = \frac{a}{b}$	$\tan B = \frac{b}{a}$			$\sqrt{a^2 + b^2}$	$\frac{ab}{2}$
a, c	$\sin A = \frac{a}{c}$	$\cos B = \frac{a}{c}$		$\sqrt{c^2 - a^2}$		$\frac{a\sqrt{c^2 - a^2}}{2}$
A, a		$90° - A$		$a \cot A$	$\frac{a}{\sin A}$	$\frac{a^2 \cot A}{2}$
A, b		$90° - A$	$b \tan A$		$\frac{b}{\cos A}$	$\frac{b^2 \tan A}{2}$
A, c		$90° - A$	$c \sin A$	$c \cos A$		$\frac{c^2 \sin 2A}{4}$

OBLIQUE ANGLED TRIANGLES

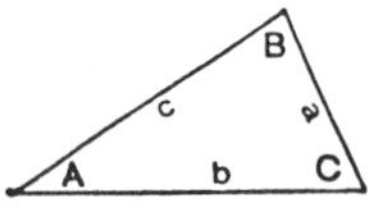

$s = \dfrac{a+b+c}{2}$

$K = \sqrt{\dfrac{(s-a)(s-b)(s-c)}{s}}$

$a^2 = b^2 + c^2 - 2\,bc \cos A$

$b^2 = a^2 + c^2 - 2\,ac \cos B$

$c^2 = a^2 + b^2 - 2\,ab \cos C$

Known	Required					
	A	B	C	b	c	Area
a, b, c	$\tan \frac{1}{2} A = \frac{K}{s-a}$	$\tan \frac{1}{2} B = \frac{K}{s-b}$	$\tan \frac{1}{2} C = \frac{K}{s-c}$			$\sqrt{s(s-a)(s-b)(s-c)}$
a, A, B			$180° - (A+B)$	$\frac{a \sin B}{\sin A}$	$\frac{a \sin C}{\sin A}$	
a, b, A		$\sin B = \frac{b \sin A}{a}$			$\frac{b \sin C}{\sin B}$	
a, b, C	$\tan A = \frac{a \sin C}{b - a \cos C}$				$\sqrt{a^2+b^2-2ab \cos C}$	$\frac{ab \sin C}{2}$

MECHANICS OF MATERIALS

FREQUENTLY USED FORMULAS

The formulas given below are frequently required in structural designing. They are included herein for the convenience of those engineers who have infrequent use for such formulas and hence may find reference necessary.

BEAMS

Flexural stress at extreme fiber:

$$f = Mc/I = M/S$$

Flexural stress at any fiber:

$f = My/I$ y = distance from neutral axis to fiber.

Average vertical shear (for maximum see below):

$v = V/A = V/dt$ (for beams and girders)

Horizontal shearing stress at any section A-A:

$v = VQ/I\,b$ Q = statical moment about the neutral axis of the entire section of that portion of the cross-section lying outside of section A-A,

b = width at section A-A

(Intensity of vertical shear is equal to that of horizontal shear acting normal to it at the same point and both are usually a maximum at mid-height of beam.)

Slope and deflection at any point:

$EI \dfrac{d^2y}{dx^2} = M$ x and y are abscissa and ordinate respectively of a point on the neutral axis, referred to axes of rectangular coordinates through a selected point of support.

(First integration gives slopes; second integration gives deflections. Constants of integration must be determined.)

CONTINUOUS BEAMS (THE THEOREM OF THREE MOMENTS)

Uniform load:

$$M_a \frac{l_1}{I_1} + 2M_b\left(\frac{l_1}{I_1} + \frac{l_2}{I_2}\right) + M_c \frac{l_2}{I_2} = -\frac{1}{4}\left(\frac{w_1 l_1^3}{I_1} + \frac{w_2 l_2^3}{I_2}\right)$$

Concentrated loads:

$$M_a \frac{l_1}{I_1} + 2M_b\left(\frac{l_1}{I_1} + \frac{l_2}{I_2}\right) + M_c \frac{l_2}{I_2} = -\frac{P_1 a_1 b_1}{I_1}\left(1 + \frac{a_1}{l_1}\right) - \frac{P_2 a_2 b_2}{I_2}\left(1 + \frac{b_2}{l_2}\right)$$

Considering any two consecutive spans in any continuous structure:

M_a, M_b, M_c = moments at left, center, and right supports respectively, of any pair of adjacent spans.

l_1 and l_2 = length of left and right spans respectively, of the pair.

I_1 and I_2 = moment of inertia of left and right spans respectively.

w_1 and w_2 = load per unit of length on left and right spans respectively.

P_1 and P_2 = concentrated loads on left and right spans respectively.

a_1 and a_2 = distance of concentrated loads from left support in left and right spans respectively.

b_1 and b_2 = distance of concentrated loads from right support in left and right spans respectively.

The above equations are for beams with moment of inertia constant in each span but differing in different spans, continuous over three or more supports. By writing such an equation for each successive pair of spans and introducing the known values (usually zero) of end moments, all other moments can be found.

COLUMNS

Concentrically loaded:

$$f = P/A$$

Eccentrically loaded:

$f = P/A + Mc/I.$ Bending in plane of principal axis. Deflection not considered.

$= \dfrac{P}{A}(1 + ec/r^2)$ e = eccentricity of load.

PROPERTIES OF GEOMETRIC SECTIONS

SQUARE

Axis of moments through center

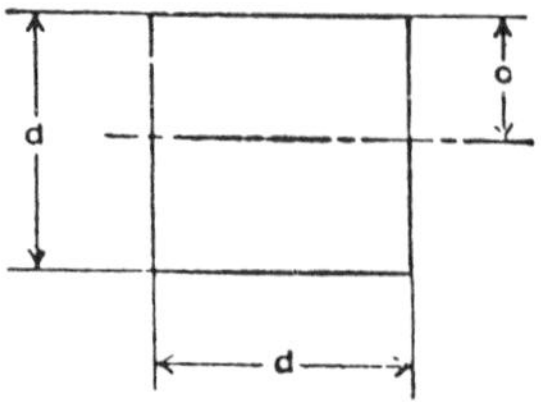

$$A = d^2$$

$$c = \frac{d}{2}$$

$$I = \frac{d^4}{12}$$

$$S = \frac{d^3}{6}$$

$$r = \frac{d}{\sqrt{12}} = .288675\ d$$

SQUARE

Axis of moments on base

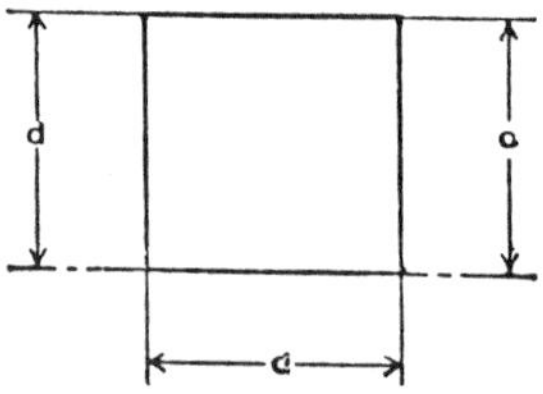

$$A = d^2$$

$$c = d$$

$$I = \frac{d^4}{3}$$

$$S = \frac{d^3}{3}$$

$$r = \frac{d}{\sqrt{3}} = .577350\ d$$

SQUARE

Axis of moments on diagonal

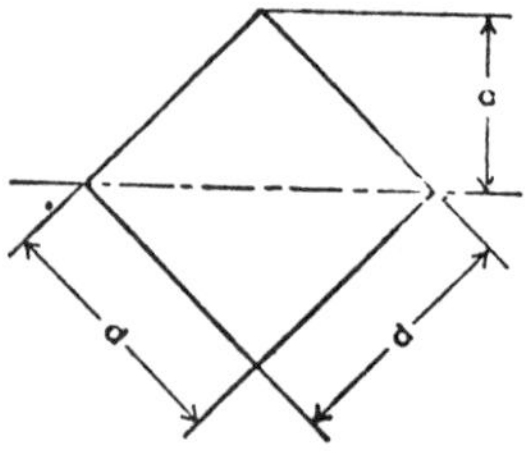

$$A = d^2$$

$$c = \frac{d}{\sqrt{2}} = .707107\ d$$

$$I = \frac{d^4}{12}$$

$$S = \frac{d^3}{6\sqrt{2}} = .117851\ d^3$$

$$r = \frac{d}{\sqrt{12}} = .288675\ d$$

RECTANGLE

Axis of moments through center

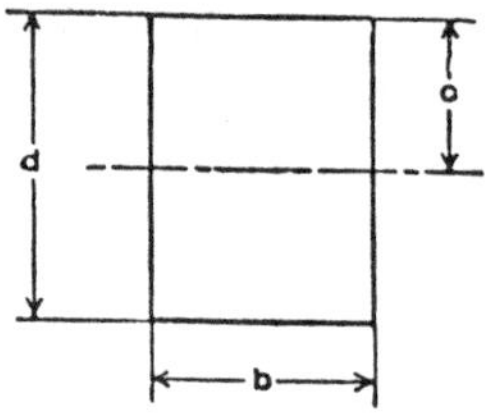

$$A = bd$$

$$c = \frac{d}{2}$$

$$I = \frac{bd^3}{12}$$

$$S = \frac{bd^2}{6}$$

$$r = \frac{d}{\sqrt{12}} = .288675\ d$$

PROPERTIES OF GEOMETRIC SECTIONS

RECTANGLE

Axis of moments on base

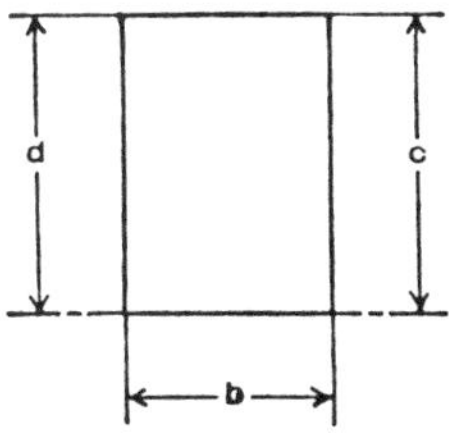

$$A = bd$$
$$c = d$$
$$I = \frac{bd^3}{3}$$
$$S = \frac{bd^2}{3}$$
$$r = \frac{d}{\sqrt{3}} = .577350\ d$$

RECTANGLE

Axis of moments on diagonal

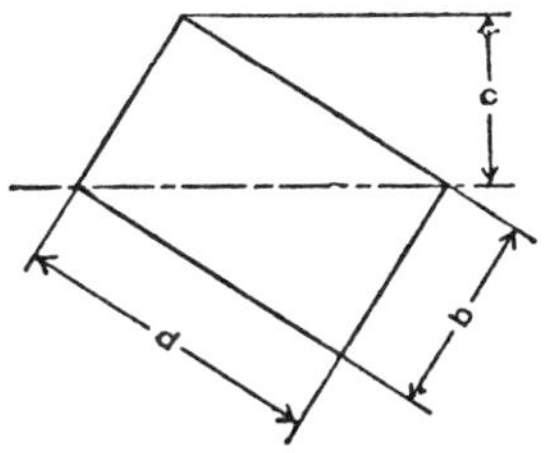

$$A = bd$$
$$c = \frac{bd}{\sqrt{b^2 + d^2}}$$
$$I = \frac{b^3d^3}{6\ (b^2 + d^2)}$$
$$S = \frac{b^2d^2}{6\sqrt{b^2 + d^2}}$$
$$r = \frac{bd}{\sqrt{6\ (b^2 + d^2)}}$$

RECTANGLE

Axis of moments any line through center of gravity

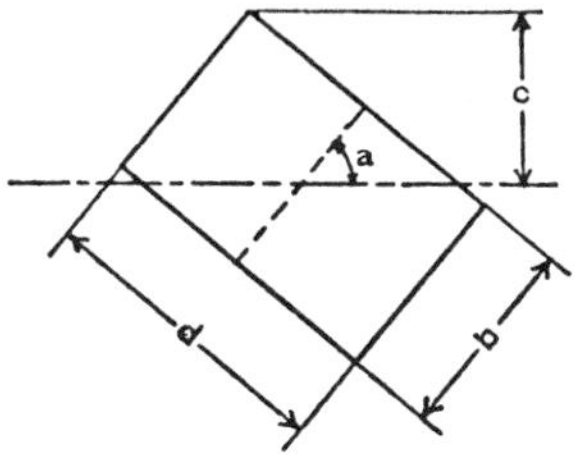

$$A = bd$$
$$c = \frac{b \sin a + d \cos a}{2}$$
$$I = \frac{bd\ (b^2 \sin^2 a + d^2 \cos^2 a)}{12}$$
$$S = \frac{bd\ (b^2 \sin^2 a + d^2 \cos^2 a)}{6\ (b \sin a + d \cos a)}$$
$$r = \sqrt{\frac{b^2 \sin^2 a + d^2 \cos^2 a}{12}}$$

HOLLOW RECTANGLE

Axis of moments through center

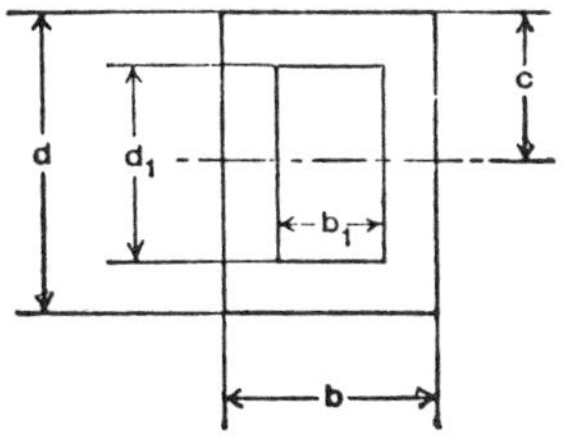

$$A = bd - b_1d_1$$
$$c = \frac{d}{2}$$
$$I = \frac{bd^3 - b_1d_1^3}{12}$$
$$S = \frac{bd^3 - b_1d_1^3}{6d}$$
$$r = \sqrt{\frac{bd^3 - b_1d_1^3}{12\ A}}$$

PROPERTIES OF GEOMETRIC SECTIONS

EQUAL RECTANGLES

Axis of moments through center of gravity

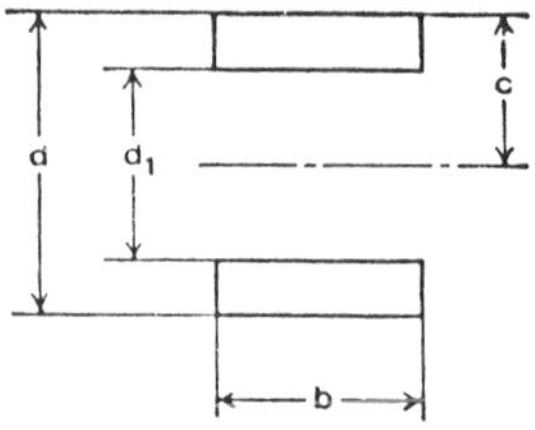

$$A = b(d - d_1)$$

$$c = \frac{d}{2}$$

$$I = \frac{b(d^3 - d_1^3)}{12}$$

$$S = \frac{b(d^3 - d_1^3)}{6d}$$

$$r = \sqrt{\frac{d^3 - d_1^3}{12(d - d_1)}}$$

UNEQUAL RECTANGLES

Axis of moments through center of gravity

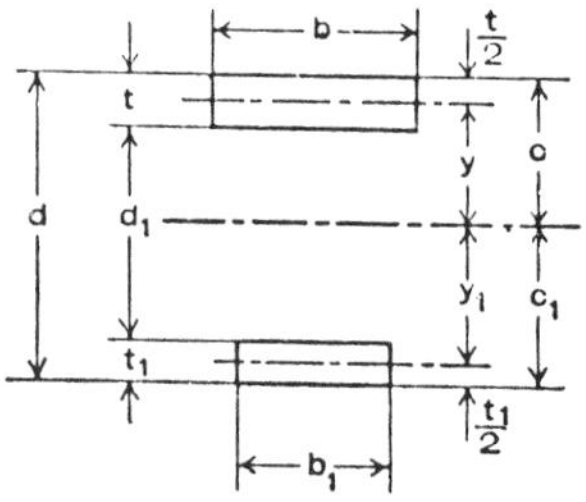

$$A = bt + b_1t_1$$

$$c = \frac{\frac{1}{2}bt^2 + b_1t_1(d - \frac{1}{2}t_1)}{A}$$

$$I = \frac{bt^3}{12} + bty^2 + \frac{b_1t_1^3}{12} + b_1t_1y_1^2$$

$$S = \frac{I}{c} \qquad S_1 = \frac{I}{c_1}$$

$$r = \sqrt{\frac{I}{A}}$$

TRIANGLE

Axis of moments through center of gravity

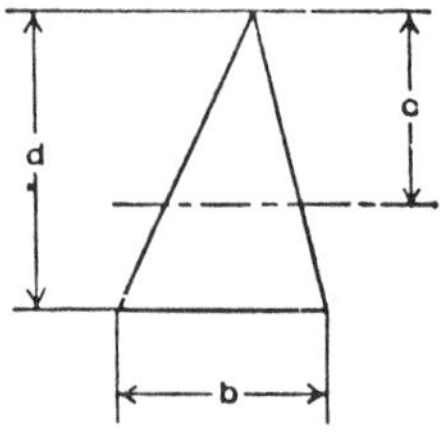

$$A = \frac{bd}{2}$$

$$c = \frac{2d}{3}$$

$$I = \frac{bd^3}{36}$$

$$S = \frac{bd^2}{24}$$

$$r = \frac{d}{\sqrt{18}} = .235702\ d$$

TRIANGLE

Axis of moments on base

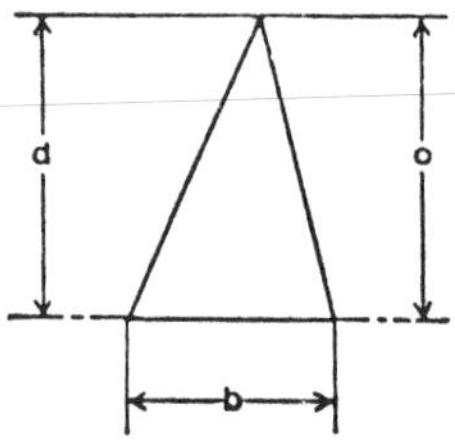

$$A = \frac{bd}{2}$$

$$c = d$$

$$I = \frac{bd^3}{12}$$

$$S = \frac{bd^2}{12}$$

$$r = \frac{d}{\sqrt{6}} = .408248\ d$$

PROPERTIES OF GEOMETRIC SECTIONS

TRAPEZOID

Axis of moments through center of gravity

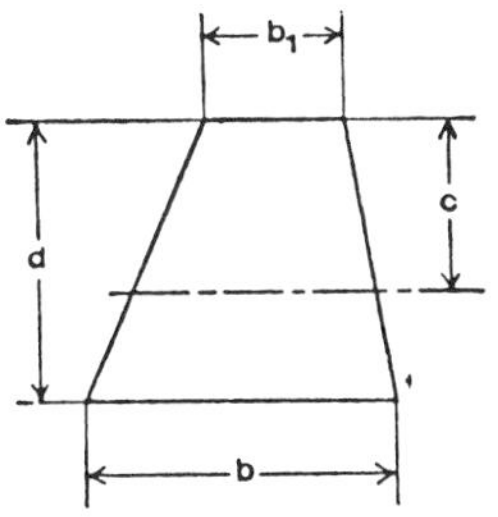

$$A = \frac{d(b + b_1)}{2}$$

$$c = \frac{d(2b + b_1)}{3(b + b_1)}$$

$$I = \frac{d^3 (b^2 + 4\,bb_1 + b_1^2)}{36\,(b + b_1)}$$

$$S = \frac{d^2 (b^2 + 4\,bb_1 + b_1^2)}{12\,(2b + b_1)}$$

$$r = \frac{d}{6(b + b_1)} \sqrt{2\,(b^2 + 4\,bb_1 + b_1^2)}$$

CIRCLE

Axis of moments through center

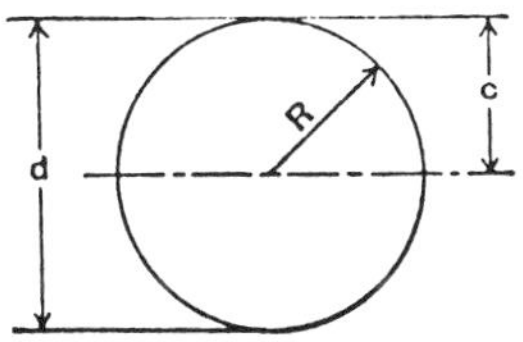

$$A = \frac{\pi d^2}{4} = \pi R^2 = .785398\,d^2 = 3.141593\,R^2$$

$$c = \frac{d}{2} = R$$

$$I = \frac{\pi d^4}{64} = \frac{\pi R^4}{4} = .049087\,d^4 = .785398\,R^4$$

$$S = \frac{\pi d^3}{32} = \frac{\pi R^3}{4} = .098175\,d^3 = .785398\,R^3$$

$$r = \frac{d}{4} = \frac{R}{2}$$

HOLLOW CIRCLE

Axis of moments through center

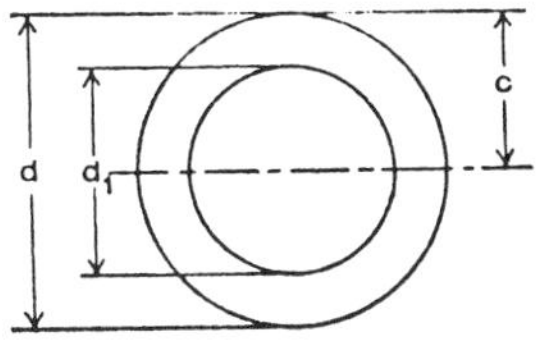

$$A = \frac{\pi(d^2 - d_1^2)}{4} = .785398\,(d^2 - d_1^2)$$

$$c = \frac{d}{2}$$

$$I = \frac{\pi(d^4 - d_1^4)}{64} = .049087\,(d^4 - d_1^4)$$

$$S = \frac{\pi(d^4 - d_1^4)}{32d} = .098175\,\frac{d^4 - d_1^4}{d}$$

$$r = \frac{\sqrt{d^2 + d_1^2}}{4}$$

HALF CIRCLE

Axis of moments through center of gravity

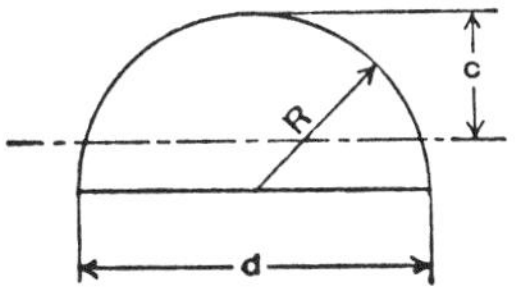

$$A = \frac{\pi R^2}{2} = 1.570796\,R^2$$

$$c = R\left(1 - \frac{4}{3\pi}\right) = .575587\,R$$

$$I = R^4\left(\frac{\pi}{8} - \frac{8}{9\pi}\right) = .109757\,R^4$$

$$S = \frac{R^3}{24}\,\frac{(9\pi^2 - 64)}{(3\pi - 4)} = .190687\,R^3$$

$$r = R\,\frac{\sqrt{9\pi^2 - 64}}{6\pi} = .264336\,R$$

PROPERTIES OF GEOMETRIC SECTIONS

PARABOLA

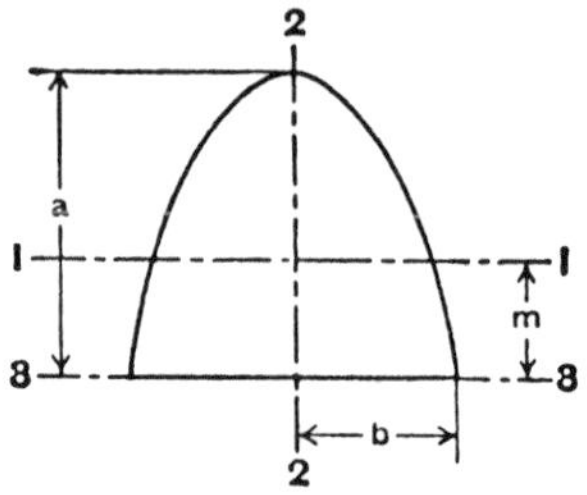

$$A = \frac{4}{3} ab$$

$$m = \frac{2}{5} a$$

$$I_1 = \frac{16}{175} a^3b$$

$$I_2 = \frac{4}{15} ab^3$$

$$I_3 = \frac{32}{105} a^3b$$

HALF PARABOLA

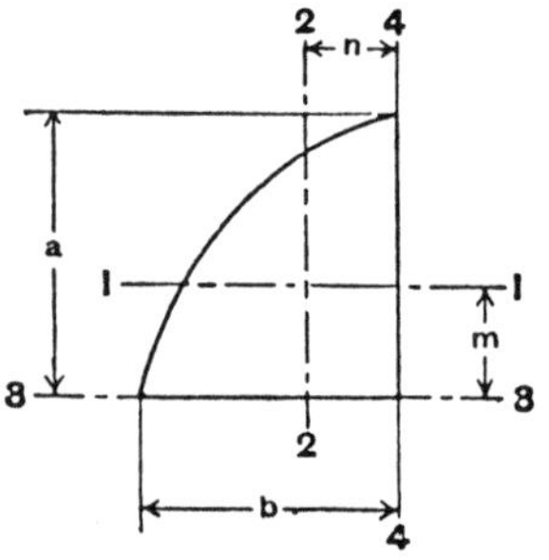

$$A = \frac{2}{3} ab$$

$$m = \frac{2}{5} a$$

$$n = \frac{3}{8} b$$

$$I_1 = \frac{8}{175} a^3b$$

$$I_2 = \frac{19}{480} ab^3$$

$$I_3 = \frac{16}{105} a^3b$$

$$I_4 = \frac{2}{15} ab^3$$

COMPLEMENT OF HALF PARABOLA

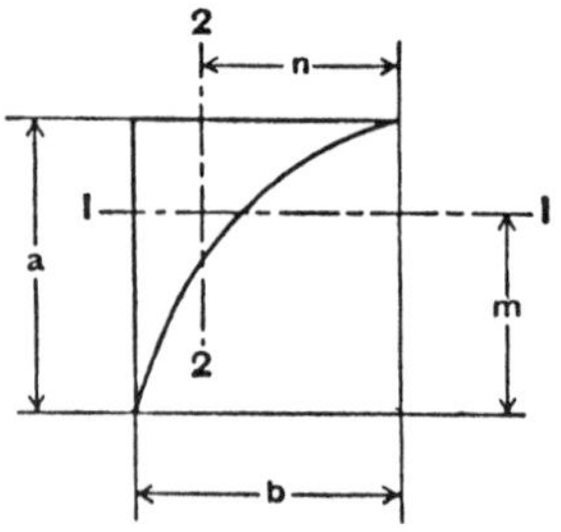

$$A = \frac{1}{3} ab$$

$$m = \frac{7}{10} a$$

$$n = \frac{3}{4} b$$

$$I_1 = \frac{37}{2100} a^3b$$

$$I_2 = \frac{1}{80} ab^3$$

PARABOLIC FILLET IN RIGHT ANGLE

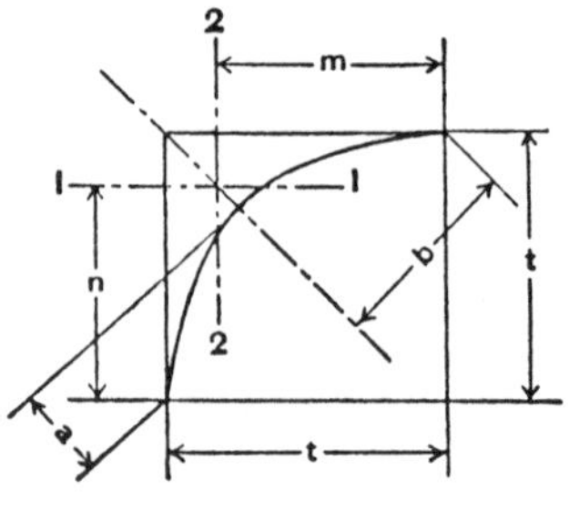

$$a = \frac{t}{2\sqrt{2}}$$

$$b = \frac{t}{\sqrt{2}}$$

$$A = \frac{1}{6} t^2$$

$$m = n = \frac{4}{5} t$$

$$I_1 = I_2 = \frac{11}{2100} t^4$$

PROPERTIES OF GEOMETRIC SECTIONS

* HALF ELLIPSE

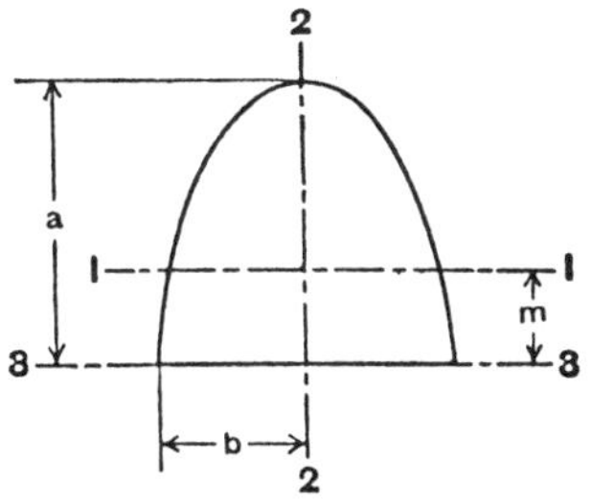

$$A = \frac{1}{2}\pi ab$$

$$m = \frac{4a}{3\pi}$$

$$I_1 = a^3b\left(\frac{\pi}{8} - \frac{8}{9\pi}\right)$$

$$I_2 = \frac{1}{8}\pi ab^3$$

$$I_3 = \frac{1}{8}\pi a^3b$$

* QUARTER ELLIPSE

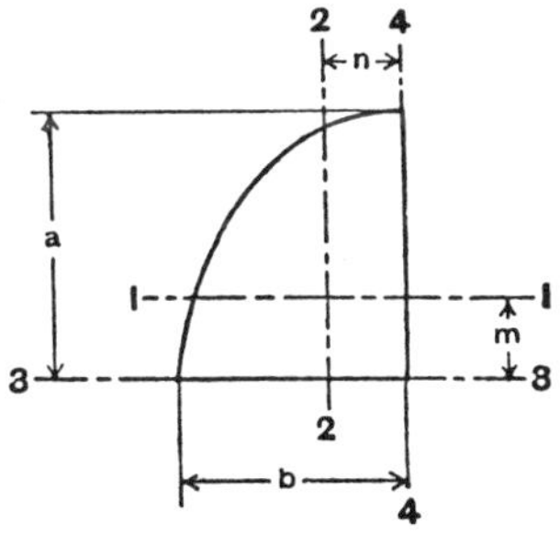

$$A = \frac{1}{4}\pi ab$$

$$m = \frac{4a}{3\pi}$$

$$n = \frac{4b}{3\pi}$$

$$I_1 = a^3b\left(\frac{\pi}{16} - \frac{4}{9\pi}\right)$$

$$I_2 = ab^3\left(\frac{\pi}{16} - \frac{4}{9\pi}\right)$$

$$I_3 = \frac{1}{16}\pi a^3b$$

$$I_4 = \frac{1}{16}\pi ab^3$$

* ELLIPTIC COMPLEMENT

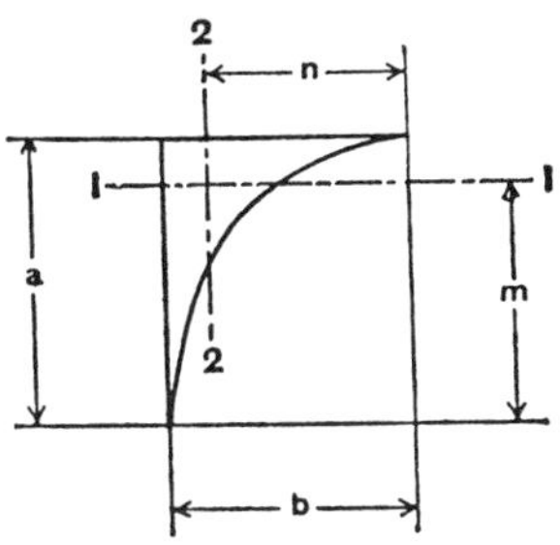

$$A = ab\left(1 - \frac{\pi}{4}\right)$$

$$m = \frac{a}{6\left(1 - \frac{\pi}{4}\right)}$$

$$n = \frac{b}{6\left(1 - \frac{\pi}{4}\right)}$$

$$I_1 = a^3b\left(\frac{1}{3} - \frac{\pi}{16} - \frac{1}{36\left(1 - \frac{\pi}{4}\right)}\right)$$

$$I_2 = ab^3\left(\frac{1}{3} - \frac{\pi}{16} - \frac{1}{36\left(1 - \frac{\pi}{4}\right)}\right)$$

*** To obtain properties of half circle, quarter circle and circular complement substitute a = b = R.**

PROPERTIES OF GEOMETRIC SECTIONS AND STRUCTURAL SHAPES

REGULAR POLYGON

Axis of moments through center

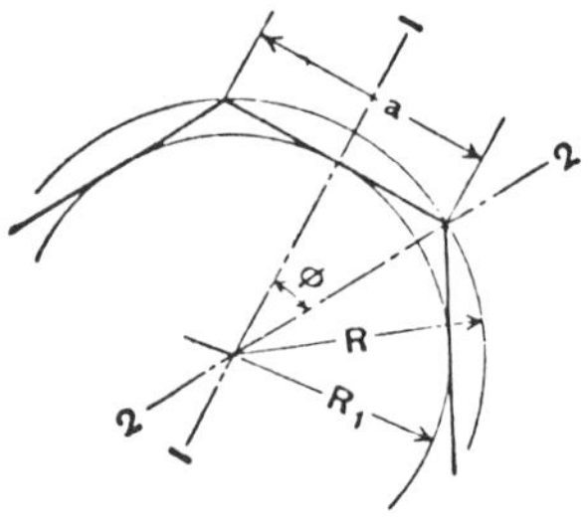

$$n = \text{Number of sides}$$

$$\phi = \frac{180^\circ}{n}$$

$$a = 2\sqrt{R^2 - R_1^2}$$

$$R = \frac{a}{2 \sin \phi}$$

$$R_1 = \frac{a}{2 \tan \phi}$$

$$A = \frac{1}{4} na^2 \cot \phi = \frac{1}{2} nR^2 \sin 2\phi = nR_1^2 \tan \phi$$

$$I_1 = I_2 = \frac{A(6R^2 - a^2)}{24} = \frac{A(12R_1^2 + a^2)}{48}$$

$$r_1 = r_2 = \sqrt{\frac{6R^2 - a^2}{24}} = \sqrt{\frac{12R_1^2 + a^2}{48}}$$

ANGLE

Axis of moments through center of gravity

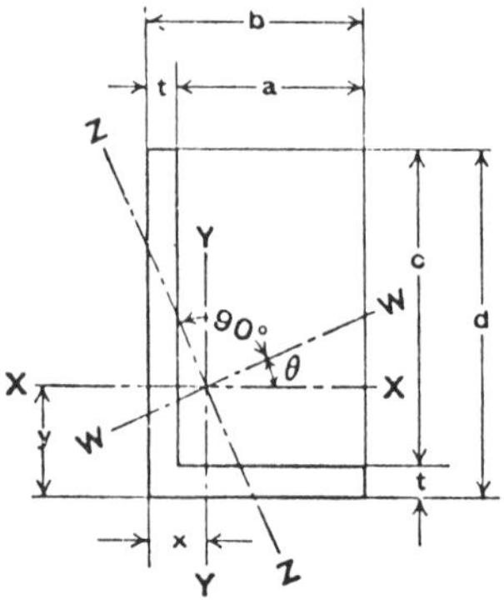

Z-Z is axis of minimum I

$$\tan 2\theta = \frac{2K}{I_Y - I_X}$$

$$A = t(b + c) \quad x = \frac{b^2 + ct}{2(b + c)} \quad y = \frac{d^2 + at}{2(b + c)}$$

$$K = \text{Product of Inertia about X-X \& Y-Y}$$

$$= \mp \frac{abcdt}{4(b + c)}$$

$$I_X = \frac{1}{3}\left(t(d - y)^3 + by^3 - a(y - t)^3 \right)$$

$$I_Y = \frac{1}{3}\left(t(b - x)^3 + dx^3 - c(x - t)^3 \right)$$

$$I_Z = I_X \sin^2\theta + I_Y \cos^2\theta + K \sin 2\theta$$

$$I_W = I_X \cos^2\theta + I_Y \sin^2\theta - K \sin 2\theta$$

K is negative when heel of angle, with respect to c. g., is in 1st or 3rd quadrant, positive when in 2nd or 4th quadrant.

BEAMS AND CHANNELS

Transverse force oblique through center of gravity

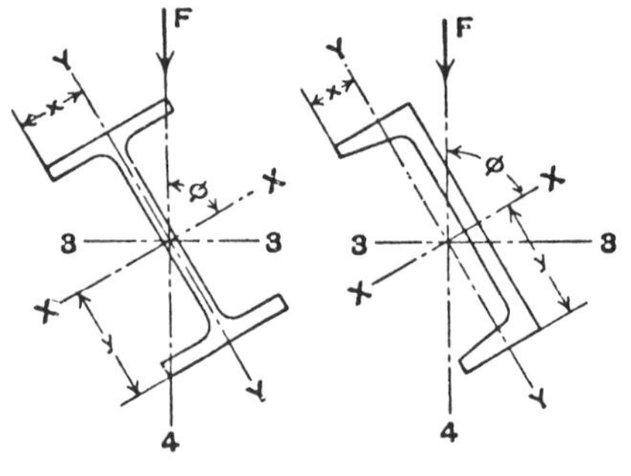

$$I_3 = I_X \sin^2\phi + I_Y \cos^2\phi$$

$$I_4 = I_X \cos^2\phi + I_Y \sin^2\phi$$

$$f = M\left(\frac{y}{I_X} \sin\phi + \frac{x}{I_Y} \cos\phi \right)$$

where M is bending moment due to force F.

BEAM DIAGRAMS AND FORMULAS
FOR VARIOUS STATIC LOADING CONDITIONS

1. SIMPLE BEAM—UNIFORMLY DISTRIBUTED LOAD

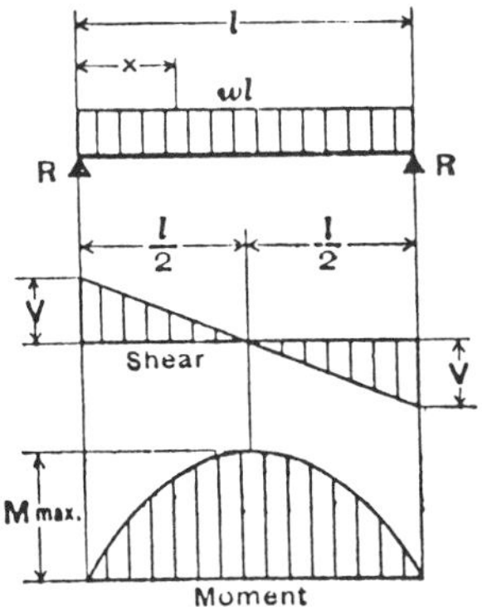

Equivalent Tabular Load . . . $= wl$

$R = V$ . . . . $= \frac{wl}{2}$

V_x . . . . $= w\left(\frac{l}{2} - x\right)$

M max. (at center) . . . . $= \frac{wl^2}{8}$

M_x . . . . $= \frac{wx}{2}(l - x)$

Δmax. (at center) . . . . $= \frac{5\,wl^4}{384\,EI}$

Δx . . . . $= \frac{wx}{24EI}(l^3 - 2lx^2 + x^3)$

2. SIMPLE BEAM—LOAD INCREASING UNIFORMLY TO ONE END

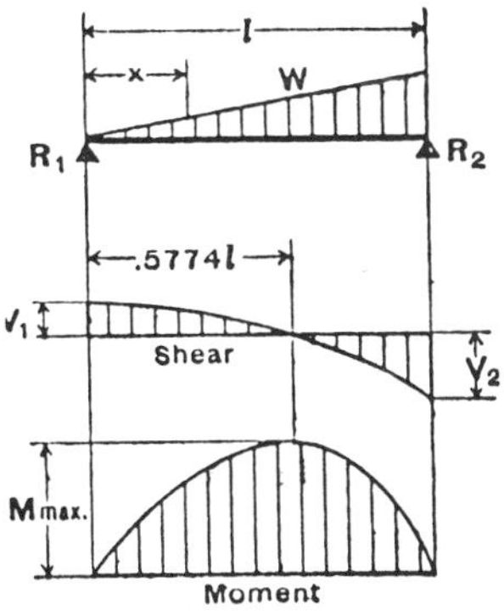

Equivalent Tabular Load . . . $= \frac{16W}{9\sqrt{3}} = 1.0264W$

$R_1 = V_1$ . . . . $= \frac{W}{3}$

$R_2 = V_2$ max. . . . . $= \frac{2W}{3}$

V_x . . . . $= \frac{W}{3} - \frac{Wx^2}{l^2}$

M max. $\left(\text{at } x = \frac{l}{\sqrt{3}} = .5774l\right)$ . . $= \frac{2Wl}{9\sqrt{3}} = .1283\ Wl$

M_x . . . . $= \frac{Wx}{3l^2}(l^2 - x^2)$

Δmax. $\left(\text{at } x = l\sqrt{1 - \sqrt{\frac{8}{15}}} = .5193l\right) = .01304\,\frac{Wl^3}{EI}$

Δx . . . . $= \frac{Wx}{180EI\,l^2}(3x^4 - 10l^2x^2 + 7l^4)$

3. SIMPLE BEAM—LOAD INCREASING UNIFORMLY TO CENTER

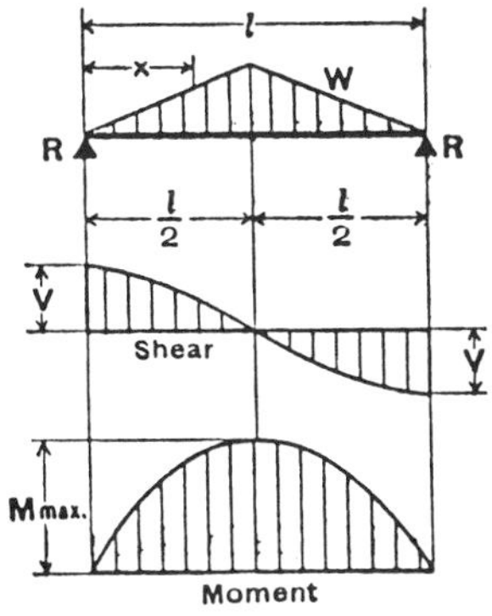

Equivalent Tabular Load . . . $= \frac{4W}{3}$

$R = V$ . . . . $= \frac{W}{2}$

V_x $\left(\text{when } x < \frac{l}{2}\right)$ . . . . $= \frac{W}{2l^2}(l^2 - 4x^2)$

M max. (at center) . . . . $= \frac{Wl}{6}$

M_x $\left(\text{when } x < \frac{l}{2}\right)$ . . . . $= Wx\left(\frac{1}{2} - \frac{2x^2}{3l^2}\right)$

Δmax. (at center) . . . . $= \frac{Wl^3}{60EI}$

Δx . . . . $= \frac{Wx}{480\,EI\,l^2}(5l^2 - 4x^2)^2$

BEAM DIAGRAMS AND FORMULAS
FOR VARIOUS STATIC LOADING CONDITIONS

4. SIMPLE BEAM—UNIFORM LOAD PARTIALLY DISTRIBUTED

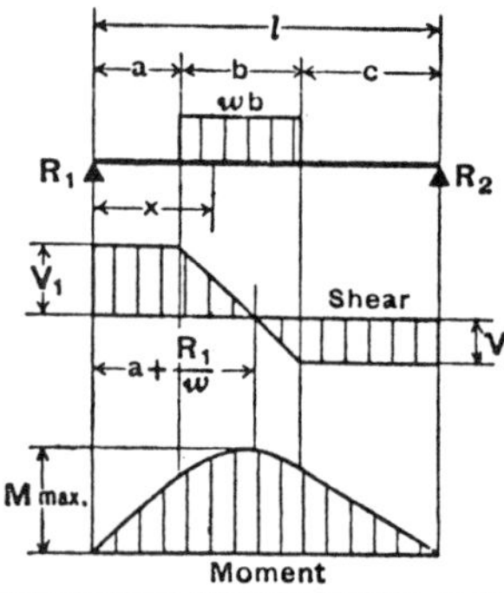

$R_1 = V_1$ (max. when $a < c$) . . $= \frac{wb}{2l}(2c + b)$

$R_2 = V_2$ (max. when $a > c$) . . $= \frac{wb}{2l}(2a + b)$

V_x (when $x > a$ and $< (a + b)$) . $= R_1 - w(x - a)$

M max. (at $x = a + \frac{R_1}{w}$) . . . . $= R_1\left(a + \frac{R_1}{2w}\right)$

M_x (when $x < a$) . . . . . $= R_1 x$

M_x (when $x > a$ and $< (a + b)$) . $= R_1 x - \frac{w}{2}(x - a)^2$

M_x (when $x > (a + b)$) . . . . $= R_2(l - x)$

5. SIMPLE BEAM—UNIFORM LOAD PARTIALLY DISTRIBUTED AT ONE END

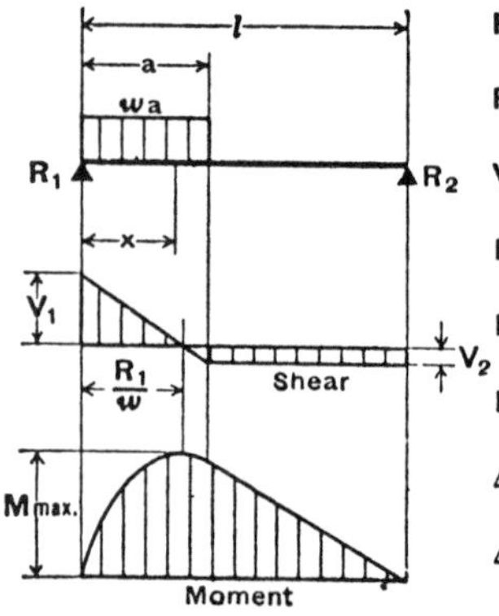

$R_1 = V_1$ max. . . . . $= \frac{wa}{2l}(2l - a)$

$R_2 = V_2$ . . . . $= \frac{wa^2}{2l}$

V (when $x < a$) . . . . . $= R_1 - wx$

M max. (at $x = \frac{R_1}{w}$) . . . . . $= \frac{R_1^2}{2w}$

M_x (when $x < a$) . . . . . $= R_1 x - \frac{wx^2}{2}$

M_x (when $x > a$) . . . . . $= R_2(l - x)$

Δx (when $x < a$) . . . . . $= \frac{wx}{24EIl}\left(a^2(2l-a)^2 - 2ax^2(2l-a) + lx^3\right)$

Δx (when $x > a$) . . . . . $= \frac{wa^2(l - x)}{24EIl}(4xl - 2x^2 - a^2)$

6. SIMPLE BEAM—UNIFORM LOAD PARTIALLY DISTRIBUTED AT EACH END

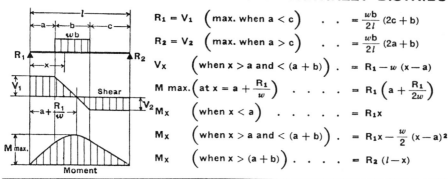

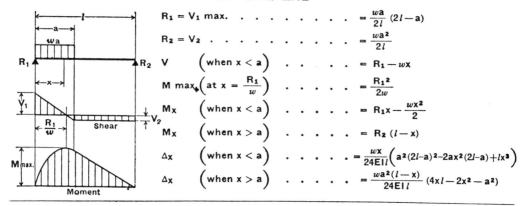

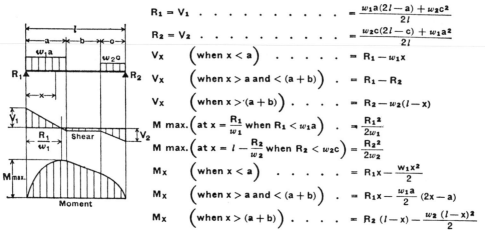

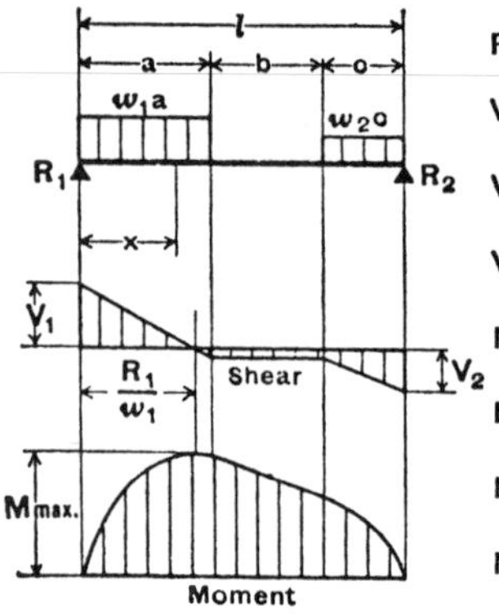

$R_1 = V_1$ . . . . $= \frac{w_1 a(2l - a) + w_2 c^2}{2l}$

$R_2 = V_2$ . . . . $= \frac{w_2 c(2l - c) + w_1 a^2}{2l}$

V_x (when $x < a$) . . . . . $= R_1 - w_1 x$

V_x (when $x > a$ and $< (a + b)$) . $= R_1 - R_2$

V_x (when $x > (a + b)$) . . . . $= R_2 - w_2(l - x)$

M max. (at $x = \frac{R_1}{w_1}$ when $R_1 < w_1 a$) . $= \frac{R_1^2}{2w_1}$

M max. (at $x = l - \frac{R_2}{w_2}$ when $R_2 < w_2 c$) $= \frac{R_2^2}{2w_2}$

M_x (when $x < a$) . . . . . $= R_1 x - \frac{w_1 x^2}{2}$

M_x (when $x > a$ and $< (a + b)$) . $= R_1 x - \frac{w_1 a}{2}(2x - a)$

M_x (when $x > (a + b)$) . . . . $= R_2(l - x) - \frac{w_2(l - x)^2}{2}$

BEAM DIAGRAMS AND FORMULAS
FOR VARIOUS STATIC LOADING CONDITIONS

7. SIMPLE BEAM—CONCENTRATED LOAD AT CENTER

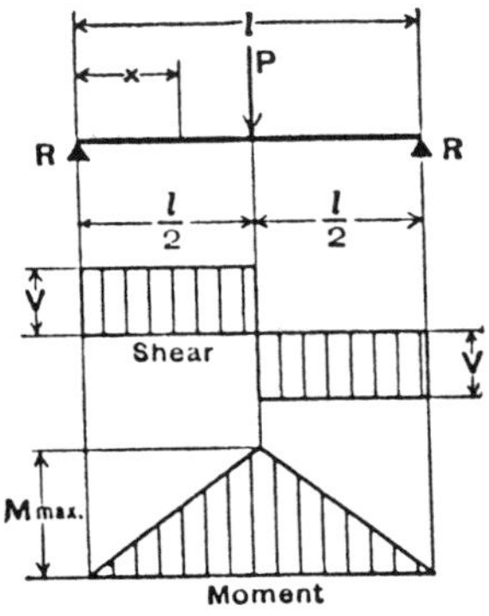

Equivalent Tabular Load . . . . . . $= 2P$

$R = V$ . . . . $= \frac{P}{2}$

$M\ max.$ (at point of load) . . . . . $= \frac{Pl}{4}$

M_x (when $x < \frac{l}{2}$) . . . . . . $= \frac{Px}{2}$

$\Delta max.$ (at point of load) . . . . . . $= \frac{Pl^3}{48EI}$

Δx (when $x < \frac{l}{2}$) . . . . . . $= \frac{Px}{48EI}(3l^2 - 4x^2)$

8. SIMPLE BEAM—CONCENTRATED LOAD AT ANY POINT

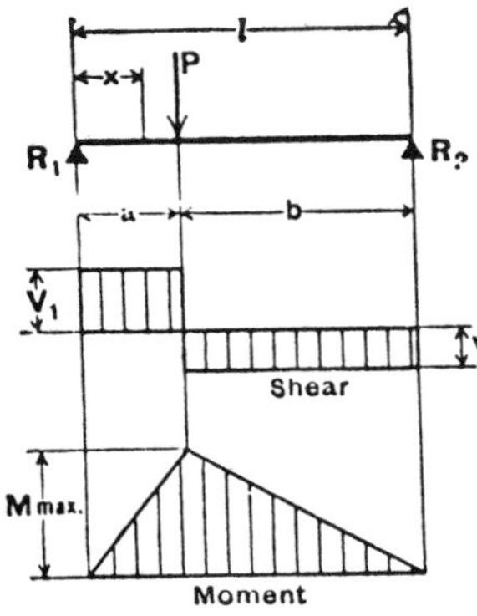

Equivalent Tabular Load . . . . . . $= \frac{8\ Pab}{l^2}$

$R_1 = V_1$ (max. when $a < b$) . . . . . $= \frac{Pb}{l}$

$R_2 = V_2$ (max. when $a > b$) . . . . . $= \frac{Pa}{l}$

$M\ max.$ (at point of load) . . . . . $= \frac{Pab}{l}$

M_x (when $x < a$) . . . . . $= \frac{Pbx}{l}$

$\Delta max.$ (at $x = \sqrt{\frac{a(a+2b)}{3}}$ when $a > b$) $= \frac{Pab\,(a+2b)\sqrt{3a\,(a+2b)}}{27\ EI\ l}$

Δa (at point of load) . . . . $= \frac{Pa^2b^2}{3EI\ l}$

Δx (when $x < a$) . . . . $= \frac{Pbx}{6EI\ l}(l^2 - b^2 - x^2)$

9. SIMPLE BEAM—TWO EQUAL CONCENTRATED LOADS SYMMETRICALLY PLACED

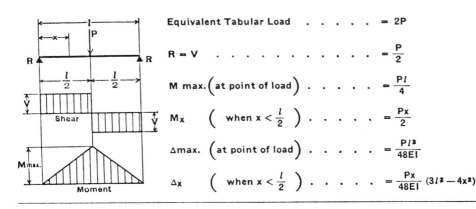

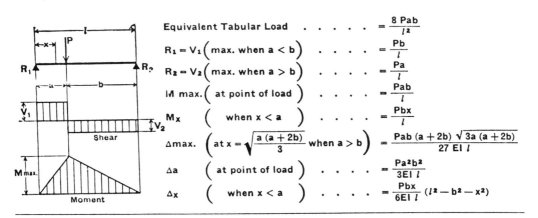

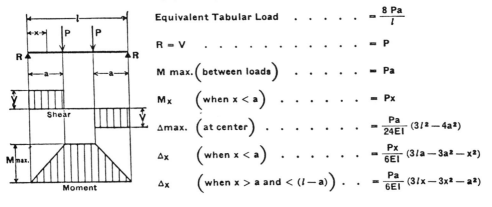

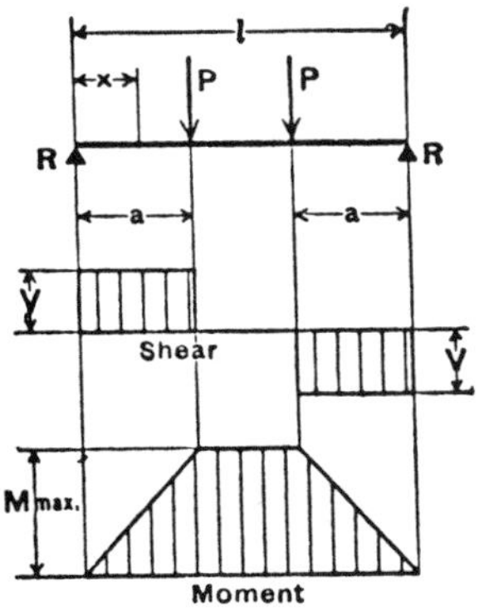

Equivalent Tabular Load . . . . . . $= \frac{8\ Pa}{l}$

$R = V$ . . . . $= P$

$M\ max.$ (between loads) . . . . . $= Pa$

M_x (when $x < a$) . . . . $= Px$

$\Delta max.$ (at center) . . . . $= \frac{Pa}{24EI}(3l^2 - 4a^2)$

Δx (when $x < a$) . . . . $= \frac{Px}{6EI}(3la - 3a^2 - x^2)$

Δx (when $x > a$ and $< (l - a)$) . . $= \frac{Pa}{6EI}(3lx - 3x^2 - a^2)$

BEAM DIAGRAMS AND FORMULAS
FOR VARIOUS STATIC LOADING CONDITIONS

10. SIMPLE BEAM—TWO EQUAL CONCENTRATED LOADS UNSYMMETRICALLY PLACED

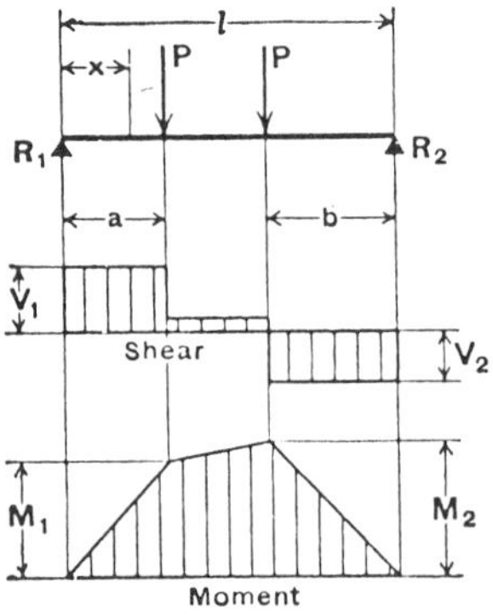

$R_1 = V_1 \left(\text{max. when } a < b\right)$ . . . . $= \frac{P}{l}(l - a + b)$

$R_2 = V_2 \left(\text{max. when } a > b\right)$ . . . . $= \frac{P}{l}(l - b + a)$

V_x $\left(\text{when } x > a \text{ and } < (l - b)\right)$ . . $= \frac{P}{l}(b - a)$

M_1 $\left(\text{max. when } a > b\right)$ . . . . $= R_1 a$

M_2 $\left(\text{max. when } a < b\right)$ . . . . $= R_2 b$

M_x $\left(\text{when } x < a\right)$ . . . . $= R_1 x$

M_x $\left(\text{when } x > a \text{ and } < (l - b)\right)$ . . $= R_1 x - P(x - a)$

11. SIMPLE BEAM—TWO UNEQUAL CONCENTRATED LOADS UNSYMMETRICALLY PLACED

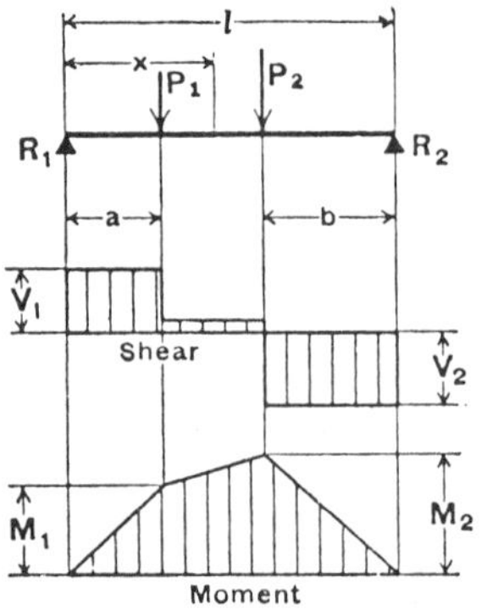

$R_1 = V_1$ . . . . $= \frac{P_1(l - a) + P_2 b}{l}$

$R_2 = V_2$ . . . . $= \frac{P_1 a + P_2(l - b)}{l}$

V_x $\left(\text{when } x > a \text{ and } < (l - b)\right)$ . . $= R_1 - P_1$

M_1 $\left(\text{max. when } R_1 < P_1\right)$ . . . $= R_1 a$

M_2 $\left(\text{max. when } R_2 < P_2\right)$ . . . $= R_2 b$

M_x $\left(\text{when } x < a\right)$ . . . . $= R_1 x$

M_x $\left(\text{when } x > a \text{ and } < (l - b)\right)$ . . $= R_1 x - P_1(x - a)$

12. BEAM FIXED AT ONE END, SUPPORTED AT OTHER—UNIFORMLY DISTRIBUTED LOAD

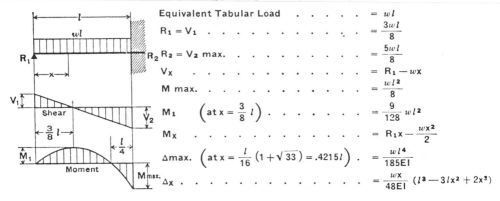

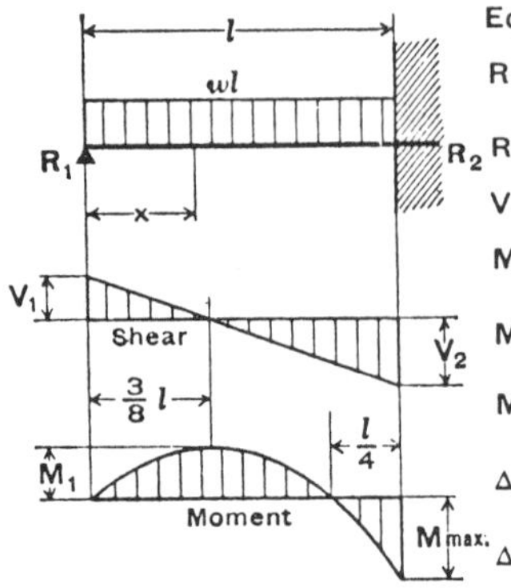

Equivalent Tabular Load . . . . . $= wl$

$R_1 = V_1$ . . . . $= \frac{3wl}{8}$

$R_2 = V_2$ max. . . . . $= \frac{5wl}{8}$

V_x . . . . $= R_1 - wx$

M max. . . . . $= \frac{wl^2}{8}$

M_1 $\left(\text{at } x = \frac{3}{8}l\right)$ . . . . $= \frac{9}{128}wl^2$

M_x . . . . $= R_1 x - \frac{wx^2}{2}$

Δmax. $\left(\text{at } x = \frac{l}{16}(1 + \sqrt{33}) = .4215l\right)$. $= \frac{wl^4}{185EI}$

Δx . . . . $= \frac{wx}{48EI}(l^3 - 3lx^2 + 2x^3)$

BEAM DIAGRAMS AND FORMULAS
FOR VARIOUS STATIC LOADING CONDITIONS

13. BEAM FIXED AT ONE END, SUPPORTED AT OTHER— CONCENTRATED LOAD AT CENTER

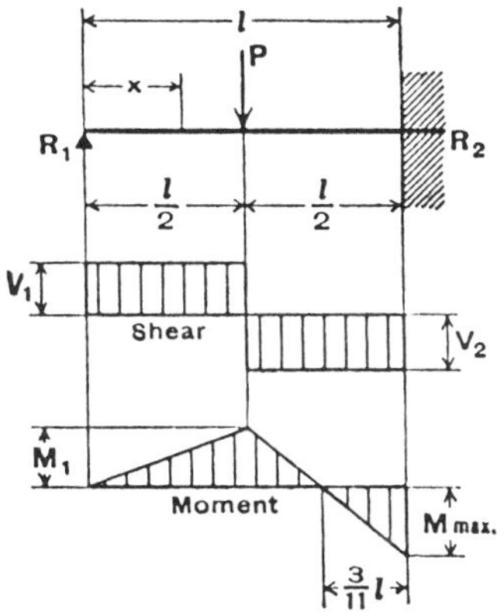

Equivalent Tabular Load . . . . . $= \frac{3P}{2}$

$R_1 = V_1$ . . . . $= \frac{5P}{16}$

$R_2 = V_2$ max. . . . . $= \frac{11P}{16}$

M max. (at fixed end) . . . . . . $= \frac{3Pl}{16}$

M_1 (at point of load) . . . . . $= \frac{5Pl}{32}$

M_x $\left(\text{when } x < \frac{l}{2}\right)$ . . . . . . $= \frac{5Px}{16}$

M_x $\left(\text{when } x > \frac{l}{2}\right)$ . . . . . . $= P\left(\frac{l}{2} - \frac{11x}{.16}\right)$

Δmax. $\left(\text{at } x = l\sqrt{\frac{1}{5}} = .44721l\right)$ . . . $= \frac{Pl^3}{48EI\sqrt{5}} = .009317\,\frac{Pl^3}{EI}$

Δx (at point of load) . . . . . $= \frac{7Pl3}{768EI}$

Δx $\left(\text{when } x < \frac{l}{2}\right)$ . . . . . . $= \frac{Px}{96EI}(3l^2 - 5x^2)$

Δx $\left(\text{when } x > \frac{l}{2}\right)$ . . . . . . $= \frac{P}{96EI}(x - l)^2(11x - 2l)$

14. BEAM FIXED AT ONE END, SUPPORTED AT OTHER— CONCENTRATED LOAD AT ANY POINT

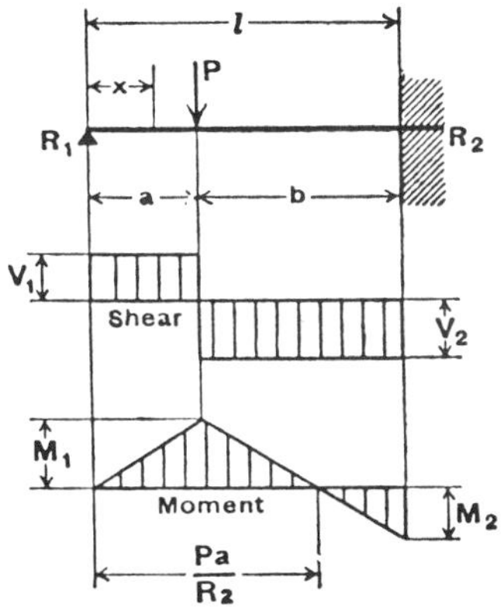

$R_1 = V_1$ . . . . $= \frac{Pb^2}{2l^3}(a + 2l)$

$R_2 = V_2$ . . . . $= \frac{Pa}{2l^3}(3l^2 - a^2)$

M_1 (at point of load) . . . . . $= R_1 a$

M_2 (at fixed end) . . . . . . $= \frac{Pab}{2l^2}(a + l)$

M_x (when $x < a$) . . . . . . $= R_1 x$

M_x (when $x > a$) . . . . . . $= R_1 x - P(x - a)$

Δmax. $\left(\text{when } a < .414l \text{ at } x = l\,\frac{l^2 + a^2}{3l^2 - a^2}\right) = \frac{Pa}{3EI}\,\frac{(l^2 - a^2)^3}{(3l^2 - a^2)^2}$

Δmax. $\left(\text{when } a > .414l \text{ at } x = l\sqrt{\frac{a}{2l + a}}\right) = \frac{Pab^2}{6EI}\sqrt{\frac{a}{2l + a}}$

Δa (at point of load) . . . . . $= \frac{Pa^2b^3}{12EIl^3}(3l + a)$

Δx (when $x < a$) . . . . . . $= \frac{Pb^2x}{12EIl^3}(3al^2 - 2lx^2 - ax^2)$

Δx (when $x > a$) . . . . . . $= \frac{Pa}{12EIl^3}(l - x)^2(3l^2x - a^2x - 2a^2l)$

BEAM DIAGRAMS AND FORMULAS
FOR VARIOUS STATIC LOADING CONDITIONS

15. BEAM FIXED AT BOTH ENDS—UNIFORMLY DISTRIBUTED LOADS

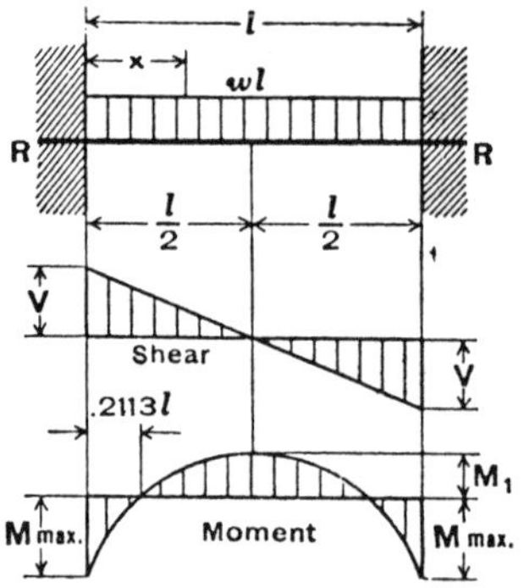

Equivalent Tabular Load	$= \frac{2wl}{3}$
R = V	$= \frac{wl}{2}$
V_x	$= w\left(\frac{l}{2} - x\right)$
M max. (at ends)	$= \frac{wl^2}{12}$
M_1 (at center)	$= \frac{wl^2}{24}$
M_x	$= \frac{w}{12}(6lx - l^2 - 6x^2)$
Δmax. (at center)	$= \frac{wl^4}{384EI}$
Δx	$= \frac{wx^2}{24EI}(l - x)^2$

16. BEAM FIXED AT BOTH ENDS—CONCENTRATED LOAD AT CENTER

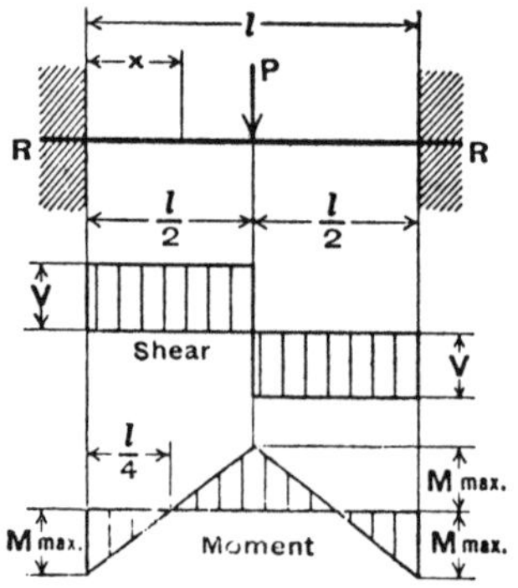

Equivalent Tabular Load	= P
R = V	$= \frac{P}{2}$
M max. (at center and ends) . . .	$= \frac{Pl}{8}$
M_x $\left(\text{when } x < \frac{l}{2}\right)$	$= \frac{P}{8}(4x - l)$
Δmax. (at center)	$= \frac{Pl^3}{192EI}$
Δx	$= \frac{Px^2}{48EI}(3l - 4x)$

17. BEAM FIXED AT BOTH ENDS—CONCENTRATED LOAD AT ANY POINT

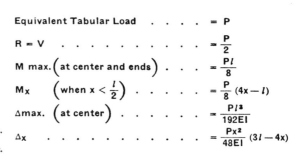

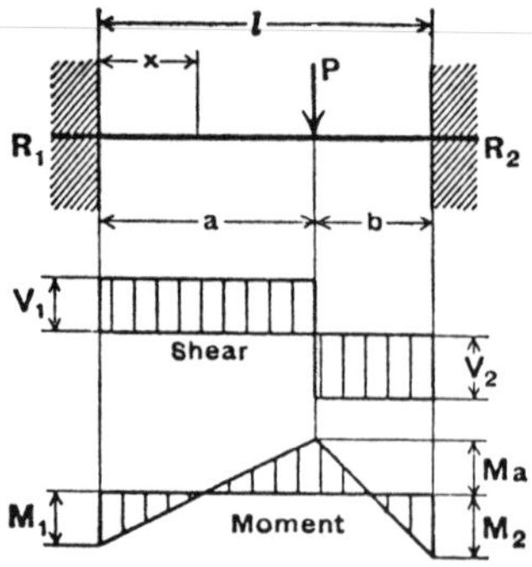

$R_1 = V_1$ (max. when a < b) . . .	$= \frac{Pb^2}{l^3}(3a + b)$
$R_2 = V_2$ (max. when a > b) . . .	$= \frac{Pa^2}{l^3}(a + 3b)$
M_1 (max. when a < b) . . .	$= \frac{Pab^2}{l^2}$
M_2 (max. when a > b) . . .	$= \frac{Pa^2b}{l^2}$
M_a (at point of load) . . .	$= \frac{2Pa^2b^2}{l^3}$
M_x (when x < a)	$= R_1x - \frac{Pab^2}{l^2}$
Δmax. $\left(\text{when } a > b \text{ at } x = \frac{2al}{3a + b}\right)$.	$= \frac{2Pa^3b^2}{3EI\,(3a + b)^2}$
Δa (at point of load) . . .	$= \frac{Pa^3b^3}{3EIl^3}$
Δx (when x < a)	$= \frac{Pb^2x^2}{6EIl^3}(3al - 3ax - bx)$

BEAM DIAGRAMS AND FORMULAS
FOR VARIOUS STATIC LOADING CONDITIONS

18. CANTILEVER BEAM—LOAD INCREASING UNIFORMLY TO FIXED END

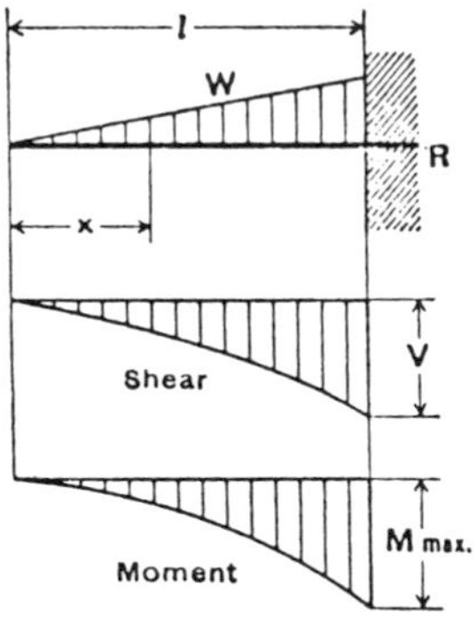

Equivalent Tabular Load . . . . $= \frac{8}{3} W$

R = V . . . . $= W$

V_x . . . . $= W \frac{x^2}{l^2}$

M max. (at fixed end) . . . . . . $= \frac{Wl}{3}$

M_x . . . . $= \frac{Wx^3}{3l^2}$

Δmax. (at free end) . . . . . $= \frac{Wl^3}{15EI}$

Δx . . . . $= \frac{W}{60EIl^2}(x^5 - 5l^4x + 4l^5)$

19. CANTILEVER BEAM—UNIFORMLY DISTRIBUTED LOAD

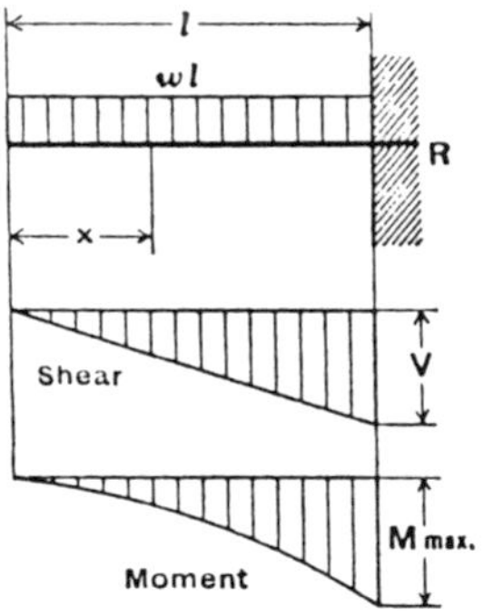

Equivalent Tabular Load . . . . $= 4wl$

R = V . . . . $= wl$

V_x . . . . $= wx$

M max. (at fixed end) . . . . . . $= \frac{wl^2}{2}$

M_x . . . . $= \frac{wx^2}{2}$

Δmax. (at free end) . . . . . . $= \frac{wl^4}{8EI}$

Δx . . . . $= \frac{w}{24EI}(x^4 - 4l^3x + 3l^4)$

20. BEAM FIXED AT ONE END, FREE BUT GUIDED AT OTHER—UNIFORMLY DISTRIBUTED LOAD

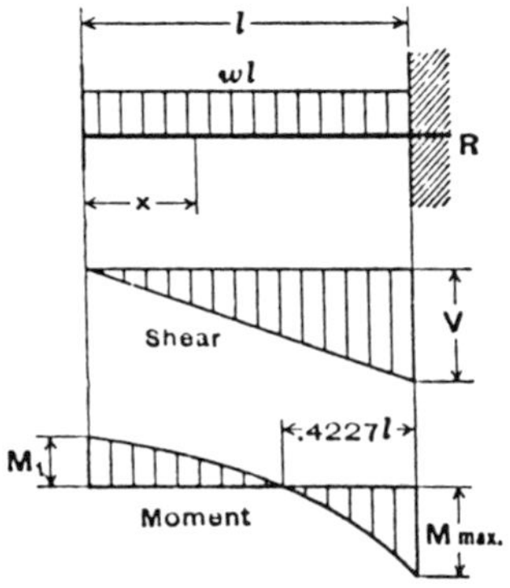

The deflection at the guided end is assumed to be in a vertical plane.

Equivalent Tabular Load . . . . $= \frac{8}{3} wl$

R = V . . . . $= wl$

V_x . . . . $= wx$

M max. (at fixed end) . . . . . . $= \frac{wl^2}{3}$

M_1 (at guided end) . . . . . $= \frac{wl^2}{6}$

M_x . . . . $= \frac{w}{6}(l^2 - 3x^2)$

Δmax. (at guided end) . . . . $= \frac{wl^4}{24EI}$

Δx . . . . $= \frac{w(l^2 - x^2)^2}{24EI}$

BEAM DIAGRAMS AND FORMULAS
FOR VARIOUS STATIC LOADING CONDITIONS

21. CANTILEVER BEAM—CONCENTRATED LOAD AT ANY POINT

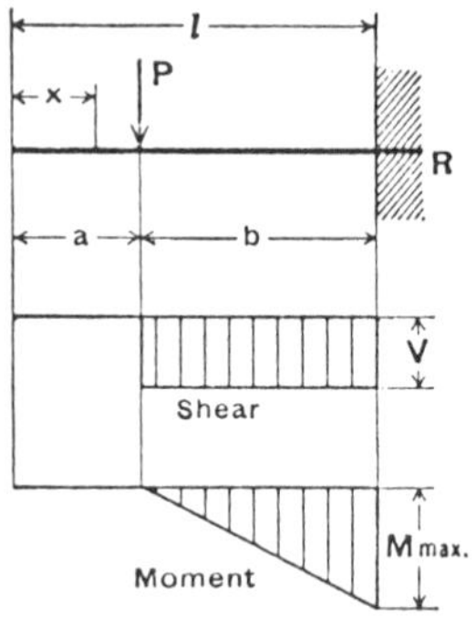

Equivalent Tabular Load	$= \frac{8Pb}{l}$
$R = V \left(\text{when } x < a\right)$	$= P$
M max. (at fixed end)	$= Pb$
$M_x \left(\text{when } x > a\right)$	$= P\,(x - a)$
Δmax. (at free end)	$= \frac{Pb^2}{6EI}(3l - b)$
Δa (at point of load)	$= \frac{Pb^3}{3EI}$
$\Delta x \left(\text{when } x < a\right)$	$= \frac{Pb^2}{6EI}(3l - 3x - b)$
$\Delta x \left(\text{when } x > a\right)$	$= \frac{P\,(l - x)^2}{6EI}(3b - l + x)$

22. CANTILEVER BEAM—CONCENTRATED LOAD AT FREE END

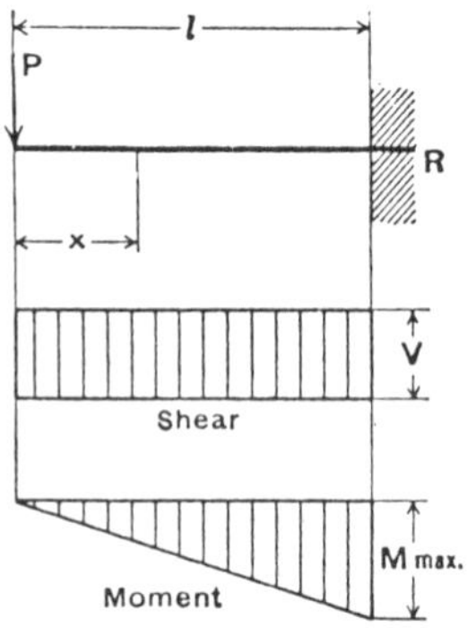

Equivalent Tabular Load	$= 8P$
$R = V$	$= P$
M max. (at fixed end)	$= Pl$
M_x	$= Px$
Δmax. (at free end)	$= \frac{Pl^3}{3EI}$
Δx	$= \frac{P}{6EI}(2l^3 - 3l^2x + x^3)$

23. BEAM FIXED AT ONE END, FREE BUT GUIDED AT OTHER—CONCENTRATED LOAD AT GUIDED END

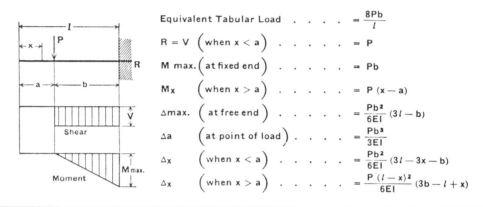

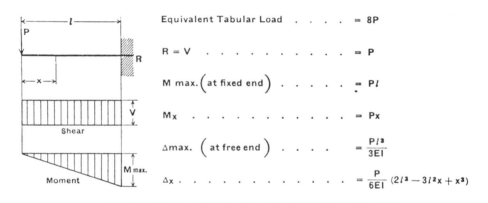

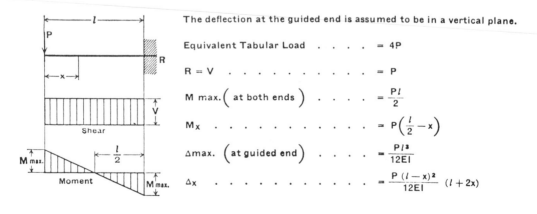

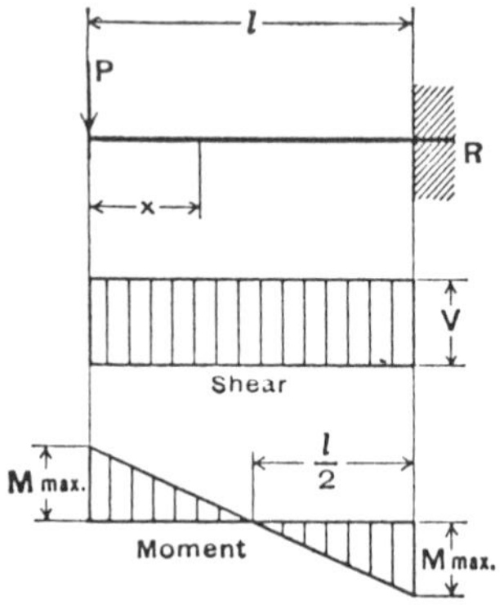

The deflection at the guided end is assumed to be in a vertical plane.

Equivalent Tabular Load	$= 4P$
$R = V$	$= P$
M max. (at both ends)	$= \frac{Pl}{2}$
M_x	$= P\left(\frac{l}{2} - x\right)$
Δmax. (at guided end)	$= \frac{Pl^3}{12EI}$
Δx	$= \frac{P\,(l - x)^2}{12EI}(l + 2x)$

BEAM DIAGRAMS AND FORMULAS
FOR VARIOUS STATIC LOADING CONDITIONS

24. BEAM OVERHANGING ONE SUPPORT—UNIFORMLY DISTRIBUTED LOAD

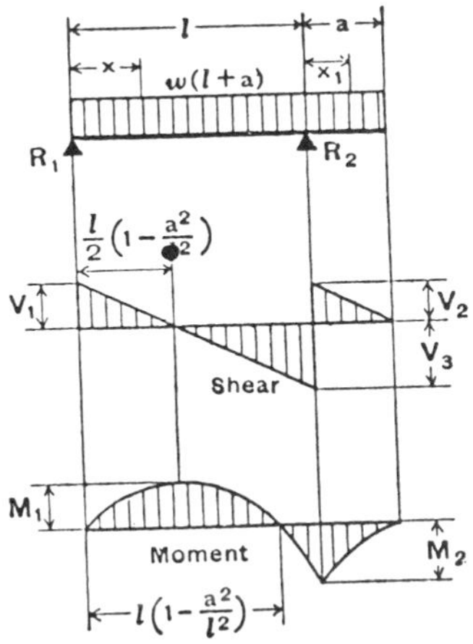

$R_1 = V_1$ . . . . $= \frac{w}{2l}(l^2 - a^2)$

$R_2 = V_2 + V_3$ . . . . $= \frac{w}{2l}(l + a)^2$

V_2 . . . . $= wa$

V_3 . . . . $= \frac{w}{2l}(l^2 + a^2)$

V_x (between supports) . . $= R_1 - wx$

V_{x_1} (for overhang) . . . . $= w(a - x_1)$

M_1 $\left(\text{at } x = \frac{l}{2}\left[1 - \frac{a^2}{l^2}\right]\right)$ . . $= \frac{w}{8l^2}(l + a)^2(l - a)^2$

M_2 (at R_2) . . . . $= \frac{wa^2}{2}$

M_x (between supports) . . $= \frac{wx}{2l}(l^2 - a^2 - xl)$

M_{x_1} (for overhang) . . . . $= \frac{w}{2}(a - x_1)^2$

Δx (between supports) . . $= \frac{wx}{24EIl}(l^4 - 2l^2x^2 + lx^3 - 2a^2l^2 + 2a^2x^2)$

Δx_1 (for overhang) . . . . $= \frac{wx_1}{24EI}(4a^2l - l^3 + 6a^2x_1 - 4ax_1^2 + x_1^3)$

25. BEAM OVERHANGING ONE SUPPORT—UNIFORMLY DISTRIBUTED LOAD ON OVERHANG

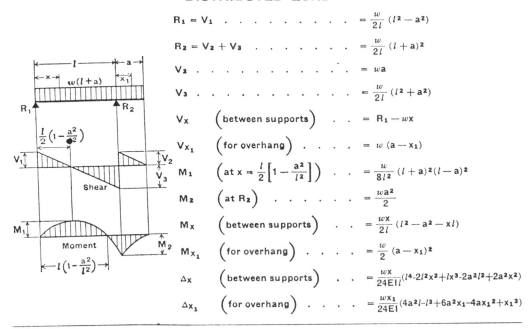

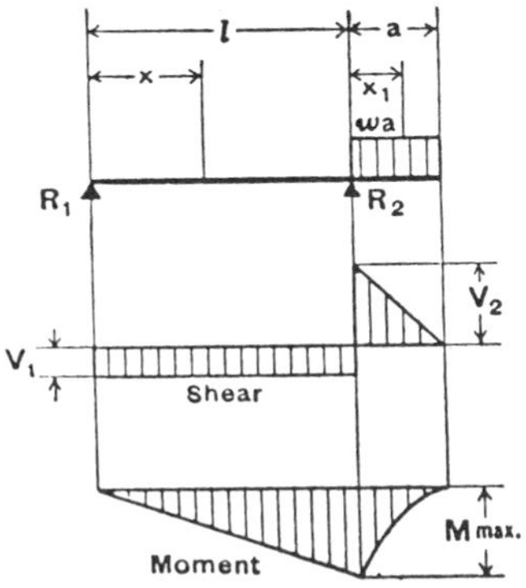

$R_1 = V_1$ . . . . $= \frac{wa^2}{2l}$

$R_2 = V_1 + V_2$ . . . . $= \frac{wa}{2l}(2l + a)$

V_2 . . . . $= wa$

V_{x_1} (for overhang) . . . . $= w(a - x_1)$

M max. (at R_2) . . . . $= \frac{wa^2}{2}$

M_x (between supports) . . $= \frac{wa^2x}{2l}$

M_{x_1} (for overhang) . . . . $= \frac{w}{2}(a - x_1)^2$

Δmax. $\left(\text{between supports at } x = \frac{l}{\sqrt{3}}\right) = \frac{wa^2l^2}{18\sqrt{3}EI} = .03208\,\frac{wa^2l^2}{EI}$

Δmax. (for overhang at $x_1 = a$) . $= \frac{wa^3}{24EI}(4l + 3a)$

Δx (between supports) . . $= \frac{wa^2x}{12EIl}(l^2 - x^2)$

Δx_1 (for overhang) . . . . $= \frac{wx_1}{24EI}(4a^2l + 6a^2x_1 - 4ax_1^2 + x_1^3)$

BEAM DIAGRAMS AND FORMULAS
FOR VARIOUS STATIC LOADING CONDITIONS

26. BEAM OVERHANGING ONE SUPPORT—CONCENTRATED LOAD AT END OF OVERHANG

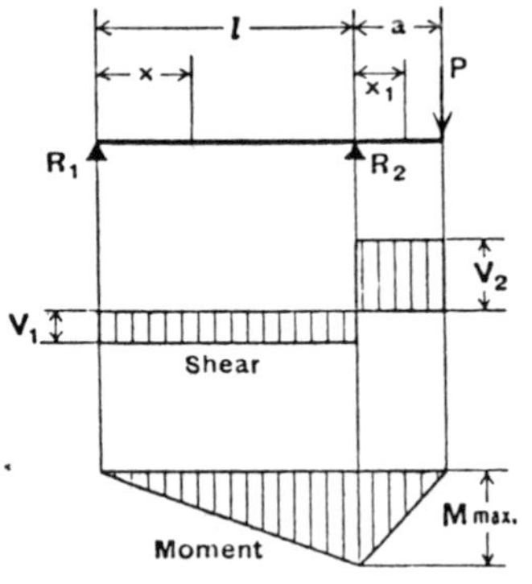

$R_1 = V_1$ . . . . $= \frac{Pa}{l}$

$R_2 = V_1 + V_2$ . . . . $= \frac{P}{l}(l + a)$

V_2 . . . . $= P$

$M\ max. \left(at\ R_2\right)$ . . . . $= Pa$

$M_x \left(\text{between supports}\right)$ . . $= \frac{Pax}{l}$

$M_{x_1} \left(\text{for overhang}\right)$ . . . . $= P(a - x_1)$

$\Delta max. \left(\text{between supports at } x = \frac{l}{\sqrt{3}}\right) = \frac{Pal^2}{9\sqrt{3}EI} = .06415\frac{Pal^2}{EI}$

$\Delta max. \left(\text{for overhang at } x_1 = a\right)$. $= \frac{Pa^2}{3EI}(l + a)$

$\Delta x \left(\text{between supports}\right)$ . . $= \frac{Pax}{6EIl}(l^2 - x^2)$

$\Delta x_1 \left(\text{for overhang}\right)$ . . . . $= \frac{Px_1}{6EI}(2al + 3ax_1 - x_1^2)$

27. BEAM OVERHANGING ONE SUPPORT—UNIFORMLY DISTRIBUTED LOAD BETWEEN SUPPORTS

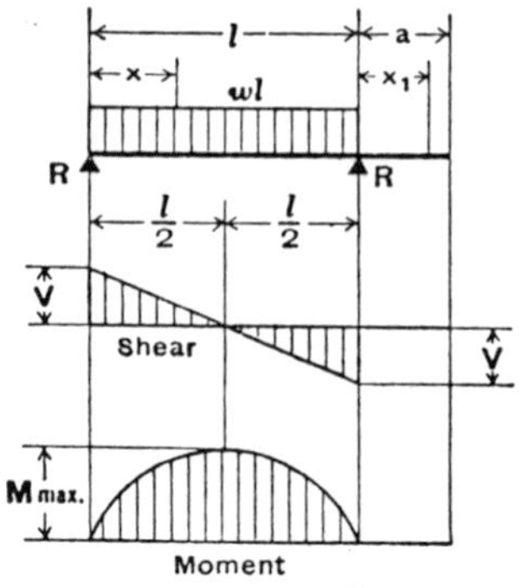

Equivalent Tabular Load . . . $= wl$

$R = V$ . . . . $= \frac{wl}{2}$

V_x . . . . $= w\left(\frac{l}{2} - x\right)$

$M\ max. \left(\text{at center}\right)$ . . . . . . $= \frac{wl^2}{8}$

M_x . . . . $= \frac{wx}{2}(l - x)$

$\Delta max. \left(\text{at center}\right)$ . . . . . . $= \frac{5wl^4}{384EI}$

Δx . . . . $= \frac{wx}{24EI}(l^3 - 2lx^2 + x^3)$

Δx_1 . . . . $= \frac{wl^3x_1}{24EI}$

28. BEAM OVERHANGING ONE SUPPORT—CONCENTRATED LOAD AT ANY POINT BETWEEN SUPPORTS

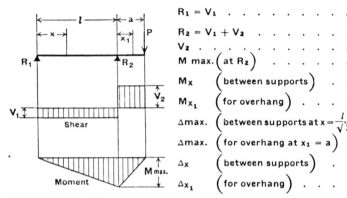

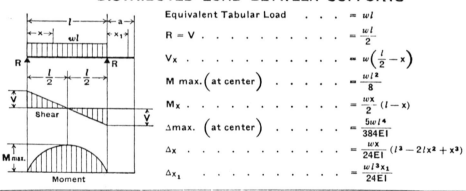

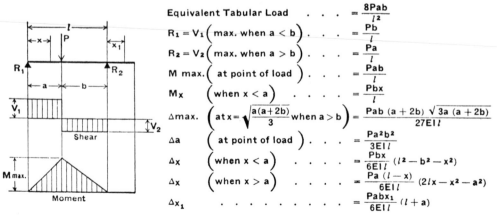

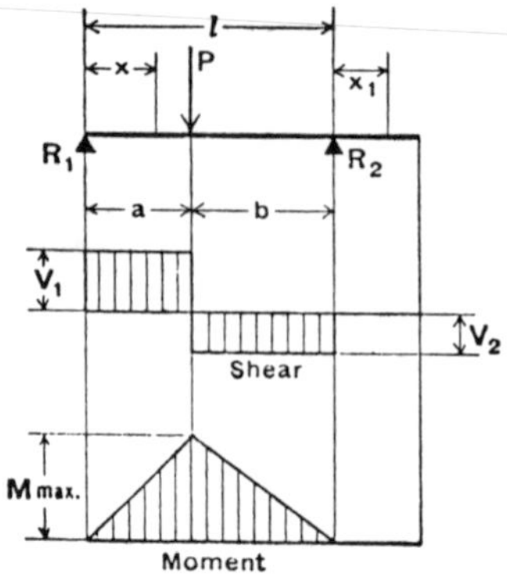

Equivalent Tabular Load . . . $= \frac{8Pab}{l^2}$

$R_1 = V_1 \left(\text{max. when } a < b\right)$ . . . $= \frac{Pb}{l}$

$R_2 = V_2 \left(\text{max. when } a > b\right)$ . . . $= \frac{Pa}{l}$

$M\ max. \left(\text{at point of load}\right)$ . . . $= \frac{Pab}{l}$

$M_x \left(\text{when } x < a\right)$ . . . . $= \frac{Pbx}{l}$

$\Delta max. \left(\text{at } x = \sqrt{\frac{a(a + 2b)}{3}} \text{ when } a > b\right) = \frac{Pab\,(a + 2b)\sqrt{3a\,(a + 2b)}}{27EIl}$

$\Delta a \left(\text{at point of load}\right)$ . . . $= \frac{Pa^2b^2}{3EIl}$

$\Delta x \left(\text{when } x < a\right)$ . . . . $= \frac{Pbx}{6EIl}(l^2 - b^2 - x^2)$

$\Delta x \left(\text{when } x > a\right)$ . . . . $= \frac{Pa\,(l - x)}{6EIl}(2lx - x^2 - a^2)$

Δx_1 . . . . $= \frac{Pabx_1}{6EIl}(l + a)$

BEAM DIAGRAMS AND FORMULAS
FOR VARIOUS STATIC LOADING CONDITIONS

29. CONTINUOUS BEAM—TWO EQUAL SPANS—UNIFORM LOAD ON ONE SPAN

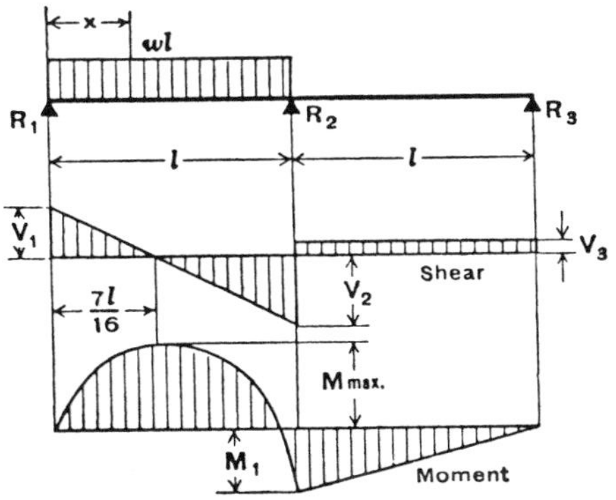

Equivalent Tabular Load	=	$\frac{49}{64}wl$
$R_1 = V_1$	=	$\frac{7}{16}wl$
$R_2 = V_2 + V_3$	=	$\frac{5}{8}wl$
$R_3 = V_3$	=	$-\frac{1}{16}wl$
V_2	=	$\frac{9}{16}wl$
M Max. $\left(\text{at } x = \frac{7}{16}l\right)$	=	$\frac{49}{512}wl^2$
M_1 (at support R_2)	=	$\frac{1}{16}wl^2$
M_x (when $x < l$)	=	$\frac{wx}{16}(7l - 8x)$

30. CONTINUOUS BEAM—TWO EQUAL SPANS—CONCENTRATED LOAD AT CENTER OF ONE SPAN

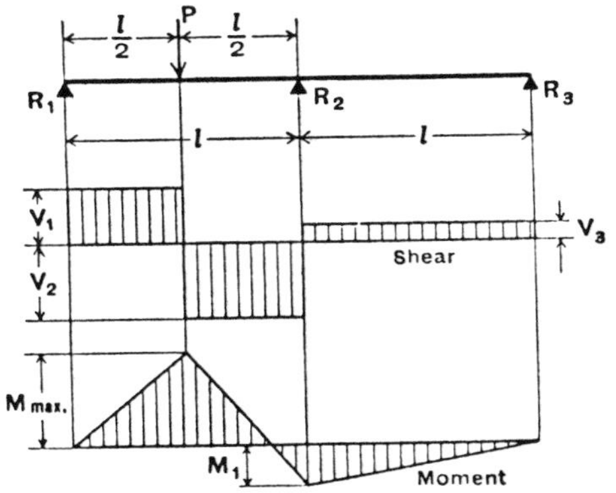

Equivalent Tabular Load	=	$\frac{13}{8}P$
$R_1 = V_1$	=	$\frac{13}{32}P$
$R_2 = V_2 + V_3$	=	$\frac{11}{16}P$
$R_3 = V_3$	=	$-\frac{3}{32}P$
V_2	=	$\frac{19}{32}P$
M Max. (at point of load)	=	$\frac{13}{64}Pl$
M_1 (at support R_2)	=	$\frac{3}{32}Pl$

31. CONTINUOUS BEAM—TWO EQUAL SPANS—CONCENTRATED LOAD AT ANY POINT

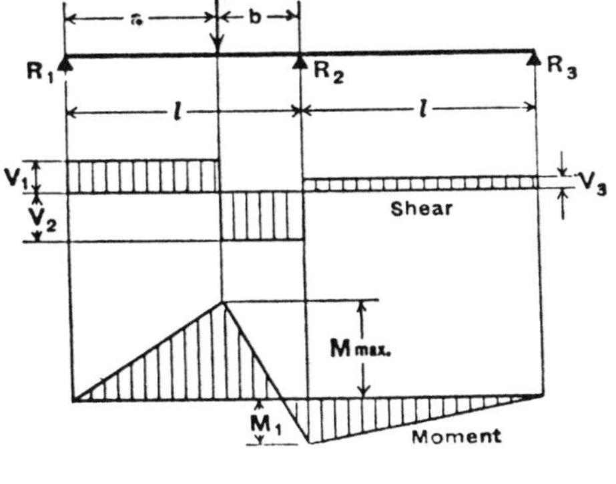

$R_1 = V_1$	=	$\frac{Pb}{4l^3}\left(4l^2 - a(l+a)\right)$
$R_2 = V_2 + V_3$	=	$\frac{Pa}{2l^3}\left(2l^2 + b(l+a)\right)$
$R_3 = V_3$	=	$-\frac{Pab}{4l^3}(l + a)$
V_2	=	$\frac{Pa}{4l^3}\left(4l^2 + b(l+a)\right)$
M max. (at point of load)	=	$\frac{Pab}{4l^3}\left(4l^2 - a(l+a)\right)$
M_1 (at support R_2)	=	$\frac{Pab}{4l^2}(l + a)$

BEAM DIAGRAMS AND FORMULAS

FOR VARIOUS CONCENTRATED MOVING LOADS

The values given in these formulas do not include impact which varies according to the requirements of each case.

32. SIMPLE BEAM—ONE CONCENTRATED MOVING LOAD

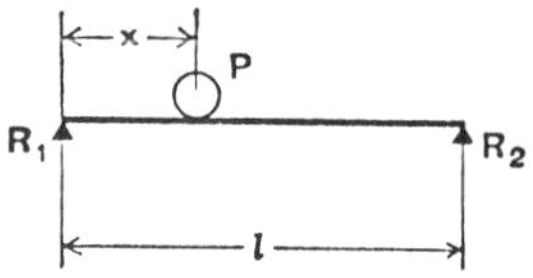

R_1 max. = V_1 max. $\left(\text{at } x = o\right)$ . . . . . $= P$

M max. $\left(\text{at point of load, when } x = \frac{l}{2}\right)$ . . $= \frac{Pl}{4}$

33. SIMPLE BEAM—TWO EQUAL CONCENTRATED MOVING LOADS

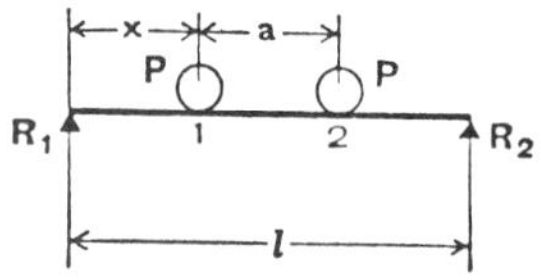

R_1 max. = V_1 max. $\left(\text{at } x = o\right)$ . . . . . $= P\left(2 - \frac{a}{l}\right)$

M max.

- [when $a < (2 - \sqrt{2})\, l = .586l$ under load 1 at $x = \frac{1}{2}\left(l - \frac{a}{2}\right)$] $= \frac{P}{2l}\left(l - \frac{a}{2}\right)^2$
- [when $a > (2 - \sqrt{2})\, l = .586l$ with one load at center of span (case 32)] $= \frac{Pl}{4}$

34. SIMPLE BEAM—TWO UNEQUAL CONCENTRATED MOVING LOADS

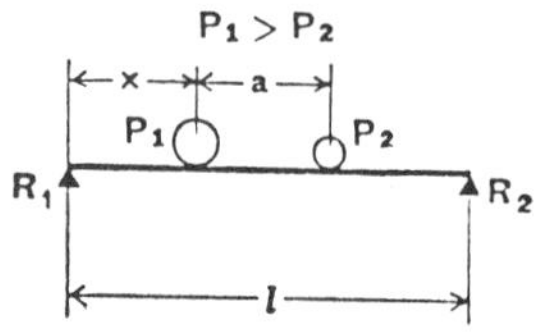

R_1 max. = V_1 max. $\left(\text{at } x = o\right)$ . . . . . $= P_1 + P_2 \frac{l - a}{l}$

M max.

- $\left[\text{under } P_1, \text{ at } x = \frac{1}{2}\left(l - \frac{P_2 a}{P_1 + P_2}\right)\right] = \left(P_1 + P_2\right)\frac{x^2}{l}$
- [M max. may occur with larger load at center of span and other load off span (case 32)] $= \frac{P_1 l}{4}$

GENERAL RULES FOR SIMPLE BEAMS CARRYING MOVING CONCENTRATED LOADS

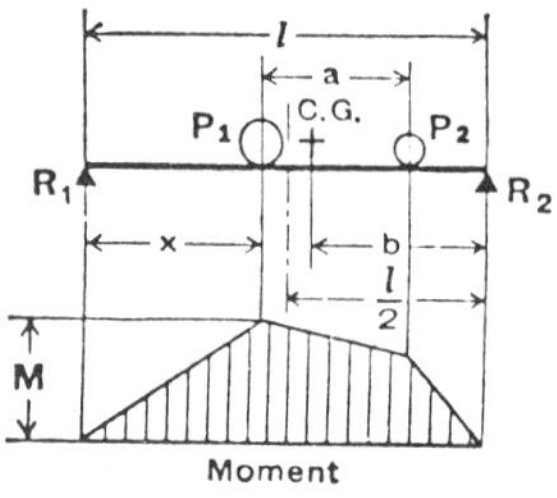

The maximum shear due to moving concentrated loads occurs at one support when one of the loads is at that support. With several moving loads, the location that will produce maximum shear must be determined by trial.

The maximum bending moment produced by moving concentrated loads occurs under one of the loads when that load is as far from one support as the center of gravity of all the moving loads on the beam is from the other support.

In the accompanying diagram, the maximum bending moment occurs under load P_1 when $x = b$. It should also be noted that this condition occurs when the center line of the span is midway between the center of gravity of loads and the nearest concentrated load.

INDEX

Numbers on this page refer to PROBLEM NUMBERS, not page numbers

Numbers on this page refer to PROBLEM NUMBERS, not page numbers

Numbers on this page refer to PROBLEM NUMBERS, not page numbers

Numbers on this page refer to PROBLEM NUMBERS, not page numbers